SECOND EDITION

THE HANDBOOK
OF MAGAZINE
PUBLISHING

COMPILED BY
THE EDITORS OF

Folio:

THE MAGAZINE FOR MAGAZINE MANAGEMENT

ISBN 0-918110-09-2

Folio Publishing Corporation, 125 Elm Street, Post Office Box 697, New Canaan, Connecticut 06840.

Printed in the United States of America

Preface

The publishers of FOLIO: THE MAGAZINE FOR MAGAZINE MANAGEMENT are pleased to publish this Second Edition of The Handbook of Magazine Publishing.

In 1977, when the first edition of the Handbook appeared, it was immediately recognized as a primary informational resource, both for people working in this dynamic industry and for students interested in entering the field.

Now, six years later, the many changes and innovations that have affected magazine publishing are covered in this updated and revised Second Edition. The best of the first edition has been retained, and to this, we have added the most valuable material from issues of FOLIO of recent years.

As the only magazine devoted solely to the business of creating, producing, marketing and distributing magazines, FOLIO is in a unique position to report on and analyze the ever-changing industry techniques and practices. This volume contains selected articles written by magazine publishing specialists and those by FOLIO editors, which have appeared in the magazine through the decade 1972-1982, a period of phenomenal growth and change for magazine publishing. Arranged in 13 sections by general subject area for easy reference, the material comprises a reference source available no where else.

The Second Edition is a practical guide to understanding the many aspects of a complex, modern industry. It offers realistic solutions to everyday magazine publishing problems. We hope that you will find it useful and informative.

Charles I. Tannen
Editor and Publisher

Acknowledgements

The editors of FOLIO: THE MAGAZINE FOR MAGAZINE MANAGEMENT are indebted to the many publishers, editors, circulation executives, art directors, production coordinators, corporate management officers, sales managers, promotion directors and consultants who have contributed their expertise in articles to FOLIO, thus making this book possible. The editors would also like to express their special appreciation to Howard Ravis for his invaluable assistance in supervising the editorial production of this volume.

Handbook Sections

See detailed table of contents on next page.

Table of Contents

Advertising management and marketing

Selling advertising

Circulation management

Circulation promotion

Single-copy sales

Fulfillment

Ancillary activities

Editorial

Graphics

Production

Printing

Management

Starting the new magazine

Contributors

Advertising management and marketing

Measuring your sales operation

By Frederic C. Decker

There is probably nothing in publishing that can make a bigger swing in the bottom line than advertising sales performance. Yet there are many publishers and their sales executives who are not sure about some very basic things in their own sales operations. And what they don't know can hurt them.

In one way or another I have posed a series of questions to at least 50 publishers and sales directors over the past couple of years. And I've probed behind their answers.

It soon became obvious that few, if any, publishers could answer with a self-assured "yes" to every one of the questions that were central to their sales success. You might want to take the test, too:

1. Do you know the real reasons why ad prospects don't buy your book?

2. Do you know the real reasons why they do buy?

3. Do you know how your sales staff stacks up—person for person and as a whole—against the staffs of your competitors, in the eyes of your prospects?

4. Are you sure your sales department compensation and incentive structures give motivation and are fair to the salespeople and to management?

5. Were your salespersons adequately trained when you gave them an account list and a rate card and sent them out onto the street?

6. Do you have an ongoing training program that is worthy of the name?

7. Does your sales department have the advantage of adequate and thoroughly interpreted intelligence back-up—through research, competitive statistics, regularly supplied market information?

(You are now not quite halfway through the questions, and you may already be saying, "Good grief, these things are elementary." You're right! But have you answered every question with an honest "yes"?)

8. Are your salespeople currently and constantly intimate with your editorial product and able to sell it cogently and enthusiastically?

9. Are realistic sales goals established? Does the staff understand them? Do they incentivize the staff?

10. Is the analysis and targeting of accounts an ongoing and constructive part of sales planning?

11. Is sales staff recruiting done with the skill and professionalism that is necessary to avoid a high incidence of costly mistakes?

12. Does management have a realistic feel of sale department morale and know what is wrong if it is low, and what is right if it is high?

13. Are sales meetings and conferences genuinely useful as information sources, morale builders, skills sharpeners?

14. Do you know which of your salespeople are promotable with greatest overall company benefit?

15. Is the sales promotional material competently prepared, and do the salespeople make regular and effective use of sales-support materials?

There's no way for any publisher or sales director to get a loud, clear and unqualified "yes" to every question. But danger signals should go up if many of the questions have to be answered with a "no" or a "well, maybe."

Effectiveness of Salespersons

Magazine people have always debated how much effect the salesperson has upon the ultimate sale. The publisher of one big magazine told me he figured that the effect of the salesperson might be about 25 percent. But the truth is that nobody knows. That's because the effect of the direct sales effort is affected by so many factors, such as the statistics that the computer digests, considerations of the advertiser's budget, how well established the book is, the marketing target.

It's my opinion that personal sales skills may be less important on a big magazine than on a small one. And it takes a better sales effort to sell a tail-end Charlie than the leader in the field. I personally think that sales competence may count for more on a trade book than on a consumer magazine, and more on a new magazine than on one that's long-established.

But no matter what kind of a magazine it may be, or what its position in the field, it is safe to say that the effectiveness of personal sales effort has a strong impact upon total sales and the cost of sales, and a massive effect upon the bottom line.

And it is also safe to say that sales effectiveness will be increased if there are "yes" answers to every one of those 15 questions.

What do you do about it?

Obviously, the first step is to become fully informed about the nature and extent of any shortfall in any of the sales management and sales development areas, any

1

weakness in staff and sales support. Once information is gathered from external and internal sources, the next step is to search it for clues and solutions. Implementing those solutions is the third step.

It is a wise publisher, I think, who considers the possibility that the first step—information seeking—can't be brought off successfully by his or her own staff people. Fact-finding probes should be accomplished without advertisers, prospects and competitors knowing that Magazine A is examining itself in the marketplace. It is better if that fact is initially kept from the sales staff, too. It is doubtful if staff people, without the discipline of outside counsel, can be fully objective in their evaluations or in their development of solutions to overcome problem conditions. Staff participation is, of course, essential in putting those solutions into action and making them work.

The easiest chore for the publisher will be finding the people to do the necessary confidential probing for facts and to help in developing the strategic planning. Publishers will find that their toughest job is making the original decision that things could be better in their sales operations, and that they really want to learn the facts and take whatever constructive steps may be necessary.

Hiring salespeople

By Dave Hagenbuch

Hiring good salespeople should be the number one item on a publisher's list of management tasks. For many publishers, however, hiring effective salespeople is an extremely tough assignment with no easy answers.

Part of the problem is that a very high percentage of people selling advertising space simply cannot sell. Far too many go out and simply bring their customers and prospects "up-to-date" on their publications. They do not *sell* a significant amount of business.

Yes, there are some truly great professional salespeople and publishing representatives, but they are the "ten-percenters." On a typical ten-person sales force, you'll find one or two stars, four average or below average salespeople, and two who should have been fired several years ago.

I once asked the president of a major publishing company with a sales team of 150 salespeople how many he considered to be real "professionals." His answer? Fifteen!

How can a publisher avoid this situation? How does a publisher go about screening and hiring good salespeople? What interviewing techniques work better than others in this area?

Planning for growth

Let me back up for a moment to discuss three preliminary steps that must be taken before the selection process can begin.

First, a publisher must plan. This is where many companies fall down. They do not have a plan for sales coverage and growth.

Second, a publisher must know exactly what type of salesperson he wants. Every publisher wants salespeople who are "intelligent," "persuasive," "creative," and "highly motivated," and many rely on the "right chemistry" to hire their salespeople. However, you're more likely to improve your batting average by establishing some fairly precise specifications covering the qualities needed to assure success on your publication.

What type of person do you want? Your magazine may need a real competitor, or someone who can take rejection better than the average. What is the condition of the territory to be filled? Does it require a lot of travel? What is the nature of your competition? The objective is to define the requirements of the job in considerable detail.

The third step is *recruiting*—a costly, time-consuming task. Most publishers use many sources for recruiting candidates. Many are turning to industry for salespeople, but there is still a lot of trading going on within publishing circles. (As a pure guess, I'd estimate that one of four salespersons changes jobs annually.)

The selection process

A publisher's hiring practices—the mechanics and approaches he uses to select his salespeople—should be developed into standard procedures that include the following items:

1) A good *application form*. Such a form should include a work history section with earning data, employment dates, reasons for leaving, and addresses and phone numbers of previous employers. You need these facts for the decision-making process.

2) An *"insurance-type"* physical. Physical fitness is necessary for sales work.

3) An *interview form*. This should be checked against the application for any discrepancies. In addition to questions on work experience and education, you'll need information on hobbies and personal references.

4) A *telephone follow-up form* or check list. Good follow-up checks to verify data are essential. The best indication of what a person will do is what that person has done. An obvious key question to ask a previous employer is: "Would you rehire this person?"

5) *Psychological tests* on aptitudes, mental ability, etc. (Be sure that such tests are incorporated in the program only as *part* of the total.) Personality and vocational interest tests can be conducted too.

6) *Credit checks.* (Before doing a credit check, find out about the legal ramifications of such an action.)

When I was vice president of sales for the Chilton Company in 1967, we did a credit check on a potential salesman and uncovered false information on his marital status and education. He was a bad risk who was about to be hired because he had done extremely well on all the tests and interviews.

Checking applicants

The best sources for checking an applicant are his previous employers. They have seen this person in action and should know his strengths and weaknesses.

You can check by letter or by sending a questionnaire, but you may not get a comprehensive reply since most publishers, sales managers, ad directors or other employers are reluctant to put anything in writing. You may prefer to make a personal visit, although this can be time-consuming and impractical.

Telephone checks are the most commonly used method of checking, but I find that few publishing executives do much more than ask a basic question or two. The form developed by the McMurry Corporation for Dartnell will serve as a useful guide (see Figure 1). It passes all legal requirements and is designed to get the kind of information you want.

You'll need to tailor it somewhat for our business and you may decide not to ask all the questions, but it's better than working off the "top of your head," so to speak. It gets you more and better information in only five to 10 minutes. More important, it is a systematic technique for getting information.

A word of caution: Never check with an applicant's *present* employer unless you have been given specific permission to do so. To play it safe, you should ask if he has any objection to your contacting any previous employers.

Making the call

The McMurry people advise planning your call:

"When calling previous employers, the approach is all-important in getting the information wanted. Obviously, no employer or personnel department is going to give out information unless they know who is calling and why the information is needed. The caller must identify himself immediately, and then make a simple statement such as : 'I would like to *verify* some information given us by Mr. Thompson, a former employee of yours, who is applying for a position with us.' Emphasizing the word 'verify' will act as an opening wedge to obtaining additional information that is not just a verification of facts given by the applicant."

Occasionally the person contacted is reluctant to reveal *any* information. If he is unwilling to talk because he is not sure of the caller's identity, ask him to call you back.

On the other hand, if the person contacted cannot give out information because of company policy, ask to speak to his supervisor and offer an explanation something like this:

"This is Mr. Jones of XYZ Publishing Company speaking. We are considering a Mr. Thompson for a job with our organization and we understand that he worked for you as a salesperson last year. Naturally, we're particular about the type of people we take into our organiza-tion and wondered if you could give us some information about the man on a strictly confidential basis. Could you verify some of the statements he has made in his application?"

If the person contacted will not release the information and if this is a particularly important interview, you should "go up the line." It may require two or three contacts, in some cases, before the right person is reached.

In nearly every instance this straightforward approach brings results. Either the person contacted will reveal what the prospective employer wants to know, or he will turn him over to someone who can.

Tests—a controversial technique

There are many opinions on the subject of testing. Some say that psychological tests and sales aptitude tests are not relevant to sales success and that the qualifications necessary for success in sales do not generally lend themselves to measurement by tests. The theory is that what people say and what they do in actual situations are often quite different.

My first exposure to tests goes back to my first job in publishing. Jay Belcher, the publisher of *Progressive Architecture,* had me take a sales aptitude test. On my follow-up interview he told me that the test indicated that I would be a "good salesman" but that I was "thin-skinned." When I asked him what that meant, he replied, "It means that if you lose a piece of business, you won't go back and fight for it."

I looked at him and said, "Mr. Belcher, will you do me a favor?"

"What's that?" he asked.

"Will you please rip that damn thing up and give me the job?"

He picked up the test, ripped it in half, ceremoniously dropped it into the wastebasket, shook my hand and said, "You're hired!"

There are, of course, many publishers who swear by tests. They maintain that testing can often flush out people who are bound to fail. One consultant, who does personality, temperament, and motivational analyses for some forty publishing companies, says that "you can't learn much in an interview with a prospective salesperson. You need to probe below the surface and do qualitative analysis."

What is this person like?

To get a comprehensive picture of your sales candidate, you should explore the following areas:

1) aptitude and abilities as evidenced by past deeds;

2) experience;

3) motivation;

4) personality and character traits as related to the demands of the sales job (*e.g.,* believability, sincerity, persuasiveness, imagination). The questions you ask or comments volunteered can give some insight into how this person would fit into your organization.

You should be thinking in terms of vocational stability, diligence, perseverance, integrity, loyalty, ability to get along with people, and attitude. A healthy attitude is like money in the bank. A poor attitude is the biggest time-waster.

Good salespeople do not fall into one distinct type. Every individual is a blend of characteristics and every asset and every liability must be considered. For example, the strongly extroverted person may be friendly but impulsive, aggressive but a poor organizer. The strongly introverted salesperson can be reflective and analytical, but

Figure 1

TELEPHONE CHECK ON SALES APPLICANT _____

Name of Applicant

_____

Person Contacted   Position

_____

Company   City and State   Telephone Number

1. I wish to *verify* some of the information
   given to us by Mr./Ms _____
   who has applied for a position with our firm.
   Do you remember the applicant? What were
   the dates of employment with your
   Company?   From _____ 19 ____ To _____ 19 _____
                                                              Do dates check?

2. What was applicant doing when he/she
   started?   _____
                                                              Did he/she exaggerate?

   When he/she left?   _____
                                                              Did he/she progress?

3. Applicant says he/she was earning $ _____
   per _____ when he/she left. Is that right?   ☐ Yes,   ☐ No; $ _____
                                                              Did applicant falsify?

4. How much of this was salary? $ _____

   How much commission? $ _____

5. How was attendance?   _____
                                                       Conscientious?   Health problems?

6. What type of selling did applicant do? _____
                                                       To whom? How did he/she get his/her contacts?

7. How did sales results compare with others? _____
                                                       Industrious?   Competitive?

8. Did he/she supervise anyone else?   ☐ No,   ☐ Yes; How many? _____
                                                                    Does this check?

   (If yes) How well did he/she handle it? _____
                                                       Is he/she a leader or a driver?

9. How closely was he/she supervised?   _____
                                                       Was he/she hard to manage?

10. How hard did applicant work?   _____
                                                       Is he/she habitually industrious?

11. How well did applicant get along with
    other people?   _____
                                                       Is he/she a troublemaker?

12. What arguments did applicant have with
    customers?   _____
                                            Does he/she like selling?   Can he/she control his/her temper?

13. What did you think of applicant?   _____
                                                       Did he/she get along with his/her superiors?

14. Why did applicant leave?   _____
                                                       Good reasons?   Do they check?

15. Would you rehire applicant?   ☐ Yes,   ☐ No; Why not? _____
                                                              Does this affect suitability with us?

16. Did he/she have any domestic or financial
    difficulties that interfered with work? ☐ No,   ☐ Yes; What? _____
                                                                  Immaturity?

17. How about drinking or gambling?   ☐ No,   ☐ Yes; What? _____
                                                                  Immaturity?

18. What are outstanding strong points?   _____

19. What type of saleswork do you feel the
    applicant would do best?   _____

20. What are his/her weak points?   _____

Checked by _____ Date _____

shy and self-conscious. Yet, they are often good detailers. Strongly aggressive types who are forceful, dynamic, and decisive may negatively impress advertisers as tactless, insensitive and overbearing.

Getting the information

Although there are as many interviewing techniques as there are interviewers, there are certain guidelines that are helpful in conducting an interview.

First, decide what kind of interview you will conduct *before* the candidate is sitting in front of you.

In the *direct interview*, you maintain full control of the interviewing. You ask direct and specific questions. The advantages are that you can get a lot of information in a short period of time. On the minus side, you lose out on volunteered comments that help you assess attitudes, traits, habits and abilities.

In an *indirect interview*, you throw the ball to the salesperson who runs with it as he or she sees fit. You can learn much by listening. At the same time, the smart candidates tell you what they think you'd like to hear. The book stores are loaded with information on how to interview for a job. There isn't much on hiring.

Then there is the *patterned interview*, which is a merger of the direct and indirect interviews. You very adroitly guide the interview and get the interviewee to talk freely about relevant topics. This technique has been used in industry for more than 20 years. It relates back to the information you get up-front through a good application form, tests and checks.

Whatever method you use, be sure to have a plan and follow it. Generally, the best approach is to get into work history and/or educational background before digging into more personal areas such as outside interests and activities.

Get the person talking

Once the applicant is in your office, set the stage by making him feel comfortable. People will reveal more about themselves when they like the person conducting the interview.

Conduct the interview in a private office where you and the candidate can talk in a normal tone of voice. Cut off the phone.

Don't rush. Break the ice and devote several minutes to small talk. This gives the candidate a chance to collect his composure. Then you can open up the interview with a question to get your candidate talking about his previous experience.

You may start with something like "You've had some interesting experiences. As a potential salesperson for our magazine (company), we're interested in learning as much as we can about you and, naturally, we'll be pleased to answer any questions you have about us. Suppose you begin by telling me about your previous jobs, starting with the first one and up through your present position. I'll be interested in the positions you held, your responsibilities, your attitudes about the job, your earnings and what you accomplished."

You may ask the inexperienced recruit about the part-time jobs. With the experienced one, you may add "How did you get into this business?"

Sample questions

There are a number of questions relating to work experience that will help you uncover the kind of person you are interviewing. Some will appeal to you and others will not, but each is designed to give you insight into your candidate.

1) "What aspect of your first job did you find most satisfying and stimulating? What aspects, on a relative basis, did you care for less?"

2) "How much travel was involved? What was your reaction?"

3) (Relating to other jobs): "How did you handle your territory?"

4) "What did you learn about yourself in that job?"

5) "How do your earnings on that job compare to what you earned on the previous one?"

6) "What were the circumstances leading up to your decision to leave that job?"

7) "What would you say were your major accomplishments on that job?"

8) "What are the things you look for in a job?"

9) "What are the major challenges you face in selling advertising space?"

10) "How do you overcome these?"

To find out about the candidate's hobbies or outside interests, ask him the following questions:

1) "What are your hobbies and outside interests?"

2) "Are you involved in any community activities?"

3) "What have you done that has given you the greatest satisfaction?" (This is a question which deals with motivation in a direct manner.)

You can also develop questions that will reveal a great deal about a candidate's personality. I recently talked to a salesperson who told me his major accomplishment was overcoming a poor living environment. You could feel his pride and sense of motivation. Also, you should ask the candidate to assess his selling strengths and weaknesses. His answers will usually yield some useful information.

One consultant specializing in placement activities says that one should look for ingredients for failure because they are easier to identify than ingredients for success.

A word of caution

There are certain questions you should *not* ask in an interview because of the appearance of discrimination. Here's a sample:

• "How old are you?"

• "What is your birth date?"

• "Do you have children? If so, how old are they?"

• "Are you married, divorced, separated, widowed or single?"

• "Who lives in your household?"

Ridiculous? You may think so, but in many states you run the risk of possible trouble if you ask these questions. Even if the employer has good intentions, if a job candidate perceives that he or she is being discriminated against in an interview, serious trouble may result. Even though the problems may arise from misinterpretation by the applicant, the employer can wind up in court.

Practically speaking, when you ask for a resumé, you'll usually have the answers to questions on age, sex and marital status.

Last call

Now that you have located, screened, tested and interviewed your sales candidates, you should be thinking of a second or even third interview with the contenders for the job. Before you make any final decision, I suggest the following:

1) Make sure the salesperson knows what you expect from all of the salespeople on your staff and what they can expect from you. Salespeople tell me they didn't know about such things as call quotas, monthly estimates

on expected space, commission arrangements, etc., until after they were hired.

2) Ask each contender to come back and tell you why he should be hired. Some publishers require a presentation based on a theoretical or real sales situation. This gives them a chance to see the candidate in action.

3) Watch for follow-up letters. People who don't follow up on job interviews become very suspect in my opinion. I'm amazed at the percentage of applicants who never bother.

4) Don't slack up on your requirements just because someone has had years of experience. Make him prove how professional he is.

Some publishers have check lists that rate sales candidates on character traits (*e.g.*, stability, industry, motivation) and assess their needs (*e.g.*, money, status, security). This is a good idea. I also suggest that you get the Dartnell form, Selection And Evaluation Summary. It lists Can-Do Factors (can he/she do the job physically, experience-wise, etc.) and Will-Do Factors (basic habits, motivations). From it you can build your own model. Too often the final decision is a hunch or gut feeling about the final contenders where emotions come into play. Much of the hiring of salespeople is in the hands of ex-salespeople who like salespeople. They're often easy to sell and that doesn't make for wise hiring decisions.

I just finished a book, *The Truth About Selling* by Samuel S. Susser, in which his advice to people looking for sales jobs is, "Tell the man you are tough, resilient, well disciplined, hard-working, and that you have an acute understanding of the human heart. He will hire you. Because he likes salesmen."

Training: why bother?

By Morton E. Grossman

Sales training, widely used in industry, is rarely used in the magazine business. Many publishers have never tried it, and most of those who have find that sales training methods developed in other industries are generally not applicable to magazines. Selling magazine advertising space requires its own approach to sales training because ad salespeople need more wide-ranging and varied information than many other salespeople.

Here's a quick review of information needed by advertising salespeople:

The market
  History
  Current developments
  Future trends
The magazine
  Editorial
  Circulation
  Rates
  Advertising
  Production
  Research
  Promotion
  Competitive media
Marketing strategies
  New business presentations
  Positioning platforms
Management policies
  Incentive plans
  Territory organization
  Reporting procedures
  Record keeping
  Billing, credit

It takes a well-thought-out communication system to transmit all this information to the sales staff. Unfortunately, for many magazine salespeople, the gap between sales potential and achievement is not due to a lack of personal sales ability, but to management's failure to communicate the complete marketing story to them. Often the best communication system for improving sales performance is structured sales training.

Structured sales training begins with a state of mind: an awareness of the need to coordinate your selling efforts with all of your other marketing efforts. Once you have this awareness you will find that sales training gives you an immediate means of meeting virtually any sales problem or opportunity.

But before you design your sales training structure, make sure you can clearly define your marketing goals. Sales training should prepare your sales staff to accomplish your sales goals.

For example, one magazine reached the conclusion that 100 additional ad pages were possible in the next year. Fifty pages could come from upgrading current advertisers and 50 could come from selling new accounts.

A sales training program was initiated, designed to attain "The Next 100 Pages." Target accounts were selected, with specific page goals for each account. Intensive sales training sessions were conducted to help each salesperson develop the best possible sales approach for each case, and to convert anticipated objections into sales opportunities.

The program worked. More than 100 additional pages were sold that year—pages that the magazine has been able to keep and gradually increase as sales training continued.

Sales meetings

The heart of any sales training program is the sales meeting. Even though you may have daily contact with your salespeople, it is in the sales meeting that you can develop and refine your marketing information package. In the sales meeting you can create and test sales strategies, and your salespeople can learn and practice ways to improve their performances.

Every sales meeting should have a purpose. The more closely related that purpose is to your marketing goals, the more successful your meeting is likely to be. Develop an underlying theme. Prepare your agenda in advance.

Here are 12 examples of what can be accomplished at sales meetings:
- Practice sales approaches—role playing
- Review basics
- Develop sales strategies
- Deal with problems and opportunities
- Work on special areas
- Work on target accounts
- Learn new material
- Integrate new people
- Foster teamwork
- Organize territories
- Ascertain sales needs
- Generate new ideas

Plan for active involvement of your salespeople in the sales training process. One consumer magazine publisher always organized sales meetings carefully, with a full agenda of lectures by the publisher, the ad manager and other department heads, and even outside speakers. The problem was that the salespeople simply sat and listened and were not required to do anything that would put the information to work for their benefit.

At one meeting, he decided to have the salespeople themselves give impromptu presentations, using material that had been presented many times. The results were unexpected: It was evident that everyone needed selling practice.

At the next meeting, lectures were cut to a minimum, and sales pitching began in earnest. Particular attention was paid to understanding the advertiser's marketing situation and how the magazine could help.

This time, the results were gratifying and ad sales gradually improved as structured selling methods learned in these meetings were put to use in the field.

Since nothing is more vital to sales success than a properly organized sales pitch, your salespeople should spend as much time as possible organizing their presentations.

The best way to learn the proper technique is through role playing. When salespeople work in teams, alternating at playing the roles of seller, buyer and observer, they find the experience stimulating and beneficial. Over the course of a few sales meetings you can see salespeople improve as they use the lessons they have learned.

Role playing also leads to new sales strategies. In the give and take of a simulated sales call, new ideas and approaches for solving sales problems are often found and can be used successfully in real selling situations.

In one sales meeting, an entire category of potential advertisers was created in a role playing session involving the manufacturer of a new type of product. Other salespeople confirmed the fact that there were many such manufacturers, and a specific sales approach was developed for them.

One of the ideas that came out of this session was for a special editorial section about the new product (which was later adopted). Today, that product area is one of the major advertising categories of the magazine, and the industry gives the magazine credit for helping it grow.

Questions frequently arise about sales meetings. How often should we have them? How long should they be? Where should they be held? Essentially, these are questions of preference, style and, sometimes, budget. You will develop your own rhythm. One publisher has a one-day mini-sales meeting monthly in the office, plus a major four-day annual meeting at a resort. Some excellent sales meetings take place in the publisher's office or company conference room.

Typically, this format works well. Frequency: at least once a year, preferably twice, ideally three times. Length: three days, give or take half a day. Place: away from the office.

Following up
To ensure the continuing effect of your sales meeting on sales performance, the next step is to provide follow-up between meetings. Sales bulletins, memos or notes within the context of your marketing goals can constantly reinforce your training efforts.

An occasional staff newsletter is one approach for keeping up sales momentum. A special interest magazine publisher uses a catchy title and colored paper that attracts attention. The major thrust is to single out salespeople who have sold target accounts and to give case histories on how the sales were made.

Useful items of market information are also put into the newsletter, as well as announcements of editorial features, special sections and incentive programs. The publisher makes this project easy to handle by avoiding rigid schedules and turning the newsletter out only when there is enough useful material. Memos are used for dated information that needs fast dissemination.

Use whatever methods you are comfortable with to communicate with your sales staff. But get into the habit of looking for and relaying ideas, facts and news that will reinforce and enhance your drive for advertising sales.

An automatic system for delivering sales materials is another obvious need. Salespeople need ample supplies of the magazine, back copies, rate cards, circulation statements, editorial schedules, survey reports, presentations, promotion pieces, media kits, fact sheets, and whatever other materials are specific to your magazine.

A great deal of time and money is often spent planning and creating sales-related materials that never reach the sales staff, especially in branch offices. To avoid this situation, make a list of all the available materials that can be used for sales purposes, put somebody in charge of distributing them regularly, and make sure the job gets done.

Sales manuals
The ultimate sales training tool is a sales manual. It should include everything a salesperson needs to sell space in your magazine: the essential concepts underlying the benefits of advertising in your magazine, the basic facts to document these concepts, and examples of strategies that can be used to achieve sales objectives.

A complete sales manual should include:
- Description of the market
- Your magazine's coverage of the market
- Selling with circulation
- Editorial selling
- How to use research

- Advertising analyses
- Selling with rates
- Competitive magazines, media
- Sales strategies and approaches
- Examples of sales letters
- Handling objections

With this textbook of fundamentals for selling advertising in your magazine, you will have a major reference system that will work for your salespeople all year long. Updated regularly, the sales manual can be your permanent marketing information pipeline to your sales staff.

One sales staff makes use of its extensive sales manual to build its own presentations for important sales calls. With the sales manual, major presentations can be quickly put together, many of which would never get done because of the time required to gather the necessary information and formulate the proper strategies.

The sales manual is also useful in preparing sales letters. When a particular point has to be followed up, a salesperson can write an opening paragraph directed to the specific account, insert the pertinent section from the manual, and write a closing paragraph. Many effective letters that have helped close sales have been prepared with the sales manual, including, in one instance, a four-page analysis of the market that convinced an advertiser to increase his schedule from six pages to 24 pages.

Whatever sales training you plan to do, always consider the people on your advertising sales staff. How many are experienced? How many are new? What are their individual sales problems? Of course, you will have to train the beginners in magazine fundamentals, but experienced salespeople also appreciate the opportunity to review the basics.

How many veterans are fully aware of the advertising sales implications of new market developments? How many can make use of all the intricacies of circulation statements, research, advertising records, editorial analyses, rate card combinations and permutations?

In most magazine sales training situations, disparity of experience within the sales staff is not a problem. Where people with less experience predominate, sales presentation structure should be emphasized. Where structure is well-understood (and this is not always the case, even with experienced salespeople), strategy development should be stressed. In either case, it always pays to train the staff in the basic magazine marketing elements. The need for a continuing flow of information and reinforcement does not diminish with experience. In fact, the need increases as the ability to make effective use of sales information improves.

What's more, beginners benefit from the insights of the more experienced, while the fresh viewpoint of be-

ginners is often a stimulus to more mature salespeople. This was clearly demonstrated during a sales meeting whose major purpose was to indoctrinate and integrate two new salespeople, both beginners.

In a session on presentation structure, the experienced salespeople were able to demonstrate the compelling build-up of a well-organized presentation, as each point bridged to the next and on to an irrefutable close. But the newcomers approached their presentations with creative and unusual openings that stimulated the veterans into improving their previous performances. The combination of youth and experience made for one of the most constructive sales meetings that magazine ever had.

Is a recession imminent? Instruct your sales staff in the values of advertising and the long-term advantages to advertisers of maintaining advertising pressure during a period of falling sales.

For example, in the face of a recession that was beginning to hit one magazine hard, a special sales meeting was held to give the staff the resources needed to minimize the effects of the downturn. Specially prepared materials were presented, including case histories of advertisers during and after previous recessions. Role playing sessions designed to meet advertising cost-cutting objections were featured. Then, a useful mini-sales manual dealing with recession problems was made from taped sessions of the meeting.

Although losses were not completely stopped, the magazine was able to increase its share of market against its competition, and held on to the bigger share when the upturn came.

Is there a development in your industry that signals increasing competition and, therefore, an opportunity to sell more space? Schedule a special sales meeting to turn the staff on to the proper sales approaches to sell additional space. Send them useful selling information through the sales manual and other communications.

When recent government deregulation signaled an end to uniform rates and a scramble for competitive advantage, one publication in an affected industry called a sales meeting to assess the advertising sales opportunities in the new situation. The sales meeting highlighted how deregulation creates a more competitive market, and how advertising in the publication could help individual companies gain additional business. Using approaches developed in the meeting, the salespeople sold accounts that had never advertised in the publication before.

Your advertising salespeople can do a better selling job for your magazine. No matter what is happening in the market, and regardless of your staff's past selling record, you *can* improve sales performance—with structured sales training.

Training salespeople

By Dave Hagenbuch

You're a publishing executive. You're responsible for the development of your people. Are you giving them the benefit of well-planned, well-executed training and development programs? And how about you? Are you developing your management talents?

During my publishing career, I've been plagued with the question, "How can an untrained publisher train an untrained sales manager to train untrained salesmen and saleswomen?" Ten years ago, at a meeting of some 400 publishers, I urged the formation of a series of association developmental programs for publishers, sales managers and salespeople. The publishers said, "Let's start with the salesperson."

In my opinion, that was not the way to go but since there were no commercial or association publishing sales management or sales programs on magazine publishing available, at least it got things moving. We formed a task force committee of volunteer publishing people, created a curriculum and successfully launched a five-day program on selling space. Two years later, the association tried it alone and the program died. We never got to the publishers or sales managers except for their participation in the sales program.

Whether you're the chief executive of a sizable publishing company or the publisher of a small magazine, as long as there are other people involved in the sale of advertising, you'll benefit tremendously by building a training program. It is unquestionably the best way to build enthusiasm and belief for your publishing effort . . . internally and externally. It's the way to meet your competition effectively and productively in this people-oriented publishing business. Publishers and sales managers who view training as a continuing need will build stronger, wiser and happier organizations.

Since the sale of advertising almost always requires a face-to-face relationship with company and advertising agency executives, the reputation of your company (or an individual publication) rides heavily on how you and your salemen and saleswomen perform. When your direct salespeople and representatives present themselves as honest, knowledgeable and efficient communicators, then the buyers will be inclined to accept your company or publication favorably. Research in communications behavior documents that a high-competence source is normally a high-creditability source. It is also clear that over a period of time, a company's reputation erodes in the absence of effective, consistent sales exposure. If you'd like to test this thesis, just remove a strong sales performer from a territory without an equally strong replacement and watch the advertising pages slide. It may not show up immediately but it's a sure bet your sales market share will decline in a year or two.

Building a Strong Sales Force

How do you build a strong sales force? How do you get full measure for your sales dollars?

First, you hire competent people. You motivate them and then, it seems to me, you accept the principle that industry accepts, namely, that salespeople need training and this includes coaching on the job.

A typical space salesperson uses only 50 to 60 percent of his or her capacity to sell. The remaining percentage represents everything from laziness to lack of enthusiasm. Usually it is not lack of media knowledge (publishers make sure of that). To develop the 40 to 50 percent of latent capacity is the challenge and major responsibility of publishing and sales executives.

Salespeople need training and retraining. While it is true that there are a few stars or "naturals" in this business who will train themselves, they are in a decided minority and usually they're the ones who respond most favorably to training opportunities.

In today's economic environment, special training emphasis should be devoted to time and territory management, precall planning (establishing objectives), presentation techniques, handling objections and closing sales. You can wrap them up in any fancy language you want but they're still the basics of good, solid selling. You can spend a lot of time on the psychological aspects of selling, but it's true that the key to successful selling is satisfying customers wants and needs; what the customers want is help in marketing *their* products and services. This means developing presentations that are clear, concise, loaded with action verbs and buyer-benefits instead of the typical publisher sales presentations that are self-oriented, self-serving, self-defeating collections of media mishmash.

A Good Training Program

What are the elements of a good training program? There are five keys. Your programs must be:

1. Educational
2. Motivating
3. Realistic
4. Pertinent
5. Productive.

Applying these elements means that you'll need to do more than just impart company, market and magazine knowledge. The objective of your program should be more effective selling by all people involved in the sales program. Emphasis should be placed on selling skills. These skills include an appreciation of the following:

• How space is bought and sold
• How to organize and plan for sales calls
• How to get appointments
• The techniques for opening up sales interviews

9

and getting the prospect or customer involved in the process

- Stimulating the customer's interest
- Overcoming any sales obstacles
- Promoting action
- Servicing advertisers and agencies.

In other words, your salespeople should have a complete understanding of the principles and techniques of salesmanship . . . and how to apply them in day-to-day selling.

You'll benefit most by concentrating on specific methods for improving sales—not what to do but how to do it. Salesmen and saleswomen look to you for leadership and guidance. They want you to coach them in how to do it. They're not interested in working for cheerleaders.

Any program that is constructive and participative will normally have a strong motivational slant to it. We're in the communications business but unfortunately, we don't often communicate with each other in an educational environment. Holding a sales meeting that doesn't have strong emphasis on training can be motivational but not educational (i.e., in developing sales effectiveness). Attending meetings where the "training" is of the motivational-film variety can be momentarily uplifting, but the question always remains, "How can I use that to sell more advertising space?"

Your training methods should be realistic and pertinent. They must be geared to the market conditions in which you are selling. Today, when publishing costs are escalating so rapidly, salespeople need instruction in the economics of the business and in the judicious use of travel and entertainment dollars. When they fully understand the necessity for tighter controls, they'll cooperate. Most salespeople are realistic.

Productive? Your program *must* be productive. Training costs money. It's expensive; but by leaving it to chance, you run the risk of having salesmen and saleswomen who are *mistrained* by customers and other salespeople. That's the worst training possible and in the end, you'll spend even more.

There are absolutely far too many below-average and average types of salespeople and publishers' representatives out there representing your magazines. If you don't believe me, please study their call reports for quantity and quality, review their correspondence, listen to their presentations for content and buyer-motivations, hear how they ask for an appointment, ask them specifically what techniques they use to close sales and review their productivity account-by-account, year-by-year. You may decide that there is considerable room for improvement.

I'm not down on the salespeople. Far from it. In their ranks are some of the most creative, honest, enthusiastic, empathetic and delightful individuals you'll ever meet. What concerns me is that the publishers and publishing executives have not given them the benefit of consistent training and development programs. How many publishing concerns have a continuing effort in this regard? What programs do the Magazine Publishers Association and the American Business Press offer? A sales day once a year? Compare what is happening in publishing to the programs in industry and you come to the conclusion that there is a special training vacuum and challenge facing publishers. Association and publishing company programs should be standard procedure in this industry.

Just as new salesmen and saleswomen need and want formal training, so do the experienced ones. They are hungry for problem-solving ideas, solutions to better organization and territory or account coverage. They want help on sales techniques, sales skills. The publisher or sales manager who won't take the sales staff off the road for training exposure is guilty of myopic thinking.

The very act of expressing an interest in developing salespeople is morale building and productive in itself.

In successful publishing operations, inspired leadership and effective communications seem to work together in a positive direction for the benefit of all concerned. When these elements are lacking, one begins to find staff morale problems. Truly inspired leadership is of the coach, not the cheerleader, variety. All good coaches train their people even if we're talking about only one or two of them.

A Plan Is Most Important

Does your training program have to be elaborate? No. The most important consideration is that you have a plan. For experienced sales personnel, it may be two sessions a year supplemented by monthly written input in capsule and digest form. Make sure that it is concise, readable, believable and relevant to publishing. You may prefer more regular meetings of shorter duration. Just don't let these become "bull sessions" or "gripe sessions" instead of training exercises. It all gets back to organizing, communicating and controlling the program based on the establishment of realistic goals and objectives.

For the new salesperson, you'll need to incorporate training in sales techniques into your indoctrination program. Consider the man or woman you hire from within the business as "new." The individual must be trained in how you run your business and what you expect from him. If you assume that he or she knows all the answers, you run a dangerous risk. Often, those people become available to you because they weren't getting along elsewhere and you'll need to retrain them.

For your training sessions, set up a program and agenda that covers two or three topics per day in a structured and participative manner. You can select subjects from books on selling, magazine articles, films, cassettes; and set the stage for an interchange of ideas.

Be sure that specific points on selling techniques are communicated and understood. The participants must leave with strategic and tactical information that they can put to use on their sales calls. If you use outside sales trainers, be sure that they know your field and can relate to it in their efforts on your behalf. There are a lot of people in training who have come from the education field and have not had any practical experience in selling and who pass out bad advice.

What is the range of subjects that you can build into a training program?

The basics:
- Market knowledge
- Publication knowledge

- Customer knowledge
- Territory and time organization
- Communications skills
- Business concepts
- Sellings skills—sales psychology, precall planning, getting appointments, opening up interviews, customer involvement, presentation techniques, comparative selling, creative selling, handling objections, closing sales, servicing.

The more advanced:
- Target selling
- Problem solving
- Specialized presentations
- Competitive tactics
- Semantics
- Listening
- Sales perceptiveness
- Self evaluation
- Role playing
- Sales management
- Publishing management.

I'm sure you'll add others to this list. Sales psychology covers buyer motivations and viewing the buyer as a business and nonbusiness person. The umbrella over your entire effort should be to develop a positive attitude and professionalism toward the business.

And P.S.: Good selling is not selling at all. It is assisting the other person to buy.

When we recently researched 600 account and agency executives in the pharmaceutical market about the selling methods employed by publishers, we found that they had a preference for sales calls in the morning of less than 30 minutes (two-thirds staying 20 minutes or less) and their biggest plea might be paraphrased briefly as, "Don't waste my time, relate to my needs and don't knock your competition."

A preference for calls in the morning does not mean *no* calls in the afternoon. The low call level in publishing is a serious problem that may be hurting your publication, too. It's not just quantity, however, but quality that you'll want to evaluate and in the field is the place to do it.

On-the-job coaching is the best training technique you can employ. What are the things you must look for as signs that someone requires special coaching? I can think of these:
- Declining sales or share of market
- A fall-off in communications
- Reports or phone calls constantly relating problems
- Too few calls
- Too much entertainment
- Poor planning.

What things might you look for when you are in the field? Consider these:
- Is this person organized?
- What about personal appearance and condition of the sales material and the automobile?
- Does the salesperson listen?
- Is the salesperson flexible, well-informed, etc.?
- How is the training exposure being utilized?
- What is the attitude of this person about your publication, your company, the customers and prospects?

You can prepare your own checklist. Obviously you do not refer to it in front of the other person but you'll want to be prepared to look for certain things.

Does all of this sound very formal? Perhaps so, but if you've decided you have a problem, you'll want to have a plan for analyzing it. When a salesman or saleswoman "levels off" that individual needs training—not a pep talk. When sales are off, you need to find the answers—not rely on assumptions.

Prior to the sales call, review the staff member's plan of action. What is the objective of the call? What material does he or she plan to use? What is known about the buyer? What problems might come up and how will these be handled? You can simply ask, "What's your plan for this particular call?"

After the call, you can evaluate it informally with the individual. After a series of calls, you should be more specific and define the problems and opportunities, suggest actions to be taken, establish a timetable if necessary and communicate what results you expect to be achieved.

What About You?

Now, let's go back to where we started. What about you? What are you doing to train and develop yourself? Salesmen and saleswomen tell me that the sales managers and publishers run the gamut from the highly effective to the totally inept. Again the publishing industry hasn't done much collectively to enhance the sales management and publishing management functions. In fact, there are far fewer educational opportunities specifically geared to publishing than those available in sales. In my judgment, every publishing executive should attend some courses in sales to stay current in that area. Then, I urge you to examine your own management techniques on locating, screening and hiring salespeople; sales organization and direction; communications; motivation; sales controls; evaluation and remuneration; upgrading personnel and the whole range of publishing management activities relating to the editorial, sales, circulation, production and the financial side of publishing. You can do this by working with consultants, building your own programs, attending seminars that are available in publishing, reading industry practices and relating these to publishing and finally, by putting pressure on the publishing associations to develop some structured programs.

Just as salesmen and saleswomen work to 60 percent of their capacity, we people who are in management need to examine our management skills with a great deal of objectivity.

When you think about the publishing business and the highly successful magazines, your mind directs you to outstanding individuals. An associate of mine would call them "Bell Cows." These are the men and women who are the leaders, the communicators, the experimenters who have helped shape the business publication field.

During the past seven years, I have had a great deal of exposure to publishing executives at all levels and to hundreds of their employees, primarily in sales and editorial. It has been an enlightening experience.

Publishers and sales managers ask me, "What do you see as key essentials for success in management?" Five come to mind.

11

1. *Inspired leadership*—the kind that is people-oriented and task-directed to promote positive action and a good working climate.

2. *Effective communications*—vital in this type of business to build staff morale and loyalty.

3. *Accountability*—at all levels of the publishing operation, backed up with job descriptions and work flow analysis subject to continual review.

4. *Effective controls*—with special emphasis on sales for increased productivity and the mechanical operation for cost savings.

5. *Good judgment*—in personnel selection, planning and timing for change.

To this, let's add one more: *Training!*

Coaching

By Dave Hagenbuch

Successful advertising space salespeople are not born. They are made—and much of their development is the responsibility of the publishers, sales managers or advertising directors who supervise them. Some training executives describe "coaching" as the most important sales training technique available to management. They say that nothing will improve a sales representative's performance more than regular coaching . . . on-the-job coaching.

Coaching is a very specific training technique designed to strengthen a salesperson's skills by putting training to work. It is done on joint sales calls when a manager has the chance to watch a salesperson working with customers and prospects, observing his strengths and weaknesses. On the spot, a manager can see if a salesperson is developing good working habits, selling habits, and sales techniques. (Please note that not all joint sales calls will involve coaching. You could be solving a "problem situation." Or, you may be sharing a new presentation with a particular sales rep.)

Before you begin to plan coaching sessions, you must be able to distinguish between sales calls and coaching sessions. As a young sales manager, I was so intent on selling the business that I was not a good coach. I felt that selling by example was the key to training. I knew that there were sales to be made and that was the goal for the day. With some maturity and more responsibility, I have learned that you learn more by listening and observing and can contribute more to your salesmen.

Who should be coached and when? The question really should be: Who needs the most help?

There are certain signs that one of your salespeople requires *special* coaching: declining sales; too few calls; a fall-off in communications; reports or phone calls constantly detailing problems; too much entertaining; poor planning; and a poor attitude or lack of enthusiasm.

Do your homework

Before actually making a joint sales call, you must be thoroughly familiar with your people, their accounts and agencies, their challenges and their abilities. There are a number of tools you can use to do your homework before you head out on a coaching session:

•Sales reports—to see what has happened on previous sales calls. Study these for content and value.

•Itineraries—to check on planning and coverage.

•Correspondence—to learn what has been communicated and how. Sales letters often tell how the salesperson sells.

•Sales and contract records—for sales results.

•Research—as it pertains to the customer.

•Your editorial and publishing programs—how they relate to the customers and prospects.

•Expense reports—to get a feel for sales costs.

Some companies maintain a coaching file for each salesperson to record the information on the coaching sessions. A fact sheet should include the following:

•Reasons for the coaching sessions. What prompted them?

•The coaching objective. What do you plan to accomplish?

•The results of the sales calls. Who was called on? What happened on these calls?

•Corrective action. This is a written record of what you and your salesman agreed needed to be done as a result of the calls and the coaching session.

•Follow-up. Was corrective action taken?

Planning for calls

The scheduling of sales calls should be left to the salesperson, but your objective should be to get exposure to different accounts and agencies over a period of time. This is also smart business. If you lose a salesperson or if one becomes ill, you can fill in for that person. As a sales manager, I made it my business to know as many people as I possibly could.

How long should the coaching session be? Full-day sessions (*i.e.*, full days of sales calls) are most effective. Several days are best. When you travel with your reps, you can see how they handle themselves in different situations . . . on calls, after hours, planning the next day's schedule, follow-up on administrative details, etc.

Coaching guidelines

Keep the following questions in mind during coaching sessions:

•What is this salesperson's attitude about his job, the company, his customers and prospects, the magazine?

•How does he plan his calls?

•Is he well-dressed? How well does he use basic sales techniques such as establishing an objective for the call and communicating that objective to the person called upon?

•Does he listen? Does he use the magazine's research and promotion material effectively?

•Does he know the editorial content?

•Is he flexible and well-informed?

•How do the customers and prospects relate to him?

•Does he close sales?

The objective of a sales call is to promote action immediately or for the future. In coaching, you have to resist the temptation to jump in and control the interview when you see the salesperson is failing to communicate. If you see a sizable sale being lost, you may have to move in and take control.

On some joint calls, you may decide in advance to share part of the presentation or to actually handle the complete call. If so, tell the salesperson what you plan to accomplish and what to look for. Training consists of teaching, demonstrating, and helping salespeople perform.

The post-call discussion

It isn't necessary to critique every call. Depending upon what transpired, a casual comment may be enough. At other times, you'll want to bring up a sales approach that may have been overlooked, or you might say something like, "Here's another way to handle the objection the agency brought up, etc."

If the salesperson really needs a constructive evaluation of the call, then go into more detail, but don't try to cover too much at one time. You run the risk of destroying his confidence. Your job is to build people, not destroy them. A good approach is to ask how the salesperson felt about the call. Were there things he would like to change if given the same sales situation again?

After you have made a series of calls with a salesperson, you are ready to present a formal review. To make your critique effective, you should be very specific:

1) Define the salesperson's problems and/or opportunities for growth.

2) Suggest action to be taken.

3) Establish a timetable if necessary.

4) Tell the salesperson the results you expect and make sure that everyone understands what is to be accomplished.

This report should be put in writing and a copy kept in your coaching file.

In addition to coaching sessions, there are many other ways you can offer constructive suggestions. Supply your salespeople with books and memos with helpful sales ideas. Check by phone on their progress; respond to their sales reports; read their correspondence and help them improve it. Continue to give them sales training exposure. Keep them informed on what the company is doing and, most particularly, what's happening on the magazine.

In setting goals for your salespeople, remember that they want to improve, they want to grow, and they want to work with managers who will help them attain their goals. They want to work for coaches, not cheerleaders. Make them reach higher than they might themselves. Let them know that you expect good things from them. Coach them honestly and constructively and watch them grow. They will. And so will you.

Motivating salespeople

By Dave Hagenbuch

One day, I had a talk with a successful salesman about his motivation.

"Well, Dave, I'm in this for the money," he said. "That's what makes me run." But as we talked more about the business, his company, and his publisher he further commented "I wonder if they really appreciate the job I'm doing."

"Are they paying you well?"

"Oh yes, but they never sit down with me and compliment me on some of the sales I've made. All they say is, 'You're ahead of budget,' whatever that means. On my previous job, we had a good team, we sold a lot of business, and we had a lot of fun; and when we did something good, the publisher called, or sent a note, or boasted to the

other salesmen about our accomplishments. I really miss it."

A research organization asked several thousand executives the following question: "What are the most serious faults of executives in dealing with their associates and subordinates?" Of the 15 to 20 reasons given, the top five were:

1) failure to see the other person's point of view (this was the most common fault);

2) failure to show appreciation or give credit;

3) failure to size up employees correctly;

4) lack of leadership;

5) lack of frankness.

In the case of the salesman I just mentioned, it was

apparent that he needed to be appreciated. He wanted some credit for his sales successes.

The behaviorial science laboratories have turned out all kinds of information on what motivates people, and some publishing companies have become more sophisticated about motivation. Much of it gets back to good old common sense.

When you consider the things that *you* like, that cause *you* to be successful, you'll often find those things that motivate your salespeople. Appreciation or recognition for the job that has been done. Praise. The feeling of being in on things; being part of a team. An opportunity to grow, to become a better salesperson or to move into management. Yes, they want good working conditions and competitive pay, but these are not major problems in publishing circles. More important are good communications and leadership.

Maslow's motivation theory

Abraham Maslow created the most quoted theory about motivation in what he called his "need-hierarchy" approach. Basically, the concept is that there are five levels of needs that people share and a person will not move up to the next level until he or she has satisfied the one preceding.

The first level deals with *physiological needs* such as the need for warmth, food, shelter and protection. Next are *security needs* which relate to the security of a job and income. Once a salesperson achieves a comfortable economic level, he wants assurance he will stay there. He doesn't want to worry about the loss of his job, his income, his home. Money is a motivation here, but as salespeople reach a comfortable level, it becomes less of a motivator.

Social needs Maslow called "love." In business we think in terms of "belonging." People like to belong to a group with which they identify. This is the sales team on a magazine.

The next level is *esteem* and this has to do with one's ego . . . such things as status, recognition, prestige and a high evaluation of oneself.

Finally, one reaches *self-actualization,* the highest level, which is self-fulfillment . . . mastery of the job . . . being as much as you can be through your work.

While each salesperson has his own needs to be fulfilled in a way that best suits him or her, we can use Maslow's thesis as a guide. Management can help people satisfy their physiological and security needs with money. Leadership can help them fulfill their social needs of belonging to a team. And working for a *cause* (goals and objectives) is an approach to self-fulfillment. As a manager of salespeople, using Maslow's concept, your challenge is to put together a combination of money, leadership and a cause that is meaningful to each individual. That's a very personal challenge, and it means getting to know the ambitions, desires, fears, and emotional make-up of each salesperson.

Frederick Herzberg developed what is known as the motivation-hygiene concept which is the result of studies to determine which factors contributed to job happiness (or satisfaction) and unhappiness. Among the leading satisfiers are achievement, recognition, the work itself, responsibility, advancement, and remuneration. The lack of certain factors—such as the lack of company policy and administration, recognition, supervision, remueration and inter-personal relationships—cause dissatisfaction.

This brings us to the question of what is a profes-sional salesperson. In my judgment, a professional is a highly motivated individual who knows what he is doing, believes in it, and loves it. In addition, he has those qualities that cause people to put him in the professional class—such things as honesty, sincerity, dependability. The old cliche that a good salesperson can sell anything is pure bunk. A professional takes pride in what he is selling and wants to offer something of genuine value to his customers and prospects.

Space peddler or professional?

A lot of salespeople are unsuccessful because deep down inside they do not believe in their magazines. They are not sold on the power of advertising or the effectiveness of the medium they represent.

At times, this happens because the salesperson isn't digging for facts or the manager hasn't helped him to truly assess the value of the publication to the reader. Often, the salesman has made no sincere effort to even read his own publication to say nothing of learning about the function of a magazine as an advertising medium, or he hasn't related the medium to the advertiser's marketing or advertising objectives and/or goals.

Is this a professional salesperson? Of course not; this is just another person peddling space. Unfortunately, there are hundreds of salespeople just "filling up" space. There are *professionals* out there, some truly *great* ones, but they are the ten percenters.

All of this presents a real challenge for management because the average salesperson is not beginning to produce the amount of business for which he is capable. Some don't care. Others become lazy. Then, unfortunately, you have those who work hard but not effectively because they do not know what they are doing. No one has properly trained them.

How does sales management motivate these different types of salespeople? Recognizing that people differ in their needs, it becomes an individual thing. One person is satisfied just to get by. Another is constantly striving for improvement. Then, there are the top producers.

Still, there are many things that you can do to create an atmosphere that is conducive to motivating salespeople. To recap, here are some motivational ideas:

1) Help your people set realistic business and personal goals and objectives. Help them become achievers by working with them toward the achievement of these goals and objectives.

2) Help them do a better job of planning and organization so they can cover their territories more effectively, more efficiently, and more productively. Get involved.

3) Use a combination of discipline, praise, and recognition to develop a more cooperative attitude on administrative details. Use your sales controls (sales reports, itineraries, sales control charts) to monitor business.

4) Keep a flow of positive communications and keep your salespeople informed. This way, you'll pull them together as a team.

5) Train them. Develop them, particularly in selling skills. It will help them grow as communicators.

6) Back them up with good, benefit-oriented promotion and advertising. Give them research—market research and media research—to document your sales story.

7) Be more than a manager. Be a leader. Be a coach. Salespeople don't want to work for cheerleaders. They

Using Sales Meetings

The sales meeting is an excellent opportunity for you to motivate your sales force to become more effective and more productive. While there is a place for motivational speakers and films, in my judgment these can serve only to complement your efforts. The primary motivation should come from you as the leader of the sales team.

Be sure that your sales meeting is informative, upbeat, educational, motivational and fun. That's quite a combination, but it comes through concentrating on a few fundamentals:

•Plan well in advance of your meeting date and communicate your plans to your sales force. I have received many calls from publishers who say "We're planning a sales meeting. Will you participate?" I say "Fine. When is your meeting?" The answer is, "Next week or the week after next." That's poor planning.

•Check all facilities for meeting purposes. Will they have the equipment you need? Is there a good atmosphere for a sales meeting?

•Establish a purpose, an objective, for the meeting. Communicate this to the sales force and make it meaningful to them.

•Develop a meeting that has a good mix of company knowledge, job knowledge, and selling skills. Make sure your meeting is structured so that everyone can participate. Get the salespeople into the act. People learn more in an active environment.

•Build in some recreation and relaxation.

•Bring in outside experts in your industry as well as your editorial and other staff people on a selective basis, but make the participation of the salespeople the major portion of the meeting.

•Screen all talks or presentations for content and timing. Prepare your opening and closing remarks.

•Check and recheck all meeting equipment.

•Stick to your time schedule. Start on time. End on time. Have regular breaks scheduled.

•Don't try to force too much information on the attendees. Avoid gripe sessions. Keep all discussions on the track.

•Open up the meeting by getting the salespeople receptive to the information you are going to give them.

•Close your meeting on a high note. If you have a long meeting, schedule a break 20 to 30 minutes prior to the end.

You can also schedule mini-sales meetings from time to time but these should be planned in advance.

Of course, traveling with your salespeople provides an excellent opportunity to get close to them and learn what motivates them. Remember that you'll need to maintain a relationship that is business-oriented. You're the coach. You're the leader. Your salespeople must respect you.

want a coach who can show them how to do it and help them do it.

8) Treat them fairly in evaluating them and compensating them.

Be a self-motivator

Now let's concern ourselves with you. How about you? Who motivates you? The things we look for in a professional salesperson apply to you as a manager and a leader as well. Sound judgment, enthusiasm, honesty, integrity, dependability.

The attitude you bring to your job will determine your effectiveness in motivating your salespeople. If you are down and lack enthusiasm, you will have a negative impact on your associates. You have to be the biggest self-motivator on the staff. If for some reason you don't have the right attitude, then change it. Think about the positives of your job, your company, your field or market, your associates. Think of the great contributions of your publication to the welfare of people. Build up your enthusiasm and watch your salespeople get swept up in it.

You show me a team of salespeople who want to win and I'll show you increases in ad pages, market shares, and profits, because the enthusiasm, the confidence of this team will build positive buyer attitudes. An important management exercise is to list all of the positive things you have to sell. Build presentations around these. Forget the negatives. They can be road blocks to success.

Sure you have to be a realist, and yes, you must make improvements in your product, methods of distribution etc., But do this in your planning time. In your regular working hours, those hours devoted to sales management, concentrate on any benefits that the advertiser can enjoy through doing business with you and your salespeople. Do this and *you'll* sell more business. Do this and your *salespeople* will sell more business. Do these things and you'll increase your own income and job satisfaction.

Motivating salespeople

By Milton F. Decker

What makes one salesperson outperform another? What is the key ingredient in getting maximum performance from each salesperson? How can a publisher or sales manager get his or her sales staff to sell more effectively, efficiently and professionally?

These are the questions most often asked by concerned publishing executives—and they are more relevant in today's uncertain and tight economy than ever before.

While there may be no one panacea that provides a simple answer for the publishing business, our research and work with a variety of publishers, both large and small, indicate that there are some market-tested steps which have helped develop a key factor that's too often neglected or overlooked by publishing management. It can be summed up in one word—*motivation.*

Much has been written and studied on the factors which go into motivating employees generally, but relatively little is available on motivating the salesperson—and particularly those whose job it is to sell a high-priced intangible such as space or time.

The problem of motivating is hardly new. In fact, some 20 years ago, the American Management Association reported on how industry was currently attacking the problem of selecting and holding salesmen. Some 143 companies selling tangible goods and services were included in a study which provided some guidelines on "the weaknesses most frequently found in salesmen."

Here are the results when companies were asked to list the number one weakness of salesmen:

* 28%—Poor planning and organization of time and effort
* 24%—Lack of motivation
* 7%—Failure to develop prospects and get new accounts
* 6%—Insufficient study of new products and applications and failure to push them
* 6%—Uncooperative attitude and failure to get along with customers.

Thus, 71 percent of all first-place mentions encompassed the five weaknesses listed above. Other shortcomings received no more than 3 percent of the mentions.

The importance of motivation is also underscored when the same group was asked about the characteristics of the ideal salesman. The need for motivation was ranked second, following the generally desired trait of "health and energy," an obvious quality essential for drive and ambition to succeed, without which there can be no motivation.

Of all the characteristics listed, it was found that *motivation was the single most important factor that differentiated the successful salesman from his contemporaries.* And because it is so vital to success, its measurement and development is highly important in terms of

your advertising volume.

It is also a characteristic we can do something about—as opposed to a number of other valuable traits such as emotional maturity and empathy, both of which are important to sales success. But emotional maturity and empathy are intangibles and if they have not already been acquired as individual traits, it's often too late to develop them. Dependability, perseverance and freedom from sensitivity are the signs of an emotionally mature person. The ability to size up a person, to know when the individual is wasting his or her time on a hopeless prospect and how the salesperson adjusts to the temperamental differences in customers are fundamentals of empathy.

But how can we instill flexibility, judgment, dependability and/or perseverance in an individual if they are not already there? These are the characteristics which we look for and hope to find in the original selection of our salespeople.

Motivation, on the other hand, can be stimulated and developed through tested techniques and proven selling principles, many of which haven't changed over the years. Yet, they're often forgotten, overlooked or neglected.

To improve the motivation of any worker, it is essential to understand the basic factors which motivate all people. There are a number of studies which have been made on the motivation of workers at various economic levels which can be applied to or adapted for the sales area.

In a recent issue of *The Harvard Business Review,* Harry Levinson talks about "the general crisis in motivation" in American industry. When asked "What is the dominant philosophy of motivation in American history?" there is near unanimous agreement: It is a "carrot and stick" philosophy of reward and punishment. Levinson claims the central image in that approach is a picture of the jackass, calling such a philosophy "the great jackass fallacy." Workers respond by trying to get more of the carrot, while protecting themselves from the stick.

Enlightened management is turning to newer managerial devices by giving more responsibility to employees, developing new compensation incentive programs, providing adequate sales training activities and helping employees overcome communication blocks in working out their own solutions.

Levinson concludes that leadership is the key. But leading is more than a matter of pronouncing cliches. Leading involves an understanding of motivation, and the way to start is by countering the jackass philosophy in their own organizations.

In 1959 Frederick Herzberg and Associates in Pittsburgh published a study entitled *The Motivation to Work.* It was based upon in-depth personal, investigative research among a panel of engineers and accountants who were asked to explain what made them feel good about their jobs. Five factors were mentioned most often in the 475 case histories on attitudes about their work. Listed in order of frequency of mention, the five factors were:

1. *Achievement.* This was mentioned by 41 percent who talked about something they had done which was successful.

2. *Recognition.* Here they told how someone recognized their good work and complimented them—a pat on the back from a customer, boss or associate.

3. *The work itself.* This factor involved work that was interesting, challenging, varied or that could be carried through from beginning to end. They got satisfaction from working at creative tasks.

4. *Responsibility.* Here people talked about jobs they

Account Analysis and Evaluation Form

Account_____Salesperson _____
Division_____Date_____

The purpose of this form is to provide some specific guidelines to help in identifying key factors affecting the account. Through rank or weight of as many points as possible, we can arrive at a better definition of what our overall sales strategy on the account should be. When complete, it should provide the basis of our sales "game" plan—both immediate and long-term.

CURRENT STATUS

Running _____Non-running _____Last ran _____
How close are we now? _____

CURRENT MEDIA PATTERN (list pages)

Ad Age_____pgs. Newspapers _____Regional _____
Vertical_____Other_____

FUTURE MEDIA PLANS_____

INFLUENCE OF DECISION MAKERS (Rate from 1 to 10)

Agency Media ___   Account Prod. Dept. _____
Agency Account _   Account Ad. Dir. _____
Other Agency ___   Account Top Mgr. _____
Comment_____

ATTITUDE OF KEY DECISION MAKERS

	Exc	Good	Fair	Poor
Toward publication	( )	( )	( )	( )
Toward our field	( )	( )	( )	( )
Toward you	( )	( )	( )	( )

Comment: _____

HOW MEDIA DECISIONS ARE GENERALLY MADE

Seasonally ( ) Calendar year ( ) Fiscal year ( )
Opportunistically ( )
Other _____

Planning period _____

OBJECTIVES OF ADVERTISING

Creative Approach (basic appeal, consistent theme, opportunistic, dramatic, etc.)

_____

Primary Audience (% men-women, income, education, etc.)

_____
_____

Other_____
_____
_____

MEDIA BELIEFS AND PRACTICES

Rank importance of following to key decision maker or promotion director

Total circulation ( )	Editorial climate ( )
Target audience ( )	Dramatic space units ( )
Lower unit costs ( )	Consistency ( )
Lower CPM ( )	Mdsing and promotion use ( )
Influence of sales force ( )	Influence of ad. dept. ( )

Other beliefs or practices_____
_____

SUMMARY OF OUR PROBLEM

_____
_____
_____

OUR BEST OPPORTUNITY (Rank)

Competitive sell ( ) against _____
Idea sell ( ) such as _____
Dramatic unit ( ) like _____
Opportunistic ( ) i.e. _____
Combination sell ( ) with whom_____
Concentration on K.D.M. ( ) _____
Influence sales staff ( ) _____
Special research ( ) Comment: _____
_____

MATERIALS AND HELP NEEDED (Rank)

Special factual presentation ( )
Editorial presentation ( )
Showmanship idea pitch ( )
Direct mail program ( )
Special promotion ( ) indicate type _____

Management coverage ( )
Other ( ) _____

OTHER COMMENTS: _____
_____

did without supervision and for which they were fully responsible.

5. *Advancement.* This meant the employee was promoted and in half the case histories the promotion was a surprise. While it usually involved increases in pay, it was separated from salary as a factor in itself in this study.

All of these factors revolve around the idea that people want to grow and develop professionally in their work. The results of the Pittsburgh study indicate that when people can realize their hopes and ambitions in the work they do, they like their work, derive pleasure from it and enjoy a high level of satisfaction with their jobs.

The conclusions of the Pittsburgh and later studies point up the fact that no matter how pleasant the working conditions or how fairly people are treated, they do not really do their best until they have the freedom to show what they are capable of doing. This means giving them the responsibility for the job and recognizing successful work, preferably by promotion which invariably brings its own monetary rewards.

The previously mentioned AMA study on selecting and holding salespeople brings these generalizations on motivating most workers more directly into focus in the sales area. That research indicated that these three points were motivating factors:

1. Remuneration and the desire to make money
2. Recognition from superiors, friends and family
3. Economic security.

In the same vein, the National Society of Sales Training Executives summarizes the general motives for success under the broad heading of "security, opportunity and recognition."

Thus, there is a preponderance of evidence to indicate that achievement and recognition of a job well done, whether in sales or on the assembly line, is almost equally important as economic incentives in motivating people.

The recruiting, training and compensating of salespeople—all vitally important in a successful sales operation—are being covered in detail in other sections of this chapter. What we are concerned with here are the elements of managing and motivating your sales staff to raise its sales effectiveness.

Now let us consider the vital area of supervision of salespeople. Here again, I feel, we can turn to some tested techniques in the field of supervision, generally that apply across-the-board and can be adapted for our use.

And when we talk about supervision, the key word is *participation.*

Douglas McGregor, professor of management at MIT, sums up the importance of participation this way:

"One theme ... recurs with remarkable frequency in reports of the experimentation of management pioneers. Its significance ... depends upon whether it is imbedded in a philosophy of management or regarded as merely another fancy technique. This recurrent theme is that of 'participation.' "

Its implications and applications can be found in more recent research such as that of the Survey Research Center and in the work of the Research Center for Group Dynamics and among dozens of other social scientists and consultants.

Certainly an idea which is so often reiterated can—and should—be applied where possible to the supervision and motivation of salespeople in the business of representing the publishing industry to the advertising fraternity.

Since all of the studies and research previously mentioned concern themselves primarily with selling in general, however, the question arises as to whether the sale of magazine space is unusual or different than other forms of selling. And if so, why? Can we realistically apply the general techniques which have been discussed to improve the motivation and performance of a high calibre group with unique sales problems?

A profile of the magazine salesperson and his or her responsibilities should be helpful in defining the type of individual with whom we are dealing. I think you'll agree that there is a definite difference in the way the salesperson has to sell and in the approach to interpreting the values of his or her product compared to other selling responsibilities.

The generally high quality, intelligence and expertise of the magazine salesperson should make the individual amenable to any logical suggestion or approach that is designed to improve the salesperson's performance.

Today's salesman or saleswoman should become a kind of committee chairperson or account manager within his or her company. This individual should be able to exploit the resources of the company in serving customers. And, in general, I feel most magazine representatives have that capability. The salesperson should also be a diagnostician.

Charles Goodman, professor of marketing at the University of Pennsylvania's Wharton School, puts it well when he says a salesperson should be:

1. A problem-identifier
2. A problem-solver
3. A prescriber.

Yet, "selling is very, very inefficient compared to what it could be," says Edward Feeney, vice-president of systems performance at Emery Air Freight. "They're calling on the wrong accounts. They're calling on accounts that give them all the business that they can. They're calling on people they think can make buying decisions when, in fact, they do not or cannot make them. They are efficient in talking about what their product does—but not in how it fills the customer's need, because they haven't probed to find out what those needs are."

While there may be no one way to find the right answer to this basic problem, there are some fundamental and market-tested steps which have succeeded where more glamorous and ideological approaches have failed. Usually they fail because they lack the one ingredient that sustains a salesperson's interest and provides the individual's motivation and *personal involvement.* Many sales-training programs and sales-development plans miss this vital point. They talk to or tell the salesperson what should be done "in 10 steps to closing a sale," etc., rather than getting the individual involved in becoming a part of the act.

Any program of sales development designed to help motivate salespeople should always include these three vital elements which are so important to a successful sales operation:

1. Provide built-in sales support and sales direction against your best prospects . . . *in terms of their objectives.*

2. Get your salesperson more directly and personally involved with your key prospects—so the individual feels responsible for his or her performance.

3. Develop on-the-job training through participation *and with sales tools* that will be accepted *and requested* by your sales force.

It sounds fairly simple, doesn't it? But after a score of years in the sales and promotional area, I've found the most difficult chore is getting management to think in terms of selling *its publication's benefits to meet its prospect's advertising objectives.*

Too often the sales ammunition provided the sales force talks about how big and beautiful you are with no regard for your advertiser's interest. An expensive and glamorous slide show extolling only the virtues of your publication can be a complete waste of time and money compared to a well-researched, simple 8½" x 11" printed presentation that answers your prospect's question, "What's in it for me?"

Elementary? Of course. But it continues to amaze me in discussions and research with publishers on their selling problems how often they neglect the basics. Or how often they are looking for the big play (or bomb) that might solve all their problems.

This is preliminary to the fact that the steps outlined below are not sensational, unusual or necessarily original. But they are neglected! Maybe it's because they represent a plain, pragmatic how-to approach that calls for thought and effort . . . with few, if any, dramatic overtones.

The obvious is often overlooked in our business—and in many others as well. But if the obvious is logical, basic and sound, it should work. They provide an effective and economical approach that should help you meet the generally agreed-upon need for motivation and participation of your own sales staff to improve its selling efficiency.

These steps are all keyed to helping your staff sell better. If you can get your sales staff to sell more professionally in terms of your prospects' objectives, they'll be motivated to sell better.

So try these motivating steps on for size. You may like them and they cost very little to develop.

1. Concentrate against your target opportunities

An obvious point. Why even mention it since it's been written and brooded about so often? But again, I am continually astounded at the lack of organization and direction so many publishers have in terms of their areas of greatest potential.

While the temptation to cover everything and everybody is always present, experience has shown that it is *always at the sacrifice of time that could be spent more profitably on extra effort against a key prospect*—a third or fourth call, a followup letter or direct-mail series.

A strange paradox is the fact that it is more often the publisher with the smaller sales staff—who can least afford the luxury of covering the whole waterfront—who feels he or she is not getting full value from the salespeople

unless they're making *x* number of sales calls on different prospects. The larger consumer magazines with sufficient manpower have found one successful formula to concentration through the Classification Manager System. In this approach one person is assigned to a major revenue area such as liquor, drugs, food and others. But even with such a setup, the need to concentrate effort against the greatest potential is still an essential element in getting more efficient sales performance from each salesperson.

The target account approach simply calls for a bit of extra planning for the most effective use of time and effort against prime prospects. Thus the first step is *a realistic evaluation of your prospects* so that a specific and total sales strategy can be developed for those major accounts selected for concentrated effort.

A list of questions (see the accompanying box) which has been successfully used to establish the criteria for evaluating key prospects provides a more intelligent basis for selection than a hit-or-miss approach.

These have proven particularly helpful for the individual salesperson handling the account. And it is vital that the individual be involved in this preliminary process right from the start. It should be a joint venture of both management and salesperson. It is also preferable to have the recommendation come from the salesperson, along with the reasons for selection.

This procedure not only helps management define where special effort should be made but places the primary responsibility on the salesperson to think more constructively about *how the individual's time can be spent more productively.*

The next step provides the platform which automatically compels the salesperson to think constructively about his or her target accounts.

2. Evaluate the sales strategy for key prospects

This is probably the most important exercise of all to get the salesperson more interested and involved in his or her accounts. Surely it's the best way for the individual to know more about his or her accounts than any competitor. Chances are ten to one they won't be doing it!

An Account Analysis and Evaluation Form is a helpful device to set up logical procedures after key accounts have been selected. (See the accompanying article for a generic outline of the more important facts necessary to evaluate an account. A bit of editing can easily make it suitable to your specific needs.)

An Account Analysis and Evaluation Form is guaranteed to make each salesperson think more professionally about each account. It forces the salesperson to do the homework necessary to be more effective than the writing of call reports on the same accounts would produce.

More importantly, however, are the corollary benefits that can increase the salesperson's overall effectiveness on all accounts. These benefits include:

• Setting a pattern for organization and work on all other calls and accounts

• Building and maintaining a higher level of professionalism in selling against major accounts at all levels

• Developing a planned program which will in-

Account Analysis and Evaluation

The answers to these questions should help provide a basis for the final selection of target accounts.

- Does the account represent sufficient immediate *and* long-term potential?
- Is it a leader in its field so that it will have an influence on its competitors?
- Is there a favorable climate at both account and agency toward your publication? (To push water uphill on a target account *may* not be worth the time and effort.)
- Is there a weak spot in their media pattern that we can best exploit?
- Is it a classification or media group which represents real opportunity for an extension of any new sales material developed?
- Can special promotion or presentations be equally applied to comparable accounts?
- Is someone else on the staff working on the same type problem? (Duplication of effort can be wasteful.)
- Do their advertising and media objectives fit logically into your story?
- Is the timing right within the next few months for extra effort?

If all of these questions can be answered affirmatively and positively, you should have the basis for a target account.

clude various forms of communication techniques against key targets

- Sharpening his or her skills in uncovering new opportunities for your magazine to interest stubborn accounts
- And above all, by demonstrating how the salesperson can use his or her limited selling time with each prospect more effectively and efficiently.

Ideally, this information should be updated monthly with additional weekly progress reports for target accounts. Without such followup, the preliminary work in establishing the plan would lose much of its value.

These two preliminary and participatory steps provide the opportunity to bring into the salesperson's work situation a variety of on-the-job satisfaction, to tap the individual's creative imagination and ingenuity and encourage the development of personal responsibility for his or her accounts. Thus, the individual sees it as his or her own work, opportunity and responsibility.

With the evaluation completed and agreed upon, the following steps are important in implementing the program and making it work.

3. Develop your basic selling proposition

We can assume that you already have established your sales approach based upon current research which should "position" your property in terms of its competition. But a review is always in order to be sure you have analyzed all the factors and available data to be certain that your own "USP" (Unique Selling Proposition) is as strong as you can make it.

In such a reexamination these questions are worthwhile asking yourself:

- Is our research up-to-date?
- Is it comparable to our competitor's so that we can favorably position ourselves—statistically and factually?
- Do we need new reader research (either subscriber or syndicated studies) to fill in any missing demographics?
- What new editorial developments or sales and merchandising angles can make our book more unique in its field—again, to position ourselves more advantageously against our competition?

Answers to these questions are often found as the following steps are executed.

4. Develop the basic selling tools

Once the target group has finally been agreed upon, experience has indicated that promotional concentration should be leveled at that area first.

All the facts available should be analyzed to find the best approach to put your magazine in the strongest position.

The content should be created and directed to the interests of *the buyer in the buyer's own field*. It should talk in terms of *the buyer's business* and the problems the buyer has in the selection of effective media.

For, *it's the content that counts*—not pretty pictures in glowing color. The research, demographics, result stories and cost factors should all be organized to help define your own USP. Some of the most important sales I ever made selling for *Life* magazine (some years ago!) were made with just this kind of approach. And there was always a wide variety of more glamorous techniques available—but they simply didn't work as well as the basic formula of facts related to the advertiser's objectives in the kind of proposal form that individual has been used to studying in making his or her own marketing decisions.

It is often worthwhile to get outside advice and a professional review of your current material. A fresh look at your selling strategy and promotional props could prove to be a profitable investment. There are dozens of competent freelancers and promotional specialists available to handle such an assignment for a reasonable fee that would not commit you beyond the needs of your specific problem.

Adaptations of the across-the-desk approach can also be readily created into slide, card or chart form, as required, as long as they factually and dramatically develop the agreed-upon Unique Selling Proposition.

5. Prepare the followup material

This important element in selling and promotion is another procedure that is too often neglected. And it is seldom planned in advance as it can be. Lack of time because of heavy workloads also limits this kind of effort—no matter how sincere your salesperson's intentions may be to follow up calls.

Ready-made material should be available for followup data after each call, such as individual proposals, thank-you letters and specific direct-mail programs for your hottest prospects, etc. They should be planned, prepared and available for most basic sales needs.

It is doubly important that this kind of effort be

made when working with a limited sales staff where complete coverage and followup is difficult to achieve. Thus direct-mail promotion must take the place of personal selling in many cases. And it always adds an extra dimension in getting better coverage of prospects fast and efficiently.

This is often the extra plus in making the sale; and we know historically that no matter how creative and hardworking a salesperson may be, he or she simply doesn't have enough time for thorough planning and follow-through on all accounts. The salesperson needs help in this area—particularly if he or she is not the creative type. Some of the most personable salespeople I know find it hard, if not impossible, to write a coherent forceful sales letter.

6. Create specific promotions and sales ideas

It is especially worthwhile in the target account area to search for that something extra—*to sell an idea* rather than just space. A special merchandising plan. An insert promotion tied to your prospect's advertising objectives. A mini-research project among your prospect's customers will sometimes uncover new angles and ideas. (Several phone calls will often suffice.)

As a salesperson digs and probes an account in depth, covers as many people as possible and all the angles, the ideas will start to come. They'll come just from involvement and *the extra interest* your salesperson shows in the account.

And don't think the advertiser won't start to recognize this extra effort.

It is in this area, particularly, where the Account Evaluation Form makes an important contribution. The whole purpose of this exercise is to *participate* in managing his or her accounts, so that the individual knows more about the advertiser's objectives than anyone in the latter's shop and certainly more than the salesperson's competitors. Thus, motivation is automatically built in when the salesperson can find new opportunities to make the sale.

7. Consider your future promotion

In addition to special presentations, specific promotional ideas and followup direct mail material, there are numerous other projects to which thought and planning should be given. Some of these I am sure you have thought of, but they are submitted as a checklist for consideration as a part of a rounded promotional program:

- Followup brochures or folder
- Editorial response and reader interest
- Advertiser results
- Complimentary copy special inserts
- Monthly media department mailings
- *SRDS* promotion on new theme
- Regular press releases
- Direct-mail promotion—against target accounts, against small accounts, against prospects in competition, against running accounts.

And don't forget the constant need to revise and update your mailing lists at frequent intervals.

Thus, the basic ingredient for the success of any program is to *organize the plan and follow the strategy.*

All the forms, formats, checklists and proposals aren't worth the paper they're printed on if some one person doesn't take the responsibility to *follow through!*

It's not tough to do. In fact, it can be fun—particularly working with each salesperson on *his or her problems and accounts.* This is the key to motivation. It comes from doing the job itself—and seeing a program develop. The army calls it O.J.T. And they've made on-the-job training work for them.

If one person can't be found or spared within the organization, again it is economically feasible to go on the outside to set up the program in its early stages. Later it can carry itself when procedures are established.

Actually, I've found this program to be especially effective for the publisher with limited manpower and a small sales staff. It's designed for concentrating personal coverage where it counts and maintaining direct-mail coverage in those areas where personal sales calls are too costly or where immediate potential is limited.

The current competitive financial climate brings pressure on both publishing management and its sales force. It may cause some to look for a new prescription, a new "something" to improve their sales picture.

One final plug for staying with the basics: Despite the fact that they are unglamorous, unoriginal and undramatic . . . they work.

What makes a salesperson run?

By Frederic C. Decker

What motivates salespeople? What makes Sammy (or Sandra) run?

I've asked that question of a roomful of magazine publishing people.

The answer always comes back like a chorus. Money! Money, they say, is what motivates salespeople.

I wish I could agree. If it were that easy, motivation—that most prized and elusive of sales traits—could be bought as readily as a sack of potatoes.

But, as many sales managers have learned, money or its equivalent is only part of the answer. And the secondary part, at that.

In his book, *Self Renewal,* John Gardner says that some people think that motivation is an ingredient that can be poured into people, like gasoline into a car.

Motivation is already within people, to greatly varying degrees. So the sales manager's job is, first, to hire salespeople whose motivation level is high and then to create an atmosphere which encourages motivated performance.

For a successful selling result give me an atmosphere built upon the intangibles discussed below, rather than one in which money in the form of bonuses, awards, contests, extra commissions and spiffs is looked upon as the magic that makes salespeople hustle.

The atmosphere of motivation is built upon:

Recognition. There is response to the prompt, enthusiastic and visible plaudits of both superiors and contemporaries. Money is a dandy *symbol* of recognition but it is applause which makes us *want* to surpass our best achievement.

Participation. People want to share in common goals. They want to be proud of their team, of the place where they work, of the magazine they work for. People want to *belong* and they don't want to turn in a performance which makes them less highly regarded within their group. An atmosphere of motivation is one in which the salesperson's contribution of experience, ingenuity and talent is welcomed and encouraged.

Opportunity. Not only must there be opportunity for growth and advancement—but the salesperson must be given the confidence that it exists and that he or she can achieve it.

Security. It is unlikely that salespeople have mistaken illusions about whether or not their company is stable so there's not much that can be done about that aspect of job security. But even the most self-confident need frequent reassurance of their own status. A measure of a sales manager's skill is the ability to communicate that confidence without continually verbalizing it.

Communication. An openness of communication upward and downward in the organization gives the salesperson the sense of being listened to and the feeling that opinions and reports are valued. Listening is the first step in communication. And communication is not always verbal. We are quick to interpret the closed door, the lift of an eyebrow, the set of the shoulders ... especially if the shoulders belong to the boss.

Accomplishment. Communication helps to give salespeople a needed sense of accomplishment, a sense of knowing where their work fits into the whole. People need to know that their work is important, beyond the limited scope of their jobs. They need to know about the goals of their company and how their own contributions help in the achievement of those goals.

Salespeople do respond to these stimuli. The degree of their response relates to their ego drive, which is a product of sheer physical energy and of what some psychologists call "a state of tension caused by unfulfilled need."

The sales manager's job is to create that environment in which the flow of energy is encouraged and the psychic needs can be fulfilled.

It takes a bit of doing. It would be easier if money could do it alone.

Sales compensation: Designing the right plan

By James B. Kobak

One of the more difficult publishing management tasks is the development of a compensation plan for advertising salespeople. Ask any publisher at just about any time about the system used currently. The publisher will almost invariably tell you that it isn't working as well as he or she would like and that a change is under study. About the only consistent feature in most companies is that the system is changed every three to five years.

This is not as surprising as it may seem. Different people may be involved as time goes on. Economic conditions are not always the same, either overall or in specific industries. Company profits can have ups and downs. Salespeople mature—and may become more or less productive. Customers change. Where a magazine is in its life cycle can be important, too.

There seems to be a need for a periodic review of any basic system. And the chances that the magazine's system can be applied to any other are very slim.

Because of the great variety of magazines and plans, I have not discussed in this piece any specifics in the way of dollar amounts, commission percentages and the like.

The basic objective of any compensation arrangement would seem to be to develop the most sales at the least cost. But that definition is not good enough. Better is this: To develop the most profitable sales at the least cost. This means that the first step is to determine which really are the most profitable pages in both the short and long run. Besides developing profitable sales, the plan must:

- Result in a living wage;
- Be equitable to all;
- Give a fair value for the services rendered;
- Result in competitive pay scales;
- Steer·salespeople to the most desirable type of sales;
- Not result in overcompensation;
- Be simple to understand and administer.

It's not easy to get all this into one plan.

Before we go too far, let's discuss just what kind of people salesmen and saleswomen are. I do not believe in the stereotype that a salesperson can be led in any direction and made to work harder just by putting a compensation carrot in front of that person. Certainly there are some people who are like that, but there are just as many who will work just as hard and effectively for a straight salary as for a commission. And there are all kinds in between.

But as long as there is just one who will respond part of the time to an incentive, we had better build one in, difficult or not.

Cash compensation method

There are a number of ways of determining the cash payments to salespeople. These vary from a straight salary to straight commission and include everything in between.

- *Straight salary.* This sounds like the simplest, and it is in many respects. But there must be a periodic renegotiation. When that time comes there must be a reason for changes. That reason normally has to do with

results; so there is not as much difference between a straight salary and a commission system as may appear.

A straight salary is best for a new person who could not quickly achieve a sales level high enough to earn a living wage on a commission basis. It might also be used for someone whose work is more of a service nature, handling a group of large customers. There are some cases, too, when selling is a team effort, or the result of heavy research and promotion, and the sale cannot be attributed directly to any one individual.

When territories or assignments are changed, too, it may be necessary to put a salesperson on a straight salary basis for a time. And there may be some people who simply work better this way than with a direct incentive.

- *Straight commission.* This is based on the sales in a territory or for specific accounts. It is at the opposite end of the scale from a straight salary. From a manager's standpoint it would seem to be the most equitable and the easiest to administer.

But it isn't that simple. The potential of different territories varies. In a time of recession the salesperson may not earn an adequate wage, no matter how hard he works, through no fault of the individual. More than once a straight commission plan has had to be amended when disaster struck (such as it did in Detroit during the oil crisis).

On the other hand, when on a straight commission, the salesperson in some instances may reap the benefits of a windfall which may not really be deserved. And the person suffers because there is no underlying certainty to his earnings.

From a control standpoint, too, there may be difficulties. When a salesperson is doing well under a commission system, that individual becomes quite independent. This can make it difficult to change territories or assignments, even though this may be best for the magazine.

- *Combination plans.* Many attempts have been made to ameliorate the difficulties which are inherent in either the straight salary or straight commission plans. These can work for a time, but must always be subject to adjustment as conditions, the company and the employees change.

And in the end, like all other compensation, any plan eventually comes down to a question of individual negotiation. The plain fact is that it is very difficult to quantify the contribution any single person makes to an operation.

Some of the combinations of salary and commission which are commonly found include:

1. *Salary plus year-end bonus* gives recognition to the results of a year, but without a specific formula being used.

2. *Draw against a commission* is an attempt to give greater certainty and to level earnings throughout the year. It does not, however, eliminate the basic problems of the straight commission. In many cases, publishers with this type of arrangement have had to allow salespeople to keep their draws even though they were not completely earned.

3. *Salary plus commission* guarantees the salesper-

son a base, no matter what, while retaining the incentive feature of the commission. This is usually paid for sales over a certain amount—called a "bogey" or "quota." Most publishers try to arrange that the salary will be somewhat around 70 to 80 percent of the total compensation, although this varies from company to company.

Bogeys are determined in a variety of ways. Most common is a percentage of sales in the territory for the prior year, although this is varied for the potential in the territory, the stage of the salesperson's development, and other factors.

Commission plans differ as much as the ingenuity of the people who create them. They can be a level percent of the sales produced by the individual. Or they can rise in steps as sales increase, under the theory that this gives more incentive to sell additional business.

Sometimes they decline in steps, a practice which at first may be difficult to understand. The reasoning behind this is that a salesperson can only handle so much business well. If you keep increasing the commission at the same or at an increasing rate, he or she will earn a great deal, but many potential customers will not be covered. The obvious move at this point is to split the territory. But if the salesperson is earning too much, there will be resistance. Since the salesperson apparently is one of the best, the choice is: (1) split the territory, give lower overall pay, and risk losing that person; (2) split the territory but guarantee the individual's pay until that person can build it up again; or (3) retain the original plan and not gain additional sales. None of these is acceptable, so you try to avoid the situation with the reducing commission rates.

Sometimes the percentage is geared to net sales less salary and expenses. This is an attempt to relate to the relative profitability of each person.

Normally you would expect that a commission based on dollar sales would be most logical, since a dollar earned for a color change is just as good as one for the basic page. There may be some instances, however, where page sales may be a better measure. This would happen if the profits from color and other charges are not in the same proportion as those from the basic page sale, if the salesperson has no influence over the advertiser's use of color, if the need for filling the magazine with pages is paramount, or if the publisher wants to avoid increasing commissions when advertising rates are increased.

In a few cases commissions are determined on a group basis. This might apply to all the people in an office, to a group who handles one category of advertising and the like.

Other compensation alternatives

Creativity is also exercised in developing alternatives to cash payments. The idea is that income taxes may be avoided, husbands or wives may be enlisted to spur their spouses on, capital gains may be received rather than ordinary income or the psychological effect of the alternatives may be better. Most common alternatives are:

• *Payment of expenses* for items which are beyond the normal travel and entertainment, but still are closely related to the business so that an individual may be able to deduct them for tax purposes. These might include club initiation fees, dues, and/or expenses, purchase or rental of an automobile and the like.

• *Fringe benefits* are also part of the compensation package, as they are for all employees. Medical, pension and profit-sharing plans are certainly all pluses to employees, but the effect on sales would be very difficult to trace, if there is one. In some cases key employees, whether salespeople or others, may be granted special benefits such as dental payments, college education for their children and other items.

• *Stock, stock options, phantom stock* and the like are sometimes given (or sold) to key employees in all departments to make them feel that they have an ownership interest and to give them a chance to gain major benefits at capital gains rates. This type of incentive is particularly helpful in getting the right people when starting a new enterprise.

• *Opportunity bonus* is a method of giving an extra incentive for developing certain types of business. An amount might be given for each new account sold, or for upgrading the amount an advertiser spent, or for selling a page in a directory in addition to space in the magazine, or for any other item which the publisher is pushing.

• *Prizes* are used in some companies to reward extraordinary performance. This might be in the form of a trip for the leading salesperson and spouse, attendance at the "winner's" sales meeting at some exotic place, a television set, etc.

Some companies deal with their salespeople as independent contractors who are running their own businesses. This sometimes is done even though they work only for one organization, although there are possible tax problems in doing this. The theory is that the salespeople feel that they are in business for themselves, will work harder and spend less. The company avoids payroll taxes. The employee can deduct part of his or her house and other expenses as business costs for tax purposes easier than the individual might if he or she were on the payroll. The salesperson also can set up an individual Keogh Plan for retirement. Compensation plans can take just about any of the forms discussed above.

A key disadvantage is a loss of a certain amount of control over the salesperson.

The true independent representative who works for a number of magazines normally is paid a flat percentage of the sales the individual generates although there are arrangements where expenses are paid separately. And in some cases a basic guarantee is included.

Setting up a plan

Simple though most plans seem in concept, in practice there is an enormous number of decisions, compromises and negotiations which must be contended with almost on a daily basis. The first difficulty comes on initially setting up the plan or in making major changes.

The problem starts with the fact that you already have the salespeople. They are being compensated in some manner now, and you cannot change their pay levels or methods without some good reason. You may have to resort to some elaborate and ingenious calculations to develop a formula which results in a good incentive, does not change present levels much and can be applied fairly to all. In some cases, exceptions have to be made for certain salespeople in order to develop a plan which will stand the tests of fairness and time.

Administrative difficulties

On a day-to-day basis there are all sorts of relatively minor points which come up. Some individuals become very picky and legalistic about their rights. At times you may wish you had never started the plan. But you are dealing with the most important item the salespeople have—their income—and they must be dealt with fairly.

24

Some of the most frequent areas of difficulty are:

• *Split commission.* Often an advertiser will be in one city and its agency somewhere else. They must be called on by different members of the sales staff. The commission is split between them, normally equally, but in some cases in some other ratio.

• *Increase in advertising rate.* With our current inflationary economy, rate increases are needed on a pretty regular basis. The questions come up: How much harder is it to sell at the higher rate? Is an increase in commission an undeserved bonanza? How should the commission be handled when it happens?

If the commission is on a page basis, there is, of course, no effect (which may not be correct). If it is on a dollar basis, the salesperson may be getting pay increases for no real increase in productivity.

The situation is handled in a number of ways, ranging from no benefit to full benefit with most publishers settling on about half of the amount of the rate increase applicable in figuring the individual's commission.

• *Increase in cost of living.* Sales personnel suffer from inflation along with everyone else. Keeping their compensation at an adequate level can be handled in a number of ways. As discussed above, they can be allowed commission on part or all of advertising rate increases, can be included in any overall company wage increases, or in some other manner. There is always a danger, however, that the cost of selling will get out of line.

• *Credit and collection.* Most publishers try to keep the sales staff out of the credit and collection process. The extending of credit and the collection of accounts is normally reserved to the home office, usually an accounting function.

From the credit standpoint, it is felt that the sales staff would be too free in granting extension. Collections do not involve a salesperson's real skill and could ruin relationships which have been built up. On the other hand, commissions normally are paid only on accounts collected, so the salesperson has a large stake in the payment. This division of duties often results in clashes between sales and accounting people.

• *House accounts.* Just about every magazine has so-called house accounts on which no commissions are given. These are the accounts serviced by the publisher or someone else who is not primarily a salesperson. Periodic review of these is needed to be sure that they might not be handled better in the normal course of advertising sales.

• *Windfalls.* At times an advertiser will embark on a blockbuster campaign for which the sales staff can take no real credit but on which there would normally be a large commission. The question arises as to whether there should be a full commission given on the sale. This is usually settled on a case-by-case basis.

• *Split territories.* At times a territory becomes too big for one individual to handle. The publisher wants to split with another person to get better coverage. This often happens when the first salesperson has done an excellent job, but just has too much to do. The problem is how to arrange the split and still not hurt the compensation of one of the best producers. Normally some sort of phased formula is arranged to give that individual several years to get sales back up to their previous level in a smaller territory.

• *Differences in territories.* Some territories do not have the potential of others because of a lack of prospects, but it is still important that they be covered well. How do you adequately compensate a person who may be doing a fine job but who cannot earn the commission the individual deserves because of the nature of the territory? This is done through a special compensation arrangement, by giving him or her a few lucrative accounts in another area, or in other creative ways.

• *New salespeople.* A new salesperson can rarely earn enough to fit into a commission plan. That individual needs a salary or a nonreturnable draw adequate for his or her existence, plus an understanding of when the employee enters the commission plan.

• *Low-profit business.* At times a publisher will accept business which does not yield the normal profit (a large insert, a remnant and the like). In this case a special arrangement on the commission must be made.

• *Non-productive work.* Some salespeople are asked to do work for the magazine on which they cannot earn a commission. This might include training a new staff member, developing promotion material or any of many other things. If this type of work becomes meaningful, an adjustment is required.

• *Sale of different products.* Although it is pretty much of an axiom in the magazine business that a salesperson is most effective when he or she works on only one product, there are some individuals who can handle more than one effectively. At times it is the only way a territory can be covered adequately. Difficulties arise because you do not want any of the magazines to be neglected. The system must take into account that one product may be easier to sell than another, the salesperson has a liking for one more than the other, and the page rates are not the same.

• *An individual's pay gets too high.* It is easy for a salesperson and family, like the rest of us, to become accustomed to spending an additional amount. Like in golf, the best we have ever done becomes "normal." Anything less is very difficult to imagine—and to live within. There can be times when the compensation of a particular salesperson seems to be higher than that individual's efforts are worth, even though the formula in the compensation plan works out that way.

Although most managers profess that they do not care how much a person is paid as long as he or she produces the business, in practice this feeling may not carry through. There is, too, always the fear that if someone earns too much, that individual may become unmanageable. The answer, when this conclusion is reached, is to change the plan—and hope you can hold on to the employee.

• *Expense account limitations.* Every company has some limits to the amount of expenses salespeople are allowed to have, whether the rules are explicitly written or not. It is difficult to set hard and fast rules because situations vary. Some salespeople can use expense accounts very effectively in selling. Others have little need for this. And, of course, filling out an expense report has become a high art form in some firms.

Most companies today require coach airplane travel, limit meal and hotel costs (with different amounts for different cities) and designate the conventions each staff member goes to. The overall approach, however, in the magazine business is not toward pennypinching in the expense area.

While everyone tries to set up a plan which will last for all time, there inevitably are times when a change is needed. This should not be done lightly or just because there are complaints.

No plan is perfect, as you have probably gathered by now. There are always exceptions and adjustments to be made. There will always be complaints. Changes require reorientation and new adjustments. And in the end, in any plan, there is some kind of negotiation with the salespeople each year no matter how carefully it has been designed.

Sales compensation:
What are <u>other</u> publishers doing?

By Karlene Lukovitz

"You've got to pay them well enough so that they stay with you, yet badly enough so that they work hard. Tell me what's simple about *that.*"

So one magazine publisher sums up his feelings about ad sales compensation plans. Though many publishers would strongly disagree with his management philosophy, few would deny that designing and implementing sales compensation systems is one of their toughest and most critical challenges.

It is also an on-going challenge: Most publishing companies change their sales compensation plans about once every three to five years, according to publishing management consultant James B. Kobak. Even publishers who have used the same basic plan for decades generally recognize the importance of re-evaluating their plans in light of changes in the economy, in sales territories, and in other factors.

Most would also agree that developing a sales compensation plan is, or at least should be, a highly individual enterprise based on a thorough evaluation of the company's financial situation and specific goals (see accompanying side bar).

"No publisher who deserves the title would adopt another company's compensation plan just because it works for that other company," says one business magazine publisher. "At best, such an approach would produce less than maximum sales; at worst, he could end up losing his sales staff *and* his shirt."

Nevertheless, publishers and advertising directors can clearly benefit from keeping up on what types of ad sales compensation systems other publishing companies are using. Publishers who are not satisfied with their current systems may find a plan being used by another company that could be adapted to their own needs; those who are basically satisfied with their systems may pick up ideas for fine-tuning them.

With this in mind, FOLIO recently interviewed 20 publishers and advertising directors from both the consumer magazine and business magazine industries to find out what types of sales compensation systems they currently use, why these systems work for them, and what systems they have found do *not* work for them. Several consultants who have helped publishers develop sales compensation systems, as well as executive search firms that deal in the advertising field, were also interviewed.

Base + commission still predominant

Almost any ad salesperson can confirm that most publishing companies still use one of the several standard sales compensation plans or a variation thereof.

And, according to publishers and consultants alike, the base salary plus commission system remains the one that is most common in the magazine publishing industry.

Why does this type of plan continue to be the front-runner? "Since it's the plan used more than any other, one has to come to the conclusion that base salary plus commission is the one that *works* best for most publishers," says Mort Grossman, president of Market Development Associates, a publishing management consultant firm.

The simple but time-honored concept behind this system is that a salesperson works best when provided enough security, via the base salary, so as not to be overly preoccupied with financial concerns, and enough of an opportunity to enhance that salary, via commissions, that he or she is motivated to achieve beyond the norm.

"A company that uses this type of plan will generally establish a fairly substantial base and arrange the commission as a supplement that acts as an incentive," notes Grossman.

"This kind of system provides a lot of flexibility for management to truly reward those who deserve it, and a lot of opportunity for the individual salesperson," says Don Mates, national sales manager for Bill Communications' *Sales & Marketing Management.* Mates sees one of the system's major advantages in its allowing for salespeople to be rewarded over the short-term. "Rather than having blue-sky expectations, they can see where they are in relation to realistic projections made for the year," he says. "Yet they know that they can basically write their own tickets in building their incomes."

Using a bogey

In most base-plus-commission plans the salesperson begins earning a commission only after he or she has brought in a pre-determined quota (bogey) of net sales or pages.

Publishers who base the bogey on net billings frequently say they do so because of a drawback in using pages: Salespeople given a page quota, they say, will try to reach that quota quickly by promoting more frequent black-and-white page buys instead of a smaller schedule of four-color pages, which yield more profit for the magazine.

Publishers who prefer the page quota, however, argue that it is not only easier to administer, but provides a better incentive because it is easier for the salesperson to keep track of his progress.

Publishing consultant David Orlow, president of Periodical Studies Service, points up another problem with net billings quotas. "If you base the quota on dollars, incentive payments are automatically raised every time ad rates go up," he says. "You can avoid this by adjusting the scale at which the plan pays off, but this can be interpreted by salespeople as an attempt by the company to rip them off."

Several publishers who do use dollar-based quotas report that they have a policy of allowing 50 percent of any dollars resulting directly from the increase to be counted toward sales commissions quotas and that their salespeople seem to consider this arrangement fair.

Another fundamental decision in developing a quota system is whether to establish one quota over which the salesperson receives a constant commission on all business, or set up a graduated commission system in which the salesperson earns increasingly larger commissions at increasingly higher levels of business above the initial bogey.

Constant commissions

Many publishers—particularly, it seems, publishers of more established magazines—swear by the method of constant commission percentage above a quota in conjunction with a base salary.

"I've looked long and hard—I've used just about every sales compensation plan at one time or another—but I keep coming back to this one," says Robert Potts, publisher of *Dun's Business Month.* At *Dun's,* salespeople receive a base amounting to about two-thirds of total income and a single commission percentage on all business above their individually determined net billings quotas.

"I can't see straight commission p'ans; a salesperson's income jumps up and down so much that you always end up putting the staff on draw—and that involves too much fancy accounting," Potts says.

"Other types of plans, such as salary plus incentives on a page basis, are all too complicated and too difficult for the salesperson to keep track of," he says.

"This plan rewards both the salesperson and the publisher well," says Potts. "Although the quota isn't based on pages, the salesperson knows he has to carry a certain number of pages in order to start making an additional 8 percent on everything he sells, so he works hard. Yet, he's got that base—that floor that he knows can never drop out from under him. With, say, an established base of $35,000 on this plan, anybody who deserves it makes $47,000, and anyone who doesn't levels out at $35,000."

Potts strongly believes that making major variations of the terms within the basic compensation plan from salesperson to salesperson only serves to aggravate counterproductive speculations among salespeople as to who's getting the best deal.

"I think all of a magazine's salespeople should be on the same compensation plan, or as close to the same terms as is possible," he says. "We do this with the exception of the bogeys, which are individually adjusted. But the ideal, as far as I'm concerned, would be if they all had the same bogeys, too. However, that may be impossible, since there are always factors such as seniority and the difficulty of the territory to be taken into account."

Although Gralla Publications also uses a system of base salary plus constant commission over quota, its philosophy on drawing up terms with salespeople differs markedly from the philosophy of Potts.

Each year, Gralla starts from scratch, completely re-evaluating the base salary, commission rate and quota for *each* of its more than 60 salespeople.

"This is an operating method that has evolved here over the years that works very, very well for us," says Larry Gralla, president of the company. In addition to producing impressive sales growth, he says, the system has several other advantages.

"With this system, the company does not lock itself or the salesperson into long-term arrangements that can prove inequitable to either of them in light of the uncontrollable effects of changing industry conditions," he says. As a result, he notes, Gralla salespeople are not subject to extreme upswings and downswings in their salaries from year to year due to fluctuations in markets. "We lower our quotas substantially when an industry served by one of our magazines is in an adverse climate," Gralla says.

The terms of each salesperson's yearly plan are based on an examination by management of several factors, including the particular magazine's share of market, industry conditions, and "reasonable estimates of the high, low and probable sales figures for that magazine for the year," Gralla says.

The method has also produced a low rate of sales staff turnover and unusually close communications between the sales staff members and management, he claims. "We discuss his or her plan with each and every one of our salespeople, which gives us an opportunity each year to talk with them about their relationship with the company, their future here, and anything that may concern them."

But there are also major disadvantages to the system—so major, in fact, that Gralla discourages others from trying it.

One problem, he points out, is that "the system is very dependent on the confidence of the sales staff in the integrity and openness of the salary administrators.

"If you don't have this very high level of confidence, you must have an on-going system that the staff members can feel secure knowing will be in place from year to year," he says. "We tell our salespeople right up front that everything is arbitrary, in that management can change all of the terms every year."

Yet another variation on the base salary plus constant commission over a quota system is employed by Gordon Publications. Rather than the usual yearly evaluation, Gordon sets individual quotas and commission percentages for its salespeople that generally remain in force for two or more years.

Ken Nelson, president of Gordon, believes that a yearly upward adjustment of a sales bogey, even if accompanied by a raise in base salary, can lead to discouragement on the part of the salesperson—which in turn can lead to sales staff turnover.

"Instead, we give each salesperson a bogey to work with over a two- to three-year period, with the commission on the increase in sales shown in his or her territory over that period of time," Nelson explains. "This gives the salesperson the chance to really build the territory and his earnings."

He adds that Gordon is a growing company that tends to hire aggressive, young salespeople with little or no prior experience and then train them. "The larger, more established business publishing companies manage to hold on to their salespeople with their yearly systems, so those systems must work for them," Nelson concludes.

Graduated commissions

As already noted, some publishers prefer a graduated or multi-level commission system along with a base salary instead of a single quota and constant commission.

"I'm a great believer in having the override for a commission that gets more interesting as the volume of sales goes up," says Peter Diamandis, vice president-group publisher, woman's group, and publisher of *Wo-*

man's Day, CBS Publishing Group.

"If, for example, the salesperson has a $30,000 base salary with a quota of 50 ad pages to sell, and he gets 3 percent on all pages sold over the 50 up to 60, he should get 4 percent on the next ten pages over 60, and so on.

"I prefer this as an incentive system because there is an efficiency in sales volume: the larger the volume, the larger the portion of every dollar that goes to the bottom line, because the smaller the cost of each sale.

"I believe that the individual always works primarily for himself," he continues. "If the commission is graduated, the salesperson makes more money as he brings in more volume, and so does the company. I love to see salespeople get rich, because it means the company is getting rich, too."

Penthouse has been using a base salary plus graduated, per-page commission system for the past seven years, but is now considering changing that plan, according to Marianne Howatson, vice president, director of sales for the magazine.

"We've kept the same basic quota each year, in terms of a specified number of pages that must be reached to start receiving per-page commissions, but each year we've built in different levels of rewards for various levels of pages sold over the quota," Howatson explains.

"But we're now beginning to feel that the system is out of date," she continues. "It doesn't seem to be responding to the needs of the salespeople. Giving them a couple of hundred dollars per page was fine when our page rates were lower, but it does not seem to be enough now in light of inflation."

Howatson had been getting input from the sales staff and from management as to how they would like to see the system changed and is now reviewing these ideas, she notes.

"The graduated commission system is, I think, especially good for a growing magazine," says one advertising executive who started out on a magazine with such a plan. "It probably creates more incentive than a non-graduated system with a single quota. Still, the single quota system is the most manageable one for a larger company. It would be very difficult to administer the levels of payments involved in a graduated system for a large sales staff."

The advertising director for one business magazine points out that publications with graduated commission plans sometimes sweeten the deal by making the commission payments "retroactive." That is, once the salesperson reaches the first quota, the commission percentage for the first level is applied to all of the pages he sold up to that quota, as well as those above it.

In some cases, all pages sold in the first level are advanced to the second-level commission percentage when *that* level is reached, and so forth, he notes.

Draw against commission

"I don't believe in salaries for salespeople," says David J. Cleary, Jr., executive vice president, general manager and group publisher of Crain Communications. "They need a constant motivator—a carrot out in front of them—and no ceiling on what they can earn. That way, they're constantly thinking, 'If I make that one extra call today, I may make a sale.'"

Draw against commission has been the predominant system at Crain for the 30 years Cleary has worked there (though, he notes, individual publishers can and do develop their own systems). In that time, Cleary reports,

he has never felt the need to alter his support of the draw system.

Cleary also says that there have been "extremely few" instances of salespeople "going into the red" on the system—that is, failing to make the page or net billings quota for the commission upon which they draw each month on the assumption that the quota *will* be reached.

At Crain (and most other companies with a draw against commission plan), draw is nonreturnable so that the salesperson never finds himself in the position of having to pay the company money. "In the few cases in which a problem has come up, we've carried the person over to the next year," Cleary says.

Actual commission percentages paid by the various Crain magazines vary widely due to the differences in the magazines' total ad revenues and so in the amounts of billings being carried by the salespeople.

Gene Fahy, ad director of Fairchild's *Women's Wear Daily,* also believes strongly in the draw against commission system. "I would guess that we pay higher total sales income than any other publication," Fahy claims, pointing out that his two top salespeople made $174,000 and $135,000, respectively, last year. Total draw can reach up to 70 percent of anticipated total income, he says.

Fahy based individual commission percentages on the difficulty of the territory, with "higher commissions on tough sells and lower ones on easier sells."

He says he has never had a salesperson fail to make his or her quota. But, he adds, he sometimes uses a salary-plus-commission plan for new salespeople in order to ease them into the job: "After they hit a certain initial quota, I might then double the commission to bring them toward what the other salespeople are earning."

"I think that newer publications need to provide bigger compensation opportunities because their salespeople need more motivation," says Mike DeSimone, associate publisher of *Regardie's Business & Real Estate Magazine of Washington.* "Draw against commission is the best way to accomplish this, in my experience. It provides the incentive to reach a goal while not allowing your salespeople to go hungry as straight commission plans can. Hungry salespeople spend their time job-hunting instead of selling and are too concerned about their financial problems to do a good job during the time that they *are* selling."

But, he cautions, the total income and number of accounts for each salesperson must be carefully monitored as the magazine grows under the draw system. "As ad rates go up, incomes can get out of hand, and you may also find salespeople trying to take on more and more accounts to hit that commission quota and start collecting the additional money sooner," he explains. "If you allow a salesperson to control too many accounts, you're going to be in a terrible situation. He'll be in the driver's seat because he knows you're in trouble if he leaves."

A salesman's view

Some salespeople contend that there is a better alternative than either the base plus commission on quota system or the draw against commission system.

"The base salary-plus-commission-on-quota plan is just too long-term in mentality—it doesn't give the salesperson the short-term, quick results that he or she needs to stay motivated," says one salesman for a major men's magazine.

"On the other hand, draw against commission

doesn't make any sense either; no salesperson has to be *on* a draw against commission system to know that he has to *make* a certain amount of business. Every salesperson knows that his bread and butter, his minimum goal, has to be to return at least as much business to the company this year as was produced last year."

Too many publishers, this salesperson contends, set unrealistic quotas that are beyond the salesperson's reach. "One salesperson I know gets 10 percent of his salary as a commission at the end of the year if he makes his quota, but the quota climbs every year. So even if he makes it one year, he knows the chances get slimmer and slimmer that he'll make it the next.

"Another salesperson was recently given a quota that includes a large chunk of new business that was promised by a particular advertiser to the magazine," he continues. "But the new business doesn't look like it's going to come through. So now he's got to meet a quota that includes the old one plus $100,000 in this 'promised' business. That $100,000 is business that has never been in the magazine before, yet he'll receive no commission on that amount even if he *does* somehow manage to bring it in."

Instead of quota systems, he asserts, salespeople should receive a good base salary and a commission on every page sold. "Nearly every salesperson I talk with agrees that working under this type of a system would make them work harder—and, as a former advertising director, I know it doesn't cost the publisher any more than other types of plans," he adds.

Such a system is not generally found except in cases of magazine start-ups, according to Elsa Ross, vice president of Gardner Associates, a New York-based executive search firm whose clients include several consumer and business magazine firms.

Geyer-McAllister Publications has such a system, however, and has found it to be quite successful, according to Arthur Spence, the company's president. The company pays a base salary plus a commission on all published ad pages, plus an end-of-the-year incentive bonus based on the overall increase in business the salesperson has produced during the year, Spence says.

Straight commission plans

Although very few of the publishing executives interviewed use straight commission compensation plans, the ones who do expressed strong advocacy of this system.

An example is Owen Deutsch, advertising director of *Chicago* magazine. "We pay a straight percentage commission on each ad page as soon as it is published," he says. "I know that some magazines have very elaborate types of compensation systems, but I believe that complicated systems are counterproductive.

"Salespeople are money-hungry—money is their prime motivator, and that's how it should be," Deutsch continues. "I also believe it is the salesperson's psychological nature to be motivated on a short-term basis. So, although this may sound rather Pavlovian, I find salespeople work hardest if they know they're going to get a certain percentage on each page, and that they're going to get it *soon.*"

On the other hand, strong reservations about the straight commission system were expressed by some publishers and consultants who have had past experience with it.

Geyer-McAllister went to its current system eight years ago when it found its former straight commission system unworkable, according to Spence.

"When business is really coming in, the salesperson can make out very well on a straight commission plan—better than on a salary plus commission plan," Spence notes. "But the obvious disadvantage of straight commission is that the salesperson can also be destitute if business drops significantly for some reason beyond his control. We stopped our straight commission plan because some of our books are erratic in their ad business and we didn't want our salespeople starving to death."

Changing over to the current plan was "a very big job" due to increased administrative work it created, Spence says. "If a salesperson was making, say, $10,000 at 10 percent straight commission, we cut the commission in half to 5 percent on all business brought in, then took that half of the old commission to create a $5,000 base for him," he explains. "In real money terms, every salesperson ended up making more that first year than he or she had been making under the old system."

Unpredictability of income from the salesperson's viewpoint, as described by Spence, is one reason that very few magazine publishers employ the system for their regular sales staffs. (Straight commission is the usual arrangement with independent sales reps or "captive" reps—salespeople who work only for one magazine but cover their own expenses.)

Another reason is the "runaway income" syndrome already mentioned in discussing draw against commission plans. A plan based entirely on pre-determined commission percentages is clearly very susceptible to this problem unless steps have been taken to prevent it.

"There may be situations in which a publisher feels a straight commission plan is best, for whatever reason," says Grossman. "If there's going to be a straight commission plan, there has to be some kind of safeguard built in. There should be an understanding between management and the sales staff that the plan will be reviewed periodically and that it will eventually change once the magazine is established."

Proper base/incentive ratio debated

Because this problem can also occur in a base salary plus commission plan, determining what proportion of such a plan should be salary and what proportion commission is a major concern for many publishers.

"Unfortunately, this decision is based as much on traditional company policy as on any other factor in most cases," Orlow asserts. "The base salary portion ranges in the industry from a low base, accounting for about one-third of total compensation, to a high base, which would be about 70 percent to 80 percent of total," he says.

"Some salespeople think that some of the larger companies that put a cap on commission earnings by saying that they can't exceed 50 percent of the base salary are just being cheap," he says. "But this cap actually protects the salesperson from the mental let-down he might otherwise experience. Sometimes a magazine's market takes off and the salesperson's income jumps from $50,000 to $100,000 if there's no incentive limit. Then when it drops back to $75,000, where it should be, he thinks he's being cheated."

Orlow says he knows of several talented salespeople who are currently looking for new jobs because they feel it's only a matter of time until they're fired. No limit was ever put on their commission earnings and they have come to realize that their employers think that they are now being overcompensated.

"These people are now looking for other jobs with

the same pay as the ones they have," says Orlow. "But there are no such jobs, and that's the tragedy."

For this reason, Orlow supports plans that put somewhat more weight on base salary than on incentive earnings. "I think base salary should be 60 percent to 80 percent of a salesperson's *total* compensation, which means that he or she can still earn up to an additional two-thirds of the base salary amount in incentives," he says.

Ross of Gardner Associates, however, stresses that setting a too-low ceiling on commission earnings can be just as big a mistake as not setting one at all. "Any plan that has too low a ceiling destroys all of the salesperson's incentive," she says. "And, unfortunately, few companies set as high a ceiling on commissions as 50 percent of the base; most set a ceiling considerably lower than that."

Many firms limit commission earnings to $10,000 or less over the base salary, according to one industry source.

"I think commissions are being reduced on magazines controlled by a certain type of management person—the type who says, 'Let's cut the sales staff's commissions and we'll improve the bottom line,'" says one business magazine executive. "But what these people fail to understand is that this will also make them lose money by cutting their growth. If you plot the growth of magazines that have been acquired by big companies,

you'll find that in most cases they are not growing at anywhere near the rate they were before they were acquired."

Ross sees a slight trend toward greater advances in salaries than in commissions as a result of inflation. "Base salaries are definitely increasing at both consumer and business magazines," she says. "With the cost of living at the level it is today, you just can't pay as low a base as some companies used to pay years ago. Commissions are also increasing, but they're increasing to a lesser extent than base salary."

Salary plus bonuses

Although they are relatively few in number in comparison with companies employing salary plus commission plans, some consumer and business publishing companies find that a salary plus bonus plan works best for them.

Some of these companies structure such plans so that the great majority of the salesperson's compensation is in straight salary, with discretionary bonuses given on an annual basis.

Such systems tend to be found mainly in large, well-established publishing companies in which much of the salesperson's time is spent maintaining and servicing existing accounts, according to several executives interviewed.

In addition to yearly bonuses, an incentive is

'Sales compensation plans must be dynamic, goal-oriented'

Far too many publishers continue to practice wishful thinking about the results their ad sales compensation plans will produce instead of using such plans as dynamic, goal-oriented marketing tools, according to publishing consultant David Orlow.

"Most publishers have hopes about their magazines' advertising but no real plans to make the hopes a reality," Orlow contends. "Compensation plans are developed with some very general goal in mind, like getting more pages, with little or nothing done about defining specific goals and designing compensation plans to motivate salespeople to work toward these goals.

"In fact, under-articulated sales goals are in my experience, the single biggest problem with compensation plans—and even with advertising sales in general. Every other industry knows that the very base of any company's success is its sales/marketing management's ability to put sales compensation plans in sync with specific sales marketing goals."

In order to acomplish this, Orlow stresses, sales compensation plans must be viewed as dynamic rather than static. "Compensation plans must change every year because both sales problems and salespeople's problems are continually changing," he says.

Orlow uses the example of establishing a new magazine to illustrate how compensation plans must change along with a magazine's sales problems and goals.

"During its first two years, a publication most likely needs to bring in contracts, so the salesperson should get an incentive on every contract he brings in as well as a base salary," he says. "By the third year, the magazine may need to concentrate more on bringing in new pages on existing accounts, and so it should modify its compensation plan to provide for upgrading contracts, and so forth."

The compensation plan must also be dynamic in

order to accommodate the changing needs of salespeople, Orlow stresses. Accommodating these needs involves recognizing and dealing with both broad, natural conflicts between the salesperson's and publisher's goals and with the individual salesperson's changing goals, he says.

"The salesperson always wants to make more money," he says. "And a good salesperson always believes he or she is worth more money and is continually striving to get it. Good publishing management, on the other hand, is constantly striving to keep costs down.

"A good compensation plan will take this conflict of goals into account and take steps to accommodate it," Orlow asserts. "But as fundamental as this concept is, many, many people who design magazine sales compensation plans ignore it."

Another key consideration also involves a set of conflicting goals, but in the mind of the salesperson. "The salesperson always wants a good floor, or base salary, but he never wants a roof on commissions. That is, he wants the most security possible along with the ability to make as much money as possible," says Orlow.

"Neither of these desires is intrinsically more important than the other; they must be balanced so that both are optimized," Orlow says. "Yet publishers are constantly putting disproportionate stress on one or the other without consulting their salespeople. These two factors *can* be optimized, if only publishers would make the effort to find out about and accommodate the needs of the individual salespeople in their compensation plans. The conservative salesperson who has a new family is never going to be happy with a high commission, high risk plan, and the daring salesperson is never going to be happy with a plan that gives him a hefty base but very little room for incentive earnings. Again, this is a factor that is obvious but very often overlooked."

sometimes provided in the form of a group bonus pot that is shared if a particular goal is met or exceeded.

"In some cases the straight salaries in these plans are quite substantial; in others these salespeople are making less than many salespeople on base plus commission plans," says one publisher. "However, the salesperson does have a good deal of security and, often, a lot of non-taxable perks such as club memberships and very high or even unlimited travel and expense budgets."

Other compensation plans incorporate smaller, more frequent bonuses.

"We like to use fairly well defined goals and keep the plan understandable—not too complex," says Grant Allan, marketing vice president of Active Markets, which publishes *Sports & Athletes* and has recently purchased *Inside Sports*. "In addition to the base salaries, we set goals for individuals by issue and for the year, as well as group goals. We believe the salesperson should work for the group as well as for himself.

"Individuals who make their page goals receive issue-by-issue, per-page bonuses," he continues. "These page goals are based on the rate card, so there are no problems with salespeople figuring out where their revenue levels should be. There is also the chance for individuals to earn year-end, over-goal bonuses, and all salespeople share a year-end bonus if the group meets its annual goal.

"We don't limit bonus amounts; we like open-ended ones that encourage people to exceed, not just meet, their goals. This has been a very effective system for *Sports & Athletes,* and it is the one we'd like to use for *Inside Sports,* too."

Travel Agent, the top business magazine in number of ad pages (6,707) in the most recent FOLIO 400, also gives frequent bonuses in addition to base salary.

Each salesperson receives a quarterly bonus, says editor and publisher Eric Friedheim, "unless, of course, the issues for the quarter were down." Salespeople can also earn additional bonuses for making quotas on special projects and issues, he says.

Friedheim, like Allan, cites the goal of productive team work as a major one for using the frequent bonus plus salary system.

"We operate as a team: Everyone fills in for everyone else whenever it is necessary," he says. "We want to be able to handle an advertiser's question or problem, even if the person who is in charge of the account is sick or out of town. With the bonus system, we don't have to worry about tensions that would develop if a salesperson on commission felt another was interfering with 'his' account, or about getting dual commission claims on the same business."

The bonuses, Friedheim says, are based on the individual's level of experience and management's appraisal of his or her contribution to the magazine for the quarter.

"We've used this plan for the past 10 years and we've had no real problems so far," he says. "With the quarterly bonus, people don't have to wait until the end of the year to know how they're doing—the cash keeps flowing to them. We don't ever intend to go to a commission plan."

Although it is clear that salary plus discretionary bonus systems work for some publishers, others warn that "discretionary" can end up being interpreted as "arbitrary" by salespeople if they sense that management is in any way holding back on bonuses despite good performance, or is unfairly favoring one salesperson over another.

"The base salary plus discretionary bonus type of plan is not the best idea, in my opinion," says Ross. "If giving a bonus, and/or its amount, is based on the discretion of management, instead of being linked only to the person's accomplishments, the bonus could end up being linked to personality," she says.

Fahy of *WWD* agrees. "In my experience, a salary and discretionary bonus system encourages selling *inside* the office rather than outside of it," he says.

Straight salary

Straight salary plans are even rarer than straight commission plans, although one publisher of a small religious magazine who was interviewed did report that his one in-house salesperson is paid on straight salary. "We do it this way because he has other responsibilities in addition to sales," the publisher explained.

T&E coverage standard

Coverage of the salesperson's travel and other business expenses remains pretty much *pro forma* in the industry.

"Just about every company pays all T&E, though their policies as to what they'll *allow* as T&E vary," says Grossman. "Some publishers frown on large, expensive lunches and dinners and big entertainment bills and tell their salespeople to keep the T&E down. But it depends on the type of business the magazine is dealing with. If it's a business that requires that the salesperson move in wealthy advertisers' social circles, there is usually much less attempt to limit expenses—and in many companies, this type of spending is encouraged."

Grossman's comments are borne out by publishers of consumer and business magazines alike: Nearly all interviewed said that they do cover all T&E for their in-house sales staff. (Independent reps and "captive" reps—salespeople who work only for one company but, like independents, generally work on straight commission—are usually responsible for their own T&E.)

Many, however, said they do try to keep expenses within reasonable limits.

"We set a budget for each salesperson by planning out for the year where each will be going and how much it should cost, and we try to live within these budgets," says Nelson of Gordon Publications. "We do encourage them to use moderately-priced hotels, but we do not put limits on their personal entertainment or expenses—and we encourage them to do business entertaining.

"One company I know of limits its salespeople to $4 for breakfast, $8 for lunch and $16 for dinner, which can be difficult if not impossible to adhere to without the salesperson reaching into his own pocket," he adds. "We don't want our salespeople worrying about things like that."

A frequently mentioned area of expense cutbacks is automobile expenses. Several publishers said they no longer provide company cars, and one said his company will no longer cover rentals. But most said they still pay for rentals and gas.

Nelson has devised a policy for handling car expenses that he says works very well. "We used to give company cars, but now we give a car allowance," he explains. "That is, our salespeople are told we will pay for gas plus all other car expenses up to a certain limit. Then it's up to them to decide how they need to use the allowance, including what kind of car they drive."

Salesperson as profit center

Yankee, Inc., publisher of *Yankee, The Old Farmer's Almanac* and *New England Business,* deals with T&E as part of its somewhat unusual total compensation plan.

"We treat every salesperson as a profit center, meaning that we focus on what amount of every dollar brought in comes down to the bottom line," says Robert Pettegrew, Yankee, Inc. advertising director. "We pay a base salary that is competitive with other publishers in the Boston area, and a 2 percent commission on net sales that rises to 5 percent if the salesperson's quota is met. We also provide a pension plan and other benefits.

"In addition, we pay expenses. But we include expenses, along with the base salary and everything else down to paper clips and heat and light used, as part of the salesperson's cost of sales. And we have a policy that each salesperson's cost of sales cannot exceed 10 percent of his or her net sales.

"For example," Pettegrew continues, "if a salesperson is billing $500,000, we cannot spend more than $50,000 on him in total. It works well, because the more the salespeople sell over quota, the more the cost of sales goes down. The more they make, the more *we* make.

"We've found that $500,000 seems to be the magic break-even point at which the cost of sales begins to diminish to less than 10 percent. At $575,000 in billing, for example, the cost may go down to 9.5 percent, and down to maybe 9 percent at $600,000."

'Oddball' plans work for some

Some publishers have developed ad sales compensation plans that incorporate parts of the standard methods in unusual ways. And some publishers' plans have very little to do with any standard plan at all.

A fairly unusual system is used by *The Blood Horse,* which, with 6,097 pages, was the third largest business magazine by ad pages in 1981's FOLIO 400.

"We pay a guaranteed base salary plus a specified amount per-page per weekly issue up to the page goal for that issue, which is the number of pages brought in for that territory for the same issue last year," says Erbert Eades, advertising director for the company. "There is a bonus if the goal is reached for the issue. Then at the end of the month we add up the plus-goal and minus-goal weeks and if the salesperson comes out in the plus column, he is paid 2.75 times the standard per page rate, retroactively, on each page exceeding the goal."

The plan also offers a year-end group bonus jackpot to be shared if the sales staff reaches the pre-determined goal of increased pages for the year, Eades says. "Last year the staff was given a goal of a 7 percent increase in pages, and brought in a 9.47 percent increase," he says. "This was accomplished despite two rate increases of 25 percent each during the year."

Spencer Longshore III, advertising manager for B.A.S.S. Publications, describes a very unusual plan that has just been implemented by the company.

"We have three magazines; two are consumer magazines—*Bassmaster* and *Southern Outdoors*—and one is a trade publication—*Fishing Tackle Retailer,*" Longshore says. "Because the page rates for the magazines differ greatly, our problem was how to get our salespeople to sell all three of the magazines instead of focusing on one or two.

"So, we decided to assign a yearly bonus figure and page goal for the year for each magazine to each salesperson. If they reach each of these goals, they get the total bonus sum; if they don't, money is deducted from the bonus in accordance with the percentage of the bonus represented by the unachieved pages."

Once the salesperson reaches all three of his magazine page goals and receives his pre-set bonus sum, he is also given a per-page bonus on every over-goal page sold, Longshore says. The amount of this additional, per-page bonus is different for each magazine (it is determined by multiplying the per-page cost of sales for each magazine by that magazine's net page rate).

Though this plan may sound complicated, Longshore says it is already producing very gratifying results. As of January, *Bassmaster* was already 25.47 pages over its goal for the period through March, he said.

Another good example of a magazine that has developed its own breed of successful ad sales compensation plan is *Working Woman.* On this plan, the salesperson receives a base salary ranging between $15,000 and $30,000 plus a per-page incentive amount that increases incrementally each time another page is sold (the amount paid per page is capped at $500 so that a salesperson who reaches this sum is thereafter paid $500 on each page sold). This system, according to *Working Woman* publisher Jim Horton, produces "killer" salespeople.

Use of multiple plans

It should be noted that quite a few publishing companies, particularly the largest ones, use more than one type of compensation plan—and some use several types.

A good example is McGraw-Hill Publications Company, which uses "various configurations" of both the guaranteed draw plus commission and base salary plus commission systems on its numerous business magazines, according to John Murray, the company's controller of marketing operations.

Other types of plans abound

There are probably hundreds of other varieties of ad sales compensation plans being used by magazine publishers; new ones are being created all the time.

In fact, there just might be more than a grain of truth in a comment made by Mike DeSimone of *Regardie's Business & Real Estate:* "When it comes to ad sales compensation, there's no system that doesn't work for somebody somewhere."

A marketing approach to sales incentives

By Morton E. Grossman

When you do your ad marketing planning, do you consider sales incentives as a tool to help you accomplish your marketing goals? Or do you consider incentives as just another aspect of compensation?

Most compensation plans for magazine ad salespeople today have a provision for incentives—usually commission, bonus, or both. However, whether or not you have an incentive plan, your ad marketing can be improved through the strategic use of *special* incentives.

To see how special incentives can motivate your salespeople, let's examine a magazine publisher's typical ad marketing objectives:

1. Increase advertising sales in general.
2. Increase sales from current accounts.
3. Bring in new accounts.
4. Renew current accounts.
5. Sell or increase target accounts.
6. Sell more schedules rather than single insertions.
7. Develop new advertising categories.
8. Sell special issues.
9. Strengthen weak issues.
10. Improve share of market.

Once a publisher has established his marketing goals, he must plan strategies to accomplish these goals—strategies based on research, promotion, sales development and training. The use of special incentives, however, is one of the most effective strategies available to a publisher, because this strategy enables him to use his sales force more efficiently and effectively.

A publisher should always consider incentives when developing his marketing plan, for properly planned incentives can stimulate salespeople to put forth the extra effort needed to achieve his marketing goals. Furthermore, the more specific the incentive, the better the results.

Let's look at that list of marketing objectives one at a time and see just how publishers have used specific incentives to further their goals.

1. *Sales increases.* This is a universal goal, but simply having an overall commission plan will not necessarily motivate salespeople to make the special effort to sell more advertising. Here's how one trade publisher learned that more specific incentives bring better results. Although this publisher was paying a commission for all sales above a given quota, he found that sales goals were not being met. He then offered a special incentive: For each sales territory, every additional page sold in the current year over the previous year earned a bonus of $100.

When the magazine met its ad sales goal, salespeople and management all agreed that it was the special incentive that made the difference. Since that time, the publisher has used special incentives to achieve specific objectives (along with other marketing strategies) with great success. In fact, he now considers incentives as a strategic option for any advertising sales problem or opportunity.

2. *Current accounts.* Accounts that are already advertising with your magazine are often the most likely prospects for additional sales. Yet salespeople often chase new accounts instead of building up customers who are likely to buy more. The following situation illustrates that the more specific the marketing goal, the more successfully sales incentives can be employed.

This publisher, finding that his magazine's young, enthusiastic sales staff was not building up the old customers, analyzed competitive advertising records. He discovered that many of his current advertisers were either spreading their advertising around a large list of magazines, or they were advertising more heavily in the competition.

Realizing that these current accounts had great growth potential, he developed sales material—a market coverage story—that demonstrated the value of ad concentration in that magazine. Still, the staff was more inclined to use the material with new accounts rather than with the magazine's current advertisers.

The publisher then decided to use an incentive plan based on percentage increases from running accounts. A 10 percent increase in an account was worth $100, a 20 percent increase earned $200, and so on. Losses were deducted.

In the first year of the program, every salesperson made money on the plan. After the third year, the program was so successful that it was discontinued (having served its purpose), and a commission plan on all business was put into effect. Today, the magazine continues to show healthy growth.

3. *New accounts.* The publisher of a monthly special-interest consumer magazine had the opposite problem: a need for more new business. His salespeople spent most of their time with large, well established advertisers and rarely called on new prospects.

To solve this problem, the publisher used the special incentive strategy. A goal of 10 new accounts for each salesperson was established, and a bonus was offered for each new account sold. Furthermore, there was a special bonus for selling 10. (New accounts were clearly defined as those which had not run for at least one year, and which ran a minimum of three quarter-pages.)

Each salesperson was asked to make at least five calls on new accounts each month. Sales activity was monitored through call reports, both to make sure that calls on new accounts were being made and to guard against neglecting current accounts.

The strategy was successful. Each salesperson met or surpassed the goal of 10 new accounts.

4. *Renewals*. One magazine had a high account turnover. Although advertising levels were kept steady by new accounts that made up for the losses, the publisher knew that significant sales gains could be realized if the defecting advertisers could be kept.

The strategy chosen was to develop sales material based on a survey of reader purchasing patterns that demonstrated the continuing value of the readers as customers for advertisers' products. Sales meetings were held in which the staff worked on structuring pitches built on the purchasing survey.

This plan made considerable headway against the problem, but the publisher went one step further. He introduced an amendment to the incentive plan: a higher commission on renewals. Within one year, there was a dramatic increase in advertising. The publisher attributes this increase to the combination of the survey, the training, and the incentive.

5. *Target accounts*. At another magazine, target accounts were chosen every six months at a sales meeting. At these meetings, selling strategies were also devised for each account.

Progress was slow, however. There seemed to be a lot of talk but little action. After analyzing the problem, the publisher decided to set specific objectives at the next meeting when the targets were to be discussed.

Account X was to be increased by three pages. Account Y was to start with a schedule of six half-pages. A bonus would be paid for achieving target on every account, and in cases where progress was short of the goal, the bonus payment would be prorated. The result: The magazine got more advertising and the sales staff made more money.

6. *Schedules*. The new publisher of a monthly dealer magazine needed more contract business. His first strategic step was to put in a special sales incentive for advertising schedules sold. A higher commission was paid on accounts running with higher frequency. Normal commission was 2 percent. For 3X, he paid 2.5 percent, for 6X, he paid 3 percent, and for 12X, he paid 4 percent.

The publisher was gratified to see an increase in advertising, but he was convinced that if other strategic approaches were used along with incentives, he would then be able to get maximum results. So his next strategic step was to make frequency discounts on the rate card more attractive to advertisers. In addition, individual account presentations were developed, working out the arithmetic showing how incremental costs dropped as frequency increased. At the same time, case histories were gathered, showing successful use of greater frequency.

When these strategies were used with the special sales incentive, growth in schedules sold was greater than ever.

7. *New advertising categories*. A publisher, recognizing that a new product area fell within the scope of the magazine's interest, decided that there was enough potential to warrant a separate advertising category that could develop into at least 50 pages a year. A list of accounts and a tentative sales rationale were developed.

The primary marketing need was for calls to be made in the category, not only for immediate sales, but also for the feedback that would help pinpoint a successful, long-run selling strategy. In order to encourage these calls, the publisher offered 500 Green Stamps for every call report made in the new category.

Within a few months, enough information had been gathered to indicate a promising marketing approach. At that point, he changed the incentive to a monetary reward for every account sold in the category, and the magazine was well on the way to its first 50 pages in the new category.

8. *Special issues*. Special issues mean additional work for salespeople and require special efforts for each individual on the marketing team. One publisher was able to motivate his salespeople and produce a record-breaking issue by taking advantage of the spirit of competition among his sales staff of four.

The goal for each salesperson was set 50 percent higher than the previous year's linage. For meeting the goal, salespeople would divide a prize of $4,000. The salesperson with the greatest gain would also win a color television set or its cash equivalent. The one-person promotion department was also brought into the effort with the offer of a color television set if the entire issue reached its goal.

The incentive spurred the extra sales and promotional efforts needed. Each of the four salespeople and the promotion manager took home color television sets.

The plan was not repeated for that special issue in the following year because the record amount of advertising helped make it a publishing event that was looked forward to by the industry. Most advertisers came back and new ones were glad to come in. However, the same plan was used successfully for another special issue.

9. *Weak issues*. Most magazines have some issues that are relatively low in advertising. One publisher felt that if three consecutive issues could be boosted substantially, annual advertising revenue would increase by 8 percent.

Commissions for those issues were doubled. In addition, the publisher provided specific promotional material based on research into readership of these issues (compared to strong issues of the year) and buying plans and actual purchasing during the time of those issues.

Although sales costs for those issues remained higher than for other issues, the additional commissions resulted in revenue gains that more than offset the rise in expenses.

10. *Share of market*. This area is often overlooked by publishers, especially when they are evaluating individual sales territories.

A territory could be showing gains and yet be losing share of market. The territory or the market in general could be growing, but the salesperson may not be keeping pace. The competition may be making serious inroads. An apparent gain in linage may make it look as though a territory is doing well when, in reality, the salesperson is doing a poor job.

On the other hand, a decline in linage does not necessarily signify poor work. The market may be down, but if the territory is down less, it is actually gaining share of market. Despite the losses, the salesperson may be doing a superb job against the competition. This, of course, pays off when the market rises and the territory rises with a larger share of market.

Realizing this, one publisher decided to base an incentive plan on share of market because he felt it was a more meaningful market criterion than sales gains or losses. This was a three book field, and his program was based on percentage points of gain in share of market.

Every percentage point of gain was worth $500 to the salesperson. In the first year, in a territory that had a 20 percent share of the advertising linage placed in the three books, share of market went up 5 percentage points to 25 percent, and the salesperson received an incentive payment of $2,500.

To complement the incentive strategy, a leadership theme was used. After three years, the magazine went up to nearly one-third share of market among the three magazines and the publisher expects to pull ahead, due, in part, to the incentive plan.

Establishing a basic plan

A publisher can use incentives profitably in just about every sales situation if he takes the time to set specific, realistic goals that relate to one another in an overall strategy. His regular compensation plan should be stable, easy to administer, easy for salespeople to understand, and fair to both management and staff.

Once the basic plan is firmly established, a publisher should identify his short-range marketing objectives and plan special incentives to work along with the basic plan. He will then be able to continually try new incentives and test innovative approaches to achieve those objectives, since one of the advantages of special incentives is that they can be turned on and off at will. There is no obligation to keep a special incentive going. Once the objective has been achieved, the incentive can be discontinued.

The entire plan should be kept simple so that salespeople can easily determine the amount being earned at any given time. If a plan is complicated—with varying amounts of points given for different accomplishments, for example—salespeople will never know where they stand. A well-constructed plan will avoid disputes and time-consuming explanations.

Furthermore, a well-constructed plan will help a publisher attract and hold good salespeople. Consider these two situations:

One multiple magazine publishing company has had its incentive plan for 20 years, and both salespeople and management are still happy with it. It consists of a base salary plus commission on net revenue above a fixed quota. The quota is permanent, adjusted only for rate increases (by 50 percent of the rate increase) and for accounts moving out of or into a territory.

Another publisher changed incentive plans frequently. First, the plan was based on a page quota. When quota was achieved, it was raised. After much complaining by the sales staff, straight commission was put in. This made the salespeople happy, especially since the market was rising. Even when the market leveled off, salespeople automatically received increases along with the rate increases. When management became concerned about the growing earnings of the sales staff while ad revenues were leveling off, the plan was changed again. Needless to say, turnover of salespeople has become a problem in that company.

Another and broader consideration for a publisher who uses special incentives is how they fit into his basic sales management approach. Here are two cases that illustrate this point.

One multi-magazine publisher has been able to reach marketing goals successfully and profitably by creating a total environment that encourages top sales performance at all times. This publisher's compensation/incentive plan includes a fair base salary commensurate with experience and productivity, plus a commission on sales. Other incentives include profit sharing, well-defined opportunities for career advancement, and personal recognition of accomplishment.

This company has a well-publicized policy of promoting from within. For the past 25 years, every opening for sales manager has been filled by a salesperson in the company who has demonstrated outstanding ability and achievement. It is well understood that when a salesperson is asked to take on extra responsibility, this is an opportunity that can lead to promotion.

Sales achievement in the company is always recognized. Management never misses an occasion to send a personal note for a job well done. Salespeople who have achieved an unusually creative, difficult or important sale are appointed as group leaders at the annual sales meeting to show others how it was done. Individual sales success stories are featured in the company house organ. Managers are highly accessible and give frequent personal attention to individual salespeople.

Within this environment, management can direct sales efforts toward its marketing goals without additional incentives. In fact, attempts at using further special incentives have not worked well. In one case, a contest was held, with vacation trips to be awarded to those salespeople who were able to get advertisers to increase ad unit size. The contest was largely ignored by the staff and the prizes went to those who happened to meet the contest requirements.

Another time, a "sale of the month" contest was inaugurated. Each month the winning salesperson would receive a small cash award, the salesperson's name would be engraved on a plaque that hung prominently in the office, and a notice would be sent to the staff explaining how the award was won. The contest lasted about three months, then died—salespeople simply stopped submitting entries.

The publisher's explanation for the lack of interest in the contests is that the total atmosphere of incentive in the company promotes maximum advertising sales in each territory without extra incentives.

Another publisher uses a different approach: a basic compensation/incentive plan of draw against commission. In addition, salespeople are encouraged to vie against each other for extra bonuses. Selling new accounts is an important goal and a contest is held each month to increase such sales. Those salespeople who bring in new accounts share in a cash bonus in proportion to the number of new accounts each has sold.

This publisher recalls that the only time a special incentive failed was when it departed from the competitive concept. A group incentive was offered for accomplishing an overall goal: in this case, a specific number of ad pages for a special issue. The goal was not reached and the publisher feels that individual efforts were not stimulated. Salespeople felt no personal pressure and blamed the failure on others.

Group incentives have worked for other publishers, however, particularly those with several titles in situations where cooperation among magazine sales staffs is necessary.

One such publisher established a special combination discount for advertisers using two of the magazines in the house. Each magazine had advertising prospects for the other, but each sales staff jealously guarded its accounts against competitors, even when the competitor was in the same company.

To quell the natural competitive instincts of the salespeople and encourage the respective sales staffs to work together, an incentive was offered which the salespeople on both staffs shared when advertisers bought both magazines. In addition, 50 target accounts were picked as prime prospects for the two-book buy and an incentive travel prize to an attractive resort was offered to both staffs if at least 40 percent of them were sold. Suitable sales aids and individual account presentations were also developed. Laying aside their mutual antagonism, the staffs cooperated with each other, and made the vacation trip together.

Experience shows that incentives motivate salespeople. But these examples show that each magazine publishing company should tailor its sales incentive plan to its own particular needs. Special incentives work best when they are designed to accomplish specific marketing purposes and are used in conjunction with other strategies designed for the same purpose.

Incentives alone will not ensure sales success, for they are not substitutes for other marketing strategies. Remember, in order to sell advertising, value to the advertiser must be demonstrated. But—if you consider incentives when developing your marketing plan, you will probably get the extra effort needed to achieve your marketing goals.

Isn't it time you took a hard look at your ad rate structure?

By David Z. Orlow

One of the basic pillars of any business is its price structure. The magazine publishing business is certainly no exception; yet, how well do most publishing executives understand and manage their own advertising rate structures?

Considerable attention in periodical publishing is given, at least in the largest consumer magazine operations, to the rate structures and pricing of circulation. But it is this writer's contention that less effort is spent by most magazines in understanding their advertising price structures than any other basic element in the business.

Just as the question of how much to charge for each product or service is critical, the relationships between the charges are equally critical and are generally the subject of thorough and continued analysis. Moreover, a good understanding of your own and competitive price structures leads to the development of modifications in your line of services and increased profitability.

Other service industries such as transportation, insurance and banking employ small legions of people with titles such as rate clerk, actuary or senior analyst who do nothing but analyze the pricing structures, the need for revision of same and the effect on profitability.

To demonstrate this lack of effort by most magazines in the area of rate structures, check out the following sample questions against your own rate analysis. This will be a preliminary indication as to whether you are as familiar as you should be with specific pros and cons.

• Given the level of four-color advertising and its potential, is my magazine best suited to a flat four-color charge or a percentaged four-color charge?

• How little can I charge my largest bulk advertiser and still be fair to my other advertisers on the one hand and my profit margin on the other?

• Should I change my fractional imposts?

• Should my magazine use standby rates?

• Does my rateholder policy accomplish anything?

Given the fact that there are numerous additional major questions which can be asked about magazine rate structures, it is apparent that an inventory of structural characteristics and the elements that affect them is a necessary tool.

Before this inventory is mapped out, it is important to keep in mind the aesthetic character of magazines together with a few basic pricing principles. By aesthetic character, I refer to the fact that our service business differs markedly from most others.

In transportation services, for example, a trip from Kansas City to Omaha for a crate of oranges would cost x dollars. If there were two competing carriers, each taking the same time and care, it would be quite difficult for Carrier A to charge a price that varied greatly from Carrier B.

Each magazine, however, carries a unique message (graphics and language) to its unique audience, and with a unique effect (information, pleasure, etc.). Even when two magazines are competing closely in the same market, it is not unusual to find significant differences in price structures. Unlike transportation companies or savings banks, the particular unique physical characteristics and aesthetic services which each magazine provides make comparison of price structures far less obvious. Correspondingly, this means that those responsible for price structure decisions can less afford to coast in a non-analytic way, simply assuming that "if anything were wrong then I'd hear about it." The burden is truly on the magazine manager to be inquisitive and analytic.

With respect to pricing principles, they are easier to list than to satisfy, as they are often in conflict and difficult to quantify. These principles would include (listed in no particular order):

1. Profit maximization. One should charge as much as necessary to deliver optimum return on investment while still delivering fair value.

2. Incentive reduction. More is less, cheaper by the dozen, call it what you will. The more your customers buy, the lower their unit rates should be.

3. Value differentiation. Some services are worth more than others—a full-page more than a half-page; four-color more than black-and-white; a cover more than a run-of-book page.

4. Class differentiation. This basic pricing principle which derived from the newspaper field and is now widely recognized acknowledges the fact that different classes of potential advertisers may have widely different purposes and values for using a particular magazine and may best be served by separate rate structures (i.e., two or more rate cards). There are many types of differentiation in magazine pricing other than the most common splits—general and mail order, national and local, or run-of-book and classified. Additional differences will be considered below.

5. Non-discrimination. The same class of customers should be charged equally for the same order.

Remembering that the value of advertising anywhere is far more intangible than anyone is really comfortable with, any analysis of rate structure requires not only that these fundamental pricing policies not be violated, but more importantly, that they be optimized.

Turning now to rate structure, which can best be described as the mathematical relationships between the rates, it is important to realize that there is virtually no such thing as a simply structured rate card. Assume that your magazine has no classified rates, no secondary rate card, prints standard magazine-sized units or any inserts—no dutch doors, digest inserts, 6-1/2" ads, banners, spines or bookmarks. We are left with the following:

• **Eight sizes**—spreads, full pages, 2/3's, 1/2's, 1/3's, 1/4's, 1/6's and inches.

• **Five frequencies**—1x, 6x, 12x plus two bulking rates at 18 pages and 24 pages.

• **Six ink use options**—black-and-white, two-color and four-color with bleeding options for each.

These minimal selections equal 240 cells of different prices for our simple card 8 (size) x 5 (frequency) x 6 (ink use).

Given the fact that a number of the cells are rather academic (i.e., 12x four-color 1/6-page) it might reduce the live cells to about 200, but the total number of cells is driven right back up again with the addition of cover rates and special position charges. In short, as publishing executives, we don't have "a price." Rather, we are operating with a complex interrelated price schedule. The assumption of the simple rate card is as misleading as the simplistic analysis of it.

Structural Grouping of Magazine Rates

Structural characteristics of rate cards can be divided between *imposts* (the variables for which one charges more) and *discounts* (those for which one charges less). One publisher's need is another's anathema,

however, and it is not surprising to find one magazine imposting while another discounts the same thing. This degree of variance being the case, it is probably more fruitful to divide structural characteristics by type or structural class rather than by whether they go up or down.

One further point is that the use of the terms "impost" and "discount" implies prices up and down as measured against a standard. Let's take that perennial favorite, the one-time black-and-white page, and use it as the standard, although the overemphasis on this "standard" inherently overstates all of our real prices and makes magazines appear far more expensive than they are.

I. Unit Size

Fractional imposts: In practice they range anywhere from near 0 percent (50 percent of the 1xBW-page for a 1xBW-1/2 page) to about 70 percent (10.5 percent of the 1xBW-page for a 1xBW-1/16, or 6.2 percent of page space). What follows is a listing of normal ranges for more prevalent units:

Unit Size	Normal % of BW Page	Normal % Impost
2/3 page	70-80	5-20
1/2 page	55-62	10-24
1/3 page	36-42	10-27
1/4 page	30-34	20-36
1/6 page	20-25	20-50

The policy problem to watch out for on fractional imposts is the "most is less" rule. It is possible to have all fractional imposts fall within the normal range as a percent of the page rate and still violate the policy. The result would be that a buyer of a larger unit would incur a higher impost than the smaller buyer. For instance, if your 1/2-page rate was 60 percent of the page (a 20 percent impost) and the 1/3-page rate was 36 percent of the page (a 10 percent impost) you would basically be doing just that. Other factors affecting a change in fractional imposting would include mechanical sizes in laying out the pages and any alteration of them, considerations about the fractional mix in space now being bought, changes in expectations about fractional mix, price resistance, etc.

Spread discounts, multiple-page single-issue discounts: Where they do exist, they are usually in the 5-15 percent range, although the current record that I know of is held by *Esquire* which offers a 38.5 percent discount for a four-color spread. Clearly the marketing hypothesis for having such a discount lies in the belief that growth in linage is achievable by trading up full-page ads to spreads. The existence of discounts for multiples beyond spreads is usually more prevalent in industries characterized by either new model introduction season for multiple model advertisers or other similar catalogue-type marketing situations.

Odd sizes (i.e., gatefolds, dutch doors, less-than-full-page inserts, spines, full pages in tabloids, floating units): The final chapter will never be written in this continuing saga. On the one hand, there are the mechanical costs and people-time costs in making sure these unusual items are not mangled in the usual systems. On the other hand, there are all of those wonderful sales possibilities for incremental dollars. Do I eat some of the mechanical costs as the loss-leader aspect of getting these extra profitable dollars or do I insist that each element in my pricing justify itself? Do I create a discount for a gatefold cover-2 in the hopes of getting my 12-page, second-cover advertiser to go to a 24-page or 36-page gate schedule, or do I charge a premium for gating with the knowledge that it costs me more? For as many positions as you can think of, there are people to be found who hold them. At the very least, be sure that your opinion and the reasons for taking it are clear to you.

II. Unit Graphics/Mechanical Production

Color imposts: Certainly color usage in magazine advertising is on the upswing as some magazine markets have shifted from next-to-no-coloration a decade ago to as high as 50 percent of linage today. Although trade professional publications generally carry less, they are also growing in coloration. Because of both this growing coloration volume and conversion to offset, it is likely that many publications which set pricing strategies years ago for coloration, especially those relating them heavily to cost, have simply outgrown their old considerations, and it is time to undergo a reexamination.

Obviously, the coloration pricing problems of one magazine can be totally different from another. The publishers who feel they have their full share of four-color space may run a four-color impost at 50-60 percent, while the publisher attempting to switch a market to four-color who also has a high raw-dollar page rate, may feel it best to set it lower at 25-35 percent. At another extreme, a trade publisher with a $700 1xBW-page rate and only occasional demand for four-color is more likely to think in terms of a flat-dollar charge to cover the incremental cost rather than in percentage terms. A further refinement of four-color pricing has even led some publishers to offer discounts based on the total amount of four-color ads placed in the contract year as opposed to the total number of all ads. On two-color charges, about the only issue other than flat price or percentage, is whether the charge is applicable to just AAAA standard colors, or whether it includes special color matching.

Bleed imposts: As magazines have shifted to offset, we have been increasingly battered with the fact that our costs for bleeding are lower and therefore our bleed imposts should go down. The general practice now is for bleed charges to run anywhere from 5-20 percent, but I'm quite sure that the average percent has slowly dropped as 15 percents have become 10 percents, etc. Moreover, because of competitive changes, some markets have virtually eliminated bleed imposts—consumer boating magazines, for example.

It is my own belief that bleed pricing must also be considered in the context of overall pricing and that bleeding advertisements do require extra consideration and service. As such, much of the retreat in bleed impost appears more as a convenient way to hide price reductions for certain types of accounts, and at the very least, should be strongly resisted.

Split-run, stop-press, slow-down, bind-in and tip-on imposts: These mechanical charges are usually phrased in flat-dollar terms and based on a cost or cost-plus basis. About the only issue is how much, if any, the cost-plus should be. You have to be careful here to revise your cost calculation at the beginning of new printing contracts since these items are quite often subject to wider cost fluctuations between printers due to differing technical production capabilities.

Insert discounts: Seven questions to consider:

1. Is the discount low enough considering the increase in paper costs in the past two years and the savings that a supplied insert allows on my paper bill?

2. Are the incremental discounts between insert sizes sufficient to give proper marketing incentive and still allow fair profit margins?

3. Are the discounts so low that I am inadvertently competing with my own R.O.P. rates?

4. Does a half-page sized eight-page insert get discounted as an eight-page insert or on a square-inch basis?

5. Must an insert be backed by a full R.O.P. page?

6. Does a discounted insert get full credit toward earning a space/volume discount in a contract year or is it just prorated?

7. Am I price competitive?

These and other questions concerning insert pricing policies can be best answered with a full analysis of cost, incremental profitability, competitive pricing and marketing opportunity.

III. Advertising Volume

Issue frequency discount: One general point about issue frequency discounts is that they tend to insure better distribution of space in low issue months. For the publisher with a seasonal problem, such as near-minimum book size, an increase in 12x discounts may tend to attract space from higher-frequency advertisers into the issues in need. While just about all publishers of 12x titles offer 6x and 12x discounts, marketing analysis may show advantages to also using 3x or 9x discount points or, conversely, eliminating current 3x or 9x issue frequency discounts. It is also important not to confuse issue frequency discounts with volume discounts which may or may not exist independently. The discount here is for number of issues used—regardless of total space used.

Another aspect to this discount is the "rateholder" policy—the smallest unit size which can be used in combination with larger units in other issues. The most prevalent rateholder unit in use is the 1/3-page, but it is not uncommon to see 1/4- or 1/8-page rateholders, and some magazine markets function without them at all. It depends on the distribution of fractional advertising and the degree and type of unit mixing that goes on within advertising schedules—and each mix would require a separate analysis.

There are no hard rules as to the amount of discount to be given at different frequency intervals, and it is the same for other volume discounts that will be discussed. The proper discount sizes to be offered depend not only on marketing analysis of sales potential and competitive practices, but also on a proper calculation of the math involved, which is also shown below.

Bulk space per year discount: Bulk space discounts are usually phrased in stage-lengths, just as frequency of issue discounts. A typical break would be discounts for 6, 12, 18, 24 and 36 pages. There is no rule, however, for the upper limits of stage-lengths. Rather, there are only considerations of incremental cost and profit to both publisher and advertiser. If, for example, a magazine is publishing in a market with a cluster of advertisers capable of using an average of six pages an issue in a 12-issue cycle, it is probably wise for the publisher to provide for discount stage-lengths up to 72 pages per year. This situation has actually emerged in markets which have been subject to particularly intense conglomeration in the past few years, and the alert publisher must watch for this type of activity to assess the rate card needs.

As to the calculation of incremental page rates, the following example illustrates the most useful type of calculations and the pitfalls of not following them. Let's assume that Magazine A has a 1xBW page of $1,000 and a 12xBW page rate of $900. Up until now, the lowest page rate available was the 12x rate of $900, but an analysis by the advertising director shows that many of the major accounts are already buying 24 pages a year and capable of moving to the 36-page level in three to five years. Further, many additional accounts now buying at the 12x rate are capable of moving to 24 pages in the same period. The ad director, however, recommends the creation of 24-page and 36-page rate incentives as a marketing tool. Your average cost for production and distribution of an ad page is $300 and the incremental page cost is $200. One of the following two plans violates a fundamental pricing policy:

B/W Full Page:	Plan A	Plan B
1x	$1,000	$1,000
12x	900	900
24 pages	790	815
36 pages	760	760

We are dealing here with a critical distinction between absolute page rates as shown above and incremental page rates. Remember the marketing problem for which the 24-page and 36-page rates are designed, and start from there. Any 12-page advertiser is now paying $10,800 per year (12 X $900). In Plan A, if your ad director asks a shift to 24 pages, the cost would be $18,960 (24 X $790) for a total incremental investment of $8,160 ($18,960—$10,800). For that incremental investment of $8,160, the advertiser purchases 12 incremental pages for an incremental page cost of $680 ($8,160÷12). Using this same calculation we can determine the incremental page cost in Plan A, moving from 24-page rates to 36-page rates at $700. A comparison of the two plans on an incremental basis shows:

	Incremental Page Costs	
Frequency from:	Plan A	Plan B
12 to 24 pages	$680	$730
24 to 36 pages	700	650

It can now be seen that Plan A violates the basic pricing policy of "more for less" in that the larger advertiser is actually paying more for the next 12 pages purchased than the smaller advertiser. In and by itself, it isn't necessarily detrimental, but it is crucial to track this dimension of price structure. For example, had the marketing diagnosis placed more stress on moving the 12's

to 24 than moving the 24's to 36, it is entirely possible that Plan A would be better even though it is slightly out of line.

Beyond these important technical considerations of incremental rates, there is also the problem of selling the incremental space. Consider the differences between presentations of those aware of incremental pricing and those not aware. In the case of Plan B, an unaware salesperson might go back to that 12-page account to sell up to 24 pages and point out that management has just established a 24-page rate of only $815. If the account will just double the space, the savings would be 9.4 percent. On the other hand, dealing with the real incremental cost in Plan B of $730 per page, it can be said that the next 12 pages are available at a discount of 18.9 percent, a statement equally true, but which would have more impact in the sales situation. Once down pat, it should greatly facilitate rate structure analysis with respect to frequency and bulk space discounts, as well as helping in the sales process.

Bulk dollar volume per year discount: Phrasing bulk discounts in dollar volume terms creates a dilemma with respect to future rate increases. On the one hand, the publisher can proportionately increase the scale of discounts each time there is a rate increase and thereby increase the attention which the rate increase gets and annoy some clients. On the other hand, the publisher can freeze the discount scale at rate increase time and thereby actually deflate the increase. A dollar volume discount could make sense in the case of a publisher who has some reason to feel that dollar commitments are waning and wants to hold them in—a minimax (i.e., minimum loss) type of game plan.

IV. Positioning in Issue

Cover imposts: Readership studies consistently show that readership is highest in the front of the issue (cover-2, for example), lowest somewhere around the middle and goes up to nearly the front peak by the back of the issue (cover-3). Yet, many publishers including some of the largest (*Time* and *Playboy,* for example) charge covers 2 and 3 at run-of-book prices. I suppose that the publishers think there is no value added, at least worth charging for, but my feeling is that the value hasn't been properly marketed. Meanwhile, media buyers chew out publishers for charging a 10 percent premium for cover-2 and cite all the top magazines that don't. In my judgment, inside covers should be imposted *at least* as much as whatever the R.O.P. special position rate imposted is, but also less than the cover-4 impost. Supply and demand is also heavily at work here and a simple analysis should lead to a comfortable and fair conclusion.

When computing cover imposts, be sure to be consistent within the comparison—holding frequency and coloration constant.

R.O.P. special position imposts: These can either be phrased in dollars or percentages, although the latter is more common. On rare occasions, two different special position rates exist for the same title (i.e. first right-hand page or center spread at 15 percent and others at 10 percent). The biggest policy pitfall to avoid is the type of discrimination where one account gets a special position guarantee and a waiver of the charge and another account plays it by the card and orders it with premium.

V. Positioning in Annual Publication Cycle

Seasonal discounts: These made a major appearance in the women's magazine field, even to the extent of being two-tier. *Woman's Day,* for example, gives a 10 percent discount for January but a 5 percent in July and August. The logical extension of this practice would call for a different rate each month, just as electronic media have different rates for each program. Deepening the 12-issue discount is a more positive way to brace up a down January, rather than by specifically selling the fact that a particular month is not worth as much. There is even less evidence of seasonality of reading in business and professional publications and less of a problem here.

Special issue discount or impost: These usually reflect instances of extreme added value and are, therefore, imposted especially with respect to directory issues. Special issues that are used as one-shot sales incentives are discounted.

Standby discount: This can be of considerable value in cases of high-frequency publication (weekly or more often), where dummying necessitates putting in more filler material than is desired. The terms usually are that if an advertiser supplies the publisher with a plate and a maximum limit on the number of insertions, the publisher may carry it in any specific issues, anywhere from zero to the maximum number of times specified. What few titles that now use it give about 40 percent off for this flexibility and it facilitates dummying. For examples check *Time* or *Travel Weekly* in *SRDS.*

VI. Positioning: Publication Life Cycle

Charter discount: Charter discounts do take a few different forms and it's important to consider alternatives in advance. There can be a dollar or percentage discount for the first issue, the first x issues or the first contract. The charter rate can also be phrased in two-for-one language. It can be the same for all affected issues, or scaled down from first to last. One thing to avoid: Charter discounts can be too generous, and when the time comes for the regular rate to take effect, the charter advertiser has trouble adjusting.

Renewal discount: This type of discount can be especially helpful for magazines in a mature phase of their space growth or for titles with high account turnover in their advertising pool. Although it's used more by consumer titles than trade, there is increased application for it in trade. It is usually phrased in a multi-year formula, for example:

2 percent discount—second year
3 percent discount—third year
4 percent discount—fourth year
5 percent discount—fifth year and thereafter.

The condition here is that the renewal will be for equal or greater space in the current year than in previous years. The things to be aware of in creating this discount are:

• The validity of the data analysis and projections purporting to demonstrate the need for it in the first place.

• The clarity with which it is ultimately expressed and sold.

Rather than try to explain my concern for clarity,

the *Reader's Digest* variant of renewal discounts as taken from *SRDS* is an example of where it is lacking:

"3 YEAR RATE PLAN"

"*Reader's Digest* guarantees 1974 CPM's and 1974 volume discounts for qualifying space units to national advertisers who run at least 50 percent more advertising pages than they have run in 1973, in each of the years, 1974, 1975 and 1976. The guaranteed 1974 CPM's and 1974 volume discounts are those in effect with the February 1974 issue. In addition, a 5 percent bonus discount on eligible space units will be earned in each of the 3 years."

Exactly what, in dollar value computations, is being offered? The potential advertiser cannot make any calculations to learn exactly what his or her discount from *Reader's Digest* will be. He or she still doesn't know in dollars and cents what his or her ad will cost. If you're going to make a statement, make it a complete one. Give all the information.

VII. Positioning With Other Rate Cards

Multiple edition discounts: This discount allows rate reductions, usually phrased in percentages, to be taken when two or more rate cards for the same magazine are used by the same advertiser, most frequently for titles with geographic editions.

Magazine group discounts: To employ such discounts you must either own a group of magazines worth packaging or be in a position to sell advertising in them, i.e., Magazine Networks, Inc. Packaging of discounts for use of multiple magazines in a group is a complicated affair and at present the only examples of simple rate structures are also poor ones.

VIII. Less-than-total Circulation

Geographic and demographic imposts: As printing and distribution technologies have improved, marketing becomes more targeted and magazines more accustomed to the idea, these types of advertising uses have flourished. It's now to the point where the Publisher's Information Bureau estimates that more than 18 percent of ad revenues for the major consumer titles it tracks is coming from less-than-national linage.

The critical problem with these types of rates is that the publishers, when establishing them, usually transfer the strategic rate structure thinking, or lack thereof, from their national card to the less-than-national card plus some percent markup. Three major factors must be recognized:

1. The very advertising pools for specific editions are different from the national pool and often different from each other.

2. The natural competitors for these editions are different and also have different rate structures.

3. The frequency of a geographic edition may be different from the title itself, further increasing the desirability of separate structural analysis.

The failure to pay attention to these factors can result in mispricing, usually more under-market than over it, and certainly poorer allocation of price incentives.

Newsstand/single copy splits: Like A/B splits below, these are used heavily by the publisher for circulation promotion and testing and were developed from the testing of cover copy and price splits for newsstand copies. Additionally, since many characteristics of newsstand buyers for a particular title can be distributed differently than among subscribers, there may be different advertising pools to draw on for each, aside from the general pool.

A/B splits: These are fitted to larger circulations and became a basic sampling or testing device designed to measure the effectiveness of copy and/or magazine audience, or to limit gross expenditure. When both A and B are used, we are dealing with a split run; when A or B, a less-than-national run. Whether the publisher chooses to offer A/B splitting on a service basis or at a premium is dependent on the analysis of the market.

Roll-out discount: This is an unusual case of an explicit provision for the removal of an impost. It is a natural consequence of selling less-than-national space and exists only with a few of the larger consumer magazines. The advertiser exclusively uses the Chicago edition three times to test a new brand, paying the geographic impost, and subsequently rolls out the brand on a national basis with at least three full-run ads. In the context of running the three full-run ads, the advertiser is rebated on the imposted part of the charges for the geo test.

Remainder discounts: In the context of the full-run form, there are remnants of unsold space from the natural effects of selling less-than-national. Remainder or remnant space discounts, like standby discounts, of as much as 50 percent may be a better last-minute alternative than a house ad.

IX. Market Classification

Discounts are commonly given for various classifications of advertising. Sometimes the conditions are such that the discount is intrinsically a discount not only for classification, but also for position and for actual copy or formal restrictions, e.g., mail order always runs in the back of an issue, "only 1-inch units," "no halftones."

In each market classification rate, pricing policy and market reactions must be considered. It is also important to watch for special terms and conditions which should apply, e.g., tie-in terms with national advertising for retail discounts, cash-with-order and pay-in-advance terms for political or classified advertising. In alphabetical order, the more prevalent discounted market classifications include: book, classified, educational, employment, fashion, financial, foreign, hotel, legal notices, local, mail order, nonprofit, personal, political, professional, publisher, real estate, restaurant, retail, travel and used equipment.

Other Dimensions of Rate Management

Having briefly catalogued the major dimensions of rate cards, we can see they are strongly affected by most of the structural characteristics of the magazine and its market environment. In turn, these structural characteristics are far more dynamic and subject to continual change than it might at first appear. The physical structure of the magazine is subject to periodic revision. The shape of the advertising pool is always changing. Competitive price structures change. Technological change alters production capabilities. "Age" of magazine is really

"aging" of magazine, and so forth.

To insure that rate structures are best fitted to current and future reality, there remain two additional management problems—the question of the mechanics of rate-card analysis and the question of delegation of responsibility for this type of work.

Just as advertising rates are laid out on a cell-by-cell basis in a rate card, the tabulation of total advertising space and dollar volume must be laid out in the same manner. By following this procedure, one is assured of "seeing" the dimensions of the advertising pool and consequently incorporates thinking about it into rate card analysis. This plotting of the advertising pool need not be revised on a monthly basis, but it is certainly advisable to update the data as part of an annual rate card revision analysis. Further, when average net advertising revenues per page experience any consistent variance—up or down—over a few issues, it is a good clue that there has been a change in structure of the advertising pool which should be understood as thoroughly as possible.

In addition to plotting the ad space and ad revenue pool this way, two other records are indispensable. The first is an impost and discount record. This consists of the computations of the percentage imposts and discounts for each cell in the card, laid out on the same grid basis. It should be done on separate sheets for your own title—for each card which each title uses, as well as important competitors. Lastly, so that considerations of actual unit dollar costs are not lost in a sea of percentages, you will find it useful to plot out, again on a cell-by-cell basis, CPM's for each card and each competitive card.

Each of these two sets of records should be recomputed each time you or one of your competitors issues a new rate card. People with some familiarity of rate structures and reasonable skill with a calculator can complete these basic up-dates for a magazine with about a day's work. Experience in working with these types of records also shows that they have considerable added value in enabling marketing people to quickly and specifically define price problems when they arise during the year.

The responsibility for advertising rate structures must ultimately reside with top management. It is the realization of the complexity and importance of this area that constitutes the first step in meeting that responsibility. Rate structure analysis is too often relegated rather than assigned and receives attention only when there is "a problem." The boss gets it by definition of title, the ad director as part of the space selling responsibility or the financial department because its people understand numbers.

Adequate rate structure analysis requires complex considerations of dimensions in virtually all functional publishing areas. It follows then, that those responsible for this area of management must not only comprehensively track changes, but work closely with other members of the magazine management group to insure optimum input and results.

Target account planning is more than A, B, C

By Milton F. Decker

"Selling is very, very inefficient compared to what it could be."

"Salesmen are calling on the wrong accounts. They're calling on accounts that already give them all the business that they can."

"They're calling on people they think can make buying decisions, when in fact, those people do not or cannot make those decisions."

"They are effective in talking about what their product does—but not in how it fills the customer's needs, because they haven't probed to find out what those needs are."

The comments above are *not* from someone in the publishing business—they were made by the vice-president of a leading air freight company—but they are certainly on target in summarizing the perennial problem of trying to improve sales efficiency. They underline the fact that this problem is faced by practically every sales organization.

Fortunately, however, there is a logical and easily applied approach to solving the problem that has proved particularly helpful in our business of selling advertising space. I call it the "target area" approach.

In its simplest terms, it is a planned program based upon the age-old principle of concentration of effort in the areas of greatest opportunity.

"Why, we're doing this all the time," people tell me.

Maybe. In fact, many sales operations do feel they use this method of concentrating effort where the greatest potential is when they categorize accounts by "A" prospects—followed by the "B" and "C" groups. Under this procedure each salesperson may have only 10 or 20 "A" accounts to concentrate on, but not at the neglect of some promising "Bs."

Or a more refined plan might call for coverage of only half a dozen prime prospects. In fact, one publisher we know had set up such a program, complete with monetary incentives and rewards. But it didn't work.

Unrealistic to cover five targets

Reason? An attempt by one person to cover even five or six accounts *in depth*—let alone 15 or 20—is simply unrealistic when combined with the normal pressure of day-to-day coverage of all his or her account responsibilities. It is equally unrealistic to expect adequate management supervision of some 20 to 25 accounts (if there are only 4 salespersons on the staff)!

This unrealistic approach, then, is *not* what target programming is all about.

The concept we've proposed here is a target account plan that completely surrounds the advertising prospect with a sales campaign mounted in depth. It can easily extend over several months, building to a climax with a major presentation directed primarily at the prospect's interests and objectives. This presentation should be researched sufficiently to include specific space recommendations and a merchandising plan or sales promotion idea.

Your management is also involved in the plan. Preliminary and follow-up calls might be made by the publisher, ad director and even the editors, if advisable. And, of course, there should be an integrated direct mail sales program to all key decision makers.

To develop a complete but workable target account program, you must first establish the basic goals and objectives of such a plan. For example, here are five goals set by one advertising executive:

1. Define and establish your prime prospects in major advertising categories.

2. Concentrate sales effort where there is the greatest potential.

3. Develop increased business from key accounts in important classifications.

4. Increase the professionalism, knowledge and effectiveness of your sales staff.

5. Involve your salespeople more directly in the planning and execution of a complete marketing plan with your key prospects.

The objectives outlined above can best be executed through a four phase plan which I have found to be the most logical and effective method of getting everyone immediately (and, let us hope, enthusiastically) involved.

Phase I—account evaluation

The obvious first step is the selection of the target prospect. Preferably there should be only one major account per salesperson—with possibly a second selected as an alternate. All too often target account planning becomes diffuse and unworkable because each salesperson is given responsibility for three, four, or five target accounts.

To avoid the selection of accounts on a subjective hit-or-miss basis, the following questions have been successfully used as the criteria for evaluating key prospects.

•Does the account represent sufficient immediate and long term potential?

•Is there a realistic chance of getting business through concentrated, special effort?

•Is the account a leader in its field so that it will have an influence on its competitors?

•Is there a favorable attitude at both the account and the agency toward the magazine? (To push water uphill on a target account may not be worth the time and effort.)

•Is there a weak spot in the account's media pattern that can be exploited?

•Is the account in a category which offers an opportunity for the application of new sales material that can be used on other important key accounts?

•Is someone else on staff working on the same type of problem? (Duplication of effort is wasteful.)

•Do the advertising and media objectives of the account fit logically into the basic selling proposition?

If most of these questions can be answered affirmatively, the basis for a target account exists.

Phase II—account analysis

Evaluating an advertiser's sales strategy and marketing objectives is probably the most important exercise of all to get the salespeople more interested and involved in their accounts. Surely it is the best way for them to know more about their accounts than any competitor.

An account analysis and evaluation form which appears on page 17 is a helpful device to set up logical procedures after key accounts have been selected. It forces the salesperson to do the homework necessary to be more effective in terms of the advertiser's interest.

There is an interesting corollary benefit from this effort which may not be apparent at first. It seldom fails to surprise a salesperson to find that his intelligent interest is so well received by the account. Most advertisers aren't accustomed to being asked specific questions about their objectives—before sellers start talking about their publication! Few salespeople take the time and effort to find out something about their account's selling strategy. Those that do are amazed at the kind of helpful cooperation and interest they get from their prospect.

Phase III—developing the plan

1. Establish your own selling strategy and your own unique selling proposition.

2. Outline the benefits of your magazine and how it fits the prospect's objectives (concentration on major areas, extension of reach, comparisons with competitors in reaching the objectives, success or result stories that apply, etc.).

3. Create a specific recommendation or new sales idea: a proposed schedule, special space or position, a unique merchandising plan, etc.

It is especially worthwhile when using the target account approach to search for that something extra—to sell an idea rather than just space. For example, an insert promotion tied to your prospect's customers will sometimes uncover new angles and ideas. (Several phone calls will often suffice.)

As a salesperson digs and probes an account in depth, covering as many people as possible and examining all the angles, the ideas will start to come. They'll come simply from the involvement and extra interest your salesperson has in the account. And don't think the advertiser won't start to recognize this extra effort.

4. Decide on the documentation and format you prefer for your major presentation to the account: slides, cards, flip charts, leave-behind sales support material, etc.

Phase IV—the follow-up plan

This important element in selling and promotion is a procedure that can too easily be neglected. After the big presentation has been made, the job is still not over.

"Leave-behind" material which supports your basic proposition should be planned.

A follow-up direct mail campaign, addressed to the key decision makers, should be created and coordinated. It would obviously continue to document the benefits of your book based upon your unique selling proposition.

If this seems like a lot of work—it is. But the benefits of a sound target program far outweigh the extra effort necessary to make it a success.

Consider these advantages—in addition to increased business—that such a plan could create:

1. It establishes a sales strategy adaptable to other major accounts in the classification. (This alone can make the extra work worthwhile!)

2. It represents "on the job" sales training for your salespeople in their developing and organizing a selling plan with the necessary sales support material. It teaches each person to be a problem-identifier, a problem-solver and a prescriber.

3. It helps motivate each salesperson by getting him more directly and personally involved with your key prospects so that the individual feels responsible for his sales performance.

4. It helps your sales force sell more professionally—and hence smarter—by knowing the marketing facts which might have a bearing on how your publication should be positioned to best influence the prospect.

5. It provides management with a program which develops the opportunity to give each individual the satisfaction of sales achievement and the recognition from management of a job well done. This can take the form of extra compensation, a bonus, special prizes, etc. While such incentives are always welcomed by the individual, our experience proves, and psychologists confirm, that recognition from others is still the most important factor in stimulating motivation.

And, just one final point.

The fundamental necessity for the success of any program is action: organize the plan and follow the strategy.

All the forms, formats, checklists and proposals aren't worth the paper they're printed on if some one person doesn't take the responsibility to follow through.

It's not tough to do. In fact, it can be fun.

The sales meeting

By Robert Potts

"Is this trip really necessary?" Those words flit through the mind of a typical advertising salesman as he sits in his tourist seat on a plane taking him—at midday on Sunday—to the annual sales meeting of his publication.

His golf clubs are safely stored, he hopes, in the cargo compartment of the plane. He left, at the airline gate, a wife, two children, a dog and a three-year-old station wagon which needs new tires and a little body work. His wife was mad as hell that he had to take off Sunday morning to arrive in time for the opening cocktail party. Her parting words hang heavy: "Why can't that company of yours have its sales meetings during the week? You're away enough. Why do I have to be alone while you're whooping it up with the boys—and God knows who else—at the Flamenco Plaza?" Another often heard variation of the same theme is: "Why isn't your publisher like the one that our neighbor Randy Smith works for? Sheila always goes with Randy to all their sales meetings."

Our hero decides he needs two drinks to help erase some of the sting of that last parting speech. While he won't admit it to her, he does *agree* with Ruth. He could just as well have flown in this evening. He doesn't need another cocktail party; he gets enough of them at the conventions and the local ad club meetings. He'd rather be on his way to Detroit where he is having trouble with that fastener account. Or better still, on his way to Dayton to put out that fire his competitor, Honey Lips Hanrahan, started with his lousy readership study.

There are, however, a lot of real benefits that can be derived from holding a well-planned, well-run, meaningful formal meeting.

For the Salesperson

Contrary to the opinion of a lot of nonsales types in the publishing business, or any business for that matter, the salesperson's life is hardly a cup of tea. It's very often lonely, anxiety-ridden and frustrating. Even the best person needs the opportunity to get together with his or her fellow salespeople on the magazine and compare notes, to refresh his or her own cognizance that they, too, have types like Honey Lips Hanrahan to worry about. And, the salesperson needs the chance to have a couple of good fights over split accounts. This kind of camaraderie and shared experience is a necessary therapy for any good salesperson. He or she also needs reaffirmation that someone back there at headquarters really cares; that the publisher and other company management executives know he or she exists—not just as a symbol of 250 pages a year—but as a hard-working, interested and ambitious human being. The magazine and the company are an important part of the person's life—reassurance is needed that the emotions, sweat and care exerted are recognized and returned in some way by the powers that be. The holding of a formal sales meeting at a better than usual location is an indication that the sales function and the people are recognized as important by management. Of course, this kind of attention is very important to any employee, but more so to a salesperson who often works for weeks, sometimes months, at a time with no contact other than the telephone and memorandums with other members of the same magazine staff. In short, the formal sales meeting, if done correctly, is a necessary ego trip for your salespeople—and a profitable trip for you.

For the Publication Sales Manager

At no other time of the year will you have such a captive audience (in an environment completely controllable by you)—untroubled by the ringing of the telephone, the interruption of unexpected visitors. At no other time of the year will you have such a perfect opportunity to communicate what you would like them to know about the magazine, the market, the competitors, the new materials and programs that have been designed to make the magazine more valuable to the reader, more effective for the advertiser and easier to sell.

For the Publishing Company Management

What better chance is there for management to talk directly with the very people whose conduct, attitudes and personal image in the field are the first line of impression that advertisers or agencies get about your company and its magazines? Often an unhappy, bitching salesperson can hurt the volume of the magazine and also other company properties because of the personal influence on a day-to-day basis with the key people at agencies and companies in his or her territory. Often, too, that same unhappy individual can poison some of the other salespeople with whom he or she shares offices or meets in the field.

I'm not referring to the occasional disloyal, treacherous individual who should be fired, but about the good, hard-working, honest person who has been temporarily disenchanted by poor communications on the part of the magazine or the company or one of the superiors. This damaging negativism can, in most cases, be turned around quickly by a little attention, a small dose of better understanding in what the company and the magazine are thinking about and doing.

How effective the sales meeting is in accomplishing some or all of the benefits outlined is directly in the hands of the people who plan and conduct the meeting. With proper care and thought about what the real objectives of the meeting are and what can reasonably be done to meet these objectives, the job will be well worth all the effort. Even if poorly planned, badly executed and done with the force-of-habit syndrome that attaches to quite a few annual sales meetings, however, there still is the benefit that accrues from getting the people together to compare notes and experiences. I think it is almost impossible—unless you definitely plan it that way, and even then I'm not sure—to hold a sales meeting that does not contribute *something* to the effectiveness of the staff.

How About the Location—What's Best?

The big resort hotel, the downtown hotel (usually selected before or after an exhibit or convention), the country club setup, the university-like private seminar establishment or the conference room at the headquarters office?

Since we are talking about a formal sales meeting, one that usually takes place once a year and lasts for more than one day, I'll dismiss the headquarters office immediately as completely unacceptable. It is too close to the telephone and the daily, sometimes hourly, emergencies that beset publishing management. Never, in 22 years of going to sales meetings, have I attended one in an office that was not interrupted frequently by notes being slipped in to management, a person called out to accept a call or people constantly moving in and out of the room. Usually all of these people in motion are management who give the distinct impression to the lower ranks, rooted to the chairs, that the meeting and the people attending it are not exactly top priority. The office meeting is bad enough for a one-day stand. It is disastrous for a two- or three-day affair.

The downtown hotel, if it is in the same city as the headquarters, is almost as bad as the office in terms of its interruption quotient. Out of town, before or after a meeting, it sometimes isn't a great deal better. From the standpoint of the meeting tied into a convention or exhibit, it should be scheduled to take place in the days *before* the industry festivities start. Once I made the mistake of having the sales meeting at the end of a three-day convention. My staff had been working, wining and dining for the entire convention period. They were, to say the least, less than totally alert. As a matter of fact, several of the opening sessions were interrupted by the snoring of one of my best salespeople. And the eastern editor, a normally quiet type of fellow, for some reason he can't explain, fell out of his chair and off the dais between the soup course and the main entree at the editorial luncheon.

The country club and the resort hotel both have a lot to commend them in terms of seclusion and the impression they make on the participants. The resort is expensive, however, and the golf course, the pool, the night club are all Loreleis, constantly calling to you and your staff. If you don't have the situation under control, you will lose them—and yourself—physically, or at least mentally, to the charms of the location. The country club, since it usually has no formal night life in or near it and because you can arrange for the bar to close reasonably early, is usually more conducive to maintaining daily alertness. There is less chance that some of the men will succumb to what my Irish grandfather used to call the "disease of the night."

The private seminar approach gives an academic feeling to the proceedings that can be very helpful—particularly if you have to cover a lot of ground in a short time and have scheduled evening meetings, buzz groups and/or preparation sessions for next day's activities.

I personally vote for the resort if you want to reward your people for a particularly good year and if the learning process is not the prime consideration. If it's a cram course, then go to the seminar house route. If it is work and play in equal amounts and the budget is a little tight, then the country club is a good solution.

The type of location should vary from year to year, depending on what the year's needs are and what kind of impression you want to make on the staff. It doesn't always have to be the Americana in Miami Beach, and it shouldn't always be a three-day crash course at some austere imitation of the halls of ivy.

Spouses can be one hell of an expensive and distracting factor at a sales meeting. But if you leave them home when you are taking the staff down to New Orleans or some similarly swanky place, you are apt to create a home guard that is working against you. One of the best ways to handle this when you select the posh resort or glamor city for the meeting, is to schedule the meeting to end Friday afternoon and have the spouses fly down for the weekend. If you can't justify the total bill, just pay their hotel and eating expenses for Saturday and Sunday and let their mates pick up the airline tab. You'll be loved for it by everyone concerned. You'll also pick up some good will that will pay off during the year.

Some words of caution about spouses at or around sales meetings:

• Don't invite just some and not others. That's really looking for trouble.

• If you have a meeting with no spouses, leave yours home and ask other management to do the same. Nothing

Strategy Checklist

This is a partial list of check points used by Dun-Donnelley Publishing Corporation in planning and arranging meetings, parties, presentations, industry functions, etc.

1. Arrange for meeting place.

2. Make up invitation list.

3. Appoint workers and committees.

4. See that committees and individuals involved know what they are to do—specifically.

5. Arrange seats, tables, etc., and make chart of arrangements.

6. Have programs, menus and seating lists printed and distributed.

7. Provide emcee with background on speakers for introductions.

8. Arrange for transportation and reservations for distinguished speakers, guests and out-of-town staff.

9. Meals:

• Order menu and number of meals necessary.

• Specify time of serving meal.

• Arrange for overflow.

• Arrange for any necessary refreshments and times of start and stop.

10. See that speakers are instructed as to where they will go, etc.

11. Assign people to take care of distinguished guests.

12. Have one person available for emcee on beck and call.

makes the staff feel more like peons than seeing that the bosses' mates are important enough to go to the meeting but not their own.

• If you do invite the spouses down after the meeting, restrict the company cocktail party or company-oriented activities to the first night. After that, let them be on their own.

A company dinner on the night the spouses arrive is a way of making the affair a pleasantly formal occasion, and it makes the spouses feel that they are really part of this second life their mates lead. It can go a long way in helping you build the "big happy family" feeling that we all hear so much about.

When Is the Best Time to Hold a Sales Meeting?

In my opinion that question should be rephrased to: What time of the year should you *not* hold the annual meeting? The period between August 1 to December 15, known with varying degrees of affection as the "mating season" of our business, is definitely not the time to tie the salespeople—or yourselves—up for two or three days.

July can be a problem because of family vacation schedules. So can June, for the same reason, though to a lesser degree.

My experience is that any time after the March issue is closed to the first of June is a pretty good time. By the closing of March, most of those little lost sheep who are going to return to your fold have their schedules decided on, and the staff is somewhat more relaxed and can afford to take two or three days out of the territory without more than the usual misgivings and anxieties. Also, this time of year is far enough ahead of the beginning of the next selling season so that the salespeople will have adequate time to digest and hone their use of the new promo, market and other data and presentation material you'll introduce at the meeting.

How Long, O Lord, How Long?

One of the smartest guys I ever worked for in this business was once asked by a newly appointed publisher how many days he could have for his sales meeting. He thought a minute and then said, "Take as long as you need to do what has to be done, but it had better be done by the end of the third day." I feel that the meeting longer than three working days is really ridiculous. Sure, you're not going to be able to cover everything, but if you carefully lay out your objectives in order of priorities, you should be able to easily get the main points taken care of within three days. The lesser objectives can be handled by ad hoc meetings during the year when you and the sales manager are traveling with the staff.

A Rose by Any Other Name May Be More Than Just a Rose

I have had the good fortune to attend a lot of sales meetings, and I've attended them at every level from junior salesperson to senior manager. The single most important thing I've learned is that the really good meetings, the great ones, weren't meetings of just salespeople. They were more like the old New England town meetings where everyone got a chance to put in his or her two cents. By everyone, I mean every editor, members of the circulation staff, the promotion staff, the accounting department, the production manager and the salespeople. A magazine is a group of people with many talents who, we hope, are pulling together to make it more successful, more profitable. Too often there is a real communications gap between the editors and the salespeople. This, of course, is a throwback to the dinosaur days of the newspaper business and the ivory tower sort of thing.

The salespeople are often looked upon—and resented—as crown princelings who are feted once a year at a meeting designed only for their benefit, the rest of the staff being rushed on and off stage to perform their specialty acts before the salesperson audience and then hustled back to the office to resume their work-a-day jobs of writing, editing, pasting up, putting together and distributing the magazine.

The perceptive publisher designs the annual meeting to be a complete staff activity. He or she has all the editors and at least the head of each staff department attend the complete meeting. The publisher rooms a non-sales staff member with each salesperson (same sex, of course). Seating arrangements, when they can be controlled, are intermixed. The publisher assigns work projects to be delivered later in the meeting to a team of editors, salespeople and other staff. At no time is any activity, panel or discussion group not made up of a mix of salespeople and other staff members. Even in the little skits and role-playing sessions, non-salespeople play important roles. The result is that everyone gets to know, respect and hopefully like each other. Editors and salespeople learn a new regard for the role of each in the publication's success story. They play together and work together like a team. Believe me, it really pays off.

I vote for dropping the old sales meeting moniker and, instead, naming the yearly get-together what it really should be called—the publication's "Annual Marketing Meeting."

Planning the Sales Meeting

What happens if you bomb in Boston? Well, if you are the director of the stage show, you make some changes and then try them out in Philadelphia, polish them up in New Haven and by the time you open on Broadway the show will be tight and right and the audience will go away delighted.

But if you are the sales manager or publisher of a magazine and your annual sales meeting opens tomorrow in the Marco Polo Suite in the hotel you are staying in tonight, your Broadway appearance starts at 9 a.m. sharp. There is no luxury of tryouts in Philadelphia or New Haven. Your show only appears once and you don't get a chance for a reprise for another 12 months.

As the sales manager or publisher, you are the director of this one-performance show. How well it goes, how much information and inspiration the salespeople carry away from the expensive, time-consuming and hopefully pleasant socio-business exercise is entirely in your hands. How well you plan, how skillfully you present and handle the various subjects to be discussed, how carefully you select and intermix the people who appear in the skits, panels and the role-playing activities will spell the difference between a dull meeting or a great one—the kind that people remember and come away from with new ideas and freshly polished skills that will pay off for them and for the magazine.

Planning Is the Key to Sales Meeting Success

Planning is not just a two-hour stint over a yellow pad deciding which subject to cover at 9 a.m., which one at 10:30 a.m., which one on Tuesday and which one on Wednesday (remember, on Wednesday the last one has to be over in time for the noon tee-off). Actually, the final timing of the agenda is one of the last things in a carefully considered meeting plan.

Long before a sales manager or publisher gets to that rather simple exercise in time division, he or she must have determined:

• The real objectives of the meeting—what he or she is trying to accomplish at this particular annual get-together

• What kind of meeting environment to create (inspirational, fun and games, back to basics, etc.)

• The subjects to cover and the problems to be solved

• The session formats that best lend themselves to the objectives and desired environment (panels, skits, lectures, role playing, etc.)

• The right location (resort, seminar house, country club, hotel, etc.)

• The dates and general time frame

• Who should be there—from the magazine, from management, from the outside—and how they should participate.

To help the publisher or sales manager do this preliminary planning, some publishing companies have formal questionnaires to be filled out and in many cases submitted by the publisher to management for discussion and review prior to the freezing of the meeting agenda, data and location. Other companies have a set outline of planning steps that a publisher or sales manager follows.

In the absence of a formal questionnaire or outline, the well-organized publisher or sales manager can obtain the same results with a logical step-by-step analysis of what he or she wants to accomplish at the meeting.

Step 1 is to make a list of the most important problems facing the magazine at the present in order of priority. This list would be reviewed with key staff people and management. Problems that can't be resolved by a sales meeting should be taken out. The items should be reordered by priority so the problem listed as Number One really is Number One. Add in, again on a priority basis, the other subjects you want to cover in addition to the necessary problem solving.

Once this list is complete, you will be able to decide on the overall framework of the meeting and pick the kind of environment and location that will lend itself to the spirit of the occasion.

After deciding the framework and location, you're ready to attack the meeting program itself. Take each problem and subject in priority order and discuss with your staff how each can be most effectively handled. Once the method of handling each problem has been decided, estimate how much time will be required to deal with each particular item. Then, figure in the amount of leisure and/or recreational time you want to allow. Now, add it all together and you'll probably find that you need about eight days to accomplish everything.

This is when the going gets tough, because either the number of subjects or the time allotted to certain ones has to be cut back. Borrow the editor's blue pencil and take another good look at the list of subjects. If there is a theme for the meeting, then toss out those low-priority items which don't really fit in with it.

If there is no theme, examine the list from the standpoint of cutting subjects that you can take care of when traveling with the individual salespeople or that can be taken care of at a regional or mini-meeting, perhaps before an industry convention.

Remember, everything can't be covered. Be hard-nosed in making value judgments of what should be dropped. It's better to have fewer subjects and cover them well than to try to cover everything inclusively. After you have cut out as much as you possibly can, reexamine the time allotments or formats for each remaining subject. Pare these down. Change the formats on certain sessions to give more time for the top priority subjects, then once again add it all together. Mix in the recreational time and take a sum. Now you are down to only four days and three hours.

Resharpen that blue pencil and repeat the whole process until you arrive at a plan that comfortably fits the time allotted for the meeting. If you have only allotted two days and everything doesn't fit, perhaps you had better go for a third day. Or, if your theme or priority list is so important that you can't knock out anything, then maybe you ought to toss out the golf tournament or that afternoon on the beach. Perhaps some evening sessions would give the extra time you need without cutting down what are necessary recreational activities.

Planning the Meeting— A Formal Approach

The questions below are taken from a form designed to help the publisher or sales manager in his or her evaluation of meeting objectives and in planning and preparation to meet those objectives. Upon completion, it is submitted to management for discussion and review.

Published with the permission of Conover-Mast Division, Cahners Publishing Co., Inc.

  A. Reasons and objectives
    1. Statement of present situation
    2. Statement of desired future situation
    3. What are the specific objectives of meeting?
    4. What are obstacles to attaining objectives?
    5. Are there any *other* ways to overcome them?
    6. What new material will be presented (presentations, sales aids, circulation figures, studies, etc.)?
  B. Planning
    1. Has agenda been completed?
    2. If not, when will it be completed and available to the sales meeting committee?
    3. What is the central theme of the meeting?
    4. How will theme be carried out (visuals, etc.)? Explain.
  C. Organizing
    1. Have all materials necessary for meeting been established? Checklist of materials, rooms, reservations, visuals, equipment, etc.
  D. Motivating
    1. What will be done to motivate the staff?
      • Before meeting (bulletins, interest-building devices, etc.)
      • During meeting
    2. Will staff members have an opportunity to contribute their ideas?
    3. Specifically how will they participate (assignments, etc.)?
    4. What postmeeting communications are planned to retain enthusiasm generated at meeting?
  E. Controlling
    1. Who will direct meeting?
    2. Who else will participate (other than our people)?
    3. What subjects will others cover?
    4. Have all participants been informed as to what their specific objectives should be?
  F. Corporate participation
    1. What corporate personnel will be invited?
    2. Will corporate personnel participate in meeting?
    3. What are their objectives?

"Casting" the Meeting

Now you have the plan. Each important subject has a time allotted to it. You and your staff have decided on the format needed for the handling of each session. This is when you get down to what showbusiness folk call "casting." Here again, talk with your staff, get their ideas on the talents and skills of others on the magazine or in the company. They may have seen something in one of your salespeople that you haven't. Perhaps your editor has noticed that the Eastern account executive has unusual sales savvy. Maybe that person would be the right nonsales type for that panel you are planning on handling objections.

When you're down to discussing the use of outsiders, really thrash this out. Inviting the media director from an important agency who will tell you and your totally bored and rightfully resentful staff what's wrong with space salesmen and saleswomen in just under two hours will make no contribution at all. On the other hand, a media person from another agency may have particularly helpful ideas on how to use circulation statements as selling tools.

Remember, the ultimate customer for what you present at the annual meeting is your own sales staff and other people on the publication. The purpose of the meeting is not to sell the media director of an agency you are having difficulty with. Sometimes it's possible that the two objectives can be accomplished at one time, but not very often. Too often we lose sight of the basic purpose of the meeting—to sell the salespeople and the staff.

The addition of readers to panel or discussion group formats with the salespeople and editors can be particularly effective in polishing your staff's knowledge of the market. I have often used readers in meetings, and when selected well and correctly used, they have made a major contribution as well as giving the staff a real sense of immersion in the industry itself.

If there is to be a formal annual dinner (and it's not necessary for your president to make a speech), you've another good opportunity to use an outsider constructively. Usually this speaker can be a sales executive of one of your major advertisers, or perhaps a reader whose speaking ability and marketing knowledge will really add to the meeting.

The use of role-playing skits and specially prepared games can be a pleasantly effective way of getting points and skills over to your staff. Plan the casting of these carefully—pick the right combination of people.

From the standpoint of casting the meeting, be sure to give everyone attending some kind of role. Outside of management, there should be no observers. Everybody plays and everybody wins when you follow this concept—especially the magazine.

Getting the Props

Now you have the program, the format, the people. The only remaining thing is the right collateral (supporting presentation material, data sheets, competitive analysis, etc.). These are the items that will be used at the meeting and carried away as part of the sales kit or sent out to the participants after the meeting to continue the learning process.

Since the responsibility for most of these items will fall upon the promotion manager, be sure to have planning sessions on the major pieces with this individual and other staff members. Even the best promotion manager is only as good as the information given him or her; the promotion manager cannot work in a vacuum. The promotion manager should participate at every planning session. Don't bring the promotion manager in after all is done and tell him or her to make up a four-pager on this, a data sheet on that and a set of foursomes for the annual golf game. The promotion manager has got to feel the spirit of the meeting so he or she can design and prepare proper materials. Believe it or not, the promotion manager often is brought in *after* the planning is done and then told to execute the collateral in the plan. The promotion manager can be the second most important person (after the sales manager or the president) in the success or failure of a sales meeting. In addition to preparing the proper collateral material, the promotion manager usually is, or should be, a jack-of-all-trades—supply officer, timekeeper, part-time bartender, room clerk and concierge of the meeting.

The last item in your planning is logistics—picking up the participants, arranging for their transportation from the airport or station, room assignments, meeting-room layout, meal planning, recreational planning, audio-visual equipment, etc.

There is a logistics rule which I'm sure is many years old, but for this article I'll call it Potts' Rule of Running Meetings, Presentations, and Parties: *Whatever can possibly go wrong will definitely do so.*

So plan well, execute well, don't overlook any detail, be sure everything and everybody is taken care of. Don't try to do everything yourself. Delegate detail. Review every phase with your staff people, however, and be sure they understand their assignments and what's expected of them. The same is true of outsiders and management participants—don't leave anything to chance.

Now all the planning and preparation is done. You open tomorrow morning in the Marco Polo Suite, the curtain goes up at 9 a.m. You have checked all the details with your staff. You have a well-thought-out program, some fun mixed in with effective meeting formats, carefully planned and staged panels made up of the right mix of people. You've got some outsiders who will really contribute to the success of the meeting and the knowledge of your staff, the location is just right for this particular meeting, everyone got in all right. Now you can relax.

After the Sales Meeting

The sales meeting is over. Only the promotion manager and secretary are left . . . packing up the props and leftover materials. The ever-present arguments over split-accounts credits were still being debated as the last salesperson boarded his or her airline limo. It's over. Everything clicked, you got your ideas over. Everyone who attended—salespeople, management and the rest of the staff—was really charged up when they left an hour ago. Those attending even gave you and the staff a plaque they put together themselves last night saying "Applause" and signed by each salesperson.

How much of what was discussed, dramatized, taught and illustrated will still be fresh in the salespeople's minds when they make their calls a month, three months, six months from now? Damn little, I'm afraid, if there isn't a thoughtful, innovative followup program to help keep the glow and enthusiasm generated at the meeting working for you and the salespeople for the rest of the year.

In my opinion, the most neglected area of sales-meeting planning is the after-period—the followup—the charging that is needed to keep the salespeople's batteries

Gamesmanship

Especially designed games can be very effective in sugarcoating the learning at annual meetings. Here is an idea I have used several times on different magazines to help the staff really make the most effective use of the sales and marketing tools that we provided them. It was a session based on a game called "You Bet Your Ass."

Two weeks before the meeting, we sent each person a miniature carnival poster announcing the game and giving the rules.

Before the meeting we made up 50 questions on all phases of our sales story that could be answered directly from the data sheets, editorial forecasts, BPA Statements (ours and theirs), survey material, etc., that were part of the salesperson's basic kit that's carried—or should be carried—in his or her briefcase. Each salesperson was assigned a number from a carnival wheel of chance that was a meeting prop. Each was given $30 in $1 bills at the start of the game. When the wheel was spun, the salesperson whose number came up was asked one of the 50 questions picked at random. If the salesperson gave the correct answer verbally within 30 seconds, he or she got $3. If the salesperson had to refer to the kit and answered the question within 60 seconds, he or she got $2. If the individual didn't beat the 60 second buzzer, the salesperson paid off $2 from his or her $30.

The success of the game was in keeping it moving fast and maintaining a carnival atmosphere. Those who had really studied their material had it properly organized. The few who failed on some of the questions and had to pay off had it very subtly driven home to them that they weren't as up to date or as well organized as they should have been. Everybody made a few bucks, some made a great deal. We all had a lot of fun and every one of the salespeople was much more familiar with our sales tools because of that game.

at top power for the months after the meeting.

There are a number of techniques that can be used for maintaining this afterglow. Here are a few of my favorites:

- The continuing series survey report or promotion program
    - The confidential "report-back" technique
    - Same-theme mini-meetings throughout the year
    - Award programs
    - The sales contest
    - The sales contest—PLUS 1

Let's examine each in more detail.

The Continuing Series Survey Report or Promotion Program

This is a way to get a lot of mileage out of a special presentation or marketing report. The principle is based on the old "what's-going-to-happen-next-time" theme of radio serial fame. Break up the results of a survey or parts of a new presentation into three, six or more bite-size chunks. Introduce the first bite at the sales meeting and follow up with additional mindfuls at carefully planned intervals. Be sure each section is important enough to stand on its own feet and is different enough from the previous one to have uniqueness. These can be packaged as the "Idea of the Month" or delivered in some other special memorable way—perhaps with a part of a gift that isn't completely usable until all the parts arrive, like a set of golf club covers or components of an FM radio kit.

The Confidential "Report-Back" Technique

Personally write each salesperson after the meeting and tell him or her you would appreciate the individual's comments and observations and suggestions on the use of specific materials or concepts introduced at the meeting. Tell the salesperson you realize it is a big job and, so that it doesn't overburden him or her, would like the report in six parts. Ask the salesperson to take one element at a time, as per the list you've enclosed, and send in the critique on each subject on a monthly basis. This not only keeps the staff up on the material, it also is a dandy feedback mechanism and new promotion idea generator for you and the sales promotion manager.

Mini-Meetings

This is an easy one. Plan regional or "before-the-show" one-day or half-day meetings with all or a few of the sales staff to review the reactions and use of the material or ideas presented at the annual meeting. Keep up the same theme as the original meetings so there is a sense of continuity. An interesting variation is to let each salesperson be responsible for planning and running a "mini-meeting" some time during the year on a particular subject. This is good experience for the staff and a good way to measure the knowledge and potential of your staff.

Award Programs

This is the Oscar or Gold Plaque technique for the salespeople who do the best job of attaining personal or magazine goals set at the meeting. You make the presentation of the award and a suitable check at a regional dinner or luncheon meeting six months after the big meeting. One of top management should make the award or, if only one or two salespeople are involved, take them and perhaps their spouses out to dinner at a special place. Bulletins on how the individual is doing should go out each month prior to the actual award. This is one of those "everybody-gets-something" ideas. But the real winners get a substantial check. Also, the presence of a trophy or plaque in an individual's office is a constructive version of the Big-Brother-is-watching-you technique. In this particular case, however, the Big Brother is the individual's own conscience and pride.

The Sales Contest (Announced at the Meeting)

This old standby still works like a charm if it is

creative, communicated well and the awards are highly visible and substantial. The secret here is to establish a competitive situation between each salesperson. Unlike the award program discussed above which is tailored to the person, the sales contest is an open game with a minimum of handicapping. A sporting theme is always a good format—Kentucky Derby, World Series or Grand Prix approach. This lends itself to the vital "where-you-stand-in-relation-to-the-others" type of report which has to come out with enough frequency and attractiveness to goad and enthuse the players.

Whenever publishers or sales managers get together, you can always get a good argument going about whether to include the spouse in a sales contest. Personally, I'm all for it.

The spouse of a really good, conscientious salesperson often feels that he or she is standing on the outside looking in on this special world that claims so much time and loyalty. Often the company becomes the target of this annoyance—and that can affect your salesperson's attitude toward the job. How can you get him or her to work for you rather than against you? That's easy. Let him or her share in some special trips, prizes or money earned by putting out that extra effort, making that extra sales call. By neglecting a spouse you are, at best, missing a real opportunity and, at worse, cultivating a highly effective fifth column working against you through voiced and unvoiced unhappiness about traveling, late nights and devotion to the job.

There are many other ways of maintaining the afterglow when the sales meeting is over. The important thing is not to neglect this vital element in sales-meeting planning. Without proper followup, the time effort and money that go into a great sales meeting can be diluted. Three months afterward, your salespeople will really only remember the fun and precious little of the details—what a waste!

The marketing function

By William Abbott

Whenever someone asks me what a magazine marketing director does, I am reminded of the story about the blind men and the elephant. If you recall, each blind man had a different idea of what an elephant is like because each one touched a different part of the elephant's body.

Similarly, very few titles are as diversely defined (and mis-defined) as that of marketing director in the magazine industry. But before examining what a magazine marketing director does—or should do—let's look at how marketing has evolved over the past three decades.

The components of marketing have become a good deal more complex as business has become more competitive. In the early fifties, Agnew, Connor and Doremus, in their text *Outlines of Marketing*, defined marketing as: "All the business activities in transferring merchandise from the place where it originated to the place where it is consumed."

Of course, life was a lot simpler in those days. Kitchens and bathrooms were white; automobiles and typewriters were black; the average vacation consisted of a trip to the nearby seashore or mountain area; the air was clean and sex was dirty.

Every generation sees itself as the one producing the greatest change. In a business sense, the generation which has dominated the past quarter-century may well lay claim to the distinction.

The fifties was the "Selling Era" from a marketing viewpoint. And this label was indeed appropriate. Business people were operating on the belief that the major functions of marketing were face-to-face selling and advertising. But industry was learning that salesmanship and advertising alone did not guarantee success. Indeed, an ever-increasing pressure to "beat last year's figures" led to a more analytical approach to sales.

The problem became one of determining what the customer wanted. The solution was to make it. And the payoff was increased buying with less selling.

With increasing frequency, business perceived customers' preferences as the key ingredient in the marketing process. Until finally, marketing, as defined in Pride and Ferrell's 1980 text *Marketing, Basic Concepts and Decisions,* had become "individual and organizational activities aimed at facilitating and expediting exchanges within a set of dynamic environmental forces." That mouthful represents quite a radical change in direction over 30 years.

Creative approach to ad sales
Stated simply, the goal of advertising marketing is to increase current business and develop new advertising. (Note that ad marketing in the magazine industry has nothing to do with editorial considerations.)

Magazines have been slow to adapt sophisticated advertising sales procedures. Not until the past decade has the publishing industry become aware of the need to identify readers' needs before presenting a coordinated sales package.

This realization precipitated a reevaluation of the entire process of selling advertising, and it became clear that two separate functions were involved: an administrative function and a creative function. Furthermore, industry people soon realized not only that each function required different abilities and talents, but also that few executives could manage both.

An advertising director is essentially a sales manager whose responsibilities and talents gravitate toward the day-to-day supervision of the mechanics of selling. The marketing director, on the other hand, oversees the creative aspects of the sales process. In a word, marketing directors are concerned about *what* sales people say; advertising directors care about *to whom* they say it.

The marketing department functions primarily as the main source of creative sales direction for the advertising staff. As such, ad marketers must be skilled in two areas: they must be analytical and creative, and they must be sales-oriented.

The ocean of publishing isn't exactly teeming with this kind of fish. Promotion directors, for example, are basically creative types, talented with copy, art or production backgrounds. It is the rare magazine promotion director who possesses strong selling experience.

The marketing plan

The job of the ad marketer is to create a marketing plan. This plan spells out where the magazine is to go and, like a roadmap, indicates how to get there.

First, the ad marketer must determine the magazine's position in the marketplace. This position is dictated by the type of reader attracted by the magazine's editorial and, in turn, by the type of advertiser attracted by the reader. In this era of specialization, most magazines have apparent target advertising categories. (Even a general interest publication has target categories: everything.)

Once the identity of the most likely prospective advertiser (usually an industry) is established, the ad marketer must determine what the advertiser wants its advertising to accomplish. To establish realistic objectives, the ad marketer will study and analyze the industry—its current business conditions, the competitive situation, new product development, sales objectives, profits.

He also examines the media currently used by members of the target industry. He analyzes why advertising dollars are invested in these media and what he must do to capture his share. If the answer is efficiency and numbers,

obviously he must at least be competitive. Does the industry react to other marketing stimuli, such as promotion or merchandising? If so, he must create programs to compete with existing ones.

The ad marketer will also work to establish his magazine as a "perceived medium" within that industry. For some magazines, the perception is obvious because the editorial content is endemic to the target advertiser's goods or services. For others, their readership may be a logical target market for specific products. And for those magazines that are not yet perceived as an advertising medium within an industry, it may be necessary to start from scratch.

Devising strategy

Once the objectives are established, the ad marketer must develop a strategy to achieve established quotas set by management. By presenting an overview of existing advertising linage by dollar volume, industry and territory, he will be able to devise tactics that will minimize attrition and secure and increase the linage of current advertisers.

When existing business is secured for the coming year and every avenue of its expansion explored, the ad marketer will then address the topic of new revenue sources. The first place to look for new business is from the list of former advertisers. An examination of background information might provide a clue to the reasons for having been omitted from their schedules.

Did the magazine fail to deliver anticipated results? Did the advertiser feel neglected or mistreated (poor positioning of his ads, lack of consistent service, etc.)? Or were budgets simply cut?

The strategy here is to re-establish contact. The effective ad marketer will get the answers and suggest remedies. He will present new programs geared to improve results. He will mollify dissatisfaction and increase personal contact.

If the budget isn't restored, he will show how dropping his magazine is not in the advertiser's best interest. These clients once felt that the magazine was effective. They will again, if the ad marketer can find out what's wrong and fix it.

Ad market strategies

By Morton E. Grossman

Writing the formal marketing plan is a well-developed and trusted procedure in most major American corporations. The plan is usually prepared once a year and is designed to answer three questions: Where are we? Where do we want to go? How do we get there?

Many magazine publishers, advertising directors and marketing directors spend most of their time working on the third question, "How do we get there?" while over-

looking the two prerequisite questions. The fact is, however, that it is very hard to get anywhere if you don't have a clear direction. And it's hard to figure out which way to go if you don't know where you are in the first place.

A good marketing plan can give you the direction you need, providing you with the perspective and the reasons for taking action. It will not only keep you from getting lost, it will also show you the way to get from where you are to where you want to be.

With this plan, you can be confident that you are justified in spending the money you are going to spend. And with this plan, you are much more likely to be right. There isn't a magazine that relies on advertising revenue that wouldn't benefit by paying serious attention to the process of strategic marketing planning.

A good manager's intuition and insight are invaluable. However, a good, factual plan will enhance an executive's ability to come up with new ideas and fresh approaches. Remember, a marketing plan is only a set of guidelines—markers to keep you on the track and speed you along. It is not a sacred book of ironclad rules to be slavishly followed.

It will enable you to keep your eye on your goals and not get diverted by the passing chances that come along or bogged down in the daily process of putting out fires. A sales staff can keep busy every day chasing after ads, answering complaints and following leads as they come along. But you will not succeed in moving ahead to where you want to be unless you take the time to make plans and follow them.

To do this effectively, the marketing plan must be in writing. Although it may consist of only a few typewritten pages, the resulting document may be the most important ad marketing job done all year and has to be treated as a major project in itself.

Assign tasks. Set deadlines. See that adequate time is allowed for gathering and analyzing the necessary information. You are creating a deliberate expression of policy that will guide you in the purposeful management of ad marketing.

Your strategic marketing plan will:

1. Analyze and define your magazine's business situation—past, present and future.

2. Identify the problems and opportunities facing your magazine.

3. Establish specific and realistic marketing objectives.

After you have gone through these three steps, you can then begin to develop specific tactics and action plans: how you will deploy your sales staff, what research and promotion projects you will undertake, what your timing will be, how you will coordinate all the elements in your plan.

Do not confuse the marketing plan with budgeting. The time to do your ad forecasting and budgeting and your marketing expense budgeting is after the marketing plan is finished. The plan comes first. It is quite likely that the plan will affect the budgeting, and that's one of the reasons why you prepare a plan in the first place.

Whoever is in charge of ad sales should prepare the plan. It could be the publisher, but normally it should not be the chief executive officer of the magazine. It could be the advertising director if this executive is also in charge of research, promotion and other ad marketing functions. Some companies, especially multi-magazine publishers, have special market planning executives, since each magazine needs a separate plan.

If a magazine deals with a number of industries or markets, there may have to be a separate plan for each market. Even though special markets or projects fall within the scope of a single magazine, the factors influencing their marketing may vary from those affecting the marketing of the magazine in general. Special marketing efforts, a major project for an anniversary issue, for example, may need a plan too.

Magazine marketing plans are generally done for a one-year period corresponding to the magazine's fiscal year. Plans are rarely done for shorter periods of time, unless there are two or more distinct selling seasons and a separate plan is needed for each.

Sometimes plans are made for 18 months or two years. The longer term plan may occur, for example, when research is scheduled late in the year and the survey results would not be available until after the end of the year. Therefore, longer term planning is done in order to include the activities and expenditures dictated by the research.

Although there is such a thing as going too far, there is something to be said for preparing an all-inclusive plan, especially when doing it for the first time. A complete detailed job will let you know what is and what isn't important for future plans. It can give you a better overall picture, and could even provide market and marketing information for selling and promotion.

A final reminder before we go into the details of the strategic marketing plan: Stick to facts and valid assumptions. Don't throw in wild guesses and unsubstantiated opinions.

Analyzing your market

In preparing your plan, the first thing to do is to find out where you are. To analyze the magazine's current situation, the first place to look is in the marketplace or marketplaces the magazine serves.

Are these growing markets or mature markets? Your strategy will be different for each case. Your best chance of changing your own market position is during a period of market change.

When the market is growing, it will pay you to spend marketing dollars to gain a larger share of the advertising dollars in the marketplace. The higher expenditure may cut into your profits, but it will be worth it when the market stabilizes, for then you will be able to hold down your expenditures and concentrate on profitability.

Growth, maturity and decline are long-term trends. You also have to look at the shorter phases of the business cycle. Is the market in a boom or recession period? Even during a long-term growth stage, there often are periods of recession followed by recovery and boom. You have to know what has happened in the past, what is going on now and what is likely to happen in the future because all of these factors affect your ad rates, the way you position yourself and the amount of money you spend on marketing. And all of these factors affect your magazine's profitability.

Next, you have to look at who the buyers are in the marketplace. This is extremely important to your marketing because your readers are the buyers your advertisers are trying to reach. In a rapid growth market, there is a preponderance of first-time buyers. In a mature market, most buyers—generally 70 percent or more—are repeat buyers.

Does your magazine reach the newcomer or the experienced customer? Whichever it is, you've got to position your magazine for advertisers to demonstrate the advantage your readership holds in the marketplace.

Consumer bridal magazines make the most of the fact that their readers are inexperienced first-time buyers, and that original sales to these customers will result in repeat sales in the future. It is a very successful strategy, despite the fact that the number of people in the bridal market is only a tiny fraction of the total market in every product advertising category they carry, with the exception of bridal wear.

Matching trends to demographics

It is important to learn the demographic characteristics of the buyers in the marketplace, both current and past, in order to discover possible trends and match them to your magazine's reader demographics. For business publications, buyers should be analyzed by size of company, sales and purchasing procedures.

What are the buying patterns? How do people get into the market and how do they progress through it? Special interest magazines are able to show that they reach customers at their peak of interest in the activity and therefore at the peak of their buying activity. You may need research to document points such as these, and that will make a difference in your strategy and magazine's expenditures.

The competitive situation in the market must be considered. Are there many small companies with small advertising budgets, or are there a comparatively few large companies which dominate the market? Your ad sales strategy will have to conform to the market's competitive conditions.

You should know the relative sales standing of each major company, their total sales and share of market. You should know their product lines, how they position themselves and whether they are in the high end of the market, the low end or somewhere in between. Then position your magazine relative to each product line.

What do you do in a market where distribution is split between mass merchandisers and specialty stores? Where can your magazine help the manufacturer with his sales to retailers? How can you help with his consumer advertising? For seasonal products, when must you lock up your advertising schedules? You have to match your strategies to the conditions of the market.

Then there is the segmentation in the marketplace. What are the major sub-divisions by product category, type, or size? Take horses. There are Quarter Horses, Arabians, Appaloosas, Clydesdales, Belgians, Walking Horses, Pacers and Trotters. There are small, light and swift breeds; and large, heavy and slow breeds. There is Western riding and English riding, thoroughbred horse racing, harness racing, steeplechasing, dressage and rodeo. Prices for horses range from a few hundred dollars to $50,000 and more. What is the segmentation in your market and how does your magazine fit in?

Technological changes in the market are important to your magazine as well as to the manufacturers. When fiberglass skis began to replace metal skis, the competitive manufacturing situation changed almost overnight. New companies appeared. Old companies who couldn't or wouldn't change were pushed out. Some big advertising schedules disappeared. New ones had to be sold. The same old magazine strategies wouldn't work under the new conditions created by the new technology.

Laws and government regulations also have a profound affect on all businesses. What impending government action will affect your market? The change in the number of citizens band channels from 20 to 40 caused a major upheaval in the CB market—and required new ad marketing strategies.

Other factors are important for some markets and magazines and not for others. Pricing. Credit practices. Geography. You may have to adopt certain strategies to cope with any of these situations.

In addition, you should have information on all of the market factors that have been important to your magazine for some time, usually three to five years. Since one of the purposes of this exercise is to learn from experience so that you can plan better for the future, it is instructive to know how things got to be the way they are. It is also instructive to compare previous market situations with previous magazine ad marketing strategies.

Finally, in analyzing the current market situation, you should try to get or make valid forecasts. This could be the most important part of your market situation analysis, because you are going to base your strategies on your best informed opinion of what is going to happen in the next year.

You may rely on experts in the field for these forecasts, but if you have done your work well on market developments from the recent past up to the present, you should be able to come up with a reasonably accurate scenario upon which to base your strategies. Do not neglect your magazine's editors and advertising salespeople for input. They are in constant contact with key people in the field, and they can be extremely helpful.

Taking your magazine apart

Now you should take your magazine apart and analyze it. What is your situation in advertising pages and revenue, rates, circulation, editorial, graphics and production? How does all this compare to your competition?

Think in qualitative terms too. What image does your magazine have in the eyes of the advertising community? Should it be changed? If so, how?

The first thing you want to look at is your advertising pages and revenue, by month, by year and for the past several years. You also want to look at your net revenue per page. And you want to look at your advertising by product category, by territory, and by rate class if you have rate categories.

Then you want to look at budgeted advertising pages and revenue versus actual performance for this year and for the past several years; in other words, compare what you expected would happen with ad sales against what did happen.

You also want to look at the same information for your magazine's competitors. And you want to see what market share each of you have, present and past.

Then you want to make a forecast for the next year; that is, what you expect will happen, not your objective. You will consider your advertising objectives when you have finished your analysis and formulated your goals.

As you can see, all of this information requires records. If you do not have records that will give you this information, you should start on them immediately. You are in the business of selling advertising and you must know what you and your competitors are doing. There is no way out of it. Keeping records takes time, and though you may know or feel you know what is happening, records are absolutely necessary. You make the decisions, but records will produce the information to help you make better decisions.

Know your idiosyncracies

Aside from the general diagnoses you can make, such as gains and losses, every magazine has specific idiosyncratic problems which will show up when you study the records.

For instance, a look at the record can show you that you have a market share problem in Territory 3, Product Category 5. Now you can practice the art of marketing. Perhaps improved selling performance is needed. Perhaps there is unusual competition. Records can alert you to this situation and give you a chance to deal with the problem. Without records, you might never have known the problem existed.

You are dealing with advertising sales, but every magazine function has some bearing on advertising. Therefore, you will have to look at the situation in each of your magazine's areas.

Naturally, your pricing policies directly affect your income. Look at your rates for the past several years. In particular, study the cost per thousand (CPM). The raw dollars you get per unit of circulation is equal to your unit price. Using CPMs you can compare your unit price directly with your competition. You may find that you have advantages or disadvantages that you didn't know about, and you should devise strategies to deal with them.

For example, if you have a competitive CPM advantage at the 12-time rate, you are in a good position to sell schedules, even if you don't have that advantage at the one-time rate. You should analyze your rates at each size and frequency. You may find opportunities to make painless adjustments that will increase your profitability.

Circulation development strategies

Circulation is a fruitful area for strategy development. As usual, you need figures for the past few years. And you need the major breakdowns that pertain to your magazine: newsstand and subscriptions, paid and unpaid, written request and source, full price and discounts. And as usual you have to compare these figures with your competition's figures.

If you have a circulation statement, analyze every category and do the same for the competition. Then correct your problems and exploit your advantages.

Subscriber or reader research is an extension of circulation. Who reads your magazine? What are their characteristics? How well do you cover the market? Reader characteristics, purchasing activity and market coverage are the most widely used concepts in magazine ad marketing because, when you get right down to it, that's what the advertiser is really buying.

Your strategic marketing plan should take your circulation department's projection for growth into account. Consider your relative circulation position now and your projected position versus the other magazines in your field.

Here's what happens when you do. Let us assume that you have the smallest circulation in a three magazine field. Your forecasts show that you will pull ahead of the other magazines in three years. You are now using a top of the market strategy but your magazine will be moving toward broad coverage of the market. How will you handle the change, beginning with your current plans?

Marketing Editorial

The editorial pages are the basic product of your magazine, yet many publishers do not make enough use of their editorial product in their ad selling strategy.

What happens once the reader buys or receives the magazine? That's what the advertiser wants to know. Therefore, take a critical look at your statement of editorial purpose. Make sure it says what you want it to say and that it convincingly reflects the magazine's strengths. If you don't have such a statement, it's high time somebody wrote one for the magazine.

What, precisely, does your magazine cover editorially? Clearly define the breadth and depth of the coverage.

What are the implications of your particular editorial mandate? If you have a new product trade publication, for example, your readers probably will not spend a great deal of time reading it. However, the magazine probably will be routed around to a great many people. Therefore, when you plan research on your subscribers, you should develop information not on how much time subscribers spend with each issue, but rather on how many other people read each copy, who they are and what they buy.

On the other hand, if you publish a feature magazine with in-depth editorial, readers will spend more time with the magazine themselves and share it less with others. In this case you should plan a strategy based not on the number of additional readers per copy but rather on reader time spent reading since this will illustrate and document reader involvement.

You have to position your magazine positively in the minds of your advertising community. You have

to differentiate your magazine from the competition. You have to define the territory your magazine has staked out for itself. And to do these things you need editorial analysis.

Keep records of the number of editorial pages you run by issue, by year, in black and white, in two-color, in four-color.

Devise a system of editorial classifications, preferably classifications that match or supplement your advertising classifications, and track them too. Do this for the competition for comparative purposes.

For magazines that have not yet developed substantial advertising sales positions, a good editorial strategy will help pave the way. For magazines that have developed positions of leadership, editorial provides a necessary rationale.

You should also consider the quality of your magazine's paper stock, its graphics, its design and format. These things make a difference to your readers—and to your advertisers.

If you have reader service, use it to show response to advertising. If you have feedback on advertising response or testimonials, use it too.

Every item can be important and can help you market your advertising pages more effectively. Once you have gone through your situation analysis you should have a very good idea of your magazine's strengths and weaknesses and you should be able to plan accordingly.

You will be in a better position to handle your direct competition, but don't forget your other competitors: television, radio, newspapers, direct mail, other communications media. Find out how much your customers are advertising in those media.

It is wise to track the other media for two reasons: It will give you a better idea of your medium's comparative standing with advertisers, and it may alert you to a problem or opportunity you didn't know you had.

Magazine publishers too often get carried away competing with magazines in their own field. In fact, it may be even more important to sell the primary value of the magazines in your field than to sell against your direct competitors. Television may be a bigger threat than the other magazines in your field.

As you plan your strategy, remember to consider the capabilities of your staff. Do you have the people who can do what you want done, or will you have to add to your staff? How much of a work load can they handle? Should you plan to stagger the work? Will your people need special training? You adjust your plans to the capabilities of the people available to you.

This stage of your analysis is crucial because your strategies are going to deal with the problems and opportunities you perceive. Take a good hard look at this area and be as objective and realistic as possible.

The matter of supply may be one of the problems you run into. Situations in which there is an undersupply tend to cut down advertising. In the motorcycle market a few years ago, manufacturers cut down on production during a recession. After the recession, production was still down even though demand was up. Dealers and distributors found themselves selling every unit they could get their hands on and, in fact, were often backordered. One magazine's successful strategy was to demonstrate the long-term growth trend of the market and convince advertisers to keep up the marketing pressure in order to reap greater share of market when the pipelines were flowing again.

Economic recession is a problem, yet a number of magazines were able to overcome this problem by consistently pointing out the value of advertising during the 1973-1974 recession.

Population and life style trends can cause problems

for some magazines. The teenage population is declining in numbers. The birthrate is down. Many people are postponing marriage. Magazines with strong stakes in these markets have to find ways to overcome these problems. In some cases nothing can be done about basic market problems. But more often than not problems can be handled if you confront them realistically and seek honest solutions.

Government regulations and legislation create problems. There is resistance to rate increases. Influential dealers may not be impressed with your magazine. Your competitor may strike a low blow. Other magazines may produce more inquiries. Whatever the problem, put it down in your marketing plan so that you can deal with it strategically.

On the other hand, there are opportunities that your magazine should capitalize on. There is the matter of oversupply: more inventory sitting around than can be moved easily. Advertising can help in this situation.

New technologies can be tremendous boons for magazine advertising. Radial tires, wide-body airplanes, aluminum tennis rackets, pocket calculators, electronic cameras—all created opportunities for advertising. But individual magazines did not automatically benefit. They had to be aware of the opportunities and sell space against them.

Market growth and new companies coming into the market are opportunities, but they do not produce advertising automatically. You have to develop strategies because very little advertising comes in over the transom. It has to be sold.

Then there are the population trends and lifestyles that represent advertising opportunities. The growth in numbers of the 25-to 49-year-old age group is an opportunity for magazines whose readers fall into that age category. Physical fitness, back to nature, trends away from high energy consumption are opportunities for magazines whose editorial thrust takes in those areas.

As many a publisher has found out, problems can be turned into opportunities and opportunities can become problems. Your strategy—and doing nothing can also be a strategy—can make the difference.

Marketing goals

This is the most important part of the marketing plan. Here is where you must choose a direction. If you have done your work well in the preceding sections, you will find that your goals will almost state themselves.

Here is your chance to make a change in the status quo. You do not want to make a forecast here, since that is merely an estimate of what you *expect* will happen. You do want to state an objective, which is what you *want* to happen.

Your objectives must be realistic. They have to be attainable, given your strategies and resources. There is no point in setting a far-fetched goal that has little hope of being achieved.

Your objectives should be as specific as you can possibly make them. You should show an actual number of advertising pages to be increased, by category, by account, by rate classification. You should show your revenue or profit gain in actual dollars. And show exactly where the increase will come from.

Some of your objectives may not be quantifiable, such as changing the attitudes of certain advertisers; but try to translate that change into numbers of pages if at all possible.

If you have worked through all of the preceding steps, you will know where you are and where you want to go. The next step is to find out how you get there.

Strategic marketing plan checklist
I.   Situation analysis
   A.   The marketplace
      1. Growth stage
      2. Buyers
      3. Buying patterns
      4. Share of market of major companies
      5. Distribution
      6. Segmentation
      7. New technology
      8. Law and government regulations
      9. Other: pricing, seasonality, etc.
     10. History
     11. Forecast

   B.   Advertising pages and revenue
      1. By product category
      2. By rate classification
      3. By sales territory
      4. Budget versus actual
      5. Competitive
      6. Forecast

   C.   Rates
      1. History
      2. Breakdowns
      3. Coverage - reader research
      4. Competitive

   D.   Circulation
      1. History
      2. Breakdowns
      3. Coverage - reader research
      4. Competitive

   E.   Editorial
      1. Platform
      2. Coverage
      3. Tracking system
      4. Competitive

   F.   Graphics and production

   G.   Other
      1. Reader service
      2. Advertising results
      3. Other media competition

   H.   Human resources

II.   Problems and opportunities

III.   Marketing objectives
   A.   Realistic
   B.   Specific

Multi-person marketing

By William Abbott

There is a lot to be said for selling to strength—knowing what the customer wants and presenting it to him on a platter. To do this with consistency, the marketer must keep abreast of changing concepts. Marketing innovations, like scientific ones, rarely evolve slowly. They usually change with the inception of ideas by individuals.

Larry Light is an advertising strategist. He earns his way in the world by engaging in deep market analysis on behalf of Ted Bates & Co. Larry rarely comes into contact with magazine people. He has no reason to. Yet what he does has an elemental effect upon magazine marketing in the same way that basic research relates to a manufactured product.

At Bates, Larry develops special presentations for clients. In the process, he tells them things about their products that aren't necessarily apparent from their position in the marketplace. His ideas are always thought-provoking and often startling. Frequently, they represent the starting point of strategic planning that will have serious impact upon advertising schedules of corporate giants with magazine budgets in the millions.

One could spend an entire career selling magazine advertising space without knowing a thing about Larry's job. On the other hand, the best magazine marketers pride themselves on their ability to match wits with their counterparts at both client and agency. In the process, they often produce marketing plans that outstrip less inquisitive competitors.

A change in the marketplace which is currently absorbing Light's attention is called "multi-person marketing." (He frankly admits that while the idea is his, it was given its name by *Advertising Age* in an article which attempted to define it.)

Choice by situation

Multi-person marketing operates on the premise that the old concept of brand loyalty has evolved into a kind of "choice by situation." In other words, in a marketing sense, *where* people are determines *who* they are and *what* they buy. Instead of having one favorite brand, consumers have a set of favorites, and which of these favorites is purchased is dictated by external conditions.

Obviously, the media marketing ramifications will be enormous if this theory is substantiated. If each consumer now favors an average of three brands instead of one, the total U.S. market of 225 million consumers will translate to 675 million for a specific product.

Advertisers' current strategies and schedules are designed to market to the traditional 225 million consumers. Broad acceptance of multi-person marketing might well expand and alter advertising schedules to include people in a number of roles, in the process making them new and different consumers. Reach will become more specialized than ever.

The process promises to benefit magazines more than any other medium. After all, magazines are the primary medium of specialization. This will be especially true of those magazines whose marketing strategists will study multi-person marketing and apply it to their plans.

So, if you would like to apply M-P-M to your next marketing plan, read on!

American industry grew up in an era of brand loyalty among consumers. In the past, a person drank one brand of soft drink and had a favorite set of items all the way from the shampoo for the hair to the socks for the feet. Somehow, this concept of brand loyalty has become outmoded.

Brand switching today, however, is not as simple as it was in the past. There is a uniform pattern of behavior, dictated by a situation or place directly linked to the brands of items we will purchase. In other words, according to Larry Light, "As a consumer, *who* I am depends upon *where* I am. What I wear, what I eat, how I feel, are direct consequences of where I am."

The one as many

A consumer whose tastes change with a situation becomes many consumers from a marketing viewpoint. So the practice of market segmentation by nose count, upon which American business has so long relied, may be effectively replaced in today's world by a count of numbers of personalities.

This obviously leads to expanding markets but with a very different connotation for the term *"market share."* In such a marketplace, magazine advertisers' strategies will increasingly relate to capturing market share on the basis of four considerations: value, time, quality and feelings.

Value. When you examine the first consideration, value, it becomes apparent that multi-person in marketing will broaden your list of potential advertisers. Previously, value had related money to price which, in traditional marketing and media decisions, related in turn to income. If a manufacturer sold a lower priced product, he advertised in media with lower income readers. As his price range increased, so did the "quality of audience" of selected media.

Today, the concept that higher income consumers always purchase more expensive products has been totally shattered by well-documented evidence that generic and "no-frills" brands are bought primarily by these consumers and "name brands" by middle and lower income groups.

The lesson for the publisher in this message is that, just because he publishes an upscale magazine, he needn't write off manufacturers of inexpensive products as advertising prospects. Because, in today's marketplace, if manufacturers are savvy, *they* won't write off a magazine on the basis of reader income alone.

Time. The second consideration, time, has perhaps had an even greater impact upon consumer practices in recent years. We want to fly to Europe on the Concorde in three hours and to microwave our food in three minutes; in the process of satisfying this urge for instant everything, cost becomes secondary. Two-income households whose members have little time for conventional home making also have more money to spend on avoiding it. Working women have ushered in an era of one-stop shopping. Credit is more available and is more freely used to make life "quicker."

Quality. Positioning a brand by quality has become tricky, mainly because people have perceived quality to have gone down as prices have gone up. The quality market segment is growing, not because there are more wealthy individuals but because middle-income people are willing to spend more in certain situations.

Feelings. Larry Light is quick to point out that in his context, feelings are something one experiences with sensation as the key. What he refers to as the "sensation generation" will pay a premium price for a premium sensation. They will spend whatever it takes to experience that special feeling about themselves.

Changing consumer habits

There is mounting evidence that corroborates the validity of Light's premise, especially in the magazine industry. One only has to examine *Vogue* magazine to be made aware of evolving consumer patterns.

In 1970, *Vogue*, which editorially is devoted solely to showing the ultra-priced end of the fashion and beauty worlds, had an average monthly circulation of about 450,000. By 1980, *Vogue*'s circulation had grown to 1,250,000, without any significant editorial change in style or content. Furthermore, most of the circulation increase was in the form of single-copy sales, a fact which precludes circulation promotions as the cause of this increase in popularity.

Are there that many more rich women in the U.S. today? Not likely! But Mary Smith, who earns $12,000 annually, while not a prospect for the $30,000 Ben Kahn sable coat on page 150, may well purchase the $400 dress on page 175. Because she wants to feel special in a particular situation, she can and will invest two-weeks' pay. So she has now become a *Vogue* reader.

Doesn't it follow, then, that a manufacturer whose product might be less grand should now advertise in *Vogue*? Its current readers do not shop at only one end of the price spectrum.

A recent study showed that some of the best prospects for Heineken's beer were to be found among regular Budweiser drinkers. In a typical multi-person marketing situation, the person who drinks Bud will be more inclined toward Heineken as a status product on special occasions.

The first element of choice is filled by the fact that the consumer is a beer drinker. Placed in this appropriate situation, probably calling for upscaling for appearance's sake (*e.g.,* in a better restaurant, out with the boss), he'll switch to the less plebian import.

Those who plan ad schedules for quality import beer accounts would do well to look past *The New Yorker.* They will find a hidden market in magazines with less impressive demographics. And advertising managers of such publications should realize that they have an opportunity to change minds by adopting a multi-person marketing approach to their sales presentations.

Of course, all products are not subject to multi-person marketing sales techniques. Items such as toothpaste or soap are still largely subject to traditional concepts of single brand loyalties because of unique qualities.

New realities in the marketplace

But the list of situation-based products is quite long and increasing. People use or wear different brands or qualities of watches, jewelry, eyeglasses (or contact lenses), hosiery, cosmetics, fragrances, shampoos and a host of other personal products. They drink different soft drinks on occasions, and different alcoholic ones to suit occasions. And the reasons for a particular choice depend on the physical situation, the consumer's multiplicity of tastes, social imagery and are psychological conditions.

Old concepts of market share have become outmoded as products proliferate. Twenty years ago, when there were 10 brands of shampoos on the market, an average market share was 10 percent. A 25 percent market-share constituted a power brand.

Today, with dandruff-frees, herbals, and a host of other highly specialized products, there are probably 100 different kinds of shampoos. Now, a 1 percent market share would be average. Today, a new product which captures a 5 percent share of a highly fractionalized market may be quite a success. In the eighties, performing five times better than average will be a significant accomplishment.

The mass exposure of television does not readily adapt to these new realities of the marketplace. Magazines, with their unique ability to segment markets, do. As advertisers accept the new concept of divided brand loyalty as a fact of life, opportunities will arise to publishers who are prepared to fit the unique qualities of their audiences into the mold.

The complexities of the marketplace no longer lend themselves to the simple solutions of mass reach. Adapting your publication's advertising sales strategies to this new marketing philosophy may even change how you position it and the identities of its competitors.

Developing new categories

By William Abbott

The scene is familiar to anyone who has spent more than a little time pursuing magazine advertising space: Someone (the publisher, the ad director, the brass in general) awakes one day to the realization that the gadget industry spends a powerful amount of money in magazines. Since *their* magazine receives none of these riches, it is decided to mount an all-out effort to correct the situation.

What procedures are followed to accomplish this goal? Nine times out of 10, the same script is enacted—and it goes something like this:

First, an editorial section on gadgets is planned and usually forced on a reluctant editorial staff (if they had felt that gadgets were suitable grist for their mill, they would have incorporated them long ago). Perhaps even a "Gadget Editor" is appointed.

Next, an expert gadget salesman is hired. Good old Joe Blatz "knows everyone in gadgets; great connections; sure to get the business." (What isn't considered is that in "Old Joe's" last three positions, two of the magazines went out of business and the third gave up the effort after 15 months, firing Joe in the process.)

Now everyone's ready to roll—and God help the guy who, not seeing the pot at the end of this rainbow, might suggest that something more is required for success.

I've lived this scenario more times than I care to recall. On occasion, the outcome has been maybe mildly successful. But in today's marketing-oriented industry, such tactics rarely work. We've become too sophisticated, too scientific, to accept any but sound business reasons for advertising decisions.

Of course, editorial compatible with a specific category of advertising helps—if for no other reason than it demonstrates that the reader is at least somewhat interested in the advertisers' wares. But in truly professional decision-making situations, editorial is a minor factor. And while it is true that some sales people are better known than others, and that personal friendships may enter into the picture in one or two instances, no one knows *everyone* well enough to sway an entire industry.

I once knew two agency execs who, every time they got a new account, would make a list of their old pals and apportion pages accordingly. Some mighty strange schedules came out of the process, and the clients' naivete is mind boggling. But these are exceptions. The rules today are far different. While it may have been true a while ago that a large percentage of advertising pages were sold in the bar car on the 5:22 to Greenwich, it isn't anymore. Style still counts, but in today's marketing climate, style must be reinforced with a lot of substance.

We work in a competitive marketplace, one in which advertisers seek solid answers to real problems about market share, distribution, heavy-user identity, buyer motivation, display and retailer acceptance. A publication not only must show an interest in an industry, it must be *part of that industry*. Its representatives to the industry must have an intimate understanding of conditions within the industry and competition among industry members. Personal relationships? Yes, but on the basis of respect earned when the customer knows that in selling him *your* product, you are also concerned with selling *his*.

Opening the door

Getting the door open must be the first objective of the marketing plan established for a new advertising category. An executive contacted by a publication that he perceives as an illogical medium for his advertising isn't apt to be readily accessible to that publication's salespeople. Therefore, the marketing plan must have a feature that makes the prospect *want* to see the seller. Since today's business executive has a voracious appetite for marketing data, providing such information is an excellent strategy for at least getting an audience. As a wise salesperson once said: "You can't sell them if you can't see them."

Information! It's the key. An authoritative study that provides usable data opens doors more readily than old Joe Blatz ever thought possible. To get that information, develop a research project—one designed to inform as well as sell. The best way to ask the right questions is to invite leaders of the target industry to suggest them. They won't mind playing expert.

When we at *Self* decided that the food industry was to be a prime target, we analyzed our market position and found a growing consumer awareness of nutrition among our audience. Obviously, this constituted an ideal market position for the magazine. But first we had to document the reality of this interest. To do so, we undertook a study to demonstrate the effects of a nutrition-conscious public on food marketing in the '80s. The study actually had two objectives: To convince the food industry that nutrition was becoming a factor in food marketing; and to open doors to food industry executives by making them aware of *Self* as a publication reaching this new, nutrition-oriented consumer.

What chance does a new magazine have to present its case to the assembled marketing wizards of, say, General Foods? None! But tell these same people that you're about to spend $25,000 on a study of vital concern to *their* business and, furthermore, that you want *them* to devise the questions—and these same folks become amazingly accessible.

Now, I don't mean that you're going to fool them. You *are* going to undertake a study. And it *will* constitute a true national sample, the results of which will be of inestimable value to them, with no dollar investment on their part. However, the study will also obtain demographic and psychographic information about your readership. The result will be a study you *and* the executives can use. More important—you've met them; they know your publication; the door is at least ajar.

One mistake frequently made in implementing this strategy is to confuse a market study with a readership study. They are not the same. In fact, nothing is as ineffective as a door-opener, or as transparently self-serving, as a study of one's own audience. Such studies are rarely accepted with interest, and are almost never believed.

Presenting your case

Now that the door is ajar, what next? The results, of course! Leading executives of an industry have submitted questions. You have collected the answers. You now have another reason to make a call, and you have every expectation that those executives will be glad to see you and the awaited results. Furthermore, common courtesy dictates that, after having accepted your hospitality in the form of the investment you've made to answer some questions important to their business, these executives will grant you the opportunity to present the case for your audience's place in the marketplace.

Psychographic and demographic surveys represent additional research tools useful in developing new categories of business. Currently, the two most visible pieces of psychographic research are the SRI/VALS study and the Yankelovich Monitor survey. Neither tells us much that we can't see by simply looking around at our friends and neighbors, or even at our own families. However, they represent strong documentation and, in some ways, answer questions about what has happened within our society over the past 20 years.

All of this can be extremely useful in analyzing purchasing patterns of the market segment which comprises your magazine's readership. For example: A trade magazine to the food industry wanting to acquire new business from manufacturers of "single serving" food products might undertake a promotion based on documentation of the explosion of single-member households in the United States during the '70s. Psychographic research reinforces the fact that this new phenomenon exists by establishing the reasons behind it. Or a consumer publication may seek to use as its strategy for breaking into a new category the idea of a changing lifestyle among its readership. Once again, proof of the change is essential, and frequently is found in psychographic research.

Demographic research is far more prevalent in the publishing industry, and its use more widespread. A recent addition to its ranks is a unique system called PRIZM. PRIZM segments the U.S. population by neighborhood. Its basic postulate is "birds of a feather flock together"—a very shaky platform indeed. My next-door neighbor, for example, is very different from me (I emphasize *different*, not better or worse), different ethnic background, social values, religion, traditions, prejudices, eating habits—different in a host of personal characteristics that dictate diverse purchasing patterns. What we do have in common is income, the one factor that determines who is financially able to live in a specific area. When you reduce it to its lowest common denominator, PRIZM merely shows market segmentation by income. If you're going after new business, it helps to prove that your readership is composed of people at an income level most likely to be attracted to the products of the industry solicited. PRIZM can be helpful in such a situation.

Use data with care

Finally, when engaged in the task of developing new categories, we may draw upon the data provided by syndicated magazine audience studies such as SMRB and MRI. Together these constitute the ultimate weapon in an advertising agency's arsenal of magazine research. However, both are primarily buying tools, not selling tools. Agencies are intimately familiar with their contents from protracted use. So, when I see an eager young space-seller charging from the office, SMRB figures under arm, I feel a touch of pity for the media buyer who, once again, will be asked to sit politely through one more recitation of dry statistics—figures which he or she has, most likely, gone over a dozen-or-so times already.

At a recent MPA seminar covering media buying, every major speaker from the media departments of leading advertising agencies pleaded with the audience, made up almost entirely of sales reps, not to waste their buyers' time by presenting already-known figures. Unfortunately, these buying tools will continue to be used as selling tools until magazine sales management instructs otherwise.

But, like the rules of French grammar, there is always an exception: The *selective* use of syndicated research can be useful in selling new categories. Data about product use, which is incorporated in these studies, will indicate the purchasing habits of your readership with respect to many goods and services, and may correlate with your research—especially as it applies to demographic and psychographic banner points within these studies.

In business there is no such thing as "too much." We are constantly striving to beat last year's figures, and new category development is one of the most effective ways to do so. The cornerstone in the construction of a case directed to an unfamiliar client who does not know your magazine must be research proving that the two of you have something in common. It's all so instinctive, so natural. In fact, anyone who has ever been married knows the process well.

Using the right tools

By William Abbott

In an earlier discussion of magazine ad marketing, I outlined the basic difference between the two functions of sales management: the administrative function (handled by the ad director) and the creative function (handled by the marketing director). I further noted how the marketing director gives sales direction to the advertising staff by creating a marketing plan and devising strategy.

Since sales techniques are an important element of the marketing plan, the marketing director must also instruct his staff in the effective use of these techniques. Selling is half art and half science. And while some people are more gifted in the art part than others, the science part can be mastered by almost anyone. He or she needs only quality instruction and the willingness to put in time and effort to learn the craft.

Consider this story:

When I was a freshman salesman I occupied a desk in a large bullpen which offered very little privacy. However, such an office arrangement has a few advantages which I didn't appreciate at the time. By overhearing my co-workers' conversations I learned quite a bit about how to sell—but I learned a good deal more about how *not* to sell.

The desk closest to mine was occupied by a journeyman I'll call Charlie. I don't know what made Charlie opt for a career selling advertising space. I do know that it was not a vocation.

Each morning Charlie arrived at 9:20 sharp, spent about twenty minutes with the Times and coffee, chatted with intimates who were equally concerned with the vagaries of the stock market and otherwise satisfied his requirement for morning relaxation before entering the fray. At 10:00 sharp Charlie plunged a hand into his desk drawer, retrieved his account books, and began his day's sales efforts, which consisted of placing telephone calls (I assume they were systematic, not random) to media buyers.

The substance of his calls went something like this: "Hello Tom, this is Charlie. Is the ABC Company going to be running with us this May? One page! Great! Thanks Tom, and if you have any special position requests let me know." Or: "Oh, they're not. How come? Budget cuts? Well, if they reconsider let me know. I'll call you next month in case the situation changes."

The sad thing about this scene is that Charlie really thought he was selling when he was speaking to Tom. And the sadder thing is that management didn't know enough to at least try to maximize his limited skills by instruction.

Selling versus marketing

Since that time, our industry has become much more sophisticated in its sales instruction, thanks to advertising marketing concepts developed over the past decade. Of greatest importance is the distinction now being made between marketing and selling.

To put it simply: Selling tries to get the customer to want what *you* have; marketing tries to have what the *customer* will want.

Given this distinction, the marketing-oriented salesperson does not ask what the advertiser will do for his magazine. Instead, he proposes what the *magazine* will do for the *advertiser*.

The first step in preparing a marketing presentation is to give some thought to the situation of the media buyer, who wants to perform his job with maximum effectiveness. In the advertising business, this generally involves producing ideas that will 1) reach more prospective customers, with the expenditure of the least amount of revenue; 2) sell more product; 3) increase market share.

Obviously, if you have the audience in sufficient number and with efficiency, you present your case to the buyer and the sale is made. However, in this situation, since you have what he wants to buy, you aren't really selling; he's buying.

On the other hand, suppose your magazine does not have such numbers and efficiency. Is your situation then hopeless?

If the answer to this question were "yes," none of us would be needed and Media Buyers with computers would rule the advertising world. However, the salesperson who addresses the problems of sales and market share will find a receptive ear.

In today's marketplace a manufacturer must do a lot more than merely reach prospective buyers with his advertising message. He must "sell the product through," and the American marketplace of the eighties is a jungle in which competition is fierce and an adversary lurks behind every tree.

Identify problem areas

The truly professional seller of advertising space understands this situation and accepts it as a challenge. To meet this challenge, he will try to identify an advertiser's problem areas and offer him assistance in these areas.

To do this, he must first make himself aware of conditions in the marketplace which surround a specific advertiser's industry: its selling structure, distribution patterns, type of retail outlets.

Second, he must identify logical consumers of the product, their probable reason for buying the product, and the pricing structure of the product.

Third, he must sort out the competitive situation: the identity of major competitors and their selling points, relative price and quality comparisons.

And finally, he must know retail sales strategy: brand awareness of the product, effectiveness and type of point-of-purchase material, the specific industry need for training of retailer salespeople.

It is the job of the marketing department to understand these market conditions and, working with the salespeople, to devise specific programs attuned to aiding the advertiser in those areas where assistance is required.

Perhaps the account needs internal sales support;

this can be accomplished by communication to its sales staff. Distribution problem? Wholesaler and retailer contact from the magazine, showing how advertising support will increase sales. Consumer identity? If you see opportunities in new markets, show how and why. Demonstrate how the competition works and produce ideas for counter-ing it.

For the fact is: Magazines can do all of the above and quite effectively. Use the tools. Work *for* your advertisers, not only with them. Make them see you as an ally, not a peddler.

Consultative selling

By William Abbott

I first met Mack Hanan in the magnificent surroundings of the Costa del Sol. It was back in 1973, after *Woman's Day* had broken records with an unprecedented gain in advertising pages during the previous year. The junket to Spain was a reward for an outstanding performance by one of the finest sales staffs ever assembled under the masthead of a single magazine.

Of course, since the primary function of sales meetings is to learn and grow in one's trade, there were intermittent business sessions between revels. Mack, a leading marketing consultant, had been engaged to conduct a course which he called "Consultative Selling." And, as I later discovered, he wrote the book.

Consultative Selling (which Mack wrote in conjunction with James Cribbin, Professor of Management at St. John's University and Instructor for The American Management Association; and Herman Heiser, partner in the accounting firm of Cooper & Lybrand) is a very fine book indeed for anyone who wants to learn to sell anything. Much of its contents provide the marketing manager with an advanced understanding of how to structure sales presentations that approach business from the same direction as the client. And while its contents must be adapted to compensate for some obvious differences between selling advertising and selling a tangible product, it is nonetheless an excellent training text for sellers of magazine advertising.

In its purest form, consultative selling involves turning a customer into a client and, as the book says, this difference is far more than semantic. A customer is someone to be sold. A client is someone to be served. In order to serve the client you must know something about his business so that you can, where practical, help him solve his problems. In addition, you must be able to identify opportunities.

The consultative salesperson is first and foremost a marketer. The entire concept of consultative selling is a reaction to changes in marketing from the era of salesmanship to the era of customer orientation.

It is the job of the marketing director of a magazine to equip sales staff members with the know-how and tools essential to successfully turn customers into clients. Admittedly, this is an ambitious undertaking, one which requires the understanding, cooperation and assistance of the publisher and advertising director. Sales training should be conducted regularly and intensive instruction given at the annual sales meeting. However, salespeople must have an educational background that will enable them to fully understand the dynamics of the marketplace.

Knowledge of the marketplace

Overall, there are few businesses whose members are better or more diversely educated than are those who sell magazine advertising space. We have a wealth of well-educated people, graduates of the nation's finest and most prestigious colleges and universities. Their backgrounds are invaluable in day-to-day business and social contact.

It is important, however, to carefully assess *what* they have studied in school as well as where they have studied it. (If I were on a sinking ship, I would prefer a lifeboat companion who was a Naval Academy graduate to an alumnus of the Harvard Business School.)

Irrespective of previous education, a person who wishes to successfully sell advertising space should have studied marketing on the college level for at least one year. If he or she hasn't, I suggest that they register for evening courses at a local college or university. (In New York, the NYU School of Commerce offers one of the finest marketing courses in the country.)

This specialized knowledge is important because in today's business climate the salesperson is going to operate in a universe where most people on the other side of the desk will have extensive marketing backgrounds. He or she must expect to be called on by people who have more than superficial knowledge of the marketplace.

Establish confidence immediately

In consultative selling, especially of advertising, the key to success is confidence. The seller must establish a "climate of confidence" between himself and the customer whom he seeks to convert to client. A product salesperson can sell as long as his customer has a minimal level of confidence in the product. A seller of advertising space can sell his service systems only if the customer has a high level of confidence in the salesperson.

And remember—initial impact is important. *You never get a second chance to make a first impression!* A salesperson who can convey his marketing expertise will be immediately perceived as an equal.

On the other hand, a customer who perceives a salesperson as lacking in marketing know-how sees incompetence, and it will be very difficult to alter this initial reading. Even if the salesperson displays other qualities, the customer will still perceive the salesperson as one who "really doesn't know the business." Confidence is as much in the eye of the beholder as it is in the salesperson's own performance.

Speak their language

The consultative salesperson understands that advertising is merely one element involved in the client's corporate strategy to achieve an objective. The client is not looking to buy "pages." Instead, he is seeking that intangible something that will make his sales greater; that will increase his market share; that will make his new product profitable more quickly. So, the salesperson who sells "pages" might as well be conducting his presentation in an exotic Caspian dialect for all the effect that it will have upon a decision-maker. Unfortunately, advertising space salespeople have developed a tendency to talk to clients in terms of pages rather than concepts because we tend to assess our successes in numbers of pages.

In order to correct this misguided approach, the marketing director must continually remind staff members that once the customer believes in the audience reached by a publication, the pages will follow. And the customer will have confidence in a salesperson if he believes that salesperson understands his advertising and marketing needs.

What are current market conditions? The competitive situation? Distribution problems? Market share? These are some questions to be addressed if the salesperson is to really make the customer his client.

He must know how to make advertising work for his client. Market conditions can be affected by developing new customers (*i.e.*, your readers). Competitors can be met head-on by reaching their customers with a sales message (especially if they are already advertisers in your magazine). Distribution can be aided by merchandising which shows advertising back-up to increase product sales in support of retailers.

The consultative salesperson knows his clients' customers. He must study the types of retail outlets in which the advertiser's product is distributed, for example. A first-rate marketing department will have opened channels of communication with retailers. The marketing director must ensure that sales personnel know how and when to use these channels.

The consultative salesperson is an innovator, bringing ideas to the client. To do this, the salesperson must first be an observer, identifying the client's needs and working with the marketing department to offer solutions. Once again, the marketing department must cooperate closely to study the client and develop programs likely to fit into his strategies and objectives. If the climate of confidence has been established, the salesperson may even plan with the client.

In the final analysis, the consultative salesperson is a business manager, delivering personal service to the client and fighting for him even with the magazine's management when ad page positioning is at issue. In other words, he must service the client on a day-to-day basis. And he must treat each account as if it were his biggest advertiser. There is no better way to build confidence.

The September-October issue of *Business Horizons Magazine* carried an article that proclaimed consultative selling as an idea whose time has passed. It stated that the technique of having salespeople act as problem solvers has too many pitfalls and that customers must now be sold aggressively rather than softly. The conclusion states: "In short, consultative selling sounds a lot better than it really is."

The writer of those words obviously never sat across the desk from an anxious product manager or account executive who was looking for an answer to some very serious problems. Aggressiveness is not what he is seeking. He wants assistance—assistance from those who have the background and knowledge to act as consultants as well as sellers.

Positioning your sales promotion effort

By Julie A. Laitin

Ten years ago, Jack Trout and Al Ries radically changed the way advertising and marketing directors plan their strategies.

"Knowing what a customer wants isn't too helpful," wrote Trout and Ries, "if a dozen other companies are already serving his or her wants. To be successful, a company must shift its emphasis from the customer to the competitor." This is the basis of what is called *positioning*.

Positioning means finding something unique or different about your product . . . something that sets it apart from your competition and makes it stand out in the minds of your customers.

If a product is truly different, it probably has an established position in the marketplace. However, since very few products are unique, a product must appear to be better or more effective than its competition.

This strategy works not only for selling products, it also works for selling space in a magazine.

To position your magazine successfully in the marketplace, take a good, hard look at every aspect of it. Does it have a unique editorial focus or a unique format? If so, it is offering something no other magazine offers.

If it doesn't, however—and very few magazines do —look for ways to describe your magazine that set it apart from the competition. Are there any words, phrases, or orientations that can set it apart from the crowd?

Keep in mind also that positioning does not necessarily depend on your magazine's strengths. Seasonality, technological advances, and government regulations can propel you to the forefront in your publishing category.

In fact, positioning can even be achieved successfully by magazines that lack a clearly defined advantage. Take, for example, the "new kid on on the block." Such a magazine can use its very newness and youth as a differentiating feature.

To successfully position your magazine in the market, you must know where to look for proof of leadership and superiority. Advertising pages, revenues, and CPM are only starting points. While most advertising, marketing, and promotion directors know some of the basic "sell" strategies that spotlight their magazines' benefits, a review of where to look may give you additional ammunition. It may also help you to rethink or reposition your present line of attack.

Advertising

• *Ad pages and revenues.* Like all people, advertisers want to align themselves with the leader. They want their ads to be where the lion's share is. And they want a growing part of the market.

Therefore, if you can show that your magazine has more ad pages and/or revenues than a competing magazine, potential advertisers will see that other advertisers are behind you, that you're delivering their market, and that yours is the best game in town.

Generally speaking, showing ad page gains in combination with revenue increases is much stronger proof of success than showing revenue increases alone. It is quite possible to be up in revenues and down in pages if page rates are increased, and, for the most part, advertisers and agencies are aware of this. They therefore look somewhat skeptically on revenue figures without accompanying page increases.

Building on its well-known "Nobody . . . Like *Newsweek*" campaign, *Newsweek* makes the most of its demonstrated advertiser acceptance by positioning itself as the consistent and outstanding leader in the field: "In 1980, *Newsweek* led the newsweekly field in total advertising pages for the thirteenth consecutive year." The magazine cites this distinguished fact as evidence of its conclusive superiority over both *Time* and *U.S. News*: "More than any other newsweekly, *Newsweek* is more efficient at bringing advertisers the audience they need. Those who can afford what they're selling." By further reinforcing this standing through a chart showing the final tally, *Newsweek* positions itself as the one "most effective selling vehicle ever to hit a newsstand or mailbox."

• *Share of the market.* Total ad pages and revenues alone, however, do not tell the whole story—not by a long shot. For example, your competitors may have more total ad pages, but you may be gaining ground on them. Thus, although their numbers may beat yours, your percentage of growth may be considerably higher than theirs.

If that's the case, look for indications that your competition is losing its share of the market. Then subtly explain this situation to your advertisers and prospects. It's a prime opportunity to show that the market is turning to you.

Which is exactly what *Sports Afield* crows with its headline, "Our competition has a right to be scared." It backs up its boast by showing *Sports Afield* up 30.75 percent in the first half of 1979 as compared with its competitors—*Outdoor Life* and *Field & Stream*—which are both

down. The ad, which then goes on to explain why *Sports Afield* is the best buy in the outdoor field, successfully positions it as the fastest growing magazine in the field.

• *Cost per thousand.* Among the first items a media buyer considers when planning a client's advertising is cost per thousand. It is, in fact, a primary determinant in media selection, since the lower the cost of reaching a selected target audience, the better the advertising investment. Therefore, if you reach a particular market at the lowest cost per thousand available, you should be telling the world, and telling them loud and clear.

Instructor does exactly that in explaining, "Any way you figure it, *Instructor*'s got the figures." Putting the spotlight on its cost efficiency, the brochure claims that "at $11.50 per thousand, *Instructor* gives you the lowest CPM of all classroom magazines." Then, emphasizing its other leading "figures," *Instructor* cites its "highest paid circulation" and "10 percent increase" in subscribers to put it ahead of its competitors by a substantial margin.

• *The advertisers themselves.* If research into total ad pages, percentage growth, market share, and CPM does not uncover areas of leadership, take a look at the advertisers you have: the number, variety, and leading companies. Do you have *more* advertisers than your competition? More *new* advertisers? More *leading* advertisers? If so, your positioning has enormously useful and broad-based applications.

This approach has been used successfully by both a large consumer magazine with a wide, upscale audience (*The New Yorker*) and a small, professional magazine with a specialized readership *(Independent Agent)*. Each magazine positions itself as a leader by dint of the leading companies that advertise in its pages.

The New Yorker's campaign shows different companies in each of its ads. The ads not only highlight the names of these companies ("Birds Eye Was Here"), they also group them according to industry: food, travel, entertainment, or automotive. By prominently displaying the leading advertisers in each of these areas, the campaign is designed to bring "me too-ers" into the magazine.

This is also what *Independent Agent* has in mind with its boast, "The Finest Companies Keep Us Company." Similar in concept to *The New Yorker* campaign, their brochure uses company logos instead of ads. Persuasive and dramatic in its approach, it underscores the strength that a successful positioning concept can offer.

• *Testimonials.* A testimonial by a leading industry spokesperson is one of the strongest forms of promotion available. If you use such an endorsement, however, the statement must be meaningful; puffery will weaken, or even destroy, its potential mileage.

Advertising Age uses Peter Bonanni's endorsement to convey three vital messages. First, from an advertiser's point of view, *Advertising Age* is a "primary *advertising* vehicle." Second, from a reader's point of view, it's "must reading." And third, it's the place where leading publishers are investing their time and money. Obviously, this testimonial is designed to position *Advertising Age* as a prime advertising vehicle for a leading industry: publishing.

In the unlikely event that the spokesperson is willing to set a dollar value on sales volume directly attributable to your publication, you've got a gem of an opportunity to display your magazine as one that not only offers exposure, but also delivers sales.

New York Magazine uses this strategy cleverly and successfully through an endorsement from Warren

Hirsch, President of Murjani International. Singling out his coverage in *New York Magazine* as the "one single event" that catapulted his company from a $50 million to a $300 million company, Hirsch underscores for *New York Magazine* the tremendous dollar potential that exposure in this magazine represents.

Circulation

•*Affluence*. If advertising pages or leading companies are not your primary strengths, then you must show that you can deliver quality circulation. This means delivering more than sheer numbers. It also means proving that your magazine reaches the people with money. The people with power. And the people who buy. Obviously, any survey figures you have will lend credibility and impact to your statements.

Barron's goes head-to-head with its major competitors in a simple, powerful ad that has a single message: "*Barron's* is richer than *The New Yorker*. Or *Newsweek*. Or *Business Week* . . . ." This headline is backed up by a Simmons study that compares the reader incomes of 141 publications and puts *Barron's* audience above the rest. Making the most of its leading position of affluence in the marketplace, *Barron's* logically argues that if it "helps (its readers) get richer," that alone is "a pretty good reason for advertising in *Barron's*."

Cosmopolitan makes sure its advertisers don't underestimate the power of a *Cosmopolitan* woman when it comes to spending. Positioning its reader at the top of the pay scale, the magazine states that she "earns more and spends more than readers of any other leading young woman's magazine." To back up the claim that she's "behind one out of every five purchases of products and services in the U.S.," the ad offers impressive figures in eight advertising categories—including cosmetics, apparel, food, and travel—to demonstrate just how powerful she is.

•*Decision-maker reach*. Besides the affluence and purchasing power of your readers, their influence on the purchasing decision is of primary importance. If you can show that your magazine reaches more of the people who actually make the buying decisions, or who influence those decisions, you'll certainly have the edge because titles and positions are vital statistics.

The *U.S. Industrial Directory*, for example, positions itself as the "one industrial directory (that) reaches 32% more manufacturing buyers and specifiers." Covering a wide variety of industrial markets, it goes to the key people—buyers and specifiers—who are responsible for making the final buying decisions. And, it delivers more of them at less cost per thousand "than any other industrial directory." Cleverly pointing out that "96% of our audience directly requests the updated *USID* each year," the ad successfully underscores its value to these prospects in a dramatic and convincing way.

•*Market coverage*. If you're the only magazine covering either a specific market or a specific segment of that market, you should give it top billing. Such exclusivity means that if an advertiser wants to reach and saturate that market, you're a "must" buy.

New York Magazine positions itself as "The Magazine of New York, For New York and By New York." Reinforcing its name and building on its regional orientation as its single most important strength, this headline is packed with promises. It offers an audience of readers who live in the most "influential" city in the country and are the "biggest spenders in the world." A product geared

specifically to their needs. And an editorial written by people with the same orientation and who speak the same language as they do. For all of these reasons, *New York* can logically conclude that it "talks to (its readers) where they live."

Rather than a regional market, on the other hand, *Parents* delivers a specific market segment: mothers. For *Parents*, this positioning strategy is especially important because it must define a market that's more specialized than its name implies; *Parents* is *not* aimed at both mothers *and* fathers. Hence the headline, "I'm a mother. I love my *Parents*." Hence too a positioning tagline that actually eliminates fathers from its audience: "*Parents* . . . the magazine only a mother could love."

Because the name works against its positioning, the copy opens and closes with the word "Mother." In fact, so strong is its need to reinforce this point that it adds the last line, "Listen to Mother," after its call-for-action (" . . . call your *Parents*") line. While on first glance this line would appear gratuitous, the magazine added it to reinforce this crucial positioning stance.

•*Market impact*. A magazine that reaches a market before any others gives its advertisers a leading edge. Two years ago, when *Instructor* was the only magazine in the field with an August issue, it offered advertisers a prime chance to get a jump on their competition: "Back to school means back to business," said the ad, and "*Instructor* puts you there first." The one magazine in the right place at the right time to help advertisers pick up new business, *Instructor* had a solid positioning lead. "August—that critical buying time right before school begins. Only *Instructor* lets you be there with its exclusive August issue." Clear and to-the-point, this offers a practical and very real advantage for advertisers.

•*Non-duplicated readership*. A magazine that delivers a group of buyers no other magazine reaches has a built-in advantage. *Scientific American* woos corporate advertisers by positioning its readers first as "the people who make the future happen"; more professional, affluent, and influential readers than anywhere else. Then, offering "virtually no duplication with *Forbes*, *Fortune*, or *Business Week*," *Scientific American* can comfortably rest on its claim that it delivers "a reader you simply won't find anywhere else."

•*Controlled versus paid circulation*. The pros and cons of controlled versus paid circulation have been argued for years. If you are controlled, you can claim a no-waste circulation of qualified decision-makers. However, this claim should be backed up with supporting facts showing the extent to which your readers go in order to stay on your controlled list. If they have to make considerable efforts to get—and continue receiving— your magazine, you should highlight the value of your magazine to your readers.

If you are a paid publication, however—and particularly if you're the only one in the field—you've got meaningful validation of reader interest. Positioning itself as one of the few paid publications among a highly competitive controlled group in the health care field, *Neurology* explains why "11,267 physicians pay to get *Neurology*." Quite simply, "It's an investment." One that "physicians want . . . and are willing to pay for." Logically, "with an investment like this, you can be sure they read it. Regularly. And carefully. So, your message will be seen by involved physicians—neurologists who prescribe drugs" in the field.

•*Auditing*. Unless a magazine is audited by an outside firm, there's nothing to prevent it from claiming higher circulation figures than it actually has. Thus, advertisers in unaudited magazines cannot be absolutely sure that what they're promised is what they'll get.

If you stand alone in your field as the *only* audited magazine, you can claim to be the only magazine of real substance. While other magazines may say they reach your market, they're doing so in name only, since without an audit, they have no third-party check. Such a check, lends stature and credibility to your name and assures your advertisers that what you promise, is what you deliver.

Which is what *Dental Laboratory Review* does by highlighting its position as the "only magazine in the dental laboratory field (that offers) BPA-guaranteed circulation." Its well-executed brochure explains how circulation is verified: "When (the BPA) knows our (subscriber) facts are right, they award us the PBA chevron and publish our circulation facts and figures." This guarantee means: "You know exactly what your media dollars are buying." The assurance this offers: "We promise you circulation . . . and the BPA guarantees it."

Readership

In addition to advertising and circulation leadership, you should also be able to promise readership. This requires more than "exposure" or "receivership." It also means proving that people who *get* your magazine are involved and actually *read* it. Quite clearly, the magazine with proven editorial readership will also have proven advertising readership.

•*Research.* One of the most effective ways to substantiate readership is through research studies that measure reader preference and reader interest. These studies should be conducted by an outside source, if possible, to avoid claims of bias and distortion by your competition.

Typically, a magazine will spend anywhere from about $3,000 to $23,000 (and up) for such studies—an indication of just how much such validation is worth.

Among the areas you should mine for proof of readership are:

Preference: Which magazine is the Number One Choice of people in the field?

Usefulness: Which magazine helps them most in their jobs or areas of specialization?

Consistency: Which parts of your magazine are best-read? Can you show cover-to-cover readership? Well-read columns or departments?

Involvement: How much time do subscribers spend reading your magazine?

Environment: Where do they read your magazine— at home or at the office?

Shelf-life: How long is it kept?

Reference value: What do they do with it after reading it?

Pass-along readers: How many additional people read each copy?

Chemical Engineering makes the most of its "6 to 1 audience advantage" in an ad that offers results of 40 different independent magazine preference studies. Not only does its research indicate that *Chemical Engineering* is preferred by a 6 to 1 margin over its nearest competitor, but it offers evidence of "2.6 readers per copy in the U.S. and Canada, and an international reach of 9.5 readers per copy." Based on 7,488 returns, these results are impressive. And while it is unlikely that readers will go through the entire ad, such numerical validation sprinkled liberally throughout the copy offers readers a sense of confidence in a magazine that offers credibility and authority.

•*Testimonials.* Another way to substantiate readership is through reader testimonials. Jerry Della Femina's endorsement of *The Wall Street Journal* is part of a marvelously effective campaign using advertising hall-of-famers: Bill Marsteller, Phyllis Robinson, David McCall, and others. The public knows these people and seeks to emulate and learn from them. The ads are gems, each highlighting a different individual with a delightful discourse on his or her success story.

If you think long copy is never read, try to start one of these ads without finishing it. It's almost impossible, since each offers some ad-ucational plums that are both entertaining and intriguing. After pulling the reader through the page, the copy winds up with some solid reasons for both reading (to stay ahead) and advertising (to get response) in *The Wall Street Journal.*

•*Reader responsiveness.* While being well-read is key to an advertiser's visibility in the marketplace, audience responsiveness is the true test of whether his investment is paying off. Any results you can point to— reader inquiries, phone calls, clipped coupons—indicate that advertisers are getting returns on their money and are points favoring you over your competition.

Fortune comes right to the heart of this matter by positioning itself as a producer of results. Addressing ad agency executives and media people, its ad reinforces the purpose of advertising: "Your client isn't in the ad business. He's in the results business." It then demonstrates the kinds of results that only *Fortune* can offer: advertising persuasiveness through an environment that encourages trust; a bigger and better quality audience response, more inquiries, better sales leads; and more orders than any other publication delivers. Backing up each claim with research figures and advertiser testimonials, *Fortune*'s message is believable, strong, and very convincing.

Today's Education's claim of "more than 60,000 clipped coupons" is also powerful. Proving that its readers react to its ads, the magazine promises a prime readership: subscribers who not only read the magazine, but also "use it to find out about products advertised (there)."

Editorial leadership

Unless your magazine is a product tabloid, one of its primary strengths is its editorial. Through editorial, you show that you know the market and its needs. Your anticipation of forthcoming events, changes, and trends is evidence to advertisers that you can adapt to meet new or unusual market situations.

•*An industry "first."* One indication of such leadership is an industry "first." Perhaps your magazine recognized a market need and was the first to fill that need. If so, you can certainly claim that your magazine offers more impact, greater readership, and longer visibility than any other magazine around.

Industrial Distribution's "Famous Firsts" uses this strategy in positioning its "*first* Survey of Distributor Costs" as an historical event. With a teaser headline bound to create interest, the piece asks, "What do Charles Lindbergh, Neil Armstrong, and *Industrial Distribution* magazine have in common?" The answer, "They're all responsible for important firsts," puts this issue not only ahead of other distributor magazines, but ahead of all magazines in the foodservice field.

•*An industry "exclusive."* Are you the *only* magazine covering a significant event? Offering a unique orientation or point of view? Providing results of a survey? Or facts on the market? Or a directory of resources? If you are, let your advertisers know. It means that you're the place readers turn when they want and need those facts.

Recognizing the value of positioning once again, *Institutional Distribution* establishes its annual equipment issue as an industry exclusive through a simple, direct question: "Will the *only* foodservice distributor magazine with a special equipment and supplies issue please stand up?" The inside headline, reinforcing the message and the medium, answers and expands upon the question: "*ID* stands alone as the only distributor magazine with an equipment and supplies issue. And September is it." Aimed at companies who sell these supplies, this position offers a convincing reason to advertise and be seen in this particular issue of this particular magazine.

•*Exclusive articles by well-known people.* Do you have exclusive articles by famous people? *Parade* hosts an impressive list of contributing authors likely to be read and sought out by many. With the spotlight on Norman Mailer, its contributors include Herman Wouk, Studs Terkel, Adm. James B. Stockdale, David Halberstam, and John Cheever, as well. Making the most of its authors and its positioning, *Parade* underscores the fact that these contributors have written articles that can be found nowhere else but "In *Parade Magazine*. Exclusively."

Other areas to explore

• *Discounts.* While your rates may be higher than your competition, and your cost per thousand also above theirs, you may still be able to stretch an advertiser's investment through frequency discounts, corporate discounts, or co-op rates.

The Communicators Network offers "The Sweet Sell of Success" through a media package that goes to "688,000 of the most successful and influential people in the world." Media Network, Inc. promises, "8 full-page 4-color magazine ads for the price of one black-and-white newspaper ad." And Hearst offers a "Corporate Buy" in getting "the quality, diversity, and sales climate of seven successful magazine marketplaces (that) reach 50 million readers."

•*Format/frequency/free merchandising services.* While competing magazines often have similar benefits, additional advertising and merchandising services can sometimes offer you the edge. Bonus show distribution, elimination of bleed charges, or TV tie-ins can all offer advertisers the something extra that makes the difference.

The same holds true of format. Size, frequency, and quality reproduction can all support your advertising story. So can better binding. And if you have more four-color editorial, better photography, or better stock, don't overlook chances to point them up. Not only do such advantages enhance the reader's appreciation of the magazine, they also upgrade the showcase you offer your advertisers.

Both *Life* and *Rolling Stone* use double spreads to tout their advantages. Directed at apparel manufacturers, *Life*'s message has a single point: Advertisers should "showcase (their) apparel advertising in the one magazine that comes in extra large." The benefit, left to the advertiser to conclude, is greater advertising impact.

Rolling Stone, on the other hand, "introduces a stock that makes playing the market easy." Better color and inks, better paper, and cleaner trim and bleed are among the investments that promise good performance, "a high yield," and "ads (that) come alive."

•*Awards.* Awards are really third-party endorsements. Use them to back up your claims of editorial superiority, as *Newsweek* does through demonstrating that it's been "Honored" with more than 300 awards since 1969. Adding impact to honor, *Newsweek* also points out that these awards "help explain one more sign of recognition: *Newsweek*'s position as "the newsweekly with the most advertising pages."

Regardless of where you find your strengths—advertising, circulation, readership, editorial—they can build a strong positioning story for your magazine. As with any successful strategy, it's essential to have a clear picture not only of your own product, but of your competitors' products as well. Armed with such insights, you can then fully assess the marketing plans that will yield the greatest returns. And only then can you show your advertisers where you fit in . . . where you fill a need . . . and where you have it all over your competition.

Creative sales promotion strategies

By Julie A. Laitin

From countering a competitive claim to announcing a new publication, program, or event, publishers rush to send out letters, postcards, and brochures rather than sitting down to plan a complete, coordinated promotion program based on their objectives.

These objectives may or may not include direct mail. While direct mail can often be the most cost-effective way of reaching many of your prime prospects, alternative promotion programs can sometimes be more effective and profitable.

Knowing what your alternatives are requires both experience and creativity. This article will discuss four objectives and ways to reach them. Keep in mind that the four objectives listed are but a few of dozens that are possible. Also remember that those suggested are meant to stimulate your thoughts.

In reaching your own conclusions, you'll pick and choose from many different and equally effective solutions that can achieve the same goal. Each solution can also meet several different and overlapping objectives.

Objective I: To establish yourself as the leading specialist in your field.

1. *Start a newsletter.* Provided you can offer truly important, helpful, innovative, and newsworthy items, a newsletter is an excellent vehicle for establishing yourself in the field. It's also an ideal showcase in which to present your magazine editors as probing, incisive fact-finders who get the inside news first—wherever and whenever it happens.

Should you opt for this kind of exposure, however, your facts must be *new* and *newsworthy.* A rehash of month-old press releases and news articles clipped from the trade press will not only fail to enhance your image, but can even harm your publication.

2. *Sponsor (or co-sponsor) an industry conference or seminar.* By bringing together your readers and your advertisers—that is, your customers and your customers' customers—you'll achieve recognition as a forum for the exchange of ideas among leading industry members.

A shining example of the potential exposure and profitability of such a project is Lebhar-Friedman's MUFSO foodservice conference, sponsored by *Nation's Restaurant News.* This annual event not only presents panels and workshops led by innovative and experienced industry specialists, it also offers plenty of opportunity for operators and manufacturers to mix and mingle. What's more, as an annual gathering that attracts leading foodservice decision-makers, MUFSO has become a prestige and "must attend" affair.

Pharmaceutical Technology has expanded this "forum" approach even further by sponsoring their important industry seminars in conjunction with the Interphex Show at the Coliseum. By organizing such a program, the publication has made their Pharm-Tech Conference not only the largest but also one of the most important pharmaceutical manufacturing conferences in the U.S.

3. *Conduct a major industry event at a critical time.* Retailing is an industry whose market weeks bring in buyers and retailers from across the country. These buyers may purchase their entire stocks for the next season or year during that one critical week.

Body Fashions/Intimate Apparel takes advantage of the retail markets by conducting semi-annual fashion shows in each city where a market takes place. Advertisers can display their garments *free* in these shows with a specified amount of advertising in *BF/IA*'s market issues. Key buyers from across the country are then invited to view the newest in lingerie and intimate apparel, reinforcing *BF/IA*'s image as a trend setter and industry leader.

To publicize the event still further, *BF/IA* also invites the trade press and local radio and TV stations, where newspaper and local broadcast coverage bring the show—and the magazine—into thousands of additional homes. This is the kind of planning, involvement, and advertising support that reaps significant rewards—both immediate and long-term.

4. *Run testimonial ads by recognized industry leaders.* Getting respected and well-known leaders to emphasize your importance to their growth and success underscores your image as a vital force throughout the industry or community. This can be accomplished through ads in the trade press, in your own publication, or through a combination of both. The endorsees may be either readers who rely on your magazine to keep them inspired or up-to-date, or they may be advertisers whose sales have profited through advertising with you.

The Wall Street Journal's recent campaign by advertising's "movers and shakers" makes marvelously effective use of this tool. Instantly recognizable names like Jerry Della Femina, William Marsteller, and Lois Corey explain why they read the *Journal,* what it's done for them, and how it helped to get them where they are.

Like any endorsements by leaders we admire and seek to emulate, testimonials not only add strength and credibility to your publication's name, they can also gain advertising and readership by stimulating the "me-too" dream within us all.

5. *Reprint market research studies you've conducted and send them to your prospect list.* Nothing underscores your credibility as a force in the market so much as your knowledge of a particular industry, market segment, or buying trend. These are the kinds of facts that your customers need—and often pay significant amounts of money to get. A major complaint, in fact, is that they never have enough of this kind of research.

By reprinting a major study that has appeared in your publication, not only are you demonstrating the kind of vital information and editorial you give your readers, but you're providing marketing information to your advertisers as well. This is a two-fold benefit and works double duty to highlight your image of strength and substance.

Objective II: To get wider recognition in order to broaden your market to both readers and advertisers.

1. *Advertise.* The most common way to introduce yourself and your benefits is through advertising. Advertising can be used successfully in many ways. For example, an ad can:

•Launch a new publication, as *Discover* has recently done.

•Announce a name change, as *Metropolitan Home* did.

•Raise your company profile for the purposes of investment or acquisition, as multi-magazine publishers such as McGraw-Hill, Penton/IPC, and Cahners are now doing.

•Draw attention to your honors and awards, as *Business Week* did.

•Highlight your circulation, readership, market share, or whatever other strengths you have.

The usefulness of advertising through print media to build recognition is two-fold: 1) You can reach a specialized market through the magazines directed to that segment you want to reach, and 2) it is generally very cost effective—enabling you to reach thousands of prospects at a relatively reasonable cost.

2. *Sponsor a sporting event.* In this era of health consciousness, sporting events are an excellent way to gain visibility, interest, and involvement. *Family Circle*—a magazine that has moved from last place in market share among women's service magazines in 1970 to second place in 1980—has made a concerted effort to upgrade its promotion to attract new advertisers.

Among its most visible sports programs is the *Family Circle* Magazine Tennis Cup, an event that is broadcast on TV and generates considerable excitement among the public at large and among advertisers as well.

So much excitement among advertisers, in fact, that the magazine actually sells combination units of print and broadcast advertising as a package to its advertisers.

In addition to the tennis tournament, *Family Circle* also sponsors both soccer- and football-oriented promotions.

Note: You can also arrange for these events to take place during a trade show. Such programs not only increase your recognition factor significantly, but can take customers out of competitive booths and bring them into your arena. Sports events are, in fact, often the most memorable item at an otherwise lackluster show.

3. *Sponsor breakfasts, luncheons, and/or dinners for existing and/or prospective customers.* Affairs like these can be simply entertainment devices that build good will and, if handled properly, good press. Or if you arrange to have a speaker, he or she can also serve to establish you as an information provider. If your magazine editors are reasonably poised and can deliver some new and useful ideas to your audience, they can build credibility and recognition for themselves—and for your magazine. Or you can bring in a specialist to talk about government regulation, advertising effectiveness, packaging and design, or any other area of broad interest.

These affairs can be the place to hand out awards, too. Here's your opportunity to stroke all those nice folks who have supported you throughout the year. Almost anything can be an excuse for an award: creativity, innovation, advertising success, or advertising consistency. The point is to put those people in the limelight so they'll stay there—*and* in the pages of your magazine.

Such events can also be used to make your magazine stand out from the crowd during a trade event. Any industry gathering, in fact, in which key buyers and sellers are assembled in one place at one time is a prime opportunity to highlight your name, offer ancillary activities, create excitement, and gain visibility.

Ten sales promotion projects that really work
By Michael M. Wood

When Mike Hanley, publisher of the *AIA Journal,* won an award earlier this year as one of the five most outstanding executives in the business press, he was asked to explain the rich success of his magazine. His answer would surprise most publishers: "Next to editorial class, I would look at our promotion."

The *Journal* has made promotion investments whose payoffs in direct sales are, I believe, without parallel in the magazine business. What follows are 10 actual promotion projects that demonstrate this often ignored potential.

1. Frequently we create single sheet promotional material for a special issue. The promotion pieces are graphically superb and unfold to create interest and command the attention of the recipient. In return for every piece mailed, we have received at least one page of otherwise unsolicited advertising. The total number of additional pages in these special issues—the result of the promotion coupled with a salesperson's followup—averages 15 per issue.

2. Once each quarter we design another direct-mail piece that hammers home a current sales advantage. These have been so compelling and thought-provoking that in two instances our competition has tried to imitate and respond to our pieces. Any publisher relishes the idea of exercising this kind of control over a competitor's sales thrusts.

3. We once did $15,000 worth of carefully mixed and carefully timed promotion in just nine weeks preceding a special issue. The result was four times the net advertising revenue that we would otherwise have carried.

4. Twice a year we design highly targeted (i.e., expensive) direct-mail promotion to motivate our most valuable prospects. In several instances, the decision-maker has been so impressed with what was sent that the individual picked up the phone and placed a call to thank our salesperson.

5. Once or twice a year we design complete magazine presentations for face-to-face selling. This is our most expensive item; but even so, we spend only about $5,000 on such a pitch. We design these with two audiences in mind—the buyer and the seller. Obviously you want to involve the buyer with magazine presentations; get the buyer jumping up and down if possible. But we feel the best way to do that is to design the pitch so that our sales staff can't wait to give it four or five times a day, 15-20 times a week. If our salespeople love it, and if it's properly directed, the buyer *will* jump up and down. We've had probably 100 sales calls where the person viewing our presentation has been so impressed that the individual summoned the company's sales director or agency account executive to check it out. They want to steal our idea!

6. All *Journal* salespeople practice target selling, which involves personalized one-use promotion. Each salesperson exhaustively studies three major accounts every year, talking to company executives from the president to the shop foreman. Each account, in the end, receives a custom designed presentation which solves a company problem our staffer has identified. The solution centers around large and creative advertising in the *Journal.* Last year, for instance, our magazine carried the largest advertisement in the history of the architectural press—32 pages in a single issue—as a result of one such target investigation and promotion.

7. At odd times during the year, the *Journal* will initiate a letter series that is mailed to unsold prospects. The series has from eight to 12 different letters, each beginning "Dear Hugh" or "Dear Fred" or whomever, and each mentions Hugh's company and products in the body of the letter. This personalized approach quadruples the expense, but the results are worth it. One series last year went to 25 people who were advertising in our field, but not with us. Today, nine months later, six of these prospects have become strong and regular *Journal* advertisers.

8. Hanley and I have begun to edit and publish a newsletter for our friends and business contacts, with columns on the advertising business, the architecture business and two other subjects.

9. We use displays in certain airports to reach hard-to-get managers in prospect companies. This can be expensive—$1,000 per month—but it gets to important decision makers where they least expect it (and most appreciate it). Billboards can be used in the same manner.

10. We run dramatic spread advertisements in the advertising press and have just begun a program in *SRDS*. We are looking at trade-off space advertising with airline in-flight magazines and travel magazines. We frequently run our spreads in our own magazine. One of the keys to success with space advertising was pointed out to me by a consultant who said: "Without merchandising—reprints, mailings, salespeople tie-ins, etc.—your space will realize only half of its potential. Smart merchandising doubles the return on your space investment."

The first year we took it over, the *Journal* spent 10 percent of *net* advertising revenue on promotion. We've stayed near that figure even with our rapid growth. That's a lot of money, but we're reminded almost weekly that it pays off. In terms of importance, here's how we rank the four columns in our promotion budget:

A. Face-to-face presentations (#5 and #6 above).

B. Direct mail (#1, #2, #3, #4 above).

C. Space and display advertising (#9 and #10 above).

D. Other (#7 and #8 above).

Finally, a word about our actual creative process. We claim just two critically important stimulants: outside consultants—John DeCesare and Fred Decker fit beautifully with us—and the confidence to make immediate decisions based on our gut reactions to the concepts we dream up.

Many executives believe their biggest failing as managers may be an inability to think analytically, according to an article in the April 1977 issue of *Boardroom Reports*. But the intuitive approach to decision making (not to be confused with fuzzy thinking or shooting from the hip) is often the most creative and reliable. A person's intuition or gut reaction usually grows out of a huge reservoir of accumulated information and experience, much of it not even conscious.

Too often, strong promotion ideas can be nitpicked and questioned to death by indecisive publishers posing as thoughtful executives. By trusting their instincts and promotion expenses, as they ask their advertisers to do, publishers can begin to put together promotion that will make their magazines rich and famous.

Getting the most from your space rep

By Milton F. Decker

"What's in it for me?"

That question is seldom the actual query, but rather the one that's in the minds of most advertising prospects. They may not specifically say it, but they're certainly thinking it when you start to extol the virtues of your magazine over your competitors'.

The agency buyer or advertiser really isn't interested in your editorial platform, your pretty numbers or your merchandising potential—but *only in how your magazine's features and values benefit him or her!* Rosser Reeves long ago translated his client's product features into consumer benefits and called it the "Unique Selling Proposition." The same selling and promotional philosophy should be the platform of every publisher's selling strategy. But too often it isn't. And to get more publishers thinking about selling their product more effectively is the purpose this article hopes to achieve.

Your customer is not interested in keeping you in business—but in how you can help keep him or her in business. McGraw-Hill's classic ad has summarized this philosophy annually since 1940. The buyer sits in a chair sternly staring at the salesperson and says:

"I don't know your company or what it stands for.

"I don't know your product or your record.

"I don't know your reputation or what you can do for me.

"Now—*What was it you wanted to sell me?*"

To find an effective approach, you, as a publisher or ad sales director, should ask yourself:

1. What are my primary values which *specifically benefit* this advertiser?

2. Does my book fill a *specific need that I know this advertiser has?*

3. What is different about my magazine, compared to my competition's, that will excite this advertiser's interest?

4. What is my "Unique Selling Proposition" (U.S.P.) to fit the advertiser's objectives?

5. Does my editorial content provide the ideal environment for the advertiser's product or service?

6. Are my market and audience research current and comparable with the competition's?

7. Do my audience and demographics match those of the prospect I'm selling?

8. Do my sales promotion and sales support material *sell benefits rather than expound virtues?*

9. How can I best "position" my medium to fit my prospect's objectives?

Answering these questions almost demands a review of your current sales support promotion.

Notice the word "support."

It's a word too often neglected when considering sales development objectives. It is my firm belief that every promotional program should be planned and developed primarily to support your sales force. It should be designed to give your sales organization the basic tools to sell more intelligently and professionally, which is the surest way to increase the effectiveness of your total selling effort.

And always remember: *If the salesperson doesn't like it, it won't be used.*

Establish Primary Potential

The first step in planning any program of this nature is to establish your primary potential. It's the old story of working the best side of the street where there's the most business that's easiest to get.

Concentration of sales promotion and sales effort against the areas of greatest opportunity also has this advantage: It automatically concentrates your thinking against specific target accounts and classifications. It helps make you tailor your case to an advertiser's problem, and find the answers to the "what's-in-it-for-me" question.

Also, by focusing on one account or classification you'll find it easier to eliminate those self-glorifying generalizations so often inherent in a "general" presentation.

To be sure you select the most logical target areas for current as well as future growth calls for continuous updating—on a semi-annual or at least annual basis—of your market and competition. It's easy to neglect this important exercise, particularly for the smaller specialized publication. But it's doubly important for the publisher with a relatively limited sales force to take the time to know the direction and plan, plan, plan a complete sales support package. It's the best, if not the only, way to equalize selling effort against competition who may have the luxury of a large sales force.

Sales Support Program

After the direction is agreed upon and the preceding philosophy is accepted, an effective sales support program should establish the following objectives:

1. To define and create the most effective sales approach for your publication in terms of the target area selected—based upon the competitive values established.

2. To develop the "positioning" of your magazine among its most logical competition as well as in the mind of the buyer.

3. To prepare the basic sales support tools and material in a presentation form that will be most effectively used and accepted by your sales force.

4. To provide a planned program for your salespeople which will help them build a higher level of professionalism and performance against major target categories and accounts.

The second step, i.e., positioning your "product," is so often neglected and is such an important factor that it's worth the devotion of a few extra words.

Publishers should all take a hard look at, and maybe a leaf or two out of, the book as it has been written by the package goods marketers. The "positioning" factor has been the key element in marketing success in the last decade among the most sophisticated advertisers. Procter & Gamble has practically built its business on positioning its new products.

In 1971 David Ogilvy, in his famous ad listing 38 points for creating advertising that sells, gave first place to "the most important decision . . . on how your product is positioned."

In the same year one of the fastest-growing young agencies, Rosenfeld, Sirowitz & Lawson, listed its four guiding principles. The first one was "Accurate Positioning . . . The Most Important Step in Effective Selling."

(For some interesting and certainly worthwhile background on this subject I suggest reading the reprint of "The Positioning Era Cometh." Ries Cappiello Colwell [1212 Avenue of the Americas, New York, N.Y. 10036] will be glad to send you one. It discusses the successful positioning of Avis as #2, Seven Up's "UnCola" campaign, *Sports Illustrated's* "Third Newsweekly" promotion, as well as the unsuccessful "non-positioning" of Edsel, Dupont's Corfam and RCA computers, among others.)

To create a successful sales strategy and sound promotional plan calls for this kind of thinking and for establishing a position that takes into consideration not only your own strengths and weaknesses but those of your competitors as well.

This is dictated by both your editorial thrust as well as your demographics. The trick is to find it. A case in point is the story of a publisher of a monthly, women-oriented magazine. He always found his audience at the lowest end of those glamour demos of high incomes, better educations and occupations, high home valuation, etc. But digging uncovered a leadership position among the percentage of readers owning homes, doing gardening and baking and it uncovered an unusual reader loyalty and response factor. The positioning solution was obvious.

The point here is that every magazine has some audience or editorial feature that sets it apart from its competition or gives it a *unique selling proposition.*

How, then, can the basic objectives outlined above best be accomplished?

Three-Phase Program

One method is a three-phase program, which is particularly effective with a relatively new publication or with one which is reviewing all the alternatives for future sales development planning.

Phase I—Analysis of current data. This important

first step is vital in establishing your competitive values through a study of all currently available statistical and selling data.

The following activities are included in this phase:

1. Selection of and agreement by sales management on the specific target area or areas of greatest potential.

2. Analysis and selection of current data and demographics to make the strongest competitive story against the target area.

3. Study of your publication's strengths to establish the competitive comparisons in terms of positioning it with its competition.

4. Review of your editorial content vs your competition's to develop such extra values as reader involvement, response, etc., which might *make your magazine unique.* Any new editorial developments or plans should also be a part of this review.

5. Examination of the latest market data to document the present and future potential of your primary markets...and how your audience will fit them.

Through this exploration you can find, if your research is up-to-date, whether you are comparable to your competition so that you can favorably position yourself—statistically and factually. You may find the need for new reader research, either subscriber or syndicated.

This exercise also often uncovers new areas of opportunity for a specialized publication in fields other than its own.

Phase II—Development of the basic selling proposition. After all of the available facts have been studied for their sales values, the selling strategy can best be developed through a basic presentation directed against a target area and the marketing objectives of your prime prospects.

Experience has proved that the most effective proposals are directed to a specific situation. They should answer what media executives usually ask for and expect in a professionally designed presentation, i.e., "helpful, factual and realistically competitive data."

An accompanying box ("What Media Executives Want and Don't Want") summarizes what 25 media executives in leading advertising agencies want and like the most, as well as dislike the most, in their magazine sales presentations.

Ideally each presentation should have these qualities:

1. *Specific direction* with the content aimed at the interests of the buyer in the buyer's own field.

2. *Comparability* which will establish your own U.S.P. (Unique Selling Proposition) and your position with the most logical competition.

3. *Flexibility* in a format suitable for effective across-the-desk presentation or as a leave-behind (preferably in 8-1/2 x 11 size).

4. *Adaptability* with charts, tables and selling points that can stand alone as direct mail pieces, or can be used as blowups, and which can readily be created into slide or card format if desired.

(The accompanying box on "The Objectives and Elements of a Target Presentation" outlines in more detail the basic presentation approach and the elements it should contain.)

What Media Executives Want and Don't Want

What media executives want most and dislike most in magazine sales presentations, ranked in order of preference.

Want Most

1. Helpful new data
2. Imaginative selling idea
3. Factual
4. Points well proven
5. Realistically competitive
6. Few hard-hitting central facts
7. Quickly grasped
8. Short
9. Visually bright.

Dislike Most

1. Too many non-essentials
2. Lacking in facts
3. Dull
4. Facts already familiar
5. Insufficient evidence
6. Long-winded
7. Complicated
8. Not related to competition
9. Dull artwork.

(Source: S.D. Survey of 25 Media Executives in 10 Major N.Y. Agencies.)

Phase III—Preparation of follow-up material. This important element in selling and promotion is a procedure that is too often neglected...and seldom planned in advance—as it can be. Lack of time, because of heavy work loads, also limits this kind of effort—no matter how sincere your salesperson's intention may be to follow up a meeting with a major prospect and summarize what was said.

Ready-made "leave-behind" material should be available for following up an important call with a specific letter, proposal or a direct mail program to your key accounts. With a relatively small sales staff, where complete coverage is difficult to achieve, it can add an important extra dimension to your selling effort.

Such material would be planned, prepared and available for most basic sales needs through the adaptability of the presentation techniques previously outlined.

This can often be the extra plus in helping to make the sale. (Our experience indicates that publishers often spend too many dollars trying to get salespeople to sell harder and insufficient time or money helping them sell better.)

There are additional ways in which such sales data can be more broadly used with a minimum of cost and effort, such as:

• Followup brochures and folders.

• Preparation of media kits for major advertising classifications.

• Monthly mailings to media people.

• Comp copy inserts based upon sales support material.

• Use of basic charts or tables in your rate card to

make it more of a sales promotional vehicle.

• Specifically designed direct-mail promotion against target accounts, small accounts, running accounts or prospects appearing in competition.

And don't forget the constant need to revise and update your mailing list at frequent intervals.

Involve Your Salespeople

Also a definite effort should always be made whenever appropriate to get your salespeople as directly and personally involved as possible. This is particularly important in the selection of your target areas and the planning of account sales strategy and specific presentation work.

This is also a most effective way to greater motivation for each salesperson. It involves participation as well as developing greater professionalism through on-the-job training. The result of such a cooperative effort usually means greater acceptability and use of the promotion by your salespeople.

One final point should be made even though it may mean belaboring the obvious: The basic ingredients for the success of this or any other sales program are organization of the plan and follow-through on the strategy. All the forms, formats, checklists and proposals aren't worth the paper they're printed on if some person doesn't take the responsibility to follow through.

If one person can't be found or spared within the organization it is often worthwhile—and sometimes more economically feasible—to get outside advice and a professional, objective review of your current material. Taking a fresh look at your selling strategy and promotional props has often proved to be a profitable investment. There are dozens of competent freelancers and promotional specialists available to handle such an assignment for a reasonable fee which would not commit you beyond the needs of your specific problem.

But regardless of whether the plan is implemented from within or with outside help, the most important factor in a successful sales operation is starting somewhere with something specific in the promotional support area. In my experience it's never failed to increase productivity . . . and in turn, profits.

The Objectives and Elements of a Target Presentation

1. *Prepare the case to meet the advertiser's marketing objectives.* The audience the advertiser wants to reach is the only thing in which he or she is interested. You must show how your values and benefits can help reach the advertiser's best prospects.

2. *Position your magazine strategically with its major competition.* The buyer of media is always interested in comparative data that will help fit the media to his or her market. Thus, as broad a comparison as possible should be made on a logical, factual basis. There should be a feeling that no magazine or demographics relating to the objectives were arbitrarily selected or excluded to make your case look better.

3. *Make it as graphic as possible.* It should be easily understood by the salespeople as well as by the buyer—and as easy to present as possible.

4. *Design each page to stand on its own.* If this is accomplished, it provides the opportunity for multiple uses of separate pages as direct-mail pieces or mini-presentations through selection of applicable data.

5. *Use charts where possible to summarize.* They should be complete unto themselves to be used as suggested above.

6. *Develop general demos and data for generic use rather than specific.* Thus they can be used interchangeably for other category presentations such as automotive, liquor, travel, etc.

7. *Use exhibits to eliminate detail for easier presentation.*

Making promotion sell
By Roger Appleby

Many publishers could cut budgets in one area with impunity—the area of advertising sales promotion. Most of it is done so badly that it wouldn't be missed.

The problem can usually be traced back to the management that budgets for promotion, hires for it and pays for it. If management doesn't know what it should expect from promotion it will place very few demands upon it.

Then, promotion takes on a life of its own. Sales brochures continue to be created each year because they have always been. Trade ads continue to run in the same group of media. Dollars for direct mail are pulled together from everywhere to assure some kind of modest effort to "help" the sales force.

Many publishers will quickly assure you that promotion never sells anything, but you've got to have it. Sales promotion—including advertising—is considered to be life insurance. The salespeople that this kind of promotion is intended to help sometime feel that the same dollars would be better spent in higher salaries or on more salespeople. And they may be right. When promotion isn't created to solve specific sales problems, it won't. The promotion effort, like the sales effort, must have a sales objective. Most promotion, including advertising, is executed according to old formulas—formulas whose validity should have been argued at their inception years ago. Many publishers who are quick to introduce new techniques in personal selling have never developed any new ideas regarding sales promotion.

Placing a salesperson in front of prospects normally fires a publisher's imagination more than other means of selling. The concept of advertising as the classic method of selling on a one-to-many ratio is a form of sales promotion he or she sells to others. The salesperson's own magazine is single-mindedly committed to selling prospects on a one-to-one basis.

Publishers and advertising sales managers in companies like this do not apply the same common sense and penetrating logic to sales promotion that they do to advertising sales. For example, the demographic data, circulation figures and other statistical information that are an important element in sales promotion pieces are, by themselves, boring. They become interesting to advertisers only when they are preceded by a profile of the entire magazine as a vehicle for their ads. Yet most promotion pieces present this information without first attempting to create interest in the magazine the figures represent.

Most publishers would never allow their salespeople to sell this way. They instruct them to sell the benefit first. They know that the question in a prospect's mind is, "What's in it for me?" Promotion is no different. The same sales logic applies in creating promotion that sells. The benefit must be "up front." The logic must be clear because the salesperson is not always present to move the prospect through the sales story.

Of course the magazine itself is the best promotion tool. But when it takes more to close the sale than either the salesperson or the product can offer, the need for sales promotion is born. Whether used on a sales call or as a direct mail piece, promotion must attempt to solve the same sales problems as the salesperson. There are no other objectives for promotion. It exists to help a salesperson sell something.

Two Major Differences

But there are two major differences between sales promotion and the salesperson's approach to selling. Sales promotion normally must deal in generalities because it must make the sales story clear to a large and diverse audience. The salesperson, on the other hand, can present the sales proposition in the way best understood by any particular prospect.

A more marked difference is the fact that sales promotion cannot adapt instantaneously to a sales situation. A salesperson can retreat, advance, approach the prospect from an entirely new vantage point, moment to moment, dependent entirely on how he or she thinks the prospect is understanding the salesperson or how he or she understands the prospect. Sales promotion presents the sales story one way—the way calculated to have the best effect on the greatest number of people.

The advantage, however, is not the salesperson's to the extent that it might seem. The salesperson is not always at his or her best. Sales promotion can present the product in its best light in the same way each time.

The advantage sales promotion has over the salesperson is its ability to communicate to great numbers of prospects at the same time while the salesperson spends 90 percent of the selling time selling to prospects one at a time. That's why sales promotion requires more disciplined thinking than preparing for a sales call. Analysis of the basic sales objectives and sales problems must be more thorough than a salesperson requires; the presentation must be carefully thought out.

It's the inherent differences between salespeople and sales promotion that make them both important. Publishers should use both to maximize their sales investments.

Bad promotion will not help sell anything. To create promotion that sells you need people who know how to sell, how to write and how to present what they write visually. If management conveys the sales objectives and the sales problems clearly enough to the promotion staff it has a right to expect results.

Here are some practical suggestions that I follow in creating and evaluating promotion, including advertising.

Tell them what you're going to tell them, tell them and tell them what you told them.

The most experienced salespeople are often practitioners of this approach. Good sales promotion almost always contains these elements. In the hands of a sales peddler or a hack writer, this technique bores the prospect because its use is obvious. But the professional copywriter knows that repetition is communication. Each time the unique sales proposition is presented it is led up to differently. Its validity is reinforced because new benefits are revealed each time it is introduced. Communication takes place when an idea is presented in such a way that it falls within a person's sphere of comprehension.

A publication usually has more than one benefit worth promoting. If there appear to be many and they all seem equally important—they aren't. One will emerge stronger than the rest. If you cannot pull one free from the others, don't trust any of them to stand alone. The central idea may still be eluding you.

For example, a product news tabloid serving a specialized market had a number of benefits to promote—most circulation, best demographics, best producer of sales leads and only publication of its kind in the field. But one saleable point stood out from the rest. It was the logic behind the product format itself. This product news tabloid serves a large industry and the readers look mainly to technology to solve their problems. In this market, technology *is* product. Therefore news of newly developed products is what the market wants most. This was the single most important idea worth promoting.

With acceptance of this basic idea by advertisers came the credibility which made the large circulation, the demographics, the ability to produce qualified sales leads easy to believe.

Less Is More

If the words in a headline instantly convey a strong message, let them stand. If the illustration carries the weight of the message, don't add to it. In sales promotion as in architecture "less is more"—that is, if the ideas you're presenting are worth communicating. If they are, offer them one at a time. Move from one strong idea to the next in a logical sequence until the unique sales proposition has been clearly stated and understood. When sales promotion is working well the prospect moves through it just as its creators intended. Too many promotion efforts are of the throw-in-everything-but-the-kitchen-sink variety. All the possible benefits are mixed together in one great glob of visual confusion. The reaction is much the same as a salesperson would get if he or she emptied a briefcase in a prospect's desk and said, "Here, help yourself."

Being "the leader" is hard work. Creating good promotion for the leading publications is also hard work, or so it appears, because relatively few leading publications have it. The problem is often twofold. The publisher is afraid to take the same risks he or she once did when there was nothing to lose and everything to gain. The people creating the promotion approach the assignment with a feeling of awe and reverence. The publication has assumed larger than life proportions. All the energy and enterprise that once went into creating the original success is now being directed towards perpetuating it. Both publishing management and the promotion staff have lost the desire to draw attention to themselves. They want only to maintain presence. To say things like, "we are No. 1" or "we lead the field" isn't calculated to upset anybody. It satisfies management. But promoting a leader is neither easier nor harder than promoting any other publication. Management and the people responsible for promoting it simply have to approach it like any other problem.

Promotion Created to Win Awards

Promotion which sells often wins awards.

Promotion which is designed to win awards often wins nothing.

Promotion designed primarily to win awards rarely sells.

The moral is simple. Concentrate on creating sales promotion that sells.

Advertising Yourself

Advertising is what you're selling. If you believe in it there's no better way to show it than to advertise yourself. Even if the investment is modest, do it properly in at least one medium, even if it's your own. Then make the ad campaign a part of your mail promotion.

The promotion list is a by-product of the salesperson's account cards. The salesperson's account cards contain the names of all the key buying influences at an advertiser's company and ad agency. Develop an effective system for picking up account card changes. This means that your promotion list can be 80 to 95 percent accurate at any given time. In principle, mail every piece of promotion that you produce. This means that you should design promotion with an eye towards using it in your mail marketing. It's purely a question of maximizing your investment in the promotion you create—squeezing every last bit of value out of each promotion effort.

How bad are your own ads?
By Roger Appleby

Let's put the myth to rest that magazine publishers know how to create good advertising for themselves because they sell advertising space. That's just as absurd as saying that bank tellers are experts in acquiring money merely by virtue of the fact that they handle thousands of dollars every working day.

In reality the advertising which most publishers create to promote themselves is below average. "Average" is advertising which is borderline and barely worth doing. "Below average" advertising is an investment in creating the wrong impression about yourself. It's the kind of advertising a competitor would gladly pay for.

Why do publishers advertise anyway? Is it meant to sell something, or is it a form of corporate self-indulgence? Certainly the origin of much of it is. "There is a special issue of *X* coming up and we ought to be in it." The rationale behind this kind of advertising is simple. "If we don't advertise it will look bad." It's not communication that they're after, merely representation. They are more afraid of the sin of omission than the one of commission.

To "be there" is thought to be sufficient reason to advertise. Why? Basically many magazine publishers believe in the power of advertising only when somebody else is doing it.

These publishers are quite sensitive about their own lack of faith in advertising. They feel guilty about selling a commodity they themselves don't believe in and would rather conceal the fact. But they can relax. Their customers are aware of it. The advertising publishers run on their own behalf gives testimony to their lack of appreciation of what advertising can do. They fail to realize that their own customers continue to advertise for one reason: It works for them. If publishers understood this they would find out how to create advertising that works and become believers too.

The reader of an ad—any ad—has the right to expect the ad to be an accurate reflection of the company that pays for it—for example, stodgy advertising is placed by stodgy companies, etc. All too often, however, it's the other way around. Ads that appear in a company's name create the wrong impression of the company, its product or service—the exact opposite of the one intended or even deserved.

Advertising is a public statement about your company's product or service. This applies to the magazine publishing industry as much as to any other industry. It needn't be self-conscious or seek the safety of acceptable cliches. Advertising language should come as easy as the sales language you use in promoting your company's product or service. Cliches are what ad makers fall back on when they can't come up with an original idea.

Customers don't buy products or services. They buy the benefits derived from using them. They make a purchase in the expectation that they will be better off as a result of the exchange. Deriving a benefit that is less than the cost or equal to it is no basis for making the exchange. That's what advertising is promoting, namely, the proposition that an exchange of dollars for your product or service will leave the customer in a better position than he or she was before.

More often than not, advertising doesn't capture the individuality, enterprise or clear superiority of one company's products over another. That's partly because advertisers have bought another myth: That successful advertising is the work of con artists and snake oil promoters.

Good advertising is honest. It is clearly presented. It asks for an action of some kind. Its purpose is to create a belief in a company, its product or service or ask for the order. It's designed to create the climate for the sale or make the sale. Either way, advertising changes attitudes. Bad advertising hardens thinking *against* that company, product or service. Good advertising increases the desire to buy.

Put the Benefit Up Front

The major problem with publishing ads is that the headline or visual in most ads doesn't give a prospective customer a reason to read it. The ads are "we" oriented. Every person worthy to be called "customer" has a mental set of "what's in it for me" each and every time he or she is asked to buy. "XYZ Publishing Company covers five major markets" is not a headline that's calculated to excite that individual. Headlines like "Look into why these firms are spending millions of dollars in our publications" or "Follow the leader to . . ." are equally boring. The first makes an unreasonable request; the second is empty rhetoric.

Of the 35 advertisements placed by magazine publishers in a recent association annual, only eight had the customer benefit *up front*. The remaining were of the "Let us tell you about our company and its capabilities" genre and, unfortunately, the capabilities portion was the usual vague exhortation aimed at no one in particular.

Establishing Points of Agreement

One of the finest ads run by a publisher was created for Dun-Donnelley Publishing Corp. by Ries Cappiello Colwell. The headline was "Life, Look and the pursuit of circulation." To most people the "point of agreement" was in the headline itself. It was reinforced by a visual showing a graveyard with two stones in the foreground inscribed with *"LOOK* Born: 1937 Died: 1971" and *"LIFE* Born: 1936 Died: 1972." "Too much circulation kills" was the message and in case anyone missed the point, the first line of body copy read: "The business press can learn a lesson from the great circulation race in the mass magazine field." This line established a point that every reader could agree with up front—one which was dramatic enough to capture reader interest. Then it moved from one point of agreement to another until the groundwork for accepting the benefit had been laid.

The unique sales proposition was simply that to "Buy a tightly-defined target audience at reasonable prices" from Dun-Donnelley was a good thing for advertisers. The fact that mass circulation for its own sake was bad for advertisers had already been presented and "agreed to" by anyone reading the ad. In this instance the benefit was in itself not sufficiently interesting to sustain reader interest and not provocative or dramatic enough to put it up front. The moral is simply this: You have the best chance of selling an idea in an ad if you have established agreement at every point leading up to it.

Six Basic Rules

There is no mystery to creating good advertising. Here are some basic rules which, when followed, lead to advertising that works.

Hire talented ad makers. Good ads are created by talented professionals. Publishers, editors and sales managers are not professional copywriters or designers. The skills required do not fall within their particular area of expertise. Remember that selling ads and creating them are mutually exclusive.

Pay whatever it costs to buy talent to create good advertising, or don't advertise. When you want a good editor or a top producing salesperson you pay the market price. There is also a going rate for fine copywriters and designers.

Undirected or misdirected creative talent creates undirected or misdirected ads. The brilliant ad that sells has a basis in fact not fancy. A clear understanding of the unique sales proposition and the obstacles that stand between it and the sales are essential ingredients in the ad-making process. Only the client knows what they are and must be sure to communicate all to the ad makers before they are allowed to begin work. Good creative people have one thing in common with the poor ones. When they begin work the same cliches run through the minds of all. To the mediocre talent, however, the cliches are the end product, while to the talented ad makers it's the beginning of the creative process. It's the point when they settle down to serious work.

Good clients run good ads. Some of the best ads that were ever created never ran because they were killed by clients. Advertising that works tends to be daring, gutsy, takes a position and contains original thinking. Today's most commonplace idea once started out as an original idea. Doing the same thing better will help you get a share of the market. Original thinking can get you market domination. Safe ideas don't excite, provoke, stop or stimulate. Everyone agrees that "We're #2. We try harder" is one of the most successful slogans of all time. But ask yourself a sobering question: "If you had been Avis would you have had the guts to run it?"

Once you've established the unique sales proposition say it in different ways. When the unique sales proposition changes, promote the new one. Stick with it until it changes. There are usually many different ways to express the same idea. Try them all. Some people grasp an idea when it's expressed one way, some another.

Once you have established the unique sales proposition promote the hell out of it. It's tough enough for the people you want to sell to retain the most fundamental facts about your company and its products, i.e., that you exist and the barebones of your product or service. That's why advertising that works keeps presenting the same great idea—Levy's Rye Bread, for example.

What's the Benefit?

Human beings are more comfortable dealing with "things" than with ideas or concepts. Concepts are ideas strung together in a coherent way. When a publisher promotes all his or her magazines in one ad, he or she must sell a benefit which goes beyond the ones which the individual magazines offer. The benefit to the customer lies in the publishing concept common to all properties.

Let's assume, for example, that a successful publisher has a string of business news publications whose proven value to the reader is the result of an international news gathering capability unmatched by any other trade publisher. The publishing premise makes it possible for the publisher to ascribe the success of each publication to this capability and to any new publication he or she might start. If the advertiser believes that customers will come to these publications when they want news, the advertiser has bought the benefit.

Sometimes the publications which a reputable publisher has have been acquired at different times and their individual identity and publishing philosophy are allowed to remain intact. It would appear that no publishing premise binds them together. This is not necessarily true. The fact that the publisher purchased a string of going publications and gave them a corporate framework in which continued growth could go unhampered is good news to advertisers who have been long-time investors in these publications. To them a corporate ad promoting continuity is what they want to hear.

There's always something worth saying in a corporate ad. Publishers and their ad agencies just have to work at it until the concept or central ideas merge to bring it all together.

The trouble with syndicated research
By William Abbott

Every year, we in the magazine industry go through our annual ritual, not unlike an election campaign, as we nervously await the results of the newest Simmons or MRI studies.

Prior to release, some data are leaked, rumors abound, and an uneasy atmosphere prevails among many magazine sales executives. After all, millions of dollars in media placement hang upon the outcome. Magazines that on Monday were perfectly acceptable will be wiped off schedules on Tuesday, and vice-versa. Fortunes will be made and others will be lost, simply because a computer fed a gaggle of numbers will thoughtlessly spit out optimization formulas based upon flawed facts.

When the studies are finally released, the winners pop open the champagne and set the promotion department to work on trade ads extolling the wonders of the survey for the following day's *New York Times*. Then they settle back like the slots player in Vegas who sees three bells fall into line, and wait for the coins to pour into the tray below.

The losers, after recovering from their initial shock, contemplate the extent of the damage and immediately attempt to negotiate with the research organization in question and advertising agencies for "adjustments" to the disastrous figures. Some have even been known to threaten litigation if adjustments were not forthcoming.

The entire scene might constitute a basis for comedy were it not for the fact that it contains the seed of tragedy. In 1974, a fine, healthy magazine named *Esquire* was almost destroyed by an aberrant syndicated study which indicated the magazine had mysteriously lost a few million readers in just one year.

How can a publication lose millions of readers in a year? It's easy to understand when you look more closely at the methodology of syndicated research.

Which method is reliable?

Many researchers believe that "open-ended" questioning is the most reliable form of questioning. Since an open-ended question leaves the answer to the discretion of the respondent without reminders such as lists and logo cards, the interviewee must know and recall the product in order to cite it. Unfortunately, syndicated researchers eschew this method for the simple reason that it costs too much to tabulate results.

On the other hand, the "screening-in" method—giving respondents the names of the magazines to be studied—is subject to error and prejudice. In fact, this procedure ranks in accuracy with the notorious Literary Digest telephone poll of 1936, in which results showed Landon defeating FDR by a substantial margin.

It is presumptuous to believe that the average reader feels as strongly about the magazines he reads as we, whose very existence depends upon them, do. And it would be naive to believe that readers do not shade their answers or answer in an irresponsible manner.

For example:

"Let's see. Was it *Family Weekly, Family Health* or *Family Circle* that I read? They're all listed. Oh well, I guess I'll check each one just to be sure."

"I'm not going to have this interviewer think I'm some kind of dummy; of course I read *Scientific American, Forbes* and *The New Yorker.*"

Or: "I'm not going to have this interviewer think I'm some kind of dummy. I never read the *National Enquirer, Star* or *Midnight Globe.*"

"Are you crazy? My wife is listening in on this interview; *Penthouse,* what's that, a real estate magazine?"

And, of course, there are always those who, given a list of 150 items, feel a deep obligation to identify a particular number of them on principle alone.

Long-term effectiveness

One of America's leading women's magazines invites its readers to submit photos of the men in their lives. Each month one man is selected as the subject of a special feature. A recent television interview show questioned six of these men about the experience. One man remarked that even though his photo had appeared over two years before, he was still receiving letters from many women who saw it recently in the beauty parlor, the doctor's office, etc.

If these women readers comprised a survey sample, they would have been asked, as part of the screening-in procedure, to specify each magazine they had read in the past six months. Although they would have correctly identified the magazine in question, it would be altogether possible that the only issue of that magazine actually read was over two years old.

This, of course, is not much benefit to current advertisers! But then, what other medium can lay claim to being effective two full years after its initial production? Television commercials evaporate into the ether in milliseconds, and the daily newspaper is usually on the bottom of the bird cage within twenty-four hours.

I recently attended a syndicated research interview at which the interviewee was my secretary. Admittedly, this young woman is not a typical respondent. Her involvement with the magazine industry is too heavy. On the other hand, her answers should, if anything, be more accurate than those of the average interviewee.

I watched as she scanned the deck of cards, each card containing a logo of a national publication. She sorted 165 cards into three groups: "definitely read within the past six months"; "definitely did not read"; "possibly read in the past six months."

The interviewer then discarded the "definitely not read" cards, and asked her to pick out those publications of which she had read at least one issue in the past four.

The affirmative pile was now much smaller and I noticed that it included *Tennis* magazine.

The young woman was then asked where she had read each magazine in the affirmative pile. When the *Tennis* card was turned face up she responded; "At the office." I interrupted to ask if she was referring to my copy. When she answered, "Yes," I realized her error: I subscribe to *World Tennis,* not *Tennis* magazine!

Such an error has a tremendous impact on the relative positions of these two competitors. At stake is a net of almost 15,000 readers: 7,500 added to *Tennis* magazine's total audience; 7,500 deducted from *World Tennis* magazine's audience.

There is no reason to believe that this was an uncommon error which will then be compounded many times over by projecting the sample base from a few thousand to millions. In this manner, a single error, omission, or prejudice for or against a specific publication becomes attributed to thousands.

Some feel that such errors can be reduced if respondents are then taken "through the book" with each designated magazine. However, in this method, the respondent must still be "screened-in" in the usual manner. "Through-the-book" accuracy can only be as good as the procedure which leads up to it.

The ABC statement

Fortunately, there is an answer to the lack of reliability in syndicated research: the ABC statement. A fine source of measurement that has been around for many years, the ABC statement was once the most important tool for magazine audience evaluation.

A magazine's ABC or BPA statement states the exact number of copies sold by subscription or single-copy over a six-month period. The audited circulation figure appearing on its ABC or BPA statement is not a make-believe statistic. It is a certified number of copies sold.

These reports fell into disuse at the urging of the magazines themselves. Besieged in the mid-fifties by the megamillions of TV, the magazine industry propagated syndicated research as a means to add numbers of readers and then urged advertising agencies to institute the use of this research. In the process, an unreliable source of measurement replaced an extremely reliable one.

An ABC statement reveals a lot more than just a magazine's paid circulation. In the hands of an astute media buyer it can provide great insight into a publication's effectiveness. In fact, it tells more about a magazine than all syndicated studies combined.

To demonstrate this value, let's compare the ABC statement of two existing magazines that are outwardly alike. A careful examination of these statements exposes the marked difference between the two.

Both are relatively new publications. Magazine A is about seven years old and has maintained a circulation close to 500,000. Magazine B, even newer, has climbed to one million circulation rather rapidly. Rates for both magazines are proportionate to circulation.

On page three of each ABC statement we find that Magazine A sells 94 percent of its copies by subscription while Magazine B sells only 48 percent of its copies this way.

Turning to page 4, *Article 5, Authorized Prices,* we find that Magazine A sold about 65,000 subscriptions, or 15 percent of its total circulation, at less than basic price; Magazine B sold 140,000 subscriptions, or 14 percent, at less than basic price. A minor advantage.

However, when ABC *Article 8, Arrears and Exten-*

sions is scrutinized, Magazine A is found to carry over 30,000 arrears (readers whose subscriptions have expired, have not renewed, yet are still sent the publication in order to maintain its rate base). On the other hand, Magazine B has zero arrears.

From the assorted data above, we may deduce the following:

While Magazine A and Magazine B seem very closely competitive, Magazine B has far more reader vitality. Not only is its circulation more than double that of Magazine A, but 52 percent of its readers pay full cover price at the newsstand each month, a higher-quality audience. While both magazines have had subscription drives at less-than-basic price, Magazine A's 30,000 arrears indicate an editorial failure to satisfy a substantial segment of its original audience.

From this evidence, Magazine B is a superior product. Yet Magazine A has a title, the components of which are found in about four other publications. Subsequently, syndicated research gives it a disproportionate number of readers per copy; many more than Magazine B. Combined with the rate differential which is based upon circulation, Magazine A looks to be a far better buy. Many agencies, therefore, buy the *less effective* magazine because it seems *more efficient*.

John Ruskin once wrote: "In this world there will always be someone who will make something of a lesser quality and sell it cheaper. And those who shop on the basis of price alone are that man's lawful prey."

Oh well. Emptor media caveat!

Subscriber studies

By William Abbott

Properly conducted, research works!
Data gathered from a well-conceived research project can be used to sell advertising in various ways. For example, research studies can establish a market position for a magazine. They can provide industry information. They can determine consumer attitudes and demonstrate the effectiveness of both advertising and editorial content. They can substantiate a magazine's readership composition. They can uncover happenings in the marketplace relevant to the magazine's primary advertiser category.

Research studies differ depending on the needs of the magazine. Some studies are subscriber oriented. Others cover newsstand audiences. A new magazine may survey its initial subscribers to determine their level of satisfaction with the product. Well-established magazines may study people who didn't renew their subscriptions to find out why. Market segmentation studies show which readers are most likely to buy certain products.

As a magazine marketing executive, I use research constantly. In a recent article, I discussed the effect of syndicated research, as done by SMRB and MRI, upon the buying of magazine advertising space. In that article, I stressed the questionable value of this type of audience study. I would now like to present research from a more positive viewpoint because, properly conducted and properly utilized, research is one of our most potent sales tools.

Subscriber studies

The purpose of a subscriber study is to identify the primary purchaser of a magazine demographically, geographically and (frequently) psychographically. Because every respondent is actually a reader of the publication, such a study is a sales tool rather than a buying tool.

The key elements of a good subscriber study are credibility and validity. The questions must be impartial and the answers must be of unquestioned veracity. A study which is suspect is useless. Since expert research techniques and methodology are the only assurance of credibility, the reputation and professional qualifications of the researcher are of prime importance.

I claim no great expertise on the subject of research, however. I merely mold the raw material provided by research experts into a viable, credible sales story. So, in order to provide an authoritative assessment of this critical marketing tool, I engaged in an in-depth discussion of the subject with one of our industry's most respected and most knowledgeable researchers, Mark Clements.

I chose Clements as my resource rather than a more heavily publicized researcher because I wanted advice that could serve an entire industry, even the most specialized publication. So-called "big name" organizations can become so generalized in their services that they lose sight of what might be considered minor points to some publishers but vital to others. On the other hand, experts such as Mark Clements are able to focus sharply on limited subjects to produce far more meaningful research. (Not that Clements has not worked for the best and the biggest; he has and does!)

Let's examine subscriber studies of three different types of magazines—consumer, trade and quasi-trade—to determine the objectives behind each study, the techniques employed by Clements to achieve those objectives, and the results.

The reader's lifestyle

Cruising World is an up-and-coming consumer magazine edited for boating enthusiasts. There was a need to know exactly who its readers were. Did they differ from those of other magazines edited for boat owners and enthusiasts? It was also important to identify some unique characteristic that would separate the *Cruising World* reader from those of the other boating magazines.

Questions were designed to establish the identity of the *Cruising World* reader: What is his lifestyle? Does he prefer big or small boats, sail or power boats? How much time does he spend on this hobby? What kind of equipment (Loran, radio direction finders, fathometers, etc.) does he invest in for his boat?

When the results of this study were tabulated, *Cruising World* was able to position itself away from its competitors with readers who were more "cruising sailors" spending an average of 77 days a year aboard their boats, far more than readers of any other boating publication. These men were found to have an average income of $58,100; an average age of 44.6 years; and 16 years average boating experience. Over 67 percent had college degrees. Eighty-six percent owned boats; 67.5 percent of these were inboards. Over 42 percent of *Cruising World's* readers were found to be managers, officials or proprietors, with another 33.7 percent professionals.

Armed with these data separating their magazine from the pack, the *Cruising World* sales staff was able to carve a niche in an already crowded field. They showed their readers to be indeed different, not reached in other books.

The reader's business position

Subscriber studies for trade publications often have an entirely different purpose. Consider the study undertaken by Clements for *National Real Estate Investor,* a magazine edited for people who are interested in the buying and selling of commercial, industrial and investment real estate.

Advertising marketing of this magazine need not concern itself with the demographics of the audience since such information has no relevance to the advertiser. The age, sex, or even income of the audience doesn't matter. What does matter is the reader who owns, develops, or manages income-producing properties. Advertisers are looking for people who might represent a financial institution active in construction loans or equity positions. (This situation is typical of most trade publications: advertisers look at the reader's business position as the sole criterion for determining the placement of advertising space.)

Therefore, in order to position *National Real Estate Investor* in its marketplace, the study brought out the following points:

•Forty percent of its readers are corporate presidents; 25 percent are vice presidents; and 19 percent are owners/partners or directors.

•Over 92 percent of its readers do not read any competitive magazines, which include *Real Estate Today, Mortgage Banker, Building Operation Management, Building Design & Construction,* and a few smaller ones.

•The average reader of *National Real Estate Investor* spends 1.8 hours with each issue; 75 percent save back copies for reference.

•Of those readers who represent financial institutions, 75 percent arrange loans, 52 percent provide consulting services, 34 percent provide property management services, and 31 percent provide real estate brokerage services.

•The typical company represented by readers of *National Real Estate Investor* arranged $56.6 million in real estate financing, enough to make a construction firm's mouth water.

As valuable as the preceding data are, they still represent only part of the study's effectiveness. Other questions are designed to inform the potential advertiser of conditions in the marketplace which affect his business. Respondents whose professional qualifications make their actions and opinions especially authoritative were questioned regarding their plans to build, renovate or develop various types of properties. Subsequently, advertisers who rely upon this market for sales of either their goods or services are provided with a yardstick for anticipated business in coming months.

Dual-nature audience

Firehouse Magazine is edited for men whose occupation, either full- or part-time, involves firefighting. The magazine was conceived by Dennis Smith, former New York City firefighter and author of the best seller, *Report From Engine Company 82,* and its audience is both consumer and trade in nature. Its readers purchase or influence the purchase of all types of firefighting equipment in their local departments. In addition, they represent a highly unique market segment as consumers of goods and services endemic to the male market.

In order to clearly demonstrate the effectiveness of *Firehouse* in reaching this dual-nature audience with an advertiser's message, the Clements organization divided the study into three segments: demographic, consumer product usage, and "influence factor."

The demographic segment provided the usual data—age, income, marital status, etc. Product-usage questions were obviously slanted toward male-oriented items: automobiles, liquor, cigarettes, insurance, stereo equipment.

The "influence-factor" segment was specially designed to document the degree of influence exercised by *Firehouse* readers over the selection and purchase of equipment such as alerting radios, mobile radio systems, ambulances, sirens, safety belts, blankets, boots, portable breathing equipment, ladders, hoses and a host of items associated with emergency situations. The study enables *Firehouse* ad director Bruce Bowling to approach marketers of a wide variety of goods and services with a practical and convincing sales presentation.

In addition to subscriber studies, there are many other kinds of highly specialized research projects used in advertising space sales. Others include trade market studies, business and sales performance studies, on-page studies, consumer market studies, advertising effectiveness studies, and seminal industry studies.

The accomplishments of these studies and methods of packaging them into highly effective sales tools will be addressed in another column.

Meanwhile, remember—when undertaking research projects, plan carefully and choose wisely.

Specialized research

By William Abbott

Syndicated types of research and other readership and subscriber studies are similar in that they all survey the composition of a magazine's audience. They differ, however, in their definitions of that audience. Some studies concern themselves with only the primary purchaser, *i.e.*, the person who actually laid out the cash to obtain the publication. Other surveys may include those within the same household who also read the publication. Finally, some studies, especially the syndicated type, will count as a reader anyone who may have seen or even thinks he has seen an issue anywhere.

There are other kinds of research undertaken by magazines in addition to readership and subscriber studies. They are equally useful and frequently even more effective. Once again, I called upon researcher Mark Clements of *Mark Clements Research* to provide examples of highly specialized research projects and their application as advertising marketing tools.

Trade market studies

Trade magazines not only serve their specific industries, they are actually members of those industries. One of the most essential strategies of their advertising sales presentations is to prove that they are preferred as reference sources by industry members.

The basic advertising marketing strategy of most trade publications involves positioning themselves, in the minds of the industry served, as superior to their competitors. *National Home Center News* is a leading publication edited for owners and operators of home center and hardware retail outlets. The publication commissioned Mark Clements Research to design a study aimed at evaluating seven publications reaching executives and buyers in the home center field. The objective was to establish *National Home Center News* as the publication most read by and with the most influence among presidents, general merchandise managers, and buyers of the retail giants in the home improvement industry. These people were asked the following questions:

1. Do you receive any of these publications? (All seven were listed.) By subscription? Office routing? In any other way? (Answer for each publication.)

2. Do you read or look through any of these publications regularly (at least three of every four issues)? (Answer for each publication.)

3. Which single magazine is *most valuable* in your job from an editorial standpoint? (Check only one.)

4. If you could receive only one of these publications, which would it be? (Check only one.)

Now admittedly, it takes a great deal of confidence in one's own product to undertake such a project. However, the publishers of *National Home Center News* were willing to gamble on the outcome. And they won!

Forty-eight percent of those who received questionnaires responded. From the tabulated results, *National Home Center News* was able to document to those manufacturers whose marketing strategy incorporated heavy trade influence objectives that it was the preferred magazine of executives who make the big decisions about buying, stocking, and displaying merchandise in the home service retail world.

The questionnaire, as designed by Clements, was simple, unbiased and very effective. Such consistent research has projected *National Home Center News* into a position of leadership in its field.

A vital business report

Trade market studies are frequently valuable sales tools as well as sources of industry events and information. For the past 23 years, *Fence Industry Magazine* has sponsored an annual "Fence Market Survey." In 1981, this study once again reported on the business and sales performance of fence dealers and erectors, manufacturers and distributors in the fence market during 1980.

Undertaken by Mark Clements Research, this study had nothing whatever to do with *Fence Industry Magazine*'s editorial content or its audience. Rather, it points a spotlight on happenings in the industry in order to update members on current conditions.

The study's first segment surveys dealers and retailers, questioning them on subjects of natural interest to all industry members: what they paid suppliers; what they charged customers; what they paid for labor; what they paid erecting crew foremen; what they paid themselves as owners or managers; how many jobs they completed using different types of fencing; how many salesmen they employed; what employee benefits they provided.

It is easy to see how anyone in the fence industry would find the study results of inestimable value in maintaining a competitive position. Indeed, this study has become a vital business report to dealers.

The second segment of the "Fence Market Survey" is equally important to manufacturers and distributors of fences. It shows the average dollar volume of these two areas of the industry, and it surveys the types of fences sold in the past year. It also covers what was paid to different industry segments and provides data on manufacturers' capital investments. With this information, a manufacturer is able to assess his own business status vis-a-vis industry norms.

Results of the study were published in the July 1981 issue of *Fence Industry* which, of course, was a resounding success in advertising page sales. In fact, there were *triple* the usual number of pages sold into the issue, and no wonder! The study contained information that was eagerly awaited by all industry segments. Against it they could compare everything—from their sales figures to their employee policies—against industry norms. And if you were a businessman with plans to enter the fence industry, it clearly defined the pitfalls, opportunities and potential.

The "Fence Market Survey" represents an excellent example of a magazine's service to the industry it represents and its compensatory reward.

Industry recognition

Another example of a Trade Market Study, this time in the consumer magazine field, is *Self* magazine's "Trends in Nutrition." With a big stake in an effort to become recognized in the food industry as a logical medium, *Self* had positioned itself as a publication editorially directed toward presenting the nutritional aspects of food products. There was general acceptance among industry members of an increased awareness of nutrition on the part of the American consumer, yet it still had to be demonstrated by fact. It was also important to determine the nature and demographic composition of those most interested in nutrition.

Self's study therefore, had two objectives: First, to identify the consumer to whom nutrition was most important; second, to heighten the industry's awareness of the magazine's position with regard to food and nutrition.

The audience sample was taken from *National Family Opinion, Inc.* and represented a true national sample of U.S. women between the ages of 18 and 64. Where did *Self* come in? Background questions designed by Mark Clements reflected over 30 demographic, geographic and psychographic characteristics, which were then cross-tabbed to reflect any segment of the *Self* audience. "Trends In Nutrition" scored an instant industry success, and the data collected enabled the magazine's salespeople to demonstrate *Self*'s effectiveness in reaching the nutrition-aware consumer. In addition, the study provided *Self* with valuable publicity, always associating the *Self* name with food, diet and nutrition—the initial objective.

The editorially-exposed study

Frequently, magazines utilize the results of studies taken among readers as editorial subject matter. This practice is based upon the very sound logic that most people like to know what others are thinking or doing. One "editorially exposed" survey of this type was undertaken by Mark Clements for *Glamour* magazine.

With its young female readership increasingly remaining in the labor force despite marriage, *Glamour* decided that they would be interested in discovering how their job attitudes compared with those of other *Glamour* readers. Three hundred readers were questioned—150 from a select panel called, "The Outstanding Working Women Search" and 150 at random, employed at "average jobs." The result was published in an interesting editorial feature appearing in the March 1982 issue of the magazine.

This survey supposedly had no advertising market value. However, reassessing its contents, it is easy to see how showing a relationship between readers and their attitudes toward the jobs they currently hold can represent a factor in positioning the publication to specific prospective advertisers.

There is a thread of similarity, therefore, which runs through all of these studies. Both *National Home Center News* and *Glamour* surveyed readers, coming up with data of value to both other readers and advertisers. *Fence Industry* and *Self* surveyed people who were not necessarily readers, but whose actions and opinions were important to advertisers. Such techniques utilized by magazines so diverse in nature show that publishing is indeed one business with many tactics effective for all elements within it.

Research:reader studies and beyond

By William Abbott

In previous columns, I described various magazine research techniques such as the syndicated type of study and the self-commissioned subscriber study. We also covered trade market studies as well as reader studies, which solicit data on subscriber lifestyles, opinions or reactions for both trade and editorial purposes. In these studies, a sample group of subscribers is targeted for questioning with the results published in a subsequent issue of the publication. I also described a study taken among selected subscribers of *Glamour* Magazine, the results of which were featured in an editorial report published in a subsequent issue. This afforded *Glamour* readers the opportunity of comparing their own lifestyles and opinions with those of their peers who constituted the *Glamour* sample panel.

The on-page study

Black Enterprise magazine has carried this tech-

nique a step further by publishing the actual questionnaire in an issue and inviting *all* readers to participate. The payoff comes in the form of an editorial feature of considerable interest to the magazine's audience.

This strategy, which combines editorial and marketing expertise, is a favorite and oft-used one by *Black Enterprise*. One example is a project called "Black America Speaks Out," a survey of readers' opinions on a diversity of subjects ranging from security and employment to education. "Black America Speaks Out" was an attitudinal study, the purpose of which was to project an image of the black executive or manager to industry while providing an interesting editorial feature to enable a very specialized market segment to understand itself.

Black Enterprise recently sponsored a new reader study called "How Do You Feel About Your Job?" Once again, results will be published in an upcoming issue, presenting a clear overview of problems, opportunities and challenges confronting the magazine's readers, black managers in today's society.

Although the primary motivation of these projects is editorial in nature, there is solid byproduct in them for *Black Enterprise*'s marketing efforts too. Reader attitudes and opinions constitute a potent sales tool.

Another example of a survey in which general reader participation represented the data source is *Family Circle*'s study of working wives. Anxious to determine the increase of working women upon the impact of family life, *Family Circle* published a questionnaire which invited married readers who also worked to reply to a series of questions, cut out the page, and return it by mail.

Results were featured editorially, allowing the working reader to compare the effects of her own job upon her family's lifestyle with those of others.

The marketing implications of this *Family Circle* project should be readily apparent to anyone concerned with the changes taking place among women in society.

In its February 1982 issue, *Family Circle* took on a more controversial subject when it published a questionnaire titled, "How Do You Feel About Abortion?" Not directly related to market research, this study will nonetheless provide an important sign of the *Family Circle* reader's place in changing lifestyles and display an element of editorial involvement in reader opinions. (In this study, photocopied returns will not be included to eliminate ballot stuffing by pressure groups.)

Consumer market studies

SMRB (Simmons) publishes product-usage statistics as part of its syndicated study of magazines. Most concede, however, that these data are not in sufficient depth to provide more than a passing idea of the buying habits of a specific publication's readership.

For example, while SMRB may indicate that the audience of magazine X is 46 percent more likely to consist of purchasers of kumquats, it provides no clue as to why, when, how many, or any other number of incidental details which are essential to the kumquat advertiser. Subsequently, many publications feel that it is essential to produce comprehensive studies of product-usage and purchasing habits of consumers within target industries.

Time magazine undertakes numerous studies with the objective of gathering information on a particular industry. These studies attempt to identify purchasers of specific goods and services, their opinions of the products surveyed, brand experience, attitude toward advertising, reasons for buying and *not* buying, price, and other related information. A textbook case of one such study involved microwave ovens.

First, *Time* identified the microwave manufacturer as a prospective prime source of advertising revenue. Then, to demonstrate *Time*'s effectiveness in reaching her, it was necessary to isolate the consumer most likely to purchase one. The most accurate way of identifying a prospective purchaser of a product is to analyze the characteristics of those who have already bought one. *Time* commissioned Mark Clements Research to implement the study, and 400 names and addresses of recent microwave oven purchasers were supplied by each of six manufacturers; Amana, Frigidaire, General Electric, Litton, Sears, and Tappan.

A post card alert was prepared and mailed, followed by a covering letter and questionnaire which contained an incentive of 25 cents. *Time* was not identified as the sponsor.

Results pinpointed the microwave oven customer as 60 percent female, 40 percent male; median age 41.4; 90 percent married; over 50 percent college educated. The study also showed that the median value of homes owned by microwave owners was $45,750, and median household income was $23,330 (twice that of the national average at the time of the study). Although this information is useful, it's all pretty general stuff.

Then the study bore in on more relevant and specialized data. For example, it showed that the greatest number of respondents had bought their ovens seven to nine months before the survey was taken. Most were countertop models without carts. The primary reason for purchasing was to shorten time in the kitchen.

The purchasing process, so vital in decision-making for marketers, was studied with the following results: One quarter of the buyers first considered the purchase of a microwave oven less than one month prior to buying it. Conversely, the same number thought about the purchase for a period in excess of a year before making the final decision. And 50 percent fell into the period between these two extremes.

Brand reputation was the most frequently cited reason for buying a particular brand of microwave. Buyers were asked to rate the importance of outside influences on their purchase. The greatest influence, over 50 percent, came in the form of advice from friends/relatives, advertising and the dealer salesman.

Two-thirds of the purchasers considered buying one of several brand choices. Price was the reason most often given for the final brand selection. A median price of $404 was paid for microwave ovens.

Nearly three of five interviewees visited appliance stores to look at the product and over half bought from appliance stores. A majority made more than one trip to shop for the microwave. Over half of these trips were made by husband and wife shopping in tandem.

As with any general usage product, relative purchase influence data are quite important to an advertiser. According to the *Time* study, buyers noted that the brand decision was made jointly by husband and wife. Six of seven married purchasers said that both partners had seen or heard advertising for microwave ovens, and 75 percent had discussed the advertising seen.

Lifestyle and usage data were incorporated into the study to assist advertising planning by manufacturers. For example, the study revealed that microwave ovens are most often used for reheating leftovers, defrosting frozen food, and preparing snacks. Most owners use microwave ovens for less than half of their total cooking.

Time has utilized this research technique in aiding its advertising sales efforts among manufacturers of a number of consumer items, such as dishwashers, side-by-side refrigerators, residential central air conditioners, and trash compactors. This ongoing program of consumer studies provides the *Time* advertising salesperson with an array of market research that makes him welcome when calling upon a member of the appliance industry.

Another example of *Time*'s professionalism is the study of 35MM single-reflex camera markets. In this *Time*-commissioned survey, Canon, Fuji, Minolta, Nikon, Pentax and Yashica cooperated by providing names and addresses of 250 recent purchasers each. The study covered not only market demographics but also profiles of primary users of various types of cameras within each household, others in the household who use the camera, darkroom equipment owned, film usage, areas of photographic interest, and magazine readership among buyers.

Another type of consumer market study was unique

in the way in which it obtained the names of interviewees. When *Time International* sought data on perceptions and ownership of videocassette recorders, videocassettes, video cameras and selected home entertainment equipment in various parts of the world, a coupon was inserted in *Time* Asia/Middle East and Latin America editions. The reader was asked to write in his or her name and if a video recorder was owned. Fifteen hundred names were selected from those returned and a letter accompanied by a four-page questionnaire designed by Mark Clements was sent to each. The returned questionnaires contained comprehensive market data when tabulated, which served as a guide to manufacturers on how to advertise to and sell the international market. And, of course, *Time* proved to be the most effective international medium to reach most prospects.

These studies differed from those cited in previous columns on the subject of magazine research. For example, *Self*'s trade market study *"Trends In Nutrition,"* while dealing with conditions in a specific industry, used as its sample a selected group of women who were not necessarily *Self* readers. *Black Enterprise*'s on-page study used readers as interviewees but did not relate to product data.

Whatever the sample source, professionally conducted seminal research, that which informs the prospective advertiser of conditions in *his* industry or pinpoints his most likely customer, will open doors.

Properly used, it is a potent advertising marketing tool.

Should your magazine use sales reps?

By S. William Pattis

Let's set the record straight at the beginning:This article is directed to *all* publishers. There are no limits as to the size of a publication in determining whether space sales should be sold through a rep firm.

You are never too big for a rep. What counts is whether he or she can do the job better. It doesn't matter if you are Time Inc. or an associate executive in Sheboygan with a publication circulating to 12,000 members. If a rep can boost your volume, you should be interested. So let's not get hung up on labels.

In listing advantages of reps, you must first recognize that a rep is not salaried. The rep's income is derived entirely from sales so in order to stay in business, he or she *must* sell space. This creates a built-in motivation that one does not normally receive from a salaried staffer. This philosophy of *earning on performance* generally prevails within the rep firm. Salespeople in a rep firm are usually provided with good salaries (often lower than a publisher's starting salary) and the big earnings come under commission plans. People attracted to plans that provide accelerated income based on performance are attracted to such jobs. Good salespeople in successful rep firms are usually the hungriest and best producers. The sort of person who is happy working at a reputable rep firm probably would be unhappy at McGraw-Hill, and the 10-year McGraw-Hill veteran generally would not make the grade with a rep firm.

Remember, also, that a publisher's representative is an entrepreneur. The rep has gone the route of working for a publisher and even possibly held a position such as publisher or advertising director. With that experience under his or her belt, the rep wanted more, so the rep went into his or her own business and brought along the know-

how. Smart publishers recognize this special type of capability and will utilize the talent to satisfy their needs.

When you work with a rep, you have a fixed commission expense. Depending upon your page rate, the present level of advertising billing and the type of agreement you work out with your representatives, you know from the outset that you will be paying 15 percent to 20 percent of your net billing. Knowledge of this fixed percent provides distinct advantages in forecasting and general business planning.

A rep can be an excellent sounding board for testing new sales ideas, investigating new markets for magazines and helping you develop new areas of potential advertising for existing publications. A rep's involvement in the advertising and marketing community is diversified since he or she serves many publishers and previous experience will often provide an edge in determining what will work and what will not. If you're going to work with reps, be sure to run your ideas by your reps while they are still in the formulative stages. Quite recently I huddled with a good publisher we represent in the electronics industry and we brainstormed over dinner for a way to create excitement at a major convention. The idea that we settled upon was essentially a copy of a proven promotion used by one of our other publishers in the premium field.

We represent a number of special interest consumer magazines and the ideas that work when we sell the importance of the photo or hi-fi enthusiast are virtually identical to what is required to sell the importance of the tennis or travel enthusiast.

A competent rep can sell a tabloid over a standard-size magazine or vice versa. The rep can sell the value of a publication with the *lowest* cost per thousand in its field and he or she can sell the quality of the book with the *highest* cost per thousand. The rep can convince an advertiser why *all* of the advertising dollars belong in the Number One book in the field and if the rep is handling the Number Two book, the advertiser will be given an equally convincing presentation on why the dollars should be spread. Does all of this sound a bit phony or insincere? Absolutely not! The rep is hired to sell the merits of the publications he or she represents, and each magazine in existence today is around because of reader wants and needs. The rep has simply had the experience in selling different types of publications and is better qualified to move into a new selling situation.

The rep is not unlike the successful trial lawyer who can handle either the plaintiff or the defendant in a given lawsuit. The lawyer is hired for professional competence and is hired to win! A competent rep will win because he or she has had the experience.

It is interesting to me how publishers vary in their interest in using these talents. One of our country's most successful consumer magazine publishers operates on a vertical basis with a publishing head over each magazine or market served. We handle some, but not all, of that company's properties. In every instance but one, the interchange of ideas, experiences and discussion of problems is excellent and is the subject of daily communication. We feed ideas, exchange views and get excellent help on our problems. We work together. We are invited to all sales meetings and are frequently asked to conduct staff meetings or sessions. We are treated as an integral part of the publisher's own staff. In one division of this highly successful company, however, such interchange does not exist. Each salesperson is treated like a soldier in a platoon. I can discuss this subject freely because this division head recently fired all of his reps. He may well succeed; only time will tell. What is sad to report is the fact that in the territories covered by the reps, this publishing head never called on a single advertiser and never met most of our salespeople who worked on his properties during his first full year of involvement with this division!

Incidentally, the performance of these salespeople exceeded that of his own staff salespeople by every known acceptable means of comparison. The message I wish to convey is that if you elect to work with reps or have inherited reps in taking over a new position, make an effort to get to know them well, listen to their ideas and provide help for their problems. Incidentally, all of us in the rep business realize that we work *for* the publisher, but we think it's to everyone's advantage when the publisher is interested in working *with* the rep.

A Sales Rep Speaks Out

Let me blow off a little steam when I say I am fed up with publishers who knock reps without ever working with a rep, and others who use reps as stepping stones for building properties only to later drop them in order to open their own offices and feed their egos: "I have my *own* man in Dallas..."

Times are changing and the realities of the 1970s are sinking in fast. Advertising is no longer being bought, it is being *sold*! If publishers want more sales, they had better investigate all options and forget any preconceived notions that a rep firm is not the best answer.

It disturbs me that in our industry so many publishers have a hangup about publishers' representatives. Let me illustrate this comment with the following:

1. Each week we receive three to five offers for representation from publishers. Invariably, one or two of these publishers begin by saying: "I really don't care for the reps, however..." The publisher then proceeds to tell me of all the bad experiences with other reps and what other publishers have said. I then proceed to match these tales because for every "bad rep" story, I have a "bad publisher" story. But what have we proven? Not a damn thing! The simple fact is that in every business there are capable people and there are incapable people. If publishers cannot be comfortable and trusting in working with reps, they shouldn't.

2. Publisher groups such as the Magazine Publishers Association and the American Business Press hold regular meetings at plush resorts like Boca Raton and the Greenbrier. Invariably, the program includes panel discussions on advertising sales and how to structure and manage a sales force. Have you ever heard of a publisher's rep being invited to participate? It is almost as if we do not exist. Last year, we sold more than 9,000 pages of advertising—many of these pages at the expense of some of these same publishers. I suspect that we could teach these publishers a bit about advertising sales as well as advertising sales *management*. Let me add that we, too, would learn a great deal through such an exchange. How about it, ABP and MPA?

3. Then there is the perennial viewpoint of the publisher who is upset because he or she is paying the rep too much money (how much is "too much" when the job is being done properly?) and feels that "progress" now dictates that the superstar rep firm be fired and the publisher open an office with a newly found unproven salesperson. The scenario that usually follows is that "El Superstar Rep" takes on the competition and drives "El Loco Publisher" into the ground. The justification in firing a rep for doing well makes about as much sense as owning a pennant-winning baseball team and firing the $100,000 star first baseman because you know the spot can be filled with a $25,000 rookie. The new ballplayer proceeds to bat .200 instead of .300 and attendance drops as the team loses more games. (Incidentally, I recognize and share the concern of a publisher who pays more and wants more; a smart rep recognizes this obligation and will deliver accordingly.)

OK, I have released some of the venom in my system. Please understand that it isn't often that a rep is provided an opportunity to talk directly to the publishing community.—*Bill Pattis.*

Finding a Good Rep

Having discussed the advantages of working with reps, let me turn to the subject of how to find a good rep. You might begin by checking the section for publishers representatives in *Standard Rate and Data*. Secondly, I would encourage you to contact the Association of Publishers Representatives at 850 Third Ave., New York City. Most reps are members of this organization and you will find that the people at APR are anxious to help and will provide a roster of members, copies of standard rep agreements, etc. I would encourage you to talk with other publishers who use reps and ask for their recommendations.

Another excellent source of information is your own advertisers and advertising agencies within the territory in which you seek representation. Your clients can often recommend the most capable people available. You should also check various sections within *SRDS* to determine how publishers of similar magazines sell space for their magazines. You will find the names of their representatives listed under their sales offices.

I must caution you, however, that some publishers will disguise the fact that they use reps and list only the names of the individual salespeople with the address and phone number of the representative. Why this is done has always puzzled me. Assuming that a good publisher's representative is well received in the territory, the publisher should capitalize on this strength, and by listing the name of the rep firm, will enjoy the benefit of the rep's acceptance while still retaining the strength and acceptance of his or her own magazine.

What to Look For

In interviewing a rep you should try to:

1. *Determine the number of full-time salespeople employed.* Discard quickly any part-time salespeople, sub reps or "working relationships" that the rep has with other reps. Your interest should center around full-time staff salespeople only, and you should meet all of the people who will become involved with your publication. Entirely too often a publisher is impressed with the head of a rep firm only to be later disappointed with the people actually working on the publications.

2. *Determine what territory the rep actively covers and with what frequency.* Equally important is to know how this coverage compares with the geographic distribution of your advertising prospects. For example, if you plan to hire a West Coast rep headquartered in Los Angeles, and if you have 12 top advertising prospects in the Seattle/Portland area, you should know the frequency of visits to that area. Attempt to get a reasonable commitment from the rep which will indicate that such an area will be covered four to six times a year, and then, of course, be sure the rep delivers.

3. *Find out what other magazines the rep handles.* How do they compare with your publications? If the rep is selling a new product tabloid in one industrial field, that might make the rep especially qualified to sell your new product tabloid in a noncompeting industry. Do any of the magazines represented compete directly or indirectly with your publication? Will the rep's other magazines complement your publication? For example, we happen to be

strong with the representation of many of the fast-rising city magazines. An additional strong city magazine from a major market will complement our present representation and will provide us with even a stronger position with our national advertisers who are interested in more than one market. A strong rep firm is a knowledge bank and you should be sure that the firm's knowledge will be exploited for your publication.

4. *Determine how the rep plans to handle your publication within the firm.* If the rep has five people and 20 magazines, you should know if he or she plans to have all five now carry 21 magazines. An alternative method is when the rep operates on a vertical basis: that is, to have your magazine assigned to a specific individual or team that is qualified to handle your publication and with whom your publication will have significant personal financial benefit. It's important that your publication be structured within the rep firm so that it receives proper attention. The people who handle your publication should be qualified and turned on by your publication and the market you serve. For example, we have two technical and industrial teams and the salespeople involved are directly out of the industry. These staffs include a former sales manager of a relay company, a former sales manager from an electronic distributing company and a former industrial sales rep. The experiences and background of these people make them ideal for engineering and technical journals, but they would be the wrong people for general interest consumer magazines.

5. *Ask the rep how he or she plans to communicate with you.* You should be assured that you will receive regular call reports, copies of all sales letters and presentations made on your magazine and periodic forecasts concerning anticipated business. Don't settle for less! If a rep is a good businessperson, he or she knows the importance of good communication with every publisher.

6. *Finally, determine if the rep provides any other merchandising or business services.* We have an in-house marketing services department to assist our staff with layouts, presentations and market research; we prepare media data material and research as needed for smaller publishers. Our offices are equipped with automatic typewriters so that we can supplement personal visits with a continual flow of personalized mail. These sales tools are important and they account for a great deal of extra business. Will your rep cover your industry trade shows? Will the salespeople involved with your publication affiliate with the industry associations within your field? It is important that you have a good understanding as to what you will receive; you must make it clear what you want.

A Proper Balance

Of course, the publisher with a small magazine, or one with modest billing, cannot expect everything, especially at the beginning when income to the rep is low. There must be a balance between your desires and the income the rep will enjoy during the early years of representation, but most of the above points I have raised are basic to the daily operation of a successful rep firm.

Once you have selected your rep, you will then be expected to enter into a written agreement. As stated earlier in this article, the Association of Publishers Representatives can provide you with a copy of its standard agreement.

We also have a standard agreement but I hasten to add that among all our signed contracts with publishers *not one* is standard. Every situation is different and the rep and the publisher should be flexible in order to work out a mutually satisfactory agreement with which both parties can live. The commission rate is generally 20 percent of net collections but for a publication with a high page rate or one with exceptionally high existing volume, the percentage rate could be less.

In situations involving foreign representation, or publications with a lower page rate, or with little existing billing, you may be asked to pay 25 percent at least for the first couple of years. If a publication is new, or not yet developed, then you may be asked to pay a retainer. Totally apart from percentages and retainers is the need to answer the basic question of "How many dollars will the rep actually receive and how much time and effort is needed to perform properly?" It is important to recognize that a rep who takes on a magazine with $5,000 in commissions cannot provide $50,000 in sales coverage. Representatives are accustomed to "investing" for a couple of

years to build a publication, however, and you will receive proper support from the rep if there is a mutual trust. You can, of course, provide the rep with an agreement that has built-in protection for continuity in the relationship geared to performance. Normally, you are expected to give a rep three months' notice in the event of termination coupled with protection for business that is on the books as of the final date of termination. Once again, these terms will vary according to the specific situation. A magazine with $500,000 worth of commissionable billing will probably be profitable for a rep from the moment he or she takes it on unless, of course, the workload demands an unreasonable number of salespeople. Therefore, the terms of termination should not carry long-term generous extended termination benefits. All in all, I have found publishers to be very fair and through intelligent discussion, we are generally able to establish agreements that are equitable to both parties. The signed agreement should not be the result of hard negotiations but rather of understanding. The publisher and the rep should not be selling one another during negotiations because, after all, they are really working towards marriage. When the agreement is finally signed, they *begin* living together.

Getting the most of your sales promotion

By Milton Decker

If your regional space sales representative isn't making all the sales calls that should be made, or if they don't seem to be as effective as they should be, it could be *your* fault.

Having been on both sides of the fence, first as advertising sales manager for a couple of publishers and later as an independent publisher's representative, I've been able to gain a perspective on the publisher-representative relationship that may be able to help you, the publisher, get better performance from your own regional reps.

First of all, let's start with the assumption that your sales representatives are competent, hard-working and trusted professionals. If they're not, you have a totally different problem and your time would be better spent finding a new rep or reps.

So, assuming that you already have good people in those market areas beyond the efficient reach of your home office, there are some things you can do to keep them running in high gear.

For Openers, Let's Get Together

Get your thinking straight about your relationship with your rep right away. Your rep's on your side; you're on your rep's side. You both—and that means *together—*

have the same job to do: Selling space. If you get that straight, everything else will tend to click into place.

Possibly the greatest single impediment to effective sales teamwork between publisher and rep is an insidious suspicion that one is trying to do the other in. If that is, in fact, the case as you see it, get rid of your rep, fast, and get another one. If it's not the case, show that you're behind your rep all the way and watch that individual respond with renewed vigor and enthusiasm.

Demonstrating that you're behind your rep means things like the following:

• Follow up promptly on all requests for market data, special rate and position information, sales supplies, etc. Where timing is critical—and it often is—an unnecessary delay on your part could kill the sale.

• Make sure that your rep has the privilege of calling you collect whenever a sales situation demands it. It's the rep's responsibility to foot all expenses in properly maintaining the sales territory, but the cost of reporting back to the office when your rep feels the need should be borne by you.

• Be accessible when your rep does call and let it be known that the call is just as important to you as anything else that you've got to do. If it's just not possible to take the call at the time, return it promptly. The rep may have to get back to an advertiser immediately with an answer that only you can provide. Be enthusiastic and encouraging.

• Keep your rep informed! Don't forget that your rep may not even be aware of much of the sales information you have access to and take for granted. Keep feeding new sales ammunition so that your sales rep has something fresh to tell clients when making the next call on them. In fact, the reason your rep may not be making as many calls as you like could be that there is simply nothing new to tell them. (This is *your* fault, not your rep's!) Remember, your rep wants to make those sales and is eager to make more calls, but he or she is not going to wear out his or her welcome and be labeled a "time-waster" because there is nothing new to say about your publication. Bear in mind that the rep's reputation with media buyers is that individual's stock-in-trade. Your rep is not going to want to jeopardize it by wasting potential advertisers' time with vain sales calls just so you can be sent some new call reports. One good way to keep your sales rep informed on a regular basis would be to send a monthly memo—kind of a newsletter—to keep your rep up with what's going on back home.

• Make sure you've supplied your sales rep with business cards and letterhead stationery. Publication's logo, rep's address. You want to be sure that advertisers associate your sales rep with your publication, not with the individual's own rep firm. This is basic, but sometimes overlooked.

• If your rep has just joined you, send out press releases announcing the appointment to the appropriate media: *Ad Age, Media Decisions, Industrial Marketing, ANNY, SAM or MAC*, and the advertising and marketing editors of your local dailies. They look for and readily use such items and the publicity will help you both.

• Remember that little things mean a lot, so how about sending along last month's *SRDS* or your slightly-out-of-date *Standard Directory of Agencies?* It'll be appreciated and will help your sales rep to scout out new prospects for you.

Serve It Up Right
Successful advertising sales consist of three parts:
1. A good product
2. A good presentation
3. Lots of legwork.
Number 1 is your responsibility as publisher; Number 3 is your rep's responsibility as a salesperson; and Number 2 is a responsibility that you share.

A good sales presentation is kind of like a memorable meal at a fine restaurant: Both the food and the service are important. The food (sales material) is up to you, and the service (delivery) is up to your rep. In fact (to keep the simile going), to the discriminating diner (media buyer), the food is really the most crucial part since that is what the media buyer came for, anyway. The service, even if not all that elegant or decorous, will be considered passing as long as it is prompt and competent.

This is in no way meant to deemphasize the effectiveness of a highly-polished, professional sales delivery. But all the flourish and eloquence in the world can't compensate for sloppy, inaccurate or meaningless sales material.

Conversely, if your rep is sloppy about appearance and inarticulate or crude in manner, the media buyer sees your magazine in that light. Of course, your sales rep is not like that or you wouldn't allow such a person to represent you. But in the same vein, if the sales material to be presented before this selfsame discriminating media buyer isn't as well-groomed and polished as your rep, then we're back to the comparison of the restaurant with beautiful decor, fine service ... and lousy food.

I have seen audience surveys and reader-preference studies that were well-executed and convincing in content, yet virtually unusable in the form in which they were supplied by the publisher. They were sloppily typed and duplicated and almost indecipherable because the relevant sales points were buried in a confusing morass of statistics. If the same data had been properly and professionally packaged, they would have packed a powerful sales punch. As it was, they couldn't be shown without almost irreparably staining the image of the publication itself and tainting the reputation of the salesperson. Being asked to present "sales ammunition" like this is kind of like having to wear sneakers with your new tuxedo.

Another mistake that publishers often make—one you should avoid—is failing to discern between trivia and treasure when it comes to defining what constitutes effective "sales ammunition." The examples shown in the accompanying sidebar should help to give you the idea.

So, serve it up right. When it comes to cooking up the sales material, you, as publisher, are the chef. How will you fix it: Rare, medium or ... indigestible?

Go Out Amongst 'Em
Learn where and just how far you can trust your rep's judgment and assessment of problem sales situations. Your rep's going out amongst 'em, getting the straight poop on where you stand with advertisers and you should be, too. If you don't, you run the risk of contracting the insidious and sometimes terminal disease known as "Publisher's Pollyanna Syndrome."

This dreaded affliction almost always attacks publishers who isolate themselves from the hard sales facts of life by having little or no contact with media buyers. Its symptoms are loss of visionary acuity and ultimate total blindness to the root causes of their all-too-real sales problems.

So get down there in the trenches every once in a while and meet some of your toughest problems head-on. Find out for yourself where the buyer resistance is coming from and why, and you'll soon learn to properly discern the difference between a salesperson's excuses for buyer resistance and valid reasons. If you're getting the former from your rep, show that you know it's an excuse by constructively demonstrating what's being done wrong. (If this situation becomes chronic, it could be a signal to change reps.) But if they are valid reasons, take them seriously and make whatever moves are required on your part to change the situation and overcome the buyers' objections. Remember that teamwork between you and your rep is absolutely vital to sales success.

Making Calls with Your Rep
Either you or your sales manager will probably want to make one or two visits with your rep in the in-

dividual's territory each year. It provides the rep with a chance to discuss sales strategy with you firsthand and also to be brought up-to-date with new information on your magazine that can be used later on sales calls. But don't overdo it. Once or twice a year is probably sufficient,

---

Trivia vs Treasure

Check the examples below to find out whether the sales material you've been sending your rep is trivia or treasure:

Trivia	Treasure
Complimentary letter from a reader.	Testimonial letter from an advertiser.
Publisher's own readership or reader-preference study.	Starch, Simmons, TGI or other valid, independent survey.
Publisher's "sworn" circulation statement.	ABC, BPA or other accepted circulation audit.
Statistically invalid sampling of reader attitudes, buying habits, demographics, etc.	Statistically valid sampling of reader attitudes, buying habits, demographics, etc.
Minor editorial mention of major manufacturer's product.	Major editorial mention of minor manufacturer's product.
Notice of major article appearing in next available issue.	12-month preview of special-emphasis issues with brief summary of each.

---

and spending much more time than this with your rep will just eat into your own productivity and partially offset the advantage of having a rep out there in the first place.

Give your sales rep at least a month's notice, if you can, before you come out. The rep has commitments for other client magazines and will appreciate the advance notice to help in scheduling. This will also allow plenty of time for notifying the most important accounts that a very important publisher (you) is coming out to see them, and, so, help to insure firm appointments. Also be sure to let your rep know just how long you plan to stay so the decks can be cleared of any other business; your sales rep will then be prepared to give you his or her time and attention for the duration of your visit.

Make sure that you do the talking on your joint sales calls. After all, that's why you're there. This also gives your rep a chance to hear how you sell your magazine and to learn some new twists or gain new insights which can then be incorporated into his or her own future calls. Consider these joint calls sales training and information sessions, with you as the instructor.

The burden of writing the call reports should be the rep's, not yours, but you both should follow up later with letters to the people you called on, briefly reviewing the points you made and thanking them for their time.

Keep a careful list of everything your rep asked you to send and other commitments for market data, etc., that you made during your calls together. Follow up on these as your very first order of business when you return to the home office. If you don't do it right away it will tend to lose its sense of priority and slip away into oblivion under the accumulated load of your other duties. Don't let this happen or you'll lose the trust and respect of your rep—and probably the time that will be allotted to your magazine in the future. After all, if you don't care, why should your rep?

Does Your Bank Sell Space?

A smart rep will have made a deal with the local bank: The rep won't lend money if the bank won't sell space. To you, the rep's publisher, this means pay the individual's commissions within the agreed-upon time limit specified in the contract. Too many publishers use the slow-pay ploy and, in effect, operate on their reps' money when their own cash-flow situation isn't what they'd like it to be. The effect of this is ill feeling toward you and a loss of respect and confidence that will drain enthusiasm for your publication, resulting in fewer and poorer sales calls—if he or she doesn't just resign your account and be done with it.

A good space rep is hard to find and should be treated fairly. Remember, your sales rep is on your side and you're on your rep's side. And that, after all, is what it's all about.

In search of the right rep

By C. Lynn Coy

I have asked many of my fellow ad reps if they always tell a prospective publisher the exact number of magazines they represent. The answer was a resounding NO. They felt publishers would not understand.

In some respects, the publisher/rep relationship resembles a courtship. In the beginning, the publisher doesn't like to hear that there are other clients besides himself. Or if there are, he or she wants to be assured that they really don't mean very much. The fact is, those other publishers provide the stability so important to the rep organization and, therefore, to all its clients.

Recently, my firm was not selected to represent a publisher simply because we said that we represented nine publishers. The representative selected said he represented three. That was the basis upon which the publisher's decision was made.

Because of this incident, and the commonly incorrect thinking involved, I have tried to construct 12 questions that should help publishers select the right representative.

How long have you been in business?

The answer to this question indicates if you are to be a "trial balloon" or if you will be joining an organization of proven stability. A new rep, or someone who has been in business only a short time, offers the apparent advantage of being able to devote a lot of time to your property since, in all likelihood, he has few other properties.

The very nature of the rep business, however, usually attracts a person, who, if new, will spend part of the time looking for additional publications, simply because he is not sure just how long you will stay around and therefore wants to protect his position. Can you blame him? He is new. He has no track record. If he cannot pick up enough magazines, the chances are that he will leave the rep business.

Do you work alone or will you cover my publication with other people?

The answer to this can be revealing. If the rep is going to sell your magazine by himself, you have to recognize the limitations as well as the advantages. Although one good person can sometimes be worth as much as two or three, you must realize that one person can do only one thing at a time.

A single rep is insecure if all his income or the bulk of it is tied up with one publisher. A publisher might feel that tying up the bulk of a rep's time is a good thing. Not so, because the representative is going to be looking for other publishers so he will not be in a position of total dependence.

If there are going to be others selling your magazine, make sure you meet them and get to know them. If they are sub-reps and a liaison has been formed in order to attract your property, your problem is multiplied since you will then have to investigate the stability and workability of this arrangement. Investigate these things in advance.

What is your track record?

If a rep firm has been in business for any length of time, it should be prepared to let you know about its performance. If the rep is new, then you evaluate ability and/or background as best you can.

How many accounts do you handle for each publication?

This is an alternate to "how many books" and gives you an idea of the work load in terms of account numbers. There are some publishers who think everyone is a prospect. If you obtain the services of a representative who works for this kind of publisher, be careful, because you will have a rep who is always pressed for time.

The number of accounts the rep is covering can be calculated into work days. You can then come up with a reasonable formula to determine just how much time he might have to cover your accounts. The "how many books do you handle?" question means little under the circumstances. Let your prospective rep know just how many accounts you expect him to handle in your behalf.

What is your time allotment by area?

Where is the rep now spending time? In the office? In the territory? The answer to this question will give you some knowledge of his work habits as well as an idea as to how much of his time you can expect. If you have the bulk of your prospects in the Philadelphia area and your candidate represents an electronics magazine and spends most of his time in Boston, you have a problem.

Do you send call reports?

As basic as this is, many publishers are hesitant to ask the question. If a rep says he doesn't believe in them—"you have to put some trust in me"—seek someone else.

Call reports serve a number of important functions basic to the publisher/representative relationship. They let the publisher know what is happening in the field.

They present an objection on paper that lets the publisher know the rationale for his not getting the business. An alert publisher will know how to use this as ammunition for a call back.

Reports serve as a printed record for future reference, as well as follow-up information. Reports also provide the record that is so necessary should a publisher have a change of salespeople or should the rep firm need the background for a change in its staff.

Reports help the representative to determine if his time is being spent to advantage on any given property. Reports can carry the updated information necessary to maintain the promotion list. There are other reasons, of course, but the fact remains that this important consideration is often overlooked.

How do you handle special issues? Do you do any promotion yourself?

Most magazines have special issues during the year. They are money-makers for both the rep and his client, yet there is generally little conversation on this subject.

What are the page rates of the other publications you handle?

If your rates are completely out of line with the rep's other publishers, it can affect the volume of work done in your behalf. If, for example, most of the rep's books are in the over $1,200 per page category and you come along with a book in the $400 per page range, you must have a tremendous growth potential, a lot of business or an easy sales story. If a salesman can make three times as much money on a call for his other books, in all probability the other books will get most of his time. It is something to consider.

What are the reputations of the publishers the rep is now handling?

Look closely at the rep's clients and find out if they are reputable, if their products are good, if they are established and if they pay their commissions on time. By all means, it is your business. If you are going to be part of that group of publishers, you want assurance that they are people with whom you can be comfortable.

Remember, the reputation of your rep is also going to be a reflection on you. Many reps will not give you the names of all the publishers they represent because they may be ashamed of some of them.

You also don't want a rep who is constantly worried about collecting commissions from his other publishers since this is bound to have an effect on the work he does for you.

Are all of your magazines audited?

This in itself is not designed to prove anything, but merely to assist you in the evaluation process. If you have yet to obtain an audit and all the magazines your candidate has are already audited, you had better be prepared to start thinking in this direction. At the same time, if none of the rep's books are audited and yours is, you may have another problem.

What is your background, and what are your associates' backgrounds?

Examine each salesperson in a firm you are considering just as you would if you were selecting your own salespeople. For example, if you are looking at a four-person team and feel one of the people is not right for your book, come right out and say so. A rep firm can make adjustments.

Do you have a typical agreement or contract under which you work?

Some firms, especially on the West Coast, have their own agreements. They may have a large number of publications and want to be somewhat uniform. Others use the Association of Publishers Representatives agreement or variations of it. Still others like to let the publisher write his own letter of agreement so he may then be more comfortable with the agreement. Find out the basic terms under which the firm is used to working.

The question, "How many books do you represent?" still has not been asked. I'm not sure it is important in the light of the preceding questions.

Selling advertising in turbulent times

By Morton Grossman and David Orlow

In an economy of rising costs, uncertain market conditions, and changing values, hard work and perseverance alone are not enough to ensure your magazine's survival, let alone raise its net revenue. Ultimately, in turbulent times like these, it is your magazine's marketing strategy that will make the difference between success and failure, and the critical question a publisher must ask himself is: "How can I position my magazine to maximize ad space sales?"

Obviously, you can't simply tell an advertiser whose sales are declining that his sales will increase if he advertises in your magazine. Advertisers know that forces beyond their control are moving the economy and that all the advertising in the world won't make people buy when they're short of money and can do without the product.

However, you can tell him that he should concentrate on going after the customers who are still in the market. And this is where your magazine comes in—for the strategy that will convince advertisers and sell ad space is the one that can demonstrate that the readers of your magazine are the people who are doing the buying.

In order to develop such a strategy, you must have a thorough knowledge of your advertiser's markets. Then, you must analyze your magazines's position in the marketplace.

And finally, to respond effectively to an advertiser's needs in an increasingly competitive marketplace, a magazine must incorporate all of this information and develop an ad marketing program with the following strategic approaches: 1) the development of a solid plan for ad sales growth; 2) the establishment of a leadership image or a unique specialization; and 3) the concentration of efforts where results will be greatest.

Let's examine each of these three goals and see how various magazines have been able to benefit by using these strategies.

Develop plan for growth

It's easy to plan for growth when times are good and ad pages are increasing. It's not so easy to plan for growth when ad sales are harder to come by—but it is essential that such planning be done.

Furthermore, growth should not be measured in total ad pages and revenue alone, but also in share of market.

It is a well-known marketing axiom that market shares are typically in flux during turbulent periods. Thus, if you ignore share of market, if you pay attention only to your own magazine's advertising sales and do not compare them to the sales of other magazines in the field (or even to other media), you may be creating a deceptive situation. It can be deceptive when your advertising revenue figures are up, and even more deceptive when your ad pages are actually growing—if you don't monitor vital variables.

Your ad revenue may be increasing by 10 percent while inflation is climbing at a rate of 15 percent. That gives you a net loss of 5 percent in real income.

But consider the situation of *Magazine X* in a business field with six other magazines. The publisher of *Magazine X* was happy with annual ad page gains of 5 percent to 10 percent. The only problem was that the field was growing at an annual rate of 15 percent to 20 percent, two to three times as fast as *Magazine X*'s rate of growth. Then, when advertising in the field began to decline, *Magazine X*'s gains turned into losses as its competitors increased their share of market.

The problem for *Magazine X* didn't start when its losses began. It started long before, when the magazine planned for less growth than it should have. The 5 percent to 10 percent ad linage increases for the magazine were really losses in share of market.

When your field is growing, your magazine has to keep growing along with it. If you don't keep up, you are losing ground.

However, if you can lose ground when the field is up and you are *gaining* advertising, think what can happen when the field is down. Lose share of market then and you face disaster. The question then is: Is there anything that can be done when the situation looks hopeless?

Consider the following: You're in an industrial field with 20 magazines. You have only 6 percent share of market, and you expect total linage in the field to shrink from 9,000 pages to 8,500 next year. The field is losing ad pages . . . your magazine is in a weak position . . . and a 5 percent loss in ad pages will be devastating to you.

In a situation like this—when your market is under attack and your position is shaky—go for growth. Even in a down market, grow in market share—and don't settle for less than real growth.

But how can this be done? Let us cite the example of a magazine that found itself in just this situation.

Recently, when the management of this major magazine assessed the ad sales efforts and sales of the magazine, they discovered that the staff lacked the sales strategies and tools necessary to confront the realities of the marketplace. To deal with this situation, management commissioned several projects.

First, a situation analysis was conducted which concluded that the market had reached its peak in sales and that profound changes were beginning to take place.

A written strategic marketing platform was then prepared, based on the finding that although the changing situation made the outlook for prospective advertisers much more precarious, there was a new opportunity for sales in reaching the policy-makers who were managing change in the industry.

Sales presentations and support materials were then prepared, based on the strategic marketing platform. These presentations illustrated how the industry's marketing climate was changing and why the magazine's readers were the key to future sales for industry advertisers.

Finally, strategic sales training in the use of this approach was given to the sales staff to enable them to carry the message to advertisers effectively.

With this positive program, the magazine is now moving ahead in share of ad pages in its field. Without a specific growth plan, it would have been in big trouble.

A consumer magazine that recently ceased publication spent its final year chasing after ads that appeared in competitive publications, while ad linage was dropping in the entire field. No marketing platform had been developed. No strategy for building advertising categories existed. No meaningful rationale for the relationship between the advertiser's market and the magazine had been formulated.

Yet all of these things could have been done at relatively small expense. And although a sound marketing strategy alone cannot guarantee success, failure is all too likely without one—especially in turbulent times.

Be alert to changes

A situation where market share is shifting can be dangerous for the unwary. However, it can be a great opportunity for those who are alert to the potential of their field through careful strategic planning. In fact, gaining share of market is most readily accomplished in turbulent times because there are more opportunities for moving share of market in your favor. When things are changing—because of new technology, new ideas or different market conditions—advertisers are forced to re-examine the validity of their prior media decisions.

The best time for gaining share of market is when ad sales are off in your field. In difficult times, a competing magazine may cut marketing efforts in an attempt to keep costs down. Another may stand pat, doing the same things that worked well during times of rising sales, ignoring current realities. This is your opportunity for real growth because you can now take advantage of any faltering on your competitors' part.

This does not mean, however, that you will have to spend more money than you have in the past, or even spend more money than your competitors. One special interest publisher, for example, forged ahead with a bigger share of market in a recession while actually cutting marketing expenses.

First, he developed a marketing platform, based on intensive market and media analysis.

This platform demonstrated that as a result of the recession the first-time buyers who had been expanding the market were becoming scarce and that most of the buying was now being done by current owners trading up—the very customers who read this special-interest magazine.

Then, a sales manual was developed for the sales staff, incorporating the platform and the supporting marketing data. Finally, several strategic sales training meetings were conducted to rehearse each salesperson's proficiency in delivering specific sales presentations. At the same time, the ad sales manager kept on top of each salesperson's progress.

As a result of this activity, ad market share increased even though ad linage was down, and the magazine lost less than its competitors lost. When the market recovered, the magazine held on to its increased share of ad pages and reaped a greater share of a bigger market. Out-of-pocket costs for strategy development and the related sales training program were modest. Time was the greatest investment.

Another situation where increasing ad linage seemed impossible involves a trade magazine carrying more than 1,400 pages of advertising to audio dealers. This constituted over 50 percent of the space in a five-book field. The magazine dominated its field so thoroughly that the concept of adding another 100 pages seemed impossible.

Well—the magazine developed a plan for growth anyway, and managed to add those 100 new ad pages. Forty pages came from the top 20 advertisers, who were in categories they had been underpromoting compared to the rest of the field. Twenty-five came from categories in which the magazine did not have dominance. Twenty pages came from upgrading one- and two-time advertisers to six-time schedules. And 15 came from a new product category in the video field that represented an emerging product line for audio dealers.

Consider your situation

In this case, the magazine was able to plan for and achieve 100 new pages of advertising. What you plan for your magazine depends on your particular situation.

For a big magazine, 50 pages, a small percentage gain, can represent real growth. (A big magazine needs 50 pages of new business to replace 50 that will be lost in the normal course of events, plus 50 new pages to show real growth.) For a small magazine, with fewer ad pages, a larger percentage gain is needed if it is to be considered anything more than a statistical variation.

In bad times, real advertising growth may be different from what it is in good times. Real growth may involve replacing declining categories with new and expanding categories. You need a good understanding of the market your magazine serves to know where your opportunities lie.

A new age consumer magazine started a few years ago assumed at that time that its primary advertising support would come from wood burning stove manufacturers. The category boomed, due to the huge influx of steel and cast iron stove manufacturers who were attracted by growing sales and low cost of production. However, a decline in sales occurred as the market became temporarily saturated and supply outpaced demand. When many manufacturers went out of business or merged with other companies, wood burning stove advertising fell to half of its previous volume.

However, since readers who bought wood burning stoves are probably good prospects for other products that conserve energy and protect the environment, the magazine realized that it could still plan for growth by developing new advertising categories such as diesel automobiles. A sales presentation was developed and two diesel accounts were sold immediately.

The four-color pages in this new category are going a long way toward replacing the black-and-white thirds for wood burning stoves. Thus, despite the down market in what the magazine thought would be its primary category, the magazine is planning for real advertising growth and implementing those plans with research, sales development and strategic sales training projects designed to sell advertising for alternate energy and lifestyle products.

In times of tightening ad budgets, there is no room for second best. In a small field, ads tend to go to the magazines perceived as the top one or two, while in a larger field the top two or three magazines will win the bulk of the business. The rest will really suffer.

In turbulent times, then, gaining the aura of leadership is what magazine marketing is all about. You must be able to show that your magazine is absolutely essential, that other magazines offer less in quantity or quality than yours, and that you offer benefits that no other magazine does.

Just because you don't think you have leadership does not mean you don't have leadership characteristics you can exploit. Leadership does not go merely to the magazine that has the highest circulation or the most ad pages. Leadership is not merely the most or the biggest overall. A magazine is a leader if, for example, it has the fastest growing, greatest concentration in a particular area or segment, or if it has qualities that are important for a specific product category.

No magazine can appeal to and deliver every segment of a market. However, it's up to you to claim your particular leadership characteristics and assert them.

In order to accomplish this task, you will have to put your analytical skills to work by amassing and interpreting evidence of your leadership. This evidence can be found in your circulation figures, advertising page counts, editorial page counts, readership studies, testimonials, and awards.

If you don't have the most circulation, you may have larger circulation gains or a greater percentage gain. One industry magazine was able to wrest leadership away from its competition by demonstrating consistent circulation gains and convincing advertisers that the market was turning to that magazine as the preferred choice, even though it had less circulation than the competition. Your advantage may be anywhere in your circulation breakdown: single copy sales, subscriptions, a region, an occupational category.

If you don't have total editorial leadership, you may have leadership in specific areas. A women's specialty magazine gained advertising leadership by showing more editorial pages in selected product areas, thus translating editorial advantage to advertising leadership. A magazine in the horse field had neither circulation, advertising nor editorial leadership, but by demonstrating that it had more four-color editorial pages, it built a quality story that created an image of leadership and resulted in larger advertising gains than the "leaders" in other areas.

If you don't have advertising page leadership, you may be able to use the pages you have run to demonstrate advertising preference. A regional magazine was able to parlay a group of "leading" advertisers into fat advertising gains across the board. The women's specialty magazine that used its edge in number of editorial pages later accelerated its advertising gains by listing new advertisers and advertisers who increased space in fact sheets issued every six months.

Readership studies
If you can't find a leadership story in your circulation and advertising records, or in comparative hand counts between your magazine and its competition, you can build documentation through readership studies. Such studies can give evidence of your magazine's ability to hold the attention of readers and give advertising a longer chance to work.

The key to conducting effective subscriber surveys lies in the questions you ask, not the answers you get. If you have a feature magazine, ask how long an average issue is read. If you have a news magazine, ask how many people read an average issue. Widespread pass-along can give you leadership in market coverage—in depth throughout companies for business magazines, or in breadth throughout market segments for consumer magazines.

Knowing which questions to ask is a matter of strategy. But strategy comes first, since the numbers you offer are meaningless by themselves. They are merely documentation for the concepts or benefits you offer advertisers.

The salesperson whose only contribution to a discussion of the market is "73 percent of our readers own sewing machines" is going to find it a lot harder to close a sale than the one who can say to the advertiser, "Sure, sewing machine sales are down this year, but they are still at a high level compared to what they were just a few years ago. Plenty of people are still buying sewing machines today. Therefore, if you concentrate your advertising in the magazine that reaches the people who are buying sewing machines now, in *Popular Sewing Machine*, you can get ahead of the competition and wind up with a bigger share of sales than ever before.

"Three out of four of our readers own sewing machines today, and you can be sure that the fourth one is planning to buy one soon. That's why she is reading about sewing machines. We have the most concentrated audience of sewing machine buyers available. A schedule in *Popular Sewing Machine* will. . . . "

The second salesperson understands the market and bases his strategy on the concept of purchasing concentration, thereby demonstrating leadership. Quoting numbers alone won't do the job.

Don't assume anything
The process of devising a leadership strategy forces you to take your unique selling points much less for granted. If there is an area in which your magazine is unequivocally the leader, you may have a tendency to assume that all advertisers know about it. Wrong. Sell it again and again, especially in turbulent times like these, when you've got to sell harder and smarter.

In the apparel manufacturing industry, there are two competing magazines: *Magazine A* with 8,000 paid circulation and *Magazine B* with 20,000 controlled circulation. According to the U.S. Census Survey of County Business Patterns, there are over 15,000 companies in the industry with 20 or more employees. Since both magazines go to top executives, *Magazine B* clearly has an advantage in reach that *A* can't match.

However, the publishers of *Magazine B* felt that they had already sold the concept of reach. They wanted to find something new to promote and were casting about for new sales points when an analysis of their marketing position demonstrated what a potentially unfruitful path this was. The magazine is now developing fresh new ways to hammer home its most advantageous sales points to advertisers.

It's a common error for magazine marketers to feel that once a point is made, it's made forever. But people forget, people confuse magazines, and there are always new people coming along. Furthermore, advertisers are not primarily concerned with your magazine—they care about their own business. When you make a point that relates to their current situation, it doesn't matter if they've heard it before.

Consider this story: A publisher who had increased frequency from four to six times a year for good and valid market reasons had gone over those reasons with a key advertiser at least five times in the past year, at lunch, dinner, visits to the office, and with follow-up letters, not to mention trade advertising and direct mail campaigns on the subject.

On the sixth call, as the publisher walked in for his

appointment in the hope of finally landing a bigger schedule, the advertiser remarked with some consternation, "What's this I hear about your magazine going from four to six issues?" The customer had clearly never paid much attention or had forgotten.

When you have made a point, make it again. Make it in new and fresh ways, but keep on making it.

Look for new interpretations

Relate your sales points to your leadership characteristics and to the unique benefits that your magazine has in light of current market conditions. Examine your circulation figures for growth, passalong or depth of penetration. Study your editorial for depth or breadth of coverage and evidence of excellence. Analyze your ad records for specific areas of superiority in numbers or rate of growth.

Mine your research for advantages in ownership, purchasing, specific market segments of readership. Look at your other activities—merchandising, reader service, trade show participation, ad readership measurement. You may find important leadership characteristics to bolster your position.

You may even find new points you didn't know you had. For example, one industry magazine that took its research as reported was able to say that 50 percent of its subscribers were top executives. But analysis of the titles and functions of those readers indicated that the figure could be closer to 80 percent if the reported arrays were reclassified in an entirely legitimate manner. This new interpretation strengthened the magazine's leadership story immeasurably.

Another example: A consumer magazine discovered an entirely new leadership point when it related its subscriber purchasing figures to total industry sales. By thus demonstrating that its readers accounted for a significant proportion of actual sales, the magazine was able to convert a "concentration of buyers" point to purchasing leadership.

If you have leadership in any area, you must work to maintain it. If you don't, you must fight to gain it. All of the material you need is available to you, although you may have to dig below the surface to find those significant benefit points.

Establish priorities

A good salesperson generates enthusiasm, even when selling to a wide variety of prospects, and is persistent in following through. Such zeal often extends to marginal efforts, simply because good salespeople won't take no for an answer and don't get discouraged. Unfortunately, however, a lot of energy can be dissipated in areas where the potential simply isn't worth it.

It is obvious that a travel magazine should spend most of its time and effort selling travel advertising and related products. However, one travel magazine's management was beguiled by the big budgets in general advertising, liquor, automotive and the like, and spent a great deal of management time and selling time chasing after these advertisers.

Three senior salespeople were kept busy in this area with very few pages of space to show for it, while two juniors were relegated to the job of selling the core travel categories. All of the people involved worked hard, putting in 45 to 55 hours of honest toil each week, and the salespeople averaged at least 20 sales calls per week. Although it always seemed as though a big new general account was going to break, somehow it never did. In the end, it turned out that their system didn't work.

It then became necessary to change those priorities, to re-channel the sales staff's energies so that they could work more in travel and related categories and less in general areas. Although each salesperson still averages 20 calls a week, those calls are different calls, and they will probably result in greater sales.

Concentrate on big payoffs

Never lose sight of your magazine's most direct path to ad sales growth. Don't fragment your efforts. Concentrate where the payoff is greatest, especially in turbulent times.

Pick your area of greatest strength and apply the maximum pressure per square inch that you can bring to bear. Keep your priorities in mind as you allocate support services. Spend the bulk of your discretionary marketing dollars in developing research and creating promotion for your top priorities. Use most of your time ordering your priorities and training your salespeople to make effective calls in major categories.

To optimize your concentration, eliminate unnecessary marketing efforts. Just because you've been doing something for years is no reason to continue it now. If you have been trying to get automotive advertising for three years but have obtained only one or two pages, admit your failure and get out now. Put that time and effort to work in areas that give you better chances for success.

Dozens of consumer magazines are after photographic and stereo advertising. All of them feel they have a good story with upscale demographics for expensive equipment. In good times there is some justification for this effort, since advertising schedules expand with rising sales. But in tough times, most of these schedules are cut to the core.

Review all of your ongoing marketing expenses and efforts and ruthlessly cut those you deem to be of little or no value today. Ask yourself if an expense is necessary. If it isn't, cut it. If you feel that it is, determine the minimum amount needed to keep it going usefully.

This single-minded effort to concentrate only in those areas where you expect the greatest return will enable you to take advantage of new sales opportunities that arise, especially in turbulent times. By staying lean you will be in a better position to go after the big chance.

When a new advertising category that fits your book appears on the horizon (for example: microcomputers in the electronics field or videocassettes in the home entertainment field), ask yourself the following: What is the most I can put into it? Who is going to do it? What is going to be dropped in favor of it?

Don't simply add a new project on to a bunch of other sales chores. Give it priority. Furthermore, don't expect that everything else that was being done will continue to be done. Decide on what is least important and eliminate it to provide time and money for the new opportunity.

Why not cut major efforts in a category that has been shrinking because it no longer fits in with the times? Or cut the category you were never able to sell in the first place. Turbulent times mean rapid change and sudden switches. Use the strategy of concentration to seize opportunities and eliminate non-productive efforts at any time.

Be prepared to use all of the marketing tools at your command. For example, a new advertising category may require differential pricing if the market a magazine delivers has different values for different categories of advertisers. The publisher of a national business aviation magazine got good results developing a used airplane advertising category by starting the category with a discounted rate card.

To the advertiser, your magazine is the market it delivers. If you need to use rate proliferation to develop new categories, do so.

You may also want to consider a separate Opportunities Budget for the new category. A major new effort may not fit into your regular operating budget. Furthermore, you may want to track the activities of a new category. Keeping a separate budget will enable you to match expenditure with result much more accurately. More important, it will allow you to concentrate your resources much more efficiently.

All of these pointers have been distilled from the successes and failures of many publishers. Their aim is to help you gain greater control over your destiny and to make more money.

To sum up, stick with the truth. Know what's going on in your advertisers' markets and don't try to fool anybody, including yourself. Plan to grow in your magazine field and to change according to the times.

Furthermore, be a leader. Advertisers want to be in the best or the most necessary magazine. Follow the money-making growth opportunities and don't fritter away your time on dreams or delusions. Careful, informed market analysis will sort everything out.

No matter what you do, however—research, promotion, strategy development—none of it can be truly effective until it comes from the mouths of your salespeople. You must develop marketing manuals for them. You must teach them the market facts they need to know. You must train them in strategic selling.

In fact, strategic sales training is the most important thing you can do to enhance your ad marketing in today's economy. If you can teach your salespeople to make relevant sales calls where advertising potential is greatest, you will be better equipped to weather the current business climate.

Selling space in a down market

By Frederic C. Decker

I should start off by admitting immediately that the title of the chapter is at least a partial fraud. Despite its implication, I will offer no magic solutions. I have never found a mystical nostrum to cure sales ills nor an incantation to stimulate sales growth. Instead, I have found that the application of basic principles will, in good times or bad, affect sales. I believe that the management which will apply those principles and use education and persuasion to get the sales staff to apply them will fare better during lean months. Some of these principles fall into disuse in some companies during lush years.

Let's start with a point which is especially applicable today.

1. Fight apprehension.

One of today's greatest sales enemies is apprehension. Some of your advertising prospects may be overreacting to worry about business prospects. Budget cuts and postponements may be a product of that overreaction.

Remember that many individual businesses and some entire industries are not hurting. Others are experiencing reduced profits but are still showing better bottom line results than they did in some other recent years.

Some of those that are still doing pretty well in this period may be among those which are the most nervous about future prospects and are holding back on advertising expenditures, postponing new product introductions, delaying budget commitments, buying piecemeal, a month at a time.

We won't kid ourselves into thinking that a salesperson has the power to turn a company full circle in its advertising attitude. But, on the other hand, the salesperson doesn't have to go around reinforcing negative thinking. There are a lot of salespeople who are spreaders of doom and gloom as they make their rounds. They may think they are making points with a prospect when they tell that prospect how poorly his or her competitor is doing. The may think they are building their own stock when they gloat about how many pages their own competitors are off.

Instead, they are reinforcing the prospect's apprehensions and pulling the string on his or her purse even tighter.

The smart salesperson looks for upbeat reports to peddle. He or she does whatever possible to instill confidence, avoiding negative gossip as well as reports of despair and disaster.

2. Combat worry.

The salesperson, as well as the advertiser, needs confidence. Confidence is among the most important ingredients in sales success. Strip a salesperson of confidence and you've got half a salesperson. Confidence is at a premium at all times.

A sales staff member needs the confidence of job security. The street is abuzz with stories of staff cuts. No salesperson is immune to self-doubt and worry. And there are a dozen ways management can tell that person he or she is appreciated and secure. Salespeople need that reinforcement, often.

A salesperson also needs confidence in the stability of the company. He or she needs to know that the company is sound, not only in its bank account but also in its policies and its attitude. This is a time for maximum communication between company and salesperson.

3. Create a sense of involvement.

During economic slumps the atmosphere of urgency and purpose sometimes drains out of a company and out of its sales department. When companies are holding back on just about everything, that "hold back" psychology infiltrates the attitudes of the last people who should hold back—the salespeople.

It's understandable. The energy and drive of salespeople are fed by their successes.

Most space salespeople, unfortunately, sound like they are trying to sell stock in their companies rather than space in their books. They dwell upon how well their book is doing (or how badly the competitor is faring). They trot out circulation figures and readership statistics. Once in a while, but not often, they even talk about the editorial content of their magazines.

But pitifully few of them approach a sales situation from the viewpoint of the buyer and what's in it for that person.

In all the work we do with sales staffs and in sales development the greatest effort is put into helping salespeople use the marketing approach. We try to help develop the technique of tackling every sales situation from the angle of what's in it for the buyer.

For some salespeople this requires a 180-degree change of attitude. For all, it means that the salesperson has to learn a lot about his or her target prospect's business, the competitive situation, the marketing strategies. Only then can the salesperson be sufficiently sensitized to present the ways in which his or her magazine can be useful in accomplishing the prospect's marketing objectives.

It isn't that difficult. It requires some structured analysis of the prospect companies by the salesperson. It requires some thinking.

We've all witnessed the infectious enthusiasm that generates itself when a special issue is being closed. The sales goal is reached a week before closing! It becomes an exciting contest to see how many more pages can be pulled in before deadline. The salespeople drive hard. They are on the phone early and late. They use every plot to wring the last possible inch of space out of their territories. It's great fun. It buoys spirits for weeks afterward.

That kind of stimulation is often harder to get. But a sense of urgency and involvement can be generated when the sales manager and the publisher spend more of their own time with the salespeople working on key accounts, analyzing prospects' needs, making calls with the salespeople and, importantly, on top prospect executives.

The salespeople are going to feel a sense of the importance of selling only when they can see it in the day by day involvement of their superiors.

4. Sell the person who can say yes.

It has always been important that the salespeople spend their time and efforts with the person who can make the decision.

With many prospects today it is not a question of *where* to advertise but *if* to advertise. The sale doesn't depend upon a tactical decision. It depends upon a policy decision.

The salesperson must have the tact and courage to move into the decision-making levels. These are, more often than not, at the advertiser's company and in the office of the ad manager, the marketing director and, sometimes, the company president.

The experienced salesperson knows that it is easier for people to say no. It is harder for them to say yes. That's because there is less risk in a negative decision. The consequences of giving a go-ahead might haunt the decision-maker for a long time. But who's to judge that person for deciding not to make a move, especially when he or she has been insulated with plausible reasons for the negative decision?

So it is imperative that the salesperson seek out the one who has not only the authority but also the sense of security and the grasp of the only view which makes it possible to make an affirmative decision on the basis of sound marketing considerations. He or she will probably be found in an office with more than one window.

5. Sell the marketing approach.

Once they get into that corner office the salespeople darn well better have something to say. They'd better be prepared to base their pitch on a solid understanding of the prospect's marketing needs and objectives. And, for proper presentation, it requires some paper work.

Using the marketing approach is a great way for salespeople to distinguish themselves from their competitors. Most of them will still be plodding along with the "I-gotta-great-book" pitch.

6. Zero in.

Two key words are "target prospect." A source of frequent wonder to me is finding that many salespeople haven't assessed the relative values of their various accounts. It pays to rank accounts and then devote attention to them in accordance with their potential.

It could be especially effective now to set up a carefully organized target account program. This would zero in on two or three at a time of each salesperson's top prospects and inundate them with a concentrated sales drive using special presentations, getting the publisher and editor involved in sales calls, calling at all levels of influence at the agencies and advertiser companies, using specially developed letters and other communications.

Even when this concentrated effort doesn't result in a sale at least two other things are accomplished. First, the prospect will have become convinced that he or she is awfully important to you. That's flattering. It will make subsequent selling efforts easier.

Second, and perhaps more important, it has gotten your salesperson thinking in terms of surrounding an account, selling at all levels and studying the account thoroughly to find the ways your magazine will advance his or her marketing objectives.

7. Prepare.

Even in the lushest times, planning and preparation are essential to sales success. They are even more important now. But it is discouraging to observe how many salespeople think nothing of walking into a prospect's office without a shred of evidence that they have given any thought to that prospect's problems and needs.

One of the best magazine salespeople I know never, no never, goes out on a call without something to place before the client which is directly pertinent to that client's advertising or marketing problem. It is always in tangible form—a chart, a clipping from a trade or professional journal, a brief memo.

I've known this salesperson to hand a typewritten agenda to his prospect at the start of an interview saying something like, "This meeting with you is so important to me that I've taken the liberty of drawing up a brief agenda, just to be sure we cover all the basic points." Impressive! And it keeps the discussion moving in exactly the direction planned by the salesperson.

Homework before a call should be exactly that—homework. Nine-to-five selling time is far too precious to be wasted upon the chores of planning the day or preparing for calls. When I was selling space for *Printers' Ink* many of my prospects were magazine publishing companies. I remember that if I wanted to see the more successful sales managers and publishers I usually had to present myself at their offices before the business day started or after it ended. They didn't want me cluttering up the hours when they could be talking to *their* prospects.

8. Work.

There's a legend in the publishing business that 85 percent of the sales are made by 15 percent of the salespeople. This might even be true.

Legend or not, it is certainly true that the very, very good salespeople are very, very few.

With one or two exceptions, I've noticed that there is one major point of difference between the best salespeople and the others.

That point of difference is work, plain old garden variety work. It isn't education or charisma or intelligence; it is well-organized, dogged work—start-early-and-stay-late work.

The salesperson who is willing to work has a tremendous advantage. His or her competitor probably isn't working as hard. The salesperson who makes more calls, better prepared and better followed-up calls, is going to get more business.

9. Use the mails.

Speaking of followup, now there's a source of frustration to most sales managers and a point of difference between top salespeople and their lesser brothers and sisters! We've got to face two facts. The first is that salespeople can multiply their impact upon an account if they'll use the U.S. mails. That warm thank-you letter gives an opportunity to restate important points. Notes between calls keep the memory green.

The second fact is that a lot of people, including salespeople, get all choked up when they have to write a letter. The most articulate and persuasively belly-to-belly salesperson often writes letters that sound like a retarded fifth-grader.

So how does the sales manager solve the problem? He or she achieves the objective through the use of form letters, form paragraphs or even a professional correspon-

dent in the department.

The important thing is to keep mail contact with the client alive and flowing. It will make a difference—because it is likely your competitor isn't doing it at all.

10. Sell benefits.

There is documented evidence that advertising increases sales, reduces the cost of sales and increases profitability. These are the days when that kind of evidence should be laid before every advertising prospect who will look at it. It may undergird the resolve of some advertisers to keep the advertising pressure up to normal levels during recession months.

When I was selling space I got a lot of mileage out of the Morrill Study which was sponsored by McGraw-Hill and available from them. It indicated a relationship between personal calls, advertising exposure, brand preference and sales.

It might also be worth taking a look, even now, at the studies of corporate profit and loss as related to advertising performance during the recession years of 1949, 1954, 1958, and 1961. These studies were conducted by Wesley Rosberg, then president of Buchen Advertising, now with Meldrum & Fewsmith, and can be obtained from the American Business Press. Both ABP and the Magazine Publishers Association have tools like this to help sell magazine space. Ask them.

Most advertisers would rather advertise than not advertise. All agencies want their clients to advertise. Ad managers hate to see their budgets slashed.

So the space salesperson who can make a solid case for the wisdom even (or especially) in a slump period is going to find receptive ears. He or she might even find an order or two.

11. Maintain communication.

Recently I had occasion to review the sales procedures in a multi-magazine publishing company. Each of its magazines was a little sickly in relation to other publications in its field. One of the first things I discovered was that there was no sales call report system and no organized substitute for one.

I also found that the general sales manager, who had no personal account responsibilities but was in direct charge of all sales activities, had a number of blanks in his knowledge of the status of important prospect accounts and he admitted to little current information about the attitudes and business climate with a number of the most important running advertisers.

The gathering of sales information is one of the salesperson's vital functions. It must be reported promptly, insightfully and accurately and then immediately studied and interpreted by management.

Only then can the "two-heads-are-better-than-one" principle be brought into play. Only then can the sales director give counsel at the time when it is most needed. Only then can the marketing and promotion people help with strategies and tactics keyed specifically to a current account problem or opportunity.

I am sure I don't have to make a case for the necessity of a system of sales call information. But perhaps I should make a case for making the system work.

It is apparent in many publishing companies that

once the call report is written nothing much happens. Either nobody reads it or nobody reads it until so much later that the information in it has become ancient history. Therefore nobody acts upon it. Nobody gives the information, help or encouragement the report may call for. Nobody does anything so nothing happens. Except that salespeople start writing reports that are less meaningful. And their calls probably become less and less meaningful, too.

12. Remember to close.

A business magazine publisher once commented to me that he wished he could give each of his salespeople a suitcase full of patented potato peelers. Then he'd dump his salespeople without money in a strange town and make them ring doorbells and peddle potato peelers to the homemakers.

Make goods

By Karlene Lukovitz

Advertising make-goods. The very words are enough to make publishers, advertising directors and ad salespeople cringe. A request for a make-good all too frequently plunges the magazine into a dilemma, and the chances of emerging unscathed are negligible.

Every make-good dilemma is different; there is no guidebook or set of rules to which a publisher can turn when faced with a make-good request. Often, he can only weigh the losses that will result from doing the make-good against the importance of keeping the advertiser and agency satisfied, and then try to negotiate the least damaging solution possible.

The consequences of agreeing to do a make-good are well-known to every publisher: The magazine absorbs the loss of revenue resulting from using space for a re-run instead of selling it for a new ad. If a partial invoice credit or other type of partial make-good is given to the advertiser, the magazine absorbs those losses. And unless the printer is at fault for the problems that caused a re-run, the publisher also pays for the manufacturing costs of the re-run.

In addition, some magazines may at times have to bear the cost of one or more extra pages of editorial material needed to preserve the magazine's editorial/advertising ratio when make-goods are given. For example, a make-good may tip the ratio just enough to jeopardize the magazine's mailing status, or it may undermine the ratio promised by the magazine in its ad sales efforts.

Advertisers' options

If, on the other hand, the magazine refuses to do a make-good, or agrees only to a partial make-good that does not fully satisfy the advertiser or agency, the consequences can be even more painful. Advertisers/agencies always have the option of delaying payment until the problem is resolved to their satisfaction. Furthermore, if they are dissatisfied with the treatment they have been receiving, they might even drop the magazine from their schedule.

"This is a business that is based on cooperation and working relationships, so it's rare for a problem to reach the point at which we would start thinking about dropping a magazine," says Paul Zuckerman, associate media planning director for Doyle Dane Bernbach. "But if we encounter too many problems, a magazine could well be dropped from the list. Generally, it's the advertiser who makes the final decision to drop a magazine, though it may be at the suggestion of the agency. There is no magazine that is so important that we cannot have a successful ad program without it."

Losing a major advertiser's business, or being dropped from a major agency's media list for several years because of disputes over make-goods, is by no means unheard of. But very few magazines have the financial security, chutzpah, or as one ad director characterizes it, "just plain lack of sense," to take principles to this extreme.

Unwarranted make-goods

"Of course we sometimes give a make-good when one is not deserved," states Technical Publishing Company's executive vice-president, Robert Dickson. "Any magazine executive who says he doesn't sometimes give unwarranted make-goods is a liar, in my opinion. We won't give in to advertisers or agencies who make unreasonable demands time and again, but within reason, if it's a good enough customer and he squawks enough, we give the customer what he wants."

A production supervisor at a major business magazine publishing company agrees. "If a good customer insists that the ad materials were not at fault and says, 'Look, you want my business? I want a free re-run,' you know what your answer has to be. You look the other way and do a make-good."

Many ad directors and other executives at consumer magazines are also frank about the subject of unwarranted make-goods. "Any ad director who's honest about it will tell you that they sometimes do a make-good to keep the business even though the reproduction of the ad wasn't bad at all," says one highly-placed magazine executive. "Unfortunately, some agency space buyers think they ought to get 13 pages for the price of 12—but publishers get wise to those individuals pretty quickly."

"You may not do anything wrong and still have to do a 50 percent make-good in order to keep the agency or advertiser satisfied," says David Obrasky, advertising director for *New York* magazine. "To win the battle but lose the war is simply not good business."

The director of operations for a general interest consumer magazine concurs: "The name of the game in make-good issues, as in most other business issues, is power," he says. "You'd have to be insane to give up hundreds of thousands or even millions of dollars in accumulative ad revenue from a long-term relationship with a major advertiser or agency over the cost of one make-good."

No figures available

An advertising director who has worked for both business and consumer magazines says he believes that business/trade magazines may tend to give more make-goods because they tend to have smaller circulations, and therefore lower per-page production costs than consumer magazines. Therefore, he says, make-goods are relatively less of a financial loss for business magazines. This cannot be substantiated or disproved, however, since no records on the frequency of make-goods or studies about make-goods are available from the Magazine Publishers Association (MPA), the American Business Press (ABP), the Association of National Advertisers (ANA), the American Association of Advertising Agencies (4As), or the Advertising Research Foundation (ARF).

Both business and consumer magazines report that they give full make-goods infrequently, but few will quote numbers. One ad director in charge of a weekly business magazine and six monthly magazines reports that the magazines collectively do about 25 to 30 make-goods per year. A production director of business magazines whose published issues total 48 per year says the magazines collectively do about 12 make-goods per year. The largest number of make-goods reported by a monthly consumer magazine was about six per year; the smallest number reported was two to three per year.

Everything negotiable

But however frequently or infrequently a particular magazine actually agrees to do full make-goods, every ad director and publisher contacted stressed that in the great majority of cases, there should be a maximum negotiation effort with the agency and/or advertiser before a full make-good is considered.

According to both publishers and advertising agencies, few if any magazines have any sort of formal policy regarding when they will or will not give make-goods. Similarly, most advertisers and agencies do not have written-in-blood policies outlining under what circumstances they will demand and expect a full or partial make-good. Moreover, guidelines on make-goods have never been established by either publishing or advertising associations.

"Every ad problem situation is different, so we like to remain flexible," says Dickson of Technical Publishing. "For that reason, we do not publish guidelines on make-goods."

Says Obrasky of *New York*: "There are certain circumstances under which full make-goods are warranted, but everything is negotiable. If it's not, the person or company taking that attitude is going to have a great deal of difficulty conducting business under the conditions that exist in 1981."

"Make-goods are certainly negotiable, though of course the bigger the advertiser, the more negotiations go his way," says the executive vice president of a biweekly magazine.

"Relationships between magazines and agencies

are based on the fact that we need them and they need us," says Jerry Wertans, director of print services for Needham, Harper & Steers, Chicago. "So sometimes we give, sometimes we take, and sometimes we caution the magazine—we do have a standard cautionary letter. But we also have a complimentary letter. If we feel a situation is negotiable, the media planner handles the negotiations, with graphic directions from the production department."

Partial make-goods for 'gray areas'

"Determining whether a full or partial make-good is due is sometimes a matter of negotiation and compromise," says Mike Walsh, vice president and media director, Atkin-Kynett, Philadelphia. "Sometimes we get a credit on the problem insertion or a credit on the next insertion, but we have no set rules stating that we should get a 20 percent credit on this type of error, or a 10 percent credit on that type of error, because many times it's a judgment call."

"Partial make-goods are important, because they can solve a problem that's not black-and-white in terms of whose fault it is," says an account executive at an agency that is among the 15 largest in the nation. "If the material is sent in late by the agency, for instance, and there is no time to correct it, then the publisher should not suffer 100 percent."

Neither are there any hard and fast rules on when a magazine should try discussing problems directly with an advertiser.

"In cases where it's clear that an agency is being forced to resist a reasonable solution because the advertiser has taken an emotional rather than reasoned stance on a problem, it may well be time to approach the advertiser—cautiously," says one former ad director. He and other ad directors stressed, however, that the agency should first be notified of the magazine's intention to contact an advertiser—both to make sure the agency does not have any objections and to get any advice the agency might have on how to deal with the advertiser. (One ad director added that he would not notify an agency first if he felt the agency had proven untrustworthy in the past or had established a reputation for being delinquent in its payments.)

In many other instances, however, it is best to deal with the agency alone, according to ad directors. "Often, if it's a good agency, it will intercede with the client on behalf of the magazine," notes Obrasky of *New York* magazine.

Try to establish some value

As to actual methods of negotiating about make-goods, at least one rule of thumb seems to apply: Many ad directors stressed that a magazine should first attempt to get the advertiser/agency to admit that the ad, no matter how flawed the advertiser may feel it is, is not *completely* without value—and therefore a full make-good is not a fair solution.

"This may seem like a rather simplistic approach, but you'd be surprised at how effective it can be, because it usually gets any reasonable advertiser to start putting things into perspective," says one ad director.

But, again, if all attempts to persuade the advertiser/agency to accept a partial make-good fail, the final decision on offering a full make-good comes down to the question of how important a client is to the financial welfare of the magazine.

Grounds for full make-goods

Despite the lack of hard rules on giving make-goods, there are several types of major errors that both advertising agencies and publishers generally agree are grounds for a full make-good, when they are the publisher's or the printer's fault:

• *Publishing the wrong ad.* In cases in which an agency has sent two or more sets of materials for different ads that are to be run in specified issues, magazines sometimes send the wrong set of materials to the printer. A few ad directors noted that they might try to negotiate for less than a full make-good if the ad published, although not the agreed-upon one, is not so timely or seasonal that it could not be argued to have at least *some* value to the advertiser. Most, however, said this error constitutes grounds for a full make-good.

• *Positioning an ad so that it faces the ad of a direct competitor.* All agencies contacted named facing competitive ads as one of the most serious errors that a magazine can make. (A position on the opposite side of a page on which a competitor's ad appears was a close runner up.) Ad directors generally agreed that, though this type of mistake is infrequent, it almost always warrants a full make-good.

Several agencies said they feel that positioning an ad near editorial material that is derogatory to the product (a cigarette ad next to an article on lung cancer, for example) is cause for a full make-good, but some ad directors said this may be negotiable, depending on the severity of the foul-up.

Other positioning matters that may or may not result in partial or full make-goods include not giving an advertiser a position which carried an extra charge or a position that had been promised. But minor complaints about positioning, such as that a competitor has been given a better position, or that the ad is right-hand, far-forward, but not *far enough* far-forward, were generally dismissed by ad directors—and most agencies said they would not lodge such complaints.

• *Reproduction of an ad that is so poor as to interfere with the ad's readability or effectiveness.* Problems most frequently mentioned by agencies and ad directors within this general area include significant over- or under-inking (to such an extent, for example, that copy is difficult to read or figures in photographs are difficult to identify); printing the ad significantly out of register; positioning an ad on the page so that significant portions of it are cut off; shooting the ad significantly out of focus; poor color reproduction (particularly when color has a great deal to do with a product's appeal, such as in food, fashion, or automobile ads); or use of the wrong color (such as in a logo).

If the use of the word "significant" in the above paragraph seems to be liberal to the point of redundancy, it is because this is the key word used by both ad directors and ad agency executives to differentiate reproduction problems that usually warrant a full make-good from those that may only warrant a partial make-good, or no compensation at all. Of course, ad agency and magazine views on how significant a problem is can sometimes differ—significantly.

Controversial areas

Amount of inking and poor color rendition were often mentioned by both agencies and ad directors as the reproduction areas that are most likely to generate serious differences of opinion.

One reason, of course, is that these two areas leave a lot of room for qualitative and speculative judgments. When it comes to four-color rendition, disputes can and

often do arise as to whether or not the shade or tone of a reproduced color is so far off from that desired by the advertiser/agency as to actually affect the appeal of or misrepresent the product depicted. With inking problems, which frequently occur in black-and-white ads as well as in color ads, the question is also whether the ad's effectiveness has been hindered—a fairly straightforward matter if copy is difficult to read, but a much more difficult determination if, for example, the relative sharpness and clarity of the details of an object are in question.

The second reason that color rendition and amount of inking are often causes of contention between magazines and ad agencies/advertisers is that the fault for less-than-excellent results can lie either with the materials supplied by the agency or with the printing job itself.

Printers and magazine production directors and consultants contend that most reproduction problems are the fault of poor pre-press materials. They say that agency production people either do not have the expertise or do not take the care to make sure that the materials they get from their suppliers conform to Specifications for Web Offset Publications (SWOP)—or, if the ad is being run in magazines printed by other processes, to the proper specifications for the processes, equipment and type of paper being used.

"Most make-goods are not deserved, because poor reproduction is caused by problems in the film supplied by the agencies," says production consultant Jeffery Parnau. "Ninety percent of agencies don't use publishers' specifications in ordering materials from their suppliers. It's very rare for an agency to order seven different sets of matched progressive proofs for the specifications of the seven different magazines in which an ad is going to run. If magazines rejected every ad that doesn't meet specs, they would have to reject almost every ad."

According to production consultant Elaine Jaffe, many problems are caused by unrealistic demands made by ad agency creative or production people who do not really know what can and cannot be reproduced well on high-speed presses.

"Production managers at agencies should have a better grasp of printing processes than they do now—they should understand every step involved in getting an ad on press and getting it off press," Jaffe asserts. "Many times, because of lack of expertise, agencies ask for things that may be achievable, but extremely difficult to do."

Some ad agencies acknowledge that their materials are sometimes to blame for poor reproduction. "Sometimes something slips by us," says the art director for one major agency. But these and most other agencies said they do check materials carefully and do go back to their suppliers if materials are faulty. Some agencies contend that printers and publishers go out of their way to find minor faults with materials so that they will have an excuse if reproduction is poor.

Printers sometimes at fault

Printers *are* sometimes the cause of reproduction problems, and they admit it. "Over-inking or poor color appearance can be the result either of poor craftsmanship of the printer or the poor quality of the materials supplied," says the president of a printing company specializing in long-run consumer magazines. "If the proofer doesn't adhere to standards, you get a muddy appearance to the color or other problems, and if he does adhere to standards and the printer doesn't go with the right amount of ink, it's the printer's fault."

The president of a printing company that

specializes in relatively short-run business magazines says: "The most common causes of those reproduction problems that are our fault are people problems, like a pressman not watching as carefully as he should."

One production director who has worked for both consumer and business magazines says he has found that printers have a tendency, for some reason, to really lay on the ink. "Sometimes you have to convince them to take it easy so that the details and subtleties of ads will start coming out."

Avoiding make-goods

In order to decrease the frequency of giving partial and full make-goods, publishers should find and have corrected as many potential causes of reproduction problems in materials as possible. In addition, they should document all problems with materials, whether or not they can be corrected, before the magazine goes to press.

Though some printers routinely inspect all film they receive for their own protection as well as the publisher's, most printers charge the publisher for inspection of ad film materials. Parnau, who recommends that publishers have their printers inspect all advertising film, says the cost of such inspections is approximately $15 to $20 for four pieces of film.

A Northeastern printer specializing in short-run magazines, however, says that the cost of doing inspections with the tools in his plant ranges between $25 to $35 for one four-color ad, and that most of his customers are not willing to pay this high a price.

"We'll definitely be doing thorough inspections on a regular basis five years from now, for as the technology improves, the costs will come down in this area," he says. "One new densitometer coming out this year may help."

In the meantime, he says, "we do review film on a cursory basis and contact the publisher if we spot a problem."

Inspect film in-house

Parnau says there should be at least one production person on every magazine who knows how to perform a rudimentary film inspection. He says such inspections should be used mainly when schedules are so tight that a full inspection is not possible, although for those publishers who are not willing to pay for full inspections by the printer and would rather not rely solely on a printer's cursory inspection, they may be of some help in spotting and preventing problems.

"It's easy to spot the big errors in film—they're almost always visible," says Parnau. "And these are usually the errors that are going to cause real problems. A magazine production person can learn to do a rudimentary inspection in a few hours by going to the printer and asking to be shown how. The only things you need at the magazine are a light table and a $20 magnifying glass called a lupe."

When a significant problem with film is found, the agency should be notified immediately—both to give the agency an opportunity to correct the film (or have new materials made) and to provide the publisher with protection against make-good claims for faulty materials. Most magazines report that they do notify agencies of significant problems with film in almost all cases.

Unfortunately, according to ad directors and magazine production people, materials are often sent late by agencies, or sent so close to deadline that there is no time, particularly on a weekly, for materials to be corrected or replaced. "Even when there is time to do something about the materials, some agencies will just say, 'We haven't had a problem with the ad on other magazines; go ahead and run it,'" says one ad director.

Document problems

When there are problems with a late ad, a magazine can protect itself legally (and, as is much more frequently the need, present a better case to an advertiser/agency howling for a re-run) if it has taken steps to document the magazine's notification of the agency and the agency's reply, according to Parnau.

When there is time for a full inspection, a copy of the printer's report can be sent to the agency. If the problem is not found until very close to press time because the materials were sent late, or if the schedule is particularly tight for some reason, someone from the magazine should call the agency, give notification of the problem, and ask if the ad should be run.

"The caller should take notes on the conversation and file them," Parnau says. "That way, if the agency has instructed you to go ahead with the materials you have, you have the groundwork for legal protection if a complaint arises and it is carried to that extreme. And if you *really* want to protect yourself, you should have a form letter with spaces in it for the agency's name, the problems with the film, and a summary of the telephone conversation. In it should be a statement to the effect that you are going ahead with the ad, per the agency's instructions, but you cannot guarantee color fidelity.

"This letter provides tremendous protection," he says, "but if you tell the agency contact that you're sending the letter, he or she may very well tell you to send back the film—in which case you've lost the ad. So, if you're going to use the form letter idea, you might want to consider sending the letter without telling the agency that you're sending it."

The fear of either panicking or annoying an advertising agency into pulling an ad insertion by notifying the agency of problems with materials was mentioned by at least two ad directors. These ad directors said they would rather risk facing a make-good demand (against which they would have little defense because they did not notify the agency) than risk losing the ad or the advertiser.

"I just can't see losing an advertiser that it has taken one of my salespeople maybe a year or more to get by turning around and telling the advertiser or agency to send new materials," one explained.

Some magazines correct film

Most magazines said that they have a policy of not correcting film, with the exception of procedures that are relatively safe and easy for the printer to perform, such as overall sharpening of film. A few magazines, however, reported that they work with or without the agency's cooperation to correct film that looks as if it might cause problems.

"Dot etching and other tricks that improve film can be done by a sophisticated graphics house before the printer makes the plates," says one magazine executive. "We try to get the agency to split the costs with us."

"When we get film from an advertiser who always complains about reproduction results, we tell the printer to sharpen up the film by etching the dots. It costs about $40, but it's worth it," says the ad director for several business magazines.

Parnau, however, says he does not advise film corrections. "I wouldn't do it," he says. "Because of the way dot etching is done, you're two more steps away from the original materials by the time you're through with it. This is likely to cause even *more* problems."

Impact on printer limited

Publishers, publishing consultants, attorneys and printers all agree that there is probably no printing contract in existence today in which the printer agrees to take any responsibility for a publisher's consequential or speculative losses—that is, losses of potential sales revenue due to having to use ad space to do a re-run, and revenue loss due to an advertiser's termination of business with a magazine. Printers pay only for actual costs involved in re-running an ad if they are to blame for the re-run.

Publishing consultant Elaine Jaffe expresses the frustration of many publishers in regard to this situation: "Printers really do try to do the best job they can, but they really get off the hook as far as make-goods are concerned," she asserts. "I feel that printing contracts should hold the printer responsible for more than just the costs of doing a re-run in those instances in which a make-good is caused by a printer's error."

Insert protections in contracts

Most printers will themselves insert a clause in the contract specifically limiting the amount of money that can be recovered from them—in instances in which they are at fault for an error—to the costs of re-running the ad, according to publishing attorney Ed Smith. However, the publisher should make certain that there is a clause in the contract stating that, if the printer is at fault, he is responsible at least to the extent of all actual, out-of-pocket costs to the publisher for having the ad re-run, that is, for costs of labor and materials, including paper, Smith says. These costs can be computed by using the space allotted to the ad in relation to the total number of pages in the magazine (or form) and figuring the ad's proportionate cost from the total cost of all pages in the magazine (or form), taking color and other cost variables into account: Costs of one page in a 16-page form would be approximately 1/16 of the total cost of the form.

Smith notes that since zoned per-pound postal rates for the advertising portion of second class publications are particularly high, it is sometimes worth trying to include the costs of postage in the contract under re-run costs for which the printer is responsible. Publishing consultant Bert Paolucci agrees that postage costs can add up, but says, "Some printers will agree to carry postage costs—most will not."

While emphasizing the importance of a written contract clause assuring credit for labor and materials, publishing attorney Stephen H. Gross says there is an implied warranty of "merchantability" in any business contract between a publisher and printer—written or unwritten. Thus, a printer is responsible for reimbursing the publisher for the cost of any work that is clearly below commercially acceptable standards, even if the contract makes no mention of such reimbursements.

"If the printer, through his own error, gives an ad a blue background instead of the red background specified, he must reimburse you for the actual cost of that error," says Gross. "But contracts between printers and publishers do not usually address judgmental areas—that is, questions of relative quality."

Gross stresses that publishers should stipulate in the contract that the printer is responsible for furnishing paper for re-runs, as well as for paying for its cost. In addition, the contract should specify that the publisher will not pay interest on an invoice during a period in which it is being contested, or at least that interest will not be paid on that part of the invoice which is contested, according to Gross.

Finally, says Gross, the contract should have provisions that help the publisher avoid incurring consequen-

tial losses on make-goods by making it possible to have re-runs done *before* the magazine is distributed. "The contract should state that the printer must send proofs of ads to the publisher within a specified period of time before going to press, and that the proofs must be sent by express, rather than regular mail," says Gross.

"The printer, in turn, will probably specify a period of time during which the publisher must respond to the proofs," he adds. The contract should also state that if the work has to be redone, it must be redone immediately and at standard rates, not at overtime or premium rates. Even if the work does have to be done on overtime, the printer should absorb that cost.

As for non-contractual safeguards at the printer, most experts advise publishers to have a representative at the printing plant during the run. Some advise this precaution so that there will be someone to tell the printer when copies are not acceptable and ask him to re-run those copies. Others say a representative should be there only to make non-technical decisions about ads—such as which advertiser should be favored in a situation in which one of two ads must suffer.

All of the attorneys and production consultants agreed, however, that although precautions are good business practice, a sound working relationship with the printer is the most valuable insurance against make-goods. Disputes between a publisher and printer over re-runs and credits should be all but non-existent if such a relationship is maintained, they say.

Quality assurance programs

Several magazine publishing companies have exemplary quality control programs that encompass stringent procedures for ensuring high-quality reproduction, both before and during the printing of each issue.

All of these programs include procedures to make sure that advertising materials are in on time, that all materials are inspected thoroughly for adherence to standards, that advertising agencies are notified immediately of problems and given the opportunity to correct the materials, and that printers adhere to industry standards.

Some programs even include follow-up critiques of each issue to analyze any problems that did occur and take steps to see that they do not occur again.

U.S. News & World Report, Inc. and McGraw-Hill, Inc. each have entire departments devoted solely to quality assurance. Other publishing companies, including Penthouse International, Ltd. and Petersen Publishing Company, Inc., have somewhat less formal but unquestionably thorough programs for maintaining high reproduction standards.

These companies have found that setting up and adhering to quality control procedures pay off in satisfied advertisers—and consequently in very few make-goods.

"We nip most reproduction problems in the bud," says James Dunne, head of quality assurance for U.S. News & World Report, Inc. "Our procedures ensure that we and our printers are usually not at fault for reproduction problems that might occur—and that we can demonstrate this to advertising agencies."

"Instead of reacting after the fact, our department exists to isolate and solve problems before they affect reproduction," says Allen C. Schulz, quality assurance manager for McGraw-Hill, Inc. "By avoiding re-runs, we believe we are not only making advertising more profitable for everyone involved, but are also establishing strong credibility with our advertisers."

Selling advertising

Selling smarter

By Dave Hagenbuch

An advertising space salesperson calls on a company. That individual represents you, the publisher and your magazine. Since the odds are that he or she hasn't been exposed to any sales training or sales development programs other than the occasional discussion with you or your sales manager after a call, the salesperson "plays it by ear."

He or she knows your publication—the editorial thrust, the circulation numbers, the rates—and knows your market. You made sure of that before you sent the salesperson off to contact any of your customers and prospects. He or she has the factual information that supports your sales story.

But does that individual know how to sell? Does he or she know how to execute an effective approach? Can the salesperson lead the buyer into a favorable decision that guarantees the use of your magazine as an advertising medium? Is he or she a good listener? Is he or she a good presenter?

Most advertising salespeople "play it by ear." They often say, "I don't know what I do, but I do it and it works." But does it? And to what degree? Is this salesperson fully tapping the potential in his or her territory? Is he or she getting sufficient pages of advertising from the accounts and agencies that have been assigned? Does the individual make any unusual sales? Is the salesperson building strong and meaningful relationships with the people called on?

A Communications Vacuum in Publishing

Industry spends anywhere from six to eight thousand dollars per year to hire and train a salesperson. In publishing, my guess is that the figure would be in the low hundreds of dollars. Most new advertising salespeople receive no formal sales training whatsoever. They are hired, go on a few calls with other salespeople or with a member of the management team and then they're on their own. A few of them create their own training programs. They become students of selling. They read. They experiment and in time become better-than-average salespeople. It happens, but too infrequently.

What about the experienced salespeople who have been selling space for three, five, 10 or 15 years? Do these salespeople have exposure to publishing sales development programs? The odds are that they don't. Individual publishers and the publishing associations have not been effective in this area of their business. Paradoxically, sales is the major income-producing vehicle for most publications.

How good is your sales force? Do you have an ongoing sales development program for your present salespeople? How do you train a new salesperson?

If a publishing company is to realize its full potential, it cannot avoid making sales training and sales development a keystone of its corporate program. This is well-known in industry and well-neglected in publishing. Just as new men and women need training, experienced salesmen and saleswomen need and want sales development programs (which is advanced sales training). Far too many salespeople fall into bad work habits, and hit-or-miss methods of training do little to improve their productivity. Consequently, it's far better to overestimate the amount of training required by your salespeople than to underestimate it.

I'm sorry to say this, but after a score of years of exposure to consumer and business magazine salespeople, I find that most space salesmen and saleswomen (1) do not plan properly, (2) lose the customers in the approach stage of a sale, (3) cannot field objections, and (4) do not even try to close sales. Is this a condemnation of publishers? Absolutely! Publishers spend far too many dollars trying to get salesmen and saleswomen to sell harder and insufficient dollars helping them sell better.

Today, a salesperson needs to be organized so that he or she can utilize his or her selling hours to full advantage. Since less than half of the individual's time is spent in actual face-to-face selling situations, he or she must be a capable planner. The salesperson must learn that the individual's job is not to sell at all, but instead to assist the buyer to buy. There may be 240 working days in a year, but less than 100 are spent in the actual buying-selling relationship by your salesperson. That individual has to be good. Organization, planning, effective sales presentations, closing techniques and communications are not inbred in salespeople. They are things over which management can exercise control.

Building a Training Program

How can you build a training program? How about sales development? What kind of programs should these be? Obviously, you must consider your budget and who will be doing the training.

Let's start with the new salesperson. Is he or she new to the business or has he or she come from another magazine? In either case, the new person will need exposure to market knowledge, product knowledge and customer knowledge. He or she must also know both the publishing and the advertising fields as they relate to your specific publishing operation. As you know, the publishing business is a six-area business: publishing management, editorial, sales, circulation, mechanical and financial. Your salespeople must be knowledgeable in all of these areas, and they should know what their relationship is to production, editorial, circulation and other publishing areas.

A magazine's specific sales story normally fits into eight key areas: market, editorial, circulation, readership, response, rates and mechanical data, advertising volume, and services (merchandising, etc.). You can infuse product knowledge of a how-we-do-it nature within this framework.

No one knows or should know your customers better than you do. Learning who they are, why they buy or don't buy and how to motivate them is essential to any effective salesperson. Call reports, correspondence and meetings with other salespeople can be valuable input, but all of these things should be planned and scheduled as part of the overall training experience.

So far, we've touched briefly on in-house information. My suggestion would be that you give the new salesperson, as well as the experienced one, complete exposure to your key staff people in each publishing area (i.e. circulation, editorial, etc.). This training should also include visiting the printer and any related services. It's amazing the number of space salespeople and representatives who have never been in a printing plant or who have virtually no knowledge about circulation development methods. My first visit to a printing plant was when I started my own publication after selling space for 10 years.

The salesperson is now armed with necessary facts about your magazine, your market, your customers and your programs; but can he or she sell? Does he or she know how to present this information to an agency person who, in turn, has to relate it to an account? In publishing, the salesperson is market- and product-oriented, but this is where most training stops. All the time and dollars invested go down the drain when your person enters the customer's office, dives in the briefcase and immediately loses the customer's attention. No one has instructed the salesperson in the elements of a good approach. That individual is licked before he or she starts. Five years from now, that individual may be doing the same thing. Is it the salesperson's fault or yours?

In analyzing what your new salespeople need to know about selling, you will be creating the nucleus of your own training program. It seems to me that there are nine basic subjects that should form the basis of such a program.

The Basics

1. *An overview of the art and science of selling space.* This should include definitions and guidelines on effective selling, how to work successfully with accounts and agencies, buyer motivations and how to grow and prosper in the publishing business.

2. *The organizational side of sales.* How salespeople organize territories, set up itineraries, cover renewal business and sell target accounts. What should be carried in their briefcase. How to organize their desks. You can develop a checklist of sales tools for them. Effective selling is organized selling.

3. *Approaching the sales call.* You'll need to teach them how to plan for a call, how to establish an objective, how to gather essential information and finally, how to select appropriate selling tactics. You'll find these elements in any good book on selling, and you can rework them to fit your sales story. The important consideration is to make sure that your salespeople know how to get and hold their prospects' attention in the early stage of the sales calls.

4. *Getting the customer involved.* In the sales situation, how do your salespeople maintain the customer's or prospect's attention? How do they sell creatively? Develop a series of ideas for them.

5. *Comparative vs competitive selling.* You and your

---

25 Objections You Better Be Prepared For

1. The agency didn't recommend your magazine.
2. The client didn't buy our recommendation of your magazine.
3. Your rates are too high.
4. We can do this job more effectively with direct mail.
5. Our sales force is on top of all of the major buyers; we don't need advertising.
6. We are going to increase our sales force and the budget is going for that.
7. We really don't need more sales; we're oversold right now.
8. We haven't the dollars for your market.
9. We're not interested in your market this year.
10. We just conducted a survey and your magazine lost.
11. We're completely satisfied with what we're using.
12. We can't increase your schedule; we like to spread our small budget across several magazines.
13. There is only room for one magazine on the schedule.
14. We can get your audience through television or mass circulation media.
15. You haven't produced any results.
16. I'll think it over.
17. We don't believe in advertising.
18. We're in so many trade shows we can't afford to advertise.
19. We are spending our advertising budget for a new 4-color catalog or a company movie.
20. You haven't had enough editorial material devoted to our type of product.
21. Business is poor so we're cutting budgets.
22. We don't have any specialized advertisements ready for your field.
23. I haven't time to see you.
24. You're too late, the program is all locked up.
25. You haven't sold us.

salespeople know the difference. Research I conducted with 300 advertisers underscores the point: Don't knock your competition.

6. *Handling objections.* You can make up a list of typical sales objections and school your salespeople in handling these. Typical ones can be found in the accompanying box.

7. *Closing sales.* How should your salespeople close business? How can they close a call? How can they close a sale? How can they get the customer to say "yes"? You'll need to spend a lot of time in this area. It's the weakest area in advertising space sales.

8. *Follow up when the sale has been made. Follow up when the sale has not been made.*

9. *Communications.* Use of the telephone, letters and other devices for selling.

These are the basics for any new salesperson. The experienced salespeople need the same type of training, but you'll get more involvement from them if you label it as "sales development."

How do you build this information into a training program? In my judgment, one- or two-day meetings on these subjects every other year is just a lick of the lollipop. Training must be continuous. Formal training is a combination of (1) information dissemination (lectures, demonstrations, manuals and bulletins), and (2) participative forms (seminars, panels, role playing, group problem solving, cases, task force methods, etc.).

For the new salesperson, the lecture and seminar approach combined with written material will give him or her the greatest information in the least amount of time. As the salesperson progresses, you can move him or her into other types of training.

Who should do the job? They're your salespeople and their basic training should be under your direction. Either the publisher or the sales manager can cover all of these basic areas. If you do not feel competent in this field, then don't hesitate to bring in outside people. A well-trained, highly motivated salesperson is a priceless ingredient in the publishing business.

Developing Experienced Salespeople

Now, let's consider the existing salespeople. The odds are that they never had any sales training. They've learned the hard way, but not necessarily the most effective way. If they started out with bad habits, they'll bring them from job to job. It is regrettable but true that many new salespeople get their initial training from some of the more experienced people who are breaking every rule in the book.

Can the experienced salesperson be retrained? Absolutely. The essential feature of most salespeople is their improvableness. It doesn't happen overnight. You'll need about two years and six sessions to see some real progress.

Start with the basics. Give your salespeople assignments on the different phases of personal selling. Then, follow up with group discussions and carefully evaluate the expertise, or lack of it, on an individual basis. Carefully note those salespeople who need more exposure to certain areas like closing sales or creative selling.

Several sessions on the basics with changes in the learning method (seminars, panels, role playing, etc.) will

prove to be productive. Then, you'll want to get into more advanced techniques like:

• *Semantics.* What are strong and weak selling words? How does this tie in with direct selling compared with sales correspondence? I'd suggest you prepare a list for review and discussion.

• *Listening.* A salesperson learns more by listening than by talking. You'll need to research this area too. There are several good commercial programs on the market.

• *Getting to higher management.* This is a subject that creates a lively discussion. It is a major selling challenge for special-interest publications. The ideas you develop with your salespeople can be profitable exercise.

• *Specialized presentation techniques.* This is more discussion in the area of creative selling. A how-to session is often most useful.

• *How to entertain customers.* How much should be done? How should your salespeople conduct themselves at a business lunch?

• *Getting maximum communications leverage.* This subject involves the use of promotion as a sales tool. Publishers waste a lot of promotion dollars by not integrating their advertising and sales promotion into the direct selling effort. Salespeople need training in working with this material.

• *Sales perceptiveness.* What is the chemistry in the sales situation? A discussion on nonverbal communications is always interesting and instructive.

Timing a Problem

The timing of training and development sessions can be a problem for some publishers. They feel for some reason that they shouldn't take salespeople out of the territory. The question is: How effective and productive do they want the calls to be? Every salesperson needs to stop, pause and be motivated to higher sales goals. Any manager who doesn't realize this hasn't spent much time working a territory.

The Sales Meeting

Sales meetings in the publishing business are often not *sales* meetings at all. They are informational sessions where the publisher or sales manager brings the sales team up-to-date on the activities of the home office. The salespeople pick up pieces of knowledge that they can use on calls, but it does little to improve their effectiveness. Sales meetings that devote the major emphasis to selling and selling techniques will bring home more pages of advertising every time and, what's more, they'll build more enthusiasm for the profession and enhance morale in the process. Most space salespeople love the business they are in. They want to learn. They want to improve. They can't wait to go shoulder to shoulder against the enemy (your competition). Give them a cause and the tools and you'll see them climb mountains.

The sales meeting (please note I did not say "annual" sales meeting) is an ideal time to build in one, two or even three days of concentrated training. Two meetings a year just add that much more impact to your development program. You can put in some recreation and company information, but for the most part you'll benefit most by concentrating on personal selling. Just remember that your salespeople will learn more in participative sessions. This applies to even a two- or three-person team as well as to larger groups. Insist that your salespeople attend and participate in all discussions (no phone calls, no interruptions). They are there to learn about selling, and the opportunity for this type of valuable training comes far too seldom. Publishers' representatives benefit by this exposure, too, and appreciate those publishers who try to assist them in growing as salespeople.

Once you have set the stage for learning, you can then do some meaningful coaching on the job. This is a complete subject in itself. Sales training people will describe coaching as the most important single technique available to management. It is a very specific activity in itself. It requires the establishment of objectives and the development of techniques. Its purpose is to implement and improve upon your sales development and training programs. In other words, it is putting training to work by helping your salespeople to grow.

When do you coach? Whenever you're out on a sales call and have the opportunity to watch the salesperson work with account and agency people. It's the best time to observe the selling strengths and weaknesses of the people upon whom you depend so much for business. It is the time to help the salespeople develop better working habits, selling habits and sales techniques.

Coaching doesn't mean that you concentrate on the newer people and neglect the others. Your most seasoned salespeople may need the most help. They could be falling into bad habits. Their morale could be low. The competition could be putting them on the defensive without their realizing what is happening.

Relate your coaching requirements to the basic content of your training program. A list of subjects matched against your estimate of the salesperson's ability in each area will give you an overall picture of coaching needs. Keeping a coaching file is a good idea.

When your approach is cooperative and constructive and you have the salesperson's and magazine's best interests at heart, you'll do just fine.

In publishing, the most vital thing that management can do is hire good people and then train them.

Steps in sales planning

By Dave Hagenbuch

Several years ago, I conducted a study of 500 advertisers and 500 agency people to find out what these customers and prospects wanted from advertising salespeople. Did they prefer any particular type of presentation? What were their reasons for buying space in a magazine? What were some of their complaints about salespeople?

When it came to some of the "don'ts" in selling, the number one plea was, "Don't waste my time." Many of the advertising and marketing executives felt that far too many calls are made simply to bring the buyer "up to date" on the magazine. These people are looking for marketing facts: specific information that they can use in their sales and advertising programs. Yes, they need media information, but basically, they want to know about the market or markets served by your magazine. Thus, it is a smart salesman who talks market and sweeps the media in back of it.

How do your salespeople plan for their calls? Are they thinking in terms of calls or *sales*?

Instead of call-planning, publishers and sales-managers should get their people oriented to sales-planning. The top producers are those people who are trained to make *sales* calls, not *call* calls.

Establish an objective

The first step in sales planning is to establish an objective. The customer or prospect needs to know *why* he is meeting with the salesperson.

The objective may be to solve a previously stated objection. It may be to get a recommendation for a program of space or to close a specific issue. It could be to present some new research. Whatever the purpose, your rep should try to make it as specific as possible and communicate the objective of the call to the buyer. I have had advertisers tell me that salespeople have called on them and they didn't have the foggiest idea as to the purpose of the call. Let's make sure this doesn't happen to your salespeople.

To establish mutual understanding, the objective should be stated in the early stage of the call. For example, the salesperson can say, "Mr. Jones, the last time we met we discussed some marketing questions. I have looked into these and would like to review them with you. Specifically, you asked me if our market would grow significantly in the next five years...."

Another example: an agency meeting on next year's advertising program for XYZ Company. One approach could be: "Thank you for this meeting. Our objective will be to outline the reasons why you'll benefit by recommending a monthly program in this magazine for 1982...."

Gather essential information

Once an objective has been established, the next step is to pull together pertinent data for the call. The information must be meaningful to the person on the other side of the desk. Please remember that the buyer is interested in *his* products, *his* marketing objectives, *his* advertising program, *his* self-interests ... not *your* media points (unless they are important in *his* eyes).

When your salespeople gather information, have them ask themselves several questions: Is this information really important to Mr. Jones? How can he use it to help his company? How can he use it to help himself?

Help your people develop sales priorities. What is *most* important for this sales call? Do we have the key elements?

Again, far too many salespeople (and publishing executives) communicate in a self-destructive manner. They talk only about what interests them. They assume that our Mr. Jones will be equally excited and enthused. They haven't learned that you sell more space by assisting the buyer to buy. When your material is essential to him, he'll do just that. Then, your salespeople will have the satisfaction of complimenting him on a wise decision.

Select appropriate tactics

How will the salesperson open up the interview? How will he get the buyer involved in the meeting? How will the presentation be staged? What is the plan for timing? What objections may come up? How will these be handled? What closing devices will be used to promote action?

The key word here is "appropriate." The verbal communications and the visual techniques have to mesh. The objective must be satisfied. The essential information must have a receptive audience. The salesperson needs to guide and control the interview to its ultimate conclusion. What's more, it must be accomplished in a manner that causes the other person or persons to willingly accept the sales proposition.

When you are considering tactics, remember that people learn more through their eyes than their ears (we get 83 percent of our learning visually). The shortest route to a person's brain is through the senses, not through reason. So be sure to have good visual presentations for your salespeople.

Establish an objective for the call. Gather essential information. Select appropriate tactics. These are the steps in sales planning.

Then when your salespeople bring conviction, desire, and a closing attitude to their calls, they'll sell a lot of business for your magazine.

Getting appointments

By Dave Hagenbuch

Ask advertising salespeople about their major problems in selling space and, invariably, you'll hear about how hard it is to get appointments. For a variety of reasons—the pressures of time, the information explosion, the desire for more leisure hours, economic conditions in certain industries—the typical executive is often "too busy" to see sales representatives, and management people at accounts and agencies are becoming less accessible.

If this is the case, is there anything a salesperson can do to get more appointments, particularly with those who make the decisions? In fact, there are many techniques a salesperson can use, and they are based on the premise that the "busy" executive will always manage to see those people who can genuinely help him sell his products more effectively.

Management people today are hungry for productive ideas, new innovations, more efficient methods, and they'll gladly spend time with salespeople who don't waste *their time.*

Let's analyze two different situations—getting an initial appointment and getting a "call back"—to see how a salesperson can open doors by developing new approaches.

Making initial appointments

In this situation, all the salesperson wants is a chance to meet the potential customer (or to service an advertiser assigned to his account list). But consider the following:

Salesperson X: "I can't get a date with Mr. Jones. I've called him six or eight times in the past two months and he just won't see me. He claims he's too busy."

Salesperson Y: "I can't get by Mr. Smith's secretary. Apparently, her boss told her to keep the salespeople away."

These situations are a normal part of the business of selling advertising space. However, salespeople can change the percentages in their favor by using techniques that will make Mr. Smith and Mr. Jones eager to see them.

Here are my suggestions to salespeople who want to improve their "appointment getting" techniques.

His interests come first

First, make a list of reasons why Mr. Smith should see you and examine them carefully. Do they speak to his interests or to yours? Do they pertain to *his* company, *his* products, *his* marketing program, or do they stress *your* media points?

The best way to get to a prospective customer is to understand and attend to whatever is on *his* mind. Mr. Smith is thinking primarily about products, markets, buying motives, and sales messages. Since he thinks about advertising only in how it pertains to these primary concerns, the smart salesperson will talk first about the market served by the magazine and then sweep the magazine in afterward.

I spent the first few years of my selling career grinding out the media points until Gates Ferguson, the advertising manager of the Celotex Corporation in Chicago stopped me one day and said, "Dave, you're a good young salesman and you're a go-getter; but you're not a go-giver. You're all wrapped up in what you are selling and that's fine, but your job is to get wrapped up in what *I'm* selling. Remember, *I'm* your customer."

His message has stayed with me: Never forget to put your customer's interests first.

Prepare for the call

Screen your list and determine the most important reason why Mr. Smith will benefit by seeing you. Remember, the first reason you give him for setting the appointment must motivate him to positive action.

Prepare exactly what you are going to say and rehearse the words so that you do not get confused or mumble. Be sure to include a key phrase that will cause him to say, "Yes, 10 A.M. on Tuesday will be fine," and make the phone call with the attitude that you will be successful in getting the appointment.

I've seen a lot of seasoned salespeople handle the telephone poorly. They don't prepare. They don't sell the meeting. They merely ask if they can see someone for a few minutes without giving solid reasons why they should be granted a meeting. That's not good selling.

To improve your chances of getting an appointment, send a letter prior to your phone call (even in your home base city). You can specify a date and time for the meeting along with your reasons why Mr. Smith should see you. Then follow up with a call: "Mr. Smith, this is Al Roberts of *Idea Magazine*. Did you receive my letter?"

If he says, "Yes," immediately ask for the date or an alternative time: "Fine, I'm looking forward to meeting with you. Will 10 A.M. on Tuesday be convenient, or would you prefer later in the day?" If he hesitates, help him by selecting a time. "How does 2:30 P.M. suit you?"

If Mr. Smith tells you he did not remember seeing your letter, tell him what it said and ask for the meeting. Being somewhat defensive about the receipt of your letter, the odds are that he'll give you the date. At least, he'll give you the chance to sell the appointment.

If you are not successful, shoot for a future meeting. Write another letter. Follow up. Persistence pays off. Use your imagination. Get to know the names of the secretaries. Ask them if they can make appointments for you.

Repeat calls

If a number of advertisers or agency people whom you have seen previously are putting you off and will not see you, it's time to reappraise your selling techniques. Be honest with yourself. It could be that you didn't do an impressive selling job on your calls. If you had, you probably would not have this problem of getting dates.

Advertisers and agencies will see professional salespeople who genuinely try to be helpful. They want and need ideas, market data, research; they want to be informed. Your job is to assist them. You are a marketing consultant.

Let's assume, however, that you do a good, professional selling job on your calls, yet you still have the problem of getting appointments. In this case, you should review your telephone and letter-writing techniques. Both of these skills can be improved with study and practice. There are all kinds of aids, books, and courses available on these subjects.

Some salespeople come off much better in person than they do on the phone. Others do not write good letters. A professional salesperson constantly works at improving all of his or her selling skills. In addition, he studies sales challenges and develops workable solutions.

If you can begin to think in terms of assisting the buyer to buy, if you can think of *sales*, not calls, if you can become a "go-giver" rather than a "go-getter," you will get all the appointments necessary to doing a professional selling job.

Your sales approach

By Dave Hagenbuch

Although a sale starts back in the planning stage, the initial contact is made the moment a salesperson walks into a customer's office. Invariably, the person across the desk will take a mental picture of that salesperson, and this picture will either last or fade, depending upon the impression the salesperson makes.

Unfortunately, many salespeople do not know how to handle the transition between the initial greeting and the selling. They find it very awkward because they don't know how to get into the selling situation. They don't know how to get immediate attention from the people they call on. Furthermore, they aren't always able to command and hold the buyer's interest during the course of the interview.

At one time or another, every salesperson faces the problem of not communicating effectively with a customer or prospect. As he or she begins the sales presentation, the account executive seems to be lost in thought; the sales manager shifts uneasily in his chair or glances at his watch; the media buyer excuses herself and picks up the telephone. To add insult to injury, the salesperson has just started the interview . . . or, has he?

When this happens to you, it is time to analyze objectively your sales approach and to develop some new techniques that will insure maximum consideration of your magazine and sales material.

First you must get his attention

It is a truism that in selling anything—space, time, products—what happens in the critical opening minutes of the sale accounts for 80 percent of that sale. And yet, far too many advertising salespeople haven't learned how to make an effective approach.

The goal of your approach is to win attention—*undivided* attention. You must have a favorable audience for your sales proposition. If you greet the customer or prospect and then put your head into your briefcase to find your sales material, the odds are you'll lose him before you start. Or, if you lead in with some meaningless remark, he may consider you to be "just another salesman."

Attention is an elusive thing. People concentrate in fleeting units of time. In fact, it is estimated that total concentration on one subject lasts only 30 seconds. Thus, getting undivided attention is not easy—but it *is* of paramount importance.

A confident greeting

To make an *effective* approach, you must start before you walk in the door. Think of something pleasant as you walk down the hall. Open the door confidently. Smile. Announce yourself. Your name. Your magazine. Shake the other person's hand with a firm grip and look directly into his eyes as if to say, "It's good to be with you. I'm here to offer you something of real value."

You may engage in some personal conversation or "small talk," depending upon the person you are calling upon. But remember—most people are pressed for time and want to get down to business. Advertisers and agency people do not like space salespeople to waste their time.

The next avenue of approach to the buyer's mind is an appeal to the senses: sight, hearing, touch, etc. Far too many salespeople overlook the fact that people learn more through their eyes than through their ears. (It has been shown that whereas people retain only 20 percent of what they hear, they are able to retain 50 percent of what they see.)

Since a good visual presentation is a critical element in effective selling, many product salespeople are instructed to get a sample of the product into the potential customer's hands at the earliest possible moment.

In selling advertising, the same technique can be used through promotional material or the magazine itself (clipped to a particular item). More often, however, the appeal is accomplished through charts, films and other devices because the buyer is not simply buying a product but making an advertising decision.

And remember, *you* must control the sales aid used. If, for some reason, the buyer gets hold of your magazine and starts reading it, wait until he is through looking *before* you say anything. You cannot sell a person who is only half listening.

In my opinion, a chart presentation is extremely effective because you can maintain control of the sales aid and the interview and still study the potential buyer's reaction to the material you are presenting.

Appeal to reason

Now that you have appealed to the senses, the buyer is ready for your appeal to his reason. At this point, your intention is to get him to consider your sales points, to evaluate them, and to make a decision.

Lead into your presentation with a buyer-oriented question or a statement that will sustain his interest. Your initial approach at this stage can even be imaginative, appealing to the buyer's curiosity. Consider these sales stories:

•I once introduced a new magazine in a highly competitive field by placing one apple and three oranges on the prospect's desk to emphasize the difference between our magazine and its three competitors. It turned out to be a most effective attention-getting device.

•When a refrigerator manufacturer in Kansas City told me he didn't have an advertising agency, I started the next meeting by introducing a series of rough layouts and some copy for a full-page color program. He appreciated the effort and we ended up with a nice program. He said it was the first time any salesperson had brought him some ideas.

•On a sales call at United States Gypsum, I brought in one of the typical readers of our magazine, a registered architect, who was designing a church using U.S.G. products. I asked him to tell the advertising manager what he was doing and why he read our publication. It was interesting to let him take over on this sales call. The advertising manager even called in one of his product managers. I deliberately did not do any selling. Fortunately, I didn't have to. The architect took care of that when he went into detail about his readership of the magazine.

Another approach that has worked well for me over the years involves the use of a visual presentation of the advertiser's advertising on a card or series of cards. I open up the meeting by saying, "Let's talk about your advertising." The immediate reaction has been one of decided interest.

Questions such as "Where do you expect this product to be five years from now?" will give you good sales information and you'll always learn a lot by listening. But remember—*you* are the salesperson and *you* must guide and control the meeting with the goal of promoting action.

Concentrate on your approach. It will pay you *big* dividends.

The structured sale

By Paul McGinnis

When was the last time you noticed that what you said was not what was heard?

Take, for example, this interchange among three people in a car traveling from Los Angeles to New York on a parched and bleak stretch of Route 66 in corn country.

"This is Thursday, right?" says the back seat passenger.

"Yeah, it's the third day, but it feels like six," says the passenger in the front seat.

"Do you want to stop at the next restaurant, or are you too sick to wait 10 minutes?" asks the considerate driver.

Since most people hear only what they expect to hear, much incoming information is either discarded or consciously compared to what is going on in the listener's mind. Because people filter everything that they hear and see, they will respond most favorably to information that is consistent with and supportive of what they already have in mind. Furthermore, people accept, consider and retain information best if it is presented in an orderly logical sequence.

Understanding the buyer

Now, let's apply this psychology to the area of ad sales. To build an effective advertising sales presentation, you must first determine who the buyer is and what he wants to hear. Then you must decide how to develop your information so that the buyer, by accepting and agreeing with each newly presented thought, will ultimately agree with your conclusion.

To accomplish this goal, you have to be keenly aware of the way your listener or buyer processes your "pitch," for any person in the buyer role is *obliged* to be resistant. It is a natural part of the position. In fact, if a buyer displays no resistance in the buying, he or she will not get full value from the seller. To carry through a successful presentation, therefore, there must be room for discussion and agreement which will lead to the next logical subject.

To achieve agreement, the seller should concentrate on the *buyer's* area of interest since the buyer must agree to and move with the presentation all the way through. The seller should not lose control of the flow of agreements, however. Certainly, if the seller doesn't know about the buyer's interests and the reasons the buyer should advertise in his magazine, the call should not be made. The "presentation" will be wrong.

Presentations miss the point when they do not sell. Although most presentations contain the right elements, elements alone, used independently or out of order, do not lead to the sale. Good presentations lead to the sale.

Good presentations show good research. They show marketing opportunity. They extol editorial value. But most important, good presentations include all salient points of fact, in a stimulating manner, and without overkill.

But where, in the course of events, do you use a fact? When is the buyer ready for the fact? Does the fact fill the need? Does it set up and arouse the appetite for the next fact?

Most "non-selling" presentations extol some important fact in order to separate their magazine from the pack. But are good facts *alone* a reason to advertise?

I recently saw the presentation of a successful special interest magazine that could have been outstanding. It showed a very wealthy and influential audience which apparently spends tremendous sums on everything you might expect these people to buy. It showed that the magazine's circulation is booming. It displayed an ad revenue chart that looked like the trail of a SAM missile. The presenter was at ease and well-informed.

Fact after incredible fact bounced off the screen and poured out of the sound speakers for over 20 minutes. The information and its audio/visual presentation were stimulating ... then amazing ... then routine ... then numbing.

The *elements* were good, but there was no orderly flow. After seeing and hearing this presentation, what does the listener do? Buy stock in the company? Wait till someone asks for a media plan of a magazine with such facts (if remembered)?

Structure is universal

The following structure is a guide to *every* presentation. It applies to the full scale multi-media extravaganza and the "informal" summary that may follow a pleasant lunch. It applies to the call stressing circulation growth as well as to the call heralding new research findings.

Every reason for the call and every item of importance is better remembered when it is positioned in its proper place in the story. Furthermore, every item of importance in the sales story must be preceded and followed by the information that puts it into the kind of perspective that points directly to the sale . . . on *every* call.

For example, you discover a strength in your readership among a certain portion of the marketplace that you know will bring a key account closer to schedule. You know their situation and you think that if they knew the rest of your story, it may even tip the scale to writing the order on this call.

You have called on this account 10 times in the past two years, however, and you do not want to bore the buyer with what you think he already knows.

However, the problem is that if you simply walk in and tell him that you can now assure him of good coverage in *this certain area*, he may justifiably wonder what the other areas were.

Proclaiming the big market

After the essential amenities of opening the call (chatter about game scores or the weather), start the presentation with a business agreement.

I believe that the best first area of agreement—and the most effective opening for a presentation—is a statement of the bigness of the marketplace that the advertiser and the magazine have in common. If it were not big enough to be worthwhile, you wouldn't be there. Your statement must be accurate, however, or the advertiser will "tune out" the rest of the pitch.

If a presentation to a CB radio account started with "CB radio sales in the U.S. were at an all-time high in 1979," it might destroy the rest of the session. A better opening might be, "CB radio sales topped x number of units of which x number were additional or replacement units, and x number were to new licensees."

The opening statements have to be recognizable, accurate and interesting to the buyer and his business. They must also be *Big*. The opening agreement must connect with the buyer in the buyer's area of interest. A presentation on the wonderful position of the magazine or publishing company (including its spectacular future promise) may be great for corporate PR or internal morale building—but by itself such a presentation does not sell space. (There *is*, however, a place for it in the structure ,as we shall see.)

Unfortunately, there are dozens, maybe scores of major and expensive presentations about very fine magazines and publishing companies that are boring and ineffective because they never develop agreement to proceed. As a result, they stumble and lose the listener. The effective presentation connects with the buyer and leads directly to the sale of space.

Stating market dynamics

After you have agreement on the dimensions of the market you have in common and agreement that this market is big, the buyer's next thought will be something like "now what?" This is the time to discuss the dynamics

of that big market . . . that it is growing.

Every marketplace has something interesting to say. Even in the depressed CB market, "the number of tranceivers sold by dealers for new car installations was up in 1979."

If the facts are well-documented and not distorted, the buyer will agree that a portion (or all) of his market is big and that there are significant areas of growth that can be documented and/or forecast. Furthermore, since the buyer has a professional responsibility to get in on this action, he will want to know more. He will want to better understand the characteristics of this dynamic situation.

Concentrated decision-making

This buyer is *still* not ready for the "media" pitch, however. It's too soon—and this is where many sales presentations get off the track.

All products in all marketplaces are bought with a certain rhythm or logic. By charting the rhythm of buying decisions, we can see that these decisions are concentrated into definable patterns.

For example, all things being equal, drivers tend to buy gasoline more often at a close but convenient station as they are *going away* from home rather than *returning* home. I noticed this some years ago when I lived in a town that had three gas stations in a four-corner intersection. Two of them were constantly changing owners while the third one was obviously prospering. The prosperous station also happened to be on the right side of the street—the side which led out of town.

Another example: The market for fine crystal has been studied by many well known and completely credible research organizations. The product's high price as well as its use in "better homes" for "fine dining" situations would tend to put it in the 35 to 49 age group of upwardly mobile affluent women. That is where the money is, that's where the atmosphere is and that's where the use is. But time after time, research report after research report, the most compressed area of decision-making, and so the most efficient market, is the bride-to-be.

Companies which sell instruments, equipment and tools to electronics technicians place more advertising in magazines that are read at home because the job environment is not a good reading environment. Companies that sell portable dictating equipment know that the executive sitting in a plane on a business trip often thinks about something he wants to put in a letter or tell his associates. The in-flight magazine on his lap has a tear-out card for a demo. That's compression.

Obviously, then, since buying activity is heavily concentrated, a seller's position in the marketplace is critical. Unfortunately, most salespeople miss this point—but it is a critical point which must be made absolutely clear to the buyer.

Market accessibility

You will not have come this far in the presentation without some questions from the buyer.

If you have done your homework, you can respond honestly and credibly. The buyer *has to* express some doubt or resistance in order to be sure he or she fully understands what has happened with the flow of information. It is in the nature of buying.

But, if you have agreement on the bigness and the growth of the marketplace, and the concept of periods of concentrated decision-making, the buyer now has to be looking for a handle. Because the well-structured presentation is laid out in such a way that it *causes* certain questions to be raised, the buyer has to be wondering, "How can I get my sales message in front of that big and growing market right there in the period of concentrated activity?" In the structured delivery, those questions are the next items to be discussed.

It is interesting that even the most sincere and honest questions can destroy many unstructured presentations. Have you ever seen a situation where a question is asked and the "presenter" pleads to have questions held to the end? Or worse, the presenter answers the question and loses his place in the pitch?

In the structured presentation, you not only know where it will end (with a sale), but you also can't lose your place. You *never* memorize it. Every question raised supports the structure, and every answer will lead to the next logical step.

Where do I (buyer) access this market which is so big and growing and conveniently compressed? Because there are many ways, this is where the media pitch enters. To deny that there are other ways to access the market will turn the listener off. But, your magazine is best for good reasons.

If you were selling one of the magazines that serves the fine at-home dining markets and you were about to call on a national floral organization, you would not deny the heavy (and expensive) use of afternoon newspapers or rush hour radio. But can a newspaper ad or a radio commercial provide a four-color floral centerpiece ad opposite a gorgeous picture and recipe of coq-au-vin and 1968 Chenin Blanc? That's the point of access in the big, growing and compressed floral centerpiece market.

Now is the time to talk about your readership, research and reader loyalty, your inquiry numbers, your circulation statement, your awards, your list of advertisers, your CPM . . . because these items now support and propel the accessibility of your reader. Your reader is *involved* with your magazine.

Offer rewards

Unfortunately, most presentations begin and end on this point. Actually, this point should only be part of the presentation, for as soon as agreement has been reached on this big, growing, concentrated and accessible market, the presentation should address the rewards of taking early or immediate action on the information.

The buyer, in fact, may already be signaling that the close is at hand, and this portion of the presentation will seal it. There may be a special position available at a justifiable premium. There may be a special issue coming up which calls for a heavier commitment. You may have a unique merchandising scheme in mind. This is the time to trot these things out.

What if you feel that you have all the agreements but find that you are gaining no ground? Obviously, you are calling on the wrong person!

Sales presentations

By William Abbott

I don't dislike presentations that include multi-media effects, flashing lights and moog synthesizers pouring forth modern music. It's just that I can't understand what they're really trying to accomplish except keeping production houses economically solvent.

If they are meant to be show biz, they miss the point because there is a pronounced difference between the audience for a show and the audience for a presentation. Shows are attended by people who are relaxed and ready to be entertained. The average sales presentation, on the other hand, is more likely to be viewed by business people worrying about business problems: the sales manager who has just discovered that sales in Oklahoma City are rotten; the brand manager who is worrying about the new product that is not gaining distribution; the account executive whose boss informed him yesterday that the client doesn't quite appreciate his creative talents. Since such people are looking for solutions, not entertainment, it's best to leave the show biz to David Merrick.

To produce a presentation that will sell, it helps a lot if you understand what makes people buy. I once knew a guy who was made director of the department responsi-

ble for supplying a large advertising staff with sales-support material. The funny thing about the assignment, however, was that he had never sold a line of advertising or even witnessed an ad being sold in his life.

This guy's first major effort in the job was supervising production of a basic presentation for a magazine that was the leader in its field. It turned out to be a 20-board chef-d'oeuvre, beautifully (and expensively) conceived. But I swear, nine of the 20 boards contained a myriad of small numbers documenting CPMs, circulation, total audience, rates, and demographics. Furthermore, there were a lot of other figures for what looked like three-quarters of the publications found on the newsstand at Grand Central.

However, here's the kicker: It was actually intended that the salesperson stand before the audience and read every one of those numbers! Never mind that any media buyer could, and probably did, get them from a book on his desk. Our newly-appointed hero just didn't know any better.

Presentation expert number two stayed away from numbers, but this one had a penchant for quotes. His presentations quoted not only market sources but just about every person at the magazine except the printer. Of course there's nothing wrong with showing opinions of experts. It was just the way they were shown: displayed on the screen with no graphic accompaniment. And once again, every word was read to the audience.

However, expert number two demonstrated a quality of mercy not displayed by expert number one. At least the presentation was on slides so the lights were out. This allowed those in the audience who may have had a spirited evening the night before to catch a few winks, and more sedate viewers to just let their minds wander unobserved.

Presentations are like roadsigns. Let's say you're driving along the Ohio Turnpike. You see an exit sign that says "Cleveland." This sign is not meant to tell you exactly how to get to Cleveland. It's simply a reminder for those who want to go to Cleveland that they should get off the turnpike.

The graphics of a presentation are like road signs. They are not meant to provide all or even most of the information that one wishes to convey. They are simply indicators to the presenter that this specific subject is what he should talk about, and he should progress from subject to subject in a smooth, flowing monologue.

Admittedly this exerts a greater demand upon the abilities of salespeople, but after all, verbalizing is what they are paid to do. If day-to-day presentations could be "canned," they could be delivered by monkeys trained to push the right button and the cost would be peanuts.

Although I am embellishing the situation, there is much truth in these descriptions. I once participated in a sales effort which required many extensive meetings with the client, a major oil company, and its agency. This was back when competition was tough and prices low. At every meeting, whenever a point was made, the advertising director of the client would look at the account supervisor of the agency and say: "I know, I know; but will it pay off at the pumps?"

Therein lies the secret of a sales presentation: to show the viewer all the good things that are going to happen to his business as a result of investing a sizable portion of his advertising budget in your magazine. Nothing else matters.

Logical progression

So what are the ingredients that constitute an effective sales presentation? It goes without saying that it must be as brief as possible yet make every valid point. Content must address the needs, goals and objectives of the advertiser and should demonstrate an understanding of his business.

It is at this juncture that a magazine's audience and its unique qualities that produce customers from that audience come into the picture. The logical progression of the sales presentation will cover every aspect of interest to the viewer in an orderly, easily-comprehended sequence. Once again, however, it must be tightly to the point. As an expert on presentations once noted: "The mind can only absorb what the rear-end can endure."

Keeping in mind the fact that the objective of a presentation is to come away with sales orders, an effective presentation should follow this sequence:

•A general positioning of the marketplace and the most current update on relevant industry conditions. This sets the tone of the presentation and establishes a climate of confidence toward the seller on the part of the buyer as a result of demonstrating that you have "done your homework" and understand his business.

•An explanation of how the editorial content of the magazine coincides with market conditions. Such an explanation will define the audience of consumers who constitute prime prospects for the advertiser's goods or services.

•A description of the special qualities inherent in your magazine's readership that relate to specific conditions within the marketplace. In this segment, numbers should be used but not accentuated. Should you have detailed statistics that you feel are vital to your sales story, present them in a "leave behind" which may be read at a later time. If figures are used, be sure that their source is one unavailable to your audience. People do not appreciate sitting through recitations of statistics they already know.

•Introduce seminal research data that fortify the established case for the inclusion of your magazine on the schedule.

•Present extra incentives to the buyer, such as upcoming special issues, the availability of positions adjacent to compatible editorial, merchandising programs, discounts, etc.

•And finally, the all-important closing.

If one follows the sequence as outlined, the result will be a well-coordinated presentation of interest to the viewer and success to the seller.

Participatory Presentations

Our industry is now witnessing the emergence of a new format which I call the participatory presentation. I saw one recently which simulated a television quiz show; the contestants were the audience. What a clever way of being absolutely sure that everyone absorbs the facts as they concentrate on finding the right answer. And of course, there were prizes for the winners.

Another form of audience participation is equally effective in presenting the results of a survey. About a week prior to the event, each invited guest is sent a booklet containing the survey questions and sufficient space for making notations. An accompanying letter describes the demographic and psychographic banner points and explains how to sort out the reactions of individual groups with similar characteristics. This format produces a far more receptive audience for a sales-oriented summation, or closing.

And the closing is what presentations are all about. After all the facts have been given, it is time to suggest that the customer take some proposed action. Ask for the order. Irrespective of how much the audience may smile, you cannot assume that the answer is 'yes.'

One way to close is to talk about dollars. Show your rates and how to structure a continuous and effective schedule by maximizing available discounts. Suggest schedules which take into account seasonal trends. In a "switch-pitch," demonstrate how adding your magazine to the schedule by replacing the weakest existing one can increase reach.

If strategy calls for it, recommend taking just one page from each of several competitors to take advantage of your attractive proposition.

Suggest action! I am constantly amazed at the number of presentations that fail to evoke a definite reaction from the viewer. Indeed, I have seen a few costing up to $100,000 that had weak closings or no closings at all. They just ended, with critical acclaim, but no business. Critical acclaim is fine for our editors. In our case, only advertising pages pay off.

113

A cure for briefcase reflex—
Selling more by showing less

By Roger Appleby

The salesperson with "Briefcase Reflex" is a gunslinger in the classic sense. He or she would rather shoot first and talk later.

For some salespeople, reaching into a briefcase for copies of their magazine, documents, charts and comparative research is like reaching for a cigarette—a reflex brought on by a minor case of nerves. Reaching for a cigarette or opening a briefcase gives momentary satisfaction. But cigarettes lead to poor health and the briefcase can lure the salesperson away from the objective—making the sale.

The professional space salesperson moves to the point of sale in a straight line with no detours. The individual establishes a time-frame, roughs out a plan of action and moves step by step toward the close. He or she knows when the contents of his or her briefcase should be introduced as elements of the sale—when graphic illustration gets the idea across better and quicker than talk. The salesperson knows how to select, remove and put back the briefcase material without disturbing the flow of dialogue.

Too often, however, a salesperson approaches a sales prospect determined to say only what he or she wants the prospect to hear, rather than what the prospect wants to know. The salesperson has the story down pat and intends to tell it all without interruption. The result is a monologue.

A monologue, by its nature, is relentless, rolling over the opposition like an invading army. The briefcase barrage provides the rat-a-tat-tat by punctuating the spoken word with monotonous regularity. In effect, the salesperson is saying "You don't have to believe me. I've got a piece of paper to prove what I say." The salesperson succeeds in building a climate of boredom, isolation and, perhaps, mistrust. The performance never varies. And when it's over the salesperson has sold only himself or herself on the credibility of the magazine.

The professional salesperson functions differently. The salesperson is, first and foremost, a good listener. The first step in making the sale is to gather information about the advertiser. Then, by listening, the salesperson can frame the right questions. No briefcase is needed. Just an active, inquiring mind.

Potential advertisers usually enjoy talking about their company, service or product. By listening, the sales pro achieves involvement, not isolation. A dialogue is established. Now the advertiser is ready to listen.

Once the salesperson gathers the facts, he or she is in a position to compare the prospect's market with that of his or her own magazine.

Now material is introduced and related to the advertiser's market objectives. The salesperson tailors the information.

This approach has a number of advantages. First, the salesperson retained the initiative. If the salesperson introduces the magazine and documentation prematurely—before evaluating the prospect—the prospect evaluates the magazine before the salesperson has determined how best to present it. It is up to the person to establish the magazine in the prospect's mind, to illustrate how the magazine can best be utilized as a component of the media mix. Allowing the prospect to form a judgment based on imperfect knowledge often means going back to correct the problem before proceeding with the sale.

A second advantage is that the salesperson has established himself or herself as a peer—discussing sales and marketing problems on the highest level. This is a far better position to begin the sale. The salesperson is removed from the peddler classification by giving his or her magazine an individual identity.

It is usually during the process of establishing the magazine that the type of salesperson I have in mind opens his or her briefcase. He or she has already made the advertiser understand the relationship between the product or service and the magazine's readers. Now the salesperson is ready to show the magazine. The advertiser has heard the logic of it.

But at times there is a definite advantage in continuing the sales call without showing anything.

If the salesperson says: "Now that I've had an opportunity to learn something about the people who buy your product and the goals of your advertising campaign, I would like to give more thought as to how our magazine can work for you as an advertising vehicle in realizing these objectives. I'll send you a copy of my magazine as soon as I return to the office and present my ideas at our next meeting. Having seen the magazine, I'm sure you will have some questions which you would like to discuss when we get together."

The salesperson has paid his or her magazine the ultimate compliment. The implied confidence that the magazine can stand evaluation unaided has created a climate for acceptance in the mind of the advertiser. The advertiser is predisposed to like it. The salesperson has established an ongoing working relationship by giving the advertiser the opportunity to examine the magazine when he or she is alone.

Advertisers know that the typical salesperson wants to supervise the examination of the magazine, ready to counter any negatives. By sending the magazine by itself, you are showing that you respect the advertiser's ability to evaluate it fairly.

The function of the salesperson is to create an environment in which a sale is most likely to take place. The salesperson can bring this about more effectively by relying on himself or herself, and not a stuffed briefcase.

It is the salesperson who provides the briefcase with its reason for being. It has no life of its own.

The importance of listening

By Dave Hagenbuch

The University of Minnesota and Brigham Young University have done some interesting and enlightening studies on listening. Because advertising space salespeople are often criticized by both accounts and agencies for not listening and learning enough about an advertiser's market and marketing problems, the results of these studies are decidedly relevant to anyone who wants to sell effectively and productively.

The facts about listening are surprising:

1) Listening is our primary communication activity. We spend 80 percent of our waking hours communicating. At least 45 percent of that time is spent listening. For executives, the average is 57 percent.

2) Listening is a learned behavior. According to Dr. Lyman K. Steil, president of the International Listening Association, "Listening is a measurable, observable, testable, and improvable behavior. Tests clearly reveal that most individuals do not listen well. Immediately after listening to a 10-minute presentation, the average listener has heard, correctly understood, properly evaluated and retained approximately half of what was said. Within 48 hours, that drops to a final 25 percent effectiveness level."

3) Listening can be improved through training or planned effort on the part of an individual.

Agency opinions about inattentive salespeople can be discounted because of the client relationships involved —agencies simply are not as objective as they should be about this subject. However, when the people at the *account* say a salesperson doesn't know enough about their market and marketing problems, it's time for the salesperson to do some honest self-appraisal.

If this situation applies to you, then a change of image that makes you more market oriented, as far as your client is concerned, is needed.

The problem

Advertisers tend to overlook the fact that at special interest consumer and business publications the average unit of sale, per space contract, is relatively low. The result is that the average salesperson has to handle a large number of accounts, which makes the job of being a specialist at each and every account quite difficult—in fact, almost impossible. Nonetheless, a salesman cannot dismiss his responsibility to know as much as he can about each advertiser. He should do everything possible to become a marketing "consultant."

How do you do this? How can you develop a presentation that sings and sells? How can you get the reputation of being "tuned in" to the advertiser's market, to his marketing, sales and advertising challenges? How can you assist the advertiser to do a better selling job in your specific field and through your magazine?

Obviously, you must know everything you can about your magazine and about the market (and field) you serve. Begin by reading your magazine thoroughly, meeting with readers, researching the field for market statistics, talking with associates—doing all those things necessary in a product and market educational process.

The goal is to know as much about the general area of marketing in your field as the people you call on.

But how do you go about learning a specific advertiser's needs? How can you tailor a presentation that is oriented to the advertising manager, the sales manager, the president and other executives?

The listening solution

To put it bluntly, you have to stop talking and start listening. This is not an easy thing, because you're a salesperson—and salespeople like to be heard. But in selling, you'll learn more by listening than by talking.

I suggest that at least once a year you put on a "listening presentation" for your primary accounts and prospects (including advertising agencies). A "listening session" involves as much preparation as any other good presentation. If it concerns a new account—an initial call—you'll need an entirely different approach than for one made to your present advertisers. (P.S.: It is the "present advertisers" who complain most about salesmen not listening and learning about them.)

Here are some ideas that may be helpful to you:

1) *Do some research.* Learn as much as you possibly can about the company through financial reports, salesmen and sales literature. You can normally obtain data from a local sales office. Salesmen will always talk about their products and companies. Most customers and prospects will appreciate it when you write to ask for current literature to use, to be of further service to them. Study competitive data too.

2) *Prepare some questionnaires.* Make up a list of intelligent questions for different types of sales situations (new accounts, established contacts, and so forth). Ask questions about the market, the products, methods of distribution, the sales force, etc.

The types of questions you ask will differ from field to field, but they must all be specific and designed to produce pertinent data for future use. For example, ask the company to estimate its sales potential in different areas. Then find out how many direct salesmen, agents and/or distributors they have to effectively cover their markets. You can relate this data to your circulation coverage, cost per potential reader, cost per actual reader (if you have good readership information), and to the company's direct selling costs. This will help show how advertising in your magazine supplements or complements their advertising program.

3) *Write for appointments* (even in your home town). An approach could be: "Dear Bill. In the interest of being of maximum service to you, I'm writing to request an appointment to probe into your marketing plans and programs. Will you be kind enough to take 20 minutes to answer a series of specialized questions and bring me up-to-date on your activities? At least once a year, Bill, I'd like to have a "listening meeting" with you, which will help me to more effectively tailor our sales efforts in terms of your interests." Ask for a time and date.

4) *Keep your date, ask your questions, and make*

notes at the meeting. Your accounts will be impressed with your interest. You'll get useful data to tie into future sales presentations. You'll increase your effectiveness and sell more business.

On your regular calls during the year, those that are not designated listening sessions, don't forget that you are there to *sell.* Listening is a *passive* activity (the odds are that very few advertisers or agency people have been exposed to listening training), but selling must be *active.* Although it's a smart salesperson who asks questions to explore and assess the needs of the buyer, on a sales call of 20 to 30 minutes, don't spend *all* your time asking questions—you'll have little time left for selling space.

Be *active* in your selling. Nothing sells better than genuine enthusiasm. When you're excited about what you are selling, the buyer gets excited. Use gestures. Keep good eye contact. Sell benefits rather than features. Tell the buyer what he or she has to gain by using your magazine. People don't buy space, they buy the expectation of some benefit. The ability to listen is important, but so is the ability to sell.

The power of the question

By Frederic C. Decker

Charles Kettering said, on the occasion of his 70th birthday, "A man must have a certain amount of intelligent ignorance to get anywhere."

Salespeople with intelligent ignorance know that they don't know everything. They also know what it is they don't know. And they know what they have to learn to be a little less ignorant about what it takes to get a specific piece of business.

Let me simplify that by saying: Salespersons with intelligent ignorance are those who make information gathering the essential first step in the sales process.

How many never seem to learn!

You don't have to look very far on any magazine sales staff to find the guys and gals who are so intent upon telling the prospect what *they* think the prospect ought to know that they don't stop to find out what the prospect *needs* to know to make a favorable decision. These are the sales folks who spend most of their interview time with their heads in their briefcases looking for research reports, reach and frequency comparisons and all the other statistical stuff that is so near and dear to the hearts of unimaginative salesmen and saleswomen and so far from the interests of most executives who make the final decisions about which magazines are going to get the order.

What *does* interest the buyer?

Salespeople are never going to know unless they ask.

They can be pretty sure that one basic question in a buyer's mind is, "How will buying this magazine make me look good?" It's probably as simple as that. Everybody has a boss and everybody wants to look good in the boss's eyes. One way to look good is to use media imaginatively; to make buys that make good marketing sense.

So how do space sellers help the buyer look good?

• They ask the kinds of questions that will produce information upon which valid and productive buying reasons can be based—reasons that help make the buyer's decision a sound one.

• They ask the kinds of questions that interest the buyer—questions about the marketing objectives of the product, its marketing problems, the thrust of the competitors, what product innovations are being made, what media mix is being considered and the reasons for it.

• They ask what the buyer wants most from media in terms of audience or in terms of the way one medium can support another. (One of our clients recently sold a big trade magazine schedule to a manufacturer who hadn't considered, before the publisher sold it, the desirability of a trade program to support a massive television effort.)

When salesmen and saleswomen ask questions about advertisers' needs and objectives several important things happen.

First, the prospect's attention is captured. Clients are a lot more interested in *their* problems than in the latest ABC or BPA statement.

Second, an atmosphere of confidence is established. Tough though they may be, the buyers of advertising space are prone to be on the defensive and even somewhat insecure in the presence of a person who is trying to sell something they may think they don't want to buy. But when they get on their own conversationsal turf, talking about their own needs and problems with someone who is informed and interested, they become different people. Through the simple act of telling a salesperson about their problems, they build their confidence in that salesperson. It is the same psychological phenomenon which takes place in the confessional or in the interview between lawyer and client or doctor and patient.

Third, sellers who know enough to ask the right questions gain knowledge they can later use to demonstrate how their magazines uniquely serve the needs of the advertising prospects. It's an old saying that reason can be found to add nearly any book to a schedule, or to knock it off. The probing seller finds those positive reasons and zeros in on them when the time comes to ask for the order.

Good questions are rarely asked without preparation. Just as the skillful interviewer first bones up on a subject, so must the skillful salesperson. To paraphrase Kettering, "He won't get anywhere unless his ignorance is intelligent," unless the questions reveal that the salesperson does, indeed, have a basic understanding of the prospect's company, its product, its marketing channels, its competitors, its history. Maybe store checks have been made to see how the product is merchandised. Certainly the company's annual report has been read if one has been published. PIB has been checked and all the old call reports have been read. Articles about the company and its people in the trade and business press have been combed. In short, the salesperson has become prepared just as would one of the editors before an interview for a marketing story.

Skill in questioning (provided they know what to do with the answers) is a major tool in all salespeople's kits.

There is recognition of that fact in a neatly framed motto I once saw hanging in a sales manager's office. It said, "Matthew VII, 7 and 8." When I got home I looked it up. It says: "Ask, and it shall be given you; seek, and ye shall find; knock, and it shall be opened unto you. Every one that asketh receiveth; and he that seeketh findeth."

Handling objections

By Dave Hagenbuch

How good are you at handling sales objections? Have you developed an objection-answering technique that works effectively?

Because of the intangibility of selling advertising space, it's extremely important that you become competent in this phase of selling. Sales objections and stalling tactics can be roadblocks or building blocks—depending upon how you handle them. You must be a good broken-field runner. You have to know when to build on objections, when to skirt around them, and when to simply ignore them.

Far too many salespeople get trapped into objection situations that block them from closing business. The agency says, "Sorry, but the budget is all locked up," or "We can use only one magazine in your field and yours is not on the schedule." The account, the advertiser, tells you "the agency hasn't recommended your magazine" or that it "didn't produce any results." These are standard objections.

The fine line between a valid and invalid objection is something that can cause an inexperienced salesperson a great deal of difficulty. He tends to accept things as they appear to be rather than to see them as they are. In the salesperson's mind, the objection too often becomes a *statement of fact* rather than a buyer's *excuse* for not buying.

The salesman then replays the objection to his management, using it as a crutch for his own sales deficiency. He hides behind an objection because he is reluctant to admit he has been rejected. It has become a "personal" thing. It's unfortunate, but true, that this quite frequently applies even to experienced salespeople.

Find the real reason
Professional salespeople can always give multiple reasons for buying, against every objection raised. They know that in most cases the reason given for not buying is not the real reason, the real objection, to their sales story.

Advertisers and agencies really do not like to say "No" to you. They are in business to buy space and it's human nature to want to be affirmative in people relationships. Therefore, most of the time, the buyer will give you a reason for not buying that *sounds good*, that's difficult to handle, or that seems to be reasonable. Your task, then, is to isolate the *real* reason why you're being blocked from the sale. You have to sell *through* the objection to make the sale or get the recommendation. Hidden objections must be brought to the surface.

Several techniques have worked well for me. One is to ask the buyer if there are any *additional* reasons (beyond the stated objection) you are not getting the business. You merely ask, "In addition to that (the objection), is there any other reason you are not buying our magazine?" (Depending upon the situation, you might temper this by using terms such as "not *planning* to use our magazine at this time?" That suggests the door is still open.) The buyer's reply to this question will often reveal the real objection. If, for example, the buyer says, "Well, the real reason is that your publisher came in here and questioned our judgment," then you know the real problem.

Another approach is to say to the buyer, "If I answer this *question* (notice I didn't call it an objection) to your satisfaction, will you then buy our magazine?" That's putting everything right up front. In fact, one of the best ways to check on your success in handling an objection is to try and close the sale.

Dealing with objections
It seems to me that there are three ways of dealing with an objection:

1) *Ignore it.* Many professional salespeople use the technique of simply continuing with the sales presentation, or overriding the objection, to see if the prospect goes back to it as a serious objection. If not, they often continue the interview and close the sale. One agency man told me about a successful salesman who "hears only what he wants to hear." I'm not recommending this sales tactic as a routine technique, but it is one approach. One that can offend too.

2) *Minimize it.* The advertising manager says, "You're too late, the program is all locked up." The salesman says, "John, I can appreciate that. Ordinarily you would not want to make a change in your plans. But this is a different situation for these reasons, etc." Or, "John, when you hear what we have for you, you'll want to 'unlock' the decision." As long as there are new ideas, sales can soar to new heights.

3) *Handle it.* Here you can either inquire or attack. Inquire. Ask the buyer a series of questions to learn what he means by "locked up." Has the program been approved by management? Have the contracts been sent? Has the advertising been scheduled? Creative approved? Film made? Will the program meet the company's marketing, sales, advertising objectives?

A series of well-directed, carefully stated questions will often uncover the fact that a *final* decision is still somewhere off in the future. There is still time left to convince the buyer or prospect that you can help him accomplish his objectives. It's also important that you clarify this unfortunate situation with both the account and the agency. A recommendation by an advertising agency is not a final decision from an advertiser. Conversely, but far less frequently, accounts will make changes upon advice from their agency.

Attack? "John, it seems to me that you've gotten some bad advice. Win, lose, or draw, will you give me one opportunity to review this with you?"

Can you honestly say that you have effectively done your sales job of assisting the account and agency to buy your medium? Have you matched your magazine to the company's objectives? If you have, then press on. After quite a few years in this business, I'm convinced this objection is high on the list of truly *invalid* sales objections faced by salespeople.

It occurs primarily because the agency wants to get the media list approved without too much interruption and the lower echelon of company executives tends to resist change. In my opinion, the technique of inquiring, rather than attacking, will serve you better in the long run, but don't be afraid to try several approaches. Before you can move on to closing business in this situation, you have to know at what stage in the decision process you find yourself. For all intents and purposes, although the door may be "locked," you may hold the key.

Satisfy the "satisfied" buyer

Here's another tough one: "We're completely satisfied with what we are using." (As the old saying goes, "Contentment is for cows.") There may be validity in this objection because it could be an affirmation that your competition has done a better selling job, or that you haven't done yours well. There also may be room to create new buying desires.

You'll need to find out what "being satisfied" means and isolate the buyer's influence in the sale. Be sure you have studied the company's financial picture, the advertising history, and the sales objectives. The advertising manager's boss, the sales manager, may not be quite so contented. Develop new information. Bring in a study of the company's salesmen and distributors, their selling methods, their challenges. This technique sold a lot of pages for me. Think of selling in its broader dimensions and open up new horizons for the "satisfied" buyer. He'll then want what *you* have.

Sales resistance is logical or psychological. Logical resistance could be such things as: 1) the prospect simply doesn't belong in your market or your magazine; 2) he can't afford it (often this is used as a dodge or stalling tactic), and 3) the agency actually can't have the material

---

Objections and Stalls

1. The agency didn't recommend your magazine.
2. The client didn't buy our recommendation of your magazine.
3. Your rates are too high.
4. We can do this job more effectively with direct mail.
5. Our sales force is on top of all of the major buyers; we don't need advertising.
6. We are going to increase our sales force and the budget is going for that.
7. We really don't need more sales. We're oversold right now.
8. We don't have the dollars for your market.
9. We're not interested in your market this year.
10. We just conducted a survey and your magazine lost.
11. We're completely satisfied with what we're using.
12. We can't increase your schedule. We like to spread our small budget across several magazines.
13. There is room for only one magazine on the schedule.
14. We can get your audience through television or radio.
15. You haven't produced any results.
16. I'll think it over.
17. We don't believe in advertising.
18. We're in so many trade shows, we can't afford to advertise.
19. We are spending our advertising budget for our new 4-color catalog or a company movie.
20. You haven't had enough editorial material devoted to our type of product.
21. Business is poor, so we're cutting budgets.
22. We don't have any specialized advertisements ready for your field.
23. I haven't time to see you.
24. You're too late; the program is all locked up.
25. You haven't sold us.
26. Your reach is too small.
27. Your inserts cost too much.
28. We don't buy regional magazines.
29. Our salespeople like to see us on television.
30. We don't buy new magazines.
31. We've always had production problems with your magazine.
32. I don't like the size of your publication.
33. People don't buy our product through print advertising.
34. You don't have the right image for us.
35. Your editorial content doesn't interest our prospects.
36. We get a better deal from your competition.
37. Your magazine is too cluttered.

ready on time.

Almost all of the other reasons given for not buying are psychological: preference for established habits; tendency to resist domination; poor chemistry with the salesperson; fear of making a wrong decision; predetermined ideas.

Be prepared

I have developed a list of typical objections for your review. You'll benefit by preparing your own answers to them. I urge you to write them down, develop several answers, and try different ways of handling them. In other words, practice improving your objection selling skills.

But all of this starts *before* you make the call. When you know what your advertisers and their advertising agencies want to accomplish through their advertising, you are in a better position to appraise the validity of the objection. When you help them accomplish their *objectives,* you'll minimize sales *objections.*

Going over someone's head

By William Abbott

The Magazine Advertising Sales Club of New York was conceived about two years ago by a group of serious-minded young people who have chosen careers selling space in magazines. These young people have displayed wisdom and understanding by following the axiom that there is much to be learned about their chosen craft, not only from each other, but also from those in our industry who have spent many years in education's final and truest arena.

Whether one is formally trained to become a surgeon or a stockbroker, he learns infinitely more about his profession after he receives a degree than any school can ever teach.

Recently, the principal speaker at a luncheon meeting was Ira Ellenthal, a man of unique experience and qualifications. Ira's name is a familiar one to those of you who read FOLIO on a regular basis. As a frequent contributor to the "Faces" section, he has profiled many of the magazine industry's leading personalities.

Ira was formally educated and trained to operate on the other side of the publishing world: the editorial field. As such, he regarded the selling of advertising space as an activity that, at best, had to be tolerated until a better system of paying the freight for editorial presentations arrived upon the scene.

Then one day Ellenthal became involved in selling advertising. This was quite a revelation, for he came to understand that the job of selling advertising space required more talent than that required by unskilled farm laborers, a prejudice held by many on the editorial floor. From then on, Ellenthal was hooked.

His recently-released book, *Selling Smart,* is an excellent choice for a beginner in the field. It relates the experiences of those who have succeeded in ad sales, magazine advertising's leading professionals, people who have earned their fame.

After Ellenthal's opening remarks, a question was posed regarding the action to be taken in the event that one's sales arguments were falling upon unsympathetic ears. Assuming that they were calling upon the lowest level in the pecking order of decision-making, should salespeople "go over heads"? Should they call upon those further up the ladder?

What followed was a stream of answers and advice from assorted pundits. Most of them acknowledged perils but basically recommended assertiveness on the part of the seller. I sat awaiting the suggestion of marketing logic from some one of the experts, but none was forthcoming. Instead we were regaled with wondrous tales of how this or that super salesperson went straight to the president of the Whammo Corp. and—you guessed it—whammo, got the business!

But our respondents missed the point. They failed to appreciate that, for the most part, they were speaking to young juniors—people many years away from rubbing elbows with corporate giants.

So, let us re-word the question: Should salespeople who would never be granted entree into the boardroom —mere mortals—go over heads?

Before I begin to answer that question, however, a word of background.

The vendor level

In approaching an account, a salesperson will usually begin at the vendor level. To product salespeople, this would be a retail buyer. In industrial sales it would be the purchasing agent. In advertising, the corresponding position is media director, media buyer or, on the account side, media manager.

The sole function of vendor level personnel is to buy. Their job is to analyze the specifications passed to them from strategy makers and seek out and evaluate alternate vendors of products that meet these specifications.

Obviously, the prime considerations at this level are price, low margins, savings and value. Retail buyers and purchasing agents seek the best product at the lowest price. Advertising buyers seek the highest number of impressions among the pre-set target audience for the amount budgeted. Their key word is *efficiency.*

Media efficiency may be expressed in two dimensions: reach and frequency. Simply stated, reach is the number of different readers who will be exposed to the advertising message. Frequency represents the number of times each reader will see the ad. Therefore, advertisements appearing in magazines which have high duplication figures will increase frequency rather than add reach.

At times, this may be desirable, since in order to be effective, advertising must be remembered. When I was a young salesman, I had difficulty keeping the two straight until someone defined them in the unforgettable: Reach is what one gives up for frequency when one gets married.

So—the advertising space salesperson's first task will be to demonstrate to the media buyer that his magazine reaches the target audience at competitive rates. If he does this, he makes the sale.

If the sale is not made, it will be for one of two reasons: a) The magazine reaches the right audience but is not efficient; or b) The magazine does not reach the target audience (*i.e.,* It does not fill the specifications assigned by strategy planners).

At this point, the salesperson's work on the vendor level is completed. Changes of such decisions are rarely in the domain of vendor level buyers.

Under these circumstances, let's return to our original question: Can one go over heads? My answer is, "In ad sales, there's no such thing," and it is not based merely on semantics. Surely the media buyer knows when a specific salesperson has no chance of making the sale. And a good media buyer will understand that alternate proposals which involve recommended changes in marketing strategy to include a new or different target market segment or merchandising programs which compensate for inefficiency, no longer relate to his area of responsibility.

Different level; different criteria

It now becomes not so much a matter of going "up," but rather a case of approaching people whose evaluation criteria are different. Therefore, alternate proposals rightfully belong on the next level and may be used to good effect. Here, in middle management, the most effective solutions to priorities set by top management are analyzed and executed. The key word among marketing directors, brand and product managers, and account executives is not efficiency; it is *sales volume.* And instead of reach and frequency, concerns are likely to be *prospects* and *distribution.*

Thus, the advertising salesperson will use seminal research to demonstrate how his magazine's readership does indeed comprise a target group of prospective customers for the advertiser's product if he will reach them with his ad message. And, at this level, if the logic is present, minds *can* be changed.

A merchandising plan conceived to convince retailers to add stock and/or display space can provide reach to millions at the point-of-purchase not even counted by media buyers. Brand and product managers however, whose very jobs depend upon movement of merchandise, understand and react to such programs.

A final word of caution: If you do call upon middle-management people, do not repeat the facts used on the vendor level. The account people know that it is the job of others to make such evaluations. If you call upon middle management using the same facts, you *are* going over heads, asking someone to declare another person's decision to be wrong. However, if the middle manager says yes *for different reasons,* only an insecure media buyer would be irked.

Why not the top?

Suppose however, that those in middle management do not succumb to your logic. What then? Do you go on to top management where you are totally unknown? And assuming that you do reach them, what arguments do you use?

It is the job of top management to allocate assets according to priorities. The making of strategy and the spending of those assets to carry out that strategy is then delegated to middle managers. The key word on the top level is *return on investment,* and concerns are for *profits* and *outlays.*

My advice at this point: Since very few media can affect these monumental considerations of a corporation, if you are not personally acquainted with the person on this level; stay away. If by chance you happen to get through, you're likely to do yourself more harm than good. Presidents of companies do not buy advertising, and good ones don't interfere with the marketing strategy of those to whom they have entrusted its establishment.

Of course, if a member of your magazine's management staff has a personal acquaintance with someone in the client's top management, it is perfectly acceptable to use it to get a hearing. I heard of a recent situation in which a publisher of a magazine not on a large advertiser's schedule, called its president, an acquaintance. The result of this call was a luncheon at which the president was impressed with the magazine's special programs (note: *not* media efficiencies). He did what any top flight executive would have under the circumstances. He arranged a meeting, which he attended, at which the magazine was given the opportunity to present its program to the corporate sales manager and marketing director. But it was their decision upon which the disposition of the presentation rested.

On the other hand, the magazine's chances for making the schedule were not exactly diminished by the fact that they knew the boss thought it was a good idea.

Following-up on 'no-sales'

By Dave Hagenbuch

In an earlier article, we examined follow-up techniques after a sale has been made.

Now let's consider the situation where you have presented your material, asked for the contract but were *not* successful in closing the sale. What do you do? How do you plan for future calls?

For purposes of our review, let's assume that you were given the opportunity to present *all* the facts about your market and your magazine to both the advertiser and his advertising agency. Also, you know that space contracts have been let and none was forthcoming for your publication. In other words, you did not get the business. How do you follow up?

The most important (and the toughest) thing to do is to ask yourself the question, "Where did I fail?" Many salespeople try to appraise their own performance and immediately assign the blame for the lost business on the agency (the media buyer, the account executive) or someone at the account. At times, this may be the case, but more often, it's a cover-up for ineffective selling.

To objectively reappraise your own efforts, you must ask yourself several questions: "Did I really do an effective selling job? Did I assist the advertiser and agency in every manner possible to make a favorable decision for my magazine? Did I document my facts by follow-up letters after each call?

"Did I establish objectives for my calls and get agreement on the points I wished to establish? Did I attempt to close the sale and specifically ask for the business . . . at both the account and the agency?"

To plan for future selling, it is absolutely necessary to find out *what* type of program will be used and *where* the advertising space will be placed. If your field was not included in the advertising plans, you probably have a "market-selling" situation on your hands. If competitive magazines are scheduled, then your job may require greater emphasis on your medium as an advertising vehicle.

You must assess the problem and get a clear picture of the job yet to be done. Be sure that you are not accepting a loss of business too easily. Advertising programs can be changed. So can contracts and schedules. New facts can be presented. New selling approaches taken.

First, you'll need to evaluate your problem. You can contact the account and say, "I understand that the *present plans* for your advertising program do not call for the use of our magazine. In your own best marketing interests will you give me the opportunity to review this with you?"

Please note that this statement does not concede anything and even suggests that the door is still open. Even if you are advised that the advertising program is all "locked up," you can request the chance to open it up for reconsideration.

At times it is possible to suggest that the advertiser can receive a better return on his investment. You might say something like this:

"Do you invest in the stock market?" (He probably does.) "If your broker suggests a change in your investment program from a stock giving you a 10 percent growth to one that has a 15 percent opportunity, would you make a change? I'm sure you would. Well, that's exactly what our medium has to offer you for these reasons: First, you'll receive 20 percent more effective circulation. Second, you can enjoy a larger volume of sales leads. . . ."

Recently I heard the president of a major advertising agency say that there is no such thing as a "locked" budget. Hurrah for him! In my own selling, I have had agencies tell me that the business was lost and the budget "all locked up" only to learn from the account that contracts had not been sent and the ads hadn't even been prepared.

On one occasion, I called the vice president of sales at a major company and asked for "just one opportunity" to meet with him and review agency recommendations that did not include our magazine. He granted the interview. We saved the business.

Then there are account executives who will override their media departments. This doesn't happen often, but a smart salesperson never loses business without fighting for it. The key is to do it intelligently.

Going back to our original proposition, the sale has definitely been lost. Here are some things you can do:

• Promise yourself you'll do a more effective selling job in the future.

• Plan to increase the number of your calls on the account and the agency. Most sales are made after five calls. Most salesmen don't make them in a given year.

• Develop a new creative approach. Always make sure that your selling is in terms of the selfish interests of the person you are contacting. You may have made the mistake of talking too much about your magazine and not enough about *his* program, *his* problems, *his* needs.

• Ask the direct question, "Why are you not planning to use our magazine at this time?" (Note that we still try to keep the door open.)

• Make up a list of the objections given to you. Be sure to write them down so that there will be no confusion as to what they are. Prepare to answer them on future calls. Also, probe and bring out any *hidden* objections so that you won't be working in the wrong direction.

• Bring your management into the problem. Ask for their suggestions. You can often benefit from a different sales perspective. You may be so close to your own problems that you lose the necessary objectivity required to handle them most efficiently.

• Make calls on other people such as salesmen, distributors and other corporate executives. They may give you a new slant on how to realize your goal.

• Start a campaign of buyer-oriented letters to create new interest in your magazine. Follow these up with better personal calls.

• Don't get discouraged. If you consider each lost sale as only a *temporary* setback and an *opportunity* for future business, you'll be able to maintain a positive attitude.

Your competition

By Dave Hagenbuch

Almost every space salesman has competition. Indeed, most magazines have both direct and indirect competition.

While we believe that the salesperson who *sells creatively doesn't have to sell competitively*, there are times when a salesperson is forced into a competitive sales situation. How he handles it and how well prepared he is to answer the questions of customers or prospects will often determine his success in leading the buyer away from the competition and into his medium.

In such a selling situation, knowledge *is* power. To be a successful competitor you must know what you are doing. You must know your market better than any other salesperson calling on the accounts and agencies assigned to you. And you must know your magazine and make sure that you sell it positively and always with the buyer's needs and motives in mind.

Relate to the buyer

A common mistake that salespeople make is being just another "media salesperson." This is the kind of individual who has all the market facts and figures, all of the research studies, all of the information necessary to do a sound selling job, but none of the sales empathy to relate this information to the wants and desires of the buyer.

Every magazine is read by a unique audience of people who are exactly the individuals that advertisers and agencies must reach to sell their products and services. Since this applies not only to your publication but to your competition as well, you can be sure that your competitors are presenting their values whenever they have the opportunity.

What does your competition sell? How do their salespeople work? Do they make regular calls? Where do they stand with the people you call on? What type of promotion material are they using? How do they react to losing business?

By knowing the strengths and weaknesses of the competitive magazines and the competitive salespeople, you are in a better position to build your own sales story. While you face competition from all types of media (radio, television, direct mail, etc.), our concern in this column will be with your *direct* competition, the other magazines with which you compete for space.

What do you need to know about your competition? Basically, you should know about your competitor's editorial content, market information, circulation, readership, response, rates, advertising volume, mechanical data, and services. (See Figure 1 for complete checklist.)

You can develop most of this information by studying the competitive magazines, their media kits, research, page counts, etc. However, there is much to be learned from your sales calls.

Several things worked for me as a salesperson. By paying close attention to what a customer said about the competition, I was able to get a clearer picture of what the customer wanted from me. Then too, a buyer's preferences tend to show up through the number of times he mentions other publications and the order in which he does. This often flags the major competition for you at that account or agency.

Don't overlook new competition. Some salespeople are so oriented to the established competition, they tend to ignore new competitors, usually because they fail to

---

Figure 1

Competitive Analysis Checklist

☐ Name of publication

☐ Publisher

☐ Frequency of issue

☐ Market served

  Definition

  Special breakdowns

☐ Market research

☐ Changes in market coverage

☐ Editorial approach

☐ Editorial history

  Date of first issue

  Changes in name

☐ Editorial staff

  Size of staff

  Chief editor (name and background)

☐ Editorial content

  Number of editorial pages

  Editorial/advertising ratio

  Percent staff-written material

  Percent contributed articles

  Special issues

  Editorial research

☐ Editorial strengths

☐ Editorial weaknesses

☐ Circulation total

☐ Circulation approach

☐ Net effective circulation

☐ Circulation strengths

☐ Circulation weaknesses

☐ Advertising pages

  Last year

  Year before

  Trend

  Advertising research

☐ Sales story of competition

  Strengths

  Weaknesses

☐ Name of competitive salesperson

  Strengths

  Weaknesses

gather sufficient information about this new entry. So, whenever a new magazine comes on the scene, be sure you get as much information as you possibly can so that you will be in a position to intelligently analyze the impact it may have on your field. Remember—it was only a short time ago that many companies in this country ridiculed the idea of foreign competition. Today, many of these companies rue the day they discounted the importance of this type of competition.

We in the publishing field have also run into a fair number of mergers during the past 10 years. Whenever one of these comes along, I urge you to ask yourself certain questions:

Will this new combination give greater strength to our competitors or will it weaken their position? (It often does.)

Will they now have research facilities and stronger personnel that will give them an edge that they have lacked in the past?

Will these factors strengthen their sales organization? Will they be more aggressive? Or will the merger have the opposite result?

Monitor personnel changes

Changes in personnel can affect your competitive situation. If you do not do so already, watch for announcements of new appointments or retirements, voluntary or otherwise, of people employed by your competition.

Do these changes indicate a dissatisfaction with what's happening at the competitor's publishing concern? Or do they indicate that the competition is adding a different type of personnel to build a stronger sales organization? Are these changes that may affect you favorably? What is the reputation of the new salesperson? Can you anticipate that he will employ new strategies or new tactics?

In our business, it pays to watch the advertising of the competition to see if it has changed. Perhaps it has changed because of a change in advertising agencies or a change of sales direction. Does this mean a more effective approach? Does it indicate that the competition is at-tempting to establish a new image?

I've always found that publishers tend to tell their sales stories as best they can in the point-of-sale reference-type media like Standard Rate & Data. You can begin to see what they think their best sales points are. Since these are often the points that they try to impress upon their salesmen, this information could accrue to your advantage or disadvantage—depending upon how the field is buying.

In competitive selling, one of the most serious problems facing magazines that have been highly successful is the business of "smugness." In this case, the salespeople have the feeling that customers should be so impressed with the firm's name and reputation that they should be half sold, or more than half sold, before the salesperson walks in. Some of these salespeople then make the mistake of not doing a good job of planning for their calls; they get lazy. Then along comes a sharp competitor who is eager to get the business and they find themselves either off the schedule or with a reduced schedule the following year. It happens every day.

There is a decided difference between *competitive* selling and *comparative* selling. Some salespeople make the mistake of indulging in such questionable tactics as name-calling and generally "knocking" the competition. It *never* pays. Advertisers and agencies resent this kind of competitive selling. (Don't forget, however, that most of them need comparative information—on circulation, editorial, readership, rates, etc.—for media decisions.)

You are far better off ignoring the competition and selling the benefits of using your publication. It's a wise salesperson who doesn't bring up the competition unless requested to do so. But, if given that opportunity, be sure you have your facts straight and back them up with solid documentation, including sources and dates. There are a lot of good magazines being published in all areas of business and leisure activities. One good way to handle your competition is to simply say, "That's a good magazine, but we have a better one for you." Then, sell what *you* have to sell.

After the call is over

By Milton F. Decker

No matter how sincere a salesperson's intentions may be to follow up on important calls, there are many reasons why he doesn't. In fact, even many of the most successful salespeople either neglect the follow-up entirely or assign it such a low priority that it just never gets done.

This often happens because there isn't enough time in a salesperson's day to plan, organize and prepare follow-up material. Or the job seems too difficult to tackle—or it seems mundane and lacking in glamour.

The failure to follow through does not seem to be due to a genuine lack of awareness of its importance, however. Here is a case history that illustrates the problem.

One of our associates was asked by a consumer magazine to prepare a direct mail sales follow-up program based on considerable readership research. The publisher felt with a small sales staff the magazine needed extra key account follow-up on sales calls.

A program was prepared, complete with a series of letters for each salesperson. It was very well received by the magazine's management. Yet, six months later not a letter had been mailed!

Easy to postpone

Why? It may have been priorities. Direct mail follow-up is usually the easiest sales activity to postpone or put off indefinitely—no matter how good the intentions might be to follow up at the time.

Some rationalize their neglect by questioning the value of sending mail to busy advertising executives. How interested are these executives in media promotion? Do they have the time to read all the mail that's sent them?

The answer to such doubting Thomases is found in a recent *Wall Street Journal* survey of all ad agency and client personnel on the *WSJ* promotion list—a universe of 7,279 names from which a random sample of 2,245 was selected.

The study found that most executives do read direct mail media promotion. In answer to the question, What practice do you follow in regard to media promotion mail addressed to you at the office? 61 percent of agency executives said that they looked at their mail. Fifty-six percent of top management said they looked at their mail, as did 26 percent of account management and 69 percent of media personnel.

Fifty-four percent of client personnel said they looked at their mail, as well as 62 percent of advertising management, 55 percent of sales/marketing management and 54 percent of top management.

The preferred types of promotional media information that was acceptable and appreciated included:

	By agencies	By clients
Original research	76%	57%
General marketing data	66	58
Editorial description and insights	59	51
Comparative audience data	56	44

Another interesting and important fact brought out by the study was the influence these executives had in the selection of media.

Ninety-two percent of all agency personnel were involved in some way "in influencing the selection of specific media in which advertising will appear." Eighty-two percent of all client personnel were involved in the same way.

Advice from Ogilvy

If more documentation on the value of direct mail promotion is desired, we can turn to one of the masters of this art form—David Ogilvy—for some down-to-earth advice. Here are a few quotes from a recent address he made in London:

"If anyone tells you that long letters don't sell, he doesn't know anything about direct mail. We sent out a five-page letter that sold 716 obsolete automobiles in six weeks. . . .

"We have used direct mail to sell $750,000 executive jets for Cessna. . . .

"When we started Ogilvy & Mather in New York nobody had heard of us. But we were airborne within a few months and grew at a record speed—so fast we had to turn down new accounts. How did we achieve this meteoric growth? By using my secret weapon—direct mail."

I could continue to document the values of direct mail ad nauseam. But these examples should suffice to provide the raison d'etre for developing ready-made material which should always be available for follow-up use. Individual proposals, thank-you letters and specific direct mail programs for your hottest prospects should be planned, prepared and available for most basic sales needs. Such material always adds an extra dimension in getting faster and more efficient coverage of prospects.

Substitute for personal selling

It is especially important that this kind of effort be made when a limited sales staff makes complete coverage and follow-up difficult to achieve. Then, direct mail promotion must take the place of personal selling. We know that no matter how creative and hardworking a salesperson may be, he or she usually doesn't have enough time for thorough planning and follow-through on all accounts.

The salesperson needs help in this area—particularly if he or she is not the creative writing type. Some of the best salespeople I know find it difficult, if not impossible, to write a coherent and forceful sales letter.

There are also additional ways, besides the letter, in which existing sales data can be re-used with a minimum of cost and effort, such as:

•Follow-up brochures, folders.

•Preparation of media kits for major advertising classifications.

•Monthly mailings directed to media people.

•Comp copy inserts based upon sales support material.

•Use of basic charts or tables in your rate card to make it more of a sales promotion vehicle.

But the most important and effective activity of all is a specifically designed direct mail promotion directed at key prospects, running accounts, advertisers appearing in the competition or small accounts which do not represent sufficient potential for personal sales calls.

Selecting target areas

In developing such a plan, experience indicates that more effective results can be achieved by selecting one or two target areas which represent the greatest potential for immediate business and growth. (The criteria for evaluating key prospects and categories are outlined in the article "Target account planning is more than A, B, C," August 1978, page 55.) This kind of approach forces the writer to think in terms of the advertiser's problems. It focuses thinking on the prospect's advertising objectives and how the publication can help meet these goals.

Such a method also helps us define more realistically our own objectives for a direct mail program.

The primary goal should be to develop a series or bank of letters addressed to a major advertiser in a key ad category. These letters are to be used by each salesperson, who can adapt them for his own use.

The sales letter series should have these qualities:

1. Each letter should be easy to read and designed to get quick interest.

2. The letter should preferably contain only one major point and never more than three.

3. Ideally, each letter should provide something factual which would be of value and interest—something the recipient might want to file.

4. The letters should all speak the language of the specific ad category and be carefully aimed at the advertiser's interests and objectives.

5. The letters should be adaptable for use in other ad

categories wherever possible.

6. The letters should be different from each other, flexible and as personable as possible.

7. A common theme should be shared by all the letters, but each letter should ask for the order in a different way.

8. Your publication's unique selling proposition must be developed.

9. Above all, the letters should be professionally designed to appeal to the most sophisticated prospect.

At best, this effort is the extra plus which makes the sale—and, if nothing else, it maintains awareness of your magazine.

Subject matter limitless

In creating such a series, the subject matter is practically limitless. Usually the plan starts with six or eight specific letters within a category—alcoholic beverages, for example.

Most of the copy might address itself to wine usage—yet be designed for easy adaptation to Scotch, gin, rum, etc. Other letters can be developed for general use on all liquor and wine accounts, depending on the data available. Subjects might include heavy usage, comparison of usage among competitive magazines, life styles, etc.

Or take the travel classification. One letter might stress passport ownership in establishing a reader's desire and inclination to travel. Another, the importance of discretionary income in terms of the affluence of your audience and its ability to afford foreign travel. The importance of occupation, education and life style are all key factors, each of which can make an exciting letter which will be of interest to the travel advertiser.

After you feel the category data has been sufficiently exploited, additional follow-up material to point out your value and leadership can be used. A list of possible subjects, depending of course upon the data and facts available, might include the following:

• Your circulation growth vs. competition
• Circulation acquisition methods
• Circulation bonuses
• Cost efficiency in terms of circulation or audience characteristics
• Reader response and advertising results
• Editorial content and vitality
• Editorial plans in the future
• Special issues
• Advertising growth
• Category gains
• New market data or research

At certain intervals in each series, it is a good idea to test readership by offering something special. It can be a complimentary copy of the magazine, a new piece of research in a prospect's field, a give-away item (book, desk pad, coffee mug, pen, etc.), or even a return post card offering to put him on your regular complimentary list.

And one final word: Remember, the name of the game is a sale, so every letter, proposal and presentation should always ask for the order. People really don't mind being sold, particularly if integrity, intelligence and enthusiasm are demonstrated.

The follow-up

By Dave Hagenbuch

"The toughest part of a sale is the follow-up after the sale has been made."

That's the opinion of one of our leading consumer magazine advertising directors. I've heard this from many salespeople on all types of magazines and these are some of the things I suggest:

• *Develop an itinerary for regular contact with both the account and the advertising agency.* These people are your customers and they determine what your business is and what it will be. You have to keep them sold and you have to upgrade their space. Evaluate their potential, estimate the number of calls you'll need for effective coverage, and then plan your itinerary.

• *Develop an overall plan for increased business.* If the account is running six pages, and your magazine is a monthly, start planning for a monthly advertising program. Weeklies should concentrate on moving 13-time advertisers to 26, and 26 to 52, etc. Catalogs should think in terms of larger units.

If you plant seeds for future business on your follow-up calls, you can often sell these increases for the next program year. For example, you could say, "Mr. Jones, we're pleased to have your advertising in our magazine. This six-page schedule is a good start. During the year, I'd appreciate the opportunity to supply you with reasons why you'll benefit through a monthly program next year."

Your plan may be to upgrade an advertiser from black-and-white to color. The future sale may be to assist the agency in thinking along these lines. Whatever you do, think in terms of service *and* future. Sell positively and expectantly, and you'll increase your business. Most accounts simply do not buy enough space.

• *Study the advertising to be sure that the account and agency are getting full value out of your magazine.* Supply them with useful ideas and marketing information. If you have a special issue and this advertiser isn't scheduled for that issue, point out the advantages of representation. Be sure the agency is informed. You may prefer to start there. Publishers do not like "switches" from one issue to another, but if you are not successful in selling additional space for the special issue, suggest a switch. After all, your job is to service your customer.

•*Help your accounts and agencies merchandise their advertising program.* Companies like to keep their salespeople, distributors, and customers informed on what they are doing. This may be part of your normal service. If so, you'll need to make sure it is being used and appreciated to advantage. People forget.

•*Make personal calls on the advertiser's salesmen and distributors.* These people will often give you ideas and support for future selling. You may have to clear these calls with the advertiser.

•*Get on a sales meeting program to talk about the company's advertising and your medium.* Be sure you use a customer-oriented type of approach in your presentation. Bragging and boast-selling can backfire.

•*Supply examples of outstanding advertising running in your magazine.* Document the readership or response, or both. It will pay you to help the people you call on to live up to what is most productive in your medium. You have to be realistic and remember that their primary interest is in what *they* are doing. Your job is to help them do it better.

•*Study the mechanical program for economy and effectiveness.* Mechanical costs are extremely high today. An advertiser can repeat a single advertisement four times before readership starts to fall off. If too many ads are prepared, dollars spent on production could be used to buy more space, more color, etc.

•*Inform* all *parties* of all *of* your services. It is embarrassing for an agency to learn from their client about a new study or another useful service available from your magazine. Make sure that your promotional material, sales letters, ideas, etc., are thoroughly exposed to both the account and the agency.

•*Take an interest in all marketing activities.* You are selling space, but your customers are involved in promotion, publicity, direct selling, and all of the things that surround a sale. By having a complete knowledge of the programs in which your contacts are engaged, you'll open up more opportunities for sales. Dollars can be shifted from one type of budget to another.

•*Reconfirm the buyer's good judgment in selecting your magazine.* Because decisions are not always made on facts, and facts are subject to interpretation, it is important that you "play back" the buyer's reasons for doing business with you. Add additional sales points, bring in new research, document results to strengthen the relationship. Advertisers and agencies want to feel that they have made good buying decisions. They need to be reminded by you.

•*Compliment them.* Praise them. Everyone appreciates honest praise. If an agency does a fine job of creative selling through your medium, be sure to tell the advertiser (at all levels of management). When you follow-up by letter, carbon everyone concerned. Any information relating to the effectiveness of their marketing effort in your market(s) should be treated in the same manner.

Publishing is a service-oriented business. When you plan the follow-up on a sale, think in terms of how you can help the advertiser and agency get maximum communications leverage out of your magazine. Think too of how you can help an individual you call on to accomplish his or her goals and objectives.

When you are gathering information for your call, ask yourself, "Is this *essential* information? How can he or she use it to help the company? How can they use it to help themselves?"

When you put your information to this test, you'll end up with something helpful to the person you're calling on and your follow-up call will be more meaningful.

Call reports

By Robert Potts

Probably no basic procedure in the magazine publishing business generates more different opinions and practice than that lowly but vital message from the sales front, the salesperson's call report.

Between those publishers or sales managers who don't require any reports at all and those who bog their men and women down with a chore that would strain the guy from Dun and Bradstreet stand those who use a wide assortment of methods and forms to extract sales call information from their salespeople.

No doubt the call report was originally intended to provide an orderly means of communication between the salesperson in the field and home base. It started as an in-

put tool for management to use to keep informed of conditions in each salesperson's particular marketplace. The collective intelligence provided by the reports from all members of a sales staff gives the manager the information he or she needs to make correct, effective decisions that will result in more sales volume and hopefully, more profitability. While that may be their basic purpose, call reports, as all of us who have made them out as salespeople or read them as managers know, provide a great deal more than just marketing information for management.

Most publishers also use call reports as a measure of a salesperson's work effort, not only in terms of the number of calls made, but also as a measure of the effectiveness of those calls. A salesperson who really knows his or her publication and its market, who is calling on the right people and who has the ability to read the reaction of the person he or she is calling on will file reports that are far different in content from those of the person who does not keep up-to-date on the marketplace or who makes the "I-was-in-the-neighborhood-and-thought-I'd-drop-in" type of call.

Call reports are one of the most accurate barometers management has to judge how well a salesperson is doing in the field on a week-to-week basis. Of course, the best proof of all is pages sold, but often it is months before the effectiveness or lack of effectiveness of an individual's effort can be measured in number of pages sold or unsold. The alert sales manager or publisher reads every call report from every salesperson. Most will be routine in nature but in among them will be particular reports that give clear indications of how the salesperson is working. Others will be early warning devices on trouble ahead in that territory. Reading these reports gives the manager an invaluable gauge to the ongoing activities of each person.

The publisher or sales manager who doesn't read every call report is not only overlooking vitally important input, but also not being fair to his or her sales staff. The publisher or sales manager insists each salesperson make out the reports and send them in but doesn't do anything with them except perhaps have a secretary count them. This is supposed to give the boss a reading on how hard the salespeople are working.

It doesn't take long for a smart salesperson to figure out that the boss isn't reading reports. As soon as the discovery is made the quality of the reports and sometimes his or her work effort go to hell in a handbasket. I know a guy, a very good salesman, who, when suspecting no one was reading his call reports sent in the *Gettysburg Address* in three-line stanzas on 13 call reports over a period of four weeks. He never did hear a word from anyone on his ploy and shortly afterward resigned and joined another company that had been courting him.

So far we have covered the value of call reports to management. It has long been my opinion that making out call reports is just as valuable to the salesperson as it is to the manager, if not more so. Most good salespeople continue to send in thoughtful, carefully done reports even after they suspect or find out that nobody back there is listening. Why? Is it just to have the number of calls made on record so the individual has ample defense if his or her territory begins to slip? Sure, that's part of the reason. However, it's a very small part. A good salesperson will continue to send in accurate reports because he or she knows that he or she will make more frequent use of these reports than anyone else in the company. They become a memory bank, serving the same purpose as carbons of letters. None of us can remember what happened at every meeting we had one month, two months, six months ago. Prior to a call, the good salesperson always refreshes his or her memory of what happened the last call on a particular advertising manager, agency or product manager.

To develop this thesis a bit let's remember that the average number of personal calls made in the publishing business is about three a day. If you multiply that by 220

working days a year, it means that the average space salesman or saleswoman is making 660 personal calls a year or 55 a month. He or she would have to be a walking tape recorder to remember accurately what happened several weeks or months later on every call made. A salesperson has to have some kind of record to refer to before making a call for the second, third or tenth time on a particular account or agency. Call report carbons are the simplest and most readily available means of doing this.

Another thing about filling out call reports is that the very act is an exercise in reviewing what actually happened on every call. This exercise helps the salesperson evaluate where he or she stands on a particular account, whether he or she really did get all points over and what to do in the way of followup.

What's the Right Form?

These are the four most popular call report formats:

1. The separate form for every call made

2. The condensed weekly (or sometimes monthly) form

3. The combination of both of the above

4. Carbons of followup letters.

Let's examine the good and bad points of each format listed above:

Separate form—This is the most widely used type and usually is in self-carboning sets or in tablet form with a slip-in sheet of carbon paper for extra copies. It is a good system in that it requires the salesperson to consider each call individually and report at reasonable length on what occurred. The forms easily separate into an original for headquarters and one for the salesperson. Sometimes they will have additional sections that can be used for carboning other headquarters personnel.

The major problem of the separate sheet system is that it takes more time than any other system, increases the volume of paper handled, and psychologically seems like a hell of a lot of writing to the person filling out the sheets and a hell of a lot of reading to the manager receiving them. Another common fault is that the separate sheet system often calls for more information than is really needed. The name of the account or agency, the date and person called on, plus space for the report, should suffice. Too often, however, the leave-no-white-space rule takes over and the salesperson is required to write the complete address, the city, product codes, advertiser and nonadvertiser codes and other statistical drivel, which makes a mountain of work out of what should be a small mound of condensed information.

Condensed weekly or monthly form—This is a format that is rapidly gaining in popularity and requires only the date, account or agency name, person called on and a one- or two-line wrapup of the present status. There may be room for 10 to 20 calls on a particular sheet; it is usually filed weekly with two or three sheets making up the whole. This form makes the job seem like much less of a chore. The drawbacks, however, are that the salespeople tend to keep their reports on all calls down to the two lines provided when more space should be used to tell management what the situation really is on some particular calls. It also makes retrieval of what happened on prior calls difficult since these sheets are usually filed chronologically rather than alphabetically by account.

Combination of both of the above systems—To solve the drawback of limited space in the condensed form a combination of both the individual call report and the condensed weekly form can be used. For the routine reports the condensed form would suffice. Where particular calls need more in-depth reporting, a separate form would be filled out. The salesperson would then file the condensed form along with the four or five separate forms together. While this combination approach doesn't solve the retrieval problem of the condensed form, it does take advantage of most of the best qualities of both systems.

Carbons of followup letters—This is a very simple device wherein an extra copy of every letter written to advertisers and agencies called on is sent to the publisher or sales manager in lieu of the usual call report. It virtually assures that a salesperson will write a followup letter after every call—something a lot of us have been trying for years to get salespeople to do. Since the contents of a letter may not necessarily give a complete picture of the problem on a particular account, a smart salesperson will add on an explanatory paragraph that appears only on carbons for the salesperson's and his or her manager's eyes alone. This is a most attractive system as it enables the chore of call reporting to be taken care of by the vital followup letter system. It also provides a filed carbon containing the all important what-happened-last-time information the salesperson needs to keep on top of the accounts.

When Should Call Reports Be Submitted?

For the sake of completeness and accuracy call reports should be made up on a daily basis. When that isn't possible a salesperson should complete the reports no later than the weekend following the reporting period. Many publishers require the reports for a week to be filed with the expense account for the same week. That is a good idea, as the filing of the expense account reminds the salespeople that their call reports are also due. In any event, to allow reports to be submitted less frequently than weekly creates problems.

Many salespeople will wait until just before due date to make up their call reports. If every two weeks is the filing period some people will have to create 20, 30 or more call reports at one sitting. Obviously, because of the fatigue factor, the quality of the last 10 or 20 reports is not going to be as good as the first 10 or 15, even if the salesperson remembers everything that went on during each call for the past two weeks—a doubtful proposition at best. At worst, those last call reports will be hastily done and may be of no value, outside of increasing the count for the period.

The other problem that can arise is that the manager gets buried every two weeks with an avalanche of reports that he probably won't be able to get through for some time.

To require reports to be submitted only once a month is to cube the problems described above. Fortunately for all concerned most publishers require reports to be submitted weekly.

Even the best salesperson will fall behind in the call report department and miss a week or two. The ineffective salesperson might miss two, three or more weeks. How do you reasonably police the staff to keep them up to date on call reports? The most extreme system I have ever heard of, short of a firing or two, was a publisher who wouldn't send a salesperson that individual's semimonthly draw if that person hadn't submitted 20 call reports for each of the preceding two weeks. I think that kind of rule is excessive and demeaning. It also tends to create some experts in that not-so-fine art of fictional call report writing and filing.

One of the most effective and dignified procedures is to send out a monthly sales bulletin that lists the number of personal calls each made during the previous month as indicated by the call reports sent in. Such a list will get the tardy call reporter back on schedule as it shows or implies that the individual is not making as many calls as his or her peers. It also will jog the salesperson who may actually not be making as many personal calls as he or she should to reexamine his working habits and schedule. If you have a salesperson who consistently lags behind the rest of the staff in the number of calls shown in these monthly bulletins, however, you probably have more than just a reluctant call report writer on your hands.

Side Benefits to Call Reports

In addition to their value to management and to the salespeople themselves, call reports serve other members of the staff, too. They are an excellent means of updating the promotion list. They are a good medium to alert the editorial department to a new product or a story lead. They are a means of alerting the sales promotion manager to the need for a new or updated market or competitive piece and, of course, they are the means of communication between the salespeople themselves in split-account situations. These side benefits can be gained by setting up the report form so they have extra carbons for other departments or by having a "route-to" line at the bottom of the report in order that the publisher's or sales manager's secretary can photocopy the original and send a copy or copies to the indicated recipients.

When followup letters are used as reports, or are sent in to the home office as a standard procedure, the better ones can be photocopied and sent to the rest of the sales staff so they can extract paragraphs that make sales or competitive points particularly well and use them in their own follow-up letters.

Minimums, Dictation and the Telephone

Should you set minimums? I think requiring a certain number of calls a week is an unrealistic practice. Some weeks a person doesn't make as many calls as in other weeks, maybe because the individual is on a trip in a particular part of his or her territory that is long on mileage but sparse on customers. Perhaps the salesperson is researching or putting together a special presentation that requires spending a couple of days in the office. Maybe the salesperson is in the office closing the magazine, which cuts down on the number of personal calls made that particular week.

If you feel you should require some kind of a minimum then I suggest a monthly figure. This is more practical as it averages out the high-production weeks with the low-production ones. I have never required minimums, but relied instead on the monthly sales bulletin technique described earlier to keep the staff's personal call averages up.

Should call reports be dictated or written out? The first reaction to this question is to say they should be dictated, as it saves the salesperson time. Very true, but it also makes it so easy to ramble on that many dictated call reports turn out to be novelettes. My personal opinion is that call reports should be handwritten because these tend to be much more concise and accurate. This makes it a lot easier for the manager who reads them and for the salesperson who refers back to them.

Should call reports be required for telephone calls as well as personal calls? There is no substitute for personal calls. Too often the telephone, which should only be a supplement to personal call activity, becomes the main working tool. Phone calls start taking the place of actual calls. Through laziness, many a good salesperson gets wedded to the mouthpiece, and his or her personal call average starts to nosedive. Usually new account selling goes down in even greater proportion. A salesperson relies on the telephone and the comfort of an office to service established accounts. The result, particularly if the competition's salesperson is out in the territory making personal calls, can be disastrous to the health of the territory. For this reason, my practice is to require the salesperson to send in call reports on every personal call and to leave it to his or her discretion whether or not certain telephone conversations are important enough to merit a call report. The report form has a box to check if it was based on a phone call. That particular report will not be counted in the monthly average. Restricting the monthly sales bulletin to personal calls keeps the salespeople out in the territory where they belong.

How do you assure the salespeople that their reports are read? There is a simple, foolproof way for a manager to do this. As the manager reads the reports, one or two should be set aside for each salesperson. Sometime during the month the manager should drop every salesperson a note commenting on some aspect of one of the calls. This should be done on a one-to-one basis, not in a bulletin. Some months you may have to invent a reason to comment to a particular salesperson on the reports, but do it, by all means. When the salesperson gets those memos from you with a compliment or an observation, he or she will give more thought, time and effort to this vitally important means of communication between the two of you.

Writing the sales letter

By Dave Hagenbuch

Most of the letters I see in the publishing business end with the line, "If you have any further questions, please do not hesitate to call me." Call you? In a sales relationship, your job is to call *them*. Furthermore, your name and phone number appear on the letter and it is quite obvious that the other person can use this information to call you.

We all know, of course, that this typical closing sentence is a nice way of saying, "I want to end this letter." However, since the goal of your letter is to *promote action*, you should close your letter with a call for action.

You can ask the agency account executive, "Will you recommend this program to your client?" or, "May we count on your recommendation?" You can suggest to an advertiser that he "schedule space in the January issue now."

When the sale is somewhat off into the future, you can leave the potential customer with a thought such as, "Let's get in business together." Or, you may suggest that this person buy space in your magazine "in your own best marketing interests."

Dr. Frank Dignan, a pioneer in letter writing, recommends that every letter should have (1) a star, (2) a chain, and (3) a hook.

Create interest

The star is your opening paragraph, designed to get the reader's attention—just as a good approach to a sale does. It may be an interesting quote, a personal reference, or a reference to something that the other person said when you last spoke together.

Think in terms of what may interest the recipient and appeal to that interest. By starting your letter with the words "you" or "yours" you will automatically be writing something of interest to him or her.

Getting the name of the company or agency up front in the letter is another way of appealing to self-interest. Mention the product or service that this person is promoting. It is amazing how many letters I read that mention the magazine in every other sentence but never mention the advertiser's product once.

Stimulate desire

The chain, the body of the letter, contains the main points, the sales appeals (benefits) that create interest in what you have to say. It should lead the reader into a favorable frame of mind since your purpose is to sell the benefits of doing business with you.

Effective selling is assisting the buyer to buy and

your letter should do just that. Whatever the purpose, keep your sentences short and to the point. Write to *express*, not *impress*. Clear language is the most direct route to effective communication. When you are trying to close a sale, use action verbs and avoid conditional words such as "if" and "should." Use the word "when"—it has a positive sound to it. "When you place space in this magazine, these are the benefits you'll enjoy."

The hook, the close of the letter, causes action to be taken. A letter without a hook is like a sales call without a close. Unfortunately, far too many sales calls are made just to bring the advertisers or agencies "up to date" on the magazine, and that's no way to sell a lot of space.

Remember, your job is to assist a person to buy by leading him into a buying decision. Otherwise, you'll end up talking to yourself and that won't get you very much in the long run. So make sure you think in terms of promoting action with your letters and your sales calls.

Your objective may be to close a sale. It may be to move closer to closing. Or it may simply be getting a favorable recommendation for your publication. The more specific your objective is, the better the opportunity to cause action to be taken.

Concentrate on your letters and those of your salespeople. They represent a tremendous source of continuing sales for you.

Dear Sir:
As per your sales letter of...

By Milton Williams

With fuel shortages restricting travel in recent memory, sales letters are going to have to carry more weight and be more effective than ever before. When was the last time you analyzed your letter-writing technique? Are your letters really communicating? Delete from them all the pat, boring, meaningless phrases that creep in when you've been in a rut too long.

Some examples of the kinds of mistakes salespeople make in letter writing recently showed in replies sent to a potential advertiser who sent letterhead inquiries to nine specialized business publications. The advertiser asked for media information and sample copies for a possible ad program promoting a new product for what we will call the "widget" industry.

Of the nine replies, four were poor, four indifferent, and one, excellent. Here are some examples:

The first publication started right off with, "Dear Mr. Smith: If developing greater sales potential is the objective of your advertising, then plan to include *Widget News* in your advertising budget..."

Does that mean if the advertiser's major goal is not developing sales potential, but building an image or developing recognition, he should forget about this publication?

Northwest Widgets made basically the same mistake—that of assuming what the advertiser wanted without asking him. "Mr. Smith, I would like to say one thing—if you are interested in reaching the northwest market—then your advertising really does belong in *Northwest Widgets.*"

Wouldn't the salesman have been better off telling the advertiser why he *should* be interested in the northwest market? And what about the phrase, "I would like to say one thing..."? Aside from being an awkward expression, it is usually followed—as it is here—by many more than "one thing."

Two publications made the insulting mistake of treating the potential advertiser like "small potatoes." An entire paragraph of the letter from *Widget Review,* for instance, went on at length about the rate structure, stressing the fact that "when full page or prominent advertisements are not scheduled, a smaller ad can be used for earning a lower per-column-inch rate on the larger space. This results in substantial savings."

What if the advertiser had been thinking of a multicolor, multipage, 12-time program?

American Widget's tone was even more condescending. The bulk of the letter was devoted to telling the advertiser what kinds of trade references and descriptive product literature the publication had to have "before accepting advertising."

Four other publications sent letters that displayed a depressing sameness. While none of them had any statements that were harmful, they were ordinary, ineffective and could not possibly spark interest. They started out with phrases like, "As requested, we are enclosing..." Or, "It is a pleasure to send you media information." They ended with pat platitudes: "If you have any questions..." and "Thanks for your interest."

Tailoring Information

But, now for the good news. One salesman took the time and trouble to call the advertiser long distance, asking him for more information so he could tailor the data he sent specifically for the situation. The letter, sent out the same day, began, "Thanks for taking time out to discuss your future marketing plans with me today." While the letter contained precisely the same kinds of market and readership information sent by other publications, the tone was friendly and every piece of information was related to this advertiser's specific needs. It was written for the inquirer: "Our editorial content, advertising and circulation are certainly right on target with the audience *you* want to reach," and "This . . . may well be of interest to *you* the first time around."

What's the difference between this salesman and the others?

● He went after the business—spending a few minutes making a phone call and establishing a friendly, first-name relationship.

● He tried to act as a marketing advisor, not just a salesman—asking what the advertiser's needs, interests and goals were.

● His letter was not much different from the others in basic content, but it was the *tone* that made all the difference. It was warm, friendly, personal.

● He expressed himself as one individual talking to another, not as a machine that sends out form letters.

Don't let the recent gas shortage lead to a sales shortage. Take the time now to brush up on your letter writing and phone techniques. They'll be invaluable in the months ahead.

Dear Advertiser: Blah, blah, blah

By Herbert G. Ahrend

I doubt if there's an ad agency executive alive who is really familiar with all the magazines that cross his or her desk. It's an impossible task. Yet publishers must not only make agency people aware that their magazines exist, they must also make certain that these ad people know—not simply assume—what type of material is published, who reads it, which advertisers use the book regularly (or at least repeatedly), and so on.

I run a small agency, by design, and decided to randomly choose two days worth of magazine deliveries as a sampling of how many publishers are reaching me. Here are just a few of the titles I received: *Smithsonian, Scientific American, Money, Organic Gardening, Modern Office Procedures, Los Angeles, Inquiry, Apartment Life, The Nation, Technology Review, Canoe, Success, Pack-O-Fun, Saturday Review, School Shop, Today's Animal Health, Pacific Search, Successful Meetings, Human Nature, Marketing Communications, The Futurist, Publishers Weekly, Yale Review* and *Esquire.*

Messages to advertisers

To call attention to their magazines and prevent them from being lost in the shuffle, these publishers use the "special message to advertisers." In its simplest, cheapest and least effective form, the "message" consists of a piece of heavy paper hung over the magazine's cover. A serious drawback of this technique, however, is that the cards may easily become separated from the magazine and be thrown away before the publication reaches the media person or account executive whom it was intended to influence.

More frequently, the "publisher's letter" or "memo to advertisers" is bound inside the covers. It is surprising that these messages—beamed from ad professionals to ad professionals—are often what used to be called "we-we" letters. These are letters which talk about how well the magazine is doing rather than what the magazine can do for advertisers. Observe this typical example:

"One Year Old and Growing Strong:
That's US
925,000
(est. circulation)

Dear Advertiser:

US has just completed its fourth consecutive quarter of steady circulation growth, and after close evaluation of our circulation numbers in preparation for our first ABC audit, we wanted you to have this advance report.

During the January-June period US had two rate bases in effect: (1) 500,000 through the February 21, 1978 issue. We will exceed the weighted average of the two rate bases (700,000) for the first six months of this year by several thousand copies. Our May 2, 1978 analyzed issue will deliver approximately 796,000 net paid circulation, with the other issues of the second quarter falling in the range of 750,000-790,000. Our third quarter appears to be off to an exceptional start . . . ."

Buried message

There *is* one important bit of news for advertisers in this message—a guarantee of 800,000 average circulation from March through December 1978—but it's completely buried in the second long paragraph on page two, in a six-line sentence which begins "As an expression of our confidence in US Magazine's continuing circulation growth . . . ." To this N.Y. Times Co. publication, I present the "light-under-a-bushel award" of the month.

Even worse—because it adds coyness to self-centeredness—is an insert, headlined "What Oui're Up To." The subhead is "Memo from the Advertising Director" (although it carries the signature of the editor), and begins:

"I am an editor, not an ad director, so the following comments won't be written in hard sell. I won't delineate the latest Spring TGI figures, which show the median age of OUI's readership down to an astounding 27.7 years old, making us the most youthful men's magazine around. I refuse to go on about how OUI caters to the young, affluent, well-educated pacesetter who drives imports instead of Detroit guzzlers, drinks everything but Kool-Aid and milk, and smokes as much as the rest of us. And as for the science (or is it art?) of psychographics, it's pointless for me to tell you the OUI reader is . . ."

et cetera, ad nauseam.

The last long paragraph starts, "But there I've gone and done the hard sell anyway. Pitched the September OUI at you with all the gumption of a junior copywriter. Ah, well—why not join OUI's other four-million-plus readers . . . ."

Hard sell? Nope. Soft sell? Not that either. Just—no sell.

Publishers' letters may be—and often are—devoted to making a single point in the magazine's favor, such as that *Go* readers are heavy users of alcoholic beverages; or two points, such as that *Americana* jumped from 11 advertisers to 109 in two years, and that it makes available a wide variety of marketing data.

Lacking in showmanship

All the inserts I've described so far are dull: They fail to employ striking graphics or any other element of showmanship. One would think that more publishers would use more ingenuity—and where necessary, a larger budget—to win the favorable attention of a jaded audience.

Money went part way along that road with its insert, which was captioned (in bold green type) "All wrapped up in money." Tipped on was a thin red plastic record of the same name, the title of the theme song from a new promotional film made for the publication.

But *Sales & Marketing Management* proves that good ideas and good taste are more important, here as in other types of advertising, than a huge budget. Its four-page, two-color insert on buff stock (which reads consecutively since the book is perfect bound) is headed "Let's Take A Walk Through This Issue."

"If your interests include sales and marketing," Ken Reiss, the publisher, begins, "a slow stroll through any issue of *S&MM* should be a rewarding experience. And this month's issue is no exception. But, before you begin, take a few minutes to skim the following paragraphs. I think they will help to acquaint you more fully with the *S&MM* subscriber's point of view, and make your brief walk through the issue even more productive."

This insert will reward the ad people who read it, and no doubt will help win *S&MM* new fans. Its final section talks about "What's Coming Up in *S&MM*." All in all, a fine job.

Greeting card approach

A few publications have endeavored to do something original. One of these is *Psychology Today. PT* tips on to the front cover of comp copies a greeting-card style folder, highlighting one of the featured articles in the issue. "What do you call a shrink who's hard, cold, calculating and A.C.-D.C.?" asks *PT's* September card. The answer, overleaf, is—"A computer." Tie-in: an article called "Terminal Therapy."

"Let them eat unsulfureted apricots," says a cartoon of Marie Antoinette on the October card, calling attention to a study of the virtues and drawbacks of the "nutritional revolution." This series of cards would not work for every publication, but is well calculated to fit the image of *PT.*

I've left to the end what I consider the outstanding example of this type of promotion. Each month *Scientific American* staples its ad, not inside, but *outside* the regular covers. No two are similar in theme or design, but they are uniformly attractive and interesting. They, too, help reinforce the impression that this magazine is an outstanding publication and one in which advertisers would be wise to contract for space.

Using readers to close the sale

By Angus Macaulay

I'm convinced, after having sold advertising space for 10 years, that constant contact with readers adds up to greater sales. I'm now a believer in reader calls, reader research, reader panels, even taking readers to lunch.

Over the years, some bright advertising people have learned that readers can help evaluate their clients' ads and provide industry knowledge, as well as verify readership data. In short, the reader can help demonstrate the value of the magazine's editorial and advertising content.

Next to taking readers on a sales call, the salesperson should take comments, statistics, tape recordings and pictures of reader activities to show the client.

I can give examples of how interaction with readers over the years has helped close sales on the three McGraw-Hill magazines I have represented: *Chemical Engineering, Architectural Record* and *American Machinist.*

The value of the reader call

Let's look first at the value of the reader call.

There was a time at McGraw-Hill when reader calls were required, but like hats and garters this practice has disappeared in the name of progress. Perhaps we should re-evalute this sales tool a bit closer. While garters are out, reader calls should always be "in."

When I joined McGraw-Hill's *Architectural Record* in the late 1960s, reader calls were still part of the traditional requirement for an advertising space salesperson. There was no option. It was required and done. Like so many traditions, the *real* value was not explained—and I was doing a half-hearted job.

The value breakthrough came when a major garage door account asked me what I thought of its new advertising campaign. I did not like the ads and wanted to sidestep the question. I responded by saying, "I don't specify your product line, but let me take your ads to the marketplace and ask the reader."

The time invested in that short project has opened my eyes forever to the value of reader call, for it was some helpful *Architectural Record* readers in the Dallas area who defused a very sticky situation at this major account. I became a more valuable asset in this advertiser's eyes. I also became a better advertising space salesman.

The ensuing nine years have taught me a great deal about the potential of a reader call in terms of advertising space sales objectives and techniques.

Readers provide product and industry knowledge

Besides evaluating advertising, readers can provide valuable knowledge about the industry.

Readers help salespeople understand the market. One of the fastest and best ways to learn the marketing and editorial mission of any publication, as well as the market it serves, is to spend some time with the reader. After all, it's the reader who is the ultimate customer of all of those editorial and advertising pages.

Usually, a new salesman for a magazine will spend a few days in the home office talking to everybody from the circulation manager to the production manager, with a side trip to the editorial department. All too often, the visit is too short to be of much value.

And bear in mind, no matter how much time the salesman spends with an editor, the editor is a creator, *not* a consumer of the product. Relying on an editor to explain all of the qualities of a publication's editorial package is a bit like having an artist be the critic of his own work.

An orientation with a few readers, in a salesman's own territory, provides a less whirlwind atmosphere, with someone who doesn't have an editorial axe to grind.

Reader calls not only provide a viable extension to the initial orientation, but in many cases, will continue to turn the new man "on" to his product and to the market it serves. Some of the greatest moments of pride for me have come when the reader has said, "you work for a fine magazine. . .," and then explains why!

Readers verify the extent of readership

Readers can also verify the extent of a magazine's readership.

Let me give an example.

In the early 1970s, *Architectural Record* published a research piece that indicated that practically all recipients of its 13th "special issue" *Record Houses* kept and used it year after year. A good client of ours did not believe this research on the special issue's longevity. So while we discussed other business, we had his secretary call six or eight local architects we had found in the Yellow Pages. Sure enough, they verified our research. We got the order!

Readers verify their own purchasing power

Not only can readers verify the validity of research, they can also verify their own buying power.

Recently, *Chemical Engineering* salespeople were bombarded with questions from our advertisers as to the value of a senior college student subscriber.

At *Chemical Engineering* we feel that students pursuing a chemical engineering degree are the future of our magazine, of our advertisers and of the entire chemical process industry.

All it took on our part was three reader calls (two former chemical engineering professors at major universities as well as a recent college graduate) to convince us to do research on the specifying and purchasing influence of new college graduates. The material ferreted out by this research indicates that the specifying clout of these young readers was incredible! As a result, young readers are now a strong part of *Chemical Engineering's* selling story.

Readers verify audience efficiency

Readers can also help you verify audience efficiency or purity. Magazines are always trying to position their readers in the minds of their advertising prospects as the most efficient audiences for the product marketing needs.

A salesman has two options when he is challenged by a competitor to prove audience efficiency: he can either shout back, which only clouds the issue in the advertiser's mind, or do what will be recognized by that advertiser as constructive help, by going to the reader for the answer. Let me cite a few examples.

American Machinist had the efficiency of its circulation challenged. The magazine has a controlled circulation directed towards production and manufacturing executives and line managers in the metalworking industries. Advertisers are made up primarily of large capital equipment manufacturers. *American Machinist* maintains no purchasing agents among its audited readers. Competitive publications do.

When challenged by competitors that *American Machinist* did not maintain purchasing readers, I simply went out and talked to half a dozen of our readers who agreed to have their comments tape recorded. They told me that "while purchasing agents do sign the orders, they lack the technical expertise to evaluate the merits of the products advertised and were mere expeditors for their companies."

Meets problem head-on

In another case, when I was on *Architectural Record*, an agency media director challenged the circulation of that magazine. He indicated that consulting engineers in our audience were of marginal value in the specification of his client's product line. It was really the architect who called the specifying shots, he claimed. My choice was either to simply emphasize the other benefits of advertising in *Architectural Record* in hopes of selling him, or do some additional work to tackle the specific problem head-on.

I elected the latter course. I showed in presentation that *Architectural Record* carried 47 percent more consulting engineers than its closest competitor. I got this media director to agree that neither of us were experts, and we listened to a 45 minute tape of five local architects (some of whom he knew) discuss the important role the consulting engineer plays in the specification of his client's product.

These readers confirmed *Architectural Record's* marketing position, and the net effect of one and a half days it took to gather the data was $17,500 worth of exclusive business.

At this point you might accuse me of playing both sides of the street, i.e., in one example I cite the purity of *American Machinist's* single function controlled group of readers versus the diversity of *Architectural Record's* paid readers. However, in both instances the reader calls were made on the audience base, i.e., production and manufacturing executives in metal-working, and architects in non-residential construction.

Reader calls belong in the media presentation

A few years ago, wanting to reinforce the editorial excellence and importance of *American Machinist* to its audience, I decided to do a presentation of a typical reader/manufacturing firm in my territory.

After looking at several companies, I targeted in on the Outboard Marine Corporation, not only because of consumer familiarity with their product line (Pioneer chain saws, OMC Stern drive, Tradewind Motor homes, Cushman vehicles, Evinrude snowmobiles, Johnston-Evinrude outboard motors) but also because so much of their capital spending, as reflected in their annual report, was solidly in *American Machinists's* market, i.e., they were a customer or prospect for virtually *all* of our advertisers.

Through OMC's public relations manager I was introduced to their vice-president of manufacturing. Over lunch he agreed to chair a five-man reader panel that approximated a cross section of our audience. The questions that we discussed included labor, capital buying/spending, federal, state and local legislation, materials and quality control, as well as some subjects that I knew would interest most of my key customers. These topics coincided closely to the editorial diet each received from *American Machinist.* With no coaching, readers cited how *American Machinist* and the industrial press helped them do their jobs better and helped them buy the advertised products more efficiently.

During this session I managed to take fifteen or twenty 35mm color slides which were later combined with other slides of their product lines and some lead pages of topical *American Machinist* editorial which were discussed during the meeting. The result of this work was *not* a synchronized multi-media presentation. Even though it was home made, the presentation was a most effective selling piece and required only ten hours of my time and a $50 investment.

After nine years I'm on my third cassette recorder and have just had my Yashica rebuilt. Whatever technique you or your salesmen employ, I'd say the recorder is the base essential.

As you can see, I've always preferred the one-to-one reader call or, at most, a panel that I have set up myself. Ed Weil, *Architectural Record's* salesman in Pittsburgh on the other hand, has joined his local industry association. He attends its local, regional and national meetings religiously and has in fact become recording secretary of the local association. This investment by Ed is one of the ingredients that has made him one of this magazine's most successful salesmen.

John Mitchell, a *Chemical Engineering* salesman, calls his New York readers by phone. He secures their permission to tape record their comments and manages to cover a great deal of ground quickly.

Perhaps the most elaborate method I've ever encountered is used by Dick Larsen, the advertising sales manager of *Power* magazine. Using the reader panel method, Dick videotapes the reader/marketing interface making the exchange much more "real" than an expensive film. He tells me that most agencies have playback equipment, and, if they or their client do not, the rental for such equipment runs about $100 per day.

Here's another method you might consider . . . at your next industry trade show, why not encourage your sales staff to strap a tape recorder to their shoulders and talk to some of the attendees?

The lead must come from you at the publishing management level. At *Chemical Engineering's* sales meetings we have five or six local readers who meet with our sales staff for a lively exchange. What does it cost? Perhaps $50 or $60 for lunch.

Readers love to talk

Any dedicated professional, whether he be in publishing or a reader in your market or mine, loves to talk about his work. With very few exceptions, I have never had an uncooperative reader. But like any customer, some cooperate more than others.

One thing I have learned is that when I found a great reader, who expressed himself well, with an understanding of why I wanted to talk to him, I kept tabs on him, neither abusing our relationship by betraying a confidence he had expressed nor making a pest of myself. Before long, I created a group of local experts that I could call on whenever I needed some reader input.

These local readers can become as valuable as a key client and should be treated as such. Their value has never ceased to amaze me. One evening my wife and I invited a group of key clients and their wives to a cocktail party at our home. A similar invitation was also extended, out of developing friendship, to three of my most valued readers. Before I knew what had happened, there were four of us representing my publication that evening!

Research: Using it as a sales tool

By Hal Duchin

Magazine readership studies have proven themselves to be critically important to publishers and to advertisers. They document and legitimatize—quantify and qualify—the values of a magazine to agencies and their clients.

And, if properly utilized, these studies should be effective tools for space salesmen and saleswomen.

There are many types of readership (audience) studies utilized in selling magazines. They range in size from large comprehensive syndicated total audience studies covering many consumer magazines to the more selective, smaller studies, either syndicated or publisher initiated. In addition, publishers will participate in sponsor studies which measure reader attitude and/or attention to advertising and to the editorial product.

Syndicated research studies of total audiences are those most commonly used in selling general and select consumer magazines. The reason: You don't have to sell the validity of the research to agencies, media analysts and line media people. It's presold. Thus, salespeople can more easily build their presentations from accepted research data.

Equally important, syndicated audience research establishes U.S. adult data bases against which the buyer can compare the performance of any given magazine to a U.S. norm. These studies also allow another important advantage—the development of intermedia comparisons within commonly accepted demographic benchmarks.

Another form of audience research, the subscriber study, is generally used as a data source when syndicated research is not available. Currently, however, advertisers and their agencies are placing more and more emphasis on subscriber studies because these provide solid data on the demographic and marketing value of the principal readers of the magazine.

To be used most effectively, the data from the studies should be analyzed and subsequently packaged to provide salespeople with a selling tool that logically and effectively positions their magazine or magazines as a must ingredient on advertising schedules. The salespeople and/or presentation packagers should know the following about the client and the product:

- The marketing problems
- Sales goals
- Target market (demographically, psychographically and geographically)
- Frequency of purchase
- Thrust of advertising campaign.

It is vital that salespeople at all times use the *language of the customer*. For example, if their potential advertiser is in the liquor industry, the salespeople shouldn't provide data on the weekly or annual consumption of liquor, if the potential advertiser thinks in terms of monthly consumption. You must conform your presentation to the language of the consumer.

Also, salespeople must be aware of whether they have to sell the potential advertiser on the validity of the study or whether it's presold. If it's *not* presold, then the salespeople have the added responsibility of convincing senior management in media and media analysis of the validity of the study. If the study is presold, however, the salespeople would be wasting a lot of time on the source—time which would be much better spent on the data itself.

To be most effective, the comparative analysis should involve, where possible, only those magazines that are currently carrying or are seriously being considered for the advertiser's program. Dependent on the magazine's strengths, the salespeople will show that their magazines can either deliver large numbers of the advertiser's customers, good concentration in the target market, good efficiency against the prime consumers, or any combination of these three.

Readership studies which document editorial response and attentiveness to advertising are used to reinforce the magazine's statistical values as they relate to the advertiser's product. To the advertiser who is sensitive to product quality, it is important that the salespeople stress the fact that their magazine or magazines complement the advertiser's product editorially.

Obviously, readership studies which provide data on audience size, quality, responsiveness and product purchasing patterns are critical ingredients in developing these effective presentations.

Since the advertiser often does not have the time, the facilities or, in many instances, the inclination to do the thorough analysis that would best position a magazine as a candidate for his or her business, it is equally important that the salespeople present their data in the most effective way.

Using as much data as possible, the specific presentation should open with a background discussion of the advertiser's problems and opportunities. The introduction should stress:

- Current industry developments
- The specific group or groups of people that represent the key market for the product
- Where and when possible the advertiser's people can best be communicated with
- The kind of advertising they respond to
- Any other information that can be developed from industry trade sources.

Because advertisers are more interested in their problems and opportunities than in any individual magazine, they will have little interest unless the salespeople can show them quickly that they understand the client's business and that their magazines can solve the advertiser's problems.

Whenever possible, salespeople should involve key media people and/or clients in the key media preparation of their presentations. Their early participation can easily turn into an endorsement of the finished product.

The salespeople use a formal tool to statistically document their magazine's ability to deliver efficiently and effectively the advertiser's primary target market.

If the salespeople can provide the advertiser with a solid document that logically provides a solution to the advertiser's problems and if they can show how their magazine or magazines contribute to that solution, the advertiser will listen. More importantly, the advertiser will buy.

Your ABC statement: a competitive edge

ABC statements are much more than statements of circulation facts and figures. They are valuable marketing tools that the astute ad salesperson can use to great advantage to point out strengths of his own magazine and weaknesses of the competition. (It is interesting that perceptions of what is a strength and what is a weakness differ among media planners, as well as among publishers.)

There is a belief among publishers that ad agencies never look at ABC statements—only total audience. However, although newer, younger media buyers may not be as familiar as they should be with the ABC statements, there are top executives at major agencies (such as Young & Rubicam) who do scrutinize them very carefully.

At a recent Magazine Publishers Association/ABC seminar, three executives told how they use the ABC statements. They represented three points of view: the advertiser, the publisher and the circulation executive. All three bring up different viewpoints about how to apply, evaluate, and manipulate the information. They make it clear that the ABC pink statement (the publisher's own six-month statement) and the ABC audited statement can be very valuable and persuasive documents in the hands of a savvy publisher or media buyer.

ABC statements are used exclusively by agencies
By Theresa P. MacDonald

The ABC statement is fundamental to media buying. Without it, we really wouldn't know what we're paying for.

Many of you have heard or stated the myth that agencies don't look at circulation statements; all they do is pay attention to total audience reports. Well, if that were all we did, we really wouldn't be able to have total audience reports because total audience reports are based on circulation numbers.

The minute a total audience report comes into the shop, we apply new circulation numbers to it. It is not used until we do this. And, obviously, we must go to the pink statements (the publishers' circulation statements) for those particular circulation numbers.

So let me dispel the myth that the agencies no longer use ABC statements. In fact, they are used extensively, for a number of reasons: for quantitative analyses, for qualitative analyses, for historical trends, for current information, and for future planning.

Another myth: media departments only look at the numbers and don't make many judgments. Let me dispel that myth also. We do use numbers. And we use them for the express purpose of making judgments.

Quantitative Information
From a quantitative point of view, let's look at the very basic information that's right up front. One of the very first paragraphs in the ABC statement is average issue circulation.

Specific issue analysis
On the subject of *specific issue analysis,* there are problems involved if a magazine is either under or over the average.

Consider the magazine that reports 18 million circulation, on average (Example 1). I would be a bit concerned if I had put an ad in that magazine and found that an issue had only 17 million circulation. On the other hand, if I were a coupon advertiser offering 60 cents off on a particular coupon, I would be very upset if the circulation was well *above* 18 million. If I get the proportion of the return I'm expecting, an extra million circulation could cost me $600,000.

Information on specific issues helps us in the area of rebates. If I'm paying for 18 million, I don't want to get 17 million, because our total audience numbers are truly determined by that rate base. So if we were planning on a total audience number, those numbers would be wrong also because we would not be applying the readers per copy against the right amount of circulation.

Geographic analysis by county
From a quantitative point of view, the ABC statement is also very important to us in terms of *geographic analysis* by county designation. Example 2 shows two books, very similar, always considered together by a particular packaged goods advertiser. Yet, when I look at the A,B,C, D county designations, I find that although the books are practically the same total circulation size, there is a very strong skew in terms of where the circulation is distributed. If my product is only distributed in A and B counties, or the major markets, I'm more likely to want to be in that book where there is more circulation going to A and B counties.

Conversely, there are a lot of products—some right in our own shop—where sales are skewed toward C and D counties or rural areas. So for those products, I may be swayed to go into that book that reaches the C and D counties.

These kinds of decisions are likely to be made when you are looking at a field with three, four or five publications in it and you can't afford all of them. When they all look equal from a numbers point of view, it's very important for an agency to look at the ABC statements to see if the circulation of the magazines is skewed in the same way as the product distribution.

Geographic analysis by region
While it may be an exaggeration that all business is local, it is true that a lot of brands are not truly national. So again, we welcome the state by state data so we can target in on our prime areas of importance. On a *geographic analysis by region* (Example 3), we see two magazines that are almost always thought of together. Without looking at the ABC statement, however, you wouldn't know that their circulations, from the point of view of areas of the country, are skewed so differently.

When you actually look at these books, you realize that one is a little bit more entertainment oriented, so you naturally have a little more circulation in the Northeast and in the West. But if you didn't look at the pink statements or the circulation statements, you wouldn't consider these elements.

This is very important, because many advertisers, considered national advertisers, do concentrate on various sections of the country. For example, we have Gulf Oil, and everybody thinks of Gulf Oil as being a truly national product, but it is weak in one entire section of the country.

Canadian vs. U.S. circulation
In the area of *Canadian versus U.S. circulation* (Example 4), we have two books that might be considered together. If we were merely looking at total audience numbers, we'd have no way of knowing how much circulation we would be wasting. If we have no distribution in Canada, for example, why would we want to pay for that portion of the circulation?

Until recently, some books have insisted that you buy total circulation. Why do I want to advertise in Canada when I have no product there? And why would I want to upset the consumer who is going out looking for our product and can't find it? These are concerns that are very important at our shop. We're very concerned with particular geographic breakdown.

Number of editions
Again, on a geographic basis, we might consider *number of editions* (Example 5). I can learn how many there are from the pink statement. These three books, very much considered together, would be considered differently if I were test marketing. The one with the most editions would be more likely to have an edition in the market where I am testing.

The same is true with *demographic editions*. Which books allow me to go after the college students? Which books allow me to go after doctors? Which books allow me to go after upper-income portions of the population?

Qualitative Information
Information provided by the ABC statements does enable us to make judgments. Planners make media decisions by looking at the numbers and making judgments based on what is deemed to be best for the particular product.

Example 1:

Specific issue circulation analysis

Magazine		
Magazine A	High	18,850,000
	Average	18,000,000
	Low	17,060,000
Magazine B	High	2,800,000
	Average	2,400,000
	Low	1,900,000

Example 2:

Geographic distribution

County	Magazine A	Magazine B
A	36	31
B	32	29
C	20	21
D	12	18

Example 3:

Geographic distribution

	Magazine A	Magazine B
Northeast	24	20
Northcentral	23	29
South	26	30
West	27	21

Example 4:

Geographic distribution

	United States	Canada
Magazine A	91%	9%
Magazine B	99	1

Example 5:

Geographic—number of editions

Magazine A	47
Magazine B	10
Magazine C	7

Example 6:

Single copy vs. subscriptions

	Single Copy	Subscriptions
Magazine A	95%	5%
Magazine B	65	33
Magazine C	38	62
Magazine D	1	99

Single copy vs. subscriptions

When analyzing single-copy versus subscriptions (Example 6), a pro or con judgment depends on the client's objectives. Some planners say that a magazine with a low proportion of newsstand sales is not a vital publication. I would not say it that way, but I would say that if a magazine does have a very large newsstand sale, it has vitality. People are coming back issue after issue and putting their money down at the newsstand.

Conversely, other planners say that a book with most of its circulation in the subscription area is very vital because, after all, the readers are plunking money down maybe two or three years before they're ever going to see that product. So they have confidence in that magazine. They're willing to put their money down before they get the product. And, in inflationary times, that's really

---

Example 7:
Basic vs. lower prices

	Basic	Lower
Magazine A	31%	69
Magazine B	8	92
Magazine C	57	43
Magazine D	**69**	31

Example 8:
Percent of subs delivered in arrears

Magazine A	0
Magazine B	5%
Magazine C	3%
Magazine D	1%

Example 9:
Subscription duration

	Less than 1 year	1-3 years	3-5 years
Magazine A	67%	32%	1%
Magazine B	47	49	3
Magazine C	0	88	12
Magazine A	**33**	67	0
Magazine B	.3	99.7	0
Magazine C	1	91	8

Example 10:
Five-year trends by classification
1976 = 100

	Total Circ.	% Sub.	% Newsstand
Group A	114	112	166
Group B	148	**229**	97
Group C	239	140	**640**
Group D	85	85	85

Example 11:
Percent subscriptions sold at basic price

	1976	1981	Cover Price
Magazine A	40	26	$1.00-$1.25
Magazine B	31	**84**	$ .75-$1.25

---

saying something—that people are willing to spend $30, $40, or $50 for magazines they may not see for a couple of years.

Basic price vs. lower price

In that same vein, what is the difference between a book that is offering most of its circulation at *basic price versus one offering it at lower prices* (Example 7)?

The magazines in this example are listed in order of circulation—again, four books, almost always considered together, again for a packaged goods advertiser. The largest-circulation magazine (magazine A) obtains 69 percent

of its circulation at lower than basic rates; whereas the smallest circulation magazine (magazine D) obtains 69 percent of its circulation at basic rates.

Some planners maintain that a person willing to pay basic price really wants the magazine and is not just being lured into a deal, so to speak. The questions here are: Does it matter whether the reader truly wants the magazine? Is the reader who takes the magazine on a trial basis because it's offered to him at a lower price a less valuable reader?

To answer these questions, we must know why a publisher would sell the majority of his magazine's subs at less-than-basic price. Is the magazine in trouble? Is that the only way it can get circulation?

So, rather than making rash judgments based on numbers, we sit down with the publisher and ask what's going on, particularly if there are wide differences between one book and another.

Inevitably, we find that there are very valid marketing reasons why a publisher does this. He may feel, for example, that letting the reader try the magazine at a cheaper rate will promote a full-payment subscriber after the trial period.

Circulation in arrears

Another indication of circulation vitality that we look at is the portion of a magazine's circulation that is in arrears (Example 8).

A person who receives a copy of the magazine when he doesn't want it is not going to read that magazine. In fact, he may get upset if he informed you that he didn't want it. Thus, many planners will just disregard that portion of circulation that's in arrears because they don't believe the person who is getting the book wants it or will even open it.

Subscription duration

Still another determination of circulation vitality is the term of a subscription (Example 9). Does it matter if a magazine sells more of its subscriptions on a three-year rather than a five-year basis? And what does it mean if it sells subscriptions on a less-than-one-year basis?

Here again, I think it's important that we sit down with publishers to find out why they are doing what they are doing. Perhaps the publisher doesn't know how to price his subscriptions because he doesn't know what inflation will do to him next year. Will he be losing money if he sells a two- or three-year subscription at too low a price? We have to realize that it isn't a matter of people not wanting the magazine for more than one year, but rather a matter of how the publisher chooses to sell.

I must admit, though, that most planners will say, "Well, if they're only buying the magazine for less than one year, they're really not committed. Do I really want to be with a magazine where the readers really aren't that excited about it?"

Magazine salespeople dealing with planners who do not understand this concept should explain to them how to make judgments based on this kind of information.

Regarding the renewal rate (which is not required on the ABC statement), some people say it is important, that a high renewal rate shows editorial vitality. Others say it simply means that the audience is getting older since the same people keep renewing.

I'm not suggesting that a high renewal rate is either good or bad. Obviously, the high renewal rate doesn't help the buyer from a quantitative point of view. The circulation numbers don't change. The difference, if any, is qualitative, and that depends on the needs and perspective of the buyer.

Historical Information

ABC statements are used not only for quantitative and qualitative analyses, but also for the historical information they yield. This information relates to either the quantitative or qualitative data.

In Example 10, five-year circulation trends by classification, we took historical data for groups of magazines to see which groups are increasing or decreasing in newsstand and subscription sales. We want to know which groups are catching on, which groups are more popular this year than five years ago.

Perhaps a particular demographic group is getting smaller so there aren't that many new magazines coming out in that field. Or perhaps a demographic group is getting much larger, so there are more books coming into that field. The pink sheets enable us to see what's happening not only to individual books, but to groups of magazines.

In this example, we see group C tends to be growing faster than the others in terms of total circulation. Group B—although it has not grown as much as group C—has grown a lot more in the area of subscriptions. Group C, we notice, has grown tremendously in the area of newsstand sales. Some planners will say that group C is the vital group, the magazines people really want.

This kind of analysis helps us determine which books are losing favor with the public and which books are gaining.

Now let's look at two books within a particular field (Example 11). Five years ago, magazine A sold more of its circulation at basic price. It's now down to 26 percent and it had been 40 percent. What does that tell me? Magazine B, on the other hand, sold 31 percent of its circulation at basic price and it's now up to 84 percent.

As a planner, I'd have to say that magazine B is much more vital, especially since the cover price went from 75 cents to $1.25 compared to magazine A, which increased its cover price from $1 to $1.25. Thus, here again, if I had the money to go into only one magazine, I would probably choose magazine B if all other things were equal—and many times, all other things are equal. This might be the one determining factor.

So much for historical data. What about current use of ABC statements?

Very often a magazine salesperson will come in and tell us that his competitor is not going to make rate base. We can, of course, talk to that competitor who could deny it, but, until the pink statement comes out, we have no way of knowing what the situation really is.

Now, if we're in a planning stage, waiting several months for a pink statement is a problem. And this is where Fas Fax comes in. Once we get Fas Fax, we can dispel any rumor that one competitor spreads about another. Fas Fax helps us on a very current basis.

The Future

All the things I've been talking about—historical trends, basic price versus less-than-basic price, newsstand versus subscription—help us determine what will probably happen in the future. We do these analyses for a specific book and for groups of magazines. We also use the data to make future projections of total audience.

We continue to need new information to update our data banks on total audience. Without the ABC statements, we cannot project what we think will happen. As you can see, we use not only the pink sheets, but the audited white statements as well. We use this information—and we teach our new people how to use it. Believe me, all of it gets used in the business.

The ABC statement can be an effective tool when selling advertising

By J. Wesley Silk

Many years ago when I started in ad sales, we had three basic tools: a magazine, a non-rubberized, non-flexible rate card, and an ABC statement. However, in all my years in ad sales in this business, never was I able to find anyone who wanted to hear about circulation for more than two minutes.

To give you an idea of what we're working with today, I relate the following: We recently conducted a series of small lunches with young people in media departments at agencies here in New York City. One of the rules for participating was that the media buyer couldn't be working in the business more than two years. Of that group, 95 percent of them didn't know anything about the ABC statement, and 100 percent of them had never heard of audited white sheets!

We in magazine publishing are fortunate in having two sources of revenue—circulation and advertising. In both of these areas, the ABC statement plays an important role.

The publisher's circulation department has the responsibility of selling the magazine to the public. The circulation director is asked to deliver a circulation level that not only meets a pre-established advertising rate base, but also delivers that rate base with profitability in mind.

The circulation director must also keep documentable records that meet the requirements of ABC auditors so ABC can verify paid circulation figures.

Every six months, the pink sheet is filled out and supplied by the publisher to the Audit Bureau of Circulation.

This pink sheet is the publisher's *best estimate* of his paid circulation for the time period reported, and is published by the ABC with the often overlooked caution printed on the cover "subject to audit." The pink sheet is not an ABC audited report. The audited white report becomes available a year to 18 months later and covers a one-year time frame, not every six months as reported in the pink sheet.

Unfortunately, that unavoidable lateness leads to very loaded use of the audited deck. If anybody wants to check on circulation figures, 999 times out of a thousand they turn to the most recent pink sheet.

No way to know

There is much room for judgment on what figures to present on the pink sheet. That is particularly true with regard to the most recent issues for which full reports on newsstand sales are not available when the information is supplied to the ABC. As publishers, we keep getting updates on newsstand sales even six to nine months after the magazine has gone off sale. The record keeping through retailers and wholesalers is still that complicated.

If the publisher tends to be optimistic, his ABC publisher's statement is going to be inflated. If he tends to be pessimistic on newsstand sales, the opposite is true. Let's be completely candid. If the circulation director is just shy of meeting his rate base, it may not be difficult for him to be optimistic about newsstand sales. Also, he may choose to be optimistic on credit collections.

Remember, we are talking about paid circulation, and except for historical data, there is no way to know, down to the copy, what the collection results will be for a specific issue. If the circulation director is short of reaching his rate base, he may rationalize that he will be able to make the base if his collections improve, say by as much as two percent. He may decide to take that view and report to the publisher that the rate base will be reached. The truth of the situation will not be known, or publicly known, until such time as the pink sheet is audited and the white sheet is released. Publishers do not release intermediate reports through ABC.

The publisher wants to meet rate base for two reasons. First of all, assuming he's making money on circulation, he needs to meet the rate base to provide the dollars expected on the revenue side of his budget. Second, if the rate bases are not met advertisers may ask for rebates. Publishers usually state their rate bases on a six-month basis. Most publishers want to meet rate base every issue because that *should* be important to the advertising community.

Advertising tool

We use the ABC statement as a competitive tool when we are selling advertising. Unfortunately, not too many people we call on want to hear about circulation. Too many decide that what's in the computer must be right, even though what's in the computer is probably from the pink sheet, and a very old pink sheet at that.

As a competitive tool, the ABC statements and ABC audits can be used by a publisher to point out his circulation strengths and the competition's weakness. Knowing the rate base promised by competition, you'll look at reports and ask:

•"Is the magazine meeting rate base for the six months, for the year, or on an issue-by-issue basis?"
•"Does the audit or the pink sheet show trends of circulation shortfalls or deliveries over rate base?"
•"Where does the circulation come from? Subscriptions or newsstands? A,B,C or D counties? Which areas of the country?"
•"How much circulation is in Canada?"
•"How much foreign circulation is there?"
•"How is the circulation being generated?"
•"Are circulation premiums or sweepstakes being used to encourage the purchase of subscriptions?"
•"Is the magazine including arrears and extensions on a regular basis, and as paid circulation to meet rate base?"

Usually, the only reason to serve the subscriber who hasn't paid is to meet rate base. Under ABC rules, publishers can continue to serve the subscriber as a paid subscriber for three issues of a monthly magazine after the subscription has expired.

The back page of the ABC statement deserves some special attention. If you check authorized prices and total subscriptions sold, you can get an idea of how the magazine is priced, and also an idea of how serious it is about its pricing. As publishers, we don't pay too much attention to the higher-than-basic price or lower-than-basic price figures, because ad buyers must know a lot more than that to make proper judgments.

In some cases, magazines are selling at lower-than-basic price and still doing one heck of a job in generating circulation revenues versus the cost of getting that revenue. That's one of the things that the ABC statement doesn't tell you—that is, revenues for circulation versus the cost of securing circulation. That well could be a key point that in a long run leads to determining advertising charges. If a magazine is not making money on circulation, it certainly is going to have to charge more for its advertising.

The duration of the subs sold is not too important. From one standpoint, the magazine that sells subs three- to five years in advance, say, has that money, that hard cash in hand for that long. On the other hand, if he's increased his price one or two years down the road, he's probably lost revenue on a long-term subscription.

Use of premiums can give you an idea of what a publisher does in order to sell the magazine. You'll have to judge whether the use of a premium or the use of a sweepstakes is a good idea or a bad idea. In our case, the use of sweepstakes invariably lowers the profile of our audience. We begin to reach a lower income, less educated audience; we get fewer home owners. That's not what *Better Homes and Gardens* is looking for. (See FOLIO, March 1982, page 64.)

Sometimes magazines are criticized for lack of research, for a confused methodology of syndicated audience research. But I assure you, the ABC statements, publishers statements and audited statements provide more and better information about magazines than Nielsen, Arbitron and so forth will ever provide for TV.

The reports from ABC can be very useful in helping buyers buy more professionally. Many magazines make sure their salespeople are fully capable of answering questions that a buyer may have on information provided by ABC reports.

And buyers should definitely ask questions of ad salespeople. "Why does your magazine use direct mail instead of clearing house operations to sell subscriptions?" "Why does your magazine invest in sweepstakes to help sell subscriptions?" "How does your magazine select the audience it directs special offers to?" "Why does your magazine sell for less than full price?"

As a publisher, I strongly encourage ad buyers to work closely with ABC statements and to ask questions. There's a lot of useful information available for the asking.

The pink sheet helps you determine your competitors' strategies

By Shirrel Rhoades

As circulation director of two ABC-audited magazines—and as a member of the ABC Magazine Committee—I may get into trouble by telling you the ways I use an ABC pink sheet.

No, I'm not going to show you some exotic way to fudge the numbers that the auditors won't catch. Most of those tricks I learned from ABC auditors anyway.

And no, I'm not going to prove to you that my competitors are using poor marketing practices, bilking their subscribers, going out of business—or even worse—although the facts are there in black and pink for all to see. I leave that up to the advertising sales staff.

But we're talking about competitive selling. So let me touch on how I use a pink sheet—to determine my competitor's circulation strategies, marketing strengths and weakness, and profitability.

A careful look at "Channels of Subscription Sales" and "Duration of Subscriptions Sold" can tell you who your competitor is doing business with (PDS agents, school plan, etc.) and can offer some solid clues as to the circulation strategies, source evaluations, and rate base strength.

Knowing the subscription sources utilized by your competitor will map out the battleground, help you make creative pricing decisions, and provide a timetable as to when you will be competing head to head.

Frequently, I use the ABC statement to create a pro forma of my competitor's business—a complete P/L of the magazine's circulation and financial performance.

It's not as difficult as it may sound, requiring only a few pink sheets, the Statement of Ownership, Management, and Circulation (which is required for second class mailing privileges), a few easily gathered facts, and a little experience.

Let me quickly walk you through this exercise. I'll use an actual case. I chose this one because the magazine has since been sold, and under its new ownership has a different operation. To further protect it, I have deliberately changed a few key numbers.

First, we must summarize certain key facts:

The figures on the magazine's circulation, the number of grace or arrears copies it's serving, and its newsstand sales come off the ABC Statement (Figure 1). The statement of ownership, management and circulation, under the heading "Returns to news agents," enables you to calculate the draw, the newsstand sales percentage, and the total draw. That statement also indicates the number of free copies, office and other copies, enabling you to get the total print order of the copies that will be manufactured.

Subscription sales

Next, looking at the back of the pink sheet, you are able to summarize the channels of subscription sales (Figure 2). One lump category under channels of subscription sales is "Ordered by mail." You can break this category down rather carefully by just using a little good judgment, particularly if you're in a competing market. You would know about how many subs your competitor would pull with a Publishers Clearing House because you have an idea of what your relative strength is. You have an idea of how much direct mail they do because you know

how much direct mail you do. And, if your numbers are looking similar, you can make some pretty close assumptions.

To determine space and inserts, you can make a simple calculation by knowing the number of copies that were served to subscribers and newsstand and using some pretty standard industry response percentages.

Figure 1

	First half (ABC statement)	Second half (ABC statement)
ABC circulation	338,000	327,000
Grace copies	500	13,500
Net circulation	337,500	313,500
Newsstand sale	31,000	30,000
Net subscriptions	306,500	283,500
Draw	75,000	75,000
Free copies	13,500	13,500
Office, other	6,500	6,500
Total print order	402,000	392,000
Total copies printed (6 months)	2,412,000	2,352,000
Total copies printed (12 months)	4,764,000	

Figure 2
From ABC pink sheet: Channels of sub sales

	First half (000)	Second half (000)	Total (000)
Ordered by mail			
Stamp (circulation agencies)	20.0	7.0	27.0
Direct mail	27.0	13.0	40.0
Space/inserts	10.5	9.0	19.5
Gift	2.0	8.0	10.0
Renewal	28.0	22.0	50.0
Bulk/classroom	8.0	9.0	17.0
Catalog	3.5	11.5	15.0
Publishers own	4.5	8.5	13.0
Independent	11.5	26.5	38.0
News	.5	.5	1.0
School	3.5	9.0	12.5
	119.0	124.0	243.0

Figure 3
Duration of subscriptions sold

	First half (000)	Second half (000)	Total (000)
+5 Years	4.0	9.5	13.5
3-5 Years	21.0	18.5	39.5
1-3 Years	43.5	58.5	102.0
−1 Year	50.5	37.5	88.0
	119.0	124.0	243.0

Figure 4
Pricing

	First half (000)	Second half (000)	Total (000)
Basic	31.5	58.0	89.5
Lower	87.5	65.0	153.0
	119.0	123.0	242.5

Figure 5
Spreading the business

	Stamp	D.M.	Space	Gift	Ren.	Cat.	Pub.	Ind.	News	School	Bulk
+5 Years								13.5			
3-5 Years					14.0			24.5	1.0		
1-3 Years		14.0	7.0	10.0	36.0	15.0	13.0				7.0
−1 Year	27.0	26.0	12.5							12.5	10.0
Total	27.0	40.0	19.5	10.0	50.0	15.0	13.0	38.0	1.0	12.5	17.0

Figure 6
Agency copy rate

Agent	Subs (000)	Remit	Term/Price	Net/Copy
Stamp	27.0	11%	7/$ 5.00	7.86¢
Cat.	15.0	65%	12/$ 9.00	75.00¢
School	12.5	22%	7/$ 5.00	15.71¢
Other	13.5	15%	60/$51.00	12.75¢
—	15.5	15%	48/$43.00	13.44¢
—	10.0	15%	36/$35.00	14.58¢
—	13.0	15%	12/$15.00	18.75¢

Figure 7
Direct mail expenses
2,000,000 mail quantity @ 2% response = 40,000 subs
$200 CPM = $400,000

Figure 8
Renewal expenses
50,000 renewals x $2.50 acquisition cost = $125,000

Subscription income
306.5 x 6 = 1,839
283.5 x 6 = 1,701
3,540

3,540 x 45¢ = $1,593,000

Figure 9
Circulation summary (expenses)

Direct mail	$400,000
Renewals	125,000
Other	100,000
Salaries	75,000
	$700,000

Figure 10
Fulfillment summary (expenses)
302.0 subs x 12 x 2.5¢ = $ 90,500
79.0 agent orders @ 25¢ = 19,750
164.0 direct orders @ 50¢ = 82,000
Misc. 7,750
$200,000

Figure 11
Distribution summary (expenses)
302.0 subs x 12 x 9¢ = $326,000
$5,000 freight x 12 = 60,000
$386,000

Figure 12
Manufacturing (expenses)
4,764.0 copies x 23¢ = $1,095,720

Advertising revenue
B/W page
$4,160 x 80% (discounted) = $3,328

456 PIB pages x $3,328 = $1,517,568

Figure 13
Pro forma

Revenues		Expenses	
Subscription	$1,593,000	Manufacturing	$1,095,700
Newsstand	226,000	Distribution	386,000
Advertising	1,518,000	Fulfillment	200,000
Other	75,000	Circulation	700,000
	$3,412,000	Ad sales	400,000
		Editorial	400,000
		G&A	300,000
			$3,481,700
		P/L	($69,700)

Renewals? That's a calculation you can pretty well make by sorting out the numbers.

Summarize all the different channels your competitor is selling with, looking at the first half ABC statement, the second half ABC statement, and then summarizing those for the year.

Next we look at duration of subscriptions sold: over five years, three to five years, one to three years, and less than one year (Figure 3). You summarize that from both ABC pink sheets, and then total it up.

Then look at the pricing—what their basic prices are, you look at prices they've sold at, you look at how much they've sold at basic, lower than basic (Figure 4). These things together allow you to do a little exercise of spreading out exactly what your competitor's business is like (Figure 5).

Spreading the business

For example, looking at the duration of subscriptions sold, knowing that there are 13,500 subscriptions sold at more than five years, it's a pretty good guess that this is some sort of paid-during-service, long-term subscription sell. And then going back and looking under independent sales, you make a pretty good judgment that this is the category of sales it would go under.

So with this information, and some judgment, you can determine how the magazine is doing business and the terms on which it's doing business.

By looking at the stamp sheets that subscription agencies send out, you know whether they're using a short-term offer, a one-year offer, or some other type of offer. Then you can categorize which group the terms fall into.

Then you do a few calculations to get the magazine's net revenue per copy. I've summarized the agency one here for a quick look at it (Figure 6). You've already determined that this particular magazine does 27,000 stamp agency-sold subs a year. Competitively, you can make a judgment of what kind of remit they're getting. It's probably about 10 or 11 percent, unless you're a magazine that has the strength to go into a much higher category. You know the term and the price that they used in that offer. By simple division, you can come up with what the net per copy would be for each source.

On the direct mail, you know that this magazine had to bring in 40,000 net subs (Figure 7). To get 40,000 net subs with a two percent response (based on a judgment factor and your own mail, what type of market you're in, etc.) it would take 2 million pieces of mail.

Judging from how much it would cost—and you might want your production manager to look at this—you just multiply the CPM times the amount of mail that had to go out and you can say, "All right, the magazine probably spent $400,000 in that year on direct mail."

Determining renewals is a similar process (Figure 8). You determine from the spreading of the terms that there were probably about 50,000 renewals sold. It probably cost them $2.50 acquisition costs, given that the cost will run anywhere from $2 to $4 at that range. So it's a simple calculation: they probably spent $125,000 bringing in renewals.

To get the subscription income, you simply take the average number of subs sold and multiply it by six to get the total number of paid copies served (Figure 8). Multiply that figure by the average copy rate—which you calculate considering all the agency business and direct business—and divide it out to get an average net per copy. In this case, the circulation revenue was probably about $1.5 million for a small magazine.

Circulation expense summary (Figure 9): We determined the $400,000 direct mail, $125,000 renewals. Just taking an estimate, the magazine probably spent somewhere around $100,000 on other things such as space ads. With salaries, the magazine probably had about $700,000 in circulation expenses.

Fulfillment expenses involve a similar calculation: the number of subs served, times 12, times the label cost that you think that type of magazine would be able to negotiate (Figure 10). You can do this either on a subscriber per year type of calculation or some other way, probably based on your own deal.

Distribution expenses: again it's the number of subs serviced, times 12, times whatever it costs for postage (Figure 11). That's a pretty easy calculation. If you are a similar size magazine, a competitive magazine, you know what you're paying to send out your copies.

Freight: again, you know what you spend to send out your newsstand copies. You can make a pretty careful calculation of what it costs your competitor to send those newsstand copies out. You've already determined from the pink sheet and auditor's statement how many draw copies are shipped out each month.

Manufacturing: We determined the total print order for the year (Figure 12). You can have your production department price it out and tell you what it would cost to print a magazine this size.

Newsstand revenue: Off the ABC statement, you have average copies sold times 12 to get the total copies. You know what the price is and you know what percentage the national distributor gives them. You can then determine their revenue rather closely.

To determine advertising revenue, you probably need the Publishers Information Bureau (PIB) figures, the rate card, and a pretty good guess as to what the magazine's discount structure is (Figure 12). This particular magazine had a black-and-white rate of $4,160. It sold mostly black-and-white ads. It seemed to have an average discount of about 20 percent. So, multiplying by 80, you get the average revenue per page, multiplied by the number of pages reported by PIB, and you conclude the magazine probably had about $1.5 million in ad revenue.

Adding all these numbers up, you simply come up with a P&L for this magazine (Figure 13). It was a magazine that was marginally at a loss, although it had some other activities that brought it into a marginally profitable position.

Nonetheless, it's a good way to look at your competitors, whether or not it's for an acquisition. It's helpful simply to see how well they're doing, what their strengths and weaknesses are, and the different circulation strategies that they're using.

There you have it. I use an ABC to give me a glimpse at the competition. As a measure of circulation, however, without some perspective and proper interpretation, it remains more quantitative than qualitative. That's why we have advertising sales staffs, Simmons, Media-Mark, PRIZM, and other tie-breakers when it comes to placing advertising. But a "strong" pink sheet doesn't hurt either.

Selling special sections

By Robert E. Dimond

They are known by many names—advertising supplements, advertorials, section twos. But basically they are the same animal: a special section of the magazine, generally on one subject or devoted to one client, supported by special interest advertising, either by a single client or a group of them.

At Hitchcock Publishing Co., where I published *Infosystems* for nine years and *Office Products Dealer* for 12 years, we called them Part IIs. They were always sponsored in their entirety by one client. They were almost always a separately published supplement that rode along with Part I in the mail. And they were always produced almost totally by the magazine staff.

From the time I introduced Part II selling into Hitchcock in 1974 until I left the company last spring to start my own venture, I was directly involved in the sale and production of 23 Part IIs. All together, they accounted for about 650 exclusive advertising pages in *Office Products Dealer* and *Infosystems*, resulting in over $1 million in bonus advertising dollars.

That's a significant amount of "windfall" advertising pages and dollars over a seven-year period—significant enough that I suggest many publishers are missing a bet by not exploring the opportunities to sell Part IIs to their prospects and accounts.

Moreover, in the case of *Infosystems*, for a couple of

years our Part II sales made the difference between black and red ink for the year. Beyond that, they enhanced our credibility, provided us a leadership stance, gave us an exciting marketing story, and helped to separate us from our competitors.

Most publishers will quickly recognize the obvious advantages of Part II sales: additional advertising pages (almost always exclusive) and bonus advertising dollars. But that is only the tip of the iceberg. The real beauty of a Part II sales and marketing program is found in its residual benefits—side effects that give surprising boosts to your overall sales and marketing program.

Before I discuss these side effects, however, I'd like to touch on what I call the "Part II Mentality" that must pervade a publishing staff from top to bottom before a Part II sales effort can be successful.

A whole new ball game

For the past several months, I've been consulting with publishers interested in pursuing Part II sales programs. One of the first things I ask them to do is to throw out all of the standard rules governing the publishing/client/advertising agency relationship. There's a different set of rules in the Part II game. Let me illustrate.

After one or two Part II sales were under our belt, I had an idea for a client that I felt represented a real spectacular. All of the ingredients added up to what I considered to be a perfect opportunity for this client to resolve a number of difficult problems facing his company at the time: image in the marketplace, some tricky competitive situations, selling a name change, etc.

When I explored the idea with the account executive at the client's advertising agency, the reception was 100 percent negative: "No way. It will never sell. The client doesn't have that kind of money in the ad budget. Besides, they're too conservative to go for that kind of program. I'm not going to embarrass myself by going in there to support that."

Generally, this should be enough to scare a publisher back to his office to hide for a month, wondering where he got such harebrained ideas. But this time it was different. This time I felt the account executive might have been underestimating the problems facing his client, the extent of his client's daring, and the potential for my proposal to help alleviate the problems.

"Is it all right with you if I take it to the client on my own, without your blessing?" I asked. "Be my guest," the account executive replied, secure in the knowledge that I would probably have my head handed to me for such an outrageously expensive proposition.

The intensity of the account exec's warnings motivated me to prepare myself thoroughly for the confrontation. The salesman on the account set up a meeting with the president of the company and his marketing director to view a table-top flip chart presentation. I acted as the researcher, designer and producer of the flip chart presentation and would personally deliver it to the client.

I spent the better part of a week researching the client's market in depth, his competition, his personnel, his image in the marketplace, etc. I cut, pasted, begged, borrowed, typed and hand-drew with color markers a homemade presentation consisting of 40 or so statements and displays.

The running commentary with the visuals characterized the firm's many problems, projected the opportunities the market was going to offer in each product area over the next five-year period, and explored what the competition was doing to get its share. Then, the presentation showed what the program we were offering could do to support the client in every respect.

The result was immediate and stunning. We walked out of there with the largest single order in our history.

As dramatic an example as this may be, it is representative of the kinds of situations you will encounter time and again in an ongoing Part II sales program. Throw out the traditional rules of the game.

Just to illustrate that this kind of thing is not the exception, permit me to allude to one other sales situation (although virtually each of the 23 has its own "story"). One aggressive, imaginative advertising director on whom I called frequently constantly drooled over the prospect of a Part II for his company. But it was an old story—no budget, corporate would never approve, etc., etc.,

On one call, after hearing this familiar litany, I posed the question: "What if I told you this program is so ideal for your firm that I would even recommend you utilize your entire next year's ad budget allocation for us to put into a one-shot supplement. I believe you'll get more out of it than the diluted program you're planning."

His response, which was not exactly a surprise to me, was: "Why, that would take not only *your* ad allocation for next year, but my *entire budget* for all three trade publications in the field." Why not?

Why not, indeed! The curious thing was that six months after the supplement appeared, the ad manager bought a follow-up suggestion to re-run the same supplement in our show issue. Two supplements in one year after contending that there were insufficient funds for even one!

A commitment to the program

A magazine with a "Part II Mentality" is one that has committed itself to a Part II sales and marketing program as a part of its day-to-day publishing efforts. The direction comes from the top and flows through every member of the publication's team—sales, editorial, promotion, design, etc., etc. Part II sales don't happen in a vacuum. They fall into place after tugging, pulling, pushing, and prodding from all members of the team.

It means that not only the publisher but every salesperson and yes, even editors, always have the Part II answer on the tip of their tongues to offer as a remedy to the countless problems and opportunities that this kind of publishing approach can treat.

I'm not suggesting that editors cross that hazardous zone between church and state to prostitute themselves in the name of sales. What I am suggesting is that when an editor is discussing shop with a potential advertiser he be ever on the alert for "Part II opportunities."

When spotting an opportunity, the editor can tactfully suggest that other companies have answered this need, or taken advantage of this opportunity, via a Part II supplement. If the potential advertiser is interested, the editor will be glad to have the publisher call on him to explain the program in detail. I believe this approach sustains the sanctity of church and state and keeps the Part II pot boiling.

If it's beginning to sound to you as though the tail is wagging the dog once a magazine is committed to a Part II sales program, I would agree with you—to a point. And what does this attitude do for your over-all advertising sales efforts? Plenty! And all of it good. That's the rest of the iceberg.

Far-reaching side benefits

Let's take a look now at the many residual benefits of a Part II sales program. I believe that such an explanation will make it clear that which end is doing the wagging is a moot point.

1. *Effect on sales staff.* If I could bottle the effects of a Part II sales program on salespeople it would be worth a fortune. One of the average salesperson's constant gripes is that he or she has nothing "new" to sell . . . that the same clients can't constantly be approached with the same old question, "Wanna buy an ad?" Salespeople love to go in with a Part II story because Part IIs are dramatic, sexy, innovative, attention-getting and versatile.

Suddenly, your salespeople are truly problem-solvers offering a unique solution to any number of different marketing problems. They can't help but feel proud of their magazine for sponsoring such a program, which has all the earmarks of a leadership posture. Any hesitation salespeople have in the early going about suggesting a project with such a hefty price tag quickly dissipates when they meet up with the inevitable enthusiasm and interest on the part of their clients. There is a snowball effect that is truly heartwarming to observe.

One of the big boosts salespeople get from Part II selling is that it provides:

2. *Access to client's top management.* Rarely is the average salesperson invited into the inner sanctum of top management to offer his routine sales presentation. Part IIs open that forbidden door and forever change the client/salesperson relationship.

It's an axiom that Part IIs must get the blessing of top management. And usually that won't happen without a face-to-face presentation to all who must bless the expenditure. Ideally, you'd like everyone in on one meeting, but practically speaking that doesn't usually happen. Therefore, Part II presentations often must be given several times as the idea is accepted by account executive, ad manager, product manager, corporate communications director, vice president/marketing director and perhaps even president. You simply accept that as part of the Part II rules of the game.

However, you can turn this into an advantage. As you work your way up through the ranks, you accomplish something else. I call it:

3. *A new intimacy with client.* Each level that you convince of the worthiness of your Part II concept then becomes a "member of the team" prepared to do battle on your behalf. In order to lend their support to the proposal, they must build a case. Consequently, you find them "getting into your magazine's story" as never before.

They tend to want to be able to spew out the publication's marketing stance as fluently as the salesperson might to his superior. You have penetrated natural defense mechanisms that always exist between seller and buyer. You suddenly realize that no matter what happens with the Part II proposal, several layers of the client's marketing team have "adopted" your magazine and accepted the viability of its sales message. This bodes well for your future relationship with the client.

A similar thing happens with advertising agency participants, leading to:

4. *Improved relationship with agencies.* Approximately half of all Part II sales begin with the advertising agency. If you have the agency's support, you find yourself building a unique partnership with the agency that didn't exist before.

Once again, the professional agency will not walk with you into the office without a thorough knowledge of the magazine, its editorial philosophy, the makeup of its audience and its specific strengths that support a Part II proposal. Chances are they have never put your magazine under such a microscope. If you hold up, warts and all, suddenly you have gained an altogether different image in their eyes. This can't hurt in your continuing battle for your share of the business, not only from the account in question, but others the agency may be handling in your field.

And even if your Part II proposal gets cut off at the pass, this new-found relationship at the agency and client levels often leads to:

5. *"Consolation" business.* As you find yourself in more and more Part II selling situations, you will be gathering supporters at both the client and agency levels. Such supporters, particularly on the client side, may not have the authority to authorize an advertising outlay large enough to accommodate a Part II, but can direct expenditures from the regular advertising budget.

After taking the Part II message "up the line" and being turned down, they may feel justified in sending other business your way, particularly if they are committed to your magazine enough to recommend a Part II. I call this "consolation business." In my experience, one such piece of "consolation business" was a $60,000 contract!

This kind of business will often lead to:

6. *Pre-empting of competitive schedules.* Whether it's Part II business or "consolation business," large doses of advertising expenditures often have the dual effect of boosting your sales and reducing your competitors' sales. Since the Part II buyer isn't always able to fund a relatively large chunk of money out of his regular advertising budget, he may have to "borrow" from dollars originally slated for your competitors. Thus, you're not only getting bonus business, you're also widening the gap between your pages and your competitor's pages even more, at least from the Part II client.

And if you happen to have only one competitor in your field, this kind of division of the advertising pie gives you:

7. *A big edge in a two-book field.* Normally, one of the big problems faced in a two-book field (or a field with two major magazines and one weak one) is that advertisers will often tend to "even out" advertising dollars for each magazine. When there are a number of competing magazines in a market, ad buyers must be more discreet and make some harder buying decisions.

Even if you're the nominal leader in the field, you often have a tough time convincing the big buyers to send more dollars your way. You have to give them a solid reason to justify breaking their pattern. A Part II is such a reason.

Whatever your relative position in your particular market, a Part II selling program can provide:

8. *A leadership posture.* A successful Part II program helps create a leadership aura about the magazine. If you're already the Number One book in your field, you're constantly searching for ways to demonstrate that leadership. If you're not, it's even more important to find some advantage that can represent some gains on Number One.

It is interesting that whoever gets to the Part II trough first in any one field generally can feed on it alone for some time to come. And exclusive Part II publishing offers prestige to its sponsoring magazine because it is a loud statement of meaningful support by the clients.

These are some of the more significant related benefits of a Part II sales program that have direct and dramatic effects on your total advertising sales program. There are others. But these should be enough to alert publishers to take a long hard look at the potential for Part II sales programs in their markets.

Recognizing and selling Part II prospects

There are certain characteristics that are common to most top Part II prospects. Naturally, there are exceptions. But I have found that most of the Part II advertisers I have been involved with have the following characteristics:

• A lot of money (although not necessarily in the ad budget). As long as the right "switch" is turned on, if funds are available in the company, ways will be found to utilize them.

• A large size. The first statement, usually but not always, points to *larger* companies.

• Far-sighted, forward-thinking management.

• "Daredevils" in key slots, willing to take risks.

• A key contact who loves innovative approaches or gets kicks out of "wowing" the boss or competitor.

• Management that tends to follow the lead of competitors. (This, of course, is in the case of a prior sale.)

• Involvement in very tight competitive battles in high stakes areas.

You and your sales staff probably recognize many companies you call on sprinkled throughout the profile listed above. Some may have combinations of two or more characteristics. But what motivation do they have to sink large amounts of budget into an "extravaganza"?

There are many "pegs" on which to hang a Part II. Some are more obvious than others. Once you've spotted a potential prospect, investigate the company well enough to determine if it has one or more classic reasons for buying a Part II.

Following are the "top 20" reasons:

1. The company is introducing an important new product or line.

2. The company is introducing a new program involving wholesalers, dealers, subsidiaries, users, etc.

3. The company is merging with another company and wants to explain what the merger will mean to employees, customers, retailers, etc.

4. The company wants to call attention to the total array of products and services offered because customers are not totally aware of broad lines.

5. The company is changing its name.

6. The company is attempting to gain greater acceptance of company name, size, importance, share of market, etc.

7. The company wants to impress or sell a program to stockholders.

8. The company wants to impress or sell a program to board members.

9. The company is looking for another form of annual report.

10. The company wants to launch sales or other types of contests among employees and/or customers.

11. The company wants to "break away from the pack" and blitz a competitor.

12. The company is looking for something that will inject new life and enthusiasm into its sales staff.

13. The company wants Part IIs to use as its employee handbook.

14. The company wants to attract new acquisitions.

15. The company wants to attract a buyer.

16. The company wants to fight a specific problem (*e.g.*, ward off effect of a competitor's price change, new models, etc.).

17. The company wants to prove the effectiveness of trade advertising.

18. The company has to satisfy egos somewhere in the organization.

19. The company wants to dominate a trade show.

20. The company wants to dramatize the effectiveness of a new product, system, etc.

Companies buy Part IIs for countless other reasons, as well, and the list will build forever. But these "top 20" give you plenty of solid openers to begin your prospecting and selling programs.

Don't get impatient or discouraged. The first sale won't be easy. But it will be an exhilarating experience when it happens. And others will follow. That I can almost guarantee.

Selling editorial

By Dave Hagenbuch

The editorial content of a magazine is the key to readership which, in turn, is the key to advertising value. When a buyer of advertising is properly convinced that your editorial material creates a good reading climate for his advertising, he will want to do business with you.

Since selling editorial is such a vital part of ad sales, the selling challenge for ad salespeople is: How do you get the reception for and confidence in your editorial product?

The answer follows logically: You must have an effective editorial presentation. And, in order to have such a presentation, you must be thoroughly familiar with your editorial policy, format, content, readership and response.

You can never assume that your advertisers and prospects are reading your publication. These people receive a huge volume of magazines and rarely have time to look at most of them. Even if they do read them, memories are short and editorial content is often attributed to the wrong source. So—make sure these people know what you are selling.

There are many kinds of editorial presentations,

ranging in cost and effectiveness. Some of these are: motion pictures, videotapes, sound-slide films, editorial meetings and seminars, recorded interviews, visual display boards, accordion folders, notebooks, tear sheets, photostats of pages, and the magazine itself.

Whatever you use, you'll first need answers to these questions:

1) What is the editorial approach or climate of the magazine? How can I make it meaningful to the advertisers and agencies?

2) What is the function of the different editorial features and departments?

3) What is the source for editorial material?

4) What do I know about the editors? Are they well-known in their fields?

5) How does the magazine stimulate readership and/or response (sales leads, letters, etc.) for this particular account?

6) Have we won any awards? What do they mean? Since these are the questions in the minds of buyers, structure your presentation to supply the answers, in advance. Make sure that your answers are directed in terms of the selfish interests of the buyers. What does all of this mean to them? Is it an opportunity for more readership for *their* advertising? More exposure? A chance to increase their share-of-market?

Remember—the universal appeal to another person is through his or her self interest. If you tell your prospective advertisers how they'll benefit because of all of your fine editorial material, they'll find a way to do business with you. Just be sure that you document your sales points with examples, testimonials, readership research, page counts, etc.

The personal touch

When it comes to the physical presentation, the poster board technique is my favorite. It is simple, inexpensive, and effective. And, if you paste one up yourself, it's *personal*.

Start by making an outline of what you want to present and some rough layouts of how you are going to arrange the material on the boards. Then cut out editorial pages which demonstrate your editorial content (example: News, Feature Articles, Editorials, Departments).

From a local art store, you can purchase 22-inch by 28-inch poster board in a wide variety of colors. (If you don't want it that large, it can be cut into a smaller size right in the store.) There are all kinds of carrying cases available too. I prefer the larger size of case and boards because they are more flexible and have more impact. They can be used for both one-on-one or group presentations.

Normally, six to 10 cards will be sufficient for a 15- to 30-minute meeting. Trim your editorial pages neatly with a paper cutter or razor blade and mount them on the boards with rubber cement. You can add to the attractiveness by mounting some of the pages on black or dark paper to give them a "frame." Make sure that each example is pressed flat on the board with no ripples or creases.

Once the physical presentation is complete, you can develop your sales talk. "Mr. Jones, the editorial content of this magazine assures you a high level of readership to your advertising for these reasons: Here is a study which proves . . . ." Know what you are going to say and have a logical order for the points you wish to make. It is also important to plan questions that will keep the listener involved.

The advantages of using visual boards are obvious. First of all, people learn best through their eyes. Second, you can study the buyers' reactions to your presentation. Third, you can work with the cards from the back of a chair, on an easel (if available), or on a conference table. You can also tailor your editorial presentation, varying it from call to call, removing some cards, adding others. And finally, it's a good device for groups. The customers may wish to bring in other people.

Through this sales aid, you are limited only by your imagination. You can add promotion material, circulation or audience information, market data, advertising and research. But be careful not to bring in too many elements. You're there to sell the editorial content which is the key to advertising value.

If you choose to work directly with the magazine itself, use some control device such as a paper clip or staple so that you can move through the magazine from section to section without fumbling. This also helps you maintain control—you don't want a situation where the buyer reaches for the magazine and says "Go ahead, I can listen" while he fans through the pages. If this does happen, stop and don't say a word until he returns the publication to you. You cannot sell someone who is only half listening. You must control the interview.

Of course, if you can work your way around the desk and share your material, that's often a good sales technique. Personally, I like to watch their eyes and look for other non-verbal signs.

Whatever you do, sell your editorial. Advertisers and agency people will say, "We use that magazine because it does the best editorial job." Or, "They have the best editors." "Their editorial parallels our marketing interests." "It's the number one magazine."

Selling editorial is vital to your success in publishing. Be sure your presentation stimulates a positive response.

Selling ad space in New York City

By Frederic C. Decker

This is for the publisher who wants to avoid the worms while getting a bite of the Big Apple—the national space placed by the agencies and advertisers in New York. This is not for the heavy hitters with the big books. They already know how to shake the tree. It is for the smaller New York-based publisher just starting up and, even more so, for the out-of-town publisher who hasn't yet made an attack upon the New York market.

There is hardly any point in trying to pin down a figure on how much advertising flows out of New York into magazines across the country. This isn't important, anyway, because there's probably nobody who would dispute the statement that if a magazine wants to sell national advertising, New York is the primary place to sell it.

Let me state some ground rules for this article. I am writing about two kinds of magazines. One is the smaller consumer-oriented publication—the regional, metropolitan or vertical special-interest book of limited circulation and which, up to now, has carried little, if any, national consumer advertising. The other target of this piece are the publishers of trade, professional or association magazines who may be just starting or who believe that there may be more profitable alternatives to the way they are presently selling in the New York market. Most of what I have to say will be for both kinds of publishers.

The following areas will be discussed:

• The qualifications of your magazine as a contender in the New York market.
• How to select your best prospects.
• Who should do the selling.
• How it should be done.
• What it costs.
• How and when results should be measured.

So now let's examine what it takes to get that bite from the Big Apple, and how to go about doing it.

Does It Belong?

First, as a publisher, you must decide if the national advertiser really belongs in your magazine. You must make an objective appraisal of the validity of your book as a vehicle for national accounts. This may be the hardest part of the entire exercise because your view of your magazine, its audience and its advertising clout may be colored by the fact that it is your baby and you are emotional about it. Unless you are very confident of your ability to be dispassionate, you may save a lot of time, money and heartache by getting an objective opinion from someone who has no ax to grind and who knows magazines, the national market and how magazine advertising is sold in it.

You will want to consider such questions as:

1. Have you established an audience large enough and/or specialized enough to be attractive to national marketers? How big is "enough"? That depends upon how specialized and unique your audience is. Few consumer product national advertisers are going to get excited about a circulation of much less than 100,000. Twice to five times that number is a safer minimum. But for professional, trade and association magazines there is really no bottom limit just so long as the magazine adequately penetrates the market it purports to reach.

2. Do you have a unique editorial niche? Whether yours is a trade or a consumer book, there is no substitute for having an editorial purpose which is easily understandable, quickly explainable and significantly different from every other magazine. The nuances of difference may not be overwhelmingly great, but they must be demonstrable.

3. Is your book professionally written, designed and produced, and thick enough to appear substantial? Subjective judgments are made by even the most sophisticated buyers of media. You'll be more apt to strike out if your book isn't professionally done and prosperous looking.

4. If yours is a new magazine, do you have the financial stamina to put up with wait-and-see advertiser attitudes for a year or more? Advertisers aren't in business to underwrite new publishing ventures. A limited number will take a chance on a new book, especially if the idea is unique, the publishing company is well known and fiscally sound and if the selling effort is expert. But many will let others take the plunge first.

5. If yours is an established regional, metropolitan, special-interest, trade or association magazine, do you have a healthy volume of endemic advertisers and is your book performing well for them?

6. Do you have or can you get basic audience profile and readership data, compiled by a recognized research firm? Do you have believable statistics on the size and purchasing proclivities of your market and the relationship of your audience to those figures? Major national advertisers are not prone to invest in marginal markets or in marginal magazines.

7. Are you audited by ABC or BPA? All advertisers want audit bureau circulation substantiation; many will refuse to consider a magazine which doesn't have it. If yours is a business publication, you would be wise to file a B/PAA Media Data Form as well.

There are other considerations, of course, but those are some of the most important. If you can't answer all of those questions with a confident "yes," then think twice about attacking the national advertiser market until your selling arsenal is more complete.

Measuring Your Market

Once you've decided you are ready, the next step is to list your target advertising prospects. You'll probably find that there are more prospects than you had imagined, so you will want to select those which are both the most logical for your book and are the largest spenders. They will make up your "A" list and all the others will be your "B" list.

With each advertiser you will want to list the key personnel as well as the agency and its personnel who work on the account. You will also want to record the pages placed in your market and in the books that compete most directly with yours. You will then have a basis for establishing sales goals and projecting sales estimates.

This is a lot of work. You will need Publisher's Information Bureau (PIB) reports for the consumer advertising statistics. For trade and professional advertising page counts in competitive books you'll have to make your own physical count unless you can get access to tabulations kept by another magazine. Sometimes they are available on a cost sharing basis.

Agency identification, indications of the advertiser's total budget and advertising personnel are listed in the *Standard Directory of Advertisers.* This covers about 1,700 of the larger advertisers and is available in either geographical or classified editions from National Register Publishing Company, 5201 Old Orchard Rd., Skokie, Ill. 60076. Agency personnel are listed in the *Standard Directory of Advertising Agencies,* also published by National Register. Your library may have copies, but, because of the high frequency of personnel changes, use only the current issues.

Now that you have decided your book is qualified to be attractive to national accounts and now that you've determined there is a big enough reservoir of prospects, let's move on to the next step.

Who Should Do the Selling?

Here we have multiple choice answers. The sales calls can be made by:

1. Staff salespersons headquartered in New York or nearby.

2. Persons from the out-of-town headquarters who make periodic forays into the New York market.

3. A commissioned independent sales representative firm which serves several publishers whose books are not necessarily in the same or related fields.

4. A sales representative firm which works solely for related magazines which may or may not be sold as a group.

5. Any combination of the above.

Let's consider some of the pros and cons of staff selling versus commissioned representatives. Although there are staunch proponents and detractors of each system, it has been my experience and that of our clients that the choice between the two depends upon many factors, the first of which is total dollar sales potential and the time it will take to achieve that potential.

Cost of Selling

Starting with the first alternative, a staff salesperson headquartered in New York, let's begin by adding up the cost. Compensation, from any of the infinite combinations of salary, draw, commissions and bonus, will run from a minimum of, say, $20,000 for a beginner to $50,000 or more for a pro with a strong track record. Offering a bigger buck doesn't necessarily guarantee bigger performance but it helps to increase the possibilities of getting a superior person.

Let us presume you get a good person near the low end of the compensation scale—say, $27,500 including payroll taxes and benefits. Add to that a minimum of $5,000 per year for luncheon entertaining, cabs and other miscellaneous expense. Then add at least another $3,000 if your salesperson will cover nearby territory outside of New York in New England, New Jersey and Pennsylvania. Hotels, planes and car rentals aren't cheap.

What office facilities and secretarial help will this person need? The most economical arrangement is the office-at-home. But its savings in dollars may be more than offset by inefficiency of location and by the very real difficulty even the most disciplined of persons may have in working hard and effectively in a home environment. So we'll add $1,800 per year for a minimum desk space and telephone answering service, if you can make a deal with a small agency or PR firm which has a surplus cubbyhole.

For a little more you can find space in one of the rabbit warrens that offer such service in the Grand Central Station area. Or go up to a minimum of $450 a month and you can have a decently furnished 10'x13' office at a place like World-Wide Business Centres on Madison Avenue where you'll have your own phone number, a listing in the building directory, switchboard service, a receptionist and use of a conference room. Secretarial service at $15 per hour, including round-the-clock telephone dictation, clerical help, telex, photocopying and similar services are available on a pay-by-use basis. There are other professional typing services, too, which provide pickup and delivery of your material and typing on your letterhead. One of these, Molly's Professional Typing Service, quotes the package at $1.20 per page. Also throw in an item of at least $1,000 per year for telephone tolls, postage and stationery.

Add it all up. Compensation for your salesperson, travel and entertainment expense and office overhead will come to about $41,500, not counting the money you'll spend coming to New York to keep an eye on things and make some sales calls.

Is it worth it? Can you afford it? Can one salesperson do the job? To help with the answers to those questions, go back to that list of prospects which you so laboriously compiled. Taking just your "A" list, how much dollar potential does it represent, how soon? And how much can you afford to spend to get those dollars?

Maybe you wonder how much you *should* afford. There is no firm answer because it depends upon the stage of your magazine's development. (You'll be willing to spend more for sales during your startup and building years.) It depends, too, upon the size of your potential. (You'll be willing to invest in direct proportion to the eventual hoped-for payout.) If yours is a business or professional magazine, you'll want to get your total cost of selling at or below the present average of around 26 to 30 percent as a percentage of net ad income. But probably that won't happen until your book has reached maturity. If you have a consumer magazine (with a higher page rate than most business books), your selling cost should be a substantially smaller percentage of your advertising income.

Clues to Coverage Needed

A study of your prospect list will give you clues as to whether it will take one or more salespersons to do the job adequately. Count the number of "A" prospects, then double that number to take the agencies into account. Then multiply by the number of persons who must be covered at both advertiser and agency. (Probably the absolute minimum will be two persons at each place. Selling, especially for a new book, must be done at every level of buying influence.)

But don't stop there. Now multiply by the number of calls per year, on the average, which should be made upon each of those buying decision-makers. Some may require as few as two calls in a year. Others may need 10 or 12. For our purposes let's say the average is five. Now divide that total by 230, the number of days in the year the salesperson will probably be available for calls. If your answer comes out at more than three, or at most four, calls per day, you either need more than one salesperson or you have selected too many "A" accounts. If, on the other hand, your answer shows that your salesperson will need to make less than three or four calls per day to cover those "A" accounts, you are lucky because you can now provide for coverage, on a less intensive basis, of at least part of your "B" list too.

(At this point please let me disagree with the management people who contend that a salesperson should be expected to make more than an average of four solid sales calls per day. I once preached the five-a-day minimum but I don't anymore. Three to four face-to-face calls in the average day are maximum in the New York market if they are to be intelligently prepared and effectively followed up.)

Selling from Home Base

Now that you have completed that arithmetic exercise you also have a pretty good idea of whether the second option is practical. If you are really serious about selling a volume of space to New York advertisers and agencies, you probably won't opt to try to do it from your out-of-town base. But supposing, for any of a variety of reasons, that is your decision. How do you go about it and what does it cost?

First, be prepared for frustrations. Sales calls in New York aren't like those anywhere else in the world. It is harder to make dates, harder to get past the secretaries on the phone. People are generally more hurried, less patient. Reception-room waits are longer, and, for that reason, dates must be more widely spaced. Dates are more frequently broken. The calling day is shorter although there are people who'll make breakfast dates or 8 a.m. office dates. These tend to be the higher-echelon folks, interestingly enough. And it is also noticeable that the higher you call on the executive ladder, the more apt you are to get a decision and the less apt you are to experience broken appointments, long reception room waits and interviews interrupted by phone calls.

You'll do well to make your appointments by phone before coming to town. I know out-of-towners who always place those calls through the person-to-person operator and reach more of their prospects more easily and get a higher percentage of appointments.

There Is No New York on $10 a Day

You will probably come to New York for a week. You will find that living expenses can be high, although they can be less than extravagant if you can be happy in a less-than-deluxe atmosphere. You can pay from $55 to $100 a day for a single with a bath at the Pierre or as little as $8.50 without a bath at the Martha Washington. The sheets are probably equally clean at both places. There are plenty of others in Midtown in the $25 to $50 range.

If you want an inexpensive place with a gym and swimming pool there is the Vanderbilt Branch YMCA for men and the Studio Club for Women, both located about midway between Y & R and Marsteller. Their rooms, without bath, go for $10 to $11. There are plenty of places that offer studio rooms with kitchenettes for the visitor who wants to beat the high cost of eating out. At least one rental agent, Manhattan East, lists them as low as $36 a day. No matter where you decide to stay, make reservations as far in advance as possible. Sometimes the town gets jammed.

After you've been coming to New York for a while you will have found some restaurants you like and you will probably get into the rut of returning to those in which you are comfortable. There is nothing wrong with that except that if there is anything New York offers in abundance it is good food in an abundance of variety. New York also offers some absolutely abominable food and service. I won't try to suggest good restaurants. There are too many of them. But I suggest you avoid most of the hotel dining rooms because of their so-so food, disinterested service and high prices. There are a few notable exceptions.

As a rule of thumb, restaurant prices are lower west of Fifth Avenue and there are many fine restaurants there. Scout restaurants in the business neighborhood in the evening when you may be alone for dinner and then take your luncheon guests to the ones you like best.

One last tip on getting around in New York: Contact the New York Convention and Visitors' Bureau, 90 E. 42nd St., New York, N.Y. 10017; 212-687-1300 and get its free kit which has a map of the city, a comprehensive hotel guide with room rates, list of restaurants with minimum entree prices, list of secretarial services, rental services of various kinds, theater ticket agents and lots of other good stuff. The special service lists are far from complete but they are at least a start. (One thing they don't list are washrooms and the most comfortable phone booths in Midtown. I've often thought I might compile such a list as a service to the fraternity/sorority of space sellers.)

Or Should You Use Reps?

There are several reasons to consider the appointment of a commissioned representative firm to sell in the New York market. Your analysis of the territory and its potential may make it uneconomical to support your own salesperson in New York. You may not want the responsibility and risk of selection of your own person. You may prefer to deal with a fixed cost of rep services rather than the variables of salaries, expense accounts, overhead and taxes.

Don't be mistaken—I do not mean to imply that appointing a rep firm is necessarily a second choice. There are many publishers happily using reps in territories which could easily support one or more staffers.

There are good reps and there are bad reps. There are those who hang out their shingles because they can't get other jobs. And there are those who are in their own business because they prefer the independence, the variety, the entrepreneurial satisfaction and the greater earning opportunity.

The trick is to find the right rep and then to make it possible for that firm to work successfully with and for you.

Where and how do you look? There are numerous sources of reps, names. The *New York Classified Directory* lists only a handful. *Standard Rate and Data (SRDS)* shows less than 40 business publication reps in the New York area and about 100 consumer publication reps. But unless you are acquainted with them they'll just be names to you.

So start by asking other publishers or a consultant. Check *SRDS* listings of other good magazines to see who represents them. The Association of Publishers Representatives (850 Third Ave., New York, N.Y. 10022; 212-421-6900) will happily supply a list of its members, all of whom have been in the business for at least two years, represent two or more magazines and subscribe to a code of ethics. One estimate given me is that about 20 percent of the reps belong to that group.

Don't overlook the fact that there are specialized groups of magazines being sold, sometimes singly and sometimes in combination, by rep firms. There is a religious group, an Ivy League college group, a couple of metropolitan groups, one or more upscale audience groups and others. There may be a group into which you would fit and which might, under the right circumstances, strengthen your own sales story.

C. Lynn Coy, a New York-based rep has written a paper entitled, "Twelve Key Questions To Ask When Selecting A Representative." Among the important considerations in evaluating a prospective rep in Coy's opinion (as well as mine) are:

• How long has the firm been in business? (Look for stability.)

• What kinds of accounts are regularly being called upon? (Look for synergism.)

• What is the business history of all the people in the firm? (Success and stability are important.)

• What are the page rates of the other books being repped? (You don't want to be grouped with higher rate books lest you get minimum attention.)

• What is the firm's policy about written reports concerning the progress made on all calls? (I would not hire a rep who didn't file detailed reports. You must have them to be able to respond with assistance and you need them for historical record.)

• Who, specifically, will handle your book? (Whether it will be one person or several, you will want to interview them personally and review their histories carefully.)

• What is the character of the other magazines in the rep's stable? (More important than the number of magazines is their quality. You, and your rep, are judged by the company you keep.)

Your financial arrangement with your rep is, and should be, a matter for discussion. If yours is a new book or has a limited market, the rep could be justified in requiring a minimum fee as a draw against commission. Some reps won't work on that basis, preferring to represent only those magazines in which they are confident of sales and financial success. I prefer that kind of rep, not because it saves front money for the publisher but because the chances of success would seem to be greater with a rep who gets paid only if he or she produces.

Don't be chintzy in dickering about the rate of commission. Human nature being what it is, reps work hardest where they can make the most money. If you have a marginal book or a low page rate, or both, you may be smart to pay above the usual 15 percent or 20 percent. Incentive bonuses for reps are not unheard of, either.

Be cautious when contract signing time comes. You don't need to accept the rep's standard contract if there are items in it which you question. Don't, however, try to make the contract so tough or onesided that it destroys incentive. It is better to err on the side of sweet reasonableness. But before signing it, check it carefully or consult with someone who has been down that road a few times before.

Once you've made your deal with a rep firm, you have assumed as much responsibility as it has. Your rep is required to sell diligently, honestly and intelligently, to keep you informed.

Your obligation includes full and frequent communication with your reps. Inform them immediately of policies which affect them. Feed them with research information, copies of editorial rave letters, news of advertiser successes, circulation growth data. Give them that kind of table-talk scuttlebutt to pass along to prospects. Keep them supplied with well-designed media kits containing current rate cards, comparability data, research reports, editorial forecasts. Get those editorial forecasts to them far enough in advance to make them useful. Give them a good presentation and teach them how to use it. It doesn't have to be elaborate—just sound, sensible and professional. If you can afford it, bring their key people, the ones on your account, to your sales meetings and to major industry meetings especially if their advertisers will be there. Visit them periodically and lend the clout of your title and the weight of your intimacy with your product to important sales calls with them.

In short, make them a part of your organization. Give them every advantage you would give your own people in the territory and expect from them the same spirit of closeness and cooperation.

Measuring Your Success

Whether you use reps, your own staff people or do it yourself from home base, you'll need a yardstick against which to measure your success.

One of the most important admonitions in this entire article is that you set goals in terms of the number of national pages you expect to sell and the time within which you expect to sell them. Break those goals into six-month or 12-month segments, perhaps, and spread them over a couple of years.

Involve your salespeople or your reps in the goal setting process so that they are a part of the decision and are committed to it. Changing circumstances or changing assessments of your magazine or the market may lead you to adjust your goals as time goes by. But only by having goals will you and the people charged with selling your space know clearly what is expected and only by having goals will they be able to measure their performance against known objectives. That's far better for them, and for you, than having them constantly wondering how they are doing—and how you think they are doing.

The Big Apple—Wormy or Wonderful?

Billions of dollars of space and time orders flow from the agencies and advertisers in Manhattan, as well as White Plains, Greenwich and the other corporate centers clustered around New York. That market is tempting to every publisher. It offers rewards to many and disappointment to others. The rewards go to those whose magazines match the needs of national advertisers and to those who sell their magazines with skill and persistence and, often, patience. The disappointments come to those who misjudge their magazines' virtues, come ill prepared to the market place or lack the perseverance and financial staying power to see it through.

New York is the center for billions of ad dollars—but it doesn't part with them easily.

Space sellers are creative people, too

By Frederic C. Decker

When one hears of a creative person in the advertising business one usually thinks of a copywriter, an art director, a commercials writer or a TV producer.

As creative as all of these individuals are, let me suggest that the unsung heroes and heroines of the creative arena may be the elite among the advertising space sellers.

I've qualified that statement by use of the word "elite." Only a few who sell space can really qualify. But those who do are those who turn in creative performances which are as demanding as any in the ad business.

Look at it this way: Writers have a valuable commodity not available to people who sell space. That commodity is time. Even if deadlines are short the copywriter usually has time to hone the copy, make changes, stop and start over again.

Not so the space sellers. Their "copy" must be created and delivered on the spot. It must be instantly responsive to the unexpected. It must be speedily adapted to the shifting moods of the interview and to unpredicted competitive challenges which must be addressed knowledgeably and convincingly. What is said is irretrievable. There can be no restructuring of a phrase, no starting of a new draft.

People who sell space have only one chance per visit, only one shot at building the chain of persuasion that advances the selling process. The spoken words must be the right words that lead toward the buying decision.

There is similarity between the copywriters' chores and those of the space sellers. Neither should approach his or her tasks before the homework is done. Just as the copywriter studies research about the attitudes, needs and motivations of the consumer, the space seller studies the advertising objectives, marketing strategies and media buying proclivities of the prospective buyer. But the writer mulls one research problem at a time while the space seller must become prepared to face three, four or five different audiences and as many different selling situations each day.

The writers ask their questions of the research material. The sellers have an advantage in that they can ask direct questions of the prospective buyer. And they should, because only then can they really know what's in the buyer's mind. Only then can they match their "copy" to the buyer's needs and interests.

The space seller's knowledge of selling psychology must be at least as deep as that of the writer. Verbal copy must be as free of cliche and awkwardness, as filled with emotional tug, as the best piece of copy for print or air.

Salespeople must produce their copy on the shortest notice. They cannot wait for the muse or the mood. And their copy is not judged by research, hunch or ratings, but by the pragmatic measurement of the dollars it produces.

That's why great salespeople are great creative people. The best.

A view from the buying side

By Ira Ellenthal

"I have a great deal of respect for the true professional," says Stewart Brown, vice president and advertising director of Max Factor.

A media executive for more than 25 years, Brown looks for several questions when evaluating a space salesperson and his presentation.

"I know it's a cliche," he says, "but advertising is only part of a total marketing plan, so I evaluate a media presentation with a primary consideration in mind: Does the vehicle fit into the solution I am seeking for the problem posed by the marketing plan?"

That kind of thinking, Brown points out, establishes the setting for what he expects from a salesperson. "For example," he says, "I expect him to have done some homework. I expect him to know his property well enough to be able to tell me how it will help me overcome a problem I might be having—be it with a product, a brand or the whole company."

Brown says he also expects the salesperson to have looked thoroughly into the industry and his company's position in it, and also to know something about the general spending levels of competitors, distribution patterns, consumer profiles, demographics and even psychographics. "In short," he emphasizes, "I expect an informed presentation."

He has more to say. "The rep who comes in to simply sell space will almost never get an order," Brown claims. "But the one who shows me how I can solve a problem will probably wind up with a schedule. Put simply, I'm suggesting that he better have an idea—*before* he comes to see me—as to why I should buy. And it better not have anything to do with his needing an order."

Brown isn't interested in presentations that focus on circulation and costs. "Let's face it," he declares, "I can read for myself—and, if all I want are cheap numbers, I'll buy television every time."

Brown's interest lies in the quality of the relationship that exists between the magazine and its readers. Says Brown: "Why do they read the book? What is their mind set when they approach it? Although I'm in the cosmetics and fragrance business, lots of female readers and a very low CPM aren't good enough reasons for me to buy a book. But there are magazines which, because of the nature of their editorial content and the thrust of their reason for being, fit hand-in-glove with the attitude I need to sell beauty products. Make that case for me and I've got to be interested."

Ruth Woolard, vice president and account group supervisor of Leber Katz Partners, a large advertising agency with headquarters in New York, also wants more than fundamental demographic and circulation data. "The profile of readers should deal with their lifestyles, with what they think, with what motivates them, and with how they relate to the book, in terms of its editorial contents or its overall concept," she explains.

Presentation should be customized

There is one sure way to arouse the interest of Fred Ellman, advertising/merchandising manager of Galaxy Carpet Mills. "After the canned portion of a presentation," he says, "let the salesperson include a customized portion about my company. Let him describe the position my company enjoys in our industry—our direction, our image, our needs—and then let him tie it all together by demonstrating why his book and my company share common goals and why advertising with him would help us accomplish those goals. Sure, it's a lot of hard work, but I couldn't possibly imagine a more effective sales presentation."

A "what's-in-it-for-me" attitude is essential to Martin Courtian, account executive at Sacks & Rosen, another New York agency. "The best magazine presentation in the world is meaningless to me if it doesn't relate to my product," Courtian says. "The salesperson has to know something about my product and who I'm trying to reach. Moreover, he's got to show me that his readers are good prospects for my product and why his book is better—not only for reaching, but for selling my prospects."

While he has heard his share of good and bad presentations, there is one certain route to turning off Courtain. "I can't stand a presentation in which the salesperson is ill-prepared or disorganized," he says. "It bugs me no end when he has a case full of papers that he constantly rifles through in order to find a piece of information."

The fastest way to make his blood boil is to interrupt Mel Sweet, president of Sweet and Company Advertising, New York, in the middle of a question he is asking. "It's amazing how many salespeople think they know the answer before hearing the whole question," he says, suggesting that the art of listening needs cultivation.

To Sweet, a good magazine sales presentation contains some special elements he can relate to that will assist his client. "One of the best space salesmen who ever lived was named Gene Bay," he says. "The originator of *House & Garden*'s color program, he remained a 'peddler' all of his life and, right up until he died a few years ago at 76, he was always a true gentleman. I thought he was wildly effective because he came to every meeting with an idea."

As much as he appreciates good ideas, though, Sweet doesn't think basic information should be forgotten. "On a first call," he explains, "most salespeople tend to think that, because I run an agency, I know everything about their magazines. All too often, I have to do my own digging, and the reason is that salespeople almost never do enough homework to present circulation and readership comparisons. It's very frustrating."

Sweet is most receptive to a nuts-and-bolts presentation that is brief. "My time and the time of the salesperson are valuable," he explains. "If there is more I need to know, rest assured that I'll keep him longer."

He also recoils when salespeople gripe about their jobs. "Believe it or not," he says, "about one in five calls include this kind of bitching. I'm neither an adviser nor an employment agency but, for some reason, that is the role in which I'm often cast."

Not far behind on his bitch-list are pitches that are keyed repetitively to special issues. "I don't want to be sold continually on a special issue basis," he says. "It's like crying wolf; eventually, it doesn't get a rise out of me."

Don't harass client

Nothing arouses Ruth Woolard's ire more than the salesperson who, once having been told in an upfront manner where he stands, becomes a nuisance at the client level. "I hate to receive the kind of call from a client in which he tells me to get a certain rep off of his back," she says. "I think behavior that creates such a situation is out of order."

Robert West, marketing manager of Carr-Lowrey, a division of Anchor Hocking, dislikes presentations that evolve into a battle of wits between seller and buyer. "Shove me into a corner and watch out," he warns. "Anyone who takes this approach need not hold his breath for an order; it's going to someone else."

Sanford Buchsbaum, executive vice president of advertising for Revlon, says, "The more a salesperson thinks about his publication as a business asset to the business he is attempting to sell, the better he, his company and my company will do."

Responsible for a huge budget, Buchsbaum wants to hear presentations that are short and concise, with relevant audience data and important non-media information. "The emphasis," he declares, "must be on the advertiser's problems, not the magazine's."

When a salesperson has succeeded in getting advertising space, Buchsbaum and others advise continued contact—but not just for the sake of keeping in touch. "I want to hear about key data that will help me increase my business," Buchsbaum says. And he also wants to know about possible problems in connection with union negotiations, paper shortages, movement of key personnel, important information on the magazine industry in general and, specifically, on a magazine's area of coverage. Finally, he is always interested in franchised position offerings.

A great believer in letter-writing as a way of maintaining contact, Ruth Woolard adds, "No one seems to write letters anymore. In most cases, I far prefer them to telephone calls, which can be extremely time-consuming, even bothersome."

She is also merchandising-conscious. While it won't be a deciding factor for her in the selection of a magazine, she says that it can help add insertions in a book. "We're paying a lot for a page of advertising and we want to get every possible nickel of value for the money," she declares.

"Helping me to merchandise my advertising is always appreciated," Martin Courtian says. "But I also appreciate a note or a telephone call about something special going on in a publication, some competitive information that might interest me or an outstanding position I've been given in a specific issue."

A word of caution from Courtian: "Anything that demonstrates a continuing interest in my account is worthwhile—but it shouldn't be overdone."

Entertainment as a sales tool

Addressing himself candidly to the subject of entertainment, Courtian says, "I'm not interested in being entertained by strangers for business reasons, nor do I want to listen to a sales presentation over a meal or cocktails. Yet, there are salespeople who are more friends than strangers and whom I enjoy meeting occasionally outside the office. While I like to think I'm pure regarding my professional judgment, I'm sure that deep down—other things being equal—the friend gets the business. Maybe that's why I'm not turned on to being entertained."

"If two publications are basically equal and I can only buy one of them," Galaxy's Fred Ellman says, "I suppose my human failings would tend to make me put pages into the book that entertains me."

Personally, Sanford Buchsbaum prefers a brief office meeting, but he also thinks that "limited, judicial use of entertainment is acceptable," an opportunity to discuss business at a more leisurely pace away from the office telephone. "In no way, though, should the salesperson expect entertainment to sway a client into giving him new business or increasing business he is currently receiving," according to Buchsbaum.

Stewart Brown recoils at the suggestion that media buyers are in business to say "no." Says Brown: "Media people are charged with the job of spending the budget, not saving it. If they say 'no,' it's because the opportunity being presented doesn't fit into the plan, or the money ran out and somebody had to draw a line."

"For the most part," Mel Sweet says, "media buying people get specific directives from account executives and other marketing people that lead them to make certain recommendations. On the other hand," he adds, "I've never seen a media salesperson who didn't think that his book would fit any set of marketing criteria. Many times, I've witnessed a salesperson describe his book in such a way that made it totally unsuitable for one of my clients. The moment he finds this out, he does a complete flip-flop and begins contradicting everything he said previously. It leads to a crisis of confidence."

Contact agency first

Sweet also offers a few words on the subject of usurpation. "I've never told a salesperson that he couldn't go to my client—ever," he says. "I do ask him to tell me what he will tell my client—so, in that sense, no salesperson has ever gone over my head. When a salesperson knows we're on the account, I resent it when he goes to the client first. It *ain't* good manners."

Ruth Woolard strikes a similar pose. "I think the agency should be contacted first," she says, "but I also think more attention should be paid to the client than to me."

Stewart Brown chips in with a lengthy—and interesting—commentary on the subject. "If a person's job is on the line, I can't condemn him for going over my head—but neither do I forget," he says. "Putting together a media plan is a difficult, time-consuming process. Once the plan is put to bed, I get very unhappy when some clown hot-shots an order out of my boss, leaving me with a budget problem to solve."

Some further candor from Brown: "Look, I've gone to a lot of trouble to do what I think is a good job. Perhaps there are books on the schedule which are marginal and bumping them won't really upset anything. But that's for me to know. After a rep has had his day in court, he ought to take the decision gracefully and try his best to make a better presentation the next time around. If the facts won't change, maybe his way of organization will. It's up to him to figure out how to make a better case for his book."

As for humor, Robert West says, "My personal feeling is that it belongs any time it can be worked in, provided it's in good taste and in keeping with the seller's personality."

"I have no objection to it, but I'm not looking to a salesperson for laughs," Martin Courtian points out. "If certain humorous touches fit into a presentation, fine; unrelated joke-telling, however, is unproductive."

"It's only for an experienced hand," Sanford Buchsbaum notes. "And it should *only* be used sparingly when the person *knows* his audience well."

The last words from the buying side come from Courtian. "Anyone who treats me as an adversary is nuts," he says. The comment serves as a reminder of a point that can't be stressed too often: the salesperson who finds ways to help the prospect will almost always help himself.

Charles Mandel

By Charles I. Tannen

Charlie Mandel is certainly not the stereotype of an advertising space salesman. Sometimes he dresses rather peculiarly and comes out looking like an absent-minded professor. And there are times he does peculiar things, like sliding into an imaginary home plate in the middle of an agency boardroom to fulfill a request for a slide presentation.

But when it comes time for serious selling, Mandel is a master. His latest success was as sales consultant for the launching of Bob Guccione's new magazine, Omni. That magazine broke industry records for first issue advertising revenues. Mandel was directly or indirectly responsible for many of the 60 pages in that issue—worth almost $500,000—plus the more than $1 million in ad contracts that were in the house before the issue was ever on the presses.

Before joining Guccione, Mandel was publisher of Madison Avenue, *a magazine which was carrying more than 500 pages of advertising a year just three years after Mandel brought it back from the dead. He is now publishing* Media People.

What makes Charlie Mandel a supersalesman? Here, from a recent interview, is Charlie Mandel on selling advertising.

On starting in the business:

"The first job I ever had was selling advertising when I was 18 years old. One day I remember coming back to the office and giving my sales manager a long list of excuses about why people weren't buying. The sales manager said to me, 'They're professional buyers. You're a professional seller. So how come they're not buying and you're not selling?'

"It's now my 25th anniversary of selling ads and I still feel that this one remark is the basis for the most constructive attitude I could possibly have."

On doing sales homework:

"Selling, to me, is building the relationship, and it all starts with doing your homework. If I'm calling on someone I don't know, I go in with my pad in hand, as if I'm interviewing him. I'm there to really find out about his plans—to find out what he's doing and how he's thinking.

"I don't want to take up a lot of a person's time with a wasted presentation that doesn't fit his needs. People are appreciative of that fact—more appreciative than when a salesman walks in and says that you have to buy some magazine because it's the best magazine in the world.

"And I'm not going to give quick answers. I'm going to go back to the office and really think his problems out. Then, when I go back to see him in a week or so, I'm fully prepared to help him.

"That's why I make two calls. I can't understand why so many salesmen are afraid to make two calls to the same person. I'm eager to call on someone twice. It's a sensational one-two punch. I'm trying to make their job easier. That's my job.

"Most salesmen lose their ability to communicate because they don't understand the needs of the person they're trying to sell. To take an absurd example, a guy goes into an office and says, 'I have a terrific women's magazine and I really would like to sell you an ad.' But the guy he's calling on is selling male products. The least the salesman should have said is that most of the readers buy gifts for their husbands and male friends.

"The reality is that most salesmen don't connect the marketing needs of the client with what they are selling. Why? Because, unfortunately, most salesmen don't want to be salesmen.

"Most salesmen also think that they're at war with the person they're selling. But I'm sitting there in his office, building a lifetime relationship. I'm going to become a part of his needs. When he thinks of new marketing ideas later on I want him to call me and tell me about them. I want him to think that I'm on his team, and in fact I am. That's what separates good and bad salesmen. The reason that a 20-year veteran is better than a new salesman is simply that the veteran knows more people and what they need."

On building relationships:

"I sold advertising for *Madison Avenue* magazine. So now, when I walk into a Magazine Publishers Association meeting, I know everybody in the joint. I know what their marketing needs are and I know what their magazine is trying to do. I know their wives' names, and how good they are at tennis or golf. That's my business.

"I hope that I've gotten each of them to the point where they are telling me the truth, even if they end up not buying. Maybe the next time I call on this person I will be able to help. But my job is to get a person to tell the truth. It's a terrific load off someone's mind when he knows that he doesn't have to lie to me, that he doesn't have to say 'Yes, I think that you are doing a magnificent job and I'm planning to put you on our 1984 schedule.'

"I love what I'm doing, and because I love it, the people receiving my sales calls get caught up in my exuberance. Usually, salesmen either bludgeon them for an order or come in with their hat in hand, pleading for an order. But I'm calling on them to make them happy, give them information and help them to build their company and mine. Since I really believe it, people respond to it."

On finding decision makers:

"Most salesmen call on people who are only authorized to say no—people who must get permission to say yes. I won't call on these people.

"If the assistant media planner at some agency loves your magazine and says he will recommend it, what does that mean? It means that he will tell his boss about your magazine. If the boss says that he doesn't think the magazine is so great, that media buyer is not going to put his job on the line for your magazine. Instead, he'll come back and tell you that they really like your magazine and that they're going to try to put you on the schedule for next year.

"I won't call on anyone who cannot say yes unless I'm doing backup work after having called on the person who can. A good salesman should be able to say to that person, 'It's a terrific idea to call on your media buyer. However, since I have something so exciting going on now, I'd just like to show it to you first. I don't want you to go through the next few weeks not knowing about the exciting things we're doing. I'll only take 15 minutes of your time and then I'll go call on everybody that you'd like me to call on.' You see, I'm doing him a favor.

"This works for both the advertiser and the ad agency, and I call on both of them. But for the most part—and especially with a new magazine—I call on the advertisers. It's their money, not the agency's money, so I may as well go see them.

"What I like to do is make a general presentation to the agency and get as many media people as they have available at the time to listen to my presentation. I want them to be informed. I'm not trying to duck them."

On maximizing the sale:

"If a guy wants to buy a page, then my job is to sell him two. A salesman's job is to maximize the buy. For in-

stance, when I called on an advertiser who told me that he was waiting for me to call because he wanted to buy a page in my October issue, I knew that my job was to convince him to buy 12 pages.

"It's my job to bring the buyer from a 'maybe' to a 'yes,' from a 'yes' to two pages, from two pages to four pages, from four pages to 12 pages.

"Recently, one of my salesmen walked into the office with a 12-page schedule he had just sold. He told me how wonderful the advertiser is and how much he loved the magazine. I said, 'Terrific, let's go back and see him.' My salesman thought I would certainly blow the whole deal out of the water. When I got to the advertiser I asked him why he bought 12 pages. He told me that he had co-op money that he had to spend before Christmas. I said, 'Why don't you buy 36 pages?' He went from 12 pages to 36 pages.

"Isn't it funny that the salesman was so happy to get the order? Actually, when the advertiser said to him that he wanted to buy 12 pages, the salesman didn't do anything. At this point, however, the salesman's job was just beginning. His problem was to figure out how to get the advertiser from 12 to 13 pages. After all, the advertiser bought 12 on his own.

"Most salesmen don't bother doing this. I guess they don't have the necessary energy.

"What I'm saying is that you have to find out the 'why.' That's the key question. Maybe, in fact, the guy would be better off with exactly what he wanted to buy. But the chances are he wouldn't be. The chances are that the selling platform I've developed is really good for the person. That's why I do my homework. I go back and think it through.

"I don't want to win an ad and lose the relationship, however. The idea is to sell ads forever. Not one-shots." Although I miss many more times than I hit, I hit many more times than most salesmen. In this business, you must be willing to miss as well as hit.

"I don't profess to be able to tell others that what I do will definitely work for them, but I know what works for me. Actually, sales calls to me are an upper. I enjoy them. I enjoy going out and saying, 'Hi, I don't believe you know me. My name is Charlie Mandel. Let me tell you what we're doing today.' That's fun.

"You see, I've been doing this for 25 years. So even if I went out one day and the first six people I called on didn't buy, I know I'd have the averages going for me. I go on the seventh call exactly the same way I started the first call. I've been doing it for so long, I know it works.

"You know what's tough? Trying to remember my expense account. Trying to figure out if I spent $8 for drinks—or was it $4? That's what kills me."

On working with editors:

"I believe that all people try to put out the best magazine they can. Vince Lombardi used to say that a quarterback would look terrible if the right guard didn't block. Everyone has to pull an oar. So as long as we're on the same team, we might as well pull together.

"Ten years ago my wife and I put up a suggestion box in the office. Although it's not new to the rest of the world, it was the first time I was aware that someone in publishing had done it. We asked our staff for comments, either signed or unsigned, and I read them before I went home each night. Before the editors went home, they also read the suggestions. Everyone realized, without my saying so, that we were all working on the same team."

On advising a new salesperson:

"Read your magazine. I mean sit down with every issue and read your magazine. Really know what's in it. If you don't understand something, ask questions. It will pay off. Most salesmen do not read their own product.

"And make eight sales calls a day. If you can't make eight, make seven. I would rather have a medium talented salesperson making eight sales calls a day than a sensational salesman making two, because in the long run the person making eight is going to develop more relationships. And like I've been saying, the name of the game is relationships."

On people who won't buy an ad from Charlie Mandel:

"There are people who say that they wouldn't buy from me, no matter what. They think that I'm doing something that is not the norm and they only want to deal with the norm. Or they think that my product doesn't fit in with their needs. Or they think that I have bad breath. Although I miss many more times than I hit, I hit many more times than most salesmen. In this business, you must be willing to miss as well as hit.

"I don't profess to be able to tell others that what I do will definitely work for them, but I know what works for me. Actually, sales calls to me are an upper. I enjoy them. I enjoy gong out and saying, 'Hi, I don't believe you know me. My name is Charlie Mandel. Let me tell you what we're doing today.' That's fun.

"You see, I've been doing this for 25 years. So even if I went out one day and the first six people I called on didn't buy, I know I'd have the averages going for me. I go on the seventh call exactly the same way I started the first call. I've been doing it for so long, I know it works.

"You know what's tough? Trying to remember my expense account. Trying to figure out if I spent $8 the other night for drinks—or was it $4? That's what kills me."

On working with editors:

"I believe that all people try to put out the best magazine they can. Vince Lombardi used to say that a quarterback would look terrible if the right guard didn't block. Everyone has to pull an oar. So as long as we're on the same team, we might as well pull together.

"Ten years ago my wife and I put up a suggestion box in the office. Although it's not new to the rest of the world, it was the first time I was aware that someone in publishing had done it. We asked our staff for comments, either signed or unsigned, and I read them before I went home each night. Before the editors went home, they also read the suggestions. Everyone realized, without my saying so, that we were all working on the same team."

On advising a new salesperson:

"Read your magazine. I mean sit down with every issue and read your magazine. Really know what's in it. If you don't understand something ask questions. It will pay off. Most salesmen do not read their own product.

"And make eight sales calls a day. If you can't make eight, make seven. I would rather have a medium talented salesman making eight sales calls a day than a sensational salesman making two, because in the long run the person making eight is going to develop more relationships. And like I've been saying, the name of the game is relationships."

Circulation management

Creative circulation

By E. Daniel Capell

Someone has suggested that a good circulation director is, in many ways, a computer scientist. With all the sophisticated tools of modern circulation management available to him, the circulation director's decision-making process should be very analytic and scientific. To this I feel obligated to reply with a resounding, "Hogwash!"

I'll even go as far as to say that the circulator that *thinks* he is a computer scientist is wasting a lot of his time, and even more of his company's money.

The *creative* circulation director is part computer scientist and part riverboat gambler, with emphasis on the latter. Creative circulation management is knowing when to be practical, sometimes illogical, and above all, opportunistic — at times very unorthodox approaches to any business problem. By definition, to be *creative* in circulation is to know when, why, and how to take the best calculated risk.

The data available to analyze in circulation is much more than the human brain can cope with. Obviously, the computer helps to track, sort out, and put all this information into a more manageable framework. Because of the sheer volume of data and the interaction of all this data, circulators tend to think the circulation business is more complicated than it really is. Circulation directors are all guilty of hiding behind the "mystique" of circulation, and in so doing, have often isolated themselves from the other publishing departments of their company.

While at times, this is not necessarily a bad management approach, in general, this isolation has tended to make the *data* of the business seem more mysterious and more relevant than it really is.

We have been guilty of losing sight of what is really important in our business. When all is said and done, creative circulation management is a *sales business*. And, there isn't a computer in the world that can replace a good salesman.

The circulation department is really the only operation in a publishing company that can actually measure every dollar that it spends.

However, there isn't an advertising sales director in the world who can tell you with any certainty how many advertising pages he's going to run next year — he just doesn't know. He can make an educated guess, but the nature of his business just does not allow for accurately predicting advertising pages.

Herein lies the major stumbling block to effective overall publishing management. Of the two major revenue streams of any magazine, one is predictable and one is not, yet both areas *must* interact to plan a magazine's future effectively.

The circulation director must not only understand this dilemma, but also constantly force top management to focus its energies on solving the problem in the best possible way. Options continually present themselves to a circulation director that are not just circulation questions. They involve issues concerning readership quality and circulation growth—questions that cannot be answered in a vacuum.

Dealing with sales-related questions

Historically, the circulation directors have preferred the security and relative predictability of circulation, and frankly have been "turned off" by the seeming lack of control of the ad sales side of the business. Nothing can be more harmful to a publishing enterprise. The circulation director must force himself to address circulation/ad sales related questions.

Here is a typical example. The question that seems to arise annually is whether or not to grow in circulation. There are really only two possible reasons for circulation growth. First, there may be the possibility of additional, pure circulation profit tied to growth. Or second, there may be a compelling ad sales reason to grow, usually an advertising rate-related change. These two reasons may both be present, but usually the question of growth is an either/or proposition: that is, to grow for circulation profit *or* to grow for increased ad sales revenue.

How does the decision-making process usually work? The circulation department, with a reasonable degree of accuracy, can calculate the cost to acquire and maintain the additional circulation in the future. The exercise is really not that difficult to do for a circulation department that has a clear understanding of its incremental acquisition costs.

Let's assume that the circulation department has completed its work, and the numbers show that over the next three years, it is financially a break-even proposition for circulation to grow an additional 100,000. That is to say, from a circulation profit and loss point of view, the increased costs to acquire and maintain the additional circulation are roughly offset by increased revenues.

The ad sales department input into the growth/no growth decision now becomes critical. Since there is no compelling circulation reason to grow, the reason has to come from advertising sales. The dilemma is twofold: how many ad pages will be sold in the year ahead under a no growth and a 100,000 growth mode, and second, how do they price the growth to the advertiser.

In our example, since circulation's profit and loss is essentially unchanged by growing, *unless* ad sales is willing to pass on to its advertisers the full cost of the circulation growth and/or to maintain its current ad page level in a growth environment, the decision is clearly one of no growth. Because of ad sales' inability to confidently predict what might happen, the decision-making process usually hits a dead-end.

Here is where the circulation director must continue to press for an intelligent resolution of the question. He must cajole, and play devil's advocate until ad sales management is *forced* to make the best possible set of assumptions. And still, even if the circulation director has made this intelligent review happen, the publisher usually makes the final decision with his best educated guess. It is the duty of the circulation director, however, in reviewing just this kind of interdepartmental question, to step out of his day-to-day role and become the prime mover in the decision-making process.

Keep authority in day-to-day management

A circulation director must also know when it behooves him (and the company) to operate his business in a vacuum. Certain questions and problems requiring immediate decisions confront a circulation director almost daily. He must have the complete freedom to act unilaterally, without interference from anyone.

Everyone in this business of publishing *thinks* he is a circulation expert. Meddling in circulation matters has become a high art form by publishers, ad sales executives, and the like. The circulation director must know when to draw the line in the face of outside interference when it concerns the inner workings of his department. He is doing himself as well as his company a disservice by accepting anything less than complete authority in the day-to-day management of his business. This can be an extremely delicate problem, and suffice it to say, this issue has probably cost more than one circulation director his job.

Let me illustrate my point with the example of arrears. A circulation director, if he is on top of his business, knows whether or not he should carry additional arrears over his operating plan. His decision must be made at a particular point in time, based on all the information about the state of his business at that point in time. Usually, when a decision to add additional arrears has to be made, it is already too late to pursue other options. The decision may seem arbitrary to the outside observer, but the decision *must* be made, or the ability to recoup a negative position will be gone forever. When a decision is called for, such as adding arrears to maintain the advertising rate base, the circulation director must act quickly and decisively, and most important, unilaterally.

There are other examples where a circulation director must be able to manage his business free from outside interference. For example, a test result may show a clear winner, yet the circulation director may decide to ignore the results. There are so many factors, past and present, that a circulation director must weigh when interpreting a test result, that only he alone has the best sense of what action to take.

One final example, and this one comes up more than anyone would like to admit: Who has final approval of outside suppliers? The circulation director must have the final say concerning whom he does business with and why.

Here, more than anywhere else, circulation directors can drive accountants crazy because cost may be the

least significant determinant in picking a supplier. The reason is simple. Service in the circulation business is crucial. Deadlines face a circulation department every day. When a major direct mail campaign is scheduled to drop on January 2, *it has to get out*. All circulation planning is contingent upon meeting a series of critical delivery dates throughout the year. Meeting those dates is the paramount concern — in many cases, delivery is more important than cost.

Freedom in dealing with suppliers that can meet deadlines is one freedom that a circulation director must never give up.

Finding and managing bright people

Crucial to a well-run circulation department is an understanding of department structure and staffing needs. The circulation director's greatest challenge is structuring and managing his people effectively. This is no easy task.

The circulation business generally suffers from a dearth of good circulation talent. This has certainly led to the job-hopping syndrome that is common to this business. Finding and managing bright circulation people should be a circulation director's full-time concern.

Why is this such a difficult task? It's the nature of the circulation business that it is comprised of many specialized functions. People become expert in their particular area of concern (*e.g.*, direct mail, renewals, ABC, fulfillment, creative, etc.). But, very few people learn the entire business, and herein lies the problem.

It is just not practical to have more than two or three individuals involved in key circulation planning sessions. Many of the functional areas in circulation use the same disciplines, but very few jobs in a circulation department give people a chance to see all the pieces come together. Advancement in the department tends to be lateral, from one functional job to another. And, it is only after all the key functions are mastered that a person is equipped to really be a part of, and participate in, management of the entire business.

Move the best people laterally first

The circulation director has two basic challenges to address. He must hire the best possible functional people available, and then have the foresight to move the best of these people laterally in order to give them the widest exposure to all facets of the business. This requires a long-range commitment on the part of the circulation director, and no less of a commitment from the staff members involved in this series of lateral moves.

The circulation director must convince the key members of his staff that the *only* way to learn this business is from the ground up. Only through a thorough understanding of the "nitty gritty" of each functional area can a person be equipped to *manage* those areas in the future.

For example, the circulation director who has run a direct mail campaign and has an understanding of all the problems and headaches of that job is a circulation director that is best prepared to run that department intelligently. Only if you have done renewal schedules, prepared an ABC statement, etc., can you be properly equipped to direct your managers of these and other functions. Nowhere is it more important than in circulation management to have an appreciation of all the intricacies of each function in the department.

None of the above is meant to overshadow the

importance of good functional people who, for whatever reason, may not be equipped to be a part of overall circulation management. Nothing is more valuable to a circulation director than a reliable, hard-working manager of a particular functional area. The security of knowing that promotional plans will be carried through correctly and on time is of crucial importance to a circulation director. The circulation director should never lose sight of, or appreciation for, the jobs performed by his functional managers.

It's also as critical to department managers as it is to the circulation director to have adequate freedom in their day-to-day decision-making. Interference by the circulation director can be detrimental to the morale of the person involved, as well as to the smoothness of each department's operation. The creative circulation director understands and has an appreciation of these interrelationships. He knows when to step in and when to give his managers freedom. Without this management expertise, the circulation director will quickly lose the respect and control of his people.

Knowing how to budget and plan

The key to effective circulation management is knowing how to construct and use the best possible budgeting and planning system. The single most important ingredient of this system should be its flexibility. Its output should provide a guide to daily operational decisions.

The planning process in circulation should be a continuous operation. The preparation of a formalized, detailed budget (once or twice a year) should be looked upon as just one exercise in an ongoing planning process. This formal budget may be more detailed, and perhaps more exact than future update plans you may run during any twelve-month period. But, these updates are in reality more important to the circulation director. They provide the circulation director on a continual basis with the information needed to make his day-to-day operational decisions.

What do I mean by a less formal, ongoing system of updates? I mean that usually eight to 12 weeks after your formal budget is prepared, enough has changed to make it necessary to run a revision. This revision may be a plan for circulation level only without an associated profit-and-loss statement. An update should reflect revisions to key assumptions only. Its purpose is to see what the short-range (six to 12 months) effect is of these key factor changes.

An update is done to see whether a *major* change in an operational decision is needed or not. Usually an update is called for because new business production is higher or lower than anticipated.

Both a formal budget and an update are already out of date when they are completed. It is the nature of the circulation business, with its countless assumptions built upon other assumptions, that change is inevitable. Only by being as current as possible, *i.e.*, knowing where you are *vs.* where you said you would be and why, can you take full advantage of opportunity management. And as I pointed out earlier, the creative circulation director must be opportunistic above all else.

Remember that the budgeting process in circulation starts with really only one "given" — the expire inventory of your subscriber list at a particular point in time. Everything else in this business is an assumption based on some historical piece of data collected in the computer. The circulation director must interpret and manipulate this history into an ongoing set of operational plans.

The overriding purpose of operational plans is usually one of maintaining a fixed advertising rate base, which is really unique to our business. What other business wants to maintain a fixed number of buyers for their product? Always remember that it is not how *many* subscriptions you can sell, but what *kind* you can sell, and *when* you sell them. You must sell those subscriptions when you need them.

Dispelling circulation myths

Effective circulation planning requires a realistic and practical understanding of this business. So before getting into the actual planning process, let's dispel a couple of current myths about our business. First, circulation in the purest sense of the phrase is *not* a "profit center." Circulators like to fool themselves into thinking that they are a profit center. Try applying the physical costs of printing and distribution, as well as some portion of editorial costs, to your circulation "profit" and see what happens. The accountants have had a field day with circulation. The various cash and deferred subscription accounting practices in this business are too numerous to mention. Suffice it to say that circulation "profit" is a very nebulous term.

It is more important in evaluating circulation performance to be consistent in your methodology of comparison from quarter to quarter, year to year, etc. Also, always keep in mind the possible ramifications that circulation decisions will have on the other areas of publishing, even though those areas may not be a part of your circulation profit and loss. For example, increasing the newsstand draw may not affect your circulation profit (if circulation is not charged for the cost of copies), but it certainly can affect your magazine's profit and loss.

Another misunderstood area in this business is source evaluation. *(See chapter on source evaluation, page 267.)* The circulation director who thinks he is a computer scientist can be tested to the limits with this one. Endless hours can be spent with source profitability models, all aimed at ranking the relative performance over time of a given magazine's subscription sources. A lot of this effort is what I like to call mental gymnastics. Remember that in circulation you can usually prove anything you want to prove.

Let's be honest with ourselves and state once and for all that most large circulation consumer magazines have inflated circulation levels. By this I mean that most established magazines are pushed well beyond their so called "natural level" of circulation. Or put another way, people are not "beating down the doors" to subscribe to most magazines. Most editors would be shocked, to say the least, if they had a working knowledge of circulation response rates. Remember, we are a business that gets excited when two percent of the people respond — and usually 25 percent of them don't pay their bills! So remember, the purpose of circulation is to deliver a fixed number of buyers as "profitably" as possible in order to support and maintain a fixed advertising rate base. Source evaluation becomes to some extent a meaningless exercise if you need all the business you can get! We all know that insert cards are the most profitable new business source, but how many more cards can we get into one issue!

Know the leverage points of your business

Starting with one given (your most current expire inventory), any planning process begins with a review of all existing assumptions used in your last plan. This exercise can become extremely complex and time-consuming.

There are certain assumptions that are less critical than others. The creative circulation director knows the important factors from the not so important. I call these critical circulation assumptions the *leverage points* of your business.

Leverage points may vary by magazine, but certain ones always seem to be important *(e.g.,* renewal percent and new business acquisition costs). To understand the significance of your own particular critical leverage points is to manage your business profitably. All the planning in the world will not improve your circulation profit if you are spending your time worrying about the wrong things. The circulation director who spends time editing promotional copy, or analyzing the effectiveness of his seventh billing effort, or negotiating a 2 percent better remit from a subscription agent is wasting his time. His energies should be directed toward improving those particular elements (leverage points) of his business that have the most effect on his company's bottom line.

Because circulation is built on so many assumptions, circulation people have become some of the most conservative budgeters that ever lived. Overselling in this business can be even more detrimental than underselling. Bonus circulation delivered over your advertising rate base, assuming no circulation profit is made on it, is extremely costly. The advertiser is not paying for it. The odds are that it is the most expensive circulation you could possibly deliver. The object in this business should be to run as tight to your advertising rate base as possible.

Perhaps more than any other reason, bonus circulation is caused by a circulation director hedging his bet, *i.e.,* creating a budget that he knows he can beat. This is a common budgeting ploy, but perhaps nowhere is it more costly than in the circulation business.

The budgeting and planning procedures of a circulation department should be the most demanding part of the operation. Formal budgets and updates will only provide meaningful results if they are approached creatively. The volatile and ever-changing nature of circulation makes it an inexact science at best. Short-range (six to 12 months) planning in circulation should be the means used to establish longer-range planning decisions. The planning process should never really stop. The more current you are, and the clearer understanding you have of the leverage points of your particular publication, the better manager you will be.

Don't over-complicate an already very complex business by analyzing every detail of your operation, or always updating all your assumptions. It is more important in this business to act quickly and decisively. Your planning process must be designed to accomplish just that.

Know long-range implications of decisions

As pointed out, circulation management is really a series of short-range operational decisions. But, associated with almost all day-to-day operational decisions in circulation, there are longer-range implications. What seems like a minor decision today can have devastating future effects on your business. The dichotomy of the business is that sometimes, because of rate base requirements, poor long-range decisions must be made. When you need a lot of business quickly, your choices are usually limited to your least profitable sources. The *quality* of business that you sell may also be poorer, producing a slow deterioration in the demographic character of your list.

Again, the key to planning in circulation is to be current and on top of your business. Presumably, you will then not find yourself in the bind of making a short-range decision with detrimental long-range effects.

Computer modeling can play an important role here in developing your understanding of the long-range effects of various decision options. Modeling should be used primarily as a planning tool. There are really two critical pieces of information generated as a by-product from any model run. Assuming the run delivers the necessary paid circulation level, the two questions are:

1. How much new business is needed to meet that level?

2. How many renewals did you sell? And of what kind?

It is risky sometimes to oversimplify this business. But, usually, as a renewal production goes up, your new business requirement will go down. In most cases, a model run that shows movement in the direction of more renewals will be the more profitable plan. If your long-range plans do not show either a reduction in new business sales and/or an increase in renewal sales as a percent of your list, then it is time to rethink your operating plan.

To again keep all this in perspective, and at the risk of oversimplification, longer-range circulation profitability hinges on the nature of the new business that you sell today. Generally speaking, the more *voluntary* the source, the better that source will renew. By voluntary *(e.g.,* your own direct mail) I mean that the decision to subscribe has been made by the consumer without any pressure. In direct mail, for example, the potential subscriber has received your mailing, elected to open it, presumably read it, and has consciously decided to act. This source of new business will sometimes renew five, even ten times better than some *in*voluntary sources. In most cases, the subscriber from an involuntary source *(e.g.,* telephone sales) may have only bought to put an end to the pressure of the sales tactic used in the sale. That sales pressure will be reflected in poorer renewal performance.

Circulation is almost always a question of short-range decisions with long-range implications. After all, every current expire group is comprised of business sold in the past. How that business was sold originally, *i.e.,* its method of sale, will determine how that expire group will renew. No amount of creative genius will significantly improve the renewal percent of an expire group comprised of people who really didn't want to buy in the first place.

Nowhere are the dynamics of circulation more misunderstood, and profit sacrificed, than in not clearly understanding this new business/renewal cycle. Longer-range profits do not come cheaply. Usually, it costs more to initially buy high quality, better renewing business. The investment is certainly worth the price.

Nowhere in the business of circulation does the circulation director play a more creative role than in the determination of which prices to raise and when to raise them. One of the tools which the circulation director uses in determining prices is testing.

Evaluating a price test

All the ingredients of the circulation planning process are perhaps best illustrated by reviewing the methodology of evaluating a "simple" price test. The traditional approach, and perhaps still the best, is to test beforehand the various rates and terms that you anticipate moving to. Let's also assume in our hypothetical example that you have enough historical data around to evaluate the effect of prior price increases. Now let's "evaluate" the current price test results on our monthly magazine:

All tests are about the same price per issue ($1.16 to $1.20) *vs.* the control of $1.00 per copy. Also, let's assume that 18 months ago you raised your one-year price from $10 to $12, saw a 25 percent initial fall-off in response for three to four months, and recovered to the $10 response level within six months. All in all, the above scenario is a pretty typical set of circumstances.

If you assume that all other factors directly related to the various offers are equal *(e.g.* bad pay, percent cash, renewability, etc.) and if you assume the rate of price recovery would be about equal for each offer, then you really have only two possible winners (A or C). Panel C, 14 issues for $16.50, is the favorite because it gives you more term and more gross dollars with a reasonable falloff in response.

Panel A, ten issues for $12, may get the nod if the shorter term doesn't jeopardize your profit because you would have to sell more new business. It shows the least fall-off and the highest per issue price. A computer, through the use of a source profitablity model, will give you all the necessary permutations on the above test using a myriad of variable assumptions. You could then verify the reasonableness of your choice.

All good and proper and scientific. And, I say also, probably wrong! The creative side of your decision-making process is missing. That *feeling for the present state of your business* is lacking. Decisions in circulation cannot be made in a vacuum. That sixth sense about your business is what separates the creative circulation director from the rest of the pack.

Consider other factors

There are, first of all, a whole host of additional factors to consider when contemplating a price increase. Most factors are not as clearly defined as the straightforward results of your price test. To cover just two of them:

1. *Competition*

What is the competition doing? What's his price in relation to yours? Have you been the price leader in the field, or have you historically followed the competition's increases?

Are your circulation economics the same as the competition's? In other words, *should* you be priced higher or lower than he is? Is your goal circulation growth, or maintenance of your current circulation level in relation to the competition? To sum it up, even though your price test says go, there may be overriding competitive factors that can only be dealt with by having a certain *feel* for your product and its position in the marketplace.

The magazine circulation business is one of the most highly competitive businesses around. Competition comes not only from a direct competitor, but from other sources that you might not expect. Depending upon the subscription channel being used (subscription agencies, for example), competition comes from *all* the titles listed on their multiple magazine stampsheet. We are all after that same portion of the consumer's discretionary income that he is willing to spend on magazines. In the subscription agency example, it's the relationship of all the prices and offers listed, not just those of your direct competition. So keep in mind the environment where your offer is going to appear. That can be as important as your actual offer.

Competition is not just limited to price and where your offer will appear. Promotional competition can be the most severe, and possibly the most damaging aspect of our business. Really new promotional packages and ideas are few and far between in circulation. But, when one comes along, the exclusivity of that idea for any one magazine has a very short life span. Creative idea "theft" is the rule in our business. Probably no one factor is as important to a circulation director as his ability to always be on the leading edge of creative promotional breakthroughs. Remember that last year's new package is probably already being used by three other people.

2. *Which price*

Always keep in mind that any price test result is only valid for the particular subscription source that was tested. All sources have varying degrees of price sensitivity. To answer the question of which price(s) to raise, based on limited source test results, a circulator's creativity is taxed to the utmost. He has to ask these questions: Was the source that was tested one of your least, or one of your most price sensitive sources? How do you interpret the test data and apply it to other sources?

In answering these and other questions, there are always more unknowns than knowns to deal with. The key to success requires a circulation director to muster all historical knowledge of his product, his source of business, his market, and his competition's current and future strategy.

If you are really on top of your business, the answers to the above questions come quickly. To the casual observer, the conclusions may even seem arbitrary and capricious.

For competitive and price reasons, you may decide to go with ten months for $12 in a subscription agency mailing. In your own direct mail, maybe 14 months for $16.50 is your choice. Your reasons could range from a choice based on clear factual data on the one hand, to the extreme of pure hunch on the other.

A good circulation director must be in command of his business so he can capitalize on a situation quickly. He must also have had the foresight to have scheduled and run his price test long before contemplating a change. If a price test is set up in reaction to a competitor's increase, then the odds are that he has already missed the opportunity. It's the nature of the circulation business that when a price increase option presents itself, you must be prepared to act quickly. Frequently, if that opportunity is missed it may be gone forever.

Be aware of 'hedges'

In circulation management, the circulation director must have a thorough understanding of the rules of the Audit Bureau of Circulations (ABC) and how they apply to his business. Knowledge of ABC guidelines, as well as any outside restraints (FTC, postal, etc.), is essential to effective rate base management.

Certain techniques, which I call "hedges," are available to the circulation director. Most of these are provided for within the framework of the ABC rules. Others are not, and some are open to interpretation. Some of these hedges are early entry, deferral, and perhaps the most misunderstood and misused hedge of all — arrears.

Knowing the complexities of the circulation business, the difficulty of delivering a fixed rate base in such an inexact environment, ABC gave circulation directors the device of arrears to help smooth out their business. ABC allowed for arrears to be counted as ABC paid circulation for ad sales purposes.

"Arrears" is probably the most misunderstood term in the publishing business. A natural distrust of the term has evolved over the years, both from within and outside of publishing companies. Arrears has been declared inherently a bad thing, a sign of circulation weakness, and something to be avoided. When used intelligently and creatively, arrears can be the most effective management tool that a circulation director has.

In the budgeting and planning process, I find it is best to first run your circulation plan without carrying any arrears. This plan becomes your base plan. Arrears can then be added to this base plan.

There are various reasons why you would want to add arrears. First, arrears can be used to carry your circulation through a particularly unprofitable new business acquisition period. Why spend a fortune for new orders, say in June and July, if historically this is your worst mailing period? If, for example, August is a better performing month, maybe arrears should be used selectively in the June-July period and then dropped in August when new business performance is expected to improve.

A creative director should spend the time to *prove* to management the positive profit ramifications of carrying arrears selectively. Only then will a large part of the negative connotation of arrears vanish.

Explain arrears to advertisers

Dealing with the ad sales community on arrears questions does not have to be as difficult as publishers always seem to make it. Point out to your advertisers that circulation has a seasonal nature not unlike most businesses. But, and here is the big difference, magazines are forced to maintain a fixed number of buyers (rate base) for a predetermined time frame (rate card). Ask the greeting card people what they would do if forced to maintain their fourth quarter sales volume in May, June, and July. Ask the suntan lotion people how they fare in January. And, how much of Seagram's business is holiday related? The problem in circulation is rather unique: We have to sell just as hard year round. Arrears is one technique available to us to help smooth out our selling cycles.

The above example is an obvious use of arrears. Just as important is its use in the ongoing planning operation of circulation. If you see danger ahead, based on current performance trends, you may elect to carry arrears as a safeguard against possible poorer future performance. The lengthy lead time needed to properly plan for arrears makes it all the more necessary to be always on top of your business. It may be better to plan to carry the arrears as a hedge, even though you may find when the results are in that it wasn't necessary.

Here again you must know the ABC rules. You may elect, *after the fact*, at the time you file your ABC statement, to not claim as paid circulation the arrears that you delivered. By simply moving the arrears carried to the unpaid circulation category, you have solved two problems. First, you sleep better at night by carrying the arrears. And, second, because you didn't need the arrears for your rate base and moved it to unpaid distribution, you have alleviated any possible advertiser objections.

Not only must you understand the "rules of the game," but also it behooves you to understand how to use those rules to your advantage. One additional point on arrears. The more this term is demystified and taken for what it really is, (*i.e.,* a planning device), the better off our business will be. Publishers and advertising agencies alike deserve to know exactly what arrears are, and why, when, and how arrears are used.

Using 'early entry' and 'deferral'

There are other hedges in the circulation business. Early entry, and its reverse, deferral, are two of the more useful techniques available to circulation directors. In tight circulation times, early entry, or advancing the start

issue of a subscription, is an excellent device to use. The gain in circulation is a temporary one, but certainly can provide you with added paid circulation in a relatively short period of time. This assumes, of course, that your fulfillment house is equipped to handle just such a contingency.

One important point to remember is that the use of early entry on an ongoing basis creates a false sense of security. You will have to sell the new business at some point, because remember, all you are really doing by starting a sub early is causing that sub to expire sooner as well. Depending on the frequency of your publication, early entry may also mean better service for the customer. In the case of some monthlies a negative effect may also be created (*i.e.,* two issues may arrive at the same time).

Deferral, or holding orders for a later than normal start issue, is still another technique available. By deferring the entry of subs, in a time of circulation plus, you can smooth out your paid circulation by issue. A warning here — watch the Federal Trade Commission 30 day rule closely; subscriber notification of a delayed start may be necessary. Deferred entry of subs also has the side benefit of pushing expire dates further out, thus temporarily, at least, reducing future new business requirements.

Remember, both early entry and deferral techniques provide temporary solutions only. They are devices to be used with care. But, they *should* be used when current circulation performance dictates they are strategically useful.

Arrears, early entry, and deferral are just some of the tools of the circulation trade. There are others like the ABC 2 percent allowance and bulk sales rules. One of my favorite circulation hedges is the actual wording you choose to use on your advertising rate card. Words like "guarantee," "average paid," or "distribution" should be selected and used with care. A thorough understanding of the rules of the business can only improve your bottom line.

There are many things that can go wrong with any circulation operating plan. Let me stress again that to deliver bonus circulation can be just as costly as missing your rate base. A working knowledge of what I call the "hedges of the business" makes it easier to run a tight net paid circulation in relation to your rate base.

Carefully select the basic subscription price

This business may begin to sound like there are enough options available to always be able to recoup any unfavorable position. That is to a certain extent true, but certainly not always. Keep in mind the most significant constraint under which we all operate—the ABC 50 percent of basic rate regulation. The magazine business may be one of the few businesses whose pricing structure is governed by its own auditing rules! ABC rules dictate what is to be counted as paid circulation and what is not. Can you imagine General Motors being told that if it sells a car at 50 percent off its suggested retail price, that car can't be counted as a properly sold unit? A little far fetched, perhaps. But, the 50 percent of basic rate sold rule points out how important it is to properly establish just what your basic price is. Pricing decisions in circulation are too often improperly thought through to their ultimate consequences.

Let me explain. In this business the basic subscription price should be a benchmark only. The important price is the one at which you are going to sell the majority of your business. Too often this very simple premise is overlooked in our business. If you are selling the bulk of your business at basic prices, that makes your basic price very important. If you are using heavily discounted offers, then your basic price is only important as a means of comparision. When raising the price, the question should always be, "Which price?" Or more important, how much of my ongoing business will be affected by the increase?

Some price increases are purely cosmetic. The overriding consideration should be the gross dollar amount of the offer that will be your primary solicitation. Consumers are not aware of, nor do they seem particularly affected by, the price per issue. Being overly concerned with copy rates is an affliction common to circulation directors. The important number to your customers is the amount they have to make out their check for.

Affecting newsstand sales

As much as it hurts me to do this, I must say a few words about the newsstand side of this business. The newsstand business is certainly the most frustrating segment of circulation. To this day, I'm still not certain whether or not it is possible for the circulation director to positively affect, in a meaningful way, his magazine's newsstand sale. My hunch is that the newsstand buyer is governed primarily by impulse. And more important, that impulse purchase is to a great extent dictated by what is on the cover. This relationship between cover subject and impulse behavior will vary in importance by the nature of your publication.

The primary responsibility of a circulation director is to see to it that his product is made readily available at the best possible mix of retail outlets. A good cover, properly displayed, will sell. What makes this side of the business frustrating is that usually a good cover, poorly displayed, will also sell! The newsstand manager therefore spends most of his time improving his distribution and displays to enhance the sale of his *poorer* selling covers.

There are other factors which make single-copy sales a difficult business for subscription people to understand. The newsstand sales system is comprised of a whole chain of middlemen, from national distributor through wholesaler to retailer. It is truly a nickel and dime business. Your particular title is perhaps one of 50 handled by your national distributor, and one of perhaps 3,000 handled by each of your wholesalers.

The circulation director, at home with the subscription side of his business, feels out of control when it comes to newsstand sales. He cannot see the direct results of his actions. He must depend on everyone in the sales chain. To run a newsstand test that is meaningful is almost impossible. The number of outside influences affecting the sale produce an impossible testing environment. When a circulation director can't believe in his test results, he certainly can't effectively manage his business.

There is still another problem inherent in the newsstand sales chain. The profit goals of a publisher and wholesaler can frequently be at odds with each other. And *both* parties can be right!

A publisher may be more interested in the number of units sold than the sales percentage (sale to draw). He is weighing his additional newsstand circulation against his most unprofitable subscription source. That can easily mean that it makes sense to sacrifice sales efficiency if it means more units of circulation will be sold.

On the other hand, a wholesaler's main expense is in the processing of returns. His goal is efficiency. The higher the sales percentage the fewer the returns.

Both the publisher and the wholesaler in the above example are, for their own very good business reasons, moving in opposite directions!

Relationship marketing: The art of courting subscribers

By Ted Bartek

Successful magazine marketing involves much more than just selling subscriptions and renewing them when they are about to run out. Instead, every single contact with a prospect or an active subscriber must be considered an integral part of the overall marketing relationship with that individual. In relationship marketing, every piece of prospect mail, billing letter or renewal notice is considered a personal contact with the individuals who compose your market. Futhermore, each contact forms an indelible image of you, your company, and your magazine in the minds of your subscribers.

Since this determines how your suscribers react to you, every message you send—the offer, the tone of the copy, the positioning of your product, the price, the tone and timing of renewals, and collections, guarantees, bonus offers, payment terms and options—should be carefully planned. Not only should they not clash with or contradict one another, they should actually enhance one another.

Before we attempt to create an integrated marketing relationship with our subscribers, however, we must understand the motivation and behavior of the subscribers in our market. Why do people do what they do? Why do they subscribe in the first place? Why do some cancel? Why do some renew?

Why do they buy?

There have been many volumes written on why people respond to direct mail copy. I won't go into all the theory. Most of you have seen much of it. It all boils down to one undeniable fact: Before *anyone* buys *anything*, he or she must believe that it's worth much more than it costs.

The job of the direct marketer, then, is to demonstrate the value and worth of a product, while minimizing the product's costs.

To expand the product's worth, he can appeal to the prospect's imagination and emotions. By highlighting factors which will improve the reader's life—becoming wealthy, getting ahead in career, being stylish, improving personal relationships, satisfying curiosity, gaining recognition, being loved, getting inside information—he can exploit the product's inherent "dream value."

This is *the key* to selling through the mail, but it should be done thoughtfully. Given the enthusiasm of most copywriters, it is not difficult to find glowing product descriptions that truly inflate the dream value of a product out of proportion to reality. Although such copy can tip the balance in favor of the sale, netting short-run success, it also can create problems in later phases of the marketing relationship.

To add weight to the buy side of the balance, the addition of product benefits and features, proof elements, explanation, demonstration, reasons why, guarantees and incentives will help close the sale.

Another way to consummate a sale is to undersell or downplay the commitment. "Send for your four free trial issues." "We ask no payment now." "This is strictly a trial . . . no need to decide now." In effect, this reduces *what it costs* in the prospect's mind, thereby lightening the weight on the "don't buy" side of the balance, and making him more likely to respond.

But this too can be taken too far. If the subscription obligation is obscured too much, the subscriber will respond out of sheer greed without any sense of his obligation to subscribe and pay for a subscription.

When a soft offer is used, the entire offer, including an honest disclosure of the subscription obligation that we want from the subscriber, should be presented. Of course, the copywriter's challenge is to present the *entire* proposition is such a way that it is understood and *accepted* by the prospect. Without the prospect's acceptance, the copywriter has not really made the sale; he's only gained the prospect's interest and gotten him to act. Part of a copywriter's job is to build enough real benefits into his sales pitch so that the prospect can digest all the ramifications of the sale, and still perceive the offer as being worth more than it costs. If he doesn't, he is merely stealing from later phases of the marketing relationship.

Why do people cancel?

Obviously, cancellations result from distortions of the order solicitation phase of direct marketing. Of course, a certain number of cancellations are randomly generated. They are expected and tolerable within limits. But significant problems with cancellations are the result of subscriber disappointment.

A subscriber becomes disappointed when the magazine he receives in the mail falls short of his expectations. To paraphrase the words of Tom Collins, a subscriber cancels because anticipation has exceeded realization.

The reasons become obvious in light of the concepts we've covered so far. Hollow *dream value* feeds a prospect's expectations, and the language of many soft offers obscures the costs of his actions—both leading to disappointment and increasing the incidence of cancellations.

The solutions are equally obvious. First, eliminate all the fluff and promises that give your prospect false hopes. Second, replace them with as many sound solid benefits as you need to sell your prospect fully enough that he can accept a full commitment to buy and still feel the balance is weighted in his favor.

Finally, word your collection letters firmly. They can be courteous, humorous, casual, warm and friendly and still be a firm request of a creditor to pay a bill he's rightfully obligated to pay. Some of the best collection series alternate between a letter that is warm and friendly in tone and one that is direct and even threatening.

But don't make the mistake some publishers make of wording collection letters apologetically because they had offered an option to cancel in the new order solicitation. Just because a publisher has given a subscriber the *option* to cancel doesn't mean that the subscriber hasn't become obligated to pay the bill by accepting the offer. He is. And you are well within your rights to encourage, even demand, payment, You certainly don't have to be apologetic about it. Collections will improve if you follow this advice. And your task will be much easier if your new order solicitations are worded with this objective in mind.

Why do people renew?

People renew for entirely different reasons than they subscribe in the first place. The cost of the magazine versus its perceived worth is no longer the issue. And it's a mistake to continue to think in those terms. People have a relationship now with the magazine and are used to receiving your issues every month. By the time they receive your renewal solicitation, they have formed a subjective evaluation of what the magazine means to them. This evaluation is based in part on the magazine itself and whether it has delivered what the reader had anticipated. It depends far less, at this point, on the attractive mental images created by the imagination of a good copywriter.

People renew when the whole experience with the magazine is greater than what they had expected. The job of the relationship marketer in getting renewals, therefore, is to enrich the experience of the subscriber while eliminating unrealistic expectations. A subscriber's experience of a publication depends on a number of factors.

Benefits delivered/benefits expected

The benefits delivered by your magazine may differ from the benefits expected by the subscriber. However, the only benefits that count in relationship marketing are the ones delivered *and received* by the subscriber, and these will be a major influence on renewals.

If your renewals are suffering, determine whether your magazine is delivering the benefits expected by your subscribers. If not, then either your subscribers are harboring unrealistic expectations or you're not delivering benefits they can reasonably expect to receive.

Eliminate unrealistic expectations. From the very beginning, you can eliminate from your new order solicitation, from your billing letters and from your renewal series all references which promise or imply benefits which you can't reasonably expect to deliver. This may sound harsh, but it's not. It will open the door to replacing them instead with expectations you *can* deliver—convincingly and dramatically.

For example, a tax publication had a renewal problem—the subscribers were oversold; they expected too much. It was unrealistic to expect to be given *so much* tax-saving advice. When the copy was toned down, it not only eliminated false expectations, it also became more believable. And that which remained—the tax advice one could reasonably expect to obtain—was more than enough to justify subscribing to and renewing the publication.

Deliver reasonable expectations. You're in the business of satisfying legitimate subscriber needs and expectations. If your renewal rate begins to suffer because you're not delivering on benefits your reader can reasonably expect, it's time to immediately take stock of your editorial platform—and realign it to *conform to the dominant* needs of your reader audience.

Positive publication concept

People expect magazines to communicate in a certain way. A political commentary is expected to be brash and irreverent, fearless in its blunt attacks on established institutions, controversial issues, and revered public figures. On the other hand, a journal covering the art of classical music would be expected to speak with the highest standards of courtesy, good taste, and decorum.

You as a relationship marketer should carry out the tone of this communication in every message to subscribers. Therefore, it's important to define *in written samples* the tone of your magazine and to check each promotion letter, brochure, renewal promotion and collection letter for it. Over time it will pay off by giving your magazine a distinct and clear image in the minds of subscribers and potential subscribers.

Habit structure

How well your magazine becomes integrated into the life of your subscribers will have a major effect on renewals. There are a number of things you can do as a relationship marketer to make it easier for your subscribers to put your publication to work in their daily lives.

Make subscribers into friends. Integrate them into your subscriber group as soon as possible. Start by sending them a welcome letter describing your magazine and its unique contributions. Explain any background or technical details they may need to understand the magazine and how they may use it to their best advantage.

I know one publisher whose major contribution is a complex system of charts and graphs for understanding and anticipating the savings of various financial markets. His magazine is useless without an explanation of the workings of these diagrams. So as part of the subscription he sends new subscribers a detailed explanation of how to read and interpret his system of financial analysis. This way they'll immediately form the habit of using his service . . . and will be more likely to renew.

But don't stop here. Continue to cultivate the goodwill you have brought into the relationship. One publisher I know sends a short note to each subscriber about two months before the renewal series begins, thanking him for his continued patronage with no strings attached. When tested against a group who received no letter, it was found that the letter more than paid for itself in increased renewals. Another direct marketer sends a small booklet about halfway through the subscription, with the same result . . . a good direct marketing relationship and loyal subscribers with the *habit of renewing.*

Another way to generate customer goodwill is to mail thoughtfully. You can mail thoughtfully by considering your subscribers and their unique needs and special circumstances. One way to do this is to time your mailings to coincide with the special personal needs of your subscribers. Promote the renewal of a horticulture magazine

across the board to all subscribers in early spring. Send your advance renewal to your tax newsletter subscribers so that they can have your renewal subscription premium in time to use it in preparation of this year's tax return. These thoughtful marketing activities improve response while promoting future good will.

The renewal series

By the time you begin your efforts to renew your subscribers, they have formed a clear perception of your publication and the part it plays in their lives. For some the image is either positive or negative—but many are indifferent. Your renewal series should be written with these facts in mind and the various phases of the series should be developed with these three distinct groups of people in mind.

Advance efforts. The first one or two efforts in the renewal series should acknowledge the receipt of the initial order and encourage people to renew right away—sometimes without even seeing the first issue.

These efforts take advantage of the initial positive mood of your new subscribers—the delight of experiencing the first issues of a publication.

This initial advantage can be further enhanced by offering an incentive for renewing early—perhaps a premium, but more appropriately the opportunity to extend the subscription an additional year or two at the same savings as the original new order, i.e., double your savings, etc.

Another appeal used in advance renewal efforts is that by renewing early the subscriber "gets it out of the way" or saves himself the trouble of receiving any more renewal notices.

Early efforts. This is the "official" beginning of the renewal series, most often five to six months before expiration. These early efforts are best approached with the expectation that most subscribers are satisfied with the product and have every intention of renewing—as soon as they are given the signal. Therefore, the objective of these efforts should be to simply signal, loud and clear, that now is the time to act. And many do act. About 50 percent of those who are going to renew will do so on these first two or three efforts.

These early efforts do not have to try to "sell" the subscription again. Attempts to persuade on these early efforts could backfire—and turn off those who are already sold on the magazine. Reserve incentives, persuasion and other high pressure tactics for the more obstinate ones who will be around to receive later efforts.

Efforts right before expiration. These efforts are most important to the success or failure of your renewal series. If handled carefully they can swing a great many borderline people into the subscriber rolls for another year. It's much more difficult to "convince" an expire to reinstate his subscription once the expiration date has passed.

You can use the "impending event"—the upcoming expiration date of the subscription—to create a sense of urgency for the procrastinators who have been putting off the decision.

And as the expire date draws closer, you can build up the sense of urgency and drama. Add to this the vision of the loss the subscriber will feel if he allows the subscription to run out. Bring up feelings about the ongoing relationship the subscriber has had with your publication and with you. Personalize the publication—"We're going to miss you," etc. That's how a relationship marketer can successfully appeal to subscribers who are indifferent.

Efforts right after expiration. These efforts should continue to play on the themes used in the prior efforts, but they can be more persuasive in tone. They should emphasize the *benefits* of the magazine . . . benefits now *lost* to the subscriber. But point out that it's "not too late, we still have your name on file and can continue your service without interruption if you reply quickly," etc.

The effort following this—"your name has been dropped from our active file"—really dramatizes the finality of the action. It also can show some feeling of disappointment on your part: "We've tried to please you. We've given you *benefit* and *benefit*. But to no avail. We must have done something wrong."

Next to last effort. In one last attempt to move some of the last obstinate holdouts, go back to the strategy used with new order solicitations. There are many reasons why these people have not renewed. Most have formed a negative impression of the value of the publication. It all comes down to the price of the subscription in relationship to the perceived value of the magazine. You can attempt to build up the perceived value by dramatizing *benefits.* And you might be able to dislodge a few more of the holdouts by lowering the *price.*

You couldn't actually lower the price per copy—for that would just reward people with a discount for waiting until the end of the renewal series (a practice which has been known to backfire on publishers on later renewal efforts to the same people).

However, the commitment—the total price—could be lowered by reducing the term offered—perhaps to six months instead of a year. This could be very appealing to those who have been resisting because of price.

Last mail effort. The last direct mail offer could be called the "last chance" offer. "Our last attempt to reach you, before we drop your name completely from our active promotion file." The use of a double post card could dramatize the offer and save money.

Last effort. The remaining expire tapes should be sent to an effective telephone marketing organization for a final attempt. Telephone renewals could be made even more profitable by attempting to sell other products with the renewal—other magazines, books, seminars, etc.

Renewal strategy

Renewals are extremely important to the long-term profitability of magazines that rely on continued subscriber support.

Thus, the structure of the renewal strategy—price and term—are vital to the success of the sales effort. Prices and terms set too high or too low will result in disaster.

Prices and terms should be set to optimize overall subscription profitability. By overall subscription profitability, I mean the highest net revenue (new order revenue plus renewal revenue minus cancellations) per 1,000 pieces of prospect mail.

In subscription relationship marketing, in most cases, the scarcest resource is neither money nor order volume. Most publishers have access to as much cash as they need to mail profitably and, despite some exceptions where rate base is a limitation, most will generate as many orders as they can profitably.

Instead, the scarcest resource is the number of names a publisher has available to mail each year. Thus, evaluating direct mail results as a ratio of profit per dollar spent or profit per order is meaningless. The objective of the game of relationship marketing is to maximize overall net profit per *available name* or, in this case, per 1,000

pieces of available prospect mail.

The biggest danger in renewal and new subscription pricing is to create too much of a spread between the two prices. If the up-front offer is effectively priced at say one-half the renewal price, the front-end promotion might flourish, but the step up to full price might kill the renewal promotion before it has a chance.

On the other hand, if front-end prices are raised so that it's not such a big step up to renew, the offer might lose its attraction to prospect names. In addition, overall profits may be eroded if renewals are lowered to a price closer to the new order price. There would not only be less renewal revenue per copy, there would also be a lower front-end response because of the lessening of the promotable discount rate.

It is a difficult question and there are no clear-cut guidelines. Each relationship marketer has to test the variables for himself.

Renewal promotion should emphasize long-term renewals. In order to maximize overall profitability per 1,000 prospect names mailed, the relationship marketer should strive to get a maximum amount of revenue from each contact with the subscriber. The best way to do this is to develop a renewal offer that stresses at every point the advantages of long-term renewals.

Such a strategy will:

•Increase average revenue per renewal (stressing two- and three-year renewals could increase renewal revenue significantly—50 percent to 100 percent in some cases);

•Increase the size of the customer base (giving more marketing depth and providing list rental revenue);

•Improve renewal cash flow (providing money this year instead of next, thereby shortening the time you have to wait to make a profit on a subscriber);

•Increase renewal profits (getting the money sooner increases profits, due to the time value of money. Will also get many people this year for two or three years who would not be willing to renew again next year);

•Lower renewal costs (by not having to mail renewal promotions to these same people next year).

Two misconceptions

There are two common misconceptions about a strategy that emphasizes and encourages long-term renewals. These misconceptions may have come about because, although they do not apply to relationship marketers, they might apply to publishers whose main marketing position is not a long-term relationship with subscribers.

Misconception #1: If we pursue a strategy of seeking long-term subscriptions, we will forgo renewal revenue at a high price in future years.

The answer to this, of course, is that the increase in profits and the reduction in costs will more than cover future renewals at a higher price. What's more, there's no guarantee that renewals gotten this year will renew at some future time.

Misconception #2: A buildup of long-term subscription commitments will lock us into a fixed sales price while obligating us to deliver copies at some future time at a higher cost.

The answer: The margin on most magazines sold in a relationship form of marketing is high—the sales price is much higher than the production cost. Therefore, the incremental cost of producing a number of additional copies on each print run is small in comparison to the time value of the high profit margins realized on the additional subscription revenue.

The ultimate in long-term renewal

The publishing industry is the one service business that assumes its customers need to be resold on its services at intermittent periods of time. Why is a lengthy renewal series—designed to re-sell subscribers on the merits of your service—either necessary or expected? In fact, it may not be the most cost-effective method of carrying on a marketing relationship with subscribers.

There are other ways. The ultimate long-term renewal is a subscription in perpetuity—a continuous renewal commitment in which the subscriber, once he agrees to it, is *assumed* to have an ongoing relationship with the publisher unless he notifies him otherwise.

This is based on the premise that the best way to renew subscribers is simply to adapt Newton's Law to human behavior: "Whatever (whoever) is in motion tends to stay in motion unless stopped or diverted by some outside force."

There are lots of ways to do it. One way is to sell continuous service on a negative option. You could guarantee the subscriber savings of a certain amount (a percentage off the regular published price as the bookclubs do). The discount price would be calculated to give the same amount of renewal revenue you get from your current renewal program, since most publishers discount their two- and three-year subscriptions. This is calculated by taking a weighted average of the renewal revenue per order of your one-, two-, and three-year renewals.

In return, the subscriber would agree to be a customer for life or until he decides to cancel. You would just notify him every year or two of his obligation to pay for another year or two of service, presenting it to him as a negative option. "If we don't hear from you in the next 10 days, we will extend your subscription for another two years and bill you accordingly at X percent off the current regular subscription price of ±X." Of course, for this to qualify as a bona fide negative option, it must meet certain FTC disclosure requirements. But it can be designed to be effective within these guidelines.

The major advantage of using the negative option to secure continuous service commitments from subscribers, in addition to the cost savings, would be an increase in renewal rates. This is based on one important fact of consumer psychology: A large number of people who would not respond actively to promotions would, under certain circumstances, allow a company to enter a sale for them automatically.

The negative option approach has been used successfully to improve the sales of bookclub main selections. Indeed, the advantage of the negative option is so great that it as much as doubles response is some clubs.

Newspapers have been sold this way for years. Once a newspaper is ordered, it continues to be delivered and billed regularly until the order is cancelled. And it can work with other publications.

Guarantees and premiums

Guarantees and premiums pull little weight in re-newal promotion where the subscriber already has a clear picture of who you are and what you can be counted on to do. Premiums can be effective, though, in later efforts to dislodge obstinate holdouts from their renewal dollars—especially if they appeal to the same emotions that resulted in the original subscription.

Payment terms, on the other hand, can have a significant impact on renewal rates. Failure to offer credit on a renewal offer can significantly reduce the results.

Amount of need satisfied

The amount of need satisfied is an important variable affecting the decision to renew or not. If a subscriber has renewed before, there is a higher probability that he will renew again, but only to a point. In general, the more his need for your magazine has been satisfied by the editorial material (including premiums, bonuses and supplements) you have sent him over the years, the less likely he is to renew.

There are a number of things you can do to improve your chances of renewing subscribers:

Reach them early. Advance renewals and renewals at birth are effective means of striking the reader when the iron is still hot. This strategy improves renewal profitability (by shortening the amount of time a new subscription becomes profitable), improves cash flow, and in many cases improves the overall renewal rate by inciting some people to renew now, who later might decide not to renew at all.

Renew them for the long term. This tendency of subscribers to become disinclined to renew as their need for the publication is satisfied is another reason to renew them for a long term. If a relationship marketer doesn't get the longest order he can from each customer contact, he may not get another chance at a later date.

Don't use premiums needlessly. Just like your issues, premiums will fill the need of your subscriber for your publication. If you have a problem with low conversion rates or high cancellations, take a look at your premium. You may be fulfilling his readership interest with your premium causing him to lose interest in your publication.

Provide good service. All of us have some expectation of service from every business we deal with. Some expectations are higher than others. We expect a lot less from a Burger King order-taker than we do from a waiter at The Four Seasons. However, most people have *very* high expectations of mail order and publishing companies and will cancel or fail to renew if these expectations are not met—to the chagrin of many publishers and fulfillment houses.

But facts are facts and we must live with them. Every effort you can make to coax more compliance out of your fulfillment house to improve customer service will inevitably result in higher renewals. It's a fact of life of a relationship marketer.

The rules of the circulation game

By J. Wendell Forbes

One of the most pressing problems facing publishers is the question of how much the public should pay for a magazine.

Public benefit is (hopefully) at the root of publishing and it follows that magazines should be made available to as large a segment of the public as possible at the lowest possible cost.

Inflation and cost increases however, stand in the way of this ideal and the customer must now pay more for his or her magazines. Few publishers, however, seem to realize the consequences of arbitrary price increases and some have missed the point that low *as possible* prices are still critical to publishing concepts. "Possible" is the key word.

A solution must be found for their economic survival by eliminating unnecessary expenditures for circulation and providing advertisers with value for their dollar. A magazine has a right to be what its management wants it to be, but it must be prepared to live with the results. Past history has proved that the industry is not served by unrealistic races for circulation numbers or uneconomical circulation methods. As a result cost per thousand becomes too high for diluted readership and total page rates begin to rival TV spot charges.

To examine this question, it is necessary to study the economic interplay among the various elements that make up the publishing formula. These elements are the advertising rate base, the cost of maintaining that rate base (circulation expense-income ratio), editorial value as perceived by the public and the amount the public is asked to pay.

This analysis makes several important assumptions:

• That publishing is a contributory enterprise that seeks as its purpose to meet the needs, raise the standards and encourage the aspirations of its audience in matters of thought, information, entertainment and service. It is further assumed that there is a desire to communicate with as large an audience as possible and that it be done at a profit.

• That the product of publishing is the reader not the magazine. It is the reader delivered, in a given editorial environment, to the advertiser who earns the advertising revenue. The advertiser pays for the right to communicate with the reader.

• That magazines are sold to the public with "reasonable persuasion." Reasonable persuasion is held to include all standard methods of selling including special techniques of direct response selling.

• That reasonable persuasion be defined in expense-income terms rather than in terms of sales techniques. A circulation expense-income ratio of 50-60 percent is judged to be a reasonable maximum.

Publishers (assuming they are in command) must produce a better product for the advertisers. New relationships must be invented. *Above all there must be a readership-editorial fit.* With a sensible readership-editorial fit, circulation selling costs will go down as people indicate a willingness to pay for a magazine they really want. Improved circulation revenues therefore come from higher prices charged the reader and lowered selling expense due to greater receptivity for the product. All this will happen at circulation levels much lower than those currently extant.

Paying Too Much

Publishers have been paying more than they should for circulation and, in fact, would not use these costly methods if they were not trying to bolster up a magazine whose involvement with its readers is sagging, to fight a competitive battle with another publication guarantee. Remove these causes and the charade would be over. No longer would circulation be "bought" with the sole intent of boosting advertising rates. Circulation would be sold with a view to demand and be governed by the more conventional rules of product demand.

When circulation prices are increased, one of three things must happen:

1. If the rate base is to be maintained, the circulation expense-income ratio will increase leaving less circulation net than before.

2. If the circulation expense-income ratio is held, then the rate base must come down.

3. If the magazine is lucky enough to have a reserve reader acceptance, then the price to the public can be increased without lowering the rate base *or* increasing the circulation expense-income ratio.

Most publications are overextended in circulation. The last 15-20 percent of their circulations are costing much more than the 50-60 percent maximum suggested. This has been caused by the numbers battle among publications and it is still very much with us. (The demise of *Life, Look* and *The Saturday Evening Post* has not eliminated the numbers race. It's just not so dramatic. It's more subtle these days.) Rate bases have been inflated with pressure-sold circulation to bring in more ad revenue and/or establish numerical superiority over the competition without regard for the cost in circulation dollars.

Some publications would continue to have a mass audience, but most mass magazines as we know them today would have far fewer readers. Each magazine has its own economics which are largely dictated by its editorial appeal. To repeat, most magazines are oversold to some extent. A magazine is free to seek its own audience level but that audience must represent a fit with its editorial content. And above all, if a publisher is to charge more for his or her magazine, increased value must be given.

The responsibility to get the magazine industry back in shape lies with the magazines themselves. Advertisers and agencies won't force the issue because it's not really their problem; they don't have a research solution. They seem willing to play the numbers game as long as the publishers are—both perhaps knowing that the end is in sight. It's like taking dope—they can't stop—the publishers can't stop—or can they?

Increasing subscription prices is not that simple, however. By charging more there will be fewer buyers and fewer buyers means less circulation. (The demand for magazines is not inelastic.) To keep circulation up, it is necessary to spend more circulation promotion dollars, thus netting little if anything from the increase.

Publishers must bite the bullet and restructure their formulas to accommodate new economic relationships. No one part of the publishing formula can be meddled with without affecting the others.

It is unrealistic for magazines to make a circulation retreat in concert, for that is an improbable thought. For one magazine to do it would take courage, because it may lose, only to have others follow and win. The magazine that does it first must be prepared to battle the ignorances that are rife in the industry and if necessary expose the foolish economics of publishing for all to see.

The Need for a Buoyant Editorial Product

The importance of editorial material in any publishing maneuver cannot be underestimated. Taking pressure off circulation sales by reducing requirements is not enough—not nearly enough. A buoyant editorial product is essential. An editorial product so in tune with its buyers that selling costs represent no more than 50-60 percent of revenues is mandatory.

If there is a need to increase circulation prices then the following steps are necessary to achieve a balanced publishing formula:

1. Increase circulation prices by 20-25 percent.
2. Plan on selling 20 percent fewer magazines.
3. Lower circulation base by 5-10 percent.

Unless the publication is badly out of balance to begin with, this should bring most of the increased circulation revenue to the bottom line. The above steps may have to be repeated in 18 months.

In truth, the starting point toward economic sanity would be to reduce the rate base and change nothing else.

This would take the pressure off circulation and permit the expense-income ratio to move toward 50-60 percent. For reasons of image this apparently cannot be done.

Assessing the impact of any size circulation magazine acknowledging its past sins and dramatically reducing its circulation is not easy. Sure, it is not hard to develop a firm, logical and hard-hitting rationale for such a move attendant with letters to agency presidents, advertising managers and full-page announcements in the general and trade press. What is hard to assess is the *true* reaction of those people who control advertising expenditures. Will those who applaud the courageous move place their orders for advertising? Will they turn their backs and continue to buy numbers because that's all they know? More than likely, they will. Reducing circulation, therefore, is not enough. (As the prices go up, readers start convincing themselves that they don't need all those magazines they are getting.) It is essential to develop and prove reader involvement. Which comes first? Reader involvement does, because it can be spotted as strength in various segments of circulation selling and it will determine how much circulation can be retained in creating a sound publishing formula.

Advertisers and agencies must recognize that publishers will be going through an adjustment period and not start predicting a magazine's demise just because its base is lowered several hundred thousand.

Magazines have a responsibility to disseminate their editorial fare as widely as possible. Hence, the rationale for low prices. The price of magazines cannot get too high or the resulting circulations, if they conform to the 50-60 percent rule, will be too low to be effective as an advertising medium.

This is not an attempt to lump all magazines into one strict set of rules. Each magazine has its own individual characteristics and requires different management actions to achieve balance. Specific applications of these general guidelines are, however, possible. Now that there is a resolve among publishers to charge more for circulation, the chain reaction thus set in motion will result in healthier relationships all around. Advertisers will be getting better value from more natural readership levels and publishers will find money in improved circulation revenues to pay for increased paper, postage and printing.

The hassle over circulation health now becomes academic since circulation methodology becomes self-policing when the 50-60 percent rule is observed.

Eight questions I always wanted to ask Angelo

By William Steiner

As a long-time top publishing executive at McGraw-Hill (he spent 17 years there, serving in such key positions as vice-president of circulation, vice-president of marketing, vice-president of production), Angelo Venezian has developed more successful circulation building programs than anyone else in the business. He was former chairman of the board of the Direct Mail Advertising Association and is currently president of the Print Advertising Association. Although his experience has been largely in the business field, his comments apply to all special interest magazines ... and that's what most magazines are these days. He is now vice-president of marketing sales for Creative Mailing Services and president of Specialized Information Co.

The following are his answers to my questions about circulation development.

How many efforts should a publisher make to get a subscription renewal?

The answer depends on determining the need to maintain a certain circulation level for audit reports and competitive position for advertising sales.

First, the cost per new subscription order for *quality* subscribers must be determined. The cost of obtaining renewals should be equal to the cost of obtaining new quality subscribers. This means that additional renewal efforts can be made until the cost of selling a renewal equals the cost of obtaining a new subscription.

In record-keeping, it's important to keep track of costs and isolate the out-of-pocket expenses.

In organizing a renewal series, it is important to isolate the unimportant areas such as students, foreign subscriptions, fringe groups, etc. They should receive just one or two notices.

Since most publishers aren't equipped to handle the exchange and other problems connected with foreign subscriptions, foreign renewals should be turned over to subscription agencies specializing in this area. Their commissions are well worthwhile, since they eliminate the specialized problems foreign subscriptions create.

What's the best way to cut the cost of request circulation verification?

Make the verification mailing look like an audit request. Send it first class with "AUDIT REQUEST" printed on the envelope. Personalize it as much as possible with computer printout or label or stencil imprint on the reply section.

Another important factor is to minimize the information on position, function, etc. There is no point in a long list of items to check when they are of little value and not used for selling advertising space. Just ask for essential information.

An idea is to mail co-op mailings several times a year to a list with verification card included. This enables publishers to enjoy extra income and carry the verification program as a piggyback.

Another idea is to spin off the labels every other month and include bind-in cards for verification with label in copies of the magazine with a reminder tip-on sticker on the cover.

How does a publisher expand or maintain his or her circulation?

The first important decision is to determine the size of the universe in terms of units and individuals.

Often publishers made the mistake of limiting the size of their universe. For example, an architectural magazine has prospects among all types of specifiers, interior designers, etc. These are groups who can benefit from the editorial service of the magazine and are also prospects for the goods and services offered by the advertisers.

Another example is ski magazines which can build added circulation among ski lodges, ski retainers, ski areas, etc., which also become potential advertisers as they become more familiar with the magazines.

Sound list-building internally or through custom list-builders and use of mailing list brokers play a very important part in developing circulation.

An often neglected area that has proven highly successful in the trade and professional magazine field is the friend's-name building program. This involves asking current subscribers to supply names of associates in their organizations and elsewhere in return for an inexpensive premium. It is important to use a premium related to the magazine's editorial area. Such a program can net an average of 10 new names for each name responding and has been the basis for major circulation increases for McGraw-Hill for many years.

Publishers who do not have the internal organization to conduct such programs on a regular basis can use outside sources to do this job for them.

How does a publisher reduce the circulation acquisition costs?

Here's a checklist:
• Use third-class instead of first-class mail.
• Use the best copy and creative talent to build promotion that pulls top results.

• Make it as easy as possible to subscribe with "bill company," "bill me" or "payment enclosed" check-off boxes.

• Mention that subscriptions are tax deductible when promoting business and professional publications.

• Use rubber stamp invoice: "Please approve for payment and pass along to your accounting department."

• Feature savings on two- and three-year subscriptions on invoices with boxes to check for longer terms.

• Nothing sells like savings—feature savings over regular price.

• Trade and professional publications can establish a high rate for those outside the publication's basic area— then subscription efforts can feature savings up to 50 percent.

• Expand your universe through sound list development and list selection.

• Take advantage of match and merge capabilities of computers—this can drastically cut the cost of extensive duplication.

Publishers should consider buying lists if they are aiming at in-depth coverage of selected markets. The cost of buying lists rather than renting them is not high and this can cut total costs.

It pays to match and undupe names to eliminate current subscribers, expires and names on the prospect list. This proves worthwhile even if the unduping isn't perfect. But don't overkill. It usually doesn't pay out to pay the cost of perfection. But it does pay very well to eliminate the largest part of the duplication.

How should a publisher evaluate mailing lists?

There are two factors, the cost per order (actual out-of-pocket costs) and actual collections (no-pays should be deducted before making evaluation).

How should a publisher locate the best lists?

Use the services of list compilers and mailing-list brokers. It is important to provide compilers and brokers with detailed and complete information so they can make intelligent recommendations.

By closely working with brokers and compilers publishers can enjoy the benefits of a list selection department at no cost to them, since the brokers are paid through the 20 percent commission they get from the list owners.

How does a publisher using more than one list decide whether it is worthwhile to purge duplicates?

There are three factors to be considered: Merge and purge costs; savings enjoyed by cutting down the total mailing quantities; the importance of not sending promotion mailings to current subscribers—especially if premiums and money-saving offers are used.

How can a publisher increase circulation income?

Constantly test all factors with the aim of producing new subscriptions at the lowest possible acquisition cost.

• Dry test various price offers.

• Increase renewal income through expanded renewal series.

• Sell more two- and three-year subscriptions through billing series and renewal series.

• Charge higher rates to fringe circulation markets such as libraries, students, colleges, institutions, government.

• Take advantage of savings available through computer capabilities to merge and purge.

• Consider selling in-perpetuity life subscriptions for sums such as $100: Based on 5 percent interest such income can prove very worthwhile even if the offer is to refund to the estate upon subscriber's death.

• Take advantage of the opportunity to add continuous flow of extra income through the rental of subscriber, expire and prospect lists. Since list brokers do the selling for 20 percent commission, this provides added income from a circulation department asset without added selling costs.

Dick Benson: What I've learned during 33 years in direct mail

By Richard V. Benson

This is my thirty-third year of selling magazine subscriptions.

Before I was fortunate enough to get into direct marketing, I did a number of other things. I was controller and assistant general manager of Western Electric Co. in Mexico. I worked for U.S. Rubber and the Standard Oil Co. of New Jersey. Three different times I worked for the government, including a year in the embassy in Chungking, China.

My first civil service job was with the Treasury Department, and it paid $960 a year. I also taught high school, was a street-car conductor, an assistant buyer in a department store, and I worked a 48-hour week in a union shop for $12.

Like most of us I accidentally got a job in direct mail. I was looking for a new job, almost any new job, when I landed in the circulation department of Time Inc.

This is my nineteenth year as a full-time direct marketing consultant. In that time I have worked for more than 40 publishers and 60 or more magazines selling millions of subscriptions. Incidentally, I have been involved with more than 150 sweepstakes. I am also co-publisher of the largest newsletter in the United States with more than a quarter of a million subscribers.

Today I want to talk about selling subscriptions through the mails.

When I went to work at Time in 1947, I believe they were the smartest direct marketer of magazine subscriptions in the industry. They were certainly the most sophisticated. (I think they are still smart, although not necessarily the smartest.) And the best thing about selling subscriptions at Time was that they had great products (in those days, Time was not run by accountants). That's the first rule of selling subscriptions successfully: Have a great product.

During my career, numerous changes have taken place. Primarily, however, I think we are all a great deal smarter. I believe we are more willing to accept the fact that there is not just one best way for everybody.

Most of what I will discuss will not be applicable to the majors such as *Time, Newsweek,* and *Better Homes and Gardens,* who need do little more in selling than express the offer in the most efficient manner.

I am going to tell you what I have learned from selling millions of subscriptions for more than 60 magazines, and selling those subscriptions one at a time. I plan to stick to the facts I have learned from counting orders and not indulge in opinion or preferences.

That is not to say I don't have opinions and preferences, but I do my best to let the marketplace tell me the best way to do things. At any given time for any given product there isn't enough money to successfully force the marketplace. You must listen to the marketplace and adapt to what it says. You must test, test, and test again.

Knowing what to test

In fact, let's talk about testing. Since there are few empirical facts in direct mail—things that always happen—the real intelligence is in knowing what to test rather than thinking you know all of the answers ahead of time.

Very few—if any—of us spend enough money testing. Some of us are purists who listen to the statisticians and never, never test more than one thing at a time. The statisticians are, or course, correct in theory, but time and money are essential factors in testing and must be given consideration if they are limited.

For example, one of our foremost agencies carries pure testing so far that in format testing (of which they are very fond), they do not vary copy or components. This leads to all formats being limited by the size and restrictions of the Kurt Volk inter-stack package with which they have been very successful.

Obviously, these restrictions do not allow other formats to be used in the most successful manner. Statistically, they are right—but they are much more apt to format test in that way than do package testing which varies many elements and has a much greater chance of success, to my way of thinking. It is impossible to deliver the whys of package testing, and they want to know the whys.

I am much more interested in getting a substantial winner and would rather spend my money on combined package and format testing at the risk of not knowing the whys.

In order of importance—and I must say the ranking changes depending on circumstances—I test 1) offers; 2) letter copy (cheaper than packages); 3) packages; 4) postage; and 5) personalization. I constantly test lists.

When I test I have my eye on the incremental cost and how I will implement. I do not have a formula for pyramiding when I implement a success.

How far I implement depends upon whether the results of the test were as experience would indicate or, as I say, went with the grain. If the test did not go with the grain, I proceed timidly. With the grain, I pyramid aggressively.

In pyramiding, I try to look at all of the collateral facts. Do I have other successes? Do I have other knowledge such as information about lists or list owners? How big is my risk?

In testing, I try to set up the sides of a test to give me a minimum 100 orders. Lists are an exception, however, and I generally go with the minimum 5,000.

Rarely have I been burned on large scale pyramiding on list tests. I have seldom had a good list turn bad on pyramiding, nor can I remember when a bad list turned out to be good on retesting.

In testing a new product or service, I tend to test more than most people. I like to do a test of 150,000 pieces which I feel will give me a yes or a no answer. Such a test will also tell me how big a universe to which I can launch. It's expensive, but life is too short to later play the game of what if and test again.

The exception is a product which I am doing primarily because I expect to make a profit from my house list. Obviously, in that case, I can test with many fewer pieces.

Twenty-five years ago when we started *American Heritage*, the selling of subscriptions by mail was still pretty much in its infancy. I remember meetings with some of the great marketers of the day where much of the conversation centered around how to reduce our $60 per thousand cost in the mail by 50 cents. Let me explain, in those days, postage was $10 and lists were $15.

American Heritage, which was one of the great innovators of subscription selling through the mails, was soon spending $110 per thousand because they were, I think, the first of the major mailers to make the very important jump from cost per thousand to cost per order.

I am sure you all feel that's unbelievable, but we really are a very young industry. For all practical purposes, *Heritage* invented the four-color brochure as we know it. They were the first to use four-color pictorial envelopes. Before the advent of computers at *Heritage*, we did merge-purge of seven million mailings by eyeball as a matter of course.

Let me tell you a couple of stories about those days. I remember making a speech in New York to the local direct mail club where I talked about having paid $50 per thousand for a list of one million and having no one believe it. The reason for disbelief was that the audience was married to a cost per thousand concept as compared to cost per order.

All of us are great imitators, but we should be careful. At *Heritage*, we started using four-color pictures on the poster side of envelopes and addressing on the flap side. It wasn't long before people were addressing on the flap side with nothing on the poster side. They thought that addressing on the flap side was the new thing we had done.

During the past 20 years there has been a radical change in attitude regarding subscription sales. Publishers are much more aware of and concerned with the leverage of net income from subscriptions. In pursuit of more income, a great number of errors of omission as well as commission have been made.

Subscription sales as basic business

As a basic tenet, let us begin with the premise that selling a subscription is no different from selling a widget. If we were going to sell a widget by mail, we would do a profit and loss sheet to establish what results we needed at what selling price in order to make a desirable profit. We would then test the marketplace to see if we could accomplish or better the desired results, either by increasing the price and profit margin, or by increasing demand and thus reducing the sales cost for additional profits.

In its simplest form, selling a subscription is no different, despite the fact that it involves a continuing sale. We must establish the average total lifetime of a subscriber, factor in renewal and billing costs, and calculate what pricing and estimated demand will contribute the most income per copy throughout the total life of the subscription.

Because we are involved with magazines which must maintain advertising and circulation bases, we must go through a second set of calculations which factor replacement costs for maintaining a level number of subscriptions through the estimated lifetime of the original starters. Once we have arrived at our best guess *pro forma*, we must then go to the marketplace and ask it which of our assumptions is correct. This must be a continuing year-to-year probe.

The important premise here is that basic economics has not changed. Prices are first of all a result of supply and demand, not a product of costs. Costs can make the difference in whether we make a profit or loss, but they are not the controlling factor as to what the market will pay. There is no economic law or rule of thumb pertaining to a specific percentage of profit. The public has frequently paid incredibly high prices for unique, low-cost items. Competition or the threat of competition is what generally keeps profit percentages down.

Magazines by their inherent editorial nature are unique and do not tend to have the same potential competition for the subscriber. Few, very few, magazines have pushed their subscription prices to the optimum point.

Some magazines have arbitrarily increased their prices beyond optimum as a reaction to cost increases or perceived future cost increases. It has been my experience that very few magazines faced with a need to increase prices for continued profits have thoroughly examined the possibility of allowing circulation to fall. Reductions in circulation have generally been done as a measure *in extremis*. It has rarely been accepted that poor management has forced circulation too high and that retreat is the better part of profit. In my 33 years in the business, I don't believe I have seen more than two or three attempts at calculating the cost of maintaining the last increment in circulation base.

With the advent of the circulation model on computers and therefore the ability to calculate any number of *pro forma* scenarios, there is really no excuse for poor pricing or poor circulation goals.

Once a *pro forma* is established and the marketplace, after testing, has confirmed that we can get an acceptable number of orders at an acceptable cost, we have then arrived at a cost per order based on what the market will pay. We can then measure our performance not only in mail selling but from all other sources as well. With this cost figure or bogey in hand, our job becomes considerably easier, and the cost of maintenance or growth is easily established.

While I am on the subject of pricing, let me tell you a few things I think I know. I believe that the same magazine sold by mail and tested at different prices will result in the same dollar revenue per thousand. That is to say that a subscription sold at half price will pull twice as many orders as a subscription sold at full price.

I believe for a monthly, an eight-month subscription sold at the same copy price will pull 50 percent more orders than a 12-month subscription.

I believe the conversion percentage on a subscription sold through direct mail at half price will be the same as a subscription sold at full price.

I believe a subscription that sold for an eight-month term will convert at the same percentage as one sold for 12 months.

I believe bad pay increases with the dollar amount of the order.

Except for having said a great product is the most important ingredient for successful mail, I am not going to attempt to rank or place in priority the other ingredients for successful subscription selling.

The importance of lists

Let's start with lists. Obviously they are vital. As I am sure you all well know, lists are primarily divided into two types: mail response and compiled. My own rule of thumb is that mail response lists are roughly twice as responsive as compiled.

That is not to say there are not exceptions, and there are, of course, many reasons for using a compiled list. But generally speaking, in most of the selling I am faced with, mail response lists are best. In fact, one of the largest mail order companies in the country uses compiled lists exclusively for prospecting.

In this wonderful age of computers, we have a great ability to segment lists. As a group, however, we do not take full advantage of segmentation. We are quite good at knowing our own list and its segments, but we know little about other lists.

Very few companies are into successfully using Zip analysis for their mailings. In my mind, the object of a Zip analysis is to identify those Zips which are least productive to our offer.

Please note: I said least, not most. I believe it is much easier to implement not mailing the worst names than finding more good names. I have found more than once that the names from Zips of 10 to 20 percent of a mailing producing the poorest results will be as much as 50 percent worse than the average of the best 80 percent.

All of you I am sure have no trouble ranking lists by results, and do not mail those lists which will not meet your required standards. The fact is you may very well be mailing Zips covering 10 to 20 percent of your names which are doomed to failure by those same standards.

Before I leave this subject, let me tell you that it is reported that the record clubs have refined Zip selection to the extent that for the past few years they have been mailing as few as 50 percent of the total Zips.

Our business goes in cycles, and like most things, some of us are too slow and some of us are too fast.

Looking at the past

I thought it might be interesting if I could identify some of the constants and some of the changes which I have seen. With this in mind, I went back to some of my old speeches to see what I have said over the years.

Here are some things which haven't changed:
•You need a good product.
•You need a special offer or exclusivity.
•The mailing package should be interesting and tell a full story.
•Booklet letters work about as well as individual pages and are cheaper.
•Long copy is better than short copy.
•Copy should preach benefits, benefits, benefits.
•A letter and a brochure should each tell the whole story.
•The letter is the most important element in the package.
•Don't sell two things at once.
•Don't write down to your audience, but do be understandable.
•Don't sample.
•Don't use humor.
•Do offer credit.

Now let's try some things that have changed at least part of the time. I used to say:
•Window envelopes produce better results than closed-face envelopes.

This is changing, particularly with our ability to match outside addressing to personal addressing inside.
•Token cards are sure to increase results.
Certainly not always true.
•Computer letters always pull more orders.

Sometimes computer letters work and frequently they do so for reasons different than we used to believe. To wit the large type MeadDigit.
•Credit alone is better than with option for cash.

Frequently this isn't true.
•Envelopes have two sides and should carry teasers on both sides.

Many times today I am more successful with sterile envelopes.
•A product which lends itself to a four-color brochure will benefit from such a brochure.

Once again, we are often more successful selling without brochures today. I mean we get more orders, we don't just save money.

Everyone knows about hot lines and how great they can be. I have clients who can mail hot lines on a monthly basis and more than overcome seasonal differences. This is fantastic. It reduces overall costs, evens out the order flow and reduces the risk of our large semi-annual mailings.

On the other hand, I have clients who have been so carried away by their discovery of hot lines that they have become totally committed and are ignoring large segments of names on their very good lists. One test recently made showed the balance of non-hot line names previously used on a given list was still substantially better than the average for the mailing.

As a group, many of us have gotten so involved with hot lines we do not pay enough attention to our best lists and other potential for total or even additional usage. I point out to you that the best 25 percent of your lists are probably 50 percent more effective than your average list, and obviously much more effective than the poorest list you use.

With this in mind, how many use a two-week follow-up mailing which traditionally pulls 50 percent as well as the original? How many of your best names mailed again as a follow-up would be better than the names on the bottom of your schedules?

It has been my experience that over the past twenty years there has been a continuous lessening of attention paid to lists. Much too much reliance has been put upon the brokers. Mailers have not worked hard enough at knowing the lists, or talking to list owners, or discovering new methods of segmentation.

Testing the offer

Much of the testing we do, and rightly so, is of offers. For me this is an exciting aspect of the business. The bad news of this testing, however, is that it frequently is done for the wrong reason. There is enormous management pressure to increase the price of the introductory offer. In my experience, most magazines find it economical to trade promotion dollars for circulation income dollars, so raising the front end introductory price accomplishes nothing in terms of contribution to copy cost since selling costs tend to increase dollar for dollar.

The basic reason for raising introductory prices should be to justify the highest renewal price the market will pay. The leverage on circulation profits of successfully increasing renewal prices is astronomical. If the price of an $8 magazine is increased to $10, that is a 25 percent increase to the customer, but the leverage on profits is fantastic.

Let me cite an actual example so that you can more clearly understand what I am talking about. I have a newsletter of my own with a circulation of more than 250,000. We recently raised the renewal price from $10 to $12 without changing the introductory price. That is a 20 percent increase to the customer. We are now losing less than 10 percent of the renewals we are getting. That is, if our renewal rate was 60 percent we are now getting 54 percent or more.

Now let's look at the income side. At a 60 percent renewal rate our cost of selling was $1.35 and our cost of collection another 65 cents, or $2 total. Our cost of product to service the order runs close to $5. Our gross profit then at $10 is $3. Our profit at $12 is almost $5, or a 65 percent increase.

I believe in cut-price introductory subscriptions.

I believe in department store pricing, $9.95—but the cents should always be higher than 50.

For memberships, even-dollar pricing often seems to be best as does annual term.

I believe in short-term offers, though never for less than eight months.

In my experience, the magic words for offers are CHARTER, FREE, COMPLIMENTARY COPY, SWEEPSTAKES, and PREMIUMS.

A charter offer is always superior, probably because it is easier to sell the sizzle of a new idea than to sell an established product. However, I do remember using a charter offer very successfully for a 50-year-old magazine. We more than tripled circulation in 14 months with excellent economics by selling a charter offer for the second 50 years.

FREE! What can I tell you about FREE! Everyone wants something FREE!

Complimentary copy offers increase both response and bad pay dramatically. I will tell you, however, that those books which have gone to comp copy offers seldom have walked away from them despite the high bad pay because the total economics continues to be better than a hard offer.

Sweepstakes: Still going strong

Sweepstakes and premiums are much the same thing, a sweepstakes being a chance to get something big for free as against the sure thing of a free premium. Let me spend a few minutes telling you what I know about sweepstakes.

If I remember correctly, the current vogue of sweepstakes came into being in 1962 or 1963 when *Reader's Digest* introduced them.

To my mind the *Digest* innovation was ingenious in that it was a pre-numbered sweepstakes. The difference from the normal drawing is that the winners were pre-drawn from the total universe of numbered entry forms instead of being drawn from only the people who sent in their entries. This innovation allowed for the very strong copy line "You may have already won...." Psychologically this made it much more difficult to discard an entry form since it might already be a winner.

I have seen a head-to-head test of a pre-drawn sweepstakes versus the conventional drawing and the results were very one-sided.

My experience with more than 100 sweepstakes has included four failures. I am not completely sure why those four didn't work, though I suspect that the prizes were not exciting enough.

On the whole, sweepstakes are tremendously successful. I generally expect a sweepstakes to increase orders by 50 to 100 percent. For many years I found no difference in the quality of the orders. Their pay-up was as good as the non-sweeps, and they renewed as well as non-sweeps.

Today, quality of orders cannot be taken for granted. There are many cases where pay-up is poorer and renewals are also poorer, but I don't know of anyone who used sweepstakes and then gave them up.

One of the interesting clear-cut trends has been the tremendous difference in response to sweepstakes from sweepstakes-generated lists as compared to lists not generated by sweepstakes. I know of one magazine where if you rank ordered the lists using 100 as par, the sweepstakes-generated lists pulled 120 and above, whereas the non-sweepstakes-generated lists were at 80 and below. No list fell between 80 and 120.

Mailing packages tend to go from A to Z, from the relatively simple package to the elaborate, multiple piece package of PCH. To my knowledge, there have been no tests of the simple package versus the elaborate. It is almost impossible to test because of the legalities. Based on my own experience and the results I've seen of similar magazines, however, I lean to the simple package.

In my opinion, there are limits to the cost per thousand of mass mail. I have had no successful experience with mass mail costing $300 per thousand or more although I do know of some successes—PCH for example.

Choosing the prizes

I believe successful sweepstakes mailers will agree that the first prize is all important. I personally believe that close to half the total prize structure should be represented by the first prize. I believe the drama and value of the first prize is much more important than the total value of the sweepstakes. When possible, I like to have a grand prize which is dramatic and easily conveyed in words and art, with the alternative prize of cash. I do not believe there is any prize more desirable than cash, unless it is tax-free cash.

There are several schools of thought regarding the total number of prizes, the total number of layers of prizes, and whether all prizes should be offered with alternatives, *i.e.*, this or that. I believe four layers of prizes are enough and the question of alternatives lies with the kind of prize structure as well as the audience. Personally, I am happy with a total of 1,000 prizes, and most times I am happy with substantially fewer. In my experience, the sweepstakes that drew the highest percentage (65 percent) had only two layers and a total of nine prizes.

I prefer a simplified but dramatic prize structure because it is much easier to convey to the reader without being too busy and without too much clutter. I believe people enter sweepstakes to win the grand prize, not because there are quantities of consolation prizes.

I use sweepstakes in the renewal series of my newsletter, and I am much more successful with a $1,000 single prize than I am with 100 watches worth a total of $3,000. I have also successfully introduced sweepstakes in the renewal series of clients.

Copywriters have tried and tried, but I do not believe they have done better than lead their copy with "You may have already won...."

There is a basic premise in selling by mail which states that if you have a premium, sell the premium and give away the product.

Nowhere is this more true than in sweepstakes. The premium, of course, is the numbered ticket, the entry form, the chance to win a prize. Copy about the sweepstakes (our premium in this case) tends to be most of the mailing package with very little said about the product.

In one case I know of, test pyramiding was done three times, finally up to a million-piece test, all clearly showing that an extra brochure selling the editorial product cost money and had no positive results. Actually, the publisher's and the editor's egos couldn't stand that result, and the last I knew, the brochure was still a part of the mailing package.

The customer's sensitivity to prices frequently tends to be much less visible when sweepstakes are used. The pitfall or trap is that should there be no sweepstakes in the future, pricing would be an entirely new ball game.

In the early days of sweepstakes, it was pretty much the rule to pay off only those prizes for which winning tickets were returned. This meant that if anywhere from 10 to 40 percent of addressees returned entries, only 10 to 40 percent of the prizes would be awarded.

FTC hearings compiled a tremendous amount of information showing that substantially fewer pieces were awarded than were merited by the percentages of entry, however. I do not believe this was purposeful on the part of the mailers but rather was due to human error in identifying the winning numbers among the entries.

After the FTC hearings, general guidelines were formulated under which sweepstakes operators awarded all prizes by means of an extra drawing from all entries for the unclaimed prizes. Recently, however, at least two of the major judging organizations are permitting the awarding of only the claimed prizes as long as it is so stated in the rules.

Perhaps even more important, it had previously been construed that you could not test prizes of equal value to different groups of people. Again, if it is spelled out in the rules, this is being allowed by at least one judging organization. I am even told the prizes do not have to be of equal value.

This latter ruling is or can be vital to a company employing sweepstakes for multiple mailings to say a house list. I am not, repeat, not making a recommendation, but as I understand it, you can take one universe of numbers, pick 100 winning numbers, mail the same people monthly, and sell the same or different products each time, utilizing a sweeps structure of 100 prizes. You can have each monthly sweeps use a different 100 prizes and make each one look like a unique sweeps—as long as the rules indicate different prizes may be offered at different times and that it is all one sweeps.

This means you could appear to have 12 different sweepstakes with a total of 1,200 prizes but actually have only 100 total possible winners and pay out only those prizes actually claimed—as long as it's in the rules.

As I am sure you well know, it is common for publishers to use a sweeps prize structure for a year and get two or more mailings from it. A multiple-magazine publisher might well use the same sweeps on all products all year. By doing this, it is of course much easier to economically justify a prize structure of six figures and above.

My own preference is to not mail the same sweeps knowingly to the same person more than once. For the same product utilizing the same list universe I prefer two separate semi-annual $50,000 sweeps rather than one annual $100,000 sweeps. I doubt that anyone has empirical knowledge on this point, but I am satisfied with what I think I know. And I do know I don't have to worry about being deceptive.

Perhaps I should say a word about economics. If you can (and I think you can) expect a sweepstakes to increase results by 50 to 100 percent, then it follows that you can lift your mailing costs including prize structure by the same ratio and still have the same net per order.

When I think about the cost of sweepstakes, I think in terms of $15 to $20 per thousand for prizes and $15 to $50 per thousand in mailing package costs, less the postage I would be paying on the returns in a conven-tional package. This adds up to $20 to $70 per thousand which, on an average $200 package, is only a 15 to 35 percent increase in costs.

You might be interested in some research I did on sweepstakes. In 48 sweepstakes, 21 had three or fewer layers of prizes and 12 had four layers of prizes. Ten had $10,000 grand prizes and 28 had grand prizes worth less than $10,000.

Think about that as compared with what most of us do. Most of us have grand prizes worth substantially more than $10,000 and we most often have more than four layers of prizes. Do we know something they don't know or vice versa? I do know I plan to follow my own advice in December and run a sweepstakes with only two layers of prizes. I also point out to you that many of us believe a fundamental truth: that one premium is better than a choice of premiums.

Perhaps I will be able to reaffirm my belief that people enter sweepstakes primarily to win the top prize. In my case, the grand prize will be $10,000 cash. I have been told that one company ran some focus groups on the size of the grand prize. My information is they found little difference in interest in a grand prize of $1 million as compared to a grand prize of $100,000.

I previously mentioned the judging organizations. I urge you to use one. They can provide few or many services according to your desires. At the least they are up to date and will keep you from breaking the law. They act as disinterested third parties and lend you authenticity. They will pick your winners. They will help you with prizes and prize structures. They will actually handle the entries if you so desire. Most important, they know the business.

New interest in premiums

For most of my career, premiums (except for reprints of editorial material) were of ill repute and only "junky" magazines used them. Today we have *Time* and *Newsweek* and *Sports Illustrated* making use of premiums and that certainly changes the image of premiums.

Despite the widespread promotion of premiums by Time Inc., however, I find very little testing of premiums by the publishers with whom I am associated. In my opinion, this is their mistake.

The choice of a premium is one of the most difficult decisions facing a promoter. Cost is clearly important, but desirability is much more important. The only fact I can give you is that a single premium is better than a choice of premiums. It is much easier to convey the merits of a single item than to diffuse the copy over several choices. Desirability is also much more important than product relationship. As in everything we do in mail, it's test, test, test.

Let me say a few words about copy and design. (Please keep in mind that I am not attempting to rank the elements of mailing. I am not a copywriter, but I have enormous regard for those who are and who produce winners.)

Most of the people I have worked with over the years do not do enough copy testing. Most of us do a great deal of testing of design, format, offers and lists, but too frequently we are dissuaded from copy testing by an ill-conceived perception of the costs.

I submit to you that letters are cheap to test and have a much better chance of producing significant differences in results than most of the things we do test. I believe words are substantially more important than design and are of course much cheaper to test. Most mailers would be ahead if they doubled their copy testing.

I suggest that it is poor economics to use other than the writers with the best track records. I have no quarrel with testing new writers so long as you use the established ones as well.

I remember a new client who had purchased an old magazine. Our first assignment was to see if we could get a new mailing. We tested packages from three of the best free-lancers. I doubt if anyone could have chosen the winner ahead of time with certainty, and actually all three writers beat the old control. But one of them produced a package that was 100 percent better.

I don't want to beat a dead horse, but should there be someone here who doesn't know that long copy is better than short copy, please learn that fact now. For most magazines, there is no such thing as a one- or two-page letter for the acquisition of new subscriptions. Four pages are standard and frequently six pages are better.

One of the fundamentals that is frequently overlooked is that when you use a brochure, both it and the letter should have all the facts. Each should be capable of standing alone and telling the whole story.

Another fundamental to which everyone pays lip service but which is often not implemented is that copy should be written by one person to one person, not written by committee, and not written to the mass of people to whom you are mailing. Remember your prospect is only interested in what you and/or your product can do for him and him alone. To say it differently: Benefits, benefits, benefits are what count.

In addition, you must remember that your prospect is not likely to be your peer demographically. New Yorkers and Washingtonians in particular must keep in mind that the rest of the country is not like New York or Washington. Too often we believe we are selling to business peers or luncheon companions. It just ain't so!

Regarding art and spectacular pieces, I believe they always have a place in the market, but I believe that they run in cycles. My own reading of the cycles tells me that today my best sales are with non-promotional-looking packages.

I am not going to go into a discussion of formats, particularly in view of the proliferation of new pieces today. I do want to say, however, that I have only been successful two or three times with a self-mailer. Given my druthers, I will not spend test money on a self-mailer. I believe when people talk about junk mail, this is what they mean.

At the other end of the scale, even though I have always believed in spending more money per thousand than most, I do believe there is, as I have said, a limit to the dollars per thousand that can be spent for mass mailings. As of today, I believe that limit is under $300.

I have purposely said nothing about billing, conversions and renewals. This is because I have had very little success trying to influence these areas. For the most part, assuming adequate systems and ignoring special offers, I believe the percentage of collection and the percentage of renewals are essentially a result of the product and not of the promotion. I have spent a lot of money in both areas and can count my big successes on my fingers and not use all of them.

Now to summarize:

• I believe in testing.

• Long copy is better than short.

• You should sell cut-rate introductory subscriptions for a short term. Sweepstakes can be a very successful ploy.

• Premiums should be thoroughly investigated.

• Lists need much more attention than they usually receive.

• More copy and package testing should be done.

• I believe in department store pricing and in credit.

One final thought: The most prevalent malady I see as a consultant is the ever present attitude of economizing, or playing it safe, and of being a slave to the budget.

There are two causes of this malady. First, there is the constant pressure from the top to stick to the budget—to economize, play it safe and not take chances. The second cause is that too many people in this business are security conscious yes men.

The simple fact is that no company has ever managed to economize its way into permanent prosperity. Selling by direct mail is a promotion business, and making gains requires risk taking. If you attempt to operate without risk, you automatically lose because you will limit gains. There will always be losses from uncontrollable causes.

To succeed at direct mail—and by my definition that means to make a profit—you must be creative, you must indulge in blue sky thinking, you must have good instincts, and you must take chances. But always test first.

Direct mail according to Freud

By Ted Bartek and James MacLachlan

Never in history have leisure, recreation and the pursuit of individual happiness attained the status they enjoy today. Psychologists explain this by pointing out that many Americans have entered an era in which the basic needs for food, water, safety and shelter are so easily satisfied that higher level psychological and social needs can be explored. This has important implications for magazine marketers.

The magazine publishing industry plays an important part in this leisure-time boom by supplying the information needed by Americans in their relentless pursuit of self-fulfillment.

Magazines today not only inform and entertain. In an indirect way they satisfy the same psychological and social needs that readers are attempting to satisfy when they pursue the leisure time activities the magazines cover.

These needs are closely related to an individual's personal identity—the image he has of himself and his aspirations. For example, a study by one psychologist showed that golfers are competitive and seek a challenge, tennis players are gregarious and look for social interaction, and bicyclists are people in pursuit of self-sufficiency and solitude.

Because of the mental nature of these needs, they are referred to as psychic needs.

Let us examine five general categories of higher level psychic needs (as presented by Dr. Abraham Maslow and generally recognized by psychologists) and see how these insights can be applied directly to improving a magazine's subscription sales effort:

•*Belonging and love needs.* This is the need to feel wanted, to belong to social groups, and to be accepted. Magazines can extend the identity of the reader in a direction consistent with his or her self-image and aspirations. For example, a subscription to FOLIO can help satisfy your need to be part of an informal community of magazine publishing executives.

•*Esteem needs.* Magazines can support a reader's need for prestige, fame and recognition. For certain individuals, magazines like *Vogue, Architectural Digest* and *The New Yorker* are symbols of prestige and status.

•*Self-actualization needs.* People can express themselves through a magazine subscription. For example, if an individual has a deep concern about the preservation of animal species, he can express these feelings by subscribing to a magazine such as *National Wildlife.* The act of subscribing in itself is a form of expression of opinion on the issue.

•*Knowledge needs.* A large number of people who subscribe to magazines are knowledge seekers—whether out of curiosity or out of a drive for achievement.

•*Esthetic needs.* Magazines can supply people with a means to appreciate order and beauty.

Meeting psychic needs

You can improve your magazine subscription sales letters by identifying the psychic needs of your magazine audience and directing your sales message to these needs. Chart I lists the various psychic needs and excerpts of actual sales messages directed to those needs.

Before you send out your magazine's subscription solicitation letter, ask yourself the following questions:

•What kinds of attitudes and opinions can readers express through my magazine? The act of subscribing to certain magazines in itself is an expression of opinion on an issue. Example: Subscribing to *Ms.* magazine expresses an opinion on women's rights.

Chart I

Psychic need	Magazine	Magazine Excerpt
Belonging and love needs —Group identity and acceptance	*Ms.*	"But something has changed. We are beginning to define ourselves, and that change is happening because women are speaking out honestly."
Esteem needs —Prestige, fame and recognition	*Quest*	"We'll print informed opinions about the 'best' wines, beaches and airlines—as well as the 'best' poets, philosophers and presidents."
Self-actualization needs —Self expression, personal fulfillment-self-renewal	*National Wildlife*	"Because it is dedicated to everyone who is turned on by riding the high country, canoeing across a mist-shrouded lake . . . all those activities and places which make us feel new again, just by being there!"
Knowledge needs —Curiosity and achievement	*Human Nature*	"If you're insatiably curious about human beings . . . if you're concerned about directions humanity seems to be taking . . . if you'd like to keep informed on the most significant discoveries . . . here's good news!"
Esthetic needs —Appreciation of beauty, order and symmetry	*American Film*	"You'll understand the creative magic of Garbo . . . Bogart . . . Bergman . . . Redford . . . Fonda . . ."

•What kinds of aspirations can my readers vicariously satisfy?

•What social groups will the readers become identified with by subscribing?

•Does my publication symbolize status in any way? Does it confer prestige on the subscriber?

•What knowledge does it convey? Does it satisfy curiosity or aid the reader in some area of achievement?

•Will my publication assist readers in the enjoyment of beauty or art?

Once you've answered these questions, build the answers into your sales message along with the usual pitch about how the magazine will inform and entertain. You'll find that the power of your sales letter will improve significantly.

Research has shown that an individual prefers magazines he perceives to be similar to the image he has of himself. By knowing the psychic needs of your audience, you'll be better prepared to write direct mail letters that strike a responsive chord.

To read or not to read

Psychology also lends insight into how your magazine prospect behaves when faced with your magazine solicitation.

From the moment your mailing piece arrives it has little chance of surviving before it hits the wastebasket. It immediately places your prospect under tension, since he is caught in the middle between read and don't read. The envelope might contain something of potential value to him. However, if he decides to read your magazine offer, he has to spend time and effort weighing the value of the magazine versus the money asked. He has to consider whether the magazine is consistent with his self-identity, and he must face the possibility of making a mistake, thereby wasting his money.

This is in sharp contrast to buying gasoline, food and many other products in the same price range which people decide on one time, then routinely purchase without much thought or effort. Magazine new-subscriber offers are all first-time purchases.

The lifetime of your mailing piece is further shortened because a magazine, unlike gasoline and food, is a luxury. Its purchase does not fill an urgent need, and its purchase can easily be postponed.

So when your prospect receives your mailing piece, his first impulse is to find the quickest way out of his dilemma. And in 95 out of 100 cases he will throw your letter away.

How, then, can we increase the chances that your prospect will open your letter and read it?

Cost benefit analysis

Understanding the concept known as "closure" is useful here.

Closure is the innate drive of human beings to reduce ambiguity in their mental environment. When the prospective subscriber picks up your mailing piece he experiences ambiguity. An easy way for him to reduce ambiguity and achieve closure is to find some reason to open or throw away your letter.

Use every opportunity available to keep the drive for closure operating in your favor: the look of the envelope, the name of the addressee, the weight of the envelope, etc.

Another concept from information theory—"curiosity"—is valuable here. Curiosity is the drive to seek novel stimuli in the environment. If, in his search for information, your prospect sees something that piques his curiosity about your magazine offer, instead of bringing closure, it will increase his desire for information that can only be obtained inside your letter. In order to obtain closure he'll have to open and read your letter.

This is certainly not news. Most circulation managers have refined curiosity-arousing techniques to a science. Nevertheless, the theory of information science confirms and explains the success of this technique. Tokens, teaser copy, sweepstakes, premiums, and perfumed letters have all been used effectively to arouse curiosity in the reader—and with it the feeling that something might be in this for him.

Turn need into desire

Upon opening your letter, your prospect will at first continue to search for closure—some information on which to act. This is your opportunity to stir desire in him for your magazine. Sales letters should create such a strong awareness of an unfilled need that the magazine is perceived to be worth much more than the money it actually costs.

Freudian psychology is useful here. When subscribers act to meet an unfilled need by subscribing to your magazine, they're acting on what Freud called the pleasure principle.

The aim of the pleasure principle is to satisfy needs and rid the person of tension. That aspect of the human psyche that carries this out Freud called the id. The id acts purely on emotion and does not respond to reason or morality.

The ego is the executive of the personality, acting on reason and logic according to what Freud called the reality principle. The superego is the moral aspect of the personality that strives for perfection. It's the role of the ego to satisfy the needs of the id while placating the demands of the superego.

A subscription offer for *New York Magazine* arrives. The id becomes excited by the prospect of reading the provocative stories but the superego complains that the stories are not practical. So the ego reads the letter, searching for ways to placate the superego, and finds that the magazine also contains a practical restaurant and nightlife guide. This placates the superego.

Since consumers often buy for emotional reasons, your direct mail letters should first involve the id by exploiting the emotional content of your magazine. Start with the reader's need for play and diversion. Point out the sheer fun and enjoyment of reading your magazine. "_____, the *one* magazine that can pack your evenings, weekends, and vacations with all of the joys that make your 35 million minutes on Earth more meaningful."

Also, captivate the id with the Big Promise. Highlight features which will improve the reader's life—becoming wealthy, getting ahead in career, being stylish, improving personal relationships, satisfying curiosity, gaining recognition, being loved, getting inside information, etc. "Put _____ to work for you, and you could save hundreds or even thousands of dollars this year."

Close the sale

Now, after you have stimulated the id with emotional appeals, close the sale by appealing to the ego. Since the ego must justify the purchase with logical reasons, mix in a barrage of factual ammunition that the ego can use to counter the protest of the cautious superego.

Convince the superego with explanations, proof, and description. Back up your promises with facts. Discuss the beneficial features of your magazine, its credentials, its physical appearance, etc. Explain the regular features, the restaurant guides, the TV listings, the timely investment advice. Describe the practical information which will help your reader's career, help him solve a problem, or help him take advantage of opportunities.

Offer proof that your magazine has the talent to deliver. Discuss the distinguished editors, the award-winning journalists, your extensive information-gathering system.

Describe your magazine physically, that it is printed on sturdy high gloss paper using modern typefaces, containing many attractive color photographs and so on.

The amount of information necessary depends on the amount of experience your prospect has with your magazine. A letter selling a subscription to *Time* magazine requires less information than one selling a charter subscription to *GEO*. (This might in part explain why *Time* sells effectively in two-minute TV spots.)

If you are unsure of how much information to give, give too much. Even in the face of strong emotional appeals, if information is insufficient your prospect has an out or an excuse to throw your mailing piece away. Don't let him attain closure from a lack of information. And since many readers just skim your letter, make these reasons stand out.

Enhance the offer

Your prospect's superego can also be won over with "special" inducements that enhance the offer. Special percent-off discounts, premiums, and subscriptions which entitle the subscriber to additional benefits are the most common. Promises of discounts on future subscriptions or related books and services can also augment the current offer.

Non-profit organizations can enrich offers by including membership benefits such as travel opportunities and the answering of questions by magazine staff people. Subscribers benefit from the knowledge that part of their subscription cost will be used to support a worthwhile organization.

It's good strategy to pile up as many enhancements to your offer as possible. Generally, in decision making, consumers do not weigh product benefits according to importance; they place greater emphasis on the number of benefits. By articulating many enhancements to your basic offer, you tip the balance in the direction of buying.

Reduce significance of the purchase

You can quiet down your prospect's noisy superego by making the offer less significant and less risky:

•*Short term subscription*. If you decrease the size of the initial commitment, you thereby reduce its significance.

•*Complimentary copy*. The ultimate reduction in term, the comp copy offer, reduces the initial commitment to one issue. In fact, it defers the actual purchase decision to the time of billing. This offer is effective in increasing response because it gives people an opportunity to examine your magazine for themselves. It relieves their fear that they might be "taken" or get "stuck" with an undesirable magazine ordered sight unseen.

But it has its drawbacks. Although initial response is heightened, cancellations at billing time can wipe this out. By this time, your initial salesletter is long forgotten and the decision is based on the first ex-

perience with the magazine itself.

•*Money-back guarantee*. This is a crucial element in magazine subscription mailings. People are hesitant to buy through the mail unless they know they can get a full refund if the magazine does not come up to expectations.

Guarantees which are simple, straightforward and believable are the most effective way of reducing risk, especially financial risk.

•*Bill me, credit card and installment options*. These techniques encourage response by reducing financial risk and providing a convenient method of payment. They seem to make the transfer of money less painful and less obvious to the buyer and he is assured that he will not actually have to part with any money until he has had a chance to examine the magazine.

•*Pre-addressed, pre-paid business reply cards*. These make it easier for people to buy from you.

Once the superego has been subdued, the emotional id will prevail. The promises of fun and personal advantage will appear realistic, and your magazine will seem to be worth much more than the money it costs.

Make your letters persuasive

The information contained in your letter will not create desire or encourage action, however, unless it is persuasively written.

Research findings explain how to improve the persuasiveness of written messages: Don't say "bird," say "raven." Would Poe's great poem be half as great if he had written, "Quoth the bird nevermore"? Since raven is subordinate to the general category of bird, it's more precise. The use of subordinate category words makes the writer seem more knowledgeable and believable.

Compare these two versions of a letter selling *National Wildlife* magazine:

When was the last time you came close to two brawling bears? Tested your strength against a rampaging wild waterway? Followed in the path of famous explorers? Watched two perky prairie animals sharing a wildflower meal?

When was the last time you came *face-to-face* with two brawling *grizzlies?* Tested your *stamina* against a rampaging *wild river?* Followed in the footsteps of *Lewis and Clark?* Watched two perky *prairie dogs* sharing a *dandelion lunch?*

The second (actual) version contains more subordinate category words and gives the message more persuasive punch.

Using messages portraying situations which form a personal connection with the reader is another persuasive technique.

The second *National Wildlife* sales message is a good example of this technique. It brings the reader right into the action. "When was the last time *you* came face-to-face with two brawling grizzlies?" The use of second person "you" immediately involves a reader in the sales message.

Contrast this with the following lead which doesn't mention the reader:

If it's boating and watersports, camping and backpacking, fishing and hunting . . . if it's the sheer enjoyment of the great southern outdoors . . .

The following re-written version is more effective in bringing the reader into the message by the addition of the word "you."

If it's boating and watersports, camping and

backpacking, fishing and hunting that you thrive on ... if it's the sheer enjoyment of the great southern outdoors that you crave ...

Tell a story

Illustrative stories and analogies increase the persuasiveness of written messages. Tests have shown that stories are more easily recalled and comprehended than other forms of written messages since stories have continuity based on a sequence of events. In fact, a scrambled story is easily re-assembled because it only makes sense if assembled correctly.

A good story starts with a question or problem. This immediately involves the reader and impels him to look for a solution or closure in the content of the story.

The following is an excellent example of the lead from a *Writer's Digest* sales letter using the technique of storytelling:

I don't have the great American novel in me. I flunked Poetry 102 in college. My first, last and only short story was rejected by 14 magazines. Talent or no, just 10 years ago I had to support myself somehow.

It wasn't easy at first, but this year I may make as much as $75,000 writing brochures, booklets, ads, press releases, TV scripts, cartoon captions and sales materials for clients across the country.

If it's closely related to your audience and your message, a story lead can be highly effective.

Use high imagery devices

Studies show that high imagery messages are clearer to the reader and make the writer seem dynamic and trustworthy. Increase the imagery of your letters by surprising your readers with the unusual. The preceding letter is an example of this. It is surprisingly personal for a salesletter and therefore creates a powerful impression.

The use of movement and action—as in the portrayal of meeting grizzlies face-to-face—is another technique to increase imagery.

Imagery can also be heightened by the use of graphic emphasis. Enliven your letters with colored ink, underlining, italicized typefaces, indenting, simulated handwritten notes, or anything you can imagine that will increase the dramatic impact of your message. There is no evidence to suggest that these devices are disliked by any audience.

Appeal to psychic needs, curiosity, the emotional, the practical. Be persuasive by bringing your readers into your salesletter. These techniques will enliven your salesletter and enable it to reflect the life contained in the pages of your magazine.

Ethics

By Eliot DeY. Schein

In June 1979, the Association of Direct Marketing Agencies (ADMA) met in Bermuda to discuss, among many subjects, direct mail ethics. The subject, unfortunately, is one that needs discussion. Fortunately, however, the ethical professionals in this business are intent on protecting their customers from fraudulent practices.

Here's a sampling of what was on the minds of ADMA attendees.

What's to stop a mailing list manager from providing, for a test mailing, a sampling of names that he knows will pull much better than an average selection from the list? The answer is clear: Nothing. In our system, it's possible to fool some of the people all the time and probably just about all of the people once.

To detect the fraudulent list manager, it was suggested that 10 names on the list be called at random to discover if they have anything in common. If, for example, they were all recent purchasers (say within the last two months), that would be a clear indication that they were hotline names instead of general file names. Or suppose it was found that all of the people who responded to, say, a standard, mass-market record company offer live in homes that cost more than $100,000. One might begin to

assume that somebody rigged the Zip Codes of the test sample, leaving only the cream of the crop.

Another member brought up the point that, since many of the lists that are ordered come on computer tape, it's impossible to select names to use in such a survey. The tape would first have to be converted to labels before the names could be read. The labels could be pulled out of the premail at the mailing house and the names called from there. But by then it would probably be too late since the list buyer is already committed to mailing them.

"O.K.," someone else said, "but no buyer would ever use that list again." Ah, but if the list tests 20 times a year and gets rolled out 15 out of the 20, that's all the list or owner really needs to turn a nifty profit.

Say they rent 5,000 of their top-of-the-list names for a test. In three quarters of the cases, those names are going to pull well enough to be used for a roll-out. If there are a million names on the list at $35 a thousand, that's $35,000 every time it's rolled out.

"But won't the industry get wise? People like us sitting here today will certainly say, 'Hey, were we ripped off by that list owner.'"

"Sure," replied a mature master of the trade, "but

you'd be surprised how many organizations have been making a wonderful living over the past years relying on the old adage that there's one born every minute."

Certainly, renting your lists through a qualified list broker would help solve this problem for your publication.

Watch for overzealous copywriters

Another unethical practice—this time on the part of the copywriter who keenly feels the spirit of competition. Direct mail copy should always be carefully perused by upper management and, ideally, by the publication's legal staff before it is mailed. If it is not, some overzealous copywriter is going to get away with mailing information that misrepresents the magazine and promises more than the magazine really delivers.

Such promises increase up-front responses, but the publisher is hurt when renewals fall apart. By that time, however, the copywriter is happily working in another publishing company at a substantial salary increase because he did such a good job for you. Ethical, no. Profitable, yes—for the copywriter, not for the publisher.

Every so often, a new publisher tries to reduce the initial need for capital by using up-front subscription money received from his direct mail test.

Although some new publishers do it and get away with it, this practice is not only unethical, it's also illegal. Any money that comes in for a subscription to an as yet unpublished magazine must be held in an escrow account, and penny one doesn't go into the publisher's hand until the first issue of the magazine is mailed.

Although this type of publisher, when he fails, gives all publishers a bad reputation, there is yet another type that is potentially more dangerous. Here's a thinly veiled true story of a publisher who launched a mailing, had more than satisfactory results, developed the capital for a roll-out mailing, produced the first couple of issues of the magazine, and then was offered a lucrative job in Tahiti.

Well, Tahiti is a very attractive place and, after two or three years of shoulder-to-the-wheel hard work, that new publisher had gotten publishing out of his system. So, although he's had 50,000 paid subscribers who had received only two or three issues of the magazine, he took their money, distributed it among his staff, and went off to Tahiti, leaving those 50,000 people high and dry with three-quarters of their money stolen, as it were.

Again, illegal and unethical, the kind of business practice that taints the legitimate people in the industry. Can he get away with it? Not according to his legal counsel. Did he discuss it with his legal counsel? Maybe yes, maybe no—but he did it nonetheless.

Then there's the midwestern publisher who made the all-time great discovery. Nonprofit postage is just about 25 percent of regular third-class postage. So he went to his local home-for-the-blind and made a deal. They would get 2 cents for every piece of cold mail he sent out on the provision that he could use their permit and they would endorse his offer in their mailing piece. (Surely it occurred to him that the postal regulations weren't set up to be taken advantage of in such a way.)

He gave the home 2 cents for each piece, which on a million mailing is $20,000 and, in turn, he saved $40,000 on what his postage would have cost him. Fortunately, the government seems to be cracking down on such violators of the true spirit of the law. But we haven't seen the end of that practice, either.

Manipulating response figures

How often does a publisher say, "The stockholders

or the investors are really important to me so I'd better show at least a 20 percent response."? Why stop at 20 percent? Why not shoot for 90 percent response to a subscription offer?

How does an unscrupulous publisher do it and still have an ABC auditable sub? Well, it's a little outlandish, but if the copy for a new sports publication says that Bruce Jenner will personally deliver the first issue of the magazine on your subscription to your home and sit down and have a cup of coffee with you and the family, it's going to get a tremendous response.

It's easy for such a publisher to impress potential investors who are impressed by percentage response figures and not by much else. He can simply break out a portion of a test mailing at half the regular subscription rate, add in a free-examination offer with an absolutely gloriously printed gold leaf direct mail package, and hype responses for that portion of the mailing. Naturally, that's the portion of the mailing the publisher talks about to the potential investors.

Well, everyone's in trouble on this one. To reproduce that mailing on a roll-out is going to be extremely expensive. The subscription income is low—it's at half-price, after all—and the investors tend to believe that the response figure shows the viability of the magazine and how much the public wants it (which is not the case at all).

The response figure shows only how exciting the package was, how low the price was, and what a bargain was available. And—don't forget—the response is in gross names and not in paid names. As soon as the magazines are delivered to this otherwise impressive group of bargain-hunting consumers, they're going to write "cancel" across the invoices they get and the net response is going to be so low that the resulting *real* percentage response from that group (since the magazine probably won't live up to the beauty of the mailing package) is going to be lower than that of the "legitimate" part of the mailing.

A few years ago, a major publication had a sweepstakes mailing with an extremely confusing order form. It was exactly the kind of unethical direct mail that gets everyone in trouble. In order to enter the sweepstakes but without subscribing to the magazine, the consumer had to punch out a die-cut circular token that said "yes." If the consumer wanted to enter the sweepstakes *and* enter a subscription to the magazine, the consumer did not have to punch out that token on the order form. Sounds simple, but in an actual field test, eight of 10 merchants in retail stores on Madison Avenue failed to punch out the token to enter the sweepstakes and not subscribe to the magazine.

This less than ethical practice was pointed out in one of the industry association newsletters, yet the same publisher with pretty much the same order form is continuing to mail that package. It's a wonder there are any renewals to that publication.

Circulation versus 'audience'

A shady publisher can also be deceptive in presenting his magazine's circulation. Circulation statements are intended to reflect consumer interest in receiving and reading a publication. There is quite a difference between paid circulation, unpaid requested circulation and the omnipresent term, "audience." For the advertising buyer, the best category of reader is renewed paid subscribers. The worst category contains those in the magazine's stated market who never requested the magazine.

Some newer-to-the-business media directors probably do not read an ABC or sworn statement the way we do, however. Certainly, there are occasions when advertising purchases are made based to some degree on the print order of a publication. So, although a magazine with a 150,000 print order that distributes 140,000 copies can say they serve 140,000 paid subscribers, they may only have 10,000 paid subs and none that have ever renewed. It's not ethical to present a magazine's circulation in this way, but it's being done.

One direct mail trick comes to mind in terms of premiums. Since a premium is designed to attract new or renewed subs, it doesn't make sense to offer a premium that's going to anger a new-found customer. Yet, some publishers and direct mail advertisers offer premiums that are such a disappointment when they arrive in the home of the new customer (whom they worked so hard to get) that the relationship between them and that new customer falters before it even gets off the ground. Think

about it. Did you ever purchase a mail order product that looked good in the catalog or ad but which turned out to be a lot smaller than pictured, a lot less luxurious than described? Perhaps it was the in-house electric circuit TV aerial that looked five feet high in the ad and turned out to be five inches high. Or the "charcoal flavor" barbeque that burned only newspapers which, upon arrival, turned out to be a piece of flexible sheet metal, a tin stand, some lengths of string to tie the newspapers together, and a rather inexpensive semi-stainless steel grill cover.

In our system, fraudulent and deceptive practices are not unknown. But if you look at the perennial successes in publishing and inspect their circulation efforts, you will see that rarely, if ever, do they set a trap or get caught in one. Their successes come from being straight with the customer and delivering the product as represented. There is no room for the people who are practitioners of fraud.

Planning a direct mail campaign

By John D. Klingel

Before long it will be time to start planning the next direct mail campaign.

There are seven major elements that have to be determined in the course of planning a campaign:

1) mailing date; 2) price; 3) offer; 4) volume of mail; 5) lists; 6) package variables to be tested; and 7) lists that will be tested.

The first thing you need to plan a campaign is a healthy respect for how sensitive direct mail response is to what, at first, appear to be relatively innocuous elements. There are a lot of things about direct mail that don't make much sense and a lot of beginners enter the direct mail marketing arena thinking they can reinvent the wheel. Using "common sense" and an overabundance of arrogance, they charge into disasters.

One of the interesting aspects of direct mail is that it is a fairly objective form of marketing and one can be almost scientific in its use. We observe, we experiment, and we objectively acquire knowledge about what works and what doesn't work. There is no need to make subjective or whimsical decisions. As a result, since this is a field where experience pays, you should never invest large sums of money in direct mail without getting competent professional help.

Timing is critical

One of the first things I learned about direct mail

was the seriousness of mailing dates and that missing the drop date was a firing offense. Direct mail response, as well as other forms of direct response, is extremely sensitive to timing. There can be as much as a 50 percent difference in response between January and March. Even a couple of weeks can make a significant difference.

I'm often asked why there wouldn't be higher response for mail that was delivered when there was less competition from other direct mail. This is a good example of how many things in direct response do not make sense. I'm not going to try to explain it. The reason isn't important, and we don't have to know the "why" in order to test and observe that it is true.

The best timing for virtually all magazines (ranked in order of response) is to mail promotion so that it is delivered right after New Year's Day, the Fourth of July and Labor Day. I have never seen or even heard of any magazine that didn't find this to be true.

As an example of the "direct response process" at work, let's assume that I am working with a magazine that has an editorial content, such as skiing, that may give it a seasonal bias. If I were launching a skiing magazine, I would start with the "tried and true" approach and mail in January or July and then test other months to see if I could mail in those "off" months.

This approach of using the "tried and true" (the approach that works most often) and testing against it is the

185

way to approach any new market. For an existing publication, we use a control (something that's been done in the past) and we test against the control in an attempt to improve the efficiency (profitability) of our direct mail.

It is extremely unwise to mail in an "off" season without testing to see if it's feasible. I recently heard of a new magazine that was planning a major campaign in November. If any time of the year is particularly bad, it's November and December. Anyone want to place bets on the survival potential of that publication?

Test before you change

The "what" you're going to mail—the package, price and offer—should be based on past mailings and test results. The basic rule (which should not be violated except under unusual circumstances) is that you never make major changes in a package without testing those changes. Minor changes in the letter and brochure copy to update editorial descriptions and new departments are not the types of changes that dramatically alter response. However, changes in the order card and outer envelope are very sensitive elements of the package. Only under the most extreme circumstances should you ever consider mailing significant quantities of an untested package.

As with the package, the price and offer should be based on past testing. These are also elements of the mailing that should not be changed unless there is careful testing or extenuating circumstances that justify the risks associated with rolling out untested prices and/or offers.

One of the first stages of the planning process is to go back to past mailings and analyze the results. This will probably require updating of past results to reflect the latest data on pay-up and renewals. The best approach, although few publications are this organized, is to review campaigns for the past three to five years—looking not only at overall results for trends but also to review what has and hasn't been learned from testing.

If you price test on every campaign, what's the trend? Is it time to retest something that was tested before? Is what was working in the past going to work in the future? Occasionally, promotion techniques that used to work can be resurrected and found to work again. The current widespread use of premiums and the complete money-back guarantee are old devices that have been resurrected.

When you update old results, there should be a very careful and complete source evaluation (financial analysis) of each list and test results. For example, each list should have a net cost per order that takes into consideration the costs of bad pay and duplication with other lists. If you can incorporate renewal data in this analysis, you should do so. All too often people fail to go back to old test results and do a careful analysis. The most unusual tactic is to evaluate tests before having final data on pay-up and then forget to go back for a final review.

If you're doing mailings for the first time, the "tried and true" approach is to use a promotion package consisting of a separate outer envelope, a four-page letter, an order card and a brochure. The biggest mistake that novices make is to use a self-mailer. A standard package with separate elements will produce more cost-effective orders than a self-mailer in almost all cases.

Forecasting response

Determining the volume of mail is largely a function of the economics of the magazine. If the magazine is total-

ly rate-base oriented, the volume of mail is determined by rate-base requirements. In this type of situation, the publication may have to mail unprofitable lists.

The procedure for determining volume calls for projecting (forecasting) response for each list, calculating the number of net subs for each list and the cost per net sub, and then ranking the lists from lowest cost per order to highest. The mailing volume is then determined by how much volume is needed to produce the required number of net paid units.

The other strategy for determining volume is to mail only those lists that are profitable. In this situation you also have to project results list-by-list and then calculate the projected profitability of each list. The mailing quantity then becomes the volume of mail that includes all the lists projected to be profitable.

One of the most critical elements in determining the mailing volume is the ability to forecast response. When there are past results, the forecast starts with the past response to a list and then adjusts the response for the following factors:

1) seasonality;
2) fatigue;
3) package;
4) offer; and
5) price.

If the last usage was in January, you may want to lower response for a July campaign. Not all magazines experience significant differences in response when comparing January to July results, but many magazines do. The extent to which you adjust response for seasonality should be based on past history. When I have to guess, I use 10 percent to 20 percent depending upon how conservative I want to be.

List fatigue

If you use the same list twice a year, there probably will be some list fatigue. The amount of list fatigue varies by list and is primarily a function of the number of new names on the list. If the list you're projecting is hot line names, there wouldn't be any adjustment for fatigue. A static list that hasn't changed since the last usage will probably show severe fatigue.

Occasionally I run into situations where a common fatigue factor can be applied to all lists, but normally the fatigue factor has to be estimated on a list-by-list basis. As with everything else, historical records are the best basis for estimating fatigue. If I have to guess, I use everything from 10 percent for a list I know has high turnover to 40 percent for a static list.

The adjustments for package, offer, and price are usually based on the test results from the last campaign. One of the tricky aspects of developing these assumptions is that test lists do not usually hold 100 percent for rollouts to the entire universe. If package A (the old control) is beaten by package B by 20 percent, I wouldn't assume a 20 percent increase in response for the entire campaign. I've never heard a good explanation for this phenomenon, but I've seen a lot of actual mailing results that seem to indicate its existence.

I've been involved in a number of tests for new magazines and have had good luck, meaning that the launch campaigns came in on budget, by assuming a 20 percent reduction in response from test to roll-out. For example, if the test shows a 5 percent response for a list, I will use 4 percent as an assumption for the launch campaign.

As an example of how the projections are put together, let's assume that we are projecting response for a summer campaign and the test results were as follows:

	Package	Price	Response	Difference
Control	A	$12	3.0%	—
New package test	B	$12	3.6%	+20%
Premium test	A1	$12	3.45%	+15%
Price test	A	$15	2.4%	−20%

To project results on a list-by-list basis, we might use the following assumptions:

Seasonality reduction	-20%
New package lift	+10%
Premium lift	+7.5%
Price reduction	-20%

Let's assume that in the January campaign, I got a 6 percent response on a list (I used the entire list) for a new magazine that's doing a lot of new subscription promotion. For the July campaign, I would break out the hot line names received since I last used the list and assume a 6 percent response and use a 30 percent fatigue factor for the names used previously.

The projected response of 3.18 percent for this list would be derived as follows:

Seasonality	6.0% x .80	4.8%
Fatigue	4.8% x .70	3.36%
New package	3.36% x 1.10	3.70%
Premium	3.70% x 1.075	3.98%
Price increase	3.98% x .80	3.18%

Science plus instinct

Obviously this forecasting is a combination of science and gut instinct. I made a judgment call in deciding not to use the entire list that the new package and premium got in the tests. In arriving at these assumptions, I take into consideration the environment of the publication in regard to cash flow and rate base. These factors determine the extent to which the forecast assumptions vary from conservative to optimistic.

When you prepare projections on a list-by-list basis using the approach shown above, you know that you're not going to be 100 percent accurate on every list. What we hope for is that by going through the detailed list-by-list projections, we achieve a reasonably accurate overall projection for the entire campaign.

If the magazine is in a situation where it mails only profitable lists, it usually pays to be conservative in developing projection assumptions. If the magazine is rate-base oriented, the projection assumptions for response are usually in the middle of the conservative/optimistic range because you don't want to be substantially over rate base and you can't afford to be under rate base.

The principal way that you improve on your projection abilities is to compare the list-by-list projections with actual results. Over time you should be able to improve upon your accuracy. No one obviously ever gets to be 100 percent accurate: there are simply too many variables and there are good years and bad years for response that are a function of the economic environment.

Executing a direct mail campaign

By John D. Klingel

For many magazines, direct mail represents the single largest investment in the future. For this reason, executing a direct mail campaign is a matter not to be treated lightly, for poor execution of a mailing is often the cause of poor response, and a campaign that doesn't go well can have serious financial implications.

Every aspect of a campaign must be well-planned. Consider, for example, the fact that direct mail is extremely sensitive to seasonality and the timing of drops. If you miss a mailing date by two weeks, you can easily lower response by 10 percent or more.

Of course, a mailing date is sometimes jeopardized by poor vendor performance: mistakes, improper scheduling, not making delivery dates, etc. However, many of the potential problems with suppliers can be eliminated by careful planning, clear communications, and good follow-up. In fact, when vendors do not perform adequately, you should ask yourself what you could have done to reduce the potential for error.

The following discussion includes a number of procedures, methods of communication, and little tricks that I've found helpful in executing campaigns.

Anticipate delays

The first trick is starting the campaign early and leaving time in the schedule for delays. Don't try to execute a campaign with the assumption that everyone will perform on time; the probability is that something will go wrong.

Since most of us plan mailing drops at the same time, suppliers (i.e., printers, lettershops, list brokers) have to schedule their time very carefully. If you're a week late getting mechanicals to the printer and the printer has many other tightly scheduled jobs, your delivery may be thrown off by more than a week. You can't expect the printer to delay delivery on someone else's job

Figure I	Magazine X	Production Chart	July 1981 Campaign

Total Drop 1,000,000

	Form	Quantity
Outer envelopes		
Control package	OE-1	960,000
New package	OE-2	20,000
Plain envelope	OE-3	20,000
		1,000,000
Reply envelopes		
Control package	RE-1	980,000
New package	RE-2	20,000
		1,000,000
Order cards		
Control package	OC-1	900,000
New package	OC-2	20,000
$12 price test	OC-4	20,000
Short-term test 8/$8.95	OC-5	20,000
Token order card	OC-6	20,000
First issue free	OC-7	20,000
		1,000,000
Brochures		
Control package	B-1	900,000
New package	B-2	20,000
$12 test	B-4	20,000
Short-term test 8/$8.95	B-5	20,000
First issue free	B-7	20,000
		980,000
Letters		
Control package	L-1	920,000
New package	L-2	20,000
$12 test	L-4	20,000
Short-term test 8/$8.95	L-5	20,000
First issue free	L-7	20,000
		1,000,000

because you blew the schedule.

The schedule I try to use for most January and July campaigns is the following:

Drop Date	12/29	7/1
Plan campaign/obtain quotes	9/1	3/1
Final copy	10/1	4/1
Order lists & printing	10/1	4/1
Deliver lists to merge/purge	11/1	5/1
Deliver mechanicals to printers	11/1	5/1
Deliver labels to lettershop	12/1	6/1
Deliver printed materials to lettershop	12/1	6/1

(For extremely large campaigns these dates may not provide sufficient lead time. For very small quantities, a campaign can be executed in much less time.)

Planning the campaign

In planning a campaign, first determine your mailing volume through rate base planning, modeling, and budgeting. Then determine the control package, offer, and price by examining past mailing results, evaluating the tests, and doing source evaluation.

In addition, determine what you want to test and plan accordingly. If, for example, you're planning to test a new package, the copywriter must be contacted well in advance since good copywriters are usually booked well into the future.

Next step: contact your list brokers and request recommendations for list tests. Prepare a production chart (Figure I) and a preliminary mailing chart (Figure II), and then contact the printers for quotes. The production chart will force you to think through clearly the number of package variations that require copy changes, mechanicals, plate changes on press, and quantities for printing quotes.

Be sure to give a form number to all promotion pieces. (Don't confuse form numbers with promotion codes that appear on the labels. They are two different things.) The form number is one of the most critical control elements in communicating with printers and your lettershop. Compare the mailing chart's use of form numbers (Figure II) with a letter of instruction to a lettershop that would say, "Put the $12 letter in with the $12 order card, in with the $12 brochure." Which method is least likely to get fouled-up?

At this stage, a mailing chart is not necessary for communications with the lettershop. However, in very complicated campaigns (the examples included here are for a very simple campaign), the mailing chart is a check on the quantities required for each version. Preparing the mailing chart early also makes it easier to figure out merge-purge instructions and to get more precise quotes

Figure II			Magazine X	Mailing Chart	July 1981 Campaign			
Panel	Promotion Key	Quantity	Outer Envelope	Order Card	BRE	Brochure	Letter
Main panel	Mixed	840.0	OE-1	OC-1	RE-1	B-1	L-1
Control panel	OTO1	20.0	OE-1	OC-1	RE-1	B-1	L-1
New package	OTO2	20.0	OE-2	OC-2	RE-2	B-2	L-2
Plain envelope	OTO3	20.0	OE-3	OC-1	RE-1	B-1	L-1
$12 price test	OTO4	20.0	OE-1	OC-4	RE-1	B-4	L-4
Short-term test 8/$8.95	OTO5	20.0	OE-1	OC-5	RE-1	B-1	L-5
Token order card	OTO6	20.0	OE-1	OC-6	RE-1	B-1	L-1
No brochure test	OTO7	20.0	OE-1	OC-1	RE-1	—	L-1
First issue free	OTO8	20.0	OE-1	OC-7	RE-1	B-7	L-7

from the lettershop.

In getting quotes from printers, specify the number of versions and plate changes. If you obtain a quote for the main run and *then* ask for quotes on test versions, the plate charges will probably be higher.

Once quotes and list recommendations are in, the next step is to confirm the quotes, order lists, and prepare merge-purge instructions. Ask the printers to provide a schedule for the precise dates by which they need mechanicals or film. Since envelopes usually require the longest lead time, those mechanicals are usually done first.

The letters of instruction for list brokers and the merge/purge serve two purposes, and they can be designed accordingly. The first purpose is to communicate. The second is to provide you with a document that can be used for follow-up. Consequently, you may want to set up the letters with blank columns (i.e., lists ordered, tapes in, etc.) so you can check things off as they are completed or delivered. This same procedure can be used with the production chart to show copy due dates, mechanicals completed, bluelines approved, etc.

A few tips on communicating and dealing with suppliers:

• *Introduce vendors to one another.* For example, the merge-purge account executive should have phone numbers and contacts for the list brokers and the lettershop. The lettershop should have phone numbers and contacts for all printers and the merge-purge house. These people often need to communicate with one another, particularly if problems occur.

• *Speak English.* It's usually better to tell a vendor what you're trying to accomplish than to try to speak his language. Unfortunately, there's too much trade slang and it can cause some real communication problems. I was recently talking to a merge-purge supplier and stated that I wanted a "loose" purge. During the course of the conversation it became clear that what I meant as "loose" they called "tight." What I should have done is just tell them what my problem was and let them come up with a solution.

• *Don't be afraid to play dumb.* If you act as if you know everything, you shut yourself off from suggestions and information that may be very valuable. You are dealing with specialists, and you're probably never going to know as much about their specialty as they do. So why try? Let them help you and let them teach you. I've been involved in more campaigns than I care to admit, and I've learned some new trick on every campaign.

• *Treat vendors as family.* Don't be afraid to show your mailing results to your list brokers and merge-purge supplier. They may have some valuable input. Showing test results to your lettershop may help impress upon them the value of tests. In any event, make your vendors feel like a "part of the team."

Once you have clearly communicated with your suppliers, be sure to follow up by constantly monitoring progress. You will find that the more you stay on top of things, the less likely it is that problems will occur. It always seems that whenever I think everything's under control, I find that it's not.

One last trick that I can pass on is the use of notebooks. For every campaign, I set up a notebook with tabs for Lists, Merge-Purge, Quotes, Mailing Chart, Production Chart, Budget, and other categories. I also keep almost all pertinent correspondence, notes and charts in the notebook so that I won't misplace key documents. It's easier to grab a notebook than to find files when questions arise. In addition, since I make sure key suppliers have my home phone number in case of emergencies, I simply carry my notebook home at night.

Timing

By Eliot DeY. Schein

One of the issues most frequently discussed by circulators and direct mailers is: "When is the best time of year to do cold mailings?"

The success of new business mail is certainly related to a number of events and activities. A red envelope may perform better than a green one. Good copy will outpull bad copy. A right-on-target list will result in more orders than a borderline list. Etcetera, etcetera, and so forth.

The ideal mailing is at best a recipe which is a pinch of this and a pinch of that, combined with the hope that the right pinches in the right places will mold the ingredients into a successful effort.

The variable that defies scientific proof and theory more than any other is the date. *When* should you mail? The experts claim that the best mailing date for magazine subscription promotion is December 31.

Historically this is the pet day for all the experts. Why is this so? Although the experts do not provide an answer, here are some points to consider.

December 31 was chosen years ago as a day to consider mailing because it was the last possible day to take a tax deduction for the cost of the mailing. One day later: a different year, a different tax situation. If a magazine found itself in a rather profitable position, it would much prefer to spend the money this year rather than next year.

Another reason: In the days of a simpler society, postal rate increases took effect on the first day of the new year. Naturally, the astute mailer would want to drop his mass mailing before the postage increase took effect. Again, the last day of the year was the last day this could be accomplished.

As a result of these two financial considerations, December 31 became the darling of the mass mailers— *Life, Look, Saturday Evening Post, Coronet*—the biggies who set the pace for just about everyone else. December 31 worked well for them, and it still seems to work well today in most cases.

No verifiable reason

The problem is not should you or should you not mail on December 31. You certainly should. The problem is trying to explain why. Postal increases don't occur on the first of the year anymore. Nor are our tax considerations quite as cut and dried as they used to be.

Actually, there is no objectively verifiable reason for the high performance of this day as a mailing date. Perhaps years ago when the ground rules were set, the biggies mailed in such volume that the American consumer began to expect the big, high-profile magazine solicitations on the last day of the year. And as the consumer is trained, so shall the consumer react.

Another possible explanation has to do with the psychology of the Christmas season. The average consumer loves to spend money and spends much of it around December 25. If a $6, $10 or $15 magazine subscription solicitation is mailed on December 31 and delivered somewhere in the middle of January, it will probably be received by the consumer at the exact moment when he has some money available and is willing and anxious to spend some—but not too much—money.

Another theory: A good part of the country is gripped by cold weather in the middle of January. What could be a better time to confront the population with the enjoyable prospect of sitting down in a nice warm living room or den and reading a magazine without the distractions of the foreboding outdoors?

Whatever the reason, December 31 stands sentinel as the best mailing day of the year. As a result, however, it has caused some headaches to rival the annual January 1 hangover.

Since the calendar has only one holiday week, the last week in December invariably causes monumental scheduling problems in terms of lead time for component production and mailing house operations.

Holiday headaches

First, because of the popularity of holiday time as a vacation time, lists must be ordered more in advance than at any other time in the year. Second, and far worse, because "everyone" mails on December 31, printers and mailing houses (who are solidly booked in the fall with orders for production of components to be mailed on the last day of the year) have a field day rejecting orders from lesser customers.

Second best

A quick shift of seasons brings us to what is commonly considered to be the second best day of the year: July 3 or the day before the Fourth of July weekend holiday celebration.

Explaining why July 3 is a good mailing day is far more difficult than justifying December 31. July 3 would seem to be fraught with disadvantages. The first one that probably comes to mind is that people are on vacation. True—and yet not true. Thirty years ago, before air-conditioning, summer vacations were a given. The only way to be comfortable in the summer was to jump into the cool waters of lakes and oceans or to head for the mountains where the thinner air was cooler.

However, this is no longer the situation. Where once only movie theaters and motels were air-conditioned, now we drive in our air-conditioned cars to our air-conditioned offices then back to our air-conditioned homes. Theaters, restaurants, stores, practically everything except sidewalks are kept comfortably cool for us. And truly, July 3 is a marvelous mailing day. How is this known? The statistics speak for themselves.

Of course, it is not the second best mailing date for *all* kinds of magazines. Two examples come immediately to mind. First, a magazine such as *Home Energy Digest*, which concentrates on keeping warm efficiently in the cold weather, will not fare as well in a July solicitation as it would in a colder month. Second, if your magazine solicitation is aimed at blue collar readers, your July 3 mailing may find your market "gone fishing" because many large production facilities close down for two weeks in July.

The autumn months

The third best day of the year is the day before Labor Day. Why is this? Unlike July and December 31, a mailing the Friday before Labor Day will find students back in school and the "work" of the year beginning to come back to normal. And normal seems to be a good condition under which to do a successful mailing.

It has also been argued that mailing the day before Labor Day can generate gift subscriptions in time for Christmas. And surely we have all seen how catalog mailers are shipping their circulars earlier and earlier in the month of September as the years go by.

The great pundits have led us to believe that the day after an election day is not a bad time to mail, either. This can only be accomplished three out of every four years, however, since November mailings in presidential election years just don't work as well as they work in other years. (The pundits feel that a presidential election creates a market that is too excited, distraught, tired or otherwise energy-drained to care about mailings.)

Test and rollouts

Whether you're testing lists, packages, prices or any combination of these, it is important to bear in mind that a mailing is (or should be) a combination of a test and a rollout. Once a mailing is set to drop, part of it is going to be used as information to develop the next mailing in the series.

The relationships between your magazine's mailing dates have a great effect on the efficiency of your mailing. If you mail on July 3 and December 31 of every year, you have approximately six months between mailings to capture and refine your information and apply it to the next mailing. If you do a September mailing, however, at best you will have only partial information upon which to base a December 31 rollout of the tested elements, and no chance at all of using any of the information for the November mailing which comes upon you very quickly.

Historically, there are some pretty poor days to mail. Remember, stay away from the mails in October and November of a presidential election year. Also, since most people must pay personal income taxes on April 15, steer clear of a mid or late March mailing which would deliver your solicitation to disgruntled consumers faced with having to raise capital for an April 15 deadline. Psy-

---

April checklist

☐ Plan your summer mailing, beginning with creative work on a test package for that mailing.

☐ Give extra attention to your July expire file (if you have been mailing early in July on a regular basis) since that file would be larger than normal. By now you are starting to receive statistics from your advance renewal and are getting ready to mail your first renewal effort to your July 1981 expirers. Take a look at that advance renewal and see how well it tracks compared to previous years.

chographically, this would seem to be the worst time of the year to mail, and statistics bear this out.

Mailing to schools

Mailing the school market—to students or teachers or administrators—requires a whole different set of rules. You cannot mail to these people in the summer. The Friday before Labor Day may be a little early for colleges and universities. And once you get past April, your mailing may fall into the hands of the custodial staff who could be getting ready to close down the school for the year.

The only way to be sure of the best time of year for you to mail is to test every day of the year and compare results. Failing that, the parameters given herein, with a little bit of logic on your part, should give you more than satisfactory results and a minimum of disappointment.

The criteria for a good mail date include the availability of the market at the time the mail is delivered, the nature of the psychology of the period of the year, the projected economic variables (which certainly do seem to have an effect), the seasonality of your magazine, and the way in which you promote.

Bear in mind, of course, that factors beyond your control can make this whole business of scheduling mail dates a matter of luck. In the past 20 years, the best laid mail plans have gone awry when, for example, pieces were mailed just before a postal strike, or delivered on the day of a presidential assassination, or mailed into or out of snowbound areas, to name just three. Because tragedy, disaster and job action can jump up and bite you when everything else seems to be going well, it makes good sense not to put all your eggs in the same mail truck . . . on the same day.

The business of lists

By Ed Burnett

Good lists are the lifeblood of successful publishing. Shakespeare may have been thinking of publishers when he had Sir John Falstaff state, "I would to God thou and I knew where a commodity of good names were to be bought."

Over 500,000 lists are in use. Over 400,000 establishments have third-class bulk mailing permits. And each permit implies a list or two or more.

Pete Hoke, editor of *Direct Marketing Magazine*, and this writer have estimated the amount of third-class bulk mail that is used for "prospecting" new customers, donors, recipients, or subscribers. If our figures (which indicate over four billion direct mail pieces) are correct, the total dollars spent on outside mailing lists for prospecting must be in the neighborhood of $125 million.

There are several ways to classify lists. Let's begin with the most obvious classification: the source of the list.

There are three convenient classifications of lists based on where the list comes from:

1. Compiled names (compiled from printed source documents).

2. Response oriented (buyers, inquirers, warrantees, respondents).

3. Originally researched (compiling at the source).

Compilers and compiled lists

A compiler provides a list of names and addresses, extracted and combined from printed sources, to reach a given market or classification. The compiler does not ordinarily work with original data, nor does he do original research. He may research sources, or research to find sources, but his product is compiled from printed sources.

Compilers work with internal sources (company records) and external sources (printed records).

The main printed sources for compiling from internal (company) records are customers, friends of customers, giftees of customers, warrantees, inquirers, respondents, prospects, sales force recommendations, house organ distribution, influentials—press and other, employees, officers, suppliers, and stockholders.

The main printed sources for compiling from external (printed) records—non-response oriented—are: 1) Rosters and membership rolls; 2) Directories and registrations (cars, phones, voters, industries, professionals, householders [city directories], purchasers); 3) Reports; 4) Announcements (births, job related activity, professional activity, social activity, advertisers); and 5) Overlay material for segregation of mailing lists (census tracts, ethnicity, surname, "clusters" [around known homemakers], professions, institutions).

External compiling itself breaks down into two kinds: 1) precompiled names and addresses provided to fit a market known to exist, or believed to exist, and 2) compilations to order—or custom compiling to specifications laid down by the customer.

In general, most external compiling operations are moving more and more toward precompiled lists. But the increasing sophistication of list use, plus the active merchandising by compilers of multiple selection factors, are blurring the lines between what is a precompiled list and what is a "custom" prepared list for just one client.

Forty lists available

There are 40 kinds of lists available from compilers (Figure 1).

Furthermore, there are lists within lists. Professionals include medical, dental, legal, architectural. Medical within professional can include veterinarians and osteopaths. Lists within MDs can be selected by staff, private practice, specialization, and age.

Who compiles lists?

There are three major compilers of most home address files: R. H. Donnelley, Metromail, and R. L. Polk. Donnelley compiles all telephone registrants, and sells a copy of the list to Metromail. Metromail provides the telephone list to R. L. Polk. Polk compiles all auto registrations in some 40 states where such lists are still available, and adds some 24 million consumers obtained through canvassing for city directories. It then furnishes a copy of the auto registration list to R. H. Donnelley.

Each of these firms then overlays basic address data with census data. They then have individualized data (length of residence, head of household, type of domicile, car ownership, surname selectivity for ethnicity). In addition, by utilization of individualized data and census data (which include median value of home, income, age of head of household, education, race, number of children, percent of ownership of home), calculated income for individual families is also provided.

By careful use of all this information, these major compilers can select names of younger families, older families, middle-class families, upper-class families, urbanites, suburbanites, exurbanites, rural families. Such selections are to the casual use of phone book data as wine is to water.

In the world of businesses, institutions, offices of professions, there are five major compilers: Dun & Bradstreet, National Business Lists, R.L. Polk, Network Marketing, and Burnett. The last four offer essentially complete coverage of yellow-page telephone books by classification. National Business Lists, R.L. Polk and Burnett overlay these with net worth ratings obtained from major credit directories, including the major file published by Dun & Bradstreet. Dun & Bradstreet, missing some data available from phone directories, includes information on number of employees, sales volume, and the chief executive of the establishment.

All of these compilers utilize the Standard Industrial Classification (SIC) system. All but Dun & Bradstreet augment the conventional four-digit SIC with a fifth digit. This adds up to 2,000 additional classifications to the 1,000 or so within the conventional SIC system. Most of these compilers now also offer all top executives at all major companies (rated $500,000 and over in net worth) selection by multiple SIC, sales volume, number of employees, and functional titles of executives.

Major classifications within the SIC system

Classification	2 Digit SIC
(1) Agricultural, forestry, fisheries	01-07
(2) Mining	10-14
(3) Contracting	15-17
(4) Manufacturing	20-39
(5) Transportation	40-47
(6) Communication	48
(7) Utilities	49
(8) Wholesale—durable goods	50
(9) Wholesale—non-durable goods	51
(10) Retailing	52-59
(11) Finance	60-63
(12) Insurance	64
(13) Real Estate	65
(14) Services—lodging	70
(15) Services—personal	72
(16) Services—business	73
(17) Services—automotive	75
(18) Services—non-automotive repair	76
(19) Services—amusement	78-79
(20) Services—medical	80
(21) Services—legal	81
(22) Services—educational	82
(23) Services—social and cultural	86
(24) Services—churches	86CH
(25) Services—eng/arch/accnt	89
(26) Services—government	91

Compiling from phone books

Alphabetic and "reverse" or "criss-cross" telephone directories (in numerical sequence by street, instead of alphabetic by name) are the major source material for the three major compilers, who stratify (break into small demographic blocks) their lists by overlaying phone, car, and city directory lists with census data. These major compilers go beyond the census tracts published by the U.S. Census (covering every metropolitan market and over 70 percent of the population) to what are called enumeration districts and sub blocks. Each of these defines the small geographic area given out to an individual census canvasser.

There are over 300,000 such "bits of real estate" which can be selected, each of which provides data in the form of medians for a reasonably homogeneous block of some 125 to 150 families.

The data available include income, age of head of household, average number of children, educational level, number of cars, male *vs.* female head of household, rental *vs.* ownership of home, value of home. For the rest of the country, these compilers, through field work and other research, have established some 40,000 to 50,000 "pseudo tracts" so that the entire population can be selected by published plus estimated configurations.

Understanding the use of medians

The key to understanding stratification is understanding the use of medians. A median is half-way from the beginning to the end. Thus, in a census tract or sub block with a median income of $9,000, half the people make more than $9,000, while half make less.

Some tracts have wide spreads; some small spreads. The art in this league consists of testing in substantial volume to determine which factors influence orders, which do not—and then selecting tracts with comparable demographic characteristics. It is a form of compiling which lends itself almost exclusively to clients with needs for large lists.

While all of us instinctively "profile" (as when we select a school or a neighborhood to live in), it is best to start without preconceived concepts when using stratified lists. That way the data can dictate the pattern to follow in an unbiased way.

From these huge files of all households, special extracts can be made to pick up, say, doctors at home addresses, pastors at home addresses, armed forces officers at home addresses, or a list of all families (the affluents) with incomes of $25,000 and over. From this source comes the very pretty list (in street number sequence) of members of boards of directors at home addresses and their next-door neighbors, by all odds the highest level income list of size in the U.S.

For a small segment of phone book names, or for saturation in a small area (as for a supermarket or shopping center), local compilers are usually utilized. (There are, in all probability, several thousand local compiling operations utilizing classified phone directories as source material.) Groups of such local specialists have banded together to furnish close to national coverage by means of so-called "occupant" lists, based primarily on phone books, plus local research for new residences.

In general, these do not yet have overlays by census tract, but a number of these lists go beyond Zip order to actual carrier-route order within Zip. And this makes possible tracted carrier routes. With the advent of the computer, and the opportunities offered through stratifying, it is probable more of these lists will feature census tract overlays.

Although demographic characteristics are usually associated with consumer files, they are equally important in business list selection.

Demographic factors to look for in both consumer and business lists are listed in the accompanying chart.

Demographic factors

Consumer	Business
Age	Age
Income	Size (Employee strength, net worth, sales volume
Sex	Income of executives
Children	Title or function
Ethnicity	Education of executives
Relation to central city	Sex
Geographic location	Classification
Home ownership	Multiple SICs
Male *vs.* female headed family	County
	City size
Single family unit *vs.* multi-family	Geographic location
Education	Size of establishment
Phone number	Corporate or non-corporate
Length of residence	Phone number

Psychographics in direct mail

Psychographics, the latest buzz word of avant-garde advertising agencies and advertising research, is

Figure 1:
40 lists available from compilers

	Business	Consumer	Mail order	Compiled
Advertisers	●			●
Alumni	●	●		●
Births		●		●
Business executives	●		●	●
Businesses	●		●	●
Canadian	●	●	●	●
Churches	●		●	●
"Clusters" around known homemakers		●		●
Contributors	●	●	●	●
Credit Cards	●	●	●	●
Data qualified by field research, questionnaires	●	●	●	●
Editors	●			●
Educators	●	●	●	●
Engineers	●	●	●	●
Ethnic	●	●	●	●
Financial	●			
Foreign	●	●	●	●
Government	●	●	●	●
Influentials, opinion leaders	●	●		●
Institution executives	●			●
Institutions (except churches, government)	●		●	●

	Business	Consumer	Mail order	Compiled
Insurance	●		●	●
Libraries	●			●
Magazine subscribers and recipients	●	●	●	●
Mail respondents, business	●		●	
Mail respondents consumer	●	●	●	
Medical membership	●	●	●	●
New businesses	●	●		
Newly established households		●		●
Newly promoted executives	●			●
Occupant		●		●
Owners of products	●	●	●	●
Professionals—other	●	●	●	●
Retail	●			●
Scientists	●	●	●	●
Senior citizens		●		●
Stratified lists by demographic characteristics		●		●
Students—high school and college	●	●		●
Teen-agers		●		●
Trade show registrants	●			●

the so-called science of reaching people not by the demographics of where they live, but rather by their lifestyles or how they live.

For my discussion of psychographics, I will be adapting from material prepared originally for Dependable Mailing Lists.

Demographics might be called the socioscience of the measurable *externals* of a life pattern, among which are age, income, occupation, value of home, location, duration of residence, head of household, and family size. Psychographics might be called the socioscience of the *internals* of a life pattern which produce measurable behavior patterns and measurable expenditures of time, energy and money. Educational level is demographic; how that education is used is psychographic. The occupation of a man is demographic; his hobbies and leisure activity are psychographic. His income is demographic; how he spends his disposable income is psychographic.

When one selects a list of boards of directors at home addresses and their next-door neighbors, that is a demographic selection based on the obvious fact that neighbors of people making $30,000 or more per year are likely to have comparable incomes.

A variation on this theme is practiced by *Time* magazine, which sends a special letter to the former home of a moved subscriber. The psychographic thinking here is that the new buyer of a given type of home is apparently inclined to lead the same type of lifestyle as the subscriber who just left. But his neighbor may have a different lifestyle, even though a comparable income, which explains why the neighbors of subscribers to *Atlantic Monthly* are not necessarily good prospects for *Time*.

The proliferation of lifestyles

The real story of our time is the somewhat fantastic proliferation of lifestyles, particularly among the young and the well-to-do, which in effect is creating a whole series of mini-markets.

Sociologists call our times the "age of alternatives, a time of doing your own thing." And we now have multiple overlapping markets of affluent, educated adults who are demanding, demonstrative, articulate, multifaceted, with a considerable cynicism concerning traditional advertising and marketing.

There are over 100 million licensed drivers in America. More people are awake at midnight in the U.S. than anywhere else on earth, maybe more than all the rest of the world put together. We are educating more millions in college than we can employ in managerial positions, which may be one good reason why multiple careers are now socially acceptable. Multiple careers affect both sexes with over half the wives already at work.

What seems to be emerging from all this is what Alvin Toffler calls "future shock"—"the dizzying disorientation brought on by the premature arrival of the future." Toffler says most travelers have the comforting knowledge that the culture they left behind will be there to return to. The victim of future shock does not. This well may be the most important disease of tomorrow.

But while "narrow casting" on an almost individualistic basis is certainly part of the future, and advertising pundits talk learnedly about the "psychographics" of their customers, the only medium which is really outfitted to use the term "psychographics" today is direct mail.

A buyer is a buyer is a buyer

To a publisher, the fact that a man or woman buys a book, a record, a magazine, or a cruise is far more important than his or her income, occupation, age, number of children, location of home, or any other demographic pigeonhole into which that buyer can be placed. To paraphrase Gertrude Stein, a "buyer is a buyer is a buyer." What someone has already bought tells us more about what else he or she is likely to buy than all the demographic statistics available per tract or block or enumeration district.

It is not chance that a good list of mail order buyers will in every case outpull a good list compiled demographically, and by a sizable margin. It pays for major mailers to concentrate on mail order buyers when they go into the marketplace and to pay the modest modern costs of unduping to increase the efficiency of each piece mailed.

A book buyer will buy more books; a record buyer will usually buy more records. If need be, such a buyer will even deprive himself of some element of comfort or reduce his apparent scale of living in order to have available the discretionary income to indulge in his lifestyle choices.

Only through direct mail is it possible now to narrow in not just on proven book buyers as a class, but on book buyers who have already bought books by mail. And while book buyers do not come in assorted sizes, they do come in assorted flavors and colors, each of which can be identified and tested individually.

There are psychiatric book buyers and history book buyers. There are buyers of novels, and buyers of biography, of mystery, and of the mystic arts. Books on science can be academic, popular, erudite, or recondite. What's more, they can be in social science, biological science, physical science, or in sci-fi. And there's an audience for cookbooks, floral books, how-to books, books of poetry, short stories, plays, adventure, discovery, sexology, psychology, child care, personal health and grooming, plus encyclopedias and reference books in dozens of fields. And there is a whole group of buyers of what the trade calls "hardware" books, books bought essentially to be seen on library tables, and not necessarily to be opened or read.

What advertiser discussing the psychographics of mass media A or B or C as markets for given types of books can "narrow cast" as does the expert user of mailing lists as markets?

The buyer of rock records, of country and western, of blue grass, revival, or Dixieland is just not the same kind of person as the so-called longhair who goes in for Bach. The Bach man may have little in common with the classical buyer who finds the classics started with Moog and not mood, who finds Bartok and Stravinsky old hat and worships strange new composers with names like Beno, Boulez, Mimaroglu, Stockhausen, and Varese.

Some record collections feature words and not music, some even sounds and not music. What's more, the stereo buyer eschews monaural, while the four-tracker knows stereo is passe. And the cartridge tape buyer may only nod at the cassette buyer, and both simply sniff at "old-fashioned" records.

Once again, only through direct mail can marketers make any such approach to what are obviously lifestyle differences. The psychographics in this case are the taste (and equipment) in the enjoyment of music.

Man is what he does

B. F. Skinner in *Beyond Freedom and Dignity* is the exponent of the theme that a man is what he does, not what he thinks. While there is an acrimonious debate on this subject, no one in direct mail is likely to argue with Skinner's position. For example, a person demonstrates charitability by his gift or his donation. The remarkable proliferation of mailings made by causes to donors of other causes is due to the fact that those who have been donors are more likely to donate than those who "should" show an interest. In its fund-raising role, direct mail is playing straight psychographics.

I can describe direct mail's use of psychographics in pithy if not very poetic terms as "the art of going where the raisins are in the rice pudding." A grower seeks out buyers of plants and seeds; a vitamin producer seeks out those who wish greater vitality; the school seeks out those who evidence an interest in self-education; the gourmet food packer seeks out those who cherish a better table.

In mail-order terms, thinking psychographically can also be interpreted as thinking peripherally. Individual lifestyles or psychographics can best be pictured not as single isolatable strands, but rather as many strands of more or less common characteristics, with some thicker than others.

Thus, the mailer selling a cultural item should test lists of buyers of a variety of cultural products. Students of the current growing cultural market calculate that there are some five million to six million family groups (within the 66 million family groups in the universe) which make up the so-called "cultural market." From a direct-mail point of view, such a market is made up of people who have demonstrated their cultural bent by engaging in one or more of the following lifestyle activities:

1. Buying books, gourmet foods, wines, expensive gifts, records, music, magazines, journals, services, art, vanity press.

2. Buying tickets or subscriptions to concerts, art shows, lectures, theatre, films, readings.

3. Donating to museums, historical societies, colleges and universities, art preservation.

4. Graduating from college, professional, or graduate school.

5. Enrolling in college, adult education.

6. Becoming a member of art societies, record clubs, amateur music clubs, museums, book clubs.

Lists mirror lifestyles

What is clear, of course, is that each element within this cultural complex can be reached via given mailing lists, which mirror in effect the lifestyles of those who have made some overt act which has landed them on specific lists of like-minded people.

Students of direct mail were students of psychographic patterns years before the "need to probe beneath the surface of human motivation" was publicized by advertising market researchers. Some of the great mail-order successes of our day have been built around service to an isolatable group with a definite specialized interest, from health to model cars to Americana to rocks to baby toys to patterns to roses to wines to astrology charts to insurance for those over 50, and hundreds upon hundreds more.

Careful mailers know that the best prospect list for a special-interest mailing is a list which parallels as closely as possible their customer files. And such mailers who use merge/purge to remove duplication are well aware of the correlation between unduplicated lists and response.

It is pretty obvious that the recent proliferation of lifestyles and the huge growing power of TV have made the road for general-interest magazines an exceedingly rocky one. But these times have hastened the development of special-interest magazines like *Psychology Today, Smithsonian, New York Review of Books, Weight Watchers, Playboy,* and *Mad,* and these in turn have produced lists which are particularly attractive to special-interest mailers.

In a recent ad directed to media buyers, *National Geographic* asks this psychographic question: "How Classy Is Your Mass?"

Most direct mail users don't have to qualify the class of their mass. They know not by demographic externals but by the solid evidence of a purchase denoting a definite internal participation in a given class of lifestyle.

Those relatively few, very large mail-order companies with lists based on sales of a plethora of products either have learned or are learning that what they really have is a group of different lists, each in effect catering to a different lifestyle group. Montgomery Ward and Sears each utilize over 170 different cells when selecting customers to receive specific catalogs and flyers. In effect, they tailor the list to fit the offer psychographically, by selecting not only by recency, frequency and dollars, but also by item and by correlations between items.

It has long been recognized that "one man's meat is another man's poison." If that phrase were to be written today, it might say that "one man's medium is another man's tedium." Direct mail is the great psychographic medium today because it seeks just those people who are most likely to be receptive to the message of the mailer.

Marketing considerations

In addition to demographic and psychographic criteria of mailing lists, we have market qualifications to consider.

Value obviously depends upon size. A list of 3,000 is not, usually, worth one-half of a list of 6,000. And this size factor is obviously dependent on accessibility, rarity, cost to reproduce, and the total size of the market.

Other factors being equal (and they rarely are), the list with the greater quantity will be preferred. Tests are made to locate lists which can be continued at a profit. Lists which are small may not even be considered for test purposes because there is "no place to go," although sometimes a smaller list may embrace a greater portion of the known universe than a larger list.

In addition to a list's size, the direct mailer must also consider factors relating to the list's coverage and deliverability: age of names on the list; cleanliness of the list; duplication factor; updating cycle and technique; feedback for update; Zip status; titles; individual names versus company names; format and discipline; method of reproduction; cost factors in selecting, handling and reproduction; sequencing of file; sequencing of crutch files (if any); and selectivity, if any, and how handled.

Mail-order list criteria

Mail-order lists contain the names of people who are buying. For mail-order lists, the primary criteria, where they can be selected, are recency, frequency, dollars, source and item.

"Recency" refers to the most recent transaction. Buyers who bought within the last six months will almost always outpull buyers who bought over, say, an 18-month cycle.

"Frequency" relates to the number of times a given individual on the file has been ordered, within a given time frame. (Time here usually implies within the last year.)

Mail-order buyers who repeatedly buy by mail are more likely to buy by mail than non-repeat buyers.

"Dollars" refers to the average order size. On well-structured files, data on dollars can be selected based on individual orders over a given amount, cumulative dollars per year, purchases in each of last "X" years, and the like.

"Source" refers to the medium or media utilized to produce the initial order. Some lists thus can be selected for newspapers, magazines, direct mail, trade shows, radio, TV, friends of friends, package inserts.

"Item" refers to the type of product or service purchased. Publishers are most interested in people who purchase books, or magazines, or services which indicate specific interests. By isolating such buyers within lists, publishers can target in on the most likely prospects for their specific book, magazine, newsletter or service.

A list broker brings together the buyer (the mailer) and the seller (the list owner). While the broker is paid by the list owner (via a universally recognized commission system, usually pegged at 20 percent), his customer is the mailer.

Professional list sources

Brokers seek to represent all lists on the market. There are 30 major list brokers in the U.S., each managing a file consisting of some 10,000 list cards filed by category. (These card files are now, slowly, being computerized so the machine can produce universes of lists covering given classifications.) Some 50 percent of the income of list brokers comes from not over 100 of the 10,000 lists they have. And most brokers have 200 customers on the average list.

Because mailers are specialized, brokers tend to specialize. Thus, there are brokers known for their acumen and special inside know-how in such fields as gardening, opportunity seekers, culture vultures, fund-raising, gifts, magazines, financial, business mail order, clothing, insurance, health, do-it-yourself.

As the cost of solo mailings increases, we see the growth of co-operative mailings. This has led to broker specialization in other response vehicles, such as package inserts, envelope stuffers, co-op advertising, and cardvertisers.

If you mail under 250,000 prospect names per year, it is probably best to select one list broker for your needs. This amount of business (about $1,300 in gross commissions annually) is not enough to get you the support and help you need from two or more brokers. But if you mail one million pieces or more, you should by all means investigate the help that can be given to you by two or more list brokers.

Reason: While list brokers work with the same lists, each broker has different experiences with various lists. Recently, for example, this office received recommendations on a given offer from five brokers for one of its clients. One hundred list cards were involved; only 11 of them were duplicated. Obviously, each broker had touched this given market in a different way. The major mailer who restricts his business to just one broker might well be depriving himself of some valuable and untouched list sources.

Understanding list management

The list manager is the one who moves lists for his client, the list owner.

It is interesting to note that some 90 percent of all major lists on the market are now in the hands of four classes of list managers:

1. *Inside list manager.* An owner or publisher who has 500,000 or more names to offer can afford to pay an internal specialist to find increasing markets for his lists, indirectly through brokers, as well as directly to list users.

2. *Independent list manager.* An independent list managing firm represents a few select lists owned by others. This type of firm does little or no list brokerage (usually only for clients who place lists with them) and thus can tap the entire capacity of the list brokerage field.

3. *List manager-brokers.* As list management has proliferated, list brokers with their unique knowledge of list sources and list users have moved into the field. More lists are now in the hands of list managers who are also list brokers than any other class of list manager.

4. *Exclusive list manager.* A few dozen lists are the exclusive properties of a few special list brokers, who offer only a split commission to other brokers who seek to use such lists for their clientele.

A good list manager could generally double the net dollars delivered to the list owner who rents his own lists. Thus, the usual 10 percent list management fee (really list merchandising or list selling fee) becomes inconsequential.

The choice of an outside versus an inside list manager is simply a matter of fees available. A list or group of lists which can bring a publisher, say, $500,000 net may have list management sales costs of some $10,000 to $12,000. It is pretty obvious that the owner of this list cannot afford the luxury of even a one person internal department. However, a firm with list income in the $250,000 (and over) range may well find it expedient to replace an outside list manager, who obviously has several arrows in his quiver, with an inside specialist dedicated only to the sales and future of the properties of the given publisher.

The proliferation of lists within the purview of list manager-brokers should not obscure the fact that one list broker does not like, for obvious reasons, to disclose to another broker that he is working with a given client. There is just too much opportunity for the list manager-broker to start a relationship with that mailer also.

Thus, with very few exceptions, it is certain that publishers who have selected firms owned by list brokers or divisions of list brokers to be list managers are depriving themselves, perhaps inadvertently, of substantial proportions of net income. A good independent list manager who promotes widely enough to position a list properly will produce from 20 percent to 50 percent more net income for the list owner than a well-meaning list manager-broker.

The exclusive brokerage relationship

The exclusive brokerage relationship works well where the list is so valuable that other brokers will place business even at the 10 percent split commission involved. However, if a publisher is seriously interested in increasing revenue from his lists, the exclusive brokerage relationship is somewhat self-defeating.

It is well to recognize there is no such thing as "No Charge" list management. While almost any list manager of consequence will computerize a list of buyers for a publisher, all of them then amortize such "front money" out of the early rentals so that the list (ergo the list owner) actually pays (as he should) for the conversion and associated costs.

If you do have someone finance placing of inquiry or warrantee or response names on tape, be certain you get in writing all the facts on the distribution of rental income. And you should be prepared to pay a modest fee for the use of money, for that is what is usually involved in any amortization of conversion costs. But look at all costs, for some "No Charge" deals involve giving up the lion's share of the net rental income from the list. All you need remember is that the list is uniquely yours, and you need to profit first and foremost.

Label fable

By Eliot DeY. Schein

How much care is enough when it comes to assuring yourself that the mailing you are pumping your company's hard-earned dollars into will go out accurately, intelligently and, one hopes, as rewardingly as projected?

For the three owners of a New York-based special interest newsletter, apparently there are times when no amount of care is sufficient to keep things from going awry.

In the two-year history of the small, but becoming-profitable newsletter, three "returning to work" young women worked their fingers to the bone and projected that sometime this year the profit picture would be worth their efforts. Their newsletter is unquestionably a quality product (as borne out by a rather high level of renewals) and surely supports their hopeful anticipation for a mid-1982 gusher of black ink. The three moved ahead to developing a springtime mailing of 57,000 pieces to interested consumers in their field.

The keystone of the mailing was to be a package and price test to an industry association list which numbered 32,000 names in their specific specialty. Getting names from this industry association was not the easiest thing in the world. And no amount of restraint could keep our heroines from celebrating the day they got the okay from the association. Their list order was accepted!

Through good research and consultations with proven talent, they arrived at their game-plan, convinced they had done everything right. They would test one quarter of the 32,000 names with their control package at the $18 annual price. They would then test a new package with a premium at $18, $24, and $29.

The results of this mailing turned out to be nothing less than tragic, and there is no amount of additional care that they could reasonably have taken to avoid the tragedy. There is a good reason for not identifying in this column their names or the name of the association or publication. Indeed, litigation has probably already proceeded.

The publisher is a wonderfully plucky sort who suggests, in retrospect, that "It's been a learning experience." In fact, the experience that she and her partners shared is one that came dangerously close to putting them out of business. Here's what happened.

Four-way split

The list order arrived at the association requesting a four-way split of the 32,000 names; that is 8,000 each on four lists of every fourth name on the file. This would be the ideal way to use a small list of this type to best advantage, or so the publishers believed. When the order was accepted, the publishers began to print the packages.

The lists eventually arrived at the publishers' address (as was their normal practice) and not a mailing house. This bit of extra caution was designed to allow the publishers themselves to review and inspect the actual labels—an excellent idea.

An alternative idea for you, if you prefer not to have a bunch of mailing lists coming across your desk, might be to ask your mailing house, upon receipt of lists, to send you a photocopy of one or two pages within the selection for you to compare and review. Taking this one step further, you may also want to make several phone calls per sample list at random to make sure the list is exactly that which you ordered.

Back to our story: So the lists arrived, and one of the publishers looked them over and found out that they were indeed in Zip Code sequence and yes, she did recognize a couple of names of people within the industry. The mailing went out, and as an additional caution, the publishers had one of their names salted on each of the mailing lists.

Imagine their surprise and collective chagrin when each of them got four packages, all different! Here's the bottom line:

The person in charge of producing the hard copy for the lists at the association either made a very bad mistake or misread the order. What was received was four sets of names covering the *same* 8,000 people! To clarify, they had four identical 8,000 name lists, which only covered one quarter of the universe. Each of the names on the list received the control package *and* the three tests!

The complaint phone calls started coming in. And as the outgoing phone calls from the publishers began to confirm, *all* recipients received *all* four packages!

Since the test package at $18 was the same price as the control at $18 (the lowest price) and the test package also had the advantage of a premium, that package has, not surprisingly, pulled very well. Of course, mailing four

---

Checklist for August

☐ By now the components for your Christmas donor mailing should be well on their way to being printed. This mailing should go out on or about September 15.

☐ You should be counting responses from your early July mailing and making your initial plans for list selection, package and offer choices for your end-of-December drop.

---

different packages to the same 8,000 recipients is—for reasons of economy and common sense—a test procedure best forgotten.

The loss in business and replacement costs to redo the other three quarters of the mailing (to the folks who never received anything) is estimated at between $50,000 and $100,000. All hopes of black ink for 1982 have been dashed, but the publishers continue to publish and to wait.

Who's responsible?

As of this writing, everyone has lost except the attorneys. It is now in their hands. Direct mail precedents of damages for negligence or breach of contract are extremely hard to come by. Does the list owner have a responsibility to deliver not only that which is ordered but that which in fact makes sense? Does the mailer have the expressed responsibility to review the material with a fine-toothed comb, and make absolutely certain that the labels received on a special selection are 100 percent accurate?

The legal answer is not simple; the moral answer is. It is the responsibility of all parties to do everything in their power to provide an intelligent, sensible and accurate result from any mailing that goes out. And it was a failure on both sides of the fence that caused this tragedy that almost put this wonderful publication down for the final count.

The list owner, in his argument, says, "We fulfilled the order as we read it." Yet when the invoice went out to the publisher for the labels, the invoice presented the counts in exactly the manner originally desired by the publisher. That is, 32,000 names in four groups of 8,000 each on an Nth name select. The publisher, on the other hand, admits that her brief, cursory examination of the labels did not reveal the duplication.

Both are surely to blame. Therefore, why should the costs be absorbed only by the publisher? Surely the list owner eventually, if nothing else, will agree to make good on the 24,000 names not yet delivered. Small solace for the publisher. Damages will be sued for and most likely not received. The postage is forever gone. The printing for the erroneous 24,000 pieces thrown out the window. The immediate revenue lost as a result of the incomplete mailing is salt in the wound.

And the fact of the matter is, while it is everyone's responsibility in the direct mail industry to make sure that every mailing is perfect, the final responsibility always seems to rest on the shoulders of the mailer. In this case, the publisher, who stood to lose the most has, in fact, suffered a tremendous loss.

If there are any further developments in this story, your columnist will pass them along in these pages. If not, you are left with a simple moral: "You can't be too careful."

Should you acquire a failing magazine's list?

By John D. Klingel

Every time there's a rumor that a magazine is going to fold, my phone starts to ring and there's someone at the other end asking whether his magazine should take over the list. My usual half-joking question is, "How much are they going to pay you to take it over?" The question is facetious because, for most magazines, it is extremely foolhardy to assume another magazine's subscription liability.

At one time, I felt that most circulation directors would never run into a situation where they would be called upon to analyze this situation, that it was a fairly rare question. Now it seems that there are few who don't run into it. In fact, at the time of this writing, I am aware of three magazines about to fold and a number of circulation directors who are studying the financial implications associated with assuming their subscription liability.

On the surface, these situations usually seem to be very attractive. They look like a very cheap way to pick up a lot of new subscribers, give the buyer a big jump in circulation, and generate a lot of publicity.

Once you start to look a little closer, however, you begin to realize that it may not be so cheap. The cost of serving copies can be staggering. As a general rule, the economics of assuming another magazine's liability don't work unless the magazine assuming the liability has heavy advertising sales. Usually the amount of income generated by renewals doesn't offset the cost of serving copies. Consequently, rate base considerations and advertising income have to be carefully evaluated.

The worst thing you can do is pick up a subscription list without first doing a very careful analysis of the financial implications. (You can do the analysis by hand, but a computer model is very helpful in these situations.)

Expire analysis by source

Since the most critical assumption in your financial analysis is going to be how well you can renew the other magazine's subs, the first thing you need is an expire analysis by source showing the copy and dollar liability by source and by issue. As you probably know, conversion and renewal rates vary by source.

The renewal rates by source, ranked from the highest to lowest percentages, will probably be in the following order:

1. Renewals—All those subscribers who have renewed at least once.
2. Direct mail and other direct to publisher sources, i.e., insert cards, white mail, gifts.
3. Direct mail agents, i.e., PCH.
4. School plans.
5. PDS and field sold.

The assumption that I generally use is that the renewal rate for the acquired subs will be 50 percent of the percentages for the sources of the acquiring magazine. I use this assumption only if the two magazines are editorially directed toward the same audience. If the magazines are positioned for different markets, I use lower assumptions.

The common mistake in these situations is to assume a high renewal rate. Even though you think you can achieve a higher renewal rate, you should be conservative in your projections. Just keep in mind that there have been a number of magazines whose demise was hastened by assuming another magazine's subscription liability.

The expire inventory, showing the number of copies due and the dollar liability, is also used to determine how many copies to serve. If the primary objective is to acquire rate base, you may want to serve as many copies as possible. If the other magazine was sold at higher rates, you may be able to push the expire dates further into the future by serving issues on a dollar-for-dollar basis.

In the more usual situation, you want to serve as few copies as possible. You have the option of serving on a dollar-for-dollar basis but this option is usually not chosen. The most common practice is to serve the liability on a copy-for-copy basis. You should contact ABC (if you're a member) and review the rules. You will need a ruling from them on whether you have to offer the subscribers a choice of a refund or a subscription to your magazine.

Renewal strategy

In setting up your renewal strategy, you will want the acquired subs to become accustomed to your magazine. Thus, in reviewing the expire inventory, you should look at how many subscribers will expire after being served only a few issues. The acquired subs that expire immediately may have been under promotion and they probably won't renew as well as other subscribers.

In addition, if you can find out which expire groups have received renewal promotion (including advance renewals), you will be in a better position to judge how well the various groups will renew. If a group has already received renewal promotion, the renewal rate from that group will be lower than from groups that haven't been under promotion.

It's also helpful to find out as much as possible about the promotion methods (sweeps, premiums, etc.) and the rates and terms used to acquire subscribers. These factors are important in developing the renewal strategy (i.e., pricing, number of efforts) that will be assumed in the projections.

Before you use a computer model to fine tune your analysis, you can do a quick and dirty manual calculation (see Figure 1) to see if it's even remotely worth the effort. This calculation is for a couple of hypothetical magazines which I will refer to as *Magazine X* and *Magazine Y*.

Figure 1

Assumptions

Magazine X	— Number of Subscribers	=	100,000
	— Number of copies remaining in subscription liability	=	800,000
Magazine Y	— Cost of printing and mailing copies	=	$.50
	— Conversion price	=	$10.00

Quick and Dirty P&L

Income — 20% Conversion (100,000 x 20% x $12)	$ 240,000
Payment to Magazine X @ $4/sub	$ 400,000
Cost of serving copy liability (800,000 x $.50)	400,000
Cost of renewing subs @ $4 per renewal	80,000
Total Cost	$ 880,000
Net Cost	$(640,000)
Net Cost Per Sub ($640,000 ÷ 20,000)	$ 32.00

Expect low renewal rate

Magazine X is going out of business and has offered its subscription list to *Magazine Y* for a price of $4 per name. Both magazines are the same editorial genre and, after analyzing the sources, my "best guess" is that we wouldn't be prudent if we assumed anything higher than a 20 percent renewal rate. In my judgment, 20 percent is a fairly optimistic assumption for most of the "real world" situations in which I have been personally involved.

For those of you who can't accept the fact that renewal rates will probably be low, consider the following bit of reasoning. What you are actually doing is acquiring a mailing list and sending them sample copies. If that technique had a high probability of success, most magazines would use that approach. They don't—since the chances of renewing someone who doesn't voluntarily order a magazine are very slim.

I have seen one exception to my overall observation regarding a low renewal rate. A few years ago *Rolling Stone* sold the subscription list for *Outside* to the Chicago-based *Mariah*. *Mariah* was able to convert the *Outside* subscribers at a very high rate because they made an incredibly smart decision: They changed the name of their magazine from *Mariah* to *Outside* and incorporated a few of the more popular *Outside* editorial features into their magazine. For the *Mariah* subscribers, it was a name change and for the *Outside* subscribers it was more like a change of ownership than a change of magazines. This was a unique situation, however, and in most cases this type of approach isn't possible.

In my quick and dirty Profit and Loss, *Magazine Y* would have to spend $640,000 to gain 20,000 subscribers. If *Magazine Y* doesn't carry a lot of advertising and must rely heavily on circulation profit, this certainly wouldn't be a very good investment. If, on the other hand, *Magazine Y* sells a lot of advertising (a rate-base oriented magazine), it might be a cheaper way to acquire net paid units than some of the other sources they are using.

Magazine Y would be buying 800,000 ABC paid copies. If I ignore the cost of renewals, I have an $800,000 cost or $1 per net paid copy. If *Magazine Y* is a large rate-base oriented magazine it might be paying more than $1 to acquire net paid copies from some sources. In that situation, these acquisition economics could be very attractive.

A computer model is almost an absolute necessity when you're studying the rate base implications. When you add the acquired subs, it tends to push the rate base up disproportionately in the first six months since expire inventories are often weighed heavily with subscribers that have less than six issues to go. This means that you either have to shut off sources (and you're probably not going to have much time) or you're going to end up exceeding your rate base. Since the excess circulation has no advertising value, some of the net paid units being acquired are wasted. If you use the acquired circulation to increase your rate base, you have to determine how you're going to replace the 80 percent that don't convert. I could continue. The key point, however, is that there are extremely complex rate base implications that must be considered.

Another type of situation sometimes arises when magazines fold—the multi-magazine offer that goes out to the subscribers offering them a choice of magazines. I've seen a number of magazines participate in these offers, and every one of them ended up with an extremely low conversion rate.

The lesson is clear: Whatever your situation, don't jump into an acquisition of another magazine's subscribers unless you have done some very careful analysis beforehand.

The end of the Nth?

By Eliot DeY. Schein

In circulation direct marketing, no process requires more attention than the simple strategy of testing. While every publisher and circulation director should be well aware that no new promotion should ever be attempted without first passing a "test," nary a year goes by without some new horror story about a promotion that was rolled out before it had been tested.

Let us all make a pact, once and for all, that nothing will ever again go out in the mails before it is tested.

Much has been discussed and written about the proper testing methods for direct mail. One of the time-honored absolute rules is to test an Nth name selection of a mailing list. For example, if mailing list A has one million names on it, and you are desirous of testing a couple of offers or packages by mailing to the people whose names are on list A, you would probably settle on selecting two cells of 5,000 names each.

Just any 5,000? Not on your life! What you want is two pure cross-sections of that mailing list. As pure as you can get.

Since most (if not all) mailing lists of that size are stored and maintained in Zip Code sequence, a test of simply the first 10,000 names on that list would be inconclusive since it would test names in the New England area only. This is not a sufficient method of testing, inasmuch as the demographics and psychographics of New England may not match the average over the entire list, nationwide. Since you will be using the results of this test to project rollout of the remaining names on the list—those that you haven't tested—you are wide open for disaster if you agree to use just the first 10,000 names available on the list.

Bear in mind that 10,000 is one percent of 1,000,000—the total number of names on the list. Imagine it this way: First, you line up 1,000,000 people represented by those names in single file along a boulevard and ask them to count off from one to two hundred and then start counting again. Then say, "O.K., now every person whose number is 50 please take one step forward." Five thousand people would take one step forward and would form your cell of 5,000. Then, ask everyone whose number is 150 to step forward, and you have another sample of 5,000 names on an Nth name basis.

In this particular case, you would be taking two 200th name selections to give you your two cells of 5,000 names each for testing purposes.

Obviously, there is no need to line up a million people in a street. You would simply ask the computer to give you two different 200th name selections of the million names, and the results that you receive would be two sets of 5,000 labels of a perfect and pure cross section.

Nice work if you can get it.

An imperfect process

Time was when we all believed that a request such as that, for that type of selection, was handled efficiently and perfectly. While the strategic principles which prevail in this attitude have not wavered from the original concept, the truth is that, nowadays, pure Nth name selections are few and far between. You will surely get 10,000 names and two cross sections of 5,000 each out of the million names on list A. However, although the chances of your getting a thousand names from each of 10 SCF's (USPS lingo for Sectional Center Facility) are pretty good, you would not be getting the pure Nth name selection you desired. Upon inspection of labels, you can sometimes determine that you did not get what you asked for, especially if the top-of-the-SCF program is used by the list manager. But most of the time (if the list is in fact checked at all), it is difficult, at best, to determine exactly what type of selection it is you have received.

Yes, there are even some cases were we come close to fraud. Where prime names, or recent addition names, are activated on a test sampling. This questionable practice would serve to increase the pull of your mailing promotion, and suggest to you that rolling out the balance of the list may be very profitable for you. An error, to be sure, and only profitable for the list owner and manager.

There are various ways of getting cross sections of mailing lists for testing, and here is one that deserves your strongest consideration. It is called Zip-Digit Select, and while it is not as scientifically pure as an exact Nth name selection, it does provide certain benefits and safeguards.

The method is simple. Since most lists, as we have discussed, are set up in order of five digit Zip Codes, if you requested from the list owner or manager (on the same list A) a cross sectional selection of two 5,000 cells, you could easily ask for all names on the list whose Zip Codes ended in, let's say, the digits 25. This would give you one set of 10,000 names (or every 100th name). If you then say, give me an A/B split on those 10,000 names, you would have two cells of 5,000.

As has no doubt already crossed your mind, there is an impurity in this system right off the bat. The impurity is that not every digit is being fully used (if at all) in every area of the country. In addition, certain Zip Codes seem to appear more in business areas than in residence areas. This method of selection is not nearly as pure as a real Nth name select. But since real Nth name selects aren't being delivered often these days, you will probably end up with a better chance of having a reasonably good test with decent projectability.

In addition, the Zip-Digit method of selection provides two very critical fail-safe conditions for you. First, its accuracy is easy to confirm upon simple inspection. If you have asked for only those names whose Zip Codes end in the numbers 25, a cursory inspection of the resultant labels will show and prove to you that that is, in fact, what you *did* get.

Duplication of names

The second advantage involves the purity of the rollout. Let me explain.

Assume you ordered the list sample on an Nth name basis and you got exactly what you ordered, a pure Nth name selection. What you have gotten, based on the sample of the million names given previously, is every 50th name, and every 150th name, out of a 200th selection. If during the time period between your test and your continuation and rollout, one person in the first 50 moved from Amherst, Mass., to Duluth, Minnesota, the purity of your rollout is forever destroyed. While you attempt to omit names previously used, there is no way really to omit them since what you would be omitting in the rollout or continuation run would be the 50th and 150th names of every 200 names.

Surely there is no way you are going to discover the flaw in this situation by mere eye-balling. You will end up with some duplication of names of people to whom you have not mailed, and some suppression of names of people to whom you have already mailed, who may, in fact, be good potential customers. (Note, there are some rather sophisticated and careful list owners who will actually delete names previously used by name, rather than by position, in the Nth name select, but these folks are somewhat rare and difficult to unearth.)

If you use the Zip-Digit system, however, when it comes time for rollout, you would ask for all Zip Codes ending in 25 to be suppressed. You would then get a run of every other name on that mailing list that fell in every Zip Code other than those which end in 25. Therefore, with the exception of the few people who have changed addresses to locations in another Zip Code, you would be mailing to virtually none of the people you had already mailed to.

In the 1982 economy, this kind of program makes even more sense than ever before. The normalized estimate of the number of people who move in the United States in the course of a normal year is 10 percent or more. This year that number will be a lot closer to 5 percent because of the economic conditions in the country (low levels of homebuilding, reduction in executive transfers, unemployment). This adds yet another advantage to the Zip-Digit selection process.

So what does Zip-Digit selection give you? It gives you, with some variation, the opportunity to inspect and

monitor a test mailing list or a continuation mailing list, to make sure you got what you ordered. It permits you to do your marketing on a numerical basis. And it provides you with absolute proof that you have gotten the names you want to mail. This is critical for making projections for rollout and saving a great deal of unnecessary money and exasperation along the way.

To review: If you want 10 percent of a mailing list, ask for a selection of that mailing list that includes a common last digit of the Zip Code. If you want one percent of the mailing list, choose the last two digits of the Zip Code. If you want one-tenth of one percent, the last three digits of the Zip Code.

As you begin to test this approach, it is a good idea to examine the initial test list to see if you have an over-abundance of residences or businesses. You may find, for example, that if the last digit of a Zip Code is one, you may end up with three times the number of business names than if you had selected the last digit of nine. Depending on the nature of your publication, the differences in types of demographics will vary, to a degree, with the last digit you select.

On national cross sections for general interest publications, for example, you should try testing with Zip Code digits three, four, five, and six. These are approximately average. For big businesses, ones and twos seem to produce a greater incidence. But, as a rule of thumb, and to get you started, try using five as the last digit. As in the example above, this will give you as good a cross section as you can possibly get for projection purposes.

The end of the Nth name selection? Could be, and maybe should be.

Renewals

By Eliot DeY. Schein

A publisher of a special interest magazine with a subscription circulation of 100,000 wanted to know the difference in subscription revenue between his then-current and "satisfactory" 60 percent renewal rate and what he would achieve with a higher renewal rate.

The renewal subscription rate used at the time was $14.95 a year. The answer to his question was simply this: he would gain an additional $14,950 per each percentage point of increase of his renewals. A 10 percent increase would elevate his subscription income by $149,500 per year. Looking at it in a still larger sense, yearly renewal income at 60 percent for this publisher was $897,000. At 70 percent (where it now is) at the same renewal price, the publisher realizes $1,046,500 per year!

With such a dramatic difference in revenue between a 60 percent and 70 percent renewal rate, one is moved immediately to inquire, "O.K. How much did it cost this publisher to achieve that income jump of approximately $150,000 per year?"

The answer may surprise you: It cost less than $75,000. And that included the first year's one-time cost of initiating the work required to increase renewal percentage.

Considering that the publisher stands to gain at least that same amount ($150,000) year after year, and that the maintenance or the continuation charges for creative and production do not increase year after year (in fact, after the first year they drop significantly), it is hard to understand why every magazine publisher in the world doesn't try to improve his renewal performance.

Preventing an emergency

Imagine if you will that your individual subscriber is a friend with a small problem, and that this problem could become an emergency. Perhaps a seam on his shirt has become slightly undone and he is unaware of it. You, as a friend, might call his attention to this problem: "Did you notice your shirt has a little hole in it?"

If your friend ignores your observation and fails to act to repair the damage, you may notice at a later time that the seam is now opening wider and wider. You now say: "You know, that's a pretty good-sized hole there in your shirt." If again no reaction, you might say: "You know, if you let that seam open up any more, it's going to split and the arm of your shirt may fall off."

As a good friend, you are not trying to *provoke* this person into taking action (having the shirt mended), you are simply becoming more and more insistent as the problem becomes more serious. Of course, ultimately you may have to ask yourself, "How many times do I have to mention the problem to my friend before I just give up and say he doesn't care if his shirt is on or off?"

The renewal series

By now you've gotten the idea. To put it into circulation terms, "How many renewal letters or efforts do you send to a subscriber in an effort to get him to renew?"

There is no simple answer to this question because people are different. Some, upon the first hint of a split seam, will run to mend the small opening; others may be sitting in rags before taking needle to fabric. Similarly, some subscribers renew immediately; others renew only after a great deal of urging.

Since subscriptions are counted in dollars earned (as well as in numbers for advertising sales purposes), the question is not "How many efforts do you use?" It is "How much can you afford to spend on renewing any individual subscriber?" The answer is based on another question: "How much does it cost to go out and find a new friend?"

Surely, the only way to determine the number of efforts in your renewal program is based on the production costs of each of the efforts. The last effort you should use, which could be the third one or the twenty-third one, is that one which represents an investment in renewals that is slightly higher than the cost of getting a new subscriber. Higher because a subscriber who has renewed once (regardless of how much prodding it has taken) is more likely to renew a second time and a third than is a new subscriber of lesser known potential.

In general, however, a renewal series consists of one advance renewal effort and five to eight additional efforts from the start. Actually, renewal efforts should begin at the moment a subscriber subscribes.

Renewal at birth

There are two basic types of first-time subscribers. First, there is the individual who has responded to some kind of solicitation and has indicated a desire to subscribe by placing an order. Then there is the preferable type, the individual who has not only ordered but has paid for the subscription.

The moment you receive the order, with or without payment, that individual is yours, your subscriber, your friend. That individual has just jumped from the overall universe into your private universe, and you now have a relationship with him that is to be valued and nurtured.

This is the earliest moment at which you can renew the subscriber, a practice that is not only recommended but, more often than not, extremely successful. The term for this "instant renewal" is "renewal at birth." While there is some argument as to whether the results of this technique are real renewals or "extensions," there is no question that achieving success with this strategy will be easy, worthwhile and productive for your magazine.

In the case of the subscriber who has ordered a subscription but has not paid, it is normally the magazine's responsibility to send invoices and letters in an attempt to collect the money for the product ordered. If, during the course of this billing attempt, you generate not only the amount previously agreed upon at the time of ordering but an additional amount as well, you are developing what is commonly known as a "billing extension."

"Double your savings"

To achieve this victory, you need look no further than the material you are sending out in your effort to get paid. The invoice (or letter that goes with the invoice, or both) should suggest the opportunity to increase the length (or term) of the subscription by increasing the amount of money remitted.

Your copy might read: "Double your savings by doubling the length of your subscription. Send double the amount shown on the enclosed invoice." Thus, if you were selling a one-year subscription for $14.97, you would direct the attention of the new subscriber to the advantageous prospect of enclosing $29.94 instead, thereby extending the subscription for an additional year.

The other type of new subscriber—the one who sends cash payment with his order—need not receive any correspondence from you for the time being. However, if you wish to develop additional up-front dollars, the technique to achieve a "cash extension" is again simple enough.

First, send him a short pleasant letter of acknowledgment "welcoming" him into his new universe. Then, give him the opportunity to "extend now, in advance, at the special introductory rate" by doing no more than writing another check and sending it back in the "enclosed postpaid envelope provided."

The advantages of this technique are obvious: In addition to the subscription income they bring in, you are now assured of holding on to these "renewals at birth" or "extenders" for a much longer period of time than you initially expected. Furthermore, you needn't take any further steps to renew them for quite a while.

Surely, your question here is: "O.K., I see the value of this technique, but what percentage of new subscribers can I expect will extend their subscriptions at this time?" Good question! Ten percent would be outstanding. Five percent of those who had paid initially is sound. Three percent of those whom you bill is fine. Remember, this is one of the few almost guaranteed "no lose" situations you have.

Advance renewals

Advance renewal promotions, the next effort after the "renewal at birth" effort, do more than simply provide revenue (usually during the midterm of a paid subscription). They are essential in their role as bellwether for the effectiveness of your renewal promotions to come. They are usually a clear indicator to help you project your renewal yield for the time period and, thus, they help establish your requirements for new subscription generation activities.

The advance renewal is just what its name says it is: An attempt to get a paid subscriber to renew his subscription well in advance of the expiration date. This is certainly a specialized promotion because, as in the example given earlier, there is no evidence on your friend's shirt that the seam is about to open up a bit. Because advance renewal is an effort to prevent the seam from even beginning to open up, it works very well with those of your subscribers who are more interested in insurance (as we'll see in a minute) than they are in their day-to-day budgets.

Unfortunately, there is not a whole lot of emergency-type excitement you can produce in an advance renewal activity. Remember, on a monthly magazine, for example, this effort is received by the subscriber with the better part of six months remaining on his one-year subscription, so your approaches are somewhat restricted.

However, we can take a hint from the insurance people because, in effect, an advance renewal is like an insurance policy: it can provide benefits to the subscriber. First, it protects the subscriber against price increases that may occur in the next six months or so. Second, it's an assurance that the subscription, when it otherwise would have expired, will continue and no issue will be missed.

In addition, a lower promotional price can be incorporated into the advance renewal. Here, you can offer real dollar-saving benefit to the subscriber because "It will help us determine our subscriber counts for the future." Or, "Save us time during the processing of the avalanche of orders that will be coming in in six months if we can process your order now." Or, "Save us the time, effort and money of sending you costly renewal reminders at a later date." Not the strongest set of benefits and reasons, you're sure to agree, but all the same, an essential part of your renewal program.

On a consumer publication, the advance renewal effort should produce from 10 percent to 15 percent response in terms of orders and reduce the projected renewal file for the full scale renewal promotion by that same percentage. (The percentages quoted here are more likely for special interest and city or regional publications.) This does save a lot of money and anxiety in the months ahead.

Another advantage of the advance renewal promotion is that it is easily trackable. Advance renewals have a wider "time window" than ensuing efforts where confusions in record-keeping often occur between efforts in fulfillment houses.

Here is an example of something that's as close as you can get to the ideal advance renewal package:

Leonard's Index of Art Auctions is exactly the kind of publication the name implies. It is issued quarterly and costs the subscriber $125 per year. The subscriber universe is made up of auction houses like Sotheby Park Bernet, Christie's and others, auction dealers, auctioneers and most important of all, those people who buy objects of art at auction.

The annual subscription cost is actually a small price to pay if the information one learns from the publication can save thousands of dollars (or, so goes the initial promotion), but certainly large enough to warrant full attention to renewing these quarterly subscribers in advance (especially during a time of high interest rates). It can, indeed, yield great profits for the publisher.

One of the main factors that brings this package so close to being ideal is the $25 savings against the $125 subscription price. This is almost a "sandbag" package. And it is chock full of exactly the type of copy and approach that you should be using in your advance renewal—whether you have a $25 savings heightening the excitement of the offer or not.

Although most magazines offer a savings to the renewing subscriber (usually because the new and renewal subscription prices are lower than the newsstand cost), this package says it all—without overdoing it.

The carrier envelope says: "Put $25 (Twenty-five Dollars) back in your pocket . . . if you act now!" This is a fine approach to use (whatever the specific savings) to get subscribers certainly to the point of opening the envelope.

Note: The white box in the upper right hand corner of the carrier envelope (see the figure) is the only unprinted part of the overall color printing of the carrier envelope's face. This was done to allow the package to go out with a third class postage stamp as opposed to a printed indicia or a metered imprint. Because most inks (as you know) are petroleum products, under certain weather and climate conditions stamps can loosen and separate from an envelope printed with overall ink coverage. This, as your chilliest nightmares may attest, could result in a mail sack full of packages without postage, sitting on an inches-high cushion of precancelled third class stamps.

The copy on the enclosed letter is 100 percent on the nose. They've gotten the subscriber's interest by saying: "Put $25 back in your pocket..." on the carrier envelope. Now read that letter. Surely you'll agree it is as close to perfection copy-wise as an advance renewal can get. (By the way, it's copyrighted as well as copywritten.)

The order form repeats the $25 savings and repeats the basic thrust of the common advance renewal: "... I also protect myself against missing even one valuable issue between my current subscription and my renewal." (Surely you try to do everything possible to have a subscription renewed without a break in service. But, it's not really a bad idea to suggest to your subscriber that this result requires some action on his or her part to achieve.)

You'll also notice that the order form's presentation of the three-year term of service comes first. And the savings of $75 is highlighted.

This package does not get into the trenches in an effort to resell the product. Instead, it is a reminder, selling the $25 savings and the continuation of the subscription without a break in service as its main thrust. After all, the publication is about saving money in the first place—or at least not paying more than you should for pieces of art—and it's only natural that this economy orientation should carry over to the index that chronicles them.

The first regular renewal effort

The first regular renewal effort (as opposed to an advance renewal) for a monthly magazine is mailed approximately three months prior to the month of expire. In other words, if the last issue on a subscription is April, the first regular renewal effort would go out in January.

The first effort should be your "block buster." Twenty percent is not an unreasonable response on this activity. In fact, there have been documented cases of better than 30 percent

The first effort is the initial call to action: "Your subscription is up for renewal and it is now time to renew." Just a quick look at the address label of any recent copy of your magazine that your subscriber has received will confirm for him the fact that his subscription is due to expire in the next 90 days.

The object of this part of the promotion is to establish an "automatic reaction" on the part of the subscriber: he should renew his subscription and keep his life going on an even keel.

Since this individual has already received eight or nine issues, there is no particular need to run the gamut of the benefits of the magazine. He knows the magazine and the ways that he personally uses or benefits from it. He has already developed his own opinion and his own realization of need. Thus, the message should be short and sweet: "It's time to renew. That's what you're expected to do, and please do it."

The artistic merits of the package (that is, the letter, the envelopes and the order form in this particular case) should relay that message. Don't expect your subscriber to guess the contents and intents of your mailing. You want the subscriber to take action—make sure that's clear!

Now, if your percentage figures from the advance renewal and first renewal efforts add up to 25 percent or 30 percent, you're in great shape. These results are ideal and mean you are well on your way toward a better than 50 percent overall renewal percentage.

The percentage response from this first regular effort alone is a good measure of the value of the magazine to the subscriber. Since the editorial content of any magazine is that magazine's salesman-in-the-field, the vitality of the editorial product must fulfill the expectations and requirements of the subscriber. If it doesn't, the renewals go down. If it does, the renewals go up—and no amount of brow-beating or idle chatter will improve the renewal percentage of a magazine that does not deliver the editorial goods.

Assuming your magazine is the excellent publication you believe it to be, and assuming as well your subscriber agrees with you, your first effort renewal will do wonders.

The second effort

The second effort is mailed a month after the first—February for that April expire. In the second effort, your main mission is to communicate an increasing need for immediate action. While not getting hysterical, you should be suggesting, a bit strongly, that time is "a-wasting" and action is required. In order to get that across to the subscriber, there are a couple of essential elements for the second effort.

The first and foremost of these elements is a very simple strategy. The second effort should appear totally disconnected from the first. This has been called the "sneak up on 'em" approach. Surely, having received a

The 'ideal' advance renewal package

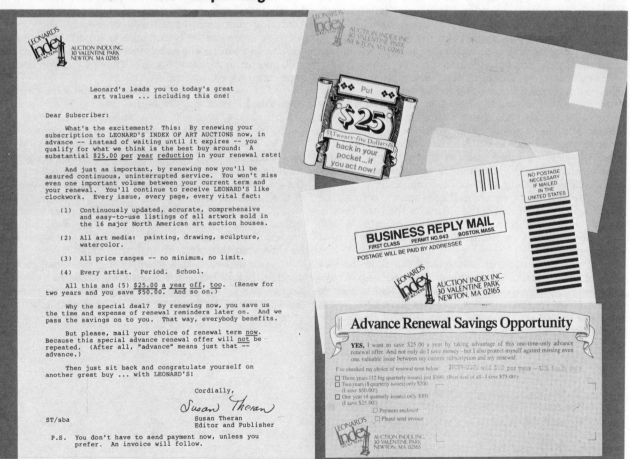

direct mail package from your magazine four short weeks ago, your subscriber is bound to recognize (through experience, and if not that, intelligence) that here's another one of those renewal letters. He knows what you're up to.

Suggest to the subscriber that this conclusion is not valid. Do not telegraph your intentions on the second effort. Instead, physically change the appearance of the package for starters. If the first effort was in a white window envelope addressed with a cheshire label and mailed via a square format third class indicia, your second effort envelope should at least be different in color of stock and style of indicia.

And even consider these variations: It might be heat transfer or direct addressed. The window could be on the opposite side of the envelope from the first effort. It could be on a different stock, maybe have no corner-card, be a different size. It could appeal to the subscriber (in, absolutely, a different typeface) in new terms and a different voice.

You certainly get the point: It should not look at all like the first effort. Other ways of dealing with this could include using an order form in a contrasting color with the envelope. Your first effort may have been white and bland, your second effort may look like a rainbow. But, by all means, make sure they look totally different. And the message, of course, is now a bit stronger, somewhat more imploring. You are now in a position of attempting to provoke the reaction. But, again, you are dealing with a friend, so don't provoke him too hard.

Subsequent efforts

The third effort mails the month prior to expiration, and is honestly your subscriber's "last chance to be *guaranteed* continuous service." It is here that you must sell the benefits of continued service. For example: "We're all vitally interested in this ever-growing field where monthly changes have occurred in the past and will surely occur equally quickly in the future. However, you have only one more issue remaining in your subscription and after that you're gonna end up being in the dark."

As with the second effort, the third and all consecutive activities should not resemble any one of the others. The sneak-up-on-'em approach should be uppermost in your mind. Vary stock, color, typography, and other physical characteristics of the packages so that your subscriber will not recognize each one as an additional attempt at selling the same thing.

The third effort should pull less than the second, the fourth less than the third, the fifth less than the fourth, etc. By now your graph should be recognizably a soft slope downward from left to right as your efforts bear their fruit.

The fourth effort arrives around the time the last issue of the magazine on the subscription arrives. It says just that: "You have now received or are about to receive your last issue of the magazine." This is panic time, and it is a time to impress upon the subscriber that he is abandoning an old friend and failing to meet his commitments to his special interest, business need or locality. The subscriber should be made to feel that he must act immediately to repair that damage.

The letter should get across very carefully that, from now on, the world will not be the same; it won't be as good. And that the magazine, in its consideration of how important the benefits are to the individual subscriber, is willing to move mountains to try and get the subscription back on the track—perhaps, just perhaps, without any interruption in service—to avoid any discomfiture for the subscriber.

The fifth effort arrives the following month and clearly asks the questions: "What is life like without the magazine?" And, "Wouldn't it be better now if you had it?" and, "Here's a chance to come back into the fold."

The sixth effort could be a personal effort from the publisher which, two months after expiration, deals with the "unhappy loss of a good friend" and perhaps a request for information as to why the subscriber did not renew. The salutation "Dear Former Subscriber" could be used and pointed to as an indication of the publisher's feeling (however erroneous) of an inability to provide something that the subscriber wanted and didn't get.

Perhaps your subscriber will react emotionally to this statement of personal weakness and take a positive step toward renewing. The sixth, seventh and eighth efforts must be exercises in attempting to provoke similar types of reactions in an effort to mop up the leftover people who have not yet renewed.

The copy on these efforts should resell the basic benefits of the magazine and describe in greater detail the kinds of things that may be missed in the months and years ahead. Basically, these are reminders of days gone by that were more pleasant when the magazine was "entering your home or office every month."

A considerable factor here is a positive irritation factor. There are some subscribers who, believe it or not, will give in and renew because they're getting tired of receiving renewal notices.

Let us take a final moment to deal with an often overlooked fact of magazine life.

Imagine yourself as a subscriber to your own magazine. One day a letter arrives from the magazine and, just by looking at the envelope, you have absolutely no idea what the people at one of your favorite magazines want to say to you. So you open the envelope and inside is the traditional letter which begins to describe the benefits of the magazine.

"But I already subscribe," you say, since a cursory glance at the order form may or may not reveal the word "renewal" or "renew." And if you miss it, you won't even be sure what this piece of mail is all about.

The lesson of this exercise: Be sure that each individual subscriber can immediately recognize the mission of any particular piece of mail. Be sure its message comes across. We are, after all, in the communications business.

Renewal strategies

By Jerry I. Reitman

What is the best way for a consumer magazine to build and maintain profitable circulation levels?

To paraphrase Vince Lombardi: Renewals aren't everything; they're the only thing. Given subscriber satisfaction with the editorial product, it is generally the effectiveness of a magazine's renewal program that will determine its life cycle.

In the art/science of direct mail, there are many exceptions to the so-called rules. This is particularly true in subscription promotion. In fact, exceptions and differences in each magazine's experience are to be expected. Since magazines serve different audiences with different characteristics, those differences may certainly show up in the renewal cycle of the magazine.

Conversions predictable

How a new subscriber was obtained and how he or she renews the first time (i.e., the conversion) is a predictable relationship, according to most circulation directors. A new subscriber obtained by direct mail, for example, is more likely than a non-mail sold subscriber to renew by direct mail. Similarly, someone who purchased a new subscription from a sweepstakes mailing is more likely to renew under the umbrella of a renewal sweepstakes.

Results can be predicted with reasonable accuracy, especially if the new business promotion copy describing the magazine did not create expectations that were not fulfilled. Promotion writers, under pressure to improve front-end response and reduce the cost of new subscriptions, sometimes make claims about their magazines which are not true. The benefits of such overstated prose are short-lived, however, and the end results are lower first-time renewals, lost income from the future, and a loss of integrity of the magazine.

Everything begins with sourcing

Sourcing means different things to different people. For some, it represents only the original new business list. For others, it represents everything that is known about (and can be coded into) the file for all direct and non-direct sources of new business. A definition which I feel makes sense defines source as "an identification of subscriptions by original source and characteristics for purposes of future promotion."

Sourcing actually starts before the orders arrive. In planning your renewal activity, decide what information has proven helpful in the past and track that information on a continuing basis.

Many publishers assign key codes to their new business mailings as they will appear on the ordering device. One typical coding system that enables a publisher to keep track of renewability by source and demographics consists of two sets of codes that are printed on the ordering device.

The first code contains six digits. The first three digits identify the specific new business list; the second three identify special tests (e.g., timing, prices, premiums). Thus, at renewal time, the circulation director knows what may have moved this subscriber to act in the first place, and what may be useful for renewal planning to this category of subscriber.

The second code consists of eight digits and is used for response analysis. Through one of several systems now available to publishers, this eight-digit code (or any practical series of numbers and letters) can be used in many ways to make list selection more effective when future new business mailings are planned. For example, the code can help certain list suppliers tell you what census tracts pull best. In addition, the code can indicate the demographics of people who live in those census tracts. Furthermore, it can indicate what segments of other lists may work.

The principal value of this code, however, is in renewal evaluation. After the renewal series has run its full course, the codes can be reexamined and evaluated. In the evaluation, a combination of first-year order cost and subsequent conversion rate (first renewal) and even second-year renewal income can be made by original source. This often leads to a different ranking of each new business source in terms of profitability. The list with the lowest first-year order cost may not be the most profitable over time!

Factors to track source by source

Ultimately, the factors you decide to monitor will depend on the values you assign to them, and how much each factor aids you in projecting overall profitability. The more factors you can measure, the more you may be able to determine what the investment criteria should be for each new business source you use.

Obviously, the mere collection of data is to be avoided; it is costly, and unless you know how you plan to use it, you may be retaining information of limited value.

Here are a few major items that most magazines would want to examine from time to time:

• Original source code, e.g., direct-to-publisher mail, TV orders, space, bind-ins, blow-ins. It can also identify indirect sources, such as direct mail agents, telephone agents, catalog agents.

• Method of payment of original order: cash or credit.

• Term of the original subscription.

• Total value of the original order.

• Payment experience on a credit order: on what billing effort did the subscriber pay for the subscription. (This is usually not possible on direct mail agency orders. Some magazines do record whether or not an order was canceled by the agency for non-payment, and then later reinstated.)

• Other products purchased (books, other magazines, records, merchandise) if offered in your billing efforts.

• Change of address activity.

• Renewal activity.

  a. On conversion (first renewal), what effort?

  b. Term and price selected.

• Extension of subscription prior to renewal.

•Renewal at birth.

With this information in hand, you should be better equipped to tailor your renewal efforts to the more economic segments of your list and provide a lower cost-per-renewal.

Renewal planning

A magazine can have many reasons for seeking out new subscribers. From a circulation director's point of view, however, there are generally only two purposes for new business mailings: attrition and growth.

In both instances, the higher the renewal rate on conversions, the lower the requirement for the more costly new business.

The planning of effective renewal promotion involves a combination of art and science. Given a solid editorial product, it is the interrelationship of these two elements that ultimately determines the results in the mail.

The basic plan should start only after some key questions are answered:

•How does our subscriber really feel about the magazine?

•What benefits has he gotten from it? What does the *subscriber* perceive as the real benefits?

•What kind of treatment did the subscriber receive? Was the subscription started promptly? Was it started with current issues of the magazine? Was it back-started? (I know of one publisher who routinely started all new subscriptions with *three* back issues. The renewal series was designed to start with an advance effort, eight months prior to expiration. Guess how well it pulled?)

A simple and effective approach

After you have answered these questions, you are ready to determine your renewal plan. The following approach, used by several publishers, may be helpful:

•Where possible, write the entire series to each major source, including a full description of each phase of the series. (For some small to moderate magazines, with a limited number of sources, tailoring the efforts by source may not be practical. This becomes particularly difficult as the expire groups become smaller.)

•Start the planning phase eight to 12 months in advance of the first effort.

•Start with a renewal-at-birth (sometimes called a collection extension). While technically not part of the renewal series, since it occurs during the billing period, it should be part of the initial planning.

•Start the series at least five months prior to expiration, and if it begins with an advance renewal, clearly identify it as such.

Advance renewals

Advance renewals have some proven values. They generate cash flow, often at levels large enough to finance other promotional activities of the magazine. They can provide stability to your active subscription file by better balancing future expire groups. Furthermore, advance renewals can provide an early opportunity to test a price increase and the potential when applied to all of your expires since some portion of the advance renewal response may be incremental to your overall renewal percentage.

If you plan to do an advance renewal, leave at least six to seven weeks between the advance renewal effort and the first regular effort. Then space each effort about four weeks apart. Depending on the term of the original order, send at least five efforts before expiration, and use

the last effort as the expiration notice (an effort before expiration is usually better than one after expiration).

Finally, continue to mail post-expiration letters until the cost of a renewal exceeds your average new business order cost. (Some magazines say an even slightly higher cost is acceptable since former subscribers tend to re-renew at a higher rate.)

Why don't people renew? There are dozens of reasons why people don't renew their subscriptions, only one of which is a lack of desire to receive the magazine.

Since the problem of inertia is high on the list of reasons, the successful circulation director will find ways to overcome the tendency to postpone action by using techniques based on the subscriber's history and point of view.

Here are some suggestions:

1. Treat conversions (first renewals) differently from previously renewed subscribers. New subscribers are probably less sure about renewing than people who have renewed before. They may have different interests now, compared to the time they first subscribed.

2. Consider involvement devices as a method of getting people's attention and getting them to act. I've heard the idea of involvement devices rejected out of hand, simply because they failed to meet a preconceived idea of what was appropriate for a magazine. That's a little like saying that if a magazine was any good, it wouldn't be necessary to send out renewal notices!

Some proven involvement devices include yes/no tokens; special opening devices (have you ever seen the paper zipper?); miniature pens and pencils; coins, tokens and medallions; unusual sizes and shapes; unusual colors and textures of materials; punch-outs; rub-outs; extra windows; promptness incentives; premium selection devices; and, what may not always be considered an involvement device, sweepstakes.

3. Consider credit offers. There are still a few magazines that do not offer credit on new or renewal subscriptions. Beyond a handful of exceptions, however, credit is a way of life. The failure to offer credit on a subscription renewal (especially when it was offered in new business) would surely reduce the results.

What are the risks of using credit in a renewal series? If the original subscription was sold with the use of credit, you are probably promoting to a credit cleared list. (Subscribers who didn't pay for the original order were long ago canceled and eliminated from the expire group.)

Pricing strategy

Few subjects have more points of view and divergent opinions these days than pricing, a vital component of the overall renewal strategy.

Some magazines offer multiple year options, at a savings, and report them to be effective. Others say they don't work and merely reduce net-per-copy income.

Moreover, some circulation directors have strong feelings about offering longer terms only at the beginning of each series, again depending on the original source of the subscription and the original term. Still others continue to offer a variety of terms throughout the renewal series.

What this suggests is that price testing to renewals remains one of the least understood and most important factors in sound planning.

Publishers who offer reduced-rate subscriptions may vary both term and per-copy rates during the series. Some magazines vary term only, offering the shorter term later in the series to give the impression of a lower price. They claim that this will attract the more price-sensitive subscriber without reducing the per-copy rate and educating subscribers to wait until the later efforts to renew.

How do you decide what is right for your magazine? As a starting point, here is one approach used in a conversion series:

•The same offer—both term and per-copy rate—that appeared in the original new business effort by source is used in the conversion.

•Upgrades (higher per-copy rates or longer terms) are limited to direct-to-publisher new business sources.

•The conversion series is tailored by original source (at least the first three efforts, or until the expire group is so small as to make tailoring by source impractical).

•The primary purpose of the conversion series should be the retention of subscribers, the highest number of first renewals, with term a secondary consideration.

In the final analysis, success in both new business mailings and renewals comes from a willingness to explore new approaches, adapt successful ideas to your magazine, and keep an open mind toward change.

Advance renewals

By Eliot DeY. Schein

If your magazine doesn't have an advance renewal program, you may be overlooking a three-pronged benefit which can go a long way toward a more solid financial position.

What exactly is an advance renewal? Not to be confused with renewal at birth (which is usually a doubling of the term of service and the price on initial invoicing to a new subscriber), the advance renewal is the first attempt to get a subscriber to renew for an additional year's service, even though that subscriber is only halfway through his subscription.

On what could be considered a normal renewal cycle for a monthly magazine, the advance renewal would go out six months prior to the month of expiration whereas the first regular renewal effort would go out three months later.

The three benefits of an advance renewal program are cash several months before you would otherwise receive it through regular renewals; the advantage of having an early forecast of how well a renewal file for that month or issue is going to do; and the opportunity to "double cream" your market since the advance renewal is mailed months ahead of the regular first renewal effort.

Creating "urgency"

By definition, advance renewals contradict one of the basic principles of direct marketing: "a sense of urgency." How excited can a subscriber get about returning an order form for a subscription that still has at least a half year to go? Since the answer is *not very*, a publisher must "manufacture" a reason for an immediate response.

In such a situation, the most frequently used manufactured reason is financial. Since prices are going up in just about every area, surely a publisher can make a pretty good case for possible increases in paper, postage and printing costs as well as salary cost for the people involved in producing the publication. The copy could read something like this: "Protect yourself against future price increases for an entire year or two by renewing now, in advance, for one or two years."

Offering the advance renewal at a price lower than the regular renewal rate is another financial reason for a subscriber to renew earlier than usual. This can boost renewal percentages on the overall series. It may also make sense because you can expect to collect money from the advance renewer three months earlier than you otherwise would have if you had waited for the first regular renewal effort. That is a fiscal-quarter's worth of holding on to that extra income.

Another technique that promotes urgency (and that can be used separately or combined with the price protection just described) is the offer of a premium. If your magazine has a yearbook or a compilation of important articles on a particular subject, offer that desirable premium as a benefit of renewing in advance, by a certain deadline.

A third method—which is useful when offering the renewal at the regular renewal rate—is to give extra issues as a bonus. By renewing in advance, for example, the subscriber will receive one extra issue added to the subscription. Even better—if cash accompanies the order, he will receive an additional extra issue (for a total of 14) on a one year renewal.

There are many ways to go with advance renewals. Publisher reluctance typically has included the following objection: "But we'll still get the same renewal percentage overall. We're just creaming our best subscribers three months earlier. We will still get the same number of renewals."

This, in some cases, may be a valid argument. However, in today's economy, who can fault the attempt to receive cash sooner rather than later?

In a strongly vertical publication (where the subscriber is in close proximity to like-minded prospective subscribers), a price reduction can be offered to the renewing subscriber only if he or she encloses the names of two or three or four acquaintances who may be interested in subscribing. If you are in a vertical market, and if you are going out with a lower price for the advance renewal anyway, why not try this simple method of list building? You can then incorporate the names of the friends in your next regular cold mail effort.

Regardless of the method you use to achieve your highest possible response on your advance renewal, you may want to reassure your subscriber about the value of the magazine. This is a point not to be overlooked. So, certainly a main benefit to the subscriber of renewing in advance is the opportunity to insure that no issues will be missed as a result of renewing later—when the deadline for expiration comes closer.

What should you expect in numbers from your advance renewal effort? Hearty congratulations if you can achieve 25 percent of your projected overall renewals from that file. For example, if you anticipate a 60 percent renewal rate, it is not unheard of for advance renewals to bring in 15 percent of the file in that one effort. And three months later, look for another peak when your first effort goes out.

An ostensible drawback is the expense of producing an advance renewal package and the concomitant testing that is required before you can have a fine-tuned effort. But considering that you are mailing to your own list of subscribers, that advance renewal solicitations are mailable third class, and that the up-front cost is minor . . . surely any renewal achieved within reasonable financial lines is much less expensive than replacing the subscription through cold mail solicitation.

TV Guide's package

Let's take a look at *TV Guide*'s current advance renewal package. The carrier envelope sports a fairly well-rendered rubber-stamp effect that says "important notice enclosed." The bulk rate indicia is lackluster and printed in a second color for no good reason. However, the inside contains, besides the business reply envelope, a letter/order form which sums up the offer in an inexpensive computer format.

The package was received on June 18, 1980, for an October 18 expiration—somewhere around 20 issues before the expiration date. What is their pitch?

The letter's opening takes into account the difficulty of converting a subscription initially generated by an 800 number phone call. It suggests that the subscriber has discovered the convenience of having *TV Guide* delivered directly to his home.

And they go on: "Because you're such a valued customer we want to introduce you to another convenience, re-ordering *TV Guide* by mail." The copy continues with, "Although this notice may seem early to you, keep in mind that it takes a few weeks to process your order and, if you're like most of us, time has a way of slipping by. Before you know it your subscription will have expired and you may miss several issues."

And the conveniences continue: "Rather than waiting to call at the last minute, wasting time looking for the phone number or forgetting to call altogether, just check the form and send it back to us in the postage-free envelope. It's that easy! This way, you'll be assured of continuing to get *TV Guide*'s lively and informative features and complete program listings week after week."

And if you need convincing that convenience is the by-word for this effort, the P.S.: "To avoid the inconvenience of receiving a bill later, why not include payment with your order now? Thank you."

Now, most publishers believe that *not* having to include payment now is a convenience and being billed later is an advantage. But *TV Guide* very skillfully tries to turn this around. This package probably works satisfactorily.

Interesting note: The $20 per year subscription renewal rate is not a promotional $19.97, nor is it in any place in this package contrasted to regular rates or savings of any kind.

It would seem to be substantially less than difficult to beat this package with other copy. There should be price differentials . . . the computer-printed signature looks too phony . . . the offer has absolutely no spark whatsoever.

In the past, this column has rated cold mail subscription efforts. The criteria used for those ratings aren't fully applicable for a renewal in which no great exposition of the product is required.

However, the *TV Guide* effort *is* well written and shows the results of a copywriter's struggle to come up with what seems to be an exciting batch of benefits when, in fact, there aren't any. And when there aren't a lot of benefits, there aren't a lot of renewals. Nevertheless, the computer innovations and the promotional use of the rubber stamp on the carrier envelope allow this package to be rated "O.K."

Advance renewal strategies

By Eugene Slawson

Why are circulation people so particular about the timing of a renewal cycle? Is there a "regular" time to start the renewal promotion, and is there a reason why a circulator would want to go beyond the regular time and start the renewal promotion earlier?

Regular renewals

What is a regular renewal series? Circulation people like to start the first effort of their renewal cycle at a time when no new names of a given expiration date are likely to come up for renewal. If Effort #1 is pulled too early, a number of subscribers in that expire group, whose names were not on the computer when the effort was pulled, will miss Effort #1 and will receive Effort #2 as their first renewal promotion. In this situation, two groups of subscribers are receiving Effort #2: one group that has already received Effort #1, and another group that is receiving Effort #2 as their first effort.

Although the length of the subscription offer within a given expiration date may differ from source to source, the timing of a first effort can be adjusted accordingly, with subsequent efforts spaced to permit the recording of most of the returns by the computer before the next effort is mailed. (The circulator may decide to start the first effort, for all sources, according to the source with the shortest term, or he may start the first effort at different times for different sources.)

A regular renewal series, then, begins with a first effort pulled late enough to cover practically all names in a given expire group. In such a case, the name count from Effort #1 can be used as a base for the computation of the rate for the whole renewal cycle (the total returns from all efforts set against the number of people who came up for renewal).

On the other hand, if many new arrivals to the expire group are promoted for the first time by Effort #2, and if their number is not known, the renewal rate based on the name count from Effort #1 alone would be distorted.

Advance renewals

As the term indicates, advance renewals are different from regular renewals. The difference is in timing: advance renewals are mailed earlier, usually much earlier, than the regular renewal series. Furthermore, an advance renewal does not replace any of the regular renewal efforts. It is an additional effort that enlarges the renewal series by one or more efforts.

But then, if a circulator's life is relatively easy when the first effort is mailed late enough, why would anyone want to go beyond the regular renewals and start the promotion earlier? There would have to be great advantages to an advance promotion to compensate for the problems it could bring.

There are, indeed, potential benefits to an advance renewal program.

•*Cash flow.* The most obvious advantage of an advance effort is the early influx of cash. Nothing improves the mood of a publisher more than an improved cash flow. And the extra profit in the form of interest from the early cash cannot be dismissed.

•*Increased number of returns.* Since the advance renewal is an additional effort, it can bring additional returns. A subscriber who renews early, adding more issues to his present term, has a better chance of developing a deeper attachment to the magazine. A renewal effort that comes later may have no effect on the subscriber who has time to have second thoughts. (There is always the option of a cancellation, but it is seldom used.) Thus, an advance renewal can save those orders that may have been lost forever.

•*Pre-empt agency renewals.* The advance effort could bring in orders that otherwise would have come through an agency as unidentified renewals.

Possible problems

The additional profits which come from advance renewals might be offset by other factors.

First, to be justified, an advance renewal effort must be financially feasible, i.e., the effort's dollar increase must be higher than the circulation and fulfillment costs. The total orders at the end of the series must be substantially higher when the advance renewal is used to cover the cost of the extra mailing.

Second, the effect on the whole renewal series must be substantial; the gains made by the advance renewal must not be offset by reduced returns from subsequent efforts. Since some of the orders obtained through the advance effort would have come later anyway, not all orders received through advance renewals are additional orders. The gain is measured by the increased rate of return at the end of the renewal series.

And finally, a very early extension of subscriptions may not be so welcome in a period when inflation forces publishers to increase subscription prices every year (or sometimes twice a year). Subscriptions sold at prices much lower than the current ones may not be beneficial to the "bottom line."

Advance mailing across the board

Some publishers mail periodically—from one to four times a year —to all names on the active file that have not been, as yet, promoted for renewal. Names with different expiration dates are included in the mailing. Such advance drops usually bring results good enough to justify their cost. It is said that about 5 percent of subscribers will respond to any renewal promotion regardless of the length of their subscription.

There are two disadvantages of such a special mailing. First, some subscribers keep on renewing, ending with a five- or even 10-year subscription. Second, since the mailing is a separate entity, not part of the regular renewal series, the returns from such a drop must be treated separately. Thus, because several expires are involved, the returns cannot be added to those forming the

Figure 1: Two simple renewal systems (Source X; Expire: July)

a) With Advance Effort

Mail date	Issues from expire	Effort	Mail qty.	First time promotion included	Returns	% per effort	% all efforts combined
Oct	8	Advance	5,000	5,000	1,750	35%	
Nov	---	---	---	---	---	---	
Dec	---	---	---	---	---	---	
Jan	5	Effort #1	13,500	9,950	3,430	25%	
Feb	---	---	---	---	---	---	
Mar	3	#2	10,250	150	1,160	11%	
Apr	---	---	---	---	---	---	
May	1	#3	9,200	30	560	6%	
			37,950	15,130	6,900		46%

b) Without Advance Effort

Mail date	Issues from expire	Effort	Mail qty.	First time promotion included	Returns	% per effort	% all efforts combined
Oct	---	---					
Nov	---	---					
Dec	---	---					
Jan	5	Effort #1	14,950	14,950	4,200	28%	
Feb	---	---					
Mar	3	#2	11,300	150	1,470	13%	
Apr	---	---					
May	1	#3	10,000	30	600	6%	
			36,250	15,130	6,270		41%

basis for the computation of the rate for all efforts combined.

The advance renewal proposed here is quite different. It is dropped to only one expire group at a time. It is part of the renewal cycle. It is mailed some time before Effort #1. And it reaches only certain subscribers, namely those with a longer term than the shortest offer.

Such an advance renewal does not differ from other renewals except in timing. It does not have to be called "advance." It could be called "Effort #1." Then, however, we would have to change the number designation of other efforts. Effort #1 would have to become Effort #2, etc. It is more convenient to call it "Advance" and leave the subsequent efforts the way they are. Should we want to introduce a second advance renewal later, we could call it "Advance A," "Advance B," etc.

Effort mail quantity and first-time promoted quantity

A small number of subscribers entering a file after the first effort has been pulled has very little effect on the rate computation.

When we use an advance renewal two, three, or more months before the first effort, however, the situation is quite different. Here we know that a substantial number of names will not get the advance effort, their first promotion being regular renewal Effort #1. If we do not know the number of these new names, we cannot compute the rate for all efforts combined, and we won't be able to see how the renewals are doing.

Thus, to enter the advance renewal program, we must have the cooperation of the fulfillment house, including their agreement to supply the count of first time promoted with every effort pulled.

Advance renewals improve returns

Figures 1, 2, and 3 show how an advance renewal can improve the cumulative returns.

Figure 1 shows two simple renewal systems: a) with, and b) without an advance renewal.

The advance renewal, mailed eight issues before expire, reached only one-third of all the July expires on file. The remaining two-thirds were reached for the first time by Effort #1.

A comparison of the two series shows that the advance effort increased the renewal rate by 10 percent.

Renewal system with subsource

In the simple renewal system, 5,000 names reached by the advance renewal received three additional efforts—a total of four. The ones that were promoted for the first time with Effort #1 received only three efforts.

If it were possible to promote the second group separately, we could check the financial feasibility of "squeezing" another effort for this group (Figure 2—a renewal system with a subsource). Only actual testing could give us an answer. But in order to have the option of testing, the two groups would have to be differentiated by a separate key. They are still the same source but they are different. They become a "subsource." We could have for this group a separate series with different timing if the test indicated it would be to our advantage.

If most of the names pulled for the first time with Effort #1 entered the file one or two months after the advance renewal, we could start their promotion six issues before expire. In Figure 2, we call these names Group 2. The names pulled at the regular time—as in Figure 1—are Group 1.

For simplicity, we have assumed that in our test the rate of return from each effort will be the same for each group—something that, of course, cannot be guaranteed since the drop dates are different. However, we have no reason to believe that Group 2, mailing individual efforts two months or one month later, has a rate lower than Group 1.

The mail quantities for the regular efforts (Efforts 1 through 3) have been arbitrarily determined with the idea that some of the returns from prior efforts did not have

Figure 2: Renewal system with a subsource

Mail date	Issues from expire	Group 1 Effort	Mail qty.	First prom. incl.	Returns	%	% all efforts comb.	Group 2 Effort	Mail qty.	First prom. incl.	Returns	%	% all efforts comb.
Oct	8	Adv.	5,000	5,000	1,750	35%		---	---	---	---	---	
Nov	7	---	---	---	---	---		---	---	---	---	---	
Dec	6	---	---	---	---	---		Adv	9,950	9,950	3,482	35%	
Jan	5	#1	3,500	100	865	25%		---	---	---	---	---	
Feb	4	---	---	---	---	---		#1	6,860	50	1,715	25%	
Mar	3	#2	2,700	20	299	11%		---	---	---	---	---	
Apr	2	---	---	---	---	---		#2	4,560	10	520	11%	
May	1	#3	2,180	---	125	6%		#3	4,160	---	240	6%	
			13,380	5,120	3,039		59.3%		25,530	10,010	5,957		59.5%

Figure 3: Comparison of both renewal systems (Figures 1 and 2)

	Figure 1 (One source)	Figure 2 (Groups 1 & 2) (Subsource added)
Number of efforts: Advance	1	1
Regular	3	3
Mail quantity all efforts	37,950	38,910
First time promotion (included)	15,130	15,130
Returns	6,900	8,996
Rate of returns all efforts combined	46%	59.5%

enough time to enter the file before the subsequent effort was mailed.

It is clear that the renewal system with a subsource brings better results.

As shown in the comparison chart (Figure 3), the number of efforts mailed and the number of first time promotions have remained the same.

The number of orders received has increased, thanks to the advance renewal Group 2, by 27 percent (2,096 more orders). The cumulative rate of return from all efforts has grown from 46 percent to 59.5 percent.

All the extra returns have been obtained in our test with only a small increase in mail quantities: from 37,950 to 38,910.

The purpose of the above discussion was to show that a circulator can substantially improve the rate of return by adding an advance renewal and separately promoting the names that entered the file after the advance renewal had been pulled.

Figure 2 illustrated the simplest case of only one advance renewal and one subsource. Should further tests and circumstances indicate that additional advance renewal efforts are warranted, they can be added and additional subsources created.

Of course, the above-described refinements of the renewal system depend on the cooperation of the fulfillment house. With each pull, they must be able and willing to supply the count of the first time promotions for each effort. They also must be able to create subsources as described above for separate promotion.

Rest assured . . . it can be done.

Sweepstakes: not just for giants anymore

By Henry Turner

There are a lot of misconceptions about magazine sweepstakes. Some publishers and circulation directors feel that they are undignified. Others believe that they are only for large circulation magazines. And still others just don't like using promotional devices.

Yet sweepstakes do work, even for prestigious magazines. They also work for small and medium circulation magazines. And, like all effective sales promotion, they put a temporary but tangible reward on a buying decision.

A sweepstakes is nothing more than a sales promotion technique that provides this additional inducement when presented as an "overlay" to the product, in this case a magazine. A consumer participates with no investment, no commitment, and no skill, and becomes involved with the sponsoring magazine.

Devices add incentive

There are many magazine sales promotion techniques and, in many cases, more care is given to the art and copy of the mailing piece for these promotion devices than to the editorial purpose and content of the magazine itself. These devices—which are often combined—include:

• A free book, or other premium, with the purchase of the magazine subscription.

• "First issue free" offers, where the customer may examine the first issue of the subscription with no obligation to buy.

• Credit offers—"Send no money now; we'll bill you later."

• Introductory offers at a reduced price compared with the regular subscription price.

• The recently popular "guaranteed subscription price for life at one-half the newsstand price."

• A two-year subscription for the regular price of one year.

• A two-year subscription, with the second year at half price.

All of these devices give the favorably predisposed person an additional incentive to make a purchase decision within those few moments when he or she reads the offer.

Some publishers fear that sales promotion techniques will produce subscribers who will not read the magazine, and who will not renew it. They must come to understand that there are always more readers than actual buyers at any given time. (Readers are considered to be those who enjoy the magazine but do not pay for it themselves.) In fact, readership figures are usually two, three or four times greater than circulation figures.

A reader, then, may buy the magazine with a sweepstakes subscription offer. If he does not like the magazine, however, he won't buy it with a sweepstakes, premium, or any other subscription offer.

Other potential buyers are those who read a particular magazine only occasionally, and still others are those familiar with the field which the magazine covers, but unfamiliar with the magazine itself. Again, a sweepstakes might be enough to commit these people to purchase.

Publishers have two other fears about sweepstakes: 1) sweepstakes subscribers don't pay their credit subscriptions as well as other credit subscribers, and 2) sweepstakes subscribers don't renew as well as other subscribers.

For the first, probably the second and possibly the third sweepstakes mailings, subscribers may not pay as well as non-sweepstakes subscribers. However, payment should improve over time as techniques are refined and net responses from each list are analyzed.

The same will be true of renewals. They will probably be lower at first, but then climb back to their former levels if they are handled carefully. Renewal sweepstakes and advance renewal sweepstakes to these subscribers must be tested, and the renewal offer price should be kept at or near the price at which they last subscribed.

Types of sweepstakes

There are two basic types of sweepstakes used in direct mail offers: pre-selected winning numbers, and the random drawing for winners. In the pre-selected number sweepstakes, the winning numbers are selected in advance. In the random drawing sweepstakes, the winning numbers are not chosen until the entries are "drawn out of a hat" after the sweepstakes is over.

With pre-selected numbers, only the numbers are pre-selected, not the names of the winners. The one who pre-selects the winning numbers, usually an outside independent organization, does not know what name will be assigned to each number. This is done at random, usually by the computer-addressing firm which prints the sweepstakes numbers and the names and addresses on the letters to be mailed with the sweepstakes offer.

It is very unlikely that all winning numbers will be returned. Since only 20 to 30 percent of all potential entrants will actually enter the sweepstakes by returning their entry, probably only 20 to 30 percent of the prizes will be awarded.

Under the regulations of the Federal Trade Commission and under the laws, rules and regulations of various states, all prizes must be given away. Therefore, with a pre-selected number sweepstakes, a random drawing must be held to produce winners for the remaining 70 to 80 percent of the prizes.

There are three advantages to the pre-selected number sweepstakes. First, you can use the magic phrase "You may have already won," which has strong appeal. Second, the number itself can be dramatized as a degree of personalization to the recipient; it is his number alone, and no one else has it. Third, it permits the opportunity to state that every respondent has two chances to win—first, if his number is one of the pre-selected winning numbers, and second, in the random drawing for all unclaimed prizes of those winners who fail to send in their winning entries.

There are three negative aspects of the pre-selected

number sweepstakes. First, the universe of numbers must be established before the mailings and controlled during the first and any subsequent mailings. This results in intangible administrative costs. Second, the numbers must be printed on all the individual entry forms—an additional printing cost. Third, all returned entries must be screened, usually manually, for winning numbers—another additional cost.

Conversely, the random draw sweepstakes is easier to control administratively. It is also less costly since numbers do not have to be printed or searched for after the entries are returned. However, the random draw sweepstakes limits the opportunities for personalization available with numbers, and restricts the use of the headline and copy points available in the pre-selected number sweepstakes described above.

Designing your first sweepstakes

Since your first sweepstakes should be as simple as possible—both to simplify administration and to keep costs at a minimum—use a random draw sweepstakes.

First, establish prizes of interest to your readers with a total value of less than $5,000. (By keeping the prize value under $5,000, you not only keep your costs down, but you also need not register your sweepstakes with the Attorney General of the State of New York, if you mail into New York, saving that expense.)

Some tips for prizes: Is there an annual convention or meeting that your readers would be interested in attending? If so, offer your readers a trip to that convention for two, all expenses paid. A two- or three-day trip should be sufficient.

To avoid paying cash for the airfare and hotel, arrange to barter advertising space in your magazine for the plane tickets and hotel bills through a barter broker. Or arrange your own barter with the airline and hotel. (Airlines and hotels should be willing to do this for free just for having their names mentioned in your sweepstakes mailing. However, they often seem to want more.)

Do you have a second publication you have been thinking about test-marketing—a newsletter, for example? Offer 100, or 1,000, free trial subscriptions as prizes in the sweepstakes. Then poll the recipients after they get their issues to see how they like it.

Look over your list of advertisers. Might any of them have low-cost products, or products being discontinued or phased out, that would make good prizes? Do any of them have new products for which they would like to receive some extra promotion in your sweepstakes? Maybe they are considering a new product which they would give as free samples so as to gauge the user's response.

Is there an individual or group, recognized as a leader in the field your magazine reports on, that your readers would like to meet? If so, arrange such a meeting as a prize in your sweepstakes.

If you also have a separate book publishing operation, you can give away your own books at minimum cost. If not, find an appropriate book that has been remaindered, and perhaps you can pick up 500 or 1,000 copies at nominal cost.

If possible, offer entrants a choice of prizes: "Which would you prefer—a trip to Los Angeles or a trip to New York?" This stimulates involvement in the sweepstakes. Go further. Ask them to write their choice on the entry card.

If you have more than one publication, all your magazines can use the same prize "umbrella," thus spreading the sweepstakes cost over more than one product. You may also join with a fellow publisher and set up a single sweepstakes for both of you. Be sure to mention in the rules that both of you are using it.

Since you're going to keep your total prize value low, don't mention total value in your promotional copy. Just discuss each prize separately.

The Federal Trade Commission has rules and regulations concerning sweepstakes which must be complied with. These regulations require that all the rules of the sweepstakes be clearly stated; that all entrants have an equal chance of winning; that all prizes will be given away; that no purchase is necessary in order to win a prize in the sweepstakes; that the sweepstakes be open for a reasonable period of time; that the prizes be awarded promptly thereafter; and that the sweepstakes mailing as a whole be fair, honest, and properly administered.

To keep the cost of your mailing package as low as possible for the test mailing, design it with economy in mind. One simple package would consist of:

• A two-page letter, front and back, 8 x 11, probably in two colors. This letter would describe the prizes, talk about the magazine, and explain how to enter and subscribe.

• An order card, 5-1/2 x 8-1/2, in as many colors as you can afford, listing and picturing the prizes, offering the reader the yes-no option ("Yes, enter me in the sweepstakes, and send me a subscription," or "No, I don't want to subscribe at this time, but enter me in the sweepstakes"). The card should set forth the sweepstakes rules and provide space for the respondent's name and address which could be computer-printed on the card, or printed on labels.

• A reply envelope for the order.

• An outer envelope.

Don't forget to say "No purchase necessary" on both the letter and the order card. And be sure to go over the copy with your attorney.

To keep the creative costs of this package as low as possible, try writing and designing the package "in-house," even if you don't have in-house copywriters and artists. Every circulation manager and subscription manager should try to write and design a direct mail package once in his career, just to have the first-hand knowledge of the mental processes that professional copywriters and artists go through.

If you are a publisher or an editor and act as your own circulation manager, you no doubt have written and designed direct mail packages before, so it should be a relatively simple task for you. Just be sure each piece will fit in its envelope, and that the size of each piece is efficient for printing.

Keep in mind that this same sweepstakes can be tested for renewals as well as for new subscribers, with only minor changes in copy.

One low-cost device now being used for renewal promotion is a $1,000 prize for each month's expires. This can be used in the first renewal promotion mailing, a later renewal mailing, or even as an advance renewal mailing.

In conjunction with such a mailing, you could offer a duplicate prize to a friend or associate of the subscriber, if the subscriber will write the name and address of the person on the reply card. Then these names can be accumulated and used in your next mailing for new subscribers, probably successfully and with no list rental cost.

The lists that work best for your non-sweepstakes mailing should be tested for your sweepstakes mailing.

All test lists should provide sufficient quantities on roll-out mailings if the first test is successful. Send the list owner a dummy or sample of your sweepstakes package and tell him your roll-out plans to be sure the names will be available if the test is successful.

For every subscription order that is produced from a sweepstakes mailing, two, three or four responses will come back saying "No, I don't want to subscribe to your magazine, but I do want to enter your sweepstakes. Just tell me if I have won a prize." This option must be equally offered as a matter of law.

The number of such "no" responses will vary, depending on mailing lists used, the mailing package, the price of the subscription offer, the terms of the subscription offer, the prizes offered, the season of the year, etc. These responses must also be processed in such a way that they have an equal opportunity to win prizes as the "yes" responses.

"No" responses have been increasing gradually over the last few years, probably indicating an increasing believability in sweepstakes. But this has also increased the cost of processing these responses.

To help cover these costs, and perhaps to make a profit on them, a recent development has been to scan or keypunch the names onto magnetic tape, making the names available for list rental or other mailings by the same publisher. Some in the direct mail industry question whether a publisher can legally use these "no" responses for such purposes, but the practice is growing.

At the conclusion of the sweepstakes, be sure to award all the prizes. Ask each winner to send a photograph and sign a release authorizing you to use his or her name and photograph in subsequent publicity about the sweepstakes winners.

Consider announcing the winners on the pages of your magazine. It lends credibility to the sweepstakes and is useful promotion for your next sweepstakes for renewal subscribers.

Christmas in July
By Eliot DeY. Schein

Gift subscriptions or donor subscriptions are in fact a real gift—especially for the publisher. Right now, a remarkable, carefully selected, response-laden market is available to buy these relatively inexpensively-generated subscriptions to your publication.

It's midsummer, however, and you are sitting there in your corner office thinking that gift time is Christmas time. You're right—but the time to plan for your donor subscription solicitation is right now. Why? Because it'll take a good two and one-half months to have the whole kit and caboodle ready to mail (third class, of course) no later than the first of October.

Start planning now

"Why the first of October?" you ask. Because if the mailing is dropped on October 1, most of it will be delivered by October 15 or 16, allowing a total of four weeks to get 90 percent of the responses back. Then, with some fast key punching on the part of your fulfillment house, you can mail your January issue (as the first issue of the gift subscription) so it arrives at the donee's home prior to the Christmas holiday.

So, although it's 90 degrees outside today and Christmas is the furthest thing from your mind, the profits from your donor subscription program will never materialize unless you start doing something about it right now.

First, you should have your copy written and the mechanicals done for the entire donor package. Getting the list is no trick—it's your own subscriber list, available certainly at your own computer house. Then, you must print the envelopes (which will take three to four weeks) and get the mailing house to insert the components.

Be sure to allow in all donor promotion the opportunity for the donor to give multiple gift subscriptions to your magazine. (A donor, we assume, is more enthusiastic than the average reader of the publication and wants to share it with friends and relatives.) A very common method of securing multiple subscriptions is the utilization of a receding scale of prices: first donor subscription, $10; second, $9; third, $8; fourth through infinity, $7 a year. (Naturally, this price varies with the price of your regular subscriptions.)

While you may decide a cut-rate offer is an advantage to you, you needn't cut it to half price. Chances are the donor will respond anyway since you are saving him or her the time and effort of conceiving of, purchasing, wrapping and shipping a Christmas present. In addition, he enjoys the convenience of having a card sent without doing anything other than responding to your original offer.

Prebill the donor

When billing for gift subscriptions, the donor should be prebilled as an acknowledgment of his order (again, use third class postage). Collections for donor subscriptions usually run at a high percentage, mainly because the donor is afraid you're going to contact the recipient or cut him off in mid-subscription if the bill is not paid promptly. A four-effort series should be sufficient to capture the lion's share of the donors' payments.

And bear this in mind: if a donor subscribes for four friends as gifts, you need send only one invoice for all four.

Over a four-effort series, this is a savings of $1.80 in postage alone for your subscription department.

Renewal of donor subscriptions is accomplished the same way. You need send only one renewal reminder next year to each donor regardless of the number of subs he has entered for friends or relatives. In addition, you have working for you the same anxiety you have with the original billing effort. The donor is going to be concerned that if he does not renew the gift subscriptions, you will send renewal efforts to the donee (which, by the way, you would do).

Keep in mind the design and production of a gift card to be sent from the fulfillment house to the recipient of the gift, preferably in advance of receipt of the first issue of the magazine. The card should be an attractive all-purpose season's greetings card, usable in lieu of the donor's sending the donee a regular season's greetings card. It should contain the name of the donor, the number of issues the donee will receive, and the name of the magazine. If possible, it should also alert the donee to the approximate time the first issue will arrive.

Four gift sub promotions that work

Let's take a look at the way *Consumer Reports* generated gift subscriptions in 1978. The package (which arrived at a subscriber's home on the 23rd of October) said that *Consumer Reports* recommends *Consumer Reports* and explained the convenience of your not having to plunge into the crowds, log the footwork, and hope for the best when you choose gifts for the holidays.

CR offered "personalized cards announcing your gift subscriptions" and asked to have your order by December 8. On the sliding-scale order form, the first gift was $11 (which happens to be the regular subscription rate), and additional gifts were $8 each. The order form had room for six names and addresses and six ways of signing the gift cards.

Prevention magazine had their handy package arrive on the 21st of October. *Prevention*'s offer advised you to "Save yourself the hassle of Christmas shopping, of wandering in and out of stores hoping just the right thing will catch your eye for this relative or that friend." Again, same story. It's an easy way to shop.

The first subscription was $7.85, the second was $6.40, and the third and all additionals were $5.70 each. "And," they said, "if you order your gift subscription now, we'll send a handsome gift card to each (recipient) announcing that a one-year subscription to *Prevention* magazine is on its way."

They also gave you the opportunity to renew your own subscription and someone else's, and gave you four handy boxes to accomplish whichever tasks you selected.

In addition, they had a premium: "The editors of *Prevention* will send you a copy of our all new holiday annual," and a copy to each person to whom you have sent a gift subscription.

When *National Geographic* sends out a donor mailing, they don't fool around. They make the most out of every penny of their nonprofit organization's postage budget. The start of the letter? You guessed it: "The hustle and bustle of Christmas will be here before you know it." Again, this seems to be the point that everyone agrees on. If you're not selling cut-rate subs, tell the reader about how much time and effort you are saving for him.

But *National Geographic* didn't just stop at gift subscriptions. They enclosed a four-color, 24-page catalog selling books, maps, globes, dictionaries, stories of the states of the United States, posters and almost anything they could think of that a *National Geographic* subscriber (or member) would buy. The gift subscription order form (four colors over two colors) had four places for the recipents' names.

The package was received in the home ahead of all the others (except the Tiffany catalog), on the 30th of September. Their effort was outstanding. *National Geographic* must have decided that no one was going to do it any better than they did. They were probably right.

The American Museum of Natural History markets a 10-time-a-year magazine called *Natural History*. The opening line of their donor subscription letter was "The answer to your toughest gift-giving problems? You already know it." (Apparently this is the tack you should take. Everybody else seems to be using it over and over again.)

The letter goes on to say that *Natural History* is the one distinctive gift that won't tire you out shopping for it. As a matter of fact, just after you've read Ann Brown's signature you go right to the "handy" order form that allows you to enter a gift subscription for yourself by pre-addressed checkbox. Each subscription is $10, whether you send one or 100, apparently. This computerized form does *Natural History* proud.

If you're sitting there saying, "Gee, why don't we have an aggressive gift subscription program for our magazine?" stop sitting there. Get started right now and develop a donor program.

Be sure to include a full-page house ad and bind-in cards and/or envelopes to work in concert with your mailing. Run these ads in October and November and use a headline such as: "The gift they'll open 12 times a year. . . ."

This whole donor promotion idea works so well and costs so little. Why not jump in with both feet for this year and every year thereafter? Call it Christmas in July.

International mailings

By Eliot DeY. Schein

Many U.S. publications at some time or another become infatuated with the prospect of making some healthy subscription profits by promoting to countries other than the U.S. and Canada. Similarly, many publishers outside of North America yearn for the opportunity to practice their tried-and-true subscription solicitation methods in what is perceived as the booming magazine marketplaces of the U.S. and Canada.

For many years, U.S. publishers have been doing a fairly reasonable job of mining for prospects in Canada, and by now they are fully aware of the variations in rules and regulations concerning this "backyard" type of international mail. For example, the Canadian postal service statutorily does not accept open-window carrier envelopes.

(A cautionary note, however. Mailers are occasionally lulled into a false sense of security by the fact that a smaller mailing of, say 5,000 pieces will slide through unnoticed, even though they contain an open window. The boom descends, however, when the larger roll-out is dropped, for that's when the Canadian postal inspectors sit up and take notice. Which means that a 100,000 open-window roll-out—based on a successful 5,000 open-window test—can be bounced at the border. And everything goes right down the tubes, including the postage.)

In addition, who among us has not been confronted on occasion by the problem of paying duty on printed materials which cross the northern U.S. border on a mission to solicit business from Canadians?

By far one of the more difficult situations concerns responses mailed back from Canada to the U.S. There is no reciprocal business reply administration machinery between the two countries. One easy way out, of course, is to have prospects pay their own way by directing them to affix their own Canadian first-class postage on a pre-addressed (to the U.S.) return envelope. Some publishers have seen fit (and profitably so) to have "postpaid" business reply mail come back to a drop, or other office, in Canada.

And, of course, you are no doubt familiar with the frequent need for cultural and lifestyle copy revisions in your direct mail packages in order to make them "Canadian-oriented."

Lucrative areas abroad

Currently the fastest expanding and, it would appear, the most lucrative area of non-North American circulation dollars (Gorman Publishing's South American controlled and paid experiences notwithstanding) is centered in several countries in Europe, parts of the Mideast, and Japan. If you are about to embark upon a direct mail subscription solicitation in Western Europe there are a few things you should know—some fine points to understand and master—in order to maximize results.

First, there seems to be a tremendous desire on the part of Western Europeans to get their hands on any publication that contains the slightest promise of deliver-

ing technical information. *Datamation* magazine and *Scientific American* have long been taking advantage of paid—yes, paid (and at a rather healthy premium)—subscribers from Western Europe.

Second, most Europeans are "trained" to expect to pay more for a subscription than for a newsstand copy of a publication—quite the opposite from the prevailing expectations of the American consumer.

Third, price sensitivity seems to be less of a factor when marketing U.S. publications overseas than it is marketing U.S. publications in the U.S.

One of the quickest methods to put your international mail on track (and perhaps one of the most hassle-free) is to use an international mailing service. The U.S. Postal Service provides one version; KLM, the Dutch airline, provides another. The service thus provided guarantees that your mail will reach the European market and that it will be mailed from a major center (either London or Amsterdam) for dropping to each particular country.

Responses should come back to a European pick-up point, which may necessitate your actually opening up a small office or at least establishing a contact and using the contact's address for your responses.

In terms of delivering the magazines on the subscriptions you have thus generated, the U.S.P.S. international service or KLM will do this by air for you (although you may want to charge a premium for airmail delivery of the publication). Failing this, there are always ships which, however slow (and sometimes unreliable), can do the job. If timeliness is a factor in your promotion, you may want to dispense with the over-the-waves medium and conduct both your promotion and fulfillment strictly by airmail.

The mail that never arrived

There is a joke (at least partially based on fact) about choosing countries in which to promote. Italy bears the brunt of the humor in this particular story. It seems that mail travels mostly by train in Italy and postmasters wait to be alerted by the railroad when a trainload of mail arrives for their specific city or town of destination.

The story goes that the postmaster goes out to the train terminal and upon discovering a freight car full of mail (and considering the concomitant labor that he and his department are going to have to exert in order to distribute it) opens the seal on the car, emerges joyfully a few moments later to say, "No, no, it's not for our town or city. It's for a town or city further down the line whose name is somewhat similar to ours."

The scenario suggests that some shipments of mail in Italy are constantly shuttled from place to place without any postmaster accepting the responsibility for delivering them. Thus, according to this anecdote, direct mail promotions (and other mail in the shipments) die on the line, as it were.

While this is meant as a humorous story, there are

218

in fact times when various situations arise wherein mail has a rough time getting either in or out of the desired hands of the residents of a certain country.

But wait. There's more. Consider the all-too-familiar fact that the U.S. has a postal service job action (slow-down or total strike) every six or seven years. It requires no great leap of the imagination to conclude that given the greater number of countries in Europe, at any given moment there can be either a national strike or some kind of postal job action which will, at best, delay significantly your attempts to do circulation promotion efficiently. It is virtually impossible to keep abreast of every country's labor and political situation at all times and coordinate the best time for your mailing drop.

Another factor concerns the demographic habits of different countries. For example, while late August is not a terrible time to have a mailing arrive to prospects in the U.S., it most certainly is in France: it seems the entire country is on vacation during the last two weeks in August (if not the whole month).

These demographic and societal factors, again, are hard to track and coordinate, and yet they often have a critical role to play when it comes to the results of your promotion. A semi-fail-safe method of combating the multitude of variables would be to mail to one country at a time, at what you have researched to be the ideal time of year, while being certain you've checked what the labor situation is in that country in advance of spending your postage money.

Know each country's peculiarities

In mailing from the U.S. to Europe, there are significant differences in weight permissible at certain postage rates. Mailing a traditional direct mail package—carrier, reply envelope, order form, letter and brochure, on the standard 60-pound stock used in the U.S.—may cost a fortune in postage between and among various countries in Europe. Lighter stock is more than advised. Another hint: the current intelligence in European direct mail advises that the response envelope be a "bang-tail" with the order form making up the tail of the envelope.

There have been many cases of European publishers trying to use European methodologies on the U.S. market. With few exceptions, their efforts have failed miserably. "Taking a shot" at the American market from a solely European base of operations can be an expensive and frustrating blueprint for bankruptcy (consider *GEO* in its early stages and the efforts of the *Financial Times of London*). The more informed European publishers pro-

duce and coordinate their mailings through professional consultants, advisors and agencies in the U.S.

A working knowledge of the vacations, habits, labor conditions, postal service situations and other germane factors in each country will go a long way toward protecting your direct mail dollar. In addition, a full understanding of the "training" of your target market is essential.

For example, in many countries in Europe, a subscription price is higher than the single-copy price because the costs of postage and handling are added on to the single-copy price. However, a non-domestic promotion to the U.S. which sports a subscription price that is higher than the single-copy price exposes the mailer's misconception of the U.S. market. This mailer, mailing to the U.S. and Canada from abroad, should come up with a subscription price that is all-inclusive and doesn't break out any "extras." The market is "trained" that way and will respond accordingly.

When it comes to mailing lists, you are in luck. In the last five years, mailing list availability on an international level has increased tenfold.

In the U.S., the mailing list business is sophisticated to the extent that a market can be targeted to include bull's-eye names only. Outside the U.S. and Canada, mailing lists are not as sophisticated as they are in North America, but they're getting there. And while it used to be impossible to get sorted mailing lists for Europe, the Middle East and the Orient, there is more than just a glimmer of light at the end of what used to be a very dark tunnel.

Mailing from the U.S. to other countries, therefore, has some degree of restriction. You will find that you will be mailing many, many small lists as opposed to selections from large ones. Do not let this bother you. The bottom line is what you are looking for.

While the problems of international mail seem to loom like an impenetrable 10-story wall, once you get your feet wet, you may just discover a remarkably advantageous and lucrative marketplace. It is worth trying and something you should practice, at least initially, with the help of people who have been there before.

Credit

By John D. Klingel

The biggest mistake that I see being made in circulation marketing involves the use of credit. For some reason, people who are inexperienced in direct marketing don't understand the importance of credit. Furthermore, some resist the concept even after it's been explained to them.

Having analyzed hundreds of credit tests with a wide variety of magazines and other products, I am prepared to make some general observations. (Please note: these are general observations, concepts that should always be tested for any given publication.)

Observation 1—Offers that produce cash with order will usually reduce response.

Observation 2—Pure credit offers are almost always more profitable than offers that produce cash with order.

Observation 3—Credit card options almost always reduce response.

Observation 4—Any attempt to reduce bad debt by asking for signatures, initials, etc., will prove to be less profitable than pure credit.

There are numerous devices and copy approaches that are used to increase cash with order. They include premiums for cash, extra issues for cash, price discounts for cash, and the simple, straightforward approach of putting check-off boxes on the order card:

☐ Payment enclosed
☐ Bill Me Later

However, I've never seen any of these approaches produce more profitable orders than the pure credit approach. Although they usually produce a higher percentage of cash with order, they also usually reduce response to the point where the costs of pure credit are offset.

But why, one might ask, would something like check-off boxes on an order card reduce response? Since the subscriber doesn't have to include payment, why should the mere existence of the option reduce response? It doesn't make sense.

But then, a lot of other things about direct response don't make sense either. Furthermore, do we have to know the "whys" of certain phenomena?

The purpose of direct response marketing is to test different marketing approaches and identify the most profitable marketing methods. For example, we know that giving potential subscribers a choice (e.g., two or more prices) lowers response, and we use this knowledge to increase the profitability of a promotion. Logic and common sense aren't necessary in the application of this knowledge.

A two-card saga

Example 1 shows order card copy for two order cards that were tested by Doug Newton at *American West*. Doug is one of a group of people who recently took over *American West*, a magazine that has been publishing since the early seventies.

Doug's first set of tests included the two order cards shown: Card A, the order card used by the previous management group, and Card B, a test of pure credit. The result: Card B pulled 60 percent more orders—not a bad start for the new management.

Obviously, the bad pay percentage and extra billing costs will be considered in evaluating the profit impact of the above test. It should be equally obvious, however, that it would take an enormous increase in bad pay to offset a 60 percent increase in response.

As I mentioned in Observation 2, pure credit offers are almost always more profitable than offers that produce cash with the order. To some extent this is a continuation of Observation 1 in that the response on offers that ask for cash with order is almost always lower than the response on pure credit offers. But the main reason for this observation is that the costs of credit for magazines are extremely low. If I were selling television sets through the mail, I wouldn't use pure credit because the bad debt costs would be very high. With a magazine, if someone doesn't pay, I've lost only a few issues. For magazines, credit simply isn't that expensive relative to its impact on response.

Example 1

SPECIAL 50% SAVINGS OFFER

THE AMERICAN WEST

Yes! Send me twelve months of THE AMERICAN WEST for only $7.50!

JOHN D KLINGEL A621E
530 UNIVERSITY AVENUE
PALO ALTO, CA 94301

☐ Payment enclosed

☐ Bill me

YOUR SATISFACTION GUARANTEED

Order card A

SPECIAL 50% SAVINGS OFFER

THE AMERICAN WEST

Yes! Send me twelve months of THE AMERICAN WEST for only $7.50!

JOHN D KLINGEL A630H
530 UNIVERSITY AVENUE
PALO ALTO, CA 94301

☐ Send no money. Please do not include payment now. We will bill you later.

YOUR SATISFACTION GUARANTEED

Order card B

A few years ago, I worked with a magazine that had always used cash-only offers. When they tested pure credit, the direct mail response more than doubled. Example 2 shows an analysis of a situation in which response for pure credit was 100 percent greater than a cash-only offer. This is an example of the type of analysis you could do if you tested credit and tracked the orders through the billing series. In this example, the pure credit orders were less expensive in the first year. However, it's possible for pure credit (versus an offer that attracts a high percentage of cash with order) to be less profitable in the first year but more profitable over the long term if it produces

Example 2

Economics of Credit

	Cash Only Offer	Pure Credit
Quantity	100,000	100,000
Response	1.5%	3.0%
Bad pay	0	30%
Net subs	1,500	2,100
Income @ $9	$13,500	$18,900
Promotion @ $250/M	$25,000	$25,000
Reply postage	285	570
Billing (3 efforts @ $220/M)[1]	—	1,980
Bad debt copies (3 copies @ $.40)		1,080
Fulfillment (extra 10¢/credit sub)		300
Total cost	**$25,285**	**$28,930**
1st year loss	$(11,215)	$(10,030)
Loss per paid subscriber	$(7.48)	$(4.78)
2nd year		
Net subs @ 40% conversion	600	840
Income @ $12	$7,200	$10,800
Cost of credit sub		**$1.12**

(1) When you use a six-effort billing series, the average number of efforts per credit sub is usually close to three.

more net paid orders in the first year.

For some reason, credit card options on order cards dramatically reduce response. I've seen credit card options tested against cash-only offers—and the cash-only offers won. I've seen credit card options tested on renewal efforts—and the response went down over 50 percent. I would never advise against testing credit card options, but anyone who puts them on order cards without testing is making a serious mistake.

There is an almost universal tendency to regard high bad pay as disastrous. Very few people see that high bad pay just might reflect promotion that is highly efficient.

At one time, I worked for a book club that increased its membership from 500,000 to one million in a year as a result of successful testing. During this rapid growth, bad debt as a percent of revenue went from 4 percent to 8 percent. Management went berserk, and for the next couple of years we tested every conceivable method of reducing bad debt. The only problem was that everything that reduced bad debt also reduced profit. The bad debt increase was a natural outgrowth of a promotion that had doubled response. Since profits had more than doubled, however, a slight increase in bad debt should not have caused a lot of concern.

I've seen promotion that was extremely profitable with 85 percent bad pay. When response is over 40 percent, you can live with 85 percent bad pay. The key is finding the most profitable methods of acquiring subscriptions, not methods that produce the lowest bad pay. And the irony is that the most profitable method is often the method with the highest bad debt percentage.

At this point, there are two things you might do: You could chalk me up as a crazy and ignore everything I've said, or you could blindly believe me and change your promotion. If you choose the first, so be it. If you choose the second, you would be unwise, for any major change in your promotion must be carefully pretested.

Remember, direct response promotion is extremely sensitive to credit. Don't make changes on your order cards—e.g., credit card options, payment with order options, premiums for cash—without being aware that they may substantially reduce profitability.

Billing series

By Eliot DeY. Schein

This is our 28th letter to you requesting payment for your subscription to Popular Skeet-Shooting *magazine.*

And, I might add, this is the last letter we'll ever send you.

As you know, PS-S magazine's staff is loaded with expert sharpshooters. Right now, as you read this letter, two of them are across the street from where you now sit.

To avoid unnecessary damage and embarrassment, please slip your full payment in the enclosed envelope. Please hold it above your head and slowly exit through your front door. Our staffers will gladly accept your payment and your good credit rating with us will *be reinstated.*

Please do it in the next five minutes. And thanks. Cordially,

Harvey Swern
Accounting Enforcement

P.S. If you have recently sent in your payment, please disregard this notice.

While the above example of a billing effort seems a little bit desperate, there is no publisher who at one time or another hasn't felt like picking up a shotgun and going after the people who ordered his magazine, started to receive it and never paid for it.

Obviously, the only way to avoid the need for billing letters is to require cash with every subscription order. However, the cost for each subscription paid up front will probably be higher than the net cost of all subscriptions if you use a charge or cash option.

Surely it makes sense, especially with a non-widely circulated publication, to allow a subscriber the convenience of charging his or her subscription. In addition, most subscribers like to see a copy of the publication before writing out a check. If the editorial quality of the publication is consistent with that which was promised in the subscription promotion, the pay rate will be higher and in most cases satisfactorily profitable.

The first step in a billing series is developing orders. When a subscription order comes in with the charge option having been selected, an invoice goes out as soon as possible. This first effort in your billing series usually contains a reply envelope and an invoice, nothing more.

Because it is only reasonable to allow your new subscribers or renewals at least 30 days to send payment, a monthly magazine will have to ship the first issue on that subscription before receiving payment.

Since fewer than 50 percent of the people you bill will pay on the initial invoice, a second effort—usually a letter from the circulation director—is sent out a month later. The third letter, another month later, is a little stronger. And the fourth letter informs the subscriber that no more issues will be sent out until payment has been made. (This is the end of the three-issue grace period that the Audit Bureau of Circulations will allow.)

Your billing series should contain between five and 10 efforts (assuming they all work at a profit, no matter how small). There are exceptions, of course. Publishers Clearing House, an atypical example, seems to turn a profit on as many as 20 efforts.

PCH's final effort threat is, "We can never again accept an order from you. This surely means that it will cost you more to ignore the enclosed bill than to pay it." They are referring to the great bargains you won't be able to cash in on in the years ahead. The envelope has a two-inch-high red rubber stamp (effect) screaming "LAST CHANCE," a theme repeated above the letter copy.

Achieving smooth response

To achieve a smooth response curve for your billing series, make a graph of the efficiency of each billing effort. For example, you may notice that the fourth effort is not pulling as well as the fifth effort. You could then substitute the fifth effort for the fourth effort and eliminate the fourth one entirely. Or, you could develop a new fourth effort.

As your billing series goes along, psychology would dictate that somewhere around the fourth or fifth effort the circulation director should advise the subscriber that any future payment problems are going to be out of his or her hands. And the next letter—drier and somewhat harsher—should then come from the accounting department.

At the point in your billing series where you approach between 75 percent and 95 percent paid, examine the results of your most recent billing effort (which may be the fifth, sixth or seventh effort) and determine whether it makes financial sense to send an additional effort. As we've said, if the cost of sending out a bill is higher than the income you project, there is no point in mailing that last effort.

It is also important to note that since billing efforts must go out by first class mail, the economies of billing are often not as favorable as those of new business or renewal efforts: A 10-effort billing series costs $1.50 per subscriber in postage alone.

There is one situation, however, when it does make sense to mail the additional effort. If you are dangerously close to dipping below your guarantee to advertisers, mailing the billing effort is cheaper than replacing those subscriptions with a new business activity. The small percentage of additional paid subscribers will keep you from going below that magic line.

The final letter

The final letter should come from the vice president of finance. There are some people who will ignore a letter from a circulation director but react to a letter from "the vice president of finance." (Bear in mind, however, that while you can use pseudonyms for renewal letters and new business letters, a billing letter must be signed by a legitimately employed person in your company.)

Since these people may be asked to renew, however, and since your magazine's relationship with its subscribers should be a warm and friendly one whenever possible, you should add the P.S. pretty much worded as in the "shotgun" letter above, offering those who have not paid a less embarrassing reason to respond to your "ultimate" billing effort. Even if a subscriber hasn't paid by then, there is saving grace, at least theoretically, in allowing him or her to think you think payment was made on the previous effort.

And remember, checks do cross billing efforts in the mail. A computer house cannot produce the list of those to be billed on a minute-to-minute basis, so a certain percentage of people who are receiving your eighth letter may have paid the bill as a result of the seventh.

Try as you may, however, you'll still have at least 10 percent of your subscribers in the deadbeat file. Make the best of the situation and hang on to the names until your next new business mailing.

Devise a special order form for the deadbeats and mail it to them as if you were offering an introductory subscription. One difference: this order form requires "Cash with order because of the unbelievably low price." Your pull on this group will usually match or beat the average of your entire mailing, without your having to pay rent for the names.

Billing and collecting money require technique and ability. Why not take a minute and ask to see your billing series? If all you get handed is a batch of invoices, without letters, your collections are probably not as good as they could be.

Take a look at the results from each effort (they should be retrievable by key) and see if you have a linear relationship of gradual reduction. If you do not, there may be an offending effort that could certainly stand removal or replacement.

Look at the copy (and this includes envelope copy as well) and see if the collecting techniques are reasonably strong but consistent with the editorial policy of your publication. If you read five billing efforts in a row, and each one has a different tone—morose, shocked, urgent, disappointed—chances are you have a billing series that can't be improved very much. If you are not moved to surprise or tears, however, it's time to get your favorite copywriter in gear to upgrade your collection series.

Collecting money, even from valuable people whom you address as dear friends, is at best a tedious process. The more often you ask for your money, the more you are straining the friendship. However, the bottom line for your publication's circulation revenues depends on how much money you collect from "Dear Friend."

Sweepstakes analysis:
The BH&G experience

By Jerry Ward

Sweepstakes promotion is widespread, particularly among major publishers, with some claiming response-rate lifts of 25 percent to 50 percent, and even 100 percent, but we at *Better Homes and Gardens* magazine, after a major sweeps test against our usual subscription direct mail program, have decided it is not for us.

Although we arrived at this conclusion 10 years ago when we tested a sweepstakes prize structure developed by our Book Division, we'd always had that nagging feeling that the unsatisfactory results might have been because the program had not been specifically designed for the magazine.

In December 1980, we had the opportunity to test such promotions again. The results for us did not conform to other publishers' experiences and revealed some interesting trends, particularly in the demographic characteristics of the sweepstakes responders.

Successful direct-mail program

It must be pointed out that *Better Homes and Gardens* has a very successful existing direct-mail program. Over 90 percent of its nearly 7,400,000 subscriptions are direct-mail sold, and even on its substantial yearly *new* business, handsome profits are made after tabulating all acquisition and fulfillment costs.

Our new prospect package control for the past several years had consisted of variations of a 9-inch by 12-inch poly outer envelope with a see-thru back dramatically presenting the front cover of our eight-page brochure. This four-color brochure, which pictures and describes our editorial subject areas, is the primary selling vehicle.

The accompanying letter is short (usually 2 pages) and stresses the offer. In our case, a two-years-for-the-price-of-one offer is the one that can't be beaten on a net per copy *or* long-term profitability basis. A no-risk guarantee is also stressed.

Because this approach has been so successful for us, and because it also collects and ultimately renews so well (no premiums, no sweepstakes), we've been reluctant to try sweepstakes. A sweepstake is very difficult (you have to award the prizes) and it can be very expensive. Trying to dabble in sweepstakes is like trying to get a little bit pregnant.

Some say you can test a small prize structure (say $50,000) and it will do almost as well as a big one (say $250,000). We had the opportunity to try this at the same time since we could adapt a $50,000 program we had just tested for *Apartment Life*. We found the size of the prize structure had a *major* effect on response.

Why, one might logically ask, would we be interested in testing sweeps at all if we had so much going for us? For a couple of reasons: Even a response rate lift as low as 25 percent for *Better Homes and Gardens* could

mean millions of dollars in additional profits and would likely be an attractive alternative even though renewal performance might not be what we've been used to. In addition, sweeps presumably have the ability to mask price. This was very interesting to us since we had doubled our subscription price from $5 to $10 in just five years and were approaching yet another move to $12. Through the judicious use of *Better Homes and Gardens'* cook books we could test a $250,000 prize structure without a cash outlay nearly approaching that amount.

We mailed a major test of a sweepstakes promotion as part of our volume mailing. The following prize structure was established:

Grand Prize (1)—$100,000 or home
1st Prize (1)—American Eagle Car
2nd Prizes (5)—RCA Televisions
3rd Prizes (75)—Kodak Cameras
4th Prizes (9,999)—BH&G Cook Books
Early Bird (1)—$10,000 maximum

Since we were new to this type of program we hired a consultant noted for his background in sweepstakes, and also contracted with the D.L. Blair Corporation to handle the administration.

We tested three different packages against our normal poly control to 25,000 name splits. We had a 9-inch by 12-inch green poly certificate approach with a see-thru back featuring the sweepstakes brochure. We had a 9-inch by 12-inch yellow poly token package with the same brochure pictured, and a 6-inch by 9-inch personalized, paper, letterlope approach.

All the bells and whistles normally employed in sweepstakes packages were used in all three packages. The offer was, of course, the same as that used in our control. (The control index number is always 100.)

The results were:

Package	Index
RSVP control	100
Certificate sweeps	109
Token sweeps	90
Letterlope sweeps	106

We tested the control offer of 24/$10 against four other prices, all packages in the token sweeps format. The results were:

Price	Index
24/$10 Control	100
12/$5	161
12/$7.50	93
12/$10	63
24/$15	55

This test showed about the same price sensitivity we see when we price-test with standard packages (no price *masking* as we'd expected).

Figure 1

List #1

Demographic		Regular Index	Sweeps Index	
Education	1 - 9.4 yrs.	90	134	
	9.5-10.4 yrs.	108	100	
	10.5-11.4 yrs.	98	107	
	11.5-12.4 yrs.	100	98	Note the trend away from higher education in the sweeps group.
	12.5-13.4 yrs.	106	98	
	13.5-14.4 yrs.	106	86	
	14.5-15.4 yrs.	71	82	
	15.5+ yrs.	62	18	
Income index	0- 79	87	118	
	80- 94	98	102	
	95-104	100	93	Note the flip-flop in income index.
	105-119	102	95	
	120-999	108	98	
Percent in professional occupation	0- 9	100	105	
	10-19	94	105	
	20-29	102	98	
	30-39	108	102	Note the smaller percent of professionals in sweeps responses.
	40-49	102	100	
	50-59	94	55	
	60-69	87	48	

List #2

Demographic		Regular Index	Sweeps Index	
Income index	0- 79	100	112	
	80- 94	102	112	
	95-104	95	98	Note the lower income skew on sweeps.
	105-119	100	100	
	120-999	100	91	
Percent in professional occupation	0- 9	98	109	
	10-19	95	107	
	20-29	105	102	
	30-39	102	95	Note higher sweeps indexes in lower percent professionals.
	40-49	83	77	
	50-59	86	93	
	60-69	186	84	

List #3

Demographic		Regular Index	Sweeps Index	
Title	Mr.	103	100	Note the decrease in male indicated responses and the increase in female in the sweeps groups.
	Mrs.	84	74	
	Miss	86	98	
Income index	-83	84	113	
	84-102	85	99	
	103-111	84	94	
	112-123	97	92	
	124-133	95	104	Note the jumps in response in the lower income indexes in the sweeps section.
	134-143	119	106	
	144-152	117	91	
	153-168	105	100	
	169-185	95	92	
	186+	116	108	

Demographic			Regular Index	Sweeps Index	
Index of social position		1	96	83	
		2	104	102	
		3	111	92	
		4	110	95	One is the top social position; ten is bottom. Note the virtual flip-flop in the index of responses between regular and sweeps.
		5	115	103	
		6	96	107	
		7	92	106	
		8	96	100	
		9	94	104	
		10	81	110	

────────────── List #4 ──────────────

Demographic		Regular Index	Sweeps Index	
Median home value	Less than $15M	84	84	
	$15M-$20M	97	90	
	$20M-$25M	116	92	Note better regular package response in higher home values.
	$25M-$30M	124	109	
	$30M+	115	92	
Percent auto ownership	Less than 70%	70	88	
	70-84	88	85	
	85-89	100	89	Note lower incidence of auto ownership with sweeps.
	90-94	112	86	
	95-96	103	107	
	97+	110	95	

────────────── List #5 ──────────────

Demographic		Regular Index	Sweeps Index	
Type of dwelling unit	SFDU*	107	99	
	Duplex	88	101	
	MFDU**	72	66	Note income flip-flop.
1970 median income	Less than $5M	63	110	
	5M-10M	80	91	
	10M-15M	113	92	Note the drop in sweeps SFDU index.
	15M+	133	70	
1970 median home value	Less than $10M	72	103	
	$10M-$20M	91	91	
	$20M-$30M	106	90	Note complete reversal in response by home value.
	$30M+	124	72	

*Single-family dwelling unit   **Multi-family dwelling unit

We mailed five different list cross sections to determine the effect of sweeps on 1) the response by universe penetration, and 2) demographics of responders. This, of course, was independent of the copy tests.

On two of the lists, the regular package performed considerably better than the sweepstakes package. On two other lists, the sweepstakes package did somewhat better. On the fifth list, the response was about the same.

Overall, the sweepstakes package did 9 percent better, but if we can't get a 20 to 25 percent better response, we aren't interested; sweepstakes have such a detrimental effect on renewals and demographics.

We found a *dramatic* difference between the demographics of responders to the sweeps approach and responders to the regular approach. Figure 1 shows the responses separated into indexes based on certain demographic characteristics. Note that the lower scale demographics generated by the sweeps appeal is evident throughout the analysis.

On collectability, we've found that sweeps will collect at only 93 percent the rate that our regular offers collect. We won't know anything about renewability until late 1982, but if the demographic characteristics are any indication—it just has to be worse.

To conclude, we didn't get the *big* lift in up-front response that others have enjoyed and we don't at all like what we are seeing in terms of collectability and demographics.

As an aside, sweepstakes programs haven't worked well at all for *Apartment Life/Metropolitan Home* either. The $50,000 program was tested for *Apartment Life* more than a year ago and an adaptation of the big $250,000 prize structure was tested as part of our *Metropolitan Home* direct-mail launch this spring. The sweepstakes fell far short of the winning non-sweeps package.

Our Family Shopping Service catalog direct-mail operation (which incidentally financed a portion of the prize structure so they could test it) also experienced similar negative results.

You can safely assume that we at Meredith Corporation feel we've given the big sweepstakes prize promotions a thorough testing, and do not expect we'll even be retesting them again in the foreseeable future. We felt, however, that others could benefit by our experience.

What's in a number?

By Eliot DeY. Schein

Direct mail is both an art and a science. And as any "with it" circulation executive would be glad to volunteer, putting numbers through their paces is very much a part of the direct mail business. And certainly any activity that is laden with numbers is going to produce certain *outstanding* numbers.

Unfortunately, some of these "star" or famous numbers are taken too literally by non-practitioners of direct marketing. And many's the time that circulation results are contrasted against the stars and unfairly judged as being under par.

Let's take an example: What percentage is the proper response result for a cold mailing? Well, ask anyone who is not too intimate with direct mail and the answer you're going to get most often is 3 percent. And sure enough, publishers, investors, and editors the world over believe that if you get 3 percent on your cold mail you're doing great—or certainly good enough—and anything under 3 percent is not good.

Well, doesn't the offer have something to do with how that 3 percent affects the bottom line? Surely, if you were selling hair combs by mail for a dollar each, a 3 percent response would not put you on easy street. But—if the product happened to be Rolls Royces at upwards of $80,000 apiece, orders coming in at 3 percent from direct mail would make even the highest overhead dealer a billionaire in no time.

Newsletters at $50 or $100 a year can make a fortune at 1 percent. And expensive-to-produce magazines might not break even on fulfillment and production at anything lower than 5 percent.

The mailing package also plays a role in percentage response. Since the percentage response is really a measurement of what you can expect to receive in incoming dollars from your mailing, the greater the response percentage, the better off everyone is going to be. But surely— if you put a dollar bill in each one of the packages as an incentive to get an order, your response percentage would go up. But your cost per thousand for putting the material in the mail would also be raised by exactly that one thousand dollars.

And speaking of cost per thousand, there's a threshold there, too. Earlier in 1981 it was $200 a thousand in the mail. How is that? Eighty-four dollars for postage, $40 for mailing lists, $15 for mailing house or lettershop services, and the balance for printing. Sounds low

to you? Okay, make it $220. (And now, the postage has gone from $84 a thousand to $100 a thousand on a third class mailing.)

Henry Cowen, dean of the creative department at Publishers Clearing House, has often said that "the more expensive the package, the more components, the more color—the better the package will pull." For some offers that's quite true. But the cost of the package must be factored in, in terms of the return on investment.

You can see that a 3 percent response is really meaningless unless you know the following: What does it cost to fulfill the subscription? How much did the package cost to put in the mail? How renewable are the subscriptions?

Renewable? Certainly, the packages with the dollar bills in them will probably attract subscribers at a higher percentage than a package without a dollar bill. But you'd better be prepared to put dollar bills in the renewal packages as well to attract these people back for more next year. Add that to your cost per sale.

Let's take a look at another number: renewal percentage. The bandied-about benchmark: 50 percent. Does that mean *your* magazine should have a 50 percent renewal? To be sure, 50 percent renewal for some magazines would represent a substantial increase from their current level; for others, it would be a disaster. So—is the 50 percent renewal figure valid? Again, it all depends on how you attract your subscriptions in the first place and how strong your editorial product is in terms of its acceptance by the readers you generated.

Modern Bride magazine, for example, has two kinds of subscribers: industrial and consumer. The industrial subscriber is the bridal salon owner, the caterer, the manufacturer, and the advertiser. The consumer is the young woman of the soon-to-be-wed couple.

The operative word here is *soon. Modern Bride*'s consumer renewals are low—and they should be. Although you can prepare for a wedding for years, after the wedding, the magazine's usefulness to the consumer diminishes greatly. A 50 percent renewal rate for, say, *Business Week* leaves something to be desired.

So if your renewal rate is 60 percent you should be happy. Right? Wrong. Why not 70 percent? It really depends on what you're charging for the renewal and how valuable your editorial product is to your reader.

Surprisingly enough, there are still some publishers

who don't have advance renewal efforts. Those who don't should probably consider incorporating an advance renewal effort halfway through the term of service. Those who do are probably looking for a famous number. How about 10 percent? If you get 10 percent on your advance renewal effort, you should then be a shoo-in for a 50 percent overall renewal percentage. Right? Depends on the *price* of the advance renewal.

The year of the big price increase at your magazine, your advance renewal package may say something like, "Renewal now—in advance—will save you money because the prices are going up in two months." Why, you may even get a *15 percent* advance renewal . . . surely a guarantee of a 55 percent or better *overall* renewal rate, one would think. But not if you raised the prices between the advance renewal and the beginning of your regular series three months later.

Here's one that everybody has a lot of fun with: What pay-up rate is expected on a hard offer? The industry "average" is 90 percent. Or is it 85 percent? Well, imagine the surprise of one Midwestern publisher who had only a 60 percent pay-up rate on a hard solicitation. Why only 60 percent, he queried, when the average is 90 percent?

Well, suppose the bill goes out after the first issue of the magazine goes out. And suppose the first issue of the magazine is not what was promised in the direct mail solicitation? The pay-up rate is going to be pretty low, isn't it? And if the original solicitation contained a cash/charge option and nobody sent cash, wasn't the handwriting on the wall?

For a soft offer, another famous number: 50 percent pay-up. Does it have to be? Of course not. None of these numbers is etched in stone. All they have to be is efficient and intelligent for the particular profit and loss statement of your publication.

Every so often, the advertising trade press announces a new magazine and discusses a test mailing that pulled a tremendous response. If that response is much higher than yours, does it mean you're sending out the wrong letters or publishing the wrong magazine? Absolutely not.

First of all, a test that sours never gets written up in advertising columns because the magazine is usually never published. Second, since average news isn't exciting news, columnists often provoke publishers into giving the rosiest side of their test results. There's really nothing wrong with that unless you are reading about a 10 percent response while holding the actual hard copy test results that read only 4 percent.

It is said that numbers never lie. But surely, 3 percent on a soft offer is not as good as 3 percent on a hard offer. Unfortunately, not many people on the periphery of direct marketing ask that question when the percentage response claim is made.

The industry average may very well *be* 3 percent with the thousands of magazines that are being sold in the marketplace.

But while the numbers don't lie, there is no predetermined average that applies to your own magazine. There is no average on renewals, or advance renewals, or pay-ups. What counts is testing and results, profit and loss, improvement of results, and deterioration of results.

And the cold hard truth is that famous numbers are for fun, and fun only. Some of them count if they are used as relative benchmarks for expectations. But the only ones that really count in figuring your profit picture are yours.

A management guide to response percentages

By Eliot DeY. Schein

You've heard it: "I got 9 percent on my new mailing." Or, "3 percent is what we need in order to be doing okay in cold mail." Or "New Publisher Achieves 17 Percent Response in Test Mailing." Well, you've heard it, or read it, but do you believe it? What do percentages on new business mailings *really* mean?

It is possible for one company to make a fortune at one half of one percent, while another loses a similar fortune at a 10 percent response rate. What's more, any direct mailer, circulation consultant, or heads-up circulation director can "rig" almost any direct mailing to provide any (well, almost any) desired percentage response result. So fear not when you hear about your major competitive magazine having just achieved a response percentage that more than doubles that of your own experience. Judging a mailing by a response percentage is worse than judging a book by its cover.

In order to judge intelligently, the elements that produce a percentage must be investigated. What type of offer is being used? If it's a soft offer (free-examination copy), the response percentage will normally be higher. The net percentage (the actual final tally on new paid subscriptions from the mailing) may match those of a hard offer when the smoke clears and the bottom line becomes visible.

Traditionally, sweepstakes may out-pull soft offers by double and sometimes even triple. In analyzing the results from a sweepstakes mailing, the simple bottom line on the first time pay-off may not provide enough information to help you determine the overall effect of the promotion. But more about that in a moment.

Consider your source of information on other magazines' response percentages when you try to determine what those percentages really are. A well-known daily newspaper advertising columnist constantly shows "hyped" percentages which, no doubt, juice up his editorial punch. A fairly recent case in point: ". . . and the new publication has managed to pull 17 percent on a direct mail viability test."

The factual result figures, however, belie this 17 percent result. In fact, not even one key, the best key, had gone that high, and the entire mailing came in at a gross of approximately 4.2 percent. There was no question that the newspaper was in error, although it's not difficult to understand how such an error might have occurred.

The scenario

You're starting a new magazine. Somewhere along the way toward that first issue, someone suggests that it wouldn't hurt your advertising sales effort if one or two major daily newspapers printed something good about your new publication. So you get in touch with the appropriate writers for the newspapers and finally come down to that all-important telephone interview.

First, you're somewhat excited and delighted by the prospect of having your name and the name of your new magazine appear on the pages of one or more of America's more successful newspapers. Second, you want to make sure your story *does* appear and that it appears in the most advantageous light. Thus, when the newspaper person says, "What can you tell me that's exciting about your new magazine?" you launch into "praiseology" of your concept, your design and the untold millions who will beat a path to your door to purchase copies of this new epic.

"But," he says, "what kind of *hard* news do you have that I can use in the paper?" You answer, "We just did a direct mail test for subscriber viability and got a response of over 3 percent."

"Well, how much over 3 percent?" asks the writer. You, in a breathless moment, say rather slowly, "Substantially."

The writer: "If you could give me the real numbers, I could do a much better job on this story. Could I say, for example, 6 percent? Because, you know, 3 percent isn't very newsy."

You: "Well, you could say 6 percent, but that wouldn't be totally accurate." The writer: "Well, then tell me how much higher to go. Accuracy is very important and this is a *newspaper*, you know."

You answer, "On one of the test cells, we actually showed a 7.2 percent overall response, but that was a soft offer and . . ."

"Seventeen point what?" interrupts your interviewer.

"I said 7.2."

"Okay, I'm going to leave off the .2 and call it 17. Is that all right with you?"

And in a split second of suppressed guilt, but sustained by hope for the future, you very quietly say "Okay" and hang up the phone.

Ask questions

This may not be exactly the way it has happened or will happen to you, but it's close enough to keep you from firing your circulation director when it seems that everyone can pull over 10 percent in the mail but you. You might just seize the moment to ask your circulation director how he or she accounts for the new competitor doing so well in the mail.

Since circulation directors, by the way, would prefer to have their own mailings do very well, they are sometimes capable of presenting percentages to management that aren't quite accurate, either. If you get responses to your questions about current results such as, "Well, one of the keys is pulling over 4 percent," or "We have a test cell that looks really big," or "Some of the roll-outs aren't doing so well, but the tests are dynamite," you need to ask more questions to get the real answers you seek.

First question: "What is the anticipated net?" The second question (and probably more important), "What is the potential renewability?" You've seen, no doubt, some pretty high-percentage-pulling cold mailings that (assuming you track them long enough) resulted in rather depressing renewal percentages.

Promises, promises

How can this occur? Any direct mail package, regardless of offer, can *promise* certain benefits—benefits that may or may not be forthcoming from your editorial product.

A recent mailing for *Time* magazine was computerized by the home state of the recipient and incorporated the state name into the list of items the potential subscriber would like to read about in the future. The line "What's happening in Wyoming?" was for Wyoming readers exclusively, "Hawaii" for Hawaiian readers, "Ohio" for Ohio readers, and so on. This is surely a clever technique. However, how does a new subscriber in Hawaii react after searching issue after issue of *Time* magazine and failing to uncover "What's happening in Hawaii?" The same goes for your Wyoming and Ohio reader and all the rest. The result: a disappointed subscriber.

One of two things can then happen. If, after the introductory subscription is over, most new subscribers have become enamored with the magazine anyway (and that's pretty easy to do in *Time*'s case), the result will be a satisfactory renewal percentage. On the other hand, if most subscribers are harboring a grudge because your package misrepresented the editorial content of your magazine, the result will most likely be a lower percentage, which increases attrition in the future and puts your magazine on a treadmill to oblivion.

Since each magazine has its own needs for circulation and its own reasons for building or reducing it, there is no one answer that can solve everyone's circulation problems.

To recap: Your essential data about how well your new business mailing did are based on three percentages and a dollar number. The three percentages are 1) the gross initially; 2) the net after a while; and 3) eventually, the renewal rate.

The gross percentage should be looked at by management as a relative percentage. Assuming that the same package and the same offer have mailed before, today's gross percentage, if higher, should prove to be a higher net. If the gross percentage is achieved by a new package or a new offer or anything different from that which you used previously, all you have in that percentage is an initial indication of success or failure.

Net percentages are much more important numbers. Unfortunately, assuming you have a cash/charge option in your offer, it will be two or three months before you will see what the net percentages really are. It is worth the wait, however, even though management often fails to ask for the figures three months down the line.

The renewal (or conversion) percentage by mailing date (and by key, if possible) for the first time out on the new subscriber is the most critical number. It shows management exactly how well the magazine is doing and provides insight into an extremely important dollar figure; namely, the income from the sub after the first renewal.

Earlier we discussed different offers, including sweepstakes. While sweepstakes usually provide a high gross, the net drop-off, surprisingly, may not be so great because some subscribers (even if they have subscribed solely to give themselves a "better shot" at the grand prize) do have a tendency to pay up. This can be true es-

pecially if the sweepstakes drawing has not yet taken place at the moment of attempted conversion from "ordered" to "paid." But watch those renewals like a hawk. Sweepstakes renewals in almost every case will not develop the high percentages of hard or even soft-offer straight mailings.

Right now would be a good time to ask your circulation department (or fulfillment house) to generate these three important figures from a mailing you did about a year ago—let's say July 1980. By looking at the initial gross response, and at the cost of the mailing, you will be able to develop a system to determine cost per order. Now investigate the eventual paid percentage six months into the mission and extrapolate the cost per paid subscriber.

Finally, take a look at the renewals that should now be pretty much crystallized for that July 1980 group and develop a cost or profit in terms of income from the initial subscription and the renewal. If you have no profit, your subscription rate or advertising rate is too low, or your editor isn't doing his or her job. If the profit is substantial, pat yourself and everyone you work with on the back because you're doing just fine.

But by all means, never again look at a 5 percent response (either yours or someone else's) and say, "Boy, isn't that great!" Beauty is in the eye of the beholder, and the person who presents and interprets the beauty is not the final authority. The bottom line is.

Offer vs. lists vs. copy

By Eliot DeY. Schein

Ever since the first stone-carved message was sent from cave to cave, a direct mail argument has festered. What's most important: the offer, the lists, or the copy?

If one caveman was inviting another to help him club a mammoth into submission (and eventually food), he would first have to decide how much of the spoils he was offering, to whom he would send his chiseled tablet, and the best way of expressing his message to assure a speedy reaction from his intended partner.

After thousands of years, things don't seem to have changed that much. Today when magazine management decides to invest in a direct mail program to generate new subscribers, the same three factors prevail as testable unknowns. In fact, when New York's direct marketing club (The Hundred Million Club) meets every year, members debate the very same questions that faced the caveman.

The offer is most important!

The price that a publisher sets for a subscription is based on break-even cost factors for the magazine's direct mail promotion, fulfillment, circulation requirements for advertising sales, and other marketing objectives. Normally, the lower the price, the higher the response.

The term can be anywhere from a three-month trial to a three-year "permanent" subscription. Normally, 12 issues for one year does better than almost anything else.

The longer term has its advantages, however. For example, there's no need to start spending dollars to renew a three-year subscriber until at least two years are up on the subscription. And, with a longer term, the promotion price can feature a relative cost comparison to the basic subscription rate. Such a comparison can be very dramatic to the consumer. But, bear in mind: If the magazine is not familiar to the consumer, a short-term trial program may provide better results.

A deadline date as a part of the offer can be effective in inspiring a quicker response (and, it is hoped, a greater response), especially in promotional programs such as sweepstakes or one-time-only "Beat the rising rate" packages.

The choice of either a "soft" or a "hard" offer can make an incredible difference in percentage point results. "Soft" packages are based on a free examination copy of the magazine being sent to the new "trial" subscriber prior to invoicing the subscriber for the sub. The offer is outlined in terms of a "free trial copy" or "free examination copy" and results in a net response which tends to be higher in number of orders and lower in percentage paid. The "hard" offer demands a subscription order (either cash or credit) and usually produces a lower gross response but a higher percentage net paid on the hard gross.

So how important is the offer . . . price, term, deadline, soft or hard, and of course the decisions regarding premiums, sweepstakes, and bonus copies?

Mailing lists are most important!

Lists are easy to come by; the proper lists come a little more dearly. As magazine management, if it seems logical to you that habitual magazine subscribers are more likely to subscribe to your magazine, you're right. Magazine subscriber lists are the best lists to use when selling magazine subscriptions. But subscribers of what magazines?

Newsweek, for example, would probably not get bang-up results from mailing to *Popular Photography* subscribers. *Popular Photography* might not get bang-up results from their offer to *Newsweek* subscribers, but for different reasons. The *Popular Photography* subscriber, for example, is generated by a cut rate offer as low as $7 for 12 issues and must have some sort of interest in the subject matter in order to be a worthwhile subscriber. The *Newsweek* subscriber is paying over $20 a year for a magazine on a general subject level.

How do you attract one to the other? Answer: Not easily!

While the *Popular Photography* mailing will attract *Newsweek* subscribers based on the offer of a low annual subscription price (relative to the price *Newsweek* subscribers are used to paying), *Popular Photography*'s special interest subject matter will not be universally palatable to *Newsweek* subscribers. On the other hand, *Newsweek*'s subject matter certainly appeals to the majority of *Popular Photography* subscribers, but the *Newsweek* price for a year's subscription is bound to be a deterrent.

It would seem that the best potential subscribers for *Newsweek* are subscribers to a current events-directed publication that charges at least $20 a year for a subscription. For *Popular Photography* the best lists are of people who have shown an interest in photography and reading about photography, and perhaps subscribers to other photography magazines.

The more recent the list, the better it is. The best mailing list you can possibly find is that of your brand-new competitor who is charging more than you are for a similar product and has a list of people who have subscribed in the last six months. Too bad these kinds of lists are not available, and even if they were, there are not enough of them around to make a substantial difference in your circulation numbers.

Someday, list brokers and sales companies are going to provide something besides those little list cards that are half promotion/half fact, concerning the list available for rental. They're going to provide a sample "control" direct mail package, or ad, or TV storyboard, showing exactly what the approach, price, premium (if any), and general thrust of the generation effort happened to be. If *Penthouse* were given the opportunity to mail a cold new-business solicitation to *Playboy* readers and didn't use a sweepstakes because they didn't know that's what *Playboy* uses in the mails, they would be wasting a once-in-a-lifetime opportunity.

Since some lists can pull two, three or four times the percentage of others, are lists the most important element?

The copy is most important!

How can there be such a great variance from package to package to package? How can there be such a great variance in cost of copy from one writer to another?

Copy consists roughly of five basic elements. The first and most important is the approach. Is it a dollar-oriented approach, short term trial, soft offer, or love of subject?

Does the introduction really catch the reader and keep him or her interested?

Is the exposition of the contents of the magazine consistent with the interests of the people who are reading the package? (Did the copywriter know which lists are being mailed to before taking pen in hand?) Are the benefits described in the juiciest, most mouth-watering terms? And is there a closing motivation that whips the reader from the request to "act now" on the bottom of the letter to the order form so that he or she will surely act?

Now, if any one of those elements—approach, introduction, exposition, benefits, closing—is weak, it can destroy even the strongest companion part.

If the envelope isn't opened because the copywriter hasn't suitably provided envelope copy that demands attention, results will falter. Or suppose the introduction on the letter doesn't keep the reader's interest level high, or the exposition of subject matter doesn't whet the reader's appetite? Furthermore, what if the benefits provided don't cause hearts to flutter? What if the closing motivation falls flat on its face? The results will tend toward disastrous . . . to a point. Obviously, the copy is the most important element!

What, then, is *really* most important? The offer, the lists, or the copy? The answer: None of the above. Try sending good copy to a good list without a decent offer. Try mailing to a good list a package with a good offer without good copy. What about a terrific offer and wonderful copy, and no one to send it to? Any one of these combinations spells failure.

The real answer is that no one of these items is most important. How they *interact* is most important: The best offer with the best copy to the best list is going to pull better than any other combination you can come up with.

And remember, offers should change when your costs and/or needs change. Sometimes it might be wise to compromise on lowering a price to develop the additional number of subs required to establish and maintain an appetizing rate guarantee.

Lists should change too. There are always new lists; there are always old lists falling by the wayside.

And copy. Take a look at your magazine. How much have the contents changed? How much has society changed? Imagine using a teaser line about energy conservation 20 years ago—or even 10.

The elements of offer, lists and copy are only ingredients in a direct mail recipe. It is the skill of the chef in selecting and mixing the ingredients that determines the response. Nothing more, nothing less.

Anatomy of a winner

By Eliot DeY. Schein

More than five years ago Alan Bennett, then in his early twenties, had an idea for a new magazine. He planned on calling it *American Photographer*, and he went through the effort and rigmarole of a test mailing. He chose a highly regarded, professional direct response marketing agency which selected the right lists, put out a proper mailing, and achieved a reasonable result.

Unfortunately, however, despite the results of his mailing, Bennett did not have enough capital to "roll-out" and develop the circulation for *American Photographer*. In fact, he had used his last dime just to do the test.

For most new publishers, raising enough capital to roll out a circulation effort and support the first couple of years of publication is extremely difficult. For people in their early twenties, it is almost impossible . . . and Bennett could not raise the required capital. In fact, he even had difficulty paying the printer and the mailing house which participated in his first mailing.

So—he took a job at CBS Publishing and cooled his heels as circulation manager of *World Tennis* magazine. A couple of years later, he found himself at *U.S. News & World Report* with the still-burning desire to produce *American Photographer* magazine.

Now, however, he *was* able to raise the venture capital (he was older and earning a wage) and he began to retest his proposed concept. In June of 1978, the magazine was launched, and in February of 1980 Bennett sold the now-successful *American Photographer* magazine to CBS Publishing for somewhere between two million and three million dollars. How did he do it?

Quality product boosts returns

Bennett did not create the multimillion dollar price tag for his publication through prize-winning direct mail; no direct mail effort is *that* good. Instead, he did it by having a superior product. (One is forced to conclude that *American Photographer* is a winner based on the observation that it has a strong position in what is indubitably a crowded market.)

An examination of *American Photographer*'s direct mail effort can still be very enlightening, however, and it is not surprising that it now comes close to matching the direct mail program of one of Bennett's chief competitors.

Bennett's first offering—which was mailed, somewhat tardily it would seem, at the end of January 1978—announced "a new, frankly elitest magazine devoted exclusively to the interests of the advanced photographer." A charter subscription order form was enclosed with a soft offer that allowed the new subscriber to cancel upon receipt of his first issue and the first invoice.

(It is interesting to note here that Bennett's unsuccessful attempt at launching *American Photographer* a few years before relied upon an illustrated promotion piece that almost should have borne the phrase "sexually explicit material enclosed." The 1978 program did *not* include promotion of that nature.)

In May of 1978 (all things being equal, a questionable time for mailing), Bennett sent out exactly the same promotion package with another soft offer, another high pull up front. Now, however, the magazine was actually being published, and despite the drawback of a soft offer and the lackluster mailing package, cancellations were remarkably low.

In December of 1978, he was able to mail on time . . . again, in terms of traditional optimal mailing dates. This time, his carrier envelope had a three-inch wide announcement of a free issue (another soft offering)—a less than solid category for ABC auditing purposes, but certainly advantageous in promotion. The order form assures that the Audit Bureau of Circulations will not accept the entire run of the subscription, unless specified in the audit report as a "free" offer.

Again, there was a decent response and a high-level conversion to "paid"—sure signs of widespread acceptance of a magazine.

In June of 1979, having learned his lesson, he mailed another version of a similar package (same three-inch wide promotion) which he changed to say: "Save 50%." Here, the order form and the rest of the material in the package worded the soft offer in a way that allowed the ABC to bestow full credit.

Was Bennett guilty of not testing sufficiently? Perhaps—but somewhere in the midst of these ultimately successful learning experiences was indeed a six inch by nine inch package with a brochure that is almost identical to the original full-color brochure used five years earlier. (Five years is a long time, and what was sexually explicit then apparently is no longer.)

Purchased by CBS

And now to update: CBS, Bennett's old employer, has purchased the magazine, based in part on a subscrip-

tion campaign that is classic in its simplicity. The only refinements between Bennett's first attempt and the current one are the decrease in the number of pages of the letter (from six pages to four), the presentation of the offer on the carrier envelope, and the more profitably auditable nature of the presentation.

Bennett could have saved a bit of time and effort by copying *Modern Photography*'s control package from the start. Instead, he tested his own, which finally evolved into a virtual "twin."

Let's compare a recent promotion from *Modern Photography* magazine with one from *American Photographer*:

Bennett's most recent #10 envelope says "save 50%," *Modern Photography*'s says "save 50%." Bennett's envelope is red and black, *Modern Photography*'s is red and black. They both have order forms.

Are there any differences? Well, Bennett uses a four-page promotion letter, *Modern Photography*'s letter is two pages. Bennett uses a business reply envelope, whereas *Modern Photography* uses a business reply card.

Are there any other differences? None. But, when the paid subscribers stand up to be counted, the *American Photographer* package will out-pull that of *Modern Photography* because the editorial quality of Bennett's magazine seems to be irresistible.

There's a lesson to be learned from this success story, but first a prediction: The renewal rate of *American Photographer* subscriptions is going to be at an all-time high level for consumer photography magazines. It will probably out-renew the Ziff-Davis publication, *Popular Photography*, and make the boys at *Modern Photography* salivate for months to come. I base my prediction on the fact that an incredibly high percentage of those who were willing to take *American Photographer*'s no-risk "free-trial" offer have converted to paid.

Back to the moral: Regardless of the quality of direct mail promotion, the circulation of a magazine will ultimately reach a level consistent with the quality of the editorial product. A publisher can get a high response from a wonderful mailing piece that will end up in a financial disaster if the magazine does not fulfill the promise of the promotion.

In the case of *American Photographer*, Bennett naively promised less in his promotion than he eventually delivered. A risky way to be successful but the odds were with him and so should be our applause.

Bennett scores the highest points for editorial and production acumen, and it's a good bet that CBS will upgrade *American Photographer*'s direct mail promotion to match the quality of the product.

Flower & Garden

By Eliot DeY. Schein

When someone tells you they've "forgotten more than you'll ever know," it's usually hyperbole. But in the case we're about to consider, it just may be an unfortunate statement of truth.

The case is *Flower & Garden*'s current control package (mailed in the December 31, 1980 rush) which illustrates—by inclusion or omission—some of the most important points of direct mail.

The circulation director of *Flower & Garden*, the Kansas City-based half-million circulation magazine, is Albert G. Glass. Glass studied under dear, departed direct-mail sage Lester Suhler at *Look* magazine and brought his many years of experience to the "show-me" state to help *Flower & Garden*'s circulation bloom.

There is no doubt that Glass succeeded. And an inspection of the control package gives sound evidence that some of the basic "Suhleresque" principles of direct marketing survive.

However, since this is a column of constructive criticism and advice for publishing management, let's take a minute or two to remind Glass about some of the principles he may have forgotten.

Please—no black

Albert G. Glass, you have a rather expensive-to-produce six-inch by nine-inch carrier envelope with two large windows—one for the address and one for the four-color art on the order form to show through.

Now, there are a couple of things you should do with this envelope: For crying out loud, *don't* print it in one-color black anymore! At least go one-color red. Furthermore, the typeface on the return address is not the logo of the magazine. It should be. And considering the concentration of females you are hoping to attract with this mailing, a sans serif face just isn't doing the job.

You have color on the front page of the letter (which faces the back of the envelope). Why not try a third window on the back of the envelope so that the four-color piece can show through, as well? Then you would have four colors on both sides showing through windows and a carrier envelope that, even though it has no selling copy on it, may say to your market, "Open me up!"

Certainly, you remember the old rule about asking "yes or no" questions in a headline or in the opening line of a letter. Yet, you say, "Dear fellow gardener: Want a garden that's the envy of the neighborhood? Bright and beautiful flowers all season long? A lawn that's velvety and green? Vigorous house plants?"

How about trying a slight change. Maybe this: "Dear fellow gardener: Now you can have a garden that's the envy of the neighborhood, with bright and beautiful flowers all season long and a lawn that's velvety and green. Your house plants can be vigorous and healthy, too!" That may work a little better.

To start your second paragraph, instead of "Try *Flower & Garden*," how about "Discover *Flower & Garden*"? And please, please, get rid of the italic typeface in the first indented paragraph. The psychology of direct mail dictates that nobody is going to believe that a letter incorporating both roman and italic was typewritten by a person (IBM typewriters with interchangeable elements are not household items).

A softer voice

Now starts a paragraph that's softer—much softer. It's a different voice, but that's O.K. You explained why: After you wrote this letter and used it for a couple of years, your friend and co-copywriter, Beth Ellington, came in to soften up the copy for the high percentage female readership dictated by the mailing lists you're renting.

The copy is soft. Remarkably soft for a half-price offer. And the four-page letter, which has four-color illustrations of flowers and plants and vegetables and fruits on every one of the four pages, adds to the softness of the copy. It's even a nice touch to have chosen a name like Betty Jackson to sign the letter. But years ago, would the moguls at *Look* have let you get away with having that signature in process blue and not blue/black?

You have to be congratulated on your order form. With two four-color spots on that as well, your reader must certainly be salivating. Next time out, why not try the words "half-price offer" in a larger typeface? And, inasmuch as you're using four-color anyway, how about red instead of black? And while you're at it, put an exclamation point after the word "offer"!

Before you have your art director go home, though, you might want him to add a dashed line over the perforation so that even the most far-sighted reader will know it is a perforation. That might save a few new subscribers the trouble of trying to *fold* the order form into the reply envelope.

No doubt the half-price offer (six bimonthly issues for only $3) is adding tremendously to the success of this package because of the relative bargain it represents. On the other hand, the reply envelope may be a hindrance because it is not prepaid and it is not printed in any color but funereal black.

An important omission: Assuming that not every person who gardens is familiar with *Flower & Garden*, why on earth don't you show a cover photograph of the magazine somewhere in the package? Consider placing it to the left of the signature on the letter.

Now you may say that putting in something as square (in shape) and hard as a magazine cover might detract from the softness of the letter. You may be right. So compromise. Take a bouquet of flowers, stick your magazine in it, and then take the picture. Or, have your illustrator incorporate the magazine cover into a hand-drawn bouquet. Wasn't that one of the original rules of introducing a magazine to a new subscriber—showing a cover? Of course, at *Look*, it wasn't necessary after a while, because everyone came to know what *Look* was like. But *Flower & Garden* isn't *Look* magazine.

So, Albert G. Glass, please accept this advice in the spirit in which it is intended: as a friendly neighborly reminder from one gardener to another that there are some basic things from the past that can help us do our job in the present. Go ahead and try these slight changes in an otherwise beautiful and bountiful package. It may perform even more efficiently!

Louisiana Life

By Eliot DeY. Schein

Thomas Marshall is a life-long resident of Louisiana, with absolutely no background in publishing. One day, he and his wife Nancy came to the conclusion that *Louisiana Life* magazine was begging to be published. They developed their concept and, throwing caution to the wind, sent out a direct mail launch promotion in January 1981.

They must have been in exactly the right place at the right time because, with zero expertise between them, the circulation promotion succeeded beyond their wildest dreams. And *Louisiana Life* today is more than just alive and kicking.

That in itself is a pretty compelling story with an adventuresome beginning and a triumphant ending. But let's examine the in-between. All along the way, the Marshalls have made some tremendous errors in their marketing, yet they managed to squeak through. And more than squeaked through—they have prevailed with flying colors.

On January 22, 1981, publisher Marshall sent a letter to FOLIO with a sample of the direct mail package "we are using for our launch." He continued in his letter: "Inasmuch as city and regional magazines are so popular nowadays and are using many of the same techniques used by the major national magazines, we thought you might consider commenting on this package in FOLIO. Obviously we think the package is good (doesn't every publisher?) but we would be very interested in your comments and criticism."

This letter was written before the fulfillment of the first issue of the magazine. And Mr. Marshall said in his letter that "early returns look very strong."

Apparently Mr. Marshall had good reason for his enthusiasm. The average response on the first mailing was 5.5 percent. This one statistic on a cash-up-front-only offer so moved the Marshalls in late January 1981 that they wasted no time in rolling out some of their higher yielding mailing lists (one as high as 10 percent) with an additional mailing of 125,000. These additional mailings, when added to bind-in responses for the first two issues of the magazine, got them 27,000 paid subscribers by September 1981.

The offer was quite simple: $12 a year for six bimonthly issues and your *entire* subscription remittance refunded if, after you receive the first issue, you're not entirely delighted. Marshall admits to having refunded some two dozen checks for $12 each.

So far so good. The Marshalls mailed another flight of packages in mid-1981 and raised the price from $12 to $15. Why did they do that? Says Marshall, "Our bind-in card response at the $15 basic subscription price was as good as, if not better than, the $12 offer. Therefore, we had no compunction whatsoever."

Possible downside?

What's missing from this entire story is the downside, although thus far there doesn't seem to be one. But the Marshalls are guilty of several infractions of direct mail and marketing law, and these very violations could easily create a downside later on.

The first and most serious infraction is failure to test. According to *Atlanta* magazine's circulation director, Elmer Dalton (a veteran professional), a city or regional publication should promote with a certain amount of folksy "home-grown" material. Dalton knows what he's talking about because he's tested every which way while bringing *Atlanta* well along the road to success. Apparently Tom Marshall never spoke to Elmer Dalton. He probably should have. But Marshall is more than satisfied with his 5.5 percent response.

How much more his response might have been with a more "down-home" touch to his offering is not going to be known for a long time, if ever. Certainly the launch package, as mailed, seems to have done the trick . . . even if it is a "city-slick" package.

Despite the many other direct mail violations—the remarkable sprinkling of flaws on the business reply envelope; the wrong signature colors throughout; the lack of benefit sell; the obvious ersatz type in depiction of sample pages; the display typeset copy interspersed with typewriter type on the letter; the clumsiness of order form—this package did have one outstanding component. The four-color brochure (usually considered essential for pre-publication circulation promotion for a magazine that is laden with four-color work) is a knockout. The color printing would even pass muster at traditionally hard-to-satisfy Conde Nast.

No testing—no information

A publisher who does not test ends up with no information to help make future promotions more effective. Publisher Marshall, who incidentally is a vigorous entrepreneur, admits the original oversight and explains it by saying, "We didn't have the time or the money to test!" Then why, after eight months of success, does he fall right back into the same non-testing syndrome?

Here's how that failure can jump up to bite him on the nose. *Louisiana Life* produced a new package for a fall 1981 mailing—somewhat of a revise of the original. There were some changes, however.

The lead of the letter was changed completely and is, essentially, a testimonial from a current subscriber. The price, as mentioned before, is up $3. The brochure now features "real" editorial. And naturally, the first issue excitement is non-existent (but why didn't they substitute "Charter Subscription Offer" or some such in an attempt to whet the prospects' appetites?).

When asked what thinking contributed to the decisions to change these elements from the original package that seemed to work so well, Marshall had no justification.

One can't help wonder at what point *Louisiana Life* is going to be damaged by the error of these ways. And one can do no more than hope that the magazine, as it has thus far, will continue to flourish in spite of the questionable strategy of the publisher.

It's always a pleasure to report on this type of success. But it's scary, to say the least, to consider that the outside professionals who worked on these mailings every step of the way would permit the total lack of pre-testing

---

Checklist for December:
☐ Check the printed samples of the components for your end-of-December mailings. Are they all there? Does everything that's supposed to fit inside something else actually fit?
☐ Check your mailing lists for December. Are they properly ordered and heading toward your mailing house?
☐ Begin to forecast responses from that December 31 mailing.

---

and package testing that has occurred. One can only conclude that the promotion program succeeded *despite* the flaws, not because of them. And further, one just has to speculate on how much more successful—and profitable—the current and future circulation and marketing of this lovely magazine could be if properly managed.

Maybe what it really means is that we have to change (slightly) a cardinal rule of direct marketing: "Every time you spend money on a promotion, you must generate not only orders but information through testing. Unless you are launching *Louisiana Life* magazine."

May its success continue. However, may this singular case not tempt the rest of us to ignore the basic tenets of direct mail subscription development which have served us so long and so well.

Sporting News

By Eliot DeY. Schein

If you make a practice of monitoring the direct mail efforts of your competitors, you have probably noticed, year after year, subtle changes in the promotion thrust, copy and methodology of those efforts. Since these changes can give you a pretty good idea of what a magazine's particular problems and needs are, it is wise to keep an eye on your major competitors' promotion efforts.

Actually, when it comes to subscription circulation, sometimes the changes aren't so subtle. For example, a magazine that traditionally uses a hard offer may suddenly switch to a soft offer, or even a sweepstakes promotion. This dramatic change is usually an indication that either renewals are down or advertising rates are going up. And, although there are other possible reasons for the change, it is obvious that the publisher has decided he needs a larger than normal number of new subscribers.

The Sporting News has been on the scene longer than most of today's popular high-profile sports magazines. To examine the metamorphosis of *The Sporting News'* direct mail activity over the past five years is to discover how that magazine decided (you'll pardon the pun) to play a little catch-up ball and how they went about doing it.

Until three years ago, *The Sporting News'* direct mail program was, at best, poor—a low-priority situation. It would seem its management had determined that inexpensive mailings were all that were needed to replace the small losses that came from a low attrition rate through failures to renew.

However, as more and more sports publications positioned themselves close to *The Sporting News*, the attrition rate increased somewhat. At the same time, the ranks of sports-oriented advertisers began to swell.

The Sporting News didn't need a crystal ball to see into the future. First, the magazine's attrition rate could not be expected to return to its previous low levels because of the competition. And second, its share of the abundant market of sports-oriented advertising could not be maximized if it accepted a downward direction in circulation.

So . . . moves were made—probably the most significant one being the hiring of Don Barrows, Jr. as circulation director. Upon joining the company, Don immediately revised the traditional (though long neglected) "control package"—a double postcard that was being sent out to generate new subscribers—and turned a not-so-wonderful track record of pull into a clear front runner.

But that's not all. He set about developing a new control package that he hoped would not only establish credibility for *The Sporting News* but also present a "hot" presentation to battle the best of the multipublisher, slick sporting magazines.

The result of his work is a startlingly consumery, "loaded for bear" package that is practically irresistible. First mailed in the spring of 1980, it combines the proper marketing elements in an environment conducive to creating high response figures.

Barrows says at this point in time, "Since our lists are quite limited, we have to go out in the mail looking for the best subscription-generating numbers, while disregarding, to some degree, production and printing efficiencies."

Efficient or not, the production of this package is not overblown and does not misrepresent the product. However (even though Barrows is reluctant to admit it), it aims at *Inside Sports*.

The carrier envelope is cherry red and measures a whopping 11-1/2 inches by 5-3/16 inches. The copy—"Want to make a sporting bet?" appears on the carrier, and the words "you're on!" appear on blue and yellow through a circular window.

In fact, these words are on the token device on the two-piece order form which is enclosed and the combination of the envelope plus the token device enables the use of four different colors on two-color printing.

The letter in the package talks sports and brings in a "sporting bet" that you "can't lose," citing how you could wind up "almost $24 ahead!" The description of the magazine (which they call a "paper") is excellent.

The second indented paragraph on the first page says that the magazine covers every major league event in the big four: baseball, football, basketball and hockey. (This begins to sound a little like the *Inside Sports* publishing plan.) The offer, 27 issues for $9.97 (the Publishers Clearing House all-time control price), is a good one.

The mechanics of the letter combines efficiency with a little bit of canny parsimony. Here's how: Nested inside the four-page letter is a one-page memo printed on both sides—a "memo from the desk of Dick Kaegel, Managing Editor."

At first glance, this extra letter seems to be very expensive—and you might ask why on earth they nested it in between pages two and three of the main letter. Upon closer inspection, you see that this was clearly printed as one piece folded in on itself and trimmed on the right-hand edge, thus providing a nesting using a continuous form technique. A brilliant way of doing something dramatic on an efficient basis.

Now to the parsimony. Barrows admits that when this letter was printed it was really printed as eight pages. The potential subscriber only got six. Where are the other two? "Aha" says Barrows. "The other 8-1/2 inch by 11 inch sheet of paper was used for office letterheads. We just printed the logo and the address and yielded the whole batch of letterheads."

Surely, if you don't mind 60-pound white smooth offset letter heads for your magazine, you might consider doing what Don Barrows did. But it did cost him a blue signature on his letter. You see, the original version of this letter was black and blue. But in order to keep faith with *The Sporting News'* red logotype that was to appear on the letterhead—and still keep the letter a two-color job—the blue lost out in favor of the red and the blue signature found itself deported to the black plate.

As if two letters (the main one from the publisher and one from the editor) aren't enough, a third letter from Don Barrows himself tries to drive home the deal. This third letter is a bit heavyhanded, carrying this warning sentence: "As circulation director, I'd sure hate to hear from a lot of free-loaders." Obviously, this is an effort to reduce the "just looking" free-examination subscribers, and although it's a little tough, it's probably effective.

The order form, as mentioned before, has a token device which says "you're on!" Since the token fits neatly in the slot, the new subscriber only has to insert the token, tear the perf and slip the order form into the almost flawless business reply envelope—*almost* flawless because, unfortunately, the business reply envelope is an eighth of an inch too short. (We all have to pay such a price from time to time if we fail to preinsert a mockup of our mailing before sending the mechanicals off to the printer.)

An oversize, entertaining, four-color brochure rounds out this package. It has art and squibs clipped from the publication and certainly presents the lighter side of sports along with the standard solid, hard-numbers news that the magazine promises to deliver.

All in all, this package is a respectable effort, making *The Sporting News* a magazine that has finally entered "prime time" direct mail.

Let's rate this package:

Letter lead strength—8
Letter content strength—8
Letter closing strength—5
Signature psychology—2
Order form—7
Business reply envelope—0
Overall believability—8
Renewal strength—5

Disasters

By Eliot DeY. Schein

Every so often you hear about errors in direct mail subscription solicitation packages. Only the gutsiest of circulation directors or publishers admit to these costly mistakes and accept the blame for some intransigence that is so silly it's almost too embarrassing to recount.

Naturally, there is no way to prevent all the little mistakes that come back to irritate and haunt all of us from time to time. Yet management can eliminate many, if not most, of these costly errors by *thinking*. One simple operation, with a little thought added, can reduce those costly mistakes and save you money.

Before allowing your direct mail package to go out, demand to see an inserted sample. Make sure all the components fit inside the carrier envelope. Seal the carrier envelope yourself and put it on your desk. Then, pretending you are a consumer just receiving your mail, open it, read it, fill in the form and order a subscription to the magazine. Take the order card, place it in the "handy business reply envelope provided" and seal it.

Now, imagine you're the circulation director of the magazine. Open the business reply envelope and remove the order form. Do you have enough information to fulfill that order? Did everything fit? Was it easy to do? Did it make sense?

Here are some reports on disasters that never would have happened if the people involved had followed this simple little exercise. Only the names have been changed to keep unemployment lines down.

Phil's attempted cover-up

First, the story of Phil. Phil was new in the job of production manager in the circulation department of a multi-magazine publishing company. One of his first responsibilities was a new subscription mailing of one million pieces for one of the company's titles. The mailing was to take place the last day of December, and all the components and lists were ordered well in advance of that date.

Phil confidently assured his management that nothing could stand in the way of getting the mailing out on time. When he checked with the envelope manufacturers, the list brokers and the mailing house (which was 60 miles away), everything was proceeding according to schedule.

One day, however, the envelope manufacturer called Phil and said that although the carrier envelopes had been delivered to the mailing house, the business reply envelopes were not converting properly and would take an extra three or four days to finish.

Phil's pride was on the line. The mailing *had* to go out on December 31. So Phil prodded the envelope manufacturer to have the envelopes ready to ship on the Friday before the New Year's weekend. He then convinced the mailing house to put on an overtime and weekend staff to insert the components.

The $250,000 mistake

Unfortunately, when the business reply envelopes were ready to ship, there was no truck available to deliver them to the mailing house that same evening.

So, while a mailing house staff stood idly by their inserting machines, Phil left his office on that cold and rainy evening with three of his best personal friends, rented a large truck with his own money and instructed the envelope manufacturer to leave the cases of envelopes on the loading platform. After six hours of truck driving, loading and unloading, the envelopes were finally at the mailing house cascading through the inserting machines.

If it hadn't been raining on that night when Phil went above and beyond the call of duty, he would have earned a hero's medal from the direct marketing hall of fame. Instead, he receives the purple heart—for on that fateful night, the rain and the dampness made most of the business reply envelopes moist enough to seal themselves under the pressure from the machines. Since most people will not unseal a sealed business reply envelope, put in an order form and then tape it back together again, this error may have cost Phil's company $250,000.

Another disaster. A major business publisher in the Midwest came up with a self-mailer, turn-around envelope. Apparently, either nobody bothered to look at it before it was mailed or they only looked at one side, because no matter how it was folded it seemed that the business reply information always backed up the outgoing third class information. How do we know this? Three days after mailing 50,000 of these, over 20,000 of them came back in, unopened, and business reply postage had to be paid for empty non-orders. Remember to *think*.

A circulation director's short cut

Here's another. The circulation director of a city publication found a way to speed up a mailing in order to achieve and maintain an advertising guarantee. It was simple. When address labels came in, they were placed on the outer envelopes of the pre-inserted and sealed direct mail packages.

This worked effectively until the publisher demanded list tests. List orders went out and keyed labels came in. But—you already figured it out. If the key number is on the label and the order form is a fill-in, you never know which key the order came from. Pity.

Every so often a mailing house misses the boat. Like the time a mailing house didn't quite load the cheshiring machine the way it was intended to be loaded. The labels were affixed to the order form face-in and the postmaster was unable to deliver any of them. Somebody wasn't thinking, or looking.

Working around mistakes that have already been made can be costly, too. Take this example.

A well-known national economics publication was assuming some of the responsibility for a recently suspended similar publication. A self-mailer was sent to the subscribers offering to fulfill the balance of their subscriptions. The format was peculiar, however, for in order to seal the response portion a gummed tab was affixed, in part, across the label.

The circulation director, knowing that the Audit Bureau of Circulations (ABC) has the right to inspect source documents, was afraid to open these responses because the source document label would be destroyed in the process. It was also going to be difficult for the fulfillment people to read any of these labels even *after* they were opened.

Two solutions emerge

With 13,000 such responses in hand the circulation director had two choices: steam the responses open or place them on a high-intensity light box, positioning a piece of graphic paper behind them and then making a photograph of the name. This would keep the source documents intact for ABC to look at.

Since steaming open 13,000 packages appeared to be the greater of the two evils, the photographic concept was attempted and worked—but at a cost that bordered on the horrendous.

Computer-generated material can cause a great number of strange and interesting errors. Naturally, whenever we go in the mail we accept the likelihood that probably over 90 percent of what we mail gets thrown out anyway, so why bother with the little problems? Well, sometimes they're humorous.

For example, a culinary arts publication sent out a computer-generated solicitation for subscribers. The computerized portion of the letter went something like this: "Dear Mr. Blattstein: How would you like the skill and equipment to prepare, develop and create 'Eggs a la Blattstein,' 'Shrimps Blattstein a la Marinara,' 'Blattstein Benedict,' and all of it with the quality and appearance of those superb dishes found in the finest French restaurant in Garnerville, N.Y."

To the best of Blattstein's knowledge and belief there was not then, nor is there now, a French restaurant in Garnerville, N.Y. Humorous? Yes. Effective? No. Wasteful? You bet!

A "test-mailing" adventure

One well-known example of a direct mail disaster is not so humorous, but it's worth retelling. Here's what happened.

A new publisher was planning a magazine for female athletes and hired a direct mail "organization" to send out 100,000 pieces of mail as a test. Two packages were used with different prices in an effort to determine which combination of creative approach and price would work best for the soon-to-be-published magazine.

The mailing pulled orders to the tune of 6.7 percent and the publisher and his marketing group were jubilant. On the basis of these fabulous results the publisher managed to generate investor capital to roll out and establish real circulation, and to develop and publish the first issue.

The happy publisher went back to the "direct mail organization" (which had never done any real direct mail marketing before) and said, "OK, now we're going to mail a million." The supplier said, "To whom?" The publisher said, "To the same kind of people you mailed the first one to." "Ah," said the ersatz experts, "you were looking for female athletes so we already mailed to every female name on the Amateur Athletic Union membership list. Who would you like us to mail to this time?"

After this shaky start, the publisher went to an experienced direct mail organization and managed to start the publication based on a lower—but projectable—response percentage.

Sit, look and think

Are there lessons to be learned? When postage costs are $84 per thousand and are sure to go up, when printing becomes more and more expensive and when personnel and creative talents are a major budget item, it does make sense to sit back, look at what you are about to send out in the mail and think about it—for just a few minutes, at least.

If even one out of 20 times you come up with an improvement you can incorporate, or see a problem you can avoid, you have invested those few minutes more wisely than you could have in any other way.

The trick is to use your time and intelligence where they will do the most good. And very often, that's in the mail.

Mail house blues

By Eliot DeY. Schein

There is a sure-fire way of throwing your best direct mail package, product, list and offer down the drain in one easy step: Simply disregard your mailing house operation.

Although it may sound silly to suggest that top management become involved with the details of getting a program out to the consumer, an inefficient, irresponsible mailing house activity can defeat even the best direct mail marketing strategy.

There is no intention here to imply that all mailing houses are dishonest or less than capable. In fact, there are many fine, reliable mailing houses which will inventory each component as it arrives, match the right lists with the right packages, keep track of the right key numbers and the right order forms, insert, label and mail your direct mail program in an efficient and timely manner. Unfortunately, however, exceptions seem to abound.

Management's fear of mailing houses varies from publication to publication. The intensity of that fear probably depends on how many times a particular publisher has been burned somewhere between delivery of materials to a mailing house and the receipt of responses from the consumer.

Where you can get hurt

The main ways a mailing house can hurt you are: failing to drop all your material on the date or dates you have specified; failing to insert and label properly; failing to key; failing to deliver to postal hands every single piece of mail you want dropped; and failing to affix the proper postage.

In testing, for example, all parts of a test should be mailed on the same day so that as responses come in, projections can easily be made in terms of relative strengths and weaknesses of the different components. Some mailing houses will not volunteer that a mailing was made over a five-day period, however, especially if they were requested to drop it all at once.

And if a mailing house sends out part of your mailing on Monday, a little more on Wednesday, and the balance on Friday, you have a five-day drop date variation. All incoming results must be adjusted for this differential or the publisher will get an error-laden view of the results.

At the end of each year, when subscription solicitations are mailed by circulation people at virtually every publication (all of whom want a drop on the last weekday of the year), mailing houses are swamped with requests to mail on the same day. The mailing house which is physically incapable of doing the job, but takes it out of financial greed, causes terrible headaches for many publishers.

A Christmas tale

When *Mariah* magazine mailed its first roll-out some years ago, the mailing house was instructed to drop the entire mailing on the last day of the year. Since the mailing house could not physically handle and inventory all of their work to be dropped the last day of the year, they got it ready bit by bit.

When they had a truck-load ready, the post office would pick up the material, "promising" to hold the loaded truck in the yard until the rest of the shipment could catch up and then be dropped into the system on the last day of the year.

Lo and behold, somebody must have goofed up at the post office: the mail went out as soon as the incoming trucks passed the fence around the shipping yard, and entered the system—anywhere from December 10 to December 24.

Needless to say, the combination of mailing half the material well prior to the Christmas holiday and the staggered and random method of dropping the mail wreaked havoc with an intelligent reading of the results from the important first roll-out of this new magazine.

The mailing house apologized, the postmaster apologized, and that was the end of the issue—except that the publisher was hurt. There is no substitute for being on site and aware of every phase of your mailing in order to avoid errors that can haunt you.

What should you do first? By all means visit or send a reliable associate to visit any mailing house you are considering. Count the labeling machines and the inserting machines. Look at the loading dock. See if the mailing house has sufficient personnel to handle your work in the time allotted.

Management responsibilities

Once you have selected your mailing house, your job is still not done. It is obvious that management cannot be on hand for the three or four days that a mailing house has material. It's impossible to keep watch every moment until the material is receipted and on a sealed vehicle heading for a bulk mail center. An inspection or two of the mailing house premises during the processing of your mailing (preferably at labeling and inserting time and at the moment the postal receipt is exchanged for your mail) is advisable.

Furthermore, demand dated postal receipts, and accept only originals. Although the Postal Service, from its pony express days, has been one of the most reliable elements of American life, not all postmasters and their staff members are 100 percent honest. In fact, a well-known veteran in the direct mail industry is obsessed with the dishonesty of some of the mailing houses he has used during his fruitful career. This pro has documented evidence of mailing houses that have made deals with underlings at the post office, of mailing houses that can get postal receipts without having mailed even half of the pieces receipted, of checks from publishers made payable to the United States Post Office which were used at the end of the transaction to buy extra usable stamps for the mailing house.

Postal problems and pitfalls

Postage—the largest expense item for a mailing—is usually given the least amount of concern when it comes to shepherding it carefully to achieve its ultimate aim.

Yet, since publishers believe a check made out to the post office is as safe as putting money in the bank, a significant amount of mail and postage goes awry every year.

Here's a story that's so incredible that, if it weren't completely documented and sworn to by a West Coast publisher of a music magazine, it sounds like something out of Baron von Munchausen.

The publisher decided to protect herself as much as possible by having her 100,000-piece mailing metered at the mailing house immediately following insertion of the package components. She gave a check made out to the United States Post Office for $8,400 (third class postage) to the mailing house, who gave it to the post office meter setter. The meter setter put $2,100 worth of postage into each of four metering machines and produced the proper receipts.

The meter is usually "on-line" with the inserting stations and metering is done automatically as envelopes are passed through. However, the machines were set for a tolerance that allowed two envelopes to go through in one pass—one on top of the other. So even though all of the pieces which proceeded through the inserting process actually passed the head of the postage meter, only the upper envelopes were struck with the postage. The lower envelopes ended up blank.

Furthermore, the weight of the sack of mail was perfect—100,000 pieces—and this was verified on the postal receipt. Of course, four days later the post office returned 50,000 pieces to the mailing house because they had no postage on them.

The publisher, whose mailing pulled very poorly, couldn't understand the disappointing performance of this solicitation. The weight was correct, the postage was correct, and the receipts were all in order. She blamed weather conditions, political timing, bad copy, bad offer and anything else she could think of, and it wasn't until a year later that she discovered only half her mail ever went out.

While this is a hair-raising story, it should remind management that no matter how open your eyes are, there is somebody out there trying to get a hold of your money without working for it. The only solution in a case like this is to try and prove the crime and sue the mailing house.

The first clue: weak response

Here's another story: A recent mailing by a sports magazine with a circulation of approximately 300,000 encountered substantial difficulties somewhere between the arrival of materials at the mailing house and eventual receipt by the consumer.

Over 500,000 pieces were scheduled to drop, nat-urally, the last working day of the year. The publisher, aware of the potential murky waters awaiting him at the mailing house, directed a high-level member of his circulation staff to be on site at the mailing house on the date of the scheduled drop.

Three weeks after the drop date, his responses looked a little weak to him. In fact, on five test cells (price variation tests) of 10,000 pieces each there was absolutely no response. Surprised by this (considering two of the test cells had lower prices than the control offer which was pulling properly), he made inquiry to his circulation people and his mailing house.

The circulation representative admitted he had been at the mailing house a week *before* the drop was scheduled, "but everything seemed to be fine." The mailing house owner finally submitted postal receipts dated on four different days. The postmaster agreed that all the trucks with numbers appearing on the postage receipts had gone through his post office yard and out to the bulk mail center. Still, those three keys showed absolutely no signs of life.

The only conclusion the publisher could reach was that at least those three keys had never been mailed. Two weeks following the publisher's mass inquiry, the first results from those keys started to trickle in, and slowly but surely the publisher got the responses (however depressed by the failure to mail on the chosen ideal date), and received what he considered to be a decent response.

The lesson to be learned from these stories is simple: The area with the least control is the area most likely to go out of control. And management probably exercises the smallest amount of concern and control over the mailing house operation for its direct mail program.

If you're lucky, you'll be in a position to notice that something "definitely went wrong," as did the publisher of the sports magazine. If you are mailing a roll-out only, all you may notice is a lower response percentage.

Protect yourself and your publication by exercising as much control over all phases of your mailings as possible. Check the postal receipts from the mailing house and check the results when they come in by zip code (your fulfillment house can give you a simple analysis of these results). Be sure every section of the country you mail to is represented. And by all means, do not be lulled into thinking that you are finished with the mailing until you count and read the results.

Some mailing house owners may bristle at the contents of this column. The reliable, honest, and hard-working mailing house managers will no doubt rejoice. Magazine management should benefit.

Third class trauma

By Eliot DeY. Schein

As soon as the postal strike of 1970 evaporated, it seemed to a number of midwestern mailers that some of their third class mail out of Chicago had gone the same route—evaporation.

More than a decade later, the United States Postal Service still refuses to admit publicly that millions of pieces of third-class mail were "dumped." However, the prevailing opinion of mailers verified by off-the-record conversations with postal officials is that the "dumping" did indeed occur. This action, apparently on the part of only two or three anonymous postal employees, cost mailers tens of millions of dollars in materials and close to a billion dollars in orders!

How safe *is* third-class bulk mail? And what can you do to make sure that your valuable investment in the mail makes it from the mail sack at the end of your production line at the mail house . . . to the mailbox of your intended customer?

In an attempt to answer this question definitively, several postmasters (of large, medium and small offices), mailing house owners and operators, and representatives of the USPS Inspectors Corps were interviewed.

It could happen again

When asked if "Chicago, 1970" could happen again, the president of one of the largest mailing houses in the country replied: "It could happen at any time, but on a much smaller scale."

The scenario goes as follows: A trailer truck loaded with third-class mail sits, overlooked, in the back corner of a depot for two months before it's discovered. Fearing embarrassment because of the incredibly late delivery that would result, some "local guy" dumps the mail rather than allowing it to go through the system any further. "This can happen today," avows the mailing house president, "and it probably has happened several times during the past year in various parts of the country."

One of the postmasters was asked what advice he would give to a close friend or relative of his who was planning a large mailing for his own personal business. His first response was, "I would tell him to choose a reputable mailing house."

Naturally, the next question was, "How does one *find* a reputable mailing house?" The postmaster suggested that, somewhere, there must be a list of "reputable mailing houses." He was informed that, somewhere, there must be a list of "reputable physicians," too. Such lists usually being less than 100 percent reliable, how then does your relative choose a proper mailing house?

"Well, I would tell him: If you can't be sure a mailing house is reputable, and if you don't have a lot of experience with a favorite mailing house over the years, your best chance is to make sure you *avoid* a mailing house that operates under 'optional procedure.'"

Optional procedure vs. weighed and verified

There are two basic types of mailing houses: the "optional procedure" and the "weighed and verified."

In an optional procedure mailing house, mail is not weighed and verified by the United States Postal Service. However, the mailing house must provide a form 3602 to the postal clerk who witnesses the loading of mail bags onto the USPS truck. *Copies* of the forms 3602 (which are now called 3607s) are also put into the truck before the door is locked and sealed.

The large risk here comes from the lack of unit tally. "The USPS clerk can easily mis-evaluate bag by bag content and be off, say, 10 percent on a large mailing," says a New Jersey postmaster. The 3602 and 3607 would be accurate to the clerk's best eyeball estimate, but the piece count could vary substantially from the receipted total. A 10 percent variation on a million-piece mailing results in a dollar error (and loss) of from $20,000 to as much as $40,000 in unmailed, yet paid for, materials alone.

Fortunately, there is a modicum of control which usually works in the mailer's favor. A mailing house that operates under optional procedure must maintain, in a permanent file, receipts from printers who have shipped components for each mailing, orders from the mailer, and receipts concerning labels or lists delivered. Furthermore, this "folder" must be made available to an audit team of postal inspectors "when and if" they come to check.

On the other hand, a "weighed and verified" type of mailing house has a scale on-premises, upon which the sacks are weighed before being placed on the USPS truck. Receipts often indicate total pounds, and it's a simple process to divide piece weight into the receipted amount to confirm actual mailing quantity within minute tolerances. The weighed and verified mailing houses seems to be the more reliable and fail-safe choice. However, a postmaster in California, discussing the reliability of the weighed and verified mailing house, commented, "You still gotta watch it."

A Missouri postmaster confided: "We must have some kind of control over big mailings because there is so much money involved. At the very least, postal clerk rotation can minimize collusion."

Spot checks "every so often"

The Postal Service Inspector Corps is a bit wary about giving out any information. But finally, a semi-talkative inspector's representative submitted the following observation: "Optional procedure mail is spot-checked on trucks at bulk mail centers. The 3607 form in the truck is compared with the mail that is, in fact, being carried on that particular vehicle. And every so often it is weighed for full verification." "Every so often" was not elaborated upon in any respect.

According to one very angry mailer in Massachusetts, there was definite proof that a mailing house he mailed from last year did not have the entire mailing ready on time. "Apparently, rather than face my wrath, the mailing house dropped the portion that was ready to mail, and dumped the balance." This was a case of mail that was metered, and, of course, the postal receipt showed the full amount. But in fact, the mailing house kept in its inventory half of the postage.

When asked about the one-and-a-half to two-month layover in a trailer truck that could inspire dumping, one inspector said that "this does not occur any more because of better check-in and check-out procedures. In case the inspectors do notice a delayed truck, we immediately call the mailer and request a 'concept of disposition.' In most cases, the mailer breathes a sigh of relief that his mail has been found and requests continuation of delivery. In some cases (for example, a time-related sale by a retailer), a mailer will choose not to accept the continuance of delivery but to receive a refund for postage from the Postal Service."

Repeat that last statement to a panel of owners and managers of mailing houses around the country and they respond in chorus: "We have never seen a refund from the Postal Service for *anything*." And one, while adamantly demanding non-attribution, even goes on to say that "the Postal Service does not take a position of responsibility in seeing that mail upon which postage has been paid is delivered. In a case where a mailer can prove that mail was dropped and not received by the intended recipient, the Postal Service will accept litigation, but to the best knowledge of the mailing house experts involved, this has never been a successful road to take." Of course, the USPS heartily disagrees with this mailer's statement.

Never relax your guard

In any case, the first step you should take in assuring that your mail does get from the mailing house to the consumer is to find a reputable mailing house that is not in collusion with a postal clerk in an attempt to skim your

---

Checklist for November:

☐ Select your mailing house for your December 31 drop (after considering what you've just read in this article).

☐ Check on the progress of your printing, especially the envelopes.

☐ Start your list merge and purge soon, if you haven't already started it.

---

postage money by not mailing some of your mail.

If your current mailing house provides you with good service, stick with it. If not, switch to another. But be sure you get plenty of references.

Second, send a representative to the mailing house on the day that your mail is scheduled to go on the truck. Although this won't guarantee a perfect mailing, it will go a long way toward making sure that you're not the fall guy. Weak-willed postal clerks and mailing house employees are less likely to succumb to baser instincts when under the watchful eyes of someone who has an interest in seeing that your mailing goes out smoothly and accurately.

And finally, get acquainted with the postmaster and make sure the clerks are aware that you know their supervisors.

If you heed this advice, you may think you can begin to sit back and relax. That, in itself, would be a mistake. For you must always keep in mind the words of that outspoken California postmaster: "You still gotta watch it!"

Other ways to get subscriptions

By James B. Kobak

Direct mail is a valuable source for obtaining subscriptions. But publishers' dependence on direct mail has been overdone.

Maybe this is because the techniques used in direct mail are well-known and have reached a high level of sophistication and predictability. Maybe it is through habit. Maybe it is because those in the magazine business have had little exposure to other methods.

Whatever the reason, the fact remains that, for most publishers, direct mail is the major source of new subscriptions while other methods are scarcely considered.

But the constantly spiraling costs of postage, paper and printing make a reexamination particularly appropriate at this time. Despite publishers' efforts to achieve greater efficiency in mailings, the never-ending climb in prices moves faster.

There is a need to develop alternatives to direct mail, both as a means to attract untouched prospects and as a cost improvement measure.

This is not to downgrade direct mail as an acquisition method—or even to suggest its discontinuance. There are many very solid advantages that direct mail offers. It can pinpoint direct mail recipients who should be interested in your magazine, who have the proper demographic characteristics and who live in the places where you want them. Direct mail results are statistically predictable. Even relatively small tests give excellent indications of what major mailings will bring. There is good public acceptance of direct mail for the sale of virtually all goods. The public has been trained to expect magazine offers through the mail and is used to shopping for them in this way.

It is true, too, that the level of skill and sophistication in the use of direct mail has been rising rapidly in recent years, to a great extent because of the extensive use of computers. We have seen "merge-purge" techniques developed to clean lists of duplicates, saving the publisher money and the consumer the nuisance of multiple mailing pieces.

Publishers have been able to refine their mailings to eliminate certain Zip codes, or carrier routes within those Zip codes or areas with low financial tract readings, or virtually anything else for that matter. This, too, has brought mailing costs down.

The use of computer letters, of sweepstakes, of tokens and other devices has been developed to a high art in the struggle to get recipients to take some action on receipt of a mailing piece. And no doubt many more good methods will be perfected.

Unfortunately, however, direct mail, like any other method, has some weaknesses:

• There are some good prospects who do not buy by mail or very rarely do. Other methods must be used to reach them.

• As with any selling method, when you have reached a certain level of saturation, the cost of acquiring more orders goes up sharply.

• Not all times of the year work well for direct mail. This limits the periods during which mailings can be made and for some publishers results in major peaks and valleys in their cash requirements.

• Some products lend themselves better to other selling methods.

• Outside events, over which a publisher has no control, can have a large impact on mailing results. These include such things as elections, hurricanes and the like, which can negate the best laid plans of publishers.

• From time to time Postal Service delivery becomes erratic, either in timing or performance, wreaking havoc with the careful plans of the publishers.

Dependence on direct mail is often caused by a lack of knowledge as to what constitutes a good subscriber. Is it one who is easy to obtain the first time? Or one who renews at a high rate? One who subscribes for three years versus one year? Or one who is demographically attractive to advertisers? One who gives a lot of gift subscriptions? Or one who buys lots of mail order items mentioned in the magazine? Or what?

The answer may be different for different magazines, but the real fact is that most magazines have never defined their good subscribers. Few have tried to rate the profitability of different sources.

While many publishers talk about such things as extensive testing and source-to-source renewal information and optimization of subscription sources, to date there has been little real benefit from this conversation. The reason, of course, is that the desirability of using these techniques has only recently been realized—and the capability of developing solid information which can be used to take advantage of them has depended on sophisticated computer routines that only recently have been put into effect.

I don't want to imply that publishers aren't doing anything outside the direct mail area. Some are doing a variety of things and others depend on completely different methods for their entire selling operation. Consider a few of the techniques used by virtually all magazines.

Catalogue agencies—Sell primarily to libraries and schools. Listing with them is easy, the remittance rate is good and they are a steady source of a limited number of new and renewal subscriptions.

Publishers Clearing House (and its competitors)—Sell subscriptions of magazines of all publishers, always at the lowest price the publisher offers anywhere. This can be a source of a substantial number of subscriptions when needed. The remittance rate is not large, but may be higher than that which can be obtained by direct mail. Because of the reduced price approach and loyalty to PCH rather than the publisher, renewals are partially developed by the publisher at normal rates and partially by PCH, again at a low remittance rate.

Telephone—Very effective in certain instances, particularly when a very personal approach can be used, such as the Norman Cousins appeal for *Saturday Review*. Rather expensive so that it is normally used where a high-price or long-term subscription can be obtained and for renewals.

Advertising in other print media and radio—Used to some extent by a great many magazines. Can be very effective as a supplement to direct mail but has built-in limitations.

Exchange advertising—With other print media. A relatively new phenomenon, developed to a high art with some magazines, virtually unused by others. Because the total expense is only the expense of running ads in your own magazine for others, the cost is much less than buying space at full rate if your circulations are relatively close. Its use is limited because only so many of such advertisements can be carried in any magazine.

Subscription cards in the magazine—These come in many different forms, from simple bind-in cards, to blow-in cards to gift offers and in some cases a whole series of multiple order forms. Most publishers include cards in their single copies, a few in subscription copies as well. They are a very good and inexpensive source of a number of good subscriptions because the subscriber has already sampled the magazine.

Gift subscriptions—Promoted both by direct mail and through the magazine. An excellent source of a number of high renewal subscriptions.

School plans—Operated by a number of organizations, these sell subscriptions through teachers to a large list of magazines. They are a good source for a limited number of subscriptions at a relatively good remittance rate.

Field selling—Field forces still exist and sell substantial numbers of subscriptions for some magazines, although a number of publishers no longer are involved with this source. Remittance rates to the publisher, of course, are very low or nonexistent.

While these sources are used by almost all magazines, a number of other publishers have developed creative programs which may be the way of the future. For instance, such efforts as these are proving successful for several magazines:

• Employ part-time salespeople. For instance, *High-*

Why Don't We

Sell subscriptions through the major sources of single copy sales—newsstands and supermarkets? Mail order catalogues and catalogue stores such as Sears, Wards and others? The Postal Service? Libraries? Delivery organizations like the milk companies, United Parcel? Book and record clubs? Retail outlets, such as book, greeting card, pattern and other stores?

Have banks offer magazines as premiums for opening new accounts or develop displays and other sales devices?

Jointly develop subscription selling devices for a number of magazines through Diners Club and American Express and newspaper supplements?

Try for gift subscriptions at logical times other than Christmas?

Put copies in buses, trains and taxis as well as airlines?

Use the same type of coupon and cooperative advertising approaches which other products employ?

Apply radio and TV broadcast techniques used by the record people to magazines?

Develop magazine centers where sampling can be done and subscriptions purchased?

Exchange advertising and lists with your biggest competitors?

Make greater use of inserts in consumer goods packages, put coupons on butter cartons, buy the back of a cereal package?

Get Publishers Clearing House to set up a workable renewal operation for all magazines?

Sell consumer magazines in business papers and vice versa?

Get newspaper delivery organizations to sell magazine subscriptions?

---

lights for Children has a network of part-timers selling this children's magazine to their neighbors.

• Use of other consumer products as carriers for subscription messages. *Sphere*, which is owned by General Mills, uses its parent company's food packages to carry subscription blanks. This costs very little.

• A number of magazines have used "free-standing inserts" in newspapers to obtain subscriptions. *Cue* has been particularly successful.

• Cooperative mailings where various products are sold in a single mailing. There are a number of organizations offering these for different companies. These range from straight syndications to the use of stuffers in department store and other billing series.

• Placement of copies with subscription cards in gathering places where people must wait. These include doctors' offices, beauty parlors, airlines and the like. A few magazines have gone heavily into these programs, but only in a limited number of different places. In many cases the copies are paid for.

There must be *hundreds* of other techniques that individual publishers are using which are not generally known. But the same sophistication, ingenuity and creativity that are devoted to direct mail techniques are not often found in other areas of selling magazine subscriptions. Some features that are commonplace in other industries are unheard of in the magazine business.

In the hope that it will spur some thoughts of other selling methods, I have set down several ideas which might lead to other selling methods. At the same time they should expand the reach of magazines and reduce the costs of obtaining subscriptions.

It may have been that in the past it would not have been possible to sell subscriptions in many of the ways suggested because of the low base rates that were charged and the extensive price-cutting that prevailed among the major magazines. This situation has now changed considerably. Most magazines have increased their prices substantially—and those that have introductory rates do not discount nearly as much as they previously did.

The margin on a subscription sale that a magazine can offer a retailer or other outlet is substantial compared with the margins received on other merchandise. The inventory problem is virtually nil. Service is taken care of by the publisher.

There is plenty of room for new ideas, new thinking and overall creativity to release the industry from its dependence on direct mail for new subscriptions.

Bind-ins and blow-ins

By Eliot DeY. Schein

One of the most efficient sources of new subscribers is right under your nose—your own magazine! It's so easy to cash in on bind-ins and blow-ins—heaven only knows why most magazines give them short shrift. For although promotion in your own book may not yield fantastic results, the proper and effective use of blow-in and bind-in cards and envelopes can definitely increase your subscription income.

Bind-ins and blow-ins are effective (especially if your magazine has higher-than-average pass-along readership or a healthy percentage of newsstand sales) because the best psychographic environment in which to promote your magazine is, indeed, your own magazine. In addition, when you compare the cost of producing and inserting bind-ins and blow-ins with the cost of cold mail, you will see that the cost per thousand for the bind-in and blow-in card is very attractive: In order to pay off efficiently, they don't have to produce 3 percent responses.

The cost to produce and insert a three-color bind-in card runs somewhere between $4.50 and $5.50 a thousand (add approximately $1 more for the insertion of a blow-in card). Of course, these prices will vary with the type of promotion material you are presenting and the intricacies of the use of color. However, since prices will also vary greatly according to quantity, it's always a good idea to plan ahead and produce more than one or two issues' worth of these materials in order to achieve relatively low prices.

The subscription generated by a bind-in or blow-in card is of course a highly renewable sub at a very low capture cost. It is highly renewable due to the single, salient fact that the card was found in the magazine—and certainly, someone who just enjoyed your editorial product is more likely to use the promotion material to subscribe and continue to subscribe.

Envelopes versus cards

Bind-in and blow-in envelopes (in contrast to cards) have a different economic structure. On the average, printing and inserting a goodly quantity of envelopes (and here again, format is all-critical) can cost $12 to $15 per thousand for bind-ins and $10 to $12 for blow-ins.

Why, then, would anyone spend more than double the money for an envelope rather than a card? The first reason is obvious: Blow-in envelopes will almost always produce a substantially greater number of cash-up-front orders than a card (although experience has shown that envelopes produce a lower percentage of *overall* response than do the still-handier cards). In fact, the envelope almost begs the question since it is designed to carry pieces of paper—checks for example.

The second reason for using envelopes is their intrinsically greater substance: They have room to carry messages and they bring credibility to the offer. Reader involvement activity is usually greater, too.

Why not do both? If your magazine, like many others, is assuming a high number of pass-along readers and is running those omnipresent, three-up, full-page bind-in cards for subscriptions, why not consider a change (or at least a test)?

Envelopes and cards in combination in the same issue of a magazine tend to increase overall percentage response. And the house ad that goes along with them may yet be another means to heighten response from either medium.

Varying the color

The publisher of a well-known city magazine admits his bind-in efforts are limited to the running of a full-page insert (which incorporates three individual cards). And although he has the color of the magazine's logo changed "for variety" each time out, he uses the same bind-in card over and over again.

Surely, the regular newsstand reader must be bored seeing the same basic bind-in card issue after issue. Moreover, because such a card blends into the magazine, it no longer can shout its offer to the prime prospect. This city publisher should certainly begin a lot of testing—immediately.

Newsweek and *Time* are constantly running bind-in and blow-in cards (in four-color), sprinkling them throughout their magazines. This concept must work for them . . . or else why would they spend the money?

You may now be saying, "Sure, if I were printing millions of copies of my magazine, I might be able to do the same thing efficiently, because the difference in cost per thousand is minimal." But isn't it worth at least a test to see what the difference would be, not in the cost per thousand for production, but in the value of subscriptions received at your fulfillment house's cage?

It is widely acknowledged that constant change and testing are necessary to maintain good results in direct solicitation for subscriptions. Why wouldn't this principle apply to bind-ins and blow-ins as well?

Where to bind them in

Traditionally, the best place to put your single bind-in card is face up over a right-hand page house ad (with coupon, of course) in the back half of the publication. This allows the reader and prospective subscriber to read and sample more than half your book before being asked to make a decision about receiving a subscription to it.

Believe it or not, a West Coast business publication (now in its second issue) put a full-page ad with a coupon (which, incidentally, was in the middle of the page on the gutter side) on the second cover of that issue. There is probably no worse place to put that kind of in-house promotion. To begin with, covers are not places for coupons of any kind. Many readers are loathe to mutilate covers. Inside front covers are the worst, because the publisher must also assume the reader knows what's in the magazine in advance. On just the second issue of publication, this hardly seems like good sense.

As a general rule vary bind-in and blow-in cards and envelopes issue by issue. Time after time, to the amazement of publishers, the mere fact of changing the graphics and approach of the cards and envelopes keeps the response from declining.

If you have a smaller magazine, that is, under 75,000, try this simple test. Go out and have a new bind-in card designed (card—because that will save a phone call to your printer to find out if he has the equipment to do a blow-in) and print cards to the tune of three times the number of copies of your print order for the next issue. Then over a six-month period, run the new card every other month. Of course, if you have A/B split capabilities, you should use them. If your circulation department is graphing the results on the bind-in card (the new compared to the old), you should see an increase almost immediately (assuming offer and editorial remain somewhat constant).

Once you see the new card is out-pulling the card you've been using over and over for years, you should then have yet another new card designed. Phase that card into every other issue, alternating it with the first test card, and continue this process as long as the response numbers stay up.

You surely should test a bind-in or blow-in envelope (or both) for your Christmas donor promotions. Your Christmas donor house ad and a bind-in or blow-in envelope (as in *The New Yorker*) will make it convenient for your readers to take advantage of your gift offer and will enable you to maximize the greater cash-up-front percentages realized from donor subscription orders in general.

And most important, be sure to key and track the order form on the ad, each bind-in, blow-in card or envelope, until you can adjust your subscription promotion effort in your own magazine. This will help to produce the most efficient results, thereby reducing your need for cold mail subs which cost quite a bit more to generate.

How to use an 800 number to boost circulation

By Jim Atkins and Dave Gotthelf

Because of the overwhelming acceptance of the telephone as an order device, there has been a vast increase in the number and variety of businesses using an 800 number. While most 800 telephone calls now go to reservation centers, rent-a-car firms and hotel/motel chains, more and more publishers are beginning to use the toll-free number in space ads for subscriptions.

There are several reasons why a publisher would use an 800 number. First, an 800 number almost always increases business. (People under 35 are more likely to reach for a phone than fill out a coupon.) Second, you get an immediate response to your ad or message. Third, because the response is immediate, you are able to tabulate the costs and results on a daily basis. And finally, you pay only for each call.

"Without an 800 number you are losing potential sales and profits," says Dennis Gougion, vice president, Budget Marketing, Des Moines, Iowa. "Clipped ads and blow-in and bind-in cards are often misplaced and forgotten. Or people don't take time to fill out a coupon. Your promotions are asking for a response right now. If you can make it easy for your readers to take action, you can immediately turn impulses into sales.

"Why not offer your subscribers a method of ordering other than filling out a card and mailing it? Use an 800 number and you give around-the-clock, seven-day service with trained operators ready to provide fast, courteous service," he says.

Although most publishers use the toll-free number in space ads for subscriptions, it can be used in many ways. For example, readers can call in classified ads. Advertisers can call and buy display ads. Stringers can call in articles. Readers can order products or services offered by the magazine. Offers, ads, packages, cards, and pricing can be tested and results obtained within a few days.

Business Week is currently using the 800 number in a way that may revolutionize the magazine business. The magazine is offering its own 800 number to advertisers. Then, for a fee, the magazine will query those who call with a series of questions developed specifically for the advertiser.

For example, prospects who respond to an ad for a truck rental firm are asked such questions as how many trucks they rent, when the present contract expires, and when they expect to lease trucks. With this information, *Business Week* can separate the callers into groups of likely and unlikely prospects. (Although an ad may pull thousands of replies, only a few hundred are likely to be good prospects.)

Because a sales call can cost up to $500 when intercity travel is involved, it is important that sales personnel see only the prospects most likely to buy. *Business Week*'s system enables a firm to concentrate on the prospects who are most likely to buy. (Bob Stone, the direct response expert, now tells clients not to use reader service cards because of the low quality of leads.)

Almost every type of business is now using an 800 number.

"The trend toward using the 800 telephone number for consumer inquiries," says Charles T. Ruppman, chief executive officer, Ruppman Marketing Services, "is a reflection of the fact that a call to an 800 number is not charged to the calling party. Increased gasoline and other transportation costs are also encouraging consumers to pick up the phone rather than jump into the car and go from store to store in hopes of finding what they want.

"There are now 45,000 subscribers to Wide Area Telephone Service (WATS) lines with companies operating their own in-house 800 service or relying on an outside marketing company."

A system approach

Telephone marketing is not a creative process. It is a system. Furthermore, there is a best way to use an 800 number in an ad, card or letter, and a best way to answer the telephone and take an order.

When a publisher decides to use an 800 number, he must plan his approach in great detail. Orders have to be taken, recorded and processed. They must be sent to the fulfillment house. Billing procedures must be followed. In addition, an up-sell effort should be programmed into the system.

Publishers can assign the responsibility of telephone marketing to a staff member; the circulation director, marketing director, or fulfillment director is often given this job. By attending seminars and reading publications in the field, this individual can become familiar with the best ways to use an 800 number in marketing.

The first step in setting up the system involves locating a telephone marketing service. Most 800 services use the same equipment. They differ, however, in the quality of their service and the ideas and counsel they offer.

To find an effective service, call magazine circulation directors or publishers who use an 800 number in their ads and ask them which service they use. Even simpler—look for 800 numbers in other magazines, call them, and test the service.

See how long it takes for the service to answer. Are they friendly? Do they try to get the source key? Do they take the order quickly? Do they up-sell?

Actually, we recommend that you use two or three services, using different numbers in your ads or cards as source keys. The telephone marketing director should check each service on a regular basis (daily or weekly) by calling each number and placing an order.

Hiring a consultant is usually unnecessary. Most of the major telemarketing firms will provide marketing ideas and how-to information as part of the service. If you get more subscriptions, they know you will continue to use their 800 number.

If you do decide to hire a consultant, however, ask him for a proposal stating the scope of what will be done, how the results will produce profits, how the results will be measured, and his fee for the project.

Testing the system

Once you have located a service, start with these simple tests:

If you have newsstand sales, start using the 800 number on the blow-in card in newsstand copies. This will bring in several hundred phone orders each month, and you can perfect the system quickly and with little risk.

If you are selling seminars or books, or if you are using a renewal series, use the 800 number in the mailing to one segment of your list.

If you don't have newsstand sales, use the 800 number in an exchange ad or a house ad. Again, you will get orders each month.

With this type of test, you can get the feel of processing telephone orders, and, as some sage at Time Inc.

always says after seeing Murphy's law in action: "The first time is to find out how not to do it."

The 800 number in your ads or in bartered space can be tested without a great deal of expense since the 800 number can be dropped in or out at any time. When it is used on blow-in and bind-in cards, planning is required since the number must be printed on the cards in advance.

Listing the number

When you put the number in your ads, cards, or direct mail, list the number this way: For fastest service, call toll free 800-111-1111, Ext. 11. In Pennsylvania, call toll free 800-222-2222, Ext. 11.

This type should be set in a box, in bold type, and double the size of the ad body type. There should be a drawing of a telephone to quickly tell readers to order by phone.

Since an 800 number cannot be used in the state where it originates, you also have to list a number for the state. This should be listed in small type under the nationwide number.

When you check mechanicals, call the number printed and make sure it is correct. At this time, you should explain you are just testing the number. Also verify the state number by reading it to the operator who answers.

Get to know the daytime and nighttime supervisors and call them at least monthly to see if there are any questions. They should be contacted the day the service is to begin to iron out any last minute details.

If the offer is to change on a specific date during the test, contact the supervisor the day before and verbally remind him of the change. In addition, phone in a dummy order on the first day of the change.

Copies of the brochure and/or ads displaying the 800 number should be forwarded to the service. A recap sheet along with detailed instructions relating to order processing should also be sent to the 800 service. If orders are forwarded verbally to the publisher and then sent, say twice weekly, the recap sheet will confirm not only the orders sent but the bill from the 800 service.

It is imperative that the service's supervisor and the operators understand all of the copy in the brochure that is displaying the 800 number. If orders are being taken for a seminar, for example, the refund policy, cancellation policy and dates, times and titles of seminars must be fully understood and easily accessible to all operators.

In-house or outside service

Although most publications use an outside service, some have in-house operations—Time Inc. has their own 800 operation in Chicago, and *Business Week* has its own in-house 800 number.

In-house operations are quite expensive, however, with the cost of a call running from 70 cents to over $10. Although you can get an 800 number in-house for about $240 for 10 hours, the cost is not in the line, but rather in space and staff. You certainly would want your number to be answered 365 days a year, 24 hours a day in most cases. Furthermore, there should be one supervisor for every 10 agents.

With a service, the cost per call will run about $1.50, depending on how much information you require. (Some services require a set-up charge and/or a monthly minimum of $35 to $200.) A telemarketing service is one of the few services that you know will be profitable, however, because almost every call is an order, and you pay only for those calls processed by the service. Thus, there is no reason for any magazine or newsletter publisher not to use an 800 number.

Warning: Be sure that the service gives you the names of the people making customer service calls and the questions or problems these people have. Otherwise, a service could bill you for unlimited customer service calls and you would have no way of checking to be sure the calls were made. In addition, be sure to provide the service with the answers to the most frequently asked questions so they can answer those questions immediately. This will save time as well as the cost of a call-back or a letter.

Complaints taken by telephone can help you avoid mistakes in the future. For example, a caller may say that the magazine is late. Furthermore, you can prepare scripts for the telephone operators so that they can question callers about what they think of your magazine. Thus, valuable information on readership can be developed for just a few cents per call.

The supervisor should constantly monitor most of the incoming calls via the use of a call director or by plugging into the operators' phones with the use of a headset. If any operator becomes edgy, tense or irritable, he should be taken off the phone immediately. If the volume of incoming calls is heavy, operators should be given a break every hour or hour and a half. Furthermore, supervisors should not work longer than a four- to six-hour shift.

Upgrade the orders

A script should be prepared for the 800 service, incorporating an up-sell or an add-on sell wherever possible. Gougion of Budget Marketing points out that nothing is more important than upgrading telephone orders.

"Once the operator has taken the information for the subscription," he explains, "he can talk about how costs keep going up. Often, he can sell a two- or three-year subscription that way. We find that about one out of five one-year subscription orders can be upgraded to two or three years.

"Operators can also sell add-on orders," he continues. "He can ask the caller if he has a friend or relative he would like to send a subscription to. Or—would he like to send a subscription to a customer as a business gift. Usually one out of every six or seven orders can be an add-on sale."

Since upselling is the best way to increase sales, everyone taking incoming calls should be trained to up-sell. Gougion also says that using an 800 number in change of address promotions can be profitable to publishers.

"We realize that getting a change of address by telephone seems like an unnecessary expense," he states. "But many changes you receive by mail require special handling, time delays, mail opening, and the charges from the postal service for getting the new address. Most important, you spend from 50 cents to $1 to fulfill each issue sent to the wrong address.

"Using an 800 number for changes of address can be a cost reducer—it is for many of our clients," he says. "Of course, we offer an extension when subscribers call in a change of address, so this actually generates more subscription sales in addition to solving customer service problems."

Advertising the number

The 800 number can be used in blow-in/bind-in cards, space ads, gift ads, renewal letters, direct mail packages, change of address house ads, TV and radio ads, and even on billboards. (When using the 800 number in any medium, be sure you always use the phrase "toll-free.")

•**Radio and television.** Dr. Tony Schwartz, the famous media strategist, says there is a problem with radio: It doesn't last.

Says Dr. Schwartz: "It's not a good medium to present something people want to study or refer back to. The most important factor: The listener's connection with the product. Why he buys it. What he expects of it. Talk to that. It's more important than identifying with the nature of the station. Radio is the opposite of print. The last line is the line that's remembered, as opposed to the headline. If you're going to give the company's telephone number, repeat it at the very end of the commercial."

Another point: The best radio time, early morning drive time, is the worst time to use an 800 number. A driver can't write down the number. Best time: After 7 P.M. or during the day if you want to reach housewives.

If you have local numbers, give the 800 number, but also remind listeners to look for the number in the phone book.

Television works for very few magazines. The only continued user of TV is Time Inc. They offer subscriptions—usually with a premium—for *Fortune* and *Time*. They also sell their continuity book programs via TV 800 numbers. (For the books, they say the best ads are ones that produce a feeling of fear in customers, such as a picture of a shark for a book on nature, or a tiger. This works because if you evoke an emotion, the commercial will be watched and listened to.)

Gougion says that in most instances magazine promotions on television are not going to be profitable and probably won't generate enough subscriptions to pay for the commercial.

"However, if you are trying to increase newsstand sales and build a better image for your magazine, going on television may be worth it," he says.

He adds this advice: "Make sure the number is flashing on the screen at all times. This gives people plenty of time to write the number down. Furthermore, since calls usually start coming in within 15 minutes after the spot airs, tell customers to write the number down and call back if the lines are busy."

•**Within an ad.** Most magazine subscription advertisements now include an 800 number.

Boldly display the WATS number near the coupon in an ad. In addition, inform the caller as to the information that will be asked for, such as source code, item number, credit card information.

Joe Sugarman, president of JS&A, runs ads that have no coupons, only an 800 number. He believes that because there is no coupon, his ads look more like a news article than an ad and thus attract more readers.

Make sure the telephone response center is fully aware of the details of an offer, including product samples or catalog copies, well in advance of the advertising being placed. Those services offering computerized on-line capability should be given advance information.

Remember, a customer will use the most convenient way available to place his order, and all other things being equal, he will buy from the company offering a toll free call option to place his order. Furthermore, if a company's fulfillment is fast and accurate, and if the customer is well treated when placing orders, he will continue to buy, and will encourage his friends to buy from you as well.

Use a benefit line when displaying your 800 number. "In a hurry?" "For faster service." "For quicker delivery." Give a reason why the customer should pick up the phone and order right now.

•**Direct mail.** Using an 800 number in direct mail is another way to get extra orders. You can put the number in the P.S. of your letter, on the brochure, and on the order card.

Because you will start getting orders within 24 hours of the date the mail is opened by the customer, you will be able to determine the exact date the mail was received in various parts of the country. Then, in a few days, you will probably be able to determine which lists will be most responsive.

Some marketers have developed ways to project total number of responses from the first two days' orders by telephone. Usually you get about 25 percent phone orders and 75 percent by coupon when you use the 800 number in a coupon ad.

Magazines can also use the 800 number in the renewal letter sent out 30 days before expiration. The offer is: "Call now and be sure you won't miss an issue." Because many people prefer to call rather than return a card, this technique will bring in extra orders.

When you send out press releases, use the 800 number near the middle of the article. Some newspapers will print the number, and you may get calls from potential subscribers.

If you sell books or newsletters or hold seminars, use the 800 number in your house ads.

The 800 number can be used for many non-selling purposes. One creative use of WATS is to use some of the incoming calls to get survey information such as demographic data. In addition, you can develop a script to find out which articles readers enjoyed and what kinds of articles they want you to publish. Such information enables publishers to give readers what they need and want.

Other information can be obtained that will show advertisers the readers' buying power. One photography magazine instructed its service to ask the following questions to callers ordering subscriptions: "How much do you spend on film each year? How much on equipment? What type film do you use? Do you have a darkroom?" This information could be developed even further by determining which readers were actually in the marke for a new camera. Such information could then be sold to advertisers.

(Note: Do not use the survey script on every incoming call. Instead, set a time to gather information, say two to four hours of calls each week.)

For ABC or BPA verification, you can set up a script to take verification information. You then only have to send out the completed verification form for signature. You have already paid for the call, so use it to gather information. Clear your script questions with ABC or BPA.

A typical call

An 800 number will usually be answered by the operator this way:

"Hello, this is Harold. . . May I help you?"

The caller will reply: "Yes, I would like to subscribe to *Winner's Digest.*"

The operator will quickly flip to a page listing the offers on *Winner's Digest.* There may be several offers in several magazines. Then, he'll ask for the source, usually an extension number.

If the caller has written down the extension number, but doesn't have the ad, or doesn't remember which TV station she was watching, the operator should try to find out where the caller saw the ad.

The operator must be trained to question callers in this situation. The questions must be planned: "Did you see it on television after 7 P.M., or did you see it in a newspaper?" Or, "Do you remember the name of the magazine you saw the ad in?"

After the source is entered, the operator will find a copy of the ad and/or a sheet or card giving full information on the offer. He'll take the name and address of the caller, try to get the caller to use a charge card, restate the offer, and usually try to up-sell, offering either a two-year or three-year subscription with a money-saving benefit for the extension. Or the up-sell may be a seminar or a book, or other product.

The up-sell script should state: "As you know, costs keep going up. But you can protect yourself against inflation by subscribing for two years for $20, or three years for $28, a saving off the regular one-year subscription of $12. Would you like to extend for three years and save $8?"

If the caller says he is not interested, he is again offered a two-year subscription at a savings of $4.

Usually about one out of four callers will give the extension, which will usually more than pay for your entire 800 operation.

Operator as friend

As advertising psychologist Ernest Dicter says: "Most consumers have a strong secret desire to be loved by their suppliers for their own sake."

Dr. Dicter adds that the advertiser (with the operator as his spokesman) must give proof through

---

Marketing and fulfillment check list

A wise driver once said, "Don't just watch the car in front of you. Watch the car in front of him, too." The same wisdom pertains to the marketing and fulfillment aspects of WATS line service. It's not enough to provide in-house WATS lines or to use an outside WATS service if it doesn't tie in with your credit card, computer and shipping needs:

☐ **Credit card processing.** If your business involves credit card charging, do you have facilities for checking each caller's credit, processing all credit card billing paperwork and sending it to appropriate banks and credit card companies?

☐ **Computerization.** If your order processing is computerized, do you have CRT screens and keyboards in front of each operator for direct, simultaneous entry?

☐ **Training.** Do you have proper facilities for training personnel for in and out WATS calls, including *all* aspects of selling, trading up, customer service, planning, budgeting, problem-solving?

☐ **Programming.** Are calls received and processed in such a way that they match your order fulfillment format, thereby eliminating the time, manpower and cost of duplicate keyboarding?

☐ **Transmission of information.** Can you receive and transmit orders with maximum speeds, efficiency and economy? Do you utilize the proper mix of phone, mail, express mail, parcel post, private shipping and delivery services, tele-copier, TWX, Telex, magnetic tape delivery or shipment, computer to computer transmission by data phone, etc.?

WATS line check list

Telephone marketing consultant Larry Schwartz, president, National Order Systems, developed this check list for 800 number users:

☐ Are the transactions so specialized or lengthy that they can't possibly be handled by an outside service company?

☐ Are there seasonal peaks and valleys that require continuous costs of recruiting, training, firing? Will deposits, installation, suspension and other equipment costs be justified?

☐ Is there enough space available at proper cost per square foot on your premises to house all the operators, supervisors, sales people and equipment that will be needed? Is there ample space for expansion when success calls for additional space?

☐ Does the number of lines you will install justify the installation and cost of Automatic Call Distributors? Will your total need for analyzing calls by duration, hour, load, blocked calls, busy signals be properly served?

☐ If you advertise in broadcast and print media, will you be able to generate daily reports of the previous day's calls by product, station or publication and hour so as to permit immediate expansion or contraction of advertising schedules?

☐ Since there is a direct correlation between speed of shipment and such factors as C.O.D. reject rate, payment rate, customer satisfaction and repeat sales, will your set-up permit the fastest possible processing of orders?

☐ Is the flow of calls sufficient to justify 24-hour lines?

☐ Are you in a good labor market where you can hire an adequate number of operators at reasonable cost?

☐ If 24-hour-a-day, 7-day-a-week service is required, are your operators and other personnel willing to travel and work nights and weekends in that particular location?

☐ Do you understand that you will have the cost of extra maintenance and security for keeping your building open nights, holidays and weekends?

☐ Have you analyzed and budgeted the full cost per call for your 24-hour and 10-hour lines, as well as your cost of overtime?

---

understanding, attitude and action that he is a friend. Thus, there should be continual training of operators to this concept. They must feel good about the job and show an interest in the customer.

The attitude of the operator should be one of wanting to help. He should speak slowly and clearly, and in a friendly tone of voice.

Contact local college acting or speech departments for help in voice training. Paul Mills, Mills-Roberts Associates, advises: "Most of us talk too high because we are lazy. You can create larger resonating cavities by opening your mouth wider when you speak. Lower your voice until it's soft and pleasant."

There should be some kind of monitoring system. This does not necessarily have to be done by management. You can give a tape recorder to operators and ask them to review their own calls. Or let a group meet each day and listen to and critique each other's calls.

You might also want to teach writing, so that orders will be entered correctly.

How to sell subs on TV

By John Hall

Sports Illustrated, Time, Newsweek, Money, Playboy, Book Digest, Soap Opera Digest, Games, Rolling Stone, Country Music. Each of these publications has aired or is airing subscription campaigns on television.

How do they do it? Can your magazine do it too? What follows is something of a primer for selling subscriptions on television.

Historically, the television direct response industry has been populated by entrepreneurs operating by the seat of their pants.

However, even though the industry lacks sophisti-cation and does not approach the precision of direct mail, subscriptions can be generated at approximately the same cost as a direct mail piece. In fact, an advertising cost of between $3 and $4 per subscription is definitely possible.

To determine whether your magazine fits the medium, take a good look at the products which are now advertised on TV with any degree of frequency. If a magazine or a product is advertised frequently, such advertising probably is profitable. So if your subscribers are in the same target audience that watches the ads currently airing, then television may be an appropriate medium for your products as well.

Once you have determined that your audience is the same as a TV audience, you must then determine whether that audience is in a low-cost programming area ($3 per thousand households is a good rule of thumb). Obviously, network programming is much too expensive. That leaves spot TV—commercials on individual local stations.

The programming areas in spot TV that tend to produce orders at a reasonable cost are weekday mornings (between 9 a.m. and 12 noon), early evening (4 p.m. to 8 p.m.), and, to a lesser degree, late evenings. Talk shows, situation comedies and movies are prime areas during the week (soap operas are too expensive), and on weekends, morning and afternoon movies have been most effective. Occasionally, early morning news-oriented programs and evening local news programs are successful.

In general, people from 18 to 50 are easy to reach, and women are easier to reach than men. Geographically there are no bounds. The right programming on the right station should produce efficiently in any area of the country. A commercial for a national magazine can run successfully both in large cities and in small towns.

Where to start

Buying TV time for direct response is a unique form of media buying that involves negotiations with the stations. Since successful negotiating depends on experience and personal relationships, find a direct response advertising firm that has extensive experience in buying direct response TV time. (Do not utilize an agency or time-buying service that does not have such experience.)

Evaluate each prospective service by talking to its clients and to sales managers at a few TV stations. In this business, a good credit rating is a must, so make sure your agency is in good financial standing. Not many agencies can handle a full-scale direct marketing campaign on TV.

Once you have decided on an agency, use it to help develop your commercial. Some agencies can do the entire commercial in-house. Stay involved, however. Developing a commercial is a highly subjective process, and since most people aren't certain why one commercial is successful and another isn't, your input is valuable. The same concepts and techniques for copy and design that make successful direct mail and space promotions can be applied to TV commercials.

A direct response commercial should be two minutes long since no one in the business has been able to do one successfully in 60 seconds. Typically, this two-minute commercial consists of one minute and 40 seconds of actual commercial describing the product and the offer and making the pitch. The remaining 20 seconds is used for a customized tag—in effect a coupon—which includes the address for pre-paid orders and the toll-free phone number for credit orders.

This tag should be customized or individualized for each station. In fact, a good time-buying agency will also set up a local mailing address for each station because a local address will elicit more prepaid or mailed orders than a common mailing address (in New York or Boulder, Colorado for example). In addition, if a major campaign is mounted it is important to utilize several telephone answering services for reasons which will be discussed later. In short, the commercial should not have a constant mailing address and/or telephone number permanently built into it.

To exploit both the audio and visual aspects of TV, fill the commercial with compelling visuals. You can flesh out the visual end of the commercial by using four-color work from the magazine—covers, spreads, and individual photos which tend to have more impact than illustrations. Show all sections of the magazine. Develop the image of a magazine that is substantive, varied, and a great deal for the money. Don't hesitate to use "supers" or "crawls," printed information that is superimposed on the screen to emphasize key points, elements of the offer, etc.

Use "hard sell"

Most commercials use hardselling copy emphasizing the importance of "acting now." Selling on TV is the ultimate in impulse sale and it is important to elicit that response on the spot—just as in direct mail.

Emphasize savings, premiums and value, and be sure the copy is simple and direct. The purpose is to make the sale, not win a prize for creativity.

Some marketers have successfully used known personalities to make their pitch. Although this certainly lends credence to the commercial, it will significantly add to the expense of the commercial and, in some instances, may distract from the message. Generally, direct response commercials use a "voice over," a spokesperson who is not seen.

Most commercials are made on videotape which allows a great deal of flexibility. Typically, once the script is approved the sound track is recorded in its entirety. Then the visuals are shot in various ways so that the director will have flexibility in melding the audio and visual aspects of the commercial to make the final product. Ultimately the visuals and sound track are put together by a computerized editing machine.

There is a great deal of flexibility in this process. As the commercial is being built—as the visuals are being added to and synchronized with the audio track—the director can create several different looks. Different visuals (shot previously) can be added or subtracted, lengthened or shortened to exactly fit the audio track.

It should take three to five hours to record the sound track and another eight to 10 hours to shoot the visuals and do the editing. The whole commercial can be done for as little as $4,000. Make sure a rate is agreed upon before you begin the commercial.

Shooting the commercial at an independent production house such as Direct Response Productions in Pittsburgh or at WAUB-TV in Cleveland is a viable alternative to producing it through an agency. In fact, these two facilities probably produce the majority of the direct response commercials. They are very inexpensive and professional, and they will walk you through the process step-by-step.

In general, the price limit for TV products is about $10. Remember, this is an impulse buy. Although there are some products being successfully sold for more, $10 seems to be the limit.

Make the offer simple; options on term and price will only confuse the issue. Payment method can be credit (bill-me) only (taken by toll-free telephone), bill-me combined with a prepaid option, or C.O.D. with a prepaid option.

The C.O.D. order is familiar to the typical TV buyer. For years now it has been the counterpart of the prepaid order for records and household products, the staples of TV direct response sales.

In one case, a magazine offered a year's subscription plus a premium record album for $9.98. The respondent could call the toll-free phone number and order C.O.D., or he had the option of sending a check or money order, thereby "saving C.O.D. postage and handling charges."

Under the C.O.D. option (exercised by 55 percent of the respondents versus a typical 60 percent of "bill-me" in a typical "hard offer" direct mail campaign) the respondent paid the postman for the entire subscription plus the C.O.D. postage and handling fees when he received his first issue and record premium in one package. Under ideal conditions the respondent receives the package within three weeks of his order and the magazine receives payment in the fourth week by the Post Office.

Testing the campaign

Unfortunately, it is impossible to test different offers or commercials at the same time on one station or, for that matter, in one market. Stations won't allow price tests because of complaints from those who pay the higher rate and see the lower offer. In addition, it is impossible to duplicate the conditions on any one station at any given time.

Therefore, most TV direct marketers run similar schedules on several stations in the same week to test the price or approach. Choosing stations which historically pull orders similarly for various offers, they will run, say, five stations at a lower price offer and five at a higher price. These marketers hope that the inherent variances in scheduling, weather, viewers in general, etc., even out over the course of a week's schedule and that there is a clear-cut difference in degree of response to the tests.

The basic test of whether your product is marketable on TV or not could be conducted on as many as 15 stations with an outlay of $10,000 to $15,000 in TV commercial time. Choose stations so that a good cross-section is represented and test different geographical areas, different programming, and different market sizes. Stations that generally reach an older (34-59) audience should be tested as well as those that reach younger (25-34) audiences.

If there is an indication of viability—if the number of orders generated per advertising dollar spent meets or comes close to meeting the criteria that have been set for generating new subscribers—run a second round of tests. Buy another $10,000 or so worth of TV time in the programming areas and on the stations and markets that match those that were successful in the initial test.

In addition, continue the stations that were successful in the initial test (eliminating unproductive commercials) and use those stations until they are no longer cost effective. This will give you some idea of the length of runs you can expect on stations in the future. As might be expected, the larger the market, the longer a station can be utilized. Some stations have been run effectively for as long as a year.

Once a test has been concluded and the viability of the product established, a roll-out strategy should be developed. As in other forms of direct response, the prime seasons for TV marketing are the quarters immediately following January 1 and immediately after July 4. In addition to the fact that consumers tend to respond more readily in these periods, TV rates are at their lowest in the first and third quarters because traditional TV advertising demand is down in these periods.

Roll-out in stages

Typically, a roll-out for a strong product is planned in three or four stages involving 20 to 30 stations in each stage. Budget approximately $15,000 to $20,000 for each stage and make adjustments upward or downward in the budget and station list of subsequent stages based on the performance of the first stage. The first stage should consist of stations that are judged to have the most potential for success. Subsequent stages should consist of progressively weaker-pulling stations.

Obtain contracts for all stations in the roll-out plan at least one month in advance of the beginning of the first or third quarters in order to insure time on prime stations. There is definitely competition for the limited amount of commercial time on prime stations in these seasons.

Typically, schedules are contracted for 13 weeks via a broadcast order which spells out all elements of the commercial time to be run. Schedules can be cancelled as late as Wednesday or Thursday of the week preceding the scheduled week (broadcast weeks begin on Monday). And, if commercial time is available, schedules on stations may be bought as late as Wednesday of the week preceding actual broadcast. Therefore, although the 13 weeks are reserved, the buyer is not obligated to run all 13 weeks. In addition, schedules may be altered in many instances. Commercials can be eliminated in areas that are not "pulling" or added in areas that are.

Direct response commercial schedules can be run in substantial volume generally from December 26 through mid-March and from July 5 through mid-October. Schedules can run in other periods, but 80 percent of all volume is usually done during the first and third quarters.

Christmas gift offers are possible but they present problems. The offer must be very strong to offset the increased TV time rates that exist in October, November and December. Delivery must be insured after Christmas. And, without a doubt, there will be problems and added expenses taking the donor/donee information over the phone.

Buying time

Typically, a TV time-buying agency will employ anywhere from four to a dozen time-buyers, each handling various products on a list of stations. In the ideal situation, a buyer has been dealing with a station for some time and has developed a relationship with the sales personnel at the station. He has a thorough knowledge of the programming and an instinctive feel for what will be successful on the station.

All other factors being equal, a good relationship with station personnel will frequently result in obtaining the best schedules. Typically, a schedule or package will consist of seven to 10 spots spread over the entire week. Sometimes these packages are fixed and the buyer gets some good productive spots and some bad spots.

When there is flexibility in the package a good buyer can maneuver for the best spots. In addition, a buyer with a good working relationship with the station will frequently be given first shot at preferred schedules. In a tight marketplace this preferential treatment can be crucial.

Another area where relationship and experience are important is in the area of "make goods," free commercials. Occasionally, when a schedule produces disastrous results, a good buyer can maneuver for "make goods" and negotiate for the best rates. A good buyer will know when the rate is too high.

Once the order for a commercial schedule has been placed, it is important that orders are monitored on a daily basis against commercials run. Hour-by-hour counts for each station, available from the telephone answering service, should be compared to the advertising schedule and evaluated, commercial by commercial. A schedule on a station that is not working should be terminated immediately. It should never be necessary to run a schedule on an unproductive station for more than one week.

The time-buying service should be able to arrange for "P.I.'s" (a "per inquiry") and "guarantees." In a P.I. arrangement, the client pays the station a certain commission per order generated. The guarantee arrangement is a variation on the P.I. theme where the client pays the going rate for a commercial schedule and the station agrees to run commercials until enough orders are generated to meet an agreed-upon advertising cost per order.

In general, arrangements of this sort are worked out with smaller stations that are unable to sell all their advertising time. However, it is now possible to make P.I. arrangements with super-stations such as WTCG in Atlanta, which transmits a signal to a communications satellite which in turn bounces the signal to cable systems across the country. (At last count, WTCG was carried in 46 states.) In two months WTCG generated over 5,000 subscribers for one magazine and over 15,000 orders for a strong record offer.

It is important that the client receive information and maintain control over the time-buying function. On Wednesday of each week the client should receive a complete recap of the previous week's activities via a "cum sheet" which lists information for each station on a weekly and a cumulative basis. The cum sheet lists each station run that week, the estimated advertising dollars expended for that week on that station, the number of phone orders and mailed-in orders generated in that week, and the advertising cost per order for that week.

The advertising cost per order is the time-buyer's bench mark, and stations should be terminated as soon as the allowable cost per order is exceeded. The client should review each station with the agency, and a decision to continue or terminate each station should be arrived at jointly. If the decision is to terminate a station the client should receive in writing from the agency an "LTC" or last telecast for that station.

On Wednesday the client should also receive from the agency a list of stations (and a budget for each) to be run in the subsequent week. This is a control list to make sure that the only stations that run are those that have been agreed upon by all concerned. In a situation where numerous buyers are buying for numerous products on numerous stations, the spending of the time-buying agency must be closely controlled by the client.

Disputes are common between station and agency and between agency and client. It is up to the agency to check affidavits from the station which detail the exact timing of commercials that ran. A station will often run commercials in times that were not ordered, and if the agency does not dispute the affidavit/invoice, the client should. The client should not pay for commercials that were not ordered.

Fulfillment

It is important to make sure that all orders reported to the agency from the telephone answering services and mail pick-up services are actually received at the fulfillment house. Since orders are often sent to the wrong place, a weekly accounting by station is necessary.

Telephone answering services are far from perfect. They frequently misallocate orders—reporting orders as being generated from one station when they actually came from another—and the ramifications of this sort of mistake can be enormous. A station performing poorly might continue to run while one that is doing well is cancelled.

Numerous telephone answering services should be used to minimize this mis-reporting problem. In addition, using several answering services enables you to "hedge your bet" and avoid problems. The snowstorm in Chicago last winter prevented operators from getting to work on one occasion. On another, the telephone company forgot to activate the line for the number being used.

Besides generating new subscribers, there are other benefits from a TV subscription campaign. The exposure is certainly important and, in fact, there have been reports of significant increases in single-copy sales.

Tests should also be made of the possible synergistic effects of TV subscription marketing with space advertising.

The 60-second subscription sale

By William Steiner

Because so many magazine circulation executives are seeking subscription building programs to replace or add to their direct mail programs, I bought lunch for Mike Fabian, March Advertising's executive vice-president, to pick his brain on how his agency makes broadcast advertising work so well for its magazine publishing clients.

Mike and his partner, Sy Levy, have developed successful subscription-building programs for their clients, which include a number of major magazine publishers, book clubs and mail order firms. They have made both TV and radio pay off as subscription producers.

The following are the answers to the questions I asked Mike.

Why should magazine publishers venture into what is to most of them an unknown area—broadcast response advertising—to sell subscriptions?

To an advertising agency selling magazine subscriptions, print is a wonderful medium—because we know so much about it. We know that everyone our ad reaches can and does read. And we have all kinds of statistics to fall back on when in doubt: Cut-out coupon returns versus four-page inserts, free-standing versus bound-in. Everything's measured and tabulated.

The same is true for direct mail. You know your customers and prospects and select your mailing lists accordingly. And aside from testing new packages and lists, you are generally operating on familiar ground.

To venture from this cozy cocoon into the alien air of broadcasting is a little like divorcing your wife of 25 years and impulsively marrying your 19-year-old secretary. Everything you once took for granted is gone and you're stuck with a set of untested assumptions and vital questions that only time can answer.

But the fact is that today you'd better venture. With the way costs are going up in space, printing and, of course, postage, direct marketers who want to expand in the years ahead must be willing to try new media and the new approaches.

Broadcast commercials were once very heavily loaded with direct mail sellers and then something happened—what?

Remember about 20 years ago when TV pitchmen were popping up on those ten-inch screens? "Mail a dollar to Charles Antell and he'll prove those hair roots aren't dead. Phone now and receive a seven-piece set of aluminum cookware *free* with your magnificent floral-patterned, genuine gold-edged china dinner service for eight. Enclose payment and get a gleaming solid chromium combination lid lifter, can opener, apple corer and screwdriver as a gift, *plus* an amazing miracle, slicer-dicer-chopper-mincer-shredder and ice crusher."

What became of those salespeople?

I suspect that larger audiences, higher time rates, growing skepticism about those fabulous offers and a steady stream of complaints combined to chase them off the air. But while they were around, the air was so polluted that advertisers with legitimate offers hesitated to try broadcast and until a few years ago, damn few did.

What about today's increasing use of TV for response advertising?

Today, of course, it's a whole new ball game. Flick on one of your local stations on a Saturday or Sunday afternoon and watch the movie. Just about every commercial is a direct marketing pitch. In fact, those record offers you see today have revived more has-been celebrities than Louis B. Mayer created in his heyday.

I just wonder how long effectiveness can be maintained when one commercial looks exactly like the other.

Just what do you feel is the big need in broadcast response advertising these days?

I used to get up at direct marketing conventions and exhort people, including magazine publishers, to get into the broadcast medium.

I'd point out that producing a commercial needn't cost an arm and a leg. As a matter of fact, a good 60-second color spot could be produced for less than four thousand dollars. I'd talk about buying time, how a good test pattern could be worked out for another five thousand dollars, or

better yet, how stations could work out a per-inquiry deal and you wouldn't have to pay for the time at all—just an agreed-upon amount per order.

Apparently the broadcast medium must have proved pretty effective for a lot of direct marketers—so much so that direct marketing as a category has in the past few years become the single fastest growing category in all television advertising.

That fact alone should go a long way toward getting rid of the myth that direct marketing is only direct mail. But what's wrong with direct mail is also very rapidly becoming the curse of broadcast direct marketing.

All of a sudden, the viewer, our potential subscriber, is bombarded by a mind-boggling sameness of appeals. Creativity? Well, these advertisers reason, we'll leave that to the other guy—we're out to get orders.

Mention the phrase *junk mail* at a direct marketing convention and you get immediate ostracism, instant leprosy or worse. But the fact is that so much direct mail, so much print advertising, and now so much television advertising has a depressing sameness about it.

While TV is indeed an exciting marketing medium, we're going to kill the-goose-that-laid-the-golden-egg unless we season our sales appeals with taste and imagination.

What guidelines would you recommend for magazine publishers to follow in building a TV subscription-producing program?

At my agency, we sat down about a year ago to see if we could develop a set of guidelines on what makes an effective direct-response TV commercial:

1. Limit your commercial to one or two simply stated points. More than that confuses the viewer and a confused viewer won't reach for a pencil or a telephone.

An outstanding example of focusing on the key point is a current book club commercial. In its print ads, this club offers the reader the opportunity to *select* four books for one dollar. On TV, this is simplified by giving the viewer four of the club's most popular titles for one dollar. There is no choice, but also there's no *time* for a choice on TV. In sum, the commercial is simple, direct and most effective.

2. Repeat the premium and offer twice. Illustrate it pictorially. Spell out your story with titles or superimposed titles. Remember, the viewer can't reread or reexamine any portion of your message. It's *not* in print.

Some of the most productive direct response commercials on the air today are record companies offering hits of the '40s, '50s, '60s, great hits of Broadway, opera, what have you. After you have seen enough of them, they are pretty dull, but notice how often they repeat the ordering information—phone number, box number, address. At least twice in each commercial. Judging from the number of record offers on the air now, they have to be working.

3. In a one-minute commercial you have 48 seconds to make your sale, excluding the response vehicles. Start the message with the first frame and don't stop selling till the last. You have no time for pointless lead-ins.

We recently tested two commercials for one of our clients. The first began by setting a mood. It followed up with the benefits. The second got into the benefits right off the bat. It was no contest. The direct approach wins every time, simply because there just isn't enough time to "romance" *and* sell.

4. Don't oversell. Don't try to cram a short commercial full of copy. 130 words for a one-minute spot, 200 words for a two-minute spot will give you plenty of time to make your point without sounding like a sideshow barker.

5. Make full use of television graphics. If you can demonstrate your product, do, but keep it simple and believable.

Recently book publishers have started using TV not on a direct-response basis, but simply to promote their books at retail. Most of these commercials show a slide of the books, with a voice-over announcer to relate the message. Frankly, it's not a very effective use of a medium that is designed to appeal to two senses—the eye and ear. But maybe times are changing. A commercial for Herman Wouk's *Winds of War* utilized old newsreel film clips to arouse the viewer's interest. While it's dangerous to draw a correlation between TV advertising and book sales, the moral is still clear: If you are going to use TV, use it to its fullest extent and don't merely adapt your direct-mail approach in a static manner.

6. If your response mechanism is a phone number, repeat it *three* times. Most viewers don't sit around with pencils in hand or a memory capable of retaining seven-digit numbers.

7. If you're running 15 spots a week, commercial fatigue will set in after six weeks. That's the law of diminishing commercial returns.

8. Testimonials are fine, if they're believable. Celebrities with a natural connection to the product make for good commercials. But unbelievable claims and celebrities with no logical product connection distract the viewer and cut down on returns.

The screen is full of celebrities today. Yet not everyone uses them appropriately. Not too long ago, Tony Martin was peddling panty hose and you had to be a genius to figure out the connection between him and the product. Perhaps subliminally we had to jar our memories to remember that his wife, Cyd Charisse, has great legs. But obviously it was a weak connection because that commercial is off the air. The one way you can tell the success or failure of a direct response campaign is to see how long it runs. On the other hand, using Chubby Checker to sell an album of great rock hits or Rosemary Clooney to promote an album of hits of the '50s is a natural—and it works.

9. Animation techniques are fine *if* they reinforce your primary sales message. As amusement only, they waste selling time.

10. Every commercial must have at least one strongly stated benefit that's believable, achievable and easily related to the consumer. A commercial without a clearly defined benefit will not do justice to the product, service or company.

Whenever possible, we try to follow our rules. More important, we are constantly testing new approaches and new techniques (that often break some of our own tenets) in order to have our client's sales message stand out from the madding crowd.

What about the use of radio for subscription selling?

In some ways, radio is even more intriguing as a direct marketing medium than television. TV is a mass medium and it's pretty tough to extrapolate any demographics about a Saturday afternoon movie or the Late Show. But radio has developed a built-in selectivity where you can break out the kind of demographics best suited to your product.

Consider this: The 6,500 commercial radio stations in this country offer their listeners an almost infinite variety of formats. All news all day, classical music, talk and interviews, top 40 hits, phone-in discussions, jazz, rock, ethnically oriented material, country music, easy-listening standards—just about everything imaginable.

Given this diversification of targeted programming, plus logical inference and a bit of testing, direct marketers can pick the kind of audience that best fits their product's specific appeal.

We've sold subscriptions to newsmagazines on all-news stations, high-brow publications on FM classical music formats, hits-of-the-'40s records on stations programming the old standards and so on down the line.

Considering its selectivity and the fact that the costs are proportionately lower than those for TV, radio is a pretty exciting medium for direct marketers and one whose full potential is just beginning to be realized.

What does the future hold for using broadcast for subscription selling?

Imagine a little box on top of every TV set that permits the viewer to order the merchandise offered by merely pressing a button. The hardware already exists.

Or think about a TV picture that, again by pushing a button, the viewer can "freeze" or have printed instantaneously, thus combining the dynamics of TV motion with the sales power of the printed word. The hardware for this is also available.

The fact is that direct marketing is at the threshold of a new and exciting era—one that offers awesome potential. It's an opportunity that has to be explored and exploited with responsibility as well as with good taste.

Subscription agents

By John D. Klingel

Agency business seems to be the least understood and most maligned source of subscriptions. PCH, which is the best known of the agents, is well known as a source that "doesn't renew very well." And I hear the same statement about school plans and other agent sources. It's amazing how many people malign these sources.

It is true that PCH doesn't renew as well as your own direct mail. That does not make it a bad source, however, and more important, it does not mean it is a less profitable source. If magazine X gets a 40 percent conversion from direct mail and is currently paying $8 over and above the $12 received for subscriptions (total cost per net sub of $20), a PCH-sold sub at $9.95 with a 20 percent conversion begins to look very good. To somewhat oversimplify the economics: in the first case you take $8 out of your wallet to pay for a subscriber, and in the case of PCH you get roughly $1 to put in your wallet. I don't know about you, but I'd rather put money *in* my wallet.

The major mistake that people make is to concentrate on a single variable (*i.e.*, renewal rate, bad pay, low response, etc.) rather than looking at the total picture. The *only* time measure of circulation profitability is to look at the profit or loss over the long term. If you want to compare the relative merits of agency sources, you have to use source evaluation techniques.

A variety to choose from

There are many different types of direct mail agents, and within categories the renewal rates and cancellation rates will vary.

The categories that have been established for the various types of agency business are predominantly based on the methods the agents use to sell subscriptions and on ABC definitions used to report channels of sales on the Publishers Statements. At times the definitions are a little fuzzy. For example, Paid During Service (PDS) and Field-Sold are often the same agents using different methods of sale; and sometimes there are catalog agents who also have a field sales force. Fortunately, the categories that historically have been used to define agency sources are also useful for defining agents economically.

The types of agents tend to be ranked economically from most profitable to least profitable sources as follows: 1. Catalog Agents; 2. Direct Mail Agents and School Plans; 3. Field-Sold and PDS.

A catalog agent is one of the most profitable sources for almost all magazines, and generally the question is not whether to use the source but how to obtain volume. I've put Direct Mail Agents and School Plans into the same economic category because for most magazines the long-term profitability from these sources is very similar. Typically, direct mail agents will be slightly more profitable than school plans (because direct mail agents usually convert better), but not significantly. The

economics of the last category are usually significantly worse than direct mail agents and school plans.

I very seldom find a magazine whose economics justify the use of Field and PDS sources. Generally speaking, a magazine will not have an economic reason to use these sources unless the net advertising profit per subscriber is extremely high. There are, however, many magazines that do have economic reasons to use these sources, and for those magazines these agents are a valuable source of business. For most smaller magazines with moderate or little advertising, the economics of Field and PDS agents would not belong in the source mix.

On the other hand, I find that most magazines can successfully use Direct Mail Agents and School Plans. Usually, these agents don't fit economically in a magazine's source mix unless the magazine is carrying a moderate amount of advertising, but I often find that magazines with very little or no advertising can make these agents work.

If you want to examine how the economics of these agents might apply to your publication, look at profitability in the following way: Assume 10 percent to 15 percent remit from direct mail agents and 20 percent or 25 percent for school plans and project income and costs over at least a two-year period using four different conversion rates: 10 percent, 15 percent, 20 percent, and 25 percent. With a good product and a good renewal series, you should be able to get a conversion between 15 percent and 20 percent. If you find that the economics don't work at 25 percent, the odds are that these sources won't work for you. I've seen magazines convert (first-time renewal) at over 30 percent, but it's rare. If the economics look good, you should test these sources by signing up for some volume and seeing how well they renew.

Direct mail agents and school plans are particularly useful to some of the special interest and extremely vertical publications that can't find large numbers of names for direct mail and are too narrowly focused for substantial newsstand distribution. Agents provide a shotgun approach to a market, whereas direct mail must be highly targeted to be effective. Often the percentage of potential readers on mailing lists is too low for a magazine to use direct mail. In these cases, agents may be much more effective than your direct-to-publisher sources.

The renewal rate and the overall economics of agent sources can be controlled to some extent with a few little tricks.

Price sensitivity. Agent sources tend to have almost perfectly elastic price curves. For example, if you lower price by 10 percent, you should get 10 percent higher volume. You may get higher volume with a lower price, but the trade-off may be slightly less qualified subs. If you want volume for rate base, you'll do better at lower prices. If you want circulation profit, *not* volume, you'll usually be better off keeping the agent rate high and limiting volume.

Conversion pricing. The highest conversion percentages will usually result when you convert at the intro rate or a lower price. This is particularly important when using short-term introductory prices. If the original rate was eight issues for $8, the subs will convert much better at 8/$8 than at 12 issues for $12. Subscribers are not as sensitive to copy rates as they are to the out-of-pocket price.

Short-term rates. When you start to analyze the economics of agency business, you will quickly see that the major cost is the cost of serving issues. In Figure 1, I'm going to use a 20 percent remit and assume that it costs $.60 to print and deliver a copy of the magazine.

Figure 1:

	8 Issues for $8	12 Issues for $12
Income	$ 1.60	$ 2.40
Cost of issues	$ 4.80	$ 7.20
1st year loss per sub	$(3.20)	$(4.80)

If you're more interested in maximizing circulation profit than rate base, the short-term offer is an interesting way to use agents to prospect the market to find new subscribers. If rate base is very important, the use of short-term offers reduces the net paid effect of the agent volume.

Early renewals. This trick doesn't work as well with short-term offers due to timing problems, but it often works with a 12-month term. The strategy is to wait until the agent-sold sub has received two or three issues and then hit the subscriber with a renewal effort (usually a special rate or premium offer). This strategy is based on two concepts: (1) people are most enthusiastic about a magazine right after they subscribe, and (2) you get to the subscriber before the agent sends out their promotion.

Alternating seasons. A general observation about direct mail agents is this: of the total subs that renew, roughly 50 percent renew back through the publisher and the other 50 percent renew through the agent. Since direct mail agents mail in the same seasons as we do our own mail (January and July predominate), one way to maximize the renewability is to go into the agency mail in January only and not in July. This trick obviously is for those who want to maximize circulation profit and aren't that concerned with rate base.

Credit. If an agent source uses credit for the original sale, it is extremely important to have a credit option on your renewal efforts.

One potential problem with agency sources is the impact they can have on your subscriber demographics. Not all magazines experience this problem, but it is possible that the demographics of the agency business will not match those of your own direct mail.

This phenomenon is quite easy to test with direct mail questionnaires, and I strongly recommend that you determine the impact of these sources before changing your source mix dramatically. Obviously, if the volume of agent business is a fairly low percentage of total volume, the agent demographics will not significantly change the overall demographics.

Catalog agents

These agents process subscriptions for libraries and institutions. They perform more of a service than a sales function in that they centralize subscription ordering and perform indexing and other services for libraries. They do not sell individual titles to libraries and are not very useful in helping you get your publication into libraries. The remit rate is almost anything you want it to be, since the catalog agent has to process the libraries' orders. Typical remits range from 50 percent to 80 percent.

Direct mail agents

These agents sell through direct mail using a catalog listing of titles (*i.e.*, a stamp sheet). They use a combination of rented lists and their house buyer lists. Although they don't try to directly renew the new orders they sold for you, they maintain an active buyers list which receives regular promotion. Since these agents use credit, you will receive some cancels (10 percent to 30 percent depending on the agent), and the cost of bad pay copies should be included in your economic analysis. The remits are negotiated to some extent, but you will usually find that the larger direct mail agents will have fixed non-negotiable remits that range from 10 percent to 25 percent.

School plans

These agents sell subscriptions through fund raising programs. Virtually all their volume comes from junior and senior high school students who sell subscriptions door to door to raise money for school activities. Roughly 60 percent to 70 percent of the subscriptions are sold in the fall and the balance during the spring. The remit rate is generally 20 percent to 25 percent, and since these are pre-paid orders, there are no cancels. For your general information, the school receives 40 percent of the commission, and these activities are usually the best fund raising activity available to schools. Selling expenses include premiums for the student sellers, which eat up another 40 percent of the commission.

Paid During Service

PDS agents sell long-term subscriptions and bill the buyer on a monthly basis. The publisher also receives a monthly payment, hence the name, paid-during service. Remits range from negative percentages (you pay them) to 20 percent. Renewal rates are usually extremely low (0 percent to 5 percent), and the term is usually three to five years. The economics of this source are further complicated by a 35 percent to 50 percent cancel rate.

Cash field

These agents use door-to-door salespeople, as do the PDS agents, but the subscription price is fully paid or billed immediately. As with PDS, the remit rates are negotiated and range from negative percentages to 20 percent. Volume from both PDS and field agents is affected to some extent by the remit, as salespeople will tend to push the magazines from which they earn greater commissions.

Telephone agencies

Both PDS and field agents use the telephone to sell subscriptions, but there are also some other methods of using the telephone. In a sponsor sale, for example, a third party sells subscriptions and part of the subscription price goes to a charity. The major use of telephone agents is to contact and sell renewals to your expires.

Rate base management

By Ted Bartek

Many publishers are finding that planning and controlling circulation to meet advertising rate base objectives is becoming increasingly difficult. The reason: management cannot accurately forecast circulation needs in time to execute new subscriber acquisition campaigns. Their timing is off, and it's either a case of too much too soon or, more likely, too little too late.

This situation can create serious problems with advertisers and subscribers. Subscriber good will is often damaged by management's desperate attempts to control circulation by backstarting, supplementing or gracing. And relationships with advertisers are often jeopardized by unexpected circulation fluctuations.

As a result, some publishers have given up trying to meet their rate base and have decided to bill advertisers on a flexible rate structure. Today, with all the unknown, complex variables that go into circulation control, is it really worth it to try to manage your rate base?

The answer is yes. In this day of computers, the task, though complex, is a lot less difficult and less tedious than it was in the past. In fact, my experience with *Forbes* magazine proves that with the right tools and an in-depth approach, circulation control is well within the scope of every magazine.

The Forbes system

Forbes magazine—a biweekly—has been having great success in controlling its circulation, averaging between 2,000 and 4,000 subscriptions above rate base on every issue. Staying that close to a rate base 26 times a year is no small task for a magazine with a circulation of 670,000. But *Forbes* has the situation well under control, thanks to a computer and a well-organized circulation control system that can accurately forecast circulation levels by taking into account all the vagaries of direct mail response, bad pay copies, cancellations, expirations and renewal rates.

Each week, *Forbes'* circulation director receives a computer-generated report which tells him exactly how many paid subscriptions the magazine will have for each of the next 10 issues—a projection for five full months. Armed with this information, he can then decide, in advance, what he has to do to make rate base for each issue.

Depending on the forecast, he may plan to vary his direct mail plans. He may produce or curtail direct mail. Or—he may decide to drop his mail earlier or later. He also could manipulate other new subscription sources such as space, TV, subscription agencies, or insert cards, selecting the least costly sources and eliminating the most expensive. Furthermore, if he plans well enough in advance, he can avoid unnecessary gracing, supplementing and backstarting.

System is flexible

The system *Forbes* uses was built on one of the many flexible programming systems suitable for financial budgeting, reporting and modeling. The basis of the *Forbes* model is the Prophit II® system offered by the Service Bureau Company, a division of Control Data Corporation. Although Prophit II® is most often used for financial analysis and planning, it is equally at home in other areas including circulation planning.

Users of this system can custom design a computer model to correspond exactly with their unique computing needs. In fact, programming Prophit II® is just like sitting down and drawing up your own work papers to solve a problem.

Using a simple, easy to learn coding system, you instruct the computer to store and retrieve data, do calculations, and produce reports exactly as you would do by hand. (The only requirement is that you understand your own problem well enough to define it on paper.) Furthermore, once you've created your computer model by defining your problem and coding its solution, you never have to reformulate your model again (although the system gives you the flexibility to change your model any time you wish).

With this programming system, *Forbes* was able to create a detailed model of their circulation system. And please note: the important word here is *detailed*—for the *Forbes* model takes every unique circulation characteristic of the magazine into consideration: its frequency; its service periods; its new order, renewal and billing procedures and timing; its fulfillment and reporting system.

How the system works

To see how this system can accurately forecast circulation levels, let's examine a hypothetical magazine—the *ABC* magazine—a biweekly planning its circulation for four issues: May 1, May 15, June 1 and June 15.

First we consider every conceivable bit of information we have that has an effect on circulation level (Figure 1).

We start with the current date—March 14. The latest computer report, dated March 7, indicates that there are 560,000 active paid subscriptions on file. This number is input into the model as the "Beginning Subscription Inventory." However, we know more than the computer does because it's now March 14, and we know that our mail room has counted an additional 2,000 new subscriptions during the week. We input this figure, and the model reports it under "New orders not yet entered on system." These new subs will be started with the May 1 issue.

In addition, fulfillment reports indicate that 5,000 subscriptions were received and processed during the first two weeks in March (1-13) and given an issue start date of May 1. These are entered and show up in the model under "Advance Starts." These reports also show the number of subscribers due to be dropped from the file—subscribers who have not renewed and subscribers who have not paid.

For the moment, we record these potential expirations in our model under the category *Offs*; if the mail were to stop today, all of these expirations would, in fact, be taken off the file at the end of the service period of the issue on which they're due to expire. However, we know that before the end of these same periods we'll receive a large number of renewals and payments from this group. In fact, we can and do estimate this figure very precisely.

Estimating renewals and payments

Estimating renewals and payments accurately is crucial to circulation planning. A renewal or payment estimate which is in error by even 1,000 an issue (a seemingly small amount for a magazine with 500,000 to 600,000 circulation) can be extremely disruptive to direct mail planning because the number of names required for your next direct mail campaign depends on the number of new subs needed (it may take 50,000 or 100,000 in direct mail to generate each 1,000 new subs).

Since direct mail planning could be off by as much as 2.5 million names over the period of a year, and since rate base objectives would then suffer accordingly, a detailed up-to-the-minute forecast of renewals and payments becomes the next step in circulation planning.

A precise method of forecasting this information requires a source-by-source, effort-by-effort renewal estimate for each expire group that is currently receiving renewal promotions—obviously, a very detailed and tedious job. Fortunately, computers are designed to do such jobs quickly, accurately, and inexpensively.

In renewal and payment estimating, again we start by recording all of the relevant information that we have. Figure 2 is a renewal estimate for subscriptions due to expire with the June 15 issue.

Source classification refers to the different categories of subscription sources—regular subs, direct mail subs, agency subs, insert card subs—which renew at different rates. For example, regular subscribers usually renew better than subscribers who subscribed through direct mail or through subscription agencies. And insert cards might renew better than direct mail.

Mail dates of various efforts are taken directly from your renewal schedule.

Quantities mailed which occurred previous to the current date (3/15, in our example) are taken directly from the most current renewal reports. Mail quantities on efforts yet to be mailed are calculated by the model, simply by subtracting renewals from the previous mail quantity.

Actual mailing quantities are input into the model from renewal reports each time the model is updated. This is a key point: We make use of actual data as soon as such data are available.

Renewals are estimated by multiplying the estimated response (based on past history of these efforts to this source classification) by the estimated mail quantity (as it now stands), thus giving us the total number of renewals.

We must keep in mind, however, that this report will not tell us *when* the renewals will be received; and those renewals which are not received until *after* the subscription has expired are too late to be counted in the paid subscription total of their expire issue.

Renewal distribution

Obviously, the late renewals will be put back on the file in subsequent issues. The next step, then, in accurate planning is to distribute the renewal estimates over the time they will most likely be received in the mail room (Figure 3).

Let's look at effort 2, mailed on 1/14/80, from which we expect to receive 475 renewals. To estimate how these renewals will be distributed over time we refer to past renewal response patterns. Future renewals can reason-

Figure 1—ABC Magazine
Circulation forecast as of March 15, 1980

Rate Base: 575,000
For Period Beginning: March 15, 1980
Actual Data Through: March 14, 1980

Issue: Service Period:	May 1 3/15 - 3/31	May 15 4/1 - 4/14	June 1 4/15 - 4/30	June 15 5/1 - 5/14
Beginning Subscription Inventory[1]	560,000	563,000	563,000	565,500
Offs				
Actual Expires[2]	12,000	17,000	19,000	13,000
Est. Renewals	500	500	1,000	1,500
Est. Expire Drops	(11,500)	(16,500)	(18,000)	(11,500)
Open Charges[3]	2,000	2,000	2,500	3,500
Est. Payments	500	500	1,000	1,500
Est. Bad Pay Drops	(1,500)	(1,500)	(1,500)	(2,000)
Ons				
Direct Mail	5,000	10,000	15,000	10,000
Renewals After Expiration	3,000	4,000	4,000	3,500
Payments After Bad Pay Drop	—0—	—0—	—0—	—0—
Other New	2,000	4,000	3,000	3,500
New Orders Not Entered on System[4]	2,000	—	—	—
Advance Starts[5]	4,000	—	—	—
Total New	16,000	18,000	22,000	17,000
Ending Sub Inventory	563,000	563,000	565,500	569,000
N/S Sales	20,000	20,000	18,000	15,000
ABC Deduction	(5,000)	(5,000)	(5,000)	(5,000)
Grace Copies	—0—	—0—	—0—	—0—
	578,000	578,000	578,000	579,000
+/- Rate Base	+3,000	+3,000	+3,500	+4,000

1. Actual Subs on File Thru 3/7

2. Actual Subs due to drop on this particular issue if renewal is not received by end of service period.

3. Actual Charge Subs due to be dropped from active file for non-payment if not received by end of service period.

4. New orders already received and counted in mail room but not in computer total.

5. Orders received in earlier service period but supplemented to later start issue.

Figure 2—ABC Magazine
Renewal estimate as of March 15, 1980
June 15 Issue Expires

Previous Source Classification	Effort	Mail Date	Mail Quantity	Percent Response	Percent Renewals
Regular Subs	1	12/14/79	5,000	5%	250
	2	1/14/80	4,750	10%	475
	3	2/14/80	4,275	10%	427
	4	3/14/80	3,848	8%	308
	5	4/14/80	3,540*	6%	212
	6	5/14/80	3,328*	5%	166
	7	6/14/80	3,146*	4%	126

*Indicates an estimate

ably be expected to be distributed in approximately the same proportion.

After assembling past data on total renewals responding to any renewal effort, we find that during the past year, an average of 2 percent responded during the second week after the effort was mailed.

When we apply this figure to our current estimation problem (multiply 2 percent x 475 total renewals), we can expect to receive about 10 renewals in the second week after effort 2 was mailed to regular expires of the June 15 issue.

This procedure must then be applied to all the remaining efforts: Total renewals received in the third week after the renewal effort was mailed average 10 percent (10 percent x 475 = 47); 20 percent in the fourth week, and so on.

Now, to find out how many renewals will be received prior to the expire date of 4/14, we simply draw a

Figure 3—ABC Magazine renewal distribution June 15 issue expires

Calendar Week (columns 1/15–1/22 through 4/7–4/14) — **Expire cut-off date** (columns 4/15–4/22 through 7/1–7/6)

Previous Source Classification	Effort	Mail Date	Renewals	1/15-1/22	1/23-1/31	2/1-2/7	2/8-2/15	2/16-2/22	2/23-3/1	3/2-3/7	3/8-3/14	3/15-3/31	4/1-4/6	4/7-4/14	4/15-4/22	4/23-4/30	5/1-5/6	5/7-5/14	5/15-5/21	5/22-5/30	6/1-6/7	6/8-6/14	6/15-6/21	6/22-6/30	7/1-7/6
Regular Subs	1	12/14/79	250	(4)* 50	(5) 88	(6) 37	(7) 25	(8) 20	—	—	—	—	—	—	—	—	—	—	—	—	—	—	—	—	—
	2	1/14/80	475	(1) 0	(2) 10	(3) 47	(4) 95	(5) 166	(6) 71	(7) 47	(8) 38	—	—	—	—	—	—	—	—	—	—	—	—	—	—
	3	2/14/80	427	—	—	—	—	(1) 0	(2) 9	(3) 43	(4) 85	(5) 149	(6) 64	(7) 43	(8) 34	—	—	—	—	—	—	—	—	—	—
	4	3/14/80	308	—	—	—	—	—	—	—	—	(1) 0	(2) 6	(3) 31	(4) 62	(5) 108	(6) 46	(7) 31	(8) 25	—	—	—	—	—	—
	5	4/14/80	212	—	—	—	—	—	—	—	—	—	—	—	—	(1) 0	(2) 4	(3) 21	(4) 44	(5) 75	(6) 32	(7) 21	(8) 17	—	—
	6	5/14/80	166	—	—	—	—	—	—	—	—	—	—	—	—	—	—	—	(1) 0	(2) 3	(3) 17	(4) 33	(5) 58	(6) 25	(7) 17
	7	6/14/80	126	—	—	—	—	—	—	—	—	—	—	—	—	—	—	—	—	—	(1) 0	(2) 2	(3) 13	(4) 25	(5) 44
	Total			50	98	84	120	186	80	90	123	149	70	74	96	108	50	52	69	78	49	56	88	50	61

Total prior to expire 1,124

Renewals after expire 757

Renewal response pattern:
*Week After Mail Date: (1) (2) (3) (4) (5) (6) (7) (8)
% of Renewals Received: 0 2% 20% 35% 15% 10% 8% 8%

line and add up renewals prior to expire (1,124) and those coming in after expire (757). When you consider that this process is repeated for every effort of every source classification for every active expire group, you begin to see the level of detail and complexity involved.

Direct mail estimate

Next we estimate direct mail in the same level of detail, key by key, based on most current plans and past experience.

There are three variables in direct mail: mail date, mail quantity and response rates. In the initial stages of direct mail planning, all three are unknown. As time goes on, the information becomes more exact. Our list broker at first gives us an estimate of the number of names he will send us on each key. Later, when the list comes in, we can get an exact count.

Although we may have a general idea of when we want to mail, the fluctuations in circulation prevent us from knowing in advance the *best* date. And although we can make an educated guess of the response we expect from a particular mailing package to a particular list, our information is by no means precise until well after the response begins to come in.

The direct mail model in Figure 4 can take into account all the most current information we have about our direct mail—whether it's in the planning stages or well under way—and that can give us a bottom line verdict on how many new subs will be available for each issue on our planning horizon. It works just like the renewal and payment estimates. We update it each week with the latest information from our list broker, lettershop, or latest direct mail promotion report. If we find out we're short 100,000 names on a key list, we let the model know. If we're getting a particularly hot response on a particular mailing, we revise our response estimate in the model. The result is an accurate forecast of direct mail for each issue on our planning horizon, given the limitation of our own knowledge.

The methodology we have just applied to estimating renewals and direct mail can also be applied to the estimation of other sources such as insert cards, space and gift subscriptions. Although agency subscriptions and single-copy sales are estimated independently of the system for this particular magazine, the system does have the flexibility to exactly represent any subscription, single-copy or bulk circulation source. In fact, the model can be designed to incorporate all the variables and assess their cumulative effect on circulation over the planning horizon.

At this point, we are now able to take action with the assurance that the best, most accurate and up-to-date information has been automatically carried through the system by the computer and is reflected in the circulation forecast (Figure 1). Now for our next step: using the model for planning.

Using the forecast

When we examine the system's forecast of March 15 (Figure 1), we find that circulation is right on target, above rate base by a comfortable margin of 3,000 to 4,000 on each issue. However, the March 23 forecast (Figure 5) a week later indicates a number of things that disturb this comfortable margin. The number of direct mail subscriptions expected between April 1 and April 14 (and started with the May 15 issue) is below estimate by 2,000. This means the May 15 issue will be above rate base only by a slight margin of 1,000. And this subscription shortfall carries through to the June 1 issue as well.

Moreover, renewals of the June 15 issue expires are coming in behind estimate by 500, and the estimate of newsstand sales of the same issue has been revised downward by 2,000. The circulation forecast indicates that the June 15 issue will be under rate base by 1,500.

With such a detailed quantitative picture of the effect these events will have on circulation totals, however, we are now in a position to plan logical actions to correct the situation.

Our thinking at this point might proceed as follows: We're now in a precarious position. We're only marginally above rate base on the May 15 and June 1 issues, with only a few weeks to take action. It is now March 23, and the

Figure 4—ABC Magazine
Direct mail estimate

					April 1		April 15		May 1		May 15	
Key	Mail Qty.	Mail Date	% Resp.	Est. Orders	2/8-2/15	2/16-2/22	2/23-3/1	3/2-3/7	3/8-3/14	3/15-3/31	4/1-4/6	4/7-4/14
Campaign 100												
101	50M	2/1	1.7	850	68	85	212	255	128	85	17	0
102	100M	2/1	1.8	1,800	144	180	450	540	270	180	36	0
103	150M	2/1	2.0	3,000	240	300	750	900	450	300	60	0
104	150M	2/8	2.1	3,150	0	252	315	788	945	472	315	63
105	50M	2/8	2.2	1,100	0	88	110	275	330	165	110	22
Total	500M			9,900	452	905	1,837	2,758	2,123	1,202	538	85

Direct mail response pattern:

Week After Mail Date:	1	2	3	4	5	6	7	8
% New Orders Received:	0	8%	10%	25%	30%	15%	10%	2%

Figure 5—ABC Magazine
Circulation Forecast as of March 23, 1980

(One Week Later)

Rate Base: 575,000
For period beginning: March 23, 1980
Actual Data Through: March 22, 1980

Issue:	May 1	May 15	June 1	June 15
Service Period:	3/23 - 3/31	4/1 - 4/14	4/15 - 4/30	5/1 - 5/14
Beginning Subscription Inventory (See fig. 1)	569,000	563,000	561,000	563,500
Offs				
Actual Expires	11,750	16,900	18,900	12,500
Est. Renewals	250	400	900 (Renewals Down 500)	500
Est. Expire Drops	(11,500)	(16,500)	(18,000)	(12,000)
Open Charges	1,750	1,900	2,400	3,400
Est. Payments	250	400	900	1,400
Est. Bad Pay Drops	(1,500)	(1,500)	(1,500)	(2,000)
Ons				
Direct Mail	3,000	8,000 (Direct Mail Off 2,000)	15,000	10,000
Renewals After Expiration	3,000	4,000	4,000	3,500
Payments After Bad Pay Drop	-0-	-0-	-0-	-0-
Other New	1,000	4,000	3,000	3,500
New Orders Not Entered on System (3/15 - 3/22)	-0-			
Advance Starts	-0-			
Total New	7,000	16,000	22,000	17,000
Ending Sub Inventory	563,000	561,000	563,500	566,500
N/S Sales	20,000	20,000	18,000 (N/S Sales Off 3,000)	12,000
ABC Deduction	(5,000)	(5,000)	(5,000)	(5,000)
Grace Copies	-0-	-0-	-0-	-0-
	578,000	576,000	576,000	573,500
+/- Rate Base	+3,000	+1,000 (Slight margins Above Rate Base)	+1,500	-1,500 (Below Rate Base)

May 15 issue closes on April 14—three short weeks.

What are our alternatives? Not many at this late date because we can't do anything with direct mail. The mailings that are generating subscriptions for the May 15 issue are completed. Any change in mailing plans now would be too late to produce subscriptions for the May 15 issue. We could grace May 1 and May 15 expires that qualify if we are so inclined. But we want to avoid gracing unless it's absolutely necessary.

We have already planned and begun to execute a large direct mail campaign, however, which is expected to generate 25,000 subscriptions that would start with the June 1 and June 15 issues. We could supplement the May 15 issue by holding it open an additional week to give 2,000 new subs a May 15 start. Let's do this. And let's do the same thing with the June 1 issue.

The June 15 issue, however, presents a bigger problem. The forecast indicates that circulation on that issue will be under rate base by 1,500. However, here we have more options. We could run extra bind-in cards in the April 1 and April 15 issues. These would supply us with an additional 1,000 subs. We could also organize a space exchange with a friendly competitor that could generate 500 additional subs before May 14. Or we could increase the size of our direct mail campaign to give us the additional subscriptions we need.

Since we need roughly 4,500 additional subscriptions in order to reach our goal of exceeding rate base by 3,000, we decide to do all three things. Bind-ins give us 1,000 additional subs, the space exchange gives us 500, and we plan to mail 150,000 additional pieces of direct mail, giving us the remaining 3,000.

We know we have to hurry with the direct mail. But exactly *when* do we need to drop this additional mail in order to receive orders before May 14? Fortunately, the programming system offers a unique feature that enables us to determine our mail date in a matter of minutes. It's called the "What If" option and it works like this.

We can try out various mail dates, without rerunning the entire forecast, and the computer will report the effect on the circulation totals of the four issues on our planning horizon. First we try an April 15 mail date because that seems to be the earliest date possible to put together the additional mailings. We run that date through the computer and we find that circulation on the June 15 issue would increase by only 1,000 subs, not 3,000, because of the lateness of the mailing date. We would have to mail a few weeks earlier to receive all 3,000 in time to give them a June 15 start. But that is impossible.

However, we do have another option open to us. We could increase the mail quantity. Again, we employ the "What If" option on the computer. What if we increased the mail quantity to 250,000? The computer reports that we would produce a total of 5,000 subs, 1,600 of which would be received before May 14. Still not enough. We need 1,400 more. But the direct mail estimate indicates that 1,600 subs would be received the week following May 14. So we solve this problem by planning to supplement the June 15 issue with 1,400 subs expected during the week of 5/15 through 5/21.

The problem is solved. Once again we have a circulation plan which meets rate base goals on every issue.

Design is crucial; operation is easy

As you can see, the application of this programming system to circulation planning offers a measure of control not usually found in circulation management. Since its accuracy depends on a very high level of detail, it is critical that every important element in the circulation equation be accounted for. Thus, problem definition and system analysis by a knowledgeable circulation person is essential to the initial design of the model. However, once it's set up, it's so simple to operate that weekly updating and forecasting can be performed in an afternoon, even by someone inexperienced in circulation.

So don't give up on rate base management yet. With the right tools and expertise, the problem can be easily managed.

Circulation reporting methods

By John D. Klingel

A good reporting system is an integral part of management control. Unfortunately, although the publishing industry seems to attract very bright and talented people, good management skills do not seem to be their forte. Many magazines don't have reporting systems, budgets, reforecasting procedures, or other management control systems. No one can run a magazine by the seat of his pants: it is simply too complex a business. And any manager who doesn't review the operation regularly (*i.e.,* through regular reports, budgets, etc.) will soon find things getting out of control.

One of my first projects in the magazine business was to design a reporting system. The package of reports was designed to be kept in a single binder that every key manager could have at his fingertips. We worked for a publisher who had absolutely no patience and hated to be kept waiting on the phone while someone groped around for numbers. When he wanted an answer, he wanted it immediately.

We code-named the reporting package the MAP Reports because we wanted a reporting package that not only told us where we had been but also showed us where we planned to go.

Before we discuss how to design an effective reporting package, however, let's look at some of the major functions that reports serve.

Presenting information

First of all, reports provide a historical record so that you can observe trends. Certain statistics, such as renewal rates and newsstand sales, are a measure of editorial vitality. During or just before recessions, it helps to be able to review what happened during prior recessions.

Second, reports can act as an early warning system. Unfavorable variances in new sub volume have implications for current and future rate base problems, cash flow, and P&L. Even a timing problem can create problems. One of the most important elements of dealing successfully with problems is early identification of the problems.

Third, reports serve as a constant check on how well actual performance compares to the operating plan. If expenses are over budget this month, something may have to be cut in future months to meet the full year budget.

And finally, reports provide easy access to key statistical data when you're performing profitability analysis or trying to analyze variances from budget. They also provide management with a common set of numbers so that everyone is looking at the same data when discussing trends or problems.

When you're designing reports for your company, you should keep the above functions in mind. Following are a few comments and suggestions for designing reports:

•Reports should be designed with a knowledge of what information management wants and needs. If management is used to looking at data in certain formats, use those formats. One of the key objectives of report design is to make them easy for management to review.

•Numbers should not be generated just for the sake of numbers. Reports should be designed so that they include only key pieces of data. Even the most numbers-oriented people get turned off by masses of numbers. In addition, if it is too difficult to generate the reports, eventually they won't be maintained properly or the only thing the circulation department will do is generate reports.

•Reporting systems should be designed with the concept of exception reporting in mind. The first thing the report reader should see is a summary. If a reader wants more data, he can turn to more detailed back-up reports. If there are no variances from plan, there may be no need to review all the details.

•All reporting packages should be accompanied by a narrative summary that highlights the key variances, results, or trends. All management personnel are deluged with data and are extremely busy. Never assume that they will notice important facts: the narrative should draw their attention to them.

•It is difficult for the eye to read many numbers on a single report. Good design of reports is just as important to the reporting package as good design is to a magazine.

•Numbers must always be compared to something if they are to communicate effectively. The usual things numbers are compared to are budgets, forecasts, prior year, and prior month.

•Reports must be timely if they are to be effective. Ancient history can be very interesting but it doesn't help solve problems if the data arrives too late.

•Different reports require different frequencies. Some types of reports lend themselves to monthly frequency while others should be generated only on an "as needed" basis. I personally find that monthly renewal reports showing response by effort are almost "too much" and that detailed renewal analysis is easier to review on a quarterly basis.

There's no way that any one report package design can fill the needs of all magazines. In the following discussion, the examples of reports and the overall reporting package are not going to be applicable to all magazines. They are intended only as examples that may help you design reports for your operation.

There are also many different ways that reports can be formatted and the formats shown here should probably be redesigned to reflect specific characteristics of your publication.

The reporting package

Example I is a table of contents for a hypothetical reporting package like the MAP reports that I mentioned earlier. The reports are kept in a three-ring binder and new sections are added and old ones taken out as needed.

The activity reports consist of weekly and monthly reports and are constantly being updated. The history reports are updated on an annual basis and are used for reference. The financial reports include the monthly updated P&L and operating statistics with the budget being updated annually. The operating reports are updated on an "as needed" basis.

This may look like a major undertaking but usually it's not. Most of the history reports are probably sitting in files gathering dust. The financial reports should be prepared as a regular function of running a business. The activity reports are where most of the work exists, and if the report package is designed correctly, even these shouldn't entail that much work.

The major activity report for subscription sales is the Sales by Source Report (see Example II). In Example I, I showed a number of reports listed under the Sales by Source Report, i.e., Direct Mail, Renewals, etc. The concept here is to provide detailed reports to back up the summary sales by source report.

Obviously, the sources that are reflected will change from magazine to magazine. I've shown a number of formats that are intended only to give you some ideas for a report package that would be suitable for your publication. There's nothing sacred about these formats. In all cases, they are formats that are or have been used by a variety of magazines but they may not be appropriate for your situation. (By the way, all the numbers are fictitious so don't waste time trying to figure out what magazine they represent.)

The various reports

Sales by Source (Example II)—On the left-hand side, the sources are broken into two major categories: renewals and new business. Under renewals, I've shown three categories under the heading Identifiable Renewals. An identifiable renewal is one that comes back on a renewal form as opposed to a direct mail or insert card order that's a renewal mixed with new business.

Some magazines refer to these as direct and indirect renewals. In the report I've shown, the indirect or unidentifiable renewals are included with the new business. Some magazines break the indirect renewals out of the new business and show them as a separate category. Note that the report shows the cut-off date and the update

Example I
REPORT PACKAGE

Activity Reports
A. Sales by source
 1. Direct mail
 2. Renewals
 3. Insert cards
 4. Agents
 5. Space (incl. schedule of future trades)
 6. Other sources
B. Newsstand
C. Advertising
D. Other income

History Reports
A. Publisher's statements
B. Sales by source (annual summaries)
C. History of direct mail campaigns (summaries)
D. Renewal history
E. Price history
F. Newsstand sales history
G. Ad sales history

Financial Reports
A. P & L for current month
B. Budget
C. Key operating statistics

Operating Reports
A. Status of tests
B. Billing and renewal schedules
C. Print-order projections

Example II
SUBSCRIPTION SALES BY SOURCE

MONTH OF July 1981

Returns Through 7/29 (Update of 8/5)

	Current Month		Year-to-Date			Previous Year	
						Current	
	Actual	Budget	Actual	Budget	Variance	Month	Y-T-D
Identifiable Renewals							
Regular efforts	6,000	5,000	50,000	52,000	(2,000)	5,000	45,000
Advance renewals	--	--	10,000	8,000	2,000	--	6,000
RAB's	300	500	3,300	3,500	(200)	500	3,500
Total renewals	6,300	5,500	63,300	63,500	(200)	5,500	54,500
New Business							
Direct mail	43,000	50,000	43,000	50,000	(7,000)	45,000	45,000
Insert cards	1,200	1,000	8,400	7,000	1,400	1,000	7,000
Gifts	100	100	1,000	700	300	50	600
Exchange ads	800	400	3,500	2,800	700	500	2,500
Catalog agents	150	100	1,200	1,100	100	100	1,000
School plans	--	--	3,000	3,500	(500)	--	3,500
Direct mail agents	1,000	--	8,000	5,000	3,000	500	4,500
Miscellaneous sources	200	150	1,500	1,050	450	150	1,050
Total new	46,450	51,750	69,600	71,150	(1,550)	47,300	65,150
Total orders	52,750	57,250	132,900	134,650	(1,750)	52,800	119,650

Example III
IDENTIFIED RENEWALS BY EFFORT

Expire and Description	Effort	Date mailed	Code	Quantity mailed	This month	To date	Gross percent
September 1981							
Effort 1	1	5/17	1EE1	3000	-	450	15.0
Effort 2	2	6/25	1EE2	2800	5	336	12.0
Effort 3	3	7/25	1EE3	2500	1	175	7.0
Effort 4	4	8/28	1EE4	2200	4	88	4.0
Effort 5	5	10/1	1EE5	2000	10	60	3.0
Telephone	6	11/15	1EE6	1950	50	117	6.0

Example IV

INSERT CARDS
November 1981

Business through 11/25/81
Update of 12/2/81

Issue	Description	Offer	Code	Quantity Mailed	Returns This Month	Returns To Date	Percent
April 1981	Sub bind-in	12/12	4401	100,000	-	780	.78
	Sub blow-in	"	4402	100,000	-	420	.42
	NWS bind-in	"	4403	20,000	1	342	1.71
	NWS blow-in	"	4404	20,000	1	290	1.45
				Total	2	1,832	1.53
May 1981	Sub bind-in	"	4501	100,000	1	710	.71
	Sub blow-in	"	4502	100,000	3	490	.49
	NWS bind-in	"	4503	20,000	1	428	2.14
	NWS blow-in	"	4504	20,000	2	340	1.70
				Total	7	1,968	1.64
June 1981	Sub bind-in	"	4601	100,000	4	650	.65
	Sub blow-in	"	4602	100,000	3	320	.32
	NWS bind-in	"	4603	20,000	1	366	1.83
	NWS blow-in	"	4604	20,000	-	298	1.49
				Total	8	1,634	1.36

Example V

AGENCY PRODUCTION

	Current month	Current year	Last year month	1980 Y-T-D	Percent change
American Ed. Service	100	700	70	500	40%
Campus	500	3,000	200	2,000	50
EBSCO	150	700	175	700	-
Educ. Subscr. Service	200	1,000	150	800	25
Publisher's Clearing Hs.	5,000	35,000	3,000	20,000	75
University Sub. Svs.	200	1,000	100	500	100
All Other	300	3,000	400	3,500	(14)
Total Direct Mail Agents	6,450	44,400	4,095	28,000	59%
Perfect	-	200	-	150	33%
Sunland	-	250	-	100	150
Quality School Plan	-	2,000	-	1,000	100
Total School Plan	0	2,450	0	1,250	96%
Alesco	70	210	50	200	5%
Black	100	300	200	200	50
EBSCO	1,000	3,000	500	2,500	20
Faxon	150	400	50	450	(11)
Instructor	50	100	100	100	-
McGregor	60	120	40	100	20
Midsouth	75	300	100	150	100
Moore—Cottrell	800	2,000	1,000	1,500	33
Nat'l Org. Pacific	100	150	200	250	(40)
Nat'l Org. Service	200	400	100	300	33
Popular	25	100	25	125	(20)
South East Sub.	10	50	20	50	-
Turner	100	200	150	100	100
West Coast Org. Plan	500	1,500	300	1,000	50
All Other	300	1,000	200	1,200	(17)
Total Catalog	3,540	9,830	3,035	8,225	20%
Total Agents	9,990	56,680	7,130	37,475	51%

Example VI
NEWSSTAND SALES

Issue (1981)	National Distributor			Direct Sales			Foreign			Total		
	Draw	Sale	Percent	Draw	Sale	Percent	Draw	Sale	Percent	Draw	Sale	Percent
Jan.	200,000	90,000	45	7,600	3,800	50	5,000	2,600	52	212,600	96,400	45
Feb.	200,000	70,000	35	8,700	4,350	50	5,500	2,860	52	214,200	77,210	36
Mar.	200,000	80,000	40	8,525	4,275	50	5,800	3,016	52	214,325	91,541	43
Apr.	200,000	75,000	37	7,800	3,900	50	3,500	1,820	52	211,300	80,720	38
May	200,000	84,000	42	9,400	4,700	50	6,900	3,588	52	216,300	92,288	43
June	225,000	88,000	39	8,800	4,450	51	7,900	4,108	52	241,700	96,558	40
July	225,000	94,500	42	9,325	4,749	51	7,500	3,900	52	241,825	103,149	43
Aug.	250,000	100,000	40	12,175	6,331	52	7,500	3,900	52	269,675	110,231	41
Sept.	250,000	105,000	42*	11,000	6,000	55*	9,000	4,680	52*	270,000	115,680	43
Oct.	250,000	112,500	45*	11,000	6,000	55*	9,000	4,680	52*	270,000	123,180	46
Nov.	250,000	125,000	50*	11,000	6,000	55*	9,000	4,680	52*	270,000	135,680	50
Averages	222,700	93,000		10,007	5,187	52	7,303	3,798	52	240,010	101,985	42

*Estimated

Example VII
RENEWALS BY MONTH
Source: School Plan
Year: 1980

Expire Month	Renewal Series Renewals						All Other Renewals							Total Renewals		
	Eft. #1 Qty. Mld.	Ident. Ren'ls		Unident. Ren'ls		Ren'ls At Birth		Advance Ren'ls		Total RAB	Unident. Adv.		Expire Qty.	Expire	
		#	%	#	%	#	%	#	%	#	#	%		#	%
JAN	1,387	261	18.82	202	14.16	0	--	40	2.80	242		16.96	1,427	503	35.25
FEB	140	33	23.57	32	21.48	0	--	9	6.04	41		27.52	149	74	49.66
MAR	90	17	18.89	9	9.47	0	--	5	5.26	14		14.74	95	31	32.63
APR	473	121	25.58	30	5.92	0	--	34	6.70	64		12.62	507	185	36.49
MAY	292	68	23.29	18	5.83	0	--	17	5.50	35		11.33	309	103	33.33
JUN	163	39	23.93	11	6.47	0	--	7	4.12	18		10.59	170	57	33.53
1st HALF	2,545	539	21.18	302	11.37	0	--	112	4.22	414		15.59	2,657	953	35.87
JUL	157	32	20.38	14	8.33	0	--	11	6.55	25		14.88	168	57	33.93
AUG	20	8	40.00	0	--	0	--	6	23.08	6		23.08	26	14	53.85
SEP	13	5	38.46	1	5.88	0	--	4	23.53	5		29.41	17	10	58.82
OCT	55	11	20.00	8	12.90	0	--	7	11.29	15		24.19	62	26	41.94
NOV	403	80	19.85	25	6.00	0	--	14	3.36	39		9.35	417	119	28.54
DEC	2,268	479	21.12	182	7.85	0	--	49	2.12	231		9.97	2,317	710	30.64
2nd HALF	2,916	615	21.09	230	7.65	0	--	91	3.03	321		10.68	3,007	936	31.13
YEAR	5,461	1,154	21.13	532	9.39	0	--	203	3.58	735		12.97	5,664	1,889	33.35

date.

Direct Mail (no example shown)—This report has an irregular frequency with frequent updates during the height of a campaign and then a time gap between gross response reports and final pay-up reports, list ranking, etc.

Renewals (Example III)—What I've shown here is one segment of a series of reports showing response by effort. These reports should be broken down by expire group and major sources, (*e.g.*, renewal before, direct mail conversions, etc.), if your fulfillment company reports this data. Usually a monthly frequency is difficult to maintain because at any given time there may be six to 12 expire groups under promotion. I personally find that I get more out of this type of report if it's prepared on a quarterly basis.

Insert Cards (Example IV)—Each major source should be backed up with a detailed report. Here I've shown an example for insert cards and agency product (Example V). Similar reports should also be designed for space ads, newspaper stuffers, package inserts, and whatever other sources you may be using.

Newsstand (Example VI)—What I've shown here is only one of many different reports that can be used to report on newsstand activity. I didn't fill in the cover description column which should contain a short description of the cover.

Renewal History (Example VII)—This example shows the renewal history for one of the sources of subscriptions. This format is fairly sophisticated. If your fulfillment company doesn't report this data, you could simplify the format. The key here is that the ability to show renewal history by source allows you to analyze trends and develop good assumptions for budgets and forecasts.

In this format, the columns to the left show the renewals produced by the renewal series. The other columns show the indirect renewals, renewals at birth (renewals obtained through the billing series) and advance renewals. The final columns show the total renewal rate for the source.

Under the heading Operating Reports (Example I), I've listed a few reports that are frequent reference reports, (*e.g.*, billing and renewal schedules and print-order projections) that may not be appropriate for reporting packages that go outside the circulation department. Consequently, these reports may be only in the circulation department report binders, and the other departments may have reference reports that pertain only to that department.

The status of test reports lists all the tests that are being planned or are in process. This report could contain a status update on other projects as well.

Source Evaluation

By J. Wendell Forbes

Selecting which sources of subscriptions to use to maintain and develop circulation in the most economical fashion is one of the most important decisions a circulation manager must make. And there is a bewildering array of subscription sources and newsstand options from which to choose.

More and more circulation managers are turning to a process known as Source Evaluation to help them make better decisions. (I am proud to be among the 400 people who invented the concept!) The logic and simplicity of this process is such that it makes for an impressive presentation to management, thus gaining confidence in (if not full understanding of) the decision process. In my experience, successful circulation directors use Source Evaluation as the basis for deciding from among all new business options, thus prohibiting emotions or preconceptions (their own or their management's) about the desirability of one source over another to influence their final judgment.

Now that circulation has been elevated from check-book accounting to an economic subculture and everybody is getting into the act, the only recourse a circulation manager has is to try once more to communicate the unique interplay of factors that affect the circulation P&L to top management.

Historically, top management has shied away from circulation details, because if they asked what the renewal percent was, they got a two-hour answer in a language they didn't understand. Whether from curiosity or necessity, the fact that publishing management is forcing itself to become more knowledgeable about circulation is an extremely important and encouraging event.

Decisions handed down by top management are only as good as the information given to them on which to base those decisions. And how information is communicated is as important as its content. In computer circles they say, "Garbage in/garbage out." In management we might say, "Garbage up/garbage down." Poor communicators are destined to live with unsound, and sometimes bewildering, directives.

The Source Evaluation System proposed here will only be of half its value to you if you use it yourself but continue to talk gibberish to the boss. It will be of full value to you if you demonstrate to your management how it works and thus gain their confidence.

Picture a chart presentation to top management that says, "Here are all the circulation sources available to us, listed in order from maximum net revenue per copy to minimum." And alongside each source is a number indicating the maximum potential subs available from that source. The circulation manager points out that he or she is currently using sources down to here, and dramatically draws a line across the chart.

The scene continues:

Circulation Manager: If we increase our base I will have to use several new sources beyond those now in use but the net per copy index isn't all that bad.

Publisher: What about renewals? I don't see them on the chart.

Circulation Manager: I'm glad you asked that question. In the process of calculating the net revenue figures, we have taken into account the complete and unique conversion and renewal history of each source, and it is reflected in the net revenue index. Hence by definition we are using sources that convert and renew well.

Publisher: What the hell is a conversion?!

Circulation Manager: I'm glad you asked that, too. It is simply the first-time renewal of a source and is treated separately from regular renewals because it can vary greatly from source to source and has a very large influence on the outcome of the evaluation.

Publisher: Now I understand all this, but what happens to your bottom line if we increase the price as we've been talking about *and* increase the base?

Circulation Manager: Anticipating your question, I reviewed our price test results and have compared our current forecast, which assumes no price or base increase, with three forecasts: 1. Price increase only; 2. Base increase only; 3. Base and price increase. And here are the results as worked out on our fully computerized circulation model. All three options have a considerable economic impact on years one and two but we believe a recovery is logical in year three and by year four we're better off on the P&L than we are now. Option three, of course, brings revenue in from another stream, i.e., advertising and option two involves servicing more copies, so we must look at the complete magazine P&L for all three options before we can make a decision. I therefore got together with the business manager and advertising director and here's what the whole magazine P&L looks like under the three options. It appears from these figures that if strategic considerations permit, we should hold our subscription price for six to nine months, go up in base as soon as possible and then consider a price increase.

And so it goes. Sounds crisp and logical and eminently understandable. The scenario is within the reach of anyone who cares to take the trouble and invest some time and discipline in developing historical experiences, accurate, current information and a way of looking at circulation—not as a snapshot, but as a panning process.

The case for modeling in magazine publishing has been made many times in the pages of this magazine. Examination of options, whether done by hand or by computer, is essential to good circulation management. If you

don't have access to computerized forecasting (and the game playing that goes with it), then at least learn how to use Source Evaluation. If you pick sources on the basis of their net revenue, the circulation mix will, by definition, produce more revenue. Net revenue per copy is a meaningful measure of not only economics but also quality of circulation because of the heavy influence that conversion and renewal percentages have on the outcome.

Referred to by many names, and formally and informally used by most circulation directors, Source Evaluation is simply a method of evaluating all subscription sources on the same basis (i.e., a common denominator), in order that they may be compared in relative value by an index of net income per copy as opposed to first costs.

The rationale for Source Evaluation is that there is much more to the cost and revenue of circulation than the first costs of a new sub. When a circulation manager buys a new sub he or she also buys the right to future renewals, insofar as they can be obtained through his or her promotional efforts. The reason the evaluation must be taken through conversion (first renewal) and renewal phases is because different sources have different conversion and renewal characteristics.

Comparative Source Evaluation permits the circulation manager to decide which is the most profitable source, fully exploit that source and then move on to the next most profitable source, and the next, as needs dictate.

If the circulation manager chooses circulation sources based on which produce the highest net revenue, he or she can't go far wrong in managing effectively.

Thus by using the arithmetic of Source Evaluation we can compare the following options:

1. A nine-month trial offer at $6.75 sold by direct mail costing $175/M and generating a response of 3.25 percent, a bad pay of 18 percent, converting at 35 percent, with 10 percent of the subs migrating from other sources and renewing thereafter at 60 percent, and

2. An 18-month offer for $13.50 sold through a school plan agency with no bad pay, a cancel rate of 8 percent, at a commission of 75 percent, converting at 30 percent with half of the subs coming back through the agent and renewing thereafter at 60 percent.

Try eyeballing these two sources and deciding which is the more profitable and you will become an instant convert to Computerized Source Evaluation.

There are two methods of Source Evaluation. One is called the *Depletion Method,* whereby a block of 1,000 new subscriptions simply runs its course (depletes) through conversion, renewal of conversion and renewal of renewal for a period of, say, six years.

The second is called the *Maintenance Method,* and in this method a level of 1,000 circulation is maintained by replacing expires with new subs from the source being evaluated.

Depletion Method
A chart will help visualize the subscription dynamics of this method:

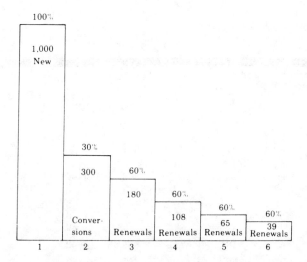

For the sake of simplicity and sanity we assume that all subs, new, conversion and renewals are for one-year terms.

Maintenance Method

The underlying calculations for the Maintenance Method are exactly the same as those for the Depletion Method. Only the subscription dynamics are charted differently. As its title suggests, the Maintenance Method is formulated to maintain a certain level of circulation replacing expirations with new subs *from the same source being evaluated.*

Here's how it looks in chart form, again assuming one-year terms, 30 percent conversion rate and a 60 percent renewal rate:

Year or Period

	1	2	3	4	5	6
New 100%	1,000	700	610	583	574	572
Conversion 30%		300	210	183	175	172
Renewal 60%			180	126	110	105
Renewal 60%				108	76	66
Renewal 60%					65	46
Renewal 60%						39
Renewal 60%						
	1,000	1,000	1,000	1,000	1,000	1,000

For convenience and ease of visualization when the new subs are converted they are entered under the second column one line down, and when they are renewed they are entered in column three, three lines down. For instance, following the arrows above, the 700 new subscriptions needed to build the circulation back up to 1,000 in period two are converted at 30 percent or 210 subs. These are then renewed in each of the following periods at 60 percent or 126, 76 and 46. The number of new subscriptions needed in each period to maintain 1,000 circulation is calculated by simply adding up the carried-forward conversions and renewals in any column and adding enough new subs to restore the 1,000 level.

Once the *subscription dynamics* have been charted for either method we must calculate the gross revenue per sub, the full cost per sub, net revenue per sub and average term per sub for each of the three types of sub—New, Conversion and Renewal.

These per sub figures are simply multiplied by the subscription figures in the charted models (either one) and the results can be filled in on this chart:

	Total Gross Revenue	Total Cost	Total Net Revenue	Copies Served
New				
Conversion				
Renewal				
Total	AAA	BBB	CCC	DDD

Gross Revenue per copy = Gross Revenue (AAA ÷ copies served DDD)

Net Revenue per copy = Net Revenue (CCC ÷ copies served DDD)

% Net Revenue to gross = Net Revenue ÷ Gross Revenue

(See accompanying sidebar on "How To Use The Depletion Method Manually.")

The complicated part of these calculations is not the charting of the subscription dynamics but the calculation of the true cost per sub of each source by New, Conversion and Renewal, and this requires more patience and persistence than skill. And you can't delegate this to the computer—it's part of the input, not part of the calculation. The gross, cost, net and copies-served calculations are arrived at by standard circulation arithmetic. For instance, the cost of a direct-mail sub is the response percent converted into net after bad pay subs per 1,000 divided into the full mail promotion cost per 1,000. (Thus: $225/M

Computerized Maintenance Method

The printout accompanying this article is an example of how Source Evaluation is handled by the computer.

There is much to be learned from studying a printout such as this. For instance, when do you recover first costs? Line 11, columns 1 and 2. What is the average term? Line 15. How many new subs must you buy to maintain 1,000? Line 2, columns 1-6. What is the return on investment? R.O.I., line 14.

The important statistic is the percentage of net revenue to gross dollars; this can be calculated for total dollars by dividing line 11, column 7, by line 9, column 7

($8,899 by $38,831). The net revenue percent can also be calculated on a per sub basis (line 13, **column 7,** line 12, column 7).

This particular example started by costing 56 cents per order more than the gross income or a revenue of minus 9 percent and ended up with a positive revenue of $1.59 per $6.92 sub, or 23 percent. When a number of sources, each with different characteristics, is put through this calculation a basis for decision making is created.

The input for this model is no more complicated than the simple arithmetic needed in the everyday management of circulation. It sure makes life simple. Use it!

Period Numbers	1	2	3	4	5	6	Cum/Ave
1. Subscription Dynamics							
2. Gross New Business	1111	849	740	682	648	631	4664
3. Net—Net New Business	1000	765	666	614	583	568	4197
Cash	1000	765	666	614	583	568	4197
Credit	0	0	0	0	0	0	0
4. Net Unident Renewals	0	0	0	0	0	0	0
Cash	0	0	0	0	0	0	0
Credit	0	0	0	0	0	0	0
5. Expires	0	1000	952	910	877	868	4609
6. Net Conversions	0	235	179	156	144	137	852
Cash	0	125	95	83	76	72	453
Credit	0	110	84	73	67	64	399
7. Net Ident Renewals	0	0	107	139	149	162	558
Cash	0	0	56	73	78	85	294
Credit	0	0	50	65	71	76	264
8. Overall Renewal Rate	0	.235	.301	.325	.335	.345	.306
Financial							
9. Revenues	5949	6419	6748	6665	6516	6530	38831
Conversions	0	1868	1429	1244	1148	1089	6779
Ident Renewals	0	0	1356	1763	1897	2056	7074
Unident Renewals	0	0	0	0	0	0	0
New Business	5949	4551	3963	3657	3470	3384	24976
10. Costs	6511	5449	4856	4535	4334	4245	29931
New Bus Exp	5933	4538	3951	3646	3460	3374	24906
Serve Bad Pay	0	17	20	20	20	20	100
Serve Req Cancels	177	135	118	109	103	101	746
Conversion Exp	0	299	229	199	184	174	1088
Renewal Exp	0	0	67	87	94	102	352
Billing Exp	0	56	68	70	70	71	336
Fulfillment Exp	399	399	399	399	399	399	2399
11. Return (Rev-Cost)	-561	970	1892	2129	2182	2285	8899
Statistics							
Adjusted Order Cost	5.93	5.93	5.93	5.93	5.93	5.93	5.93
Conv Cost/Net Conv	0.	1.28	1.28	1.28	1.28	1.28	1.28
Ir Prom Cost/Net Ir	0.	0.	.63	.63	.63	.63	.63
Tot rpc/tot Net Rnwl	0.	1.28	1.04	.97	.95	.93	1.02
New Bus Exp/Net Ord	5.93	5.93	5.93	5.93	5.93	5.93	5.93
Tot Ord Cost/Net Ord	5.93	4.84	4.46	4.32	4.26	4.21	4.70
Bill Exp/Cdt Ord Col	0.	.51	.51	.51	.51	.51	.51
Tot cost/net order							
Current period	6.51	5.45	5.10	4.98	4.94	4.89	5.34
Overall	6.51	5.98	5.69	5.53	5.42	5.34	5.34
Tot cost/net sub year							
Current period	6.51	5.45	4.86	4.54	4.33	4.25	4.99
Overall	6.51	5.98	5.61	5.34	5.14	4.99	4.99
12. Total rev/net ord							
Current period	5.95	6.42	7.08	7.32	7.43	7.52	6.92
Overall	5.95	6.18	6.47	6.67	6.81	6.92	6.92
13. Tot ret/net ord							
Current period	-.56	.97	1.99	2.34	2.49	2.63	1.59
Overall	-.56	.20	.78	1.15	1.40	1.59	1.59
14. Return on investment	-.09	.03	.14	.21	.26	.30	.30
15. Average term (copies)							
Current period	12.00	12.56	13.40	13.70	13.83	13.95	13.20
Overall	12.00	12.28	12.64	12.89	13.06	13.20	13.20
16. Copy value							
Current period	.50	.51	.53	.53	.54	.54	.52
Overall	.50	.50	.51	.52	.52	.52	.52

*Courtesy Policy Development Corporation

How to Use the Depletion Method Manually

1. Calculate true cost per net new sub by source (include bad pay, cancels, premium, return postage, fulfillment, etc. Also include impact of collection extensions if used by increasing gross and average term.)

2. Calculate true cost per net sub converted from the original new source. (Effectiveness of mail at the conversion stage is less efficient than in renewal stage and this fact should be acknowledged in the calculation. Include all costs noted under 1 above if applicable.)

3. Calculate true cost per net sub renewed from conversions. (Mail effectiveness is much higher on renewals and will result in some pretty low cost figures. Include any and all elements mentioned above if applicable.)

4. In the conversion and renewal phase, migrated conversions and renewals must be accounted for. (Migrated conversions and renewals are those that come from sources other than your direct to publisher renewal promotion.) This is done by calculating the weighted average of the cost of conversions and renewals direct to the publisher (the greater proportion) and the cost of conversions and renewals that come in from other sources. Thusly for renewals:

	Points	%	Cost	Wtg. Avg. Cost
Direct to Publisher	45	75	$0.60	$0.45
Migrated	15	25	1.00	$0.25
Total renewal %	60	100		
Wtg. Avg. Cost				$0.70

Therefore 70 cents becomes the true cost of the renewal. The same method is used for conversions.

5. Without going through the cost calculations which are fairly straightforward, if tedious, the following assumptions are made (assume all one-year subs).

Per Sub	New	Conversion	Renewal
Gross Income	$6.00	$6.00	$6.00
Cost	5.00	2.75	.70*
Net Income	$1.00	$3.25	$5.30

(*See item 4 above.)

6. The depletion dynamics are illustrated by the following diagram. It starts with an assumed purchase of 1,000 net subs from the source being evaluated. Conversion rate is 30 percent and renewal rate is 60 percent. Use net subs in all cases.

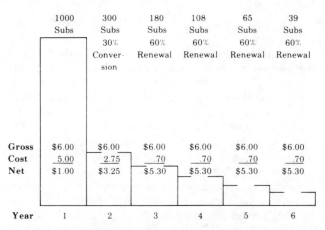

Depletion Dynamics Chart

÷ 3.7 percent or 37 subs per 1,000 = $6.08 per sub.)

As with anything that is portrayed as simply as this, there are a number of pretty important caveats. In this case it is the need for reliable statistics, either in hard or estimated form. If you are to evaluate each of several sources you must have statistics that are unique to each source (else it would be a pointless exercise). A conversion percentage for each source is mandatory as is a pure renewal of renewal percentage. Pressure should be brought to bear on your fulfillment house to provide these statistics. It should be pointed out, however, that any statistic required for Source Evaluation should already be available from the normal requirements of even the most casually run circulation department. It's just that we now put them together and create Source Evaluation.

Results of Source Evaluation

The results that may be expected of Source Evaluation are as follows:

● Each source will now have an index of profitability. The index is the net revenue per copy that takes into account conversion and renewal activity over a period of six years (or fewer but never less than three for a one-year original source).

● If each source is put on descending order of profitability and the estimated potential from each source alongside, you will have a handy and accurate basis for deciding on which sources to use.

● The array will become infinitely more valuable if you break out the direct-mail portion by list or some other form of stratification and calculate a Source Evaluation Index for each level. It is a fact that an overall response of 3 percent is made up of some segments at 5 or 6 percent and others at 1 or 2 percent. This type of thinking will lead you to all sorts of exciting refinements in your direct-mail program. Most certainly you will soon discover that you should cut off direct mail at a certain index, utilize another source and then go back into direct mail if necessary. Remember, the S/E Index reflects the whole economic character of a source so you don't have to pause at each decision point and wonder about renewal performance, front end costs and the like.

● Using Source Evaluation will make you so conscious of conversion percentage that you may end up with an obsession. Apart from upfront costs, the conversion percentage has the most leverage on results. In fact, a good conversion rate can smother high front end costs. No longer will you treat conversion and renewals as those nice

7. The calculation develops as follows: (All sub counts and costs are net of bad pay, cancels, etc.)

	Conversion	Revenue			Cost		Net	
Year	Ren.%	Subs	Per Sub	Total	Per Sub	Total	Per Sub	Total
1	—	1,000	$6.00	$6,000	$5.00	$5,000	$1.00	$1,000
2	30	300	6.00	1,800	2.75	825	3.25	975
3	60	180	6.00	1,080	.70	126	5.30	954
4	60	108	6.00	648	.70	76	5.30	572
5	60	65	6.00	390	.70	46	5.30	344
6	60	39	6.00	234	.70	27	5.30	207
		1,692		$10,152		$6,100		$4,052

Copies served: 1,692 x 12 = 20,304

Gross per copy: 10,152 ÷ 20,304 = $0.50 100%

Cost per copy: 6,100 ÷ 20,304 = 0.30 60%

Net per copy: 4,052 ÷ 20,304 = $0.20 40%

8. The punch line of this analysis is that new business which originally netted 16.7 percent ($1 on $6), when credited with its future earning ability, will net 40 percent over time including original costs. This, then, is the index that is to be compared with other sources and thus aid in the circulation source selection process.

9. There are, of course, other considerations beyond the net per copy. If direct mail works well for a given publication but upfront money is not available, other sources requiring no upfront cash must be considered. If there is a sudden need for circulation, some sources are more quickly turned on than others.

10. Source Evaluation is an organized way of looking at circulation. But one cannot be superorganized in one facet of his or her business and expect success. All aspects of the circulation operation must be well managed. Areas such as the budgeting function, what-if games, statistical and cost analysis, and testing are all input to Source Evaluation and full computerized forecasting.

11. Anyone who blindly follows a formula without knowing how it works deserves the predictable consequences.

12. Source Evaluation doesn't control costs or improve responses, conversions or renewals. It simply tells you which source is better than another and, by indirection, tells you that you must *do something* to alter the input and improve results.

trouble-free subs that seem to come in automatically at long term and low cost. You will soon realize that conversions and renewals can be very responsive to testing techniques and that a 15 to 25 percent improvement is not beyond reason (depending on where you start from).

• You will also become more aware of individual source characteristics. You will learn that you can trade off high upfront costs for high conversion performance.

• You will also be more sensitive to the costs of bad pay.

• Source Evaluation permits evaluation of promotional concepts before going to the expense of testing. For instance: Will the free copy act work for you? What response will you need before cancellation to match your regular direct mail offer? Is it reasonable to expect this needed response percent from the free offer?

The list goes on and on. Each opened door leads to another with a big question mark on it. Evaluating subscription sources and knowing what goes into the evaluation and where the pressure points are will most certainly contribute to more intelligent and perceptive circulation management.

One last repetition: If you go to the trouble of setting up a Source Evaluation System be sure to "sell" it to the boss. Nothing will give your management more confidence than knowing that you look at things this way. Even if management doesn't fully understand, they will sleep a little better. So communicate—use charts, overlays, give actual demonstrations on a computer console, draw diagrams. Management will be grateful, your life will be easier and your magazine more profitable. And please do remember: Do not expect one reading of this article to make you an instant expert. Each magazine has its unique characteristics which must be accounted for on the input side. Only a thorough understanding of the concepts behind Source Evaluation will permit you to accurately and comparatively account for these differences.

History repeats itself

By Eliot DeY. Schein

There's gold in them thar files—and it's all locked up in those musty old records from your past direct mail activities.

While these days we bandy about a cost-per-thousand in the mail (third class) of $250 to $300 for a major mailing, there is a tendency to disregard the information we receive along with the orders.

Although there is no way to go out and generate orders for subscriptions without coming up with at least some information, in many publishing companies, that byproduct falls by the wayside and isn't used to its full advantage.

Years ago, *Esquire Magazine* (one of the earliest customers of Neodata Fulfillment in Boulder, Colorado) had available critical pieces of information that most publishing companies did not have. They had a track on their renewals by initial source of generation. This information facilitated a substantial number of interesting and viable strategic marketing approaches. In fact, under the astute guidance of then circulation director Irving Mayer, *Esquire* was able to take long strides toward the maximization of their "in the mail" promotion dollar.

What was most impressive about these historical data at *Esquire* was the fact that they got to the circulation department at all. Heretofore, outside of one or two small pockets of numbers-oriented publishing companies, this kind of detailed information was ignored because of either a lack of effort or a lack of marketing insight. Imagine, if you will, the additional cost of circulation promotion for magazines that failed to avail themselves of these kinds of hidden data.

In the 1960s, there were no retrieval methodologies or retrieval systems to do the job. Today there are no excuses. The electronic data equipment now exists to provide a wealth of information. It is incredible, however, that most publishing companies seem to continue to ignore this information.

One of the reasons cited for this disuse of background data is a resistance on the part of some circulation directors to change. "O.K.," they say, "Computerized fulfillment has now made it substantially easier to generate our labels to fulfill our magazine on a timely basis." These circulation directors continue: "Our renewal and billing promotions are more than simplified by an automated program of developing and retrieving the proper names of the proper subscribers at the proper time."

The invaluable commodity—information concerning source generation—is still falling by the wayside in alarming chunks. Let's examine some of the areas where information exists that can help save you and your company a fortune.

Renewals by source

As indicated earlier, renewals by source are more than worth the effort to track them. Surely, up-front results by dollar income from a cold mailing are the most crucial and exciting (assuming they're good) statistical tallies to cross anybody's desk. But how much is a subscription worth in its entirety?

The financial people usually do not count subscriptions for longer than the first term or year. However, subscriptions should be counted as long as they remain subscriptions . . . and that can be through several years of renewals . . . in some cases, decades.

What, then, is the overall value of a new subscription? It depends on the historical tracking of the relationship between how much it costs to initiate and how much revenue it actually brings in over the course of its life. And the numbers needed for this simple formula come directly from your renewal reports and promotion budget.

To determine the numerical solutions which can guide you to greater efficiency, it is necessary to break down every key number used from the point in time at which you have the historical data. This information is then used to project out individual source characteristics to potential in terms of renewability and thus gross worth.

Mailing list information is by far the most accessible and most important of the source variations. If you watch renewals by mailing list, you may find that a list that did not bring in a wonderful response in the initial stages is, in fact, the most profitable mailing list you've

---

SAMPLE PROFITABILITY FORMAT BY ORIGINAL DIRECT MAIL SOURCE CODE — PAGE 1

KEY	LIST	PKG	OFF	GR%	NET%	#1R	#2R	#3R	#4R	#5R
=====	======	=====	=====	=====	======	=====	=====	=====	=====	=====
5601	AMEX	AA	17	4.35	3.72	43.6	54.9	61.7	60.8	60.7
5602	CCAT	AA	17	3.51	2.54	43.8	51.7	66.3	68.4	66.4
5719	CHIL	AA	17	3.87	2.23	84.2	85.3	91.6	89.7	88.3
5624	AMEX	AB	17	5.51	2.93	71.3	77.2	74.9	75.8	77.1
5625	AMEX	AC	17	5.61	4.91	33.8	35.9	36.7	34.8	34.2

ever used. (In order to ascertain this, of course, you have to keep good records and follow renewals by list for a number of years.)

Another variable in your direct mail promotion is the package you have mailed. It is conventional wisdom that a package that offers a potential subscriber a variety of benefits from his or her subscription to your magazine should pull a higher percentage response than one that doesn't offer as many benefits. However, if the benefit-laden package presents a somewhat overblown view of your magazine, the resulting negative psychological effect on the part of the new subscriber most often results in a diminished likelihood of renewal. This may very well mean that the direct mail package you think is doing a good job for you is in fact robbing you of back-end income.

Tracking renewals both by list and by package gives you an even keener insight into what your most valued subscriber reacted to, and why.

Net percentage more informative

Many circulation people make roll-out assumptions based on gross percentages. To do this invites disaster. There are a number of highly touted mailing lists being used by publishers with total abandon because of their high gross percentage response.

Net percentages (that is, the percentage of pieces mailed that resulted in paid subscriptions) are substantially more informative because they deal with real sales and have positive impact on your bottom line. Once you take your net percentage and historical information based on list performance and package performance, you can then correspond them to the renewal percentage by initial mailing key. To do this you will be in a position to maximize your profits on the back end. You will also find that what may appear to be a more costly approach in terms of your initial promotion will result in more actual cash-per-subscriber via a higher renewal percentage.

To simplify the effort of all of the above, do it by machine. There are various computer programs available (or soon to become available) that will eventually be used by virtually all circulation directors.

One of these, which is currently getting set to jump from the drawing boards into reality, is a list, package and

offer program that can be constantly updated by key, day or week. Assuming you start one of these now and include renewal percentages for each key spread over the next five years, you will have a template from which you will be able to generate your future mailings for the greatest efficiency and profitability.

Old information—new format

The illustration shows a sample report. Assuming you have been keeping track of all of the information contained therein for the past number of years (as we all should have been doing anyway), it would be a rather simple procedure to translate that information into this new format.

The first column identifies that portion of a mailing by key number (or cell). This is helpful in determining when the mailing took place, from which mailing house, what the economy or other market conditions were at the time. It also serves as a cross-check for information verification. Assuming your key numbers are consecutive (as most are), you'll no doubt have a pretty good handle on this information by inspection alone.

The second column deals with the list mailed. In this sample illustration, the lists are abbreviated for simplicity. Next, the package and offer mailed are inserted (again with in-house coding), followed by gross percentage, net percentage, and renewal percentage for five cycles after initiation.

If history repeats itself (and it usually does), a careful review of a printout of this nature can give you the ammunition you need to hit your most profitable targets where they will count the most—on your bottom line.

Efforts analysis

By John D. Klingel

As much as I've preached about the need for careful financial analysis, I still find that most magazines don't analyze their costs per sub. Although most publications keep good records of gross response, bad pay, and net response by promotion code, few publications calculate the net cost per order with billing, fulfillment, the cost of bad debt copies, and other direct promotion costs charged to the subs acquired.

Another similar mistake that I often see is an er-

ror of omission: not going back after final pay-up to re-check conclusions drawn from analyzing test results prior to final pay-ups.

The reason for not doing the analysis is usually quite simple: it's a lot of work. Effort analysis is extremely time-consuming, and most people find the number-crunching tedious. Yet, effort analysis is an essential part of good circulation management, and if you're not doing it, you're probably not running your circulation department correctly.

Many circulation people try to get by through "off the top of the head" analysis by eyeballing returns and doing quick mental calculations. In many cases, this approach works and serious mistakes are avoided. But sooner or later, sloppy analysis leads to mistakes. No one can do the analysis in his head. It's simply too complicated.

Increasing need for circulation homework

During the past few years, the need for thorough analysis has dramatically increased due to changes in our cost structures. The costs of credit—first class postage and bad debt copies—have increased substantially. So have the costs of reply postage and list rental fees. In the old days, a list producing more net subs than another list almost always turned out to be more profitable because the costs of credit were relatively insignificant. Today, credit is relatively more expensive; and lists with lower response and higher pay-up are looking better and better.

The changing economic environment is just one of many reasons that circulation people should acquire the discipline to do effort analysis. Circulation is responsible for investing large sums of money in sub acquisition. And these dollars can't be invested correctly without doing a lot of homework.

One way to make the job easier is to get a personal computer (I personally prefer the Apple). Every circulation department should probably have a personal computer. They are amazing little tools and there are numerous ways they can be profitably used in a circulation operation. Although it takes some work to get used to them, it's not that difficult. The key point here is that there are ways of making the task easier so you shouldn't let the difficulty of number-crunching stand in your way.

Figure I represents a format that you can follow in doing an effort analysis. It will probably work for most situations, but you may have to adapt it slightly for your magazine. This format can be adapted to a spread sheet for analyzing mailing lists or other large numbers of efforts. In the January 1981 issue of FOLIO, I discussed the concept of list ranking using the procedures that follow. Each of the following alphabetical headings corresponds to the lettered sections of Figure I.

A. This is descriptive information for reference.

B. These data should come from your merge-purge or lettershop reports (quantity mailed) and your fulfillment reports. If your fulfillment company doesn't provide this information, get a new fulfillment service.

C. The package cost should come directly from vendor invoices. These costs should include printing, paper, lettershop, and merge-purge costs. No fixed costs (i.e., copywriters, mechanicals, photo fees, etc.) should be included. You should use variable costs only. The cost of printing and paper should probably not include make-ready costs as these costs are incurred no matter what quantity is mailed. When you get quotes from a printer, always ask for the cost of additional Ms (thousands). The additional Ms or end-of-run cost is a better reflection of the variable cost than the average cost. In the example, I used a package cost of $90/M times the quantity mailed.

D. Postage can be included in (C) if every list was mailed at the same postage rate, which is the usual case. I used $110/M in the example.

E. List rental charges vary by list; and in the case where a list is an exchange list, the low list rental cost will

Figure I
July 1981 Campaign

(A) List	XYZ Hotline Names
(A) Package	Burnett Control
(A) Price & term	$12/12 Issues
(B) Quantity mailed	25,000
(B) Gross response	3.8%
(B) Gross subs	950
(B) Net response	2.28%
(B) Net subs	570
(B) % bad debt	40%
(B) Bad debt subs	380

Costs

(C) Promotion —printing, paper & misc. [25 x $90]	$2,250
(D) —postage [25 x $110]	2,750
(E) —list rental [25 x $64.30]	1,608
(F) Billing costs [2.5 Aug. efforts x $260/M x 950]	618
(G) Bad debt copies [3 x $.40x380]	456
(H) Reply postage [950 x $.23]	219
(I) Premium cost [570 x $.50]	285
(J) Order entry [950 x $.35]	222
Total Costs	$8,519
(K) Cost per net sub [$8519 ÷ 570]	$14.95
(L) Revenue per sub [$12 for 12 Issues]	$12.00
(M) Net revenue per [$12.00 - $14.95] sub	$(2.95)
(M) Net revenue per [$2.95 ÷ 12) copy	$(.25)

be a significant factor in the cost-per-sub for an exchanged list versus a rented list. Another factor that can significantly affect the cost per sub is the purge factor. If the list is 30 percent duplicated with other lists and the rental fee is $45/M, the true cost-per-net-name mailed is $64.30/M. I arrived at this by dividing $45 by .70 (100 percent—30 percent).

F. To calculate billing costs, you have to calculate the average number of bills sent to a credit order and refer to your printing invoices for the average cost of a billing effort. The average number of billing efforts is usually found by analyzing the lettershop or fulfillment reports of quantities mailed by effort. Effort 1 always goes to 100 percent of the credit orders. Effort 2 might be received by 70 percent, with 40 percent getting Effort 3 and 20 percent getting Efforts 4 and 5. If you add the percentages (100 + 70 + 40 + 20 + 20) and divide by 100, you get the average number of efforts (250/100 = 2.5).

In the example, I used an average of 2.5 efforts (which is fairly normal) times a cost per bill of $260/M, which includes printing, postage, and lettershop. The cost of billing is calculated by multiplying the average efforts (2.5) times the cost of printing, postage, and lettershop ($260/M) times the number of credit subs (950). I assumed here that the orders are 100 percent credit. If there was significant cash with order, I would use only the number of credit orders to compute billing costs.

The average number of bills sent to each list as I've calculated it above is a little oversimplified in that it assumes that each list receives the same number of bills. This is probably not true, since lists with a high bad debt rate probably require a higher number of bills. Your fulfillment company may be able to run a special report that would give you a total bills-by-list analysis. This level of sophistication becomes important in situations where lists pull extremely high front-end response and have high bad pay.

G. The cost of bad debt copies is the cost of printing and mailing copies to the bad debt subs. The copy costs should be based on the incremental or end-of-run costs. In the example, I've assumed that all credit subs receive three issues and that the incremental cost per copy equals 40 cents. The reason that only the bad debt copies are included is that these copies aren't included in the calculation of paid subs for ABC purposes and are consequently considered a cost of acquiring net paid subs. This cost should include the label rate from your fulfillment company.

H. Reply postage is a function of the number of orders received times the reply postage rate. In the example, this calculation came to $218.50, which I rounded up to $219.

I. If you're using premiums, cash incentives, or any promotion methods that generate additional costs, these costs should be included in the calculations. In the example, I used a premium cost of 50 cents which includes the cost of manufacturing the premium (i.e., printing a booklet), an envelope, postage, and inserting cards. I also assumed that only paid subs receive the premium.

J. Some fulfillment companies charge an order entry fee as well as a per label rate. The label rate was included in the cost of bad debt copies. The cost of entering the orders was assumed to be 35 cents in the example and multiplied by the total orders.

K. The cost per net sub is calculated by dividing the total costs by the number of net subs.

L. The revenue per sub is the price or average revenue per sub if more than one rate is offered. If you want to, you could also include some value for list rentals or other income that helps offset acquisition costs.

M. Net revenue per subs is derived by subtracting the net cost per sub from the net revenue per sub. This is a purely optional step since there are different ways that people like to look at the data. A lot of circulation people convert everything to per copy figures. There is no right or wrong way. It simply depends on what you're used to and the various ways in which the data can be used.

Additional costs

Magazines that don't carry much ad revenue may want to add the cost of sending copies to the paid subs into this analysis. In the chapter "Source Evaluation," from *The Handbook of Circulation Management* (published by Folio), I discuss the more complex analyses involved in source evaluation and the various reasons we use the concepts to make decisions. In this article, my primary objective was to explain the mechanics, rather than theory and decision-making.

In creating an example of effort analysis, I obviously can't cover all the various situations in which you use this type of analysis. If you're analyzing insert cards, you have the cost of printing and binding; agents have different costs; and different types of direct mail offers (*e.g.*, sweeps) have other costs associated with them. All you need is a little common sense to figure out what additional costs were created by the promotion effort you're analyzing.

The approach that we use to analyze efforts and sources is based on a very simple objective. We want to identify the additional (incremental) costs that were created by a promotion effort or a source of subscriptions. If I'm using direct mail and try to decide whether to use a particular list, I don't assign fixed costs of the campaign such as copywriters and creative. If the list in question consists of 20,000 names, I want to know what it is going to cost me out-of-pocket to mail those additional 20,000 names. I don't incur any additional creative costs, and the printing cost isn't the average cost per piece but the end-of-run cost to keep the press running for 20,000 more pieces.

When you analyze a source or an effort, you don't want to allocate fixed costs to that effort. If you can add more business and the incremental revenue (the price you charge) exceeds the incremental costs, you are ahead. For that reason we analyze efforts and sources with incremental costs.

Personal computers move into circulation
By John D. Klingel

Recently, Duane Kelly, owner of a small trade publication called *Pacific Fishing*, asked me about using one of the models available on time share to do his budget. I looked at the lack of complexity in his subscription sources and pointed out that the model was a fairly complex tool for what his budgeting required.

Then I told him that although I had never used an Apple computer to do budgets, I thought that with an Apple and a software package called Visi-Calc he could get the job done and probably use the Apple for other things as well.

Three weeks later I visited him, and there on his desk were an Apple and a finished set of budgets. He told me that after our conversation, he had gone to his local computer store and purchased an Apple, a disk drive, a printer, and Visi-Calc. In five evenings working a few hours at home, he learned how to use the computer, determined how to use Visi-Calc to do his budget, and did his budget.

I found it extremely interesting that someone with no prior experience could successfully learn to use a personal computer in such a short time. I've had an Apple in my home for two years, having purchased it in the vain hope that my kids would learn how to program, and with some vague notion that I would start to learn something about the mysterious world of computers.

Although aware of Visi-Calc, I had no idea of what I would use it for or that it was a fairly powerful tool. I also operated under the mistaken belief that most of the applications I envisioned would require my programming the computer.

My misconceptions, as it turns out, are fairly typical of business people. Most people don't know how easy personal computers are to use. They don't know all the things they can be used for. And they aren't aware of the software (programs) that is available.

At the risk of sounding "born again," this article will discuss a number of experiences that have made me extremely aware of how useful a personal computer can be in a circulation operation, as well as in many other departments of a magazine.

No prior experience

Just after my experience with Duane Kelly, I was visiting *Personal Computing* magazine, which had just completed a massive test mailing in which we had tested over 150 different lists. Now that pay-up data was available, I wanted them to calculate the cost per net sub for each list—a rather massive number-crunching job for those of you who haven't ever done it.

I suggested that since their magazine was about personal computing, they should be able to figure out how to get a computer to crunch the numbers. So, as a kind of test, we assigned the task to a recently hired person with no prior computer experience. In about a week, he had learned how to use an Apple and the Visi-Calc program, and we had the list analysis completed.

Although the Visi-Calc system had done the job, Bob Lydon, the publisher of *Personal Computing*, informed us that there was other software that could be more appropriate for the type of analysis we were doing. Like many others who are learning how to use personal computers, we experienced the problem of not knowing the most appropriate software to use. Programs called PFS:File and PFS:Report can keep list history and rank the lists in addition to performing the calculations. Both of these programs are available off the shelf from any computer store that handles Apple computers.

Using a personal computer requires a lot of patience and a willingness to experiment. My kids use our Apple only to play games. They have never read the instruction manual for the computer nor do they read the software instructions for the games. They simply turn the computer on and experiment with the keys until they get it to do what they want.

Obviously, it helps to read the manuals, but often one has to be very patient and try various approaches until one method works. Unlike kids, most adults freeze when they sit down at a keyboard and are afraid to touch the wrong key, fearing that they will destroy the computer.

Although the software programs available for personal computers are fairly easy to use, they are not as simple and easy to operate as some of the modeling, accounting, and promotion systems available to publishers on time share. So as enthusiastic as I am, I will caution you that you have to have patience, be willing to experiment, and be willing to spend the time required to learn how to

use a personal computer. However, the benefits that accrue as a result of taking the time to learn how to use personal computers far outweigh the effort.

Another major frustration to the computer novice is that salespeople in computer stores are sometimes difficult to talk to, they are often not totally familiar with the hardware, and they frequently cannot give you good advice on which software would best serve your needs. These factors have generally slowed down the use of personal computers in all businesses.

So, if you are interested, find a computer store with salespeople who can talk to you about business applications in plain English. My favorite salesperson at the local Computerland has an MBA and describes herself as not knowing much about the technical aspect of computers. The technical people in the same store drive me crazy because they talk over my head. So at first, if you don't find someone you feel comfortable with, keep trying until you do.

What usually gets people interested in computers is finding out how they can be used and what software to use. In what follows, I will share with you some of the things I've learned. I'm by no means an expert, but I think all of us can learn more as we go.

Applications justify computer use

The following is a partial list of ways you can use a personal computer in a circulation department.

1. *List analysis.* As I've mentioned, you can analyze lists, store list history, and do projections for future campaigns.

2. *Budgets.* When we prepare monthly budgets, we sit and manually post numbers in each month, add the rows across for the annual amounts, and add the columns for the monthly totals. On the computer, you still put in each month (or the computer will spread one-twelfth in each month if you so instruct), but it will add the row and columns for you and then print the report. You save on the clerical time involved adding and balancing as well as on typing. In addition, you can change the budget, do variable budgeting, or reforecast with greater ease.

3. *Print-order projections.* Projecting net paid for future issues (see my article in FOLIO, December 1980) is an easy application for Visi-Calc or the many other electronic spreadsheet programs. If you do print-order projections, you know how many times you end up revising numbers, erasing previous projections, recalculating future suspends, etc. With the computer, you can go in and change one group of starts and it will automatically calculate the future issues.

4. *Schedules.* Many circulation departments have to submit detailed schedules to their fulfillment houses showing start issue assignment, bill key assignments, renewal drops, and other information. We need mailing charts for the lettershops and production charts and I could go on and on. By putting them on the computer, you can update them easily and the printer types them for you.

5. *Reports.* When reports are repeated on some regular basis, the computer makes it easier to update them and then it types them. Let's take flashcount reports on a direct mail campaign, for example. If you enter the list name, quantity mailed, and key code into the computer and make it permanent, all you have to do is then enter the quantity received. The computer calculates the percentage return, totals, and types the report. The

same approach can be used for your regular circulation reports or any other reports.

6. *Newsstand.* Petersen Publications is using personal computers in their circulation department for a number of newsstand sales studies and for maintaining sales history by wholesaler, as well as for a number of other applications.

7. *Cash flow projections.* Computer models are not designed for short-range detailed cash flow projections (i.e., by week for the next three or six months). This type of control is particularly important on start-ups, and I understand that the circulation department at *American Health* is using a personal computer for this, as well as for other applications.

8. *Inventory control.* One of the many time-consuming functions of a circulation department is projecting billing and renewal usage by effort. You could also use a personal computer to keep issue inventories.

9. *Filing.* We keep a lot of paper and record a lot of numbers in a circulation operation. Much of this is done better with a personal computer, and it's a lot easier to store a floppy disk than reams of paper.

10. *Efforts analysis.* In an earlier article, I addressed the need for and methods involved in performing this analysis. If you're analyzing a lot of efforts, you can set the formulas up one time and the calculations are done by the computer.

11. *History.* With PFS:File you can store data by form number or type of form, etc. Then, for example, when you want to see an old invoice to find what something cost the last time, you can easily retrieve the data.

12. *Time management.* You can use your computer to dial the telephone for you by storing frequently called numbers or even your entire phone directory, for that matter. If the line is busy, you can instruct the computer to keep calling until it gets an answer. You can also instruct it to call a number at a specific time so you don't forget an important call. It can handle your appointment calendar, remind you that it's time to plan the Christmas campaign, and buzz you when it's time for a meeting.

13. *Customer service.* You can use the personal computer for personalized correspondence, just as you use a word processor, by storing commonly used paragraphs. You could also use it for other form letters or correspondence where standard paragraphs are frequently used, such as ordering stock or getting printing quotes.

14. *Accounting.* You can use a personal computer for light accounting functions such as billing and accounts receivable, for list rentals, back issues, T-shirts, and other by-products. And then there's the accounting that's involved in list and space exchanges.

15. *Communications.* At *Personal Computing,* we're using our Apples to send data and messages between the publisher, the circulation department, and myself, all of whom are in different parts of the country. We can store data, tell the computer to phone after midnight when rates are cheaper, and go home. In the middle of the night, the Apple calls another Apple, the other Apple answers the phone, and the data is transferred. Nobody has to be at either end. The whole process is extremely simple to execute.

I'm sure that the above list of applications could be expanded tenfold. What has excited me is that there are enough applications that save time and effort and that aid in circulation decision-making to justify the use of personal computers in a circulation department. They can be extremely profitable tools and we're going to see their use increase tremendously.

In addition to the magazines I've mentioned, *Business Week* is using a number of Apples (they call them apple polishers) in its circulation department. The president of Newsweek personally uses an Apple to analyze budget variances and for other financial control purposes. Jim Romaly at Ziff-Davis has been using a Tandy TRS-80 personal computer since 1979. And I'm sure that many other magazines are using them.

Computers are becoming "user friendly"

When computers were first marketed to individuals, there were all kinds of blue-sky predictions about how everyone would soon be using them. But the problem was software. The typical business person probably never will learn or have the patience to write his own programs. Computers have become easy to use and the next generation of computers will be even easier. There is no real need to write your own programs because there are so many good software packages available in computer stores.

In the next decade, we are going to see enormous changes in the use of computers, electronic communications, and information handling. In 10 years, direct mail may be an obsolete method of marketing and methods of selling and communicating with subscribers may be totally different. Personal computers will help you understand how to use the new technologies and make you more aware of how they may be used in marketing and communicating with subscribers.

I've used the term "personal computer" for a very specific reason. Think of a personal computer as you would your desk, phone, or calculator—it's a tool. It's meant to handle your personal computing needs. One of the current circulation users described his usage by saying, "I use it to do everything I used to do by hand."

Computer models are, in my opinion, not something you should try to do on a personal computer, and I'm continuing to use one of the models available on time-share for financial projections. When you're modeling, there are often calculations that are done off the computer to calculate input (i.e., postage per copy, advertising, commissions, printing costs per copy, etc.) and these calculations are potential applications of the personal computer. Another potential combination of model and personal computer is to store your reports on the floppy disks instead of trying to store reams of computer paper.

One last comment about personal computers that's extremely important: You probably shouldn't impose these machines on managers. It's very important that managers request personal computers or you will find they won't get excited about them. If they are not excited about what they can do with them, they won't make the time and personal commitment needed to maximize the computer's potential. But by all means, if they do show an interest, get one in your office and start learning about what it can do.

Games

And then when you have had a bad day, you can play games on your personal computer. There's "Destroy the Post Office" when your campaign is under budget;

there's "Bomb the Fulfillment Company" for daily frustrations; and "Beat the Control" where you pit your creative test ideas against the computer's. For the serious game aficionado there's chess (seven levels of difficulty), backgammon, blackjack, war games, dungeon and monster fantasy games, and an endless variety of others.

If you are interested in getting involved with personal computers or if you're currently using one, I would like to hear from you. I will be happy to act as a central clearing house of users, letting you and others know how other magazines are using personal computers. It may be possible in the future to arrange program swaps. This way magazines can also trade notes on software and hardware and learn from one another. So drop me a note if you're interested. My address is 4090 Amaranta Avenue, Palo Alto, Calif. 94306. Many of the programs that *Personal Computing* has developed for print order projections and list analysis are available for swap or for some minimal fee.

The undeliverable dilemma

By Henry Turner

It is generally recognized that we are a mobile society. This social phenomenon has an effect on the magazine business in terms of a magazine's "undeliverables"—subscribers who are not receiving the magazine and can cost a publisher a considerable amount of money.

Most general interest magazines find that approximately 20 percent of their subscribers change addresses every year. Magazines with substantial numbers of subscribers in their late teens and twenties have an even greater percentage of address changes: These subscribers leave home to go to college, often move at college, leave college after several years, change apartments, change jobs, marry and move again, divorce and move again.

Many subscribers forget to notify magazines of their new address. Some may remember after they move, but do not have the addresses of their favorite magazines. Others may say, "I think I only have a couple of issues to go anyway, so I won't bother."

Still other subscribers may forget to notify the Postal Service, while some intentionally fail to file a change-of-address form to avoid a certain creditor or creditors.

When the Postal Service is unable to deliver your magazine, they return the front covers with your address label, marked "undeliverable," to your fulfillment house. The fulfillment house, in turn, keypunches these names into its computer, telling it to suspend service on these names until it gets new addresses.

How undeliverables cost you money

These undeliverables are costly for the following reasons:

•If your magazine is a monthly, you probably addressed and mailed a subsequent issue before you received the first undeliverable notice, so you have wasted the paper, printing and delivery costs of two copies. If your magazine is a weekly, you probably wasted even more copies.

•You have invested subscription promotion monies in acquiring these names. Unless you get the new addresses, that investment will have been for naught.

•These copies should be deducted from paid circulation, which means the names must be replaced at additional promotion expense.

•Lost subscribers mean lost renewals.

•Subscribers at new addresses are very valuable because they buy more of certain kinds of products than other subscribers.

What can be done to minimize those undeliverables, and maximize circulation profits with new addresses of subscribers? What can a publisher do to get those new addresses, get them early and keep getting them no matter how often subscribers move? The following is an 18-point program involving and coordinating all your promotion, circulation and fulfillment activities:

1. Put "address correction requested" on the outer envelope of all third class mailings of renewal promotions and house list promotions.

2. Evaluate your first class mailings (which cost 6.6 cents more than third class). Although first class mailings guarantee forwarding, you do not get the new address for subsequent mailings. First class mailings should say "first class" on the outer envelope, and preferably carry a stamp rather than an indicia or metering.

3. Ask for a change of address in all renewal mailings.

4. Put change-of-address information on the wrapper if your magazine is wrapped.

5. Carry a change-of-address coupon in every issue. Make it more conspicuous in May, June, August and September.

6. Test a change-of-address card, rather than a subscription order card, in May, June, August or September. If your frequency is more often than monthly, alternate a change-of-address card with a subscription order card in these months.

7. Test blow-in or bind-in cards in newsstand copies as follows: "Moving soon? *Mag* may not be conveniently available on the newsstand at your new address. Don't take a chance on missing *Mag*. Subscribe now at your new address, and tell us when you will be there. *Mag* may be the first mail in your new mailbox! Don't know your new

address? Subscribe now at your old address: if in the same town, the Post Office will forward free for three months to your new address."

8. Test an occupant mailing to the old address (but not to a student's address who lived at home).

9. For an "address correction requested" mailing that is returned "moved, left no forwarding address," do not purge from the file. Mail it again three to six months later.

10. For magazines returned undeliverable, test a first class letter to the subscriber, telling the subscriber what has happened. Ask for the new address, and ask for a renewal.

11. For bills returned undeliverable, continue the billing series through to the end. This assumes that the Postal Service will eventually get the new address, and the first class bill will be forwarded.

12. Consider identifying student subscriptions on your subscriber file. Test an "address correction requested" mailing in May and September.

13. Three months before your seasonal house list mailing, run your house list against new listings on a large compiled list. To the "hits," send a cheap "address correction requested" mailing. Put the new addresses you get back on your house list file, and include them in your best seasonal mailing.

14. Ask the college subscription agencies to give you the home addresses of the students who subscribe to your magazine at their campus address. Put this home address in your file for subsequent promotion.

15. Ask your telephone subscription agency to test your undeliverables for renewals. If the agency is reluctant, negotiate a special commission arrangement with them.

16. If you promote subscriptions to students, ask for their home addresses and key them on your subscription file. If the campus address is undeliverable, send the magazine to the home address. Or send a first class letter to the home address, asking for the new address. (This could also be done with open credit orders when bills are returned as undeliverable.) Find out how many changes of address you receive now for students during the summer months.

17. Use an "800" number in your magazine for changes of address. As more magazines use an "800" number, more people will become used to the idea, and the industry will benefit.

18. Explain the importance of your changes of address to your fulfillment house (in case they don't already know). Monitor their performance in this area to make sure changes are entered quickly on the file. Study their system for entering changes to see if you can think of ways to improve it.

Gripes

By Eliot DeY. Schein

Efficient direct mail marketing requires an array of specialists (copywriters, list brokers, printers, circulation managers, fulfillment house personnel, mailing house personnel, post office workers), each of whom must perform a specific task in a professional manner. Because direct mail is such a highly specialized effort, however, there are many possible sticking points which can stay a publisher's direct mail from its appointed (or projected) rounds.

Each individual specialty has its own pet peeves, and each individual specialist similarly has one or two candidates for number one status on the hit parade of pestiness.

To provide an insight into the problems that direct mail itself can create, I questioned representatives of just about every segment in direct mail marketing about their biggest problem in the mail. Some of the answers will surprise you. Some may even shock you. And some will probably sound like the ones you would have given if you were part of the poll.

The post office
The United States Postal Service came out wanting in this little survey. John Mitchell, circulation director of a national magazine, said his biggest problem was: "Third class mail doesn't move fast enough."

Pete Mattimore, an account manager for a major fulfillment house, says: "The U.S.P.S. doesn't accommodate December 31 drops with extra service."

Joe Jenkosky, the subscription manager for Times-Mirror, says his biggest problem is: "Getting the mail out. So many people are mailing at the end of the year, and the number of facilities available (and the lead time required to engage them) is insufficient. The result is a major difficulty."

Printing and production
Jenkosky continues: "Because today's direct mail is so sophisticated and requires so much advance planning, it's harder and harder to track production processes before you mail." What Joe is talking about was amplified by a printer and manufacturer of direct mail (who preferred not to be quoted by name).

This well-known practitioner says: "My biggest problem is when things are late. There are so many components necessary to complete a package for mailing: computer list tapes, brochures, BRE's. We can be all ready with our part, but if some other company holds everything up, we have to play catch-up and work overtime in order to try to meet the mailing date."

Another printer, Walter Simson of Rolls Offset, apparently has other problems, because he says his biggest hassle is: "Collecting money. My 30-day customers are trying to extend themselves to 60 days, and 60-day customers are now getting to the point where I don't want to do business with them. With my volume, I've had to spend a lot of money on expansion and equipment update, and my capital requirements have tripled in less than 18 months. If everybody paid in 30 days, I would need only half the amount of working capital I now need."

Well, Walt, let's listen to a publisher of a national magazine who says: "My biggest direct mail problem is anticipating the amount of the bills. Sure I know the economy is such that everything costs more, but I have trouble when I start budgeting what you have to pay the suppliers: the computer house to prepare lists, the cost of lists, printing and mailing house operations, and so on. Granted, direct mail is pulling for us better than ever, so it's not that the money doesn't come in to pay for these bills. It's the fluctuations in the budget that give me a pain in the belly."

Creative services

Obviously, this publisher is buying top quality services and is therefore getting a good response (which contributes to his cost headache). But Linda Wells, a copywriter who provides him with one of these services, has a different problem.

"My biggest problem is getting adequate information about lists and offers from the client before I write the package. When I have this information, I can write a package that works better. Also, the earlier an art director is assigned to the project, the easier it is to take advantage of teamwork. In both cases the publisher is the winner if these problems could be solved."

Sounds like Linda's biggest problem is the publisher. His response to her statement: "A publisher needs a lot of lead time to get out a good direct mail package, and frequently the test that determines the selection of offers and lists is going on when the copywriter is assigned the project. Therefore, it's often impossible to know which lists and offers one is going to use in advance."

You might think the direct mail art director gets away scot-free and doesn't have a problem in the world. Not so, says Ken Beck. His biggest problem: "Postal regulations. Very often the regulations change while you're designing a package. Dimensions, BRE requirements, size requirements. Clients who are permit holders get postal regulation up-dates all the time and they assume the post office gives the art director the information, too. However, the post office doesn't know who the art director is."

What was the United States Postal Service's reaction to Ken Beck? "Easy enough. All he has to do is let us know he wants the information. We'll be glad to put him on our mailing list."

Take heed, art directors and everyone else. If you're not getting up-to-date regulations from the United States Postal Service, the information is available for the asking.

Fulfillment

One direct marketing manager of a major multi-magazine publisher's major magazine said his biggest problem was: "Fulfillment. Our forecasts are a nightmare because we're on an antiquated computer information system designed for smaller magazines in this company.

Unfortunately, the computer system didn't grow when the magazine did, so we aren't getting the benefits of up-to-date circulation data."

The fulfillment manager's computer consultant chimes right in by saying: "Unidentified payments are my biggest problem. Attaching the person to the payment or the order is difficult. All too often you have one name on the file and then a different name comes in."

Surely if this computer consultant got together with the direct marketing manager, they could try to figure out a way to solve their problems. In the meantime, the fulfillment house has to search for the name on the main file which may be spelled differently from the name on the input document (which may have been a hand fill-in by the consumer).

Lists

A well-known list rental computer expert says his biggest problem is: "Fulfillment houses who are in the list rental business. They don't know the craft of list rental fulfillment. They should be willing to give up the list rental business to do what they're good at. They don't track well, they don't eliminate dupes well." He went on to say: "They have their own profits at heart—not those of the list owner or publisher."

For years, fulfillment houses have been trying to provide extra services, much to the chagrin of the list brokers and creative people. Fulfillment houses produce their own billing formats, determine the mailing dates. Are they equipped with the marketing expertise needed to handle this, however? Are they qualified to eliminate duplication between lists? These questions must be answered to management's satisfaction.

But look what the list brokers seem to be doing: "My biggest problem is the list broker who offers to analyze direct mail results for a magazine as part of a so-called service. (In return, the broker becomes responsible for all list orders from that magazine.) Magazine circulation staffers should do their own analysis; it should not be done by an unqualified list brokerage company. Offering this service is just a sales technique to get the magazine's list business." This quote from a list broker whose company is apparently not offering that service.

And finally,

Management

One of the world's all-time savvy senior circulation directors insists that management is his biggest problem. "My biggest problem is making my direct mail efforts pay-out reasonably. I can't convince management to release the funds because the pay-out is too far away from the allocation, renewals are too long in coming to spark management to become an investor of today's dollar."

So who doesn't have a problem? It seems that everyone involved in direct mail effort has some legitimate grievance. However, one interesting fact emerges from this survey: In interviews with more than 20 direct mail practitioners in the magazine industry, not one said his biggest problem was response percentages. Not one said that getting the consumer to pay for a subscription was a problem. No one, it would seem, has any major difficulty with renewals.

Magazine direct mail does what it is supposed to do. In fact, it produces sales and income so efficiently that the biggest problems in mail have yet to stop any conscientious publisher from using the medium to its fullest potential and at its most sophisticated level.

Certainly, the more complex the medium, the greater the possibility of problems. But as long as the bottom line isn't the major problem, there's no problem.

Managing non-paid circulation: theory and craft

By William Strong

Very little has been written about controlled circulation, except when it pertains to conversion to paid circulation. In fact, since conversion to paid circulation involves change and excitement, quite a bit has been written on that subject. Unfortunately, almost nothing exists on the subject of the circulation manager's day-to-day activities with controlled circulation. This, then, is an effort to address a very important but poorly documented circulation management activity.

First, why controlled circulation? For one thing, it requires less of an investment for start-up than paid circulation. Competitive considerations may also indicate the controlled route. Controlled circulation, by its nature, has the potential for more complete universe coverage and it has the capability of providing deeper initial penetration of the marketplace.

The circulation management activity on a controlled circulation publication starts with goal setting in concert with the publisher, the editor, and the advertising director. For whom is the publication being edited? How many of these people are there? How many constitute a market for the advertiser? Where are they located?

The source of controlled circulation

Competitive pressures in the marketplace, plus the available budget, will soon determine the kind of controlled circulation necessary: 1) direct request; 2) direct request from recipient's company; 3) written communication; 4) lists and directories; 5) interviews; or 6) a proper combination of all sources.

Competitive marketplace situations will also determine whether or not an audit is necessary and may even help determine in which audit bureau to seek membership. Most publications join either BPA (Business Publications Audit of Circulations, Inc.) or the Business Publications Division of ABC (Audit Bureau of Circulations Inc.).

Recently, another factor, introduced by the Postal Service, affects the decision about the source of controlled circulation. As of October 1, 1982, in order to continue to qualify for second class rates of postage, a controlled publication must have 50 percent "request" circulation. There is some thought, too, that audit bureau membership will satisfy the Postal Service's audit requirements.

Undoubtedly, then, this Postal Service regulation will affect the decisions made by controlled circulation publications in the areas of source of circulation and the necessity of auditing.

When these considerations are carefully thought out, and when editorial is satisfied that the correct kind of reader is being matched with the editorial, and that a real editorial need exists, it's time for the advertising sales area to be heard from. How many readers are necessary? What will we need to know about the reader?

The advertising sales area will also have a voice in determining the kind (source) of circulation to be obtained and membership in an audit bureau. (Some publications join both audit bureaus.)

A plan of action

Once the goals have been set, the circulation manager can start mapping out a plan of action to achieve the circulation goals. He starts by providing budget information to the publisher. On a new controlled circulation publication, he would probably submit a figure for the original list-building activity, and then annual figures for the cost of maintaining quality controlled circulation, fulfillment, etc.

Next comes list building. The goal-setting activity provided a blueprint for the circulation manager. He now knows the kind of reader that the editorial product will serve, how many individuals constitute the advertising universe, what kind of circulation (source) is required by the marketplace, and what kind of audit he will be trying to satisfy. He'll also be aware, by this time, of any budget constraints.

There are a number of ways of building the initial controlled circulation list. Most circulation managers begin by accumulating all the current rosters and directories available in the field. They also obtain manufacturers lists, names of customers provided by the publication's advertisers. The desired readers are then manually selected out by individual name, title and function. These names are then computerized, merged and purged, and a scan of the computer print-out, alphabetic by company, reveals any holes in the circulation universe which have to be plugged through further list-building activities.

If the plan calls for the use of outside or rented lists, the usual method is to make a "prequalification" mailing asking potential recipients if they wish to receive the publication and if they would provide the required business or function data. Those who return a properly filled out response card then go up on the qualified controlled list as "direct request." Those names that went directly onto the qualified controlled list from rosters, lists, and directories are mailed a similar qualification form and, as returns are processed, are upgraded from "lists" to "direct request." (All names not initially needed should be held on to because they can be reverified and used as replacements down the line.)

Although the initial list-building effort is laborious, it is critical to the success of the publication. If sufficient time is given and everyone cooperates, the new controlled circulation publication can start off in great shape. By producing alphabetic-by-company print-outs after every update and going over them not only with circulation people but with the publisher, editors and space salesmen, gaps can be filled and the first issue can be mailed off with the best possible market coverage.

Off and running

Once the list is built and publication has started, one can really begin to practice the craft of controlled circulation management. How to keep what you have . . . how to better what you have . . . how to work as efficiently and economically as possible . . . these are the challenges.

And the solutions come through good organization, good two-way communication with the ad director and publisher, and tight control over the circulation operation. Working with a good qualified controlled list requires the same kind of organization and systematic planning as is required by a good renewal program on a paid publication.

The issue statistics from the computer keep you informed about your controlled circulation: a classification breakdown by title and industry; a breakdown by source; an aging analysis. The budget tells you how much money you have for the year.

At this point, the circulation manager's next step is to develop a well-thought out, properly executed annual program (quite like a renewal series).

First, he knows that he needs "request" circulation, at least 50 percent, to satisfy the USPS requirement. Second, the advertising department will let him know the additional requirements dictated by the marketplace. Furthermore, for magazines that are established, he also needs a determination of what percentage of the circulation should be under one year old. Then, with these figures and using the money available, he puts together a program to reach qualified readers, asking them if they want to "request" the magazine. That program can include direct mail, "outserts" or protective covers, and perhaps telephone interviews followed by a mailing.

The number of efforts and the kind of reverification procedures that will take place are dictated by a publication's marketplace and the style of its circulation manager. Furthermore, a controlled circulation publication that wishes to convert to paid circulation (or has a desire to have *some* paid) would plan accordingly in determining the nature of its controlled circulation maintenance program.

Typically, a good qualified controlled circulation operation calls for several reverification efforts during the audit cycle. Three efforts are customary, although some annual programs have even more efforts.

An annual program might include a combination of techniques: some direct mail, perhaps a protective cover or two, and maybe some telephone work at the end of the cycle to salvage those readers who have been most reticent about responding to previous efforts.

Building the list

New-name procurement is a critical aspect of a controlled circulation operation and one that requires excellent organization. Many circulation managers maintain a source card on each list available, complete with a record of 1) when the list becomes available each year, 2) how to order, 3) how the list performed last time out, 4) cost per usable name obtained, and any other information that might help in subsequent list building.

Some circulation managers have to go beyond the traditional methods to get the kind of coverage or penetration their publications require. For example, although they may be able to locate the name and addresses of companies they wish to cover, they may not be able to find the names and titles of the functions which their publications editorially serve.

In this instance, a circulation manager's list maintenance activity involves two steps. First, he can call a key employee in the company—perhaps the personnel director—and get the names of the people he is seeking. In this case, the names he obtains would show as a source "telephone interviews." He could also mail a census-type questionnaire to the recipient, requesting a list of all individuals (and their titles) who should receive the publication. If the form is properly worded, the individual who signs the form qualifies under "personal written request from recipient," while the individuals whose names have been listed will qualify as "written request from recipient's firm." This type of effort is extremely effective in cases where the goal is penetration of specific firms.

If a circulation manager wants more of the circulation to show under "personal written request from recipient," he must take the second step. He must take all the names obtained from the telephone interview and the additional names provided on the census form and send them a personal reverification form to complete and return.

The qualification form

Let's, for a moment, examine the qualification form itself. The audit bureaus mandate that the form contain a question essentially like the following: "I wish to receive (continue to receive) name of publication . . . YES ( ) . . . NO ( ) . . . date . . . signature."

The form will also have to elicit all of the information necessary to classify the record, unless you are using an acceptable secondary source such as Dun & Bradstreet, state directories, etc. It will have to obtain all the additional information you wish for your records for sales purposes and/or to satisfy the requirements of the comparability program to which your publication belongs. (More about comparability later.)

Usually, the response form is positioned as an opportunity to send in an annual renewal (no charge) to the publication. If a publication plans to try converting to paid at some point, the circulation manager may want to position the form as an opportunity to obtain or extend a "complimentary, trial subscription."

When designing the qualification form, a circulation manager must be sure that fulfillment people and art and copy people are also involved in its creation. Most circulation departments have had the experience of having a form that either is not in compliance with audit bureau rules or, by its design, does not lend itself easily to good fulfillment. These problems can be easily avoided by seeing that everyone involved screens the form for compliance and practicability.

In addition to reverifying existing records and verifying new records, a circulation manager must be constantly alert to capturing the names of new people entering the field who should be readers of the publication. Invaluable for this activity is a record-keeping aid that records the time of the year each qualified maintenance activity has to be performed, the source of names, the response rate of the various kinds of efforts to implement, and the cost. Such a "program" is the one sure way of maintaining a high-quality controlled circulation file at the most economical cost.

Many publishers look at annual reports which show the cost per year for maintaining a controlled circulation recipient. An interesting adjunct to this report would be a section that would show the value per controlled circulation name on the file. This figure would be the sum total of revenue—produced through advertising sales, list rentals, sale of books and other merchandise to magazine recipients, and paid subscriptions, if any—divided by the number of qualified names on the active file.

The annual cost of maintaining a controlled circulation name is going to be directly related to the source and age. It goes without saying that a controlled circulation list where the source of all names is business directories and where the names are allowed to age to the maximum allowed by the audit bureaus (36 months) will be much cheaper to maintain than a list that is primarily one-year direct request. Again, it will be the competitive pressures of the advertising sales marketplace and the USPS 50 percent ruling that are determining factors.

Budgeting the maintenance program

After the initial list-building activity has been completed, it is a relatively simple matter to fairly accurately budget the cost of the annual qualified controlled circulation maintenance program. The publisher and ad director will join in setting the goals in terms of circulation size, amount of direct request, and the amount needed in the one-year column. These goals should be stated in terms of target figures for the June and December audit bureau publisher statements.

The cost data that a circulation manager has been maintaining by effort will enable him to fairly accurately estimate his budgetary needs to achieve the goals set for the coming year. Most publishing companies generally provide the circulation manager with monthly P&L statements which enable him to stay on a fairly straight course in terms of spending. Furthermore, the issue update statistics let him know whether he is on course for goal attainment.

Time should be budgeted as well as money. If a plan for controlled circulation activity has been followed, there should be time for some list "tune up" (probably about mid-way in each January-through-June and July-through-December audit period) to ensure the best possible publishers' statements.

This "tuning up" process would include making mailings to upgrade records in terms of business and industry classifications. It would also include running special computer printouts by individual name so that a manual check can be made to eliminate any duplicate records that may have crept into the list-building process (both audit bureaus are very sensitive to excess duplication in the file). A manager who has allowed sufficient time in his planning so that he can sit back in March and September and take a good look at what he has will find "tune up" opportunities that will result in a higher quality statement.

Audits and comparability

In addition to the basic audits offered by both ABC and BPA, there are additional auditing services available through these bureaus which satisfy unique needs in the marketplace. There are unit audits, passalong reader audits, buying-influence audits, and various other kinds of supplemental data audits.

Both auditing organizations also have comparability programs that involve advertisers, agencies, and publishers. These programs encourage publishers serving readers in similar markets to report reader data in a uniform format.

BPA calls its program "Comparability": ABC's program is usually referred to as the "Uniform Industry Agreement." Dialogue is now taking place between the two auditing organizations to get further uniformity in terms of reporting data and in auditing procedures. All of this is done with a desire to better serve the media buyer.

Systems design and personnel

No discussion of the circulation manager's role in controlled circulation would be complete without some attention paid to the following two items:

First, systems design. Controlled circulation has some unique "store and retrieve" requirements. Your computer record will have to accommodate additional fields to house source and aging information as well as a greater amount of demographics information than the usual paid circulation record requires. Your computer system has to produce reports that will enable you to do a good job of managing the controlled circulation file.

Second, a high priority should be placed on the proper training of the circulation fulfillment people working on a qualified controlled publication. Even in a multi-book environment, it seems to make some sense to assign specific people to specific titles; working with the same publication all the time enables a person to become familiar with the field and familiar with the classification requirements of the publication. Accuracy and speed of handling seem to be improved with this concept.

For additional information on controlled circulation I refer you to the audit bureaus: Audit Bureau of Circulations (ABC), 900 N. Meachum Road, Schaumburg, Ill. 60195; Business Publications Audit of Circulations (BPA), 360 Park Avenue South, New York, N.Y. 10010.

A number of associations in the field regularly provide information on controlled circulation, such as the ABP Circulator, the newsletter published by the American Business Press Inc. as a membership service. Meetings, which cover subjects such as controlled circulation management, are put on from time to time by the Circulation Managers Committee of BPA, by the Business Publications Industry Committee of ABC, by the Circulation Managers Committee of American Business Press, and by such organizations as the National Business Circulations Association (NBCA).

Direct response
for controlled magazines

By John D. Klingel

I was recently asked to give a talk on direct response testing to a group of publishers in Monterey, California. When I arrived at the conference, I was dismayed to find that my audience was to consist primarily of publishers of controlled circulation magazines. Since my talk on testing is designed for people who use direct response to obtain paid subscribers, I was concerned that my three-hour presentation would have no relevance for them.

As I was going through my usual pre-speech jitters, however, it occurred to me that controlled circulation magazines do use direct response and that testing could play a very valuable role. And, as it turned out, the talk went extremely well, judging from the questions asked and the reactions of the participants. What captured the most interest was the use of reader service cards as an example of testing various approaches that might change the number of inquiries generated.

In the discussions during the Monterey conference, and in additional conversations with controlled circulation magazine publishers, it became apparent that very few people in the controlled circulation magazine world ever try to adapt direct response techniques to their business. Since I have only a little experience with non-paid books, I'm sure that I'm not aware of all the potential. However, I want to share with you a few ideas that demonstrate how creative marketing approaches and testing can pay off in almost any type of marketing. For those of you who don't work for controlled circulation magazines, what follows is a good example of how direct response principles can be applied in a wide variety of situations.

Bingo cards

The term "bingo card" is slang for a response device that is used to generate inquiries for advertisers' products and services (see Example I). In front of advertisers we call them "reader response cards," "reader action cards," or some other suitable term.

This device provides readers with an easy way of obtaining additional information about advertised products and services by simply circling or filling in numbers on a card. The advertiser is then sent a list of names and addresses of the inquirer.

The profit from these cards is usually derived directly or indirectly from advertising. In many markets, advertisers base their ad buys largely on the volume of inquiries generated or the quality of leads generated. Some advertisers judge the effectiveness of a magazine by the total number of inquiries generated. Other advertisers judge effectiveness by the number of inquiries that result in actual sales and thus are interested in the quality of leads, not the quantity.

An advertiser who mails catalogs to inquiries may want volume. An advertiser who uses salespeople to make personal calls on inquiries usually doesn't want volume. A salesperson who consistently gets 10 leads from Maga-

zine B with one sale is probably going to tell the advertising manager in the home office to put the ad dollars in Magazine B.

For some magazines, the advertisers break neatly into one of the categories above. For others, the market is a mixture of some advertisers who want volume and some who want quality. Fortunately, the magazine publisher has some degree of control over the responsiveness of the bingo card. For example, making inquiries pay reply postage will often reduce the number of inquiries, and, in general, a reduction in volume will often improve the quality of responses. Note that I specifically said "often," not "always."

Following is a partial list of reader service card variables that can be tested to determine their impact on volume and quality.

Reply postage. As noted above, a business reply card will usually outpull a card with a "place stamp here."

Number of cards. Example I shows a reader service card format with three separate cards. As a general rule, the more cards, the more response. There's usually considerable pass-along readership, so why not provide cards for everyone? Why limit yourself to three cards? Maybe six would be even better. If some segments of your distribution have greater pass-along, you can put additional cards in those segments. And why not steal another page out of paid circulation tricks and try a blow-in reader service card?

Listings. Example II shows an example of advertiser listings that are positioned close to the reader service card. These listings are provided only to advertisers in the issue and are in addition to the little statement that accompanies each ad, that is, "For additional information circle 101 on the Reader Action Card." Compared to running a card with no listings, the listings will often increase response dramatically. In the education field, some advertisers have gotten close to 15,000 inquiries from magazines distributing roughly 250,000 to 300,000 copies. In the example shown here, the listings are grouped by subject area for easy reader reference. For many magazines, it's impossible to break advertising into categories but, if you can, I think it's a neat trick and a valuable service for readers.

Copy. When listings are used, the advertiser can, to some extent, control response by the wording of the listing and what's offered. In Example II, a number of listings start with the word "free," an almost certain way of increasing response. In the education field, most advertisers are looking for volume. If the advertisers want to be more selective, they can charge for their catalog (note the space on the bingo card for cash items) or try different ways of wording the listing.

Write-ins versus pre-numbering. Some bingo cards are set up so that the responder must write in the numbers. There's a very strong likelihood that the circle-the-

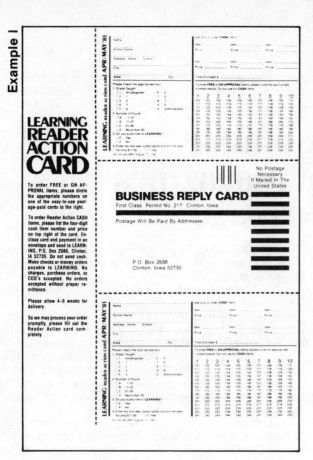

number approach will be more responsive than the write-in approach. In general, the easier it is to complete the card and mail it, the higher the response.

Limiting the number of inquiries. One way to reduce volume and perhaps improve quality of responses is to limit the number of inquiries the reader can make; that is, circle no more than 10, etc. You can also make the reader pay for each inquiry.

Asking for demographic information. If you ask the responder to fill out demographic information, you take the risk of reducing response. Consequently, don't ask for any information that isn't being requested by your advertisers or that you are not planning to use in some profitable fashion, such as building a mailing list, promoting the inquiries, etc.

So much for specifics. The point is that with a little creativity you can find numerous ways of improving reader service card performance. And for a lot of magazines, improved reader service card results translate into bigger ad dollars.

It is interesting that advertisers are even less sophisticated than controlled circulation magazine people in using direct response techniques. In fact, most do not service their inquiries effectively.

If you've never checked to see how your advertisers respond to inquiries, take your own reader service card and fill it out. Then keep track of how many respond and how long it takes to get back information. One paid circulation trade magazine made a lot of friends in the advertising community by putting on seminars and publishing marketing memos designed to teach advertisers how to service these inquiries more effectively.

Another area where controlled circulation people use direct response is in obtaining qualified subscribers. Since there is virtually no difference between a paid subscriber and a qualified subscriber (other than the fact that you don't have to collect money from the qualified sub),

there should be no difference in the promotion that is sent to each. Yet most promotion put out by controlled circulation magazines doesn't look anything like that put out by paid circulation magazines. It's usually ugly, with little or no copy, and it is generally printed in the cheapest manner possible.

Most controlled magazines look only at what the promotion costs and not what the return is per dollar spent. Cheap is not always best, and as we know in the paid circulation field, an expensive four-color package often produces more profitable orders than a cheap package.

Understanding the economics

The trick in almost all direct response media is understanding the economics. For a controlled circulation magazine, the goal is to produce qualified subscribers for the least cost.

Let's assume that a controlled circulation magazine is testing two packages: Package A, their usual dull-looking self-mailer, and Package B, a more traditional direct mail package with an envelope, letter, order card, etc. And let's assume that Package A, the self-mailer, costs $100 per thousand, and that Package B costs $250 per thousand. Both packages are mailed to two randomly selected groups of 10,000 each.

Figure I, an analysis of the hypothetical results, indicates that the cost per qualified sub is the same, but Package B produced two and a half times as many subs.

If Package B had pulled 10 percent, the cost per qualified sub would drop to $2.50. If package B pulled only 3 percent (300 qualified subs), would the 50 percent increase in qualified subs justify the increased cost per sub?

This type of analysis is referred to as source evaluation in the paid circulation business. Although conversion and renewal rates make the analysis more difficult, the concepts are the same. (In a future column, I will discuss the ranking of sources for paid circulation magazines. The

Figure I

	Package A	Package B
Cost/M	$100/M	$250/M
Quantity mailed	10,000	10,000
Cost	$1,000	$2,500
Response	2%	5%
Number of qualified subs	200	500
Cost/qualified sub	$5	$5

concepts that will be discussed in that column can also be applied to controlled circulation magazines.)

Paid subscribers

There are a few other paid circulation magazine tricks that can be used by controlled circulation magazines. There's no reason why a controlled circulation magazine can't sell subscriptions for a high price where the acquisition cost is low and a highly profitable sub is obtained. If the paid subs aren't appropriate for advertisers, simply exclude them from your rate base.

Insert cards in your own magazine tend to produce highly profitable orders. Yet I seldom see a controlled circulation magazine promote paid subscriptions through the use of an insert card. In fact, most controlled circulation magazines make it almost impossible to subscribe. I recently heard of a controlled circulation magazine with a waiting list of three people for every one receiving the publication. That situation certainly seems like a ripe opportunity for some additional profits.

And what about space trades between controlled circulation magazines? Competitive as well as non-competitive paid circulation magazines trade space. If controlled circulation magazines trade space with competitors and promote for qualified subs, they might find that the cost per qualified sub is lower than some other method being used. And controlled circulation magazines in different fields could trade space for paid subscription promotion.

It probably wouldn't pay for a magazine in the agriculture industry to trade with a magazine in the aerospace field, but a trade between an electronics magazine and an aerospace magazine might be quite profitable. And how about trades between controlled circulation magazines and paid circulation magazines?

Enough of specifics. The key point is that when you observe the methods used by paid circulation magazines, try to understand the concept behind the technique and then ask yourself if there isn't some way you could employ a variation of the concept in your business.

One last parting trick—if you want super reader service card response, take a close look at Number 1 under Reader/Language Arts in Example II.

Circulation promotion

The 'art' of direct mail

By Denison Hatch

The only difference between a work of art and a work of advertising is that the artist wants to sell the painting, while the advertiser wants to sell the subject.

A direct mail package is the only truly participatory art form. You find the envelope in your mail box, and immediately have the option of participating or throwing it away. If you elect to go ahead and read it, *you* make it all happen. You open the envelope, and generally you will find several pieces inside—usually a typewritten letter, a printed illustrated circular or brochure, an order device, and a method for getting the order back to the sender—either a reply envelope or reply information printed on the back of the order card. You savor each piece at your own pace.

Artistically, direct mail is (as it should be) extremely interruptive. It jerks the eye all over the place . . . highlighting benefits . . . showing the product in a number of different focuses. There is a rhythm to direct mail—a kind of beat you might find in Mondrian's *Broadway Boogie-Woogie,* where your eyes climb multi-colored ladders, then skitter across to a splotch of red, slide down a bright brass firepole, and land with a thump on a subhead that leads you off in another direction—perhaps to the back of the page or to another piece in the mailing.

There is reason for this seeming clutter, summed up in the simple three-word dictum: "Neatness rejects involvement." (If you walk into your office and your desk is absolutely clean, you'll sit back, have yourself another cup of coffee, and then get around to digging into your work. If your desk is piled high with papers, you can't help but start reading the top one . . . and foraging around, immediately involved. Clutter invites involvement.)

The direct mail artist—the person who conceives, writes, and designs the work of direct mail art— knows direct mail is an impulse sale. Once the envelope is in the prospect's hands, it has to be startling enough to interrupt the day's normal routine and the person's thought processes. What's more, it has to keep on interrupting until the order device is acted upon then and there. If the mailing is laid aside, chances are it won't be picked up and reconsidered, and the sale will be lost. Thus, if it is too neat, it will be rejected.

Not only is direct mail the only participatory art form—where the viewer/reader savors, touches, considers or rejects each piece at his or her own pace—it is the only one in which the artist can use many words and pictures to tell the story. In addition, unlike the novelist who must decide at the outset whether to use the first or third person and then stick to it, the direct mail artist has the luxury of using all three persons.

There is "you" copy, "me" copy, and "it" copy. The "you" copy talks about all the benefits to you . . . why you should buy or subscribe to this product, because it will make you rich or beautiful or smart or live longer or whatever. The "you" copy naturally falls into the format of the letter, the personal discussion between me (the writer) and you (the prospect). In the letter, you sell the *experience* of owning the product more than you sell the product itself. Since letters between people are either handwritten or typed (never typeset, which is used for mass—not personal—communications) and since handwriting is difficult to read, the letter in direct mail should *always* be in typewriter type.

The "it" copy describes and shows "it"—the product. This tends to be what goes into the circular, where the third person is used throughout, with copy and illustration so thoroughly intertwined they are as one. This is akin to Cubism, introduced in the early years of the century by Picasso, Gris, Leger, and Braque. It drove the art world somewhat crazy. But Cubism wasn't a very complex idea. The artist simply depicted a bottle or a nude or a still life or a chair from a number of different angles; so the Cubist painting has a unique four dimensionality—the three basic dimensions plus time.

This is what a direct mail circular is designed to do—show the object from all possible angles, using "it" copy and art. (Some mailings have been tested with and without the circular. They have proven more effective in both numbers of orders and bottom-line cost-per-order when mailed without, rather than with, the circular. This reaffirms the power of the word "you" and the effectiveness of "you" copy and the letter format.)

The "me" copy tells the prospect what this product or service has done for "me." It's the endorsement . . . the publisher's letter . . . the words of praise from the user.

The direct mail artist, then, has at his command all communications techniques that can be reproduced on the printed page—words in all parts of speech, plus illustrations (photographs, paintings, tables, drawings, graphs—anything).

The result: a multi-faceted package that assaults the prospect visually, that all-at-once charms, amuses, informs, excites, delights, intrigues, stimulates, and emotionally turns on the reader/viewer.

Every part of the package is designed to tell a piece of the story. Nothing should tell the whole story. No copy on one piece should be repeated verbatim elsewhere; otherwise, the prospect will say, "I've seen this before," and lay the thing down. The entire effect of these various pieces should be to bring the focus of the prospect down to the most important single part of the package—the order device—which can use all three persons at once ("Reserve IT now" . . . "YOUR personal guarantee: if YOU decide at any time YOU are dissatisfied" . . . "Yes, please rush ME the item and bill ME at the low, low price of . . .").

The direct mail artist has made the product or service so real that the prospect not only believes it exists, but simply has to have it. The more he studies and sifts through the various parts of the mailing, the more real the object for sale becomes. Ultimately all the verbiage, wild artistic jumble, and parts of speech melt into the background as this object or service shines forth like a holograph in the prospect's brain, three dimensional, touchable, perhaps even smellable. *He must have it!* (Or at least try it under the risk-free money-back guarantee.) And so goes through the trouble of ordering it.

In direct mail, the artistry is all the more consummate if the product does not yet exist—such as a new magazine not yet published, and which, in fact, won't ever be published unless enough people subscribe as a result of the test mailing.

This is why the direct mail package is the "ultimate trompe l'oeil," and why the writer/designer is a true artist.

The success or failure of this art form is precisely measured in terms of response and cost-per-order. No other writer/designer in any field is as much under the gun to produce actual results. He isn't in the business of creating warm feelings about a product shotgunned out to the millions in the hope that a few hundred thousand will remember when they get to the store. He has no help from a supersalesman at the dealership or some strong in-store

or point-of-purchase back-up. No sweet-talking rep is going into an outlet to persuade the manager to put the product on the counter in return for an extra discount.

The direct mail package goes out with no help from anybody (except, hopefully, a canny list broker), and if the replies don't come back, the sender is out of business, and the artist is out on the street with him.

Thus, where many in general advertising consider direct response the ugly little step-sibling of the business, it is actually the aristocrat. And its creative efforts are authentic works of American art.

It is astonishing that so-called knowledgeable connoisseurs spend thousands of dollars for a print of a Campbell's soup can or a few runny blotches on rice paper . . . frame the thing . . . and call it art. Then they throw out these fascinating art forms that come into their mail boxes—free!

Actually, direct mail art is not free. It costs a great deal of money to create—perhaps an average of $20,000 per package. This being the case, all a serious collector needs to do is acquire 1,000 pieces of direct mail, and he has a $20 million collection—probably with a number of originals by the major artists of the day—Jayme, Wells, Burnett, Stagg, as well as many new artists coming along.

No other graphic art form in the world is as easily accessible . . . as powerful . . . as demanding of a viewer's time . . . as effective with its message as direct mail—the ultimate trompe l'oeil!

Do you know your primary audience?

By Herbert G. Ahrend

In some instances, the failure of many circulation promotion pieces to give the reader a worthwhile reason for buying the publication results from the lack of a clear picture—in the mind of the publisher as well as in the mind of the copywriter—of the person they are addressing.

Too often there is an effort to "cover the waterfront" with a single appeal or copy approach, when special attention to the particular interests or needs of actual or potential groups of readers might significantly increase the number of orders per thousand. Worse yet, tradition—or simply persistent erroneous assumptions—may result in an appeal based on a completely inaccurate concept of the most easily reached new reader.

The American-Scandinavian Foundation, publisher of the 60-year-old—but very contemporary—*Scandinavian Review*, recently sought to determine where the most likely prospects for member-subscribers were to be found. The eventual approach taken and reasoning involved can be useful to many other publishers. Here's how the campaign developed:

Initially, there were two obvious questions to be answered: "Whom do we want to reach?" and "How do we reach them?"

First—after considerable brainstorming—it was determined that there were, in general, three types (or

categories) of people who were worth approaching:

1. Those with deep-seated interest in serious aspects of life in Scandinavia, such as health care, governmental innovations, etc.

2. Those with a serious interest in less serious aspects of Scandinavian life, such as saunas, skiing and sex.

3. Those with a more general interest. (Naturally, this group had the least-clearly-defined criteria; two prominent characteristics of these people were above-average intellect and income.)

We then proceeded to plan and design a distinctive mailing for each of these three groups.

Category 1

"He who doesn't learn from the past is condemned to repeat it," in 36-point dark blue type, stood alone on the 6" x 9" envelope of the package for the more serious-minded readers. The four page (11" x 17" two-color, two-sides) letter began:

"THE PART OF THE WORLD THAT COMBINES
A SENSE OF HISTORY WITH
CONTEMPORARY SOCIAL PROGRESS
HAS SOMETHING TO TELL AMERICA . . ."

This copy appeared above a reproduction of an early

Renaissance map of Scandinavia; and just below it, in red, was this:

"AND WE'D BETTER START LISTENING."

There followed a list of "Did you knows" covering subjects as varied as Norway's successful techniques for wiping out unemployment and Sweden's paid maternity leave for *men*. Overleaf, the copy continued by inviting the reader to "discover the real issues" in the pages of *Scandinavian Review* describing its contents more fully and presenting other benefits of ASF membership.

The 22" x 17" brochure declared that "In the Days of the Vikings The Scandinavians Provided World Leadership" and continued inside with "And They Still Do!" The headline on the full-cover, full-size spread asked, "Are You Aware How This Affects Your Quality of Life?"

Category 2

"POSTER ENCLOSED!" proclaimed the red teaser on the 9" x 12" bright yellow envelope for the mailing to the second group. The word "NOW" in 5"-high blue letters stood alone on the front panel of the outward side of the poster, followed as the piece was opened with the words, "From the Wonderful Lands that brought you . . ." Then, following a list ranging from Bergman films, sauna baths, Ingemar Johanson and the Vikings to Liv Ullman, Saarinen's chairs, *Peer Gynt* and skiing, ending with the word "Comes . . .", a 1930's Hollywood-style poster within announced a

"SCANDINAVIAN FESTIVAL"

"66 years in the making . . . cast of twenty million . . . starring The Arts, The Folklore, The Food, The Society, The Scenery, The Beaches . . . from the Smash Best-Seller SCANDINAVIAN REVIEW." The accompanying four-page letter began, "You're invited! You're invited to a Scandinavian Festival.

"Come along with me to excitement you've never dreamed of, brought to you from the peoples of the Lands of the Midnight Sun—through the fascinating, colorful pages of SCANDINAVIAN REVIEW . . ."

Category 3

The third package carried as a teaser "What do you have in common with . . ." followed by the names and addresses of ASF members with distinctly non-Scandinavian names, from every part of the United States. The letter opened with, "Answer one easy question, please—"; then repeated the query and the list from the envelope, but with the addition of their very varied occupations. It continued: "Unless I miss my guess, the answer is: 'A little bit of Scandinavia is a part of you; the Scandinavian spirit of discovery, of adventure.' That's why they've enjoyed, and I'm sure you too will enjoy discovering SCANDINAVIAN REVIEW, and all the other exciting benefits your membership in the American-Scandinavian Foundation will bring you . . ."

The brochure, 8-1/2" x 22" with a short flap fold, continued the theme: "Because 'There's a little bit of Scandinavia in every one of us' . . .

"You'll find the Scandinavia that's part of you, vividly portrayed, clearly presented for your enjoyment in ' the fascinating pages of SCANDINAVIAN REVIEW . . ." It contained the pictures of and quotations from the ASF

members who had been listed on the envelope, and other reasons for subscribing.

Of course, there were many other aspects to the tests. For example, in each category we tested three different emphases. One batch stressed a particular—and more expensive—category in the foundation and included a valuable book in the offer; a second emphasized the benefits of a foundation membership without stressing one category over another; and the third emphasized the benefits of the magazine itself.

The response to each of the various packages clearly indicated the direction in which future appeals are being concentrated.

The size of the total test audience was 100,000.

When the mailings were about ready for printing, the ASF received an unsolicited, handwritten note from the President of Iceland, congratulating it on the publication of its latest "magnificent book." Naturally, this became the basis of a short "lift letter."

Successful 'Lift Letters'

I've been happy to observe the recent tendency toward greater originality in such "lift letters," which have all too often seemed to be taken verbatim from the old standby: "If you've already decided not to subscribe . . ." Two excellent examples have crossed my desk recently. One is from *Boardroom Reports,* headed "Office of the Publisher" and with the first phrase in imitation handwriting in brown:

"A personal invitation

" . . . because *Boardroom Reports* really is as good as the long letter says it is.

"I hope that you will send for the free pilot issue. It has become a must for executives in these competitive and complex days.

"Here's how you can improve your competitive edge . . ."

That, plus the brown "signature," is all. I wonder how many people will read that and subscribe, without ever unfolding the very well written six-page letter. (No, I am *not* attacking long copy. The more complex the proposition, the longer the copy must be, as a general rule.)

The other lift letter with a difference comes with a four-page mailing from *Forbes*. The letter— alone in the package—is on ivory stock, a 3-5/8" x 6-5/8" memo form; and after the opening, "If you have every thought of trying *Forbes,* there's a good reason for doing it now . . ." it pushes for prompt action on the ground that a price increase has already been announced. Furthermore, accepting this offer (which is strongly based on price) "will guarantee that you have the right to extend your subscription at today's rates, before your trial finishes."

Incidentally, the *Forbes* letter neatly handles the matter of avoiding complaints and potential violation of governmental regulations caused by late delivery. Here's what the letter says in the penultimate paragraph:

"An acknowledgement of your order will be mailed to you directly. The acknowledgement will advise you when your subscription will start, and that issue will be in the mails within thirty to forty-two days after we receive your order."

How your promotion stacks up
By Herbert G. Ahrend

Over the course of the years, I've received some highly effective promotion pieces. The three reviews below illustrate the broad range of responses as well as underline some very important concepts in promotion.

Manfred Holck, Jr., publisher of *Church Management: The Clergy Journal,* doubled the number of paid subscribers as the result of a recent mailing to 100,000 churches which drew a 3.1 percent response.

The emphasis in the letter, and on the reply card, focuses heavily upon the free bonus—a technique which is often dangerous, since it can both distract attention from the publication itself and attract gift collectors.

Here, however, it fits perfectly, for the gift is *Tax Planning for Clergy,* a Prentice-Hall booklet written by the magazine publisher himself. This gift not only serves a useful purpose for the prospect, but also, in and of itself, demonstrates the authoritative nature of the magazine.

This is the way the letter starts, with the headline in red 24-point type and a large picture of the cover of the booklet filling the upper half of the first of four pages:

"USE THE ENCLOSED REPLY CARD TO SAY YES . . . to this CHURCH MANAGEMENT: THE CLERGY JOURNAL No-Risk Trial Subscription Offer and get this important booklet ABSOLUTELY Free!

"Dear Friend:

"I am writing you this letter in the hope that the enclosed reply card will be in your outbound mail within 24 hours or at least within 10 days.

"Do this, and I will see to it that my valuable new booklet, *Tax Planning for Clergy,* is immediately mailed to your office as a gift.

"You may already know about my annual cassette tape, *The Minister's Income Tax,* the step-by-step, line-by-line instruction guide used by thousands of clergy each year to fill in their Form 1040 tax return.

"You may also know about my biweekly financial newsletter for clergy, *Church and Clergy Finance.* And you know about my books, *Making It on a Pastor's Pay, How to Pay Your Pastor More* and others.

"Each year I produce *The Minister's Income Tax* cassette tape in order to show clergy exactly how to fill out their tax return. Clergy who have used *The Minister's Income Tax* report it saves them valuable time besides saving them money.

"My new booklet, *Tax Planning for Clergy,* takes you beyond just the mechanics of filling in Form 1040. It tells you how to plan your taxes, how to avoid the taxes you don't owe, how to keep your tax bill to the legal minimum required by law."

Ten separate benefits which the booklet provides, each bulleted, occupy the second page and are followed by:

"All you need to do is to sign the enclosed postage paid reply card and drop it into the nearest mailbox. *Tax Planning for Clergy* will be mailed to you at once.

"At the same time we will enroll you as a no-risk trial subscriber to the professional magazine for clergy and church business administrators, *Church Management: The Clergy Journal.*"

Now *that's* what I call dramatizing a gift offer and getting full mileage from it.

The remaining two pages of the letter go into detail about the magazine and its contents (it's pictured on the center spread) and offer a no-obligation trial subscription. The final paragraph repeats the offer:

"But see for yourself. Mail the reply card. Allow me to send you *Tax Planning for Clergy* as a thank you gift. And allow yourself the privilege of a 15-day no-obligation study of your first issue of *Church Management: The Clergy Journal.*"

A two-color, 11" X 17" folder promotes the magazine, a newsletter and a variety of books written by the publisher on church and clergy finance, cassettes and a seminar. Effective and not too cluttered, considering the number of items.

The business reply card devotes two-thirds of its space to:

"IT'S YOURS FREE!

"A valuable booklet that could save you money.

"We're holding a FREE copy of this practical tax booklet just for you.

"No strings . . . . No obligations . . . . A plain and simple GIFT."

This mailing certainly deserved its success. It might have done even better, however, had the no-risk trial offer (i.e., cancel if you're not satisfied with the first issue) been repeated and played up on the card. That offer is contradicted by the contract printed on the card, which the prospect is asked to sign and which promises only pro-rata refund on cancellation.

One query: Why include a "no" box on the card? Have there been any complaints from people who thought that it meant they could receive the free booklet without subscribing?

doing it! is a non-profit publication which offers "practical alternatives for humanizing city life." Making that phrase immediately visible on the face of its self-mailer helps assure that the target audience will read further.

The mailer is unusual in size and appearance. It bears the earmarks of a "homemade" package. But I do not say that critically; for this publication's particular audience, it might well constitute a "plus." *doing it!* has made effective use of a single color, a dark chocolate brown.

The magazine offers a no-obligation trial, but that fact is not mentioned in the letter. Indeed, the letter might confuse a reader—it makes NO request for subscriptions. In fact, the last paragraph says, "Whether or not you subscribe, I would appreciate your comments." But it does offer to send a brochure.

The brochure is evidently about the Urban Alternatives Group, the nonprofit educational and research organization which publishes the magazine. It would have been more effective to separate the "word about us" (the UrbAlt Group) from the subscription copy and to repeat the offer of the UrbAlt brochure on the reply form. As it is, the appeal to work with the group dilutes the subscription appeal (to the extent that it is reduced to "I hope that you will join us not only by getting the magazine, but also by working towards change together with others in your community") and vice versa.

The promotion probably worked well because it gives so complete a picture of the contents and purposes of the publication. But it could certainly have been made to produce far more had the offer been made more explicit both in the letter and in the reply form area.

Failure to think through the terms of an offer and to phrase them clearly are common faults in subscription promotion. And a poorly presented offer can vitiate all the effort and expense you put into the promotion.

New Directions for Women is a feminist news quarterly which has attained a circulation of 30,000 in five years. Editor Paula Kassell informs me that the magazine aims "primarily to reach women throughout the United States who are not yet feminists." Its major effort should go to improving the renewal percentage; and that might even involve some changes in the publication as well as the letters. For, while the publication is a good one, the fact that it's a tabloid, printed on newsprint, gives it an ephemeral appearance. This discourages readers from filing the issues for later reference which in turn adversely affects the renewal rate.

Design and format questions aside, *New Directions For Women* would do well to extend the renewal series beyond three letters. Publishers too often give up on renewals long before they should. Mailing to expires should continue *beyond* the point at which the cost of each renewal equals the cost of getting a new subscriber. Yes, beyond, because a person who has renewed once or twice is far more likely than a new subscriber to renew again.

Some might consider the promotion letter for *New Directions for Women* too coy—I like it. It begins—below the letterhead and a "flagged" diagonal sentence at the upper right—by referring to recent improvements, with this:

"RECIPE

1 cup crushed ego
1 teaspoon job discrimination
1/4 teaspoon chauvinism
1 well-beaten path to the washing machine
1/2 teaspoon grated nerves
1 pinch from a man on the street
1 dash from the dentist to the babysitter

"Mix all ingredients, one on top of the other, and stir violently. Cook until you feel a slow burn and add one last straw.

"Serves: 53 percent of the population.

"Dear Friend:

"Women are becoming aware of the ingredients that make up their daily lives, and many questions are rising to the surface.

"The staff of NEW DIRECTIONS FOR WOMEN is dedicated to finding some answers and creating a newspaper that will affect every woman who reads it. NEW DIRECTIONS FOR WOMEN believes that when women understand sex discrimination, they will reach for the tools to combat it. That is why we are trying to reach the woman who recognizes herself as a person, with her own rights, even though she may have heavy responsibilities for others."

A good start; it selects the audience and should hold interest. However, I think that the next few paragraphs—filled with the paper's history and praise of the staff's dedication—will lose momentum. If you want to keep them in, move them further into the body of the letter. Keep the momentum up at this point with the survey results on the quality of your readership (the reader of the letter will identify with the others) and the list of articles which were praised by subscribers.

The idea of using a premium to encourage long-term subscriptions is a good one. But the separate blank which appears on the premium announcement sheet is a mistake. Why make people take the trouble to fill out TWO blanks, neither of which has the full data on it? I'm not quibbling about a minor point. Just such small irritations can cause an almost-sold prospect to toss the whole thing aside. Remember, it's essential to make *clear* exactly what action you desire the reader to take and to make it *easy* to do so.

Twenty tips

By Eliot DeY. Schein

Every industry has certain proven basics that seem to provide success for its products or services. The magazine subscription direct mail industry has its basics, too. So here, for top management, is a look at how circulation promotion people are taking advantage of a score of proven ideas designed to increase response and profits.

1. One-to-one.

Be sure your creative people write one letter to one person at a time.

A letter shouldn't begin: "All of you photographers out there . . ." This opening indicates that the writer hasn't realized that each recipient is (ideally) receiving only one piece and is primarily interested in him- or herself. Direct mail is a personal medium, and letters are sent to individuals, not groups. The letter should have said, "You're a photographer . . ."

2. The blue signature.

The effectiveness of direct mail is substantially increased when the reader can psych himself into believing the letter is being sent specifically and exclusively to him. That psychology should be fostered and nurtured and not destroyed by an obviously "printed" signature.

While on large mailings it is impractical to sign each letter by hand, there are machines that can do original signatures. Not up to the additional cost of machine signing? Then print in a color commonly associated with a hand-signed personal letter. Blue-black ink seems to do the trick.

3. The scrambled indicia.

The indicia are the printed postage devices on outgoing envelopes. They are used instead of stamps or postage meter imprints for most third class mail, and they are too often given short shrift. Keeping in mind the goal of personalizing letters, advise your art people to angle, screen and use whatever tricks are permissible to make those indicia look like they came out of your postage machine, one envelope at a time.

4. Order forms that work.

This is more a warning than an idea: You have invested a great deal of money, time and effort into producing and mailing a carrier envelope that gets opened, a letter that gets read, and a brochure that entices. Be sure to have an order form that is easy to use and that fits into your return envelope.

The best way to check this is to make believe you are a consumer. Open up your own package. Does the order form have the information necessary and the mechanical sizes and conditions required so that the order can come back without any additional work on the part of the consumer?

5. P.S.

One of the most highly visible and highly read parts of any letter is the postscript under the signature. Take full advantage of this device to reiterate your basic selling message, emphasize a benefit, drive home a no-risk guarantee. It also provides the necessary transition to the order form and helps close the sale.

6. Coordinate your package.

A direct mail package should look like it's "all together"—color coordinated or connected by some graphic device. Consistency provides a sense of structure and security for the reader, so keep the package components looking like they belong together to avoid an assortment of conflicting pieces.

7. Envelope teaser.

The carrier envelope has two main jobs. One, to contain the package components. Two, and often overlooked, to get itself opened by the consumer so the offer can be made. An effective device is teaser copy on the carrier envelope that lures, prompts, provokes and, generally speaking, makes the reader anxious to get inside.

8. Use typewriter type.

Another strong psychological component of sound direct mail strategy: The letter should look like it was typed on a typewriter. (You will probably have to *set* type to make it look like it was typed.)

When was the last time you received a business letter that was typed in Helvetica medium? It was typed on a typewriter as your direct mail letters should appear to be.

9. Reader involvement.

Stamps, order form tokens, and spaces to initial are fun to use. If you have a magazine that has enjoyment or pleasure as any part of its selling proposition, you might want to add to the fun and enjoyment promised in your package by involving the reader in the fun of ordering.

Most recipients of your package will try your reader involvement device to see how and if it works, and that gets the ball rolling. It may be a ticket to put into a theater ticket-takers slot, or a roll of film to be put into a camera. Just make sure your reader involvement device is not too complicated.

10. No "yes" or "no."

Whatever you do, be sure that the consumer you have spent your time and money to reach cannot say "no" to any question in your direct mail package. An effective technique is to ask the question "Which would you prefer?" and give two answers from which to choose. That way, either answer will be "safe" and will not preclude a sale.

To start a letter off "Do you like fly-casting?" begs a yes or no answer. A better start would be, "Which of these two answers would you give if you were asked about fly-casting?"

11. Write simple copy.

Write to the lowest reading level of your potential market. The simpler the copy, the greater the percentage of people you're mailing to who will be able to comprehend it. Since lower reading level people cannot relate positively to graduate school-level copy, make sure your copywriters don't show off their expertise in complex diction in your direct mail.

12. Surprise renewals.

As your renewal series gets to its third or fourth effort, the subscriber should not be able to look at the carrier envelope and recognize it for what it is—another renewal effort. If the carrier envelopes are different sizes, shapes and colors, and if they have different postage devices, your renewal series may begin to pull better immediately. Take your subscriber by surprise.

13. Publisher's credibility.

When you are reaching people who may not know of your magazine, you are asking for an order "in the blind." And just as a substantial looking retail store makes consumers more confident, direct mail that establishes your credibility makes potential subscribers more confident. Say who you are and what guarantees of fulfillment you are making. Once credibility is established, it's easier to get the consumer to take a chance on ordering your product.

14. Be a scout.

All circulation directors should subscribe to all magazines competing with their own. They will then receive the competition's billing series and renewal series. In addition, by varying the way your circulation director spells his name (to serve as a key), he can receive the rental history of the competitors' mailing lists.

Watch your competition's changes in copy, offer, and editorial content. See what seems to be working for them. It will help you decide what may work better for you.

15. Ask for the order.

No matter how luxurious and refined your package is, don't be afraid to nail down the order within the package. The consumer should not be given a chance to say, "Maybe I'll look for it on the newsstand to see if it's the kind of magazine I want."

Your package should contain all the information necessary to aid the consumer in making a "buy or no-buy" decision. And certainly it should end requesting that the order be placed *now*.

16. Forget exotica.

In tests over the past 14 years, red and black printing has out-pulled every other two-color combination. If the graphics people you use are getting tired of red and black, it would be better to change graphics people rather than to allow them to change your colors. No—mint green and purple will not pull better than red and black.

17. To thine own self be true.

Your direct mail package must be the representative of your magazine. For example, if your magazine contains full-color editorial, you should use slick full-color printing. This will, of course, aid initial responses. But it will also prepare your new subscribers for the product they are going to receive.

The closer the direct mail package comes to describing the actual publication (both physically and editorially), the closer you come to having an audience highly refined and fully receptive to the product he or she will actually receive. This can result in only one benefit, but a big benefit it is—better renewals.

18. Sign here.

One of the most successful mailings ever produced was for a business school. The signature block included the name Jacqueline Landers—a non-existent person. There is no question that an easy, believable name will pull better than a difficult name of a circulation director or publisher.

Note: In your billing series you are legally required to use the name of someone who really exists and works in your company.

19. Third-class renewal.

There's no profit in using first class mail for your renewal series, unless for some reason you are interested in instantaneous renewals or in wasting money. Renewal letters can and should go out third class.

If you have a publication with a subscription circulation of 240,000 for example, you are averaging 20,000 subscribers per month added to your renewal promotion file. At a 50 percent renewal after six efforts, assuming each effort pulls 10 percent or lower, you may be mailing an average of three efforts per subscriber. At current postage rates, the difference between first class and third class in one year on this hypothetical renewal series alone is more than $60,000!

20. Always test.

Test something every time you put a mass mailing through the post office. A new package, a different offer, a new price, a new color, a new signature, a new postage device. Whatever it is you are testing, incorporate it into your mass mailing. It is relatively inexpensive to test one or two new ideas with each mass mailing you make. Your production people, your mailing house and your printer will all operate more efficiently if you add 100,000 test pieces to a one million piece mailing instead of waiting to mail the 100,000 pieces of test material separately. It is much more efficient, and the information you get will help make your next mailing an even greater success.

Go for a second sale fast

By Herbert G. Ahrend

Never again will you be as likely to get favorable attention and additional orders from your readers as immediately after they've decided to subscribe.

That's why it pays to try for conversion of short-term trial subscribers right away. One effective technique to achieve this aim is offering to credit the entire payment for the short-term sub against a reduced rate, a one- or two-year figure, provided the reader takes action within a given time. By this method you can frequently increase your total number of conversions and renewals. It's a formula which has been proved over the years by such knowledgeable publishers as Kiplinger.

It's also a good idea to sell a second product to your subscribers immediately, when you send an acknowledgement of the subscription. This may prove more profitable than offering both the subscription and the other item in the same mailing. This subject came up in a recent discussion with Len Latimer of *Songwriter* as a result of the comments I made on his mailings. I had remarked that the claims made for a newsletter overlapped and clashed with those made for the magazine, resulting in a reduction of the believability of the entire package. I was interested to learn from Len that the inclusion of the newsletter offer brought in a considerable number of profitable subscriptions for it, but had apparently cut considerably the number of orders for the magazine.

You will generally find that you will cut the number of sales of the primary product when you include a second item in your prospect mailings. Of course, if the second item is profitable enough, this may prove to be more than acceptable. But why not get the maximum number of subscriptions the first time around, and then offer the other product when you thank the subscribers for their support?

Unless your additional item is a natural that a large percentage of your list will want as soon as they are informed of its existence, you'll probably find that your lowest cost method of selling it is to approach your current subscribers. Many publishers have found that newsletters related to their basic magazine are an extremely profitable source of additional income. The material in them can often be obtained as a byproduct of the editorial work in putting together the basic publication. There have even been cases—*Newsweek* is an example—where a department has been extracted and expanded for sale at many times the basic magazine price.

Your Bounce Back Can Be Anything

The product you use as a "bounce back" need not, of course, be a newsletter. It can be a book or a series of books, whether made up of material from your publication, or simply of related interest. There's really no limit to the number of things you can sell. I received a mailing recently in which the effort is made not only to reactivate former subscribers, but to sell T-shirts with the magazine's logo.

According to Ed Ferman, publisher of *Fantasy and Science Fiction,* such a mailing did not do as well as he had hoped. Frankly, I'm not surprised.

The mailing falls into the category which Henry Hoke, Sr. used to call "we-we letters." It starts:

"Dear Reader:

"I'd like . . ." and it contains 11 "I's," "we's," "our's" and "us's." True, there are eight "you's" and "your's," but the emphasis on the first person is overwhelming. Then, too, the letter starts with a price offer before promoting the contents, and pushes the T-shirt in the post script, which ends:

"Send us a check for $9.98 and have your reading *and* wardrobe set for summer!"

Personally, that's an offer I can refuse. The reply form, printed in dark blue on pale blue stock, says, "Special Summer Offer," but does not mention that this is "the best deal we've had in years," as the letter claims, and does not have a single box to check for *both* the "reading and wardrobe." The *F&SF* logo, which the letter says is imprinted in white on navy blue, is almost lost on the photo because it's printed on blue stock.

I'm curious to know whether this mailing sold many T-shirts. I confess to still being amazed at the eagerness with which many people pay to act as walking billboards for all types of things, from sneakers to beer to bookstores. It could be that Ed had a good idea in the T-shirt, but I think there should have been a combination price to give the impression to the former subscribers that they're getting a special deal. I also feel that the appearance of the mailing worked against its success. The monotone blue of the entire package is not up to the high standard which *F&SF* has always maintained editorially.

Season of Amazement

But perhaps this is just my season for being amazed. For I can't understand why a magazine of the quality of *Harper's* uses an envelope which screams "FREE ISSUE . . . May we send it?" in inch-high type, orange against red, and no indication of the publication which is being offered, except for the small line—"Harper's Magazine Co."—in the postal indicia.

The reader *Harper's* wants is probably unimpressed by an offer of an anonymous free issue. If he or she does open the envelope the reader will probably be equally unimpressed with the blown-up heading on the letter.

"Why are we offering you this opportunity to get our current issue *free* and, if you like it, to try eight issues of HARPER'S at the *lowest price available?*

"There must be a good reason..."

If there is a good reason, why not say so, either on the envelope or in the heading? It isn't until the inside of the four-color brochure, printed on unnecessarily heavy-coated stock (considerably heavier than the reply card, in fact), that any headline offers an indication of an actual benefit:

"...provocative viewpoints and quotable commentary on everything worth talking about in today's world."

My guess is that most readers will not take the trouble to find it. This mailing may pull a large number of curiosity orders, but they won't be the type of people who will renew and re-renew, and those are the people who provide the life blood of any magazine.

Free-issue and half-price offers are still popping out of the woodwork all over the place. There are many occasions on which they are appropriate—for example, when a new magazine is convinced that it can secure loyal readers if only it can get the exposure. But, please remember that the purpose of direct-mail solicitation is to get the type of subscribers who will stay with you. Keep in mind that free issues or half-price offers alone are not adequate to describe and sell your product.

Here's a piece used by *New Times*. It's a computer personalized form, 6-3/8 x 3-1/2", which reads in full:

"Dear _____ _____:

"No elaborate sales pitch. 20 issues of NEW TIMES for only $5.77...the lowest price ANYWHERE for the feature news magazine of colorful, irreverent, in-depth journalism. Use the pencil to subscribe today. GEORGE A. HIRSCH."

The envelope says "Pencil enclosed for your reply," and a reverse block in turquoise at the head of the form reads, "Special Half Price Order Form." The young lady who gave me this piece wrote on it:

"H: For your file of 'Horribles'?" (Is *New Times* really well enough known to get away with this?)

Now comes the "funny coincidence" department. A mailing from *Newsweek* in bluish green. A computer personalized form, 6-3/4 x 3-1/2", heading "1/2 COVER PRICE LIFETIME GUARANTEE," and reading in full:

"Dear Mr. Ahrend,

"No Big Sales Pitch. Just a big offer. Use the pencil to subscribe to *Newsweek* and get it at half cover price—now and later, as long as you wish, even for life! See details on back, then mail this form. Dan Capell." Sounds pretty much the same, doesn't it?

But it isn't. When *New Times* has one of the forms returned, all it has is a 20-issue trial subscription. The *Newsweek* piece offers a choice of 25 weeks for $12.50 or 48 for $24.00, but the printed explanation of the "life-time guarantee" on the back of the personalized form makes it clear that this is virtually "till forbid" authorization. Here's the first paragraph of that form:

"As a lifetime-guarantee subscriber, you will be notified each time your subscription nears expiration, and billed for a one-year extension of service at half the newsstand price which is then in effect. As long as you authorize an additional period of service each time such authorization is required, your half-cover-price guarantee will remain in effect. Thus you can continue to subscribe at one-half what others are paying at the newsstand for as long as you wish—even for life."

There are also two other significant differences in favor of the *Newsweek* piece. *Newsweek* has a check box for credit-card use, and another one reading "Check here if this is RENEWAL."

Reason To Open

If everything I've written so far has given you the impression that I favor packages in which the envelope gives you a good reason to open it, you're right. The *California Journal* has sent me two packages. One is a 6 x 9" paper envelope printed in red with nothing but a line drawing probably representing a man trying to push a boulder uphill at night; and the other is in a plastic envelope, one side of which is clear, permitting a view of a map of California and the slogan, "Don't let California get away from you...", while the other side shows the dome evidently being blown off the State House, with the query, "Hey, what's going on in there?"

For the reasons cited above, I favor the plastic. Its message selects the audience far more than does the sketch on the other, a sketch which is repeated on the cover of the folder inside, along with the slogan, "It doesn't have to be an uphill battle..." The first inside fold carries a printed letter against a benday. I prefer to see the letter as a separate unit. The inside of the folder is good, with attractive cartoons and comments on what is going on in Sacramento.

The other piece also has its letter hidden inside the folder. Once again the inside spread of the folder is the most attractive part of the entire package. In this case, plastic was tested against a paper envelope with the same materials. The plastic out-pulled slightly.

California Journal has one practice which might well be adopted by other publications which are in a logical position to do so. It has three rates—an individual rate, $15 a year; a library or government rate, $30, including a quarterly index; and a corporation or association rate, $50 a year, which includes not only an index, but also an "annual binder and our Quick Query Service, which provides spot research on matter related to state government and politics."

Tricks of the trade

By Eliot DeY. Schein

In the February 1980 issue of Folio, this column presented 20 tips for increasing the efficiency and effectiveness of your direct mail. Because of an overwhelmingly positive response from publishers, managers and circulators, 20 more tips were carefully put together to help you achieve even greater success.

1. Stand out in the crowd.

With direct response a booming industry and everybody putting *something* in the mail these days, the competition to be noticed and read is fiercer than ever. Try using a bright, boldly-colored envelope—like orange or magenta. On coated stock, the effect is even snappier. And strangely enough, it works just as well for formal products like newsletters and business magazines.

2. Double your color.

If your mailing piece includes a full-color brochure, test using a carrier envelope with a large window positioned against some of the color work. It's a relatively inexpensive way to heighten the impact and excitement of your package.

3. Combine components.

If your product warrants a full-color brochure in addition to a letter, but costs are putting the squeeze on you, try combining both elements into an "illustrated letter." Admittedly, in years past, this has been a no-no, since a letter with color pictures on it violated the credibility of a letter that was supposed to have been written *by* someone *to* someone. However, in recent years, and perhaps due to the advent of a new visually-oriented generation, the "illustrated letter" can, on occasion, outpull a standard letter.

4. Re-evaluate your mail.

Check your direct response promotions to see whether your copy has wandered away from the tried-and-true basics. The basics may seem old-fashioned . . . or hackneyed . . . or cornball . . . or stale. But they work. Consider the power of "HALF-PRICE". . . "LAST CHANCE" . . . "LIMITED TIME" . . . "NOW" . . . "NEW" . . . "SAVE" . . . "SALE" . . . and "BARGAIN." They worked then. They work *now*. Don't put them out to pasture too soon.

5. Stick up for your magazine.

Chances are, you offer some sort of guarantee on the enjoyment and acceptability of your magazine, usually a money-back. It may be old hat to you, but to your prospect, the guarantee implies credibility and reliability. It is important ammunition: Don't bury your guarantee—use it to help sell.

6. Let the parents in on it.

If your magazine is oriented toward young people, test enclosing a "second letter" addressed to the parents.

Such a letter can help reinforce vocational advantages, discuss the value of the learning experience, and emphasize the benefits of character building. Since the parents usually sign the check, it makes good sense to win their confidence.

7. Repeat the high points.

Since the average consumer has little time to read your direct mail package, highlight your major selling points or benefits so that they are easily identified in the letter. It's an especially good idea to summarize these benefits on your order form, where many readers go directly for a quick idea of your selling proposition.

8. Pennies from heaven.

In today's economy, your costs—and,as a result, the prices you charge—are increasing. However, the consumer's ability to pay is decreasing. Therefore, you have to soften the impact of your prices.

One way is to state the price, repeatedly, in terms of "pennies per day," or "just a quarter a week," etc. Quoting your benefits at these rates can make your deal sound like a positive bargain.

9. Hit 'em at home.

If you publish a business, trade or industrial magazine, you can increase circulation nicely just by decreasing pass-along readership at the plant or office. All of your promotional pieces, from new business to billing to renewals, should encourage delivery at the individual's home. To help make the point, you can cite the advantages of on-time delivery, reading at leisure, and no borrowed or cut-up copies.

10. Name calling.

In your direct mail, don't be afraid to mention your competitors by name and tell how you believe you are better. Today's consumer has already been conditioned to this approach by general advertising and is receptive to it.

Competitive advertising not only shows off your advantages, it also says that you are confident about your magazine. In addition, if your competitors happen to be bigger than you are, you enhance the perception of *your* size by association.

11. Who's on your board?

Almost any magazine can create a board of advisors to be used in its promotion pieces. Usually they can be drawn, without much coaxing, from regular contributors to the magazine and notables in the magazine's special sphere of interest. It's a beautiful way to add respectability and an aura of strength and authority.

12. Something of value.

On your new business mailings, test the inclusion of a pertinent chart, map, table, graph, schedule, calendar or the like. For little or no extra cost, this device can provide you with certain benefits.

Right off the bat, it connotes that your product is useful and valuable. Furthermore, it increases reader involvement with the package and it provides you with a must-open teaser for your carrier envelope.

13. Controlling the control.

You should make it an ongoing campaign to continually test and refine your control package. Don't be satisfied just because it wins. Try to make it cheaper and even more efficient.

How? Try eliminating one color from components. Test it without the brochure, on less expensive stock. Do an 11 inch by 17 inch one-sheet instead of 3 or 4 nested pages. You may be surprised to discover that you can eliminate some costs without compromising results.

14. How big is your building?

Ask your fulfillment house to create a special street address for you. *Firehouse* magazine is 82 Firehouse Lane, Boulder, Colorado. *Jewish Living* is 1 Jerusalem Avenue, Marion, Ohio. This technique can help decrease the impersonality of a fulfillment house address, increase your magazine's credibility, and help spread the magazine's special personality throughout your entire mailing piece.

15. Stimulate your reader.

With the increased use of computerized letters, especially ink jet, how do you stimulate a quickly jading audience? Try hyping your computer package by programming some easily available information into it.

Ask your copywriters to incorporate into a letter information such as the number of women . . . homes . . . cars . . . doctors . . . universities (or any information easily accessible from government statistics) in the potential subscriber's state. A simple one-time programming operation can bring an important new twist to your package.

16. Hardening results on soft offers.

How can you depress cancellations on your "soft" offers when the subscriber can quit with no cost or penalty after the first issue? Of course, fulfilling your promises with a good product helps. But so does designing an invoice with broad diagonal bars in the background (or some other pattern) so there's really no clear space to write the word "cancel." Believe it or not, this device does seem to give the subscriber pause and a chance to reconsider his decision to cancel.

17. Satisfying the FTC.

Since you obviously can't fulfill an order within 30 days if you're doing a viability test mailing on a magazine that doesn't yet exist, the Federal Trade Commission says you must provide the customer with an option to cancel for a refund. Turn this minus into a plus by offering, along with the refund option form, an explanation that the magazine will take a while longer to produce in order to ensure a superior product. You can also include an additional form for gift subscriptions.

This technique demonstrates to the customer the quality you intend for the magazine and your intent to ultimately publish. You might just be surprised how it can decrease "cancels" and actually produce gift subs!

18. Change your bind-in.

To maximize the effectiveness of bind-in and blow-in cards and envelopes, change them as often as you can. Over-used cards lose their impact, fade into the background, and become fixtures. Cards with different copy and art work gain attention immediately and register the message. It's an additional expense, to be sure, but one that's more than likely to pay for itself.

19. Double your bind-in.

How can you double your number of subscription bind-in cards for just pennies extra? Print and bind them two-up, attached at a perforation. They can be side by side, or top to bottom. It can help draw in those extra subs, especially if you're a publication with high pass-along readership.

20. Control your lists.

When selecting lists for a test, ask your broker to get you the control package for major lists under consideration. Gauging their compatibility with your package and offer can help you zero in on the lists with the most potential.

If the control package that was used to generate the lion's share of a list you were considering renting happens to be a sweepstakes package, you'd better consider the possibility of mailing a sweepstakes offer yourself. Or else be prepared for what could be substandard performance.

Is your opening question turning them off?

By Herbert G. Ahrend

When should you use a question as your first paragraph?

Only when the answer which it will normally elicit is one which will start the reader on a chain of thought that leads to a desire to subscribe.

Never use a question which can be answered with a flat "NO" (except in the case of highly controversial publications or issues where it is clear to the prospect from the outset that his or her vehement "NO" is in accord with your own opinions).

Never use a question which can cause the reader to say, "Huh? Don't *you* know?"

This little lecture was inspired by a promotion letter just given me by a resident of Delaware County, N.Y. Delaware County is situated southwest of Albany, just a couple of hours drive from the Adirondacks. The letterhead reads: "Adirondack Life, The Magazine of Life in the East's Last Great Wilderness."

The letter begins:

"Dear Reader:

"What are the Adirondacks?

"According to the dictionary, they are a 'mountain range in NE New York, part of the Appalachian chain.' Many geologists might differ with that last assertion, for they know that the Adirondack mountains are far older than the Appalachians—that they are, in fact, among the oldest mountains on earth. . ."

Are you still reading? If you are, you're probably far more polite than most of the recipients of that letter. But for the benefit of the curious, here are the next two sentences:

". . .But lovers of the region would simply say that the dictionary definition is too barren to do justice to the unique qualities of a magnificent area.

"What are the Adirondacks?"

Why in the world is such an opening directed toward people who probably are fully aware of most of the facts listed alongside the eight bullets which follow the repetition of the opening question?

As the young lady who gave me the letter stated: "I love the Adirondacks, and I might be interested in subscribing to the magazine, but I found the letter boring and I didn't read very far."

It's always possible that I will receive a note telling me that this letter is the most successful the publication has ever used, since flukes do happen. Nevertheless, I feel certain that it would have pulled better if what is now the last paragraph on page one were the first paragraph. Here it is:

"Only one magazine deals with the entire Adirondack area in all its aspects—its people, its politics, its history, its wildlife, its beauty. That magazine is ADIRONDACK LIFE. If you love this beautiful land, then you will want to own ADIRONDACK LIFE, the bimonthly regional magazine that captures it all in articles and photographs."

The eight bulleted items could better be used inside a box at the bottom of the last page, or even as a separate enclosure.

The purport of everything I've said to date is similar to the dictum enunciated by the late Henry Hoke, who founded The Reporter of Direct Mail Advertising, the publication which his son Pete has expanded so brilliantly into today's Direct Marketing. Henry's oft-repeated thesis was that most letters written by amateurs (and many written by professionals as well) would be stronger and more effective if the first paragraph were blue-penciled. Next time you're really stumped by a promotion letter, try that technique and see.

All too often writers strive for a quite unnecessary and extraneous effect in the first paragraph. By the time they reach the second paragraph, they're in their stride and are telling their story naturally.

A Good Opening Question

Of course, it is possible to get into the story with a good question. Following are two examples of such promotion packages. Each starts with a question which focuses the reader's attention in a direction the writer wants it to go.

"Dear Songwriter,

"Have you ever heard a tune on the radio and thought to yourself, 'I can write a song as good as that'?"

Now, this is a question which is bound to get attention from people who have unpublished songs among their papers. . .and those are exactly the people to whom Songwriter Magazine appeals. Len Latimer, the publisher/editor, has been averaging 6 to 10 percent returns, with approximately 50 percent cash with order—an exceptionally high return, but it's an exceptionally good letter. Here's how it continues:

"Well, in fact, maybe you already have.

"But what do you do with it? What are your chances of getting published. . .how do you approach the right people?

"Do you need a lead sheet. . .how about a demo? And, how do you protect yourself?

"You can learn how to do it with SONGWRITER MAGAZINE.

"It gives you the vital, hard-to-find information you need to know.

"Perhaps you haven't heard of us since we only started publishing a year ago. Yet in that short space of time, over 20,000 of your colleagues are reading SONGWRITER every month!

"Yep!. . .Someone 'went and done it' . . .

"Developed a classy, knowledgeable, monthly magazine about songwriting as it really is. . .backed up authoritatively by music pros. . .a magazine that explores the art and craft of songwriting. . .a magazine that interviews the top writers and industry executives. . .a magazine that teaches, informs, inspires and entertains you.

"With this letter I would like to invite you to try it out on us. . .to examine a current issue without risk, obligation or commitment. But more about our special offer later."

Songwriter does not give away its profits. The offer is simply the first issue for a two-week examination. There's also a bonus of a useful "Music Directory" for cash up, permitting an interesting twist in the mailing. "Yes" and "Yes special bonus" slots in which to insert the "Yes" token, instead of "Yes" and "No." And they have increased their average order by one-third by adding flyers offering related books, back issues and a six-page monthly newsletter at $10 for six months "introductory rate."

My only major criticism of the mailing concerns this last offer. In my opinion the claims made for Tunesmith (the newsletter) overlap, and clash with, those for the magazine. This results in a reduction in the believability of the entire package. For example, I tend to snort when I find such a paragraph as this in a piece printed in two colors on coated stock:

"What exactly is TUNESMITH? It's a six-page, monthly newsletter from the publishers of SONGWRITER MAGAZINE, available only to a small number of songwriters on a first-come, first-serve basis. The circulation is limited because we simply do not want our contacts swamped with songs. That's how we're able to keep them as contacts."

Another Good Example

You may feel that my next example does not truly

start with a question, since a quotation appears above the salutation. Yet I think it may properly be included; the quote (of which more later) seems an entirely separate element. So here we go:

"Dear Reader,

"Does our name sound dull to you?

"Sometimes people think the 'CoEvolution Quarterly' is a pretty dry-sounding name for a magazine.

"Until they find out what it means.

"The *CoEvolution Quarterly (CQ)* is a magazine produced by the staff of the *Whole Earth Catalog.*"

I think that's a great way to introduce *CQ* to people, such as myself, who never even heard the word "coevolution" previously. (It means an evolving "relationship, stably dynamic, unpredictable and sure," in which two or more species "progressively evolve in close response to each other—coevolve.")

After a number of paragraphs reviewing the extraordinary range of material in this unique publication, the letter proceeds:

"We're eclectic. We don't pretend to be anything else. You have to be, to survive these days...

"If a magazine can be noncommercial and professional at the same time, we could be it. The *CQ* is an experiment in magazine publishing. An experiment because it's a forum for ideas you won't find anywhere else...

"I'd like to invite you to participate in this experiment with us. I think we can promise you your money's worth in innovation, controversy and access to tools that can help you stay one step ahead—or several paces behind. That depends on whether you're engineering a space shuttle or chinking a log cabin.

"Either way, I think the *CQ* could be valuable to you. I hope you'll give us a chance. I'm looking forward to hearing from you."

Now, about that introductory quotation to which I referred earlier. Jeanne Campbell, *CQ*'s circulation director, writes me:

"My formula is this: When I mail to subscriber lists for other 'sympathetic' magazines, I elicit some favorable comment about the *CQ* from either the editor or some figure that particular audience theoretically believes in. I excerpt the statement on the outer envelope and run it in full at the head of the cover letter."

A mailing to Esalen Institute members, she adds, incorporating a statement by Michael Murphy of Esalen, "got a whopping 4.7 percent response" the first time, and only 0.2 percent less, the second.

Direct, Forceful, Clear

I also received a copy of *The New Harbinger*'s promotion letter for comment. It's direct, forceful and clear and offers a strong guarantee in a postscript: "We will refund your *entire subscription price* at any time."

Here's the opening:

"Dear Colleague,

"I'm writing to tell you about a new publication that I think you will find interesting, provocative and, most important, useful in your work as a co-operative educator.

"First, a confession: It's not *really* a *new* publication. It is *The New Harbinger: A Journal of the Cooperative Movement,* and we have been publishing it since 1971. If you've never heard of us before, you can consider us new. Until this year, we never really tried very hard to tell the rest of the movement what we were doing."

The response, from a "narrow list," was over 4 percent. One point worth noting is that the reply card carries an extra box with this legend:

"Occasionally we exchange our mailing list with other organizations. If you do not want your name given out, check here."

If you are not yet incorporating this option in your mailings, I urge you to do so. You'll be helping the public image of the entire direct-response field, and, I firmly believe, yourself as well. Many large firms are finding that only from one-half of 1 percent to 2-½ percent object to the renting of their names. It might well be, too, that you'll get more subscriptions as a result of this gesture.

25 ways to build action into your mailing
By Herbert G. Ahrend

Sometimes the best of us overlook the obvious—such as asking for the action we want and making it easy for our prospects to take that action.

The worst example I've ever seen was the gaffe of an ad agency which sold, for its own account, four-color syndicated Christmas cards. They mailed an elaborate brochure, complete with reproductions, but without their name and address. If any of the following seems too elementary, consider that one is not meant for you. All are tested and proven techniques and may give your mailing just the extra lift for which you're looking.

1. *Start at the beginning. Ask for action on the envelope.* Use an imitation rubber stamp with a message such as "reply requested by (date)." *The Wall Street Journal* for many years used a purple boxed phrase, "Air Mail Reply Requested." *Reader's Digest* once printed, to the left of the address window in bold red type, "Please Let Us Know...."

2. *Offer a bonus for action before a set date.* If you adopt this technique, be sure to allow adequate time for production and mailing; avoid the twin dangers that the recipient will get your offer after the deadline or that the date will be too far in the future to achieve its purpose. Many mailers use a phrase such as "if you act within the next ten days" for this reason, but that may not ring true with sophisticated readers.

3. *Ask the readers to select their own subscription terms.* *New York* magazine dramatized this proposition by placing random numbers, from 33 to 207, on punch-out gummed discs, white against vivid red, on the stub of the order card. *The Wall Street Journal* used a bold caption which said, "86¢ a week...and choose your term."

4. *Or ask the reader to "check the savings you want."* A similar technique, which involves complications in fulfillment and renewal, is to put the emphasis on the savings available for one-, two- and three-year subscriptions and ask the prospects to check which amount of savings they want.

5. *Use a token.* Make the reader take some physical action. Tokens have become far more elaborate since *Reader's Digest* first employed them two decades ago, but the purpose remains the same: To "get the reader into the act." Your chances for a "yes" answer are improved, once he or she is involved. An early *Digest* piece, from 1960, used half-dollar sized (even to the thickness) gold-paper-topped tokens which had to be ripped off the stub and deposited in a slot on the card.

6. *Use a "reservation certificate."* That same *Reader's Digest* mailing also displayed this technique in its infancy. The words "Reservation Certificate" appeared in red in an overly fancy typeface. But no further effort was made to give the card a more distinctive appearance. The explanation for this appeared on the stub and said, "Because we are holding a reservation in your name, we should like to hear from you whether you accept this offer or not."

7. *Don't forget "bill me later" and credit card options.* Insisting on payment with the order nearly always cuts response drastically. If a lack of facilities or staff to handle billing hampers you, make sure you offer at least the bank cards and, if your publication appeals to the business or professional person, American Express.

8. *Put a deadline on acceptance of the offer.* Although this technique is not the same as that described in item #2, since you withdraw the offer after the deadline rather than give something extra for acting before it, it is subject to exactly the same pitfalls.

9. *Use a transferable label.* Ask the potential subscriber to peel the label off the carrying envelope and place it on the order device. In addition to securing the potential subscriber's participation, this also assures accuracy and readability of name and address.

10. *Use a "cash voucher" or a "check" as your order device.* These are two of many variations which may be employed to dramatize savings. Verisimilitude is important. The late Les Suhler, the circulation genius who originated the check for *Look*, told me that on several occasions banks actually cleared *Look's* $3 discount "checks," although they bore no bank name and were clearly marked "non-negotiable."

11. *Enclose a pen or a pencil.* The popularity of this idea seems to run in cycles. It's effective especially when you ask the recipients only to check one or more items and to sign their initials or name.

12. *Add a buck slip regarding a special bonus or stressing a major element of your offer.* Kiplinger has been among the most consistent users of this device.

13. *Use a sweepstakes offer—but if you do, play it up.* *Show* magazine, for example, used a second window on the envelope, through which a registration number appeared. The copy above and below the window was as follows: "A $15,000 European vacation may *already* be YOURS—if the number below (registered in your name alone) is the one that has been drawn. Note: You will forfeit any prize unless you mail back the enclosed certificate. So please see the details inside."

14. *Add a "handwritten" note to your letter, your envelope, or both.* *Newsweek* once added a blue handwritten message above the window of a mailing with a first class adhesive stamp—then 3¢—"Your final newsletter—see note enclosed." The added feeling of a personal communication will prove effective.

15. *Similarly, use an imitation rubber stamp at the top of your letter.* Here's how the *Journal of Commerce* used it year after year: "ACT AT ONCE to obtain latest all new 1961 edition NEW PRODUCTS and NEW SALES IDEAS FREE."

You'll notice that some of these ideas date back two or three decades. The chances are that their first uses were even years before that. A good idea never really wears out. It may need updating due to changing times but it can serve at least as an idea-starter.

16. *Offer a full refund guarantee.* The risk of obtaining an excessive number of freeloaders is really slight with quality lists. Moreover, if yours is a quality publication, the longer a person reads it, the less the likelihood that he or she will ask for a refund.

17. *Tip on a routing slip* asking that your letter be passed on to all those executives, by title, to whom your offer applies.

18. *Make an alternate trial offer* for those who are unwilling to commit themselves for a long term.

19. *Use a postscript to urge fast action.* The P.S. can be the second most important paragraph in the letter. Here's the P.S. *The New Republic* used 10 years ago to "sell" the alternate short term proposition which I just mentioned:

"P.S. On the attached card you will note that there is an alternate low-priced offer. If you'd like to give us a try (before going 'all-the-way') enclose $2 in the envelope. We will be glad to send you 18 issues of THE NEW REPUBLIC FOR YOUR APPROVAL. Later, if you wish, you may send on the $3 for the remaining 30 issues."

20. *Build holiday business by offering deferred billing.*

21. *Tip stamps at the top of the letter for the reply.* For maximum response, use an extra window on the envelope to reveal them. Caution: Be sure your lettershop merely tips them on. Pasting them on heavy-handedly will guarantee failure.

22. *Hint at higher rates to come.* Here's how *Skeptic* handles this: "Buy yourself up to three years of immunity from the *Skeptic* price increase. Renew your subscription now, in advance, at the old, low prices!" (I'm rather skeptical of the letter which accompanied that card. These two sentences would turn me off: "I'm not saying that a price increase is in the works. I *am* saying that no prudent individual would bet against it..." But then, they're probably betting that most people will not read that far down into the letter.)

23. *Make your guarantee prominent.* Whether it's for a full refund or simply a refund for the unexpired term, get maximum mileage by playing it up. *Art in America* has used a bold brown and white guarantee, die cut so that it stands two inches higher than the reply form to which it is attached.

24. *If you offer a free trial, make sure that your reader is aware of it.* The principle here is the same as in the last case, get maximum mileage from whatever device you utilize.

...And—a special bonus idea:

25. *Don't forget to ask for the order!* You'll never get action if you don't ask for it.

Cashing in on the news

By Herbert G. Ahrend

"What's new?"

That hackneyed greeting expresses the interest that most people have in the world around them. It can refer to current events, to underlying trends in the economy, to activities in a particular industry. On a more personal basis, it can refer to fashion, personal affairs, emotional entanglements.

Since "What's new?" can be interpreted in many ways, it is a question that can serve you well when preparing your next subscription promotion mailing.

The longtime champion in using current trends to sell subscriptions is, of course, the *Kiplinger Washington Letter.* Who has not received *Kip's* warning of "Boom and Bust Ahead"?

The first use of that famous phrase is shrouded in the mist of time. It's fascinating to observe the subtle changes which Stan Mayes, assistant to the president of The Kiplinger Washington Editors, Inc., and his staff have made in his superb sales letter to suit changes in the economic climate.

For instance, here's the way it started in December 1975:

"Will YOU Be Ready for the New KIND of Boom Ahead?

*"*The next few years will bring better times . . . new growth approaching boom proportions. And with this growth, more inflation.

"But the new boom won't be as free and easy to ride as the boom of the 60's. You will need reliable facts, forecasts and analyses on which to base your plans and preparations to cash in on THIS boom. You'll get the information you need for this type of planning in the *Kiplinger Washington Letter* . . . and the enclosed form will bring you the next 26 issues of this helpful service on a try-out basis. The fee: Less than 54 cents per week . . . $14 for the next 6 months.

"During the depression, in 1935, the Kiplinger Letters warned of inflation and told what to do about it. Those who heeded their advice reaped rich rewards.

"Again, in January of 1946, the Letters renounced the widely-held view that a severe post-war depression was inevitable . . . ."

By October of 1978, when different experts offered widely varying economic predictions, the letter—now localized for the Northeast—began:

"Is Business Headed for

More Boom and Inflation?

"Business during the 1980's will climb to the highest level this country has ever known. And with it . . . inflation.

"That may be hard to believe in the Northeast where high taxes, unemployment, welfare problems and soaring costs add up to a heavier burden than business faces elsewhere.

"Northeast governors have made this clear to President Carter . . . and now it's vitally important for you to know what Washington will do, if anything, to help business in the Northeast. By preparing now, you'll reap big dividends for your foresight, and avoid the blunders others will make.

"You'll get the information you need for this type of planning in the *Kiplinger Washington Letter* . . . and the enclosed form will bring you the next 26 issues of this helpful service on a 'Try-out' basis. The fee: *Only . . .*"

It's also worth noting that the envelope also appealed to the Northeastern businessperson's fears and insecurities. A bold red envelope carried this message against a white arrow:

"WHAT'S THE OUTLOOK FOR BUSINESS IN THE NORTHEAST?"

The arrow itself pointed to a pull-open tag on the short side of the envelope, inscribed *"PULL HERE FOR DETAILS."*

Three months later a smaller, more personal-looking envelope with the reply form (also personalized) still reflected economic uncertainty, but the postscript to the envelope teaser added a more positive note. Here's the way the envelope read:

"WILL THERE BE BOOM & MORE INFLATION AHEAD?

" . . . and what YOU as an executive can do about it."

The letter itself made a similar change in the basic boom and inflation pitch, as follows:

"Will There be BOOM and More INFLATION Ahead? . . . and what YOU as an executive can do about it.

"The next few years will see business climb to the highest level this country has ever known. And with it . . . inflation. Not a boom, but steady growth accompanied by rising prices.

"Those who prepare NOW for the growth and inflation that lies ahead will reap big dividends for their foresight . . . and avoid the blunders others will make.

"You'll get the information you need for this type of planning in the *Kiplinger Washington Letter* . . . and the enclosed form will bring you the next 26 issues of this helpful service on a 'Try-out' basis. The fee: *Only . . .*"

Magazines with a well-defined political point of view can also personalize their subscription promotion mailings. Here's how *Reason* uses the news to encourage subscriptions:

"Dear Reader:

"As you read today's headlines you are probably sometimes gripped with the feeling that something is terribly wrong with our world, something the news media seem unable (or unwilling) to notice. You probably especially get this feeling when you observe that:

• *"Taxation* at all levels now claims over 40% of your income, and total federal liabilities now are $5.1 trillion ($115,000 for every man, woman and child).

• *"Inflation* continues to destroy the value of your dollar, while the government (which caused inflation in the first place) continues to print excess paper money and spend more billions.

• "*As crimes of violence* return our streets to the Dark Ages, our police spend half of their budgets 'protecting' us from marijuana, prostitution, and nude bathers.

• "*Experts still tell us that the way to solve social problems is with massive federal spending programs*—ignoring the total failure of the 'Great Society' and hundreds of similar government boondoggles.

• "The federal government embraces 'consumerism' while at the same time keeping food prices high with farm *subsidies*; enforcing airline *price-fixing* via the CAB, and dozens of similar absurdities.

"*What's going on?* Why do these conditions reoccur year after year? Why don't the news media question these things, the way they seem to seize on every business failing pointed out by Ralph Nader?

"There *are* answers to these questions, and they're available in a unique magazine that asks embarrassing 'why's.' Its name is *Reason*.

"*Reason* is a monthly analysis and commentary on current events and issues. Unlike 'Establishment' media, *Reason* asks fundamental questions about what's going on in the world."

Business publications, as well as general consumer publications, can and should take advantage of political developments to catch the attention of potential subscribers. *Marketing and the Law* makes the connection in this effective manner:

"At this very moment, there are *over 200 separate bills* dealing with sales, advertising and marketing before the Congress! And that's only part of the problem facing the businessman/executive as he goes through his day.

"Apart from the Federal government's Big Eye and local regulatory agencies, competition is keener, consumer groups are more organized and the public is going to court with increasing frequency with both real and imaginary complaints.

"And there's the law . . . and the businessman's relationship with distributors, retailers . . . his suppliers, salesmen, purchasing agents . . . his problems of collection . . . his bid for governmental contracts.

"In short, there is a *growing significance of the law* as it affects everyday sales, advertising and marketing decisions . . . AND . . . knowing the legal pitfalls has become very much part of management's job. Not the fine points, of course. But a business executive just can't have a lawyer at his elbow every working minute.

"*Marketing and the Law,* issued twice a month, is designed to help you stake out the danger areas when setting your marketing policies."

Events in an individual industry provide an excellent topical tie-in for subscription promotion. Here's how *Housewares Review* capitalized on interest in the Chicago housewares show: "ANNOUNCING HOUSEWARES REVIEW TEN-MINUTE SHOW PLANNER!

"Whether or not you plan to attend the Chicago Housewares Show, be sure to see the July issue of HOUSEWARES REVIEW with its special 24-page 'Show Planner.'

"*If your subscription is received in time we guarantee to ship the Show issue immediately upon publication.* Please see the enclosed *order card.* The 'Ten-Minute Show Planner' presents a select group of 'top notch' show items in picture form with concise descriptions, resources, exhibit booth numbers. This folder represents only a small sampling of what the complete section will look like.

"If you plan to attend the show *this 'Ten-Minute Planner' is a must!*

"If you do not plan to attend, this special section will *bring the top new items to you in picture form.*"

The use of topical subject matter in circulation promotion has been tested and proved over many years. For example, back in 1955, *Life* pictorialized the subject of inflation on a sheet of graph paper with a red line, presumably representing the cost of living. It was surprinted with the following:

"Dear Reader:

"Let's talk about the *low* cost of living.

"Sure, newspapers cost 50 cents a week. And five pounds of potatoes sell for 30 cents. And a bus ride's as much as 23 cents.

"But you can still buy a picture-packed issue of LIFE at your corner newsstand for only 20 cents. And when you *subscribe* to LIFE (at the special introductory rate I can offer new subscribers), you get 39 *weekly issues of LIFE for only $3.99*—saving you $3.81 under the single copy price!

"That's a mighty low price for all the living you can experience through the big picture pages of LIFE!"

Even further back, on April 3, 1944, *Fortune* presented a truly classic example of a current event tie-in, with this letter promoting the current issue:

"As the Pacific offensive gathers momentum, your special interest in our postwar relations with other countries has probably made you realize, more acutely than most, the great lack of sound and current information on Japan.

"So I felt that you would like to know in advance about the publication of the first really comprehensive report available since war began. The entire contents of FORTUNE's April issue are devoted to:

"JAPAN— A MILITARY POWER WE MUST DEFEAT—A PACIFIC PROBLEM WE MUST SOLVE.

"You will doubtless be as surprised as I was that so much new information could be unearthed and such an *up-to-date, completely detailed* study made of this enemy during wartime . . . ."

What skills are needed to turn current events— whether in the world arena or in your industry—into reasons to subscribe?

First, you need a thorough knowledge of your publication and your audience's primary interests. No one can write effective circulation promotion without a comprehensive understanding of the product. If you're new at your job, or if you're an agency copywriter or a consultant with a new account, immerse yourself in the periodical's style and contents.

Second, develop a sharp eye for detecting new trends. Read six months' or a year's issues, cover to cover. Do that, and you're virtually certain to find several subjects appearing frequently which may well serve as the foci of promotion mailings or ads.

Recurring subjects for a TV trade paper, for example, include the expanding but still undefined role of cable systems *vs.* regular broadcasting, and the efforts to create "superstations" and satellite-linked nets.

In the banking area, you might zero in on the tempest created by Citibank's nationwide credit card promotion or the expanding automatic, teller-less "branches" (and the proliferating, often successful, attempts to "knock them off"). Or, you could tackle the big question of whether the "checkless society" is truly just around the corner, and what its effects on society as a whole will be.

If you've tried reading back issues, and still can't sort the important trends from the unimportant, make friends with one or more of the editors. Although some editors may feel superior to "mere" promotion people, most of them today know that the relationship of the two departments is a symbiotic one: your promotion will probably not succeed if they're not doing their job well, and they may not continue to have the money they need unless you're good at your task.

Don't be afraid to ask any questions at all about the field in general, as well as the particular aims of your own publication. Find out what distinguishes your publication from the competition, what special trends they see developing, and what special features are planned for future issues.

And—*don't* limit your reading to your own field. The broader your general knowledge, the greater the possibility that you'll perceive trends *before* others do. With a greater understanding of national and world events, you'll be better equipped to recognize both the dangers and opportunities in current development.

Window watching

By Eliot DeY. Schein

Most brand-new publishers believe that the concept of their magazine is so wonderful that the world will, literally, beat a path to their doors to pick up (for money, of course) copies of the magazine. However, once they learn that circulation is more a combination of hard-gained newsstand and subscription sales, this through-the-transom fantasy quickly disappears. And after a certain amount of trial and error, the subscription route surely comes into focus as being mainly the job of the direct mail medium.

Managers of established publishing companies who have been through remarkable testing cycles over the years have come to the conclusion that direct mail is the most efficient method of achieving new and renewal subscriptions. Taking this one step further, the direct mail package (in its present format), regardless of magazine, starts with one common element—the carrier envelope.

It is widely acknowledged that envelope copy is the "prime mover" of the direct mail subscription solicitation. One only need be on a number of divergent mailing lists to be able to sit back and observe the parade of different messages, formats, colors, teasers, sizes, shapes, indicia, and offers sporting themselves upon envelopes from just about every savvy publisher in the business.

If we accept the premise that the envelope is to direct mail as the "door-opener" is to the house-to-house salesperson, it must follow that the more consumer benefits visible to the recipient, the more envelopes opened. And clearly, order forms for subscriptions can't be returned from packages that were never opened.

In an effort to put as much up-front emphasis as possible on your direct mail carrier (or outer) envelopes, consider using techniques that will make your envelope, and thus, your package, stand out from anything else that arrives in that day's, week's, or month's mail. One of the easiest (and, in large runs, inexpensive) techniques of "using the carrier envelope for all it's worth" is window creativity.

Imaginative shapes

Windows are interesting elements. Since the United States Postal Service refuses to permit circular, trapezoidal, or other creative shapes of envelopes, all mailers are pretty much "stuck" with a rectangular shape. However, when it comes to window configurations, sizes, and combinations, the United States Postal Service seems to give direct marketers a free hand, at least to a degree.

Approximately 15 years ago, Ziff-Davis Publishing Company produced a renewal envelope for *Boating* magazine that had a window through which the address of the recipient appeared. The window was in the shape of a whale. This theme was carried through on the order form by three different-sized whales with check boxes in them, each one representing a different term of service. Naturally, the larger the whale, the greater the term.

Another Ziff-Davis publication, *Travel Weekly,* was marketing one of their annual publications with an address window die-cut in the shape of an SST plane.

Unfortunately, custom shapes cost lots of money and probably should not be tested unless a printing and die-cutting efficiency can be achieved through use of great volume. Today we have various formats and types of die-cut windows that are being used in control, as well as test packages, for some of our major magazines.

Additional windows

Another common technique used by magazines that contain a great deal of color editorial is the picture window which is usually on the reverse side of the envelope from the address window. This allows, as in the *House Beautiful* example, a full-color brochure to appear on the so-called back of the envelope and permits a feeling of four-color work on the carrier itself, even though the carrier is not printed in four colors. This technique allows your four-color printing to do double-duty and to present to the consumer an effective excitement which, one hopes, will cause more envelopes to be opened, and, therefore, more order forms returned ordering subscriptions.

In the case of the *Sport* magazine envelope, a smaller window is die-cut to the upper right of the address window through which the expiration date of a sweepstakes entry shows. *Sports Illustrated* uses a long, skinny additional window. *Time* magazine uses the picture window format we have just discussed.

Additional windows can also be used to allow token devices to appear through circular or rectangular shapes as part of the overall design of the envelope. One of the more creative examples of this technique is *Fortune* magazine's "instant free money" package, which sports an obliquely situated window larger than the actual address window.

The variations and permutations are endless. The envelope from a combined *Ladies' Home Journal* and *Redbook Magazine* offer has a window that could probably best be described as being in the shape of a smile or elongated T (or whatever you and Rorschach care to make of it). Not inexpensive, to be sure, but perhaps extremely effective. And when *Newsweek* sends out its "credit card calculator" free offer, a picture of the calculator is shown through a large window on the left side of the carrier envelope.

"How much profit does it produce?"

Now you ask: what is the best way to go about testing the creative use of additional windows on my "door-opener" or carrier envelope? "Timidly" comes to mind as an immediate response. Unless you have

money to burn, you will quickly discover that the cost of die-cutting additional windows for a sample quantity of mail may seem prohibitive.

On the other hand, to quote Henry Cowan, the famous practitioner of the complex and effective Publishers Clearing House-type mail, "It is not important how much the package costs to produce. It is important how much profit it produces." Cowan would have us all using multiple windows and colors and componentry until the United States Postal Service was required to give strained-back insurance to all mail carriers.

So when do you know if it is worthwhile to attempt a fancy window? Unfortunately, as in other variations in direct mail, you must test. And biting the bullet on what may seem to be a rather imposing up-front expenditure may just be something that can add profits to your circulation picture.

On the minus side, it's expensive. On the plus side, it is not as expensive as it used to be and, for goodness sake, if *Time, Newsweek, Sport,* and *House Beautiful* are using this technique almost 100 percent of the time, shouldn't you give it a try? The answer is, surely you should. And maybe now is the perfect time for you to start setting aside a little "hope chest" of circulation development dollars in order to test customized die-cut windows in next December's direct mail.

By the way, the whale window envelope package for *Boating* did not work very well at all. However, the SST window envelope package did wonders for the *Travel Weekly Annual.* There are not apparent reasons for the disparity in results, but there is every reason to test.

Don't neglect your best prospects: Your subscribers

By Herbert G. Ahrend

Publications both large and small constantly spend every penny they feel they can afford to attract new subscribers. Why, then, do so many of them take the loyalty of those readers for granted, to the extent of expecting that they will renew merely because they are sent a cold, impersonal bill?

"Our renewal rate's O.K." is the response I've grown accustomed to hearing, even from publishers and circulation directors who should be aware that it's a heck of a lot easier and cheaper to hold a present subscriber than it is to convince a new one.

All too often these otherwise alert executives are not even fully aware of the exact procedures they employ to hold their readers. And if they're mailing two or even three bills and statements, they believe they've done all they need to, or can. As one publisher put it, "If they haven't renewed after three bills, we're just not gonna get them back."

Wrong!

True, more bills will not do the trick; but a friendly, informative series of letters which can maintain and rekindle the subscriber's original interest in your publication *will* improve your renewal percentage by a significant amount.

Even a single friendly letter will help. That's been the experience of Mary L. Powers, circulation manager of *Practical Horseman.* Powers' comments in a recent letter started me on this train of thought. Here's the way she states the case:

"I am trying to reach them on a somewhat personal approach, as well as point out a few of the good qualities of *Practical Horseman* magazine ... I started this promotion a short time ago and already I feel that it is going to be worthwhile. I get very nice letters back from the subscribers telling me how much they appreciate the fact that we CARE about them and that we are interested enough to go one step further than the regular renewal notices ...

"In today's hustle and bustle world oftentimes all it takes to regain a subscription is a show of interest and a gentle reminder to the subscriber that the subscription has expired."

The letter which has been working for her begins, "WE MISS YOU!" and contains a lot of information about upcoming features—information which should, and does, convince the specialized reader that he or she should not miss any more issues. It's informal and personal; a few too many we's, otherwise fine; and it's proving to be effective.

Perhaps you're thinking that only a small publication could make such an approach pay; but that's not so. Of course, the almost "clubby" association among people who share a common hobby or sport helps, but every publication has a bond with its readers. You must make the most of that bond in your renewal efforts.

Remember, each subscriber costs you a considerable amount of both effort and money to obtain. For many publications, the new reader acquisition cost is $4, $5 or much more. And you didn't get that reader by simply sending a bill! So why do you assume you can hold the reader with a bill alone?

Why Drop Others?

Of course, there are a great number of publications, especially in esoteric and specialized fields, which can renew 50 to 70 percent (and occasionally even more) by that technique. But why should the other 30 to 50 percent be permitted to drop by the wayside? A proper renewal program can bring in many of them at costs as low as 50 cents each.

You should not stop trying to renew any subscription until the cost of each renewal becomes significantly *higher* than the cost of a new subscription.

The reason for this is that the renewal-on-renewal rate is nearly always higher than the conversion, or first renewal, rate.

You will, therefore, hold a significantly higher percentage of readers who renew, than of new readers; and you can consequently afford to spend more to make sure they do not lapse.

"But," I hear some of you protesting, "doesn't the fact that they have not responded to the first or second or third renewal effort show that they've lost interest in my book?" Not at all.

There are any number of reasons why a person who would really prefer to continue receiving your magazine may not reply to any one mailing. My old friend Marv Barckley of Publishers Clearing House has compiled a far-from-exhaustive list of 10. Here are just a few of Barck's reasons for nonresponse:

• "Got spectacularly good (or bad) news in another letter, and never got around to reading yours."

• "Momentarily wanted something *else* selling for the same price as your subscription, more than the subscription."

• "Resented the impersonal nature of your notice."

• "Momentarily reacted negatively to some feature of your last issue."

And, the clue to many, many failures to renew: "No reason at all. Just not motivated to take positive action."

When the time comes for your readers to renew, do *your* renewal mailings motivate them to take positive action?

Your renewal series should create this motivation by showing your reader that he or she will gain more by extending a subscription, than by keeping the money in his or her pocket or spending it on something else. The series should speak in a tone of voice appropriate to your publication and your audience. And, it should take into account the source of the individual name.

There are many ways in which the source of the name affects your ability to renew the subscription. If it was originally obtained through a mailing stressing one aspect of the field you cover, it can be more easily renewed when you emphasize future features in that area in your letters. And a similar technique should be used to appeal to subscribers who originally came from specialized mailing lists.

Furthermore, not all sources of subscriptions are equally valuable in terms of mail renewability. Don't make the mistake of assuming that because your renewal mailings do not pay off on the average after a certain number of appeals, you should discontinue all renewal efforts at that point. On the contrary, what you must do is to break down your list by its sources and determine whether certain segments are worth further cultivation.

On one occasion when I was called in to improve renewal response for a major consumer publication, I found that all renewals, regardless of source, were sent six letters. But analysis disclosed that field-sold and PDS (paid during service) names were not profitable beyond the first or second notice, while subscribers who had originally responded to the publisher's own full-rate mail subscription efforts could justify 12 renewal letters.

Your publication's financial health depends to a large extent on the length of time over which you can hold your reader, and that, in turn, depends upon the nature of your renewal efforts. Don't take them for granted.

No, not even after you've obviously lost a reader should you stop trying to reinstate that subscription.

Your expires constitute one of the most productive pools of potential subscribers. They should be cultivated and resold periodically.

Former Subscribers Profitable

One publication which has found promotion to former subscribers profitable is *Missouri Life*. The letter which James P. Thompson, general manager, sent me for comment begins exactly as does Powers'—"We miss you." It then proceeds to make a special offer to win them back, and outlines many of the features the reader is missing by not reading *Missouri Life* regularly. Some of the copy portrays "the magic that cannot be found outside the State of Missouri":

• "...take an excursion to places that you've seen, but never really known before..."

• "And all of those places that you have always wanted to visit, but have never had the time."

• "Time. Perhaps that is what *Missouri Life* gives you most of all..."

• "Time. That's what *Missouri Life* gives you. Time to enjoy Missouri like [sic] you've never enjoyed it before."

• "For only $10 per year, or $17.50 for 2 years, you can enjoy *Missouri Life* in your home or office. This is a savings of $5 for 1 year, or $12.50 for 2 years, over the newsstand price of $2.50 per issue."

Both this letter and the publication's prospect letter have a number of good points, but both could benefit from revision. Why, when the magazine's art and photography content is stressed, is there no folder, but merely a one-color letter with no illustrations? And why is there no offer at all in the subscription letter except for the low-pressure P.S., which makes no mention of the price, or even of the frequency of publication?

The psychology of direct mail

By Eliot DeY. Schein

Cashing in on the positive nature of mail as a marketing medium requires an understanding of how letters are perceived by consumers.

Basically, letters are associated with positive information, and the warmest reception from a consumer is reserved for checks and refunds. A close second is personal mail from friends or relatives. Unfortunately, business mail is ranked rather low on the list, just a small step ahead of requests for payment.

Given this ranking, it seems to make sense that your direct mail will be better received if it resembles a check or refund. However, you seek more than a good reception; you seek responses. And a phony check or cer-

tificate can easily depress response if it causes the consumer a disappointing let-down. The same risk is faced with mail that appears to be personal but isn't.

Fortunately, direct mail can be designed and written to elicit initial positive consumer reaction while keeping disappointment to a minimum if sales logic and psychology are taken into consideration.

Do you write one on one?

First of all, do you do everything you can in your current direct mail promotions to allow the reader to believe that you (or your circulation person) have actually hand-typed at least the letter portion of your direct mail piece? Every component in your direct mail promotion must at least appear to be a direct appeal to the one individual who at any given moment is being reached by and, one hopes, is reading your package.

There are various techniques dictated by various psychologies and applications of logic which have become an unquestioned part of direct mail strategy. For example, the blue signature, which faithful readers of this column have heard discussed many times, is important because your readers should not stray from the belief that you actually hand-signed the letter in blue ink. What's more, the reader wants to believe that he or she is so important that you personally took the time to correspond. So, while nobody is really trying to fool anyone by printing a blue ink signature on a million pieces of mail, the prevailing psychology dictates that any other signature color can be at once jolting and revolting.

Every dedicated direct mailer, when asked about the one most important concept of successful direct mail, will answer with the term "one on one" (or "one to one"). Definitely, a critical concept to keep in mind at all times. You are not mailing a million pieces of mail; you are mailing one piece at a time to one individual or family. One-on-one copy keeps that critical point in mind and uses the second person singular—the word "you"—wherever possible.

Surely, the recipient of your promotion piece (who, remember, did not ask to be the recipient) is more interested in himself than in what you have to sell and who you are. Direct mail is no place to let the writer's ego go unbridled. It is a place to massage the reader's ego. After all, the reader is the target and the hoped-for customer.

You may have already won...

There are some brilliant psychological phrases that are used over and over again (with some variation) in certain types of direct mail promotion. For example, you're probably familiar with the direct mail phrase, "You may have already won." How does this differ from "You may win"? Quite simply, "You may have already won" means psychologically, of course, that if you, the recipient, do not return the response vehicle, your prize may be sitting there with your name on it, unclaimed, because you didn't take the one or two seconds of effort to return the response card. "You may win" means that nothing has yet happened, and by not sending in the response there is no way you can win, and therefore you have nothing to lose.

No risk

The term "no risk guarantee" is not quite as blatant, but it does have a lulling effect on the consumer. In magazinedom, a no risk guarantee is simply a guarantee that the unused portion of the subscription monies will be returned if the subscriber decides to cancel at any time during the life of the paid subscription.

This would not be a good tactic to attempt if you were selling refrigerators. Who wants a dirty, beat-up refrigerator returned for credit? Yet more and more, we see this "no risk guarantee" being parroted by other merchandisers.

For example, in automobile accessories, the term "limited warranty" has practically the same meaning as a no risk guarantee. With automobile batteries and tires, no risk guarantees have been around for years. What these thinly disguised pre-sale soothers mean is that if the item or product fails to function for the period of time it is expected to function, it can be traded in for partial credit

toward the purchase of a new product. Pretty close to the way a "no risk" offer is presented, you're sure to agree.

...and it's free!

Another bit of psychology requires the generous use of the term "free." Free is highly touted as one of the most effective words in marketing and, linked with the words "examination offer" or "examination copy," it is almost irresistible to consumers.

For example, we use the term "free examination copy" as the lead line in our direct mail to suggest to the consumer that he or she not only has nothing to lose (as in "no risk guarantee") but, even better, may be getting something for nothing.

Deep down inside, publishers hope that the magazine product being fulfilled as that free copy (pardons, please ABC) will be so welcome in the hands of the reader that it would be absolutely impossible for any new customer to cancel after having seen the wonderful product. The fact is, in most cases, cancellation percentages resulting from a "soft offer" such as this frequently fall below the 50 percent mark.

Colorado vs. New York

If all of these so-called sales tactics are part of the intelligence or logic of direct mail, here's an idea that, to the best of the writer's knowledge, was never before tested. The sense of the test was based on a bit of logic and psychology; but first, the research.

A batch of aunts, uncles, nieces, and cousins (naturally, of more than above average intelligence, and even street smarts) was questioned on the major magazine publishing centers of the United States. It is not surprising that, after New York, in very close second place, came Boulder, Colorado. It seems that over the past 20 years, as Neodata broadened its base of magazines for computer fulfillment services, Boulder has become (in the mind of the general consumer) a place where magazines come from.

The idea spawned as a result of this research was masterful in its simplicity: Rig a return address in Boulder for a test mailing for a new magazine in order to increase that new magazine's credibility in the eyes of the potential subscriber. So the order went out: Get a college student at the University of Colorado at Boulder to open up a post office box and have responses sent to that box number. The student can then clean out the box every day and mail the responses back to the publisher.

An argument concerning these logistics and their efficiency ensued, and a better way was advocated: Ask Neodata what they would charge to receive and pay business reply mail for the responses generated by a test mailing of 100,000 pieces. At the same time, have some of the pieces of cold mail bear a New York return address as a control.

A test such as this (for the first time in anyone's knowledge around here) took place just last summer. Because the new magazine was concerned with sports, sporting apparel and equipment, there was no question in any pundit's mind that the Boulder responses would beat the pants off of those coming in to the Madison Avenue address being tested against it.

They reasoned that consumers had undergone a psychological shift to Boulder as a center of magazine publishing, and that Colorado seemed like a terrific place to participate actively in sports of all kinds.

The pundits were all wet. All of them. The results, when all was said and done, showed unquestionably that the responses could have gone totally to either place without any change in pull. (The next test, of course, is to pit Boulder or New York against New Orleans or Peoria.)

It is one thing to go with the tried and true and almost unquestioned concepts and tactics of direct marketing. It is another to be in the forefront of current market trends and psychology and try to create new techniques to take advantage of them. In the case of the Boulder versus New York test, the difference was, at best, negligible. In the other cases—blue signatures, one-to-one copy, "you may have already won," no risk guarantee, and "free examination copy"—the tests have proved over

and over again that those concepts are the way to go. At least for the time being.

One last word on the New York/Boulder test. You might say something was ventured, but nothing was gained. That may be your feeling as to the bottom line of the test (which, incidentally, was not that costly). However, there was a gain, a significant one. The test was made by people who believed in the possible logic of it and were willing to invest the few extra cents to see if they could add another rule to the ever-changing book of rules, concepts, logic and psychology of direct mail.

The circulation/advertising partnership

By Herbert G. Ahrend

Looking for new ways to cut circulation promotion costs and make each dollar more effective? You're missing a bet if you're not working closely with your publication's advertising department to develop new techniques of cooperation beneficial to both.

Note the advice of Rosalie Bruno, the dynamic vice-president, circulation, of *Architectural Digest* and *Bon Appetit:*

"Circulation can provide advertising with more than just a rate base and a set of demographics. It can also provide the opportunity—beneficial to all concerned—for additional promotional co-ventures.

"We are now offering advertisers the ability to ride along in our direct-mail packages. To our standard control, we have added a Bonus Pack, a recipe packet. Each recipe represents and uses the product of an advertiser.

"*None* are direct-response devices. They are totally supportive of the editorial product; this, I think, is the key to their success."

Perhaps at this point, you're saying to yourself: "Surely I can see the advantage to advertising, but where's the gain to circulation promotion?"

According to Rosalie Bruno, it's twofold. First, there's an additional incentive to the reader to open the envelope; the teaser, "Bonus Pack Enclosed," appears in bold capitals on the back of the 6" x 9" carrying envelope.

But secondly, and of greater importance, the cost of the mailing is reduced. The advertisers assume the entire cost of production of the recipe card on their product *in addition* to a reasonable charge per thousand for the privilege of "riding along" in the mailing. Thus, if five advertisers purchase cards, the net cost per thousand in the mail is reduced significantly.

This is particularly important in the case of *Bon Appetit* or of any other publication with a specialized appeal.

It lowers the breakeven point on the mailing, hence, allowing the use of many mailing lists which simply would not be profitable without the cost contribution from the advertisers.

Her basic mailing itself is a winner. The offer is a free copy, no money up front, with the other 11 issues sent for $7.95 unless the prospect writes "cancel" and returns the bill. The reader is asked to punch out a token on the stub and insert it on the order card.

The four-page letter, conversational in tone, reproduces the token on the upper part of the first page, with this lead-in:

"Enjoy food and drink? Enjoy discovery? Want to sample new dishes, new cuisines? Want to add more *life,* more *style,* to your lifestyle? Here's the token that can help you."

The body of the letter instructs "dear reader" to "first, fill a pitcher with ice." It then proceeds to give a recipe for sangria and tells the reader to sip it while perusing the letter, which also contains the recipe for *Bon Appetit*'s chilled avocado soup. Not until page 4 is the offer outlined.

The colorful folder, which measures an unusual 5-9/16" x 7-1/2" closed, has one word captions on its three major photos: "EAT," "DRINK," and "BE MERRY." The latter two are on a short flap which, when lifted, proclaims: "ANNOUNCING *Bon Appetit.* ELEGANCE IS BACK." The second side (measuring just over 11" x 17" flat) has a column of four-color photos down the center and hard sell copy on contents and benefits flanking it. Although there is a guarantee of "complete refund or credit" for unmailed copies in the event of cancellation, there is no offer on the folder; simply "to subscribe return card today." Thus the same folder can be used with tests of many different offers, should the occasion arise.

This is one of the most tastefully executed blends of circulation and advertising promotion I have seen. But Rosalie Bruno hasn't stopped there. She's exploring many other avenues of close cooperation and interaction between the two departments. "I have found this interaction to be extremely stimulating," she writes me, "and we have only just begun.

"For instance, I have just instituted a bimonthly circulation newsletter which goes to each salesman and updates him in all circulation activities. This vehicle not only keeps the ad salesman informed, but allows him to relay specific questions back to circulation and get an immediate answer."

I wouldn't be at all surprised if she also received some good promotion ideas from the salesmen. When they know what is being done and why, they take an interest; and who knows better than they how the publication is regarded in the field and what its strong points are?

One of the lessons which Rosalie's achievement teaches us is that we should not sit back and be content with a winning promotion package. Always strive to find new ways to make it even more successful.

Bon Appetit's way is to look beyond the mailing package itself, to seek cost-sharing ideas. But more often than not, you can take even the most productive package and improve the returns by seemingly small changes in format or copy or both.

An Improved Package

An example of such improvements comes from *Empire State Report*, a monthly publication which provides articles and features on key developments in New York State politics and government.

For many months it has been mailing to selected lists a well-above-average package consisting of a four-page, two-color letter with a bold heading offering the next issue "FREE OF COST OR OBLIGATION—when you sign and return the enclosed charge card"; a four-panel, two color, two-sided folder declaring "You can't tell what's happening in the Empire State without a PROGRAM," continuing the theatrical theme with cartoons of "The Cast of Characters" (Daniel Moynihan, Bella Abzug, *et al.*) with quotes headed "The Critics Loved It"; a business-reply envelope and a business reply card with a stub. The stub has a guarantee on one side and "Send for your FREE issue today!" on the other. The response area itself, which is pre-addressed, is headed "THIS IS YOUR EMPIRE STATE REPORT CHARGE CARD" and has a blue or green wavy-line background simulating safety paper. All this is mailed in a brown kraft window envelope with considerable resemblance to those used by the New York State Government in mailing numerous official forms.

How has it been improved? Two ways. Minor changes in the copy assure that both the letter and the folder carry the most recent possible examples of the types of stories found in the *Report*, as well as cartoons of the most important currently talked-about politicians. Governor Carey has replaced Nelson Rockefeller, for example.

But I will bet a Dewey button against a dried-out campaign cigar that the change which brought about the greatest increase in response was in the mechanical, not the copy.

In the earlier version, the text on the "charge card" was in about 6 point news gothic condensed and was virtually unreadable against the comparatively deep wavy blue lines. Inevitably, some readers must have been given the feeling that the publishers were trying to hide some of the terms of the agreement. Now, the type is 10 point sans serif and the wavy lines are a much lighter blue. Result: A clean looking card which no one would hesitate to check and return.

Such "unimportant" details can affect your returns just as much as poor copy or bad lists. Don't let your good ideas be hurt by poor execution at the typographer's or the art studio. And above all, as *Empire State Report* has done, keep on trying to increase even a satisfactory return. Look at your mailing package as if you had just received it in your mail and eliminate any disturbing elements.

Where's the Letter?

Of all the promotion pieces I have reviewed, there is one general remark which applied to a large percentage of them: *"Where's the letter?"* In circulation promotion, 90 percent of the time it is better to use a letter without a folder if you have to economize, than a folder without a letter. Yet altogether too many publications attempt to attract new readers with nothing but a cold, printed piece—one which frequently fails completely to portray the particular virtues of the periodical.

People want to do business with people, not institutions. When they agree to subscribe to a magazine, they are buying the editor's outlook on the world, the editor's point of view, the editor's style. The more they know about the publication, the more loyal subscribers they will be. For all these reasons, the individual communication which a letter embodies is more effective in encouraging people to subscribe than any other format. Oh yes, of course, we can all point to outstanding exceptions where striking artwork or particular timeliness has made a printed mailing pull remarkably. But I still stick to my position: As a general rule, the letter is the most important single element of the circulation promotion package.

It is the letter which conveys the nuances, the feeling, the true quality of the publication. It goes without saying that the letter must truly represent the magazine. Truth in advertising *does* pay in the long run; many a tombstone in publication graveyards could read, "It got lots of trial subscribers, but the renewals were lousy."

Among believers in the power of the letter, count Claretian Publications, a nonprofit organization serving the religious field. It has forwarded to me a number of promotion packages which are simple, dignified, yet friendly; all of which rely heavily on the letter. They are generally straightforward and direct, offering a quick, clear portrait of the particular publication concerned. As an example, here's the opening of one:

"Dear Friend: CONTEXT is a newsletter. A true newsletter. It provides readers with 'inside' information and advance knowledge. Religious news editors of major newspapers and news magazines subscribe. They know how much is reported and commented on in CONTEXT before it's printed anywhere else."

That letter is directed to busy people; it talks their language, tells them quickly and clearly what CONTEXT is and how it can be useful to them. And I'm sure it works.

A sample issue accompanies the letter, which is printed in deep blue on both sides of a single sheet. In addition to the response card and a business reply envelope, there's also a card for friends' names and addresses—a good idea for building the mailing list. My only (carping) criticism is that the differing shades of blue clash, irritatingly to my eye at least, and that the red of the friends' card makes it stand out too prominently. On the whole, the Claretian mailings serve their purpose well, at comparatively low cost.

My dear Russell Baker:

By Eliot DeY. Schein

My dear Russell Baker:

Your column in the February 22, 1981 *New York Times Magazine* section was illuminating and enjoyable. You started your column, "My dear Paula Collins" and went on: "As circulation director of *Harper's Magazine*, I realize you are entitled to hector decent people through the mails on behalf of your publication. And if you want to call it 'The Battlefield of the Mind Since 1850,' it's all right with me, though why the mind needs a battlefield is another question.

"Give me peace of mind any day, and let *Harper's* keep the carnage of mind for them as likes a good rousing headache, I say. And speaking of peace of mind, how do you think anybody can maintain it with letters like yours popping through the mail slot?

"I refer specifically to the envelope containing your invitation to enjoy the mental battlefield at a trial price of $7."

Mr. Baker, you comment on the teaser copy on the carrier envelope, which is, "Should you be punished for being born with a high IQ?" You say that you were "tricked" into opening the thing for the sales pitch. "Fair enough," you continue. You once sold magazines yourself and you agree it's a brutal business. You recognize that a person with any IQ at all would have read the question and realized that he or she was dealing with a sales pitch. "A person with the faintest scintilla of intelligence would have said to himself, 'What nonsense. I was born with such a low IQ that I didn't even know my own mother was my own mother for the longest time' . . . and chucked the envelope unopened into the trash."

Your article ends with the following paragraph:

"My vanity was hooked by that 'high IQ' flattery. Still, should you be punished for turning up on the mailing list of *Harper's Magazine?*"

Mr. Baker, there are a few things about direct mail that maybe you ought to know. In this particular case, it all started back in the summer of 1978. It was outdoors, on a grassy knoll overlooking the Hudson River from the west bank, in a small pre-Revolutionary War town called Snedens Landing.

There a man sat, pencil in hand, by the name of Don Staley. Don had been challenged to write a direct mail package for *Harper's Magazine*. And *Harper's Magazine* was challenged to pay Don Staley about $5,000 for the privilege.

According to Mr. Staley, an avowed neophyte in direct marketing: "I felt at the time the most important thing was to put something on the envelope that would get people to open it." Well, that's certainly the prime responsibility of the carrier envelope in any direct mail package. And he came up with the high IQ line as the teaser.

For more than two years, this package has been the "control" over at *Harper's Magazine*. And it brings with it some interesting history. For example, at the time it was first mailed, *Harper's* was still owned by John Cowles of the Minneapolis Star Tribune Company. Cowles just happened to be on one of the mailing lists selected and received the package for his first real look at it.

Cowles rejected it out-of-hand. He blue-penciled it to death. Criticized Staley's lack of command of the language and demanded of publisher Jim Alcott that a *Harper's Magazine* editor modify the package to be a little more grammatically in sync.

Through testing brilliance and a rather heads-up understanding of direct mail, Alcott tested the new modified package against Staley's original not-so-perfect version. The original beat the pants off the modification.

Cowles must be given credit for being astute when it comes to grammar, but who said that a salesperson in print has to be grammatically correct? Apparently not the buying public.

On or around December 31, 1980, one million people in the United States were sent this selfsame direct mail package that you received, Mr. Baker. The lists that were used to do this mailing were selected in hopes that the recipients had high IQs. And, as we have discussed, the package was designed to be attractive to those people. And after all the testing, it certainly is.

Perhaps if you were familiar with what goes into a direct mail package of this nature, you would appreciate the next package you receive in the mail.

On this mailing alone, the United States Postal Service bill for postage was more than $84,000. The cost of the mailing lists exceeded $40,000. The cost of the printing and computerization at Kurt Volk & Company had to be greater than $115,000, and the team of people involved includes upwards of 20 direct mail professionals and a few thousand letter carriers.

When you consider how many people are employed just to reach you with a direct mail package, your first reaction to receiving the package has got to be, "Boy, this is good for the economy." It's also good for *Harper's* because it should yield approximately 20,000 new subscribers. Which leaves—of course, you figured it out—980,000 who did not subscribe. So be it. That's the risk to be taken and it is expected.

The bottom line is this: You received the package. You were attracted by the envelope. Then, when you opened it, the intended job for that package was done.

Certainly, whether you subscribe or not is critical to the magazine. Perhaps the direct mail package did not exactly appeal to you, personally, in the way it sells the benefits that accrue to being a subscriber. However, it's a sure bet that you have either subscribed to *Harper's* before, subscribe now, or will subscribe in the future. Because it's the kind of magazine a person of your caliber would doubtless enjoy reading.

There is an important consideration in direct marketing and direct mail. It is called the "common denominator"—everyone's a consumer—philosophy. Here's what it means: Regardless of how important and famous a surgeon might be, when he or she takes a walk down the aisle of the supermarket, any purchasing decision is likely to be based on a sale price, good packaging, or just downright pleasure-preference selection.

In direct mail the same holds true, and the job of the envelope that you seem to resent is to get itself opened. This envelope did the job . . . be the recipient a doctor, lawyer, Indian chief. Or yes . . . even a Baker.

PCH sweepstakes
By Eliot DeY. Schein

Sweepstakes! That's the name of the PCH (Publishers Clearing House) game and it works like a charm. The package is a monster—from its 7-1/4″ x 11″ double window, die-cut carrier envelope to its three-fold, four-color, double gatefold bonus brochure.

"Your choice of a yacht and vacation home or $100,000 cash," shouts the usual offer—"Plus unbeatable values on a multitude of your favorite magazines." We've all received them at one time or another, so there's no need to describe this direct mail piece. But there are some details you may have missed.

For one thing, the rubber stamp-like messages are all off-center and mottled to suggest that real rubber stamps are used (we all know the messages are printed). The certificate/order form is a masterpiece of mechanical production. While most of the computerization is done in-house by PCH, the certificate printing is rife with screens, shadows, printed watermarks and handwriting—every advantage of five-color flat printing is here! The bank officer's signature even looks as if his pen started out dry and then began proper ink flow. They simply don't miss a trick.

Letter rumored to be group-written
The letter is a 10-1/2 x 13-3/4 behemoth, signed by Robert H. Treller (whose signature is becoming almost as much of a household name as that of the late, beloved circulation master Lester Suhler) and is rumored to be written by committee. That is, there's an "opening" expert, an "offer" person, a "body copy" specialist and a "closing" genius, all of them putting their best efforts in the able hands of the "transition" master who really knows his stuff.

Tom Owens, creative director of PCH, pleads "no knowledge" of cooperative copywriting. But he agrees it is not uncommon to have the order form, letter and brochure penned by separate individuals.

Back to the letter: Treller's familiar scrawl highlights the best information for the consumer to read, all done in carefully screened ersatz pentel. The only reference to magazines is about the low rates . . . there's no hint of content, editorial premise or benefit. Apparently, the consumer should know all the magazines by name and doesn't need to know any more than that to order.

Two four-color brochures enclosed
Enclosed with the letter are two main, four-color process prize brochures. They're wonderful—with the exception of a glaring typographical error in the description of the Sony videotape unit. "Start your family on your own TV," the message reads. It should probably read "Star your family. . ."

The package is huge, chock full of excitement, and it embodies just about every technique in the book of good salesmanship. But how valuable is PCH to a publisher?

For some, PCH is a bonanza for subs. Others are better off targeting their own mail to their own markets. For many, PCH is a good solid source as an adjunct to a full and varied circulation program.

At an average remit rate (cash to publisher from PCH) of 10 percent of the bare-bones reduced rate collected for a subscription, your basic publisher isn't going to get rich. But "direct mail sold" subscription circulation will accrue (the Audit Bureau of Circulations accepts PCH-sold subs as if a publisher did his own mailing). This looks great on an ABC statement, and advertisers will, for the most part, assume these subscribers are really interested in reading the magazine.

However, many have probably subscribed through greed rather than the thirst for good reading material, and these subscribers are generally not as desirable an audience as the advertiser might wish. On the other hand, if the alternative is a 100 percent attentive readership which fails to meet a circulation guarantee, the publisher's choice is obvious.

Sweepstake subs don't renew well

Another consideration is the renewal rate of a PCH subscription. When the publisher tries to renew these PCH-sold subs a year from now, he may see a 10 to 20 percent reduction in renewals. Why? Subscribers generated through a sweepstakes promotion just don't renew very well unless a publisher chooses to renew by sweepstakes (John Veronis at *Book Digest* has a very handy sweepstakes renewal program). Certainly, without specific editorial content promotion, with a cut-rate offer, and the vision of free vacation homes and prize money running through readers' heads, you can't expect full consumer commitment to a magazine's subject.

Also, it's fair to assume that some PCH package recipients enter a subscription order simply because they think it will increase their chances of winning a sweepstakes prize. These subscribers are obviously unaware that sweepstakes contests are carefully monitored and that a subscription purchase has no effect on their chances whatsoever. However, PCH-sold subs do renew better than most outside agency sources, and PCH does help maintain that guarantee to advertisers.

On the plus side, for some publishers, it's a lot less expensive to accept 10 percent cash, avoiding a direct mail promotion at $200 per thousand or better. And for the new magazine, PCH has a special "first year" program that remits 25 percent to the publisher! But beware. It had better be a magazine with a very descriptive title (such as *Games*) because those little stamps afford only 48 characters of descriptive copy.

Furthermore, PCH will highlight, feature or otherwise pump up a new entry, but they don't accept everyone and they don't test each offer by list; so when the 25 percent remit comes in, a publisher had better be ready to do a test mailing of his own anyway. For relativity, if not ten other good reasons, and certainly, by the looks of the PCH "factory" in Port Washington, N.Y., PCH is doing just fine selling other people's products and getting its share of the income for doing the job of locating, selling, billing and rewarding hundreds of thousands of subscribers per year. Let's see how their package rates:

(Scaled from 1-10 with 10 being excellent and 1 being poor; renewal strength refers to projected renewability based on capture technique.)

PCH Sweepstakes Package

Postage device	8
Carrier envelope	10
Letter lead strength	10
Letter content strength	9
Letter closing strength	9
Signature psychology	10
Order form	9
Reply envelope	5
Overall believability	10
Renewal strength	2
	82

Big apple sweepstakes
By Eliot DeY. Schein

If this one hadn't worked like a charm, nothing would have. The psychology of the Big Apple Sweepstakes is so carefully and beautifully rendered for its market that this is truly an example of *New York's* market involvement as well as a sweepstakes subscription sales effort.

Mary Clark Zogott, circulation director, teamed up with writer Chris Stagg and art director Al Sandler to entice, provoke, encourage and otherwise entrap recipients of this 8-3/4" x 11-1/2" Big Apple Sweepstakes broadside. First prize: a Mercedes convertible. (This prize wouldn't work in a national mailing.) And the 537 other prizes are apartment-dweller-oriented, presented in dot-retouched color and so very indicative of the magazine's attitude toward life.

Chris presented the auto in such glowing terms, one just has to read on. And Mary's other prize selections are everything the magazine's typical potential subscriber lusts after: a projection TV system (the 5 foot model that even fits into a studio apartment); Pioneer's 8-piece stereo (in a shelf alignment that solves the space problem; a telephone answering device; plus 25 gourmet baskets (from Bloomingdale's, where else?). And last, but most crispy, bushels of apples (billed on the brochure as the most appropriate selection for a prize). Brilliant.

It's obviously not just another sweepstakes. Rather, it's a wonderful example of a professional team working together to develop, unify and produce a package with the ultimate secret ingredient—good thinking.

Compared to the costly efforts of *Reader's Digest* or Publishers Clearing House, the Big Apple Sweepstakes offers only about $40,000 in total prizes—but it is the choice of prizes that makes the difference.

The package for working cityfolk

The carrier envelope is in muted olive to give greater drama to the four-color car photo that's aimed down toward the label and silhouetted almost properly. The indicia leaves something to be desired, but the early-bird prize—dinner for four at the ultra-expensive Palace restaurant—gets a good play.

Inside, a letter that's not as much a subscription solicitation as it is an auto sales brochure. (If you have them salivating on the envelope, why shut off the Pavlovian fluids in mid-stream?)

At the top of page two we see the first subscription copy: "You see, the Mercedes. . .is, in a way, symbolic of *New York*, and all our magazine can mean to you." Then, on to some short general remarks about magazine content, back to the car, and then to the close which has a deadline date. The letter finishes off with Mary's signature (in blue, of course) and a reminder about the early-bird dinners.

This short, easy to read letter is perfect for working cityfolk who just came home to the mailbox. Chris ends the letter with "So get up early tomorrow to enter." That hits the target perfectly. In spite of a heavier-than-necessary sprinkling of first person pronouns, this letter does the trick.

Note: The prizes should go to the people who spot the line, "For only only $9.95" in the third to last paragraph. Who said that great thinkers are great proofreaders?

By the way, $9.95 is the regular subscription rate for 29 issues, but Chris makes a strong comparison with the newsstand rate and develops a 65 percent savings story bewildering enough to hook a healthy percentage of readers.

The four-color broadside brochure (sporting the same car shot that was retouched for the envelope) displays the additional prizes and presents the very necessary content description copy. Eight previous covers are reprinted in color (to establish credibility, as if there's anyone on the mailing lists who never heard of *New York* magazine). The brochure also highlights the 35 cents per copy cost, contains the rules and reiterates the early-bird feast.

The giant-sized order form pushes the offer, shows the car again and contains a punch-out token (not quite the shape of the real thing) which the reader is supposed to place in an unmarked slot in the "return this portion" part. Sexy, it is—obvious, it isn't. And how do you put this melange into either of the business reply envelopes?

Either envelope? Yes—a Yes and a No envelope. Both postpaid. Which means *New York* intends to solicit the No people with another effort no doubt waiting in the wings to mail when the list of No's is complete.

"I'm puzzled"—a wonderful approach

But don't go away folks, there's more! A little publisher's letter from Joe Armstrong. He says "I'm puzzled." Seems Mary told him they wouldn't get 100% response and he can't understand that. So, he drives home the point that whether you subscribe or not, your chances of winning are the same. As long as there's nothing to lose, how can you hold yourself back from entering the Big Apple Sweepstakes?

It's a wonderful approach. He doesn't ask for an order, he just asks for an entry. Why? Because no matter how many times you assure them it's not so, most people feel that if they subscribe, they have a better chance of winning. So Joe's letter will develop more subscriptions—at least enough to offset the cost of printing his letter. And, as you remember, they're saving up the No's for another mailing. This little letter is perfect for maximizing response, both Yes and No.

Let's see how top-level this package rates:

New York's Big Apple Sweepstakes

Postage device	5
Carrier envelope	8
Letter head strength	7
Letter content strength	4
Letter closing strength	8
Signature psychology	9
Order form	8
BRE	6
Overall believability	9
Renewal strength	3
	67

(Scaled from 1-10 with 10 being excellent and 1 being poor; renewal strength refers to projected renewability, based on capture technique.)

Approving copy

By Eliot DeY. Schein

Assume you're responsible for a new business cold mail package and you receive the copy for that package. What should you look for as you go over that copy?

First, you must keep in mind the purpose of a new business cold mail package—namely, to pull the highest possible response percentage, on an efficient cost per thousand in the mail, of new subscribers who will be as renewable as (or more renewable than) your current new subscriber file.

Then, you must ask yourself several questions.

Are you testing the new package against a pretested and successful package? If this is the case, the new package should be as different as possible from the old one, both from a copy standpoint and graphically. (Naturally, refinements in a control package can be tested at any time, but here we're talking about a brand new approach.) If the new one is too close to the current control, it may not be worth testing.

Is the copy you have been given indicative of your magazine? (Indicative not in the physical sense of paper stock or the quality of photography, since obviously it is a direct mail package and not a magazine, but indicative in terms of the way it has been written.) Will it scare away your prime prospects with overly-aggressive, elitist writing? Or, on the other hand, will it capture too many unrenewable people with too many soothing promises?

Is the copywriter's language up to the mental level of your readership? At the same time, is it on a level low enough to appeal to the masses to whom you are going to mail it? Obviously, the greater the percentage of recipients who can understand the words and concepts in your package, the greater the percentage you may expect to respond.

High-blown phraseology and vocabulary usually serve only to impress magazine management with the letter writer's command of the language. But direct mail copy is not designed to impress. It's designed to communicate . . . and get results. Generally speaking, the lower the levels of vocabulary and phraseology, the easier the package is to read.

The editors' role

Now that you have checked over the copy, let the editors take a look at it. (Editors certainly deserve the courtesy of seeing the promotion material before it goes out.) Of course, many editors don't want to take the time, but they can play an important part in a package by reading it over and making corrections for accuracy concerning subject matter.

It's usually dangerous for editors to get involved any more deeply than this, however. Just as direct mail copywriters are not editors, editors are not salespeople. Because a copywriter has only two to four minutes of reader involvement to make a subscription sale, he or she must capture an entire year's worth of a magazine on an envelope and three or four pages of a letter. (Some successful letters are much shorter, some much longer.)

Writing to sell is not the editor's trade—it is the direct mail copywriter's trade. Unfortunately, many editors do not perceive this distinction clearly. Given the opportunity, they may try to edit the sell copy as if it were editorial copy. That's when the fur begins to fly—and the response begins to drop.

What's more, editors are also very good at grammar. But the flow of a direct mail package is sometimes interrupted by eye-twisting grammatical technicalities. Thus, an editor who corrects a split infinitive in the copy for a direct mail package may actually be making the package more difficult to read.

There's no question that editors are the ones to check that the information in the package is accurate and that the use of the "in" words of the subject matter is proper. (A grossly misused term or an inaccurate "fact" may lead the reader to question the magazine's knowledge of its subject.) But when you consider that, more often than not, the offer and list selection together have more to do with the total response than the perfect accuracy of the copy, don't press the point if your editors don't want to be bothered looking over the direct mail package.

Should your circulation director participate in approving the copy? Definitely. It is essential that he scrutinize the copy in terms of ABC or BPA and USPS rules and regulations.

The circulation director should also make sure that the mathematics of the offer pricing work out. In addition, he should check the format for useability (for example, for in-house generated computer forms) and overlay the mailing lists that his department has selected against the level of copy that has been written.

Approval by committee

What about publishing companies that meet to approve copy by committee?

The publisher wants the copy to be of the highest level because an advertiser or potential advertiser may see the direct mail package and feel that the level of writing in the subscription solicitation package doesn't match the demographics touted in the ad promotion material.

The editor wants to have more about the contents of the magazine and a little less "hype" because the magazine is not full of hype.

The circulation director wants to make sure the package pulls as much as it can in terms of renewable subs in order to make his or her job easier for the next year.

And the production manager sits there saying: "Please approve this package already. I'm not even sure I have enough time *now* to produce it in order to meet the mail date."

Incidentally, let's not give the production manager short shrift. While the production manager's office is not a profit center, it can easily be the biggest profit-saving center of your circulation program. Believe it or not, there are packages designed that cannot be inserted by machine. The production manager can spot this, saving a last-minute frenzy of hand-inserting which wastes time and money. In addition, your production manager can often trim a fourth of an inch here or an eighth of an inch there, or reduce one color on an order form, thereby saving you a bundle in the process.

Remember, the new package must do better than the control package. How does it do better? It either *pulls more* subscribers per thousand mailed or it *costs less* to put in the mail and pulls the same number of subscribers. (Ideally, it will do both.)

Of course, insofar as almost all copy passes before various department people at any magazine, there is always some "approval by committee." However, where there is a formalized procedure (and, rest assured, there often is), such procedure not only tends to encourage criticism as different interests vie for supremacy, it actually legitimizes the pocket veto.

Copywriter responsible for quality

The quality of the copy in direct mail is first and foremost the job of the copywriter. If the copywriter is informed about the lists to be used, if he has been given a back-up file of previously tried promotions with the resulting scores, and if he has been given the mission of adjusting the circulation upward with this new package, it might make sense to let the package go as written. Whatever your magazine's experience has been in direct mail, there is sure to be a copywriter out there who can do a better job writing a direct mail package than can the combi-

nation of yourself, your editor, circulation director, production manager and administrative assistant.

No question about it—management spends more time reviewing copy for a new package than it spends on list selection and offer development combined. The reason: It is easier to be a critic of something "everyone" can do. Everyone knows that list selection and offer development take real skill, but the copywriter is "just writing a letter."

The truth is, the copywriter in direct mail has to combine skill with creative ability. And the proof of the pudding is that there are more marketing people than copywriters and more list people than copywriters in the direct mail world. Always has been, and it is likely to remain so. (You may conclude from that paean that it requires a great deal more to be a successful direct mail copywriter than the writer is usually given credit for.)

Who approves your copy? Be it yourself, your editors, your circulation director, your production manager, your space salesperson, or the American Academy of Grammarians, the person who *really* approves your copy is the recipient of your package. And if you have adhered to the precepts of good direct response promotion—a professional, heads-up writer who quickly and sweetly translates your magazine's identity into copy that sells a good product at a reasonable price to an accurately selected list—you'll get that approval. In the form of mailbags of new subscriptions.

Innovations

By Eliot DeY. Schein

About 15 years ago, a certain printer decided to increase the effectiveness of mail. Using his own special brand of ingenuity, he linked a fifth station to a four-station roll-fed press and used that additional station to emboss copy on-press.

This embossing technique was used successfully and is still being used by Ziff-Davis to promote practically every one of its magazines.

Now, for the 1980s, that same printer has already produced effective technology to die-cut and vacuum on-press as well as emboss, consecutive number, print five different colors including day-glow, and convert bind-in envelopes with lightning speed.

Innovation was one of the themes of 1979's New York Direct Marketing Day, and innovation in direct mail is a joy to behold. In recent years, we have seen the development of the so-called standard computer letter which uses all the information available about the prospect to "personalize" a piece of mail that could not be more direct. And as our technology continues to develop rapidly, the signs of amazing high-speed presses, compu-

ter capabilities and downright unbelievable human ingenuity are around for all of us to see.

While the so-called "standard" computer letter for consumer use seems to be a thing of the past (its effectiveness apparently having waned in the late seventies), new technology has appeared. In a process called MeadDigit, computerized input is attached to a special printing device which shoots droplets of ink against the material to be printed, thus allowing the option of multiple sizes, a variety of type faces . . . and, apparently, a most effective personalized vehicle for *Time* magazine (among others).

Time Inc. pioneers the process

The Time Inc. people have been testing and retesting MeadDigit-produced order forms and letters for a couple of years. And certainly they deserve a lot of credit for taking what was then an expensive production medium and refining it to fit in with an entire direct mail package.

All of the pre-printed type on the *Time* package is dotted and probably was originally typeset by being

317

printed by a Mead machine. Then the fill-in parts were ink-jetted in during the press run.

One of the lines of copy on the first page of the *Time* letter is: "In fact, we've been the leading news magazine every week since March 3, 1923." Certainly one of the leading news magazines in terms of technological innovation in direct mail.

While being one of the leaders of the pack, Time Inc. has also managed to make this pay out. And due to continued use and the general cross-pollination of information among circulators over the years, *Quest 80* has just launched a new package which uses this very same technical process.

Quest's ink jet artistry

Included in the package are two pieces of ink jet artistry. One is a "Certificate of Recognition" which bears the full name of the recipient three times in four different sizes; three times all upper case, once upper and lower case.

This certificate folds in a remarkably strange way so that the last name only partially shows through a north-south window to the left of the address on the carrier envelope. According to Vicki Mateulewicz, associate publisher of *Quest 80*, this was done to tantalize the reader when he sees part of his name showing through that window. Mateulewicz goes on to say that this is now the control package for *Quest 80*. Apparently the new technology works well.

The other piece of personalized ink jet copy is thrown into a table of contents as one of the articles to be contained in the magazine. The ink jet fill-in doesn't come close to matching the type face, nor apparently was it supposed to. The name and address are also printed on the "acceptance form" and on a graphically paper-clipped buck slip which shows through the window.

No question that the Mead process is a favorite of the people at *Quest 80*. The mystery of their package is how they got the order form/brochure to show through the additional two open windows in a strategic manner. The question is: Did they really design that certificate to show only a third of the last name of the recipient through the vertical window?

During the seventies we saw the computer letter, the die-cut window envelope with die-cuts in the shape of whales or jet planes, and the dawning of the MeadDigit program. But according to John O'Donnell of *Smithsonian* magazine, "The versatility (of another kind) of equipment is amazing." He's talking about the IBM 3800 laser printer which uses laser beam technology and computer hardware to produce not only the new *Smithsonian* control package but also an incredibly believable piece of personalized mail.

The machine is faster and certainly more versatile than the Mead. And the appearance of the printing done by this machine belies the technology in that there are no dots and the addressing looks like typing—*for real*. The *Smithsonian* laser control package is a remarkable piece of work and just a sample of what we are to expect in the decade ahead.

Looking into the future

According to the innovators—people like our printing genius, the Mead group, and the IBM folks—we ain't seen nothing yet. The examples of material we see here are only the tip of the electronics technology iceberg. For example, electronic mail is already a reality in some sophisticated quarters.

Will the ink jet and the laser go the way of the old computer letter? To be sure, they will. And similarly, it's certain that they will be replaced by more sophisticated examples of ingenuity and innovation. As we get further and further into the electronics age, current methods will undoubtedly be shoved out of the way by that which is yet to come.

Is trade publication promotion different?

By Herbert G. Ahrend

"Circulation promotion for trade publications is completely different," a friend of mine said recently. "We can't use what works for the consumer magazines."

Well, he's wrong.

Of course, the two types of periodicals are not the same and have varying circulation promotion problems and needs. The two major distinctions between the two types of publications are that trade and professional magazines can make a strong case based on career help; and that, since their circulation is often miniscule in comparison with mass-circulation consumer magazines, elaborate four-color process mailings for trade publications may be out of the question.

But apart from these factors—one positive and one negative—most of what works for consumer magazines can be—and increasingly is being—employed profitably by trade and professional publications.

The day is long past when the trade publisher could merely announce the availability of his or her periodical and expect to have the checks for subscriptions subsequently pour in. Yet I could name dozens of publishers who have not significantly altered their promotion mailings for one, two or even three decades.

To gather subs at the lowest cost, today one must (a) dramatize both the periodical and its benefits to the reader; and (b) divide one's audience into segments—whether vertically or horizontally, by industry or by job function—and appeal to each identifiable group in terms of its own interests.

These two principles, you will note, apply equally to both consumer and trade or professional magazines.

Dramatizing Career Advancement

But in applying them to business publications, you have a big benefit to offer, which the consumer magazine cannot provide. I've already mentioned it—career advancement. It can be dramatized in many ways. Here are just a few of those I employed for *Chemical & Engineering News* and other American Chemical Society publications some time back, when I was consultant to the ACS:

"YOUR KEY TO THE FUTURE

"Everyone dreams of finding the magic formula that will be his key to personal success. But it is the men who come to grips with reality who are the leaders of today, the well-rewarded successes of tomorrow.

"These leaders are not 'marked' by Fortune or Good Luck. They have simply taken stock of their own abilities and sought out all the practical means of broadening and advancing themselves.

"And most of these successful men have embarked upon a personal advancement-through-reading program. They are not just abreast of their job, but on top of it.

"Such men are at the forefront of the industrial world. They are the decision-makers—on whom such tasks depend as keeping America's industrial lead or deciding on the production of a new chemical. These leaders must keep ahead of developments and trends in their own specialized industries; and they must know what's going on in all interrelated industries.

"In fact, they must have a knowledge of a grip on the entire chemical and process industries' world. That is why the reading program is so vital—for those who want to advance, as well as for those who want to stay on top.

"*Chemical & Engineering News* is *the* weekly periodical, whose technically trained staff is organized to gather data from all over the world concerned with chemical and engineering activities. You get the current news, pointing up trends of the future, whether your particular field lies in industry, education, commerce, government, finance or research.

"All of these divisions—and many more—are covered by *C&EN,* which is printed on high-speed presses so that you receive the *latest* developments in all departments every Monday morning."

And the following letter had a large four-leaf clover at the top:

"IT'S NOT ALL LUCK!

"Look at the men who win advancement to top engineering and managing positions in the Chemical Process Industries.

"You'll find most of them have four things in common—four qualifications which you might portray as the four leaves of a four-leaf clover.

"Of course, luck is one element—but it's not all—not by a long shot!

"Intelligence is another—

"Education and professional training is a third.

"Men with all three of these qualifications can be found almost as often as the common shamrock. But the good executive is rare—as rare as the four-leaf clover.

"The vital fourth leaf—the element which makes for success—is *keeping up in your profession, keeping ahead of the field.* And *that* is where *Industrial and Engineering Chemistry* fits in.

"*I/EC* is the only professional periodical you need, to get and stay ahead. *I/EC* blankets the entire CPI, to bring you data in depth, pinpointing the trends that will determine the future developments of importance throughout the field."

Another Approach

Here's another approach we used for *C&EN:*
"THIS CAN BE YOUR GOLDEN MOMENT
"Your GOLDEN MOMENT is now—the moment of

decision, *your* decision, which will determine your whole future.

"For what you do now may decide how far and how wide will be your company's importance in the chemical and industrial world.

"It is up to you to cut your own path in your personal advancement.

"This is your Golden Opportunity to join the 100,-000 decision-makers in the chemical and engineering spheres, by returning the enclosed form to receive the one magazine on which you can depend for brief, accurate, easy-to-read news—*Chemical & Engineering News.*

"*C&EN* is *your* weekly news publication ... designed especially for men in management positions, whether or not they have had technical chemical training ... designed specifically to present to you a quick but complete picture of all the significant developments and trends in the chemical and interrelated fields."

For Top Management

As an example of market segmentation, here's an approach I developed for *C&EN*, to appeal to top management:

"The 'BOSS'S—EYE VIEW
OF THE WHOLE CPI!

"As a 'boss,' you *know* the Chemical & Process Industries—you know how fast they're changing.

"Of course you must—and want to—keep abreast of and ahead of these changes. But your executive duties take up so much of your time ...

"That's why *Chemical and Engineering News* is YOUR weekly news publication—designed especially for you, who are in top management; to give you, whether or not you have technical training in chemistry, *a quick but thorough picture* of developments in the entire field.

"*C&EN* will carry you along the main highways of CPI activity and into the off-the-road locations where tomorrow's news is being made. Every Monday you will receive the complete, accurate, *latest* panorama in the news magazine of the CPI.

"When you subscribe to *C&EN* you actually are hiring the services of an entire top-notch news bureau—with a large editorial board reaching from San Francisco to London, and field staffs located throughout our Continent and in Europe ...."

Combined Appeals

The career advancement benefit, which cannot be employed in promoting consumer publications (although "women's service" magazines use it in appealing to those women who feel that homemaking is their career), can be effectively combined with many appeals used widely in the consumer field. For *Columbia Journalism Review*, for example, I blended it with the "free gift" appeal, in a mailing to editors.

The address side of the 6″ x 9″ envelope carries the message: "A gift for you—1 of the 3 essential tools of your trade," while the reverse, against an overall light blue tint, blows up a part of the typewriter-type letter beginning:

"How well are you now doing your job? In these challenging times, and more than ever in this election year, you need the *Review*'s critical analyses and insights. The *Review* helps you achieve those high standards which an increasingly alert public demands ... helps you avoid blunders from too trusting a reliance on 'official'—or any other—sources" followed by a partial listing of recent *CJR* articles, and the words "(continued inside)."

An 8-1/2″ x 18″ two-color folder carries the teaser, on the short flap:

"The 3 essential tools of your trade:" Visible on the right part of the page below are "1. Your curiosity; 2. Your typewriter; and 3.——" with a line directing the reader's eye to the part hidden by the flap. Lifting it, the reader sees "*Columbia Journalism Review.*"

Premiums and Inducements

Another big advantage possessed by many trade publishers is the availability of directories and other special issues, which may be used as premiums or as inducements to begin a subscription immediately.

Bob Birnbaum used this technique way back when he was circulation manager of *Modern Packaging*, with a letter beginning:

"I'd like to send you—for your *personal* reference use—a FREE BONUS copy of the 836-page 1957 *Modern Packaging* Encyclopedia Issue."

And the idea still works! If your book has one or more special issues or special features of particular value to your readers, promote them to the hilt.

Other consumer promotion devices which work extremely well for business publications include:

● Cut-price offers, especially when accompanied by a cut-off date

● Free trial or free first issue

● Money-back guarantee

● Free booklet connected in some way with the particular field; especially strong is a "self-premium," a booklet made up of articles from the publication itself

● Short-term introductory offer; it's wise to test several different prices and terms

● Reader's choice of length of subscription at special introductory rate

● "Subscribe now before the price goes up" offer (if valid)

● Guaranteed refund at any time during the life of the subscription.

Single-Copy Sales

The shifting single-copy marketplace

By Frank Herrera

With rising costs of printing and distribution, and with fluctuations in rate bases, publishers are beginning to pay much more attention to circulation. They are asking "Why do we do it this way? Isn't there another way to do it?"

Publishers are taking a long-term view of the balance between subscriptions and single-copy sales. As cover prices go up, the economics of a subscription become more palatable to publishers.

The single-copy sales picture is changing rapidly, especially since there are fewer traditional outlets available. Publishers who become involved, however, will find plenty of opportunity to improve efficiency (cut waste) in the dwindling markets and room for expansion into new outlets.

Despite the economic climate, the single-copy industry has shown remarkable growth. In 1980, single-copy sales totaled approximately $2.1 billion. Now we are estimating sales at about $2.4 billion for 1982. Part of the growth has been from increased cover prices. Although cover prices have not kept up with the Consumer Price Index, they have been steadily increasing since 1975.

From 1975 to 1980, the cost of buying a magazine went up 70 percent for the newsstand buyer and 65 percent for the subscriber.

Until 1981, there was a steady growth in the sale of single-copy units. However, in the second half of 1981, the Audit Bureau of Circulations reported that single-copy sales for the top 200 titles were down 4.3 percent. Since total circulation went up four-tenths of a percent, it was obvious that publishers, concerned about protecting their rate bases, were moving their losses in single-copy sales over to subscriptions.

Single-copy circulation for a lot of the big magazines dropped in 1981. In fact, of the top 30 magazines, only three showed an increase in single-copy sales. *TV Guide*, for example, was down 8 percent; *Woman's Day* was down 9 percent; *Reader's Digest* was down 11 percent. These are significant drops for magazines that sell millions of units.

Lesson from books

At the same time that magazine single-copy sales are decreasing, the proportion of wholesaler business represented by magazines is going up. Books have become a declining portion of the wholesaler's business. This is partially a result of publishers selling more copies of books through direct channels than through wholesalers.

Although wholesalers claim that Waldenbooks and other chains are taking the business away from them, wholesalers have pretty much given up on books. They do not give books the same kind of attention they give to magazines. It's almost an emotional reaction on the part of wholesalers. They feel that book publishers have betrayed them by going direct.

About five years ago, 60 percent of paperback books were sold through wholesalers and 40 percent through direct channels. Today, it's exactly the reverse: 60 percent are sold through direct channels and 40 percent through wholesalers.

As more and more of the book business goes into direct markets, publishers create more and more products for the direct market audience, which is a slightly more intellectual audience. At the same time, they produce fewer mass market books. This pushes more sales into direct markets and fewer sales into wholesalers.

This trend should serve as a warning to wholesalers; the same thing could happen with magazines if chains decide to buy direct. If wholesalers don't start energizing themselves, performing more services, they could be in long-range trouble.

Magazine publishers should also look at the situation that has occurred in the book industry; namely in "skyrocketing" cover prices. Because of rising author costs, as well as production costs, the book publisher has been forced to increase the cover price. The consumer reacts by buying fewer books. The publisher then has to raise the cover price again to cover his costs and the consumer buys even fewer books. This vicious circle has created a terrible marketing problem.

Less than 10 percent penetration

In this country, there are 153,000 retail outlets that take magazines and/or books. Some of these outlets are checkout only. Some of them are *TV Guide* only. Some of them have mainline racks. Some have books and some don't.

If we consider, however, that there are 1.9 million retail outlets that sell items to consumers, we can see from a marketing perspective that the wholesaler system has less than 10 percent penetration of the total market.

Admittedly, these other markets are not as lucrative as supermarkets. They're not going to take 500 titles, or even 200 titles. A lot of them are only two-and three-title stores; others are perhaps 20-title stores. Wholesalers have to keep those accounts open, however, because the supermarkets are getting more and more restricted. They will eventually tighten up on the number of magazines they sell, just as they've done with every other product category.

The basic retail outlets for magazines and books at this time are supermarkets, drug stores and convenience stores. Thirty-five percent of the business is handled through chain and independent supermarkets; 14 percent through convenience stores; 30 percent through chain and individual drug stores; and 20-25 percent through discount, variety and other outlets (newsstands, offices, airports, train stations, etc.). Adding up the 35 percent, 14 percent and 30 percent, we find that almost 80 percent of the business is done in three categories of stores. Those three categories of stores are now 75 percent to 80 percent chain-owned, not individually-owned.

The danger of concentration

The retail business is concentrated in the hands of a very few, which creates a situation fraught with danger. If, for example, a decision is made not to handle magazines or books, you're in big trouble. This has happened with Grand Union, Colonial Stores and Weingarten. These chains are all owned by the same man —Jamie Smith in England, who decided he didn't like magazines in stores. The result: the magazines were out in 30 days. The checkouts were left, but all the mainline racks in about 500-600 outlets were gone.

A big chunk of business—gone in 30 days. If they decide that motor oil or greeting cards should go in your space, you're out. That's the danger of dealing with chains.

Another problem we are experiencing with supermarket chains is that the number of supermarkets is declining. According to Food Marketing Institute, supermarkets have been declining at the rate of about 800 stores per year for the last three years. Many supermarket chains are closing down smaller, less efficient stores and opening up bigger stores.

This trend toward fewer and larger supermarkets can only hurt the magazine and book business because it limits display. Having more magazines in one big store is not as effective as having fewer magazines in a lot of stores because you lose customer exposure. The more times consumers see your magazine, the better chance you have of selling it.

However, there is opportunity for increased penetration in the marketplace with other untapped accounts that can easily sell magazines. With only 81 percent of convenience stores, 51 percent of drug stores, and 50,000 out of 174,000 food stores selling magazines, wholesalers should be encouraged to broaden their horizons by expanding and opening up these potential markets.

Chains more selective

With 350 publishing companies producing 2,380 titles for newsstand sales, publishers are facing great competition at the newsstand.

Furthermore, chains are becoming more and more selective; some are restricted to 100 titles while others are only taking 80. This is alarming because it leaves no home for the remaining titles. It would not be healthy to end up with only a few major titles. The magazine business needs a variety of titles to provide a breeding ground for the big books of the future.

When supermarkets learn that 34 magazines produce 50 percent of their sales, they're going to say, "Let's keep just those 34 magazines. We don't need the others." And they'll probably narrow it down even tighter than that.

What happens to the other magazines in this case? Without the other magazines, the system doesn't need wholesalers—or national distributors for that matter. If the industry cuts down its title selection to only 34 magazines, those magazines could sell direct to the chains. And in all likelihood the chains may only want to be serviced on a direct basis in order to take advantage of a possible better discount. That's the danger.

Building an alternative

Since wholesalers may not be able to deter what's going on in supermarkets, they should begin to work on an alternative—building another basket as a hedge against the breakdown of the supermarket system. Remember, 25 years ago supermarkets didn't carry magazines. If wholesalers continue to let the business be concentrated in the hands of a few, they are going to pay the price some day.

Wholesalers have to expand and open up those other 1.9 million outlets to ensure a home for magazines. Specialty retail outlets—health food stores, boating stores, any store—which can sell one magazine or five magazines. Eastern News, which sells direct, does it all the time. They service art stores, museums, health food stores, marinas and specialty book stores.

The normal trend is to sell one or two titles that relate to whatever product is sold in the specialty store. Within a short period of time, the specialty store usually discovers that the magazine business is not so terrible and decides to buy five, 10 and sometimes even 20 titles.

Wholesalers shouldn't look at what a specialty store is selling; they should look at the kind of people who shop in the store. The person who's into boating probably also likes wine, entertainment, travel. He may have a wife who cooks or sews. His interest is not so narrow as to be confined to just boating. And he probably spends a lot more time in that kind of specialty outlet than in a supermarket.

Wholesaler mergers hurtful

Not only is the number of supermarkets declining each year, so is the number of wholesalers. In 1969 there were 620 wholesalers, 202 were owned by 51 owners, and those 51 owners accounted for 57.7 percent of the wholesaler business.

These statistics show that approximately 180 wholesaler agencies disappeared. What has in fact occurred are mergers. And what usually occurs when there is a merger is that fewer copies are sold. The two wholesale agencies sold more total copies before the merger than after the merger.

There could be several reasons for this. One reason is that the small wholesaler may perform some inefficient service to hold on to clients. He may service an account that is remote, or he may go in two or three times a week, even if it doesn't make economic sense. Then, when the more sophisticated company makes the acquisition, it eliminates those accounts that are not profitable. The result: We now have not only a concentration of retailers but a concentration of wholesalers as well. And concentration is certainly not always best for magazines and books, which are impulse buys.

The computer: monster and blessing

The big monster, which is both a danger and a blessing, is the computer. With the computer, distributors and publishers will eventually be able to do everything from one place. They could tie into every supermarket in the country that has a computer. The computer will be able to provide the number of copies sold in the last 10 minutes, for example.

Now every distributor has a sophisticated computer system that eliminates all the routine work done by clerks with green eyeshades—analysis, market penetrations, distribution, high-lows, etc. It's managed by exception, basically. The computer does all the work and says, "Hey, I've got these five towns that look strange. What should I do?" The manager just looks at the printout and tells the computer, "Do this, this and this."

Many wholesalers have computer systems that do this for them. The Council for Periodical Distributors Association will give you a number of 330 computerized wholesalers. However, the problem with that number is that computerized means everything from billing by computer to total marketing. I would guess that perhaps 100 wholesalers have sophisticated computers that do marketing, special allocations and distribution.

Some wholesalers have very sophisticated systems that show what *products* are selling by what store. One wholesaler in the Southwest gives a sales analysis that breaks down information by type of store, number of stores, the chain, the section of town, the dollar volume done in the store, and the kind of people that go there. If we suggest putting *Town & Country* in all the supermarkets in a certain town, he'll come back and say, "No. You don't want *all* supermarkets. Only some of them have the kind of shoppers that would buy *Town & Country*."

This wholesaler—Weiners in Texas—has arrived, and maybe three or four more are close to it. The others, when it comes to computer technology, are still driving Model T Fords.

Single-copy picture changing

When we look at magazine circulation trends from 1970 to 1980, we find that single-copy sales were up 29 percent during that decade, whereas subscription sales were up only 9 percent. The reason for this was the cost of subscriptions. Single-copy sales were more profitable.

Post office costs were the big killer from 1970 to 1980. The average mailing cost of a second-class piece went up 514 percent. That sounds like a staggering number as a percentage, and it is. But during that same time, the wholesaler cost to publishers went up 260 percent (wholesalers get paid a percentage of the cover price). And during that decade, the average magazine cover price went from 60 cents to $1.50, which meant the amount paid to the wholesaler just skyrocketed.

As it is now, the wholesale cost in dollars has gone up *more* than postal costs have gone up. In 1970, the cost to deliver a magazine was five or six cents. Now it's 30 cents. That's 24 cents more. On the other hand, with a 60-cent magazine in 1970, the cost of single-copy distribution would have been 33 cents. With the current price of $1.50 for that same magazine, the publisher's costs are 93 cents, 60 cents more.

So although the percentage increase for the postal costs looks horrible, in absolute dollars to the publisher, the single-copy cost of delivering the magazine has gone up even more.

Let's look at the newsstand copy and where the money goes. For example, take a magazine that sells for $1.25. Twenty percent goes to the wholesaler, 20 percent to the retailer, 7 percent to the national distributor, 6 percent retail display allowance (6 percent rather than 10 percent because most magazines don't pay on 100 percent of

sale), and 2.4 percent shipping expense. That leaves 44.6 percent to the publisher. Out of that, the publisher must pay for production, selling, and general administration before he can take a profit.

It is here that rising costs are hitting publishers today. Let's see what that 55 cents (44.6 percent of $1.25) must cover. This kind of magazine is probably going to cost somewhere between 40 cents and 50 cents to produce. Taking 40 cents off this price leaves the publisher with 15 cents for selling, administration, profit, etc. But—that's on copies sold. If it costs him 40 cents to produce every magazine, and he has a 50 percent sale, he's spent 80 cents on production alone just to get 55 cents back because he only sold one copy. That's not cost-efficient.

Newsstand economics volatile

The economics of the newsstand is *extremely* volatile at this time because of the rising cost to the publisher and the return factor. Publishers cannot afford a 50 percent return anymore. In the case just mentioned, the publisher has to experience about an 80 percent sale to break even. On the other hand, he does get advertising revenue which offsets some of his costs. But in evaluating your income—single copy versus subscriptions—subscriptions begin to look better because you're selling every copy.

Let's look at a fictitious magazine to get a better idea of newsstand economics. The cover price is $1.50; subscription price $16 for one year and $40 for three years. The circulation is one million copies. The various sources for subscriptions are field service agents, renewals, television, inserts and blow-ins, PCH, direct mail and direct single-copy. Now, the net revenue per copy: renewal generates $1.33; television $1.33; direct single copy $1; inserts, blow-ins 90 cents; direct mail 90 cents; etc. The net revenue for the single-copy sale would be 67 cents.

When you look at the profit per copy per category, you see that only three categories are really profitable on a per copy basis: renewals (which are the most profitable), direct single-copy, and newsstand. None of the other subscription sources are profitable on a per copy basis—and this is what the wholesale community has always hung their hats on. Publishers can't get all the renewals they need, so direct single-copy and newsstand single-copy are their best vehicles. And direct does not produce that many sales.

Long-range planning

Broken out over a five-year period, you see the bad sources begin to renew, and all of a sudden you have five categories that are profitable. On 100 copies, you see that inserts and blow-ins are the most profitable, at $687, and your newsstand is not so profitable. When you get sophisticated publishers doing long-range planning as opposed to one-year planning, you start looking at the business differently.

Take a look at magazines like *Playboy*, which just six years ago was sold by single copy. *Playboy* now has 50 percent of its circulation in subscriptions. That's a result of long-range planning and the fact that their cover price got so high. Now, since they don't have the ups and downs of the single-copy marketplace, they have stabilized their circulation.

As cover prices go up and publishers increase the remit of the offer, there will be an advantage in subscriptions that we don't have at this time.

Add to that this bit of information. I have a field subscription force that sells three- and four-year programs. Right now we are selling 90 percent of our three-year subscriptions at about the current newsstand price. The logic defies me. But the rationale is that people are so concerned with inflation that they'll buy now to protect themselves for three years.

As the cover prices go up and the frequency of increases goes up, consumers are becoming very much aware of the purchase. A magazine selling for $1.50 or $1.95 is no longer an impulse buy. It's a decision buy. And the higher the price goes, the more decision is going to be involved.

At some point, circulation will begin to dwindle because people are going to shop for value. They will realize it's more cost-efficient to buy a subscription than it is to buy at the newsstand.

Reading audience increasing

On the positive side, the reading audience is increasing. The number of college graduates—your best reading audience—will increase 61 percent from 1980 to 1990. The number of upper-income people is also increasing. The group earning $25,000-plus will increase 135 percent from 1980 to 1990, making the potential reading market bigger than it's ever been before.

It will be the responsibility of the publishing community, now more than ever, to understand not only the consumer's interests, but also his buying habits, in order to deliver the right product to the right place at the right price. All segments of the industry—editorial, advertising, production, and circulation—*must* work in concert to maximize these opportunities or languish in the frustrations of poor, inefficient sales.

Are consumers trading down?

By Ronald T. Scott

There seems to be general agreement about the decline in the newsstand sale of magazines in units as well as dollars. Because I am usually skeptical of free-floating opinions, I have been doing some unscientific research on unit sale of magazines. This research involves discussion with national distributor personnel as well as the owners and managers of various wholesale agencies, all of whom I see and speak to as a continuing part of my daily work schedule.

What I have found is that our statistics are virtually useless. They have been distorted by inflation-powered cover prices, by regional pockets of severe unemployment and/or extremely high growth rates, and by the uneven rise and fall of product lines (i.e., the weakness in the high-priced men's sophisticates and the strength in some high-priced specialty titles). They are further distorted by the increased speed of returns flow as a result of computers, optical scanning and telecommunication of data from the local wholesaler.

There are two points to be drawn from this research: 1) We must be very skeptical of the statistical information we now possess; and 2) at least one of our many trade associations ought to get working with a professional research house on building a reliable set of statistics as a crucial service to its members and to our industry.

If statistics can't help us, how do we begin to understand what is happening to the buying patterns of our elusive consumer in these challenging times? How do we sort out a strategic plan for marketing and merchandising our product in the short term?

Well, as unscientific as it may sound, my approach to the problem is to "surround" it with information I obtained from my discussions with national distributors and wholesalers on which we can rely.

For example, we are rather certain that the men's sophisticate category, which represents as much as 20 percent of some local wholesalers' volume, has slumped as much as 12 percent in sales. We are fairly confident that there were few major cover-price increases in the last quarter of 1980 and the first quarter of 1981. We have reason to believe that a number of specialty magazines with significant newsstand sales are growing at a steady rate. We also know that a number of titles which depend to a significant degree on checkout line display for their sales have suffered significant decline in circulation.

Further, we know that discretionary income (the money left over— if any—after we have paid for our basic needs) is shrinking rapidly. We are reasonably confident that while leisure time is growing, the funds to fill that leisure time with activities are shrinking. And we can be reasonably confident that our competitors for that reduced leisure time money have also been raising their prices.

As a result of this exercise in "surrounding," can we determine the buying patterns of our consumer? Is our consumer buying fewer magazines? Or, is our consumer buying different magazines?

Preliminary information from owners and managers of local wholesaler agencies seems to indicate that unit sales are *not* down and, indeed, may well be rising. If this is true, how do we account for the drop in dollar sales at the wholesale level in most of the country?

To a substantial degree, this drop in dollar sales can be attributed to the men's sophisticate category. If 20 percent of a business drops 12 percent, that business has lost 2.4 percent of its total volume. If we add to this the reported drop in sale of some of the major supermarket checkout titles, I believe we have identified even more of a drop in sales than our consensus indicates. But, then, what is the explanation for the indications that units are not down?

The title of this column poses the question: Are consumers trading down? I believe the answer is yes. I believe the consumer is trading down in magazines, in books, in clothes, in foods, in almost all categories. The rise in importance of generic foods, off-brand basic clothes, and virtually unknown and unpromoted household items seems a clear indication of this trend in other consumer products. It may well be that the success of Harlequin Books can be attributed more to a thinner book offered at a lower price than to the fine marketing skills of its sales people. I think that we can easily conclude that our consumer is trading down, and will continue to trade down, as long as his discretionary income is under such heavy pressure.

If these conclusions are correct, publishers should determine whether fewer pages per issue and lower cover prices for the consumer could be a way to build back volume and widen profit margins.

As long as we continue to operate in a world economy best characterized by the word "stagflation"—stagnation of growth combined with high inflation—we will have cost pressures. Thus far, our response has been to pass on our increased costs to the consumer in the form of higher prices. We may well have reached the point where the consumer is no longer able to absorb these increased costs, even when he wants to. The only viable option that remains is to reduce costs by reducing the quantity of information and entertainment that we offer.

The consumer marketing cry (exemplified by the shrinking Hershey Bar) was "less for more." The new cliche may well be "less for less."

Adjusting for the economy
By Ronald T. Scott

The selling of consumer magazines, whether through newsstands or subscriptions, has always been subject to the health of the national economy and probably always will be. Magazines are essentially leisure time products, purchased with discretionary income which remains after the basic needs of the consumer are satisfied—after the rent is paid, the food and clothing bought, and primary needs and wants satisfied.

Thus, it is not surprising that magazines are suffering in today's recession. As consumers began to have difficulty meeting basic needs, the amount of money available for leisure time activities was pinched, and it is now clear that magazine sales in general began to decline almost in concert with the economy in general.

Specific patterns occur when sales begin to fall, however, and most good national distributor or publisher information systems can provide early warning signals of declining (or rising) newsstand sales.

When several publishers told me that they noticed these early warning signs of softening sales, I placed a series of telephone calls to local wholesalers in various sections of the country.

Since national statistics are only general indicators of economic activity and basically provide only an average economic level, the information I received was diverse. In some sections of the country, sales were indeed dropping dramatically. Other sections were showing a slowing of previous rapid growth; still others were stagnant and, somewhat surprisingly, some sections were enjoying accelerated growth.

When I questioned these same local wholesalers about specific categories of magazines, the responses fell into the same pattern. Some categories were failing rapidly; others were slowing in growth patterns; others were steady; and some were still moving upward at a rapid pace.

Early indicators

By reading the early indicators carefully and correctly, and then by sampling regional and category trends, publishers can evaluate the position of their magazines well in advance of potential crises.

I use a five-step evaluation of each magazine when sales weakness is apparent: 1) product value, 2) competitive product value, 3) product category trends, 4) regional distribution patterns, 5) profitability.

Product value is rated in terms of number of pages, type of paper, number of color pages, ratio of advertising pages to editorial pages, cover price, cover design and packaging. The purpose of this review (and of those which follow) is to correct any publishing extravagances which might have crept into the magazine during the high sales periods. I have rarely been involved in such a review in which no area of savings was detected, and it is a good exercise even in good times.

After completing the product review of one's own titles, the next step is to review the most current issues of competitive titles, using the same criteria. It is especially important to look closely for changes from the standard format which a competitor may be testing, so that we can follow the test and its results.

The third review is a sales analysis of these competitive titles. Such an analysis will determine whether the field is stronger or weaker than the general magazine market, and whether our title is running in pace with the field.

This review leads logically into an analysis of regional sales patterns of magazines. A publisher can then make adjustments in the number of copies allocated to various wholesalers, based on these regional factors.

The final step—after a new print order, or pressrun, for newsstand copies is completed—is the calculation of a new breakeven percentage or profitability index.

When a publisher systematically evaluates his magazine, he is usually able to reduce costs, trim staffs, and ultimately produce his magazine more effectively and efficiently, while reducing the risks inherent in a declining economy. Rarely have I seen such an evaluation damage the editorial vitality of a magazine since most cost sav-ings are in areas that were marginally productive at best, supported only by the apparent good times which the magazine had been enjoying.

The most logical response in a recession, then, is the orderly evaluation of each product to bring costs into balance with potential sales. Furthermore, publishers must reevaluate the allocation of copies based on the un-even impact of a recession on various sections of the coun-try and continue to watch those early indicators for the in-evitable upturn in economic activity.

The magazine merchandiser

By Ronald T. Scott

Over the past 15 years, most wholesalers have made great progress in developing communications with their retailers, and specifically with the buyers of their major chain retailers. Their objective has been to develop an at-mosphere in which the chain retailer feels comfortable with the magazine department.

To that end, wholesalers have been using profes-sional sales representatives to keep chain buyers current and informed about magazine and paperback profits, turns and return on inventory investment. These representatives provide computer sales reports and other statistical information, which chain buyers in particular need to monitor the success of their magazine and paper-back books department.

One innovative local wholesaler, Charles Levy Cir-culating Company of Chicago, has taken these services to their retailers a step further. This company is constantly monitoring the universe of titles to ensure that merchan-dise at retail is reflective of changing consumer trends.

More than two years ago, Levy began distributing computer magazines in the greater Chicago area. This year, it is looking for magazines in the health and nutri-tion field—a special interest field it believes is the next to experience tremendous growth.

Such innovative merchandising efforts place Charles Levy on the cutting edge of new magazine marketing and merchandising.

Magazine Merchandise Director

These efforts are due largely to the fact that for some 10 years Charles Levy has had a unique position for a local wholesale agency: Magazine Merchandise Director. This position is unique in that the director—Harvey Wasserman, who has been Levy's Magazine Merchandise Director since the position was conceived by David Moscow, President of Levy—has no operating re-sponsibility; that is, he is not concerned with receiving, scheduling and delivering products.

Wasserman's job is simply to select products for the retailers serviced by Levy. For example, when Was-serman first determined that computer magazines were indeed a potential growth field, he bought on consignment the first computer magazines directly from the publisher. (At that point, none were being handled by national distributors.) Levy then tested these computer magazines in selected accounts, including their own book store chain. The test result showed that computer magazines sold especially well in bookstores and in other retail outlets with traffic that was college oriented, or where the store's demographics included substantial numbers of people of above average income *and* education levels.

Levy was thereby able to supply its retailers with a better product mix by responding quickly and efficiently to the needs and wants of consumers in a new area.

Responding to a decline

A second example involves the romance magazines which were popular five or six years ago. In this case, computer reports on this category of magazines began to show a decline in this field in almost all types of outlets serviced by Levy. Wasserman's response to this decline was to reduce the number of copies allocated to most stores and, in many cases, reduce the number of titles in that category. At the same time Wasserman replaced this reduced romance field volume with a variety of female oriented titles, ranging from shelter magazines to titles targeted for a working woman, to other special interest women's titles.

A third example, and one similar to the computer story, is the speed with which Levy moved on widening distribution of video magazines when this field began its growth, some one to one-and-a-half years ago.

Wasserman considers himself a part of Levy's marketing team. It is his job, he says, to be sensitive to the ebb and flow of consumer interest in new and old products, and to constantly monitor the product mix for each of the retailers Levy services.

The objective of the Magazine Merchandise Director is to build confidence on the part of the retailers that Levy has the ability to deliver the right products to each store in the right quantity, and that Levy has the ability to change both titles and quantities in concert with changing consumer needs and wants. It is not enough, Wasserman says, to convince retailers to increase the amount of display space they should devote to magazines. It is just as important to be constantly working on merchandising the product to reflect the retailer's focus. It is as important to sense trends in the consumers' changing interests as it is to read the detailed computer printout by title and issue by retailer.

What makes Levy's Magazine Merchandise Director unique is his ability to focus on a single aspect of magazine merchandising—product mix—without having his attention diverted to the other technical aspects of wholesaler distribution.

As local wholesalers have continued to improve the quantity and quality of information available to them, the need for concentrated expertise and sensitivity in selecting product mix becomes more obvious.

We should expect to be doing business with more and more people like Harvey Wasserman as publishers, national distributors, wholesalers and retailers begin to realize the opportunities for marketing and merchandising magazines more effectively, efficiently and creatively.

Charles Levy's example, through its Magazine Merchandise Director, is one that will be followed by others, and they are due much credit for their leadership.

Decade of the merchandiser

By Ronald T. Scott

Now that the retailer environment is dominated by the chain retailer, there is a definite need for a new type of communication link among the four segments of the distribution channel: The publisher, the national distributor, the local wholesaler and the retailer.

The marketing departments of the publisher, the national distributor, and the local wholesaler have been responsible for selling the chain retailer on the value of magazines, comics and paperback books as an important consumer product line for their stores. And these departments have grown larger and more professional over the past 10 years.

Dealing with the chain buyer

The chain buyer with whom we now deal is, in most cases, concerned with that catchall category of consumer products called general merchandise: cosmetics, hair products, health aids, deodorants, shaving products, greeting cards, film, records, stationery, pet accessories and toys. Whether it fits our self-image or not, these are the consumer products with which we must do battle each day for the consumers' discretionary income and, almost as important, for the general merchandise buyer's attention and commitment.

The general merchandise buyer, like all other category buyers, is under enormous pressure to meet preset profit objectives based on the amount of selling space for which he is responsible. And the information on which he makes his buying decisions—information both internally generated and that furnished by his suppliers—is getting better.

The publishing industry faces a unique problem, however, caused by the nature of the product it markets. Because we handle an enormous variety of individual products (3,000 magazine titles and 400 new paperbacks each month), and because of the returnable nature of that product, the reporting of net sales to the buyer is a complicated procedure. Furthermore, because the Universal Product Code has given us the ability to record sale and return information in a more orderly and efficient manner, most publishers, national distributors and local wholesalers are providing chain buyers with more sales information than ever before.

In my discussions with chain buyers, I get the impression that they are both pleased and confused about this explosion of information they are now receiving from their local wholesaler, national distributors and publishers: They are pleased by the effort to inform, but confused by the volume of information they receive.

And this may well be our biggest problem. We have increased substantially the quantity of information we now provide the chain buyer, but we are providing him with a lot more information than he can handle.

I believe that the solution lies in the creation of a new service—magazine merchandising. For while the magazine marketing department gets our product into the product mix of chain retailers, it will be the magazine merchandising department that will keep our product in the stores and see that it continues to grow in importance. It will achieve this objective by providing the chain buyer with specific information about his changing needs and wants.

Putting information to work

To give you an example of how the first of these two functions would work, let's examine publisher A who has been carefully building the circulation of his specialty magazine over the past several years. Although his primary emphasis has been in the subscription area, he has also been developing modest single-copy sales through the national distributor-local wholesaler-retailer channel and has gained the approval of most major chain retailers for the display of his product. Furthermore, through the efforts of his national distributor—and using the records of the local wholesaler—he now can identify the special type of retailer who can sell high volume with a low return factor.

Given the present state of the art (without the capability of a magazine merchandiser), our publisher would instruct his national distributor to have his field sales people prepare a new distribution at each local wholesale agency they visit, based on the specific retailer profile he has. This new distribution would increase allocations to the target retailers and reduce or eliminate allocations to the less efficient retailers of this magazine. The national distributor would agree to do so and over a period of months, the directive would be executed.

The publisher will sell more copies of his magazine at a more efficient level, the national distributor will have a more profitable client, the local wholesaler will have higher sales and fewer returns to process and record, and the chain retailer will make better use of his precious display space.

However, with the press of day-to-day activity in the context of 3,000 titles and millions of copies of magazines, this damn good job of service merchandising would go almost unnoticed. In only a modest number of cases would local wholesaler executives be aware of this new merchandising effort, and only a chain buyer or two would know of the publisher's efforts to improve the retail product mix and target only the efficient stores for this particular magazine.

Now let's see how this task could be accomplished faster, more efficiently, and with far greater effect on the retailer if there were a magazine merchandiser communication link.

More efficient marketing

After our publisher had identified his prime retailers, he would meet with his national distributor's magazine merchandiser and staff who are in constant contact with the magazine merchandiser at the local wholesalers. Together, they would further define the target retailer. Then, the national distributor's magazine merchandising staff would contact their counterparts at each local wholesaler and instruct them to make a new distribution based on the new target retailer profile.

Because most wholesalers are now using computers for record-keeping, they could see immediately that the new distribution is based on sound information and makes good business sense. The new distribution work would be accomplished in weeks rather than months. And the local wholesaler magazine merchandiser would have a very good story of service to tell the general merchandise buyer the next time they sit down to review the magazine business.

To give you an example of the second function—how the local wholesaler magazine merchandiser can find out what the general merchandise buyer's needs are—let's examine the situation of a chain buyer who has just received his quarterly reports from his local wholesale suppliers which indicate that for the prior quarter he had a 9 percent increase in net sales on magazines contrasted with a 6 percent increase in net sales in his entire department. Although he is very pleased with the performance of magazines, he is faced with a directive from his superior stating that he must reduce inventory levels in his department by 5 percent due to the rising cost of money to finance his inventory.

Our general merchandise buyer has a problem and we need to be aware of it—fast. If that quarterly report is delivered by the local wholesaler magazine merchandiser who is prepared to offer suggestions on how he could balance his increasing sales volume with his need to reduce inventory, the magazine industry has a chance to come out ahead of its competitors. If we do not have a knowledgeable representative there to help our chain buyer work his way through that mass of numbers, however, we can be in trouble—trouble like reduced title lists, smaller display fixtures, or heavier premature returns.

There are literally hundreds of additional examples of how a communications link among a new group of magazine merchandisers can improve the efficiency of our distribution channel. At the present time, there are only a few national distributor and local wholesaler executives who perform this critical function, and they indeed are providing an important barometer of the needs and wants of chain retailers. More important, however—they clearly illustrate the need for this vital service.

Striving for efficiency in single-copy sales

By Melissa Lande

If you are a publisher—particularly a small publisher—and you are considering a single-copy sales launch, I suggest you visit a couple of wholesale distribution agencies first. At each agency, pay particular attention to the thousands of magazines being shredded and transformed into bales of waste.

If you can fathom the reality that *your* magazine will share the same fate, and you feel that you can sustain these losses for the sake of, say, the subscription business that single-copy sales will attract, or high profits on a low sale of a high ticket item, then take the plunge. But if this *is* your attitude, resign yourself to the fact that you will not necessarily be in a position to command performance (or respect) from your national distributor (ND), the 400-plus independent wholesalers who receive allotments from your ND, or the thousands of retailers who display and sell your product to the consumer.

A troubled economy has taken its toll at each of these levels, and the result is very little sympathy for the publisher who wants to throw copies out into the marketplace to see what happens. Gone are the days of speculative distributions.

Publishers of the 2,000 or so magazine titles currently in single-copy distribution are already aware that efficiency is their single biggest problem. And there is no solution in sight.

Publishers want to know why wholesalers aren't (by publishers' standards) enthusiastic about selling their magazines. They want to know why national distributors are asking for such high brokerage fees, why they seem unable to effect consistently high sales levels. They want to know why chain retailers seem to look down on the magazine business with condescension (after all, it's such a dynamic, fast-turning product category). They want to know if it's possible to increase the sales of a given title, particularly a small title, while being "victimized" by a system wracked with problems.

Wholesalers, national distributors, and seasoned publishers all agree that a joint effort is necessary if publishers are to be served most effectively. Unfortunately, that's all they agree on. Each sector of magazine distribution has been touched by the faltering economy in a different way. The result: differing ideas about how to increase sales and cut waste. In addition, each company, individually, has been affected by the economy in a unique way, so that views, even within each sector, do not match. There is an industry stalemate. No player can make a move without putting his own king in check.

And all this has a direct bearing on the small publisher fighting to break into or stay in the single-copy sales market. It will greatly benefit him if he has an accurate perspective on the problems that the industry and its various sectors face today. While he may feel victimized by the system, he should realize that without an understanding of the industry's internal workings, he cannot contribute to his own—or his industry's—growth.

While the various sectors of distribution have not been able to agree on an ultimate plan to solve the waste problem, it's not in the publisher's interest to find a culprit.

Wholesalers: the war on waste

Those bales of shredded magazines have become a part of the daily routine at many ID (wholesale) agencies, and they're costing the wholesaler money. After all, the wholesaler isn't shredding magazines because he's mean; in fact, most wholesalers are as frustrated as any publisher about the problem of waste.

Wholesalers, severely squeezed by many economic factors, are currently "waging war" on waste. True, they don't have to invest money in the fully returnable magazines they distribute, but their operating costs have skyrocketed so dramatically that many have been forced to take a hard attitude on the issue of waste.

Stanly G. Budner of the Delmar News Agency in Wilmington, Delaware, has tried on many occasions to explain to publishers the reason for high returns. "Our problem dated from the Arab oil embargo in 1973 and 1974, when the percentage of returns dramatically increased. Because consumers had to pay more for gasoline, heating oil and other necessities, there wasn't as much disposable income available for magazines—impulse items with a relatively lower priority. Because many publishers increased cover prices at the same time, demand slackened and newsstand returns shot up. In previous recessions, our sales always held firm, maybe because our products provided many hours of value at a low cost. But today our products are more expensive. Compared with TV, which is universally available and free, they aren't such a bargain any longer.

"The tail seems to be wagging the dog," Budner elaborates. "And it's not the top-selling titles that have caused the problem. It's the titles of lesser quality and production."

Citing figures taken from a study prepared by the Market Research Division of Warner Publisher Services, Budner points out that IDs have been distributing 164 sophisticate titles imitating *Playboy* and *Penthouse,* 138 car and van titles, and 146 crossword titles.

"Yes," he says, "new titles are the lifeblood of the industry, but did we need so many in the same categories? Yes, new publications deserve a chance, but isn't there some reasonable time after which we should not have to continue to take 60 percent returns from proven nonsellers?"

Budner believes that the waste problem has no one single solution because it is caused by inefficiencies found on all levels of distribution. One problem he names is an overall lack of communication—both in words and numbers—between wholesaler, retailer, national distributor and publisher. Also, he says, since there is a basic inequity between the publisher's breakeven and the wholesaler's breakeven, it is possible for the publisher of lesser quality titles to make money at a sale below 40 percent, while the ID cannot. In addition, the ID is negatively affected by competition between national distributors for the sales volume of lesser quality publications. This, he feels, has made it relatively easy for untried titles and inexperienced publishers to enter the single-copy marketplace. (National distributors, who are highly selective about taking on new publisher clients, will dispute this.)

Says Budner: "I can understand the frustration of the smaller print publishers, many of whom want to do something about these problems. But I feel they can't be the ones to initiate solutions, and, what's more, I think they are afraid because they don't really trust the system.

"In pursuing their own interest," he continues, "publishers who over-allot do not seem to understand that they are wreaking havoc in my agency. If they ship a mere hundred titles more than I need, with 1,900 titles per month, that spirals to 190,000 copies out of my warehouse that I must handle at no profit. Multiply that times 400 wholesalers. If I am a good guy and distribute all of the copies shipped, I am then penalized with higher expenses, not to mention the ill-will that my retailers feel toward me."

Over-allotment, coupled with the rising cost of wages, insurance and gasoline (while being interviewed, Budner signed a $10,000 check to cover his monthly gasoline bill; that $10,000 used to buy six months' worth) will force many wholesalers to continue a policy of withholding copies, a step, he says, "which has occurred in many cases." He believes, however, that proper communication between the various sectors of the industry can result in the establishment of proper allotments. He cites Macfadden, Playboy, Penthouse, and Playgirl as examples of publishers who have cooperated by cutting allotments—without losing sales.

Roy Newborn of Altoona News in Altoona, Pennsylvania, and president of the Council for Periodical Distributors Associations (CPDA), a non-profit national association representing wholesalers, has done much to open this communication, which everybody agrees is needed. As a spokesperson for wholesalers, he urges publishers to find out more about the mechanics of a wholesale agency before passing judgment.

"To understand how we work, publishers should visit several wholesalers. I think they would be amazed at our operations," he said. "Let them come to Altoona. Visit my agency. I beg of them to tell me how to do a better job.

"What we do need," he says, "is to discuss allotments with national distributors and arrive at figures we can defend to our retailers when we send out copies."

One reason for premature returns by retailers, Newborn points out, is the cash flow problem. "The wholesaler has the obligation to give every publisher the right to distribute—providing he doesn't look for distribution that requires putting out far more copies than dealers can handle. If we jam racks with more copies than a dealer needs, we create an untidy situation both visually and financially. The dealer dollar means too much to us for that."

Newborn also points out that dealer money is becoming harder to collect. Given this situation, if the wholesaler tries to force more copies on the dealer than the dealer can handle, he will probably cause further strains on an *already delicate* relationship.

Publishers, he suggests, should examine their own editorial and circulation strategies. "There are percentages for everything, and when they're out of line we have to withhold copies. A publisher is like a mother—her child could be the homeliest in the world, but you can't tell her that. To put it bluntly, many publishers aren't hitting their editorial targets."

Robert Bartles of Verham News Corporation in West Lebanon, New Hampshire, believes that withholding among wholesalers will continue as long as there is a surplus of product. "High returns and waste lead to overreactions," he explains, "so withholding is sometimes indiscriminate. Because he has been burned so many times by over-allotments and lack of controls, the wholesaler can become less sympathetic to market needs.

"Since we are only asking for the right to process returns cheaply, we want more controls from national distributors. We have already instituted scanning, an affidavit system, and instant destruct equipment. I feel that I've taken all the steps available to me to make returns more efficient. The next step is for national distributors and publishers to trim the product. Individual title analysis is meaningless with this surplus."

Edward E. Elson of the Atlanta News Agency in Atlanta, Georgia, believes that the efficacy of distributing small draw titles relates directly to demand by consumers. "Until the best markets for a title are determined, it is extremely difficult for an ID to distribute it without risking wasted copies. These copies are a waste for the publisher, entirely, and handling them is expensive for the distributor.

"Lack of sales," continues Elson, "is an extraordinary expense that the distributor is not willing to undertake unless he is subsidized to do so. The ID feels that his role is making copies available for sale. It's up to the magazine to sell itself. With limited circulation and a lack of information about where copies should be allocated, our risk of failure is high. Few people are willing to underwrite expensive losses.

"The problem with distributors goes further," he says. "Even if the narrow-interest magazine is successful in the single-copy marketplace, what happens if it sells out a limited number of copies? The distributor still has the problem of the same overhead and expense for this periodical with very limited sales potential. The same effort can be more profitable by furthering the sale of a more popular general title."

On the other hand, Elson points out that the perceptive distributor knows that a full line of periodicals is essential to his overall economic prosperity, and that it is necessary to carry a full line of magazines in order to have the opportunity to sell the widely circulated general magazines. "It is shortsighted to judge each title on its own economic merits," he says. "Titles must be looked at collectively if the wholesaler and retailer are going to maximize their profits."

Elson should know. Besides being a wholesaler, he is the largest retailer of magazines in the U.S., with exclusive airport concessions in Atlanta, Chicago, Pittsburgh, Houston, Boston, Milwaukee, and other major cities. He also holds the retail concession for magazines in most of the hotels in chains such as Hyatt, Hilton, Western, and Sheraton. Looking at magazines as a retail profit center, Elson states, "The narrowly defined title that is not normally single-copy beneficial can be a recognizable source of income for the retailer, but not to a distributor."

According to Gene Maday, vice president for marketing at Mid-America Periodicals Distributors Association, the average retailer sells 350 titles, while the wholesaler handles 2,000. Maday points out that wholesalers have invested heavily in improving the industry, investing in two retailer-directed marketing groups: Magazine and Paperback Marketing Institute (MPMI) and the Periodicals Institute (PI). MPMI offers management information centers, financed by wholesalers, which can be used by any retailer in the country. The Periodicals Institute is supported by wholesalers, publishers, and national distributors. It functions to create better magazine displays, more space at retail for periodicals, and a stronger brand awareness for magazines (as well as paperbacks and tabloids) at the consumer level via the Family Reading Center.

Says Maday, whose involvement with MPMI goes back many years, "Eight years ago, a Family Reading Center offered about eight feet of display space for magazines and 12 feet for paperbacks. MPMI worked very hard to situate them in the 92 percent of the supermarkets that have them today. We keep pushing for more and larger Family Reading Centers because we feel that more cover displays will help alleviate the waste problem. But we also know that distributions need reevaluations periodically. IDs aren't warehouses. They need more help from publishers. The bad money is driving out the good."

National distributors: a realization of the problems

Wholesalers argue that national distributors are responsible for many of the industry's inefficiencies. They take on too many publisher/clients, it's said, and they over-allot titles. But to generalize about national distributors as a group is difficult. In reality, the fewer than 15 companies in that business represent a far-ranging variety of titles, billings, and marketing strategies.

Since each national distributor must serve the interest of his specific corporate management, their willingness to speak out on sensitive issues varies as well. Understanding national distributors requires understanding the economic and corporate policies for each company.

To help increase sales and eliminate waste, some national distributors have allied themselves with the Periodicals Institute. These national distributors contribute to the institute's mission of expanding Family Reading Centers, cooperating with wholesalers and publishers in the process.

Some NDs support the International Periodicals Distributors Association (IPDA), which also has publisher members. For nine years, IPDA has worked to improve publication sales through programs that deal with institutional consumer advertising, calculating publications mixes, providing information to all segments of the trade on merchandising, the creation of a national distributor/wholesaler telecommunications network, and marketing seminars.

In terms of solving the efficiency problem, IPDA's telecommunications network, currently in the testing stage, may blaze significant trails in cutting down overallotments. According to IPDA's chairman, Emerson Egbert (also president of Pocket Books Distribution Corp.), quoted here from an article in IPDA's *Profit Ways Magazine*, "The network will permit the national distributor to be much more responsive to the sales histories of the various publications. It will create a situation where there is less of a chance of selling out on fast-moving titles, and it can bring down returns by greatly reducing over-allotments. Essentially, the telecommunications network will bring about a more sophisticated sales tracking record.

"Specifically, returns processing will be greatly accelerated once this program is fully operative. Currently, when a wholesaler has completed returns counts, it takes a considerable length of time to transmit this information to national distributors. The telephone batching service that IPDA is testing will permit the wholesaler to transmit, overnight, returns information to the national distributor.

"This method of transmission carries the added advantage of eliminating data entry errors at the national distributor level. The system's future applications include the transmittal of title allotment information."

As service organizations for publishers, national distributors serve as conduits of communication, and they work constantly to keep peace with the ID community.

The retailer's viewpoint

Three chain retailers, representing top supermarkets that carry magazines, were surveyed for this article. Because of corporate policies, they asked to give their input anonymously . . . and spoke on pertinent topics to the overall efficiency situation.

Retailer A
On efficiency: We get tired of prematuring copies, or refusing them. Some of our stores operate very efficiently in terms of merchandising because the ID provides great service. In other stores, magazines get dropped off twice a week, and I'm still trying to get someone in here to train my people. I think the ID is forced to spend too much time on bookkeeping, when he could be servicing good titles, and that comes from overallotments.

On positive aspects of product category of magazines: Though the industry is slow to change overall, the use of scanning in the ID agencies is encouraging, and those wholesalers who are becoming more service oriented are encouraging, too.

On bugs in the system: Publishers who operate with a 30 percent sale, the me-too kind, hurt the system for everyone else. When we premature, we ourselves are bugs in the system, because the wholesaler has given us too many copies. That's his fault, except that he can then say that's the national distributor's fault for overalloting. We don't have enough control over the titles sold in our store.

On Family Reading Center: We know that without a Family Reading Center, the retailer suffers a drop in overall magazine sales . . . that dollar amount would be reduced without Family Reading Centers.

Retailer B
On efficiency: The industry is inefficient simply because there is a lack of communication between the national distributors, wholesalers and retailers.

On positive aspects of product category of magazines: They provide high turns, they are guaranteed (we never get stuck with unsold copies), and our customers' needs are fulfilled.

On bugs in the system: RDA is the biggest bug, because it leaves room for open abuses, which retailers do take advantage of.

On Family Reading Center: They're a great idea, but we never really know what's on display there. We spend a lot of time authorizing titles, and then find magazines that shouldn't be there at all. There should be a plan.

Retailer C
On efficiency: The system is a slave of the computer, which doesn't take into consideration that each issue is a new item, so there's often a lack of adequate copies when a given issue comes along with punch.

On positive aspects of product category of magazines: Magazines play a role in one-step shopping that is important. Our stores are getting bigger, and every year we get a higher percentage of business. Our people are conscious that publications are an important category. We've matured, and we know that it's an important part of our mix.

On bugs in the system: We tend to believe the wholesaler before we'll believe the publisher or the national distributor, since the wholesaler is in the trenches with us. Some publishers hand you something that turns out to be a real stiff.

On Family Reading Center: We think magazines are an important category and we are looking for more volume. We divide our magazines about 50-50, front end/Family Reading Center.

Still, wholesalers seek drastic cutbacks in the allotments that the hundreds of ND field reps arrive at.

To further stimulate sales, national distributors have become increasingly more aggressive in selling to the retail chains. (One myth discovered while interviewing a retailer is that the ND has no stake in the sale, that he makes money on every copy distributed. Contrary to this belief, the ND makes money on sales, just as the wholesaler and retailer do.) Some scuffles have occurred when the ND has called on a wholesaler's retail chain; some wholesalers feel that too many people calling on one chain could hurt their relationships. Still, many national distributors and, of course, publishers continue to expand the number of hard sales calls, with either an implicit or explicit message to wholesalers—"sell harder!"

There lies the rub. With numerous investments centered on waste control, the wholesaler replies, "Cut back! You can do it without losing sales."

Says Patrick Flaherty, vice president of marketing services for Warner Publisher Services, "One of the biggest factors in our business today is that the retailer has become a dominant factor. Five to 10 years ago, fewer than 50 percent of retailers carrying magazines authorized them; they were supplied on the ID's recommendation. Today, more than 70 percent of the retailers in the U.S. and Canada work with authorized lists, and during the next five years, more than 90 percent of magazines sold will go to retailers with authorized lists. The retailer wants more control, and those lists put him in the driver's seat, so to speak.

"You see a situation now," explains Flaherty, "where the publisher, national distributor and wholesaler may all call on one retailer because of the control that retailer exercises. A new magazine is lost if a solid marketing program isn't instituted at the retail level. And publishers are unwilling to place their current or future destinies in the hands of wholesalers—or certain wholesalers—when the retailer is so dominant."

According to Flaherty, Warner has recently instituted numerous programs which incorporate promotion and marketing efforts. He names a number of point-of-purchase promotional/marketing programs with special retail incentives. For instance, Warner tested, then rolled out, a program where 90 copies of the 1980 Old Farmer's Almanac were offered in a specially designed point-of-purchase display. Citing test results that indicated the display was boosting sales 250 percent, the marketing department sold 9,000 displays nationally.

John Martin, president of Select Magazines, Inc., believes that efficiency can be achieved if retailer-oriented action plans are developed. "Depending on the magazine—checkout versus mainline—each situation must be analyzed by area, retailer by retailer, wholesaler by wholesaler, to develop such a plan. Our fundamental thrust is to sit down with each publisher and develop the kind of marketing plan a company like Procter and Gamble would expect."

Continues Martin: "In some cases, a distribution analysis is fundamental to draw and sale; other times, we may focus on developing merchandising, racking and incentives, particularly for checkout titles, since front-end merchandise requires unique handling."

Jim Mayor, vice president and director of chain marketing sales for International Circulation Distributors, part of the Hearst Corporation, always keeps the retailer's cost effectiveness in mind. He believes that one of the best ways to merchandise the smaller circulation magazine is to find special interest accounts that match its demographics. From there, he urges the creation of a total program for the retailer. Careful targeting, believes Mayor, plays an important role in selling magazines, now and for the future.

Recently, Mayor and his marketing division launched three unique marketing programs that signify Hearst's commitment to his approach. The "Relaxation Station" is a special fixture created to encourage people to buy magazines in liquor and gourmet stores. It combines the retailer's specials of the week with gourmet magazines. "Extraordinary Worlds," another fixture, carries six science-related magazines, and is placed where people with science interests are found (e.g., college bookstores, retail accounts situated in electronics-industrial towns). "The Q Factor," featuring magazines of quality, is targeted to consumers who can afford high ticket items, such as *Geo*, *American Film*, *Quest*, and *Art News*. It is being placed in upscale bookstores.

Such programs won't solve the efficiency problem per se or sell massive numbers of magazines, but they do open new points-of-sale, and they do expand the sales opportunity for magazines that would otherwise be lost on mainline racks.

In discussing efficiency, Mayor comments that "a modern national distributor must be a full service distributor who explores all facets of circulation for client publishers and is capable of handling subscriptions, wholesale distribution and direct accounts. These factors shouldn't be farmed out to different systems because the publisher is concerned with the whole picture."

William Hall, director, CBS/Fawcett Marketing Services, is emphatic about aggressive marketing to retailers. He feels that such action is necessary to increase sales opportunities for magazines.

Regarding efficiency, Hall builds a strong defense for national distributors, particularly those that are owned by volume publishers. "I resent the label of national distributor," he says. "We are publishers— and we're in the business to control how copies are being distributed. The wholesalers tell us that they should set allotments. Now, on an individual basis, this isn't so bad, but if they all did it, it would mean that the IDs would be determining the publisher's print order. Can we afford that? With a final sale, yes. With returnable sales, no. We're taking too much risk."

He continues, "The wholesalers want us to print fewer, and allot fewer, so they can get the business down to where they can handle it. Strategically, it's not wise of them to want that. If wholesalers ever get the business down to where they can handle it, what's to stop retailers from deciding that they can do the job themselves?"

In a recent speech to Atlantic Coast Independent Distributors Association (ACIDA) wholesalers, Hall elaborated: "The cost of money is a serious problem for national distributors. Today, money is at least 10 percent higher than it was just a couple of years ago, and that's costing distributors around $50 million annually. If you don't think the cost of brokerage is going to rise dramatically with the next round of contract writing, then you must believe in a free lunch.

"Moreover, I haven't mentioned travel and entertainment costs. They are rising, for the whole industry, at about 15 percent per year, with airfare and gasoline leading the way. That means travel and entertainment costs will double every five years.

"So," Hall asks wholesalers, "Who is going to finance the new magazines that are going to rescue your fortunes in the eighties? Not national distributors, not at

18 percent money we're not. Can we load these soaring costs onto the consumer by simply raising cover prices? Absolutely not."

Hall believes the answer to the efficiency problem is not in withholding, which has a cyclical effect, but in full-cover display. "We must all become marketers, not merely warehousemen, fleet operators, and distributors. You cannot gain enough efficiency in internal operations to survive if you don't protect sales—and margins are not going to increase enough to save you because they cannot."

With full-cover display, sales of special interest magazines can be 60 percent or better, Hall believes. But this is not so in situations where only 25 percent of the cover is shown. "The result of full-cover display for all titles on the mainline rack will be increased sales *and* increased efficiency," he says. He points out that in 1970, there was virtually no supermarket space for greeting cards. Today, in outlets that carry both greeting cards and magazines, greeting cards have more total space. He asks wholesalers: "How many of you service supermarkets with 60-foot magazine departments? How did the greeting card companies do it? They were better salesmen than we were!"

Hall has invited wholesalers to talk with his executives directly about allotments, pointing out that perhaps reps aren't always astute enough. "We will be reasonable," he says, "but we're not going to allow you to put our publishers out of the newsstand business in the name of efficiency."

Publishers: sharing a profitable goal

What happens to a magazine once it has been authorized by a chain? With the exception of checkout titles, most land on the mainline racks. According to Nigel Heaton, director of circulation, marketing and administration for Petersen Publishing, whose single-copy livelihood depends on mainline fixtures, very few magazines ever get full-cover display.

To combat this situation, Heaton launched a campaign to change the covers of his magazines. Previously they were designed for full-cover display. "We decided it was easier to change the package than the 40,000 outlets where they are carried, so we did a study to determine what our display positions were. Then we revamped cover designs to fit their alleged positions on the racks. We worked it so the cover lines could be seen from those positions, thus making full impact on the consumer."

After the redesigned titles went on sale, Heaton visited some retail displays and was horrified. "All of our work went down the tubes," he said. "Nobody was minding the store. I saw messy racks, some containing more than the one issue that was supposed to be on sale, and more. I believe that if you stripped down a mainline rack that's been neglected, put magazines back in their proper display positions by group, and took out the unauthorized titles, I am certain that you would find bare wood— and room for the full-cover display of additional titles. In the old days, field reps would get permission to strip and re-do racks for all titles. Today a field rep checks a dealer only for his titles. He isn't concerned with maximizing square footage for the dealer."

Heaton regards the mainline fixture and display as a prime source of concern to the industry—the place where efficiency efforts should be concentrated. "I think that it's time for all the panels that spend so much time on the RDA problem to address the point-of-sale issue instead," he says. "Many of us are finding it advantageous to increase our subscription efforts, which has got to affect our single-copy marketplace."

According to David Maisel, circulation director for *Rolling Stone*, efficiency isn't being generated because every faction has a self-serving plan, and because economics vary so much from publisher to publisher. "We'll get efficiency, along with increase of sales, when all the factions can sit down together. A definitive, overall plan must be drawn up that allows for efficiency to be improved in stages."

Maisel believes that there's a need to refine computer systems used by wholesalers. "Even if wholesalers use a formula that helps them achieve a 60 percent net sale, retailers can be hurt, unit sales can be lost, and a negative curve could result. There needs to be a much greater understanding of the specific needs of all titles."

He continues, "My goal is the same as a wholesaler's. I want more sales, fewer returns. I've effected my draw cut and my units are up, yet we were treated like a monthly by the system, even as a biweekly." By devising a formula for his publication which protects and weighs retailers, Maisel has succeeded in increasing his units. He says that many formulas have been developed by individual publishers to accommodate limitations in the system.

From his vantage point, Maisel believes that overall efficiency can be approached if the whole industry devises a multi-phased plan that includes analysis of national averages for publications, categorization of publications, and the prioritizing of retailers. Such a plan, he says, could be effected by the whole industry. But, he cautions, the problems won't go away overnight.

The future: dawn of a better decade?

If you are thinking about pursuing the single-copy route, it will be rough sledding unless you can afford to sustain a loss. Says John Harrington, executive vice president of CPDA, "You shouldn't regard single-copy sales as a beast unto itself: It's part of the whole circulation picture—and if a new publisher doesn't see it and use it that way, he'll never succeed. Single-copy sales can grow and can be used as a way to test locally. But don't expect it to be a money-maker right away. Right now, small publishers may be better off going to subscription mailings where they can predict responses better."

If you are already in national distribution with a small magazine, keep informed about the economic problems that are currently affecting your wholesalers and national distributors. Also, keep informed about plans being formulated by specific companies, or the whole industry, to solve the efficiency problem.

If you are an entrepreneur with a hot idea and limited funds, don't expect to make a pet rock out of single-copy sales. Reconsider your timing. Consider what Bill Hall told wholesalers last April at the ACIDA meeting: "Brace yourselves, gentlemen. This is a tough period we are living through, with no quick and easy solutions to the problems we face. The problems are rooted in national economic issues, they are not merely publishing industry phenomena."

It may be small comfort, publishers, but wholesalers and national distributors are also feeling the bite. Just about everybody understands that in order for the industry to grow, it must become more efficient.

Information superiority

By Ronald T. Scott

The newsstand magazine industry stands on the threshold of a new era of increased efficiency and productivity. In an industry long noted for its lack of timely information, we now have more information than we are prepared to handle.

Certainly, the concept that information superiority is the key to market superiority is basic to this industry. But we must understand that it is the quality of that information which ultimately leads to market superiority.

Less than 10 years ago, the typical independent wholesaler kept records on sale and return by retailer for about 200 titles. That is, there were only about 200 titles out of a total list of some 3,000 titles on which a publisher, national distributor, wholesaler or retailer knew exactly how many copies were actually sold at each retail outlet. On the remaining 2,800 titles, the only records available were the number of copies delivered to each retailer, the total number of copies delivered, the total returned, and the net sale by individual wholesaler.

One of the important tasks of a national distributor was to get more of his titles on that select list of titles on which sale and return information by retailer was kept. Distributions by retailer for titles not on the list were made by using the records of a title similar in consumer interest which was on the list.

Information now abundant

Today, over 380 independent wholesalers keep their records on a computer, and 122 of them use a scanning device to record the returns from their retail accounts. These 380 independent wholesalers represent over 90 percent of the newsstand magazine volume, and all are capable of recording sale and return information by retailer for every title they distribute. The 122 independent wholesalers who are scanning their returns are also keeping records of sale and return by retailer on every title they distribute. The result has been an explosion of information on magazines—information which has never before been available at the wholesaler level.

There has been an equally powerful explosion of information available to the national distributor and the publisher as a direct result of the explosion at the wholesaler level. Because of improvements in input devices, such as scanners, the local wholesaler is not only recording more information, he is also recording it faster. Thus, the time frame for return reporting has been shortened. And because information on titles by individual retailers is available on almost all titles, reports from national distributor field personnel are more detailed and more current.

Furthermore, several national distributors are currently testing information transfers via telephone lines from a local wholesaler's computer directly into the national distributor's computer. This will further decrease the time frame of information flow and increase the amount of information available.

At the other end of the channel of distribution, retailers are demanding—and getting—more current and detailed information on the titles they carry, the returns they are getting, and the return on inventory they achieve. As the Universal Product Code is used by more and more retailers to speed check-out counter productivity and to record sales, the information available to general merchandise buyers will be more extensive.

Using information efficiently

While I am convinced that the availability of this important information has put the newsstand magazine industry on the threshold of a more productive and efficient era, I am not convinced that we are well prepared, yet, to use the information productively and efficiently. Since one of the more awesome characteristics of a computer is its ability to manipulate the information stored in it into an almost infinite variety of reports, I am concerned that we are creating more reports than we have the ability to handle.

In his landmark book, *Management: Tasks, Practices and Responsibilities*, Peter Drucker spends a substantial amount of time on the concept of the "knowledge worker" replacing the production worker in the advanced economies of the world. Since there is no doubt in my mind that the future of the newsstand magazine industry depends on the development of a force of knowledge workers, let us define what a knowledge worker is, what he does, and why he's important.

The critical tasks of a knowledge worker are to analyze information and to make decisions based on the analysis. He must be prepared by training and experience to understand which pieces of information are important and which are unimportant so that he can make the proper decisions at his level of authority and responsibility.

There are several levels of authority and responsibility for knowledge workers. To illustrate these levels in the newsstand magazine industry, let us examine magazine "A" at the time when the February issue has just come off sale and the March issue is placed on sale.

At the local wholesaler level, information on sale and return by retailer is available on the issues prior to February (which is just being processed). If there is no knowledge worker available to analyze this information, the local wholesaler will instruct his computer to use a mathematical model to adjust individual retailer allocations, basing that model on an overall sales efficiency ratio (or percentage of sale) that he wants to achieve with his retailers.

Most retail allocations are prepared in this manner today—that is, based solely on yesterday's information. This method is unquestionably better than methods used prior to the computer, but there is an even better method. A trained knowledge worker could analyze the available information on prior sales and add current and future information. Such an analysis could improve both sales volume and efficiency.

For example, what if national sales trends are different than those indicated by the local wholesaler's prior sales? What if new chain approvals have been received but not yet entered into the local wholesaler's records? What if individual retailer consumer traffic patterns are changing faster than the mathematical model's ability to adjust allocations? Or what if a paper shortage dictates fewer copies available to cover existing sales?

Knowledge workers needed

The information necessary to respond to any of these situations is available now, but a knowledge worker, not a mathematical model, is needed to respond correctly to them.

At the national distributor/publisher level, faster recording of information is providing more and faster feedback on sales trends. Yet publishers are not using this information to adjust newsstand press runs and determine allocations to individual retailers. It still takes up to six months for increased allocations—for example, a new authorization of a title by a major retail chain—to affect a press run. It still takes almost as long for a publisher to adjust press runs, either upward or downward, to reflect clear national sales trends.

Despite better and faster information flow, we still make too many intuitive press run decisions. We need trained, experienced knowledge workers to analyze information such as national sales trends, new authorizations, seasonal population changes, declining regional economic activity, major industry strikes, increased retailer competition, and a host of additional factors.

As general merchandise buyers at retail chains receive more information—not only from magazine suppliers, but most other suppliers as well—they have less time to analyze and interpret it. And although the newsstand magazine industry has made great strides in supplying information, we have a long way to go in using the information as a real sales tool. We need the knowledge worker to provide the general merchandise buyer with an interpretation of the volumes of information we now have available.

Understanding wholesalers

By Ronald T. Scott

For many publishers, the most mysterious and incomprehensible link in the newsstand distribution chain is the local wholesale distributor. Why do we need these local distributors? What do they do? How do they do it? Is there a better way to perform these functions?

Since these are questions which have been asked many times by many people, this column will try to answer those questions by outlining the basic functions of the local wholesale distributor. In the process, I hope to dispel the myth of the local magazine wholesaler as a mysterious shadow operating from a rented garage using second-hand trucks, and show the wholesaler as a vital link in the newsstand distribution chain.

Wholesalers service 145,000 retailers

There are approximately 145,000 retail outlets selling magazines and paperback books in the United States and Canada. Given the present economics of distribution, the nation-wide network of approximately 500 local wholesalers services these outlets and performs certain functions which could not be performed as efficiently in any other way. In fact, in most cases the local magazine wholesaler runs a multi-million-dollar business, maintaining an office complex, a large warehouse, and a fleet of delivery trucks.

The first step in the process begins when the wholesaler receives magazines in bulk from the publisher or the national distributor. He or she delivers these magazines to the individual retailer and takes back the unsold copies, billing the retailer for the new issues and crediting him for the unsolds. He then collects from the retailer, keeps sale and return records, and reports them to the publisher or national distributor. Finally, he pays the publisher or national distributor for the copies sold.

Maintains timely delivery

By receiving magazines in bulk quantities and collating the variety of titles in a weekly delivery to individual retailers, the local wholesaler provides some economy of transportation. However, his critical function in this process is the timely delivery of dated consumer merchandise to these 145,000 retail outlets. Because most magazines are topical, they are of interest for a limited time only, and it is an extraordinary system that can place a weekly or monthly magazine on sale in almost every retail outlet in the United States within a day.

Publications receive more attention

In addition, because the local wholesaler is delivering a large quantity and variety of magazines and paperbacks on a regular basis, these publications receive more attention from the retailer than individually-delivered titles would.

In the area of record-keeping and collections, the local magazine wholesaler provides a vital service to both his suppliers and his customers. When a retailer sells a magazine to a consumer, he begins the process whereby the publisher receives his payments. The local wholesaler, who bills and credits the retailer with a weekly statement, collects his payment from the retailer and, at the end of the month, pays the national distributor or publisher.

It is obvious that without the local presence and weekly transaction between the local wholesaler and the retailer, the process of reconciling sale and return transactions—and the entire billing procedure—would be much more complicated. It is not difficult to imagine the chaos which would result if every publisher, or even every national distributor, had to bill and credit all 145,000 retailers for the magazines on their newsstands.

Alleviates retailer workload

There is little question in my mind that a substantial number of retailers would no longer sell magazines if they were to receive them from a variety of sources (mail, UPS, truck) and had no local distributor to prepare them for display and sort down the unsold copies before returning them to a number of billing agents. (Those few retail chains which have advocated direct warehouse shipments should very carefully analyze the costs they are creating.)

Wholesaler speeds information flow

Publishers maintain, and properly so, that they must wait too long for sale and return information on their publications. However, it is not the local wholesaler who is holding up this information flow. While I have previously discussed the potential improvement in this information flow with the increased use of the Universal Product Code, it is important to note that the local magazine wholesaler has a vested interest in quickly processing unsolds.

Processing provides the data for the current statement on which to collect from the retailer. Faster processing also enables a wholesaler to take a deduction from his statement from his national distributor. Obviously, this information flow would be much slower without the wholesaler's weekly contact with his retailers.

The local magazine wholesaler, then, is not a shadowy figure: he is an operator of a multi-million-dollar service business which forms an important link for the successful magazine publisher.

National distributors

By Ronald T. Scott

I am frequently asked about the financial arrangement between a publisher and a national distributor. There seems to be an increasing number of magazines being started with inflated newsstand revenues in their projections. There's also a growing feeling among existing non-newsstand publishers that perhaps they are missing opportunities by not being on the racks.

Obviously, the publisher who is considering entering the newsstand business should understand its financial arrangements. How does the national distributor determine his offer to a publisher? What does he charge to distribute a magazine? How does he pay the publisher?

It must be understood, of course, that the national distributor is in business to make a profit selling magazines, just as the publisher is. And his desire for profit and the psychic rewards of successfully launching a new star within the world of publishing is as great as the publisher's.

Knowing this, the alert and aggressive publisher can be prepared to sell the national distributor on the importance of his new magazine so that he can bargain for the best financial and sales arrangements possible.

When a national distributor is approached by a publisher of a new magazine for the newsstand, that distributor must make several value judgments about the magazine. Is this magazine capable of achieving significant newsstand volume? Is it comparable to other newsstand magazines which are already successful? How much effort will be necessary to help this magazine achieve its highest level of success? Are the financial rewards worth the effort?

The national distributor's answers to these questions form the basis for his economic decisions regarding the commission rate and advance payment rate he should offer the publisher.

The national distributor works on a commission ranging between 5 percent and 12 percent of the cover price of the magazine. A magazine with a suggested retail price of $1.50 is traditionally billed to the local wholesaler at 60 percent of the cover price, or 90 cents. The national distributor's commission must also be deducted from the 90 cents.

If, for example, this commission is 8 percent of the cover price, the publisher must deduct an additional 12 cents from the 90 cents, leaving a net 78 cents per copy sold. (These calculations do not include the retailer incentive known as the Retail Display Allowance, which is normally 10 percent of the cover price for those copies sold through retailers who apply for the allowance and submit sales figures for the magazine.)

Evaluating a magazine's potential

The national distributor will determine his commission bid by evaluating the magazine's potential and the commitment of resources—field sales personnel, marketing personnel, executive time, financing—required to do the job. Obviously, the more optimistic his evaluation, the lower the commission rate.

In deciding what advance payment (payments made to the publisher for future sales) he will offer the publisher, the national distributor bases his decisions on his judgment of the potential sale of the magazine. If 100,000 copies of the first issue of the magazine in the above example were to be distributed and billed, the publisher's gross billing to the national distributor would be $78,000. In most cases, the publisher expects to receive an advance payment of some percentage of this $78,000, ranging from 15 percent to 50 percent of the gross billing.

If the national distributor feels there is a high risk of poor sales on the initial issues, or if there are few titles of comparable editorial content on which to base an estimate, he will offer a low advance payment. The lower the risk or the more informed the national distributor is of similar magazines that are successful, the higher the advance offer will be. If the national distributor offers a 20 percent advance, he is offering to advance $15,600 of the $78,000 gross billing, before the magazine has been placed on sale.

It is important to note that this advance payment is a loan to the publisher against the collection of sales by the national distributor and is, in essence, a bank function. While there is in most cases no specific interest charge for the money so advanced, there is usually some correlation between the size of the advance payment and the commission charged by the national distributor. Generally, the less advance payment needed, the lower the commission rate.

Risk vs. commission rate

I wish to note one other important factor which the national distributor will evaluate to determine the advance payment and commission rates he will offer. This is the financial health and capital resources of the publisher of the magazine.

The healthier the publisher and the greater his capital resources, the lower the risk for the national distributor if the sales of the magazine do not equal the advance payments made. Since this advance payment is, to a large degree, a loan against receivables, the lower the risk, the lower the implied finance charge which is built into the commission structure.

The publisher of a new newsstand magazine who wants to be in a position to bargain for advantageous advance payments, low commission rates and firm commitments from the national distributor for sales and marketing efforts must understand these financial arrangements. He must understand the factors which the national distributor will use to determine his offer to a publisher. And he must prepare a well-organized and carefully documented presentation of the editorial concept of his magazine as well as a profile of the consumers who will be interested in buying it on the newsstands.

It is, then, the responsibility of the publisher to stimulate the national distributor's interest in and enthusiasm for his magazine, for it is only the publisher who "knows" what he has created. The publisher's success in generating this interest and enthusiasm is the key to making advantageous financial arrangements with the national distributor.

Choosing a national distributor

By Melissa Lande

"All national distributors are alike."
"Some national distributors don't tell the whole story."
"One field force runs circles around the others."
"One national distributor can really launch a new title."
"National distributors are a necessary evil."
"Magazines wouldn't survive without them."
"National distributors. Can't always work with them—can't distribute without them."

Opinions about national distributors certainly do run the gamut, depending on whom you talk to. These personal opinions have recently been expressed by various people in the newsstand industry: publishers, wholesalers, retailers, and even national distributors themselves.

At best, the newsstand industry is an industry that's known for its incomparable delivery capabilities, outrageous personalities, charitable works, and back-slapping friendliness. At worst, it's known for polarized factions and a prolonged plunge into data processing. ("This industry is light years behind the fulfillment indus-

try," claims one publisher.)

But no matter what people say, the newsstand industry always manages to get copies of magazines out. The system works, and the national distributor is a vital part of that system.

If you decide that your magazine warrants a mass market distribution—and if you have facts that suggest a potential sell-through in specific markets—you must realize that choosing a national distributor is a complex project that requires research into many variables. Furthermore, you will have to make decisions based on both objective and subjective factors.

Before a publisher even begins his research on choosing a distributor, however, he must understand the concept of mass marketing, the changing wholesale and retail markets, and the economic climate of this country.

The distribution system

The national distributor oversees and administers the distribution of magazines from publisher to

337

wholesaler, and, in turn, to retailer. He must keep tabs on the 150,000 points-of-sale that constitute the mass market of the U.S. and Canada—newsstands, supermarkets, convenience stores, drugstores, variety stores, and other chain outlets. To do this, he must work very closely with about 500 independent wholesalers who service these retail outlets, market by market.

Interfacing with local wholesalers is a very important function of a national distributor—particularly for small publishers who cannot afford additional field services—and it takes a lot of data and time to convince wholesalers and retailers that they have a winning magazine on their hands.

The national distributor's field reps work at wholesale agencies around the country every day, and some maintain offices at large wholesale agencies. National distributors have been known to jump through hoops for the million-seller title in their lines. And they've also been known to perform less than adequately for smaller publishers.

The wholesaler is the man with the truck. He's also the man with the power. However, he's a man without time—especially for a new publisher.

Magazines are shipped to him every day from printers, and he works with established publishers and national distributors on allotments. While his men divide up the magazines and deliver them, he handles the returns, the endless paperwork, and, in many cases, the task of integrating new computer systems and scanners (UPC) into his system. Furthermore, he may face union difficulties.

Chances are, you will not find it easy to talk with an independent wholesaler without the entree provided by a national distributor. Though the wholesaler appreciates new entries, he doesn't have the time or facilities to wet-nurse your publication. And unless you're handing him a surefire hit, he's not going to wander far from the national distribution system, which, in many ways, has been designed for him.

Finding a distributor

Years ago, all national distributors might have wooed the fledgling magazine with newsstand "potential." But don't expect too many free dinners from national distributors this year. Choosing a national distributor isn't what it used to be. Finding one that welcomes your publication sounds more like what you're going to have to do.

Though you won't have as many choices as you would have had a few years ago, you should still exercise careful consideration and take the time to learn about each one. Since a national distributor can play many roles—banker, marketer, billing department, administrator, promoter, hand-holder and psychiatrist—you'll want to find one who will best suit your needs. Otherwise, you could find yourself screaming for attention.

Furthermore, since many people in the industry believe that 20 percent of newsstand titles account for 80 percent of the dollars generated, your new magazine is likely to be left in the lurch. You will want to blame your national distributor for this, but you must be realistic about the marketplace.

Gather the facts

Publishers should examine a national distributor's size and position in the industry, his financial reliability, title compatibility, management information services,

and his position with wholesalers. Publishers should also be aware of each distributor's marketing and computer capabilities, the organization of the main office, the company's traffic services, how returns are handled, its list of existing clients, promotion and advertising, and the company's flexibility and intuition.

Take note of how many field people each distributor has in relation to the number of titles he handles. Although the chart cannot evaluate the effectiveness of the field force, it does indicate how many people the national distributor thinks are necessary to do a good job.

Use this chart as a frame of reference and start asking questions about each service that's listed. For instance, Select Magazines recently announced a S.M.A.R.T. (Select Magazines Automatic Reporting Technique) computer system, which will, they say, "knock the industry on its ear." Kable News has been involved with computer operations since 1959. What does each system do? Most national distributors consider telecommunications the key to the future, but it's up to you to determine how far along they've developed their own. Ask for sample print-outs to see what reports and data your magazine would be getting.

Evaluate services

Promotion and marketing services also require a "subjective" evaluation. In many cases, you will be in a better position to evaluate the competence of these departments if you actually meet with the people who run them, the people with whom you'll be working closely. Ask for introductions before you sign a contract.

About five years ago, Warner Publisher Services (then Independent News) started blazing promotional trails in the industry when it designated its in-house promotion department as an independent company in its own right: Publishers Advertising Associates. PAA President, Mark Greenberg, says, "We provide supplementary services to clients like *Playboy* magazine, who are heavily involved on their own. To smaller clients, we function as their total agency—conceptualizing programs, buying time, inserting ads, billing, and following up."

Today, Warner isn't the only national distributor with its own in-house agency and versatile creative services. It's becoming more and more apparent that promotional think tanks are scoring lots of points in the industry. Point-of-sale displays, retail kits, trade and consumer advertising are all areas that are keeping today's distribution promoters among the busiest people on the national distribution level.

Of course, field and sales services should be scrutinized carefully, since each national distributor has a different method of delineating responsibilities. And since the industry is constantly changing—and has recently experienced personnel shifts, it's important to ask about each company's internal sales "machine."

Because national distributors take pride in their circulation expertise, it's in this area that they're best known. However, they also happen to serve as bankers to newsstand publishers—and although money may not be everything, when it comes to getting small, independent publishers onto the newsstand, the money advanced by a national distributor can come in pretty handy. Handy enough to pay the printer, to pay for paper, to stay in business.

Traditionally, money has been discussed behind closed doors. Standard deals were made, giving publishers a 25 percent advance against the estimated net sale, plus shipping. The national distributor, in turn, got a commission of 8 percent to 10 percent of the cover price.

Today, there are no standard deals for publishers—they bounce all over the ballpark. However, most national distributors are more cautious than ever about bankrolling a new, small magazine because they face a static domestic economy and a high magazine attrition rate—and they have been burned too many times.

Frank Herrera, vice president of distribution for Hearst Magazines (and the former president of Independent News), warns the new publisher to be very careful. "We may issue upfront money without charging interest," he says, "but you can be sure, *that* money will be absorbed and charged back to the publisher somewhere along the way. No one gets anything for nothing—and if that money costs us money, the publisher will pay. We may figure the money into the brokerage, or some other cost, which may not seem very obvious."

Herrera tells the newcomer to expect a low advance and a high brokerage, and advises him to always add a clause to contracts with national distributors specifying that commissions be adjusted after six months, based on the magazine's performance. His final message to the small publisher looking into mass newsstand distribution this year: "Don't!"

Joy London, a veteran of magazine distribution, now an investment counselor for Alan Patrikof Associates, contends that new publishers should seek independent relationships with their national distributors, as well as with their printers. "If you can't find proper financing," she says, "don't expect to live off your national distributor. If you depend on him to bankroll you, you'll pay for it in the end."

London emphatically points out that her company will not express interest in magazines that sell only through single copy sales. "Categorically, we won't touch them," she says. "Too much risk."

Chip Block, Publisher of *Games* magazine, offers a financial tip for starry-eyed entrepreneurs. "Sell out as soon as you can to a large company!" he laughs.

Block ought to know, since he did just that when he delivered his brain child *Games* into the hands of Playboy Enterprises. "It may look as though there are a lot of successful new magazine launches on the newsstand, but take another look," he says.

Block points out that last year's great new successes were all accomplished by major publishers, who have established field operations and plenty of clout. He cites *Self* (Conde Nast), *Omni* (Penthouse), and *Inside Sports* (Newsweek) as prime examples, and reveals that *Games*'s own newsstand activity has greatly increased since Playboy took over its single copy sales responsibilities. "When we were publishing independently, we were going nowhere fast on the newsstand," he says. "Since Playboy has taken over, we've more than doubled our sale on the newsstand."

The area of personal relationships—simpatico—cannot be too heavily stressed. In fact, a successful marriage of publisher/national distributor carries equal weight with "objective" factors. Since the newsstand business still operates on the basis of personal relationships, there has to be an intuitive feeling between publisher and distributor to insure a smooth working relationship.

Most publishers who were interviewed for this article believe that most distributors are pretty much alike, give or take a few services. However, since their personnel and corporate "styles" vary significantly, it's important to meet as many people as you can from the companies that interest you. Do they understand your title? Does their "company image" match yours?

One publisher tells about the national distributor who didn't "want" him, but was obliged to take on his title because of other agreements with the mother company. "We had the normal distribution problems that can be expected for a specialty magazine that distributes under 75,000 copies on the newsstand. But we also had the problem of not being wanted. Although that national distributor warned us ahead of time, we went ahead with him anyway. I suppose we got what we deserved."

Anne Getson, a consultant, speaks of her distribution experience. "There should be a rapport between publisher, national distributor and product for any distribution deal," she advises. "You should understand your product and its relationship to your national distributor."

"A deal should never start out with bad feelings," claims Carol Shaw, who, along with her husband, started what has been called one of last year's surprise successes, *Big Beautiful Woman*. Although both Shaws have versatile backgrounds in the entertainment field, they had no publishing experience. "We had no idea how to find a national distributor," reveals Mrs. Shaw, "and at one point, I even used *The Yellow Pages*."

Through one of their show biz friends, the Shaws learned about PDC, which was then a subsidiary of Filmways. "We liked the people there, and since we've been there, we've gone from 50,000 to 300,000 on the newsstand."

Since Flynt Distributing Inc. has assumed distribution of PDC titles, was Shaw concerned? "We do not expect problems, and don't think we should look for trouble. When you make a deal, you'd better feel great about it and not look for problems when there aren't any. Period."

Mother Earth News surprised the industry by waiting almost 10 years before searching out a national distributor. Like the editorial content in its pages, *Mother* wanted to do it herself. However, when she had gained as much marketplace acceptance as she could on her own—and when the paperwork started to pile up—Ted Black, her vice president of single copy sales, knew it was time.

His prime consideration in making a selection was "environment." "It was important for us to settle in with a national distributor who made us feel proud, who welcomed us into his family, and who accepted our uniqueness," he explains.

Some publishers base their decisions totally on personal relationships, past experiences and personal recommendations. Chip Block said he placed *Games* with Curtis because he knew and liked Curtis people.

Be persistent

Since making the right decision on a national distributor is so important, use as many resources as you can. Meet as many people in the business as possible. Go to shows, industry events, conventions.

Talk to other publishers and even retailers to learn from their experiences. Most publishing colleagues in newsstand distribution have no qualms about sharing information and the benefits of their experiences. In addition, there are consultants available who help new publishers with national distribution. It's important to specify how he/she can help you before you begin. Consultants may specialize in various ways. Some make deals. Some open doors. Some work with your numbers. Some are promoters. And some do all of this. Find out what you're getting.

Since getting into the closed door isn't easy, it's important to be persistent. National distributors want tangible evidence that you're not just another magazine to come down the pike. If you don't have evidence to impress them, create some. Perform tests in specified market areas, and bring the results to national distributors.

Above all, be persistent. Because you need the national distributor more than he needs you, you must keep selling him all the time.

Once you start penetrating some of those closed doors—you should record your impression of each national distributor.

Prepare an evaluation report for each company. Determine the number of weekly, bi-weekly, monthly, bi-monthly, semi-annual, annual, and one shot titles which each distributor handles. Determine wholesaler dollar billing and ranking.

Evaluate the personnel of each company. Note the number of employees in marketing (headquarters and field) and the number of employees in operations (head-quarters, supervisors, district managers, metro sales reps, district clerks, and part-time checkers). Also determine the number of employees per title.

For each distributor, note your immediate and projected impressions. Try to determine where your magazine ranks with his other titles. Actually list the other titles, their frequency, price, average single-copy sales and annual billing. Analyze where your magazine will stand in the national distributor's mind.

Finally, summarize your findings, listing the pros and cons of each company. *Rolling Stone*'s David Maisel, who developed the format for the evaluation report mentioned here, points out that the process doesn't end here. "Once you've cut your deal, you have to realize those pros and cons will still be with you," he says. "Then, it's up to the *publisher* to come up with specific plans that will utilize the national distributor's strong points."

Maisel stresses that the publisher who views the national distributor as just a billing and collection agency will receive just that— and nothing more. "Publishers have to guide the way, and they have to be as specific as possible."

If you understand the variables—and the high stakes—you will start out on the right foot.

The supermarket battleground

By Ronald T. Scott

In 1978, total domestic sales of weekly and monthly magazines, digest-sized books, children's coloring books and pocket-sized books amounted to $2,468,640,000. Of this amount, $670,900,000 was spent in 187,910 grocery stores, which had total sales of $162,640,000,000. That is, 27 percent of all book and magazine sales as defined above were in the nation's food markets and small grocery stores. And yet, those sales represented only 0.41 percent of total food store sales. (My source for these statistics is the 32nd Annual Consumer Expenditures Study of *Supermarkets* magazine.)

These statistics illustrate the fact that while the food store is a very important retail outlet for magazines, paperback books and related items, these consumer products are not nearly as important to the food store business. However, since the revolution in scanning and computers began in the food store, that is the place where the publishing industry will fight its first fierce competitive battle of the 1980s.

It is clear that the merchandising information tools of the future are the Universal Product Code (conceived and executed by the Supermarket Institute, a predecessor of the Food Market Institute), scanners and computers. And those who have seen or used the computer programs which are part of the scanning revolution at the food market level and at the independent wholesaler level will tell you that they are powerful and effective.

I have used a simulated computer program that enables a general merchandise buyer, for example, to determine his daily profit on one pound of regular grind coffee in each of his stores, in each of his regional divisions, and throughout his chain. And he can use this information to determine his profit in a number of ways: profit per linear foot and/or cubic foot; profit as a return on inventory investment; profit per sales dollar; and profit compared to other consumer products that compete for his display space.

More important, however, is the fact that a general merchandise buyer will have this information instantly retrievable on a CRT display screen—not at a later date on a computer print-out. Simply stated, a food market will record the date and amount of the merchandise it receives and create an inventory number for that merchandise. Then, as each item is scanned at the check-out, the inventory number is adjusted, leaving a net sale for the number of days on sale.

As a sales history develops, the general merchandise buyer will be able to determine which products are profitable to keep and which should be reduced in quantity and/or in allotted display space. He will be able to determine an optimum inventory level that will protect his daily sale and keep his inventory investment at the lowest possible level.

Food market executives are aware of the importance of this information flow, and they see the future profits of scanning quite clearly. They are proceeding slowly and carefully in building their scanning stores, however. While they are sure that scanning technology works, they also know that they must test the new in-store systems and procedures leading up to the scanner check-out in order to maintain complete control of their businesses.

The use of scanners and computers is definitely increasing, however. In fact, the Food Marketing Institute reported that at the end of October 1979 there were 1,297 scanning stores in operation. In the month of October alone, 105 stores converted to scanning check-out lines.

It is anticipated that the food market industry will have 2,500 scanning stores by the end of 1980. It is important to note that almost every important chain of food markets has a goodly number of individual stores that have converted to scanning. Furthermore, one regional chain, Ralph's Markets, has already begun to sell to its vendors information on sales which it collects from its scanner stores. More of this is sure to follow.

If publishers are to remain competitive in food markets, they will need carefully trained salespeople with well-documented information. Fortunately, such information is now being developed by the independent magazine wholesaler.

As I have said more than once in this column, one of the primary functions of the independent wholesaler is record keeping. Wholesaler records—the data on the sale and return of magazines by individual retailer—can be used by salespeople to document the current success and to forecast the potential success of a magazine when they are making sales calls on general merchandise buyers.

There are now 325 independent magazine wholesalers, representing close to 85 percent of the U.S. and Canadian magazine volume, who are computerized. Of these, some 140 wholesalers are using scanning to process unsold copies from their retailers and to maintain current sale and return information by title and issue for each of their retailers.

There is no question that the information will be available. However, is the publishing industry ready to invest the time and money to prepare for the challenges which the food market industry will present in the 1980s?

Dealing with delivery

By Ronald T. Scott

It is a constant source of amazement to me that publishers who keep the most meticulous records of the status of every page of every magazine while it is in the production stage keep little or no record of its delivery status once it leaves the printer—especially since this information is readily available.

Unfortunately, too few publishers realize that when a magazine is consigned to a freight carrier, destined for the local wholesaler for newsstand sales, a lot more than the cost of freight is involved.

The two most critical factors that can affect the sale of a magazine on the newsstand, and in which freight plays a critical role, are timely delivery and secure delivery. In order to illustrate the importance of these two factors, let's examine the steps taken by the local wholesaler in scheduling and delivering a magazine to the newsstand.

Well in advance of the shipment of a magazine by the printer to the local wholesaler, the national distributor sends an advance notice to the local wholesaler, indicating the issue date, coding, quantity of copies allocated, and the on-sale date of the issue. This advance information is recorded by the local wholesaler who will use it when he begins to schedule his magazine delivery for the on-sale date listed on the notice.

When the local wholesaler begins this scheduling process (usually seven to ten days prior to the on-sale date), he reviews the files of all of the magazines which indicated this on-sale date to determine if the allotment has been received and if the delivery was complete.

Timely delivery is essential

It is at this critical point that the factors of timely delivery and secure delivery play an important role in the potential sale of a magazine on the newsstand. If a magazine scheduled to be a part of this newsstand delivery has not been received, it will probably not be scheduled for its designated on-sale period. And if only some of the allotted copies are delivered, either fewer retailers will receive copies or all retailers will receive fewer copies. Any one of these possibilities can be devastating to the sale of a magazine.

To illustrate a non-delivery situation, let us say that the publisher of magazine "A" has notified the local wholesaler that the magazine should be placed on sale on January 15, 1980. Let us further assume that when the local wholesaler begins his schedule review on January 7 he notes that he has not yet received magazine "A."

In the case of a major magazine title with high volume, the local wholesaler may well call either the publisher or the national distributor to find out if the magazine is on its way. In the case of the vast majority of magazines, however, the title is simply dropped from that week's schedule and returned to the files for review the following week.

Although this would seem to be an arbitrary and unfair decision, the potential confusion caused by the billing and non-delivery of that title to as many as 1,000 retailers is a more serious consideration.

There would be massive paperwork for both the local wholesaler and the retailer which would probably delay payment by the retailer, complicate the record-keeping function of both, and further confuse the retailer when the magazine is delivered the following week. Furthermore, the reaction of retailers to non-receipt of a magazine for which they have been billed strains the carefully developed service relationship between wholesaler and retailer.

Unfortunately for the publisher of magazine "A," the local wholesaler really has no other choice; he must schedule the magazine for later delivery. And it is important to note that the cause can be traced directly to late delivery, not inefficiency by the local wholesaler.

Now let's suppose that magazine "A" arrives on January 9. Since it is too late to make the January 15 sale date, it is scheduled to go on sale on January 22, which it does.

On February 4, the local wholesaler reviews his schedule of magazines to go on sale February 12, which is also the next on-sale date for magazine "A." When he finds that it has been delivered to his warehouse, he schedules and delivers magazine "A" as requested. However, when the new issue is delivered on February 12, the previous issue comes off sale with only three full weeks of sales time, rather than the four weeks the publisher wanted and needed.

There is little doubt that the sale of the issue that went on sale late will be less than it could have been had it been delivered on time.

In the case of inefficient delivery, let us say that magazine "A" is received before January 7 when our local wholesaler makes his scheduling review, but that the freight carrier has noted a shortage in delivery—that is, the advance notice from the national distributor to the local wholesaler indicated an allotment of 3,000 copies, but only 2,700 were delivered.

Our local wholesaler (or national distributor field sales manager) had prepared a distribution of these 3,000 copies to 600 retailers, but now there are only 2,700 copies on hand.

At this point, the wholesaler has three options: He can choose not to schedule the magazine on sale and wait for the 300 copies. He can reduce the number of copies per retailer. Or, he can reduce the number of retailers getting the magazine .

Very few local wholesalers or publishers would reschedule the entire delivery on the hope that the missing copies will be found and delivered. And obviously, since the other two options are not going to increase the sale of that issue of magazine "A," we again have a situation where freight movement has had a negative effect on newsstand sales.

Watch for warning signs

Publishers should be aware of these two hidden costs of freight and become sensitive to the warning signs which indicate that a problem is building.

If newsstand sales begin to fluctuate on an issue-to-issue basis with no apparent relationship between these fluctuations and cover packaging, editorial emphasis or economic conditions, a careful look at delivery dates is in order.

If a publisher begins to see a pattern of freight shortages appearing on his statement of accounts from his national distributor, he should take a hard look at the freight carriers involved.

Local wholesalers keep careful records of the delivery date of every issue of every magazine they sell (this is critical to their scheduling review), and this information is available through the national distributor on request. Furthermore, every signed delivery receipt from the freight carrier carries the date of delivery, and this information is also available.

I have personally "solved" seemingly unexplainable fluctuations in newsstand sales efficiency by analyzing the delivery dates to local wholesalers and correcting freight movement procedures. And I have seen sales levels rise after dismissing freight carriers with long records of delivering shortages, weeks after the magazine has been placed on sale and when the copies are no longer of value.

With the cost of delivering magazines to local wholesalers for newsstand distribution escalating as fast as many other costs, publishers and printers alike are searching for more economical ways to ship. But it is important to remember that the on-time delivery of all the copies consigned to each local wholesaler is critical for successful newsstand sales.

RDAs: Who's watching the stores?

By Karlene Lukovitz

Many magazine publishers do not know the details of their own Retail Display Agreement (RDA) programs. Consequently, they may be unaware that a general lack of effective RDA monitoring procedures is costing them millions of dollars annually.

This current state of affairs is drawn from reports by sources within the magazine distribution chain ranging from retailers to publishers' representatives.

Individual publishers pay out RDA sums amounting to thousands, and in many cases, millions of dollars each year. Yet many of them—perhaps the majority—do not always know which retailers are receiving their retail display allowances (in the form of a percentage or flat sum off cover price per copy sold), or even the number of retailers to whom they're paying these allowances.

This situation has developed as a result of the extremely rapid and largely uncontrolled growth of RDAs since the 1960s. Before that time, publishers offered retail display allowances (usually an extra 10 percent above the standard 20 percent off cover price per copy sold) only to a small number of selected outlets and chains as an incentive to provide better display for their magazines.

But new Federal anti-trust regulations (specifically, the Robinson-Patman Act) forced publishers to offer display allowances to all retailers in a competing market area who would agree to meet the terms of allowance contracts. At the same time, retail chains began to materialize all over the country. Thus, publishers found themselves having to pay display allowances to a constantly increasing number of outlets—a trend that still continues.

A 1978 estimate of publishers' RDA expenditures put the total at about $78 million. This figure is not surprising, considering that at any given time there are between 2,000 and 3,000 magazine titles distributing at least a portion of their circulations through the approximately 145,000 retail outlets that handle magazines—and that the great majority of these magazines offer some kind of RDA program.

Moreover, one publisher's RDA consultant estimates that total industry output in RDA payments increases 10 percent to 15 percent annually.

Most publishers have turned over the administration of their increasingly unwieldy RDA programs to their national distributors. But RDA administration is becoming more difficult for national distributors each year because more and more independent retailers and retail chains are signing RDA contracts with their client publishers.

As a result, although national distributors always report the total RDA sums they have paid to retailers in their regular statements to publishers, they infrequently give breakdowns on the burgeoning individual stores and chains included in these totals.

In general, publishers seem not to be very concerned about their lack of direct control over their RDA programs: National distributors have done an admirable job of handling administration and marketing and protecting their clients' interests in the single-copy arena over the years.

But even national distributors have a limit to their resources, and their efforts in the primary areas of distribution administration and marketing drain their resources substantially, so that effective monitoring of the RDA programs (whose administration alone already strains their operations) is difficult.

The hard fact is that—with a few exceptions—publishers and their national distributors have no effective system for monitoring retailers' RDA claims.

In theory, publishers should be doing two kinds of ongoing monitoring in regard to retailers' RDA payment claims: 1) monitoring of displays to see that retailers are, in fact, giving magazines the preferential display called for in RDA contracts (usually full-cover exposure or a specified portion of cover exposure); and 2) auditing of retailers' RDA claims forms to determine if the numbers of sales of RDA-eligible magazines reported on the forms is accurate.

Monitoring displays

The first aspect of RDA monitoring—policing retailers' performance of display requirements outlined in RDA contracts—is generally conceded to have become both logistically unfeasible and largely futile.

Under anti-trust laws, publishers are required to make at least spot checks of retailers' compliance with RDA display requirements. Publishers with RDA programs do attempt to comply with this anti-trust guideline by conducting spot checks through their own national distributors' field forces.

But for the majority of publishers, there is no way of conducting checks that have any practical significance for maintaining proper display of their magazines in all or even most outlets. Very few publishers have field forces large enough to make regular rounds of thousands of outlets. National distributors' field forces, though large, are responsible for performing a host of services for the 200 or more titles that many of their companies represent—so display monitoring for RDA purposes is often their last priority. Moreover, even large distributors' field forces would find making regular, systematic checks a herculean task.

The larger issue involved in RDA display monitoring, however—and the major reason most publishers' magazines are not getting proper display—is that retailers cannot accommodate all of the magazines with which they have RDA contracts. Most retailers simply do not have enough space on their display fixtures to give all their RDA magazines full-cover exposure. So, in a convoluted way, it is somewhat fortunate for retailers that few publishers can enforce retailers' compliance with display terms of RDA contracts.

In short, RDA programs have come to be widely viewed solely as a means of getting magazines authorized by retailers and into the stores by increasing retailers' gross profit margins. The idea of getting preferred display in return for a display allowance has been all but abandoned.

There are exceptions to this prevailing laissez-faire attitude about the "display" part of Retail Display Agreements. There are a few publishers who have displays checked on a regular, systematic basis and withhold RDA payments to retailers who do not comply with requirements.

These exceptions, however, are almost exclusively publishers of top-selling magazines which occupy the few coveted display pockets at checkout counters. These publishers have the clout to insist upon correct display because their magazines are so profitable for retailers. In addition to selling very well, these magazines often offer retailers more lucrative types of RDAs than the 10-percent-off-cover RDA offered by an estimated 80 percent of magazines.

Checkout magazines tend to offer more profitable RDAs because they are battling among themselves to get the best positions at the checkout—and are willing to pay retailers more to secure those positions. For example, several checkout magazines offer retailers flat per-pocket RDA sums ranging between $3 and $5 per quarter. Some also offer one-time or renewable flat promotional allowances.

Moreover, most of the top single-copy magazines have either the resources to conduct regular, thorough checks of displays themselves or the influence with national distributors to make sure their magazines' displays get checked. Many of these publishers are their own national distributors; some can afford to employ large field forces that supplement the beleaguered sales forces of their national distributors.

Still, the fact remains that most publishers gave up long ago on making more than nominal attempts to monitor the display aspect of their RDAs.

Auditing of RDA claims

Barring any realistic hope that their magazines will get preferential display, it would seem that publishers who offer RDAs should at least be certain that they are paying display allowances only on copies that actually have been sold.

But even this dollars-and-cents aspect of RDA monitoring has been largely ignored by publishers and their national distributors over the years. From all indications, only four national distributors offer services which could even loosely be called claims "auditing" services, and these distributors launched the services relatively recently. The other national distributors, according to various industry sources, may or may not make some attempts to check retailers' addition on claim forms and/or have their regular sales field forces make spot checks of wholesalers' records to verify the number of sales claimed on retailers' RDA forms.

As with most other aspects of RDAs, there are no hard data on how much the magazine publishing industry may be losing on payments of retail display allowances for copies that were never sold.

John Ryan, president of Progressive Magazines, an independent firm which has been auditing RDA claims for publishers for four years, estimates that fully 50 percent of all RDA claims filed by retailers have at least one error in them.

Ryan further estimates that publishers could be saving "a minimum" of 25 percent of their total RDA payments if they caught incorrect claims with proper auditing. Using the 1978 $78 million estimate of publishers' total output in RDA payments, an overall 25 percent reduction would represent $19.5 million in annual savings for publishers.

Reasons for losses

Some of the RDA money being lost by publishers is the result of intentional overclaims by a few chains and independent retailers. Sometimes these overclaims are blatant enough to be caught with or without auditing systems; there are undoubtedly many other times when bogus claims go undetected. "Horror stories" of retailer overclaims that were detected somewhere along the line circulate sporadically through the publishing and distribution industries.

Reese Coppage, president of the Duval-Bibb Company, a wholesaler agency that also prepares RDA claims for retailers, says that occasional "reprehensible" cases of overblown RDA claims cause shock waves among publishers.

"There's no doubt that some retailers do attempt to rip publishers off," Coppage says. He cites instances in which claims have been filed for stores in areas in which the magazine title in question was never distributed. He also says publishers and national distributors have sometimes found that total RDA claims for an issue actually exceed the print run for the issue.

Bill Schnirring, publisher and editor in chief of Convenience Store Merchandiser, recently cited a case of a "respected convenience store chain" that submitted an RDA claim for five times the chain's actual draw and 10 times its actual audited sale for one magazine.

But although incorrect RDA claims usually overestimate, rather than underestimate, a retailer's or a chain's sales of RDA eligible magazines, almost no one, including publishers' auditing agents, would contend that most of these faulty claims are intentional.

Those involved in dealing with RDA claims say that excessive claims are the result of flaws in the existing systems for handling RDAs—flaws which force many retailers/chains to *estimate* their sales totals on RDA-eligible magazines rather than base claims on actual sales figures.

Under most current RDA payment systems, the retailer or the chain's management is responsible for collecting the sales data on which claims are based. But the supermarket, convenience store and drug store chains whose outlets now account for the great majority of single-copy magazine sales made in this country face extremely frustrating and sometimes insurmountable circumstances surrounding their attempts to obtain sales data.

Reliance on wholesalers for data

The main problem is that wholesalers, who have no legal involvement in the RDA contracts made between publisher and retailer, are in most cases the only ones who have the data retailers need to make their claims. This situation is a by-product of the setup of the entire magazine distribution system: With the exception of a relatively small number of direct sales agreements between publishers and retailers, wholesalers are responsible for the record keeping on their retail customers' magazine draws, returns and sales.

Most chains and independent retailers rely on sales information maintained by wholesalers because it would not be cost-justifiable for them to set up adequate systems for maintaining their own magazine sales records, according to Larry Bershtein, former marketing director of the Wawa Food Stores chain.

"Retailers carrying hundreds of titles can't possibly keep track of the number of copies of various magazines they get on a weekly or monthly basis without the help of wholesalers," says Bershtein, who now heads Professional Management Associates, a firm that helps retailers prepare RDA claims and collect payments. "For one thing, checking deliveries of magazines to stores is scattered because of magazines' varying frequencies of publication and other factors. Monitoring magazine deliveries and recording draws would take at least one full-time person in each store—and retailers are not about to spend money to maintain such employees."

A survey of more than 4,500 supermarkets (accounting for more than one-fifth of national supermarket sales) conducted by the International Periodical Distributors Association (IPDA) in November 1978 illustrates retailers' continuing reliance on wholesalers' magazine sales data for RDA claims filing.

Eighty-four percent of the supermarkets reported that they use wholesaler records to obtain data for RDA claims; 53 percent of these stores said wholesaler records were their only source of data. Approximately 25 percent reported that they also use some information supplied by national distributors; 19 percent used in-store records as aids; a very small number said they get some information from consultants or publishers (each of these two sources was mentioned by about 3 percent).

It is true that a growing number of retail chains are installing Universal Product Code (UPC) computer scanning systems that allow nearly total automation of inventory-keeping on all merchandise, including magazines. But these chains remain in the minority.

Until computerization and UPC scanning become established practice at the retail level, retailers will continue to rely primarily on wholesalers' magazine records when filing RDA claims.

There are two major problems involved in retailers' heavy reliance on wholesalers for RDA claims data. One is that most chains cannot or will not bear the expense and inconvenience of gathering data from all of the wholesalers who service their stores in various areas around the country. The other is that those chains who do attempt to gather all the necessary sales data find that wholesalers' records are often incomplete.

Regarding the first problem, chains long ago learned the pitfalls involved in attempting to gather sales data on their numerous RDA magazine titles from all of the wholesalers (often between 10 and 20, for large national chains) servicing their stores.

Chain management could send representatives to area wholesaler agencies to gather sales records. But this would be a costly operation that few, if any, chains consider worth the effort.

The chains could ask all their wholesalers to forward the data. However, this method would also involve considerable expense since "only a handful" of wholesalers are still willing to provide this service at no charge, according to one RDA consultant to chains.

In addition to their costliness, both of these alternatives are unacceptable to chains because it would simply be too difficult to coordinate and keep track of reporting being done by so many different representatives and/or wholesalers.

Records don't exist

Moreover, even the most persistent and committed chain would inevitably come up against the second major problem with getting data for claims from wholesalers: in many cases, the records do not exist.

Although the number of wholesaler agencies whose operations are computerized is increasing rapidly (more than 300 of the approximately 500 agencies in the United States and Canada were computerized as of late last year, and more than 100 of these had installed UPC scanners for faster returns' processing), a significant number of agencies still do not have complete records on all of the magazine titles they handle.

According to the owner of one large wholesaler agency, probably one-third to one-half of all wholesalers do not have Order and Regulation (O&R) on all of their magazine titles. O&R is the term for recording of draws, returns, and net sales of titles by individual stores.

"There are probably only about 20 wholesalers who are fully automated and have O&R on all their titles," says another wholesaler. "Most agencies record their total draws on each title, but most don't have the capabilities to keep records on allotments and records on return and sale by individual retailers for many of their titles—especially new titles or titles that are not very big sellers. Instead, they keep bulk records that are adequate for getting their own credits from national distributors but inadequate for chains trying to determine their stores' sales so they can make out RDA claims forms."

Pay others to prepare claims

Most chains still prepare their own RDA claims despite these obstacles to data gathering, but some have set up agreements with independent consultants, national distributors, or wholesalers to have the claims done for them. These agents gather the needed data and fill out RDA claims in return for a percentage of RDA payments collected by the chain.

It is clear that the number of chains opting to make such agreements is growing, though no reliable total is available. The IPDA supermarket survey gives some indication of the strength of the trend: 25 percent of supermarkets reported that wholesalers did some or all of their RDA claims (about 50 wholesalers now offer such services); 13 percent were using national distributors; and 13 percent were using independent consultants (many supermarkets were using a combination of two or more of these sources).

Still prepare their own

Still, well over half (59 percent) of the supermarkets surveyed by IPDA said they were preparing some or all of their RDA claims themselves—and self-preparation remains the norm among supermarket, convenience, and drug store chains.

Unfortunately, because of the obstacles already explained, most chains that handle their own RDA claims have given up on attempts to gather sales data from all, or even most, of the wholesalers who service their stores.

Instead, the chains make estimates of total RDA payments due them by projecting sales data obtained from a limited number of wholesalers or stores. These estimates are sometimes reasonably accurate, but often they are far in excess of the true RDA sums.

"Of course it's true that chains have to swear on their claim forms that their magazine sales figures are completely accurate," says a veteran chain merchandising executive. "But it's also true that almost all of them are actually doing projections. Chains only want what's due them, but if many of the records aren't available, how can they be expected to produce completely accurate claims?"

Errors in chains' RDA estimates can happen in a number of ways, according to Ryan of Progressive Magazines.

"In most cases, retailers are not even aware that their methods of making estimates distort their sales," Ryan says. "Many of them take figures from their largest wholesaler and project these over all their stores. But this inflates their figures because these wholesalers cover major cities with large stores that would naturally show more sales than other stores.

"Sometimes, when figures for a particular title aren't available, chains make estimates on the basis of figures for a similar title," Ryan continues. "Also, they don't realize that due to holdups in distribution or computer record errors, some of the titles they have authorized for their stores sometimes never reach stores in a particular region. Still other errors result because the records that chains do get from wholesalers sometimes don't yet reflect all returns from all retailers in an area—they are not net sales figures. All of these things can produce estimates that are inflated to one degree or another."

The head of a wholesaler agency that has been preparing RDA claims for chains for more than eight years says that reliable estimates can be done, but most chains do not have the skills or resources to do them. "There's nothing wrong with estimates as long as there is no intent to defraud and they are based on current available data plus accurate sales history records for stores," he says. "The problem is that most chains don't have access to that kind of data that wholesalers have—or the experience to make good estimates."

If publishers had effective systems for auditing retailers' RDA claims, it would not be so alarming that inaccurate methods of estimating magazine sales for RDA claims are apparently in widespread use among chains. But such auditing systems, with a few exceptions, do not exist.

Lack of auditing

Most publishers have their RDAs handled by their national distributors, and most of these distributors do not audit or even monitor the accuracy of RDA claims. For the most part, national distributors simply check payment sums against number of sales claimed on the forms as they process claims for payment. (A few do augment this with spot checks of the accuracy of the number of sales claimed.)

Existing alternatives to this predominant method of handling RDA claims can be summed up as follows:

•Among national distributors, Curtis Circulation Company has a staff of professional auditors in locations around the country; Kable News Company, Inc. and Independent News Company, Inc. audit claims by com-

puter using statistical sales parameters; and Select Magazines, Inc. has a system in which wholesalers fill out claims for retailers as a method of reducing claims errors and speeding payments to retailers. (Select is also in the process of setting up an EDP system that will automatically process and audit RDA claims.)

•About a dozen publishers audit their own RDA claims (some of these use national distributors for other services, others are their own national distributors).

•Nine publishers (125 magazines total) use Progressive Magazines, which, from all indications, is currently the only independent RDA claims auditing firm in the country.

National distributors' systems

Curtis Circulation Company is the only national distributor that could be said to offer auditing in the true sense of the word. Because Curtis does use professional auditors in the field, it is generally acknowledged by retailers, RDA consultants and wholesalers to be the best RDA monitoring system available among national distributors.

Despite (or perhaps because of) Curtis' generally good reviews on its RDA claims auditing system, the company will not reveal details of the system. Stewart Freedman, general counsel for the national distributor, says Curtis "prefers not to give details for competitive reasons."

Nevertheless, information supplied by Freedman and Curtis clients who use the auditing service provides a general picture of the system.

Freedman stresses that Curtis' auditing program does include monitoring retailers' compliance with RDA display requirements, as well as auditing the number of sales claimed. He verifies that Curtis employs a staff of certified auditors (a Curtis client says there are about 15) located around the country. Beyond that, he will say only that the system's activities "are centered on the retail level" and that audits are "assisted by a sophisticated computer data base."

A Curtis client reports that Curtis auditors take true random samples of retailers' RDA claims, then go to wholesaler agencies to audit sales records on those retailers. He also says the auditors "double check" the claims of retailers who have made incorrect claims in the past.

The circulation director of one top single-copy sales magazine, whose total RDA payments fall between three and four million dollars annually, reports that the Curtis claims auditing system has saved the magazine "hundreds of thousands of dollars a year."

He adds that magazines using the Curtis system share its costs (his magazine's costs are in the low five-figure range), but that these costs are "nominal" in comparison with the amounts the magazines are saving by not paying incorrect claims.

But despite his publishing company's satisfaction with the Curtis system, he says the company plans to supplement the Curtis audits with its own field force audits in the near future.

Kable News uses a computer auditing system that examines every retailer audit claim according to pre-set statistical sales parameters. The parameters, essentially national sales averages, are derived mainly from Kable's data base of wholesalers' records.

Kable's computer flags those RDA claims that exceed the sales parameters for a title. These claims are sent for in-house "executive review" to determine if a field audit is warranted. Such field audits are sometimes deemed necessary if the retailer in question has a history of "chronic overclaims," according to Robert Urish, vice president/general manager of Kable.

Claims requiring field audits are sent to members of Kable's regular sales field force, who go to the wholesalers' records to check the actual recorded sales of the retailers in question.

Urish reports that "the retailer, on his own initiative, may exercise the option of substantiating his claim by supplying sales support information from his wholesale suppliers."

According to wholesalers, this means two things. First, it means that Kable's data base and field audits include only a limited number of wholesalers—so retailers might in fact be able to show that their sales claims were accurate by obtaining data from wholesalers Kable does not have included in its records.

Second, according to wholesalers, it is Kable's policy to send out a "corrected" RDA payment check that is in line with national sales averages if Kable's field check of its wholesalers still leaves the claim in question. Thus, a retailer does have the option of disputing a payment reduction "on his own initiative" if the payment reduction is noticed.

Urish reports that "the accuracy and reliability of the (Kable) computerized auditing procedures have been validated time and again by the results of field audits." He also says that Kable may soon use a group of accountants for field audits of questionable claims instead of its regular field force.

But wholesalers and retailers' representatives say computer parameter auditing systems are often unfair to individual retailers.

"For example, if our records show that a retailer sold 25 percent of copies received, but the computer system has determined that the national average for retailers is 15 percent, Kable will just reject the claim and send a check for what they claim is the 'right' amount," says one wholesaler who prepares RDA claims for retailers.

"I don't see how such a system can make sense. National averages are made up of individual figures that vary above and below these final averages," he says.

Independent News, which also has a computer parameters RDA claims auditing system, was not mentioned by those who object to the parameters method in general. Herb Kasak, vice president of information systems for Independent, claims his company's computer auditing system has been steadily refined over the approximately five years it has been in use. "We're currently broadening our data base of sales history for each retailer," he says. "Our parameters will be more flexible in that we will be able to set parameters by issue, as well as by title."

Kasak also says that, though questionable claims are checked first at the wholesaler level by Independent's regular field force, Independent representatives always contact retailers directly to see if they can explain any discrepancies before a final decision on the check amount is made. "Sometimes it turns out that the retailer is right, and we then pay the full amount claimed," he says.

Select Magazines has a "fast pay" RDA system that is used mainly by publishers of major checkout magazines, such as Meredith Corporation and Reader's Digest Associations, Inc. (Both of these companies are part owners of Select.)

Under the "fast pay" system, Select pays wholesalers (about 10 cents per entry) to complete RDA claims for the retailers who have RDA contracts with publishers using the fast-pay program. Select representatives go to the wholesaler agencies to make checks of their methods for filling out the claims.

"The costs to publishers using the fast pay system are quite high," says David Miller, Select's vice president-director of sales. "But it's worth it for publishers of checkout magazines who want to pay retailers within a few weeks but who also want to be sure they are not paying on incorrect claims."

Miller explains that chains receive print-outs showing sales breakdowns and RDA payments for all of their stores along with their checks for the RDA sums due them, so "there have been very few complaints from retailers."

He reports that the Select Magazines Automatic Reporting Technique (SMART), an EDP system which is scheduled to be completely operational by this fall, will allow for total automation of all RDA procedures, including auditing.

SMART will store four years' worth of sales data from 500 wholesalers in the United States and Canada, including data on 80,000 retail outlets. In addition to incorporating sales parameters (based on averages of retailers' previous claims plus national sales averages) for automatic RDA auditing, SMART will allow publishers to call up claim forms on their video display terminals for examination.

Publishers checking own claims

Wholesalers and chain RDA consultants estimate that there are about 12 publishers who handle their own RDA programs. Some of these publishers always handled their own RDAs; others set up their own RDA systems because they felt they would have better control than national distributors who handle RDAs for publishers.

Three of the publishing companies administering and auditing their own RDA programs are publishers of major tabloids: *National Enquirer, The Star* and *Midnight Globe*. Because these magazines offer flat quarterly allowances each quarter per checkout pocket (instead of a percentage off cover price), they do not have to audit RDA sales claims.

All three of these magazines report that, instead, their field forces make on-going checks to see how many eligible checkouts a chain or independent has. The field forces send in reports updating the checkout data on all stores, and the magazines automatically send out checks for the current number of eligible checkouts each quarter.

U.S. News & World Report is an example of a magazine that offers the traditional 10 percent off cover price RDA and handles its own administration and auditing. It is also an example of a magazine that enforces its full-cover display requirement for RDA payments, according to vice president/circulation Samuel J. Keker.

U.S. News uses Select Magazines for its distribution, but has always done its own RDA administration and auditing. "We wanted to make sure that we could carefully police the performance of ever retailer we have had an RDA contract with," Keker explains.

Because *U.S. News* does enforce its full-cover RDA display requirement, it has RDA contracts only with stores large enough to accommodate the requirement, Keker says.

The magazine's relatively small number of RDA

contracts is handled by a manual claims auditing system. Members of the *U.S. News* sales field force go to wholesaler agencies periodically and gather print-outs on the magazine's sales by individual outlets. These are used to update the magazine's existing records of sales history for each outlet.

Using the accumulated sales data on each outlet, *U.S. News* has assigned each outlet claims parameters. Clerical workers identify an outlet's parameters through a system of codes and check to see if the outlet's current claimed sales fall within the parameters. If not, a field person is sent to the wholesaler agency handling the outlet to check the sales records for the period in question.

Sterling Publications and Ideal Publishing Company are examples of publishers who used to have national distributors handle their RDAs but now use an independent computer service firm to handle their own. Both companies use Computac, which sends out claims forms to retailers, processes them as they come back, and also prints out RDA payment checks.

But the publishers make their own determinations of how RDA claims are audited. Ideal reports that it has had Computac apply fixed parameters based on regional and national sales averages to every retail claim. But Ideal gets reports on claims and can override a claim rejection if the chain has had a good past record or for other reasons.

Stewart Nerzig of Sterling Publications reports that Computac "asterisks" claims that "fall way above our national sales average." But claims monitoring is done in-house using "no firm guidelines," he says.

"We were doing random audits, mostly through our 10 regular sales managers and with some help from our national distributor," says Peterson circulation director Nigel Heaton. "But we started to find that our claims payments were climbing, apparently because more chains were having wholesalers or consultants prepare the claims for them. When we finally found we were paying RDA allowances on well over 50 percent of our magazines' total sales—a very high percentage for us and for any magazine—we went to Progressive."

Progressive Magazines

Progressive's president, John Ryan, contends that very few magazine publishers can afford to do proper claims' auditing on their own. "Based on the money we spend to audit RDAs, I would say that only magazines with the very largest single-copy circulations could afford to do this properly for themselves," he says.

"Publishers who take RDAs out of the hands of their national distributors without having systems for getting the data they need to audit claims—and so use arbitrary measures—will sour retailers completely on RDAs," Ryan continues.

Progressive, whose sole business is auditing retailers' claims for publishers, has 50 professional auditors stationed around North America. These auditors go to wholesaler agencies and collect draw and sales data on each retail outlet that is included in RDA claims for Progressive's client magazine titles. The auditors then send the data on to Progressive's New Jersey headquarters—often before retailers' claims have arrived there.

A number of "reliable" wholesalers also send printouts of sales data to Progressive on a regular basis, according to Ryan. He adds that Progressive will soon have an on-line hookup with Data Processing Systems of Tampa, Florida, that will allow Progressive to have instant access to records of more than 70 wholesalers.

In addition to its large force of professional auditors, Ryan claims Progressive has several other advantages over national distributors' auditing systems. Since Progressive's publishing clients receive breakdowns on the names, locations, draws, claimed sale, audited sale and recommended payment for each retailer *before* retailer payments are made, they are able to have approval rights. Furthermore, Progressive guarantees that audit reports will be based on data from no fewer than 75 percent of the total number of stores in any chains. If data on all stores cannot be obtained, the company pro-rates on the basis of its own audited data on the 75 percent or more stores, not on the basis of national sales averages.

Progressive also sends publishers special reports that can be "massaged" into marketing/sales tools. These reports include: which stores/chains have and have not authorized a title; comparisons of retailers in terms of their sales and other data; and a title's number of RDA copies sold and the dollars they represent by issue.

Progressive's nine current publishing clients are the Laufer Company; National Lampoon, Inc.; Lopez Publications Inc.; Playgirl, Inc.; Quinn Publications, Inc.; McMullen Publications, Inc.; Consumer Guide Publications; Family Media, Inc.; and Peterson.

Dick Stanton, circulation director of McMullen Publications, supports Ryan's claims of the effectiveness of Progressive's auditing methods. "We started with Progressive in the spring of 1979. It looks as if we're megabucks ahead already, and we haven't lost any retailer accounts as a result," he says.

The new power of chain retailers

By Ronald T. Scott

The increasing power and authority of the chain retailer is rapidly changing the way magazines are sold in the single-copy channel of distribution.

The chain retail operation, a relatively new phenomenon which began in California in the late 1950s, slowly but steadily rolled across the continent and began to dominate retail sales in the 1960s. By the late 1970s, the chain retailer finally emerged as the single most dominant force in single-copy sales of magazines.

I define the chain retailer as a structured multi-unit retailer of consumer products. A chain retail operation can best be categorized by its primary product: food, drugs, discounts, convenience, books, etc. Of course, magazines are, or have the potential to be, an important factor in many chain retail operations.

The most significant difference between the chain retailer and the independent retailer of days of old is that the chain retailer has reserved for himself the decision about which products will be sold in his stores and has developed an organizational structure to deal with this decision-making process.

To understand the extent of the power of the chain retailer in his dealings with suppliers of consumer products, it is necessary only to remember that the supermarket industry was successful in demanding that products carry the 10-digit Universal Product Code as a primary condition of sale.

Purchasing by product category

Most chain retailers have organized the purchasing function by product category; that is, one buyer is normally responsible for a group of products exclusively and he is allotted a specific amount of selling space for these products. Each buyer is judged by how well he manages his selling space. In fact, his job, his salary levels, and his promotions are determined to a large extent by how well he manages his selling space in terms of predetermined budget levels and sales and profit objectives.

The professional manager (or buyer) charged with responsibility for the product category which includes magazines considers his present position as an intermediate step in his career. He knows that his opportunity for advancement will be judged by his ability to select that optimum product mix of merchandise which will produce the highest return on inventory investment, the maximum gross profit, and the most dollars per cubic foot of selling space.

In the minds of these rising professional managers,

magazines must compete for selling space with greeting cards, disposable cigarette lighters, shoe laces, motor oil, panty hose, and health and beauty aids.

Success at the checkout

Magazines are just a small part of the merchandise sold in chain retail stores. Although more than 50% of single copies of magazines are sold in supermarkets, magazines represent less than one half of one percent of supermarket sales.

Furthermore, our RDA incentive program puts us at a disadvantage since it cannot be calculated as profit when the sale is made. Instead, it can be calculated as an addition to profits only when (and if) it is collected. In fact, some chains actually credit RDA payments to general and administrative revenue rather than to the buyer who decides which magazines to sell on the theory that the administrative cost to collect RDA must be repaid. Surely, the profit-oriented buyer is not happy to see 50% of his gross profit credited to another department.

It is surprising, then, that magazines have come to dominate the selling space of the most competitive real estate in a supermarket—the checkout display. But the fact is—in competition with such giants at the checkout as Gillette, Wrigley, and Bic, the single-copy industry has been aggressive and innovative—and extremely successful. In the two most critical merchandising areas, profit incentives and display fixtures, the checkout merchandising programs are almost unlimited in their diversity of approaches.

Weak main floor sales

Unfortunately, in the area of main floor selling space where we compete with less powerful forces, we have been rather mediocre in our merchandising techniques. Chain buyers, calculating precisely the average dollar expenditure per customer for their primary product (e.g., food), select every other product to appeal to the consumer as an unplanned (impulse) purchase. Magazines, with their incredible diversity of product and the excitement engendered by their ever-changing editorial and advertising, are the almost perfect add-on purchase which the chain buyer needs. However, our approach to merchandising the main floor (or main line) display fixtures has barely changed in the past 10 years.

It is true that our information systems are in the process of developing the statistical data we need to speak the language of the chain buyer, both at the national distributor and local wholesaler levels. In addition, both the quality and the professional training of personnel at these two levels have improved greatly. And our investment in trade organizations like the Periodical Institute, IPDA, CPDA and local wholesaler joint marketing groups has increased at a rapid rate. We are, indeed, learning the language and techniques of our competitors in this changing retailer environment.

But all this investment in time, people, computer programs, information systems and better communications with the retail trade has, at best, allowed us to maintain a toehold in the chain retailer's mind.

Publishers must realize how *much* the retail environment has changed. They must realize that they have a product with a great deal of potential, and that capitalizing on that potential requires innovation, more creative merchandising techniques, more exciting display fixtures, different forms of incentive programs, and even better people.

The innovative packaging and display of panty hose, the mini- or purse-size books of Dell and Globe, and the cross-merchandising techniques of HP Books cook book line are all classic examples of meeting the challenge with exciting programs.

As far as incentive programs are concerned, everyone associated with the ubiquitous RDA understands (if not acknowledges) its inadequacy. The announcement of Ralph's Grocery chain (which operates 89 stores in Southern California, all with optical scanners) that it would use its own scanner data for filing its RDA claims is a clear signal that the shell-game of RDA is running out of time.

The retail chain buyer is the new king of the hill, just as publishers, national distributors, and wholesalers have been at various times in the long history of magazine publishing. His demands for more profit, volume and service are voiced in new terms and backed by computer printouts, CRT screens, and mathematical formulas.

Our most important asset in this changing environment remains our product. Magazines are exciting, innovative, challenging, colorful and certainly more fun to talk about than shoe polish or kitchen utensils.

In the titanic battle of the checkout, magazines have come to dominate the selling space, because magazine salespeople have spoken the language, met the profit objectives, and made the chain buyer look good.

With such a success story behind us, and with similar potential for success on the main floor fixture before us, I am looking forward to the enterprising publisher who will seize the chance to lead magazines into this new area of opportunity.

Adjusting to the new reality
By Ronald T. Scott

In my last column, I described the attitudes and operating procedures of the new King of the Hill, the general merchandise buyer of the chain retailer. This buyer and his power are bringing about major changes in the way publishers view retailer relations. They are also effecting major changes in most of the other traditional ways in which single-copy sales efforts have been conducted by publishers.

In the past, publishers looked to national distributors to use their influence and persuasion with wholesalers to develop the best possible retailer mix for each title they published. Back then, the wholesaler's primary customer was the independent retailer, and the wholesaler had the flexibility to allocate copies of almost any title to almost any retailer as he saw fit. The independent retailer, for the most part, was relatively unsophisticated, possessed few records on what did or did not sell, and rarely complained unless he was grossly over-allotted titles and quantities.

In those "good old days," pressure for more sales from more retailers flowed smoothly from the publisher through the national distributor, to the wholesaler, and on to the independent retailer.

Now, the chain retailer has driven most of the independent retailers out of business. The old-fashioned forced allocation of magazines has come into direct conflict with the decision of chain retailers to decide for themselves which products will be sold in their stores. The result is infinite friction within the single-copy channel of distribution.

The publisher who increases his press run without having first secured authorization from chain retailers is, to use an old cliche, pushing on a string.

Everyone in the chain of distribution has adjusted to the new power of the chain retailer—everyone, that is, except the publisher.

Adjusting to the change

The local wholesaler, who perceives himself as pinned between publisher and retailer, has opted to direct his talents and resources toward satisfying the demands for service and information of the retailer. He has done so on the basis of his vested self-interest: If he does not make serious efforts to satisfy the chain retailer, he will have few customers to whom to sell his large supply of magazines.

So the wholesaler has added computers to provide the chain retailer with faster, more accurate data. He has established marketing departments for the sole purpose of developing better chain retailer communications. And he has used his more detailed computer-generated information to improve the chain retailer role.

The national distributors have also responded to the new reality. The management information systems now in place at most national distributors contain more information on chain retailers than ever before, better information on wholesaler performance levels, and more timely information on sales trends, regional biases, field representative effectiveness, and myriad ways to manipulate this information into usable reports. Marketing departments staffed with people who speak the language of the chain retailer and of the publisher are in place at both head office and regionally.

As an industry effort, trade association activity has increased substantially, especially through IPDA, the national distributor trade association; CPDA, the wholesaler trade group; and Periodical Institute (PI). PI, whose membership includes publishers, national distributors and wholesalers, devotes its full attention to retailer relations.

While all of this effort is quite helpful, most publishers have not yet attempted to understand this new marketing environment, and then to use the new tools available to them. By making an effort, publishers can realize solid gains in distribution efficiency. For example, when I was retained as a single-copy consultant for *Early American Life*, a magazine with over 300,000 subscriptions and a very small newsstand sale, we began a study of how to increase its single-copy circulation. Two problems were immediately identifiable. First, *Early American Life* had no RDA program. Second, the magazine usually ran only one or two rather passive cover lines on its covers.

In consultations with both publisher and editor, we were able to increase the information on the cover without reducing the integrity or ambiance which the editors had developed for it.

Next, we introduced an RDA program through our national distributor. It was agreed that the press run would not be increased until retailer authorizations were secured so that new retailers were available to sell the increased copies. We asked the national distributor to make his early chain retailer calls at the regional chain level rather than at the national chains. We felt that we had a better chance with the regional chains and that we could use the sales information from the regional chains to sell the national chains.

A 50 percent increase in press run was ordered on the second issue after this twofold program was introduced. And we now believe that a press run increase of 67 percent over this second issue within one year is a reasonable objective.

To achieve this 150 percent increase, we have set issue-by-issue target press runs for the issues involved. This gives the national distributor the opportunity to schedule his sales calls in a manner consistent with his other responsibilities. And it gives the publisher the opportunity to set his budgets and his rate base objectives well in advance of actual printing and shipping dates. I have no doubts that we shall meet these objectives because all parties agree that they are realistic and attainable.

In fact, the emergence of the chain retailer as a powerful force in the single-copy sales channel has changed the way in which we must do business. And with the new rules and the new tools have come opportunities for increased newsstand sales with higher levels of efficiency.

Chain authorization

By Ronald T. Scott

In the new chain retailer environment of the eighties, the primary objective of a publisher is to motivate his national distributor to secure chain authorizations for his title.

As I illustrated in my last column with the *Early American Life* example, a publisher must have some real focus and discipline to this policy of motivating his national distributor. Specific types of chain retailers, or specific areas of the country, or even specific chains must be targeted in advance, and reasonable amounts of time must be allowed to accomplish these tasks.

While securing chain authorizations is the primary task, the second step in the process is of equal importance to increased single-copy sales: the allocation of copies to the newly authorized retailers by every wholesaler who services the chain. This can be a relatively complex exercise in the case of a major chain authorization.

Many challenges remain

Consider, for example, the national distributor who secures authorization for the 7-Eleven chain. He must temper his feelings of elation with the understanding that there are many challenges still to be met, for a headquarters authorization from 7-Eleven only places the title on the 7-Eleven master list. Distribution requires an additional authorization at each of seven regional buying offices. (And there are numerous cases where only some regional offices approve a specific title already on the master list.)

But to continue our example on an optimistic note, let's assume that our national distributor is successful at *all* the regional offices. Excitement is everywhere! We have just added some 7,000+ convenience store outlets for our magazine.

Temper that excitement again, however, for in the highly structured and complex world of the chain retailer operating in a geographic area of 40 or more states and being serviced by as many as 400 wholesalers, there is still plenty of work to do.

Some national distributors have reached the advanced stage of computer development where they can identify the individual wholesalers who service any individual unit of a chain retailer. This information is of critical importance to our publisher because the only way copies of his title will be allocated to individual 7-Eleven retail units will be when his national distributor field representatives prepare new distributions at individual wholesale agencies in which they allocate copies of the newly authorized title to 7-Eleven stores.

The missing link

Unfortunately, no wholesaler system (to my knowledge) has an organized set of systems and procedures through which to accept a notice of a newly authorized title and then to allocate copies of the title to the authorized chain retailers. As long as this "missing link" exists, it is incumbent upon publishers to maintain pressure on national distributors to have their field representatives prepare new distributions at individual wholesalers who service chains.

It is important to note that publishers must be aware of and sensitive to the other demands and commitments to which national distributors are subject when they request field representative distribution work. For example, if our publisher did get 7-Eleven authorization approved at all regional offices, the most effective and efficient procedure for getting the distribution work done is to meet with the national distributor circulation executives and develop a program of priorities for the field work.

Almost all national distributors have two types of field representatives: a city representative who has responsibility for a single wholesale agency, and a traveling representative who may be responsible for from two to 20 or 30 wholesalers depending on population density and geography. Obviously, the national distributor has the ability to respond more rapidly where he has a city representative; and if his computer indicates that the wholesaler with a city representative services a large number of 7-Eleven units, he is motivated to make this a top priority.

Any national distributor's ability and motivation to respond to a new authorization has a direct relationship to the number of retail units serviced by a given wholesaler and the availability of a field representative to do the work.

Setting deadlines

The primary objective of this meeting with our national distributor is to set such priorities and the time frames in which they are to be accomplished. Setting priorities without mutually agreeable deadlines can be a serious error, since other publishers with equally pressing requests will be demanding services, and priorities will be changing every day for our national distributor.

We began this exercise by motivating our national distributor to get us a major chain authorization from the new king of the hill, the retail chain buyer. We followed up by getting regional office authorization. We then met with the national distributor circulation executives to set priorities for field representatives to allocate copies to individual retail units within mutually agreeable time frames.

The last task which our publisher must accomplish is a carefully timed follow-up with the national distributor to be sure he is meeting the priorities within the time frame. This scenario, repeated chain upon chain, is the key to rising single-copy press runs, increased efficiency of sale, and a successful newsstand magazine.

What about selling direct to retail?

By Ronald T. Scott

Certain highly successful consumer products have had a long history of successful direct selling. Can this very profitable way of selling apply to magazines as well? Why has the publishing industry been so reluctant to sell magazines directly to chain retailers?

The advantages of such direct sales seem obvious. By cutting out the middleman, a publisher could make more money per copy sold. Furthermore, by dealing directly with the decision-making executive of a highly valued retail customer, he would have the opportunity to directly influence display position and volume.

Certainly, there is no justification for remaining with the existing system just because it has served the industry well in the past. Previous channels of distribution became antiquated and fell into disuse. In fact, the existing channel of distribution (national distributor and independent wholesaler) replaced the national distributor system simply because it could perform the desired functions at a more efficient cost, and for no other reason. A less efficient system was replaced by a more efficient one.

To analyze the question of direct sales versus the existing system, let us examine the two critical functions now performed by the national distributor-independent wholesaler system which would have to be performed by the retailer in direct sales to him.

The first critical function involves record keeping, the recording by title and issue, the sale and return information for each retailer involved in the sale of a specific magazine. Today both the retailer and the independent wholesaler use the Universal Product Code (UPC) although the retailer is using UPC to record sales and the independent wholesaler is using it to record returns.

There is a logical reason for this: The retailer has only a few fully returnable products on which he must keep timely records. Furthermore, a magazine is his only product which becomes obsolete on a seven- to 30-day cycle and is replaced immediately by a new product with the same short life-span.

On the other hand, almost every product handled by the independent wholesaler is fully returnable, with a new issue replacing the obsolete one with this rapid frequency. There is little question that the retailer, especially the large chain retailer, is capable of building such an exception system to handle magazines. The real question is whether he can afford to build and maintain such a system for the relatively small volume that magazines represent.

Supermarket's consumer expenditures study shows that sales of all magazines, paperbacks, comic books, newspapers and children's books amounted to 0.43 percent of store sales. I find it hard to imagine a chain retailer building and maintaining an exception system to quickly process and record returns for less than one-half a percent of store sales, or for even two percent of store sales for that matter. Let's suppose, then, that the chain retailer does not build and maintain such a system. Would it significantly hurt the publisher to get returns back more slowly than he does now?

I have a client who uses a national distributor to distribute his monthly magazine both through an independent wholesaler and directly to variety chains. Let's examine the flow of returns on the same issue from both systems to see the trade-off the publisher makes on return flow.

On November 15, 1979, the September issue of this magazine was off sale for eight weeks, and the national distributor had rendered reports of sales to date for both systems. Over 90 percent of the anticipated returns were already recorded and reported from the independent wholesaler system, but less than 10 percent of the anticipated returns had been recorded and reported from the direct variety system. The result: the publisher knew within one or two percent what he had sold through the independent wholesaler system, but he had almost no idea what he had sold through the direct variety chain system.

Let me hasten to add that this difference was not the fault of the national distributor, who has an excellent processing, recording and reporting system. In fact, no one is at fault. Simply put, the chain retailer in this case did not have enough economic interest in the product to commit the resources necessary to do a better job.

Timely delivery is critical

The second critical factor is timely delivery: the delivery of the product to a retailer for placement on a display fixture on the proper day.

The task of placing some 14 million copies of each issue of *TV Guide* on the display fixtures of some 150,000 retailers within three days of printing borders on the miraculous. That this is done 52 times a year for additional hundreds of millions of copies of monthly magazines adds to this impressive logistical accomplishment.

Again, I do not doubt the ability of chain retailers in particular to perform this logical task. The important question still remains: will the retailer commit the necessary people and resources to the task? Every business manager today must constantly establish priorities and

decide how to accomplish his goals with the limited time and resources he has available.

Here again, I find it hard to imagine a chain retailer making a sustained commitment to the exception procedure of immediate stocking of display fixtures with new magazines and the processing of unsold copies of now obsolete magazines, when magazines represent such a small part of his volume. Furthermore, since timely delivery is such a critical factor, assigning this function to a less experienced and less committed party is very risky.

Some time ago, *Profitways,* the journal of the national distributors trade association, interviewed Joel Novack of CBS/Fawcett, which publishes *Woman's Day.* With the approval of *Profitways,* I would like to quote from that interview:

The direct approach

Q. You are basically new to our publications distribution industry. You've come into it with an ability to maintain a fresh viewpoint. From that vantage, what are you seeing?

A. One of the most interesting proposals I've witnessed—from chain store executives—is their increasing desire to go "direct." In effect, to circumvent the wholesaler.

Q. That is not uncommon these days. How do you react?

A. I think we are luckier than most publishers, and certainly than many other national distributors, in that we have the advantage of a perspective of 20 years of experience with "dual distribution" of *Woman's Day,* which is sold direct and also sold through wholesalers. We are able to compare the results of both sequences of distribution. We can deal in actuality and not in theory.

Q. The results? Everyone would say "direct" for bottom-line, of course.

A. They would be wrong. In spite of the fact that we might be eliminating the middleman—the wholesaler—and dividing margins between the retail chain and the national distributor, our experience over all these years is that the efficiency factor, when we deal directly with the chains, is below that of dealing with the wholesaler. And that is with what is considered a "store book."

Q. Why is that?

A. Whatever the reason, those chains with which we deal directly have a lower sell-through percentage than those chains serviced by wholesalers. We suspect that the reason is that the wholesaler, in spite of all we say about him and his lack of efficient business operation, does something more than the chain does. They are at least making an attempt to dress the racks and see that they are full. Very often, when we deal direct, copies of *Woman's Day* go into the back and never see the light of day until it is time for them to be returned for credit. And this, as far as CBS is concerned, has to in some way enter the equation as we entertain the growing request for direct service on titles.

Dollars and sense

Q. This selling-direct or through wholesalers—is there a unit movement equation?

A. What I can give you is a percent-variance that is sufficient enough so that the added increment that we make on the cover price from selling direct is negated by the drop in efficiency. That means that, assuming for the sake of discussion, we gain 5 percent by selling direct, the sell-through percent drops sufficiently to totally wipe out any economic gain we might have achieved.

Furthermore, even rate-gain-maintenance comes into question. If we sell too many copies direct and the rate-base that we guarantee the advertiser drops, we are in serious trouble.

Q. This logically affects the question of direct sales?

A. Of course. Now, it becomes the job of those supermarkets clamoring to go "direct" to demonstrate that they are capable of handling this product in a manner as profitable for us as wholesalers, if they hope to eventually get a serious audience for their future direct requests.

Q. Would you assume then that this situation would project itself through the total magazine spectrum? Would it also apply to paperbacks? Can "cherry picking" work?

A. It would seem to me that when store magazines, which probably get the most attention of any of our kind of product, are treated the way they are by the individual stores, it would follow that another published product with lesser personal interest would fare, at best, half as well. There is, of course, no documentation of this premise.

Mr. Novak's comments stand by themselves as clear evidence of the results of over 20 years of "testing" direct to retail selling of magazines.

There is much that needs to be changed and improved in the national distributor-independent wholesaler channel of distribution, and we must continue to seek such improvement. But there is a qualitative difference between improving a system and changing to a system which on the surface holds great promise but which can also be most disastrous.

Direct to retail:
the controversy continues

By Ronald T. Scott

I have received some interesting comments on one of my columns ("What about selling direct to retail") which contrasted two methods of magazine distribution: the traditional national distributor-wholesaler channel versus direct to retailer distribution. The column clearly stated my opinion that the national distributor-wholesaler channel is far superior to direct to retail distribution, and I gave detailed reasons for my belief. I concluded by indicating my belief that while the national distributor-wholesaler channel was better, there were still areas in which this sytem could be, and should be, improved.

Most of the comments on that column centered on the improvements that ought to be of primary importance to the national distributor-wholesaler channel of distribution. This column will discuss five specific areas which I believe must be closely examined, for these areas are critical to the continued growth and improvement of this system. Three of these areas are primarily concerned with the retailer environment and two are concerned with the wholesaler environment.

The retailer environment today is dominated by the chain store, and chain store management is professional, profit oriented and aggressive. Although they are interested in the magazine industry, they are also frustrated by it—and nothing frustrates them more than the ubiquitous Retail Display Agreement (RDA).

Chain retail management cannot understand the reasons for the tedious and complex RDA requirements, especially in light of the clear incentives provided by suppliers of other products, who operate under the same laws as publishers. There is no single improvement in the national distributor-wholesaler channel of distribution that would do more for the publishing industry than the end of the RDA.

I fully realize that there are serious economic consequences which must be faced and solved before the RDA can be replaced by a different form of economic incentive for retailers. I also realize the complex legal implications of such a change. But in comparing these problems with retailers' negative reactions to the RDA, I am convinced that as long as the RDA remains the keystone of our economic incentive program, the publishing industry will continue to fall far short of its potential volume in chain retail stores. It is no surprise that those magazines that offer checkout incentives and wider incentives through wholesaler billing are, on average, growing faster and more efficiently than RDA titles.

Improving authorized list usage

The RDA challenge leads to the next area in need of improvement: the authorized list. Most chain retailers display only those magazines which they have authorized for their stores through a sales call by the publisher, his national distributor, or the local wholesaler. There are two points to be made here about the authorized list.

First, I believe that most retailers maintain an authorized list because it gives them a handle on the RDA claims they must submit to improve their profit margin. I further believe that retailers would be less likely to maintain authorized lists if they had a less complex method of receiving an incentive on their magazine sales.

Second, if we have to live with authorized lists, we must do a better job of coordinating our sales calls to chain buyers. Publishers, national distributors, wholesalers and retailers are often confused about who represents whom. And the great variety of people (representing a diversity of interests) now calling on chain buyers does our industry no long term service by the confusion caused at buyer offices.

There is still another aspect of authorized lists that

can be improved. For most publishers, the struggle to gain the chain retailer's acceptance of their titles is time consuming, costly and frustrating. But publishers now realize that gaining a spot on an authorized list is no guarantee of display and sale in that retailer's stores. At times it seems more difficult to get copies distributed to a chain's stores than to get the authorization. We must make a more concentrated and consistent effort to allocate copies to retailers who authorize titles than we now do.

The last two areas that need improvement are in the wholesaler environment, and they are both concerned with the handling of allotments of titles by wholesalers to retailers. When a publisher, through his national distributor, changes his allocation of copies to his wholesalers, the reaction (in terms of retailer allocation) is often inconsistent and erratic.

Despite the increase in the number of titles on which full sale and return records are kept by retailers, we still seem to have difficulty coordinating a publisher's allotment response to the marketplace with the

mathematical formulas used by wholesalers to allocate copies to retailers. Although we have reduced the time differential between the publisher's and the wholesaler's records, we still have not been able to reduce the return ratio on their titles.

Coordination on allotments could probably be improved if publishers had a better understanding of the mathematical formulas used by wholesalers to allocate copies to retailers. Because a substantial number of different formulas are used by wholesalers, it is difficult for publishers and their national distributors to allocate the appropriate number of copies in coordination with the sale and return goals of individual wholesalers.

In my opinion, the appeal of direct sales to retailers stems from frustrations on the part of retailers and publishers—frustrations caused in part by the changes brought about by the computer technology we are now learning to use effectively. However, if we can alleviate some of the frustrations that now exist, we can greatly improve the efficiency of the most effective mass distribution system in the world today.

Working within the system

By Ronald T. Scott

Discussion and controversy continue over the ability, or lack thereof, of the single-copy distribution system to efficiently sell the highly specialized consumer magazine. How, say the skeptics, can a system geared to selling over 12 million copies a week of *TV Guide* and two and a half million copies of *Cosmo* a month still be sensitive to the needs and wants of a specialized magazine aiming for 50,000 single-copy circulation?

There is a simple reply to these skeptics: The single-copy distribution system was no more or less sensitive to *TV Guide* (when it was an impossible dream competing with daily newspaper TV listings) or to *Cosmo* (when it was close to failing in the late fifties), or to any highly specialized magazine.

The single-copy distribution system is rarely sensitive to any magazine until it reaches into the many hundreds of thousands of copies per issue. So, if any magazine is to be successful on the newsstand, its publisher and circulation people must be sensitive to the system.

The single-copy or newsstand channel of distribution handles a greater variety of consumer products than any other system in the world. There are 3,000 active magazine titles and 400 new paperback books flowing through this system each month. The only logical response to the massive variety of products is a set of systems and procedures for recording, processing and marketing which are highly structured and carefully controlled. Any less disciplined response to this massive volume and variety would produce chaos.

Publishers must adapt to system

The publishing companies that understand the need for the existing controls and adapt to the system rather than battling it are the most successful with their newsstand circulation.

Let me give some examples. Every publisher is frustrated by the length of time it takes before he can determine the circulation results of each issue of his magazine. Why, some ask, does it take months and months after off sale before he gets his final sales information?

However, the question itself is naive. Within 45 to 60 days off sale, there is enough information available for most publishers to determine the relative success of any issue of a magazine so that packaging and editorial can be adjusted to meet consumer interests. A simple chart comparing current return flow with final sales of prior issues is usually sufficient for a relatively accurate determination of sales efficiency.

Publishers must wait so many more months for a final sales accounting because the information flow which produces this final accounting is financial in nature, with all of the normal financial and accounting controls. But publishers who understand the difference between the need to know the relative circulation success of a particular issue and the need for accuracy in final accounting will not fight the system. Instead, they will make it work for them.

A second example: the apparent slowness of the single-copy system to respond to a major chain approval of a publisher's specialized title. Why, says the publisher, does it take so long for a print run increase after an authorization is secured?

The key to answering this common question rests with the publisher and his circulation people rather than with the system itself. If a publisher is active and aggressive in his dealings with his national distributor, the response time can be reduced dramatically. If he is not, there may never be an adequate response.

Our publisher must always remember that his title is being circulated in an environment of 3,000 magazines and that the local wholesaler from whom that print run increase must come gets dozens of chain approvals each week. Furthermore, the wholesaler's economic motivation to respond quickly to that chain approval is substantially less than that of the publisher and his national distributor; the increase in the number of copies per local wholesaler is small compared to the overall increase which the publisher will get.

The appropriate response to a major chain approval is to get the national distributor field personnel to prepare new distributions at the local wholesaler in a prompt and orderly manner, rather than wait for the slower response of a crowded system.

The competitive environment

A final example—in the area of cover design, or packaging. It is of crucial importance that our publisher understand the environment in which his magazine is competing for the attention of the consumer. The standard display fixture from which magazines are sold today is a virtual cornucopia of ideas, information and entertainment. In fact, it is crowded with magazines all attempting to catch the moving eye of the consumer.

Publishers of successful newsstand circulation magazines understand that their magazines must earn a place on that display fixture and that each step up in display position is the result. By understanding that all magazines compete for the consumer's roving eye in a crowded environment, the publisher can design his packaging to meet the demands of this environment. If his design is good, circulation will increase and the system will work for him.

As I have said more than once in this column, the single-copy channel of distribution works for those who understand how it works and who then work within its constraints.

Faster data

By Ronald T. Scott

There is a well-tested theorem of marketing which says, "Information superiority is the key to market superiority." The publishing industry has not been noted for its superior information systems. In fact, these systems have been very slow in providing information about the marketplace and the basic facts on which to make critical decisions for the future.

Today, the sale and return information—which flows from the retailer through the local magazine wholesaler and the national distributor to the publisher—is adequate. Unfortunately, however, the length of time it now takes for that information to make the journey is much too long. Publishers need faster information more than they need more information.

The Universal Product Code (UPC), by now an accepted symbol appearing on the covers of most magazines (with less esthetic damage to the artistic integrity of the cover than the ubiquitous subscription label), can provide the aggressive and alert newsstand-oriented publisher with faster and more accurate response to his or her magazine.

In another I discussed the origins of UPC and touched briefly on the effect of this code on the single-copy sale of magazines. In this column, I will cover certain practical results of UPC and some exciting and profound implications for the future. For when these codes are used

on magazines to record sale and return data by title and issue from individual retailers, they can dramatically increase the speed with which sale and return data are reported to publishers.

Current recording method too limited

The critical factor in this process has always been the speed and efficiency of recording the data on the sale of each magazine by retailers. This recording of retail sale and return data is one of the primary functions of the local magazine wholesaler who deals with approximately 3,000 active magazine titles (for which he has at least three active issues at any given time) and from 700 to 1,000 retail accounts.

This recording function, using the existing manual systems, has been slow and inefficient and has limited the number of titles receiving complete data control to less than 200. The remaining titles have little or no record of sale by retailer, slowing the information flow which the publisher needs. In fact, the only record maintained on these titles is of total allotment received by the local magazine wholesaler and the total number of returns processed and forwarded to the appropriate national distributor for credit.

Because there is no appropriate way to check individual retailers in order to verify the credit claim of a local wholesaler, most national distributors and publishers require wholesalers to return the front cover, or a part of it, in order to verify and extend credit for unsold magazines.

Even if the local magazine wholesaler is using a computer, however, this entire process involves the tedious manual sorting of thousands of magazine titles and issues, the physical transportation of the front covers of these magazines to the national distributor warehouses, the verification of the quantities claimed, the key-punching of this information into the national distributor computer systems and, finally, the reporting of the data to the publisher.

UPC speeds credit verification

It is this tedious credit verification process that is the cause of the slow reporting of return information to the publisher. However, if a local magazine wholesaler used the UPC symbol to record the sale and return of each issue of each magazine by individual retailer, the credit verification process would be much faster. This is because this verification can be done by matching the wholesaler's credit claims against credits given by him to his individual retailers on all magazine titles. (This credit verification procedure is now used by almost all publishers with their national distributors.)

As this column is being written, one national distributor is receiving the sale and return data from more than 20 local wholesalers within a few days of the recording of that data. In addition, the data is being transmitted electronically from the local wholesaler's computer directly to the national distributor's computer. When this system is fully implemented, a publisher will be able to receive sale and return data a full 30 to 60 days sooner than it is currently being received. And when the publisher makes decisions, they will be based on information from at least one or two additional issues.

Revitalizing sales

By Ronald T. Scott

What can a publisher do to revitalize weak newsstand sales? Is it usually a hopeless cause? Or is it possible to rebuild the sales of a magazine that has fallen on bad times?

As the former president of a national distributor and as a single copy sales consultant, I have faced this situation many times, and it seems to me that a publisher in this situation has at least as good a chance of achieving success as a new entrant to the newsstand market.

In most cases, when a magazine's newsstand sales are declining, the consumer is sending a clear message: I do not perceive sufficient value in what I see to spend the price you are asking. The challenge is obvious: to change that perception so that the consumer will buy our title.

The first step on the road to better newsstand sales is to evaluate the assets and liabilities of the magazine involved. There are certain basic assets of an older title. First, an older magazine has already been accepted by most, if not all, independent wholesale distributors. Second, there are already consumers who are buying each issue, even if there are not enough of those consumers. Third, there are some, though probably not enough, retail chain authorizations in effect. Fourth, there is a national distributor who is familiar with the title, the publisher, and his organization. And, fifth, since certain changes in cover packaging, editorial emphasis and distribution patterns have already been tried and found wanting, some options do not have to be tried again.

An older title also has some serious liabilities. While the title is accepted by the local wholesaler and does not require pre-selling, the local wholesaler's sale and return records do show a poor sales percentage and may already indicate withholding of copies. The national distributor, meanwhile, is probably also familiar with the title and some of his salespeople may have already tried (and failed) to improve the sale and become discouraged.

Studying the competition

Once the analysis of assets and liabilities has been completed, it is time to evaluate the problem in terms of your competitors—both the successful and the unsuccessful. Since your magazine is on the newsstands it has a track record, and there is a wealth of information available from the national distributor's salespeople and field reports.

These reports contain historical sales data on your magazine and selective competitors. Analyze a good sampling of these field reports to determine which retail chains have authorized your title and how these authorizations compare with the competitor's authorizations.

Is there a correlation between volume and sales efficiency on the one side and the number and type of chain approvals on the other? Are there regional variations in sales? Has the national distributor lost some interest in the title because of the poor sales? Is the return flow from the local wholesaler faster on later issues than earlier ones, indicating an increasing problem of undistributed copies? Are certain competitors' sales increasing, while yours are falling?

If a thorough examination is done, you will see definite patterns which will begin to explain the reasons for the sales decline. In the case of one publisher, this analysis clearly indicated that although his title was selling as well as his competitors' titles at the retail accounts, his competitors had more chain authorizations and, hence, more sale.

In another case, the national distributor's field personnel were comparing one title to another title in the same field, but the second title appealed to a different segment of that consumer interest group. Since almost every magazine will have a different combination of factors, it is critical to do the investigative homework.

Listening to distributors

After the homework is completed and some tentative conclusions have been drawn, sit down with the national distributor's salespeople and get their opinions and their help. Although these salespeople are not skilled in publishing, they are skilled in marketing and merchandising magazines and they can be of great assistance in these two areas.

What kind of feedback are they getting from their field salespeople and the local wholesalers? What are their evaluations of the entire field in which your magazine is competing? How difficult is it to sell magazines like yours to retail chains? How do your competitors sell these chains successfully? What suggestions do they have to bring sales up? Why do they think sales are down? What do you have to do to help them get sales up?

There is a great deal that can be learned from these meetings with your national distributor. In fact, it may be necessary to schedule a second and third meeting with the national distributor, because some of the questions will require further thought and research before conclusions can be reached.

A visit to selected local wholesalers can also be quite helpful. The local wholesaler and his salespeople are on the firing line with the retailers and have current sale and return information available on your title and your competitors' titles. Here again, it is important to remember that although the local wholesaler is not a skilled publisher, he is skilled at marketing and merchandising magazines. As long as the opinions are given and taken in that context, they can be quite valuable.

Preparing an action plan

At this point, an action plan must be prepared to deal with the situation. This plan must be simple, with a small number of variables working at the same time.

If, for example, the analysis shows that your title is losing sales to a competitor whose magazine has more pages and a lower cover price than yours, a somewhat different cover-packaging approach, and about the same chain authorizations, we probably should not take the gamble of both reducing price and increasing pages. This might not be the answer anyway.

We seem to be in relatively good shape in retail outlets. But what about that cover treatment? Does it reflect changing editorial emphasis? Or is it changing packaging? Is our target consumer price-sensitive, or subject-sensitive? Is advertising an integral part of the editorial thrust of the title, or is it secondary to editorial?

Ultimately, we should choose to answer a limited number of these questions, so that we can understand the consumers' answers: Yes, it was packaging. No, it was not price. Yes, it was the number of pages. No, it was not the packaging.

If the problem is partly an editorial or art problem, some publishers prefer to communicate with their editorial and art staffs themselves. Others prefer to bring together the newsstand circulation people and the editorial and art people for a series of discussions. And still other publishers want their national distributor's representatives to be a part of this exercise.

All three approaches have been successful, and choosing your approach is a matter of individual management style. But in one form or another, the action plan which emerges from the analysis must be used to recreate the enthusiasm, interest and hope which characterized the magazine when it was successful.

Rebuilding the newsstand sales of a magazine with declining sales is possible. In fact, a publisher with such a magazine usually has a higher chance of success than the publisher of a new title, where everything must still be learned through experience. The wise publisher will use both the history that he has and the people who have experienced it. When he does so, he begins the rebuilding process to successful newsstand sales.

Field representatives

By Ronald T. Scott

The role of the national distributor field representative seems to be attracting substantial attention these days. While this is certainly not the first time we have had attention focused on field representatives, this is probably a most appropriate time to review the cost and effectiveness of field representatives.

Some of you may be unfamiliar with the term "field representative." When I first entered the publishing circulation business over 20 years ago, a representative was called a "roadman." Today, the terms defining this representative vary from sales manager to marketing coordinator. Whatever his title, however, this person represents a national distributor or publisher in a defined area of the United States, working with the individual wholesalers and/or chain retailers within that specific geographic area.

What is causing so much of the debate today is that publishers, national distributors and wholesalers are realizing the enormous cost these people now represent. In the July 1980 issue of FOLIO there is a chart of the 13 largest national distributors. One column on that chart is headed "Number of full time sales representatives" and another is headed "Part-time sales representatives." The total of these columns indicates that 1,244 full time representatives and 414 part-time representatives are employed by the 13 national distributors.

It is safe to assume that each of these full time field representatives will cost the national distributor a minimum of $30,000 a year in salary, benefits, and travel and entertainment expenses. That comes to $37,320,000, even before we've added in the cost of the 414 part-time field representatives and all of the field representatives employed by publishers directly. So—it is indeed time to take a very close look at just what the industry receives for its investment of $37 million a year.

The computer age

In the dark ages, before the introduction and acceptance of computers, service bureaus, digital codes and optical scanners, the job of the field representative was critical. He had to dig out and organize into meaningful reports all of the information on the sale of magazines at the wholesaler level and report it to publishers as quickly and efficiently as possible. He had to continually review and update individual allocations of copies to each retailer within a given wholesaler's primary marketing area, and review the allocation of copies by the national distributor to each wholesaler in terms of current sales.

The field representative's role was critical because much of this information was unavailable to the national distributor for several months after it was available at the local wholesaler level. Unfortunately, the primary functions of a field representative today are no different than they were prior to the computer and the information revolution of the late seventies.

Today, both national distributors and publishers receive current accurate information on their own and competitive titles directly from the wholesaler via a computer printout. Since the accuracy of the information and the speed of its transmission from local wholesaler to national distributor and publisher is today much greater than before, there is in my opinion no greater waste of a field representative's time than that time allocated to the accumulation of information.

Distribution work—the constant revision and updating of individual allocation of copies to retailers—continues to be necessary, however. Unfortunately, field representatives often spend as much time accumulating statistical data from which to prepare distribution as they spend on the distribution itself, and this is a massive waste of both time and money.

I believe that we need every field representative we now have in the publishing business. In fact, we probably need more field representatives. However, since we don't need field representatives who perform unnecessary tasks, we must change the way we view the field representative.

In today's competitive economy, the single copy sales industry needs professional marketing and merchandising people. How can the industry attract good people, however, when the field representative room at the local wholesaler agency is dirty, crowded, noisy and inefficient? And how can it attract quality field personnel when the basic training program is a week in the field with an already tired and discouraged, but more experienced representative?

As others have pointed out before me, we need better training of field representatives, we need better conditions under which the field representatives work in wholesale agencies, and we need more productive assignments for field representatives.

The environment in which the field representative operates today is far different from that of yesterday's "roadman." We have begun to recognize the challenge by changing the terminology. Now let's change the function.

Field reps in the computer age

By Ronald T. Scott

In a recent column I asked the question: "What are we getting when we spend $37 million on field representatives?" The logical follow-up to that question, and the theme of this column, is: "What *should* we be getting for $37 million?"

Because telecommunications will be a fact of life within the next few years, the transfer of information—one of the most boring, time consuming functions—will soon be an obsolete part of a field representative's job. Of course, field representatives will still need to search out and record information on products competitive to their titles, but there is no reason why the information on those titles cannot be supplied to them by national distributors or publishers well in advance of visits to any wholesaler agency.

I believe that we can calculate a saving of one workday per wholesale agency visited by each field representative when this information transfer is a fact of life. With some 1,244 full-time field representatives averaging one agency call a week, this information transfer alone should make 64,680 work days available for more productive pursuits (52 weeks x 1,244).

What shall we do with this enormous amount of time being used to produce hundreds of thousands of pages of ancient history? And what shall we do when technology enables us to free up an additional workday per week for these 1,244 people, when wholesaler computers are able to collect and print out competitive information in advance, when a field person can give the wholesaler advance notice of the day on which he will call on that agency?

It seems to me that we can use this time—which we are already paying for—in three important ways. First, we can train personnel to understand the product we are selling. Second, we can train personnel to analyze the market in order to make better allocations of copies to retailers. And finally, we can have representatives spend more time in the field, working to develop additional retail outlets.

Understanding the market

No one can effectively sell a product that he doesn't understand. This is especially true in today's market with its ever-increasing emphasis on market research.

We, as an industry, are just beginning to understand all of the sociological and psychological factors (e.g., demographics, personality profiles) involved in sales of consumer products.

Unfortunately, we spend very little time training our first-line field representatives to understand what these terms mean and how they apply to individual magazine and book titles.

If this situation continues, if we do not begin to train our people, we will be at a great disadvantage when competing for retail display space and consumer purchases. Thus, it is imperative that we develop ongoing programs that will train people to understand what we are talking about, how it applies to individual titles and marketing areas, and how to keep abreast of the marketing situation in a rapidly changing environment.

Once people are trained in using today's information, they will be more intelligent, more disciplined, and certainly more efficient in the work they do at individual wholesale agencies in the allocation of copies to individual retailers.

Expand retail outlets

There are literally hundreds of thousands of retail outlets in the United States and Canada which could and should be handling our product as an integral part of their selling to consumers. Since these outlets generate consumer traffic able and willing to buy our impulse items, our product would be profitable for them. Such a relationship would also be profitable for us, for in addition to selling more copies, we could also open our channel of distribution to a wider variety of specialized products for these retail outlets.

When I looked at *Fortune*'s 50 largest retailers a short time ago, I noticed that we do a minimal amount of business with Sears Roebuck (#1). We do fairly well with Safeway (#2), and a fairly good job with K Mart (#3), but we do very little business with J. C. Penney (#4). We do well with Kroger (#5) and A & P (#6), but very little with Woolworth (#7), Federated Department Stores (#8) and Montgomery Ward (#9). We do a good job with Lucky Stores (#10).

These top 10 retailers account for $94 billion in sales of the $161 billion sales of the top 50 retail companies in the United States. Since our potential for additional sales of our product with these retail giants is incredible, we should direct our field people toward these opportunities.

There is a great deal of conversation today within the single-copy industry about the cost of field personnel and the reception of field personnel by wholesalers and retailers. There is more conversation about the need to attract better people and to train them better. What we must begin to realize is that as the current functions of field representatives become obsolete, a great deal of time will be available. Our success in the future depends on how we make use of this vital resource.

Data interpretation

By Ronald T. Scott

In previous columns, I have touched on the increases in information becoming available at the wholesale and national distributor levels as a result of computer and optical scanning input of data. At the present time, all national distributors and 355 wholesale agencies are using computers to improve the sale of magazines and books, and 226 wholesalers are now scanning for input of data.

Chart #1 is a listing of 68 computer printouts presently available at a standard wholesaler magazine and book agency. In this column I will analyze and describe four of these reports. These four have been selected because all four can be used by publisher field personnel and national distributor field personnel to enhance the volume and efficiency of sale of their magazines.

The four reports we will analyze are the Draw/Net Sale Report (Chart #2), the Dealer/Title Comparison Report (Chart #3), the Retail Dealer Sales Analysis (Chart #4), and the Chain Billing Analysis (Chart #5).

The Draw/Net Sale (Chart #2), also known as the O&R file, is a record of eight issues of the draw and net sale by individual retailers. Starting from the left, the first column is the retailer number, the second column is the number of copies allocated to each retailer on issue 0012, the first issue. The second column, P/R, is an adjustment column, and the third column is net sale, that is the number of copies sold after returns have been credited.

This Draw-P/R and Net Sale category is repeated for eight consecutive issues ending with issue 0020. At the bottom of this report is the bulk record summarizing the individual allocations by retailer, that is, on issue 0012 the sum of the copies is 5,141, sum of the returns is 366 and net sale is 4,775, or 92.8 percent. This report is now available in almost all wholesaler agencies for all titles and issues distributed through that wholesaler agency.

Less than 10 years ago, the average wholesaler agency with a modest computer installation (if any) and no optical scanning capability had such Draw/Net Sales reports available on only 200 or 300 of the 2,000-odd magazines distributed. Now, a publisher or national distributor can use this report to follow the sales results of each individual retailer and adjust allocations based on each one's success or lack of success.

The report is a clear and accurate record of consumer response to the products being offered for sale at each individual retailer outlet. However, it tells only part of the story of how well a magazine could sell.

Compare allocation

The Dealer/Title Comparison report (Chart #3) adds a new dimension to our ability to analyze the sale. In this report, we are able to compare the allocation of copies to selected retailers (in this case, 13 competitive titles).

We are able to determine that dealer 01610, an Eckerd Drug Store, did not receive copies of *Modern Screen* and *Movie Life*, did receive three copies of *Movie World*, did not receive copies of *Movie Stars*, etc. This report, which is available at most wholesaler agencies, gives salespeople the opportunity to compare their magazines with competitive titles in terms of retail coverage and volume of sale.

The Draw/Net Sale Report indicates less than adequate sales, whereas the Dealer/Title Comparison Report tells us *why* the sales are inadequate: our title is not going to the retailers who are selling the high volume of our competitive titles. This report enables us to measure sales results by retailer against those titles most likely to attract the same type of consumer.

To carry the scenario even further, the Retail Dealer Sales Analysis (Chart #4) is an analysis of the sale of the selected group of titles within an existing chain, in this case the A & P Food Stores. This report analyzes for comparable issues the relative success of 13 titles by issue in this one chain, giving us a further opportunity to understand the Draw/Net Sale numbers in Chart #2.

This report may very well show us that a particular chain is an excellent outlet for our type of magazine and that we are allocating far too few copies compared to others. On the other hand, it may show us the reverse—that this particular chain is not a good outlet and that we are allocating far too many copies.

The Chain Billing Analysis (Chart #5) is the summary by quarter of the business done between the wholesaler and individual retailers compared to the same quarter one year ago. The report is expressed in dollars, not in units, and each chain is summarized after the listing for each individual store.

Chart 1   LIST OF COMPUTER PRINTOUTS FOR WHOLESALE MAGAZINE AGENCY

TITLE LISTING	SALES DISTRIBUTION REPORT
DETAIL TITLE FILE LISTING	AGED TRIAL BALANCE
TITLE FILE UPDATE REPORT	STATEMENTS
RESTRICTED LIST	COLLECTION REPORT
DEALER LIST	CANCEL & SHORTAGE REPORT
DETAIL DEALER FILE LISTING	QUARTERLY SHORTAGE AND CANCEL REPORT
DEALER FILE UPDATE REPORT	REPORT OF DELINQUENT ACCOUNTS
PUBLISHER FILE UPDATE REPORT	HOLD LIST REPORT
ORDER REGULATION STATUS REPORT	CHAIN BILLING ANALYSIS
THE ORDER REGULATION FILE STATUS BY DEALER	RETAIL SALES REPORT
EFFECT ON AFF DAVIT COPIES DROPPED	ROUTE BILLING ANALYSIS
ORDER REGULATION FILE UPDATE REPORT	RETAIL SALES ANALYSIS
RECEIVING REPORT	QUARTERLY BOOK ANALYSIS REPORT
INVOICE MASTER REPORT	ACCOUNTS PAYABLE TRANSACTION PROOF LISTING
SORTED INVOICE MASTER	INVOICED A/P TRANSACTION PROOF LISTING
RECEIVING REPORT BY PUBLISHER	ACCOUNTS PAYABLE LEDGER
DRAW/NET REPORT	ACCOUNTS PAYABLE SALES ANALYSIS
INVOICES	ACCOUNTS PAYABLE SALES & INVENTORY REPORT
BILLING ERROR REPORT	TITLE DISTRIBUTION REPORT
AMOUNT BILLED REPORT	TITLE DISTRIBUTION SUMMARY
ROUTEMANS DAILY SETTLEMENT SHEET	TV GUIDE RETAIL SALES REPORT
GALLEY REPORT	SPECIAL FORMULA ANALYSIS
RETURN ERROR REPORT	O/R DISTRIBUTION INQUIRY
BULK RETURN POSTING REPORT	DEALER/TITLE COMPARISON REPORT
CREDIT MEMO FROM SINGLE ENTRY	CHECK UP REPORT
DAILY TRANSACTION LOG	RETAIL DISPLAY ALLOWANCE REPORT
BULK RECORD REPORT	ABC REPORT
DETAIL BULK LIST	BULK SALES HISTORY BY TITLE
BULK EXCEPTION LIST	BULK SALES HISTORY
TITLES NOT CALLED-IN REPORT	BULK SALES HISTORY—CATEGORY SEQUENCE
BULK FILE UPDATE REPORT	BULK SALES HISTORY—PUBLISHER SEQUENCE
STATEMENT OF BULK RETURNS	CHAIN DISTRIBUTION COMPARISON
PUBLISHER LIST	DEALER DISTRIBUTION REPORT
ACCOUNTS RECEIVABLE BATCH PROOF REGISTER	DEALER PROFIT ANALYSIS

Chart 2

DRAW/NET 18067 TV GUIDE SOUTH   CLIENT 199

PREV ISS	PUB	TITLE	ISSUE	TITLE NAME	TOTAL BASE	RECEIVED	DISTRIBUTED	BIN	BUNDLE	DATE	FREQUENCY
0000	070	18067	0021	TV GUIDE SOUTH	5,549	4,608	4,608	8	100	06/04/79	5

DEALER NUMBER	0012 DRW	0012 P/R	0012 NET	0013 DRW	0013 P/R	0013 NET	0014 DRW	0014 P/R	0014 NET	0015 DRW	0015 P/R	0015 NET	0016 DRW	0016 P/R	0016 NET	0018 DRW	0018 P/R	0018 NET	0019 DRW	0019 P/R	0019 NET	0020 DRW	0020 P/R	0020 NET	CUR DRAW	BASE	DTE	F	DEALR NUMBR
00001	50		44	50		48	50		50	50		44	50		50	50		48	50		50	3		3	44	53	104		00001
00002	486		483	487		484	487		487	500		458	511		511	503	300-	0	505	10	515	35		35	461	559	609	4	00002
00003	260		235	262		238	263		263	263		247	259		259	250	50	100	242		242	17		17	253	306	104		00003
00004	70		64	71		63	71		71	70		64	68		58	62		62	63		63	4		4	63	75	104		00004
00005	50		44	50		43	50		50	50		43	50	40-	10	50	30-	0	50	10-	40	3		3	42	51	104		00005
00006	31		30	31		30	31		31	31		27	32		32	29		29	30		30	2		2	28	33	104		00006
00007	534		524	537		524	541		541	550	40-	448	558		558	542		542	550		550	38		38	600	688	104		00007
00008	35		29	35		31	34		34	34		32	34		34	31	6	37	28	18-	10	2		2	29	35	104		00008
00009	24		21	24		21	24	20-	4	23		23	22	20-	2	19	9-	0	18	20	38	1		1	14	17	104	H	00009
00014$	71		70	72		67	74		74	74		74	73		73	68		68	66		66	5		5	66	80	609		00014
00015	490		446	491		436	491		491	486		436	480		480	458		458	450		450	31		31	500	594	104		00015
00016	64		61	62		56	64		64	66		14	52		66	63		63	62		62	4		4	57	69	104		00016
00017	216		196	217		197	217		217	216		200	215		215	205		205	205	5	210	14		14	200	254	104		00017
00018	22		21	22		21	22	12-	10	22		21	22		22	20		20	20		20	1		1	16	19	104		00018
00019	55		52	50		50	50		50	50		48	50	10-	40	50	10-	160-	50		50	4		4	48	58	104		00019
00020	129		119	129		115	129		129	127		117	126		126	121		121	120		120	8		8	124	151	104		00020
00021	55		47	55		47	55		55	50		46	50		50	44		44	50		50	3		3	45	55	104		00021
00022	33		29	33		29	34		34	35		32	34		34	30	10	40	29		29	2		2	28	34	104		00022
00025*	50		46	50		44	50		50	50		50	50	50-	10-	50		50	50	150-	50	3		3	43	42	104		00025
00101	544		504	545		487	544		544	541		491	550		550	532		532	529		529	37		37	244	297	609	4	00101
00102	324		310	322		307	323		323	326		296	331		331	318		118	324		324	22		22	300	391	104		00102
00103	100		92	100		92	100		100	100		85	100		100	100		80	100		100	7		7	90	108	104		00103
00104	100		96	100		95	100		100	100		85	105		105	100		100	100		100	7		7	92	111	104		00104
00105*	577		537	581		544	582		582	581		581	580		580	557		557	550		550	38		38	600	720	104		00105
00109	45		41	45		41	44		44	43		38	43		43	39		39	41		41	3		3	39	47	104		00109
00110	27		27	28		28	26		26	25		22	26		26	22		22	22		22	2		2	25	30	609		00110
00112	24		21	24		21	23		23	22		22	22		22	19		19	20		20	1		1	20	24	104		00112
00116	224		218	217		211	213		213	215		190	220		220	211		211	221		221	16		16	222	267	104		00116
00117	205		175	207		173	211		211	211		198	200		200	186		186	160		160	11		11	200	232	104		00117
00120	118		73	115		97	113		113	111		91	112		112	100	60-	0	100		100	6		6	SUSPND		609		00120
00121	42		39	42		39	43		43	43		39	43		43	37		37	39		39	3		3	37	45	104		00121
00122	24		22	24		22	23		23	23		20	23		23	20		20	20		20	1		1	21	25	104		00122
00125	62		59	62		59	62		62	62		56	63		63	59		59	60		60	4		4	57	69	104		00125

ISSUE	DEALERS	DRAW	RETURNS	PU/REORD	NET SALE	PERCENT
0012	33	5,141	366		4,775	92.8
0013	33	5,140	380		4,760	92.6
0014	33	5,144	0	32-	5,112	99.3
0015	33	5,112	406	90-	4,616	90.2
0016	33	5,168	10	56-	5,102	98.7
0018	33	4,944	1,294	283-	3,467	70.1
0019	33	4,924		7	4,931	100.0
0020	33	338			338	100.0
0021	33	4,608				

35 BUNDLES   1,108 LOOSE COPIES

DRAW/NET REPORT

THIS REPORT SHOWS THE DETAIL DISTRIBUTION OF EACH TITLE LISTED ON THE INVOICE MASTER. IN ADDITION IT SHOWS THE DRAW, PICKUP AND REORDER AND NET SALE FOR PREVIOUS ISSUES WHICH IS VITAL FOR ACCURATE REVIEW OF DISTRIBUTIONS. IF THE SPECIAL FORMULA IS BEING USED TO CALCULATE THE NEW BASE, THE INFORMATION IS SHOWN AT THE BOTTOM OF THE PAGE.

IT CONSISTS OF -

PREV ISS - DATE OF THE ISSUE SELECTED TO MODIFY DEALER BASE

PUB - NUMBER USED TO IDENTIFY PUBLISHER

TITLE - NUMBER USED TO IDENTIFY TITLE

ISSUE - CODE ASSIGNED BY AGENCY TO IDENTIFY ISSUE

TOTAL BASE - AVERAGE NET SALE OF ALL DEALERS RECEIVING DISTRIBUTION OF THIS TITLE

RECEIVED - NUMBER OF COPIES RECEIVED FROM PUBLISHER

DISTRIBUTED - NUMBER OF COPIES ACTUALLY DISTRIBUTED

BIN - THE LINE LOCATION OR PICKING SEQUENCE OF TITLE

BUNDLE - NUMBER OF COPIES IN BUNDLE RECEIVED FROM PUBLISHER

DATE - INVOICE DATE

FREQUENCY - THE FREQUENCY OF DISTRIBUTION

DEALER NUMBER - NUMBER USED TO IDENTIFY DEALER

CODE - A $ INDICATES A SELLOUT DEALER, AN * INDICATES A HIGH RETURNER AND A X INDICATES A SPLIT INVOICE.

DRAW - NUMBER OF COPIES DRAWN FOR THAT ISSUE

PICKUP/REORDER - NUMBER OF COPIES PICKED UP OR REORDERED FOR THAT ISSUE

NET - NUMBER OF COPIES SOLD THAT ISSUE

BASE - NEWLY CALCULATED NET SALE

DATE - LAST TIME MAINTENANCE WAS DONE TO THAT TITLE FOR THAT DEALER

FRZ - IDENTIFIES DEALERS WHO HAVE DISTRIBUTION FROZEN. THE NUMBERS PRINTED IN THE FREEZE COLUMN DETERMINES THE TYPE FREEZE.

    P - IS A PERMANENT FREEZE (REMAINS FROZEN UNTIL MANUALLY CHANGED)
    B - IS A COPY FREEZE (THE DEALER GETS THAT EXACT NUMBER OF COPIES)
    1-7 - IS A TEMPORARY FREEZE IN WHICH THE NUMBER DENOTES THE NUMBER OF ISSUES THAT THE BASE WILL REMAIN FROZEN.
    H - HIGH DRAW FOR BASE B
    L - LOW DRAW FOR BASE B

DEALER NUMBER - IDENTIFIES DEALER AND IS PRINTED ON BOTH SIDES OF REPORT FOR EASE OF READING.

Chart 3

DEALER/TITLE COMPARISON REPORT FOR CLIENT 199   DATE 02/15/79

33480 MODERN SCREEN	33660 MOTION PICTURE	38520 PHOTOPLAY	57300 TV MOVIE SCREEN
34200 MOVIE LIFE	34320 MOVIE MIRROR	38415 PHOTO WORLD	
34800 MOVIE WORLD	33295 MODERN MOVIES	45780 SCREEN STORIES	
34500 MOVIE STARS	38340 PHOTO SCREEN	57660 MOVIE TV GOSSIP	

DLR	DEALER NAME	33480	34200	34800	34500	33660	34320	33295	38340	38520	38415	45780	57660	57300
01610	ECKERD DRUG			3		2	2			3	6			6
01612	ECKERD DRUG	2				4	6			3	7	4	3	4
01613	ECKERD DRUG		5	7		3	5			4	5	4	2	5
01614	ECKERD DRUG	4	6			4	5			1	6		3	2
01616	ECKERD DRUG	8	8	7	6	8	9			8	10	6	6	7
01617	ECKERD DRUG	4	3	5	2	4	4			5	10	5	2	6
01619	ECKERD DRUG	3	4	7	4	4	4			2	6	4	3	6
01620	ECKERD DRUG	3	5	6	4	6	7			4	6	5	3	6
01621	ECKERD DRUG	6	11	11	6	8	20			16	12	5	15	19
01622	ECKERD DRUG	6	9	7	5	10	10			11	13	6	3	9
01623	ECKERD DRUG	5	8	10	66	8	13			8	9	5	7	16
01625	ECKERD DRUG	2	4	6	3	4	4			6	9	2	2	5
01626	ECKERD DRUG	7	2	8	6	5	6			3	10	6	4	12
01628	ECKERD DRUG	3	5		4	4	4			4	6	3	4	6
01857	EMERSON BK STORE	5	3	7	4	3	3				12	6		7
02101	PANTRY PRIDE	3	6	6		8	6			8	10	6	10	14
01635	ECKERD DRUG	7	8	6	2	12	13			6	8	5	8	11
01637	ECKERD DRUG	3	3	3		2	2			4	6	4	4	5
01638	ECKERD DRUG	3	6	6		5	6			8	7	4	7	11
01639	ECKERD DRUG		5	7		4				5	6		3	5
01851	ECKERD DRUG								4					4
01855	ENCHANTED FOODS			7		13	11	4		5	12		4	
02102	FOOD FAIR	4	5	9		4	6			4	10	4	2	6
02103	PANTRY PRIDE	3	4	4	2	8	6			6	14	5	3	13
02104	PANTRY PRIDE	5	3	4	5	6	9			11	6	4	3	2
02106	PANTRY PRIDE	3	4	6		4	4			4	10	2	2	3
02107	PANTRY PRIDE	3	2	6	5	6	8			11	7	4	6	10
02108	PANTRY PRIDE		3				2			2	3	5	2	3
02110	FOOD FAIR	2		3		4	3			4	6	5	2	
02111	FOOD FAIR	5	7		6	9	17			6	16	5		11
02112	PANTRY PRIDE	3	6	6	2	4	3			5	6	4	3	3
02113	PANTRY PRIDE	3	3	6	5	4	6			7	5	4	3	5
02401	J M FIELDS	3	5	2	4	7	5			3	5		3	
02402	J M FIELDS	3	5	2	4	7	5			3	5		3	
02403	J M FIELDS	3	5	2	4	7	5			3	5		3	
02404	J M FIELDS					5	4			4	4			
02451	FOUR WINDS	3		3		4	3		4	4	5		4	
02453	FOODWAY			4			2		4	1	4		4	
02576	GATEWAY BK CORNER	4					3		4	3	6	6	4	
02579	GULF SUNDRIES			4			3		4				4	
02586	G & M MKT								4	3	2		4	
02701	GRAY DRUG	4	7	6	3	4	9			3	4	3		7
02702	GRAY DURG	3	8	7	3	3	9			3	3	3		7
02751	HOLIDAY INN			3		2				3	3			
02752	HANDY MARKET								4	3	3		3	
02753	HANDY MKT					4			4		6		4	
02754	HOLIDAY CAMP GRND								4	4	3		4	

DEALER/TITLE COMPARISON REPORT

THIS REPORT ENABLES YOUR AGENCY TO SELECT A GROUPING OF SIMILAR TITLES (EXAMPLE - MOVIE MAGAZINES) AND THE DEALERS WHO RECEIVE THEM FOR A COMPARISON OF TYPE SALES.

THE REPORT CONSISTS OF A GROUPING AT THE TOP OF THE REPORT OF TITLE NUMBER AND TITLE NAME. THE BODY OF THE REPORT CONTAINS

      DLR - NUMBER IDENTIFYING DEALER

      DEALER NAME - IDENTIFIES DEALER BY NAME

TITLE NUMBERS ARE LISTED AND EITHER THE AVERAGE NET SALE OR BASE CAN BE LISTED FOR ALL DEALERS THAT HAVE DISTRIBUTION OF THE CORRESPONDING TITLE.

Chart 4

RETAIL DEALER SALES ANALYSIS   FOR CLIENT 199 FOR 05/08/79   DEALER 99920   A&P FOOD STORES

BENT WIGGLY 08091   PUB 35

ISSUE	RETAIL	DLRS	DRAW	RTRN	NET
004	1.00	10	40	6	34
005	1.00	10	44	7	37
006	1.00	10	43	8	35

HB COLONIAL HOME C8224   PUB 35

ISSUE	RETAIL	DLRS	DRAW	RTRN	NET
031	2.00	10	47	6	41
005	2.00	10	43	4	39
1979	2.00	10	51	9	42

COSMOPOLITAN 08233   PUB 35

ISSUE	RETAIL	DLRS	DRAW	RTRN	NET
001	1.50	12	422	42	380
002	1.50	12	415	39	376
003	1.50	12	397	20	377
004	1.50	12	424	34	390
012	1.50	12	450	40	410

GOOD HOUSEKEEPIN 08345   PUB 35

ISSUE	RETAIL	DLRS	DRAW	RTRN	NET
001	1.25	12	220	29	191
002	1.25	12	215	31	184
003	1.25	12	235	28	207
004	1.25	12	240	39	201
012	1.25	12	230	33	197

HARPERS BAZAAR 08390   PUB 35

ISSUE	RETAIL	DLRS	DRAW	RTRN	NET
001	1.25	10	40	10	30
002	1.25	10	38	8	30
003	1.25	10	36	8	28
004	1.25	10	41	5	36
012	1.25	10	42	10	32

HB HOME DECOR 08412   PUB 35

ISSUE	RETAIL	DLRS	DRAW	RTRN	NET
003	2.00	11	50	5	45
004	2.00	11	48	6	42
091	2.00	11	48	6	42

HOUSE BEAUTIFUL 08458   PUB 35

ISSUE	RETAIL	DLRS	DRAW	RTRN	NET
001	1.00	12	140	17	123
003	1.00	12	145	19	126
004	1.00	12	142	15	127
012	1.00	12	150	18	132

POPULAR MECHANIC 08638   PUB 35

ISSUE	RETAIL	DLRS	DRAW	RTRN	NET
001	1.00	10	110	18	92
002	1.00	10	110	17	93
003	1.00	10	120	20	100
004	1.00	10	117	19	98
012	1.00	10	115	19	96

PRIVATE PILOT 08642   PUB 35

ISSUE	RETAIL	DLRS	DRAW	RTRN	NET
002	1.25	10	30	9	21
003	1.25	10	28	10	18
004	1.25	10	27	11	16
012	1.25	10	28	10	18

```
SIMPLICTY HOM CA                                    SOAP OPERA DIGEST                                      SPORTS AFIELD
08760                        PUB     35             08769                            PUB     35            08780                            PUB     35

ISSUE  RETAIL  DLRS  DRAW  RTRN   NET               ISSUE  RETAIL  DLRS  DRAW  RTRN   NET                 ISSUE  RETAIL  DLRS  DRAW  RTRN   NET
 001    1.25    11    46     5    41                 CO2     .75    12    280   81    199                  001    1.50    12    95     11    83
 003    .00     11    42     5    37                 003     .75    12    275   79    196                  002    1.50    12    95     1?    85
 092    1.25    11    50     7    43                 ?04     .75    12    270   90    180                  003    1.50    12    100    12    88
                                                     005     .75    12    280   95    185                  004    1.50    12    100    12    88
                                                     006     .75    1?    282   91    191

SPOT A WORD                                                         RETAIL DISPLAY ALLOWANCE REPORT
08794                        PUB     35
                                                   THIS REPORT LISTS THE QUARTERLY ACTIVITY BY CHAIN OF THE DEALERS REQUESTED.  IT GIVES
ISSUE  RETAIL  DLRS  DRAW  RTRN   NET              THE TITLES DISTRIBUTED, THEIR ISSUES, DRAW, RETURN AND NET.
 001    .75     12    48     7    41              THE REPORT CONSISTS OF
 002    .75     12    5C     9    41
 003    .75     12    50     8    42                   ISS - IDENTIFIES COVER DATE OF TITLE
 0?4    .75     12    45     8    37
 011    .75     12    44     7    37                   RETAIL - IDENTIFIES COVER PRICE OF TITLE

                                                      DEALERS - IDENTIFIES NUMBER OF DEALERS DRAWING TITLE

                                                      DRAW - IDENTIFIES NUMBER OF COPIES DEALER RECEIVED

                                                      RETURN - IDENTIFIES NUMBER OF COPIES THE DEALER RETURNED

                                                      NET - IDENTIFIES THE NET SALE OF TITLE
```

Chart 5

CHAIN BILLING ANALYSIS REPORT FOR CLIENT 199   DATE 12/31/78   DATA PROCESSING SERVICE   QUARTER 4 CHAIN 05

		THIS QUARTER THIS YEAR			THIS QUARTER LAST YEAR			CHANGE		THIS Y-T-D		LAST Y-T-D
		NET SALES	PCNT	AVG/WK	NET SALES	PCNT	AVG/WK	NET SALES	PCNT	NET SALES	PCNT	NET SALES
DEALER 00162	MAGS	2,202	68.6	169	1,236	71.0	95	966+	78.2	4,385	73.0	1,236
WINN DIXIE	BOOKS	805	46.3	62	931	87.9	72	126-	13.5	1,978	56.8	931
STORE 207	NEWS	1,391	90.3	107	237	66.9	18	1,154+	486.9	2,616	90.8	237
	TOTAL	$4,398	67.8	$338	$2,404	76.2	$185	$1,994+	82.9	$8,979		$2,404
DEALER 00136	MAGS	1,951	60.1	150	1,866	70.0	144	85+	4.6	4,234	66.9	2,818
WINN DIXIE	BOOKS	273	23.9	21	8-	.9	0	281+	3512.4	638	29.0	231
STORE 225	NEWS	193	71.5	15	173	69.2	13	20+	11.6	376	76.3	307
	TOTAL	$2,417	51.9	$186	$2,031	54.6	$156	$386+	19.0	$5,248		$3,356
DEALER 00319	MAGS	1,354	63.2	104	1,492	68.3	115	138-	9.2	2,778	65.3	2,273
WINN DIXIE	BOOKS	342	28.6	26	362	93.1	28	20-	5.5	806	35.9	486
STORE 20	NEWS	375	80.0	29	380	85.6	29	5-	1.3	630	75.2	640
	TOTAL	$2,071	54.4	$159	$2,234	74.0	$172	$163-	7.3	$4,214		$3,399
DEALER 00127	MAGS	1,173	64.0	90	781	46.9	60	392+	50.2	2,294	63.6	1,132
WINN DIXIE	BOOKS	367	39.0	28	24	3.9	2	343+	1429.2	488	27.1	144
STORE 237	NEWS	272	75.8	21	172	67.5	13	100+	58.1	506	76.6	277
	TOTAL	$1,812	57.8	$139	$977	38.4	$75	$835+	85.5	$3,288		$1,553
DEALER 0075	MAGS	94	35.7	7	102	34.0	8	8-	7.8	357	52.7	304
WINN DIXIE	BOOKS	165	53.4	13	40	33.1	3	125+	312.5	228	47.8	37
STORE 15	NEWS	41	41.4	3	46	70.8	4	5-	10.9	86	52.4	63
	TOTAL	$300	44.7	$23	$188	38.7	$14	$112+	59.6	$671		$404
* * * * * * *	MAGS	6,774	63.3	521	5,477	64.0	421	1,297	23.7	14,048	67.3	7,763
* TOTAL CHAIN *	BOOKS	1,952	36.7	150	1,349	45.1	104	603	44.7	4,138	40.6	1,829
* * * * * * *	NEWS	2,272	83.0	175	1,008	73.7	78	1,264	125.4	4,214	83.7	1,524
	TOTAL	$10,998	58.6	$846	$7,834	60.6	$603	$3,164		$22,400		$11,116

THIS REPORT IS QUARTERLY AND IS PRINTED BY CHAIN AND IN DESENDING Y-T-D NET SALES. IT IS DESIGNED AS AN AGENCY SALES TOOL IN PROMOTION OF PERIODICALS TO CHAINS. IT LISTS DOLLAR SALES, PERCENT SALES, PERCENT OF SALE TO TOTAL DRAW, AND THE AVERAGE WEEKLY SALES FOR THE QUARTER. ALSO A CURRENT QUARTER SALES BREAKOUT OF MAGAZINES, BOOKS, NEWS AND MISC IN DOLLARS AND PERCENT OF SALES TO TOTAL DRAW ARE PRINTED.

IT CONSISTS OF

DEALER - THE CODE NUMBER ASSIGNED BY YOUR AGENCY TO IDENTIFY THE DEALER

NAME - THE NAME OF THE DEALER

STORE - THE NUMBER ASSIGNED BY CHAIN HEADQUARTERS TO IDENTIFY THE STORE

THIS QTR NET SALES - THE NET SALES FOR THIS QUARTER BROKEN DOWN BY MAGS, BOOKS, NEWS & MISC (ORDERS PLUS REORDERS MINUS RETURNS AND PICKUPS)

PCNT - PERCENT OF SALE TO THE TOTAL DRAW

AVG/WK - AVERAGE WEEKLY SALES FOR THIS QUARTER

THIS QTR LAST YR NET SALES - THE NET SALES FOR THIS QUARTER LAST YEAR BROKEN DOWN BY MAGS, BOOKS, NEWS & MISC (ORDERS PLUS REORDERS MINUS RETURNS)

PCNT - PERCENT OF SALE TO THE TOTAL DRAW

AVG/WK - AVERAGE WEEKLY SALES FOR THIS QUARTER LAST YEAR

CHANGE NET SALES - THE DIFFERENCE IN THE NET SALES FROM THIS QUARTER THIS YEAR AND THIS QUARTER LAST YEAR

PCNT - PERCENT OF SALES TO TOTAL DRAW

THIS Y-T-D NET SALES - THIS YEAR TO DATE NET SALES FIGURE

LAST Y-T-D NET SALES - LAST YEAR TO DATE NET SALES FIGURE

This report is valuable for a number of reasons. First, it is concrete evidence for today's chain retailer who demands to know the productivity of the display space he has allocated to any product line. Second, for publishers and their salespeople, it indicates which chains are efficient in the sale of magazines and which chains are not. It is therefore an indication of where to increase and where to reduce the allocation of copies.

These are four reports out of 68 that are available.

They are not the only reports that are important, but they are an indication of the kinds of data that are beginning to emerge. This information becomes even more valuable as the consuming public segments into more and more specialized areas, and as the number of magazines increases to meet the more specialized demands of this public. It is important for publishers to learn how to use this information properly.

Testing

By Ronald T. Scott

Despite the wide use of testing in other areas of circulation, surprisingly little attention is given to testing in single-copy sales. In fact, it seems to shock many publishing executives when I propose single-copy testing. Few seem aware of the various tests that are now being done in the single-copy channel of distribution.

The tests I am currently familiar with include the following: cover price test; chain potential test; a newsstand potential test; and a regional newsstand potential test. Before I describe these tests, it is important to note that it is the recent improvement in record keeping at both the national distributor and local wholesaler levels that has enabled us to test effectively in the single-copy channel of distribution.

Thanks to the computer and the UPC code, almost all wholesalers now have complete records on the draw and sale of each issue of each title by individual retailer. This makes available detailed information on individual retailers for analysis by wholesaler, national distributor and publisher. The ability of national distributors to extract this information from wholesaler records and to manipulate this data within their own computers gives us unequaled opportunities to analyze test data and project it to national levels.

Testing cover price

The first test involves a very successful, highly specialized magazine with single-copy circulation contributing 25 percent of circulation. The title is presently cover priced at $1.75, and, as is normal, the subscription prices are based on a percentage of the single copy price.

The publisher, a prudent businessman, is anticipating cost pressures over the next several years which will require him to consider raising his single-copy cover price and his subscription prices. In anticipation of these potential cost pressures, a program was devised to test several cover prices with selected wholesalers. When the results are in for four issues of testing, a number of comparisons will be made: First, the level and efficiency of sale on the higher cover prices will be compared to sales and efficiency levels of prior issues in the same primary marketing areas. Second, sales and efficiency levels of the test wholesalers will be compared with those of wholesalers having the current cover price and similar demographics in their primary marketing areas. And third, cover prices will be compared. (This comparison will indicate the optimum cover price trade-off with volume.)

By analyzing the results of these tests along with those of subscription price testing, this publisher will be in a position to determine the amount of revenue that should be paid by the consumer, whether single-copy buyer or subscriber, in view of rate base considerations and advertising revenue stream.

Testing chain retail sales

The second test involves a magazine which has modest but profitable newsstand circulation. Currently, the magazine has no retail display agreements and no substantial chain authorizations. The question is: What is the potential for this title if we try to increase its newsstand circulation by these methods?

For the test, three wholesaler agencies were selected, representing a fair spectrum of demographic interest, and arrangements were made with local wholesalers (through the cooperation of the national distributor) for a sufficient number of chain retailers to display and sell the magazine over a period of four issues. By obtaining from these local wholesalers detailed records of draw and sale on these chain retailers, the impact of chain retail sales can be projected to a national level. The sales potential for this title, should it decide to move forward with an RDA, can thus be closely estimated.

Newsstand potential

The publisher of a magazine presently distributed directly to selected retailers was intrigued by the possibility that there might be more newsstand circulation available to him through the mass market system. Three wholesale agencies were selected and, with the cooperation of his distributor, organized tests were planned in which the magazine was distributed by local wholesalers to a wide variety of retailers, including chains, for a period of four issues. Once this test is completed and the detailed draw and sale data by retailer are analyzed, the publisher will be in a position to project these test results to a national level, to make the appropriate calculations of risk and reward.

Regional newsstand sales

The last test involves a magazine which may have mass market appeal in a single region of the country only. In this case one wholesaler in that region was selected with the cooperation of the distributor, and a wide variety of retailers are now being tested to determine if there is regional potential and, if so, at what level and at what cost.

Publishers should take better advantage of the opportunities available through testing at newsstands. These opportunities certainly did not exist 10 years ago, or for that matter even five years ago. Most national distributors and wholesalers, well aware of the good business sense of testing, are more than eager to cooperate with testing efforts. The new accessibility of detailed, accurate and timely information throughout the single-copy channel of distribution now makes newsstand testing a viable alternative to the old method of changing price or distribution on a national level and hoping for success.

Through a combined analysis of single-copy and subscription tests publishers can now obtain more solid information than ever before—information enabling them to make reasoned economic decisions. Rest assured, the single-copy channel of distribution is ready and waiting for publishers to wake up to the possibilities.

Inside Sports: A lesson in testing

By Ronald T. Scott

It seems about time for me to add my two cents to the continuing analysis of *Inside Sports* and its newsstand success (failure?).

I am particularly intrigued by the initial testing of *Inside Sports* on the newsstands and the subsequent multiplication of the test results which set the rate base for advertisers. The consensus seems to be that failure to meet the rate base rather than lack of circulation was the primary reason for the decision by the Washington Post Company to sell *Inside Sports*. If this is true, then the validity of the newsstand test and its interpretation are crucial to *Inside Sports*'s fate.

Frankly, it was a poorly constructed test. First, only a single issue was tested. Second, the single issue was promoted heavily. And third, the single issue received well-above-normal service levels.

Of these three serious flaws in the *Inside Sports* test, the most important was the reliance on a single issue. All that one can learn from the first issue of any new magazine is whether the consumer is interested in the concept. Even that is somewhat suspect, however, for the on-sale period will vary from retailer to retailer since there is no subsequent issue to trigger retailer returns of the first issue. In the case of *Inside Sports,* without a subsequent issue to trigger retailer returns, the first issue of the magazine undoubtedly had on-sale periods ranging from three- to six weeks, thus distorting final sales results as much as 5 percent.

By heavily promoting the test issue of *Inside Sports* without designating control areas where little or no promotion would be done, *Inside Sports* further distorted its results on the high side because it was not prepared to sustain this intense promotion on a market-by-market national scale. The same analysis applies to the service levels provided for the test issue; that is, they could not be sustained on a market-by-market national launch.

Test three issues

To properly test a monthly magazine on the newsstands, it is necessary to test three consecutive issues. A test of the second issue tests the execution of the concept and the consumers' desire to keep buying. A test using the second and third issues disciplines and controls the on-sale periods.

Just as important as conducting a three-issue test is the need for control areas in which no special promotion and service activities are conducted. For example, I have often used Phoenix, Arizona and San Diego, California as pair test cities because the demographics of the population are relatively similar.

In these tests, one of the two cities would receive promotion and concentrated sales and service activities, while the other would have no promotion and only average sales and service effort. Analyzing the results of two cities tested in this manner will add a bit of realism when it comes time to evaluate all of the test results.

Thanks to the widespread application of the Universal Product Code and the ability of local wholesalers to create retailer sales and return records by title and issue, we have fully entered the age of testing.

Figure 1 is a listing derived from the records of four wholesalers for a selected group of retailers for a three-issue test of a magazine (magazine A), compared to the same three issues for two established competitive titles. As you can see, it is possible—indeed easy—to determine from these records a number of relationships:

1. A ratio of draw/sale for certain types of retailers among the three titles.

2. Net copies sold for each of the three titles in different types of retailers.

3. Since we know the percent of total national single-copy sales represented by the four wholesalers involved in the test, we can project a national sale for the test title.

Forecasting results nationally

Today, given the industry's ability to extract detailed information from local wholesaler records and to use that information in standard testing procedures, we are able to test accurately and to forecast test results to a national level. And it is this—the forecasting of test results to a national level—that is the most difficult and critical part of testing.

I have one basic and firm rule about interpreting and projecting test results: I have rarely seen test results exceeded by the actual launch of a new magazine title. In addition, there are two corollaries to this rule: First, use the lowest reasonable multiplier when projecting test results into potential national sales. And second, beware of optimism. Even with the best-designed test, the results are going to be on the high side because the best people and the most intense attention are always devoted to a test.

Inside Sports used a poorly designed test and an op-

Figure I	Three issue average					
	Magazine A Test Issue		Magazine B Est. Title		Magazine C Est. Title	
Retailer	Draw	Sale	Draw	Sale	Draw	Sale
Alpha Beta	8.7	7.7	18.3	13.7	24.3	10.7
"	4.7	3.3	12.7	8.7	5.3	3.7
Big Bear	5	2.7	6.7	4	4	2.3
Albertson's	5.3	4.3	7	5	4	2
Foodbasket	6.7	5.3	14	8.3	6	4
"	8	4.7	0	0	10	55
Von's	5	3.3	7.3	3	4.7	1.3
Sa-Von Drugs	5.7	3.7	15	9	11.7	4.3
7-11	2.7	2.3	8.7	6.3	0	0
"	3.7	2.7	5.7	5.3	0	0
Norm's Liquor	6.3	3.7	5.7	5.7	20	14
Fleet A.S.W. Exchange	11.3	9.3	33	29.3	18.3	12
N.T.C. Main Exchange	16	13.3	60	29.7	11	6.3
Ballast Point Exchange	25	13	20	14	26.7	9.3
South Bay Bks.	13.7	8	5	3.7	17.7	16.7
Waldenbooks	15	9	20	12	10	8
"	15	12	0	0	0	0
Family Mart	6	3	26	11	4	1
Albertson's	7	4	20	8	0	0
Dobbs House	50	27	60	34	55	26
"	3	2	10	4	7	3
"	3	2	10	6	9	5
"	3	2	10	3	8	3
"	3	2	10	7	6	3
Kash & Karry	5	4	12	6	7	3
Albertson's	14	9	30	20	23	11
Walgreen Drug	8	4	7	5	0	0
Lazurus	8	4	50	19	7	3
Stop-n-Go	3	2	5	2	1	0.3
Kroger	5	4	8	3	5	4
"	9	5	14	10	8	5
"	11	8	25	16	20	16

timistic projection. These two factors caused them to set an unrealistic newsstand rate base, and their troubles multiplied from that point. It is too bad, because they did prove something interesting. *Inside Sports* is the first sports magazine to sell substantial quantities on the newsstand on a consistent basis. Although that would seem to indicate a solid editorial product, unfortunately they were unable to obtain as large a market as quickly as they had projected.

I believe *Inside Sports* was on the right track in testing its newsstand potential, and I believe testing will soon become a common occurrence. The increased ability of both national distributor and wholesaler to record and interpret detailed retailer sale and return data has made testing a more advanced art. But take note: testing will always be an art and not a science. And testing will always require a firm respect for both the flexibilities and inflexibilities of the single-copy channel of distribution.

In failing to understand this, *Inside Sports* made some bad judgments. However, all the post analyses may serve to advance the state of the art.

Competing with TV

By Ronald T. Scott

Back in the fifties when television first emerged as an important factor in communication, a number of magazines tried to match the large numbers of viewers being delivered by television through massive subscription and single-copy circulation. The more successful of these—*Life, Look* and *Saturday Evening Post*—reached such a level of success in the numbers game that they went out of business.

These magazines (and a number of others which managed to survive because they were *not* successful at building circulation numbers) were competing with the three large television networks in what I call Phase I of the electronic communication evolution: very large audiences selecting from a rather limited number of subject categories. Essentially, both television and magazines chose to appeal to a mass audience.

Economics, as usual, decided the battle over the delivery of mass audiences in favor of television, which had free transportation of its product through the air. Furthermore, the only charge to the consumer who wanted to watch television was the one-time charge for his TV set.

When the magazine industry lost the battle of mass circulation numbers, it responded by proclaiming the era of special interest magazines. We, as an industry, proceeded to reduce our emphasis on the mass interest areas and increase the number of consumer-oriented magazines offered through both the subscription and the single-copy channels of distribution. (It is interesting to note that along with this change in emphasis by publishers, consumers began to narrow their range of interests. They were becoming overwhelmed by the quantity of information being made available by the computer and the television set.)

As an industry, we have been quite successful in combating the television competition by carefully designing our consumer products. Over the past 30 years, however, the definition of a special interest magazine has been changing. The circulation numbers (which could be called successful) have been growing, and I fear that this could be a dangerous trend as we enter Phase II of the electronic communication revolution.

Phase II is simply the addition of a substantial number of options to the existing three television networks. These options are spreading across the country in the form of cable hookup, satellite transmission, cassettes, and local and regional programs.

These television options, which are now or soon will be widely available to consumers, are not going to compete for mass numbers with the three major networks. Instead, they are aimed at more specific audiences, and they are going to enjoy most of the same economic advantages that the TV networks did in Phase I.

In effect, Phase II presents the same kind of challenge to publishing that Phase I did—with a zero or two less involved in the numbers. With each cable hookup, the competition for the consumer and his discretionary income grows more fierce, and competing for audience numbers grows more difficult.

Does all this mean that the publishing industry is in its last stage of existence and that we had better start learning how to survive as television producers? (I remember that same doomsday prediction during Phase I.) I think not—but we *are* going to have to rethink our audience numbers again. And we are going to have to take a fresh look at the methods we are using, or should be using, to secure and service specific limited audiences.

The costs of transporting our product either by truck or mail are rising rapidly, while those of television are one-time investments. The costs of securing an audience are rising rapidly with no plateau in sight.

In the single-copy channel of distribution we'd better be prepared for an increase in the number of titles as we become even more specialized than we are today, and we can expect that in five years the average circulation per title will be less than it is today.

Now that the single-copy channel of distribution has begun to use electronic recording and manipulating of data, we are *technically* prepared to handle more titles with lower circulation, but I am not sure that we are *psychologically* prepared to meet this challenge. As we continue to refine the information we are now capturing, and as the economic resources freed by electronic data collection become available for marketing and merchandising services, we will be in a position to meet this challenge, as long as we are aware that it is a challenge and that there are profitable responses to it.

We are beginning to use demographic data better in selecting the specific retailers who have the consumer traffic for selected titles. We are beginning to move in the direction of expanding retailer coverage to include more specialized types of retailers, and we are beginning to use the data we are accumulating in more efficient and effective ways.

We must continue to improve in all of these undertakings as our industry is further fragmented by the electronic communications revolution. Magazines have proven almost infinitely adaptable to changing consumer wants and needs, and it seems to me that we will again face an adjustment which we are capable of making.

The international market

By Ronald T. Scott

A sometimes neglected and often misunderstood area of newsstand circulation involves the international marketplace.

Under the right circumstances, newsstand circulation outside the North American continent can amount to more than 10 percent of a magazine's circulation. And, for a number of reasons which will be discussed in this column, international newsstand circulation has traditionally been more efficient and profitable than domestic and Canadian circulation.

The structure of an international newsstand circulation system resembles our domestic system, but there are eight important differences: cost of shipping, timing of delivery, timing of sale and return information, timing of payments, method of allocating copies, retail pricing, exchange rate factors, and the annual Distripress Congress.

Shipping paid by customer

The first two critical factors involve freight movements, and it may come as quite a surprise for some to learn that in almost every case freight costs from the United States to the customer are paid by the international customer—not the publisher. The publisher pays freight costs to a point within the United States, designated by the international customer. At that point, the customer is responsible for the method of shipping and the costs of such shipment to his place of business. In most instances, the international customer consolidates the shipments of a number of publishers through an international freight forwarding agent and ships via ocean freight.

By choosing ocean freight as the shipping mode, the international customer sacrifices time for lower costs. Shipping via the less costly but slower ocean freight means that the international customer will receive and place his merchandise on sale well after the on-sale date of the magazine in the United States.

There are some problems with this slower delivery system, especially when a magazine has timely information or entertainment in a particular issue. But since almost all magazines are shipped in this manner and arrive at the same time, no competitive advantage is gained or lost, and the international consumer is accustomed to this delayed arrival of most magazines.

A publisher always has the option, of course, of negotiating an exception system—allocating shipping costs and method of shipping for a particularly timely issue or magazine if it is in his economic interest to do so. For those publishers with exceptionally timely magazines and substantial consumer interest within a particular country or group of countries, there are the additional options of licensing, joint ventures, or establishing a separate publishing entity within the specific area.

For most publishers, however, freight costs and method of shipment are the responsibility of the international customer.

The obvious result of the longer shipping schedule of magazines to international customers is a slower flow of information and payments in international sales. This slower pattern is offset by the normally higher sales percentage and the consistent sales levels which are normal in international sales. The reasons for this are best illustrated through an examination of the method of allocating copies of magazines to international customers.

There are virtually no forced or unsolicited shipments of magazines in the international market, either on new titles or on established magazines. In new title introductions, the international distributor presents the title to each of his customers in person (through his traveling representatives) or by mail. In these presentations, the international distributor explains the consumer market desired, the competitive magazines targeted, and the editorial and packaging strengths of the magazine. The international customer then responds by setting his own allotment which cannot be changed without the agreement of the international customer.

The international customer has insisted on this order-only system because he has agreed to bear the freight cost on all magazines he orders. He is able to absorb the cost of freight because American magazines are sold outside the United States at substantially higher prices than the suggested cover price printed on the magazine for U.S. and Canadian sales. Anyone who has visited Europe and purchased an American magazine there is aware of this increased cost.

The other important factor contributing to higher cover prices internationally is the unstable exchange rates among major currencies during the past few years. In the early 1970s, President Nixon removed U.S. gold reserves as guarantor of U.S. dollars because U.S. dollars held abroad exceeded U.S. gold reserves. This decision was a major factor in the substantial and rapid changes in relationships among the major currencies.

In most cases, the publisher does not bear the risk of currency adjustments because most arrangements between international distributors and international customers specify payment in U.S. dollars. But rapidly changing exchange rates can have a great effect on magazine cover prices from one country to another since the international customer needs more or fewer units of his national currency to buy the U.S. dollars he needs to pay the international distributor for the magazines he has sold.

Distripress sets trade standards

International newsstand circulation has one additional unique factor—the annual Distripress Congress. Distripress is the trade association of publishers, importers, exporters and suppliers involved in worldwide publishing. Distripress members are from all six continents.

Once each year, Distripress holds a working convention to discuss magazine allotments, trade terms, and all of the critical factors of business which distance makes difficult to discuss in person during the remainder of the year. These discussions are formal in nature, and a convention hall is set aside in which each member has a table with his firm's name and his nation's flag displayed.

Through the Distripress Congress, publishers involved in international sales have the unique opportunity to debate, discuss and resolve most of the business matters which will smooth the following year's business.

International newsstand circulation, then, is characterized by a slower but more stable pattern of business. The vast distances to which magazines must be shipped create a longer time frame in which to do business, but sales are more efficient and the cost of doing business is lower.

Such sales can add more than 10 percent to a publisher's newsstand sales volume, and international newsstand circulation can be and is, for most publishers, profitable circulation.

A guide to international distribution

By Tom Tully

Mention International Distribution over lunch at a publishing conference and you might get a knowledgeable nod, a few comments, and half a dozen blank stares: INTERNATIONAL DISTRIBUTION!?! Visions come to mind of foreign mail regulations, customs inspection, exchange rates, currency, multiple documentation, long distance expenses, loss of on-site control, interpreters, and unsophisticated postal services. Pushing the fog aside, however, we *can* take the capitals out of international distribution.

Who needs a foreign distribution system? Today, consumers, businesses, and technological industries are setting sights beyond U.S. borders in order to increase exports and revenues. Advances in communication are creating easier access to new markets in a shrinking world. But before they can sell their products overseas, manufacturers must deliver their marketing, advertising and promotion campaigns. Publications sold to subscribers directly or via newsstands, promotional letters, brochures and other printed matter are a major medium for international marketing. In addition to resources, scheduling, and the costs involved in choosing a distribution system, publishers contend with the inevitable cultural, economic and political disparities between countries.

Foreign distribution is by no means an easy nut to crack. But if you know what you're dealing with, if you are well-informed and well-equipped, you are on your way to international "Savoir Faire."

Approaching international distribution

So one day you're happily planning your delivery in the U.S. and the next day you're expanding to mail to 10-, 20-, 30-, or 40,000 foreign subscribers. You are now going to distribute overseas!

Your approach to international distribution depends on the nature of your product (content, size, weight), the total number of subscribers, the volume to each foreign country, the time frame for delivery, and, of course, your budget. Generally speaking, the greater the volume and the denser the concentration in particular foreign markets, the more efficient your distribution system. Ten thousand foreign subscribers concentrated in Europe will afford you volume discounts, centralized services, and other distribution options not possible with a foreign distribution of 2,000 scattered throughout the world.

Whatever your circulation spread is, your distribution network will fall into one of the following categories:
1) The USA as home base.
2) Ocean freight from the USA.
3) International hub delivery from a major foreign distribution point.
4) Direct air freight to individual countries.
5) Combination international hub and direct air freight.
6) International printing and distribution.

From the U.S.A.

The United States Postal Service provides several methods for distributing magazines and other printed materials abroad. The least expensive and slowest method is surface or sea mail. Via this system, foreign-destined publications are transported from all over the United States to one of three major foreign distribution centers located in New York, New Orleans, and Oakland, California. Mail is containerized at these centers and loaded onto ocean vessels which transport the material to your destination daily, weekly or monthly, depending on the country to which it is going.

Because of this varied schedule, delivery standards for surface mail are not published or guaranteed. Since delivery of your publication could take two or three months if you miss a monthly sailing, this distribution method is generally used by monthly magazines that have small foreign circulations.

A much faster, more expensive method is that of Air Printed Matter (APM), which delivers your publication within approximately three to five days at about five or six times the cost of surface mail. Air Printed Matter provides air service to your destination where, as with the surface method, your mail is processed and delivered through the local postal system. However, unlike surface mail, which is usually packaged in inexpensive sleeve

369

wrappers, envelopes are recommended to protect foreign mail sent via Air Printed Matter.

The obvious gap in the cost and delivery times between these two services has prompted the development of a middle ground service at a middle ground price. As members of the Joint Industry/Postal Service Task Force, McGraw-Hill and other major publishers developed between 1978 and 1980 the lastest system: International Surface Air Lift (ISAL).

ISAL offers speedier but slightly more expensive delivery: it delivers your publication in about one week at two to three times the rate of U.S. surface mail by airlifting to the destination and surface processing through the local postal system. There are some restrictions involved in using this method, however, such as special handlings, minimum weight requirements, limited origins, and a specific list of available destinations. Nevertheless, ISAL is a great alternative for the publication and promotion mailer. Since all printed matter outside of personal correspondence is eligible for this service, and the restrictions are loosening, even smaller, more tightly budgeted publishers may soon find this expedient method within their reach.

If your magazine were an ounce heavier or lighter, which method would you choose? Surface mail and Air Printed Matter are costed by the piece in two-ounce increments from four to 32 ounces. ISAL is based on total weight and costed by the pound. Your true cost per copy is computed by adding total overall costs which include handling, wrapping, enveloping, transporting, follow-through, and monitoring. The lighter the weight of your piece, the more desirable the ISAL method becomes.

ISAL: hope for the future

ISAL began with three origin cities (New York, Chicago, Houston) and eight direct destinations (Australia, Brazil, England, France, Germany, Holland, Italy and Japan). In October 1981, ISAL expanded to include 35 countries, with France and London as transit points for onward forwarding.

The Postal Service is currently posing a 750-pound-per destination minimum on all direct shipments except for users who meet the minimum criteria by combining their material. With the growth of such user support, the ISAL program will be able to provide a worldwide distribution network by which its users can reach the most inaccessible places within a reasonable time and cost framework.

Rates are twofold: per pound and per sack. The rate per pound is based on origin/destination mileage and the rate per sack is $1 for 22 to 66 pounds. In addition, you receive a 10 percent discount if you make up direct sacks to one addressee (M Bags) because terminal dues are not applicable.

If ISAL is right for you, then take the following preparatory steps before launching off:

First, in order to meet eligibility requirements, determine the number of pieces and the weight per destination of your shipments.

Second, get your free ISAL mailing permit.

Third, make sure your printer and postal traffic manager understand the method by which the publications or printed material you are sending are to be prepared. Also, ensure that the necessary paperwork involved in indicating the pieces, weight, origin, destination, applicable postage, and other tracking information is prepared and that the printer makes you aware of any additional charges this preparation will incur.

Fourth, review with your fulfillment house any label separations—by country—that need to be made and any city sorts you desire in order to improve delivery service when your material reaches the host post office at the other end.

Finally, arrange to transport your shipment to an ISAL AMF (Air Mail Facility) where it will be received, verified, and processed.

Your ISAL shipments are called in and bookings are confirmed through a computer tracking terminal in Washington, D.C. This system can monitor and trace information on the actual flight and arrival time of your material. However, it would also be useful for you to implement your own mail monitoring program as a back-up to pinpoint actual delivery.

For example, branch offices of McGraw-Hill report on actual delivery date and condition of materials on receipt. If branch offices are not available, you can record delivery standards by return post card responses or selected first class sampling letters. *Business Week, Aviation Week* and *Electronics* are usually delivered within five to seven days. Delivery to the London area is accomplished in three days about 75 percent of the time.

ISAL is a program worth investigating and supporting when you consider the service, price, monitoring capability, and the one-vendor approach it provides via air freight, terminal dues, customs, and postage—all in one rate. Also appealing is its acceptance of all printed matter—separate or mixed—and its potential for developing into a worldwide distribution system.

Ocean freight

There are many advantages to hiring a private transportation service to handle your international distribution needs rather than operating through the U.S. Postal Service; more and more publishers are choosing this route. This method affords the user greater control over the operation and provides faster service since shipments can be made directly to your ports of exit. For example, you would be informed of all scheduled passenger lines and cargo lines to your desired destinations and therefore would be better equipped to plan the most direct and economical routes.

International hub delivery

The gap between news making and news reporting is rapidly closing as publishers are improving their electronic transmission of publication editorial film to outlying printing plants. However, modes of transportation and distribution have always been the time catcher of international publishers. Once the magazine is produced, it can be delivered to foreign countries overnight by air transportation via international hub delivery. This service provides sorting, wrapping, enveloping, and labeling services as well as customs handling, local post office deposits, return of undeliverables, address changes and other special handlings.

International hub delivery is already offered in Amsterdam (KLM, Bleckmann & Bleckmann, Smeets, WTC Air Freight) and in London (Mercury Mailing). Many of the companies with this service also handle advertising promotion letters, brochures, and catalogs. Each vendor provides for each publisher's particular needs.

Some distribution services cater to limited geographical areas. Japan, Hong Kong and Singapore, for example, provide economical hub service to Asia by utilizing economical labor and lower postage rates. Some services offer Surface Air Lift (SAL) or Accelerated Surface Post (ASP), which forwards shipments by air or surface mail.

International hub delivery provides for your printer to carton your bound magazines so that they can be transported by truck to the nearest international airport. Your product is flown to its destination where your foreign handling agent clears customs. Mailing labels with instructions are sent ahead or with the magazine shipment. At the agent's facilities, copies are sorted, wrapped, enveloped (using stock which has been supplied or ordered in advance), addressed, and deposited for forwarding at the local post office.

Distribution via international hub delivery is achieved in two to three days in many key cities. Costs range from 70 cents per copy for a four-ounce magazine sent via surface mail to $5 for a 12-ounce magazine going air mail. This covers all postage, handling, air freight, trucking, customs and handling services. Air freight charges range from 50 cents to $2 per pound, depending on your total volume and airline weight break categories.

Greater volume discounts can be secured if you consolidate and containerize your packages either on your own or through a freight forwarding agent. This may also provide you with improved service through regular frequency and bookings of easily handled airline containers. Remember, airlines love printed matter freight due to its density and adherence to an air cargo manager's dream: high weight, low volume, more money.

Direct air service

If the density of your circulation and the delivery time call for more immediate action, individual direct air service to the various countries may be an answer. Your magazines can be cartoned as bound copies or be pre-addressed and wrapped depending on the service you have contracted. McGraw-Hill maintains direct air service to Israel, Brazil, Colombia, Mexico, Venezuela, Argentina, Japan, Hong Kong, Malaysia, Singapore, Thailand, India, Philippines, Taiwan and Indonesia. Depending on distance and time changes, air freight publications arrive at their destination within one to three days.

If you choose to use direct air service to a number of countries, consider including label splits by country in order to aid your printing plant. Also search for a good trucking firm and air freight forwarding agent to sort your material out correctly and make out the proper documentation.

Be prepared to deal with a number of vendors, foreign currency and exchange rates. Names of vendors can be obtained through recommendations by fellow publishers, freight forwarders, airline and other transportation customer service representatives. In addition, you can check *Who's Who in Distripress*, the directory of foreign publishers, and distributors/agents.

Combination international hub and direct air service

As your international market expands geographically, you may find that a combination of international hub service and direct air shipment suits your needs perfectly. If you have a concentration of copies in Europe and the Far East, for example, you could provide direct air service to selected Far Eastern countries and develop a special hub delivery system for Europe. This would service the majority of your market on a two- to five-day basis. The balance would be forwarded via surface mail from the hub point for delivery within one to five weeks.

Though you have already invested money in air freight to get copies to the hub point, this service is much faster than the one- to three-month service you would probably receive from the U.S.A. via surface mail. You may also elect to forward mail from your hub point via air mail for three- to five-day delivery. Remember that service standards are not always published or guaranteed, so develop your own testing and sampling measures.

As your circulation in a particular country or area grows, you may want to expand your services to another direct air delivery point. Europe and the Far East have a variety of vendors for hub or direct air service to various countries around the world. The South American and African countries offer direct air services, but no major hub service. As the market grows in this hemisphere, hub service will become available to fill this gap. In the future, we may see the development of European, Asian, and Latin American hubs in a three-pronged fist-and-fingers type of global coverage.

International printing and distribution

Some publishers will always consider foreign circulation a section or edition of an American magazine. But others in the general business, consumer, management, plastics and computer industries have developed publications which are large enough to consider international printing and distribution. McGraw-Hill's *International Management* and *Modern Plastics International*, for instance, are printed in and distributed from Europe. After comparing printing, paper and distribution costs in the United States with those of an international operation, the *MPI* publisher decided to move operations to Switzerland and establish a worldwide distribution point out of Amsterdam. *International Management*, which is printed in three languages, maintains two printing and distribution points—one in the Netherlands, the other in Ireland.

The key to developing an economic overview of the bottom line costs of publishing, whether on a domestic or an international level, is in evaluating the interrelationship between printing and paper costs, the location of your operation, and the costs to distribute to your distribution area.

Too often, decisions to relocate or make major changes are based on a limited study of printing, paper or distribution costs. For example, without taking in the total overview, you might make the mistake of spending $100,000 to meet the delivery standards of a new plant which saves you $50,000 in printing costs. The bottom line, of course, is that you have lost rather than gained $50,000.

Evaluating vendors

Know what your needs are and be demanding. Ask the appropriate persons for a step-by-step rundown on the procedure for physically distributing on an international level. These might include the freight forwarders, airline cargo representatives, transportation sales people, postal service operators, and management people; also, other publishers, circulation managers, distribution directors, foreign agents, and the Department of Commerce. Cover all bases. Make personal visits to various facilities, talk with the people, and observe first-hand the workings of their operations. If the firm does not have a branch office in the United States, long distance phone calls, telexes and air mail letters may have to do, but they can still be effective.

Establish your own units of measure and itemized checklist of services by which to evaluate the bids you receive from vendors. Reading them can make your choice difficult; often vendors submit different units for measuring their service and rates. You may want to request that mailing, addressing, labeling, stamping and wrapping rates be submitted by cost-per-thousand, cost-per-piece, or cost-per-pound. Be sure to note any additional handling charges for airport pickup, customs clearance, mail sorting, local post office delivery, telegrams confirming the handling of shipments, and other services. The currency and terms for exchange rate should also be clearly stated.

In the case of a language barrier, find an in-house interpreter or an outside firm to translate the written communications between you and your vendor so that there is no mistaking your needs and specifications. Request references from the vendor and check them out. Compare how the product and service requirements of his firm compare with yours. If this does not apply to your situation, then consider making sample test mailings before you commit yourself to a major change in your distribution methods.

Solicit numerous bids

Of final priority is rate negotiations. Solicit numerous bids to find out the general market price for services. While it is fairly common practice to reject the highest bid, it is also important to be wary of the lowest bid. Vendors often bid low initially to gain your business and then within six to 12 months raise their prices or introduce new service charges.

Whether you choose to work by contract or simply by a letter of agreement, establish rate stability. It will be much easier for you to plan and forecast if you know your rates may change quarterly, half-yearly, or annually. Also, determine which rates are negotiable. Some costs are established and less controllable, such as the postage in certain countries. Others, like pickup, delivery, and wrapping, are more flexible. Use this information as leverage in your negotiations.

Understanding your specific needs

Having done your homework on the available vendors, services, and related costs involved in distributing your product internationally, you are ready to decide if this is a desirable route for you to take. If so, it is now time to choose which method you will use.

Your goal is clear: get the best service for the most attractive price. Your delivery target dates, budget, circulation makeup and the weight and classification of your pieces will dictate the right method for your product. Does your product require daily, weekly, or monthly delivery? Perhaps you can live with a three-week delivery schedule on a normal basis, but twice a year you require faster service for your promotion mailing or convention issues.

At these times, you could air mail your copies from a hub point rather than via surface mail. Consider where your mail is going. A density of copies sent to Europe or the Far East affords you hub or direct service. If time is a priority and your market is in South America, then direct air service or air printed matter from the U.S.A. is appropriate. If time is flexible, surface mail via a European hub point may be the answer, providing one to five weeks delivery service.

Consider the category of your publication. Determine if you are eligible for the publishers' periodical rate or if you must pay the printed matter surface rate. Do you meet the requirements for International Surface Air Lift? If so, you may want to improve on ISAL service by making sorts according to city. Examine the restrictions of each method and see if you can overcome them or obtain exceptions.

Are you in a position to negotiate rates with air carriers? Do you mail in quantities that afford you container air freight or special commodity rates or will you be charged for minimums, extra consolidation handlings, and delays? Make sure there is an appropriate backup system and that you have contingency plans in the event of labor strikes and inclement weather conditions. More important, have a contact who will advise you of such problems and line up alternatives should a vendor go out of business.

Once you are satisfied that your vendors meet your requirements, be ready to implement the project. Inform the appropriate people in your operations groups of who will be handling the distribution. Ensure that they fully understand what service is being contracted and how the product will move through the system. Also, make sure you are sufficiently staffed to properly document and trace your shipments. Now that your system works on paper, you are ready for start-up.

Implementation and control

Set a target date for implementing your project and maintain tight control of it from the outset. Run through all procedures with vendors and staff and prepare in advance written instructions and guidelines for each party to follow.

Your control over a successful start-up of your international distribution scheme will be greatly enhanced if you have developed a rapport with vendors who thoroughly understand all of your requirements. Do not forget your vendors after the initial start-up. Continue to meet with them and update the status of service. This will solidify your working association and be an asset when problems prompt you to ask that special favor.

Within the system itself, you can achieve quality control over the air and ocean shipments of your freight as well as the actual mailing operation. Computer tracking terminals can trace freight shipments going to foreign destinations by identifying their airway bill numbers or ocean bills of lading. In order to monitor the operation, you may require the service to log in the number of pieces, their weight, the number of mailing labels and arrival date, and the date for actual deposit into the local post office.

These reports can be telephoned, telexed, or air mailed back to you as they are confirmed. Your overseas branch office may add names to the regular mailing list of those to receive copies through the system and report back to you on the delivery time and condition of your product. Enclose a response card with your product or mail it to a selected group of your readers for feedback. If it is within the policy of your company, offer them gift incentives or discounts on their subscription renewals.

Set performance guidelines

How well your material is handled depends solely on the performance guidelines you set for your vendors. Ensure that each knows his place in the assembly line process.

For instance, on airfreighting shipments, inform your trucker when the product is expected to be ready at your printing plant and give the trucker's schedule to your freight forwarder. Check to see that the airline has scheduled space for your product and also a backup flight. Make sure that your foreign agent is aware of this schedule as well as your delivery requirements and your delivery checkup system. Responsibility begins when each vendor knows that the next vendor in line is depending on the successful completion of his part of the job.

Open communication and support must come from you the user in order to reinforce this high standard of service. Begin with supplying each vendor with a 24-hour emergency phone list of your distribution personnel. When they call up about a problem, ensure that your staff is well-equipped to provide the necessary decision-making to resolve it. If you do not insist on such control, your vendors will make their own decisions about these matters without regard for their impact on the bottom line.

Set priorities for decisions that must be made about common problems. For example, you might devise a formula for your trucker to follow in the event of printer delays that jeopardize air freight shipments: for a projected delay of less than two hours, you tell him to follow his regular pickup schedule; for a four-hour delay, have him send one truck to pick up two hours later than the normal schedule and another backup truck to pick up the balance.

Maintain good records

It will be the time-consuming but all-important responsibility of your staff to maintain records. Require proofs of mailing from your foreign agents, bills of lading from your printer indicating the pieces and weights of all outbound shipments, and airway bills from the airlines matching quantities on the bills of lading. The key to resolving the inevitable problems incurred due to lost shipments, damaged cartons, and product shortages will be keeping good paper trails. These will also be a checklist to audit your invoices for services performed.

Monitor the cost control area carefully to examine such factors as the cycle of payment most advantageous to your firm's cash flow. Some of your vendors may operate on a short cash flow and require a short turnaround on payment. You may want to develop an advance deposit system or a priority payment list for them, but negotiate bills weekly, bi-weekly, or monthly as appropriate. The waiting period might be shortened if they accept payment at a branch office in the United States.

Set up separate accounts for your vendors so that you can identify their individual per-issue and cumulative charges. Decide on a standard currency to be billed in and a method for itemizing your bills to indicate the different services supplied. Since price increases do not always occur across the board, you may want to separate the charges for sorting, labeling, wrapping and postage. You may also want to negotiate a flat monthly exchange rate or accept the daily exchange rate posted in major newspapers.

Keep informed

Familiarize yourself with the cultural, economic, and political aspects of the countries you will be distributing to in order to enhance your overall expertise in international distribution. Knowing the temperament of the people you work with may improve your ability to communicate with them and gain their cooperation.

Be aware of any working standards which might affect or conflict with your own—such as their labor relations or holidays. Keep informed about the inflation rate in each country and how this rate fits into a historical perspective. This will enable you to better forecast rate increases.

Educate yourself on how closely the government monitors business and the policy on competition with foreign importers. Canada, for example, does not allow regional advertising to target exclusively to the Canadian market. Canadian postage rates are considerably higher for publications that do not originate within its borders.

From a broader perspective, be aware that terminal dues, which have recently increased postage rates in many countries, may greatly affect your foreign distribution costs. Terminal dues are those charges paid by one country to another in order to equalize mailing costs incurred when it receives more mail than it sends. In 1981, the international currency for terminal dues increased from 1.5 to 5.5 gold francs per kilo of excess mail. (Forty U.S. cents is equivalent to one gold franc, about $1 to a pound.) Since the United States is a major exporter of mail, increases in terminal dues caused a dramatic rise in its foreign surface, air printed matter, and ISAL rates in January 1981.

The Universal Postal Union (UPU), the postal organization which sets standards for international mail, convenes every five years in order to set terminal dues. Every three years it tests the volume of mail flow. In July 1981, the UPU revised Article 23 of its bylaws to state that "a member country shall not be bound to forward or deliver to the addressee letter-post items which senders resident in its territory post or to be posted in a foreign country with the object of profiting by the lower charges in force there." This change was spearheaded by objections from France, Germany, and Norway, but no other objections of any magnitude have arisen since. Nevertheless, for appropriate decision-making, it is important to be informed about international issues like terminal dues and Article 23.

New opportunities and developments

Once your distribution system is established, continue to look for new opportunities and developments. Competition will provide an incentive for you to keep your service the best available. Let your vendors know there are others soliciting your business. On the other hand, do not develop a reputation for changing vendors frequently. Commitment is necessary on both sides in order to develop support and a high grade of service.

Deregulation in the trucking and airline industries should allow you to be more demanding, and reaching for the stars can often get you to the moon. Keep abreast of developments by attending seminars and trade shows, joining postal committees and task forces. Subscribe to trade journals that have an international emphasis and follow legislation that affects international distribution.

Services can be expanded or developed only when publishers make their needs known. The ISAL program was a direct result of an industry need voiced through the Joint Industry/Postal Service Task Force. Major mailers are currently developing a committee to discuss the impact of terminal dues and possibly create a forum to present publisher views to the UPU in 1983.

Influence is often difficult to measure, yet managements clamor for results. Patience and perseverance may be the only weapons that can succeed when changes require major institutions and industries such as worldwide postal services and transportation groups to cooperate and coordinate programs.

Is it all worth it?

While the United States grapples with a recession, American business must continue to look to the future in order to survive. The foreign market has been established and publishers have already developed international distribution systems. Examples are McGraw-Hill's *International Management* and *Modern Plastics International* publications. Many McGraw-Hill publications air freight 80,000 to 100,000 copies weekly for international hub or direct air service. Some of these include *Business Week International*, *Aviation Week and Space Technology*, and *Electronics*.

These publications enjoy a healthy advertising revenue as a result of their investment in international distribution. The market coverage in some industries has expanded to the point that publications are printing European, Asian and Latin American editions to focus editorial and advertising input in these areas. *Business Week International*, for instance, prints an international edition and a European edition in each issue, an Asian edition every other issue, and a Latin American edition once a month. *International Management* publishes an English edition with sections for Europe, Africa and the Pacific, a Spanish edition, and an Arabic edition.

Yes, international distribution is complex, but not necessarily confusing. Define your goals, recognize your problems, investigate your options, anticipate the future. With patience and perseverance you, too, can be an international distributor.

An international success story

By Ronald T. Scott

Every specialty publisher would love to double his newsstand sale in less than a year, but very few realize that this can be done without adding a single copy to United States or Canadian circulation. *Astronomy* magazine, however, is a good example of a magazine that went from zero to 15,000 copies in circulation through the international single-copy channel of distribution, all in one year.

In back of this amazing success story is a lot of planning, a lot of organizing, and a lot of discipline.

Astronomy is a highly specialized magazine designed to appeal to the advanced amateur astronomer. Before the magazine considered an increase in newsstand sales, its circulation had more than doubled, from 40,000 to 90,000 copies, including a sale of 6,500 copies on the newsstand through Eastern News Distributors.

When the publisher realized that there was substantially more potential for newsstand sales of *Astronomy*, he began to explore the possibility of increasing newsstand sales through Eastern. However, when the opportunity for international sales was mentioned, his response was enthusiastic and he decided to develop a plan for increasing newsstand sales through both channels of distribution: domestic and international.

Sensitivity to the market

The first step in the plan was a thorough analysis of the magazine. After several conversations, the publisher, the editors and the graphic design people all agreed that the magazine's cover did not reflect the exciting material inside the magazine. Faced with the challenge of designing a cover that could communicate what was going on inside the magazine without violating the magazine's quality and ambiance, they developed a new cover treatment. Now, *Astronomy*'s covers are informative and exciting, yet they manage to preserve the integrity of the magazine as its creators envisioned it.

Once it was clear that there was an exciting product to present, the publisher decided to try the magazine in the international market. At the Distripress convention in Torremolinos, Spain, the product was shown to a selected group of international wholesalers from a variety of countries to determine their interest. The reaction was uniformly positive.

Now, two critical factors were in place: a more exciting presentation of the product and a positive reaction from a sampling of the marketplace.

International distributors contacted

At this point four international distributors were contacted and told the story. Ultimately a contract was signed with Boarts International. An information package was then prepared for Boarts so that their salespeople around the world would have a basic and clear understanding of the product and the types of consumers it would attract.

Boarts then went to work soliciting orders from international wholesalers throughout the world, using its foreign-based sales personnel as well as the mail. This was followed by a well-organized presentation during the next Distripress convention in San Francisco. The results were very good, exceeding the expectations of both those at *Astronomy* and at Boarts.

At this point, *Astronomy* has been offered in the international market for less than one year, and is already selling 15,000 copies. Their objective during this first year has been to build volume and to determine the level of sale within the 31 countries where *Astronomy* is now being offered for sale. During the second year they will be concentrating on adjusting, revising, and fine tuning the efficiency of sale, and targeting countries that have reasonable potential.

Astronomy fits the classic profile of a magazine with high potential for international consumers. First, it is aimed at an audience with a high level of education, an audience therefore more likely to speak at least two languages, including English. Second, it is aimed at an audience which is relatively affluent and therefore able to purchase a high quality, high priced product. Finally, it is aimed at an audience with a sufficient amount of leisure time to devote to a specialized area.

But *Astronomy* is also indicative of the kind of successful and profitable sales volume available to United States publishers in the international market if they prepare an organized and disciplined launch. There are many special interests that flow across national boundaries and leap the barriers of language, and there are literally thousands of new special interest markets being developed as a result of these trends. Furthermore, there is in place an international channel of distribution which is capable of matching these special interests with the incredible variety of products that serve these interests.

This opportunity for significant increases in newsstand circulation of specialty publishers is waiting, ready and able to deliver. *Astronomy* magazine is a classic example of a coordinated effort by publishers, editors and graphic design people seizing that opportunity.

What's your international newsstand potential?

By Douglas Learner

Imagine your magazine on the local newsstand in Sydney . . . or Bangkok . . . or Cape Town. Does the idea excite you? Does the prospect of international sales and the money it can bring in appeal to your business instincts?

If you are a publisher who has not yet become involved in international sales, you probably know very little about the sales potential in overseas markets. Unfortunately, many publishers who begin to consider such involvement become frustrated at what seems like such a complex subject. For such publishers, however, there are a number of international distributors in the United States who are well-versed in the intricacies of foreign distribution.

"American publishers who do not look into foreign single-copy sales might be overlooking a great opportunity," says Ronald T. Scott, a publishing consultant specializing in both domestic and international single-copy sales. Scott explains:

"First, the international market is basically a newsstand market. Rather than buying subscriptions for home delivery, the prospective reader purchases his magazine at the local kiosk.

"Second, the highly specialized foreign magazine does not do well in its own country because there is usually not a large enough audience to support it," he continues. "Two percent of America is a huge market, but two percent of France isn't much.

"On the other hand, there is a distinct market overseas for American special interest magazines," he says. "People in the international market who have an interest in specialized magazines are generally well-educated, affluent, and multi-lingual. Chances are they speak English.

"Finally, there is little risk for the publisher who does get involved overseas because of the nature of the international distribution system."

Each country a different market

The key to understanding the international newsstand market is to realize that it is really many different markets, with each country a different market.

"You cannot compare, for example, Europe and America," says Heiner Eggert, vice president and circulation director, newsstand sales for Gruner & Jahr's *Parents* magazine. "Each European country is completely different from every other European country. The people are different, the attitudes are different, the lifestyles are different."

William Yokel, circulation manager for *Scientific American,* says that each country has to be handled separately. "There are no distributors that reach across national borders," he comments.

To Paul Hamrock, manager, newsstand sales at *Business Week,* "it's like there are 50 wholesalers, only each wholesaler is a different country."

How the system works

Each country has its own distribution system, usually consisting of two or three national distributors (foreign distributors) that supply magazines to local distributors. These foreign distributors obtain their U.S. titles through an international distributor who represents U.S. magazines.

For each title, the foreign distributor pays the international distributor a price roughly equivalent to the amount paid by a U.S. wholesaler. The publisher will then be paid by the international distributor. (A publisher's contract with the international distributor should spell out that he's to be paid in American currency, advises Scott.)

Magazines to be shipped overseas are sent to a port —usually New York, Philadelphia or San Francisco—where they are collected by a freight forwarder and separated by country. The magazines are then shipped overseas, with the foreign distributor paying the freight costs. Once overseas, they are distributed for sale throughout the distribution network by the foreign distributor. Returns are handled as they are in the United States, with either affidavits or cover strips, depending on the foreign distributor.

Low-risk venture

The foreign distributor's handling of freight charges is the reason for the low risk involved for a magazine publisher. The only cost incurred by the publisher is the cost of printing the magazine and having it trucked to the port for shipping.

There is an added advantage for a U.S. publisher: Since the foreign distributor pays for freight and duty on the magazines even if they do not sell, he works hard to maintain a high percent of sale. This creates a "built-in safeguard" in the system, according to Ed Ham, senior vice president, director of international sales at Curtis Circulation Company, because the foreign distributor will not take a greater number of copies than he knows he can sell.

Most U.S. magazines sold on foreign newsstands have a sales percentage between 65- and 70 percent, and a 90-percent sale is not unheard of.

According to Lee Selverne, executive vice president of World Wide Media Services, Inc., an international distributor handling approximately 920 magazines, the high percent of sale overseas—as compared to 37- to 40 percent in the United States—results in a "much higher percent of billed price" for the publisher. Of course, figures will vary from magazine to magazine, depending on cover price, percent of sales both domestically and internationally, and the payment agreement between the publisher and distributors.

Davis Publications, Inc., for example, receives roughly a 20 percent greater net per copy on newsstand sales overseas than it does in the United States, according to Don Gabree, circulation director of newsstand sales at Davis. Davis publishes 25 titles (some are annuals) including *Ellery Queen's Mystery Magazine, Alfred Hitchcock's Mystery Magazine* and *Isaac Asimov's Science Fiction Magazine.*

But the "built-in safeguard" of the international distribution system, and all its benefits, do not come free. According to Scott, it is achieved at the expense of growth.

"International newsstand sales grow much slower than do U.S. newsstand sales," he says, "because the risk of distribution is taken by the foreign distributor who isn't willing to take risks. There is a real trade-off between sales efficiency and growth. In the United States, growth is gained at the expense of efficiency."

The problems

One unavoidable part of the overseas newsstand distribution system is the delay caused by the transcontinental travel and occasional slow distribution in a foreign country. Because of these delays, it can take up to a year for complete returns of an issue to come in. (Some international distributors advance publishers a percentage of expected revenues.)

The situation in Australia exemplifies the extremes a magazine publisher involved in foreign single-copy sales can expect, according to Scott. "First of all," he says, "shipment of the magazine from the U.S. can take four to six weeks. Once in Australia, it may then take another four weeks for distribution throughout the country. The magazine, therefore, may not even go on sale until 10 weeks after the U.S. on-sale date."

For a monthly with a four-week on-sale period, returns cannot possibly begin to come in for almost four months after the U.S. on-sale date. For bimonthlies, the delay is even longer.

Margo Waite, circulation manager of *Cruising World,* which has been distributed overseas since 1975, visited Australia last February and found the November issue of *Cruising World* still on sale. She says it usually takes nine months before she is able to get a good idea of how an issue performed, and over a year to get final figures. Fortunately, she says, the sales performance of magazines sold overseas does not fluctuate as much as it does domestically because of the high sales percentage maintained by the foreign distributor.

Though the time lag causes problems in getting final sales figures, it does not hamper sales as it would in the United States. The real problem, according to Yokel, comes from irregular on-sale dates within a country. "You want your magazine to appear on the newsstand at the same time each month for regular sales," he says. "Unfortunately, delays can be caused by a number of factors, such as missed connections, bad weather, and labor strikes."

For a weekly, the problem is compounded by the need for timeliness. "For a weekly magazine, timeliness is as critical as regularity," says Hamrock. "We should be on sale on a Monday or Tuesday. If it is delayed until Thursday, half our sales are lost."

Getting involved

According to Scott, every publisher should consider the foreign market, although not every magazine will sell well abroad. Thus, before seeking out an international distributor, a publisher must do his homework.

First, a publisher looking overseas should "find out where the market is," says Scott, "just as he would before launching a magazine in the United States. Because of his lack of knowledge of the overseas market, a publisher should take special care to see that standard business practices of seeking information are carried out before making plans and decisions.

"The publisher should sit down with the people at his magazine and ask, 'Are there pockets of people abroad who would be interested in our magazine?' Such information is not difficult to obtain—researching foreign membership in trade associations is one possibility."

Second, a publisher must consider his editorial content. In general, a magazine covering a subject that transcends national boundaries will sell well. Specialized magazines with an affluent and educated readership have excellent potential.

"Not only does a publisher have to consider the editorial content and the potential market, he must also consider the local competition," according to Alan Pardo, president of Boarts International, Inc., which handles over 360 magazines overseas, including *Business Week* and *Scientific American.*

"Women's service magazines tend not to sell proportionately as well in the foreign market," he adds. "Women tend to buy the locally-published product because it deals directly with their concerns."

In most cases, magazines sold overseas carry the same editorial content as their U.S. counterparts. However, a publisher should be prepared to make editorial changes if it is in his interest to do so, according to Scott. "*Astronomy* magazine, overseas for about a year with 14,000 copies, publishes sky charts as an editorial feature," he says. The magazine found that, to sell in the Southern Hemisphere, it would have to publish an additional chart, viewing the stars from that part of the world. The staff of *Astronomy* determined the cost of printing the extra chart and figured out how many copies would have to be sold in the Southern Hemisphere to make it economically worth their while to print the chart.

According to Robert A. Maas, president of Astro-Media Corp., publisher of *Astronomy,* the southern hemisphere charts were not printed because he was able to get only a modest number of additional orders, "and the net profit from these orders would not pay for the editorial, printing, and insertion costs of the monthly chart." Maas adds that the feasibility of adding the charts to *Astronomy* is periodically considered.

Choosing the distributor

Homework done, the publisher must seek out an international distributor, keeping in mind what the distributor does and how well he may be able to represent the magazine overseas.

Representation involves selling the magazine to foreign distributors, dealing with these distributors to maximize sales, and adjusting the draw from market to market.

According to Selverne, a publisher new to the international system "should speak to someone with credentials, someone who knows the markets." This theme is echoed by many publishers and newsstand directors within the publishing world. "It's like a lot of things," says Maas. "You have to pick people you trust."

When choosing an international distributor, a publisher should carefully examine the prospective company, its reputation, and the people involved, according to Davis Publications' Gabree, who details the items to be considered:

• The company's size, and the number of magazines they represent. ("The larger the company, the more influence it has in the marketplace.")

• The number and quality of their field representatives.

• The experience of the reps.

• The company's reputation and length of time in the marketplace.

• The respect given to the company from wholesalers.

• The financial position of the company.

• The quality of the home office personnel. ("The people directing the traffic.")

John Boyd, general manager at Technical Publishing Group, a subsidiary of the Goldhirsh Group that recently introduced *High Technology* and reintroduced *Technology Illustrated,* recommends that publishers get estimates of anticipated success in particular countries from the prospective international representatives. These figures should then be compared with a publisher's own research and with estimates from other distributors. "It's a difficult decision," he says. "You don't have all that much information to go on. It is a little bit like shooting in the dark—it's scary."

When introduced on international newsstands, *High Technology* and *Technology Illustrated* had a combined draw of 70,000.

The solicitation

Once a publisher chooses an international distributor, the next step in the process is the solicitation: the effort by the international distributor to sell a magazine to a foreign distributor. (Once distribution has begun, the solicitation also becomes the effort to sell more copies to each distributor when sales merit the increase.)

To sell the publisher's product, the international distributor obtains from the publisher a "sales package" which consists of sample copies of the magazine and information about the magazine's sales history in the U.S. This package is relayed to the international distributor's field representatives, who contact the foreign distributors. (International distributors who do not have a field force use solicitation letters to sell each magazine.)

The key, says Pardo, is for the international distributor to locate the right foreign distributors for the magazine. To do this, the distributor will base his selling efforts on sales histories of related magazines in various countries. "You use your knowledge of which particular markets work best with a particular product," he says.

"We can deal with small numbers or large numbers as far as circulation," he continues. "However, most of the publications we distribute overseas must be distributed selectively in each market. You may have foreign distributors who specialize in imported publications, and, in some cases, you may even have distributors who specialize in imported magazines in one specific language.

Such a distributor would be more desirable than the mainline distributor, who is not equipped for small volume, much the same way a large distributor in the U.S. is not equipped for small volume."

Publisher involvement

The initial solicitation should not be the end of the publisher's involvement in selling the magazine, according to Scott. "The first solicitation is only the beginning," he says.

After the first solicitation the publisher should discuss the results with his international distributor, questioning the results in much the same manner a national distributor would be questioned: "Of all the countries you service, how many are buying the magazine?" "Did they order enough copies?" "Did they order too many copies?" "Who didn't buy?" "Of those who didn't buy, who should have bought?" "Why didn't they buy?" "When should they be solicited again?" "What should be done differently in the solicitation?"

Through questions like these, Scott says, a publisher will get the most for his money with the international distributor. "If you're not involved with the international distributor, you're going to get minimal service."

Pardo agress with Scott. "Some publishers are more involved than others," he says. "Many leave the whole process to us and we report to them regularly on the magazine's performance. We like a publisher to be involved since his input can help our efforts."

Once distribution and overseas newsstand sales are under way, the international distributor works to adjust the draw of each country to optimize sales. This adjusting is done country versus country in much the same manner as it might be done county versus county in the United States.

Furthermore, with modern communications technology, the international distributor can adjust a country's draw quickly, to accommodate specific situations, according to Curt Rome, mass market sales director at Feffer & Simons, Inc., which represents over 225 magazines. "For example, the July issue of *Popular Science* had a cover story about an airport in Saudi Arabia," he says. "For that issue we increased the draw in Saudia Arabia from 400 copies to 1,000 copies."

Publishers receive a computer print-out of a magazine's sales on a country by country basis. With this information, the publisher is able to make suggestions to the international distributor concerning draw or representation.

"If we see an area that is not being represented, we'll suggest it," says Waite. "Sometimes, though, there will be a reason why we're not there." Recently, *Cruising World* ceased distribution in a country and was told by its international distributor, Boarts, that the political upheavals in that country were the cause. "I knew about the political problems there," she adds, "but I never thought it would affect magazine sales."

"The only way a publisher can cause critical problems that may lead to failure is by being overly aggressive," says Scott, "by pushing circulation too hard. It is better to do it in a controlled manner, letting the marketplace ask for more."

Selverne says that publishers must "realize that marketing concepts in foreign countries are different than in the United States."

"U.S. publishers have got to take the time to discover the special patterns of distribution in each country," says Yokel. He recounts an episode a few years ago of a publisher who insisted that copies of the magazine be placed on checkout racks in a particular chain of supermarkets in Australia. Against the advice of the international distributor, the publisher forced the issue and, as a result, lost a different retail outlet that took years to regain.

Distripress
One way to meet foreign distributors and gain a greater insight into their markets is to attend the annual Distripress convention of international publishers. The convention is a working meeting of Distripress members. (The convention is open to Distripress members only.)

"Almost all the time at the convention is taken up with meetings between publishers and foreign distributors," says Scott. "You visit with people, show them new products, existing products, look at sales figures, and alter your allocations.

"It is a convention where you can actually write down dollars and cents made," Scott continues. "For example, you can come away and say 'I just increased my allocation in Zimbabwe from 50 copies to 500 copies.' "

If a publisher can not attend a Distripress convention, his international distributor must represent him. "But," says Scott, "the vigor with which he represents you usually depends upon how closely you're associated with him. He represents a lot of magazines, so if you don't go to the convention you have to meet with him beforehand to set up goals and priorities. You want to try to get your magazine on the top of his list."

Benefits
What benefits can the publisher who becomes involved in the foreign single-copy sales market expect?

First, and probably most important, is an increase in "profitable circulation," says Scott. Although most magazines sold overseas have a small circulation (a circulation of 5,000 per title was estimated by Selverne), the overseas copy is more profitable than the domestic copy.

Second, an increase in circulation has a positive effect on ad revenues by increasing the rate base. In addition, the foreign circulation can be presented to advertisers as an added attraction of the magazine in a sales pitch. Foreign circulation can be very valuable to many advertisers.

If the overseas newsstand circulation is large enough, advertising can be sold for the foreign edition alone, thus opening the magazine to advertisers who may not have a reason to advertise in the American market. At *Scientific American,* an advertiser can purchase an ad page in the American edition, the international edition, or both. "That's where we make the profit," says Yokel.

The placement of the magazine on the newsstand, in and of itself, says Scott, is also a plus from the standpoint of product promotion.

At *Astronomy,* Maas expects the sale of editorial-related products, such as posters and calendars, to increase as a result of the international exposure. He also mentions the sale of reprints or reprint rights as possible profit-making activities. In general, he says, the public's continuing awareness of a magazine's ancillary activities overseas helps to increase sales.

Overseas newsstand sales can also help increase foreign subscriptions (which will also raise the magazine's rate base). These subscriptions, from insert cards, should be high-priced subs because of exchange rates, says Scott.

A U.S. publisher can also sign a licensing agreement with a foreign publisher for production of a foreign-language edition of his magazine. Such franchising deals are usually struck once a magazine has established itself overseas, according to Pardo. Such deals usually give the foreign publisher the responsibilities of ad sales, circulation and editorial, he says, while the parent publisher receives a licensing fee.

With the potential opportunities for success in international newsstand sales so great, and with the risks so small, many publishers who have gotten involved are both enthusiastic about future prospects and a bit more realistic in their outlook.

"I think it's easy—there's nothing to it," says Maas in a statement echoed by many publishers involved in foreign newsstand distribution. "I had no idea what the potential market for a magazine like *Astronomy* was, and I imagined large numbers of people all over the world wanting to read the magazine. Now, finding out that there are not many magazines that sell a lot of copies overseas, I'm happy with our draw."

"Even if a publisher does not have a *national* distributor," says Selverne, "he should contact an international distributor. He could be sitting on a gold mine."

Distripress

By Ronald T. Scott

The Distripress convention, the annual meeting of the international publishing and distributing industry, is one of the most fascinating and productive conventions held anywhere in the world.

Imagine listening to international publishers and salespeople switching from French to English, German, Spanish, Dutch, as if it were—as it is—an every day occurrence. Imagine the circulation directors of European distributing companies buying German magazines in the first half hour, Dutch in the second, French in the third, English in the fourth, and Italian in the fifth. Imagine a convention where you can personally conduct specific detail business with customers from as many as fifty countries without even leaving the room.

This is Distripress, the international publishers convention. In 1980, the Distripress convention was held in San Francisco and it attracted over 1,200 registrants with representatives from more than 50 countries. It has indeed become a major event in the international single-copy circulation industry.

Unprecedented opportunity

If you are a publisher or a distributor, there are two important reasons to attend Distripress. First, it gives you the opportunity to discuss your publishing plans for the next 12 months, and to learn from customers the challenges and opportunities that will be available in their countries during the next year. There is an enormous amount of information to be gained from the sometimes casual, sometimes formal meetings with the experts on foreign publications from each of the countries.

The second reason for attending Distripress is that it gives you the opportunity to review with each foreign customer the success (or lack of success) of each of your magazines circulated in his country during the past year. This information, along with your own sales records, is a good indicator of changing customer interest and specific changes in allocation that should be made to take advantage of recent sales trends.

To many, Distripress, with its emphasis on practical business rather than speeches and seminars, is one of the reasons that international sales of U.S. magazines have usually enjoyed a much higher percentage of sale than these same magazines enjoy in the U.S. We realize that this convention is the only opportunity we will have to talk with the wholesaler from Japan, so there is an urgency to doing business at a Distripress convention. Furthermore, each year Distripress becomes larger with more active participants and, as a result, more substantial business is done.

Cover price a threat

Several themes ran through the Distripress meeting, some of which could pose serious difficulties for American magazines in the international marketplace.

The primary concern of international distributors of American magazines has been the substantial increase in U.S. cover prices when compared to those in most of the rest of the world. As U.S. cover prices continue to increase dramatically, we become less and less competitive in the international marketplace, and this is having more and more of a dampening effect on sales volume.

It seems to me that two responses to rapidly increasing cover prices are beginning to emerge. First, there is a trend toward licensing rights and editorial to foreign publishers. The second is to price magazines for the international marketplace with a different cost basis than that used in the domestic market.

In the licensing area, there are certain categories of American magazines where American expertise is predominant, and foreign publishers will better serve their own marketplace by licensing access to this expertise, rather than attempting to organize and develop their own. While most of these licenses are for foreign languages, there is also a trend for licensing to a publisher in Great Britain, giving that publisher all marketing outside the U.S., Canada and U.S. possessions.

In the pricing area, some publishers are beginning to realize that if they don't find a better cost basis on which to price their U.S. magazines for international distribution, they will ultimately lose their international marketplace.

International publishers and distributors are still concerned, of course (as they have been since 1973), with the increases in ocean freight shipping rates. These increases are tied mostly to increases in the cost of fuel and to fluctuating currency exchange rates, and they have made future buying decisions even more speculative.

Indeed, there are changing social and economic trends in almost every country which is a member of Distripress. Most of these changes can be opportunities for U.S. publishers and U.S. magazines. And there is no better opportunity to learn about the rapidly changing international marketplace than the productive, fascinating Distripress convention.

Fulfillment

The future of fulfillment

By Willis R. Rivinus

In an era of instant gratification, magazine fulfillment seems to be moving backward. ("Please allow up to eight weeks for delivery of your first copy," printed unobtrusively on most subscription order blanks.) Furthermore, the impersonality and inflexibility of computers constantly bedevil the subscriber who has a problem.

Time was when service was faster and real people solved fulfillment problems. But, in all fairness to the fulfillment manager, that was before computers replaced Addressograph plates. That was before publishers mailed hundreds of millions of promotion pieces almost simultaneously around December 26 with the resulting huge order entry load. That was before they promoted gift mailings with their complex record-keeping requirements. That was before publishers distributed multi-magazine offers with combination pricing. That was before as many people took as many magazine subscriptions. That was before the consumer became so accustomed to sending in for free trial copies.

The fact is: magazine subscription fulfillment is vastly larger and more complex than it used to be. Fifty million subscriber records on a computer file that would fit into your kitchen. On-line access to every one of those records 24 hours a day. Mail processing which runs into the hundreds of thousands of pieces a day. On-line management inquiry for statistical information. At a cost which is actually declining every year!

But, so much for the present. What of the future? What will fulfillment be like next year? In five years? What trends are evident in consumer purchasing? In fulfillment management? In magazine promotion? In equipment? In ancillary services?

Every phase of magazine fulfillment is due for change—order entry, cash flow, initiation of a new order, the customer record, customer service, label preparation, billing and renewal lettershop, equipment, management control, ancillary services, and more. The question is not whether these will change. No one in the business doubts the change. The real question is how, where and when.

As I look into my crystal ball, and as I talk with some of the most perceptive leaders in the field, I see six primary trends for the immediate future. These are the leverage points where publishers and circulation directors can expect dramatic changes to improve or hurt their business.

Equipment improvement

New developments in equipment are driving the immediate growth of the fulfillment industry. Changes in equipment are revolutionizing order/payment entry, customer record maintenance, and customer name printing. This is where the greatest effort and investment are being applied by the manufacturers at the fewest control points, the fulfillment centers. This is where the fulfillment director can expect to cut present costs for present work in half, improve his ultimate performance time in some cases by weeks, and significantly expand the services he offers.

Order and payment entry are undergoing major innovations. Turn-around documents and optical character reading are the order of the day. White Mail is great and represents found money, but if those multi-million piece publisher mailings in January and July weren't machine readable and machine processable, the whole industry would come to a halt in just a few days.

Many fulfillment operations are already scanning more than 75 percent of their new orders and payments, and that percentage can only go up. A 30 percent increase in mail volume, subject to better initial selectivity and higher postal rates, with 90 percent of it machine scanable is predicted in the next five years.

New mail processing machines are entering the market to automate the mail opening, outserting, editing, posting, balancing, microfilming, batching, and depositing functions into one continuous pass. IBM has one. Charter Data Products has another. All such machines are designed to simplify and speed up the processing of large volumes of orders or remittances. Standard orders or exact payments are entered automatically. Only the exceptions are processed by hand.

More and more of the subscription agencies are clearing orders on magnetic tape, saving large amounts of handling and processing time. As computer costs continue to drop, more clearings will take place on tape.

Some of the larger service bureaus are setting up satellite input stations to receive and enter orders which are then fed at high speed to a central computer which acts as the data bank. Charter Data Services has input offices in Bergenfield, N.J.; Toronto, Canada; Harlan, Iowa; and Long Beach, Calif. Thus, the publishers can maintain closer control over the input and the mail workload is distributed where there are ready labor markets.

And what of the future trends in computer main frames? Bigger, faster, less cost per transaction—the same trends which have been evident in the computer field for the last 20 years. As Frank Brooks, chief of the in-house fulfillment operation at Rodale Press points out, "Computer power is becoming steadily less expensive than people power."

Order entry is important, but automation has had a major impact here already. The main frame computing speeds and expanding storage capacities are also significant, but the improvements, though great, are less dramatic. It is in the output printing areas that I see the biggest changes in production and service time coming. These changes will primarily affect subscription copy mailing and the preparation of bills and renewals.

The paper mailing label as we know it today is going to disappear—from the promotion piece, from the subscription copy of a magazine, from the billing or renewal notice. A.B. Dick has already discontinued manufacturing and servicing its high speed line of label printers. Meanwhile, the opportunities for direct addressing on the magazine are really impressive, and they are already being pioneered by the catalog marketers. The subscriber name and address can be imprinted, by jet or by laser, directly on the magazine as it moves through the bindery line. Behind the scenes the central fulfillment computer has selected the name, analyzed the mailing details of routing, bagging, and labeling, and is communicating directly to the bindery line—at a time saving of more than a week in many cases.

With jet or laser printing, procedures can be simplified, time- and people-consuming steps can be eliminated and customer input can be processed faster. The master customer file can accept new orders and updates up to 5 p.m. one day. The bindery line can start printing and mailing the new issue at 9 a.m. the next day. Overnight, the fulfillment computer has performed the selection, calculated the statistics, and transmitted these instructions to the bindery printer's computer. That's automation.

When it comes to preparing bills and renewal notices in the lettershop, consider the following scenario (which is already technically feasible if not yet in full operation): As input to the renewal mailing machine we see a magnetic tape listing of names and addresses to be billed, a blank roll of paper, and a set of control codes. The machine is programmed to read the name, ascertain which promotion effort the person is due, pick up some personalization data, laser print the letter and the order card, fold, cut, insert with a waiting business reply envelope into a waiting window outer envelope, sort, tie, and bag for mailing, all in one continuous operation. Each letter is different. Yet the output for a day's processing is in Zip and carrier-route sort, ready for delivery by the post office. File maintenance will be closed in the morning; bills will be mailed in the afternoon.

The traditionally labor-intensive lettershop effort is automated, streamlined, and simplified. Then when the subscriber claims that "the check is in the mail," he is probably right because the records are up-to-date in the fulfillment center. The potential for time and money-saving is so significant that this development is merely a matter of time. And, the high-speed computer-drive jet or laser printer is the cause of it all.

Software sophistication

Directly allied to the development of fulfillment hardware is the increasing sophistication of the computer software. The customer record will expand, yielding publishers greater marketing opportunities. At the same time, the system software will steadily improve, yielding greater operating flexibility.

The master subscriber record will change as the cost of computing power comes down steadily. The first change which has been promised by Postmaster General William Bolger is Zip+4. The 9-digit Zip code is a foregone conclusion at this point, regardless of the political and economic skirmishes that may accompany its introduction. Thus, the subscriber record will expand by four digits, in addition to any carrier route identification. The publisher will ultimately benefit from greater market segmentation of his file, if not also from faster postal delivery.

Telephone numbers are next. If a publisher uses the telephone as part of his billing and renewal effort, or if he pursues telephone surveys with any regularity, the home number is very handy. It is of further value in a promotional merge/purge. For instance, the man of the house may have one magazine in his name; the woman may have a service title in her name; the teenage children might have additional subscriptions. Here the phone number would be more effective and simpler than any matchcode to ensure only one mailable name per household.

Many multi-magazine publishers are converting from a complete file of names for each title to a central data base listing each name only once with appropriate codes for each title and expire date. In this way the publisher can build a status and historical record with easy access for address changes and payment problems. This is particularly important if the publisher issues combination offers—two titles for a special discounted rate—or if he also sells books to the same customer.

Many consumer magazine publishers collect demographic data. All business magazine publishers do. If a publisher kept this information as part of the subscriber record and tabulated it, he could improve the accuracy of both his advertising and circulation marketing efforts. He could also use this information to improve the thrust of his editorial content.

Looking off into the future, I can visualize real benefits to having mammoth data bases combining the subscriber files of a number of independent publishers. One of the most important benefits would show up in the improved efficiency of promotional mailings. Granting the need for controls and safeguards, if a circulation promotion director could use demographics to select subject interest and recent purchasing behavior in a related field, he should be able to target his prospects with far greater effectiveness than at present.

The savings in wasted mail or lost targets should more than offset the revenues in list rental which might be missed. As John Murchake of *Kiplinger* says, the objective will be fewer pieces mailed, better returns from those that are mailed. A second benefit would involve more immediate and complete change of address updating. The process of building these data bases is already under way at Metromail and R. L. Polk among others.

Programming managers see the growth of mixed format records, with fixed length records for the name, address, and critical code data and a variable length record for historical transaction data. This innovation, while more complicated to program for, allows for better processing speeds when the master file is scanned repeatedly for file updates. It also allows the publisher the equivalent of his childhood dream: a three by five card with the status and full history of each subscriber.

As important as these master record changes are, there are innovations in system software that will have as much or more impact on the publisher's bottom line.

It is traditional for the fulfillment center to buy a big computer and then staff it with ever-increasing numbers of systems and programming personnel. Now, however, I am beginning to hear of major publishers who are willing to sell their entire computer fulfillment systems to other publishers for a fraction of what it costs to develop those systems. Why? The seller may be in the process of rewriting his whole system and wish to defray his costs. Or he may otherwise be willing to turn a cost center into a profit center. The buyer gets a proven system with virtually none of the people-problems.

Some professional fulfillment managers, including Doug Florenzie who manages this function for *The New Yorker* and is also president of the Fulfillment Management Association, see a new trend developing in packaged fulfillment systems for small to medium-sized publishers. With the proliferation of mini-computers and the standardized packaging of software systems, it has become possible for these publishers to acquire a turnkey fulfillment system for about $50,000. Such systems allow the publisher to give customers personal attention and faster service.

Important new suppliers in this field include Scribe Data Systems of Boston; Donald Grenier Corporation of New York City; Publi-Comp of Forest Hills, N.Y.; STC Systems Inc. of Maywood, N.J.; T & B Computing of Ann Arbor, Mich.; Software Inc. of Cherry Hill, N.J.; Automated Resources Group of Upper Saddle River, N.J.; and Computing Information Services Inc. of Phoenix, Ariz.

Such package systems offer distinct advantages for some publishers. They are simple and inexpensive, allowing the publisher the ultimate in responsiveness and flexibility to control his whole subscription list in-house.

However, there are some inherent drawbacks to these in-house mini-fulfillment systems. Although their very standardization may be ideal for some publishers, it could be very inconvenient for others. In addition these systems require a level of computer/systems/fulfillment operator which may be difficult to find and keep.

On the one hand, the publisher may gain complete physical control of his list and system. On the other hand he may not be able (or may not want) to do any more with it than when the file was maintained at a service bureau. These systems can ultimately be more expensive to acquire and to operate in an on-line mode, particularly when the publisher begins entering special requests beyond the capability of the system or its operators.

There is a parallel trend for small to medium-sized publishers to process input and output documents in-house while their master files are maintained at a service bureau accessed by telephone. Orders are received and bills are sent at the publisher's location so that he can maintain direct personal overview of his workflow and insure that customers are receiving prompt service. Since this is the labor intensive part of the business, he can borrow staff personnel to handle peak loads. The expensive computer with its sophisticated software is here maintained by professionals who simply charge by the processing hour consumed. For magazines with high levels of consumer contact, this can be an efficient and economical method of operation.

The large fulfillment service bureaus, such as Neodata, Charter Data Services, Fulfillment Corporation of America, Fulfillment Associates, are not worried about losing business. They see their future in understanding and satisfying the demands of publishers—demands which become more voluminous and more complex every year.

They look forward to increased automation and ever more powerful computers spread over a number of clients as their way to expand service and contain costs. As Roger Loeb of Neodata sees it, the cost of computer hardware is coming down at the rate of 90 percent every decade, while the cost of people is doubling every six years.

At that rate, the service bureau has to develop ever more sophisticated software to improve the decisions of the circulation manager on one hand and reduce clerical labor on the other. But, there is no question that personal service for the smaller publisher at a large fulfillment service bureau is a perennial problem.

Subscriber personalization

The combination of expanding computer power, coordinated laser printing, and the competitive forces of the marketplace is going to force much greater personalization in the mail. (A personalized appeal to the consumer results in a greater response in orders and payments.)

The most immediate developments are due in the lettershop where billing and renewal notices are prepared. To begin with, it will be possible to open payments in the morning and prepare billing or renewal notices in the afternoon for all those who did not pay.

Then, I foresee personalized letters reading something like this:

"Happy Anniversary, *Jack Doyle!* (name and address). You have been a faithful subscriber to *Popular Mechanix* for the last *six years* (initial order date). We know that you have a special interest in *metal working* (bought metal working book) so we want to alert you to an upcoming article on *making a brass hatrack* scheduled for our *January* issue (article selected from a table of subjects scheduled for one to two months after expire date).

"Mr. Doyle, as of *November 8* (the date of printing the letter) we have not received your renewal payment. We know that you appreciate a *price break* (initial buy through PCH; subsequent renewal on a step-down), so we have a unique deal for you if you respond by *December 8*" (30 days from letter date).

Taking the possibilities a little further, we can expect to see "Never underestimate the power of *Jill Abrahams*" printed on a little inscription box on the cover of her copy of *Ladies' Home Journal.* We can expect to see "This is the last copy of *Good Housekeeping* on your current subscription, *Judy Gelman.* Please call 800-123-1234 with your renewal today." And, future copies of *Redbook* may have the unique sweepstake number printed on the cover and on the bind-in card at the final assembly step before they go into mail sacks. The marketing possibilities are intriguing.

Customizing the subscriber's mailing label is only one short step from customizing the editorial content of the magazine, based upon psychographic characteristics identified in the master record. For any issue of *Games* magazine, publisher Chip Block proposes to include appropriate personalized signatures relating to puzzles, anagrams, riddles or whatever. Regional magazines could tailor both editorial and advertising content on the bindery line to suit the demographics of a neighborhood. All of this individualization will be driven by data in the subscriber master file plus some sophisticated controls.

List rental selectivity is going to improve as mailers will demand greater levels of detail. No longer just Zip-select and 90-day hotline. Why not regular renewers (two or more sub records) who live near the water (based on Zip table) and who have high income potential (match to census table) for a subscription promotion to *Yachting?*

Faster customer service

Magazine customer service is bound to change. What other mail order marketer tells his new order prospects up front that they can wait six to eight weeks for delivery of a standard product? No "thank you for your order." No "sorry we are out of stock but here is a premium." No teaser to keep them interested. Just wait. And then the publisher wonders why the pay-up rate is declining.

The initiation of a new order is the most critical period in the life cycle of a subscription. As in fishing, this is when the hook is set. This is when the customer's loyalty is first established. In recognition of this importance, publishers will demand that the first issue of a subscription be sent out the day the order is received, ABC rate base balancing notwithstanding. Some fulfillment centers will even be able to wrap the invoice with the first issue to credit orders. This speed-up of the cycle, even with the additional postage required, will improve the cash flow, reduce the number of unpaid copies served to people who decide not to pay, and generally reduce the consumer bad pay problem of the magazine industry which, on some "soft offers," exceeds 48 percent. I expect this change within three years.

Most large publishers are installing 800 telephone numbers to take orders, changes of address, and resolve complaints. The call comes in to an operator who is equipped with a video display terminal which is normally on-line to the master subscription file.

This system is ideal for answering problems which would otherwise be time consuming and expensive to solve by batch processing with mail response. It is somewhat less efficient for entering orders or changes of address which could be processed more easily in batched mode. The In-WATS system is here to stay.

Better control and forecasting

Improvements in controlling and forecasting the business are among the most exciting and rewarding developments I see coming in fulfillment.

The publisher's sense of mystery and frustration in managing his circulation file will slowly subside as the management information system becomes more comprehensive, intelligible, and automated. Computer fulfillment systems are now beginning to provide on-line management reports on video display terminals rather than on reams of tab paper. These systems allow the circulation manager to do simple comparisons and ratios as he goes along. The next step is to automatically connect the historical data in the fulfillment master file to the future projection techniques supplied by Kobak Business Models, Policy Development Corporation, and others. Then the actual trends which are evident in response patterns, pay-up percentages, renewal rates, and circulation mixes can be simply extended into more realistic five-year plans and "what if" marketing games.

There is no reason why the computer, which has been faithfully tracking historic subscription data and accumulating it into statistics, cannot extend the performance trends forward to create a decision environment for the publisher and circulation manager.

Will we make the ABC rate base for the half year on our present course, given the plans we have currently under way? What is our projected cash flow for the next couple of months, based upon historic trends? What should our print order be for the upcoming issue? The steadily expanding computer, with a little help from its friends, will integrate all the existing accounting/circulation/purchasing fulfillment information, enabling publishers to make intelligent decisions. The fulfillment information system is the heart of the corporate management information system.

Today, circulation activity is analyzed in simple two-dimensional reports, such as list results by price and term. In keeping with the trend to mail and manage smarter, future circulation managers will call upon their fulfillment computers to analyze results statistically. As the data bases grow and the variables per subscriber increase, circulation professionals will deal in cluster analyses, regression analyses, and linear programming techniques to find the really profitable directions of the business. These techniques have been around for a long time. Now managers can use them effectively and economically.

No discussion of a mail-intensive activity is complete without some reference to trends in the U.S. Postal Service. A couple of trends seem predictable as far as magazine publishers are concerned.

With a heavily unionized national workforce of about 600,000, it is hard to believe that any Postmaster General will be able to significantly reduce the labor cost component of delivery. That means that postage cost containment will have to come from the mailers who do more of the sorting and specialized handling before the post office receives the mail. And that means more sophisticated counting and decision-making by the fulfillment center.

We may well come to see large first- and third-class mailers making consolidated shipments to secondary postal entry points to speed deliveries, just as publishers do now for second-class shipments. We may also see fulfillment service bureaus combining the billing notices of two or more clients over a day or two to create giant Zip strings which are more efficient for delivery. All with the blessing and even the financial encouragement of the Postal Service.

Financial changes

Cash flow is the life blood of any business. The faster cash enters the business account, the sooner it is available for the publisher to use. Obviously, daily order entry using automated remittance processing machines is going to help. Daily deposits are mandatory, even for the smaller publisher, with the funds going into some sort of interest-bearing account. There is no reason why the publisher should not be earning high interest just as any prudent money-manager does.

Don Ross, president of Charter Data Services in Des Moines, suggests one of the more interesting sophistications for the future. He is already depositing receipts daily, and many of his clients are using electronic funds transfers directly from Des Moines to consolidation bank accounts in New York, Jacksonville, or elsewhere. Why not have the funds be deposited directly from the receiving cage to the regional Federal Reserve Bank, thus saving from one to three days of transit time? Both the funds and the check paper could move faster.

Other payment innovations are becoming popular. More and more consumers are paying their bills with the use of credit cards—American Express, Diners Club, VISA, Master Charge. The consumer thereby consolidates his expenses while still maintaining control and full records.

For the publisher and his fulfillment center, the credit card can be a benefit in many ways. Yes, there is a discount for the service which is payable to the card company. But in return, the publisher is relieved of billing and collections. The card company in effect guarantees payment, almost as fast as the magnetic tapes can be processed. The procedure becomes automatic with credit authorizations and all payments cleared by the card company.

Credit card payments, telephoned authorized bank payments, and video terminal interaction are all interesting developments, but I do not expect them to have a significant impact on fulfillment in the near future.

Five years, maybe 10 years from now, Americans should be exploring a payment method that has long been popular in Europe–the pre-authorized payment–which effectively speeds up the flow of money. Now, the consumer must send a piece of paper to the publisher who then must cash it and return the check through the banks to the sender. With the pre-authorized payment method, the consumer simply notifies his bank at the beginning of the cycle to pay the publisher.

This reversal of the paper flow speeds the money flow and simplifies the paperwork. There are even provisions for delayed payment if the consumer wants to enjoy the 30-day free-trial offer. For the publisher, this process could virtually eliminate the ever-increasing bad debt and bad check problems.

Conclusion

The innovations in fulfillment are exciting. They are intriguing. They are tantalizing. But, as Bob Frankel, director of fulfillment operations world-wide for *Reader's Digest,* points out, these innovations are worthwhile only if they represent a positive financial contribution to the magazine.

Sure it is great to have a VDT operator taking 800-number calls and entering new orders on-line as a service to customers. Just remember that the VDT operator can probably enter 60 to 80 orders in a hour. The same computer operating in batch mode can update more than a million files in the same hour. Sure, personalization is fascinating and technically feasible, so long as it does not offend the subscriber and turn him off.

To the extent that change can be introduced at the relatively few fulfillment centers in America with their skilled, motivated personnel, change will come rapidly. Computers are easy to change. The more people there are who have to change, the slower the rate of change. The willingness of the vast number of customers to change or accept change can make or break the best of technical innovations.

Ultimately, fulfillment is a personal service business. Tom Lagan, fulfillment director at Publishers Clearing House, is particularly sensitive on this point. To be successful, he says, the fulfillment center must be imaginative, prompt, and sensitive to the needs of both the circulation marketers and the consumers. Amen. One thing is certain over the next 10 years—fulfillment will change as much or more than any other aspect of magazine publishing.

Moving fulfillment in-house

By Douglas Learner

It has been said that the subscription list represents the lifeblood of a magazine—or its Achilles heel. It follows, therefore, that fulfillment holds some of the greatest opportunities for a publisher while also creating some of his or her greatest worries. Will mailing labels get printed on time? Will new subscriptions get started quickly? Will renewal letters get mailed on schedule and thus not interrupt the magazine's cash flow?

For most publishers, the responsibility for these and related questions is placed in the hands of a fulfillment house. Many publishers, however, have begun to look at in-house circulation fulfillment systems as an alternative. In-house fulfillment is capturing publishers' attention today—just as in-house typesetting did a decade ago.

In the past year the number of vendors offering in-house circulation systems has swelled and new systems seem to be entering the marketplace all the time. Concurrently, the cost of computing hardware has dropped, making in-house systems affordable for small publishers. With prices beginning around $25,000, the systems are available for magazines with circulation as small as 10,000, and are applicable to magazines with circulation in the millions as well. Most turn-key systems are designed for a maximum circulation of close to a quarter of a million.

In-house fulfillment systems offer a publisher or circulation executive greater control over his or her subscription information than is available from a fulfillment house. "Control," in this case, is defined by publishers as the ability to quickly manipulate subscription data when, and how, they choose. In the fulfillment operation there are two areas where this control is cited by publishers and consultants as most beneficial: the entry of subscription additions or changes, and the setting of priorities for the system.

Order entry control offers the publisher a solution to the "please wait six or eight weeks for delivery" dilemma that plagues many magazines today. With an in-house system, an order is entered into the computer as soon as it arrives, and the subscriber receives his first copy sooner than if the order had to be transmitted to a fulfillment house (assuming the magazine does its own caging). The same speed of entry also applies to renewals, cancellations and address changes. The result is more satisfied customers—which is one thing a publisher can never have enough of, especially come renewal time.

"Our complaint volume has dropped dramatically

as a result of moving our fulfillment in-house,'' says David Ahl, publisher of *Creative Computing,* which installed its in-house fulfillment system three and a half years ago. ''We've installed terminals next to our 800-number phones and we're able to give customers better service than before. Complaints are down, as a result, to less than 5 percent of what they were. That in itself justified the purchase of the system to us.

''We had been living with a four-to-six-week turnaround using a fulfillment house,'' Ahl continues. ''Putting in the in-house system brought the turnaround time down to a week-and-a-half at most, and usually it is virtually instantaneous.''

Even if a publisher does not offer 800-number service, the ability to quickly enter information into the computer can be a benefit. ''If you want to change an address, or check an expiration date, or enter a new subscription, you can do it yourself, immediately,'' says Evonne DeFrancisco, circulation manager for *Model Airplane News,* a 25,000-subscriber monthly.

''We bought the system because of the control it offered. Our fulfillment house made a lot of errors, and that created more work for us because we had to correct them. Bringing our fulfillment in-house is the best thing we've ever done.''

Setting priorities

The second area of control a publisher gains with an in-house fulfillment system is the opportunity to decide when each project is to run on the computer. If the publisher uses a fulfillment house, he must work into *its* schedule. With his own system, *he* sets the priorities. This can be especially helpful, for example, in generating a mailing list that must meet a promotion deadline. And with an in-house system there is the added benefit of not having to pay extra for a rush job or for the generation of a special report.

''A small, poor magazine tends not to do those things that cost extra at a fulfillment house, such as list generation, extra billing series and extra reports,'' says Matthew Nemerson, publisher of the 27,000 circulation *The Washington Monthly,* which installed an in-house system in July, 1980. ''It wasn't that the cost for the extra reports was so great,'' he adds. ''It was more psychological; we were aware that we were spending extra money each time we had to fill out a request form, and that made us more reticent to make the request. In-house, there is no added cost for reports, so when you get an idea you just do it—you're always playing with the system.''

''There is absolutely nothing we can do with our system that we couldn't do with a service bureau,'' says Ahl. ''But we feel we have more freedom to experiment than we would if we were paying a per transaction fee.''

Software the key

The key to the control gained by publishers with an in-house system, however, lies not so much in the immediacy of having a computer on the premises, but in the software that runs the computer hardware. For any fulfillment operation, be it an in-house system or a service offered by an outside bureau, the software is its greatest asset. It is the software that instructs the computer to manipulate subscription files and tells it how to create the reports a publisher and circulation director need to manage a magazine.

''The software is far and away the most important thing in an in-house fulfillment system,'' stresses Shirley Mackey, a publishing consultant. ''You have to be aware of what you are looking at and what you need. I've had people coming to me claiming that they were cheated by a software vendor, when they really just cheated themselves. The software vendor was representing exactly what he had to offer, but the publisher didn't realize what he was getting into.''

The software needs of any magazine, a reflection of its fulfillment needs, will vary from one magazine to another. As an extreme example, let's consider two 10,000 circulation monthlies. The first is ABC audited and offers multi-year subscriptions, billing on two different credit cards and gift subscriptions. Its billing and renewal series consist of four and five letters respectively, and there are over 50 source codes to be tracked.

The second magazine is unaudited, offers only prepaid single-year subscriptions, and has just two letters in each of the billing and renewal series. And it does not bother to track subscription sources.

Obviously, the fulfillment software needs of these two magazines are different—and we don't even know what kind of reports the publishers or circulation directors of each want.

Because the fulfillment needs of each magazine differ, it is impossible for a single in-house system to be ''right'' for all magazines. A publisher looking for a fulfillment system (software and computing hardware) must therefore consider all of his present and future fulfillment needs, and purchase the software that is best for his magazine.

While every publisher or circulation director will have questions that pertain specifically to his or her magazine, Jim Fischer, circulation director for Gralla Publications, has four questions that should be asked of any fulfillment software supplier. ''If you get any sort of hesitation from any of these questions,'' he warns, ''be wary.''

First, he said, ask for a list of clients currently using the system. Such a list will let the publisher know if, in fact, other magazines are using the software or if he is to be a guinea pig for the software developer. The client list also gives the publisher a list of possibly similar magazines to call for references (or warnings).

After asking for the client list, Fischer recommends asking for three specific publishing features: the ability to create deferred income liability reports; ABC/BPA auditing report capability; and gift subscription donor recipient tracking. These features are common sticking points for new system suppliers, according to Fischer. He adds that even if the publication does not presently need these features, future growth may make them a necessity.

Some publishers may be tempted to design their own fulfillment systems. Most consultants and circulation directors warn against this move, unless the publisher has a great deal of expertise and confidence about both computer programming and circulation fulfillment. Consultants also caution about efforts expended to ''reinvent the wheel,'' and suggest publishers with a programming bent purchase a basic ''off-the-shelf'' package and build on it to design a system that meets their specifications. In this case, an on-staff programmer is a necessity for system design, troubleshooting and maintenance.

Customizing software

A publisher in the market for an in-house system must realize that buying circulation software is different from selecting a fulfillment house. The fulfillment house designs its software with the greatest possible capabilities in an effort to appeal to the greatest number of magazines. When searching for a fulfillment house, a publisher will usually choose from a variety of reports and list maintenance possibilities.

With an in-house system, however, a publisher may have to customize the software in order to get all the features he wants. "One problem with purchasing a fulfillment software package," says Frank Brooks, director of systems and operations at Rodale Press, Inc., "is that these packages sometimes address only narrow, limited applications, and the publisher ends up adapting to that software or paying to make changes." (Some in-house system vendors offer this customizing as part of the cost of their system, while others offer it for an extra charge.)

Rodale has its own fulfillment operation which it designed seven years ago. It handles over nine million names, according to Brooks.

Though Brooks warns about the possible limited and limiting nature of software packages, he does not disdain their purchase. "If we had to design a system at Rodale again," he says, "we would seriously consider buying a software package because a lot of the work is already done. In some cases it is easier to modify a system than to start from scratch.

"There is another type of control you get with your own system," Brooks adds. "When you are in-house you can change things whenever you want (and have the money). Most service bureaus are reluctant to change their programming for just one customer."

To plan for such changes, Mackey recommends that publishers make sure the software they purchase is well documented (explaining how it tells the computer what to do) and that it is not written in esoteric computer language. These precautions should be taken, she said, in case a publisher decides to bring in an outside programmer to make changes, in case he is forced to bring someone in because the software supplier has gone out of business, or in case he should decide to add a programmer to his staff. Without these precautions, a publisher can end up with a fulfillment software package that no one can understand or work on.

Service contract

A software service contract purchased from the software supplier is viewed as a necessity by everyone involved with in-house fulfillment systems. The contract provides a publisher with service maintenance on his software should any problems develop, as well as providing him with all software updates and changes that are developed. A service contract for the hardware should also be purchased—usually through the hardware manufacturer, although some system suppliers will offer service contracts on both software and hardware.

"You can skate along for six months without a service contract—not having a problem—and figure you're ahead of the game," says Nemerson of *The Washington Monthly*, "but all you need is one system crash or burned-out board and it costs you. Labor costs are high, and replacement parts are outrageously expensive. On top of that you have to put up with electrical engineers who don't know the system probing around saying, 'I don't know what's wrong,' when you're thinking, 'I've got renewal letters to send out.'"

Purchasing service contracts for system software and hardware from the system supplier, if possible, can be preferable to having two separate contracts should a problem occur.

"The biggest single problem we have had, and it persists to this day, is finger-pointing," says Ahl. "When the system fails, and it does do that occasionally, the software people say the problem is the hardware, the hardware people say it is the software, and last time they both said it was the power line. As a user I don't care who is at fault, I just want to get the problem fixed.

"We recognized the problem of having service contracts from two different suppliers when we put the system in," adds Ahl. "And all our fears have been borne out."

System problems are further complicated because most publishers don't have a back-up system, as do fulfillment houses, according to publishing consultant Willis M. Rivinus.

Safeguarding

Problems resulting from a "crashed" system can range from missing a deadline for renewal or billing letters to wiping out all transaction information recently entered into the computer. To avoid losing information, Mackey suggests that publishers installing in-house systems set up a schedule for periodic dumping of all information in the computer onto storage disks. This way, should the computer go down, it won't take all the information with it.

The dumps can be conducted hourly, daily, weekly or monthly, according to Mackey, depending on how much risk the publisher wants to take, and the likelihood that a problem may occur. She noted that power outages and surges can knock a computer out of commission, so a publisher in a remote area, for example, might want to dump more frequently during thunderstorm seasons.

Publishers should also make copies of all subscription records and store them in a location away from the computer, thus guarding against loss in case of fire or other disaster.

Finally, Mackey said, publishers not dealing with a vendor who will supply both software and hardware should buy their fulfillment software first, and then buy hardware that is compatible. "It can get very expensive," she says, "if you buy the hardware first and then find you can't get any software to run on it."

System costs

The cost of an in-house fulfillment system varies, depending on the system supplier, the complexity of the software, and the size of the magazine's circulation. A larger magazine will logically need more computer size, and computer size, in terms of memory, means more money (the difference in cost for a 10,000 circulation magazine and a 250,000 circulation magazine can be $100,000).

There are limits to how far a computer can be expanded to handle additional subscription information. Publishers, therefore, should make sure that both their software and hardware are expandable to at least handle foreseeable growth.

"In general," says Ahl, "a system will not expand gracefully if you haven't planned for it in advance." Ahl found this out with his own system, which was designed for a maximum of 250,000 names when Ahl had 50,000 names. Since then, Ahl's publishing efforts have expanded to a point where he is about to exceed his system's capabilities. "When we had 50,000 names and planned for 250,000, that seemed like a lot of growth," he says. "But we've just bought a magazine with a circulation of 220,000, and to add that to our 170,000 names is a major job that requires a lot of additional machinery. And they are all expensive alterations to make—costing perhaps as much as the original system."

Return on investment for an in-house circulation system is difficult to generalize: it is dependent on the cost of the system, the amount of money a magazine is currently paying to a fulfillment house, and the costs for operating and maintaining the system. These costs will vary for each magazine, just as fulfillment software needs vary.

When determining the cost of a system a publisher must not forget to include the cost of service contracts for his software and hardware. A general rule of thumb in the computer industry is that *annual* maintenance costs, for both software and hardware, are between 10 and 12 percent of the *total* system cost. Thus, a publisher who installs an $80,000 system should expect to pay between $8,000 and $10,000 a year in maintenance. A publisher should have the costs of the service contracts quoted to him before purchasing a system, so he knows what to expect.

Staffing, for in-house fulfillment

Staffing is another concern to publishers installing in-house systems. If a magazine has its own caging operation, chances are it already has the people on its payroll who will be able to operate the system, according to Mackey. The caging personnel will also have a better working understanding of fulfillment than the complete novice. While software is user-friendly, and requires no computer knowledge or programming ability to operate, a person familiar with subscription sources and ABC audit reports, for example, is more valuable than some one whose only knowledge of subscriptions comes from receiving *Time* magazine each week through the mail.

"Data entry is a pretty boring job," says Nemerson, whose circulation director at *The Washington Monthly* also handles the data entry. "When you're a small magazine and there aren't a lot of people on your staff, you have to be careful that your circulation director doesn't get burned-out at the terminal. It can be hard for him to be creative when he spends all day looking at a video display."

The costs of installing an in-house fulfillment system go beyond system and software customizing costs, additional staffing and service and maintenance contracts. Publishers determining the amount of their expenditure should also include the cost for making and storing security tapes or disks, for the conversion of a fulfillment house's tapes to the in-house system (some vendors offer this service for no charge), for training operators (again, sometimes offered at no charge by the vendor), and for any additional overhead costs such as space requirements, environmental controls and utility costs.

Combining fulfillment with other operations

A number of in-house fulfillment systems are expandable to include other publishing functions, such as accounting, rate card analysis, word processing, typesetting, advertising billing and so on. In many cases, each additional function can be added to the system's software for a set fee, and there is no need to expand the hardware. As a result, the entire system becomes more economical for the publisher.

A publisher purchasing a complete publishing system, or adding software to a fulfillment system, should be as cautious and careful as he is when purchasing a circulation fulfillment system, according to consultants and publishing executives.

Making the decision

The decision to move in-house with fulfillment "often becomes a large emotional/philosophical decision" rather than a straight business decision, according to publishing consultant Rivinus. "It is a business deal and the publisher must look at it as a business deal," he says. "Different publishers have different experience and different views on how to do certain things. Someone new to publishing may be more apt and able to look at the decision to move in-house from a straight business standpoint, while someone who has been here a long time may be more set in his ways.

"One of the big problems is that publishers don't really understand what fulfillment is," Rivinus continues. "It's not glamorous like editorial or advertising. The result is that many publishers don't have a good grasp of what it takes to do circulation fulfillment."

Rivinus's view is seconded by many circulation executives and publishing consultants, including Mackey. Because of the size of the dollar investment and the risk involved, she said, publishers should make doubly sure they know exactly what they are getting involved with.

"With a fulfillment house you can change companies if you're not getting what you want," says publishing consultant John Klingel. "But what do you do if you have the system in-house and it doesn't work?" Klingel said he "wouldn't touch in-house fulfillment with a ten-foot pole" because of the complexity of the task involved. "I wouldn't even go into business with a fulfillment company that has less than ten years' experience," he adds, "because they haven't had the time to shake out all the problems."

"There are a lot of trade-offs between in-house and service bureaus," says Rodale's Brooks. "Someone has to sit down and think about all the variables involved; the size of the company; the added overhead; in-house as compared with service bureau costs. You also have to consider those added benefits provided by in-house fulfillment but not by a service bureau."

"If you are going to move in-house with fulfillment you have to be intellectually ready to go into computers," cautions Rivinus. "And you have to ask yourself if moving in-house will be the best way to get your fulfillment done. It is like printing in some ways: Does the publisher want to get his own presses? Fulfillment, of course, is on an intermediary ground."

For some magazines in-house fulfillment may be an answer to a host of problems. But it is not for everyone. If the publisher has the money to invest in a system, and if his fulfillment costs are high, and if he is not afraid of computers, and if the thought of running his own circulation fulfillment operation doesn't send a shiver up his spine, and if he is ready to brave the expense and possible annoyances of maintaining a computer system, and if he is able to get software that will handle his fulfillment needs, and (finally) if he is able to get a system that will allow for future expansion and change without incurring great costs, then an in-house circulation fulfillment system may be just the thing for *that* publisher.

Three in-house fulfillment case histories

It is difficult to generalize about the purchase of an in-house circulation fulfillment system, just as it is difficult to generalize about signing a contract with a fulfillment house. Potential problems vary, as does the quality of service. Truly, one man's wine may be another's vinegar. The following case histories of publishers who have moved their fulfillment in-house show some of what was involved for three magazines.

Creative Computing. It was 1978 when David Ahl began to look into an in-house fulfillment system for *Creative Computing* magazine. Introduced four years earlier, the 30,000 circulation monthly had recently encountered a number of problems with its fulfillment house. According to Ahl, the fulfillment house handled mainly business magazines, and had difficulties dealing with a gift subscription promotion as well as a recent change in the magazine's frequency from bimonthly to monthly.

This was all the incentive Ahl needed to start looking elsewhere.

The major fulfillment houses wouldn't carry his

magazine because of its small size, so Ahl talked with people in the industry about purchasing an in-house system. "Almost uniformly they told me to use a well-established circulation fulfillment house," he recalls. "They said, 'You don't want to do it in-house.'

"But as computer people publishing a computer magazine," Ahl continues, "we figured if anyone could do it we could. We knew enough not to try to write the software ourselves: we wanted a turn-key system."

After talking to a half-dozen software houses, Ahl chose a system from Scribe Data Systems, Boston. "In general, the framework was there," he says. "We needed some additional programming, for things like ABC auditing and gift subscriptions (which have since been added to Scribe's software, according to Ahl), but their system was very close to what we needed." Ahl said he purchased Scribe's first in-house fulfillment system.

Creative Computing had a circulation of 40,000 when the system was installed, and Ahl had just purchased another magazine with a circulation of 10,000. The system has a capacity of 250,000 names, as mentioned earlier.

Ahl paid $80,000 for the system: $55,000 for the hardware and $25,000 for the software. He also purchased service contracts for both the hardware and the software: the hardware through Scribe, the service contract from the hardware manufacturer.

Since installing the system, Ahl has put an additional $24,000 into it, bringing his investment to $104,000 (he notes that at current prices he could probably buy the original hardware for about $25,000). A fulfillment house would have cost him about $2,000 a month, "but that's not really a fair comparison," according to Ahl, "because the system we have in-house does so much more than a bureau, particularly in maintaining our lists, which would probably have cost us an additional $700 a month.

"Of course," he reasons, "with the rather dramatic growth we have had here we've come out ahead. The outside cost for fulfillment is based on a per transaction fee, while our inside costs are relatively fixed. Our cost per transaction actually goes down as we have acquired more magazines."

Ahl said his system, like most in-house systems available today, is very user-friendly. "But I do think that people today feel a computer is something to be feared and something you need expertise to operate," he says. "It is more a question of confidence. We don't have any programmers on our staff, and we haven't found it necessary. But we have the confidence that we can deal with any state-of-the-art technology."

With the growth of *Creative Computing* to over 85,000 circulation, and the acquisition of more publications, Ahl now has four magazines and mailing lists totaling about 170,000 names. His recent purchase of *Computers and Programming* (formerly *Elementary Electronics*), however, has him investigating fulfillment alternatives for his company as he has outgrown his original system.

Model Airplane News. "Programming is just beyond my comprehension," says Evonne DeFrancisco, "and I was very leery of getting a computer for that reason. I kept thinking 'There are a lot of fulfillment houses out there and I'm considering getting involved in this way!' I was really worried, but the system is easy to use and it gives us control over all our information."

When *Model Airplane News* purchased its in-house system about a year ago from CADO Systems Corporation, Torrance, California, it left behind a fulfillment house that DeFrancisco said consistently made entry mistakes. Those mistakes made added work for the magazine's staff, and brought complaints from subscribers. So, for a cost of "under $50,000," DeFrancisco purchased the system, and now estimates a return on investment at a little over two years.

The monthly does no billing for subscriptions, nor is it audited. But both these features are parts of the fulfillment system, and DeFrancisco likes the fact that the system's capabilities outstrip the needs of the magazine, allowing room for growth. The in-house system also offers features not provided by the fulfillment house, such as four renewal letters rather than only two from the fulfillment house.

The only problem the magazine experienced with its in-house system was an inability to convert the fulfillment house's tapes onto the in-house system's storage disks. As a result, the magazine had to enter all files into the computer by hand, a job which took about two months, according to DeFrancisco.

The Washington Monthly. The fulfillment system used by *The Washington Monthly* is unique in that it is leased—rather than owned—by the magazine. There are two reasons for this. First Matthew Nemerson didn't want to purchase a system at a time when many new systems are appearing in the marketplace and advances in computer technology are commonplace.

The second reason for leasing was a matter of economics: the magazine did not have the money to pay for a system. This follows in line with the major reason Nemerson gave for acquiring the system. "Our fulfillment costs were going up," he says, "and we were getting somewhat unreliable service from our fulfillment house. So we decided to go in-house to save some money."

At the time of the move in-house with a Scribe system, *The Washington Monthly* had a circulation of 20,000, and fulfillment costs were $1,500 a month, Nemerson said. The magazine in March 1982 had a circulation of 27,000 and was paying $1,400 a month for their lease (Nemerson said he was able to get a favorable lease back

when interest rates were low). Service contracts cost the monthly another $350 a month. The magazine had been doing its own caging when it used a fulfillment house, so no additional people had to be hired to operate the system.

"Considering the fact that our circulation has grown," says Nemerson, "I would say we're paying about what we would have had to pay for a fulfillment house. But we've got a lot of control over our data now that we never could have had with a fulfillment house."

As mentioned earlier, Nemerson said that possession of an in-house system has increased the availability of information about his magazine's circulation. It has also brought some frustrations. "We got into this advanced technology and found out that there was a lot more efficiency to be had for no more money," he says. At the same time, though, we can see what we could do if we had more money. There is a great temptation to get better software which would further increase our efficiency, but we don't have the cash. Unless you go into in-house fulfillment with capitalization, you're always going to be frustrated."

Another source of frustration for Nemerson was not completely understanding what the system had to offer when it first arrived. As an example, he said that *The Washington Monthly* never coded subscribers by sex. "It would have been easy to do, and we could have done it, but we never thought to. If you don't do the coding from the beginning, you don't have the information to work with."

Nemerson said he has learned a valuable lesson from this about operating an in-house fulfillment system: "You have to understand how the computer thinks, and use it to its fullest, not just learn which buttons to press in order to run the thing. It really kills you when you don't use all of the system's capabilities.

"Take the time to go to the software people and get a full day's demonstration on a system that is up and running before you start your own system," he continues. "Don't wait until yours is up, because by then you'll probably be backed up with order entry and you won't have the time to really learn the system."

From circulation manager to computer scientist

By Mark Miller

It's time to throw out the 25-column work pads. The computer has made circulation planning the science it was always meant to be.

Until recently, very few of us have been able to know positively that we were taking the most profitable short- and long-term approaches to our circulation planning. What has stood in the way has been the difficulty in calculating the large overall mathematical interaction that takes place because of everything from bad debts to future renewals.

Some of us have devised pat formulas for six-month periods based on past performance and, with additional input, have extended them a few more periods just to get an idea of the impact of those projections.

Too frequently we embark upon circulation budget speculation overemphasizing short-range effects of our current promotions. On one hand, the advertising director urges increased prices and circulation levels to match or exceed competition and show vitality. On the other hand, the publisher is concerned with the most profitable long- and short-term approaches to the magazine's circulation. You, as circulation manager, can now, at last, arrive at an answer to profitably balance the scale.

If you were to sit down and manually calculate the myriad factors and permutations that affect profit by circulation source or by promotion source and combine them into an optimum circulation plan that achieves the rate base at the best profit both in accordance with your short-term and long-term goals, it would take days or perhaps weeks. If you add the task of compensating for sources that overproduce or underproduce, mailings that fly or bomb, months would be required. So, in general, we've built plans based on what appears to be the most profitable approach, usually a shortsighted one at best.

Circulation Planning Optimizing Computer Models

An option offered on the market today is a circulation planning optimizing computer model. The computer takes over all the cumbersome mathematical calculations that used to take us hours. Sounds great? It is. The circulation manager can finally be a creative scientist.

Once you have chosen from the circulation models available you build your basic circulation plan. The recipe starts out with the following few, but extremely important, basic ingredients that you have always used when planning:

1. Expire list and deferred income.
2. Renewal percentages by source, promotion and term.
3. Basic sources you have been using from month to

month, their anticipated production and remit rates and their starting pattern.
4. All the bad debt and cancellation information you can gather on your production sources and promotions.
5. Your incremental paper, printing, delivery and fulfillment costs.
6. Your newsstand print and net, including trends and planned future growth.
7. Your duplication percentages.

Once all the raw data has been inputted into your model and you have gotten back your first three-to-five-year projections showing circulation gaps compared to the future rate base—with your thinking cap squarely on your head—your fun begins.

At this point an unending list of questions should be bouncing around in your head, a few of which you have always been meaning to get to but have never had the time and patience to attack:

● What is the long-term net income per sub year of each of my sources and promotions based on renewability, bad debts and cancellation rates?

● What are the true incremental costs or savings of raising or lowering my rate base today and three years from today?

● At which point do I trade off subscriptions and add newsstand copies or how does the net income per subscription year relate in the short- and long-term to my newsstand sale at various levels of sale?

● What is the profit pecking order of my sources? In other words, which agents should be remitting what in terms of their service and their competition?

You can even evaluate the profitability of using arrears to fill temporary circulation gaps. The trick in any evaluation is to take both the worst set of assumptions in your data and the best set of assumptions to establish your profit-loss range and risks involved in any decision you might make.

Instead of taking days, it now takes minutes to arrive at an answer. In fact, it takes longer to think up the question and feed in the relative data than to get an answer. Alternate plans can be devised just in case those mailings bomb or sources overproduce.

Beyond just planning your short- and long-term circulation and related profit, if your model has a circulation optimizer, you are really cooking. The next step, and big question, is, "Have I built the most profitable circulation plan in terms of my long- and short-term goals?"

This is where the terms optimization of circulation

391

and financial planning come in. This phase of your planning allows you to take those sources or promotion plans which you wish to evaluate and which are available for your future use and feed them into the computer.

The computer helps you to get right down to the nitty-gritty. It looks at every effort you have given it and evaluates its short- and long-term profitability and the cost of replacing its expires which may be cheaper in some months than others. It also takes into account the cost of saving bad debt copies, the fulfillment entry cost, billing cost and all the other little details. Then it does the same thing for extra newsstand draw and arrears and finds the most profitable plan that meets the rate base—month by month, effort by effort.

It tells you when to go to which source, when to drop those mailings and make those inserts to achieve the best short- *and* long-term profit, and at the same time achieve your rate base. Of course, one of the great benefits is that you can reoptimize your circulation as those promotions become actuals so that you ultimately end up with a rolling optimized circulation financial plan—a mouthful to say, but the impact on the bottom line will make it every bit worthwhile. Some of the interesting results you might discover are as follows:

1. Perhaps you should mail out more than you need next spring and over-deliver during that six-month period, because in the next six-month period the best promotion or source will not yield nearly enough income to match that from your spring mailing, even after you consider the loss for the extra paper, printing and delivery you took in the first half. Also, you have more renewals a year or two later and now less net production.

2. With an outside source you might be better off using a one-year offer than a two-year offer.

3. The upper or worst part of your mailing might not be as good as an outside tape to tape source when you add on the fulfillment entry costs.

4. Sources which give good up front yield might not give the best overall long-term profit due to renewability and bad debt factors.

You might even find your most profitable rate base if you work closely with your ad manager in developing and optimizing various rate bases.

The function of manually planning your circulation and magazine profits can be greatly improved through the use of the computer. Beyond just a better understanding of your circulation, the whole concept and layout of information required to build a circulation model as well as the results really force you to understand your circulation. That alone is sufficient reason for every circulation department to try computerized circulation planning and optimization.

Effective utilization of your fulfillment house

By Mary A. Staples and David W. Webber

The relationship between a magazine and its fulfillment house is like modern marriage: Great expectations, mutual adjustment and, often, growing irritation and divorce. Sure, there are bad fulfillment houses; and magazines do outgrow the system they are using. But there are also a substantial number of divorces caused by magazines' failure to understand the realities of the fulfillment business.

The basic fulfillment service consists of the following:

1. Accurately recording the names, addresses and subscription terms of a magazine's subscribers.

2. Billing credit subscribers.

3. Providing mailing labels for the subscribers to an issue.

4. Mailing renewal notices to subscribers due for renewal.

This basic service required to run the magazine can be provided using computers, addressograph plates, typewriters or mud tablets. Most fulfillment houses have discarded the last three options and use computers. If you are willing to pay for more than just this basic service—and many publishers aren't—the fulfillment house can do a lot more for you. Since the entry of names and addresses is by far the most expensive part of the operation, it's folly to draw the line with this basic service. Your fulfillment house can handle your collections, provide you with very valuable information—in its fulfillment reports—and supply a good account representative who will help you understand and use the reports.

(Before going further, we feel compelled to remind you that fulfillment houses are entitled to make a profit, too. If you insist on cutting their prices too much, you will either forego the extra services that can make money for you or you will have to settle for lower-quality basic services. If all you want to pay for is the basic service, say so. There ain't no such thing as a free lunch!)

A good fulfillment house can give you reports that can make a considerable difference to your bottom line. The reports can tell you if you are sending too many—or too few—renewal notices to some classes of subscribers, how much profit you make from each source and so on.

For example, suppose the last renewal letter in the series costs $150 per thousand and has a 1 percent response at $8 per subscription. Every thousand letters sent costs $150 and brings in 10 subs at $8 each, for a loss of $70, or 7 cents per letter sent. If you have a 50 percent renewal rate, half your subscribers get that last letter so that you are losing 3-1/2 cents per subscriber over the course of a year—not much less than your monthly fulfillment bill.

On the other hand, if your last renewal letter had a 10 percent response, you could probably get more renewals—and at a profit—by sending another letter.

Only your fulfillment house can give you this information—if you ask for it and if you know where to look.

In helping hundreds of magazines build circulation and financial models over the last few years, we've noticed that magazines, in a large number of cases, uncover major surprises in the process of preparing information for the model. These surprises have ranged from discovering that four grace copies were being served instead of the two that policy dictated, to discovering that no renewal notices had been sent out for several months because the fulfillment house had "forgotten."

In most cases the information used to discover the error was contained in fulfillment reports that had previously been ignored.

This brings us to the second service you should make sure you receive from your fulfillment house—namely, whatever reports you need to make sure that nothing is going wrong.

Ask your account rep to help you set up a short, hand-prepared, monthly statement culled from your fulfillment reports which gives you the key indicators about your magazine. Included in the information which should be presented are the following:
• New subs and renewals received and income per copy.
• Percentage of new subs that are credit subs.
• Number of billing letters and renewal letters sent.
• Percentage of payments received from last month's outstanding credit.
• Percentage of renewals received to date from each expire group now in the renewal series.
• Number of grace copies served by each expire group receiving them.

Review the report monthly, and if any of these numbers look unusual, investigate further. This report will help you spot, among other natural phenomena:
• Backlogs in processing new subs and renewals.
• Billing letters not sent or too many sent.
• Renewal letters not sent or too many sent.
• Grace copies served or not served.

There are no magic numbers which you must have to the exclusion of all others. Just make sure that the numbers you get will reveal the important mistakes, that they are easily extracted from the fulfillment reports you get and that there is no more than one double-spaced piece of paper in your report.

Get help from your account rep in setting up the report and the procedure for preparing it from the fulfillment reports. Your rep should know all the types of reports available from the system. He or she should also understand your magazine and be able to tell you what information is easily available and suggest alternatives for that which is not.

Every month you gaze into your crystal ball and set a print order. Set it too high and you lose 15-35 cents per extra copy. Set it too low and you are in trouble for taking too long to start a subscription.

To help you determine this accurately you need a good expire report showing you how many subs expire with each issue. If you have expires broken down by source, and you know the renewal percentage by month in the series by source, you can estimate how many more will renew before the issue is served. You should have a very good estimate of what your new business will be (if you have done your testing correctly); and if you know how many of those will really be renewals, you can make a very good print order estimate.

Some magazines have used models to do the arithmetic described above and were able to cut their print order and effect a significant savings. But don't wait to build a model. You can do it with a calculator.

For longer-term planning you need your expire and renewal information to determine how much new business you need to maintain your rate base next year. A good expire will also tell you your income from the expire inventory for each issue—the base income for next year's budget.

Make sure that you get an expire report every month and that you use it to estimate your press run. If you don't trust yourself, make an estimate; then add some fat. Compare what actually happens against your original estimate to find out how accurate you were.

If you were wrong and you don't know why, ask your account rep.

At least once a year you should be reviewing your sub sources to see which ones are costing too much.

To do this you will need the following from your fulfillment house for each source or major effort:

For new subs—
• Number of subs received.
• Percentage of credit and bad debt subs.
• Percentage of credit payments received by month after receipt of the subs and the average number of billing notices sent.
• Percentage received by term and income per copy.
• Percentage of the subs received that were really renewals.

For first time and subsequent renewals—
• Direct renewal percentage and percentage

renewed through other sources.

• The credit, bad debt and billing information as for new subs.

• Percentage of expires receiving each renewal letter and the average number of letters sent per renewal received.

This information can be used to determine the profitability of each sub source, taking into account billing costs, cost of bad debt copies and profits from renewals. You can also spot sources that are bringing in too many renewals at new sub prices and take some action—list purges, a "please renew" box on an insert card, using agencies in alternate years, making advance renewal mailings to agent sources and so on.

The main point is that your fulfillment system has the information and you can get it—if you ask for it and know how to read the reports. If you don't know how to read the reports, your account rep can show you.

Your account rep is one of the most important parts of your fulfillment service.

A good rep can make a bad fulfillment house look good; a bad rep can be a disaster. A good one will never let you run out of renewal letters, will know how many subs you are expecting, will let you know all the reports in his or her system and will know which ones are useful to you.

A good rep will take the time to get to know you and your magazine and should be used as a staff adviser (but not as a number juggler—the rep doesn't have time). Your rep will not only know what information is in each report but why it is reported and what you can use it for. If you want a piece of information that is not reported anywhere, a good rep will try to understand why you want it and suggest something that is reported that can be used instead.

When shopping for a fulfillment service try to get each company under consideration to tell you who your rep will be and spend some time with that person. Talk to some of that rep's customers, not the fulfillment house's customers. If you are not impressed, ask for another rep or look for another fulfillment house.

If you are in the process of selecting a fulfillment house, don't choose the one that buys you the most dinners; choose the one that will do the best job.

One magazine we know sent a form letter to lots of fulfillment houses stating its volume, service needed and report requirements and asked for prices and report samples. It got several responses and was able to choose rationally and carefully.

If you don't know what you need because you are new to the business, there are several good circulation consultants who can help you. Use them; they will save you money in the long run—not necessarily by getting you a better price but by making sure that you have the information you need.

Bear in mind that fulfillment houses can and do change dramatically over a two-year span, both for the better and the worse.

And remember, there are no shortcuts to good fulfillment service and no major cost savings that everyone has overlooked. A fulfillment system is more than just a computer program and your local service bureau simply cannot do the job properly if you have more than 25,000 subscribers. There are several good, well-established companies around. Find the one that is right for you, get a good rep, understand the reports and ride off into the sunset.

The compleat fulfillment service

By M.J. Block, Jr.

I suppose that there are more foolish mistakes that a circulation director can make than attempting to be the fulfillment manager; I just can't think of any offhand. The circulation director who spends too much time on fulfillment is cheating his or her publisher.

Of course, the fulfillment function is the heart of the circulation operation. Why, then, do I say that concentrating on this function is detrimental to the efficient operation of a circulation department? For one, a reliable fulfillment service is something for which the publisher should be willing to pay a reasonable price. The circulation director should be concentrating on the marketing and financial functions in order to build his or her department's contribution to profits, not on fulfillment.

There are some qualities which a circulation director should demand from his or her fulfillment operation which will enable him or her to spend a minimum amount of time on this activity. These qualities are reliable service, flexibility, responsiveness and efficient, user-oriented processing and communication of information to the publisher.

Reliable Service. Between the circulation director and the customer stand the printer, the Postal Service and the fulfillment house. It is incumbent upon management to make each of these as efficient as possible. In the case of fulfillment, there are areas of concern which should be understood and evaluated by the circulation director. These include caging, electronic data processing (EDP), label production and billing-promotion (B-P) generation.

1. *Caging.* The manual processing of orders, payments and other correspondence is critical to the fullfillment function. Control is the key element. The circulation director must have confidence in the processing and output of the cage. It is imperative that the trained personnel in the cage be aware of quality control and that the caging system, especially when batching is involved, have a quality control function and audit trails built-in.

2. *EDP.* The circulation director must understand how data is processed. The entering of information, the file maintenance function and the nature of the file itself are critical. Here, again, quality control is important. Equally significant is the quality and nature of information retained on file. Order integrity is a necessity today. This means that the customer must be identified by a discrete current order and discrete past transactions, also.

3. *Label production.* The maintenance of a file and the consequent production of labels is a basic fulfillment function. The circulation director must be satisfied that labels are generated in a reliable manner after file update. The timing is important in allowing the proper interval between the production of labels and receipt by the printer for affixing.

4. *Billing and promotion generation.* Part of the file maintenance function involves the generating of tapes and/or labels for billing and promoting subscribers. Timing is important and reliability is critical.

There are important policy decisions to be made to insure reliable service. The nature of the matchcode, the processing of service correspondence and the relationship of mail opening date to first service are among these decisions. There are many more. The circulation director should take an active role in making theses decisions.

Flexibility. From beginning to completion of each fulfillment cycle, flexibility should be the key note. In a business of constant financial and marketing change, it is essential that fulfillment both facilitates alterations in procedure and does not hinder change.

If the publishing strategy is changed, the fulfillment service activity must be able to change and to inform management of the potential effects of the changes on the fulfillment operation.

Responsiveness. A fulfillment service may have the greatest system in the industry. It may be cost efficient. It may produce wonderful reports. It may still be unsatisfactory. The key factor is, of course, people. The attitude of fulfillment personnel is very, very important. If these people are responsive and positive, it creates a wonderful relationship with the circulation director, particularly if such an attitude is reciprocal.

A circulation director whose fulfillment personnel have the attitude that "we can do it, it will take *x* amount of time, and will cost *y* amount of dollars" has a great asset.

Management reports. There are some basic reports that almost every fulfillment house supplies. Included are promotion, financial and production reports. In general, these reports should have a summary page and an accumulated data column (from week to week or month to month) to facilitate the use of information. These basic reports provide the bread-and-butter information that a circulation director uses to measure the relative effectiveness of various promotions, the status of the subscription inventory and the value of the subscription file.

That's Fine, But

Now, if a circulation director has a fulfillment service which provides everything that I have listed, he or she will not have to attempt to be the fulfillment manager. All of this should be what I will call "basic service." The circulation director can concentrate on marketing and on financial strategy with a minimum of time spent on fulfillment.

But, there is more. Most fulfillment service includes the above characteristics and procedures to varying degrees of satisfaction. But there is a lot more you can get from your fulfillment house.

A very few fulfillment houses go beyond basic service to provide information which can lead to greater circulation profits. The concept of "management information service" (MIS) has gained acceptance by a number of sophisticated publishers.

The MIS provides the circulation director with data which tells not only "what happened," but "what would happen *if* . . ." Generally, MIS contains the following elements—recapitulation and projection of key indices, simulated modelling and various types of planning tools, such as print order projection.

Key indices, such as payment percentage by source, renewability by source and month of expire, average term sold and subscription net per copy, are presented on a continuing basis as a barometer of performance. Trend curves can be established to project the impact of changes on plans.

Much has been written about modelling. I will not belabor the point except to say that the use of models to project the effect of different assumptions and variables can be of great help in budgeting and planning.

Another feature which MIS may incorporate is a set of planning tools. I include a print order projection, an earned income projection and a balance sheet. A circulation director can set the print order for the next issue, estimate subscription income and produce an end of period balance sheet direct from the computer.

The fulfillment service is going to become more and more important to publishers in the future. The computer can be used in many ways to build profits. For example, most magazine publishers are among the relatively few businesspeople who know exactly who their customers are and what their customers' buying patterns have been. Both publishers and fulfillment services will learn to use census data and other information to identify subscribers' demographic and psychographic characteristics.

The fulfillment function is of supreme importance to publishers. It will become even more important. The circulation director should be able to depend on the fulfillment house to provide reliable basic service. The circulation director must not attempt to be the fulfillment manager, nor should he or she have to do so. Creative use of information provided by the computer has proved and will prove to be the basis for profits for magazine publishers.

My good customer J0026824R06JIBD23C

By James B. Kobak

Consider the condition of the potential subscriber way out there in some obscure Zip code area in a Nielsen C or D county or, if the subscriber's lucky, in an A or B.

He or she sends in some sort of card asking if you will accept the individual as a subscriber. Often that person trustingly sends money, too.

Then he or she waits to see what will happen. The potential subscriber might even forget that he or she subscribed—it takes that long to get the first issue. Often the first contact with you is the return of the canceled check. Aha! You do love the potential subscriber after all.

But he or she had the misfortune to send in the order on the wrong day of your updating cycle—and the fulfillment operation is behind schedule. And if you don't need the individual to meet your circulation guarantee you might start that person next July when things are slow. He or she will never know what happened. The person may even think someone has sent him or her a gift when the magazine finally does arrive!

This sordid saga could go on in the same vein through virtually all the steps in most magazines' dealings with their subscribers.

The Abused Subscriber

Most publishers just don't think of subscribers as customers. But they are. And probably the most valuable ones they have. Consider the position of the subscriber:

• The subscriber doesn't know when the first copy will be sent.

• The subscriber doesn't know when the last copy will be sent.

• If something goes wrong, he or she doesn't know how to ask for correction.

• The copies come with some weird hieroglyphics above and sometimes below the name and address.

• The subscriber is never sure he or she is paying the lowest possible price for the subscription.

• If the subscriber moves and tells the magazine, he or she has no way of knowing he or she was heard from unless, through some legerdemain, copies start arriving at the new place.

• If the subscriber does ask for a correction, an enormous time period elapses before that person hears anything—and sometimes he or she never does. So the subscriber writes again and again.

• Sometimes he or she continues to receive issues after the subscription has expired. We are servicing the subscriber in arrears, but he or she doesn't know that.

• The subscriber may have a subscription which won't expire for 20 years, but doesn't know it, so continues to send in money. No one says anything.

• Sometimes you ask the subscriber to renew when he or she has just received the second issue.

• Often you ask the subscriber if he or she wants to renew before new higher rates are put into effect. But the person is never sure just what this means.

• Since the person is a long-time loyal subscriber, he or she is allowed to pay more for the subscription than a new subscriber.

• If he or she pays promptly, the subscriber gets no benefit from it, but pays the same amount as those who wait three months.

• The person wonders what other things you are doing with his or her name and address.

• If the person lives in some undesirable (for advertisers) area, he or she may never even be asked to subscribe.

My thesis is simple: Subscribers are customers—and should be treated like customers. In fact, they are probably the most important customers you have.

Circulation As A Marketing Function

Many readers of FOLIO know that I have advocated for a long time that the circulation director be renamed marketing director. Fulfillment should not be a dirty word either in sex or in magazines. And subscription fulfillment should be treated as a major part of the marketing function.

Let me first explain *why*—and then give some examples of *how*—this might be accomplished.

Subscribers are important for a number of reasons: They pay you money so that they can read your magazine and they pay in advance—which helps your cash position. If they renew, they pay you again and again—and the expense of obtaining that renewal is much less than that of obtaining a new subscription—gifts, bind-in cards used by readers other than the original subscriber, etc. They form the loyal readership which you work so hard to sell to advertisers.

Philosophically, of course, we all know these things. But let's be severely pragmatic, and compare the basic economics of an increase in the renewal rate.

This example was only carried for two renewals, but the difference in income is obviously enormous.

And don't forget—this same thing happens not just once, but every year that you are able to keep the renewal percentage at a higher figure.

A magazine is a creative product which develops a dialogue—a warmth—a real communication—between the editors and the readers. Why shouldn't this feeling be continued through all the communications with the readers? Sometimes it seems that people renew in spite of the material we send them.

Subscription prices have been going up for many magazines over the past few years and, with the cost increases which are obviously going to take place in the future, they will continue to rise. The thoughtful and friendly handling of subscribers becomes even more important than before.

In the accompanying sidebar I have listed a few "Why Don't We's" in handling our customers. These are designed to stimulate thinking on ways to develop a real relationship with subscribers. The obvious response I will get is "It costs too much. We just can't afford to keep these other communications going to the subscribers."

Aside from the answer that you cannot afford not to, let me point to tangible benefits which will offset the additional costs of communicating more often with subscribers.

The most costly parts of a fulfillment operation are the entering of new subscriptions and answering complaints. Increasing the renewal rate reduces the number of new subscriptions which must be entered. Helping the subscriber understand what is going on reduces complaints.

Each renewal notice and each collection effort costs money. Isn't it better to communicate constructively if you can increase the speed as well as the percentage of replies from the customer? You will probably send no more pieces than you do now—but they will be different ones at different times.

The case, I believe, is obvious. The benefits are enormous.

Renewal vs New Subscription: The Basic Economics

Suppose we have 10,000 subscriptions which are expiring. What happens if we can increase the rate of renewal by just 1 percent (100 subscriptions)?

Subscription price $10.
Cost of obtaining a new subscription is $10.
Cost of obtaining a renewal is $2.
Renewal percentage for the first renewal is 40 percent.
Renewal percentage for subsequent renewals is 60 percent.

	Renewal	New	Difference
Income from 100 subscriptions	$1,000	$1,000	
Cost of obtaining 100 subscriptions			
New @ $10		1,000	
Renewal @ $2	200		
Net	$800	$800	
At time of next renewal income from 60 subscriptions @ $10	$600	$600	
Cost of obtaining 100 subscriptions			
First renewals @ $2 (40)		80	
Second renewals @ $2 (60)	120		
New @ $10 (20)		200	
	120	280	
	$480	$320	$160

Solving your postal delivery problems

By Charles L. Pace

In 1981, publishers of second class matter mailed over 9 percent of the total 110 billion pieces of mail processed in the United States. By truck, by rail, and to a lesser extent by air, literally tons of magazines arrive daily at post offices and bulk mail centers throughout the country for processing and delivery.

Needless to say, with changes occurring so frequently throughout the entire circulation and distribution process, delivery is becoming an increasingly difficult task. Publishers receive frequent complaints from subscribers that copies were damaged, or late, or never delivered at all.

If publishers are not responsive to these complaints, they risk getting repeat letters, telephone calls, and, ultimately, cancellations. Unfortunately, however, few publishers know how to proceed with a subscriber complaint.

Develop simple procedures

Since reorganizing a legitimate postal problem and knowing how to handle a postal follow-up require skill and persistence, publishers need to develop procedures to deal with their customers' delivery problems. These procedures need not entail excessive administrative costs, however, if the publisher regards good recordkeeping an essential ingredient in the process. A simplified complaint procedure is essential, and any step that proves to be impractical should be discarded.

Some post offices feel that publisher complaints are nonproductive, claiming that the post office delivers the copies when it receives them without holding any back. However, if the customer requests, the post office will establish a "watch" or conduct an investigation. Unfortunately, all too often, the replies from the post office are bland and tell very little.

In many cases, however, it is the publisher who is at fault by not providing the post office with the facts needed to conduct its investigation properly. The post office needs specifics in order to correct a problem and perhaps even find lasting solutions. Therefore, although publishers may find it somewhat time-consuming, they should consider submitting the following information with their requests for follow-up:

- Name, address, suite or apartment number if known, city-state, and Zip Code of the subscriber as shown on the address label (match code is unnecessary).
- An explanation of the problem.
- Mailing point of entry, time, date, and postal routing if known. If using your own transportation, indicate the name of the carrier.
- Frequency of issuance.
- Anticipated delivery day of week, or, in the case of monthlies, approximate date.

- A sample of the bag label if available is usually helpful, or method of shipping.
- A copy of the magazine cover is desirable but not absolutely essential. (This would be an aid to the post office for the smaller, lesser known titles.) Page dimensions also assist.
- Degree of mail makeup: Carrier Route, 5-digit, 3-digit City, SCF, or State.

Postal watches or tracers as they are sometimes referred to, are normally requested for three issues for a daily or weekly but normally only once for a monthly because of the span of time between publication dates.

Absolute rules on filing a complaint are difficult to establish, but there are some general guidelines to be followed to achieve the best results.

First, send the complaint to the attention of Customer Services. There is no form required. The typical letter would be addressed: Postmaster, Attn: Customer Services, U.S. Post Office, City, State, and Zip Code. The Zip Code for post offices is found in the National Zip Code and Post Office Directory. Cities with multiple codes will have their own Zip Code for postmaster; the smaller offices will just have the 5-digit Zip Code.

Some publishers have developed over the years their own network of contacts at post offices and frequent communication with those officials at the operational level has made communication easier and more acceptable for both in solving day-to-day problems. However, for those unfamiliar with postal parlance or the internal operations of a post office, it would be preferable to present the problem to the Customer Services.

Second, include in the body of the letter the dates you want the watch performed so that the post office can return that same letter with all the information you requested. This letter can also be used to notify your subscriber that action is being taken on his or her complaint.

In order to save time, effort, and unnecessary cost of handling complaints, you should review with postmasters on a regular basis those areas you hear from most often. In your analysis, determine where the problem came from, whether it is at the plant or at the postal installation itself. Sometimes it's a question of reassessing delivery standards because of other factors.

While not a 100 percent scientific way to evaluate a complaint without a knowledge of the distribution system, you can take your postal zones on the mailing statement forms 3541 and 3541-A and apply the Zip Codes you are mailing to establish the approximate delivery dates you should be getting. For example, if you were mailing from Chicago to Denver, you will find that Denver falls into zone 5 and the service standards are five days for preferential mail and seven days for non-preferential. The service standards for all eight zones are available in the front of the Zip Code Directory.

Of course, if the publisher or his agent delivered the mail to the facility, this information will have to be adjusted for the zone at which he is depositing: the closer you haul it, providing for less handling, etc., the shorter the time span.

Publishers can be as brief and concise as they feel is necessary for the postal watch.

A publisher of a weekly may wish to include detailed information covering all the particulars cited in the earlier example in his effort to solve a late delivery problem. He also may want the post office to know that he is doing certain "extra" things on behalf of achieving better service and, as such, expects to receive service. The publisher of a monthly may have an altogether different situation. He may be more interested in correcting damage or missing issues. Each situation is going to dictate the method for your follow-up.

Most delivery problems for second class involve late or missing copies. The missing copies occur for no one particular reason: address labels falling off and damage in the mails are probably the most frequent causes. Protective covers or wrappers would help solve some of these problems but the cost can make this prohibitive.

Top-copy damage will involve the subscriber whose copy in a given town is marked up because it is the top copy in that bundle. Some damage will occur when copies are rehandled several times in the system, i.e., SCF packages or State separations that do not package directly because of smaller volumes. The likelihood of this repeating itself is lessened with better makeup and drop-shipping close to the final destination, not always easy to accomplish. The deeper the system penetration, the fewer handlings for the Postal Service.

Case histories

Let's look at some case histories of problems to see how specific situations were handled by other publishers.

Case History #1

Problem: The subscriber writes, "What I like about your competition is that it's always delivered on Monday. The same for the other publication, except that it comes a day later. What I don't like about your publication is that sometimes it comes Wednesday, sometimes Thursday, sometimes Friday, and once in a while on Saturday. Someday, like the ten o'clock scholar, it may not come at all!"

Solution: The publisher had recently moved to a new plant and was having production problems that consistently delayed this subscriber's area. While there was no immediate solution to the problem, he was able to reassure the subscriber and the post office that his delays were due to this new move which would soon advance copies to the original delivery day. By asking for their understanding during this transitional period, the publisher gained credibility with the subscriber and the post office.

Case History #2

Problem: A complaint was filed with the publisher by the customer stating he was receiving his copies later than his friends who also received their copies at home. The subscriber did not plan to renew.

The publisher, without checking the subscriber's subscription record, sent a letter to the post office for correction. The postmaster's watch determined that the subscriber's Zip Code was incorrect and that the copy was be-

ing rehandled several times at the central post office.

Solution: A frequent complaint received by post offices is an incorrect Zip Code. A check of the file against the Zip Code Directory, while time consuming, would have determined an incorrect Zip Code and saved a postal watch.

Case History #3

Problem: The subscriber's copy of the magazine arrives one to two days after the issue appears on the newsstand. He writes to the publisher asking why his copy is habitually late.

Solution: Before filing a complaint, the publisher looked at his schedule of mailing, since in all likelihood the newsstand copies would have been shipped ahead of the subs. The publisher's schedule in this instance could not be advanced ahead enough to compensate for the time loss.

However, in further checking his schedule, he found that the subscriber could receive a one day improvement if he directed the copy to his office instead of the suburban home. The subscriber accepted this change of address and it satisfied him.

Case History #4

Problem: A letter was filed in the customer's behalf because of frequent late delivery. The postal carrier became annoyed with this subscriber and attempted to intimidate him by using abusive language.

To the customer's credit he again contacted the publisher who this time sent him a Consumer Credit Card to file with higher authorities. His local post office had tried to dissuade him from filing a complaint—even going to the extent of saying that they had no form to give him.

Solution: Admittedly this is an exception to the general rule, but the post office is now aware of the carrier problem and disciplinary action or transfer will likely occur.

Case History #5

Problem: The publisher changes his dispatch times from the plan so that connections to the downstream post offices are missed. The result: Service is one day later. The post office was never notified of this change and files a complaint with the publisher.

This is an all-too-frequent occurrence among publishers who have not coordinated their publication's production change with the Postal Service and are continuing to file reports based on false information.

Solution: The solution in this case would have been to notify the postal areas about the change you made and to ask their cooperation in delivery.

Case History #6

Problem: The publisher receives a complaint from the subscriber and, without bothering to investigate at his end, sends a complaint to the post office. In addition, he fails to provide any information about the publication, saying only it was arriving late.

Solution: Here is a problem that occurs quite often because no facts are given the post office to conduct its investigation. The post office has to write back and get the desired information before it can proceed. The publisher should have checked his end and given all data before filing the letter.

Case History #7

Problem: The postmaster writes that the mail makeup is poor and is costing both of them time in delivery. The post office insists that some of this mail can be made up into 5-digit districts to improve service by 24 hours.

Solution: The publisher finds that he can change his sack parameter to a lower copy minimum and avoid those extra handlings in the system. This soon corrects the problem for that area while allowing him more level B 5-digit districts.

Benefits

As can be seen from the above examples, there are many benefits to establishing a good post office strategy:

● It gives you the chance to present your side to the post office.

● The post office becomes aware of problems and can initiate steps or actions to correct them.

● Problems that may not be postal related come to the forefront.

● You avoid the potential loss of a subscription that was costly to obtain.

● It allows you to look at areas for improvement.

● You keep score on how well you are doing in delivery.

Benefits, however, extend far beyond that fact that you are solving problems more systematically. You are also gaining knowledge about the Postal System that can work to your advantage.

Conclusion

The Postal Service usually accepts any constructive criticism of their service that publishers can offer. All too often, however, the publisher has not done his homework that would enable the Postal Service to follow up properly. Incorrect or insufficient information will deny the post office its opportunity to complete its investigation and possibly correct the problem, besides avoiding a loss of time and further irritation to the customer.

In addition, post offices cite industry problems that can delay mail: improper mail makeup (incorrect presort, package or bundle identification missing, bundle breakage); incorrect Zip Codes; mislabeled sacks or bundles; unlabeled sacks.

There is fault on the Postal Service side as well: It could do more to follow up in tracking complaints through the system to correct publishers' problems and in educating Customer Services to respond sooner to problems. Sometimes the Postal Service is extremely slow, and sometimes it fails to respond at all. This is annoying and consumers time.

Post Offices type far too many personalized replies to customers when an acknowledgment that the problem was being looked into or had been corrected would have been better. In addition, postal standards are minimum standards, and should not be used to establish a norm in delivery.

Of course, we must also recognize that postal managers must work within budgets, just as publishers do, and budgets can become the guiding factor in establishing the criteria on how they will operate their facility. A situation in which a postal manager is graded according to how well he stays within budget can pose problems for the customer.

We must be ever vigilant, even when we are told that everything is okay. Furthermore, if we are not satisfied with the results we see, we must not be afraid to go to a higher authority—perhaps to the district or regional level.

I believe that most postal people want to serve the public well. However, if the Postal System is to remain responsive to our needs, we must do our part, even prodding it when necessary, to keep it as a viable institution.

The cost of reader service– Less than meets the eye

The cost of running a good reader's service department, like the report of Mark Twain's death, has been greatly exaggerated.

A study by *Sales Management* magazine showed that a letter personally dictated by a correspondent will cost a company $3.50. A magazine's reader service department can be organized and run for less than 50 cents per letter, including the cost of personally dictated letters where needed.

To accomplish this goal of good but inexpensive reader service means cutting out the administrative trappings and empire-building that sometimes occur in reader service departments.

For example, a reader says he or she paid a bill for which that person is still being dunned and requests that you stop the billing. Give him or her what is asked for— mark the account paid. No look-up. No request for a cancelled check. It would cost more to look it up or ask for a cancelled check than it would to allow the amount right away.

Experience shows that people are basically honest; you can lose a lot of money antagonizing 98 customers in order to catch the two who are dishonest. Now you must capitalize on what you have done by telling the reader that you have that person's word for it and marked the account paid. He or she will love you for it and because of the pleasant memory you left with the person, will be more likely to renew.

Too simple an example? Good reader service is based on simplicity. It's when it becomes complicated that it costs exorbitant amounts of money. Nothing is more expensive than employees' time. Complicated rules and regulations devour that time. Let there be just one simple rule: The customer is always right, even when wrong.

Good reader service is simply good business and the fact that it is a pleasant system to administer does not diminish the return; you will find it helpful in progressing toward your goal. That's the first step: To define your goal.

At the beginning of your reader service improvement program you may find yourself something of a freak in the magazine industry. But if you are successful with your system, if you are able to do a favor for readers each time they write to you, then you will be making a big investment in the future.

In a few short years your competitor who is getting by with a minimum of reader service will be analagous to an apartment dweller who is just paying the rent: He or she will be able to look back on no equity from the money spent. For a little more money, you will have built a home. The number of satisfied readers grows surprisingly fast over the years, depending on the number of opportunities (synonymous with the number of letters) which a magazine receives per week.

Who wouldn't like to have just 50,000 customers, much less 5,000,000 customers, whose last memory of your company is a pleasant one because you did them a favor and did it in a warm, friendly and gracious manner? You may find that they are money in the bank, that you can then sell them anything you care to—in addition to magazines. You will have converted your readers to customers; when they have found they can trust you, they will transfer that allegiance to other products because you have given them reason to expect the same kind of service that they received from you before.

Long-range Planning

So most of the planning for a reader's service department is long-range planning. And once you have set down your goal, you will need people to accomplish that goal.

The first person you select, the reader service manager, should have a feeling for good customer service and be able to transmit it to others through enthusiasm and good judgment. This manager should be consistently for the reader at all times rather than for the company. Otherwise people in the department will always be looking up the account or demanding proof of payment.

And you must be sincere in encouraging the manager to be on the side of the reader. If you're really not believed, the department will only give the concept lip service. The better the leader is, the better the people will be.

Office productivity is quite difficult to measure: The motivation should come from the employees. If they feel they are performing a service by being ombudsmen for the readers, if they can feel proud of their company's concern for the customers, then that kind of loyalty to an idea will be a tremendous motivational force. All the salary increases in the world cannot produce that kind of incentive.

People who work for a company naturally tend to want to protect that company in business dealings, perhaps because they feel they justify their employment that way. You know this is true when they say, "How do we know this customer isn't trying to cheat us?" What they're really saying is: "Let me spend 10 dollars in look-up time so we won't have to make an adjustment of three dollars."

Your reader service manager and the staff will be efficiently trained if they always take the reader's part instead of the company's. Then the incredible plethora of bureaucratic paperwork can be avoided because you have taken away its justification. The goal is always the satisfied subscriber.

The key is to eliminate every step in the operation that you can. The consultants on clerical operations will kill me for this, but don't make a separate operation out of even the dating of the mail. Every additional stop along the maze of office flow is a potential enemy of good reader service. Readers aren't interested in flow charts—they simply want an appropriate and reasonably rapid answer to their letters.

If it were possible to eliminate all the desk drawers in an office, the chances of speeding up the flow of mail would be considerably enhanced. And each separate step in an office is a "desk drawer," a resting place into which letters can be pigeonholed.

Motivating Your Employees

In evaluating the shortest distance between two points don't underestimate the potential of properly motivating employees to handle more than one function. For instance, the first person to handle a letter in many offices can be a mail reader; a person who quickly scans the letter to determine what the customer wants. In 50 percent of the cases, the mail reader can also be the last person to handle the letter.

When a customer requests the expiration date on a subscription and encloses a label, why in the world should not the first employee that opens the letter be able to answer it by filling in the correct expiration date on a form letter, hand addressing an envelope and mailing it out on the same day? It is appropriate to the inquiry and the average reader can scan all the mail and address envelopes at about 40 pieces per hour. Not bad, especially if half of the letters have been answered on the first handling. Four mail readers can process about 1,000 letters a day, answering half with simple form letters and, more important, categorizing the other half by the nature of the complaint so that they can be answered more efficiently by the next department.

Here is where to spend money. Invest heavily in obtaining mail readers with good, sound judgment and common sense. They control 50 percent of the image you want to convey to your readers. In addition, having read the complaint they will categorize it by type of complaint such as a cancellation, a replacement, etc., in order to facilitate intelligent processing.

The next step in the flow might have to be a look-up in a file, but this should be avoided like the plague. From the standpoint of satisfying the customer, many look-ups are useless: They may serve as pacifiers to the correspondents who feel better after seeing a file, but very often they make the same adjustment for the customer whether they "look it up to be sure" or not. Get rid of look-ups which are excuses for not taking a direct action.

Finally, the flow ends with the correspondent or adjuster who creates the personal letter or types the personalized adjustment document. With a good system only 10 to 20 percent of your answers need be personal letters (where the reader has a multiple complaint or when the letter is from a government agency). A higher percentage will involve typing a refund or a label or other paperwork necessary to give the readers what they want. Suffice it to say for now that I finally came around in favor of dictated letters when I found they encouraged what I wanted in a letter—a warm, friendly, natural tone of one human being talking to another as if they were sitting together.

Form letters are as desirable as any other letters which guarantee a consistent, friendly attitude toward the reader. However, check-off form letters are an abomination. They tell the reader that you were too lazy to write or keep in stock separate and appropriate form letters, so you lumped them all together into one confusing, inappropriate form which serves chiefly to alarm the reader about the many different ways his or her subscription can get fouled up.

The key to successful form letters is to have copywriters compose them—preferably direct-mail copywriters. Once written, each will convey your company's image to thousands of readers at a very small cost per reader. At his or her leisure, an experienced professional can write in a warm, friendly, understanding tone better than a harried correspondent can bat it out on the battle line.

One of the problems with form letters is that amateurs are writing them. Some even apologize for them: "We have chosen this method of giving you a quick answer . . ." There's no need to apologize if you have given it your best shot. If you send it in a hand-addressed envelope, that's OK too. People don't receive many hand-addressed envelopes any more and when they do, they tend to open them first.

Furthermore, the reader service manager should be encouraged to be aggressive in protecting the best interests of the reader.

If coupon handling by advertisers lags behind, the manager should give them hell because it's the magazine which gets blamed for the bad service. When computer scheduling pushes change of address processing to 70 days, the manager should be backed up in efforts to change the schedule. When more money is needed to improve service, it should be asked for without hesitancy.

Further, the manager (and the boss) should be encouraged to investigate the magazine's other resources and systems to search for opportunities for improvement of reader service. They should look for the unusual, the unique, the kind of thing that readers normally would not expect a magazine to do for them, but which will make a lasting impression on them for that very reason.

Ancillary activities

The cable TV connection

By Barbara Love

There is a great deal of excitement in the magazine industry about cable television. Everywhere, it seems, people are asking questions: What opportunities does cable TV present for magazines? How can magazines take advantage of those opportunities?

There is much confusion about the deals being made or what deals should be made because there are no rules, no standard arrangements. It is possible that a publisher could expect to pay for distribution on cable TV and find out someone will pay him, or vice versa. These are pioneer days in cable TV, and a period of research and development for magazines.

"Cable TV is a jungle," says Bruce Pennington, a management consultant in corporate communications. "It's such an infant medium, people are doing all kinds of crazy things."

To help publishers learn more about cable TV, FOLIO talked with two dozen experts in cable—publishers, cable TV programming network presidents, ad agency executives and consultants.

A perfect fit

Cable TV was developed in the early 1950s, but it did not become an important communications medium until recently when two developments took place: an increase in channel capacity in the coaxial cable in the early 1970s, and the first utilization for cable of a first satellite in 1975. These developments provide both capacity and efficient distribution of programming.

Cable television began to change quickly and dramatically. It soon became apparent that cable could benefit from the expertise of magazines, since magazines have editorial resources to come up with program content for special interest audiences.

Magazines, on the other hand, quickly grasped the tremendous potential benefits of working in cable. First, exposure on cable TV can build the magazine's name among new audiences, thus promoting subscriptions and single-copy sales. Second, additional profits can be made on advertising sold on such programs. Everyone agrees that cable TV and magazines are a perfect match.

Magazines can benefit in other ways as well. William J. Donnelly, vice president-director of resources management, Young & Rubicam, points out that cable TV does not involve postal costs. "When you add another person to the audience, you don't add to the distribution costs. It costs the same to distribute a program with a high rating as one with a low rating. The fulfillment costs are the same. There's no paper and postage. That's why

broadcasters can make a lot more for the money invested than magazine publishers."

If for no other reason, magazines may get into cable TV to protect their franchises. "Sometimes advertisers take the back cover just to prevent a competitor from getting it," says publishing consultant Bob Birnbaum. "Some people are getting into cable TV programming for the same reason.

"Cable TV now competes with magazines head on," he adds. "If magazines don't supply the information cable TV needs, someone else will. That somebody will say, 'Let's hire an expert,' and perhaps hire away the editor of one of those magazines."

Some roadblocks

There are some roadblocks publishers must get around when thinking of cable TV. One is the unfamiliarity with the terminology and the whole world of electronic communications. In this fast-developing new world, publishers have to deal with discussions about satellites, transponders, "infomericals," programming networks, and program production. They also have to learn about an almost overwhelming number of options available to them as the new technology accelerates.

David Auchincloss, former publisher of *Newsweek*, now a publishing consultant, compares the publisher's entry into electronic communications with Alice in Wonderland. And Roger Christian, a journalist with expertise in this area, says understanding this subject today is like trying to hold a 40 ton amoeba.

Another roadblock is secrecy. Since everything is new, people who know things aren't talking. "At this stage, those in cable TV are treating it as a trade secret," says David Lee, vice president of Magazine Publishers Association. "Publishers are spending money on research and development and are trying to protect their shot at the market," says Lee, who is developing seminars for publishers on the emerging media.

No discrete technologies

While much attention is being paid to cable TV (and that is the subject of this article), experts warn that it is dangerous to consider cable TV in isolation. They argue that publishers must consider the whole cluster of options. Once a magazine enters the world of cable TV, it can also consider exploiting, with some modifications, commercial TV, pay cable, video-discs, videocassettes, two-way cable, video text, and other options.

"There are no discrete technologies," says Les

Brown, editor of *Channels of Communications*. "They all interact."

"It's difficult to break out cable," Donnelly concurs. "I keep arguing that 10 years from now all the electronic communications vehicles will be fully present, and it's the impact of all of them that will be meaningful."

Lenore Hershey, president and editorial director of Charter Publishing Development, Inc., agrees that other technologies must be explored. "There are so many things going on," she says. "There's not just cable to look at, but videodiscs, videocassettes, teletext—all things I hadn't heard of six months ago." Hershey, who still holds the title of editor in chief of *Ladies' Home Journal*, notes that much of what she's hearing about cable and discs is "contradictory and confusing."

Programming possibilities

Given that warning, a publisher would then have to consider if his editorial franchise is one that will interest cableTelevision operators. Is there a need for the kind of program he would do?

Unfortunately, although opportunities will open up in the future, right now the situation is tight in some areas. Thus, a magazine with a high quality product that can produce a high quality program may find it tough to sell that program if it is similar in content to programs currently on cable. This is true even if the program is better than all the others.

There is already a proliferation of sports and women's programs, and networks with news and movies have wide penetration. In fact, one agency executive recently discouraged some well-known news people from going into competition with Cable Network News, indicating that since what is being done is "good enough," cable operators won't replace it.

"It's not like the newsstand where you can just put another magazine out there," says Neal Orr, president of Cable Program Services, Inc. "The problem with cable is getting space on the magazine rack."

Clear concept needed

If a magazine feels there is a need for a program based on its content, the program concept must be carefully planned.

"A magazine should study the things it does well and see how it could directly translate those things into video," says Orr. "The magazine shouldn't simply clone itself for television. It must look for other things. For example, you can do more how-to-do-it features on TV than you might be able to do in print."

Management consultant Pennington says pilots done for magazines have generally been talk shows. In his opinion, such shows will not give cable operators a big enough audience since viewers can watch elaborate programs on network.

As with magazines, the content of the program is considered critical to the program's success. "Even with all the new technology, the crux of the matter is the creative idea," says Hershey. "You can't just put a magazine on TV. You must translate the material into new forms."

Program formats differ

Program formats built around magazine subject matter are likely to be different from the conventional program format seen on commercial TV. The "magazine format" on TV, perfected in the program "60 Minutes," is being used on cable by some magazines. With this format, time is broken up into segments on different subjects.

Consumer Reports has a series on pay cable TV designed in this way, with segments of one to five minutes on different subjects.

Other programs incorporate what is called the "infomercial" (similar, in some ways, to what magazine publishers know as an "advertorial"), although the publisher may retain control. In an "infomercial" an advertising message is built into the program material.

On cable TV, it is possible to use sponsors' products in a highly visible manner; on commercial TV, such product references would be routinely edited out. Thus, if you are doing a series on golf or skiing, for example, it is logical and appropriate to use the sponsors' products—golf clubs or skis, in this case—in the program itself.

In addition to programming, publishers can and do use cable TV to advertise their magazines, much as they do now on commercial TV. But these promotions may include editorial material. *Success Unlimited*, for example, airs lengthy (10-minute) spots on cable TV which promote subscription sales, but also give the viewer information.

Thus, the lines between an ad and program content can become very blurred.

Cable program networks

A number of cable program networks or services have sprung up recently to feed cable operators. "The networks have been proliferating like mad," says Leslie Grey, senior editor of *The Home Video Report*.

The networks have bought transponder time on satellites. Some networks have bought 24 hours a day, every day, and others have bought as few as three hours per week. Some are in the business of packaging programs, and some will also sell advertising. Again, everything is negotiable.

Among the more widely-known cable networks are Entertainment and Sports Programming Network (ESPN), which reaches 7.5 million homes; USA Network, 6 million homes; and Cable News Network (CNN), 4.9 million homes.

Many of these networks are interested in joining with magazines. "We are open to discussing ideas with magazine publishers," says Jay Campbell, president of Modern Satellite Network (MSN). "We believe cable lends itself to a magazine format and has the same kind of specialized audience."

Campbell says joint cable TV ventures between a network and a magazine can be profitable even with small audiences. "Magazines would provide the editorial and some capital, and the network would provide the production expertise, the satellite network and some capital," he says.

Who pays who what?

Who pays for what depends largely on advertising. If the magazine sells the advertising, the magazine would pay a share of that money to the network for satellite time. If the network sells time, it would give a percentage of the ad monies to the magazine.

A magazine could charge a network a price for carrying its program. Occasionally, a magazine will give away a program to a cable network. The magazine might then sell all the advertising and keep the bulk of the ad revenue. Often, time within the show to promote circulation is struck into the bargain.

While it is not usual for a magazine to pay for time on a cable network, it does happen. *Model Railroader* paid the standard rate card fee of $5,000 a year to be available to MSN's 3.4 million subscriber homes. But the film that the magazine put on the air could be considered an "infomercial" for the publishing company. It had no sponsors and included many references to the magazines and books the company puts out on model railroading.

If advertising is to be sold, Campbell feels that the magazine is in a better position than the network to do the selling. "It's more appropriate for a magazine to sell ads on a program that has strong magazine links," he says. "The magazine space salesperson is the appropriate one to deal with the cable TV buyer."

Cable TV networks collect money from the cable TV operators they provide with programs, as well as from ad monies. This charge to the cable operators is about $2 to $5 per subscriber.

A noteworthy exception is Hearst/ABC Video Services' Alpha and Beta networks. According to Ray Joslin, vice president-general manager of Hearst Cable Communications Division, cable operators are not being asked to pay the network any monthly fees.

Pay TV

Another option, of less interest to most publishers because there are no ad revenues, is pay cable TV. Home Box Office (HBO) is the largest of the pay TV networks, with 5.2 million subscribers. Others include Showtime, The Movie Channel, and PRISM.

There are benefits to being on pay cable TV, however. A magazine can cut a deal for a flat fee to produce a show. This means there are no out-of-pocket costs for the show and the magazine gains exposure from the show, listings of the show, etc.

Both *Ms.* and *Consumer Reports* have worked with HBO. *Ms.* was reportedly paid between $100,000 and $150,000 to produce a documentary for HBO, and *Consumer Reports* produced four half-hour programs for the network.

"We do not have the funds to develop a program of our own," says Richard Cross, associate director of Consumers Union. "We need a source of funds; HBO pays us as we produce the programs."

N.J. Nicholas, Jr., vice president/video of Time Inc. and chairman of the board of HBO, repeats what is said so often in the area of cable TV: "There is no standard financial deal." But he does indicate that in all cases HBO pays a flat fee for production. How much is paid? "Each project is evaluated as to its financial worth, what it will cost, and what kind of talent will be on it," says Nicholas.

"Magazines don't make money with the deal, by and large," he adds. "But they don't lose any either. They look on the programs as promotion. The programs prove their franchise."

Nicholas says HBO is exploring 15 or 20 ideas related to magazine concepts (a program based on *Sports Illustrated* is scheduled; one based on *Money* is being considered). "However, for every 20 ideas, we're lucky if one makes the air," he says.

Do-it-yourself networks

A magazine or magazine publishing company can set up a network itself, using its own sales force to make deals with cable operators.

These kinds of deals aren't set either. When asked what deals are being made, one consultant responded, "You name it. I heard of one deal where a cable operator, who owned land, agreed to pay the program supplier by giving him permission to hunt on his property."

While some people say it's easy for a magazine to set up its own network, others say it's difficult unless the company plans to offer a full channel of programming. Cable operators have 12 or 20 channels, and will have as many as 120, so they have a great deal of time to fill, these people contend. "They do not want to deal with half-hour shows," says Grey, of *The Home Video Report*. "They want to deal with groups that can fill up a whole channel."

The National Association of TV Programming Executives has been encouraging cable operators to come to see shows, Grey says, but cable operators are saying they don't want to look at one-half hour or hour shows. Instead, they want to buy services.

The result is that if a publisher has a half-hour show in mind, he may have to go to a network or service. If that publisher has in mind programming to fill a channel, however, he could go to the operators directly.

"Advertising agencies and publishers still don't understand the concept of selling cable operators a channel," says Grey. "They still think in terms of programs. That's okay for broadcasting, but not for cable."

Hearst/ABC is getting together a joint venture and forming its own networks. But, in this case, the group is willing to take on a good chunk of time for the cable operators. Its Beta network for women will be on four hours a day, five days a week.

The Hearst/ABC Alpha and Beta networks will reach audiences of 3.5 million and 3 million people respectively.

To have a network, a firm must have transponder time, and transponder time is very tight right now. Hearst/ABC indicates they would like transponder time in the evening, but so far it can secure only four hours during the day. (Executives insist the type of women the network will reach are not housewives.)

"Because transponder time is in short supply, we can lease only four hours a day today," says Joslin. "There are a limited number of transponders out there now. Three years from now an abundant supply is expected because the FCC has allowed for more satellites in space."

Two revenue streams

Most magazines have two revenue streams—advertising and circulation. The situation with cable TV, however, is different: non-pay cable TV relies mostly on ad revenues, pay TV on subscribers. Cable TV will soon be able to provide two streams together, however, because the emergence of networks that will both charge subscribers and take money from advertisers is around the corner.

One such service is RCTV, a cultural/entertainment network scheduled for 1982. What's more, this network is the type that will be looking for "quality programming you would think of as magazine programming," says Grey. And Public Service Broadcasting is starting a pay TV service on cable in 1983 that will take advertising—not just sponsor identifications, but 30- and 60-second commercials.

These and other networks that plan to charge subscribers and advertisers will challenge the concept that you can't put commercials on programs that people pay for. This attitude no doubt grew out of early sales promotion for cable TV, which promised viewers programs free of commercials—if they would pay the freight. But the change in attitude to two revenue streams for cable is not unrealistic when one considers that magazines and newspapers have two revenue streams.

Young & Rubicam's Donnelly argues for what he calls "video publishing," which parallels in cable the two revenue stream concept. He feels cable networks aren't going to make any money on cable TV for five or 10 years if they rely totally on ad revenue. "I doubt if it's economically viable right now, under any set of circumstances, for a cable network to rely totally on advertising dollars and make money," he says. "The base won't be there."

For the sake of discussion, Donnelly points to a universe of 20 million cable subscribers. A product on a network can go to say 5 million. "When you ask what percent of the subscribers will be watching your program, the answer is, 'Not much,' " he says. "Say the program gets a 2 rating; of 5 million households, that's 100,000. If time costs $10 per thousand, that means you're selling time at $1,000 per clip. Can you make an hour program and cover your costs by multiplying by 9 or 18? There's not a lot of money out there. And this is almost the best case, not the worst case."

Donnelly says magazines should get dollars from ads and pennies from subscribers (indirectly from cable network or systems).

"We don't need any more controlled circulation networks," Donnelly adds. "We already have three big ones —ABC, CBS and NBC."

Advertiser acceptance

Advertisers are looking closely at cable TV. "Everyone wants to be in the vanguard," says Rick Busciglio, senior vice president-director of broadcasting, McCann-Erickson. "It is no longer a situation where major advertisers are waiting around on the sidelines. The big names are all into cable."

For example, it is reported that Bristol-Myers signed a 10-year $25 million advertising contract with Cable News in 1980. In March, it signed a $40 million contract with USA Network to produce and sponsor a health show. And it is reported that in November, Anheuser-Busch signed a five-year $25 million advertising deal with Entertainment and Sports Programming Network.

Both ESPN and CNN claim about 70 national advertisers each. ESPN has Exxon, Volkswagon, and General Telephone and Electronics among its advertisers. CNN has General Foods, Johnson & Johnson, Merrill Lynch, American Cyanamid, Nestle, General Mills, Sunbeam, Hanes Hosiery and Time Inc. on its ad roster.

Incidentally, ESPN reported advertising revenues in excess of $7 million in 1980 and claimed that figure would quadruple in 1981. CNN reported it took in about $4.4 million in ad revenues during its seven months of operation in 1980.

In 1980, cable advertising revenue reached $35 million, according to *The Home Video Report*.

Common wisdom in the business (based on a remark made by Donnelly in 1973) is that advertisers will become seriously interested in cable TV when penetration reaches 30 percent of TV households. As of February, 25.5 percent of TV households have access to cable TV. The 30 percent mark is expected to be reached in early 1982.

Latest estimates by *The Home Video Report* put 38.9 million U.S. homes within reach of cable television, about half of all the nation's TV homes. About half the homes passed by cable are subscribing to basic cable TV; of those who pay for basic, about 46 percent are opting to pay more for pay TV.

Advertiser attractions

Perhaps the most important attraction of cable TV for advertisers is its ability to reach special interest audiences that match product users. (Commercial TV does not have this capability whereas magazines have made it their trade.)

But there are other benefits for advertisers—bene-

fits that stem from the fact that ad rates are very low. Some people compare the cost of network cable to the cost of local radio, where costs are low primarily because audiences are small.

Advertising sells for as low as $100 for a 30-second spot, depending on the time of day and the network, and possibly the number of affiliates that pick up the program.

Because the cost of advertising on cable TV is so inexpensive, advertisers can afford show sponsorship. This is of great interest to advertisers, according to McCann-Erickson's Busciglio. "I can't afford sponsorship of a one-hour special for my clients on CBS," he says. "That would cost $1.5 million. Very few clients have that kind of money."

This close identification with a program is a central theme in ads put in the trade press by ESPN.

Advertiser concerns

Cable TV audiences, however, are still relatively small potatoes for national advertisers. "During an average minute, CNN reaches 50,000 homes," says McCann's Busciglio. "A local radio station reaches 50,000 people. Compare those figures with '60 Minutes' on commercial TV which reaches 17 million people. It will be a long time before cable TV is a potent force."

What's more, the cable TV industry suffers from audience measurement problems. Traditional methods of measuring television audiences don't work for audiences watching cable TV because they do not take into account the secondary and tertiary characteristics of the audience, which are so important to advertisers.

"We want to be able to measure the cable audience," stresses Busciglio. "Right now there is just no proof of penetration. Just because a certain number of homes subscribe to a service doesn't mean they're watching. Those people also watch NBC, CBS and ABC."

CNN and ESPN have both been working with A.C. Nielsen which calls about 800 homes in various systems to determine how many people are watching a particular program at a particular time. However, since the research services aren't geared to gathering information on cable, such measurement is costly and unreliable.

Audience measurement is so bad, in fact, that CNN claims that 80 percent of its audience is not counted.

Hearst/ABC's Joslin is not worried. "A new measurement system will be developed," he says. "Where there's a need, someone will step in and fill it."

Because of the audience measurement problems, ad rates are even lower than advertised on rate cards, a consultant points out. "I've bought cable TV time for incredibly low prices—prices that are a fraction of the rate card price," he says. "Since cable networks are not sold out, it's a buyer's market. And because there's no effective evaluation of the audience, the seller has to accept what the advertiser offers."

Ad agency activity

The advertising agency side of the business has also gotten caught up in the excitement over cable TV. Ad agencies are setting up units and divisions to explore cable TV for advertisers, in many cases making ads for cable, exploring program concepts, and producing programs.

Among the agencies that are considered to be ahead in cable TV know-how and interest are Doyle Dane Bernbach, Young & Rubicam, Ogilvy & Mather, and McCann-Erickson.

Like networks, ad agencies will also work with publishers on program ideas and deals. Like the networks, they are very flexible. "There are no formulas, nothing is established," says Mike Drexler, vice president, executive director, media and programming at Doyle Dane Bernbach. "We're breaking new ground."

Nevertheless, he provides one possible type of agreement: "The magazine would provide the editorial material for a program that would be titled after the magazine. We, in turn, would produce the show, provide sponsorship and handle distribution via cable network or local cable systems. A certain amount of commercial time could be made available for circulation promotion. Depending on other factors, the magazine could get a percentage of sponsorship dollars."

Healthy skepticism

Because of all the problems and the excitement over a newly-found medium, some people are skeptical about cable TV.

"Cable TV is the most talked about thing in the world," says Busciglio. "It's novelty money. There's very little actually being spent on it."

Donnelly sends out the same don't-believe-everything-you-hear message. "Publishers have to be very careful to watch what's really going on," he says. "Cable and program suppliers are financed by press releases and are about as fleeting sometimes. A lot of people are announcing things, but we see very little evidence of things happening. Some of what we hear is real, some less real, some unreal."

And Charter's Lenore Hershey: "It is very easy to rush into projects in cable TV. Cable TV is the big hype of the moment. It's very exciting and very visible. The imagination is so stirred by cable that one is tempted to spend loads of time and effort to be there. But it takes a lot of evaluation to see if you're reaching the right number of people with the right message and constructing programs worthy of the magazine. We are considering several things related to *Ladies' Home Journal* and *Redbook*, but I think we'll go slowly."

No threat to magazines

One final concern that everyone seems to have: Will cable television hurt magazines? Almost everyone says no.

"Absolutely not," says Doyle Dane's Drexler. "No advertiser will replace magazine ads with TV ads. The audiences may not be the same. The advertisers may or may not be the same. A cable show may get new advertisers not using print at all, or a print advertiser not using the magazine."

Hershey says she doesn't think readers will turn off magazines. "People will be so tired of looking at the tube, magazines will be a pleasant interlude."

Auchincloss feels TV and cable are good for magazines. They expand new markets, he says. "Television's strength is in delivering live events live, whereas the printed word is far superior in organizing, analyzing and interpreting the stories behind events." He contends that "the demand for our magazines has been greatly broadened by what we too often regard as an adversarial medium—television."

Moving into cable TV

By Douglas Learner

Cable television programming has generated great interest in the magazine industry. Some publishers are enamored with the glamour of transmitting their editorial message into millions of homes, while others view cable from a defensive posture, hoping to stake out a claim before their competition does. For most, though, the potential for profits has been enough to spark curiosity: A number of publishers are currently developing programming, while a far larger number of publishers are scrutinizing these efforts to see what happens.

But developing cable programming is quite different from publishing a magazine. Cable is a new industry to publishers, involving new technology, new procedures, new terminology, and perhaps most important, new kinds of managerial decisions.

Imagine the difficulties facing a cable programmer who decides to start a magazine, based on his cable show's editorial idea, with no knowledge of how the magazine industry functions.

Publishers are finding themselves in a similar position as they move into cable.

Fortunately, the three basic questions facing a publisher contemplating a cable programming venture are the same questions he would face starting a new magazine, or any new business: Is there a market for the product? Can I deliver a quality product that people will buy? Can I establish a business structure that will enable me to produce the product so that I can make money?

Testing the waters

A cable programming venture begins with the idea for a show, just as a magazine begins with an editorial idea. (Many such analogies can be drawn between the cable programming and magazine publishing business.) Idea in hand, the publisher must find out if there is enough interest in the idea to sustain a cable show. To do this, obviously, he must approach the right people.

When starting a magazine, the "right" people are

potential subscribers and advertisers. In cable they are network programmers and advertisers. (A publisher works with the cable networks to get a show on the air. He is not involved in establishing a viewing audience.)

The standard operating procedure when selling programming is to begin with a treatment of the show. A treatment is nothing more than a written description of the show's theme—two pages are enough—and an accompanying verbal presentation. The treatment is taken to network programmers (more on choosing a network later) and prospective advertisers or their agencies.

At this point there is no need to spend any money to produce a sample or pilot of the show, according to David Fox, of Fox/Lorber Associates, New York, a cable consulting firm. "If people don't like your idea," he says, "having it in video won't help."

If people do like the idea, the next step is the creation of a sample reel. A sample reel is an eight- to 10-minute production highlighting the content and format of the proposed show. This, too, is taken to networks and advertisers. With luck, the publisher will be able to set up a deal with a network, and maybe even sell a little advertising, based on this sample reel.

There is no need to produce a pilot of a show, according to Fox, because the show can be sold without it. He estimates that most buying decisions by network programmers are made in the first three to five minutes of viewing a reel. A sample reel also has a decided advantage over a pilot, he maintains, because its brevity will make the show seem faster-paced than a full-length pilot.

That brevity is also an aid to the pocketbook. A 30-minute pilot can cost a publisher $30,000 to $60,000, depending on the amount of gloss put in the production, Fox says. Of course, the pilot can be used for the first show in the series if the series is aired, but there is the obvious risk of making the pilot and not selling the series. A sample reel, on the other hand, can be made for under $10,000.

"Unless someone has very deep pockets," he says, "a sample reel is probably the best way to present a show."

To draw an analogy between the selling of a program and the creation of a magazine, taking a sample reel around to networks is similar to sending a direct mail test package to potential subscribers. In both cases, the goal is to make sure there is a potential market for the product before a large investment is made.

The cable industry
While the publisher is looking for cable network interest in his idea, the cable network is looking for potential viewer interest.

That is where the cable network will make its money—it is through an understanding of how the cable industry operates that the attraction of magazine-based programming becomes apparent.

A cable network provides its programming fare to local operators in exchange for a negotiated amount or percentage of subscription revenues. The local operators use the networks' programming (they might carry 10 networks or 100) as an inducement to get subscribers. (Cable franchises are auctioned off by municipalities, and carry with them exclusivity in an area.) The cable network and, in some cases, local cable operators may also share in the revenue produced by selling advertising time on the show. This depends on the deal between the network and the programmer (more on striking the deal later).

Because of the cable industry's set-up, a program produced by a magazine provides the cable network and local operator with a name that may already have mass recognition. "A strong magazine has the type of awareness cable needs now," says Fox. "A lot of cable networks are start-ups, while the magazines have existed for a long time. The association adds viability to a network. And if there is an editorial match between the show and the network (the premise behind narrowcast), it affords the cable network fantastic promotion."

Two-way promotion
This promotional value works both ways. While the cable network can promote itself by capitalizing on the recognition factor of a magazine's title, the magazine receives the promotional value of having its show seen in perhaps five million to ten million homes across the country.

"Essentially, the show softens up the prospective subscriber," says Jeff Cox, director of electronic publishing at Rodale Press. "When a viewer sees the magazine on the newsstand, or receives a subscription promotion in the mail, he says: 'I like this magazine's television show—I'll buy the magazine.'" Rodale currently produces a cable show, "Rodale's Home Dynamics," that is based on its *Organic Gardening* and *New Shelter* magazines.

Magazines that produce shows for pay cable networks (which usually do not accept advertising) have found this promotional value to be the only benefit from cable.

Ad revenues
The most lucrative benefit of cable programming is the profit potential from advertising revenue on basic (advertiser-supported) cable.

An advertiser on a special-interest, or narrowcast, program receives the same advantages as an advertiser in a special interest magazine: greater efficiency of ad dollars; audience targeting for the ad message; and the association of the ad with related editorial material. Because the content of a magazine's cable program is based on the magazine's editorial, advertiser contacts are already established for a publisher. Plus, the advertisers are already familiar with the editorial product.

Advertising expenditures in cable are increasing. In 1981 the amount was approximately $110 million, and the outlook for 1982 is between $150 million and $200 million. It is predicted that by 1990, annual ad dollars for cable will be between $2 billion and $3 billion.

The narrowcast medium
The narrowcast idea in cable is analogous to the idea of special interest publishing, and special interest magazines are thus viewed as a "natural" to help meet the cable industry's programming appetite. "Magazines have a wealth of editorial knowledge and expertise that can be used to create programming for cable," says publishing consultant Bob Birnbaum who worked with *American Baby* magazine on its cable series. "This is where magazines can translate their special interest appeal into video."

There also appears to be a desire for such special interest programming among cable subscribers, according to researchers at the Gallup Organization. Gallup recently completed a study of American cable viewers to ascertain what the market wants to view. The report was privately commissioned by a consortium of publishers, cable programming concerns and cable system operators, and cannot be released publicly due to contractual obligations.

But Gallup's executive vice president for sales and marketing, Dean J. Maitlen, offers publishers a hint of its findings with his comment that "there is strong potential for transferring the appeal that exists for special interest magazines into programming for cable television."

Searching for a production company

Once a publisher has determined that interest in his program idea exists and feels confident that there is a potential to make money from it, he has to establish the means of producing the show.

The search for a production company is much like the search for a new editor: reviewing past work; discussing ideas for future projects; evaluating creative potentials. And, as in the hiring of a new editor, the choice of a production company is often a key to the quality of the final product. "It becomes obvious that there is as wide a range of production quality in video as there is on a magazine rack," says Rodale's Cox. The key is to find the production company that will produce a show with quality consistent to the level of the magazine.

Harold Levine, Chairman of the Board of Levine, Huntley, Schmidt, Plapler & Beaver, Inc., New York, recommends publishers avoid production companies with experience producing high-budget commercials. "Look to the independent contractor," he says, "to small producers who have been satisfying major corporations with good industrial films, personnel films, and have been making effective documentaries for public television, foundations and universities."

Birnbaum suggests publishers limit their search to production companies with experience producing shows similar to the one the publisher has in mind. And rather than going door-to-door looking, he recommends the use of a firm that specializes in matching programmers with production companies. Such a firm will assist a publisher through the search, the interviews, the negotiations, and the preparations of a contract, he said, for a standard fee of 15 percent of the production cost.

If a publisher seeks a producer on his own, he must be prepared to evaluate production bids. "You have to be familiar with the kinds of costs it takes to produce a cable show," says Cox. "A good way to do that is to find a film-maker whose work you like and ask him to come in as a consultant for a few days to look over the estimates.

"The expertise is out there," he says of people who know production. "If you don't feel you know enough to make a proper decision, use it."

Quality a major concern

While cost is of course an important consideration, the quality of the production a publisher is buying should be a paramount concern—just as in magazines.

"Cable production is not so much a question of the expediency of getting a picture on the screen—that can be done easily and poorly," says Bruce Boyle, publisher of Meredith Video Publishing, which currently produces a cable show based on the Meredith Corporation's *Better Homes and Gardens* and is planning another on food and entertaining. "The trick is delivering not only quality programming, from the standpoint of content—which publishers understand intimately—but to deliver a show that will attract viewers and advertisers."

The key to that quality is for the publisher to maintain editorial control over the production of a show.

Deborah Moses, a programming developer at Consumers Union, which produces a series of specials based on *Consumer Reports* magazine for HBO, says the key is

communication. "We work very closely with our production company," she says. "I scrutinize their scripts very carefully and then discuss them with our editors and staff engineers to make sure everything is clearly explained." She also checks with Consumers Union's lawyers to make sure nothing is libelous.

"You don't lose editorial control if you work with your production people," agrees Cox, who came to video publishing at Rodale from a managing editor position at *Organic Gardening*. "I make sure the initial scripts from the production company are consistent with the quality of information this company is known for. I also look over the rushes of each day's shooting and make any necessary changes." He has had to make few such changes, he says.

"If you know exactly what you want—and you should if you're going to spend the money—then you can tell the production people and they will give it to you."

"There is a lot that can be lost between the concept and its execution," says one publisher who admits that his magazine "lost control of the show by giving it away" to a production company to produce. "It is imperative that a publisher maintain *complete* control over production," he says. "The woods are filled with production companies that will approach a publisher and say, 'We have a super idea. All we need are your editorial ideas, use of the magazine's name, and money. Just leave the rest to us.'"

Cox and Moses agree with others involved in cable production that the terms for a publisher's editorial control should be written into the production contract. But, like a contract with a printer, the publisher never wants to have to go to the drawer and pull it out—by that time conditions have already deteriorated severely.

Making money on cable

The enthusiasm of network acceptance of a magazine's cable idea, and the excitement of interviewing and previewing production companies, should not keep the publisher from considering the bottom line. Not everyone can be a Michael Cimino or a Francis Ford Coppola, after all.

To make money on a cable program the production cost for a half-hour show should be between $12,000 and $15,000, according to Richard Lorber, of Fox/Lorber Associates. (Fox/Lorber has worked with Cox at Rodale Press on that company's cable efforts.) Production costs can easily run to $20,000 or more for a half-hour show, Lorber adds, so publishers should be especially careful when scrutinizing production estimates.

The "American Baby Magazine Cable TV Show" is a good example of how a publisher can make money on a half-hour show that costs over $12,000 to produce. The American Baby series includes 26 segments, to be seen on the Satellite Program Network over a 26-week period. Each segment will be aired twice a week. When the series completes its 26-week run, it will be repeated during the next 26 weeks. Thus, each show will be aired four times during the course of the year.

There are six minutes of ad time on each show, so total ad minutes for a year is 624. At $500 for a half-minute ad, and $900 for a full minute, ad revenues from the show will be between $561,600 and $624,000.

Alan Goldberg, publisher of *American Baby* Magazine, did not reveal his cost of production for each show, but he did say the show would make money. (The ad revenues he can expect from the show far exceed the $390,000 it would cost to produce the series at $15,000 per show. The $390,000 figure, though, does not include developmental and administrative costs associated with the show.)

According to Lorber, an ad rate of $500 for a half-minute ad is about average in the cable industry.

Joint venture possibility

Though it is possible to produce cable shows using a production company on a per hire basis, many publishers and consultants suggest publishers look for a joint venture with a production company. Such a venture will reduce a publisher's out-of-pocket expenses and financial risk.

"In the basically precarious world of cable television, it makes sense to go with a production company that will assume part of the risk," says Lorber. "The partnership also enables the publisher to better collaborate with the producer in developing the best possible programming by allowing the producer to work with the publisher, rather than for him."

A contract for a joint venture should "spell out everything," according to Lorber. In addition to the above-mentioned editorial control, the contract should cover such points as the distribution of profits (usually a 50/50 split, he says), marketing, distribution, ad sales responsibilities for the show, and what each party contributes to the effort.

In a joint venture, Lorber says, the publisher will usually contribute his magazine's name and editorial resources, while the production company is responsible for all production facilities and work. Though it would seem that the publisher has a lesser investment than the producer, Lorber said, his role is invaluable. "The magazine's name and content are usually the elements that make a show salable," Lorber says. "The name itself has to be worth a lion's share of the production costs."

Another contract consideration is aftermarket potential of a show in the form of network syndication, foreign sales, videocassettes and videodiscs. While these sales may not be in a publisher's current plans, it is best to have the possibility covered in the contract, Lorber said.

Choosing a network

The establishment of a joint venture and the beginning of production will usually not begin until the publisher reaches an agreement with a network to carry the show. The choice of network can affect a show's promotion and ad sales potential.

Currently, much of cable's narrowcast programming is shown on general interest networks, which predominate in the industry. The trend, though, is toward narrowcast networks which will show only programming pertaining to the network's "theme."

The advantage of a narrowcast network, such as the planned children's programming network or health network, is that it offers "audience preselectivity," according to Birnbaum. This preselectivity will provide publishers with a more finely targeted audience than currently available, he said, which will help the ad sales efforts.

When choosing a network "you should try to get on the largest possible network, taking into consideration the network's editorial environment," says Fox. A larger audience has a greater appeal to advertisers. A larger audience also means more people will become aware of the magazine through the show.

The other major consideration in choosing a network is the financial arrangement between the network and the publisher. Here there are no rules, and few precedents to follow.

At one extreme, the publisher receives a large payment from the network for the rights to the show. Period. The publisher does not sell ads, nor does he share in the revenues generated by the ads that the network sells.

Some networks operate only in this fashion, according to Fox. These networks are usually owned by large corporations, he said, and are more concerned with maintaining an image (by choosing who advertises) than with making money now. The purpose of creating such an image is to position the network for future profits when ad expenditures are greater.

At the other extreme, a publisher pays a network to air his show, and is allowed to sell advertising and retain all ad revenues. Most networks have a standard rate for buying time, ranging from about $500 to $1,500 for a half hour. (These rates are low because the network's main revenue comes from deals with cable operators and their own ad sales operations, and because audience size is not large enough to demand a higher price.)

Between these two extremes are infinitely many deals to be made: No fee is paid by the publisher who turns over a percentage of ad revenues to the network, the network sells the ads and turns over a portion of the revenues to the publisher, the ad sales responsibility is split, with the publisher selling four minutes of ads per half-hour show, for example, and the network selling the rest. It is even possible to barter with the network, offering the network advertising in the magazine promoting the network in return for a desired negotiating point.

This deal making can be a marketing man's dream, says Meredith's Boyle, but it can also be his nightmare because there are no guidelines to follow. "The variations are almost infinite," he says.

(Occasionally, the production company chosen by the publisher will have connections with a cable network and can provide the publisher with air time. This was the type of arrangement used by *American Baby* Magazine, which went into a joint venture with the Don Kirshner Entertainment Corp. to produce its series. In such a situation, Birnbaum says, the publisher should check the financial and ad sales arrangement with the network to make sure it is to his liking.)

Proceed with caution

Most everyone involved with cable television agrees that it is not a business to jump into quickly. Three years of development work preceded *American Baby* Magazine's cable series which began this past March. At Meredith Corporation and Rodale Press the involvement in cable is on a research and development basis only —they do not expect to make money now. They are learning for the future.

And *Sunset* magazine sits poised on the edge of cable involvement with over $1 million to invest in cable programming, waiting to see if there is money to be made. "We're conducting several studies and making preliminary plans for entry into cable," says Paul Fillinger, executive producer/general manager of Sunset Films. "Until the advertising support looks like it is more viable—when the audiences are bigger and advertisers are willing to pay more—we're in a position of wanting to move into cable but having no way to make money in it."

For these publishing companies, and many more, the opportunities for cable programming are alluring. The industry is perceived as wide open by programmers, advertisers, networks and cable operators alike. And the entry level costs are low when compared to network television. These costs will most likely not remain low, however, for as audience levels rise and audience measurement procedures are perfected, ad rates will no doubt grow, and greater programming quality will be expected.

On the other hand, publishers must be careful not to jump too quickly into an unknown industry that is fraught with risks. As one publisher put it, reciting a motto he carries with him in his cable exploration: "When you're on the cutting edge of technology, it's best to stay behind the razor."

Should you also publish a newsletter?

By Robert Luce

During the latest period of recession and economic uncertainty, McGraw-Hill re-evaluated its product mix in an effort to better adapt to the ups and downs of the economic picture. Finding that newsletters have a remarkable survival quotient when times are tough and uncertain, the publishing company decided to increase its efforts in specialized newsletter publishing.

What McGraw-Hill realized is that although businesspeople will dispense with a lot of "frills" when times are tough, they are reluctant to give up the kinds of information on their particular industry that they get from newsletters.

And what this suggests, of course, is that specialized magazine publishers who are not in the newsletter business may be missing an opportunity to diversify—to slice up their information and tailor it to specific specialized markets. (Incidentally, information in newsletters can be sold at a higher price word for word than information in magazines.)

Newsletter diversification is certainly not a guaranteed road to increased profits or greater stability in an uncertain economic climate. Yet, when times are tough and bottom line profits are threatened by lower ad revenues and increased cost, the prudent publisher should seriously consider the option of newsletter publishing.

But how does a publisher make the decision to diversify in this direction? Where is the target audience? What subject has the broadest appeal for that audience? What are the costs and the marketing problems? What is the competition? How should it be priced? What internal resources can be allocated to a newsletter operation? When do the profits show up?

Magazine publishers don't often ask these questions, however. Many of them often fail to see the unexplored possibilities in their own businesses (even though they deal with advertisers who diversify their product lines, with businessmen who are constantly developing new products, with companies that deliberately create products that come in "standard" and "deluxe" options). Their attitude is similar to that of Henry Ford, who once said that his customers "could have any color they want, as long as it was black."

At the opposite end of the scale are those publishers who are hell-bent to explore book publishing, book clubs, and newsletters without a sober evaluation of the risks or the practicalities of diversification.

I don't intend to lobby for the newsletter as the logical offshoot of a magazine publishing operation. However, consider the following: Is publishing a newsletter a worthwhile project in terms of your own magazine?

Establishing relationship with reader

To answer that question, we must first establish what a newsletter is. Basically, a successful newsletter is a one-to-one communication between the editor and the reader. When W.M. Kiplinger wrote his newsletter, he had a specific reader in mind: He was writing to a relative in Ohio ("Dear George") who was a small-business man.

The further a newsletter gets from being "one-to-one"—the more it becomes a report, a digest, a bulletin—the less effective it is in establishing an important long-term, intimate relationship between subscriber and editor. And it is that relationship that is the key to a successful newsletter.

To establish that relationship, the publisher of a newsletter must make the reader believe that:

• He is receiving useful inside information he can't get elsewhere.

• He is getting opinions and judgments he can trust.

• He is learning how his business, or his investments, or his career will be affected. (He knows that the editors understand his business and his needs and are able to interpret what is happening in meaningful terms.)

• He is getting the answer to that important question: "So what?" ("If the F.T.C. levels a charge against the clothing industry, or if the price of raw materials for plastic tubing is rising faster than other prices, how will my business be affected?")

• He is saving reading time because the newsletter highlights and condenses the information that is important.

• He is learning not only what has happened, but also what will happen. (Forecasts and predictions are the stock in trade of the good newsletter.)

• He is receiving unbiased information from an expert with no ax to grind.

• He is getting value for his money. (Newsletter prices of $200 to $500 are not uncommon.)

Now, having defined what a newsletter is, let's look at some magazine publishers who are publishing newsletters which are simply logical extensions of their basic information function—particularly in very narrow specialized fields.

McGraw-Hill—perhaps the most outstanding example—now publishes 22 newsletters. Most of them are extremely specialized, and most of them have small cir-

411

culations at extremely high prices. It is safe to conclude that if the management of McGraw-Hill felt that their magazine bottom line profits were in any way adversely affected by their newsletter group, they would not have proliferated to nearly two dozen separate newsletters.

Newsweek has its *New Products and Processes* newsletter. London's *Financial Times* has spawned *World Insurance Report*, *Euromarket Letter*, and *European Community Information*.

The Cahners Publishing Company is fast developing a list of specialized letters—*The Oil Spill Intelligence Report*, *Trade Show Week*, *The Chain Report* (on the food service business), *The Early Warning Forecast*, a financial service, *Food and Restaurant Advertising and Marketing*, and a recent acquisition, *Hazardous Materials Transportation*. Ziff-Davis publishes, in addition to its galaxy of popular special interest magazines, *Aerospace Daily*, *Aviation Daily* and *Business Aviation*.

Diversifying an information bank to make more profit from it is not limited to the publication of newsletters. Kiplinger now publishes a magazine of *personal* business—*Changing Times*. And even *The New York Times* has taken a leap into modern information dissemination with its InfoBank that stores decades of information.

Starting your own newsletter

The point of all this is that if you think about your own "information bank" long and hard enough, you may well come up with an idea for a new publication. And then, the question to ask is: "Is the newsletter the most efficient and most profitable way to go?"

Let's assume for the moment that you have isolated an idea and a concept for a newsletter. Let us also assume that it is a subject on which your editors are expert, that readers have a real need for information on this subject, and that readers can afford to pay for it.

Your next step, then, is to decide whether to buy an existing newsletter or create your own.

The simplest way, obviously, is to buy an existing newsletter that either meets or comes close to your specifications. Such a newsletter can then be adapted, refined and improved to fit your own special audience and your own editorial expertise. (You can get a directory of newsletters or a list of members of the Newsletter Association of America and begin your search right there.)

Unfortunately, although there are literally hundreds of newsletters, it is not easy to find one that matches your specifications, has the potential for growth, and is available at a price you can afford. However, if you can bring it off, you will avoid a good bit of grief in the long run.

You will not only acquire a subscription list, you will also acquire the know-how that built it, marketing expertise, and a host of information about such key matters as renewal and conversion rates, list rentals, and price and offer tests that have been successful or unsuccessful in the past. This is information that may come dearly if you begin from scratch.

If you decide to create your own newsletter, there are several ways to do it.

You can create the product on a test basis—running through several pilot issues—until you are satisfied that the product is editorially sound and can be sustained on a weekly, biweekly or monthly basis.

For that period of time, the newsletter can even be supplied free to a select list of prospects and advertisers as a goodwill gesture and as an aid in creating a favorable image of the parent magazine in the advertisers' minds. To cite an example, Cahners' monthly *Early Warning Forecast* was published for several years as an exclusive service for its own executives and advertisers. Some years ago, a nominal charge was made ($12 dollars!) and now the annual subscription is $100 (and there are no "freebies").

If the reception to this "pilot" stage is positive, you can then "go public" and invest the money to promote and sell the newsletter on a subscription basis. The transition can be made gradually by retaining a "comp list" of favored readers and selling the newsletter to the rest of the business universe you are aiming at.

There are several advantages to this approach. First, you are able to find out exactly how much time and editorial talent has to be set aside to produce the product. Second, you get feedback from readers. Third, you gain a certain amount of promotional mileage from your complimentary list. And finally—perhaps most important of all—you do not invest any money on the promotion of a new and unknown product. You keep your list small and your postage, printing and mailing expenses at a minimum. Furthermore, you can keep strict records of exactly how much overhead expense you can expect *before* you add marketing costs.

Another way a publisher can start a newsletter is to publish it between the issues of the magazine. One publisher with a monthly magazine decided to bring out a new newsletter—also a monthly. Eventually, by virtue of the newsletter, he was able to double the subscription price of the magazine—after all, the subscriber was getting 24 issues a year instead of 12, and the interim newsletter proved to be a highly successful part of the service he provided to his readers.

Now that we've examined some alternative ways to go, let's assume for the sake of simplicity that you decide to do what most magazine publishers who start newsletters do: start from scratch and immediately go into the marketplace with the new publication.

Think positively—you can afford to

Remember the compelling advantages that you have over most of the people who attempt to enter the newsletter business from scratch. First—you are already an authority on the subject. Second—your own subscription list will undoubtedly be your most profitable source of subscriptions. Third—you have in-house editorial expertise. Fourth—you have in-house production and fulfillment facilities. And finally—your own promotion and circulation departments can probably set up the promotional program for testing the new publication.

In short, your start-up costs are considerably lower than those incurred by others who attempt to launch new newsletters. Since your mailings will be directed in part to your own lists, you will save from $35 up to $125 per thousand on list rentals. And, if you spread your existing overhead to cover the newsletter operations, you are bound to be ahead of the game (but keep close watch on those costs to be sure that you are making fair allocations within your budget to the start-up costs).

Remember, too, that launching a newsletter is generally far less expensive than launching a new magazine. Newsletter staffs are smaller, and printing and fulfillment costs are infinitesimal in comparison. Yet revenues per subscriber, even without advertising, are high.

Newsletter economics

Unless you are extremely fortunate, or unless your

concept is brilliant, you can expect to face at least a two-year break-even point. The first year will be excruciating: testing the concept in the marketplace, testing prices, testing offers, testing lists. There will probably be many disappointments along the way, but there will probably be some triumphs.

Since you are marketing not to a mass audience, but to a very select one, you cannot expect the kind of response you normally get from your own circulation promotion. As a rule you are dealing with response rates of 0.7 percent at best, depending on your offer and your price per subscription.

The crunch comes in your second year at renewal time. Here again, your expectations should not be too high. The accepted bench mark in the newsletter business is a 50 percent renewal rate in the second year. Anything below that signals trouble. Anything above that is a positive and very respectable reader response.

In the third year you should begin to break out of the red ink and reap the rewards of reader loyalty. At this point you can expect to have a 70 to 80 percent renewal rate. This means that you only have to spend enough money to replace 25 percent of your subscription list each year, plus whatever you want to spend to increase the list.

Other profit sources

Is it possible for a newsletter to accept advertising?

One very clever approach to this problem has been extremely successful for the newsletter *Trade Show Week*. This newsletter regularly contains paid inserts which are reprints of ads that have appeared in other publications. Most of the ads are from convention centers, hotels, and other concerns who do business with those responsible for selecting trade show and exposition sites. The advertising revenues from this insert program offset virtually all the costs of production and mailing.

The business magazine publisher can take this same approach. He can offer his regular advertisers the opportunity to run special inserts of existing ads in the newsletter, thereby increasing his revenues.

Does this violate the integrity of the newsletter as an "unbiased" source of information? In my judgment, because the ad is an insert, separate and distinct from the letter itself, the average subscriber will separate the two, both physically and consciously.

Another source of revenue for newsletters is international sales. Since foreign investment in the U.S. is growing by leaps and bounds, foreign concern about the U.S. economy and business policies has increased considerably, and airmail editions of U.S. newsletters have become a necessity for many foreign subscribers.

Furthermore, airmail editions are profitable from a business standpoint because the airmail edition carries with it a different price structure. You must, of course, add foreign postage (unless you have the ability to print and relay camera-ready copy) for mailing from Europe or perhaps the Far East. But with the exchange rate as it is, you can add to your subscription price an increment above and beyond your raw costs of foreign delivery and thereby increase your bottom line profits.

Still another potential source of revenue—and one of the most profitable—is the seminar. Using your editors and other experts in the field, you can conduct seminars in various cities throughout the country and charge $250 to $600 per attendee, depending on the length of the seminar.

Many newsletter publishers also issue directories, annual surveys, and special reports. Since these publications often accept advertising, they can become profit centers in themselves. In addition, they can be useful as bonus or premium offers to new subscribers or as an incentive to renewals.

A final word. The newsletter business is growing, and highly competitive. It is different from the magazine business, both in concept and execution, and its economics are special.

But—as with any other kind of publishing—if it works, it can be highly profitable. As my former friend and boss, the late W.M. Kiplinger, put it: "The secret of the newsletter business is to produce a product for a dime, sell it for a dollar, and make it habit-forming."

Launching a newsletter

By Stephen Sahlein

Few businesses are as gratifying and lucrative as publishing a successful newsletter. Few ventures are as torturous and expensive as getting knee-deep in a newsletter that never should have been started in the first place.

Even the best evaluation process can't guarantee success. But if asking the right questions doesn't assure your picking a winner, it can unmask and eliminate losers.

Magazine publishers have the advantage of knowing their market, but the disadvantage of years in the trade magazine business, which in many respects is the *opposite* of the newsletter business.

For instance, magazines usually strive for the broadest perspective and coverage. Newsletters thrive on narrow coverage. And the coverage itself is different. Trade books provide *news* of an industry. Newsletters give *key information*. The distinction is not just a semantic one. News content in a magazine is determined by the importance of the event. Key information in a newsletter is determined by its importance to the reader.

Which leads to the distinction that most differentiates a newsletter from a magazine: A newsletter does not so much report *on something;* rather, it reports *to someone.* In fact, many newsletters still use a salutation: "Dear Client" or "Dear Reader."

A major event such as a leading company's failure or turnaround usually gets feature or special-issue coverage in a magazine. A newsletter will have been covering developments of interest to its special readership for months. When the news breaks, it will have a paragraph or two just to assure readers that it's aware of the event. Big news is not necessarily inside news. Often, I've heard newsletter publishers or editors complain about a major news event: "Well, we have to say *something* about it."

Similarly, a small change in the wording of some government regulation that merits lead-story treatment in a newsletter will end up in a magazine only if the gaping hole in the *Briefs* section is even uglier than the "dull" regulation piece.

Unfortunately, these distinctions usually take on real meaning only after you've been involved in both newsletters and magazines. However, there are specific questions you can ask about a newsletter idea, and there are guidelines to evaluate it.

The checklist below assumes that you can do some of the general market research required for any kind of new publication. The questions and guidelines are gleaned from my experience in starting four newsletters in four different fields for four different publishers (all succeeded and are still in publication); my involvement in numerous other start-ups that never began publication; writing for over 20 newsletters; and working with clients on start-ups.

From my involvement in so many successful newsletters and, yes, some failures, I have learned the hard way which questions to ask, which rules of thumb to follow.

Not every question or guideline offered here applies to every idea. However, until you've been through one or two start-ups yourself and have learned which parts of the checklist to apply to a particular idea, I recommend using the whole checklist for each new concept.

Newsletter idea evaluation checklist

1. *Is the field a growing and changing field?* This rule of thumb may seem obvious if you haven't been mulling over a newsletter for the cobblestone road industry. Still, the question should be asked. *Growth* is self-explanatory. A newsletter on some area of high technology has a much better chance in today's market than one for, say, the black and white television industry (which is shrinking) or the milk industry (which is probably fairly static).

Change can mean many things. An industry may have found a whole new market. It may be coming under government regulation, or it may be in the process of being deregulated. Or perhaps the industry is becoming national or international instead of local.

2. *Can you describe the idea in 25 words or less?* Or at least in a few sentences? I have talked a few people out of starting newsletters for no other reason than their difficulty in describing exactly what the newsletter would cover. A show-business axiom applies here: If the joke doesn't pay off, there's something wrong with the set-up. If it's difficult to describe the newsletter idea, there's something terribly wrong with the concept. So, when someone comes to you saying, "I have this fantastic idea for a newsletter, but it's a little hard to describe..." *beware!*

Think of the successful industry newsletters you've seen. You can probably describe what they do in a few words. Many describe themselves in a two- or three-word title: *Newsletter on Newsletters, Beer Marketer's Insights, Home Computers, Hazardous Materials Transportation.*

When I say this, people usually ask: "What about the *Kiplinger Letter?*" No, I can't describe it in a few words. But is it an exception? It sells because it is a name, an institution. In my opinion, The *Kiplinger Letter* would fail if it started today under a different name.

3. *How big a market do you need?* The answer to this question depends on your reply to another: How much income do you need? If you require $150,000 a year for a profitable operation, you could start a newsletter in a market of 10,000, provided you can get that 10 percent of market most publishers hope for at a subscription price of at least $150.

Some publishers have succeeded in even smaller markets, but there is usually a reason. For example, there may be one or two Fortune 100 companies whose headquarters and nationwide offices provide literally *hundreds* of subscribers. Or there is a big but hidden secondary market. Or the newsletter gets a lot more than 10 percent of its market. Response rates to small, very well targeted markets may run well above the usual 0.5 percent to 2 percent range. I know of three newsletters in small markets that have 4 percent to 5 percent responses to mailings.

4. *Carefully scrutinize newsletter ideas that "everyone in the industry can use."* If "everyone can use it," chances are no one can.

Newsletters report specialized information to a targeted audience. If industry people outside your targeted market can use it, or if the primary market turns out to be different from the one you'd anticipated, that's fine. But a publication should address people with a strong common bond. It may be that they sell to the same market, are in the same industry or industry segment, have the same job function or level of responsibility. It's the special, focused quality of your publication and market that enables you to charge a high price and results in high renewal rates.

Broader, all-inclusive newsletters usually charge $35 to $50 (*Kiplinger* and *Boardroom Reports* are two examples), which may not be enough in a small market.

5. *Is the market identifiable?* Suppose you want to do a newsletter on international trade. In different companies different job titles might handle this function. It might be Marketing at one firm, the International Department at another, Sales at a third. This could make it difficult or impossible to find a productive mailing list. Failure to find good lists could make the newsletter prohibitively expensive to market.

6. *Does the market perceive its need for information as you do?* Beware of associates bearing newsletter ideas of "must have" information. If people *must have* the information, they either have it already or they don't need it. After all, they're making a living without your newsletter. What you can provide is very useful or important information that will give them an edge on competitors, enable them to stay ahead of the regulators, or simply help them make better decisions in important areas.

7. *Sell to sellers, not buyers.* Everybody in business buys something and sells something. Magazines are usually directed at buyers because they are a larger market.

Newsletters should appeal to the selling interest.

Magazines succeed if they find a large enough market to interest readers and advertisers. Ads are sometimes as important to readers as the editorial content.

Newsletters require a different approach.

Let's say you have a magazine for widget retailers that reports on merchandising and marketing. The ads keep storeowners informed of the latest available equipment, packaging, warehousing and distribution alternatives. Your newsletter should go not to the stores, but to their suppliers—the equipment manufacturers, wholesalers, and so on. It should tell them what their customers are doing.

Sellers can *make* money on the information you give them. Buyers can at best *save* money.

There are exceptions. Successful buyer letters usually cover items that are bought on a regular basis, cost a lot of money (either singly or in volume) and require expert evaluation. Examples include oil, stocks, gold, and office equipment (computers).

If you can produce a letter of this kind, you may have a great opportunity. There is no harder news than statistics—particularly prices. However, any publisher interested in a price publication should keep one eye on electronic publishing, the ideal medium for this information.

8. *Is the original idea the best one?* Give your idea some time to develop. It may evolve into a bigger and better one—or into a narrower concept. Narrow ideas sell for a higher price (which would you pay more for, *Publisher's Update* or *Circulation Insider*?), are easier to promote and produce, and renew better because the information is always 95 percent on target. The broad idea you first came up with may become a nice extra, a series of "Other Industry News" items on the back page. You'll find out if the idea can grow as you talk about it over a period of a few weeks or months.

9. *Go for "good" ideas—avoid "great" ones.* The great idea is unique. Nothing like it has ever been done before so there's nothing remotely like it on the market—and the market is huge.

Unfortunately, I've found that when there's absolutely nothing like it on the market, there is no market—or at least no identifiable one. Or the market knows about the subject but isn't interested in it.

The good idea usually has the ring of common sense, which makes it sound undramatic. Initial response to the good idea is positive, but not enthusiastic. Typically, someone will say, "Isn't there something like that already on the market?" That may well mean that the idea makes so much sense people feel there *must* be something like it already being published.

For example, when I was with Harcourt Brace, my job was to expand the newsletter division by coming up with new newsletters. One product we had was *The Real Estate Investing Letter,* a broad publication covering all kinds of real estate investment. I kept in touch with our outside writers and subscribers to keep on top of general trends that did not necessarily show up in each issue.

I began hearing fairly regularly about investment in single-family homes (the kind you see in the suburbs) and condominiums, which offered low risk and immunity from the growing specter of rent control, a major concern of investors in residential property. I decided we should do a newsletter on rental house and condo investment.

There was nothing very sensational about the idea. It made sense. "Isn't there something like it on the market?" someone asked. There was, but it was very small, very regional, and really more of a journal than a news-letter. The subject was covered elsewhere in bits and pieces. But there was no national newsletter covering rental house and condo investment in depth.

When *Rental House & Condo Investor* was introduced in November 1980, it had a sensational reception.

10. *Other publications in the field are a good sign.* It means there is a market for your idea. Newsletter publishers frequently talk about their publication's *niche.* The rental house letter described above is a good example. At the time, there were at least 15 to 20 real estate newsletters being published, showing a large market willing to pay for information on the subject.

An excellent place to check out what's already in the field is *The Newsletter Yearbook Directory,* 44 West Market Street, Rhinebeck, NY 12572 ($35). Since new newsletters crop up almost daily, make sure you also talk to prospective subscribers to see what they read.

11. *"Sooner," "better," or "more comprehensive"— is not enough.* If you discover a publication that already covers exactly what you intend to, you'll have a hard time competing, unless it's a market with enough room for two.

Occasionally, people try to start directly competing newsletters, sure that they will succeed because they will be superior to the other letter in some way. They may go in at a lower price. In a business newsletter, however, price is not so important since subscribers aren't paying for it—their company is.

Slightly better coverage, writing, graphics, etc., usually are not enough to pull someone away from another newsletter they find reasonably useful. And publishing information sooner doesn't mean much unless the reader needs it sooner. Sometimes the idea of publishing in a single newsletter material put out by many periodicals seems appealing. But in my experience, a digest is not enough.

You've got to have something in the newsletter that is both new and important to the reader. If you do, you have a good chance of success.

For example, Commerce Clearing House and The Bureau of National Affairs both put out comprehensive weekly looseleaf services on product safety covering all legal, regulatory and legislative developments, including decisions by the Consumer Product Safety Commission (CPSC). David Swit started Washington Business Information Inc. with a successful four-page weekly newsletter called *Product Safety Letter* (it's now six pages, $337). The reporters talk to people at CPSC to find out which products the commission is looking into long before it selects those it will investigate and act on. The newsletter gives affected industries a big jump on the CPSC and on the looseleaf services that report CPSC decisions after the fact.

12. *If others have tried the same newsletter and failed, drop it.* It's very tempting when you're excited about an idea to think that someone else failed because he was stupid, inept, incompetent or inexperienced. Not true. If it failed, it's usually because the *idea* didn't sell—not the publication.

Here, too, there are exceptions. A newsletter can fail because of poor timing. If someone had tried a cable television newsletter in 1955, it would undoubtedly have failed.

A newsletter can also fail if the publisher is unable to handle the promotion. It's not unusual for someone with great ideas and great industry connections to start a newsletter with no understanding of how to market it. The newsletter may carry its invaluable information to 46 subscribers and renew at 100 percent—but it can die for lack of direct-mail knowhow and capital.

13. *How will you price it?* You can test prices on a new product. However, you first have to decide how much you need to make a go of it. There are three factors to consider:

a) The prices of other newsletters in your field. If they are all $140, you may be limited to that price range.

b) The salary (which means level of responsibility) of your potential subscribers. If you go to vice presidents of marketing whose average salary is $55,000, you can charge anything you like. If you go to managers who make under $25,000, $65 a year might be high.

Sometimes income isn't the only factor. For example, a small-business person who makes a good income may see the subscription price coming right out of his pocket. So, although his treasurer might readily spend $225 for a newsletter, he might balk at $150.

c) The size of your market and what chunk of it you think you can get. After you determine this number, divide it into the minimum revenue needed for a profitable operation. It will yield the minimum subscription price you *must* charge to succeed. (Most publishers hope for no more than 10 percent of their market even if they eventually get more.)

Let's say, for example, that your market is 10,000, you estimate getting 1,000 subscribers, and you need $150,000 to make a profitable operation. Your minimum subscription price, then, is $150 ($150,000/1,000).

14. *How often must you publish?* The profits in newsletters are in the renewals. Weeklies usually renew best; biweeklies (or twice monthlies), second best; monthlies, third. However, a good monthly can have a top renewal rate of 80 percent or more.

If you have a choice, start monthly and stay there for a year. By the end of your first year you'll know what your renewals are and you'll have ironed out the kinks. If renewals are good and you have enough material, you may want to come out every two weeks and jump the price.

If the area which you are covering has fast-breaking news, you may have to come out weekly. Before you get started, know whether your operation is flexible enough to meet production demands. Will your production people be able to get the letter out every Friday? Or are there lots of "departments" with "priorities" that simply won't bend for this kind of operation?

15. *Can the editor's job be learned?* Most trade-magazine readers are at least as interested in the ads as in the copy. But in a newsletter there is nothing but copy. If publishing it depends on having someone with 10-years' experience who knows everyone in the industry —like the magazine editor who's been with you a long time—you may end up hostage to the editor. If the editor leaves and is extraordinarily difficult to replace, what will happen to your publication?

One way around this is to offer the editor some equity (if the newsletter succeeds), or at least a percentage of revenues or profits. This kind of incentive will also make a big difference in the editor's performance.

16. *Don't ask prospective subscribers, "Would you buy this?"* Naturally, you want to find out how much the market needs or wants the information. Better questions are, "Could you use more information on this?" or "Would this information be useful to you?" It's futile to ask, "Would you be interested in a newsletter on this subject?" People who ask this question are generally averse to risk. They ask this question to "make sure."

Once you've used this checklist to see if you're headed down the right path, the only way you can "make sure" you have a winner is to do a direct mail test. And sometimes even the test isn't the last word.

This is not to undervalue the importance of talking to your market, an essential part of the research. You want to find out not only its main concerns, problems and needs, but also the language it uses to describe them. This language should be used in the promotion, if possible. Everyone knows when someone else is "talking my language." Interviews with prospective subscribers may also provide you with story or column ideas, or change your original concept.

For example, one client came to me with a broad newsletter for a particular market (I can't mention the idea because it is not yet in publication). I told him that in my opinion the idea was too general and had only a fifty-fifty chance of success. He decided to proceed anyway.

I spoke on the telephone to half a dozen prospective subscribers in his market and asked what their primary concerns were. Specifically, I asked: "In the course of your business, which laws or regulations do you find yourself most preoccupied with —which ones most concern you?" If that didn't get a good answer, I would rephrase it: "If you had a million dollars to spend on consulting advice on the various laws and regulations, which ones would you want more information on?"

Nearly everyone talked about a special series of tax problems. Some of these were to have been in the newsletter as originally conceived. I recommended that the newsletter be renamed with "Tax" in the title and to leave the more general subjects for the inside pages. This new slant gave the newsletter a better focus and injected "smell of money" into the publication—something that had not been there. I think that with the new angle, the newsletter stands an excellent chance of success.

Showing people a sample issue may help you iron out some kinks before publication, but it's not going to give you a go or no-go signal. Too often pride gets in the way. People may feel: "You think you know my business better than I do? Thanks, but I have all the publications I need." Or people want to be polite: "It's very nice. I really like it." Or their enthusiasm for your *idea* influences their opinion of the product itself. I was involved with a newsletter where many people who read a sample issue said, "Please let me know as soon as you go into publication." Despite the apparent pre-publication, pre-test interest, the newsletter did not test well and staggered along until it was sold.

17. *Does it need more than $10,000 to test?* It shouldn't. I'm a strong believer in starting small. For $10,000 you can get everything you need for a solid test in an industry market. Not a statistically accurate random sample, since few newsletter markets are large enough for this, but a response that gives you enough information to help you decide whether or not to proceed.

The $10,000 can get you everything you need for a solid test: a good consultant, a strong, four-part direct mail package, and a market test of anywhere from 5,000 to 20,000 names (depending on how much is left after you've paid for consulting, copywriting and production costs).

18. *Know the economics.* To give you an idea of what you can expect of a successful newsletter over the first four years, I've drawn up a projected budget for a successful industry newsletter: *Widget Insider.* It sells for $150 per year, comes out monthly at eight pages, and is aimed at a primary market of 40,000.

XYZ Publishing Co.

Four-year budget for (the successful) *Widget Insider* newsletter

	1st year	2nd year	3rd year	4th year
Number of promotional pieces mailed	10,000 (test) 30,000 (first mailing)	120,000	120,000	120,000
Percentage return on mailing	1%	0.8%	0.6%	0.5%
Renewal percentage	--	60%	70%	80%
Number of subscribers	400	1,200	1,560	1,848
Subscription income	$60,000	$180,000	$234,000	$277,200
Expenses				
Mechanicals, printing, paper and postage	$ 7,200 ($1.50/issue)	$23,760 ($1.65 @)	$34,070 ($1.82@)	$44,352 ($2.00@)
Promotion	9,000 (30K at $300)	39,600 ($330K)	43,560 ($363K)	47,916 ($399K)
Cost of Test	10,000 (includes 10K)	---	---	---
Fulfillment	2,000 ($5 per name)	6,600 ($5.5)	10,296 ($6.05)	12,307 ($6.60)
Misc.	2,000	2,200	2,420	2,662
Salaries				
Editorial	20,000	25,000	28,000	31,000
Production	4,000	10,000	13,500	16,000
Marketing	6,000	12,000	18,000	21,000
Total direct expenses	$60,200	$119,160	$149,846	$175,237
Gross profit (loss)	(200)	60,840	84,154	101,963
Overhead	7,000	7,700	8,470	9,317
Pre-tax net (loss)	$ (7,200)	$ 53,140	$ 75,684	$ 92,646

To keep the example simple, promotional mailings go only to the primary market, once the first year, three times per year after that. Since the same lists are used over and over, response rates to the mailings drop each year. However, for the same reason (a well-defined, relatively small market), renewal rates rise quickly. This kind of response and renewal pattern is not unusual in a well-targeted industry letter.

All costs rise 10 percent per year except salaries, which rise by much larger percentages. As the newsletter succeeds, more and more of the editorial, production and marketing people's time is required. I am assuming that the first year the newsletter requires 80 percent of one editor's time and 100 percent thereafter, with some contributions from other editors. (I would advise trying to "stretch" a current editor—if you have one who's good enough—in preference to hiring someone. This holds down your start-up costs and avoids the unpleasantness of firing someone you recently hired if the idea doesn't sell.) Although you would probably raise your newsletter price at least 10 percent per year, I have kept it constant in this example.

Graphics are minimal (as they should be). The newsletter is typewritten and photo-offset in one color.

As you can see, the big number is the renewal percentage. Between the third and fourth year, the response rate to the mailing drops 16 percent, and total costs (total direct expenses plus overhead) rise nearly 17 percent. Even though the renewal rate goes up only 14 percent, *net profit rises over 22 percent.*

Ready to go

I didn't use the example of a successful letter to offer you a pipe dream. Remember the evaluation process? It's supposed to weed out losers. If it didn't, then the $10,000 test should.

This is an important point. Before you start your test, decide the rock bottom response rate you'll accept from your test mailing. Make it a little on the low side. If you don't, you'll be tempted to ignore or readjust your stop sign if it flashes. Set your minimum response rate low enough to assure that you really will stop if you get the wrong number on the mailing.

Don't set two numbers—a go and a stop. Nine times out of 10 your response will fall somewhere in between. What will you do then? It's awfully hard not to go forward on a "maybe" signal.

Which brings me to my last and in some ways most important point. Whatever you do, don't make your new newsletter a *project.* Projects have a life of their own. They have a way of becoming disconnected from the original plans, the budgeted investment and long-term projections. Problem projects are assigned to people to "see what's wrong," "come up with some ideas" or "work on it and let me know what you think."

It would be better to think of your new newsletter—however repugnant this may be—as a trip to Las Vegas. You hope to make a bundle, but just in case things go wrong, you've done the sensible thing and set yourself a limit. If luck and circumstances go against you and you lose your ten thousand, you won't be stubborn and throw away more money. Instead, you'll pack your bags and go home—and try again next year.

Getting into books: The market

By George Duncan

Increased revenue may be the most obvious reason for magazine publishers to go into book marketing, but it isn't the only one. Take the case of *Sail* magazine, which, until its recent acquisition by Meredith Corporation, was published by Bernard Goldhirsh.

In 1973, *Sail* was just three years old when Goldhirsh decided to try his entrepreneurial hand at book marketing. He had acquired a book in England called *This is Sailing*, a book which he felt contained the same kind of "how-to" sailing expertise that his magazine was providing.

Goldhirsh knew, of course, that magazine buyers are not necessarily book buyers, but he was anxious to see how his readers would respond. He knew that he stood a good chance of added income if he could find the kind of books his readers wanted.

Goldhirsh was looking for more than the increased revenue, however. He was looking for a way to extend his young magazine's fledgling authority and influence within its very specialized market. Books, with their traditional sense of authority, are a natural means toward that goal.

Furthermore, there is the matter of service. Most magazine publishers recognize a responsibility to serve their readers by providing as much information and expertise as possible, and publishing books is an effective way to accomplish this goal.

Before marketing *This is Sailing*, Goldhirsh and his book division manager, Bob Mamis, explored in detail the pros and cons of both a continuity program and an open-end type of book club format. After a thorough investigation, they decided that the start-up costs and staffing requirements for either format were more than they were willing to take on at that point.

"We would have needed a hefty editorial staff as well as a marketing staff," says Mamis. "Since we felt that would be too cumbersome, we established a four-person book division instead, and it has stayed that way ever since."

This is Sailing was launched with full-color, full-page ads in *Sail* and was accorded trade (bookstore) distribution through W.W. Norton Co. The book was an instant success—eventually becoming a mail order "best seller" with more than 100,000 copies sold—and it's still a reliable performer on the *Sail* Books' back list. The company's new division was under way.

Magazine publisher's advantages

Clearly, *Sail*'s success story exemplifies the natural advantages that most magazine and newsletter publishers have even before they enter the field of book publishing:

First, most magazine publishers already have a fairly good picture of their readers in terms of demographics, psychographics and other factors. They know their market—and a firm knowledge of one's readers is absolutely essential to any successful book marketing program. (In *Sail*'s case, being sailors themselves, the staff also had a "gut feeling" for what their readers might be most interested in. However, gut feelings are a risky basis for establishing anything more costly than what Mamis was working with at this point.)

Second, magazine publishers have direct access to their market and have experience in selling to their readers.

Third, magazines have a "built-in" authority. Loyal readers will trust the magazine as a source of reliable information. In fact, the more specialized the subject area, the stronger the bond becomes, and it naturally influences anything else a magazine may offer them, be it books, newsletters, seminars, cassettes or whatever.

A defined market; ready access; authority; and a common area of interest and expertise—these are the main advantages almost any magazine publisher enjoys up front. They are the "edge" in deciding whether to take a stab at book marketing.

Of course, there are pitfalls to be aware of when entering the book marketing field, just as there are when entering any new business. (Unfortunately, success in one area doesn't necessarily guarantee success in another.)

For one thing, good books in any particular specialty or subject area are difficult to find. Publishers rarely catalog their books by subject, and you'll have to invest a fair amount of your own or staff time searching for likely titles among the various directories, press releases, trade publications and publishers' catalogs.

Second, the most successful books are the ones you publish yourself, and "growing your own" is both costly and time consuming. Furthermore, pricing, author and publisher negotiations, book manufacturing, trade distribution and other aspects of book publishing are very different from magazine publishing.

In addition, it takes time to build a profitable book marketing division, even on an individual title basis—*Sail*'s early success notwithstanding. Clubs and continuity programs are even more complex and require considerable investment of both time and money from title selection testing and promotion to fulfillment.

Profit margins, moreover, can be dangerously thin, especially when books are discounted (which, in mail order selling, is often the case).

Finally, your readers may subscribe to your publication precisely because they prefer the easier-to-read magazine format to the greater detail and depth of material they'd have to deal with in books.

With all that, however, the lure and promise of book marketing is difficult for a magazine publisher to ignore and, as noted above, there is the matter of a publisher's responsibility to provide whatever service his readers may require. So perhaps every publisher owes it to himself and his readers to at least investigate the possibilities of book marketing.

There are three categories of book marketing for a magazine publisher to consider:

1) Hardcover and/or paperback books marketed on an individual basis through direct response and/or trade

distribution.

2) Hardcover and/or paperback books marketed through direct mail as book club or continuity programs.

3) "Softcover" books—magazine format one-shots, annuals, buyers' guides and the like which may or may not carry advertising and are marketed through direct response, mass (newsstand) distribution or controlled distribution.

This article will examine the first of these categories.

The Country Journal Bookshelf

Bill Blair, publisher and co-owner with Dave Ketchum of *Blair & Ketchum's Country Journal* in Brattleboro, Vermont, is a good example of another publisher who succumbed to the "lure and the promise" of book marketing.

His magazine, *Country Journal*, is a how-to guide for the landed gentry, catering to its readers' love of and interest in gardening, cooking and preserving food, woodburning, animal husbandry and the like. The income level and educational level of its readers are high, and circulation is around 225,000.

Although Blair regularly makes reprints of important articles available at a nominal cost, he wanted to provide an additional service to his readers through a book offer.

In the April 1980 issue, Blair ran his first double-spread *Bookshelf* featuring 26 books ranging in price from $4.95 to $29.95.

This initial selection was culled from a list of 250 titles, all personally read and evaluated by special projects director Jeff Seroy and other members of the staff.

"Our goal was to present as wide a selection as possible consistent with price and quality," says Seroy. That is to say, they wanted to keep quality as high as possible for books in a modest price range. Titles included both hardcover books and trade paperbacks in "how-to" and public policy subject areas.

Sales averaged 1.5 to 1.75 books per order with an average of almost $20 per order on Master Charge and Visa, $14 to $15 on cash orders. Credit cards were used generally for the more expensive books, while lower price titles brought cash with order. "We could detect some resistance around $20," said Seroy.

Most encouraging, however, is that the *Country Journal Bookshelf* was breaking even by the June issue.

Furthermore, although Seroy had anticipated a 50 percent turnover in titles for both the July and October ads, he found that only 40 percent of the list changed for July and—even better—only 30 percent of the list changed for October. These figures indicate higher sales than anticipated on the majority of the titles.

Ten titles of the original 26 did particularly well. Only one book on the April list was published by *Country Journal*. The others were all put out by other publishers, although Blair does plan to publish his own titles gradually.

"Ad response has a half-life," says Seroy. "By the end of April, for example, we had roughly half the sales we were going to realize from that ad. We received half of that again the following month and so on." For that reason, it's important to keep some inventory on hand for several months following any ad.

For publishers who may be anxious about tying up capital in a large initial inventory, however, it may be comforting to know that *Country Journal* began with no more than a dozen copies of each title and reordered as

necessary. All fulfillment is handled in-house.

In addition to publisher Bill Blair's desire to provide this service to his readers, he had had some earlier indications that his readers might respond well to a book offer.

First, he knew his demographics were high in the areas of education and literacy. What was more significant, however, were the results of several mailings that had been made to the *Country Journal* list by the Cooperative Book Service, a subsidiary of the History Book Club. Blair felt that these results were strong enough to support an initial effort. (It is interesting that *Country Journal*'s extensive book reviews had never been ranked very highly in readership surveys.)

Finding titles

To find likely titles, Seroy sifts through more than 75 publishers' catalogs. "Front list titles (new books) are fairly easy to come by," he says.

The standard resource for new titles is *Publisher's Weekly* magazine, especially the Spring and Fall issues in which the major publishers showcase their new books. Another source is R.R. Bowker's *American Book Publishing Record*, a monthly that lists new books by subject, together with publication dates and all related information. (Digging out publishers' backlist titles, however, takes a lot of personal contact with publishers' "special sales" people.)

"There are also many good books being published by smaller publishers, especially for our readers," says Seroy. One such major source is a distributor in San Francisco called Bookpeople. Another source on the East Coast is Pushcart Press.

Discounts on books range from 40 percent to 50 percent, although higher discounts can sometimes be negotiated, particularly for a successful title you're ordering in quantity. Some publishers also have co-op advertising plans which provide cash allowances based on advertising space allocated to their titles. These allowances have the effect of increasing the discount.

Magazine publishers who wish to learn about the discounts, allowances and special plans that various publishers offer can do so by joining the American Booksellers Association for a nominal fee. Members receive the association's annual *Bookbuyer's Handbook* which lists the policies of most U.S. publishers. The association's magazine, *American Bookseller*, also provides information on the better-selling books in various subjects.

In the months ahead, *Country Journal* will be carefully tracking sales, focusing in on their readers' price and subject preferences. These preferences will then form the basis of *Country Journal*'s plans to publish their own titles.

Two business publishers

The situation of CW Communications differs from *Sail* and *Country Journal* in two respects: First, as publishers of *Computerworld*, the weekly tabloid of the computer industry, they are business rather than consumer publishers. Second, they placed their Computerworld Books division in the hands of outside consultants.

When company president Walter Boyd decided he was ready to test the book marketing waters, he brought in former Crain Publishing senior vice president Mike Hartenfeld and his partner, Mel Brisk, who had also been at Crain and, before that, at Quadrangle.

An early experiment in marketing books that were

essentially reprints of articles from *Computerworld* indicated good possibilities.

Repackaging editorial material from previous issues, in fact, is one way to determine reader interest in books generally. Costs are minimal and acceptance of such books is often high. (One of *Sail* Books' most consistent sellers is a volume called *Sail Trim*, a compilation of magazine articles that is clearly sold as such.)

Although *Computerworld*'s experiment heightened their interest in book marketing, in the case of *Sail*, their first plans would have required more additional staff than the company was ready to commit—so they let it ride for a while. Finally, however, publisher Boyd got together with Hartenfeld and Computerworld Books was launched with full-page ads in *Computerworld* and *Computer Business News*, another CW Communication publication.

Initial ads featured 15 to 17 books with fairly long copy about each one. Titles ranged from books on computer software and similar technical subjects to general management and personal business and investment. Later, the ads were trimmed to about 12 titles each. The full list includes some 125 titles from about 30 publishers.

Prices for these books are higher than the prices for most consumer books (some close to $60), with an average of $23. All books are sold on 15-day money-back guarantee, cash-with-order or bank credit card as well as "bill me." Orders are running 42 percent prepaid versus 49 percent "bill me," with an average of one and a half books per order. Returns, Hartenfeld reports, are negligible.

Operation on computer

The entire operation was put on computer after a brief period of manual fulfillment. Now the computer generates labels for drop shipping by the publishers, eliminating the need for costly inventories of books. *Computerworld* found publishers quite willing to accommodate them on that score. (In fact, The American Booksellers Association recently initiated a program known as SCORE whereby stores can order a single copy sent directly to the customer when the order is accompanied by the store's check for the book, less their discount. It seems that drop shipping is becoming an acceptable way of doing business for many publishers.)

More than labels, however, Hartenfeld's computer has been set up to provide valuable tracking information on prices, titles and number of insertions per book relative to sales. From this data, he plans to develop *Computerworld*'s own book publishing program.

One difficulty encountered by *Computerworld* (which other business publishers might take note of) is the tendency of some book publishers to treat business titles as "textbooks" and allow only a 20 percent discount. It has taken time, sales success, and Mel Brisk's best efforts at *Computerworld* to convince these publishers that it is in their own best interest to allow a trade discount of at least 40 percent and preferably 50 percent or more since the books that give the most profit are the ones which will receive the most exposure and, ultimately, the most sales.

These efforts are paying off now as *Computerworld* gains greater leverage through increased sales.

Even with that, however, *Computerworld* promotion manager Jack Edmonston points out that "the best you can expect to do selling other people's books is break even. The profit is in publishing your own. No magazine publisher should even consider book marketing unless he is prepared to eventually publish his own books."

Other criteria Edmonston suggests are 50,000 to 75,000 minimum circulation, inexpensive fulfillment capability, reasonable discount from publishers, and, of course, some indication of your readers' interest.

A free market study

If the best you can do selling other people's books is break even, why do it?

First, it's a way to get your feet wet in book marketing without risking a complete bath. Learning about book margins; finding sources for books and book information; writing book promotion copy instead of magazine promotion—all of these tasks have their own idiosyncrasies to which the magazine publisher needs to become acclimated.

More important, however—selling other publishers' books is the most reliable way to determine whether there is a viable book market among your readership. It's a sort of "hands-on" book marketing laboratory—a free market study—assuming you at least break even on the deal. At worst, you have a limited downside risk.

Selling other publishers' books can be considered the price of developing a profile of the kinds of books your readers want to buy and the prices they are willing to pay. Obviously, having such knowledge is essential before you commit yourself to the more risky business of publishing your own books. But even that needn't be a major risk, especially for business publishers, as in the case of one magazine we all know.

FOLIO: the book publisher of magazine management

FOLIO took the book publishing plunge in 1976 with *The Handbook of Magazine Publishing*, essentially a book of reprints of articles from the magazine—again, a proven technique for many publishers.

In this case, FOLIO saved considerably on production costs since the type was already available on disc, courtesy of FOLIO's in-house typesetting capability.

The book is supplemented by annual updates which are also sold separately as the *Folio Annual*. The supplements, previously published as separate sheets and shipped shrink wrapped, were actually cheaper in a bound and perforated format. Appropriate coding for placement in the *Handbook*'s various sections was included.

After the *Handbook* came another successful venture: *The Handbook of Circulation Management*. This time, FOLIO editor and publisher Charles Tannen tapped a "who's who" of industry experts to contribute chapters (for a royalty) to this how-to compendium of magazine circulation. It's just one small step removed, editorially, from a reprint book and sells just as well, but without annual updates.

Six more books and monographs, all of the information/how-to genre, are now planned. To publish these, Tannen found short-run printers at FOLIO's own Face-to-Face Publishing Conference—people who could offer a good price on as few as 1,000 copies of a book, bind as they sell, and drop ship with labels supplied by FOLIO's computer.

The monographs are typewritten rather than typeset, since typesetting would have made them too expensive to produce. Typewritten books are another slight edge sometimes enjoyed by business publishers. Readers want the information, not fancy books as such.

The only non-FOLIO book which FOLIO offers at present is Jan White's *Graphic Idea Notebook*. But even here, Tannen had an "in." FOLIO had previously published, as a continuing series, the pages of this book. Since they owned the original negatives for the book, they were able to negotiate a highly favorable deal with the outside publisher.

"I see FOLIO as an information company," says Tannen, "not just a magazine company. I want to get information to the customer in any way I can, whether it's a book, a magazine, a seminar."

Direct mail marketing

Thus far we've discussed promotion achieved primarily through the magazine "bookshelf"—full-page ads in the publication itself. This is partly because it is difficult to make direct mail pay with the 40 percent to 50 percent margins you're working with when you're selling other publishers' books. When you publish your own, however, direct mail becomes as viable a medium for your books as it is for your magazine, if not more so.

FOLIO, for example, has done quite well, with an average 2 percent return on self-mailers promoting their books at special pre-publication prices. Modest discounting works well for *Sail* Books, too, as we'll see.

In addition to FOLIO's 10,000 circulation, the magazine mails selectively to their larger database of some 50,000 industry executives. *Sail* Books also tests and mails outside lists in addition to their subscriber base.

Three main formats for direct mail promotion are inserts, direct mail packages and self mailers, both solo and of the mini-catalog variety.

For an insert, *Sail* Books mails a single sheet, coated stock 3-3/4 inch by 7-1/2 inch flyer. The front side features a black and white photo of the book against a color background with two paragraphs of sell copy. The reverse is black type on white with the regular price and discount as a headline, the book's contents spelled out, and a coupon below.

Sail Book's direct mail packages usually sell three or four new titles, also at a discount off "retail" prices. A two-page letter, a two-color 8-1/2 inch by 11 inch flyer with pictures of and from the books, and an order card typically pull 6 percent to 8 percent on *Sail*'s house lists, an average 2.5 percent on outside lists. One mailing to buyers of a particular book pulled 16 percent—a good example of what properly targeted direct mail can do.

FOLIO's self-mailers are 11 inches by 17 inches, folded to 8-1/2 inches by 11 inches, and packed with sell copy. Self-mailers of this type are generally more effective with business markets than they are with consumers who prefer the more personal approach of a letter.

Full color is seldom required to sell what are basically information or "how-to" books, either business or consumer. The exception would be cooking or art books where color plays an important role in the subject matter itself.

Growing your own

As the example of FOLIO books demonstrates, publishing your own books needn't be a major financial commitment, but it will take some investment. The cost of printing a short-run hardcover book under ordinary circumstances (400 pages, 4,000 copies, six inches by nine inches) went just over $8,000 in 1979, according to *Book*

Production Industry.

The best advice is to proceed slowly until you've determined, by whatever means, that you have a market for books. Then, develop a few titles of your own.

Keep your subject matter as close as possible to your magazine's editorial content. Reprints of previously published material are an excellent place to start, especially for business topics, how-to skills and information areas.

If you're starting fresh, try to use authors who are already well known to your readers, either through your own magazine or through the related industry. In dealing with authors, stress the benefits they will get by working with you, a leading authority in the field. Royalties, rather than large advances, are the expected method of compensation in these areas.

Also, announce wherever appropriate that you're looking for manuscripts and assign someone knowledgeable to read and review them.

You'll want to keep good records of all your costs so that when it comes time to price your books, you'll have an accurate account of what's gone into them. Pricing should be at least four times cost including manufacturing, acquisition, staff salaries and overhead, royalties and promotion—even more in the case of book clubs where titles are developed more slowly and tested at various stages.

Consider outside help

No matter how well it goes, you're going to find that publishing your own books is more of an energy-draining, time-consuming effort than you thought.

Computerworld's Walter Boyd even goes so far as to caution would-be publishers, "Don't try to do it yourself," which may be good advice.

The book business is not the magazine business, and your first concern must be your magazine, the goose, not the book publishing egg, no matter how golden it may appear. There are many knowledgeable consultants who can help you get a book division started without a major disruption of your primary business, and what you save in time and error may more than pay the consultant's fees and costs.

On the other hand, although it does require planning, setting up a bookshelf market test need not be an overwhelming process.

Book marketer Henry De Weerd, Rodale Press vice president and veteran of Rodale's highly successful Organic Gardening and other book clubs advises, "Know your audience cold. Get some books with shelflife or coffee table life (for consumer markets)—some unique niche that only you can service—and go after it. As long as you stay within your own boundaries, within your own market segment, you won't have to worry about anyone competing with you because no one will be able to do it as well as you can."

His warning, however: "If you do it in a sloppy or careless manner, you leave yourself wide open for someone to come in and do it right."

Starting a book division

By William Dunkerley

When *Reader's Digest* magazine published its first book in 1950, no one thought that the company would eventually be among the top 10 in the U.S. hard-cover book publishing. Nor did the founders of the American Radio Relay League, a non-profit publisher of an amateur radio magazine, believe that the sale of books would one day become a major source of revenue. They were all surprised over something which should no longer be a secret: Book publishing can be one of the most lucrative and easiest-entry side-ventures readily available to the magazine publisher!

How is it readily available? For one thing, book publishing is a relatively easy industry for anyone to enter. (Perhaps that explains why there are nearly 15,000 book publishers in the United States.) And for you, a magazine publisher, it's even easier. Since you're already in the business of producing a publication product— your magazine—you have these distinct advantages:

•You own editorial material (articles) which can be repackaged into books.

•You have the know-how for processing editorial material.

•You know more than a thing or two about transforming a manuscript into a printed page.

•You are in contact with good writers in your field, potential book authors.

•You have the insight into your market which comes from publishing a magazine.

•You have in your magazine's pages and mailing list a relatively inexpensive advertising medium for promoting the sale of books.

That's an impressive list of advantages. But how do you get started in book publishing?

There's quite a difference between producing your first book and being headlong into the book business. For the latter you'll need a whole product line of books, a system for producing them, marketing them and delivering them.

But for now, *what about that first book*? What'll it cost? How do you price it? When will it show a profit? Questions like these are just a few of a slew of interrelated factors to consider.

Cash-flow requirements

When you publish an issue of your magazine, expenses are usually paid in part by drawing from a pre-paid subscriptions account. In contrast, the publication of a book typically involves a number of up-front expenses—art, photos, typesetting and layout—before any revenue is obtained. They're likely to be on a pay-as-you-go basis and represent fixed, pre-publication expenses. Printing, too, is an up-front expense, perhaps the largest.

Editorial expense is one category, however, where you may find some flexibility. On one hand, you can buy a manuscript for a fee, just as you would buy an article manuscript for your magazine. On the other hand, if you compensate the author through royalties, the fixed editorial expense becomes a variable one which accrues as

sales develop. (How much of a royalty to pay varies with the field and the clout of the author. Ten percent of the title's net revenue, however, is a typical figure.)

Most of your up-front expenses, though, can't be deferred and will have to be recovered through sales. Thus, it's not hard to see that the faster you get your book on sale, the sooner you'll begin to recover your up-front money.

How long does it take?

Producing a book can take anywhere from months to years. Traditionally, the idea for a book begins with an author. He or she completes the manuscript and then submits it to a publisher. Upon acceptance, the publisher assigns an editor to work with the author, make appropriate revisions, and prepare the manuscript for production.

Next, design decisions are made, followed by typesetting, illustrating and layout. An exchange of proofs with the author also may happen along the way. Finally, the book goes to press. Elapsed time for the entire cycle can be several *years*.

Short-cycle publishing

There's a shorter way. A recent management technique has emerged called the "managed book" or short-cycle publishing. It works like this:

The publisher arrives at a decision to publish a book (having considered such things as marketability, design, price, size, etc.) and recruits an author.

Then, the book is planned, a detailed content outline is drawn up, and a length is established. Next, specific page allocations for each chapter are made, a storyboard of chapters is assembled, and deadlines are set for the completion of each chapter or section.

If that sounds like dealing with articles in a magazine, it should. The approach is similar. It allows a number of functions (editorial, typesetting, layout) to be performed in parallel.

The traditional approach took so long because these functions were performed in series without tight control. Now, with short-cycle publishing, a new title can be put on the market in four to eight months. That's quite a time savings.

Breaking even

Before making the final decision to publish a book, you must figure out *when* you will break even. The longer it takes, the longer you will be out-of-pocket the amount of capital which went into the venture—and the higher your interest expense will be. This is a real consideration whether you've borrowed the money from a bank or from yourself (in which case it's an opportunity cost).

To do a break-even analysis, you'll have to forecast sales volume, set a price for the book, and identify what your expenses will be.

Let's say a book has a projected average rate of sale of 500 copies per month and is retailing for $7 net. The author's royalty is $1 per book, allocation for advertising is $0.50 per copy, and the cost to process an order and ship the book is $2. That leaves you with $3.50 per book as the net margin on a sale.

From that money you start paying for the fixed expenses.

In this hypothetical case, the fixed expenses are the following: $3,200 for editing and proofreading; $5,480 for typesetting and layout; $2,000 for pre-publication house advertising; and $7,300 for printing 10,000 copies. That's a total fixed expense of $17,980.

Dividing that number by the net margin on a sale, $3.50, we see that selling 5,137 copies (about one-half of your inventory) will produce the revenue to cover the up-front expenses. That's your break-even point. With sales at your forecast rate of 500 copies per month, it will occur after 10 months. That isn't a bad bet.

If you had found that it would take selling 90 percent of your inventory to break even, watch out! That's a bad risk. But, what do you do if that *is* what your figures tell you?

One solution would be to increase the price. Demand for a book tends to be somewhat inelastic, especially if the book has no direct competition. And even if some consumer resistance to price does develop, you could possibly make back your up-front money quicker by selling fewer books at a higher price.

Return on investment

Another key financial indicator to look at when deciding whether or not to publish a book is your return on investment. It is useful not only in making the decision to publish, but also in choosing among possible ventures. It may also indicate if you'd do better to leave your money in the bank!

Using the forecast, costs and revenues from the previous example, we see $17,980 going into the venture. When all the printed inventory has been sold, the total net margin will be $35,000 ($3.50 x 10,000 = $35,000) or $17,020 above the up-front investment and not a bad return ($35,000 - $17,980 = $17,020). (Unfortunately the picture wouldn't be that rosy, since our example does not consider such expenses as overhead or taxes, nor does it allow for returned books or free copies. It also does not include the cost of direct mail promotion, which, according to DM/MA, is approximately $300 per thousand. The effect of these factors would be to reduce the return on investment.)

Thus far, we've been constructing a financial model of a book or product. Now let's extend this modeling into the marketing realm. To plan for a viable finished product, the forces of the market place must be taken into consideration.

How great is the demand? In what form will your book be best received by the consumers? Content, design, size, shape, color and price— all should be considered with the perspective of the market in which the book will be sold.

Before committing resources and funds to the development of a book, some objective market reading should be obtained. Did the subject score high on your magazine's last reader-interest survey? Are other survey data available?

Many times the idea for a book subject will come from important authors, from staff, or from your own intuitive judgment. Although each of these sources is a valid point of origin, be sure to test or verify the idea. If it were easy to know which books are destined to become best sellers, there would be nothing but best sellers on the market. Or, so it would seem.

Positioning the product can have a great impact upon its market performance. When you have a topic for a book in mind, look around to see what's on the market. Do you want to position your entry to go after market share against an established good seller? Or, can you fill a void in existing literature and make your money that way?

A model price

Price is both a financial and marketing factor in planning a new book. It has to produce the revenue to pay the bills. If the price is pleasantly low, it can increase the attractiveness of your book. Conversely, an exorbitant price may create buyer resistance.

Positioning and perceived value are key operants. A big price in a little league is sure to stand out—unfavorably. That is, unless the perceived value warrants the big price and justifies the introduction of a super-star entry in the competition.

A book can even lose consumer appeal if it is priced too low! There's a textbook example about a cassette-recorder head cleaner. In a marketing test, it was placed on sale in different outlets at two different prices. The cheaper of the identical units did not sell as well as the higher priced unit! Why? Consumers felt that a device "that cheap" probably wouldn't perform well. The price had a negative effect on the product's perceived value.

Certainly, a book with its contents available for inspection is less an enigma than a cassette head-cleaner gadget. But don't price a book too low; the prospective buyer might assume the price is an indicator of low value.

There are a number of rules of thumb for determining retail price from manufacturing cost. Some say multiply by a factor of seven, others say five. And these multiplication factors can be a useful starting point.

Don't use them as hard and fast rules, however. There are some definite pitfalls. For example, the unit manufacturing cost when printing 50,000 copies will be quite different from that of the same book on a 5,000 press run. Using the seven-times rule, the retail price for the short-run version will be a lot higher than the long-run product. Is one worth more than the other when placed on the market? The consumer won't think so—they both look alike.

Consider these factors when setting price:

1. Unit cost. Include all costs. Manufacturing, editorial, production, cost of capital, allocation of overhead expense, etc.

2. Ball park prices of competing or similar products.

3. Perceived value of your product.

4. Elasticity of demand. How much price resistance will there be in the market segment you're aiming at?

5. Discounts given off retail price. What will the average net revenue be from a sale?

Manufacturing considerations

How many copies of your book should be printed? To make that decision, consider your sales forecast for the first year as your print order. For discussion, let's use a sales forecast of 30,000 copies per year.

You have a quote for web-offset printing of $18,602 for that quantity with an adjustment factor of $552.40/M for greater or lesser quantities. As an alternative, let's also consider meeting the demand forecast by making three printings of 10,000 each costing $7,554 ($18,602 - [$552.40/M x 20/M fewer copies]).

The total cost for one year's inventory using this

approach would be $22,662 ($7,554 x 3 printings = $22,662). That's $4,060 more than the cost of printing 30,000 copies at one time. Most of the extra expense is because you're now paying for three make-readies rather than one.

Obviously, if you print 30,000 copies at one time you save $4,060. In addition, you won't risk a stock-out between printings.

However, there are disadvantages to printing all 30,000 at one time. First of all, you'll have an unnecessarily large inventory if your forecast was overly optimistic. Second, you lose early opportunities to revise subject matter. And finally, your initial capital requirements are $11,048 greater.

Another factor to consider is the appropriateness of the equipment on which your book is to be printed. The web-offset quote used in the above example may be appropriate for the 30,000 press run, but not for 10,000 copies. A sheet-fed press, usually with lower make-ready costs, might do well here. The Cameron Belt press is also an interesting alternative for short-run book printing. Although it has unfortunate limitations with regard to halftone reproduction, its economy for short runs (as small as 2,500) is excellent.

Generally, the objective in setting a print quantity is to put the least amount of money into inventory while keeping in mind economics of scale, avoidance of a stock-out, availability of capital, and the timeliness of the content.

The quality (and therefore cost) of materials and processes that go into your book are another manufacturing consideration. They contribute to the book's perceived value.

A book intended to sell for $3 can get away with using a pulpy, ground-wood sheet. Not so one retailing for $35. You shouldn't have a high price tag on a book when its visual and tactile messages say $2.98! On the other side of the coin, putting high quality materials into an inexpensive book may be money down the drain. It's the old rule of diminishing returns. Try to match the aura of perceived value with the price tag.

Whether to go hardcover or softcover, to use multicolor printing or high-quality paper—these questions must fit into the formula, too. The manufacturing materials and processes—combined with the value of a book's contents—will establish whether cost and perceived value are in consonance.

Valuable contents

What is the best way to present the subject matter of your book? This is a question that must be carefully considered. As a magazine publisher, you have certain built-in advantages for source material.

There are certain types of books which naturally lend themselves to both publishing and marketing in a magazine environment. They can make the jump into book publishing painless and profitable. Here are a few examples:

The *anthology* is an obvious type of book for the magazine publisher to consider. It can be made up of a collection of articles which appeared originally in your own magazine. (Some publishers reuse the magazine mechanicals to keep editorial and production costs low.) These articles can also be augmented by new material to bring subject matter up-to-date and to fill in subject gaps.

An anthology appeals to regular readers in that it provides a handy compendium of information on a popular subject. To non-readers, it's just like new information—and might even serve to promote subscriptions.

Directories can be another avenue for exploiting your position as a magazine publisher. Accurately compiled and well-organized lists can make very successful publications. Consider information which might be extracted from your subscriber data or solicited via the pages of your magazine. Who's Who lists, resource people or services, lists with statistical data—and the lists go on!

The *executive report* is an interesting alternative to the traditional book. When you have information aimed at a selective audience, a profession, workers in an industry, or some other particular interest group, you might well have the makings of an executive or special report. These publications—which often appear in loose leaf or spiral binding—provide timely, well-targeted information.

Usually, the executive report has a limited production run. Since economy of scale is not achieved from a relatively short printing run, unit manufacturing costs are high. But because of the exclusivity of content, such reports can sport high price tags.

The format for executive reports, however, does offer a few economies. Illustrations are used only as needed for content amplification— not for decoration. And, it is acceptable to present text from a typewriter rather than typeset copy.

A *multimedia package* can be produced by pairing a book and an audio cassette in a simple container. This technique can be very useful when there is an aural aspect to the subject, such as a cassette with bird calls to go with a bird-watchers guide.

Step-by-step instructions can be given on cassette for applications where it would be difficult to read and perform the instructions at the same time (e.g., photographic darkroom procedures). An introduction to a subject can be presented by the voice of a well-known personality or expert. Chapter summaries and study questions can be recorded on cassette to convert a text into a self-study course.

Handbooks containing reference or how-to information are usually popular and, if revised periodically, can enjoy a long lifetime of sales. One-shot books, such as *annuals* containing year-in-review and introductory information about a field, lend well to opening new avenues of distribution, including newsstands, in some cases.

Try to get double or triple duty from a topic. Your subject may lend itself to presentation in more than a single type of book. One technical publisher took a back-list standard text and revised it graphically to create a new appearance. At the same time, a second product was created by packaging the book together with an audio cassette for sale as a multi-media package. And, finally, a third new product was created by assembling transcripts of the tape's chapter summaries into a handy pocket-book format.

In all three cases, the basic information was the same. The form of presentation was varied, however, to go after different market segments and to achieve economy in editorial expense.

Keep your options open to all the kinds of books you might publish. Hardbacks, paperbacks, talking books on cassettes, books with fold-out charts or diagrams, or even books on diskettes for use in a microcomputer. There's quite a range of possibilities from which to choose.

Special issues

Four years' lead time to prepare an issue of a magazine? That might seem pretty long to you. But to Eugene Weyeneth, the publisher of McGraw-Hill's *Engineering News Record,* four years is just about the time his staff needs to ready *ENR's* 100th anniversary special issue. According to Weyeneth, the key to success for *any* special issue is its complete planning—early.

ENR had a natural topic for a special issue. For other magazines, it's really up to the editors to decide what becomes a special issue. Once the idea has been pinpointed and the issue has been created, publishers find that these specials pay off immeasurably in both reader interest and increased ad pages. So it's no wonder that magazines are continually looking for new angles around which they can create special issues.

ENR's 100th anniversary issue and, in fact, all viable special issues depend on the needs and wants of the magazine's readership. "We want every scrap of useful material that we can offer our readers," declares Weyeneth.

Endorsing his philosophy is *Hospital's* Rex Olsen. "We think a special issue is one in which we can do more by studying one subject in one issue than by spreading coverage of it over many issues. We can attack more sides of a subject and cover it in depth."

Specials Add to Workload

Time is often a major problem since specials frequently require double or triple the amount of copy a regular issue does. Knowing just how much time should be allotted to get the issue together is normally the publisher's job. After meeting with the entire staff—editors, salespeople, production people, promotion writers—the theme and work time for the issue can be set. The publisher as coordinator can then draw up department deadlines.

To find out what readers need and what the special issue can provide, information is sometimes ferreted out with telephone surveys before and after publication of a special. But the original idea for the special usually comes from the editor's contacts in the normal course of work in the field.

Readers love special issues if they're pertinent to their immediate needs. Olsen of *Hospital* says, "Timing an issue to appear when interest in the particular subject is at its peak or still growing is difficult, especially when you have to plan so far in advance. If the subject is of past interest, any amount of attention assigned to it will probably be fruitless. It is necessary for the editors to see developments far in advance." Anticipation bordering on clairvoyance is the key to success.

No matter what the editorial focus of a special, it is mandatory that it be above the standards of regular issues. After all, the rationale for a special issue is to provide a keen-edged focus on one specific topic, in contrast to the more diverse fare offered in regular issues. If it is to be a success with advertisers, it must meet with high acceptance by readers. The editorial material must be written with a long shelf life in mind. Specials, by their very nature, are reference tools for readers. And this is a great selling point to make to advertisers: An ad in the special issue will be seen again and again as readers consult the issue throughout the year.

Engineering News Record, anticipating that its 100th anniversary issue will be around for a long time after publication, is using a plastic paper for the cover to make it more durable. The single copy price is a hefty $5.95. It is even offering a $10 hardcover edition.

Depending on how extensive editorial coverage will be, additional help might be necessary. At *Coal Age* a special thirteenth issue compelled the editors to hire a writer in Denver and use additional contributing editors.

Regardless of the subject matter of a special, it is important that it does not drain time from the normal operations. Work on it must be done gradually, most publishers and editors feel. "Almost the entire staff puts some time into the special issue every day," says one publisher, "but that is time that fits into the regular routine." This is a major reason for a publisher to begin work on a special many months, even years, before it is to appear.

All this, of course, requires extra money, as does the increased promotion, production and sales effort. Some publishers devise wholly separate budgets—above and beyond the ones for the regular issues—and treat the special as a magazine unto itself. A special usually has heavy impact on the fiscal year before, during and after its appearance. To take into account the special-issue ad linage along with regular ad linage would give a very distorted picture.

Selling to New Advertisers

A special issue is a golden opportunity to sell more space to both regular and new advertisers. All magazines report a heavy amount of one-shot advertisers cropping up in special issues. A number of publishers find that new ad contracts come in later because of reader response to ads in a special issue.

Extra revenue is not produced only from new advertising. Publishers can bank on continuous orders from readers and advertisers for back issues and reprints.

Appliance magazine is well aware of the extra revenue that can be produced from a special. One January 10,000 additional copies of a special on the Maytag Corporation were ordered by Maytag for its own promotional use. And according to *Appliance's* publisher Dana Chase, inquiries from other companies about doing editorial in-depth profiles on them have paved the way for future specials.

A single advertiser paid for an entire extra thirteenth issue of *Hardware Retailing,* a magazine that does more than one million pages in reprint business yearly, mostly from specials. Other magazines such as *Advertising Age, Hospital, Purchasing*—in fact about every magazine questioned by FOLIO—experienced high demands for reprints from special issues.

Promoting Special Issues

How should extra money be scheduled for a special issue ad promotion? What difference is there between this promotion and that for a regular issue?

A special published for many years becomes an industry tradition. Usually the staff sits back and lets the space orders flow in. It's up to the salespeople to go after *new* business and pry loose ad dollars held by suppliers who aren't in the habit of advertising. The most popular methods used are direct mail promotions and a blitz of personal sales calls. *Hotel and Motel Management* uses both, as do *Advertising Age, Chemical Engineering* and most other magazines who put out special issues.

"Before you start any promotion campaign for a special issue, you have to rev up your sales staff to sell it more intensely. But they still must not forget that it is only one issue during the year," advises E.P. Blanchard, Jr., ad manager for *Chemical and Engineering News. CEN* recently featured a 50th anniversary "blowing-our-horn" issue that was promoted with all the dazzle and hoopla of a Pillsbury Bake-Off. The extensive ad space effort included a giveaway of 50 extra copies for every page of advertising placed. Customers also received a commemorative metal medallion and a lacquered wooden plaque embossed with a letter from the American Chemical Society and a copy of the ad. This was all touted in advance with a brochure mailed and handed out by salespeople.

More sales-producing gimmicks: *Electronic News* put ads on 119 billboards for 27 advertisers who had taken space in *EN*'s special show issues. Each billboard showed the name of the company and at what booth they would be found at a forthcoming show. A reminder to look for the company's ad in *EN* was also displayed. Cahners Publishing Co. offered any advertiser in any of Cahners' books the opportunity to appear in a thick supplement that went exclusively to the top 12,000 corporate executives and government officials. The supplement contained editorial from four of Cahners' magazines that were running a feature called "Keep America Competitive."

In spite of all the special issue direct mail pieces sent out by business magazines, few seem to attract much attention. Some advertisers complain that many magazines don't give enough advance notice of forthcoming specials or that they announce them in such lackluster mailing pieces that they are easily overlooked and thrown out. But if the promotion is eye-catching and persuasively written, it can be the clincher in pulling the advertiser into the issue.

If salespeople are allotted enough time to sell far ahead of the deadline, special issues will not interfere with their normal sales call schedule. Extra time is vital because they are selling space to the long-shop advertiser *plus* the regulars.

While most magazines reported that they start heavy sales legwork about four to eight weeks ahead of a closing date, many others begin work a year ahead. Timing of promotion campaigns can be critical. Aggressive selling is best done when a salesperson can show the poten-

tial advertiser why an ad is worthwhile.

For Martin Rosenblum, vice-president of Fairchild Publications and ad director for its *Electronic News,* there is no better time to sell than when a trade show or convention issue is coming up. Then the opportunities for getting new advertisers are at their peak. Rosenblum not only goes after the ad for the imminent show issue but also resourcefully negotiates ads for the following year's show issue. He points out to the potential advertiser that it is physically and mentally impossible for a buyer at a housewares show, for example, to meet with 2,000 exhibitors. But by running an ad in the show issue, the exhibitor insures against being overlooked.

Rosenblum is convinced that a special issue must be sold early—preferably six months in advance. "Lock it up before the competition does—and while the exhibitor is still planning for the show."

Farm & Power Equipment plans its issue schedule a year in advance, timing it to fall before July, the traditional beginning of the ad budget year. "You have to work far in advance to be on the minds of advertisers when they are planning their budgets," says a spokesman at *F&PE.*

A Special Issue Is...

Everybody who produces special issues seems to come up with yet another definition of what makes the issue a special one. There are, however, some standard definitions set down for the industry.

According to *Standard Rate & Data Service (SRDS),* the special issue is "an entire issue, distributed within the announced publishing frequency and devoted to homogeneous subject matter related to the basic publication. It is an *extra* issue within the subscription cycle."

By this definition, though, *SDRS* has limited its listing of specials to a scant 200 per year. But even a quick study shows that the special issue is flourishing almost to what would seem the threshold of saturation.

The trend toward business magazines' publishing special issues has swelled to such proportions that about two years ago *Industrial Marketing* magazine started to list free of charge advance notices of forthcoming special issues. The job of tabulating the information for this now regular feature has become so burdensome that two people are needed on an intermittent basis to compile the data.

George Young, *IM* editor, says that when the magazine first started the listing, it sent out questionnaires to all magazines listed in *SRDS.* "Now we don't even have to send out forms. Publishers are glad just to forward necessary information to us automatically." He adds that *IM's* definition of a special issue is when one issue of a magazine has at least 25 percent of its editorial content devoted to one subject—admittedly a less rigid criterion than that established by *SRDS. IM* listed an estimated 1,600 special issues in the past year—and these are only for the industrial classification magazines.

What *IM* considers to be a special issue is called a *special feature* by *SRDS* and listed in a separate classification. These are issues that are devoted in whole or in part to a particular subject and are published as part of the cycle of regular issues.

With readers and advertisers quite receptive to specials, many publishers devise yearly schedules with nothing but specials. This ploy doesn't often work. A special is only as special as a magazine makes it. Some magazines run special feature issues every month, using the word *special* like salt. This waters down the special's intrinsic value. The fewer special issues offered during the year, the more response these few will receive. At *Advertising Age,* Lou DeMarco says that many readers ask for repeats of well-received specials, but the magazine avoids this because it would glut the year with too many specials and detract from the appeal of each one.

Why Special Issues?

Any publisher expecting to make pots of money from a string of special issues will find that advertisers soon will lose interest because intense reader interest will have waned. Keep special issues special and not specious by spacing them far enough apart from each other, advise some successful special-issue publishers.

A special issue should mean in-depth coverage of a particular facet of the industry that makes it stand out from the other issues during the year. It should say to the reader: "Here. We have done extra work and research to meet your needs and put it all into one jam-packed issue."

Existing reader interest and gratitude will be strengthened. And an issue that is read by readers is bought by advertisers.

With editorial discrimination and foresight—understanding what readers want and need—publishers can continue to produce special issues that not only reach out to readers but also ring up ad sales. And that, after all, is what publishing is all about.

Five Types of Special Issues

1. *The Desk Book or Buyers Guide*—It seems as if every industry has one of these. It appears as one of the regular issues and, with a few exceptions such as front- and back-of-the-book features, is composed entirely of directory listings. It is designed to be kept as a permanent reference tool by the reader and is one in which the most ads are sold. Depending on the extent of research it contains, it proves to be a valuable reputation booster.

2. *The Trade Show Issue*—Usually this is an issue which, like the type above, is produced on an overrun. Whereas the directory issue overrun is used for the continual demand for extra copies throughout the year, the extra copies of the trade show issue are given away at the particular exhibition to promote the magazine. Trade show issues are of two varieties: Souped-up regular issues that cover the show in general and show directory guides with news coverage left for the following issue. They are scheduled as regularly as the trade shows appear and usually fall into a predictable niche that readers almost expect.

3. *Research Topic Issue*—Defined as any issue with more than 25 percent editorial devoted to a particular report, this is the approach that can be of most value to readers, having the greatest amount of impact on the industry served. Advertising usually falls around the particular subject of the in-depth focus. Here the emphasis is on high editorial achievement—a promotion for the magazine in itself.

4. *New Products Issue*—This could be considered just one more researched topic special issue but more and more magazines are devoting entire issues to the rapid advancements in their field; thus it has become a class in itself. Not only does coverage of new products attract strong reader interest but it draws advertisers (after all, it's their products being reported) like bears to the honeypot. Editors must be wary, though, because news of a product *is* per se free advertising and copy should not be simply verbatim news release material. It can be a quick way to lose credibility with readers.

5. *Anniversary/Special Occasion Issue*—A substantial editorial reason for an anniversary/special occasion issue must exist, for this type of issue is of hard-to-recognize value to advertisers and usually must be heavily promoted. Its very reason for existence is often entirely fabricated (i.e. a need for it which did not exist is created) and does not affect the industry as much as it does the magazine.

Making your seminar work for you

By Robert Sbarge

A number of innovative magazine publishers have recently ventured into the sponsorship of educational seminars for their readers. Some have succeeded, others have failed.

If you've been thinking of entering the seminar arena, it's probably because you recognize—as other publishers have—the benefits it can offer your publication:

• Enhancement of its competitive leadership position with both readers and advertisers.

• Significant income from a new profit center.

• Important content for future issues.

• First-hand contact and interchange with readers.

Some of these publishers who have not succeeded have, in fact, invited failure. Too many rules were broken, too little commitment was made to time and thought and too many decisions were made on the basis of ego instead of reality.

To avoid many of the critical problems which can arise, there are some guidelines to help you oversee the successful execution of a professional program.

First of all, as publisher you already control a set of assets which favor a successful outcome:

• Your editors' expertise and overview of the industry.

• Direct access to leaders in the field for utilization as speakers.

• Credibility with your audience.

• Your circulation mailing list for promotion of the program.

• Your capability to promote the seminar in your magazine.

Successful execution of any seminar requires thoughtful planning and the dovetailing of many complex factors. Timing is critical and content is paramount, along with effective promotion and the ultimate delivery of the program presentations themselves. And, risk money is at stake. It is, indeed, a full-time job that requires undivided attention and thorough followup.

Consequently, the first question to face is whether or not you can delegate this responsibility to someone on your staff whose regular duties can be assumed by someone else. In addition to this time commitment, you should consider the person's ability to research content, structure program format, plan the budget, contact and negotiate for hotel and meeting space, develop promotion strategy, identify and commit speakers and handle on-site logistics and problems which arise during the seminar.

A viable alternative is to use the services of a seminar management company on a fee basis or a joint venture "share the risk and profit" basis. If you decide upon this course, you will want to list its responsibilities and yours, agree on the means of monitoring its progress, specify those areas in which you *must* have final say and determine exactly your liability in case the project must be aborted along the way.

Planning the Theme, Objectives and Content

A seminar offers the opportunity to accomplish goals that are impossible to attain with the printed page— for example, face-to-face communication, exposure to new ideas, interaction and exchange, all keyed to a period of time that permits meaningful learning experience.

Topics should be selected and methodology employed which capitalize upon successful use of these factors. Additionally, the seminar audience and your program can be defined as narrowly or as broadly as you like.

Prospective attendants choose among many competing seminar offerings—from national, state and local associations, from commerical sources such as the American Management Association, from your competition and from the program you are planning. All of these will be judged by the criteria of greatest take-home value measured against time and money spent.

This competitive environment requires careful evaluation so that *your* program, when marketed, will appear to be relevant to the attendants and will emphasize the "special voice" of the industry which is yours.

The early definition of theme and objectives will immediately suggest possible program speakers. There is great, but often fatal, temptation to go for "big names," to select by reputation alone. This is, perhaps, the biggest trap of all to avoid, especially if the reputation is derived from authorship of popular articles or books in the field. Frequently, people believe that the selection of a prominent name will help sell the program and there's certainly some validity to this view. Unfortunately, however, some of the country's most effective writers are also some of the poorest verbal communicators to ever grace a podium.

The impact of verbal communication can make or break a seminar. So, unless you are a gambler, never commit a speaker unless you or someone you know has personally heard him or her speak before an audience. There simply is no way to recover from the disaster of a poor speaker.

In balance, a seminar is successful because the attendants learn, because they go away armed with meaningful information, new techniques or proven methods which can help each one when he or she is back at work. Speakers who bring this kind of substance to a program are the ones to include in your program. It's the message that's received that counts.

There should be an early understanding *in writing* with each speaker as to topic, role in the program, fee, expense reimbursement, means of travel to and from the seminar, time and place of participation and special equipment requirements. It's useful to let each program speaker know the complete program content and roster of speakers.

Last minute cancellation by a speaker is always a real possibility. This situation is particularly prevalent when dealing with government officials who may suddenly be called back to official duties. In order to be prepared, advance planning for back-up speakers or program substitutions is necessary.

As the time of the seminar approaches, someone should confer with speakers to probe into their presentation and suggest changes for improved relevancy or effectiveness. This tack achieves other goals: It pressures program participants who may have fallen behind in their preparation and assures you that all the components are progressing according to plan.

Seminar Structure and Schedule

Some common session formats are lecture, lecture-discussion groups, panel and case method. A well-structured seminar will utilize a combination of these formats to best convey information and to maintain maximum interest by the audience.

A lot of factual information can be conveyed in a limited time by *lecture*. About 40 minutes is the limit anyone should be required to sit and listen to one speaker. A planned question-and-answer period following the lecture allows for clarification, provides a change of tempo and may offer new viewpoints.

Many speakers like to engage the audience in *discussion* by presenting a brief formal statement. Then, through interchange with the audience of provocative questions and answers, they elicit aspects of the topic that closely relate to the problems and interests unique to the attendants. The essential ingredient of the lecture-discussion format is an informal atmosphere in which members of the audience feel free to question the issues and state their opinions.

Discussion groups require stimulating topics and effective discussion leaders. One topic or a variety of subjects may be assigned to each discussion group. The latter allows participants to choose an area of particular interest to them. At the close of the group sessions, each table or group leader reports to the total audience on the nature of the discussion and conclusions reached. If the discussion leaders do their jobs well, everyone in attendance will be an active participant.

The *case method* technique is popular with many speakers because it generates the audience's participation but keeps it within the limits of the case situation. Printed material can be mailed in advance but more often the printed "case" is distributed for reading at the start of a session. The cases are open-ended situations which the au-

On-site Checklist

Arrival at the seminar site by the staff person responsible for the program should be one day in advance to correct any errors in arrangements. Items, as applicable, that should be brought include:
- Printed program schedules
- Printed roster of attendants
- Name badges
- Writing pads and pens (unless supplied by hotel)
- Marking pens, cellophane tape, paper clips, etc.
- Evaluation forms (to be completed by attendants at conclusion of the seminar)
- Extra sets of advance reading materials
- Copies of all hotel correspondence and agreements covering confirmation of facilities and services.

General Hotel Arrangements (as applicable)
- Check all reserved hotel accommodations and guest room lists
- Arrange with hotel all procedures for checkout and guest bill payments as you do not want to be responsible for registrants' unpaid bills
- Check hotel lobby posting of your meeting and events as scheduled
- Supply hotel with envelopes which contain detailed schedule of events including locations, list of fellow attendants, information about speakers, etc., to be distributed to attendants upon registration
- Meet hotel staff assigned to your program and know how to reach them quickly in case of emergencies.

Meeting Rooms (as applicable)
- Table and chair arrangements
- Sound system, volume controls, etc.
- Air conditioning and heating controls
- Lighting controls
- Electrical outlet locations
- Pencils and pads placed on tables
- Blackboard, chalk, erasers
- Flip pad, easel, markers
- Pointer
- Lectern
- Water, glasses, ash trays
- Projector and other equipment, operators
- Correct distractions such as glare, phone noise, piped music, etc.

dience must digest and then, through discussion, decide what the problems are and how they should be solved. Good cases do not have a single "approved solution." Participants benefit by exposure to the experiences and thinking of their colleagues.

Controversial subjects or those with conflicting viewpoints can be treated most effectively in a *panel* format. Under the guidance of a moderator, panel members state their opinions and then discuss the subject among themselves. Questions from the audience should be encouraged to challenge the panel members' views.

Whatever your final seminar format, it's vital to consider the individual needs of the attendants. Most, if not all, of them may have a unique problem that they hope they may be able to solve by attending your seminar. Give them the opportunity to pursue this goal.

Also, don't minimize the importance of informal interchange among all conference participants—the attendants, the speakers and your personnel.

Set Date

Consider national and religious holidays, industry conventions and trade shows (national, state and local), school vacations and the business cycle of your industry in deciding on your seminar dates.

While the length of the seminar—probably one to three days—should be determined by content, consider the desirability of weekend vs. weekdays, beginning of the week vs. end of the week or a combination in terms of what best fits the audience. Keep in mind that you're asking participants to give up either family time or business time or both to join you.

Select Location

Should you choose a central geographic location (either nationally or regionally), a downtown city location, an airport access location or an isolated "retreat-type" location? Is a resort atmosphere helpful or detrimental?

A one-day program might suggest a location with a nearby airport, easy to get in and out. A downtown city site may mean losing local attendants for part of the time to demands of their office and the others to the competitive activities of the city, either business or social.

An isolated location may be ideal for a program several days long in which attendants should be captive to themselves as a group and to the in-depth content of the program. A resort area allows a balance between serious education and recreation.

Most major hotels have conference facilities and staff specialized in servicing conference needs. Also, autonomous conference centers exist, and some academic institutions encourage professional groups to use their facilities. In considering which facilities to use, the factor that should, perhaps, tip the scale is the cooperative attitude of the meeting or convention staff employed by the hotel or conference center.

Before executing a final written agreement with the hotel or facility, determine the following:

• The availability of the specific number of rooms for overnight accommodations and meeting rooms for the required dates.

• The daily rate per person for rooms, single or double occupancy.

• The charges, if any, for meeting rooms, which should always be specifically identified and committed by name, and for audiovisual equipment and operators, athletic facilities, etc.

• The charges for coffee during breaks, as scheduled in your program.

• The penalties of cancellation or "no show" for rooms.

• The deposit payment requirements.

• The menu selections for all meal functions, cocktail parties and other social events.

The physical setup and size of your meeting rooms will depend upon the type of session you plan. "Classroom" style encourages the educational atmosphere and provides table space for participants to take notes. This setup is the most popular.

"Theatre" style, with rows of chairs, accommodates the most people in a given size room. Other alternatives are possible and a good hotel or conference staff can point them out. Consider the degree of formality or informality and the amount of interchange desired when setting up the meeting room.

Promoting the Seminar

Successful seminar promotion techniques include letters, mailing pieces, advertisements, editorial support, phone campaigns and others. As publisher, you have all of these techniques available and at attractive costs. Selection of which ones to use will be determined by seminar objectives, audience analysis and cost.

Seminar promotion results are as varied as programs and audiences. Generally, however, direct mail outpulls ad coupons, often ten to one. Some magazines have been successful using space ads only whereas most benefit from employing both.

Promotion lead time of 60 to 90 days satisfies most personal scheduling requirements. When a national audience is involved, requiring participants to travel from greater distances, this lead time is imperative.

To encourage early registration and ultimate success, first promotions should contain as much complete information as possible. It should describe subject content, speakers, the time schedule and costs including registration, meals and any others which may be involved.

Budget and Registration Fees

Early determination of theme, length of program, speakers and promotion campaign enables one to prepare a realistic preliminary budget. Only after this is done should the registration fee be set.

Expense items will include speaker honorarium and expenses, promotion (including printing, envelopes, lists, postage and advertising production), travel and expenses for a staff planning trip, staff travel and expenses during seminar, meeting room charges, supplies (notebooks, pens, printed materials, etc.), gratuities, meals and/or other hotel expenses and your operating overhead allocations, including staff time.

The total estimated expense divided by the projected number of registrants identifies the breakeven number of registrants and the actual cost per attendant.

In setting the selling price, many first-time seminar sponsors add too low a profit margin which is often consumed by unexpected additional expenses. Price, generally, is *not* the determinant in seminar attendance. The opportunity to learn and obtain valuable information is what the registrant wants and he or she is willing to pay for it. In this respect, a 35 percent margin is not uncommon.

A second budget to consider is the risk budget. The key ingredients in this are promotion, staff planning overhead and any financial commitments to hotels or others which cannot be cancelled.

You might also consider the possibility of running the seminar even if you will only break even or incur a slight loss. The other potential benefits—for example, the experience of running a seminar, the good will created, material obtained for future issues, etc.—may be worth the slight loss.

Historically, the majority of seminar registrations arrive within the first month of promotion exposure. And, since a lead time of 60 to 90 days is in effect as suggested, a "go" or "no go" decision can be made well ahead of the seminar dates and deadlines for payments of deposits and other irreversible financial obligations. From the point of view of the magazine, this is the most important aspect of ample lead time.

Seminar sponsorship offers the business or professional magazine publisher a new type of communication service which utilizes his or her present staff, expertise and information facilities as a base from which to profitably grow. In this world of knowledge explosions, rapid technological changes, altering marketplaces and professional obsolescence, seminars can help fulfill professional needs of readers. Magazines, with their basic stores of data and information, can be in the forefront of this continuing education activity.

Keep those postcards coming in

By Stephen M. Curran

Publishers are constantly on the lookout for additional products and services to add to their sales portfolio and which will fit in with their respective audiences. One area they might look towards for additional sales potential is loose-deck or postcard booklets. Direct reponse postcards, in whichever form, can be used to attract new advertisers to your publication.

About a year-and-a-half ago, our firm looked to direct-response postcard programs as a door opener to marginal or infrequent advertisers in a relatively low-reader response industry. We worked toward converting these prospects into display advertisers by using such a program as a sales tool. In one case, a publication we represent initially experienced a 61 percent increase in direct-response postcard sales during the six-month period from early 1976 to our second mailing that year; in the next six-month period, from late 1976 to early 1977, a 72 percent increase was experienced; and from early 1977 to our latest mailing, an additional 78 percent increase was recorded.

The steady increase in direct-response postcard sales during this 18-month period produced bottom line profits for the publication as well as ourselves; but, more important, it opened a lot of doors and presented tremendous opportunities. During this same 18-month period of direct-response postcard sales increases, our share of the market for this industry also increased and total display advertising sales rose approximately 22 percent as well.

That's significant! Significant, because advertisers were being lost due to lack of inquiries even though the publication covered an industry where there were historically relatively low inquiry readers. One of the ways we felt we could show audience interest—even though we had all the other tools to show circulation, readership, reader-service cards—was through the use of the direct-response postcards.

Direct-Response Postcard Format

For those unfamiliar with loose-deck postcards or postcard booklets, they are simply business-reply postcards with one side of the card displaying an advertiser's message along with room for name, address, phone number or any other information the advertiser may desire. The reverse side of the card carries the return business address of the advertiser and the advertiser's mailing indicia.

The stock used, of course, complies with U.S. Postal Service requirements regarding business reply cards.

Getting Started

Probably the best place to start in putting a postcard program together is with your printer—getting some prices, finding out what facilities are available for such a program, what the printer's capabilities are. You should shop around to see who specializes in postcard mailings. Not all printers have the capabilities.

You should also check with publishing colleagues, your publisher's representatives who may be handling similar programs and your professional associations to see what information is available.

Once you have some prices and background relating to sales, mechanicals, closings and the like, you then have the potential of an additional sales tool for opening, or reopening, some formerly closed doors.

The Mailing List

Direct-response postcards are mailed directly to a publication's entire or partial mailing list, depending on the audience and preference of the publisher.

Design-book audiences or heavy-responding end-user book audiences, as examples, would certainly be potentially well-responding audiences compared with, let's say, certain retailer/dealer book audiences.

If a publication's comp lists were added to the well-responding audience list and thus to the rate base on the advertising in the mailing, gross revenues for the publisher and the representatives would normally go up. But the cost-per-inquiry for the advertiser would also, in turn, go up, making the program a much tougher sell the second time around.

Of course, if the advertising in the postcard mailing warranted the addition of the comp list, revenue for the publisher and representative would be up and the cost-per-inquiry for the advertiser would be down. Command decision! The direct-response postcard mailing program is not a one-time shot, and that list, or that portion of that list, is a vital initial consideration.

Pricing

What to charge the advertiser is an important point to consider, to say the least. Some say get whatever the market can bear; with that attitude, however, you can miss out on a large chunk of that volume market by pricing yourself out of the market. The newer companies, which use direct-response postcards exclusively to merchandise their principals' products, normally use an in-house agency and look at a breakeven point of one cent per card after frequency, agency and all the other discounts are taken. They don't always make that breakeven price.

One practice of publishers that turns off final decision makers to postcard programs is refusing to give standard agency discounts on them. By refusing to do so, they continue to lose business.

Another practice which discourages potential postcard users is giving two prices. Normally one price which is much lower is given to a display advertiser in a publication, with little or no consideration given to size or frequency. A second price normally much higher is given to nondisplay advertisers. Some publishers do offer the nonadvertiser what they consider a "break" by offering, let's say, a three-time frequency rate for cards coupled with a low cost one-eighth page display ad, bringing their cost for the direct-response postcard down below their one cent breakeven point. However many postcard merchandisers consider themselves pioneers in the field and they often wouldn't even consider running a display ad at any price.

The practice of setting two separate prices for the same product also raises some legal questions which, at some point in the future, will come to litigation.

By establishing a uniform price for all advertisers for the same product, prospective advertisers normally not willing to test the marketplace with display advertising are more encouraged than discouraged to test it with direct-response postcards. Additional incentives can be added, by bulk or by frequency, to postcard advertisers, however. Volume postcard merchandisers and advertisers will run when the price is right. And the right price for volume advertisers will not have a maximum ceiling on discounts for a specific number of cards or disregard standard agency discounts or have higher prices for non-display advertisers than for display advertisers. These practices create barriers for volume advertisers, not incentives.

Frequency

When figuring this pricing, consideration should be given to how many successful mailings you could make a year. Before you establish your frequency you should know:

1. What part or all of the list you will be using.
2. Advertising prospects for that list.
3. How your competitors may react.
4. Other considerations in the marketplace.

The trick is to get the first one off the ground successfully but you should try to plan for a minimum of two per year. For instance, your first mailing could be tied in with a trade show package deal, containing invitations to booths or hospitality suites along with contests for those showing up; or it could be tied in with special buying seasons, offering catalogs, special discounts, personal sales calls, etc. The uses of postcard programs are endless but they depend on the marketplace.

A Different Sell

Selling postcard programs to advertisers is much different than selling display advertising, though much of it is still in the story line.

Advertisers seek a barometer by which to gauge their advertising program. All too often they gauge the success or failure of their ad program by inquiries, even though a benchmark study or some other means may be much more practical.

But if inquiries are the barometer, even though the successful program does not warrant them, an advertiser will drop out of a publication if there are none.

Promotional activities will move to direct mail, premiums, trade shows, etc., where some "tangible" results can be seen. After all, that ad manager or ad agency must justify those ad dollars being spent.

These nondisplay hardliners are the best prospects for postcards and for moving them back into display advertising using postcards as a vehicle. If the advertiser had an advertising program which did not warrant inquiries, but did use inquiries to gauge the success of the campaign, approach the advertiser with the fine points of your program initially; then, after having sold the program, go back to the basics and what is trying to be accomplished with the campaign.

Selling Points

Direct response postcards are direct, quick, convenient and inexpensive.

A normal size deck will contain approximately 50 postcards, as an example, and should be a successful and a profitable co-op for the publisher and advertisers. As far as cost-per-card or cost-per-thousand, that much will depend on the printer's capabilities.

The advertiser should be told that the message on the postcard stands alone and does not have competition with other ads, editorial or even folios. The respondent can assess his or her interest in each advertiser's card and respond if he or she wishes, which is possibly one reason for the high quality and high inquiry counts from postcard mailings.

The best position in a mailing deck is in the front half of the deck. Of course, the very first card in the deck is the best position of all. A premium should be charged for this position or at the least, it should be used as a closing incentive for an advertiser.

The cards have flexibility; advertisers can offer informational literature, special deals, personal calls by salespeople, discounts or almost anything that can be said within the physical confines of a postcard.

Inquiries from the respondent are sent directly to the advertiser with no third party acting as a clearing house for the responses as with bingo cards. And, in spite of the technical progress made by services fulfilling reader service card inquiries and forwarding them to their respective advertisers, these postcards are much hotter leads for the advertisers.

They can be processed in the advertiser's morning mail and given directly to the salespeople for prompt followup.

Because these cards are so quick and so direct, inquiries by the respondents are more likely than not to be still in their mind when the salespeople make contact.

With the postcards going directly to the advertiser, the respondent has a feeling of confidentiality; he or she feels that more personal attention will be given than by using a bingo card. And if the advertiser is on the ball, depending on the quality of the lead, that respondent should be receiving *very* special attention.

Cost-of-Sale

In many cases, the cost-of-sale for 50 display ads may seem to be equal to, or less than, the cost-of-sale for 50 postcard sales. But actually the cost-of-sale for postcards should be much less and become much lower for future sales. In many cases, just letting the prospective advertiser know you have such a program available opens new lines of communications. It is all in how it is presented and how it is followed up.

Advantages

The directness and simplicity of postcards have tremendous advantages for everyone:

1. It brings in additional revenues without the solicitation of press releases to test the market, a practice that is sometimes abused.

2. It allows the advertisers the opportunity to test a publication's audience at a relatively low cost to the advertiser.

3. It supplies enough traceable inquiries converted to sales to rekindle interest and even support display advertising in the publication.

The actual selling of the postcard is not as important as the benefits the program can later deliver when handled correctly.

Once it can be proven that the audience is out there, an advertiser may go a little further out on a limb to get those ad dollars for display advertising. A direct response postcard program can open the door.

Editorial

Are editors necessary?

By Henry A. Grunwald

The editor's job has sometimes been likened to that of an orchestra conductor. There he stands at the podium, or sits behind his desk, waving his arms in all directions. At his downbeat, reporters report and writers write and words pour in from near and far and pictures are assembled and headlines are written. And all these disparate elements come together harmoniously—we all hope—until they are finally formed into one symphonic whole. My predecessor as editor in chief of Time Inc., Hedley Donovan, once put it this way: "The music, the news, is provided out there by Carter and Sadat and Begin and Reggie Jackson and others, who perhaps are the equivalent of Brahms and Bach and Beethoven. The editor doesn't make the news, except occasionally, but he does interpret it and shape it, as the conductor does. Above all," Donovan concluded, "he selects what's going to be on the program, which is one hell of a power."

Being an inveterate armchair conductor, I naturally like this comparison very much and enjoy seeing myself as a sort of Toscanini or at least a Solti of the press. But I was deeply shaken one day when I talked to a violinist and found that the fellow didn't think a conductor necessary at all. He thought most of the gyrations on the podium were done for show, and that most orchestras could play the score perfectly well on their own. And quite a few people feel the same way about editors. They suspect that most writers and reporters could do very nicely without all the arm waving by some maestro. In fact, some even feel, and I am horrified to report this, that editors just louse up good ideas, mess up stories and repress individuality. So I thought I'd talk today about the question: Are editors necessary?

I know that you can hardly bear the suspense of trying to figure out what my answer to the question is going to be. My answer is, yes, editors are necessary. You may disagree. Or you may agree and in fact even consider the point obvious. Either way, I mean to offer some supporting evidence simply by telling you what, in my experience, an editor does.

Of course there are different kinds of editing. To borrow a phrase from economics, there is micro-editing and macro-editing. The first has to do with words and meanings, style and structure. It involves the age-old battle to get meanings clear and structure as logical as possible, and to encourage a style that is attractive without being ornamental for its own sake. The purpose of journalism with very few exceptions is not self expression. If you want self expression, become poets. It's all right to show

off in your journalistic writing and to be a little dazzling, if you can be, but never at the expense of clarity and communication. An editor can truly help a writer to say what he means. Something that may be perfectly clear and understandable in the writer's mind is not necessarily so when it reaches paper. There may be a few writers who don't need editors. Perhaps the definition of an artist is someone who can edit himself. But even literary artists have required editing. The sprawling novels of Thomas Wolfe might never have been rendered readable except for the help of a good editor, Maxwell Perkins. Even T.S. Eliot was not beyond editing; his friend Ezra Pound slashed the hell out of the first version of *The Wasteland*. And journalists are not artists. We are craftsmen, and usually craftsmen in a hurry.

An editor serves his writer when he, in fact, represents the reader. The editor must ask all the questions that the reader is likely to have and he must ask them with the relentless insistence and single-mindedness of a 5-year-old. This is what Harold Ross obviously had in mind when he said: "Editing is the same thing as quarreling with writers." My own favorite maxim about editing comes from another profession. The great architect, Mies van der Rohe, used to say that "God is in the details." I don't know about God, but an editor certainly must be in the details.

An editor also must know his audience. In that respect I always admired General Charles Taylor, an early editor of the Boston *Globe*, who was an unabashed provincialist and wanted each citizen to see his name in the paper at least once a year. When he was informed that the rival Boston *Herald* had signed up another London correspondent, General Taylor cried: "Then, by God, we'll have to get another reporter in South Boston."

An editor should be a guardian of the language, uncompromising enemy of cliche and jargon and faulty grammar and bad syntax—all sins which are widely committed these days even by college graduates and even, I dare say, by graduates of journalism schools.

Speaking of language, may I slip in here a special plea on a subject about which I am somewhat obsessive: the use of the word "media" in the singular. I don't like the word "media" anyway, but if we must use it, let's at least use it properly. "The media is" is an atrocity. It should of course be "the media are." I am not just being pedantic when I insist on this. Correct usage here makes a philosophical difference, because the media used in the singular evokes one big, undifferentiated blob, suggesting that all media are the same. But even as I say this, I am aware of the fact that I am probably fighting a losing battle. I am reminded of Horace Greeley, who clung to the plural use of the word "news" long after others had collectivized it. Once Greeley cabled a correspondent: "Are there any news?" The reporter cabled back: "Sorry, not a single new."

Anyway, language aside, an editor should have an engineer's eye for the structure of a story. I find that I sometimes have to read a story many times and, as it were, live with it for a while before the true or the most effective structure becomes clear to me. Often in such a case a story has to be taken apart and reassembled. But an editor fails completely if he merely rewrites a story himself.

This practice of rewriting has not been unknown at *Time* magazine, though it is much less frequent than legend has it. A good deal of writing, however, goes on in the margins of *Time* copy where criticisms, comments and suggestions for revisions appear in great profusion. Composing marginal notes is itself an art form. Eric Hodgins, an editor of *Fortune*, could be devastating with the observation: "This story *subtracts* from the sum of human knowledge." A former managing editor of *Time*, T.S. Matthews, would write: "This is Choktaw. Now try it in English." I myself have occasionally been guilty of referring to words or sentences I specially hated with the marginal notation: "Ugh, ugh." One *Time* writer memorably characterized this as the "American Indian school of editing."

In a sense I began my editing career at *Time* many years ago when I was an office boy. I used to read copy while delivering it, and from there it was only a step to try to improve it. I took to rewriting cover stories to show my elders and betters how I thought it should be done. This practice of mine was not uniformly popular. Once, according to *Time* legend, I was standing in a writer's office peering over his shoulder as he sat at his typewriter. I was somewhat startled to find that the words he was typing were as follows: "Kid, if you don't cut this out, I'll break every bone in your body." It is said, though I personally do not remember it, that I left the office in a hurry but muttering as I walked out: "Cliche."

I was a *Time* writer for many years before I was made an editor, and for a long time after that I wasn't sure that I didn't prefer writing. But I distinctly remember the moment when I decided that I really might settle down contentedly to being an editor. I happened to be sick at the time. I was at home and had some copy sent to me from the office. I recall reading one short piece that was so perfect that I jumped out of bed and started walking around the room in high excitement. Maybe it was my temperature. But I felt really happy—as happy as if I had written the piece myself.

The moral of this story is that an editor, to a certain extent, must be self-effacing. (They'll be quite startled if they hear this back in the Time & Life Building.) There is always the danger that, like some critics, the editor will get his or her kicks simply by criticizing or changing copy as an exercise in ego-gratification. This is dangerous and wrong. But when editing is done in the proper spirit, you will find many writers who appreciate it—maybe as many as one in a hundred. A former colleague at *Time* insists that once a letter he had written to his mother was taken to his editor by mistake along with a batch of copy. The editor automatically edited the letter and the writer grudgingly admitted later: "Mother liked it a lot."

So much for micro-editing. Let me move on to macro-editing—the matter of setting an agenda and a tone, or, to revert to my opening image, deciding what the orchestra should play and how. An editor must assume an often contradictory role either by restraining emotions or stirring them up. Sometimes he must calm things down and keep his staff from chewing up the score. More often he must allow himself to get excited and in turn excite those around him. He must be something of a showman and react viscerally to the drama of events. "Stop the presses—tear up the front page" is the oldest cliche of all newspaper melodrama. I have stopped the presses and torn up a cover many, many times; I have torn up entire issues and started over from scratch—and I've almost never been sorry afterwards.

Such decisions are made in the mind of course, but before they happen there, they happen almost literally in the arteries. I have found over the years that my pulse beats in a certain way to a big news event—or for that matter to a question or a major problem. Occasionally, cooler heads around me have had to pull me back and keep me from getting carried away. I wish somebody had pulled me back when Henry Kissinger declared that "peace is at hand" and I ran a 16-page special section on the end of the Viet Nam War just three months too soon. But most of the time I have found my pulse beat a pretty good guide and few things in my trade are more exciting than to be able to communicate that beat to a group of reporters and other colleagues and to work together on some unfolding drama in the news.

I don't mean to suggest that all of what I call macro-editing is dramatic. Much of it involves quiet and painstaking and sometimes tentative reflection on future trends in the news, or on where a publication is heading, or even where society is heading. In short, it involves strategic thinking. Let me give you two examples:

When I became managing editor of *Time* in the late 60's, there was a good deal of talk that the newsmagazine as a form had become too rigid, too impersonal and that it was just about done for. I think my colleagues and I were able to redefine *Time* by breaking some of the conventions, some of the rigid formats, both physical and intellectual, by encouraging much greater variety and individuality. (And I must say we had quite a bit of stimulation from our competitors.) But we were able to do all this without changing the basic nature of the newsmagazine and in fact reaffirming its validity and usefulness. One part of this effort had to do with a prophet who is not much remembered anymore these days—Marshall McLuhan. He taught among other things that this is the age of television, in which the viewer is bombarded by images in no particular order, and that therefore what McLuhan called linear organization—the A-B-C, 1-2-3 structure of the conventional book or the chronological story was dead. Moreover, he suggested that print itself was dead or dying.

I was convinced that McLuhan was wrong. I believed and still believe that the orderly, linear presentation of printed information is absolutely essential to understanding, and that the newsmagazine in particular is more useful than ever, because it rationally organizes an ever more complex and chaotic world. I think that belief has been proven right and the continued success of newsmagazines is only one piece of evidence. Another minor but significant piece of evidence is the fact that, increasingly, television news uses linear and print devices to support and organize its nightly welter of images—captions, lists, chapter headings superimposed on the picture.

A different kind of strategic thinking has to do with

the relationship between the press and society. The American press is rightly proud of the role it played in Watergate. But I think we must increasingly realize that the adversary relationship between the press and authority—the journalism of suspicion—can be pushed too far. We must never abandon muckraking and our investigative role. But neither must we shy away from positive stories, constructive stories, stories that are not Pollyanna-ish but are not dictated by knee-jerk cynicism either. The press should be seen by America not merely as the tireless sheriff who unmasks evil—and sometimes shoots from the hip. It should also be seen as a force that helps understand and build and defend the community. Balancing these functions is one of the most important jobs an editor can perform.

An editor must also be a target. I don't mean this in the literal sense, although it used to be literally true, especially on the frontier, when editors were regularly horsewhipped, tarred and feathered, shot by vigilantes or attacked by Indians. There is a good deal of nostalgia in certain circles for those good old days. In our time, the attacks take different forms. They come in the guise of pressure from advertisers, from interest groups, and I am sorry to say, more and more in recent years, from the courts. An editor must protect his staff against all these pressures. He must serve as a target for such attacks, and thereby as a shield to the people who work for him. Most of the time this is no fun, but it is absolutely essential if reporters are to function.

An editor must also be a target in another sense—a target for his own staff. I am sure you have already discovered that to be able to curse your editor and blame him for everything that goes wrong is immensely bracing and downright therapeutic.

Editors make such good targets because they obviously have a great deal of power. In fact, many people think they have too much. Carlyle observed enthusiastically, "Isn't every able editor a ruler of the world?" It's a terrifically flattering idea to bask in, until one realizes that our critics actually believe it. One sign of this is an angry question that is hurled at us very often: "Who *elected* you, anyway?" The answer obviously is—nobody, in a formal political sense. The real point about this question is the apparent assumption that anybody in this society with any kind of power *should* be formally elected. That is simply not so. There should be quite a few power centers that are *not* part of our political system, power centers where students, for example, choose their schools and to a degree their teachers, where worshippers choose their church and hence their pastors, where customers choose their products and therefore, however indirectly, vote for one entrepreneur over another, and where readers choose a publication and therefore cast their ballots for an editor.

On this matter of power, an editor has to do a kind of intellectual balancing act. He certainly should be aware that he *has* power and that, as a result, he must bear a great deal of responsibility. On the other hand, he should not become intoxicated by Carlyle and get up every morning and look in the mirror and ask himself: "How am I going to use my tremendous authority today for the benefit of the nation and the world?" Or worse, of course: "For my own benefit?"

We have all heard that power corrupts. I happen to think that the *lack* of power corrupts more—but that's another speech. There is very little conventional or monetay corruption in the American press today. It is sometimes suggested that the celebrity status which some editors and indeed some reporters have reached is somehow corrupting because it puts them more or less on the same level as the people they write about and thus undermines their neutrality. I suspect there is something in that, although I would not necessarily make it a firable offense to have dinner at Elaine's.

The real danger of corruption for journalists comes with intellectual arrogance and closed minds. An example of that would be the late Col. Robert Rutherford McCormick of the Chicago *Tribune*, of whom it was said: "He never cites authority, since he is *it.*"

In short, editors should retain a certain becoming sense of fallibility. I have every confidence that in the years ahead you will richly contribute to that sense of fallibility in the editors who become your targets.

But in the end, you know, we may have different jobs, different approaches—and different expense accounts. But as journalists we are really all on the same side. Let me conclude with a piece of folk wisdom which a recent essay in *Time* says is so corny that audiences wince when they hear it. But I will use it anyway. There are three statements about life in general which must be greeted with the utmost skepticism. The first is: "The check is in the mail." The second is: "I work for the government and I have your best interests at heart." The third is: "I'll respect you even more in the morning." Now there is a fourth statement that one might add to these others: "Editors exist to help journalists." Many of you may feel equally skeptical about this statement, but after many years as an editor, I really believe that it is true.

Grow your own: The art of developing top editors

By Milton Gralla

Where will you find your next great editor in chief?

It is the wise publisher who considers this question, for in publishing life today, one thing is certain: With magazines enjoying an era of growth and prosperity, and with greater recent emphasis on editorial performance, outstanding editors in chief have become increasingly scarce.

And since a publisher never knows when he'll be in the market for that talented, experienced, versatile, motivated editor capable of breathing life into a magazine, it makes sense for him to be ready for the day when, through a slow or sudden rift, piracy, chance, or act of God, he finds himself looking for a new editor.

When that day comes, a publisher can search outside, using ads, agencies, head-hunters, word of mouth, personal contacts, and similar traditional procedures, or he can be ready with one or more strong candidates for the job within his own company.

The first alternative gives publishers a much wider range of choice, but it also raises some serious questions and problems.

•How certain can a publisher be of an outsider's performance? Does he or she have any faults or any weakness that will turn up later? Will he or she be compatible with the magazine's methods, its staff, its readers?

•How will a loyal staff feel when an outsider is brought in?

•How long will it take to find a new editor, and will the magazine suffer in the interim?

The second alternative—promoting a fully prepared replacement from within—avoids these three problems. However, this alternative assumes that a company already employs people with the varied skills and leadership qualities needed by a successful editor. Can a publisher rely on the chance that he will have such people? Or is it possible to "grow your own?"

In an attempt to answer these questions, I did some research to ascertain which method was used to acquire the editors in chief of each of our 14 business and trade magazines. I found that only two of our 14 editors in chief were hired from outside at the top job level . . . and both were hired more than 10 years ago before our editorial development program was in force. On the other hand, eight editors originally joined us at the very lowest assistant editor job level our company offers, three joined us at middle job levels, and one came along with a recent magazine acquisition.

Since our company has prospered greatly in the past 10 years, and since much of that prosperity is probably due to our emphasis on editorial and journalistic performance, my advice to publishers is to develop editors rather than recruit them. Our company has established a program for developing editors, and although I'm not certain that all of our methods will work for all other companies, they have worked for us during a growth decade when there was a need for strong editors.

Seek future "stars"

At the entry level we will not hire someone who is qualified to fill only the job at hand. We patiently seek future "stars."

We look for people with high school and college newspaper experience and evidence of other student activity. We look for people with leadership capabilities, people with initiative, people who are self-assertive during an interview. We also look for photographic experience and high scores on our inhouse journalism test for job applicants.

Once hired, a new assistant editor goes either into a trainee pool, floating to various magazines, or onto a specific magazine staff. In either case, he is "tracked" carefully and given immediate writing assignments.

Trainees also attend a series of workshops, conducted by our vice president and associate editorial director Howard Rauch. Rauch also reads and evaluates each new recruit's manuscripts for several months.

About twice a year we conduct an "ideal story" workshop for new junior editors. We analyze the elements that make a magazine article or story appealing to its audience, and then we give each editor two assignments.

The first assignment—due in 30 days—is to study several back issues of his or her magazine, select an "ideal" story, and describe the qualities that make that story ideal. Every response is evaluated, and the non-respondents do not go unnoticed.

The second assignment invites each junior editor to submit one of the "ideal stories" that he or she writes in the 90 days following the workshop. There are no further reminders. We study every response, make note of the stars, and give cash awards to the two or three best. We also silently notice the non-respondents.

During the course of their work, junior editors are given a variety of assignments to help them gain both experience and exposure. These include assigned articles, "initiative" articles, and anything else from exhibitor visits to collecting business cards of future story sources.

Editors are also given the opportunity to travel periodically. For editors on our business, trade and special-interest magazines in particular, there are countless events—shows, conventions, seminars, association activities—where they can meet contacts, interview, learn, and grow.

Another useful editorial development tool is our company-wide "story-of-the-month" contest. Each month (excluding the summer months) all junior editors are invited to submit their best stories for management recognition and cash prizes. (Upper-level editors are excluded.)

Contest judges are Rauch and myself, and we evaluate entries separately before learning the opinion of the other. We judge each story on the basis of its accuracy, timeliness, audience appeal, exclusivity, and photographic or visual elements.

The contest has several beneficial results. It reminds all junior editors of the specifics of the "ideal" story and the company's recognition of editorial performance. It helps us encourage and spot future stars. And it raises Gralla's company-wide editorial performance.

Public speaking skills important

In our continuing series of editorial development workshops, one other is worth some mention: our voluntary workshops on public speaking.

At the lower or middle levels, an editor is adequate if he can write and generate outstanding contents for the magazine. But today's truly successful editor in chief must also have self-confidence, identity, leadership capabilities and an "image" among the power centers of the magazine's audience and advertisers.

Since public speaking fosters those qualities, we have developed a series of three two-hour workshops which combine theory with actual practice. We cover everything from moderating seminars to delivering formal talks to large groups.

The results have been gratifying. The more confidence they have, the more Gralla editors, even at the middle level, have volunteered for podium appearances of every description. They moderate seminars, give golf and tennis awards, report to business groups on our surveys and research, present fresh slide films. And—they are invited back more often than not.

We encourage this activity, and we don't restrict it to editors in chief. Where we control or create a convention program running a few days, we involve editors of various job levels. This gives the middle-level editor valuable exposure, and prepares him or her for the eventual mantle of top editor. Furthermore, any podium appearance by an editor furthers the magazine's interests in many ways.

Still another builder of executive editorial qualities is our "field editor" job level. In this assignment, a mid-level editor is freed of all inside editing and production responsibility and assigned to full-time story development for a related group of magazines. Thus, promising editors can travel more and get experience writing for several magazines instead of concentrating on one field or one audience.

Currently, we have several field editors in New York, two on the West Coast, and one just getting started in Chicago. The more editors we promote to this job level, the larger our pool of promising editors who've had exposure to a number of our magazines.

Another factor in preparing mid-level editors for the top is our intentional effort to build their images. They get frequent bylines and, when appropriate, they're identified and quoted in our newsletters and promotional material. Sometimes our magazine pictures them moderating a seminar, conducting an important interview, or otherwise getting involved in an industry activity.

Creating the right environment

In addition to outside travel and inside nurturing, editors need access to research, a generous free-lance budget, and periodic reader-interest studies for personal guidance rather than promotional use. They want positive dollar evidence that management's commitment to editorial excellence is sincere rather than lip-service.

You can sometimes fake this commitment in presentations to your advertisers, but you can never fake it to your own editorial staff. It pays to spend—to invest in whatever back-up your staff needs. Without such an environment, future stars often fly the coop.

A less tangible but quite vital element in establishing a creative atmosphere is the nature of the power structure within the publishing organization. Your most valuable present and future editors may not endure in a situation dominated by a totally business-oriented publisher—a person with no editorial experience who gives heavy-handed orders to an editor in chief.

We have two thoughts on this matter. First, editors should get a better-than-even shot at becoming publishers. Among our publishers, co-publishers and associate publishers, the most recent count shows that 56.5 percent came from the editorial side and 43.5 percent came from the sales side.

Second, when a sales manager becomes a publisher, he should be given no direct authority over the editor. Our editors report only to the company's editorial executives—Rauch and myself.

Editors can grow and thrive where they report only to executives with editorial background and where they have a chance at command.

It takes time, patience and commitment to cultivate editors whose attitudes and standards are compatible with your own. But why put a magazine you love in the hands of a stranger if there is a better alternative?

Editorial training

By Loy Wiley

A marketing professor I know always tells his students, "All life is sales."

I wouldn't go that far, but certainly magazine editing is sales. An editor who doesn't realize that—who thinks he has only to perfect his craft as a wordsmith—is an ineffective editor.

The craft matters, of course. It matters a lot. But what matters even more is the ability to anticipate and meet the needs of potential readers. The effective editor must be able to analyze suggested topics and unedited manuscripts and then give them a focus that will make them irresistible to the reader.

But where do you find editors who have these skills?

As president of an independent magazine editing company, in a city better known for cash register manufacturing than magazine publishing, I've had to grow my own editors.

Learning as I've taught, I've developed the following guidelines that serve to heighten my editors' awareness of our readers' needs while helping them develop their craft.

1. *Start at the finish line: reader satisfaction.* Since the goal of every article and department of your magazine is to satisfy readers, make that goal the basis of your editors' training.

Explain to your editors from the start that their job is to turn people into readers by presenting each author's viewpoint in the form that will most appeal to a potential reader.

Tell them to imagine themselves as the typical reader when they analyze each manuscript, and to ask themselves, "What do I already know, and what do I want to know? What interests me most about this article?"

Also tell them to put themselves in the reader's shoes when they are considering what to explain and what to gloss over. Beginning business editors tend to overexplain basic concepts to the reader—because very often the editors themselves are learning the field.

Hammer these points home to your new editors by walking them through an issue of your magazine: What do the titles tell about the topics and their focus? How do the title blurbs attempt to attract the reader? What is each article's appeal to the reader?

2. *Start small.* Even an experienced editor will need to edit several articles before he learns to do things your way. Save everyone frustration by giving one-page articles or departments as starters.

3. *Vary assignments.* The hardest part of being a beginner is that every part is hard. When your beginners' eyes become glazed and their coats lose their shines, you've pushed too hard. To avoid this situation, vary assignments by scheduling low-key work between articles.

4. *Tailor the deadline.* All editing deadlines count back from the printing deadline, of course, but you have some leeway you can use to good advantage.

At the beginning, let new editors set their own deadlines, so that the deadline becomes a goal instead of a threat.

As you get to know your editors better, you'll see which ones produce best under pressure and which ones need an all-the-time-in-the-world atmosphere. Use this knowledge to get their best efforts: If one editor needs time, get him on a long-deadline schedule. If another needs pressure, give him the manuscripts just before they're due.

The real secret to managing deadlines is to insist on them. Once you and an editor agree on a deadline, that's when you should get the article, finished or not. Your goal is to build dependability as well as creativity.

5. *Limit research.* If your editors have to verify facts in each article they edit, you're going to find that some of them get bogged down in the research stage. You'll know this is happening when they ask to extend the deadline with the excuse that "I'm still not clear on some things."

The real problem, invariably, is good old editors' block: They don't know how to approach the article, so they want to delay the approach.

The cure is a gruff but helpful order: "Don't open another book, except a dictionary or grammar book, until you've completed your first draft. If you haven't checked a fact, just write a note in the margin to check it after you've finished the first full draft."

Forced to face the real problem, most editors beat the block.

If an editor continues to have this problem, tell him to limit his research to three hours until the first draft is finished. Works like magic.

6. *Let them flounder for a while.* The beginner's second complaint (after you've locked up his library card); "This article doesn't seem to be going anywhere." Or, "I have a lot of stuff I can't fit in."

When an editor makes this kind of vague but decidedly uncomfortable comment, listen to him. Discuss the article. Make suggestions. But don't take the problem away yet. Let him struggle with it.

Only after an editor has come back a second and third time with "floundering" complaints should you offer to take a look at the manuscript. Then, give the manuscript—with comments, changes and criticisms—back to the editor to be re-edited. Even if you have to give it back two or three times, it will be worth it. Finally, you're going to be able to return an edited copy and tell the editor: "Good job. I like it." Every little ego-saver helps.

7. *Insist on a one-sentence theme.* You will find that the problem for most floundering beginners is clarifying the theme. When a beginner gives you a theme sentence such as, "Time management is an important managerial trait," help him state the theme to meet the reader's needs. Sharpen his focus with a theme such as, "You increase your efficiency with these seven time management techniques." This will usually get his creative juices flowing again.

8. *Emphasize the positive.* Black and blue are better than red where a rewriter's ink is concerned. The beginning editor feels pain enough without getting back a bleeding manuscript. Put away your red pen when you rewrite.

Even more important, dig through the manuscript to discover the strong points of the beginner's editing job. Discuss these before you point out his weaknesses. This will help the beginner save face when you discuss your criticisms.

9. *Emphasize the rules, not the changes.* When you go through a revised manuscript with an editor, try to emphasize the general rule behind each change.

If you and your beginning editor both feel overwhelmed when you look at your heavily penciled revision of his editing attempt, pick out a few problems that occur repeatedly and review them. If you don't know where to start, look for a basic problem that invariably occurs again and again, even with fairly experienced editors:

• The article isn't directed at any particular reader or reader need;

• Series aren't parallel;

• Continuity is lost from paragraph to paragraph;

• Anecdotes and examples are boring.

10. *Insist on basic English skills.* Everyone in your department should have a good grammar book (I like the *Harbrace College Handbook)* and stylebook, with instruc-

tions from you to read them often.

When an editor makes the same mistake twice, don't correct it. Instead, send him back to his grammar or stylebook for the answer. He'll learn grammar, and he'll begin to see the patterns behind your changes.

I learned this the hard way as a beginner when my first managing editor (whose seemingly mercurial expectations, slashing changes, and caustic remarks were making me reconsider the advantages of selling life insurance) handed out a fat packet of loosely typed sheets with a cover sheet splashily titled: "Secrets of Our Magazine Revealed."

At last, we gloated, we'll know what he wants, and the bloodbath revision sessions will end.

What a humiliation, then, to see that each of his "personal quirks" was basic English grammar. Beside each of our little linguistic cripples, he'd typed a concise and readable version, followed by the source: the page number of a college grammar book.

The bloodletting was immediately reduced, we began to learn the rules, and we soon realized that he had not been capricious in his criticism.

11. *Hand out correction sheets.* Although most training has to be one-on-one, handing out typed sheets of everyone's corrected sentences and paragraphs—with the before on the left and the revision on the right—can be very helpful. New editors will realize that others are making the same mistakes. In addition, it enables you to reinforce the pattern to your changes.

12. *Insist on column width.* For some reason, one of the hardest habits to break in beginning editors is thrift: They're determined to fill every page by starting at the top, setting their margins at 0 and 100, and typing all the way down until the paper falls out of the typewriter.

To break this habit, have them type on copy sheets, with numbered lines and preset column widths that are marked with bold, black vertical lines.

Using the column width helps an editor break the copy into short paragraphs and subsections because he will have the reader's view of the material from the beginning. This, in turn, will maximize the readability and visual appeal of the article.

13. *Insist on clean copy.* It isn't cost-efficient to expect editors to type clean copy, but be sure they send it to the typing pool before you see it and mark it up. Revising dirty copy is like pruning trees in the dark: You may do some good, but you'll have to wait to find out how much.

14. *Insist on time sheets.* Unless you explain the purpose of time sheets, an editor will look at a time sheet as a golfer looks at a sand trap: It's an obstacle a good player can avoid.

But time sheets are invaluable to you, the manager. If everyone in your office keeps a time sheet listing the hours spent on each article, you'll know immediately what each article has cost in editing time, typing time, and supervisory time. You'll also know how much an editor has progressed.

Some editors are able to reduce the time spent on a

feature-length article from 160 hours to 35 hours in their first six months. That kind of progress is dramatic and profitable, and it should be rewarded. Point out that you will reward it if you're aware of it, but that you can't see their progress unless they hand in accurate time sheets week after week.

15. *Encourage group support.* Beginning editors can help each other a lot by talking about themes, analyzing each other's leads, and so on. With a little encouragement, they'll become a good team. Without such group support, they'll tend to look on each other as competitors.

16. *Listen with your ears and not your mouth.* This is a tough one, because listening *seems* to take a long time. In fact, if you'll listen to your sessions with your new editors, you'll probably hear yourself asking questions, then answering them. Kind of silly if you think about it. After all, you know you know the answers.

You'll save time in the proverbial long run, by letting your editors think through and articulate solutions to editing problems and by repeating the same questions until the editors can internalize the answers.

17. *Encourage practical ideas.* Heaven help you if your editors bring you every idea their fertile brains hatch. Train them early to analyze the pros and cons of their ideas, to discard the bad ideas, and to accompany the good ones with recommendations for implementation. If an editor suggests an article on crocheted snake snoods, he should accompany his suggestions with evidence of reader interest, a suggested focus and theme, and a choice of author.

When you start getting only the ideas that have withstood your editors' careful thought, you'll start getting good ideas.

18. *Encourage responsibility.* In a small editorial department or company, managers tend to keep decision-making centralized because it works. Unfortunately, when the department or company is ready to grow, no one is capable of taking over some of the old projects.

Look for the ability to assume responsibility and encourage it in all your editors. You'll probably find it's unrelated to editing skills. The editor who is struggling with leads may be a budding policy-maker.

19. *Encourage expertise.* If one of your editors excels at titles and subheads, ask for his advice in this area and encourage others to do so. If one editor has a particular interest in a topic that interests your readers, encourage him by giving him money to attend workshops and time to stay current on the topic. Your magazine will be stronger, and so will your editors' self-esteem.

20. *Go to lunch.* I've gotten many of my best training ideas from my editors, and many of these ideas came out during beer and hamburger lunches. A no-agenda working lunch is a good keep-in-touch technique every few months.

21. *Enjoy.* Editors are a self-critical and compulsive lot. If you'll give them training, a goal, and a deadline, they'll produce—that kind of motivation doesn't need policing. Give them room to grow. Then relax and enjoy them.

The Editor as manager: How do you rate?

By Bernard Weiss

Last year, FOLIO published a terrific article titled, "How good are your editors?" (December 1980). That question could easily be turned around: How good are *you*, as an editorial boss?

When someone becomes managing editor, he or she usually is technically and editorially proficient. That's part of the job. The other part —even more important—is to be a *leader*, a *manager*, a *supervisor* of creative talent. A managing editor may have one of the toughest jobs in the company, simply because the people who are managed are the company's most valuable asset. These creative people probably require more skillful management than does any other asset—financial or physical—in the corporation.

Recently, during a coffee break at an editorial management workshop, a young woman told me she had just been promoted to Editor. Then she complained: "My new job really stinks! The whole staff wants me to help them solve problems. It takes all my time. I can't do my work!"

Lacking experience and training, she had not yet realized that being Editor *means* managing people— helping them solve problems, teaching them to write and design more creatively, encouraging them to develop the editorial and graphic skills that, in turn, would help her publish a more successful magazine. I reminded her that one of her major functions as Editor is *to remove obstacles that prevent her staff from doing well.*

To be successful, an Editor must develop and exercise certain managerial qualities that enable him or her to become a firm but professionally respected creative director.

Here are seven such managerial qualities; they are characteristic of successful Editors with whom I have worked. How do *you* rate?

Rapport

Do you spend enough time with your staff? Remember, your relationship with your people is the basis for nearly all their effort. For many writers and designers, especially those who are young and lack experience, the relationships that develop with their immediate supervisors are the most important facets of their jobs—more important than money, in many cases.

As a senior, experienced manager, you should plan to commit most of your working day to being with fragile people who need help, and with *any* who are the workhorses of your team. This expenditure of time is important to both your success and theirs, because failure to look after marginal situations will surely cost more time (and dollars) when problems develop.

Consistency

Do your people know what to expect of you? Are you firm and disciplined, enthusiastic and sensitive, aware and thoughtful? If so, be that kind of person every day. Even if you're insensitive, or undisciplined, or laid back—be *that* kind of person every day.

The editorial manager who is mercurial—one who is alternately disciplined, then lax; attentive, then insensitive; thoughtful, then thoughtless—will drive a creative staff mad. Moreover, the staff will take advantage of chinks in the managerial armor; they'll wait until those days when they can get away with less-than-excellence, a sloppy manuscript, or an unreasonable extension of deadlines. Whatever your managerial style, practice it consistently.

Caring

Do you really care? Are you really interested? Concerned? In today's publishing climate, the successful editorial chief is not a dictator who rules by authority of his title and seniority. He's a respected professional who leads by example, demonstrates and teaches, helps and coaches, supports and energizes the staff.

Most successful Editors I've met fit this pattern. They are skillful and dynamic professionals whose staffs are loyal because they find their Editors credible, trustworthy, sensitive and responsive to needs, *even before those needs become apparent.*

Decisiveness

Do you act with conviction? Failure to make decisions—even wrong ones—is probably one of the most serious flaws in managerial personality. Are your decisions occasionally bad? Unpopular? Don't fret. As a professional, you must learn to trust your editorial judgment and to make tough decisions without fear or guilt, based on the circumstances and the facts available to you at the time.

No Editor is perfect; all have made mistakes. And the occasional wrong, poor or unpopular decision will be accepted by your staff if they understand that you made the decision with a sense of professional responsibility and a careful evaluation of the situation. As Mark Twain put it, "Do what's right. This will gratify some, and astonish the rest."

Sharing

Do you give credit? Are you complimentary? Most creative people are intelligent people, and brains are like hearts: they go where they are appreciated. Acknowledge success frequently, and quickly. Give more than your share of credit. You needn't exaggerate; just be certain that everyone knows the name of the genius behind the great cover (special issue, investigative series, etc.).

Almost all of us in the creative professions need frequent recognition and acknowledgment; it fuels the fires of inspiration and helps us get ready for the next effort. It also takes the sting out of the discipline that every Editor must impose from time to time.

Courage

Do you have the courage to hire clever, bright and imaginative people, give them direction—and then leave them alone? The courageous Editor is a trusting Editor, one who relaxes the reins, encourages creative freedom, helps develop and refine ideas, and offers an imaginative writer or artist real opportunities.

All of this requires more courage than most of us are willing to generate: the courage first to hire and live with exceptionally talented people (who may be more talented than ourselves), then the courage to step back and let them go free, and *then* the courage to step forward to give them the time, money and human resources they may require to maximize their potential. Are you *that* courageous?

Maturity

Do you take more than your share of blame for occasional failure? The mature manager is one who expects an occasional failure because he recognizes that every truly creative effort involves an inherent risk. He encourages writers and artists to try risky new approaches in copy, design and other creative functions, and conveys to them the philosophy of acceptable failure: better to have tried and failed, than never to have tried at all.

Maturity also means that you are willing to accept the risk at a higher level than any individual on the staff: "As your Editor, I have more to lose than you do—and as your boss, I can protect you better than I can protect myself. So, if you'll take the risk, I'll take the responsibility."

Test Yourself

If you've read this far, and done so with introspection, then I encourage you to take the short self-evaluation quiz accompanying this article. It will help you consider some of the job-related personal characteristics that contribute to success as an editorial boss, assuming your basic editorial and technical proficiency are beyond question.

How effective are you at managing your staff?

Take this simple test. Give yourself 5 points for each "Yes" answer. A score of 75 or better is passing; 70 or under suggests the need for management training to help you function more skillfully as a true managing Editor.

Yes No

☐ ☐ Do I give realistic assignments and allow reasonable time for completion?

☐ ☐ Do I respond quickly and thoughtfully to manuscripts, art, etc., submitted for review?

☐ ☐ Have I communicated to staff my concept of my magazine's role in the industry?

☐ ☐ Does everyone working here recognize and understand our magazine's objectives: service, professional, financial—long-term and short-term?

☐ ☐ Do people on my staff have a positive attitude regarding their contributions to the magazine and, through it, to our readers?

☐ ☐ Do I challenge my staff to try new creative approaches? Am I tolerant of occasional failure?

☐ ☐ Does everyone feel that he or she has plenty of opportunity to learn from his or her seniors, and opportunity to grow in this organization?

☐ ☐ Do I maximize personal strengths and minimize personal weaknesses?

☐ ☐ Am I aware of the effect my decisions and actions have on my staff?

☐ ☐ Do I know what motivates every individual in my employ?

Yes No

☐ ☐ Am I honest in offering criticism to those who are not working up to par?

☐ ☐ Am I free with praise, when warranted?

☐ ☐ Do I encourage my staff to come to me with suggestions, opinions, ideas, comments and criticism of our work—i.e., am I "approachable"?

☐ ☐ Am I able to resolve most creative conflicts in a constructive way?

☐ ☐ Am I tactful and discreet when working with my staff?

☐ ☐ Am I responsive to staff problems even before they become critical?

☐ ☐ Do I offer my people every opportunity to succeed, even if it means helping them find jobs elsewhere?

☐ ☐ Do I have a clear understanding of my role and my responsibility in this company?

☐ ☐ Do I have a specific plan for personal self-improvement, and personal improvement of every individual on the staff?

☐ ☐ Do my superiors know and understand the work that is being done in my department—our accomplishments as well as our problems?

_____   _____
(Date)   (Score)

(File among personal papers to be reviewed on_____)
(Date)

How good are your editors?

By Robert Sgarlata

As publishers become more and more concerned that their magazines run efficiently, editorial performance evaluations are gaining greater importance. Management wants its editors to know what is expected of them, and they want proof that editors are living up to those expectations.

To achieve those ends, editorial supervisors are being asked to evaluate the performance of editors and writers periodically. Since there is still a great deal of experimenting going on with evaluation, there is no consensus among publishers about the best format, frequency, or questions to be used. Everyone does agree, however, that the creative nature of an editor's job makes it difficult to quantify performance.

The business and consumer magazine executives who shared their evaluation approaches with FOLIO spoke in terms of supervisors evaluating editors. Those supervisors—the immediate superiors of the editor being evaluated—range from senior editors to president of the company. Those who are being evaluated can also be anywhere on the editorial ladder, and include writers as well as editors.

What is a performance evaluation?

An editorial performance evaluation is an appraisal of how well an editor is doing his job. It generally describes the editor's strengths and weaknesses and is shown to both management and the editor himself. (At large publishing companies, these evaluations are usually conducted formally, whereas smaller companies use an informal approach.)

Conducting evaluations is a matter of smart management practice, according to Sey Chassler, editor of *Redbook*, and president of the American Society of Magazine Editors. "Management has to know if its editorial staff is running efficiently," he says. "The way to find out is by periodically evaluating every editor on the staff."

Why evaluate?

In addition to determining how well an editor is doing in his job, evaluations enable management to upgrade job performance in the following ways:

•*Inform editors how they are doing in the eyes of their supervisor.* "One of the most common complaints I hear from editors is that they never know how they are doing," says Bernard Weiss, president of Bernard Weiss & Associates, publishing consultants. "The reason is that editors find it easier to edit than to manage people, so the managerial function usually loses out. Periodic appraisal prevents this from happening."

Although editors shy away from the bad news that can come with evaluation, in the end they appreciate the effort by management to help them improve. "People can do better only if they know what is wrong," says Edward T. Thompson, editor in chief of *Reader's Digest*. "An editor can go through life thinking everything is fine, then a problem crops up. Evaluations create an ongoing communication about the problems an editor has and how he can correct them."

"Editors really do need to know what you think of their work," says Richard Dunn, editor of *Purchasing World*, a Technical Publishing Company (TPC) trade magazine. "Editors have fragile egos and always fear the worst, but deep down inside they want to know what their bosses think. The supervisor should be just as concerned that the editor is aware of the areas that need improvement."

•*Enable management to maximize the strengths and minimize the weaknesses of editors.* Editors are, of course, individuals, and therefore each editor will have his own particular strengths and weaknesses. A heavy producer of copy may be a poor researcher. An exceptionally good writer may miss deadlines. And an excellent researcher may be a poor writer. There is room for improvement in every editor, and performance evaluations can pinpoint any weak areas and enable management to strengthen them.

"Evaluations are a learning process for finding out if the right person is doing the right job," says Paul W. Kellam, editorial director of *Inc.* "We use them to discover editors' strengths that can be developed to benefit the magazine. If there is a problem, evaluations will tell us where the root is."

•*Reveal individual problems and solutions.* "Our evaluations tell us a great deal about the person we are dealing with," says James Autry, vice president and editor in chief of Meredith Publishing Group. "In a creative environment it is important to recognize individuals and their needs."

Because evaluations reveal personal characteristics of the editor, the solutions to similar problems may be different for different editors. Meredith Publishing Group, which has its editors take an active role in their evaluations, solves problems using such diverse approaches as giving some editors bigger budgets and sending others to encounter groups.

•*Set goals and deadlines.* Whether or not problems exist, the supervisor and editor can use the evaluation to set new goals and determine a time period during which the goals should be achieved.

"Goals can range from asking the editor to do background research on a subject to creating a new department for the magazine," says *Purchasing World*'s Dunn. "The specific goal will depend on the editor's abilities as revealed by the evaluation. Then the supervisor can set a deadline for results. At the deadline, the supervisor and editor can meet again to evaluate that specific goal."

When an editor demonstrates major problems, the goals and deadlines can be used as a guide for terminating employment. "Setting termination deadlines is one of the unpleasant aspects of evaluations," says Ralph R. Schulz, senior vice president/editorial for McGraw-Hill Publications. "But if an editor has a persistent major problem, evaluations help you put a limit on how long you will wait to see improvement."

•*Reestablish objectives.* Evaluations provide an opportunity to reaffirm an editor's job objectives. "You hire

444

someone as your features editor, and six months later that editor is producing more news items than features," says Dunn. "An evaluation allows the supervisor and editor to compare how each perceives the job. Maybe the editor should be on the news staff, or perhaps he just drifted away from the objectives. Evaluations enable everyone, including management, to come back to ground zero from time to time."

•*Establish superior/subordinate relations.* Because many supervisors come from the editorial pool itself, it is necessary to set the proper tone between new supervisors and their former peers, according to Dunn. "The performance evaluation accomplishes this," he says. "It is difficult to make the transition from working with someone to managing that same person. Having the new supervisor conduct evaluations makes it easier for him to assume, and former peers to accept, that new role."

•*Discover stars.* Evaluations uncover the stars on a magazine's staff by documenting superior performance and revealing individual career goals. "Knowing how well an editor does his job and what his long-term goals are lets me know who is ready to take on new assignments and responsibilities," says Howard Rauch, vice president/associate editorial director of Gralla Publications. "Evaluations tell who will fit where in the company—in short, who will be the managing editors of the future."

•*Determine raises and promotions.* Finally, performance evaluations are a tool for determining salary increases and promotions. While all companies use performance evaluations in determining salary increases, many conduct them separately from salary reviews.

At Charter Publications, where performance evaluations are not conducted during salary review, evaluations include salary recommendations from the supervisor. These recommendations are used by the personnel department to determine actual salary increases at the end of the year.

At Gralla, performance evaluations are turned over to the personnel department, where all of the information about editors' duties and salaries at a particular level is entered into a computer. The resulting salary comparison charts ensure that all editors doing the same work are making the same salary.

In addition to helping determine salaries, evaluations aid management in granting promotions and internal transfers. "Evaluations tell us who has the potential, desire and proper talents to fill a vacant position," says McGraw-Hill's Schulz. "Finding bright spots in the evaluations expedites the decision-making process."

There are some editors who warn against connecting performance evaluations with salary review or promotion, however. "Evaluations are a problem-solving tool," says Dunn. "When conducted in relation to salary, they become a score card. The editor is scored in terms of performance, and the score interpreted into dollars. Such evaluations become one-sided, with the supervisor saying, 'This is the way I see things.' Two-way communication breaks down in that atmosphere."

Salary reviews are only a happy by-product of evaluation, according to *Inc.*'s Kellam. "Of course, the editor who performs well should be rewarded. But helping editors reach their highest level of performance is the real reason for doing evaluations."

What is evaluated?

Most questions on performance evaluations cover what the editor is expected to do and how well; how well the job is actually getting done; the editor's recent achievements; areas of strength or weakness; what the editor can do to improve; what new goals he should try to achieve.

Other areas of evaluation cover the editor's technical abilities. These questions focus on those aspects of the editor's performance that are more measurable than those mentioned above, such as the editor's ability to meet deadlines, his command of the language, the cleanliness of his editing, his ability to take directions, and his dependability, initiative, punctuality and attendance.

The specific questions asked by each company differ, with some companies excluding important areas, such as original contributions, adaptability, and willingness to accept difficult assignments. At the same time, some companies ask questions about personal characteristics, such as the editor's relationships with fellow employees and his appearance.

According to Meredith's Autry, however, rating an editor's appearance is not acceptable. "Such traits really have no bearing on an editor's ability to edit," he says. "'Part of the reason we have standardized evaluations is to avoid criticism based on personal bias rather than professional qualities."

One magazine uses reader response to articles as part of its performance gauge for editors. After each issue of the magazine is published, *Inc.* mails a questionnaire to 250 subscribers asking for their reactions to specific articles run in the issue. Questions include how interested the reader was in the subject, how useful the information was, how well the article was presented, and whether the reader finished the article.

When the returns from the questionnaires are in, the performance of individual editors must be separated out, however, for it is dangerous to depend on raw response alone as a criterion for evaluation, warns *Inc.*'s editorial director Kellam. "The subject of an article is very important," he says. "If the reader was not interested in the idea to begin with, assigning the article was a managerial mistake and cannot be held against the editor."

Formal evaluations

While all companies evaluate their editors on basically the same criteria, the evaluation process can be either formal or informal. Most large publishing companies find formal evaluation most useful because of the number of editors who must be evaluated.

In a formal system, the supervisor uses a questionnaire answering the same questions for all editors.

"Using the guidelines of a standardized form ensures that all editors are appraised on the same criteria," says McGraw-Hill's Schulz. "Editorial evaluations are meant to pin down an individual's value, but that value must be found in terms of a norm. Once we have pegged an editor in terms of the norm, it is easier to compare him to other editors."

The first point that should be covered in a formal system is the job description. Very often, a job description can clear up any confusion about an editor's duties.

"In the atmosphere of an editorial department, it is easy for people to have differing perceptions of the same job," says *Purchasing World*'s Dunn. "Having the supervisor and editor reach an agreement about expectations guarantees they will be talking on the same plane during the evaluation."

A job should be flexible enough to change during the course of evaluations, however. As the supervisor and editor become more attuned to one another's needs, they may find it necessary to restructure certain aspects of the job. At one corporation, each editor writes a brief descrip-

Editorial performance evaluation

Name:_____ Title:_____

Period of evaluation: From:_____ To:_____

Job description:_____

_____

_____

How well the job is done:_____

_____

_____

Specific   achievements:_____

_____

_____

Specific   problem   areas:_____

_____

_____

Improvement program:_____

_____

_____

Deadline: _____

Supervisor's signature: _____

Editor's signature:_____

Date: _____

Copy and use this form

tion of his job every six months and discusses it with his supervisor.

Job descriptions are the jumping-off point for evaluations, for having agreed on the editor's duties. The supervisor is then able to gauge performance. In a formal evaluation, both open-ended questions to be answered in paragraph form and check-lists or rating systems for documenting the editor's performance are used.

The open-ended questions cover broad areas of concern (such as recent achievements) about which the supervisor can comment at length on his impressions of the editor. These questions allow for the ifs, ands, and buts that are necessary when discussing an editor's creative abilities.

"Taking numbers or comments on a page at face value is not enough," says *Readers Digest*'s Thompson. "There is much more to evaluating editors."

One outstanding problem in the magazine industry is trying to give the qualitative work of an editor a quantitative value, according to *Inc.*'s Kellam. "Everyone is trying to objectify editorial performance," he says. "But since much of an editor's work is creative, its quality cannot be judged on an objective standard alone."

Publishers obtain objective ratings for editors by using either a check-list system or a numerical rating system. (Some companies use both.) Although editors agree it is difficult to give an editor an objective rating, they do acknowledge that in some technical areas such ratings can indicate how well the editor measures up to the supervisor's expectations.

The check-list system used by many publishers uses the ratings "excellent," "good," "fair," and "poor" to evaluate items such as writing style, quantity of articles, and editorial judgment. The supervisor simply checks the rating that coincides with the editor's performance for each evaluation item.

The numerical rating system is similar to the check-list system. However, because the numerical system has 10 possible ratings with finer increments, such as "Good: no serious problems, but improvement desirable," and "Good: sometimes excellent," a supervisor has more flexibility with this system.

Editors receive an over-all rating based on the average of the supervisor's objective evaluation and the comments on the open-ended questions.

To alleviate the problem of objective rating, companies that use formal evaluation systems direct their supervisors to discuss their appraisals with each editor individually. In this meeting the editor is given an opportunity to offer his impressions of the evaluation and discuss problems and goals. Some companies even have space on the evaluation form for the editor's comments.

"You can try being dictatorial, but that is not productive in a creative environment," says Meredith's Autry. "To make problem solving work with creative people, you have to take a humanistic approach. Let every editor take part in discussing expectations, short-falls and solutions."

Besides letting editors participate in writing job descriptions and discussing their evaluations, Meredith has each editor write a "standard of performance" every six months. The editor states his goals for the coming six months and how they might be achieved. These forms are submitted to the supervisor and discussed at the time they are written. "Standards of performance" are not part of an editor's record, but before new ones are written the editor and supervisor review the old form to check successes and failures.

"We do not consider anyone incompetent if they fail to meet the goals," says Autry. "We find out what we can do to help. Using this method has increased editorial productivity because it individualizes jobs, rather than categorizing them."

Some companies take editor participation a step further, letting the editor help write a portion of the evaluation itself. "Having the editor help write the answers to some open-ended questions gives the results more depth," says *Purchasing World*'s Dunn. "Working together, the supervisor and editor can create an evaluation which has both the managerial and individual points of view. Without both points of view the evaluation will not be helpful to the editor's growth."

Gralla publications goes even further by letting its editors evaluate their evaluations. Editors in the training program fill out a questionnaire at the end of a training cycle with a magazine.

After indicating which magazine he worked for, the trainee comments on what kind of assignments were given; which he liked and which he disliked, and why; and whether the trainer's attitude toward training was good or bad.

The training program is very important to Gralla in terms of evaluating supervisors, according to Rauch. "We want to know which editors are good trainers and which are not," he says, "and the trainees are the best people to tell us."

Informal evaluations

Some publishers prefer a less formal evaluation process. For the most part, these are publishers who publish magazines that have small staffs, where the supervisor and editor are in constant contact.

Editors for Communications Channels, Inc., which publishes 16 trade magazines, are evaluated by the chief editors on a totally subjective basis. Once a year their chief editor simply writes two or three paragraphs explaining how he feels each editor is doing. The evaluation is discussed with the editor only if there is a specific question the chief editor wishes to bring to the editor's attention.

"Our editors are very close to the people who work for them," says editorial director Doug Shore. "Having 40 to 45 editorial employees, I don't think quantitative forms in triplicate would be very effective."

Currently, most publishing companies conduct total evaluations once a year. However, many publishers feel that multiple evaluations are more productive.

"Evaluating editors every six months ensures that one of the evaluations will not fall during salary review," says *Purchasing World*'s Dunn. "More frequent evaluations would not be fruitful, however, because there would not be enough time for improvement between evaluations."

Other publishers do not agree with Dunn, however. Their companies perform some type of evaluation every month, week, or even every day.

The frequency of evaluation should be tied to the magazine's frequency, according to consultant Weiss. "Conducting a performance evaluation once a year without other forms of evaluation is barbaric," he says. "For monthly magazines, semi-formal evaluations should be done quarterly, a weekly magazine should do appraisals every month or so, and quarterlies should conduct evaluations every five or six months. An editor is only as good as his last performance, so some form of appraisal should be conducted as close as possible to the last performance."

The most common form of mini-appraisal is known

447

as coaching. Coaching, conducted on an on-going basis, augments annual evaluations.

Every supervising editor must perform coaching or that supervisor is not doing his job, according to Dunn.

"Coaching is not the complete dissection of an editor's work, but rather a status check," he says. "It enables the supervisor to see how an editor is progressing toward a specific goal. And, when done on a regular basis, it reinforces the feeling that supervisors are interested in their editors."

Gralla Publications handles coaching in a formal manner. Every month for at least three months, new editors submit a file of raw, unedited copy to associate editorial director Howard Rauch. Rauch reads every article in the file and jots down his initial reactions. The editor is then called in to discuss Rauch's criticisms.

"I often begin with goofs such as typos, misspellings, and missing quotation marks, simple problems that can be corrected right away," says Rauch. "Gradually the comments deal with more difficult problems such as knowledge of the subject and ability to capture the magazine's style."

The editor receives a copy of Rauch's comments, and Rauch keeps a copy for reference the next month. "Any editor doing evaluations must write the comments down and see that the editor has a written copy," says Rauch. "No one should be expected to commit critical comments to memory."

Rauch continues the monthly reviews until an editor is performing satisfactorily on his own. Particularly talented editors may reach that point after three months. The average editor is critiqued for six months, and Rauch says some editors could be reviewed monthly for eight months.

Contests and prizes

Billboard Communications supports its evaluations with weekly and monthly contests for the best news, feature and interpretive stories. Winners are chosen by the circulation director and two editors, based entirely on a subjective evaluation of the articles.

Every six months the contest results are compiled into a study of the winners and their characteristics. The studies are used as unofficial performance standards. "Having these standards enables us to make qualitative judgments in terms of quantitative criteria," says Walter J. Heeney, vice president of Billboard's Amusement Business Group. "For example, we have found that the editors who produce the greatest amount of copy most often win the awards."

Although it would seem that conducting evaluations and their support systems could take all of a supervisor's time, most publishers say the entire process takes about an hour per editor.

How long does evaluation take?

"The supervisor should know the editor well enough so that filling out the evaluation does not take much time," says Chassler. "The discussion with the editor is usually brief because he most often agrees with what the supervisor has to say."

A number of brief evaluations during the entire year would be more productive than one all-encompassing review, according to Weiss. "Instead of doing one 60-minute session every year, I suggest performing six 10-minute sessions throughout the year," he says. "More frequent discussions of the problems make the experience less ominous, and all reviews can be compiled into a progress report at the end of the year."

Editorial performance rating

1. Unacceptable. Editor must show immediate improvement.
2. Satisfactory. Performance acceptable, but needs improvement.
3. Satisfactory. Performance acceptable, but improvement suggested.
4. Satisfactory. Performance acceptable, showing improvement.
5. Good. No serious problems, but room for improvement.
6. Good. Always meets expectations.
7. Good. Sometimes excellent.
8. Excellent. Exceeds goals and standards, is highly motivated.
9. Superior. Exemplary performance.
10. Outstanding. The best possible performance.

Responsibility	Rating
Command of language	_____
Writing style	_____
Clarity	_____
Accuracy	_____
Thoroughness	_____
Deadline observance	_____
Dependability	_____
Quantity of articles	_____
Ability to take direction	_____
Contribution of original ideas	_____
Technical knowledge	_____
Punctuality and attendance	_____
Supervisory skill	_____
Willingness to accept difficult assignments	_____

Copy and use this form

Care and feeding of writers

By Bernard Weiss

The story is told of a New York magazine editor who developed a new technique for motivating his writers. Every year or so he would circulate to his staff the resume of an unbelievably well qualified job applicant. In the upper right corner the editor would write: "Looks great. Willing to start at $75 week. Call for interview."

Motivating writers is one of an editorial executive's most challenging tasks. It's debatable whether any editor can have much of a direct motivating influence on writers, however, since creative people are usually self-motivated. But what the editor can do is provide a stimulating environment or office ambience, personal recognition for effort expended, and professional rewards for tough assignments that are done well.

If these management responsibilities are fulfilled, writers and other creative people will usually respond positively. They'll work hard, learn to improve themselves, and strive with enthusiasm to achieve personal and professional goals.

Psychological theories of motivating creative talent abound. Some are gaining wide acceptance, even though they have strange labels understood only by those who have been textbook-schooled: Frederick Herzberg's Satisfiers-Motivators Model and Douglas McGregor's Theory X and Theory Y, for example. "I never believed in those high-brow theories," one senior editorial executive told me recently at his retirement dinner. "In my office, the only technique that ever worked for me was Theory Y, S and T: Yelling, Screaming and Threatening!"

Here are some other, more practical suggestions that have proven effective at motivating writers.

Do your writers know what happens to their copy after it leaves the editorial offices, before it gets to the reader? Many publishers authorize newly-hired editorial employees to visit art studios, photo labs, type houses, computer centers, printers and binderies as part of their orientation. Usually, the editorial policy in such companies is to make writers responsible for following their articles through the production process (reading their own galleys, coordinating art and graphics, reviewing page proofs, etc.). How many of your writers have thrilled to the sight of their first cover stories spinning off a four-color press?

Do your writers talk with their readers? At one farm journal, every writer on the staff must talk to five readers a month, obtaining their responses to recent issues, soliciting future article ideas, learning what's happening in the real world. Many trade, professional and industrial magazines have boards of editorial advisors representing cross-sections of readership. The advisors are available for brief conferences with writers by telephone, and pre-publication review of manuscripts by mail.

An educational publisher authorizes its editorial staff to spend 15 working days a year in field visits to nearby schools, as well as attendance at conventions preferred by its magazines' readers.

Do your writers ever receive special praise or recognition? Do you hand out paychecks personally to your staff? If you don't, you should, and you should also take a moment with each individual to comment on some recently completed writing project that's earned your notice.

There are many ways to recognize special effort. For a particularly difficult assignment done well and on time, writers for a Chicago-based business magazine are rewarded by their editor with dinner for two at a classy restaurant and a pair of theater tickets. One newsweekly publisher sends lavish fruit baskets to the homes of any staffers who spend nights and weekends trying to make impossible deadlines for late-assigned cover stories. The president of a sports publishing subsidiary will frequently order a box of cigars, a bouquet of flowers or a bottle of superior champagne for any writer in the company whose article earns two or more letters of favorable comment from readers.

Are awards, certificates and other forms of public recognition given to staff members for outstanding achievement? Displays of awards are common in lobbies and reception rooms. Why not provide duplicates or miniatures for writers and art directors to exhibit in their offices or homes? Enter all the contests and competitions for which your publication is eligible.

If no competitions are offered for your particular publication or industry, start one internally. Ask your art department to create an award for the single outstanding creative contribution to each issue. Give the prize a funky name. Present the award at an informal staff party. Invite family and friends of the winner. Take photos for the company bulletin board or house publication. Past winners should judge future competition. Skip an award every now and then if nothing in an issue merits special recognition.

Do you seek fresh ideas and new concepts from your writers and artists? Although a formal procedure (e.g., requesting memos, treatments or outlines in writing in advance of each issue's planning meeting) is helpful, it may not be necessary. Depending on the degree of structure and organization in your department, you may be able to accomplish the same objective by simply asking each of your staff from time to time:

• What do you think we ought to be doing next?
• Have you got something special in mind?
• Suppose I were to turn you loose from your regular assignment for the next two issues. What would you do with this opportunity?

Remember, the best way to motivate creative people is to find out what they want to do, then tell them to do it.

Are outstanding members of your staff asked to share their techniques with others? There's a dual benefit here: ego gratification and wide recognition for the talented individual, plus in-service training for your staff. A medical publisher recognizes that one copywriter on the staff is extremely skillful at writing journal abstracts; that copywriter trains all new staff writers and, over a period of time, has gained a considerable measure of peer respect for having done so.

The editor of an engineering magazine convenes an in-house training seminar each month. The leader of each seminar is someone on the staff who is extremely clever at, for example, writing photo captions, headlines and cover copy; interviewing difficult subjects; scheduling long writing projects; developing sources of visual material to accompany manuscripts; etc.

Are you responsive to your writers' requests for help? Sensitivity is an important quality in any manager with responsibility for directing and motivating creative effort. Given a chance, you can often motivate a creative individual by simply being available to him and responding to his requests for help with deadlines, or advice on handling an assignment.

Such moments offer you additional opportunities to be supportive, take a sincere personal interest in someone's welfare, train him for more challenging assignments, and offer general encouragement.

On a more intensely personal basis, be sure to respond to your writers' needs for prompt review of their creative performance. These are wonderful opportunities to motivate people. Creative people hunger for professional recognition; they want to know how they are doing, and they are acutely aware of your attitude toward their copy or art.

Therefore, the sooner you can respond to a manuscript, the better. Praise is a marvelous motivational tool. Criticism, when presented properly, is too. But remember, criticism should be like a shot in the arm, not a kick in the backside.

The art of being on time

By George A. Glenn

What's the cost of late copy? Besides possible overtime charges in the production, art, editorial and print departments required to handle such material, other penalties are even more severe:

• Poor on-time performances cause last-minute rushes. Staff members can be drained of creative talent in the effort to meet last-minute pushes to get the job done.

• The art department, in an effort to catch up on deadlines, limits its creative effort.

• Copy is sent through without proper proofreading, causing error-riddled galleys. The blame is usually put on the printer, production staff and editorial department.

• The chance for errors on final page proofs increases as poor on-time performance problems begin to back up into the finished page.

• The constant hassle of running to complete editorial assignments at the last minute causes department upheaval and often harsh words. Staff morale can be damaged regularly as months of poor on-time performance pass by. If overtime is demanded regularly, staff members often start looking for new job opportunities.

• The opportunity to plan and get into the next issue seldom occurs because issues are constantly bumping into one another.

• Often the editorial staff becomes so exhausted playing catch-up that the after-issue letdown prevents everyone from thinking clearly about the next big push.

The list of negative repercussions resulting from poor on-time editorial performance goes on and on. There are few, if any, positive points to be gained.

There are many excuses for being behind on editorial schedules but only a very few that will hold up in the editorial court of order.

Conditioning and Discipline

My contention is that every editor deserving of the title can meet deadlines; and better than that, those deadlines can be met easily. There's no big secret. The key is in conditioning and disciplining oneself to think "on time."

For many editors, conditioning and discipline don't come easy. It's often not a case of resisting discipline but one of not knowing how to go about it.

It's much like the sandlot baseball player who tries to make it in the majors. He may be able to hit an occasional record home run, he's built like an athlete and looks like a baseball player, but he hasn't learned how to bunt, run bases, hit in the clutches and field a long drive. He's afraid of a fast-running base runner and doesn't like to hear jeering crowds. He can't stand reading bad reports about himself in the newspapers and hasn't learned how to deal with the press. He has the potential but he hasn't been conditioned, trained and disciplined. If he wants to be a pro, he learns how and he works at it.

But where does an editor start if he or she really wants to become a pro in the business magazine profession? And more importantly, why *is* it so important to be on time? Many editors ask this question when they feel that quality or credibility may be sacrificed in meeting deadlines. Being creative, well-organized and in command of every situation are the signs of a professional editor. They are the signs of an editor who can think efficiently. Nothing fazes such an editor; no editorial problem is too big to solve. Such an editor usually creates a smoothly running staff that knows what it's doing and how to get the job done at all times.

I have come to the conclusion that the biggest obstacle in building an on-time attitude is the editor's "state of mind." When I was in training, one editor told me to think of time as a measure of productivity. "How much can be done in 60 seconds? Sit back and count off 60 seconds and experience how long it is. Then ask yourself how much you could have done in that time." He was right. I could have made a phone call to a reader; given a brief assignment to a staff member; typed 50 words of copy; proofread half of my monthly column; written an answer to any of those countless wordy memos.

Conditioning Begins

So I began to condition myself that way. My mind began to approach problems mathematically.

An illustration: I began to look at each issue first as a mathematical challenge. How many pages of manuscript are needed to fill an average issue? How many feature stories are needed per issue? How many department inches are required? How many special reports are planned for each issue or throughout the year? How many pages of copy and what number of features and departments from each staff member are necessary each and every workday to meet a deadline? How many pages should we expect from outside writers?

That may sound rather academic and mechanical, but I've found that knowing the answers to questions such as these is the first step in conditioning.

In my experience, it has become quite evident that many editors do not know how many pages of manuscript they send out on the average. More do not know the productivity rate of their staff members. Of course, an editor should be aware that a staff member might be working on a research project in a given month or on an in-depth study which will not produce as much copy as would come from an editor writing department copy on a daily basis. But even there, an editor can be aware that a certain staff member who works on difficult assignments usually takes so many days to complete such an effort. That editor plans his or her schedule accordingly.

We have seen editors who could turn out up to 35 pages of copy each day for a month on a special project where all material was in hand and ready for writing. Others can turn out only 17 pages under these conditions. On the average, however, we have found that you should expect an editor to turn in slightly more than four pages of copy daily. If this were a goal, most publications would be on time without any problem. What really happens in most cases is that the editorial staffs will attempt to write their four-pages-a-day-average all in the week just before deadlines. This means that they are trying to write up to 80 pages in five working days.

There's where the problems arise. The editor who comes in late, has an unforeseen appointment, must attend a meeting that goes to half a day instead of one hour or has a breakdown in equipment is in major deadline trouble.

Therefore, I have found that the first point in developing the art of being on time is thinking mathematically about production checkpoints to assure on-time performance. This means a knowledge of publication mathematics and a conditioning and discipline to think in terms of the mathematical factors in developing good production and work habits.

A second factor in the art of being on time is scheduling. Certainly every editor must have a month-by-month schedule of deadlines to meet. This should be prepared for one calendar year at least three months before the new publication year begins. Separate schedules should be prepared for special sections and special reports.

All staff members should keep such deadlines posted by their desks for ready reference.

More than scheduling, a yearly editorial calendar of major features should be planned by issue and by the year. The editor should frame out approximate length of such features; diagram how such material is to be gathered; assign major features three months prior to the new publication year. This should be set in type, dramatized and sent out to staff members. It should also be posted at the desks near the schedules.

A calendar can be flexible, but having the major features pinpointed helps day-to-day planning. Above all, if there is a change in the master plan, every staff member should be alerted and a substitute feature should be plugged in.

There are always features that can't be planned in advance and late-breaking stories that can't be anticipated, but if an overall major editorial plan is made, the late-breaking unforeseen stories will be that much easier to program in and meet deadlines without major interruptions.

The third point in the art of being on-time comes in creating self-discipline techniques. I have a personal built-in list. The point is not so much whether my personal guidelines are used, but whether an editor develops an individual set of discipline goals. I find them vital no matter what other planning and programming methods are followed. Here's my personal list:

1. Come into the office with a plan for yourself and your staff.

2. Check the staff daily to determine progress or problems.

3. Solve those problems and create alternatives immediately with staff members.

4. Periodically check outside writers before deadlines to determine progress and problems.

5. Following early morning staff checks, handle mail quickly along with interoffice communications. Then move directly into your portion of the daily plan. Know exactly what you must do.

6. Plan trips at times when the staff is writing and all assignments are made.

7. Check the staff daily—every other day when on trips—to uncover problems and chart progress.

8. Abbreviate lunches unless valuable stories and leads are unfolding from them.

9. Plan trips so that full working days can be put in.

10. Try to cover several stories in any given outside city.

11. Check staff travel plans to ensure good use of

time. Have staff members report back by phone to you daily.

12. Plan schedules so that the staff is on board for production chores—proofing, dummying and making final okays.

13. Try to make each staff member totally responsible for copy to completed page proof.

14. If you have a small staff, pitch in and help on everything.

15. When an issue is complete, don't relax. Get into the next one.

16. Cut insignificant office chatter down to a minimum.

17. Don't write when you can phone and if you can't answer a question or gain information by phone, keep the memo or letter you must write short.

Gearing Up

Of all these points, I would consider an editor's ability to gear up for the next issue to be one of the most important. Mental slowdowns are the worst kind of time-wasters.

Not all problems can be solved in a standup position. If the answers don't come fast, move to the next problem if you can. Sometimes solving an unrelated problem triggers new solutions to a harder-to-solve situation.

The fourth ingredient in building the skill of being on time can be found in a few useful tools:

1. A bulletin board chart by month showing features, departments and assignments helps keep the mind focused on a target.

2. A monthly editorial plan sheet, detailing features and departments with assignments for the editorial staff issued well before the current issue closes, helps put the wheels in motion.

3. A set daily production goal for staff and self helps and conditions everybody. See that those goals are met. Find out why they are not being met and remedy problems fast.

4. Good programming for artists is also important. They should be checked regularly to maintain an on-time performance.

5. Printed schedules, programs and calendars furnished to all staff members and posted in a prominent place, preferably near the desk, are also good reminders.

Some editors are natural born time clocks. All they must do is refine and perfect the art of being on time. Others—as I have found, most—have to work at it. Once the editor develops a respect for time, staff members will follow it. There is no question in my mind that on-time and quality editorial do go hand in hand.

Planning, programming and constant checkbacks are the major keys. Does it all pay off? And more important, do the points made in this article really work? They do.

Using the various guidelines mentioned above, we will now see how such a program worked for a publication that had serious deadline on-time problems.

Publication X had been operating with a staff of two. Editorial planning was done from month to month.

Deadline schedules were seldom met. For some months, more than 100 pages of copy were sent up after deadline dates. Editorial costs, as a result, were far above the average. We considered carefully whether or not we could continue to publish this magazine.

The decision was that we had an obligation to the industry. We were needed. Therefore, we would continue publishing the magazine.

We knew that structuring good editorial on-time procedures would play a major role in this publication's revitalization.

Our first decision was to bring in an editor whom we felt could respond to the needs of this publication. We looked for a person with writing talents, a good grasp of urgency and the ability to learn good magazine organization.

We found such an editor and gave that person the challenge to turn out an interesting trade publication with consistent quality.

A study of the content indicated that one good editor could handle the publication and meet all the necessary deadlines.

In order to come up with a more exciting publication and help the new editor organize time and content, we developed a clear editorial concept. The market was studied; readers were interviewed; advertisers were asked their opinion concerning the magazine's needs.

Reader research was done on a face-to-face basis. Based on our field findings, we redesigned the publication's directions to mirror the day-in-day-out functions and problems of the readers. The magazine was departmentalized from cover to cover with each feature, section and department clearly labeled as to function. Each issue was to have a reader "Profile" feature; an "In-Store-Merchandising" feature; a "Fashion" page; a "Special Report" and so on. Fifteen such groupings were made.

The new approach represented a clear editorial profile of those features and departments in which readers said they were interested. For the new editor it represented a major step in organization and building on-time performance.

Graphically, the magazine was then completely redesigned around this concept. It spelled out exactly what the editor had to deliver each and every month. Each feature was slotted to perform a function for the reader.

With an organized editorial concept and redesign to complement it, an editorial calendar defining the major features and departments planned for each month was programmed. This was another aid to the editor in planning assignments and writing.

A desk file system was set up to correspond to the new feature and department categories. Each file folder was made in duplicate and labeled by feature and department grouping. One set of folders is used to hold fresh copy, photographs, related clippings and other materials pertinent to developing each feature while the second set holds corresponding galleys, engraver's proofs and other printed material necessary for dummy.

A simple log-in, log-out book is used to keep track of all editorial matter to be set.

With the system and deadline charts to follow by the year and month, the new program was in order. All that was needed was copy.

Initially, copy was generated from freelance writers on an assignment basis. The new editor wrote departments and local features.

For the first two months an unusual number of freelance articles was assigned to build a backlog of material that would not be dated in three months. Fortunately the cost was billed into the last two months of the year against the old budget. By the time the new design and editorial package appeared in print, twice as much copy as was needed was already in type and on dummy. Some had been set in bogus pages.

The backlog then freed the new editor to move out into the field, hold meetings in conjunction with the publisher to explain the new editorial philosophy and develop new features and in-depth industry special reports.

Each presentation made to advertisers was backed by a strong visual approach showing the new format, its function, benefits and future outlook.

The purposeful organization was a convincing story. Advertisers regained their confidence in the magazine; the publisher had renewed confidence in the editorial direction; and the editor felt free to create in an atmosphere of organized work flow.

Another stage in the reorganization is a recently introduced program which disciplines the editor to maintain constant contact with readers for their input. Three reader calls are made daily; each is recorded and weekly reports are made from the editor to the publisher. Leads, story material, feature story interviews and reader feedback have resulted from this system. Close to 60 readers are contacted by phone each month.

The system establishes the editor's daily plan. There is no guesswork. One hundred percent on-time performance has been maintained for five straight months. A backlog of editorial material is always on hand yet the bulk of editorial stays fresh and current because the editor has time to manage the publication and stay on top of industry happenings simultaneously.

Now conditioning has taken over. The editorial direction and makeup of the book dictate what must be done every day.

There is a definite correlation between organized on-time editorial performance and success of a publication. In this case it may well have saved a publication. Costs have been brought into line; editorial quality has been revitalized; advertising has almost doubled in four months; and best of all, the publication is showing a profit for the first time in several years.

It's creativity that makes an editorial department sparkle. The best way I know of to establish a creative environment is to provide the editor with the time needed to come up with fresh ideas. That means building a system that keeps you on schedule, preferably ahead, with time to spare for those bigger creative endeavors that all editors wish they could undertake if they "only had the time."

Every art must be worked at and practiced. I contend that the art of being on time is no exception.

Thirteen steps to editing a successful magazine

By A.C. Spectorsky

The late A. C. Spectorsky, associate publisher and editorial director of *Playboy*, had very definite ideas on what makes a successful magazine. *Playboy* founder Hugh M. Hefner concurred and the two of them proved the validity of the formula they devised. Following what Spectorsky called a "Baker's Dozen: 13 Publishing Precepts," *Playboy* rose from a circulation of under a million in 1956 to 6,500,000 at the time of his death.

FOLIO is proud to present Spectorsky's "Baker's Dozen," 13 points that we believe apply to all magazines — consumer or business, large or small.

1. The reader must come first. This may sound insultingly simple but it is perhaps one of those utterly simple truths that is so familiar as to be largely ignored. Certainly, in my 30-odd years of experience in communications, it has seemed abundantly clear that if the publisher makes the audience the primary concern, genuinely so, all else that is good will not necessarily follow but will certainly have a clear path. Just as surely, without this primacy of audience, all else is doomed; or if not doomed, then certainly unsuited to the shoals and storms and variable winds of the subcultural archipelago that comprises today's society and determines its climate.

2. Surveys, statistics, demographic breakouts, computerized evaluations and all the other wonderful paraphernalia of communications analysis can be a detriment rather than a help if they are used to guide action, rather than to validate on-going imaginative and creative publishing. Reliance upon surveys is precisely how one becomes a follower rather than a leader.

3. The ethical and moral posture of the responsible publisher must be that of a gardener, not a miner. His or her role is to cultivate, not exploit. Happily, self-interest is best served in this way.

4. In a permissive society, the successful publication leads its readership, rather than following it—a point I just made in speaking of the statistics trap. Putting it another way: Stimulate, don't tranquilize. A useful corollary to the leadership principle is that it is important for the leader to stay within sight of the troops. There are still plenty of straits out there. Too many neophyte publishers—zapped-out and far-out or trying to appear so—have experienced the thrill of a first issue and the sudden grim reality of its being the last.

5. As to the relationship of publisher and reader, it should never be a "we-they" relationship; it must always be a "we-all" relationship.

6. Today's society is a turbulent one, a maelstrom of identity-seeking individuals. Therefore, no matter how specialized or pinpointed your audience, it is essential to address the whole person. As I said earlier, this is a time of affluence, but it is not merely or exclusively financial affluence. Greater leisure and wider horizons, combined with financial affluence, have created an audience that has time and attention for all of life, an audience that feels less and less guilt about material possessions—or the total abandonment of them. An audience that has the time and attention to sample and savor, accept or reject, varieties of living in all aspects: Physical, intellectual, emotional, spiritual, very much sexual.

People today are more whole and more far-ranging in outlook than they may ever have been before. I am talking about the death of the Deprivation Syndrome or the Self-Punishment Mystique. The intrinsic virtuousness of thrift, self-denial, discomfort and economy may no longer be assumed. Today, the measure of medicinal efficacy is not how bad it tastes. The successful publisher in this society must address himself or herself to the whole person as he or she grows and evolves and seeks fulfillment in less regimental ways.

7. Publishing today demands flexibility. But never buy flexibility and adaptability at the cost of personality. A publication must attain and project a consistent personality or each issue becomes merely a disparate miscellany within covers bearing the same title. Variety is fine but it must stem from a consistent, readily-recognized editorial viewpoint. Otherwise, continuity of attention and interest—and reader loyalty—are lost because the competition for attention from all media has never been greater.

8. Be courageous. This again sounds very sweeping and very obvious. Yet I am sure that all of us can recall situations in which vacillation, doubt, a failure of nerve, an unwillingness to risk, have led inevitably to one more proof of the "Peter Pan Law." The "Peter Pan Law" says that prompt and decisive action will pan out, whereas caution and timidity will peter out.

9. To assure failure, attempt creativity by committee. The fact is that a magazine is not a democracy. An over-structured organization becomes rigid, brittle, inflexible. But the alternative is not lack of control. Tight control is what is needed, not ingenious, postfacto explanations for accidents or disasters achieved by a voting majority.

10. To survive and thrive in the self-examining and identity-seeking society, a magazine must be partisan. That is, it must be zealously and in all things pro-reader. We live in a semantic deluge of judgmental directives, scolding, sermonizing. The high moral posture of a great many publications too often results in the reader feeling inadequate, inferior, depressed, even despised. Were I an advertiser, I do not think I would be satisfied that this psychological climate would be the ideal one in which to present my product—unless I were in the business of selling suicide kits.

11. In publishing, the very cheapest expenditure for the largest return is a high-priced editorial content. I mean high-priced in terms of assembling and rewarding a creative editorial staff. I mean high-priced in payments to contributors. For these two groups of people are your senses—your eyes, ears and your voice—in relating to the society within which your audience resides. And I mean high-priced in terms of a high ratio of editorial content to advertising. High-priced, too, in charging a reader a full, fair price for your magazine. This is the kind of publishing that leads to the happy situation of selling magazines, as opposed to buying bargain hunters. And it does not demean authors by selling their work at bargain prices.

12. Have fun at your work and produce a product that you, yourself, can enjoy. The pleasure will show through and create a happy feeling in the reader. And second-guessing will be precluded. As everyone knows—or should—trying to second-guess the reader breeds condescension on the part of the publisher and suspicion on the part of the audience.

13. Finally, bear in mind that the greatest peril for a publication may exist at the very moment of its greatest success, when it is most susceptible to relying on self-duplication. A good publisher is an innovator, not a curator. A successful magazine must be a process, not an artifact. It must constantly evolve, not just keep pace, to retain leadership. The history of publishing is strewn with the remains of embalmed publications that knew they had a good thing going and kept it going the same way while the world went by. For every hallowed institution in the magazine business today, there are a dozen unmarked graves.

On the other hand, shun radical editorial and graphic revolutions—they usually ensue on intimations of fiscal and financial catastrophe and they almost invariably fail by alienating the last remnant of loyal readers.

Some magazines don't die, they just fade away. They pass the point of no return and reach a fade accompli. This moribund condition is brought about by the hardest sort of work—and sheer busyness—invested in the wrong places: There are special deals and high-pressure pitches to advertisers, accompanied by cascades of cut-rate subscriptions to subscribers and consumer advertising aimed at an already alienated public. This, too, means buying readers instead of selling magazines. It seems abundantly clear that it is the product itself that should have been the prime focus of all this expenditure of time and money and effort. Yet, in times of crisis, the opposite is too often the case: The icy wind of an economy drive afflicts the magazine itself, parasitically battering on the staff at a time when it most needs help. I don't mean that one should protect incompetents or encourage self-pity— the sure sign of entrenched underachievers. I refer to brainless business-office cutbacks. This is what is known as the Human Sacrifice—or Body Count—theory of publishing. It has one virtue: It does not discriminate between personnel and clientele; staff and circulation go down together.

It is my experience and my belief that these 13 publishing precepts can be found to have been operative in the most vigorous, successful, enduring publications in the contemporary history of publishing. Alternatively, misplaced cynicism, misdirected efforts, failed nerve and greedy calculation have characterized the winning entries in the casualty sweepstakes. And tinkering or surface retouching will not reverse the flow of traffic toward disaster. In point of fact, these acts of desperation too often make a magazine look like its own retouched passport photo—and as everyone knows, when you look like your passport photo, you aren't fit to travel.

Confronting the editorial mystique

By Philip Wootton

It was Edward Weeks, long-time editor of the *Atlantic Monthly,* who enunciated the shortest and truest formula for magazine success: "One man, one idea." The proof is all around—Ross at *The New Yorker,* Luce at *Time,* Thompson at *Smithsonian.* These men are (or were) their magazines and under them the distinction of publisher versus editor blurs. Lacking such transcendent talent at the helm, however, the great majority of magazines rock along with an editor and a publisher locked in formal and often uneasy harmony.

One of the ills afflicting this relationship is a tendency of some publishers to regard their editors almost in the light of the men mentioned above—as geniuses, or nearly so. This is useful promotionally and helpful to the publisher's ego. "Look what I have here." But it does not wholly protect the editor from being fired (wrong kind of genius) and tends to make communication between the publisher and editor an all-or-nothing affair impeded by the mists of editorial mystique. It also creates a poor atmosphere in which to solve the problems of a magazine in trouble.

With the possible exception of cereal or laundry detergents, magazines (omitting editorial) are among the most analyzed and surveyed of products. Consider the following scenario.

A subscription magazine of medium circulation in the consumer field suffers a dismal response from its latest direct mail piece. New orders are going to fall far short of forecasts. Lists are analyzed frontwards, backwards and upside down. A cry goes out for new promotion

writers. Production is asked to cut 10 percent out of its budget. Ad sales are analyzed. New promotion is produced. And a quick survey is made of the hours the sales staff spends in the office compared to being out on calls.

All this time the conversion and renewal percentages—the two sure measures of the public's enthusiasm for the magazine—are no higher than the barely acceptable levels of two years before, a clear indication that something is very wrong with editorial, the core of the enterprise.

At this point the temptation to fire the editor, as the quickest and simplest solution, becomes very strong. But that is all it is: quick and simple, not necessarily good. To get out a magazine at all, whatever its faults, editors have to be constantly in the thick of things—and the editor who can keep unfailing sight of the forest and not get lost in the trees is the exception.

Publishers often don't know what to do about their editorial product. They don't realize that the editorial component of a magazine, like its other elements, can also be analyzed to discover why the only thing a magazine really has to sell is not selling. This must be the publisher's job. His is the overall responsibility and he must wade in, editorial mystique and genius theory notwithstanding, and find out what is wrong.

All magazines are different and each has its own problems. However, there are certain analytical and curative procedures which apply pretty much across the board. These should be attempted, with attendant diplomacy. Good editors are hard to find and the prospects of getting a better one are never more than 50-50.

Since the final arbiter of what is a good (i.e., successful) magazine is the reader, the publisher must play the role of a perceptive and constructive critical reader. This task can be divided in two—format and content. Begin by using a simple device, known only to a few publishers.

First, find a big room with a soft wall and a lockable door. Then, pin every page of the latest issue of your magazine up on the wall in normal front-to-back sequence—a big long line of pages, ads and all. Then lock the door, sit back, and gain some perspective by staring at this display for at least an hour a day for a week.

Format problems revealed

If your magazine is in editorial trouble, your own common sense and good taste should begin to reveal some format problems. In fact, it is surprising how the mistakes stick out.

The crucial point is this: In several hours of concentration the pinup will reveal, sometimes with embarrassing precision, what the reader has been learning little by little (and largely subconsciously) over six months or a year.

If you see too many type styles, confusion between departments and features, diagrams that must be painfully deciphered, jumbled photographs and mysterious illustrations, plus other evils of disorganization, you can be pretty sure that these same things will first confuse and then annoy the reader. When the time comes for renewal or buying another newsstand copy, a small inner voice may resist.

A magazine format that is too complex gets in the way of clear and easy communication. This rule is not universal, however. Some women's magazines make a virtue of editorial clutter. Among them it is not uncommon to find an avalanche of bits and pieces of editorial material mixed in with another avalanche of ads. By and large, however, simplicity and clarity are the key words in magazine appearance, and two consumer magazines with exceptional reader loyalty, *Smithsonian* and *Scientific American*, exhibit these qualities to an outstanding degree.

Besides revealing any tendency toward clutter and confusion, the pinup of a magazine often demonstrates that a large proportion of its audience is being short-changed. It must be assumed that only a certain percentage of the readers of most magazines are fully committed readers in the sense that people *read* magazines such as *Harper's, The Atlantic,* partisan political journals, specialized trade publications, and expensive insider newsletters.

Possibly as much as 50 percent of a general magazine's audience consists of people who never read the magazine thoroughly. Instead, they look at the pictures, read the headlines, subheads, intra-article teasers, picture captions and initial paragraphs of some of the features. They then dip briefly into the departments and short takes. Beyond this they rarely go.

However, these kinds of readers can be loyal subscribers and regular newsstand buyers who provide a substantial economic underpinning to a multi-million-dollar enterprise. The proof of this lies in the success of—most obviously—*National Geographic Magazine,* and the quasi magazines produced by Time-Life Books.

It follows, then, that the elements upon which these part-time readers depend—headlines, subheads, picture captions, opening paragraphs, etc.—must be nothing less

than gems of efficient and provocative communication. This quality must be unassailable, an integral and unvarying constant in the magazine's format.

Then and only then can the casual (but invaluable) reader absorb headlines, look at pictures, read captions, scan a few columns, and derive a sense of full value received in the course of an hour. Then and only then can the wise publisher rest easily knowing that he has done his best to win the ultimate battle, which is for a reader's time.

The pinup technique can also reveal the crying need for a new, or at least a consulting, art director. Displayed nakedly on the wall, many magazines look as if they had been laid out by someone used to designing a number of unrelated exhibits in a commercial art gallery. In such a magazine, each story appears as a discrete piece with a definite beginning and end, wholly unrelated in feeling to what comes before or follows after.

A magazine should flow from front to back, moving the reader along through all those fascinating pages and their accompanying ads. However, it is also important to grab the reader's attention with each story—stopping him with headlines, illustrations and compelling design. Obviously, this poses a dilemma and, possibly, a need for outside help, someone who can provide a nice (i.e., expert) balance between stop and go.

If some publishers tend to think too reverently of their editors, many think not at all about the wonders of type, that most basic element without which their industry, after all, could not exist. Big type, small type, thin type and fat, bold type and pretty type, used carefully and with taste and logic, can do miracles in organizing a magazine and, at least subliminally, charming the reader.

Readers are easily dismayed by getting lost, by not receiving definite clues as to what is very important, less important, and what follows what. Readers want clues to the stories that are clearly light-weight and put in for amusement or a change of pace, and they want clues to departments or special features they have become used to finding in issue after issue. Many subscriptions have been cancelled on this point alone.

Good type design, by creating a sense of pace and establishing location, is essential for readers' peace of mind. It can also do something else. Used under strict rules and conventions, good type design can bring a magazine together as an aesthetic whole, while helping to establish the all-important distinction between editorial and advertising, to the benefit of both.

Five easy improvements

If you, as the publisher of a new or faltering magazine, are discouraged after a number of sessions in the pinup room, take heart. Let me suggest a small kit bag of "quick fixes" which will help make a start toward improving almost any magazine.

1. Take 100 to 200 words out of each major article.

There is more logic to this technique than immediately meets the eye. Most magazines must operate within a finite number of editorial pages. Within those pages even the dedicated reader (as opposed to the casual peruser described before) will rarely read every piece. If even only one or two touch him closely and fascinate him to the degree that he will talk about them and recommend them to friends, you are doing well.

It follows, therefore, that the more articles you have in each issue, the better chance you have for catching the special interest of each reader and adding still more dedicated fans. If your usual number of features is eight, shortening them all will get you nine or maybe 10, and your fascinated reader quotient per issue will go up.

Aside from this mathematical achievement, it is obviously better to leave readers wishing for more at the end of each article than bogged down somewhere in the middle. Even the best editor tends to let articles run longer than necessary. By press time his eye is no longer fresh enough to see the advantages of cutting.

2. Increase the size of body type.

Editors who want to cram in more words soon learn that the easiest way to do this is by using smaller type. Thus the magazine appears with smaller and smaller type and the readers become more and more irritated.

Putting items one and two together will automatically result in shorter articles. This, in turn, will force tighter editing, a goodly number of gutsy verbs, and a minimum of flabby adjectives (and, possibly, a new copy editor).

3. Polish up the opening paragraphs of each article.

There is an old carnival expression, "First you got to get them into the tent." Editorially, you have three chances to do the equivalent—the main head, the subhead, and the opening paragraph. Pictures and their captions act as flags and bunting. It is the opening paragraph that must give the reader the final shove into all the paragraphs that follow and it had better be a pretty attractive piece of writing.

To accomplish this there is no surer guide than the old journalistic rule of who, when, why, what and where. All too many magazine pieces begin with paragraphs of flowery scene-setting and absolutely no clues as to why the reader should work his way downward. In all too many magazines, the really provocative information promised by the heads and subheads does not turn up until page three, and by this time the reader has either given up or forgotten why he began reading the piece in the first place.

4. Clean up the diagrams; add more pictures.

Charts, graphs and maps, if appropriate to an article, should be colorful but utterly simple in design. Embellishment and decoration, while often appropriate, must be confined to the peripheries and never in any way interfere with the information being conveyed.

Somewhat beyond the scope of a "quick fix" is the development of a chart, graph and map style for your magazine as a whole. Nothing will help your format more, but it requires expert work by a talented person. So, too, does any substantial addition of pictures because they must be good pictures properly used. The additional dollars required must pull their full weight.

5. Establish white space uniformity and a caption style.

Size of page margins and the use of white space throughout the magazine should be a matter of consistent design. Couple this with an orderly style of picture captions, and another step will have been made toward producing a magazine that gets its information off the pages and into the reader's mind quickly and easily. (And remember, never, never have a picture without a caption. Why deliberately mystify the reader?)

There are some magazines which have sufficiently talented art directors so that they get by pretty much on format and design alone. Reading such a magazine is like skating on thin ice; so long as it is gone over quickly everything is fine, but there is not much substance below the surface. The opposite kind of magazine is also familiar, crammed with important and provocative information which must be dug out with a pick and shovel.

Analyzing content

Since the trick, obviously, is to put good format together with good content, the second part of a program of editorial improvement is to analyze content, the basic information carried by a magazine. It is the more important part of the task. News of the Second Coming, after all, would be little affected by the format in which it appeared.

Content is also a more difficult problem for the simple reason that it more deeply involves people: finding them, managing them, inspiring them. A magazine's content directly represents the skill, imagination and intelligence of the people who put it there. Short of a hospital emergency room, it would be hard to imagine a more labor-sensitive organization than an editorial staff—or one more clearly dependent on sheer creativity.

Every month, or week, or two weeks, as the case may be, that staff starts with 50 to 80 pages of blank white paper which it must somehow fill, on a rigid timetable, with fascinating words and arresting illustrations, all presented in an attractive framework.

Question: How do you analyze so vital and delicate a matter as editorial content in its infinite variations, let alone improve it?

Answer: Begin by asking two crucial questions, the answers to which are applicable alike to existing magazines and the plans for new ones.

The first question is this: Is the magazine *for* someone or *about* something? The answer to this contains the nugget of truth central to editorial success or failure: To be fully successful, a magazine must be *about* something. Magazines can certainly be *for* someone—yachtsmen, golfers, runners, investors, executives, housewives — but, first and foremost, it must be *about* something of interest to these people.

In recent years, with the improvement in audience survey techniques, more new magazines have been started for someone rather than about something. Almost without exception, however, these kinds of magazines get into editorial trouble because a truly viable product must be based on a certain subject or subjects. Stated baldly, the first concern of a successful magazine must be journalism, not marketing.

This does not mean for a moment that marketing, in all its facets, is not vital; few magazines can survive unless marketing techniques are employed skillfully and extensively. However, the question is one of priority and emphasis, of a basic mental attitude on the part of the magazine's proprietors who must first decide that there is something very important (fascinating, unique, surprising, exciting) that needs to be said. Then, and only then, should they go about the intricate task of finding those who will most want to hear about it.

As stated earlier, the basic thing a magazine has to sell is its editorial product. If a publishing enterprise primarily sells a particular audience or a special set of demographics, trouble is probably on the way.

Is it interesting?

The second crucial question to ask about a magazine's content is very simply this: Is it interesting? How can a question so patently over-simplistic be asked? How, indeed, can it possibly be answered?

The answer, or most of it, can be found in a now-familiar place, the big locked room with all the pages of the current issue (or latest dummy) pinned on the wall. As publisher, you must slip back into your role as the intelligent, inquiring and critical reader.

Look carefully at those pages. Read and think about every story, every paragraph, every illustration. Page by page, ask yourself if you are interested. You will soon find yourself able to say that some things are distinctly more interesting than others. Mark the less interesting items with a red pencil. The chances are very good that your deletions will closely parallel those your audience would make.

Once you have completed this exercise, you are ready for the last and most important step. Ask the editor and one or two of his staff to join you in the pinup sanctum for a thoroughgoing discussion of your red-marked pages and paragraphs. If your editorial people respond with imagination and ingenious suggestions for making things more interesting (which is what happens nine times out of 10), you are on your way. But if they do not, you must in due course send them on their way—out the door.

Whichever way your editors react, here are a few devices which have often helped to make magazines more interesting.

1. There is nothing to equal hard digging for information to produce unique and compelling stories that will fascinate your readers. It is the oldest trick in the business; good reporting means good circulation. There is a specific and relatively easy way for a publisher to get a big part of this job done. Pick (or hire) a bright and, above all, imaginative editor and give him responsibility for something called Special Projects.

It should be his job to put into each issue a clearly remarkable story, a small (or large) tour-de-force of journalism which reflects unusual imagination, a lot of work, or a stroke of insight or smart timing. It must be clear that this editor's career will stand or fall on the success and energy with which he can produce the kinds of stories for which awards are given and about which newspaper articles are written. Tough on the editor, but a simple and effective strategy for the publisher.

2. Another tool for increasing the interest quotient of your magazine is the use of surprise writers. These are essentially switch hitters, people of some public reputation writing about something you and your readers hardly expect. To take an extreme example: Thoreau on the Industrial Revolution. Or, more up-to-date, Thor Heyerdahl on mountain climbing. Recently John Kenneth Galbraith did a fascinating piece on Swiss watches that contained nothing about their politico-economic significance.

3. A time-honored technique is that of doing stories about (or interviews with) people in some degree pre-sold by other media to your readers. No matter what your magazine is about, there is always someone out there about whom your readers already know a little and can be counted on to want to know more. It is, of course, a narrow line; your pre-sold subjects must not be over-sold.

4. Put in some controversy of greater or lesser intensity in at least every other issue.

5. Almost every magazine can justify a certain amount of service information for its readers. Although this is often opposed on grounds that it is inelegant or interferes with the higher purpose of the publication, service information passes the test of being interesting if it is accurate, not easily obtainable elsewhere, and not overdone. Clearly identified and internally-promoted departments that tell your readers something that will enhance their lifestyle, their fortunes, their intellects, their health, their skills or their attractiveness will also win their gratitude.

Such departments have the added advantage of giving the readers something they can count on finding in the next issue, and the next, and the next. Each time they find their old friends, chalk up a quantum of loyalty for your magazine.

6. That vital question "Is it interesting?" can and should be applied to photographs and illustrations as well as words. New illustrators will inevitably create new interest. In looking for them, there are no better places than the medical magazines, fashion magazines, and their attendant advertising. Fresh photographic approaches are often found in the more expensive photography books and, again, in fashion pictures.

7. The most important picture in any magazine is, of course, the one on the cover. This is a genuine never-neverland which has defied years of surveys, psychological analysis, group therapy and fierce argument. Three things which seem to work for a cover picture, however, are a large pattern, bright colors and provocative billings. All else is a matter of luck and guesswork.

8. Finally, if you still find yourself in the pinup room marking too many pages in dull red, you obviously need some fresh spark. One way to get it, short of tearing up the staff, is to create a board of editors or consultants or advisors or any other flattering designation. Choose the people carefully and then pick their brains for ideas. A weekend "retreat" for brainstorming will probably be worth the cost—but hold at least one session before you put any names on the masthead.

When all is said and done, a successful magazine publisher must 1) get a reader to buy his first issue; 2) induce him to read it; and 3) leave him happy enough to come back for more. That's all there is to it—necessarily complicated by the myriad, wrenching details of circulation, promotion, advertising, manufacturing, distribution, and general management, to say nothing of cash flow, capital demands and even profits.

In all this, the buck stops with you, the publisher—a busy, responsible, and sometimes impatient person. Yet none of the specific editorial or attitude changes discussed here can or should be effected quickly. Take your time—you can, or should, afford it.

Magazines have a nasty way of pushing the proprietor into experimenting in public; and haste is waste, or even disaster. Try things out in dummy or mockup form, then mull over the results thoroughly before rushing into print. Taken altogether, the matters discussed here will, with any luck at all, eventually improve your magazine.

And remember, never let the image of your ideal reader grow dim in your mind. He, the customer for your product, must come away from each issue with the feeling of having been stimulated but not satiated, of having his life enriched, his psyche encouraged. But above all, he must come away from each issue with some regret that he has finished it and some feeling of anticipation, no matter how small, for the next one. Think of the magazines which give you these feelings, then imitate their technique—although not too closely. Give your editor a chance to exercise his own creative variations.

One last word: Keep your priorities in rigid order. Your first purpose must be to inform (and entertain) well and truly. If you do this unequivocally, the money will take care of itself.

Copy editing and writing

By Howard J. Taylor

Editor's note: The following article is adapted from a booklet, "Writing and Copy Reading," written by Taylor for the Copley Newspapers. The author comments upon some very basic—and too often forgotten—editing and writing techniques. Though written for newspaper editors and writers, the article is just as relevant to editors and writers in the magazine industry.

The purpose of this is to round up a few points of writing and copy reading. It is not intended as a complete catalog.

Although some consider many of these points elementary, they emerge from copy or from stories that have actually appeared in print.

The American Press Institute (API), in a note on writing, says this: "The average reporter—not the good one—has little respect for the basic tools of his craft, the words he works with. He is impatient of distinctions in meaning. He regards as academic (a somewhat dirty word) any insistence on precision. Although he began his career because He Wanted To Be A Writer, he resists the discipline all writers must follow. As a consequence, much of his writing is full of errors ranging from small imprecisions to outrageous misuses."

Thus "imply" is used when "infer" is meant and "following" when "after" is meant and "over" when "more than" is meant and "aggravate" when "irritate" is meant. "Claim" is used when "say" is meant, "refute" when "contradict" is meant and "flaunt" when "flout" is meant.

Words like "authored" and "chairmanned" and "hosted" are used, as are phrases like "strangled to death," "accused with treason" and "had his leg broken."

Minute points? Yes, yet minute detail determines the whole and spells the difference between the average writer and the craftsman.

News should be written simply, directly and crisply. It should be written so any reader, regardless of education, can understand it. It should be written straight away, without backing into the phrasing.

Statements of fact should be hung specifically on their sources when qualification is necessary.

Pretentious language should be avoided. Colloquialisms and vernacular should be used only when the tone of a story calls for them.

Short words, short sentences and short paragraphs are best.

Kenneth L. Simms, formerly managing editor of *The San Diego Evening Tribune,* made this point in a memo on newswriting:

There are even "little" big words:
- "Encounter" when "meet" would have said it.
- "Inevitable" when "sure" would have done.
- "Accelerated" when "speeded" would do.
- "Purchase" when you might say "buy."
- "Commence" when you might use "begin."
- "Employment" or "position" when "job" would do.

A reader is in trouble when a sentence contains too many ideas.

Here's an example (from the body of a story about a 50-hour revival meeting at a college):

"Authorities at the ancient school located about 35 miles west of Chicago which was founded as a church college in 1861 at the start of the war between the states and now opens its doors to youths from all denominations, including some from overseas, said they would let the demonstration run its course."

Hub Keavy of the Los Angeles AP, an able craftsman with words, wrote this advice:

"News writers are forever being advised to use simple sentences. They might better be urged to use simplified sentences. A simple sentence has one clause. It can be admirably direct if the subject matter also is simple. But it isn't versatile. It won't always tell as much as we need to tell at once. A sentence can be compound or complex and still be a good sentence if it isn't too long. All the clauses and phrases have to be arranged properly. If they are, the sentence will be clear and will have impact. These are the chief objectives in news writing."

That in itself is an example of lucid writing. His longest sentence is 18 words. Other lengths in it are 4 words, 6, 8, 9, 10, 12 and 13.

The API has made surveys of the relationship between sentence length and reader comprehension. One publication with an average of 17 words in its sentences had a reader comprehension of 97 percent. Another with average wordage of 33 had comprehension of 31 percent.

Excess words get into stories. A writer must sharpen his or her perception of verbiage. Here is an example from a wire-service story (the words in caps are excess baggage): "Doctors transferred two of the students to the nearby Fort Hood Army Hospital FOR FURTHER CARE after INITIAL treatment at the Killeen Clinic. Those LISTED BY CLINIC PHYSICIANS AS SUSTAINING WOUNDS SUFFICIENTLY SEVERE TO BE SENT TO THE ARMY HOSPITAL were Bobby Watts and George Chastain." That's 20 wasted words.

Another wire-service lead: "Detroit—Production of smaller automobiles by the auto industry's 'Big Three' of General Motors, Ford and Chrysler appeared today to have moved a bit closer to the realm of certainty." It might have said: "Detroit—Smaller automobiles by General Motors, Ford and Chrysler seemed more likely today." There are 12 words against 29, and has anything been lost?

Mental tanglefoot sometimes ruins a lead. Hub Keavy offered these examples:

"A law designed to force the American Red Cross to label blood plasma shipped into Louisiana according to race goes into effect July 30."

Read it again, if you want to find out what it means. And newswriting should be so lucid that no one is forced to read it again. Hub rephrased it thus: "After July 29 blood plasma shipped into Louisiana by the Red Cross must be labeled according to race."

Another: "A young couple and their two infant sons were overcome by ammonia fumes last night when a line through which liquid ammonia was being pumped from a tank car into a storage line burst."

Revision: "A young couple and their two infant sons were overcome by fumes last night when an ammonia pipe line burst."

Another: "The chief prosecution witness at the trial of the accused slayer of a prominent druggist hanged himself in the jail cell today."

Revision: "The state's chief witness in a murder trial hanged himself in jail today."

Another: "The biennial general council of Congregational Christian Churches, in session here, today sent a telegram to House Speaker Rayburn and House minority leaders urging full support of the administration's foreign aid program, now before Congress."

Revision: "The biennial general council of Congregational Christian Churches today indorsed the administration's foreign aid program."

It may seem unnecessary to explain what a lead should do. But, to repeat what we all know, a lead should:

• Tell the reader what the story is about.
• Make the reader want to read on.
• Put the story in focus.
• Create the proper mood, if there is a mood.

Here are two leads that capture the reader's interest:

"Attention women: Want to drop 130 pounds in nothing flat?"

"Ever go chasing girls down a railroad track?"

Use the active voice—"Lightning struck the house" is better than "The house was struck by lightning" (passive). In the active voice the subject does the acting. In the passive voice the subject receives the action.

Use concrete words—"The snow was six feet deep" is better than "There was a heavy snow."

Put sentences in positive form—"He rarely came to the beach" is better than "He did not often come to the beach."

Stories about violence should be written with restraint. A writer should avoid the breathlessness that tries to impart hectic (and usually exaggerated) emergency to the situation.

For example, instead of saying "All available ambulances were immediately dispatched to the scene of the tragedy and the victims were rushed to nearby hospitals," be calm and say "Ambulances took the injured to hospitals." The latter is more effective and the professional tone of the article will be enhanced if you underwrite instead of overwrite.

Adjectives and superlatives sometimes are used in a mistaken belief they strengthen and lend color to a story.

Actually, they weaken a story.

For example, "an explosion" is better than "a violent explosion," because all explosions are violent. It's better to tell precisely what happened: "An explosion today destroyed a 10-story building." It's more effective to tell the facts specifically and without jabbing the reader in the ribs. Then the reader will decide for himself or herself that the explosion indeed was devastating.

By the same token, don't describe a slaying as "a brutal murder," or say that "the night watchman was viciously beaten by the burglars" or that "the girl was savagely raped."

None of those crimes is committed with gentleness and it is a mark of immature writing to doll up the circumstances with such ornamentation.

Similarly, I often wonder why we call all homicides "murder." "Murder" is really a technical term; "slaying" is a better basic word, even when the slaying is premeditated.

Thus, "an investigation" is better than "a thorough investigation" or "a sweeping investigation" or "an all-out investigation." If it's a genuine investigation, it won't be superficial.

Related to the foregoing is the subject of clutter. Clutter words are used by everyone in ordinary speech, but ought to be kept out of print.

They are a waste of space because they contribute nothing, and worse, they give the copy a juvenile tone. For example:

"He said he had not yet received the report." Why the "yet"? If he hasn't received it, obviously he hasn't receive it "yet." So you don't need "yet."

"Construction work already has begun." Why "already"?

"The witness denied any knowledge of the robbery." Why "any"?

"The senator is now serving his third term." Why "now"?

"The house burned down." "The factory will close down." Why "down"?

"The flight set a new record." If it's a record, it's new.

"He disclosed for the first time." If it's a disclosure, it's for the first time.

"He strangled to death, he suffocated to death." That's the same as saying "He drowned to death."

"He served as toastmaster; he served as vice-president." Make it "He was ...."

"The President has a bad cold." "Police said he was badly injured." That implies some colds and injuries are good. What's meant is that the President has a severe cold and that the injuries are severe.

The person who has been injured sometimes "remains critical in a hospital." The individual is not "critical"; it's his or her condition that's critical.

Saying "Fire broke out" sounds like the fire had been confined in a cage. Why not "Fire started"?

Use precise words. "Tipped" is sometimes used for "informed," "spotted" for "saw," "combed" for "searched" and so on.

Those bits of jargon should be avoided.

Some additional examples where specific words would be better than manufactured cliches:

"Names will not be released until next of kin are notified." "Testimony released today showed...." This sounds as if the names and the testimony had been held captive and finally set free. Use "made public" or "announced" or some other specific word.

"The convicts staged a three-hour riot." Save "staged" for events that take place on a stage. Instead, say the convicts "rioted three hours."

"The Navy today unveiled a new plane." Use "unveiled" for activities in which a veil literally is removed from an object—"Mayor Dail unveiled the statue." The Navy "exhibited" the new plane is more accurate.

"The Community Chest launched its funds campaign." Save "launched" for vessels and use "started" or "opened" or "began" or some other precise word.

Inept synonyms should not be used in an effort to avoid repetition of key words in stories. For example, words like "hike" or "boost" or "jump" should not be used for "pay raise." "Slash" or "cutback" should not be used for "reduce."

If you're writing about cats and dogs, it's better to repeat those words than to call them "felines and canines." And never refer to a banana as "an elongated yellow fruit."

Beware of word pairs that are often confused and misused:

Anticipate and expect: Literally, "anticipate" means to take up, use or introduce before the proper or normal time. It's not a synonym for "expect." "Anticipating rain, he put a roof on his house" is correct. "GOP anticipates Democratic support on tax bill" is not.

Between and among: The marbles are divided "between" two persons, but are divided "among" more than two persons.

Each other and one another: Use "each other" for two persons and "one another" for more than two.

Argument and quarrel: An argument is a point of view or its presentation. Thus people are injured after "quarrels," not after "arguments."

Compare to and compare with: Similar things are compared with each other; dissimilar things are compared to each other. You compare John Smith with Richard Jones and you compare John Smith to a sturdy oak.

Infer and imply: You imply by what you say and you infer from what you hear or see. "His words implied his readiness. The audience inferred he was ready."

Claim and say: "He said he was innocent" is correct. Strictly speaking, you can claim an estate but you can't claim that Los Angeles is larger than San Diego.

Unnamed and unidentified: "Police today sought an unnamed man who ..." He's not unnamed; he has a name. He's unidentified.

Injured are and dead were: Use "The injured are..." and "The dead were...." This is because the injured are still with us here on earth, while the dead are not.

In that connection, it's preferable to repeat the auxiliaries in such parallel forms as "One man was killed today and one was injured." When the form of the verb "to be" (is, are, was, were) is not parallel, however, the auxiliary must be repeated: "One man was killed and two were injured." It is wrong to make it "One man was killed and two injured," because that is saying "One man was killed and two WAS injured."

Say "Ten persons burned to death" or "Five persons drowned" instead of "Ten persons were burned to death" or "Five persons were drowned." The latter implies someone burned them at the stake or held their heads under water.

Problems often arise with "ly" adverbs that precede adjectives. Do not hyphenate such things as "a recently enacted bill" and "a firmly established precedent."

An adverb ending in "ly" should not be hyphenated to the adjective it precedes, in forming an adjectival phrase. Thus it should be "a firmly (adverb) established (adjective) precedent (noun)"—no hyphen.

It's an over-simplification, however, to say that adverbs are never hyphenated to the adjective they precede. Adverbs that don't use "ly" are hyphenated as in "a well-done steak," "an ill-advised act" and so on.

Adverbs using "ly" are not hyphenated to adjectives because the normal grammatical relationship is established without the hyphen. You can see the difference that would exist if you omitted the hyphen in "an ill advised act." Also, "well" and "ill" are not always adverbs, while "firmly" always is.

Mouth-filling strings of compound adjectives force the reader to go back and retrace the meaning of a sentence: "The strikers presented a 20-cents-an-hour wage-increase demand." The compound adjective is too big to swallow. Instead, say "The strikers asked a wage increase of 20 cents an hour."

A story read: "The strikers are seeking a 25-cents-an-hour wage hike, contending that a 10-cents-an-hour jump, which gave them $2.10-hourly pay-scale, is insufficient." That's really making life tough on a reader.

Likewise, a string of titles preceding a name is difficult to digest. A story said: "Signers included former Salt Lake City mayor Albert Sprague." Say "Signers included Albert Sprague, former mayor of Salt Lake City" to make it easier on the reader.

Note the difference between definite and indefinite articles. "John Smith, the organ grinder," implies that most readers are acquainted with him and that he's an organ grinder. If he's not that well known, say "John Smith, an organ grinder." That is merely a reference to a man named Smith who is an organ grinder.

In general, an article should be used in a combination consisting of a name and an occupational identification. "John Smith, an organ grinder," is preferable to "John Smith, organ grinder," because the latter suggests he's the only one in town.

Indeed, the absence of articles is sometimes so noticeable in stories that it jars the reader. A recent story ended this way: "Date of the meeting has not been decided." It would be better to make it "The date of the meeting ...."

By the same token, if an "A" or a "The" will start a lead more naturally, don't hesitate to use it. Arbitrary omission of articles often makes stories objectionably abrupt.

Likewise, don't hesitate to use a name to start a lead, if it will read better that way. We had a lead recently that said, approximately, "Formal announcement was made today by Joe Doakes that he would be a candidate for re-election ..." That's labored. "Joe Doakes today announced ..." is much better.

Quotation marks are another problem area. Avoid orphan quotes. These are used in a mistaken belief they lend special meaning to the words that are quoted: "Many of Washington's soldiers went 'over the hill' during the winter at Valley Forge." The futility of using orphan quotes is that if the reader doesn't know the special meaning, putting quotes around the words won't explain it. If you have the feeling that you need orphan quotes around words (or italics to emphasize a point), it's evidence that the sentence ought to be reconstructed.

Illegitimate quotes pop up all the time. In a story about a teen-age killer, one wire service wrote: "Her step-father had urged Starkweather to 'stay away' from the Bartlett home." Any special meaning to "stay away"? No. Do the words add flavor that help characterize the step-father? No. It would make as much sense to quote "step-father" or "urged" or "home." Another wire service said: "Authorities said Starkweather had signed a 'confession.'"

A wire service wrote: "Police said Young had been 'despondent.'" Another story said: "Haynes pulled a pistol and ordered Russell to 'walk to the back of the store.'" Another: "Company dealers report a 'slight upturn' in the auto market."

A reporter, writer or copy reader should take a second—and a third—look at quotes like those. In none of the examples were quotes proper.

Quotes and sources should be handled in such a way that the reader knows immediately who is being quoted. Thus the source would be buttoned up at the first natural break in the quote: "Thousands of South Koreans are still held by the Reds," Gen. Clark said. "They must be returned."

Sometimes the source is located in an awkward place: "Thousands of South Koreans," Gen. Clark said, "are still ..." Doing it that way makes the quote difficult to read.

It is necessary to introduce the source only once—at the first natural break—in a block of continuous quotes. It is wrong to sprinkle re-introductions through the continuous quotes and, as sometimes happens, to wind up the final paragraph with a "..." he concluded.

If the running quotes are interrupted in any manner, however, the source should be re-introduced when the quotes pick up again.

It's almost always better to start with the quote than with the source. Thus, say: "Thousands of South Koreans are still held by the Reds," Gen. Clark said. Don't say: Gen. Clark said, "Thousands of South Koreans ..."

In connection with quotes—either direct or indirect—be sure to specify the circumstances. Tell whether the remarks were made in an interview, a press conference, a speech, a radio or television appearance, a statement (a handout can be called a statement), in a letter the man wrote to his grandmother. Explaining the circumstances helps to orient the reader.

When it comes to hanging a statement on a source, there's nothing better than the word "said." Almost every other speech verb has an editorial implication—asserted, charged, insisted, denied, reiterated, pointed out and so on. Don't worry about repeating the word "said" in a story. By all means, avoid the word "stated." It's stiff-necked.

Take pains to use restrained language in connection with speech verbs in stories about controversies. Some writers run wild with "fiery rebuttal," "blistering accusation," "ripped out a counter-charge," "devastating rejoinder." Be calm. Make it: He said, "..."

Avoid the editorial "we," "our," "us" and so on in anything except direct quotes. Say "Sen. Brown said this country's exports have increased," not "Sen. Brown said our exports have increased ..."

Don't neglect to hook up the lead with the second paragraph:

"A San Diego woman yesterday awaited word from a Cascade mountains wilderness area where her husband has been missing since Sunday.

"Mrs. Charles Dickens, 2659 Fairfield St., said she has given permission for bloodhounds to be used in the search."

As that stands, there's nothing to tell the reader that Mrs. Dickens is the woman referred to in the lead. Such gaps should be bridged, with the second paragraph reading, approximately: "The woman, Mrs. Charles Dickens ..."

The editor as a dictator

By Benedict Kruse

The year was 1952. I was mostly writing feature articles for business publications and industrial public relations clients and averaging some 50,000 driving miles a year.

There were plenty of subjects to cover. We were coming into the cycle of change to be later identified as future shock—change so rapid and drastic it defied normal comprehension. Word volume became a problem. Between interviewing and driving, there wasn't enough time and strength left for the typewriter. It was the writing—the actual grinding out of copy—that developed into a horrendous backlog.

What was needed was more creative time. Then, one day, I discovered that it was natural to sit and arrange a whole story in my mind while I was barreling down the highway—only to find the whole thing eluding me by the time my weary carcass was dragged to the battered typewriter.

One solution which came to mind was to dictate the story in the car, while the ideas were flowing. Here, obviously, was an untapped potential for new writing time.

In 1952, it took some doing. Portable dictation units had not yet happened. There were no cassettes. The rig I eventually developed required drawing current from the cigarette lighter, running it through an inverter and operating a recorder designed for household current. As crude as it was, this solution proved a point. Productivity went way up—enough to add 30 percent to my income.

The productivity consideration was paramount at the beginning. But, after several months, it became apparent that quality was also improving. This had been a concern at first. The natural assumption was that quality might suffer. I had expected to have to step up rewriting and editing efforts. But it didn't work out that way. After just a few weeks of adjustment, the copy became more cohesive, flowed more logically. Dictation became a first-rate tool rather than just a shortcut.

Another pleasant surprise came through resolution of questions about the safety of dictating while driving. Rather than causing a distraction, the process made for a greater alertness. Drowsiness brought on by the humdrum of the open road was overcome.

Like any other spontaneously derived success, the technique for dictating in the car—and later in planes—went on to evolve its own new applications. To meet common-but-special situations, the dictation method was adapted to writing collaboration. An acquaintance was commissioned to write a 45,000-word book on management uses of data processing systems. We collaborated in dictation, using a technique which I have come to call synergistic writing. The manuscript was completed in 47 hours. (Synergistic writing will be described later.)

Experience has also led to the development of principles for using dictation techiques.

To dictate, I have found, you need to be in an alert, energetic frame of mind. If you can't bring yourself "up" to remember what you have said and plan sequences of words and thoughts rapidly, you are better off using a visual writing technique. In my case, if I find myself very tired and still have a deadline which can't be slipped, I work most effectively by hand writing the manuscript. The slowest technique provides the best match to my capacities at moments like these.

Recorder Not A Crutch

But care should be taken not to use a recorder as a crutch. Too many writers relax, let down, when they record an interview. They are lulled by false security that they have everything on tape. In practice, the recorder should free the mind from the detail of concentrating on writing notes. The writer can respond interactively to the interview subject, thinking his or her way ahead of the situation to challenge what is being said, to come up with more probing questions. This sounds logical, natural. But it is done too rarely.

An important next lesson comes with recognition of the fact that the tape recorder is not a journalistic or publishing cure-all. The electronic method must be adapted to fit the medium. For example, take the basic assumption that the dictation of copy or the recording of interviews is a quick and easy way to get into print. This assumption can lead to trouble. The writer with a notepad can begin to pick out facts and write immediately. The writer with a recorder frequently has to listen to the entire interview before he or she can begin writing. Similarly, the story written on a typewriter is ready for immediate editing. Dictated copy, though it may be completed sooner, still needs to be transcribed. Thus, for short or quick jobs, the traditional approach may still be best.

Part of the recognition that these techiques are tools calls for avoiding use where they don't fit or belong—as well as avoiding overuse. For example, the recorded interview may not fit every situation. It's a matter of presenting the information in the clearest and most interesting form for the reader. Thus, if an interview involves one person with a clear-cut message, a narrative article can probably tell the story more concisely and with greater clarity.

The interview format is more effective where multiple subjects are covered or more than one person participates—the kind of situation where a seasoned writer is hard pressed to find a lead. Also, if you really plan to use an interview—rather than a stylized format which puts words in the subject's mouth—the subject should be screened first. Recording is a method for use with articulate people who express themselves clearly and concisely.

Planning the Entire Story

Another element of effective use of electronic journalism techiques lies in planning the end product as early as possible. All of the techniques covered here involve tradeoffs in the allocation of creative time. The electronic method, hopefully, shortens the cycle to first draft—which normally occupies the bulk of any editorial effort. In exchange, however, the writer or editor can expect to devote more time to the processes of polishing and revision.

The better the end product is conceptualized in advance, the smaller the penalty in editorial effort following first draft.

Electronic Flexibility

There are no easy answers or firm rules for where and how to apply these techniques. One of the beauties of these methods is that they are so adaptable and flexible.

The writer making the transition into dictation should begin by understanding the processes. Consider a 1,700-word magazine article covering a business system, a product application or a personality interview. Assume the necessary interviews have been conducted and the facts are in hand.

My own habits, when working at a typewriter, have been to start by digesting the information at an overflow level and developing a lead. I personally do this by instinctive feel. The lead is the hardest writing task. So I concentrate on this until I am satisfied that the importance of the story has been stated in terms which will attract the interest of the reader. Then I usually take time to review the notes again. From this second review, I will build a continuity—either mentally or by scribbling a sequence of topics too rough to be called an outline. As I write, I refer back to my notes. The process works partly because I have a written manuscript to compare with my notes at all times.

The conventional process could be described as building a story as you go. In my case, given a typing speed of 80 words per minute, the bulk of the time is spent in going back over what has been done and reviewing notes to keep building the product.

In dictation, I have found it necessary to change the order of things. It has proven best to review thoroughly at the outset. I must have the story firmly in mind before I begin writing. If you do this, your mind will work faster, in better continuity. The reason is simple: It has been estimated that a trained mind can form thoughts at 450 or 500 words per minute. Through dictation, the ideas can be converted to words at about 150 words per minute. This, of course, is not a continuous process. The mind creates in spurts. Working at a typewriter, productive speed is halved. With a pencil, things go even slower. Thus, the slower you write, the more mental restarting and reshuffling must be done.

To write through dictation, then, I frequently begin by scribbling a first version of the lead by hand. Handwriting has become something of a habit because I frequently do this work in places where I don't have typewriters, but the process works just as well by starting on the typewriter.

Once the lead has been roughed in, a preliminary outline is constructed. This serves primarily to sequence the continuity of the story. It is not detailed. It is highly informal and personal.

Visual Dictation

Dictation then follows the established sequence, with the prewritten lead serving as a primer to get the thoughts flowing. In the transition from typing to dictation, my biggest single problem lies in visualizing what I have done. To help this process, I dictate the spellings of all proper nouns and technical terms. I supply all punctuation and capitalization. Figures are given literally, digit-by-digit. I find this helpful even though the persons who handle transcription are more than competent to capitalize and punctuate the copy. It is worth the effort for the visual value.

From this style of dictation, I get a far cleaner first draft than I was ever able to generate when I typed. I find I can read such a draft more objectively than something I typed myself. I do this reading as though the manuscript had been written by someone else. Special care has to be taken to look for repetitious use of words—one of the major stylistic problems of dictation. Paragraphing also has to be watched carefully. Paragraph restructuring is a frequent requirement.

For an article of 1,700 words, first draft writing time by dictation is generally under two hours. Editing time is at least an hour, with one to two pages of inserts a general requirement. A far-from-small benefit from this process is that I find myself fresh and relaxed at the conclusion of the writing process. By contrast, I'm generally pretty well wrung out at the conclusion of four to six hours of typewriter time for the same assignment.

One of the obvious prerequisites for making the transition to writing by dictation is to take a critical, practical look at available equipment and come up with a machine which is comfortable—one that minimizes mechanical mental blocks. This is a personal thing. It resolves itself readily with a little practice.

This familiarity with dictation techniques and equipment, in turn, can be important in moving on to recording interviews. The key factor in developing interviews for print lies in planning. The writer should avoid the temptation to simply walk in and turn on his or her recorder. Rather, there should be an informal interview to precede the formal recorded session. The writer should ask enough questions to fully grasp the scope of the subject and focus on the key points to be covered. Notes on a few key questions can establish the general sequence of the interview in advance. For magazines, random recording of interviews can be both wasteful and confusing.

Electronic journalism techniques can also serve as a bottleneck breaker for a universal editorial problem—the need to develop authoritative articles under bylines of persons with expertise or experience relevant to a magazine's readers. Often, the person with the credentials lacks the skill, the time and the inclination to do the actual writing. Conventional collaboration can be slow, tedious and expensive. In dozens of situations, problems of this sort have been solved through a technique I have come to call synergistic writing.

Synergistic Writing?

The synergism occurs because the technique is designed to produce a product of combined efforts which is greater than the sum total which could be realized through separate efforts of the participants. Through careful matching, a qualified writer and subject are brought together. The topic to be covered is reviewed in general and outlined.

Then segments of the outline are discussed in detail, with the writer making notes. The writer then dictates while the other person listens and interacts. Errors or misconceptions are cleared up before they are committed to paper. Almost invariably, the writer's presentation will trigger new thoughts by the listening expert. These are applied to create a dimension greater than would be attained individually.

A recent experience offers a good illustration. The product manager of a company in the data processing field had been asked by a leading electronics magazine to do an article on design and software principles. A deadline was accepted. But under the pressure of other responsibilities the writing chore was put off. Finally, I got together with the product manager on a Thursday in Los Angeles. The article was due for mailing to New York the following Monday.

A 3,500-word draft was dictated collaboratively in about three hours. It was transcribed, edited and returned for review the following day. The product manager then took it home over the weekend, revised a few paragraphs and had the manuscript ready for final typing on Monday morning.

Any editor who has sweated out delivery of key technical articles and has gone through the approval process where articles have been staff written on the basis of submitted materials will realize the value of this technique immediately.

This has not been offered as a catalog of writing techniques. Rather, the intent has been to introduce a principle for increasing productivity and satisfaction in the preparation of manuscripts for print editor as it is to the broadcaster—provided methods adapt to medium.

The craft of business reporting

By Chris Welles

Public interest in news about business and the economy is at an all time high, and business stories increasingly are making page one and the lead spot on TV newscasts. Unfortunately, the demand by the public for knowledgeable reporting about business is much greater than the supply of knowledgeable business journalists. The imbalance is especially glaring in press coverage of large corporations. Far too many reporters and editors, for instance, are unaware of the numerous, easily accessible public documents that contain vast quantities of information about internal corporate affairs. Many do not know even of the existence of 10-K and 10-Q reports, let alone where to obtain these documents.

Perhaps more than any other field, covering business presents special challenges and requires special skill. You may have won prizes and acclaim covering state legislatures or sports teams, but that does not necessarily prepare you for covering corporations.

What follows are some informal tips from a reporter who, after close to 20 years in the field and 150 or so magazine articles, is just beginning to feel comfortable in a line of work whose frustrations almost continuously threaten to overwhelm its pleasures.

The first thing to understand is that while you are certainly familiar with the names of many corporations and while you probably work for a corporation, the corporate culture presents several obstacles to the inquiring reporter that are probably not immediately obvious. Corporations are very different from such public organizations as hospitals, schools, libraries, police departments. By public I mean that they receive their funding from the public in general, usually through taxes.

Public organizations open

Let's look at the "culture," as the business schools term it, of public organizations as against that of corporations, which are essentially private organizations. Public organizations, to begin with, have and feel an obligation to serve the public. (What I am saying applies to public organizations generally but not necessarily to all public organizations. There are numerous exceptions.) They feel an obligation to be open to public inquiry about their activities and to be responsive to you, as a reporter, when you're doing a story on them.

Public organizations tend to be relatively democratic. They have hierarchies, of course, and do not take votes on every policy issue. But those at the top do delegate a great deal of authority and responsibility and are usually responsive to the feelings and opinions of individuals in lower echelons. At universities—with which I am familiar, having spent five years teaching at the Columbia Graduate School of Journalism—it sometimes seems as if the faculty has more power than the deans.

Employees of public organizations, while they are loyal to the organizations they work for, typically feel high loyalties—usually to their craft or profession. As a result, there is a strong tradition of dissent within public organizations. It is quite common for officials of public organizations to resign over policy disputes —and frequently to do so quite publicly. The first thing many government people do after they resign is call a news conference and lambaste their former bosses. Most dissidents do not resign, of course. But they do get their complaints out through the time-honored tradition of leaks. Many of the most widely heralded scoops in

465

Washington are less the result of laborious digging on the part of the reporter than of a phone call and some clandestinely photocopied documents from a disaffected minion in the federal bureaucracy.

I don't mean to denigrate entirely the industry and enterprise of reporters who cover the government and other public organizations, many of whom regularly overcome formidable obstacles. But I think that it is incontrovertible that gaining regular access to the workings of public organizations is considerably easier than covering corporations.

"Public" a misnomer

Most corporations are referred to as "public" in the sense that their stock is owned by investors. But the term is a misnomer. Corporations are really private organizations. Many of them engage in worthy and commendable charitable activities and other good works, but their basic purpose is to pursue the very private end of making money for their employees and their shareholders.

This predisposition powerfully affects their attitude toward responding to requests for information from the press. Many corporate executives quite sincerely do not feel that the public has any particular right to know how they run their business.

Executives, to be sure, know the value of good publicity. Most major corporations have skilled public relations departments whose basic job is to enhance the corporation's public image. When the company comes up with a dramatic new invention or has enjoyed record earnings, the PR people will be quite anxious to talk about it. But they will usually be much less forthcoming, and perhaps not forthcoming at all, if earnings were down sharply or the chief executive was just fired.

Thus, a reporter seeking more details of an unpleasant event from the PR officer is unlikely to get very far with the argument that the corporation has a duty to disclose the details of what happened. A more effective argument is that you, as the reporter, have obtained information about the unpleasant event from outside sources, that you want to get the company's side, and that it would be in the company's interest to have its side represented in your story.

Corporations, at least those which are "publicly" owned, do release detailed financial information, but rarely much more than is required by the Securities and Exchange Commission. As I'll mention later, though, that information can be an enormously valuable resource for the financially sophisticated business reporter.

Another charactertistic that distinguishes corporations from public organizations is their authoritarian command system. Power resides quite clearly at the top—and necessarily, for it would be quite difficult to run an efficient corporation as a democracy. There has been a trend recently—largely a response to Japanese competition—to give lower level workers more say in management. But senior executives are unlikely ever to relinquish their control over major policy matters.

This authoritarian structure helps shape employee attitudes. Relative to the employees of public organizations, corporate employees feel a stronger loyalty to the corporation. Not only would they view public complaints as disloyal, they would be afraid that if the company found out they would be fired. Of the hundreds of corporate executives I've interviewed over the years, no more than a tiny handful were willing to offer even muted criticisms of their companies—even when promised

anonymity. Needless to say, corporate executives rarely resign for reasons of principle. And when they do, they virtually never talk about their decision publicly.

From the standpoint of the reporter seeking information, then, corporations can be secretive, protective, closed organizations. I have written stories on several companies that, despite my pleadings, refused to talk to me at all. In a couple of cases, notably Harcourt Brace Jovanovich, the publishing concern, senior executives were officially directed not to return my calls. Though I am naturally disappointed in such instances, I try not to hold it against the company. More than likely, they have their own very good reasons for remaining silent and I don't feel they have an obligation to talk to me.

Conflicting interests

The almost inherent disparity of interests of journalists and business executives—one group wanting to obtain information and the other often wanting to withhold it—has been a major contributor to the growing antipathy between the two sides. That antipathy, among other things, has created still further obstacles for business reporters.

There are other sources of the bad feeling, of course. The two groups see each other in much less than accurate stereotypical terms. Too many business executives regard reporters as left-wing intellectuals who would like to put corporate executives in jail and destroy the entire free-enterprise system. Too many reporters view business executives as avaricious radical-right conservatives who have their hands deeply inside the cookie jar and would have no qualms letting the poor starve to death. Business executives complain continually that business reporters don't understand business, that they only print negative news, that they get facts wrong and take quotes out of context. Business reporters complain that business executives lie to them, attempt to exert political and economic pressure on their publications, and commit such overt hostile acts as withdrawing advertising in response to an unfavorable story.

Both sides, in my view, have a good case. Speaking for my profession, I must concede that the performance of the business press far too often has been woefully anemic—which is the main reason I spend about half my time at the Columbia Journalism School running programs to educate business journalists. Business journalism has been improving greatly in recent years, but it will be a long time before the performance will be as good as it ought to be.

In the meantime, business reporters will continue to find many corporations no more than marginally cooperative.

How, then, does the enterprising business journalist go about getting the information to write his or her story?

Start with documents

The best starting place is documents. A veritable wealth of documents is available on business. Some of them are rather arcane. A few years ago, I was researching a story on the business empire of Reverend Sun Myung Moon. I knew he had several corporations in Korea, but I could find no available information on them other than their names. After much asking around, I discovered that for a relatively modest fee—$65 each—one could request through the Commerce Department "trade reports" on most foreign companies engaged in export. Within two weeks, I received a complete analysis of Moon's concerns, including sales, earnings, management, and stock ownership.

The major source of the most useful information on companies, though, is the Securities and Exchange Commission. Literally the first thing I do when I am assigned to write about a company is to obtain three basic documents: the 10-K report, the annual report, and the proxy statement. The 10-K, which is required to be issued annually, is a complete description of the company and its financial results. Though tedious to look at and even more tedious to wade through, it is a gold mine of useful information—if you know where to look.

The annual report is a kind of public relations version of the 10-K. It is not actually a SEC-mandated document but, at least in the case of most large companies, is overseen by the New York Stock Exchange. The first part of the annual report tends to feature elaborate art direction and uplifting prose whose purpose is to put the best possible face on the company's performance the previous year. Material omissions of embarrassing facts are not uncommon. A recent Warner Communications report, for instance, failed to mention a widely publicized bribery scandal. The back section of the annual report contains the financial statements. Having been audited by a reputable accounting firm, these data, which closely parallel the 10-K, are quite useful.

A brief word about financial statements: It is a theory of mine that many people who love words are afraid of numbers, and that includes many business journalists who love the drama of big business and finance but are terrified at the thought of digging their way through a balance sheet. Such a phobia can be extremely debilitating, for no single body of information is more crucial to the understanding of a corporation than its financial statements.

My students at Columbia have told me that the lectures on understanding financial statements were the most useful of the entire course. The long, grey columns of numbers are actually far less formidable than they seem and, phobias aside, are quite accessible to anyone with a normal intelligence. As a quick and comprehensible guide, I strongly recommend an excellent book called *Understanding Financial Statements* issued by the New York Stock Exchange and available for a nominal charge.

The third of the "big three" documents, the proxy statement, is generally very thin, but more than makes up for its lack of heft with an abundance of good reading. A SEC-mandated document, it is sent to all shareholders prior to the annual meeting. It contains, among other things, the salaries and stockholdings of most senior executives. And under off-putting headings like "certain transactions," it contains details on potentially incestuous dealings between the company and its management and the company and its directors. If an outside attorney is on the board, the proxy may disclose that the attorney's law firm is receiving many thousands of dollars in legal fees—a fact of some relevance if other outside directors become interested in replacing the chief executive.

While these three documents are the most useful, there are literally dozens of other SEC-required releases, such as the 8-K report, issued in connection with an important event such as a merger; a 10-Q quarterly version of the 10-K; and the prospectus, issued to buyers of new issues of securities. The SEC, further, generates much information in the course of its many investigations. Once in working on a story on economist Eliot Janeway, I learned that he was involved with a company called Realty Equities, which had gone bankrupt. Janeway, who had a large stock interest in the company, claimed that he had little other connection with it. The point was important because of the image of financial sophistication that Janeway carefully cultivates. The SEC, it turned out, had conducted a major investigation of Realty and, through the Freedom of Information Act, I obtained access to some of the records. Janeway was not implicated. But he had been in fact intimately involved with Realty's management and, in the end, lost over $2 million before taxes on the deal. He later conceded Realty was the largest single stock investment he had ever made.

IRS data

Many kinds of non-SEC material may also prove valuable. Non-profit organizations are required to file a Form 990 with the Internal Revenue Service that includes such illuminating data as income and expenses and officers' salaries. Unlike most IRS documents, 990's are available for public inspection at IRS offices.

Though few reporters take the time to examine them, the often voluminous records generated by lawsuits are a rich resource. Corporate litigation is increasingly common, and even suits over minor points produce numerous depositions and corporate documents. For a story I wrote on Kennecott Corp., the copper concern, a few years ago, I found in the files of some litigation minutes of board meetings, internal financial projections, and other material that gave me important insights into the company's decision-making on some crucial issues.

Congressional hearings are often useful. Many reporters attend hearings, but few bother to obtain the hearing record when it is published several months later. Those records often contain appendices, answers to written questions, and other submitted material that can bear importantly on a story.

I always make it a point to consult the trade press when I am doing a story involving an industry. Many trade publications, in my view, are excessively sympathetic to the industries they cover, but even those that are can be worth reading. I once wrote a story involving the efforts of the cosmetics industry to block safety legislation in Congress. The best account of the industry's lobbying effort, I found, was in an industry magazine. The magazine, of course, applauded the industry's success. I took a somewhat different view.

Investment publications can be a great help. Value Line is perhaps the most convenient and useful guide—so much so that I keep a recent volume next to my desk and consult it almost as often as the dictionary. It provides regularly updated reports on about 1,700 major companies and, on a single page, capsulizes all of the financial data you are likely to need for quick reference. Standard & Poor's and Moody's also publish good services. Wall Street brokerage reports can come in handy as well, though the quality of the research varies widely and the conclusions tend to be excessively bullish.

How can you obtain these documents? The SEC material can be obtained from regional SEC offices, where it is usually stored on microfiche, or from a variety of private services. One such service I use in New York, called Disclosure Inc., can provide copies of virtually any SEC document for 35 cents a page and will even deliver the material anywhere in the city within a matter of hours if necessary. Most companies themselves will send you their annual report, 10-K's, and proxies just for the asking. Though some confidential material is occasionally withheld, courthouse files of corporate litigation are open to the public.

A phone call to the appropriate committee will usually get you a copy of most congressional hearings and studies. (If that fails, try the Government Printing Office.) Many industry organizations, not to mention business school libraries, maintain excellent collections of trade magazines. There are several good indexes, including the *Business Periodicals Index* and the *F&S Index of Corporations and Industries.*

Wall Street brokerage houses will usually hand out their research reports gratis to the press. Value Line and the other investment services are the only documents you may have to shell out real money for. Value Line sells for $330 a year. But an eight-week trial subscription, which gets you the entire volume, is only $33.

Be gracious

Obtaining documents can also involve some ingenuity and tact, especially if you need them in a hurry. Access to material in places like court houses, congressional committee offices, and libraries is often overseen and controlled by clerks or their equivalent. These people rarely have the power to prevent you from getting what you want. But they usually have the power to determine how expeditiously you get the information. Many reporters and others treat clerks as functionaries somewhere between servant and slave, and the clerks understandably often resent it. Asked in a brusque way, to fetch a certain file, they will take…their…time. On the other hand, if they are treated politely, graciously, as an equal, they can do often wondrous things to help you.

Once I needed a Form 990 and called up the regional office of the IRS where it was on file. The woman who answered the phone explained I would have to submit the request in writing. That was the rule, she said. I could, of course, have argued with her angrily and at length that I was a member of the press, that the rule was ridiculous, that the taxpayers paid her salary, and that she had better shape up and send me the document. The net effect of that, of course, would have been zero. Instead, I explained politely that I was under a terrible deadline, that I needed her help, and wasn't there some way that I could get it faster. She sent it out to me Express Mail the next morning. And the following day she called me up to make sure I received it.

Two investigative reporters I know, Ron Barlett and Jim Steele of the *Philadelphia Inquirer,* do a lot of courthouse work. They not only maintain an elaborate file of key clerks, but they send the clerks Christmas cards every year. It pays off.

The same tactics apply to secretaries. Rudely treated, a secretary can make it almost impossible to get through to her (or, rarely, his) boss. Politely treated, she can become your advocate. I recently was trying to arrange an interview with an extremely busy lawyer.His secretary became quite sympathetic to my efforts to get some time with him. One day she called to tell me that he was taking a limousine to the airport that evening and that if I wanted to go along, she might be able to set it up. I did, she did, traffic was slow, and I had a great interview.

People sources

Quite similar approaches can bring results in your dealings with interview subjects themselves. First, though, let's go through the kinds of people sources that can be helpful in business stories. Though aware of the predisposition to secrecy, I always contact the company if I'm doing a company story. Unless the story sounds negative, you can usually get some cooperation, and sometimes a lot of cooperation. For a story I wrote recently on the chief executive of Merrill Lynch, the head PR person promptly arranged nearly 10 interviews—with virtually every senior executive at the company. At other companies, the PR staff may be obstructionist even on a benign story. But it's always worth a call.

By far the most important sources on company stories are former executives. Unconstrained by the fear of being fired if word gets out that they talked to you, they can be extremely forthcoming about their former employer. Even if they have been gone for some time, they usually keep up with the gossip and have a good idea of what's going on. They also keep up with other former employees and can give you names.

Using information from former employees, though, can be very tricky. The majority of them left the company because they weren't happy there or they got fired. Their information, thus, tends to be biased toward the negative. As a reporter, you have to separate the useless invective from useful impressions. The most valuable information you can get from them, though, is not opinions but facts—facts that you can then try to verify through other sources. It is not very helpful when the source tells you the marketing manager was incompetent. It is helpful when the source describes the particulars of how the manager botched the campaign for a new product.

Many other kinds of people should be on your call list: competitors, because nobody knows Macy's better than Gimbels; suppliers, because you can bet the rubber companies keep up on what is going on in Detroit; managers of institutional portfolios, because if you've got several million dollars of your clients' money in a company, you maintain a very close watch. Plus: management consultants, bankers, security analysts, congressional staff people, regulators, and many others.

Once you've singled out the people you want to interview, how do you get them to talk? This is an especially difficult problem in business stories for the reasons mentioned earlier: corporate sources are usually very reluctant to get involved.

It is often assumed by people not in the field that the most adroit reporters deal with sources the way prosecutors deal with witnesses for the defense. This assumption is reinforced not only by movies about the press but by shows like *60 Minutes.* Mike Wallace grinding away at the perspiring bad guy has become a regular piece of Sunday night theater.

Instill trust

I've gotten a few good pieces of information that way. But very few. Far far more effective is to treat sources the way you treat the courthouse clerks. If you sense a hesitancy, you try to get them to relax, feel comfortable with you. Instead of demanding information, which would instantly make them tense, you explain you're involved in a difficult story, that it is very hard to find out how the company works or the person you're writing about thinks, and that you need the source's help. Most people are predisposed to respond favorably to someone who, in a non-threatening way, asks for a little help.

You have another thing going for you. Most sources feel flattered to talk about things they know about. And they like to talk about themselves. They really would like to talk to you, and usually the only impediment is their concern over whether they can trust you if they talk frankly. You can usually assuage those concerns with your manner of approach.

Once sources start talking a little—start them out with very very easy, non-anxiety-producing questions—they will usually keep on talking. The following has happened to me often: the source says he doesn't really know anything and he's very busy, but if I insist, he has time between 11:15 and 11:30 the following morning. I show up at 11:15. He starts talking and talking. At 11:30 he tells his secretary to hold all his calls. At noon he is still talking. At one o'clock, I've got to leave because I've got another appointment, but I can't shut him up.

I should add that how you listen makes a lot of difference to how long and well the source will talk. The best way to listen is with great interest and sympathy. Sound as if you are totally caught up in what he is telling you. Sources have a great deal of trouble terminating a conversation with someone who seems to be hanging on their every word.

Usually with sources on company stories, you have to promise not to quote them by name in your story. Or if you want to, you will have to clear any quotes first. I have no trouble with such a bargain and find it reasonable. But a word of caution: keep the bargain. Too many reporters do not. In my experience, the word gets around about those who do not. People I ask for interviews, even after they have agreed to a date, often check with friends to see if I am trustworthy. If I were the sort of reporter who treated promises of anonymity casually, I'm certain I would find a lot of people I had interview dates with suddenly calling with the news that they had to go out of town and wouldn't be able to make it.

A final word on sources: It is also a common misperception among non-reporters—a misperception furthered by the Woodward/Bernstein Watergate saga—that reporting is often a matter of finding a Deep Throat, the incredibly knowledgeable, super wired-in source who knows all there is to know, who can save you countless hours of digging around looking for other sources.

The Deep Throat notion is probably even less true in business journalism, considering the complexity of the subject matter, than in any other part of the field. In all my years of writing business stories, I've never found such a person. I've run across some very helpful people. But when I've gone back and examined how much of my stories came from a single individual, I've found it rare if any one person accounts for even as much as 5 percent of my information. Even if I located someone who seemed like a genuine Deep Throat, I would still have to interview a lot of other people to be sure I could believe what he said.

In short, there is no short cut, no substitute for talking to many people, consulting many documents, digging through lots of leads, and generally working your tail off. But of course, if it were easy, it wouldn't be any fun. And there would be many more people doing it, which would mean that those of us who do do it would get paid a lot less. Not, I should say, that we're getting paid very much right now. But then that's another story.

The fog index

By Douglas Mueller

What makes a magazine successful? There may be many factors, but one characteristic of all best-selling publications—magazines, books or newspapers—is that they're relatively easy to read. The ones that achieve boxcar circulation numbers can be understood by a broad segment of the public.

By contrast, those with writing mostly at the college graduate level, with marathon sentences and clusters of long, hard words, sharply limit the audience available to them. Most adults have real difficulty reading them; others won't take the trouble.

Your initial reaction may be: "But our audience is literate; they are college educated. Our subject matter is complex. We're not going to use 'baby talk' that turns off readers of our magazine."

Simply consider the following:

• Every successful magazine of general circulation in the U.S. can be read with ease by anyone who has completed 12 years of education.

• No book that sold a million copies or more in the past 100 years (fiction or nonfiction) requires more than 12 years of schooling for easy reading. Most best-sellers require nine, or even less.

• Every business day *The Wall Street Journal* covers the most complex subjects—finance, taxes, business trends—in language understandable to anyone with 11 years' education. With 1.9 million circulation, it is the largest-selling U.S. daily newspaper.

The lesson for publishers and editors: Monitor the skill of your writers. Do they turn in crisp, clear copy that makes even complex subjects understandable? Or is their writing pedantic, foggy, filled with unnecessary complexity?

Big profit dollars may ride on the answer. Magazines written at a level understood only by college graduates have a potential audience of 20 million, or 16 percent of U.S. adults. However, those magazines that can be read by people with only some high school education have a potential audience of 121 million, or 83 percent of U.S. adults!

One way to measure writing and relate it to years of

Table I

The top ten U.S. magazines
(By 1980 average circulation)

	Circulation* (millions)	Fog Index
1. Parade	21.6	7
2. TV Guide	18.4	6
3. Reader's Digest	18.0	9
4. Family Weekly	12.4	8
5. National Geographic	10.6	10
6. Better Homes & Gardens	8.1	9
7. Woman's Day	7.7	7
8. Family Circle	7.4	7
9. Modern Maturity	6.7	9
10. McCall's	6.2	8

*(Source: Folio 400)

Table II

Fog index of popular magazines

	Fog Index	Reading level By grade	Reading level By magazine
	17	College graduate	(No popular general maga-
	16	" senior	zine is written at a level
	15	" junior	higher than 12)
Danger	14	" sophomore	
line	13	" freshman	
	12	High school senior	Atlantic, Harper's, Time,
	11	" " junior	Newsweek, U.S. News, Wall Street Journal
	10	" " sophomore	National Geographic
Easy	9	" " freshman	Reader's Digest
reading	8	Eighth grade	Ladies' Home Journal
	7	Seventh grade	Parade, Woman's Day
	6	Sixth grade	People, TV Guide
	5	Fifth grade	Comics

(Source: Gunning-Mueller Clear Writing Institute)

Table III

Educational Attainment
(U.S. citizens 18 and above)

Education attained	Share of population (millions)	Share of population (percent)	Combined population (millions)	Combined population (percent)
College degree	20.4	13.9%	20.4	13.9%
1-3 yrs. college	24.4	16.7%	44.8	30.6%
High school degree	52.7	36.0%	97.5	66.6%
1-3 yrs. high school	23.4	15.9%	120.9	82.5%
5-8 yrs. grade school	20.6	14.1%	141.5	96.6%
K-4 yrs. grade school	4.9	3.4%	146.4	100.0%

(Source: Statistical Abstract of the U.S., 1980)

schooling are the readability "yardsticks" developed by educators in the 1930s and 40s. Originally used to help writers of textbooks, these include scales by Gray and Leary of the University of Chicago, Edgar Dale of Ohio State, and author Rudolph Flesch. One drawback is that all are relatively complex and time-consuming.

Eliminate "fog"

In 1944 my late partner, Robert Gunning, one of the pioneers of the "plain talk" movement, came up with a shorter, simpler method. He used it in his work coaching news writers. He called it the "fog index," an apt name for a method to measure "fog"—our code-word for unnecessary complexity in writing.

Earlier scales required you to count syllables, prefixes and suffixes, and personal references, in a passage of writing. The fog index—which gives the same result—calls only for average sentence length and the percentage of hard words.

Table I shows the fog index of the top ten U.S. general magazines. Sales range from 21.6 million to 5.5 million copies per issue. None has a fog index higher than 10—meaning they can be read easily by anyone who has completed 10 years' schooling, the high school sophomore level.

Does this mean these magazines limit their audience to the "mass market"; that people with college training don't read them? Certainly not! All readership studies testify that all of these magazines have a large number of college-educated readers.

Instead, the evidence points to two conclusions:

First, the obvious conclusion: There is a high correlation between high readership and low fog index. Table II shows that a low score makes the magazine easily understandable to a much larger number of adult readers.

Second, the experience of publication editors, plus studies by educators, both show people prefer to read and get information at a level *below their capacity*. Even a Harvard professor prefers to get information without strain.

This is proved by the success of such magazines as *Time* and *Newsweek*—and especially by *The Wall Street Journal*. All these publications are for sophisticated readers. All have a *majority* of readers with college training.

Yet all are written with a fog index no higher than 11—consistently, every issue. All deal in complex, difficult concepts, but in terms easily understood by anyone with a high school junior-level education.

The Wall Street Journal is a special case. Its run-of-paper fog index of 11 is helped by what may be the most readable front page in the U.S., with a score averaging 9. Consider these recent page 1 leads:

WASHINGTON—"The nation's attic," otherwise known as the Smithsonian Institution, resembles a lot of attics: It is overflowing with who-knows-what.

Corporate profits in the second quarter soared far above those in the recession-hit period a year earlier. However, the road ahead looks rather bumpy.

DETROIT—It's as if the Army, in a cost-cutting move, decided to cut off financial support to West Point. That's what General Motors Corp. is considering doing to General Motors Institute, "the West Point of the Auto Industry."

WASHINGTON—Every Wednesday, Treasury officials visit the Federal Reserve Board for lunch and informal talk about the economy. But the lunches aren't as relaxed as they used to be.

The *Journal*'s practice of explaining complex issues in simple terms began in the 1940s, when the paper decided to transform itself from a financial to a business paper. In the process, its circulation rocketed from less than 50,000 to more than a million in a decade.

Bernard Kilgore, put in charge of the paper's editorial output, gave orders to chase fog. "Write for the expert," he told his staff, "but write so that the non-expert can understand."

Kilgore hired Gunning to coach his crack front-page staff, then other writers on the *Journal*. The paper's fog index gradually dropped from 14 to 11, its present level.

Cutting through the fog

Gunning's method of coaching writers was deceptively simple, and unique. Furthermore, once a writer was exposed to it, the training "took." No refresher course was needed. His training sensitized the writer to elements in his copy that made it hard reading. For example:

The physician reports:
Lacerations and contusions were suffered by the victim.

The Senator reveals:
I can anticipate a disposition among my colleagues to expedite additional labor legislation.

The businessman writes:
Kindly advise if your information gives confirmation to the conclusions outlined herein.

The social worker warns:
Unless due regard is given to the development of the child, the result is likely to be irresponsibility, moral laxness, and inability to cope with the complexities of life.

The reporter translates:
The victim was cut and bruised. The Senator says to look for Congress to pass new labor laws in a hurry.
Tell me if you think I'm right.
Children raised without proper care are likely to turn out as bums, crooks or idiots.

Computing the Fog Index

The Gunning Fog Index[SM] is based on the count of long words and the average sentence length of a sample passage. A formula, described below, translates this into the approximate number of years' schooling needed to understand the prose tested: The higher the fog index, the harder it is to understand.

Here is how to find the fog index of a passage:

1. Select a sample of 100 to 150 words, ending with a period. Divide the total number of words in the sample by the number of sentences. This will give the average sentence length of the sample.

2. Count the number of words in the sample having three or more syllables. *Don't* count words (a) that are capitalized—even the first word of a sentence; (b) that are combinations of short, easy words (like "bookkeeper" or "butterfly"); and (c) that are verb forms made into three syllables by adding -es or -ed (like "created" or "trespasses").

Divide the total of such long words by the number of words in your sample to get the percentage of long words. For example, 19 long words divided by 125 words in the sample gives you 15 percent in the passage.

3. To get the fog index, add the average sentence length and the percentage of long words. Multiply this total by 0.4. The answer corresponds to the years of education needed to easily understand the piece of writing. In this step *only*, ignore all numbers following the decimal point; a fog index of 11.7 is shown as 11.

(Anything over 17, score as "17-plus," meaning it is above the reading level of a college graduate.)

It is important not to over-use the fog index. Use it only occasionally to spot-check your writing. Don't write to achieve a good fog index score. It makes for short choppy sentences. Like these.

Writing cannot be encased in a system. You can't make rules to write by. Rules are a substitute for thought, and you can't write without thinking.

So never try to write by this or any formula. And don't think you have written clearly just because your fog index is low. Consider the following passage:

'Twas brillig and the slithy toves
Did gyre and gimble in the wabe;
All mimsy were the borogoves,
And the mome raths outgrabe.

Although it has a fog index of only 7, a reader has a hard time making sense out of it.

Before he retired in 1957, Kilgore attributed "about half" the *Journal*'s circulation increase to improved readability.

What about the fog index of other leading publications? As seen in Table II, most U.S. general magazines score between 7 and 11. The only two that consistently score as high as 12 are *Harper*'s and *The Atlantic*.

People are usually surprised by the relatively low fog index of the magazines they read. The fog index of most business writing—letters, memos, and business and technical reports—usually ranges between 11 and 17 or more, averaging 14.

"The fog index of your favorite magazine can be your goal," I tell business and technical writers. "If you consider 12, the highest score you'll find, as your top limit, and try to keep your writing below that level, you'll write much more readable copy."

Measuring reading level

How can magazine publishers and editors measure the reading level of their publications—and then, if necessary, take steps to improve it?

The first step should be a thorough measurement of its fog index. This can be done by one or two editorial or administrative employees. They should cover a single magazine issue in one to three days.

This should be done carefully. Pick passages to be tested at random. Select three or four samples of 100 to 125 words for each major article. If one sample tests 11, another 14, another 9, and a fourth 10, the fog index for that article is 11, the average.

The instructions for calculating the fog index should be followed to the letter, so your scores are accurate and comparable with the magazines listed.

It is also important to *avoid* what you might think is the next, obvious step: To distribute the instructions to your writers, telling them to keep a check on the fog index of their own copy. This smacks of "formula" writing, usually abhorred by good writers. It can damage staff morale and the quality of your magazine's writing.

In our seminars we do encourage writers to use the fog index—but to use it very selectively, as an occasional check on their progress.

"Never post the fog index formula by your typewriter," we tell them. "If you do, you will be tempted to 'beat' it by writing short, choppy sentences. They are as bad as long, rambling ones."

Be sure you analyze at least two issues of your magazine thoroughly before coming to a conclusion about its fog index. It's a good idea to keep separate scores for staff-written articles and for those by outside contributors. Often the staff writing will score better. If so, better editing of contributed material may be necessary.

Now that you have your analysis and an accurate

estimate of your magazine's fog index, what comes next? Will an improvement in readability have a material effect on your success?

Widen your audience

Table III, the educational attainment of U.S. adults, may give you a clue. It's not a scientifically accurate method. However, you can match your fog index to the level of education and get an estimate of how many readers in your market the magazine can reach.

For example: Suppose your magazine is aimed at a special interest group—gourmet cooks, home gardeners, or sports car buffs, for instance. Suppose you decide your total potential market is, let's say, a million U.S. households.

You have determined that the fog index of your magazine is 13, the college freshman level. The table indicates you should be able to reach half that potential market. This doesn't mean you're selling half a million copies; only that the magazine can be easily read by half the market. If that satisfies you, nothing may need to be done.

But remember the success of *The Wall Street Journal, Time* and other publications which consciously hold down the reading level. They gained a larger share of the market available to them.

Remember, too, that your 13 score is higher than that recorded for any successful general magazine. Its content still is relatively hard going even for college-trained readers.

Remember, it's not a question of what people *can* read. They can read almost anything with enough motivation. High school English students struggle to wade through Chaucer's prose to get a passing grade. All of us knit our brows at tax-return time, coping with language from the IRS, like this sample from the 1980 edition of *Your Federal Income Tax:*

... decrease the basis of your property by the amount of depreciation you claimed each year on your return, or that you could have claimed, whichever is more. If you claimed more depreciation than you should have, you must decrease your basis by the amount you should have claimed plus the part of the excess claimed which resulted in a decrease in your tax liability for any year ...

Can you understand this if you try? Of course. But the real question is, What will people read *without* intense concentration? Remember, editors of the most successful publications have elected to make them easier to read, to widen their audience.

Now, look again at Table III. Note that by bringing down your fog index to the high school freshman or sophomore level, you raise your potential market to 80 percent or more of its potential. If your potential market is a million adults, the magazine will be easily read by 800,000 —a potential increase of 60 percent.

In fact, the potential may be even greater, as successful publishers have found. By lowering the fog index from 13 to 9 or 10, you pick up a bonus by attracting casual readers from the high end of the scale who might now find your magazine more interesting and become subscribers.

"Ten Principles"

All right, we'll assume you have decided to make the effort to go after a lower readability score. What can you do to achieve it?

When Gunning first offered his services as a writing coach to newspaper and magazine publishers, he said the training was based on three premises:

• Writing is an art. But writing to *inform*—the mission of all non-fiction publications—comes close to being a science as well. There are tested ways to make it work.

• Much that is written and published today is heavy with "fog," or unnecessary complexity. It is harder to read than it needs to be.

• Professional writers who command a large audience, or who have wide influence, instinctively follow *principles of clear statement* that promote easy reading. These principles can be taught to anyone who writes.

Key to the training was Gunning's own "Ten Principles of Clear Statement." By presenting them on slides, then giving examples, class exercises and discussion to bring them to life, he focused reporters' attention on them and made them literally unforgettable.

The results were dramatic, and immediate. Fog index studies of a paper's front page for a week before the seminar showed an average of 13 to 15, with many examples exceeding 17, college graduate level. In the first week following the seminar, the fog index typically dropped to 9, 8 or even 7. In some cases reporters tended to over-react and use short, choppy sentences.

Reader reaction was always favorable, and inevitably circulation was increased, so publishers were delighted.

Between 1944 and 1952, Gunning worked with the staffs of over 100 major newspapers. Later he was hired by the United Press (now UPI) to survey the daily report of the wire service. More than half the news on the UP wire tested above college reading level.

Two months later, further tests showed only 10 percent of the daily report tested above college level. More than half was below 12, the danger level—a big improvement. Following this work, the Associated Press hired Dr. Rudolf Flesch to survey its report, and improvement was made there also.

Gunning's work with newspapers and magazines trailed off in 1952 for two reasons: One, he had covered nearly all major dailies in big cities, and repeat visits were not needed. Two, he recognized that a much larger market existed elsewhere. Of the millions of words put on paper each day, most are in the offices of corporations and government agencies.

So from the mid-1950s until the late 1970s when he retired, most of Gunning's work was with people in over 200 major corporations (from Alcoa to Xerox) who use writing in their work.

How publishers can help

Publishers can expose their writers to the Ten Principles of Clear Statement either through coaching by a qualified teacher, or by distributing books which list them. Then they can assign qualified editors to work with writers on a daily basis, coaching them.

Here is an introduction to the Ten Principles of Clear Statement, condensed from Gunning's hardcover book. Any writer who makes these his own will have the same set of tools used by every successful professional writer.

1. **Keep sentences short—on the average.** Sentences must vary in length to avoid boring your reader. But the average length should be short. Fifteen to 20 words per sentence is a good average.

Compare these two sets of statements:

Experiments initiated to determine when corrosion

began showed that the metal corroded upon contact with the saline solution.

Experiments showed the metal began to corrode when it touched the saline solution.

Applications from four departments for financial assistance in development of training programs were voted approval by the board of directors.

The directors granted four departments money for training programs.

The first sentence in each set is difficult reading for college graduates. The second sentence is easy reading for almost anyone.

2. Prefer the simple to the complex. This principle does not prohibit the use of a complex form. You need both simple and complex forms for clear expression. At times, the complex form may be best.

So if the right word is a long word, go ahead and use it. But if a shorter word does the job, use the shorter word.

Of the ten principles, complexity is the one most violated. Nearly anyone facing a sheet of blank paper begins to put on airs. We use three words where one would do. We can't resist the gingerbread of four-syllable words. We write "utilize" when we could just as well write "use," or "modification" when the word "change" would do.

3. Prefer the familiar word—but build your vocabulary. You need all the words you can master. Perhaps you can get along with a working vocabulary of 10,000 to 15,000 words. But if you want to succeed in our complicated society, you'll be better off with 30,000.

However, the intelligent person uses his large vocabulary only to give clear, exact meaning—never to show off. "Big men use little words; little men use big words."

4. Avoid unnecessary words. Nothing weakens writing more than extra words that don't convey meaning. Read your copy critically; make every word carry its own weight. Note how 17 words do the work of 38 in the example below:

Before:

It is the responsibility of each and every department head to properly arrange the affairs of his organization in such manner that each salaried employee, including himself, may receive the full vacation to which he is duly entitled.

After:

Each department head must see that he and each salaried employee under him gets his full vacation.

5. Put action in your verbs. "The fullback hits the line." That is writing with an action verb. "The line is hit by the fullback." In this sentence the verb is passive; the electricity is gone. This same idea translated into typical organizational prose may sound like this: "The hitting of the line is an activity engaged in by a player acting in the capacity of fullback."

6. Write the way you talk. Actually, we recommend that writers try to write *better* than they talk; to eliminate pauses, repetition of words, and too many connectives. But the goal is to achieve a conversational tone.

7. Use words your reader can picture. Abstract terms make writing dull and lifeless. Choose short, concrete words your reader can visualize. Examples:

Abstract:

In industrial communities, the principal motivation for the purchase of curtains is practicality.

Concrete:

In factory towns, people buy curtains because they wash well.

Abstract:

Experts accused the city transit company of inefficient management and high operating costs, and cited poor scheduling, excess manpower in the maintenance department, and purchasing of buses beyond actual needs.

Concrete:

Experts charged the city transit company was wasting money by (1) having buses at the wrong places at the wrong times; (2) hiring too many people for upkeep; and (3) buying too many buses.

8. Tie in with your reader's experience. The reader probably won't get your *new* idea unless you can link it with an *old* idea he already accepts. The meaning he gives your words is determined by his past experiences, and his own goals. Consider this experiment conducted by *Fortune*:

A cartoon chart of "The Four Goals of Labor" was clipped from a labor newspaper and photostated. A new legend was attached: "From June 3 newsletter of National Association of Manufacturers." Twenty AFL-CIO members then were shown the ad and asked if it was a fair presentation of labor's goals. Four grudgingly said it was and two couldn't make up their minds. The remaining fourteen damned it as "patronizing," "loaded," "paternalistic," "makes me want to spit."

9. Make full use of variety. Avoid stilted patterns of writing. Use different arrangements of words and phrases. Good writers work within a strict discipline of simplicity, but they use enough variety—sentence length, structure and vocabulary—so the simplicity is not noticeable. As a result, the reader never thinks of the writing as choppy or childish.

10. Write to EXpress, not to IMpress. Fancy language is the bane of most organizational writing, but it is also found in trade magazines and in the writing of most nonprofessional writers.

Remember, few people are fooled by fancy language. It's been a long time since I've heard anyone say, "I can't understand what he is saying; he must be highly intelligent."

There are the 10 principles. And, in case you've been wondering, the fog index of this article is 9. You might try fog-indexing it yourself. You'll find passages ranging from a high of 11 to a low of 6. That doesn't include our example from the IRS manual, which (typically) is hard reading for college graduates.

The art of the interview

By Howard S. Ravis

Ask a group of editors and writers to discuss the "how-to's" of conducting an interview (we did just that) and you'll get as many different answers as the number you asked the question of (and we got just that).

Some of the editors and writers interviewed for this article disagree with each other. One swears by the tape recorder; another uses it only as a last resort. One recommends an almost ruthless self-policing of the interviewer to talk as little as possible, while another says, "Don't be afraid to do some talking yourself."

It all proves a basic point (which we really didn't have to survey anyone to know): There is no one "best way" or "best technique" for conducting an interview. What there are, though—and what is included in this article—are many techniques you can use to increase your chances of getting that "good" interview.

The editors and writers sharing their techniques in this article are (listed alphabetically):

• Jim Browne, editor of *Urban Georgia*, published by the Georgia Municipal Association and former editor of *The American Soft Drink Journal*.

• Bob Donath, senior editor, *Advertising Age*.

• Nora Ephron, senior editor of *Esquire* and noted freelance writer.

• Harold Littledale, communications consultant specializing in the areas of education and industrial training and former editor of *Teacher* and *Training* magazines.

• Stephen G. Michaelides, editor of *Restaurant Hospitality*.

• Norman Schreiber, freelance writer, whose work has appeared in *Playboy, Saturday Review, Gallery, Modern Hi Fi and Music* and other magazines.

• Ron Scott, assistant editor of *People* and former writer with *Life*.

• Lewis Young, editor of *Business Week*.

* * *

I've never really given much thought to the topic of interviewing or what special techniques I might use in any of my interviews. To me, it has always been a very special thing—a very natural and enjoyable experience—and I think it should be with every individual who sets out for an interview.

Also, I don't think you should ever go into an interview with the attitude that it is a "job." Interviews should be treated as a personal hobby; after all, we have the power to find and bring out that beautiful and special story in our subject to share with our readers. That alone can, and should, generate the excitement you need in obtaining a successful interview. All that is needed is a little organization, curiosity and genuine interest to learn.

When I first began my career as a reporter back in Oklahoma, I recall the day I first read Max Ehrmann's poem "Desiderata," which includes these lines: "Speak your truth quietly and clearly; and listen to others, even the dull and ignorant; they too have their story."

Keeping these words in the back of my mind, I have always entered an interview realizing that no matter how important the person, no matter what his or her status, fame or job might be, each of us has that special, unique, human story to tell. I don't believe you can successfully tell the story if either you or your subject is influenced by ego.

It is the interviewer's task to eliminate egos, establish a mellow mood and let the interviewee know you are a friend. I say "friend" because I strongly believe that if you want that personal, "down-to-earth" interview with a human touch, you need to treat your subject as your friend. It works for me, and one of the rewards is that, usually, the friendship initially established is lasting.

If I had to devise a formula for interviewing, it would be as follows:

1. Be organized.
2. Keep it personal and natural.
3. Treat it as a hobby.
4. Be curious and eager to learn.
5. Eliminate the ego—in yourself and in your subject.
6. Offer your friendship.

Jim Browne

* * *

The more I've thought about capsulizing something intelligent about the "art of interviewing," the more individual techniques skitter from view to reveal a rather simple quintessence. So instead of commenting on techniques, let me try commenting on the underlying substance of interviewing.

If you can't make people laugh or cry, sing or despair, love or hate—or if you can't share those emotions—you've got no business writing in the first place. So don't sweat interviewing. Forget it.

Beyond the routine of asking questions that get simple, factual responses, if you can bring empathy to the interview and gain the interviewee's trust, you've licked 98.7 percent of the problem already. The best techniques generally require manipulation of that trust, based on reasonably sound readings of the source's prides and fears. Even when you're seeking facts only, such manipulation may be called for in the interview.

The worst you can do is let your subject control the interview. At best, you pick away at the acceptable "on-the-record" fantasies and the cover stories that the subject might even have convinced himself or herself are true. Quote accurately. Finally, it's sad to even have to write it, but too many reporters forget: Don't make promises you don't intend to keep. If you promise to go "off the record," you've locked yourself into a box. Try for "not for attribution" status instead on sensitive information, if necessary to protect your source.

Reading the emotions of the source is vital; learning how profoundly emotion can affect an otherwise factual conversation is surprising, especially to young reporters. They create, for the reporter at least, lasting impressions that are the education in this business.

Bob Donath

* * *

The following are excerpts from an interview with Nora Ephron that appeared in *Random Folio* (Copyright 1974 by Random House, Inc.).

How do you prepare for an interview?

...One of the first things I do is try to find everything that has been written about the person or subject. I use the public library. If I'm doing a piece about someone in the theater, for example, I look up every production the person has been in and find others who have been in the same production and call them all. You know, for personal stories. I usually see all secondary people *before* interviewing the person I'm writing about. What other people tell you is useful in making up questions for the interview.

Do you use a tape recorder for your interviews?

Very rarely. I find that there are few people worth listening to twice. And you know it takes time to make written notes from a tape. So I take quick notes by hand and find that I quote people pretty accurately. Also, I type up my notes immediately after the interview. Then, the way people talk is very fresh in my mind. If I miss a detail in the notes, I can usually remember it right afterwards.

When do you use direct quotes?

I use direct quotes when I feel there is no better way to say it. A lot of writers use direct quotes endlessly and have the people say the dullest things which would read better if the writer said them in his or her own way. I never make up a quote—ever. If a person says something on the same subject at different moments in the interview, I will sometimes move the quotes together. If there are a lot of "ums" and "ahs" and the person leaves off a word at the end of a sentence—the way people *do* talk—I will put in the last word to make the statement whole.

Do you let the people you interview read your manuscripts to check the accuracy of their quotes?

I never let them take a look at the manuscript, but I will very often read to someone his or her quotes over the phone. When I interviewed Henry Kissinger for a story for *McCall's,* I even had to read him my paraphrases of his quotes, but that was a deal I was glad to make because I would never have had the interview if I hadn't made the arrangement.

* * *

I want to put in a good word for sloppiness—not a lot of it, just enough to bring your interview to life.

The nice, tidy Q&A is fine. You ask all the right questions, get all the expected answers and write a blameless story. It can be a bloodless one, though, without a ragged edge or two.

So begin with your prepared questions, but be ready to dump the script. Your subject may have something far more interesting to say than you could ever plan.

That was the case in an interview I conducted with the late James E. Allen, Jr., when he was U.S. Commissioner of Education in the first Nixon administration. The topic of our interview was education funding in the 1970s—whether it was going to rise, level off or fall.

Education had passed through an innovative and federally engaged decade in the 1960s. But now as the war in Vietnam wore on, federal spending priorities seemed more and more focused on the military establishment and less and less on the needs of children and their schools.

I was (and continue to be) disturbed by this situation. Evidently Jim Allen was too, for, from some general questions about U.S. spending priorities, we improvised ourselves into a lengthy discussion of Vietnam and a declaration by the commissioner that we should "get on with the business of ending the war."

That may not sound like much in these days but it was a courageous statement then, by a ranking official in an administration where moral courage was seldom in evidence. And to me, providing a forum for the commissioner to speak out on the fighting was my own personal brick in the anti-war wall.

Of course, some interviewees—especially those running for public office—will say exactly what they feel safe in saying and nothing more. Getting an impulsive remark out of them is frustrating and unlikely. So you shouldn't be too hard on yourself if your interview with the current big name in politics turns out to be a dog. Just cut it to the bone and leave out the hoary jokes.

But even among politicians you will stumble onto a live one occasionally and the trick then is *not to get in the way.* Forget your prepared questions for a while. Let your subject talk. You'll be thrice blessed: by your subject, your editor and your readers.

Harold Littledale

* * *

I have three rules of interviewing that I never break:

1. Never go in cold.
2. Use a tape recorder.
3. Listen, listen, listen.

Number Two above makes Number Three a cinch. I will never understand why some writers in a one-on-one situation still use notepad and pencil. It's difficult to take notes and concentrate on what the subject is saying. Furthermore, even if you argue that you need not note everything, much of the sense and substance of a good interview results from questions triggered by the subject's answers to other questions. The tape recorder lets you keep a conversational flow going in the interview (much like the easy chitchat at lunch or a cocktail party) and, because your head isn't buried between your legs, you can work with facial expressions to help break down the defenses of the subject.

I try not to ask questions that can be answered with a simple "yes" or "no." The only time I'll violate this rule is when I must have an opinion about a sensitive matter that is so sensitive that I know I'll never get a narrative response. In this instance, the question contains the answer and all the subject need do is say, "yes," or "no." In trial law, this is called "leading the witness," and is a no-no.

Stephen G. Michaelides

My attitudes are my gimmicks. A good interview is a performance wherein you play the part of yourself. The single responsibility of the interviewer is not to ask good questions nor to develop a good rapport with the interviewee, nor is it even to get a good lunch in a decent restaurant. I interview people to get information. This is called research. I will do whatever I can—within the confines of civility—to get information.

The first thing I have to do is respect my subject. Most people do not readily consent to being interviewed. They're shy. They have been burned by the press or they know somebody who's been burned. They're busy. They're suffering from severe personal problems, etc. But one of the PR people told them this interview is helpful to the team. Or, they have some favorite project that they want more people to know about. Or they feel constant publicity is helpful.

Basically, the interviewer and the interviewee have a tacit agreement. The interviewee is an invited trespasser. I always imply my understanding that I am trespassing. If a subject says something of a sensational nature that might create discomfort if made public I ask if I can write about it. Sometimes they say yes, and sometimes they say no. I tell them an interview is an artificial situation. They assure me that it isn't; but they know that I know. I give them time to talk about what they want to talk about. If there's something they don't want to discuss, we don't discuss it. I treat them with the respect and curiosity that one pays to an interesting stranger at a party. Ultimately, we move to an area of information that is fresh for both of us.

One of the most important qualities I bring to an interview is my phenomenal *ignorance*. Looking knowledgeable to your subject may make him or her a little more secure, but it also encourages elliptical answers, loosely defined terms and hopelessly vague generalities. Having the subject overexplain, until you've really captured that person's views and not your assumptions, is rewarding. Furthermore when I explain that I want to be certain I understand their important points, they tolerate my ignorance and feel more secure because they recognize they will be represented accurately. (Do you notice how such ignorance suggests respect?)

Then there is spontaneity. What this really means is listening and reacting. This is probably equivalent to "brainstorming." My subject will say something that gives me an idea. I will phrase the idea as best as possible and the subject will react.

As vital as spontaneity is, there are certain questions that always seem to help me know more about the subject. "Are you more like your father or mother in temperament?" This has a double purpose. I learn how my subject views himself or herself, more accurately, I feel, than if I were to say, "What are you like?" Secondly, it opens up the area of my subject's childhood, which is very rarely touched upon in interviews. A recent addition to my repertoire is, "What are the occupational hazards of _____?" Doug Henning told me that it used to be that when he said he was a magician, people laughed at him. Also he has a lot of scars from working with animals. A sculptor told me about burns that come from welding and

about the special glasses and shoes he wears. Also, I'm very much interested in the transitions in people's lives. When a subject says, "I decided to change jobs and get into this new area," I ask why. What was happening in this person's life to cause a change? What preparation or prior interest did this person have about this supposedly brand new area? Finally, at the end of the interview I ask, "Is there anything I haven't asked that I should have?" Basically this question is a form of courtesy. I am serving notice that the interview is over. I am also telling them I am aware that they have needs which they would like to be served. Usually, they'll say no or they'll sum up what they have said or they'll make some wonderful but irrelevant humanistic statement. Once in a while, they'll even provide me with some more useful information.

One more attitude is useful to mention. I make my subjects aware that I am working. This is how I earn my living. I'm willing to flatter. I'm willing to be silent. I'm willing to look dumb. I'm willing to expose myself. All for the purpose of gathering information that can be used in a subsequent article. Usually, I'm proud to say, my interviews develop into intense enjoyable experiences where all parties are expected to work hard.

Norm Schreiber

We deal basically with people rather than issues, so when we go out on a story, we take a different approach with the subject than many other magazines. Say, for example, I'm going to see Governor Carey. I'm not going to see him about a program he's backing. When I go to see Governor Carey I want to see what he's like as a human being. The approach taken in talking to someone to find out what he or she is like is really a lot different than if you want that person to talk about an issue or a program. That can be a tough job. Some people don't like to talk about themselves, some people do and will go on for hours and hours and hours.

I do as much homework as I can beforehand. I try to find out if the person is a talker or is quiet, what that person's interests are.

I like to go out and talk to the people I'm interviewing as if they're "normal human beings," knowing at the same time what the goals of the interview are, what points I want to cover. And if I have the time, which I usually do, to leisurely go about getting all those points covered. Unless I'm pressed for time, I'll let them ramble. If it gets to the point where I'm nearly falling asleep I'll try to steer them back as gently as I can.

I don't like to use a tape recorder usually, except for a "formal" interview or one in which I'm covering a complex or technical area. I find that a tape recorder in the center of a table or a desk can be intimidating. I usually use a pad and pencil. The first thing I do after the interview is go back and transcribe my notes or talk them into a tape recorder, because I think you do lose the recall after a certain amount of time.

As I'm doing the interview I start formulating in my mind which way the story is going. I remember important phrases I want to make sure I include in the story when I start to write. And if I do this right away I can pretty much recall what they said.

I think it's more important to get the gist of what the person said or what he or she meant than the actual quote word for word.

Ron Scott

* * *

The art of interviewing is the art of getting information says Lewis H. Young, editor-in-chief of *Business Week*. During the past year Young has carried that art to the offices of the presidents of France and Venezuela and to U.S. Secretary of State Henry Kissinger.

The results were newsmaking.

The State Department explained that *Business Week* got such candid answers from Kissinger because of the questions asked, and President Carlos Andres Periz of Venezuela reported that the magazine's questions were the best he had ever been asked in his political career.

Young agrees that it takes time to develop interviewing expertise. "You learn from not getting answers. Probably the most important thing to learn is that the name of the game is getting information, and any way you can get the information honestly and ethically is the best way."

Young is something of a diplomat with a notebook. Unlike a number of modern reporters, he's against arguing with a source as a way of checking information. "If you feel that what somebody's telling you is not completely true, the trick is to ask the same question different ways."

Once an interview has been granted, *Business Week* goes through exhaustive preparation. The questions are paramount. "The thing I like to do is zero in on what our interests are. By knowing what you want when you go into an interview, you know whether you've gotten the answer that will be of interest to your readers."

To prepare themselves before an interview, *Business Week*'s reporters go through everything they can—speeches, stories, what the magazine has done on the subject. Then, when *Business Week* gets to France or to Venezuela or even to Kissinger, a lot of time is spent in reporting before the actual interview.

In Venezuela the magazine team talked to 30 people before interviewing the president. They got information from cabinet officers, from U.S. businesspeople in Caracas, from Venezuelan businesspeople. They talked to government people and to the opposition political party.

Next the reporting team sat down to refine the questions. "We try to ask questions that cannot be answered yes and no. We ask, 'What does this mean?' or 'How did this come about?' So you set up the areas and you ask very specific questions about them and you don't ask questions that will get a baloney answer such as, 'What do you see as the future of South America?' Rather, we'll ask, 'Why is Venezuela getting less out of the Andean Pact than it is putting in?'—that kind of thing. We spend a lot of time on the questions." For the Kissinger interview, Bob Farrell, Boyd France and Young spent almost an entire day refining their questions. "We went over them and over them.

"Now in the Kissinger case I must have asked him four different ways what the United States could do about forcing the price of oil down, and the first three times, he gave me brush off answers and the fourth way I asked it got a response.

"Much of what you get out of these interviews is luck and timing," continues Young. "And I would not be candid if I did not say that." He feels that some of Kissinger's revealing answers resulted because the Secretary and the State Department had decided the time had come to say something firm.

Establishing rapport—the other difficult aspect in interviewing—becomes easier with thorough preparation and research. "You build rapport with your personality," says Young. "If you come in with confidence because you're well briefed and you know what you're going to do, that in many respects will help you with rapport. And people feel more at ease with you if they think you know what they're talking about."

How did *Business Week* set the tone of the interview with Kissinger, whom Young had not met previously?

"We didn't do much ground setting because I didn't know how much time I was going to have and I wanted to get as many questions asked as quickly as possible and not waste time telling jokes and pleasantries and laughing it up. So I started right off by saying: 'We're going to concentrate on economics.' And he shot back: 'And then after we do this, you'll write a piece in which you say I know nothing about economics.' ('Because we had,' explains Young.) I shot him back a rejoinder: 'I hope we write a piece in which we say you do know something about economics and then I asked him the first question. Kissinger later commented: 'You guys really get down to business, no small talk!'

"That's another reason why you spend a lot of time laying out the questions, so you go from one area to another. You have to ask other questions in your plan because you don't know the answers, and the answer often triggers questions. You get off the schedule of questions, but it's more important to get answers that are going to illuminate than just to ask the questions.

"And that's terribly important," emphasizes Young. "A lot of interviewers make the mistake of thinking that their questions are important. They're not, except as a means of getting information. See, the key to the success of a good reporter—and I guess the late Frank McGee of the *Today* show illustrated it best—is to get interested in what you're reporting.

"Another thing that's terribly important in an interview and this is a cliche, but I say this to our young reporters: 'I never learn anything when I'm talking. The less you talk in an interview, the better off you are. When you interview somebody, that person doesn't want to hear your view of anything.'

"There's one other rule that we try to enforce. When you interview somebody, he or she should not know the thrust of the story. He or she should not be able to say that person's going to do a negative story on our company or that person's going to do a puff story on our company.

"That's one of the reasons why you should not argue and say to someone 'I don't think that's true. I think you're doing that wrong.' If the person gets an idea of what you're thinking, he or she may mislead you."

(This article on Lewis Young is adapted from one that originally appeared in the *McGraw-Hill News*.)

How to run a roundtable

By Bernard Weiss

Editor's note: Many editors believe that the way to organize a roundtable discussion is by recruiting a few leading experts in a field, making room arrangements, hiring a stenographer and then hoping for the best.

Often the results are as haphazard as the planning.

But there are techniques that virtually guarantee success. Although the following methods were developed specifically for *Patient Care,* a journal of family medicine, they can be applied just as easily by any magazine.

It's early Friday evening, and the guests are arriving, quizzical and curious, occasionally encountering with relief a familiar face but more often entering into that kind of polite conversation that gives one a chance to size up the others.

Soon the talk becomes more serious. Someone's asking each guest to define his or her role and position, to give the others a chance to see what that person's really thinking and doing. The atmosphere becomes warm and friendly, even though sparks fly from time to time. Gradually, wary defenses drop and each guest begins to say what's really on his or her mind.

Come Saturday morning, the barriers dropped, the group opens up in earnest and for six hours probes and challenges, supports and disputes, digresses and returns to purpose. Stimulated but word-weary, the guests depart for home in late afternoon, unlikely to meet one another in similar close contact ever again.

This isn't another version of an encounter group. It's a generic description of a roundtable discussion conducted by *Patient Care,* the journal of practical family medicine. *Patient Care* is published 21 times a year for more than 102,000 doctors, who read in nearly every issue the edited results of at least one roundtable discussion. The magazine's staff has conducted some 75 roundtable discussions over the past five years, in most major cities of the United States and in Canada and Mexico.

The roundtable technique, though not original with the editors of *Patient Care,* provides a unique blend of authoritative and balanced information on almost any medical subject that is changing and therefore open to differences of opinion. The topics, often suggested by readers or a board of physician-editors, must meet these criteria:

1. Is the subject a common problem?

2. Is the proposed agenda focused on up-to-date information that is truly helpful to the reader?

3. Is the discussion likely to yield valuable opinions or information not found in other literature?

For each roundtable, from five to seven active participants are selected based on the appropriateness of their specialties to the topic, their reputation among their peers and their practical (as opposed to academic or textbook) approach to medical care. The participants are also screened to achieve a balance, reflecting differing points of view, specialties, geographic regions and variations between the idealistic and realistic approaches. More than 500 physicians, psychologists, nurses and educators have been our guests during the past six years.

About one-fifth of the doctors have been family practitioners, primed to keep reminding the specialists of the "real world" of medical care and its day-to-day problems. Essentially, the family doctors try to pin down the specialists for answers to their problems.

Each participant begins his or her involvement six to 12 weeks in advance of the roundtable, helping to prepare the agenda by working with the *Patient Care* editor assigned to the session. The editor will have constructed a preliminary agenda by inviting family doctors to submit questions in advance on this basis: " . . . if you had a seat at the table, what would you ask the experts?" The experts on the panel review the preliminary agenda to eliminate questions to which answers might be found elsewhere and questions which are repetitious, invalid or inappropriate. They also help the editor organize the questions into a logical sequence for discussion.

Even so, the panelists often are not fully prepared for this free and open exchange that takes place behind closed doors. That's why we take time Friday evening to let each guest slowly put his or her cards on the table—and look at everyone else's.

During the roundtable, the panelists are either seated at a large table (it's not always round) or in chairs and sofas in a hotel suite. They are not seated randomly, but are assigned positions based on what our editors have learned of them.

For example:

• Physicians with weak voices or who speak quietly or mumble are seated near the microphones.

• Strongly opinionated panelists who are likely to have contrary views are seated across from each other with a microphone between them.

• The moderator is assigned a seat from which he or she can easily maintain eye contact with everyone.

• A devil's advocate, whose job it is to help the moderator, is seated directly across from the moderator.

• Panelists in the same specialty or with similar interests are not seated next to each other. (They tend to whisper among themselves and we'd prefer they talk to the group.)

• The doctor who wants to show slides is seated next to a projector across from a screen.

• The medical school professor is seated near the blackboard.

We try to start the meetings at around 9 a.m. with a 15-minute break for midmorning coffee and a 45-minute break for lunch. To save time, we usually serve lunch in an adjacent room or a private dining room but always in the hotel. From experience, we've learned to keep the lunches light; heavy meals lead to heavy eyelids during the afternoon. Adjournment is about 3:00 p.m. The moderator, also a physician and member of the *Patient Care* Board of Editors, has the burden of keeping the meeting moving, keeping the discussion on the practical level and making sure that the problems and questions on the agenda are satisfactorily answered. The adept moderator asks needling questions in a polite manner and isn't ashamed to ask "dumb" questions representing problems of the many readers who would also have liked to be at the roundtable. To help our moderators, we have prepared a checklist of helpful hints, and we routinely remind moderators—and devil's advocates—to look over the checklist before the meetings begin and during the breaks.

The editor usually sits next to the moderator, passing notes with the editor's own questions and suggestions.

We regard our roundtables as a technique of research—a technique which is intended to obtain for medical education purposes the best thinking available on a topic of current interest and a technique which affords the contributors and researchers an opportunity for personal interaction and exchange.

In a sense, a roundtable transcript can be considered raw research data. As much as 70 percent of the raw material in a transcript is either heavily edited or rewritten (the transcript itself serving as a source document). Occasionally, a good interchange or a short, heated debate may be left intact, to be published verbatim.

Also, as in any technique of true research, we aren't always sure of what we'll get. At a roundtable in Washington, D.C., a transcribing service delivered worthless gibberish, and we had to hold a second roundtable. At a roundtable in New Orleans, two friendly panelists excused themselves and disappeared for the remainder of the discussion. A roundtable in Chicago ended abruptly when the moderator announced he had to leave to catch a plane. The ideas for many of our best articles were developed after roundtables strayed off course and yielded unexpected content.

And finally, if the roundtable can be regarded as research, then a roundtable transcript can be regarded as a preliminary research report. A copy of the transcript goes to the moderator, who marks it up: "Must use," "omit," "need more data on this," "convert this information to chart form," etc. The editor relies on this guidance in tearing apart a transcript and organizing a tight article. When it is written, edited and copied, all the members of the panel review the first draft and offer their comments. As many as 20 non-participating physicians also review the

Guide For Moderators

Make the most of a preliminary warm-up session. Get each panelist to tell a little about himself or herself and the individual's specific interest in the topic to be discussed. Let each person talk briefly about what he or she considers to be the most significant problem involved. Go through the agenda with an eye toward adding or subtracting or moving parts around for better organization of the discussion. Let the staff editor help carry the ball in questioning so you, as moderator, can sit and size up the participants—that is, get an idea of who is most forward and who is most reticent; who will interact best with whom; who is going to be most difficult to pin down, etc.

Always ask specific questions addressed to specific participants. For opening questions at the actual meeting, try to let one or two participants know in advance that you will be calling on them first for these particular questions. Remember that a general question frequently yields little information. In fact, questions addressed generally to the table may get no answer from a participant who is not best qualified to handle that question.

Keep the discussion on the track. Be tough about this at the start. The first time a participant departs from the subject or goes on too long, interrupt that person quickly and remind that person and the others in a nice way that time is limited and you want to make every moment count for those who will be reading the results of this discussion.

Get a clear expression of opinion from the panelists in any controversial area. Make it clear that you want to reflect differences of opinion and the reasons for them. When a consensus is possible, ask each panelist to signify his or her agreement or disagreement verbally, explaining why if he or she disagrees. Do not settle for shakes of the head or hand raising. These won't show up in a transcript. If different points of view are expressed, look for the balance that should be reflected in the final report.

Eliminate repetition. If a panelist wishes to go back and reiterate a point that he or she made earlier, cut that person off quickly. Also cut off any other panelist who starts repeating what has been said before simply for emphasis. Let the individual indicate that he or she agrees with a specific comment and then move on. A good way to handle this sometimes is to ask if anyone disagrees. If no one voices disagreement say for the record: "We can therefore assume that everyone agrees with the statement by Mr. . . . ."

Make sure all the good comments get in the transcript. This means urging participants to repeat for the record any "pearls" dropped during the coffee or luncheon, making sure that panelists speak only one at a time and insist that no sideline conversations are going on that should be entered into the record.

Keep everyone in the act. Try to draw out any participant who hasn't spoken for 10 or 15 minutes. You must control those who have a tendency to respond to every question. Directing questions specifically to a given expert helps.

Maintain your role as moderator, not participant. Know your subject, but avoid interjecting advice or experiences as your own. Raise questions or attribute ideas to another person, thus allowing panelists more freedom to challenge you. Don't be afraid to run a tight meeting; the participants will appreciate it and so will your readers.

draft "cold." With comments in hand, the editor then revises, rewrites and polishes for publication.

So, obviously, a roundtable must be carefully planned, starting with the topic. The more controversial the topic, the better; bland subjects are covered more effectively through telephone or personal interviews. Guard against cancelled hotel space, misinformed hotel staff, the star panelist who drops out the day before the meeting and not enough copies of the agenda. After the roundtable, stay in touch with panelists—information presented at the roundtable may be obsolete before publication.

We usually convene a roundtable in a hotel suite in either an easily accessible city (our guests are drawn from all over the country) or a resort or resort hotel. The guests and the moderator are paid a $100 honorarium and we pay their first-class fare, hotel, meals and miscellaneous expenses. As a rule, spouses are not invited; if they come, it is at their own expense.

The meetings are tape-recorded or stenotyped. We have paid from $300 to $800 for a verbatim transcript which may run more than 300 double-spaced pages (by the time it is edited, the published equivalent is usually fewer than 50 pages). Also we usually retain a photographer to shoot candids.

All told, our out-of-pocket expenses for a roundtable of modest proportions range between $4,000 and $5,000, not including our staff time, travel and entertainment. The yield is at least one, often two, and occasionally three feature-length articles in *Patient Care*. Though the bulk of the raw source material for those articles is found in the roundtable transcripts, some follow-up interviewing by phone is usually necessary to fill information gaps, to clarify inconsistencies and ambiguities and to bring up to date any topical discussions which aged between the roundtable meeting and the date of publication (sometimes there is a 6-8 month interval).

The cost of gathering this editorial material is high, but is justified as an effective device of continuing medical education. In effect, we are providing a bridge between the producers and teachers of medical knowledge and the first line users of that knowledge.

Eight ways to fight 'puff'

By Milton Gralla

One of the toughest problems for all of us in the magazine business is the advertiser who tries to use his big ad program as a blackjack to gain undeserved publicity.

Whether you're a business or consumer magazine publisher, editor or ad sales manager, you've probably had many encounters with this type of pressure.

Sometimes the advertiser's "big story" has valid news appeal to your magazine's audience. More often it's something secondary like a dealer trip, a 20th anniversary, a new factory, a sales meeting, or something of limited value to your readers.

But when you explain your standards of reader interest and value, or use the other routine defenses against "puff," some advertisers charge right through. They continue to flaunt their ad programs and demand attention.

Welcome to the tightrope! At one end you may commit an act of editorial prostitution and pacify an advertiser. However, this might erode the credibility of your magazine and you may lose the respect of your readers. At the other end you may say "no," offer no alternatives, and risk losing a valued customer. You can't win! Or can you?

I have a third alternative. Over the years I've learned some defenses that can help keep publishers, sales managers and editors off the tightrope 90 percent of the time. These defenses are basic, but they really work. Here are a few.

Don't let p.r. agents distort your view

Sometimes an advertising or public relations agency gives a client a distorted or downright dishonest view of your magazine's cool reaction to a story idea. When your editor cuts or discards the story, it's too late to explain your standards to an outraged customer.

That's why we prefer to confirm any preliminary conversations with intermediaries in writing, and send a carbon copy to their client. Thus unreasonable expectations are not raised, our editor's request for useful story suggestions gets more attention, and the client knows what's going on.

Control and educate salespeople

Some of the worst problems occur when good advertisers first try their "big story" ideas out on their ever-faithful friend, your advertising salesperson.

One of our absolute rules is that salespeople may never promise that anything will be published. They must convey any advertiser's ideas to the editor, and then step out of the picture.

Also, our salespeople may never be placed on the publicity mailing list of any advertiser or agency. If this is offered, they must explain that all publicity should be mailed directly to editors, to avoid delay.

Internally, no salespeople are ever given the authority to order an editor to publish anything—even a one-paragraph new product report in the back of the magazine.

Finally, we make a consistent effort through sales training to familiarize all salespeople with editorial practice and value. The salesperson who has fully absorbed our magazine's editorial philosophy is much less likely to stick his or her or our neck out when a major advertiser tries out a "big story" idea.

Avoid expensive free trips

A free trip for an editor or publisher often has that old publicity tightrope at the end.

The typical free trip may be occasioned by a new factory opening in Europe, a sales meeting in White Sulphur Springs, a plane-load of outstanding retailers spending a week in Hawaii, or some similar "news event" at any attractive destination.

You're never asked directly for publicity when you're invited for the free ride. But if you don't come across afterward—look out!

Our editors must have written permission from the editorial director to accept any such offer which includes air transportation and/or lodging. They're also advised that productive use of their time has more value than costs saved by accepting free trips.

These guidelines help most editors duck most of the time-consuming joy-rides and the puffs or problems which might follow.

In addition, editors also are required to decline or obtain management approval to accept any gifts or favors worth more than $25.

Publicity tipsheet avoids problems

Our editors and salespeople have a one-page sheet of "helpful tips on effective publicity." These tips are simple guides to getting publicity in our magazine.

When an advertiser complains about publicity or puts pressure on a salesman, the salesman offers the advertiser a copy of this "idea sheet" to demonstrate that he really wants to help the customer. It gets the salesman off the hook, and it often gets the customer on the track to creative publicity approaches instead of non-productive pressure.

A "maybe" is better than a "no"

If we don't want a story on "Jones Observes 20th Anniversary," we may ask Jones for an interview on "My 20 Favorite Business Tips" based on his 20 years experience.

If the "big story" is an annual sales meeting, we may dig deeply to find newsy talk or fresh ideas that have valid appeal to our readers.

If a contest has been concluded, we may try an exclusive interview with the winners, again looking for unpublished new ideas that serve the needs of our audience.

No matter what the subject of the puff, a few imaginative questions may help produce a more useful angle.

Before saying "no" to mediocre ideas, tell your customers "maybe," ask for specific information, and then

it's their job to deliver.

Give back-up in other areas

Some advertisers exert pressure for publicity only because they have the vague feeling a magazine "ought to be doing something for me." They don't know what else to ask for, so their demands for publicity are constant.

The magazine that offers back-up services for contract advertisers gets less of this unreasonable publicity pressure. Services that have worked well for us include daily news hotlines at major trade shows, custom mini-research jobs, distributor and sales rep assistance efforts, and other standard merchandising activities.

Is the editor's boss a non-editor?

Serious trouble can develop when the editor's "boss" is a publisher who came up from the financial, advertising, or non-editorial end of the business, and that publisher starts meddling in individual publicity decisions.

Ideally, we've found, editors should be responsible only to superiors with specific journalistic or editorial experience. In some companies that's not possible and, in such cases, the publisher must keep hands off.

In our own company, which has 13 national business publications, we probably have a somewhat unusual structure of editorial responsibility.

When the editor has demonstrated enough leadership to earn the added title and function of publisher, there's no problem. He makes editorial decisions with little interference.

But where the ad sales manager has earned the role of publisher, he's still given no authority to alter his editor's decisions. The editor is responsible only to the company's associate editorial director and to myself as editorial director. In this way we are able to avoid editorial pressure by executives with no editorial training.

What to do when all else fails

Sooner or later, every act of caution fails, and we find ourselves firmly on a tightrope with no possible compromise.

Let's suppose a major advertiser is insisting on unreasonable and unjustified publicity, time is running out, and the usual defenses have failed.

We know we must either run an embarrassing puff or lose the good will and possibly the ad program of an important customer.

Here's the philosophy we recommend.

A good magazine has many advertisers but only one reputation. If it loses one advertiser, it still has many others.

What does a magazine do if it loses its one reputation?

What about the editorial page?

By John Peter

Question: Should you have an editorial page?

Answer: Perhaps.

As a consultant, working on launching a new magazine or improving an existing one, I have found that the question is inevitably raised. If it had been asked some years ago, the answer would have been much simpler: Yes. In the early days, magazines had editorial pages with the same certainty as newspapers. Magazine editors, like preachers, were expected to sermonize from the editorial pulpit. There were some great ones at it, like S.S. McClure of *McClure's,* Edward M. Bok of *Ladies' Home Journal* and George Horace Lorimer of *The Saturday Evening Post.* They believed in the editorial page with the same fervor they believed in the family, free silver and national destiny. Readers did, too.

Ask editors the same question today and you'll get all kinds of answers.

'Here to Stay'

For example, John L. Cobbs, editor of *Business Week,* believes it's here to stay. "There's never been any serious idea of doing away with the editorial page. We've never thought that any aspect of the magazine is beyond question or improvement. But I don't think there has been any serious sentiment in favor of discontinuing the page in modern times.

"I also don't believe the editorial page is dying out. It all depends on where you look. *Time* and *Newsweek* have never had an editorial page, as such. Without getting into invidious comparisons, one of the reasons that we feel that we want an editorial page is that we want to make a very sharp distinction between what we state as our judgment and opinion and what we state as objective reported fact. I think you will find that a typical *Business Week* story is very little editorialized. Since it is necessary for a magazine in many areas to state where it stands, our editorial page serves as that outlet," he added.

"We have a meeting on Thursday morning of a group of our more senior people. We ask the editors if there's a particular article in the magazine coming up that looks like it has interesting editorial possibilities. I ask the writer of the article to sit in with us, if he or she is not a member of the group already. Then we simply have a rather informal, but very frank, discussion for as long as is necessary—both what is going to be in the magazine and what's in the news generally, as well as any ideas that a member of the group might present," Cobbs explained. "At that point, I take brief notes on the meeting and later consult at some length with the editor in charge of each of the stories we're interested in. We come to tentative conclusions on what editorials we're going to have. These are

modified as the week goes along.

"Late Monday night or early Tuesday morning I consult with the editor-in-chief, Lewis Young, and we determine the subjects we're going to editorialize on in that issue.

"I regard the editorial page as the clearest, most lucid and most effective statement of a position that we can make. We don't carry the kind of editorial that exhorts our readers to do this or do that. What we do is give them our best judgment of what ought to be done in a particular situation."

'Not Necessary'

If you talk to Don Berg, managing editor of *Medical Economics,* he would tell you it's not necessary. "We've never run an editorial page in the traditional sense that we preach or take a position on issues. What we do if a position should be taken is to encourage our writers and our editors to draw conclusions within the stories themselves. In other words, we're not simply a reportorial service where we present the facts and let the reader make up his or her own mind. We attempt to reach a conclusion for the individual within the article so we feel there isn't any need to have an editorial page.

"In the medical field there aren't too many that do have the traditional editorial pages anymore," says Berg. "There are one or two and I think they, too, will eventually drop them."

Managing editor David Hollander observes that *New Times* has never felt any necessity to include an editorial page among its contents. "There aren't very many news or news feature magazines that have such a page. *Time* and *Newsweek*—the ones that come most readily to mind—certainly don't, nor does *The New Yorker, New York, Rolling Stone* or *Esquire.*"

As a matter of record, it was in the more sophisticated and cynical atmosphere of the post World War I period that editorials began to disappear. Harold Ross, avowedly publishing for "a metropolitan audience" and "not editing for the old lady in Dubuque," never had an editorial page in *The New Yorker.* Henry Luce, ardent advocate of group journalism, reinforced the trend, creating *Time* without one.

Coincidentally, it was *Time* that spawned the best-known version of what has most frequently replaced the traditional editorial. The Publisher's Letter is an informal, personalized report on the story behind getting a story in the issue.

New Times has such a letter from its publisher, George Hirsch. "As far as I know," comments David Hollander, "the feature is well read, although there's never been any survey on it. The page is in the front of the book. It's the first thing you come to after the table of contents. The name of the publisher's column is 'Behind the Scenes,' which is a name that was selected before I started working here. It's short and usually written fairly breezily and doesn't run more than two columns or a page.

"But I want to stress that this is not a publisher's comment. This page has never, to my knowledge, dealt with taking a position on any issue. Sometimes the positions are implicit because of the articles which are being written about. For instance, if we have a cover story on how aerosol cans are a threat to the ozone layer, in some way that is taking a position. But that doesn't appear in the publisher's note. That's in the magazine," he explained.

Tennis magazine runs a page called "Notes From The Publisher," but is now in the process of altering the page. "One reason why we're changing the page," notes Jeff Bairstow, managing editor, "is because we've had a change of publisher. It will now be written by the editor-in-chief so it's not really a column by the publisher anymore. The intention of the new column is to be a kind of behind-the-scenes column which will tell people interesting things that are happening to the magazine in editorial terms. It will tell about some of the people involved in the magazine, about the problems and strange things that happen when one goes out to get a story.

"It runs two columns in each issue. It won't be an editorial in the sense of pontificating or taking a lead in the tennis world."

Sam Burchell, managing editor of *Architectural Digest,* says, "We don't have the editorial page in the sense of the kind of editorial that appears in the newspaper. We do run a feature called 'People Are The Issue' and that is the nearest thing we have to an editorial page. That is, there are 10 or so lines at the beginning which the editor-in-chief generally writes on some topic or subject. It's a comment, but it's not an editorial. It is followed by some brief biography of the material appearing in the issue."

Business and Trade Publications

It is among business and professional editors that you will find many of the true believers in the editorial page.

For example, William Patterson, editor of *Food Management,* says, "A good trade magazine is a magazine that is trying to be the focal point of the industry it serves. It's trying to reflect what's happening in the industry within its pages. In terms of its editorial page, it's trying to give direction in a more personal and subjective way. I think a good editor is someone who really knows his or her field and cares about it. The editor is in a strong enough position that he or she can make statements which are controversial because they have been substantiated by the editor with the readers and the advertisers. The editor has conveyed to the readers through the years that he or she has worked on the publication the individual's own sense of intelligence and integrity. And the editor has also conveyed to the advertisers a genuine concern for the industry," he said.

"If you've got a sense of fairness and intelligence in what you're doing, if you've built up credibility—then you can speak."

Patterson admits to discretion, however. "What we do is take issues that are of genuine concern to the industry and we talk about them. Other issues we don't talk about or I find an angle from which I can talk about them."

A good number of editors in the business press have come to be dubbed the "Mr. Industry" of their field, such as Jerry Svec of *Ceramic Industry,* Anderson Ashburn of *American Machinist,* Charles Jones of *Boating Industry* and Gene Beaudet of *Iron Age.*

They are the recognized brokers for industry know-how as well as rallying leaders. The American Business Press considers this role so worthwhile that it has a special editorial category in its annual Jessie H. Neal Editorial Achievement Awards. Recent award winners include *Engineering* editor Kerry Gibbens, Philip Schreiner of *Buildings,* James O'Connor of *Power,* Dr. Irvine Page, editor of *Modern Medicine* and Robert Jones, editor of *Industrial Research.*

Cousins' Viewpoint

If you searched today's magazines for a widely-known editor in the great tradition, it would be hard to find a better one than Norman Cousins of *Saturday Review.*

Cousins feels the answer to whether you have or do not have an editorial page relates to your theory of editing a magazine. One is that you try as conscientiously and as accurately as you can to find out what your readers want and then you give it to them. You can find this out in a variety of ways—market research surveys and other sampling devices. Then you try to gear the magazine to what your guide sheet tells you your readers want," he explained.

"The second theory of editing is that you put out a magazine to please yourself and, if you're lucky, you'll find a number of people who will respond to those tastes. If not, get out of the way and let someone else try his or her tastes out.

"I tend to favor the second theory. The trouble, it seems to me, with asking readers to help you write the magazine is that they decide to be helpful far greater than their capacity to do so. Sometimes they just don't know. I doubt that a brain surgeon would ask his or her patient how to operate. So an editor, I think, has to deal with things that wouldn't even occur to the reader.

"The most important job in editing is to think ahead of your time and to try to bring things into consciousness of the reader that the individual may not have thought of otherwise. I can't think of any compliment that can be paid to an editor that is greater than for a reader to say, 'You know, I never even thought about that.'

"In the context of that approach to editing, the editorial page represents a sort of a culmination. The editorial page gives the editor a chance to have a point of focus between the editor and the reader. The editorials need not be confined to cosmic events or opinionating about subjects in the news. It also has to be a form of communion between editor and reader and a place where he or she can stress doubts, not just certainties; where the editor can sketch common problems, problems held in common with the reader," Cousins added.

The answer to the question, "Should you have an

editorial page in your magazine today?" depends on what kind of magazine you have.

Clearly, if you have a magazine of advocacy, such as *Ms., Consumer Reports, Audubon* or one that follows Norman Cousins' approach to editing, you are expected to take a stand on issues of concern to your readers. If yours is a trade or association magazine, your job is to state the organization's view for the members. If your magazine is a professional or business publication there is also a strong case to be made for the editorial page.

It provides a regular spot where the editor can address the problems of the industry. It personalizes the publication and builds the reputation of the editor as an authority in the industry or profession. This is important from both a reader and advertiser standpoint. A photograph and signature of the editor reinforces recognition.

Relaxed Informal Style

The trend in writing the editorial page is towards a more relaxed and informal style. Preaching is out. Even the pregame pep talk is disappearing. Editors like Ed Walzer of *Progressive Grocer* recognize that their readers are as bright and professional as they are. They approach readers in the same relaxed, no-nonsense tone they would in meeting them person to person. They often discuss more than one topic, as they would in a face-to-face conversation.

Editorial pages in many business publications consistently place at or near the top in readership. For example, Patterson's page scores 92 percent on reader research studies.

A while ago, a reader challenged Bob Bierwirth on his outspoken editorials in *Product Design and Development.* "Your choice of subjects in a technical publication is inappropriate. If you don't believe me, survey your readers." Bierwirth took up this challenge. He asked his readers to vote by circling a number on the reader service card. "Down with Bierwirth" was #774, "Write on Bierwirth" was #775. Brother Bierwirth writes on with over 3,000 engineers voting 5 to 1 in his favor.

Recognition, readership and reader response are the real test of an editorial page. If you don't get it, you don't need it.

Sixteen hints for the new products editor

By Dick Barnett

Each day's mail brings in more of those new product releases to add to the ever-growing pile. What can you do with all of them? Here are 16 different hints on how to best handle a new products department.

1. Read your mail. A goodly portion of the ever-increasing batch is product news and occasionally there is something of value. You can save time by checking the product pictures, not for the quality of the photo but for the interest value of its subject matter.

2. Public relations people aren't all that bad. If you do choose to use a product a PR agent's been boosting, he or she can cut a lot of red tape for you. They can be of enormous assistance in the shooting of the product, for example, and they understand deadlines. Of course, some can make things downright difficult. Be wary of claims, but don't be overly suspicious; it's the minority that try to pull the wool over your eyes.

3. Take in the merchandising and premium shows in your area whenever you can. You will have to weed through an awful lot of garbage and burn some shoe leather in the process, but the half-dozen or so usable items you'll find make it all worthwhile. This is your chance to talk directly with the exhibitors who promote products of interest to your readers; if they talk future plans, you might even get a scoop. Visit the press room before you leave the show; you may learn about something you missed in your travels.

4. Attend press conferences as often as time permits. At one fell swoop, they give you the opportunity to meet the people behind the products and provide tips on usage, sometimes hints of future introductions. If you can't make a conference, have the sponsors send you a press kit.

5. Check with your ad salespeople, if they don't check with you. They can often provide good leads on upcoming products from their clients.

6. Visit department stores in your vicinity and check out the sections relevant to your magazine. You may spot an unpublicized item that would really turn your readers on. Store displays can also spark ideas for product department themes and gift roundups.

7. Read the specialized publications in your field. Chances are that the technical products being introduced to these special groups haven't yet filtered down to the consumer level. If you have a general-interest audience, why not let it in on some of these products too?

8. Samples help you deal with interesting but questionable items. This is particularly important when you deal with mail-order items, since you can't go to a local store and check them out. An advantage of soliciting samples is that you have them on hand for photo sessions. The main reason is that you won't be letting your readers in on something that a first-hand look would show to be worthless.

9. It is obviously important to check what your competition has been running in the way of new products. Needless to say, featuring a "new" item six months after they do can be mighty embarrassing.

10. If you're on a tight budget, keep in mind the tons of free photos coming in the mail every week from manufacturers, distributors and PR agencies. Most photos from mail-order houses—often the majority of your mail—are of poor quality. But if you see something good—even though the pictures are poor—ask the manufacturer or distributor for new pictures.

11. Remember that in-use product shots are far more interesting than pictures of the item standing by its lonesome. They also give your reader an idea of the size of the product. This works both ways, of course; a small product that might be lost in a busy shot comes across better in a clean closeup. Ultimately, your style, format and budget combine to make the final determination.

12. When writing new product copy, keep your distance. Use expressions such as "is designed (made, meant, supposed) to"; otherwise stick to the undisputed facts like size, color and price. What you're supposed to be doing is informing your readership about the product; you're not the press agent for it.

13. Really impressed with a product? Don't try to sell it with superlatives; you may sound like you sold out. But a personal-use report might be warranted. This is the logical follow-up on a product that really sells you—and may do likewise to your readers.

14. Before using a product feature from your holdover (or overset, or whatever you want to call it), update it by checking with the manufacturer involved. Addresses may change, prices change (usually upward)—and sometimes products are discontinued or businesses go bust.

15. Keep careful files on the new products you use in print and save all your correspondence, just in case there are any questions or complaints from the manufacturers or PR agency once the issue is published.

16. Sending tearsheets or photostats is standard. You might even want to send an entire issue featuring a product to the people who make it or represent it. They usually get good mileage from editorial publicity and plug your publication in the process . . . at no extra cost to you!

More tips for the new products editor

By Edward McCabe

If you must process a number of new product items each month, the game of discovering what the thing is, how much it costs and how it is used can be most stimulating. My personal approach hinges on the 10 points which follow:

1. Look at the order form *first,* if one is supplied. In this copy the manufacturers have been forced to reveal what they truly have to sell. You will discover how many different models there are, the number of colors, sizes, price and so forth. After you have absorbed this, proceed to the release text.

2. What is the prime source? Many new product "releases" actually are offers to sell and the material has been sent to you by reps, jobbers and others. Very likely you want to identify the prime source—and tracking this firm to earth can be as difficult as following a hard news story. At some points it appears that half the distributing community is in league to stop you from finding out.

3. There are two major premium shows held yearly—one in Chicago and another in New York. If you actually can attend either show, well and good. If not, the *Directory of Exhibitors* is a useful reference guide. The

New York show is run by Thalheim Exposition Management Corp., 98 Cutter Mill Rd., Great Neck, N.Y. 11021. The Chicago show is held by Hall-Erickson, Inc., 7237 Lake St., River Forest, Ill. 60305. In addition, many specific product shows publish exhibitor directories—*National Housewares Exposition* and *National Hardware Show,* for example. Since most of these shows gravitate either to the New York Coliseum or Chicago's McCormick Place, a list of the shows held in both places can be useful. A simple query to the manager of each exhibition usually gets you advance press registration and the valuable exhibitor guide.

4. Advertising specialty and executive gifts should be clearly set aside in your mind from other new products. The ad specialty is an item usually made to be customized in some fashion and then be given away by a firm to potential customers. The executive gift, which may also be customized, often is purchased in bulk for existing customers.

5. Is a thing really new? The number of "truly new and useful items" at most premium shows is so small in number that they are talked of widely by exhibitors. A single hour of questions, posed during the next-to-last day of any show, will reveal the "truly new items" to you in plenty of time to actually see them.

6. If you attend a trade show, carry with you a rolled sheet of gray cardboard, a camera and make your own new product shots using the card for background and an electronic flash as light source.

7. If you must use handout pictures, and if they truly are bad, consider silhouetting alternate items in copy. This can at least create some interest on the page.

8. Some items are hard to describe. Mentally run through how the item is used in practice and the copy may come smooth: "User fits widget into accessory slot of standard widget and holds in upright position to cut holes from one-half to one inch in diameter."

9. How much or how many is being offered? If you ever have struggled to unravel a bad catalog description of something you wanted, consider what a spare thing of beauty is the good description! Invariably the catalog price is followed by notations such as "each," "ea.," "doz.," "pkg. 50" and so forth. It is wise for common sense and legal reasons to spell out how much of a thing is offered. Otherwise, readers may expect an entire, room-size rug for $14.95 un-

less you have specified "ea. sq. yd." Usually it is standard practice to quote the polite fiction of "retail price" with an item. Although wildly inflated, your legal department can point out the pitfalls of quoting for-real-in-store prices.

10. What is a trade name? Learning to step with assurance through this minefield can be painful. "Fiberglas" with one "s" is a trademark. Fiberglass with two is not. It is unwise to describe a camera as being of the "Instamatic-type" unless you long for a tart rejoinder from Eastman Kodak Co. Releases from the prime manufacturer usually bristle with phrases like "registered trademark," and in some cases even the symbol and colors of a company constitute "trade dress" upon which others may not infringe. The new products editor who makes an honest error in copy may be asked to mend his or her ways, but it seldom goes further. When reading such "reminder" letters, bear in mind what companies have at stake. Talk of "nylons" as stockings in the years which followed World War II caused DuPont to lose a valued, upper-case Nylon trademark. Consequently those firms which have widely used trademarks are vigilant about their use—and with cause.

The care and feeding of stringers

By Jules Abend

You, too, can become a mother.

Make no mistake, ladling out generous portions of symbolic chicken soup with the loving care of a mother is the key to keeping nonsalaried stringers ready and eager to take on your occasional news or feature assignment. Finding and keeping a few good stringers is not vastly different from maintaining a large network. You just use a smaller pot of soup.

I, however, as manager—news operations, need a cauldron. McGraw-Hill World News has a string of nearly 200 nonsalaried foreign and domestic correspondents. In addition, there are 20 foreign and domestic news bureaus staffed by 80 salaried correspondents.

But small pot or cauldron, the main ingredient is the same—Tender Loving Care. Usually these people are at the end of a long string. They feel isolated and out-of-it. My job is to establish a relationship that builds confidence. They have to know that somebody at headquarters is watching out for them and protecting their interests.

The same is true on a single magazine. If the editor is not going to manage stringers personally, the responsibility should go to a senior staff member. If the string is fairly large—25 to 50 correspondents—and active, it is a

full-time job. In either case, passing the duty off to a secretary (unless he or she should really be an editor) or a clerk would be disastrous.

Whoever has the responsibility should be a journalist with knowledge of the type of story you cover, who your readers are and the events of our times. A smattering of geography wouldn't hurt either. This person should be active in the editorial process of the magazine, suggesting stories that the correspondent could produce.

Getting back to the mother angle, this editor should have a large tolerance for just about anything. He or she should be expected to cope with letters (correspondents' letters are about as long as their stories) demanding more money for such and such a story, or asking that checks be deposited in a Zurich bank or explaining that compensation for mileage is not adequate because the transportation got sick on the way back from the story and had to see a vet.

Believe me, this is just about the most important aspect of keeping stringers working for you—answering their letters and trying to help them when you can. But even if you can't help, respond promptly.

It is better for the person who is managing the

string to become angry with family and friends than with a correspondent—especially if that correspondent is in the midst of working on an important story.

But nobody's perfect. Here's an example of what can happen when you blow it.

A McGraw-Hill correspondent in an exotic place had a major story to produce for one of the more important magazines. This man was, and is, an old retainer. He was a month late with the story and hadn't answered my cables. Finally, I heard from him; he had been sick. "Why didn't you inform me?" I asked. And back-and-forth. I got sore and gave him an ultimatum. I asked him for assurance that he would produce the story by a certain date or I would find someone else to do it.

Bear in mind that my cables were going into his newspaper office where they could be read by others. He was humiliated. He wired back: "Find somebody else." There was nobody else. He had me. I assessed the situation for almost a minute before cabling my humble apologies, telling him what a fine journalist he was, the best on the subcontinent, no, the whole continent, and asking him to please, please complete the assignment. He was mollified. I could have avoided the incident. I forgot the chicken soup. As I said, nobody's perfect.

I have also found that concepts of ethical behavior for a journalist vary tremendously. Don't be shocked or indignant when a correspondent from Africa suggests that he or she also be allowed to sell space and subscriptions. Simply explain how you separate the editorial function (I hope) and let it go at that. Don't write the person off. You may need that person.

Good stringers cannot live by chicken soup alone—plan a budget for retainers, travel, expenses and emergencies. Money is important. Not necessarily a lot of money, but enough to enable them to function properly.

I'm not saying that each one should receive a retainer or that all retainers should be equal. That's up to you, the rationale for making retainer payments varies. The two most popular are: The stringer is a good person and prolific, so he or she deserves a regular retainer. The stringer is a good person in a rather desolate, unproductive area so let's pay something regularly so he or she will be there when needed.

To me, both are valid, as is the theory that if a man or woman is a productive correspondent who earns a substantial amount of money he or she doesn't need a retainer.

I can absorb all of these philosophies and work with them without a feeling of conflict. I have to. So many of the decisions concerning retainers are arbitrary. To be sure, the good consistent stringer will get more consideration when budgets are reviewed. But then again, you may offer a retainer to a person not known to you just because you need a stringer.

One thing that you should do is graph the earnings of the correspondents who do receive monthly stipends. If you see that a correspondent in a productive area hasn't earned very much, some action is needed. For example, if you are publishing a mining magazine and see that your person in Phoenix, Ariz., who is receiving $50 a month from you over-and-above earnings, hasn't filed anything on copper in a month, you should know that something is wrong.

Some acceptable, realistic measure should be developed for a proper retainer-to-earnings ratio. I consider earnings of three times retainer about right. That is, if a stringer is getting $50 per month from you, he or she should be earning an additional $150 if that person is in a productive area.

This would be averaged out annually, but checked monthly and quarterly. At the six-month mark, I feel that it is proper to write and try to bolster those who are lagging. You understand that sometimes nothing is happening, even in productive areas. But you don't want to pour the company's money down a nonproductive well.

If there is no response to your constructive criticisms, then you have no choice other than to let the laggards go and replace them.

Now that you have a budget for retainers, travel, expenses and incidentals, you need a policy on payments. And you should try to build into it safeguards against inequities which will arise.

Let's assume that you pay three dollars a printed inch, and that a stringer produces a first-rate story 15 inches long. Theoretically, he or she would earn $45. But the story was briefed to five inches. What should be done? The correspondent should be paid $45 anyway.

How would you do it? You can simply pay the stringer on the basis of what the story was worth originally, by translating the typewritten manuscript into magazine inches. Or you could have an alternative, as stated policy, which would take some of the subjectivity out of the decision and cover a wider range of situations. For example, you can tell the correspondents that on assignment they will be paid either at space rates, or for their time, at the rate of, say five dollars per hour. Let me emphasize that there is no magic formula to determining equitable payment. So much of this is flying-by-the-seat-of-your-pants. While the figures used here are hypothetical, you really cannot go much lower and hope to come up with many good people.

As you get into it, you'll find that stringers tell you what they get from other publishers. So you will have some guides. Just remember that correspondents aren't coolies. You are using their material.

If you use hourly rates you have three guides to work with: The original manuscript, the printed version and the time-claim. It should help you to make a more equitable decision.

Time as a measure does another thing. It takes the guesswork out of those jobs that you know wouldn't amount to anything in inches. If you want a person to cover a meeting, he or she knows that he or she is going to get $35 to $40 per day even if nothing is printed. Also, if a correspondent is assigned a story, does a good job, but the story is killed, you have the individual's time as a guide to payment.

You have to make it clear, however, that you reserve the right to determine payment by hours or space. If you want to apply this concept, you should have time cards printed and distributed to the correspondents. The cards should be designed to have the correspondent's name, assigning editor's name, story slug and number of hours on the job. It might also carry the sentence about your reserving the right to determine method of payment.

It has to be understood, too, that the freelancer may not file time on speculative stories, that he or she will be paid space rates for any over-the-transom material unless an editor goes back for more information. At that point it becomes an assignment.

Pay policies, aims and goals, as well as editorial style and picture requirements should be written down for all to see. This could take the form of a correspondent's handbook. It can be an inexpensive, mimeoed affair, or an elaborate production, but something to which correspondents may refer.

In addition to outlining payment for editorial material, it should be specific regarding travel and other expenses. And it should tell how you will pay for pictures. If you want them to supply the illustration, will you pay $10 for each glossy taken and used? Do you prefer that a professional photographer go along on the job? At what rate? Fifty dollars per day for black-and-white? Spell it out.

Even with a clearly defined *modus operandi*, finding freelancers can be a problem. I have my own approach and I'm not always successful.

I had been looking for a person to represent us in New Delhi for months without success. Then the Pakistani war erupted and I had no one to cover it. Fortunately, there was a good man in Singapore who went in and filed stories for *Business Week* and *Chemical Week*, but we were a week late as a result. And when the Singapore man left New Delhi a week later, I was still unprotected.

If you are looking for a correspondent domestically, check the *Editor & Publisher Yearbook* which lists every U.S. and Canadian newspaper and their key editorial personnel by name. It also has a good representation of foreign newspapers.

The *Yearbook* is a valuable tool for me. I use it to find new domestic correspondents. And I use it to find people in an emergency. If something happens—for instance a bridge failure in a town where I don't have anyone—I use the *E&P*, find the local newspaper and the managing editor's name, call and ask that person to suggest a staff reporter for the job. In this case, the story would be for *Engineering News-Record*, a construction news weekly. I would forego the usual space or time rates and offer what I think is appropriate for the job.

In addition to the *E&P*, there are other good ways to find people. If you are a member of one of the wire services, you can request stories from their reporters, depending, of course, on the situation. Keep your eye on the bylines in the publications you read. If you like somebody's work, get his or her name and address from the publication and contact the writer. It is somewhat more difficult to find reliable foreign correspondents. I usually rely on my people in nearby cities or countries to make recommendations.

Of course, there are always the resumes that come in unsolicited. They should be acknowledged, even if you are not planning to do anything in that part of the country or world immediately.

When you find a new correspondent in an area that you want covered, you have every right to ask that person for some background. It would be wise to send the individual a prepared biographical form asking for all the details. Ask for the office phone and Telex number if he or she is a domestic news reporter. And give the news reporter an opportunity—on the bio sheet—to tell you whether he or she wants to be contacted at the office or at home. You should ask for a list of publications, if any, for which he or she freelances. As a rule, I try to find correspondents who work nights. Then, if there is a story that needs covering, or an interview, it is easy for the person to work for you during the day, when most business is conducted.

When the person returns the completed bio, the information should be transcribed onto a file card for immediate retrieval. You should follow up after you get the bio. At this point it might be time to send the individual that handbook or policy guide. That guide, by the way, would also give your Telex, address and filing instructions. You don't want him or her to wire a 4,000 word feature unless the circumstances are very unusual. Spell it out.

Follow-up is very important. As I said earlier, it is the personal touch, the letter writing, that pays off. This is the chicken soup concept again. Relationships with stringers are tenuous at best. When you find a good person, you want to do everything possible to cement that stringer to you. As part of the continuing communication between you, he or she should receive your publication regularly, as well as notes of praise when warranted.

Remember, the correspondent is usually only as good as the assignment. Don't kid yourself into thinking that newspaper reporters and magazine editors are a breed apart. Some of the best correspondents I have were taken out of the *E&P Yearbook*. What they need most is clear assignments, like anybody else. If you frame a vague assignment, don't blame the person in the field for responding with a poor story. Again, spell it out. Be concise. Cover all the points. Give background. And include length wanted and deadline.

Sure, everything is risky. So when dealing with a new person, think far enough ahead and put some leeway in the deadline.

As soon as you make an assignment you should file your carbon for follow-up. If you want a fairly long feature, and give the person a month to produce it, you should tickle the person at the end of the second week by phone or cable to check on progress. If the writer seems uncertain, it is up to you to be firm, but gentle, and ask if he or she expects to meet the deadline. You have some rights and the freelancer has obligations. If he or she has been writing for you for some time, you should know what to expect.

On a fast-breaking story with an as-soon-as-possible deadline, keep that carbon of the assignment in front of you, and call, even if you know that the person is good and will come through. You should ask the individual to confirm the receipt of your assignment on the initial wire.

You should also be prepared for some failures, even if your assignment is superb and the stringer is excellent. There just may not be a story.

I cannot make any distinction between news and features, where contributors are concerned. I must use the same people for both kinds of jobs. It would be impossible to weed out the good writers from the mediocre ones, the news-oriented people from the feature writers. Virtually all the material supplied is rewritten to some extent. All I look for is clear, concise copy. If a correspondent has a flair, all the better.

As you know by now, attempting to maintain a string is hardly a precise science. No matter how you try to create an orderly, predictable atmosphere, something will pop. You have to be flexible and handle each situation—or crisis—as it arises.

No matter how well you plan, there is always the exception. A correspondent cabled to inform me that he could acquire certain documents, the contents of which would not be released publicly for several days. One of the publications, an aggressive magazine whose stock-in-trade is hard news, was interested. The timing was such that it could publish the information and beat its competition by two days.

I told the man to go ahead and file. To my surprise, he wired back asking for more than $1,000 "petty cash" to buy the documents.

I pulled myself together and huddled with the assigning editor, who said to forget it, the story was not that important. Unfortunately, by the time I got the negative cable out, the man had already contracted for the papers. They were on the wire. He insisted on being paid. We argued. He won. The magazine used the material.

But the question is: Were we cornered into the position where we had to pay? Or, did he simply assume that we understood that buying the materials is the way you do business where he comes from? I dunno. I do know that if I could have reached him that day I would have given him chicken soup, ladle and all.

Evaluating your editorial product

By Jim Mann

When was the last time you analyzed, assessed, evaluated or assayed your editorial product? No, I don't mean that read-through you give the magazine when each issue comes out. That's a soul-satisfying and somewhat useful exercise, but hardly qualifies as an in-depth evaluation of the product.

What I'm talking about is a scientific analysis to determine whether the product possesses the qualities it is supposed to have and to what extent it possesses them.

No one familiar with magazine publishing is surprised that few editors take the time and trouble to methodically analyze what they do. Editing is a pressure business and it is impossible to analyze anything with your nose to the grindstone. Even in editorial policy sessions, the inclination (and need) is to look forward, not back; to act rather than analyze; assault rather than assay.

There is also serious subconscious resistance to scientific editorial analysis and evaluation. Good editors have enormous confidence in their highly-developed instincts. Their jobs require a constant stream of rapid-fire decisions in the face of constantly changing circumstances. Scientific analysis, particularly post-factum analysis, seems to challenge their entire method of operation. Their reaction is similar to that of Picasso when asked by a visitor to explain his "Three Musicians." The question was presumptuous precisely because a reply was impossible.

This is one reason why the editor should not be asked to perform the editorial assay. He or she is too involved to muster the required objectivity. There is serious danger that the scientific approach required for an assay may interfere with the instinctive approach needed for effective editing. Besides, an effective assay requires extra time—a luxury granted to very few editors.

(While the editor may not be the best person to make the full evaluation of the product, he or she—and the staff—should be involved in some type of critiquing session of each issue as soon as possible after publication. It can be a most fruitful exercise and is most beneficial while the details of the issue are fresh in the editors' minds.)

Who, then, should conduct the assay? Naturally, the first inclination is to look in-house—perhaps a resident editorial director who acts as counsellor to staff editors. Henry Luce performed that function for Time Inc. magazines in the decade before he died.

Or what about the publisher? Many publishers—especially owner/publishers—are convinced that they assay their editorial product regularly. Many do. But most are so involved in the day-by-day financial, advertising, production and personnel problems that editorial assays become superficial.

This can open the way for a gradual editorial drift, a hardly noticeable condition that can send a magazine into shoals of red ink if not onto the rocks of bankruptcy. Every publisher should see that his or her magazine gets a formal assay at least every two or three years—whether the publisher or someone else does it. If there is no one inside the company to conduct it, the publisher should call in an outsider—but it should be done. It is more important to the magazine's vitality than the annual visit to a doctor for a physical checkup is to the publisher's good health.

What is the basic protocol for a successful assay? There are as many approaches to this job as there are people doing it. But any genuine assay has to include the following four areas:

I. Definition of Publishing Purpose and Objectives

No editorial assay is valid unless the evaluator understands the objective of the publication's owners. And it is not enough for the owners to say they are publishing to make money. They must understand why they are publishing their particular type of magazine, whom they wish to reach, what is the general message they want to convey or service they wish to render—and how all that is supposed to result in making money or, at least, paying the bills. Also, is the editor's viewpoint the same as the owners'?

Ability to define a magazine's *raison d'etre* is essential to publishing success. In the five years before *Life* met death there was no agreement at Time Inc. as to precisely what the magazine was supposed to be doing. During that period I posed the same questions to a half dozen Time Inc. executives: "What is the purpose of *Life*? Precisely what unique reader-need does it fill?" No two gave the same answer. And all the replies had the troubling smell of rationalization—concepts created more to camouflage confusion than to organize a team in achieving specific goals.

II. Determination of the Publication's Ideal Editorial Positioning

This requires a study of actual and potential readers. Unfortunately, the usual readership studies are not much help here. Most editorial research attempts to measure how much the audience reads in the publication or how it reacts to what is already published. But a magazine's success depends on selecting for its readers what they will want tomorrow, not what they wanted yesterday. When a publication starts to follow its audience, you can be certain it is in decline. Successful editors position their magazines far enough ahead to keep their readers reaching for it, not so far as to lose them. The explanation of *Ms.* magazine's triumph is not that there are 400,000 radical feminists in the United States, but that there are more than 400,000 women ready to be led by a small group of dedicated feminists.

Only by analyzing the possibilities for positioning can the assayer appraise the owner's publishing objectives. The market must be large enough to sustain the publication and the editorial must be unique enough to attract and hold the necessary share of that market.

III. Investigation into the Staff's Comprehension of, and Attitude Towards Both I and II

All the members of an editorial staff need not (and should not) think alike. But they must work as a team. Different ideas, thought processes and manners of expression should all contribute to common goals. Otherwise the publication develops a schizoid personality certain to bewilder, frighten and eventually alienate readers.

The investigation into staff comprehension and attitude should include the advertising sales force as well as the editorial people. The sellers of a magazine's advertising space play a major role in the construction of the publication. While editors and circulation-promotion staff are positioning the magazine in the minds of readers, the sales force is positioning it in the minds of advertisers. It is important that all three work in tandem.

IV. Evaluation of Editorial Performance

Once the goals are clearly defined and acknowledged, it is possible to examine factors like editorial mix, manner of presentation, graphics, sources of material and the interplay of editorial and advertising. Frequently this will be the least important part of the assay. In the very process of interviewing staffers on the publication's objectives and positioning, the assayer will trigger an avalanche of new editorial (and sales) ideas. Investigation by a competent assayer, whether that person be the publisher, editorial director or consultant, acts as a catalyst in the magazine's talent pool. Most of the final observations and recommendations will be anticipated by the staff as they participate in the assaying process. And in the end this may be the *real* purpose of an assayer—to act as a catalyst.

Periodicals are growing things. They must march ahead of the crowd or be trampled by it. So they change from issue to issue—or should. Unfortunately, the attitudes and approaches of individuals frequently fail to keep up with, not to say precede, the march of time. Any magazine with three-fourths of its senior personnel in harness more than three years needs a shakeup. Some publishers achieve this by firing key people and hiring fresh talent. That can be expensive and risky. Smart publishers do their shaking up by conducting regular assays to fire their editors' imaginations.

How to take your magazine's temperature

By Jim Mann

It has been pointed out often enough that magazines are living things and, like all living things, they are born, go through all the uncertainties and perils of youth, reach their prime, go into decline and die. Like all analogies, this one, if you pursue it far enough, begins to limp. Some magazines never reach their prime and others are reborn again and again.

It might be useful to think of a magazine as a fire. It starts as a spark in the mind of some editor/publisher with its success measured in the amount of heat and light it generates. Depending on how it is fueled, the spark can remain very hot for a very long time; it can flare up, die down and flare up again; or it can slowly cool off until it dies.

It is certainly easy enough to recognize when a magazine is hot. Readers snap it up. Advertisers fight to get in. The staff soars on the exhilaration of success.

It is much more difficult, however, to understand what made the magazine hot—or how to tell that it is getting there.

It is most difficult of all to spot the signs of cooling off soon enough to do something about it.

There is a strong inertial factor in magazine publishing that can be treacherously deceiving. Long after a magazine starts to cool off, advertisers will continue to buy space and readers to renew their subscriptions. The bigger and more successful a magazine has been, the longer it takes to die—and the more easily the staff is lulled into believing that everything is all right until it is too late. Precisely because advertisers and readers are so slow to abandon a once successful magazine it is very difficult to get them back when you finally have lost them. The same inertial factor that disguises decline in its early stages makes it doubly difficult to stop decline once it is well underway.

The following 10 "tests" were developed as an early warning system for publishers, editors and anyone else interested in the progress and prosperity of publications. Each "test" is helpful in a different way. Some are thermometers to check whether your publication's temperature is rising steadily (i.e., whether the magazine is on its way to becoming a hot book). Others are more like barometers that forecast drops before most readers, media buyers and, unfortunately, publishers and editors realize the magazine is in trouble.

Since no business is as full of exceptions as publishing, all of these tests can be misleading if used alone. It is by combining all 10 (or as many as apply to your publication) that they become really useful.

Test 1: Is your publication's style or personality full of surprises yet unmistakably recognizable?

A hot magazine is always unique. There are seemingly healthy magazines today that are very difficult to identify once you have removed their covers. This is particularly true of some of the established women's books and is fast becoming a fact among some of the top men's books.

A really hot magazine manages to look different even from its imitators. It is continually changing and the imitators are always two or three issues behind. To say that a magazine which is always changing remains unmistakably recognizable may sound like a contradiction, but it is always that way with a truly successful publication. A hot book is so attuned to its audience that readers have no difficulty in recognizing it even though today's issue always represents an advance beyond yesterday's. This is "style" or "personality" and it is as vital a factor in great magazine publishing as it is in great art.

Style in art, like personality in people, is the continuum out of which growth and change constantly evolve. It is much more than faithfulness to tradition in format and presentation.

Test 2: Has the publication's editorial recently caused waves?

If it has not, the magazine, in all probability, either has not yet become hot or is cooling down. Magazines make waves in many ways. The most common is the breaking of an important news story. But just as significant is a highly controversial article or a strong editorial stand.

Creating a splash signals editorial vitality only when it is the editorial matter that causes the waves. If the noise is generated by the magazine's publicity or business departments more than by its editors, it is pseudo-excitement and may even be a symptom of trouble. For instance, bidding the highest price for an already controversial book is not editorial excitement.

Test 3: Can you summarize the publication's editorial purpose in a very short paragraph?

If you cannot summarize in writing precisely what your publication is trying to do, chances are the staff lacks a clear idea as to where it is going or what it is trying to do—and is not working very well as a team.

Editors frequently resent this very old method of testing their singleness of purpose. They justifiably see their job as complex and difficult, dependent on highly developed skills and finely tuned instincts. But the very complexity of the job and the subtlety of the required instincts can be used to camouflage confusion and indecisiveness. Editors of hot books always know precisely where they are going. The average reader's assessment of what the editor is doing may not be as clear or precise, but the one thing that will not characterize it is doubt.

Test 4: How many feature articles in your latest issue could have been published intact in a competitive publication?

If most of the articles in the issue could have appeared in a number of other publications, your magazine is probably no more exciting than the rest of them. A hot book has a way of attracting (seeking out?) material that contributes to its overall purpose of direction—and making it its own.

The single most frequent cause of *rigor mortis* in magazines is the "discovery" of a successful formula coupled with the decision to stick to it.

Test 5: Disregarding news-related subject matter, is the publication's current issue very similar to the corresponding issue two years ago?

If so, the magazine has become self-refrigerated. Communications media, like plants, must grow or die. And growth means change. A successful publication has to change to stay abreast of its audience since audiences change all the time. A hot publication does more than stay abreast. It leads its audience.

One of the most common phenomena in publication mismanagement is the widely publicized change. This is always a mistake, tantamount to a public admission that the magazine has not been changing organically and that changes are being grafted upon it. It tells loyal advertisers and readers that the editors think they were foolish in backing a loser and challenges them to resist rather than rediscover. It forces prospective advertisers and readers to become judges with a wait-and-see attitude (and expectations that are seldom fulfilled). Most important, it destroys a magazine's strongest loyalty-building opportunity—the feeling among readers and advertisers that the new star on the horizon is their own personal discovery and not something somebody else had to point out to them.

Effective change is organic and constant with a relationship between magazine and audience much like the naturally enriching experience of two people in a successful marriage.

Test 6: Is your publication's paid circulation growing at a slower rate than the population of its market area?

New magazines grow considerably faster than established publications, but a hot book will never slow down to a growth slower than the U.S. population's (if it is a national magazine) or the population of its distribution area (if it is regional).

If the population rises at a percentage rate greater than that of the magazine's circulation growth, one of two things has happened: Either the magazine is targeted to an audience that is static or shrinking or the magazine itself has slipped off target (sometimes because the editors' aim has shifted without purpose; more often because the market has moved and the editors have failed to adjust their sights).

What about magazines which have recently made substantial cuts in their circulation guarantees? A cutback may be part of a publisher's strategy to warm up a cold book, but you can be certain that the publication has

not become a hot medium until its circulation resumes an upward curve and sustains it.

This test, of course, cannot be used for free-circulation publications.

Test 7: Are there wild fluctuations in single-copy sales?

If the flame is constantly flickering, the magazine's fire is not only cooling down but the publisher is probably poking the embers in desperate efforts to get it burning again. A hot book burns with a steady flame. Its single-copy circulation will run at a constant and growing number (with seasonal adjustments). Wide variances from issue to issue indicate that the editors are reaching for readers via cover subjects, headlines or sensationalism—pulling in suckers, not readers.

Single-copy sales are a dangerous measure of success. For most magazines a sudden spurt in newsstand sales means that some editorial offering interests a large number of people outside the magazine's core audience. This is great when the feature is of equal interest to the publication's basic readers, but very dangerous when it is a departure from the magazine's usual appeal; and disastrous if this, in turn, motivates the editors to edit for the accidental rather than the essential reader.

Furthermore, single copies can be sold by cover lines and pictures, leaving buyers disappointed after purchase, frequently turning them off forever. Cover subjects, headlines and sensationalism can contribute to the making of a hot publication, but only if the target market *is* composed of suckers and the technique is used with consistent brazenness.

The single-copy test must be used differently for different magazines. *Woman's Day* and *Family Circle* depend 100 percent on this type of circulation whereas single-copy sales mean little to *National Geographic* or *Smithsonian*. But wherever single-copy sales account for 5 percent or more of total circulation, they are a valid gauge to be used in conjunction with other tests of publishing health.

These last three tests indicate more than the fact that a magazine is starting to cool down; they are often signs of serious trouble.

Test 8: Is your advertising sales staff spending a lot of time in pursuit of advertising unrelated to the editorial?

This type of publishing schizophrenia occurs when management loses sight of what the magazine is all about and communication dies between the editorial staff and the advertising sales force. A magazine works efficiently as an advertising medium only so far as it simultaneously serves the reader's editorial and advertising needs. The ads are most effective when they are directed to the same zone of interest as the editorial. They can still work, though not as efficiently, when they are tangential to the editorial interest. They are even less effective when they must depend on triggering different but genuine zones of interest in the same reader.

What motivates a publisher or ad director to send the sales staff in pursuit of "foreign matter"? The publisher has misjudged the advertising income that can be expected from the magazine's proper advertising market, the sales department doesn't understand the magazine's purpose and audience or the sales staff is trying to hide its incompetence in exploiting the proper market by running off in new directions. Finally there is the greedy publisher whose magazine has reached the top of its market. Many a good magazine and a few great ones lost their footing at the top of their class precisely because they were not satisfied with what they had and began to overreach.

Test 9: Does the publication have a high percentage of subscriptions sold at less than full price and/or made up of arrears and extensions?

This is another very old method of testing a magazine's health. But it still works. A hot publication does not need to offer bargains in circulation. If the subscription list is inflated by arrears or extensions, you can be sure the advertiser does not receive the same guarantee of readership quality that he or she gets without giveaways.

A similar test can be used as a stand-in for the above for controlled-circulation publications: "Is the magazine selling a high percentage of its advertising space off rate card?" Here again the need to cut prices is a sign of weakness—even though it is done to meet the competition. A hot book does not have to stoop to selling on its knees.

Test 10: Is there a high percentage of the publication's subscribers who have read nothing in the latest issue a week after they have received it (two days after, for weeklies)?

This is a difficult test to use with precision without incurring major expense. But the regular practice of asking friends and acquaintances or using a limited telephone survey can alert you to trouble. The readers of a hot book cannot wait to get their hands on the magazine. They require an exceptionally important reason for setting it aside.

If most of your readers are not in a hurry to read your magazine, something is wrong. Editorial excitement is dying, if not dead. The greater a publication's frequency, the shorter the permissible gap between delivery and first reading. A weekly is in real trouble if most readers fail to look at it within a couple of days, while the majority of a "hot" daily's readers will open the paper within minutes of the time they get their hands on it.

How to measure readership in depth without going bankrupt

By Jeanine Katzel and Leo Spector

What makes a good readership study?

The ingredients are easy to specify. Most editors of magazines that have been involved in readership surveys or profiles would very likely agree that, to be truly meaningful, measurement of reader reaction should:

- Query a representative sample of readers
- Survey the sample directly
- Ask simple, unambiguous questions
- Elicit candid, impartial responses
- Cover specific key points as well as provide perspective on the total product
- Permit easy scoring and uniform interpretation of results
- And, most of all, be relatively low in cost.

The ideal readership study would have all of these attributes. But, of course, what is ideal often is not what is realistic. In an attempt to find a method for keeping a finger on the reader's pulse, *Plant Engineering* magazine searched for a way to determine reader interest that would come as close to the ideal as possible.

The result is the Editorial Quality Audit (EQA). It is an approach that combines the economy of direct mail with the in-depth probing features of an interview. It is simple in concept and low in cost. The program—which is handled entirely by members of the *Plant Engineering* staff—has two major objectives: To measure the readership of all feature articles and to monitor editorial performance. First developed and tested in 1967, the EQA program was fully operational by 1969. Although some refinements have been made in the original plan, the basic concept and operation of the program have remained intact.

Understanding of the purpose of the EQA program may be helped by some background about *Plant Engineering*'s staff organization. Eight senior editors are responsible for developing articles in specific subject areas, operat-

493

ing as independent agents to obtain and prepare feature material. One reason for establishing EQA was to find out how well they are accomplishing this task. Because the program also is intended to uncover what the reader thinks of the magazine, we knew at the outset that two criteria were essential to make the program work—impartial, candid and conscientious panels of quality auditors and an article rating sheet precisely prepared to elicit useful and unambiguous responses.

The nucleus of EQA is the reader panel. *Plant Engineering*, which is published every other week, uses nine panels of 25 readers each, for a total of 225 members. In 1975, the panels rated nearly 300 feature articles.

When it was initiated in 1969, the program had 96 members—six panels of 16 members each. They rated 144 articles, almost half the feature material in the magazine that year. Major changes have come in the refinement of the questionnaire and in the size of the panels. The 25-person panel size was established as the result of a pilot study conducted in 1970. Analysis of the ratings showed that among panels ranging from 10 to 60 members there was close correlation between those of 15 members and larger. Overall article ratings of the 15-member teams were within a few percentage points af the larger panels. The size was set at 25 to assure at least 15 usable returns for scoring purposes.

The auditors, as they are called, are required to make specific judgments on each article in terms of nine qualitative characteristics. The characteristics, carefully developed, are designed to pinpoint the most important attributes of a feature article. In preparing the form, the magazine tried to avoid journalistic jargon and to relate the wording to the readers' experience—clearly, simply and with no room for misinterpretation.

To each question on an Editorial Quality Audit Rating Form the auditor answers "deficient," "fair," "good" or "excellent." Each choice is assigned a numerical value— 1, 2, 3 or 4 points, respectively. For example, Characteristic 3 asks the auditor if the "text is organized in logical sequence." If the auditor judges that point as "good," the article receives three points. Each attribute is considered in similar fashion.

The auditor rates nine individual characteristics. Because the last one—which asks how useful is the article—is considered critical, it is double-weighted. In essence, then, the score of one article is composed of 10 elements. Each auditor reviews approximately six articles per quarter, or about half the contents of an average issue.

Auditors are selected from a random sampling of the *Plant Engineering* circulation list. Initially, panels were built from lists of readers requesting tear sheets, reprints, etc. However, that source frequently supplied names of persons who were not direct recipients of *Plant Engineering*, since the magazine has a strong pass-along readership. Because the circulation list offers a more representative selection of potential auditors, it is used instead. A preliminary mailing invites a random sample of readers to participate. Each person receives a letter of invitation and an acceptance form. To let the prospective auditor know what is involved, *Plant Engineering* also sends along several articles so that the recipient can perform an actual audit before accepting.

Those who wish to participate are queried further. They are asked for detailed information about themselves and their work. On the basis of these data—type of product manufactured, plant size, experience in plant engineering and age—panels are formulated and balanced to assure as representative a cross-section as possible. Although all auditors perform plant engineering functions, the panel members are not limited to those bearing the title "plant engineer."

At this point, the success of the program lies in the hands of *Plant Engineering*'s ready-made group of critics. But the work isn't all theirs. As the forms come in, those from the same panel are bundled together to await tabulation of the vote. The first 15 fully completed forms to arrive are used to compute the final score. A perfect mark by one auditor would be 40 points, derived from "excellent" ratings that carry a weight of four points each on the first eight characteristics and the double weight of eight points on Characteristic 9. If an auditor fails to score a characteristic, for whatever reason, it is automatically scored. "2." Such a ground rule is necessary to provide uniformity of scoring.

The scoring process is routine. Results are carefully tabulated, checked by a second person and then checked and approved by the editor or managing editor. A percentage score is determined for each category and then for the article overall. The final result: A good indication of how the article was regarded by readers.

Because EQA is used as a barometer of article readership and editorial performance, the ratings of each article undergo thorough evaluation. Guidelines have been established for interpreting the scores: Below 65 percent = poor; 65 to 75 = fair; 75 to 85 = good; 85 and above = excellent. No article has achieved a perfect score. None is expected to.

The scoring scale is designed to be tough. When auditors accept an assignment, they are urged to be brutally frank in the evaluation. They usually are. Less than half a dozen articles a year attain a rating of 85 or better. Editors who author or edit an article that reaches this coveted height are awarded a plaque and a check. Articles that score under 65 are given special attention to learn why they bombed and articles over 85 are also studied with extra care to see why they did well.

Each quarter, the "marks" of every editor are gathered and a sort of "report card" is issued. The editor receives the file of rating sheets on each of his or her articles to study. Through the results the editor learns how well or poorly the article performed and, more importantly, why. The aim of the compilation is to help the staff analyze and understand the work it does, thus providing a solid base for improvement.

One trend revealed by EQA is that subjects of limited interest routinely score lower than articles with broader scope. As an example, the use of product case histories as feature stories was eliminated after they consistently scored low in EQA. Composite scores of all editors are averaged each quarter, giving an overall picture of total editorial performance and serving as a tool for monitoring trends.

It is understood that editors, like everyone else, do not like to be rated. However, because the EQA program is believed to be objective and fair, *Plant Engineering* uses it as a measure of performance. It is part of an overall rating procedure and is one factor considered in salary reviews and performance analysis. It is necessary to emphasize, however, the EQA is only one of a number of criteria used to judge editorial progress.

The goal, of course, is to produce a better product—to let the *Plant Engineering* staff know what its readers want, what they think of what they are getting and what kind of job the editorial staff is doing. From the picture sketched by the ratings, editorial planning and performance can be more effectively monitored—and directed.

One of the most startling advantages of the EQA program is that it has no apparent disadvantages. Among its many benefits are the concrete comments it supplies. The form offers three opportunities for the auditor to supply more than numerical ratings. Characteristic 5 on the rating sheet, which concerns article length, asks the auditor to indicate whether the article should have been longer or shorter. The all-important Characteristic 9, "The article is useful to me in the performance of my plant engineering duties and responsibilities," directs the auditor to go one step further. If the auditor rated the article fair or poor on this point, he or she is asked to explain the reason for this disfavor by indicating (a) if the article is outside the auditor's job responsibility; (b) if he or she has no present problems on this subject; (c) if it is not pertinent to the auditor's plant situation; or (d) if it is just a poor article. Finally, the auditor is encouraged to comment on any aspects of the article not covered in the rating.

Comments are received frequently. Some are long, some short, some complimentary, some critical. Coupled with the numerical rating, the written comments provide our editors with a further amplification of the auditor's rating.

Once the initial orientation is complete, the program operates in simple fashion. Each year, auditors are given the option to renew their participation or withdraw from the program. Those who leave are replaced with new members, solicited and oriented in the same way. No payment is offered. The appeal at the outset is "help us do a better job for you." However, each year small gifts are sent. In the past, the tokens have included sets of attractive framed prints and books of universal interest. In addition to the variable costs of the gifts, expenses average approximately $200 an issue for postage, paper and personnel time. This amount represents the rating of about 11 feature articles; *Plant Engineering* publishes some 290 articles a year in 26 issues. Tabulation of the final score takes about a half hour an article.

Some unexpected benefits have been reaped from the program. It has provided a base for experimentation by the editorial staff. If an editor suggests a new approach to an article or a new kind of article entirely, he or she can try it out on a panel and see what kind of reaction it receives. The editors are afforded some degree of flexibility by having a ready-made testing ground for new ideas and an objective means for settling differences of opinion. As a specific example, a reader panel was used to prejudge a new department, "FeatureFacts." Sent to an EQA panel before it was ever seen in print, this section had a successful tryout before taking its place in the magazine.

Overall, the EQA program functions as an excellent educational tool. The magazine has undergone no dramatic facelift as a result of the program, but a general upgrading of staff performance has been noticed. Everyone is more conscious of the elements that contribute to article readership. Those editors scoring low in the program do try harder, proving the motivational effect of EQA.

The editors strive to fulfill the criteria of the rating sheet. And since the characteristics of the form have been refined until they capture the essence of a good article for *Plant Engineering*, this effort can never be bad.

Although not a panacea for eliminating the problems of measuring reader interest, EQA does offer numerous distinct advantages. It works for *Plant Engineering* and the easily adaptable system can be custom fit to the needs of almost any magazine.

Regionalizing your editorial

By John Fry

Can a national consumer magazine intensify reader loyalty, improve subscription renewals, and increase newsstand sales by regionalizing its editorial content?

Is regionalization the way to combat growing competition for readers' time and money from city, state, and regional magazines?

And is it a way to give a special imprimatur to your magazine that makes it unique and editorially visible to advertisers?

The answer to all of these questions is a qualified 'yes.' Qualified, because not all special interest magazines, which account for most of consumer magazine publishing, have an editorial content that can be geographically sub-divided. But many do. And then it becomes exciting for the editors to explore vistas of split run covers, special sections, and other printing and binding variations that enable a magazine to carry an increased amount of information relevant to where readers live.

Most publishers, of course, are familiar with regionalization for the simple reason that they've been offering regional editions and Zip Code breakdowns to advertisers for years. Frequently, space imbalances between regions have resulted in magazines filling a split run unit of space with remnant ads or public service advertising. Occasionally, the filling is done with inexpensively developed regional editorial, such as a local calendar of events. Such regional fillers have even marked the beginning—the first tentative steps—toward editorial material geographically focused.

For many publishers, however, the beginning of editorial regionalization has started with reader research. A questionnaire is mailed to subscribers. Typically, it contains an open-ended query: "What more would you like to see featured in the pages of our magazine?"

Invariably, the most frequent response to this question is: "Tell me more about what's going on in my region."

At this point, the publisher or editor has grabbed a tiger by the tail. The reader clearly has communicated that he would like something of a regional nature in his magazine that you're not providing. And clearly, the cost of supplying the editorial service he wants won't come cheaply.

Nevertheless, as pressure grows to increase cover prices and subscription rates, a publisher must think of improving editorial service to the reader.

The best kind of price increase is one accompanied by an evident effort by the publisher to give the reader more for his money. The improvement can take a variety of forms: more four-color, more editorial pages, better paper stock, or a better package such as a heavier-weight, varnished cover.

One of the most visible and substantial ways to improve the product for the reader is to fine-tune part of the editorial to regional interests. And it need not involve expensive costs of additional pages and paper with concomitant increases in postage and distribution.

Two key elements in deciding whether your magazine is a logical medium for regional editorial are research and editorial intuition. These case histories from my own experience may be helpful.

Outdoor Life

A national magazine for hunters and fishermen, *Outdoor Life* has a circulation of 1.7 million.

Important to the magazine's readers is knowing about good hunting and fishing areas that are within reasonable driving distance of where readers live—accessible at least for weekends and economical vacations. Such places number in the thousands.

In 1968, *Outdoor Life* began running a four-page section in five regions of the country. Produced on inexpensive uncoated paper (colored yellow, it came to be known as "the yellow pages"), each separately produced section told readers in the Midwest, Northeast, South, West and Pacific coast about promising places to camp, fish and hunt in their area. The reader in California could find information about trout fishing in the Sierra, whereas the subscriber in Massachusetts could read about the outlook for striped bass fishing on Cape Cod. The success of the yellow pages led to an expansion of the section to eight pages.

The effectiveness of *Outdoor Life*'s regional sections is not precisely measurable. No regional program ever will be. But during this period, the magazine has maintained a wide leadership in newsstand sales and a healthy subscription renewal rate. In 1977, *Field & Stream*—*Outdoor Life*'s principal competitor—started an eight-page regional section in several issues. *Sports Afield*, another competitor, elected not to go regional in its editorial, but reduced circulation from over a million to a level of 500,000.

Research by *Outdoor Life* in the mid-1970s quantified what the editors well knew: Most readers define their interests and outdoor activities by the species of fish and wildlife they pursue. Whitetail deer hunted in the East and Midwest do not exist in the West. Southern quail do not prevail in New England. The quail hunter of Georgia may be a woodcock man in Vermont. Salt water fishing information holds little interest for the landlocked fresh water angler in Michigan. And so on.

Against this background, *Outdoor Life* a year ago created a new form of regional features. Using the central 32-page, offset-printed feature well form, regionally slanted articles have been created in two-and four-page self-contained building blocks. They are designed to split run. Thus a four-page Southern largemouth bass fishing story may be printed for Southern readers, where the same four pages are used for a Northern pike story in the Midwest and Northeast, and a four-page Pacific salmon feature in the West.

Outdoor Life creates separate covers that feature the unique editorial regional content of each issue. Cover blurb copy changes in each region. Occasionally, the cover illustration will be different. The November 1980 cover used five separate visuals, each focusing on an animal unique to the region.

It is too early to say how successful the new regional feature program has been. Advertisers have been sold heavily on the uniqueness of the editorial strategy.

Ski Magazine

Experience and intuition of the editors, as much as research, turned the editors of *Ski Magazine* toward regionals.

Ski, with a circulation of 410,000, is the oldest publication in its field. The magazine's three main areas of editorial coverage are advice on selection and purchase of downhill ski gear, techniques of skiing, and where to ski.

Most special interest magazines find no marked regional difference regarding information on technique (skill) and equipment (nationally distributed products). (There are exceptions, of course—boats immediately come to mind.) But if information about where to participate in a special interest activity is important to readers, regional information can come into play.

Both *Ski* and *Skiing* (Ziff Davis) magazines have carried regional forms for many years, largely to meet the advertising requirements of medium and smaller-size ski areas that had neither the need nor the budgets to reach skiers on a national basis. Filling the columns around these ads were short, regionally slanted feature articles, executed without any larger editorial plan.

After *Ski*'s acquisition by Times Mirror in 1973, the new management sought editorial improvements that would distinctly benefit readers. One that the editors could instantly agree on was a special where-to-ski regional section.

There are approximately 900 lift-served ski areas in the United States and Canada. But of these, less than 20 can be classified as national vacation destination resorts—that is, resorts like Aspen, Vail and Sun Valley whose trails and vacation amenities are of interest to skiers from Maine to California. The vast remaining number of ski areas generally are reached by skiers in their own cars, usually for a six-day ski week or a weekend or day. *Ski*'s editors know that while Catamount Ski Area in the Berkshires is of interest to a New York City subscriber, it is of almost no interest to a skier in California. Similarly, June Mountain in California holds little interest for the Eastern skier.

The editors of *Ski* divided North America into three regions—East, Midwest and West—and created an eight-page, putty stock section for each region. For every issue in which the special regional report appears, the editors effectively produce 24 pages of material.

Each regional section contains up to a dozen "capsule" reports on medium- and small-size ski areas. The reports are written by freelance and staff writers who ski at each resort and report their impressions along with basic information about the facilities. The reports are invaluable to skiers scouting for new places to ski.

In addition, the regional sections usually have a "handy facts" wraparound that covers basic skier information ranging from listings of ski nurseries for children to illuminated night skiing.

Cover tip-ons, tied to the regional section inside, contribute to the improvement of *Ski*'s newsstand sales in months when the regional sections are published. As an example, the 52,000-copy newsstand sale of the February 1974 pre-regional issue grew to 101,000 copies with the regionalized February issue of 1979, while total circulation of *Ski* remained the same at 400,000.

"This increase of newsstand to 25 percent of total circulation in February, once a soft month for single-copy sales, would not have been possible without the pulling power of the regionals," says Dick Needham, editor.

The cost

There are as many ways to look at the cost of regional publishing as there are editorial formulas for doing it. For convenience, though, let's assume the following situation.

A publisher wishes to add a valuable new editorial feature to his magazine, possibly in conjunction with a price increase to subscribers and single-copy buyers. A side-benefit will be to improve the advertising competitiveness of the magazine by giving salespeople an important new ingredient to talk about in presentations.

We'll assume that the editorial improvement involves adding eight pages to each issue. For a magazine with a distribution or print order of 500,000, the cost, including editorial expense, for eight black and white pages might be $16,000 per issue, or $2,000 per page. For a monthly, the 96 additional pages per year would come to $192,000.

Although the addition of eight pages of new national feature or department material looks attractive, the introduction of a regional flavor to the magazine may look even more exciting to the publisher and the editors. What would it cost?

The mere allocation of eight pages to regional coverage—say, four departments of two pages each on a geographical section of the country—probably would cost little more than devoting the same space to nationally oriented articles. But then the effect on the reader is rather minimal.

What about devoting all eight pages to one region, then doing the same for the others? After all it takes no additional paper and only a small increment in printing and bindery charges to do it. And readers in any one region could then get eight full pages of information on their region that didn't exist in the magazine previously.

The major additional costs in implementing full regional sections or splits lie in editorial art, photo and, to a lesser degree, additional composition and makeup charges. To compare costs with normal magazine publishing procedures, consider your first eight pages of regional as basic. Each additional region is extra. Thus, a magazine offering four regional sections of eight pages each must prepare 24 additional pages of editorial material per issue.

In the accompanying chart, I have shown the cost of doing four regionals at $28,000 per issue, including all editorial and composition charges. This is $12,000 more than publishing "normal" nationally run pages. But also note that the cost of producing these individually tailored pages for readers in each region is only $875 per page, because the total cost is now spread over 32 pages.

The uniqueness of offering a special regional section may justify a decision *not* to add editorial pages (hence no additional paper and printing costs), but rather to substitute the regional for some other less valued part of your magazine. In this case, the additional cost, as noted above, would be about $12,000 per issue for a half-million distribution magazine, or $144,000 per year compared with $192,000 for adding eight pages to each issue. The costs I've cited here would also take into account copy changes on the cover to reflect the regional coverage.

While the costs look substantial, they seem less so

when comparing the alternative consequences of, say, a $2-a-year subscription price increase without editorial improvement. If the introduction of the regional editorial heads off any significant decline in newsstand sales, subscription renewal or cold mail response to new subscription offers, then the additional cost will turn out to be a fraction of the additional revenue realized.

Organizing editorially

Regional programs of the kind described above require almost all of the time of a staff editor at the home publishing base and a clear line of direction to regional field editors and stringers.

The entire effort can be directed centrally from the home editorial office, but a better solution is to retain a field editor in each region. After all, if the purpose of a regional editorial program is to bring your magazine closer to readers where they live, it makes sense to draw on the knowhow of editors who live in the geographic areas involved. They, in turn, know the stringers or correspondents who can deliver the best information to you.

Just as your national editorial content is planned a year ahead, so should the regional plan. Think of the regional section as a magazine within a magazine. Field editors should be subject to disciplined planning and should submit timely, clear outlines of content month by month.

Make sure everyone is aware of the number of readers in each state so that content remains relevant to the largest possible number of paying subscribers and single-copy buyers. I have found it useful to send ABC statements to field editors showing the magazine's state-by-state circulation in their regions.

Budget from the grass roots up. Figure on the payments to be made to local stringers, plus the amount you will need to pay the field editor both for his own reporting and the organization and direction of stringers. Allocate salary for the staff person responsible for pulling the sections together. And finally, budget for multiple pages of photography, artwork and maps.

Promoting regional

It is possible to do "blind" regionals—regional material run in such a way that the reader is unaware he is getting anything but his regular magazine which happens to devote space generously to news of his region. But, as a general rule, you should promote the special regional to the reader, indicating with headlines and blurbs that it is a bonus or special reading dividend.

Emphasize state or city names in headlining regional material. People tend not to think of themselves as Northeasterners or Westerners, but rather as being from Massachusetts or Oregon. Tests of the newsstand effectiveness of regional cover tip-ons have tended to confirm that single-copy sales are definitely helped by the inclusion of state names in headlines and blurb copy.

Covers: The possibilities are endless. You don't even have to publish special regional material inside the magazine in order to capitalize on the regionality of certain features inside. In fact, you don't even have to change the cover illustration in order to promote. If the cover can be designed so that type changes are limited to the black plate only, the cost is small and the dividends on the newsstands can be considerable.

Nevertheless, promoting regional on covers may pall eventually if, in fact, the editors are not really delivering anything of substance on the inside pages. On the other hand, if you have it, flaunt it.

The competition

Recent years have seen a further proliferation of regional magazines—not only city and state magazines with general coverage, but also special interest magazines covering regional aspects of recreation, sports and shelter. Such magazines represent competition to nationally distributed special interest magazines despite the fact that many are poorly edited and designed by comparison. They attract reader time and dollars as well as advertiser budgets.

One obvious way to counter this competition is to feature regional content in part of the national magazine. One problem, however, is that editorial regionalization of the magazine often does not mesh neatly with advertisers' ideas of the regional markets in which they want advertising to run. When they can be made to mesh, though, the regionally slanted advertising and editorial can run together. The editorial becomes an ideal environment to attract advertisers aiming at a particular region.

To regionalize or not?

While research may indicate reader interest in regional subject matter, such research is not necessarily a mandate to produce it. In the final analysis, editorial judgment must determine whether the reader will be valuably served.

If such a determination is made, however, regional content has benefits that inevitably will improve a magazine's circulation strength and demonstrate its editorial vitality to advertisers.

The cost of regionalizing
(Cost comparison for a single issue, 500,000 copies distributed)

8 pages national feature coverage		8 pages covering 4 regions (2 pages per region)			8 pages each for 4 regions		
Paper, printing distribution (PPD) & editorial cost	Cost per page	PPD & edit cost	Cost per page	Cost per region	PPD & edit plus add'l. composition & editorial	Cost per page (32 pages)	Cost per region
$16,000	$2,000	$16,000	$2,000	$4,000	$28,000	$875	$7,000

In praise of criticism

By Bernard Weiss

"If you are not fired *by* enthusiasm, you will be fired *with* enthusiasm."

This grave admonition—on a red and white wall poster—greets everyone who walks into the office of an ex-magazine editor who is now president of his own small publishing company. He deeply believes that nothing worthwhile is ever achieved without a substantial measure of enthusiasm. He therefore surrounds himself with bright, cheerful, energetic, ambitious—and enthusiastic—employees.

Recently, however, he had a jarring experience. He regarded as a personal insult the sudden resignation of one of his top people, an exciting and talented young art director in whom he took great professional pride. "I can't be what you want," she told him on the day she made her good-bye rounds. "I'm only human. I can't *always* be enthusiastic about my job, this magazine, or your company."

The poster is still there; the president's attitude hasn't changed; the world continues to turn and the art director has been replaced. But, in reflecting upon that experience recently with me, the publisher searched for explanations and realized that he had a few things to learn about management:

Editors and art directors, like the rest of us, are human beings. They are not always excited by or enthusiastic about their work. Sometimes the work is dull. Sometimes they make mistakes. Failure and bad judgment are not uncommon in a creative environment. Perfection, after all, is merely a goal—rarely an achievement. It is the process of becoming.

Living with imperfection

Perfection in a creative job is particularly difficult to achieve—and to assess—because it is so difficult to define and identify. A good example is playwright Neil Simon, who has been spectacularly successful in the theater and films. Simon readily admits that he can—and would, if possible—rewrite most of his award-winning scripts because they are far from perfect. "As successful as *Murder by Death* was," he admits, "I could have rewritten 35 percent of it and made it better." When he rehearses a new play, Simon rewrites many of his scenes almost nightly, and must fight the temptation to continue rewriting scenes after the play opens.

Therefore, when an editorial manager reviews creative performance in order to offer criticism or constructive suggestions for improvement, he or she should consider these questions:

• Is the individual already doing his or her best?

• Does he or she have the capacity to change (improve)?

• Is he or she *likely* to change, with my help, based on what I can offer?

• Can I be satisfied with less than optimum performance?

• Is it possible, by realigning responsibilities or changing assignments, to take advantage of an individuals's strengths and minimize the deficiencies, thus maximizing the opportunities for a successful result?

The fact is, if people are already doing their best under your direction, then nothing you say or do as their manager is likely to make any difference in their performance. Experienced executives and supervisors know that constructive criticism works only when a subordinate has both the capacity and the desire to do better. And even then, it only works sometimes. (See accompanying chart.)

Let's assume here that you are that senior editorial executive, and that your staff has both the capacity and desire to do better.

How to offer helpful criticism

Of course we all know the familiar "rules" for criticism:

• Be sure you have your facts straight.

• Don't be critical when angry; emotional agitation may prompt you to exaggerate the problem, or lead you to say something irrational or not wholly true.

• Offer criticism privately, quietly, professionally.

• Be specific.

• Avoid multiple criticisms; tackle just one thing at a time, on a priority basis.

Most of these rules, which can be applied in most business situations, also have valid application in a creative office where individual sensitivities and fragile egos are put on the line, with every performance. It is in the creative environment, where the delicacy of human relations is the basis for nearly all good productive effort, that great care should be taken when criticizing job performance. In other words, the manner in which criticism is offered is just as important as the actual substance of the critical conversation.

The astute publishing executive is therefore keenly aware of how his critical remarks to creative staff are prepared, transmitted and received. Here are some suggestions, based on my personal experience and the trials and tribulations of my associates, colleagues and clients:

Don't hint of criticism, then fail to follow through. This technique can only heighten anxiety levels that already exist when a fresh creative effort is being evaluated.

One editor of my acquaintance often violates this principle. He will dash down the corridor, bump into someone on his staff and call back as he hurries away, "Joan, I got your manuscript. I don't like the lead. We'll talk about it later, okay?" Joan, of course, is left standing in the corridor, frustrated and anxious.

Alternative: "Joan, I have your manuscript. I'm busy now, but I'll read it this afternoon or this evening. Can we meet tomorrow morning first thing?" At least Joan will be able to sleep tonight.

Be aware of your biases; do not let them interfere with sound judgment. All of us have biases and prejudices. Some of us dislike fat writers, sans-serif type or bearded photographers. Biases are normal cultural phenomena. We can't avoid them, but we can accept them and work around them.

For years I was hung up on dirty hands—particularly, dirty fingernails. Every time I sat down with my art director over a display of boards or sketches, all I could see was the accumulated grime of charcoal, rubber cement and cigarette stains on his fingers—and especially the caked paint under his nails. I was able to deal with this, however, by using the first 10 minutes of every art conference for idle chatter. This enabled me to come to grips with the subject matter—to force my eyes to look at the sketches, not the art director's fingernails. Eventually I learned to judge the art director's work (at which he was a success), not his ability to wash his hands (at which he was a failure).

Criticize the work—the result of a performance—rather than the individual. Concentrate on the actual result. A critical remark directed at the individual ("You don't like white space, do you?") is likely to be perceived as a personal attack, without regard to the product of creative effort. A critical remark directed at the product of that effort ("It looks kind of tight. How about some more white space . . . here. . . or here?") is more likely to be perceived as being based on a sincere attempt to seek improvement.

Suggestion: When reviewing a manuscript or layout, sit down with the writer or artist and put the papers or sketches on the table between you. As you converse, direct your speech and focus your eyes upon the physical creative product. This minimizes any tendency to wander into the minefield of personal criticism.

Avoid the word "you." When "you" creeps into a conversation in which someone's performance is being evaluated, your remarks are likely to be interpreted as personal criticism, which can be destructive to the creative effort. Keep your remarks impersonal, non-threatening.

Suggestion: Try substituting the impersonal, passive voice grammatical form. Instead of, "*You* missed the point in this paragraph," try, "The point in this paragraph was overlooked." Instead of, "*You* didn't finish the photo captions," say, "The photo captions are incomplete."

Share responsibility. Usually the failure of an assignment can, at least in part, be attributed to the immediate supervisor. Some common examples of supervisory culpability include: Not enough time allowed to complete the assignment; not enough direction given to avoid wasted effort; assigning too great a challenge for the individual at this particular point in his or her career. Whatever the reason for failure, an editorial manager can usually assume at least a part of the responsibility.

The mature manager should acknowledge responsibility and, moreover, communicate the shared responsibility with the subordinate. Use of the word "we" is helpful in this regard. When you acknowledge joint responsibility, the relief of writers or illustrators is usually visible, if not audible, because now they know they can count on your help in rectifying the error. They have the assurance of knowing that the project is a team effort—not an individual burden and that you are available for more guidance, if not assistance.

Suggestion: Instead of saying merely, "The point in this paragraph was overlooked," why not add, "Let's see if there's some way we can work it in." Instead of simply, "This article is six days past deadline," try, "Let's see if we can adjust the schedule. If you get started on the rewrite immediately, I'll try to work out something with the production department."

Start with the negatives, end with the positives. Everyone who leaves your office should do so with the feeling that although there may be problems, there is a way of dealing with them. The immediate future should be regarded with optimism, not despair. I usually recommend that editors follow up their negative or critical remarks with supportive statements. For example, offer some modest praise for an important aspect of the work—ideally, something about which there was anxiety or doubt in the beginning, but which now appears so well done that it merits special mention.

If there's nothing worthy of praise, you can usually rely on the old standards: "I know it's a tough job, but I've got lots of confidence in you . . . I'll support you and help you every step of the way . . . don't hesitate to interrupt me if you have any questions or run into any problems . . . I want to help you succeed. I know you can do it."

Avoid words like "all," "none," "always," "never"

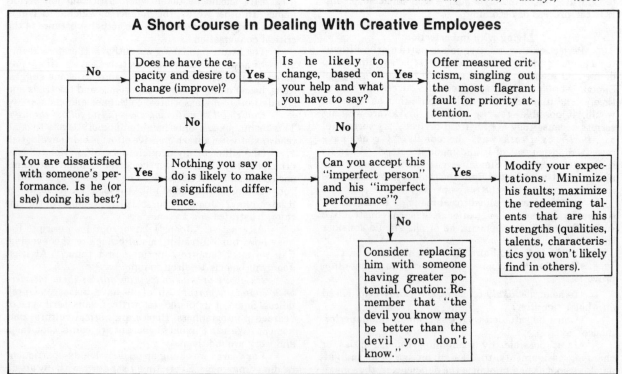

A Short Course In Dealing With Creative Employees

and "*invariably.*" These absolutes are easy for someone to refute. The editor charges, "You're *always* missing the deadline." The writer fires back, "That's a lie—I made the deadline twice last year!" The editor has no defense against such a retort. Or, "These mechanicals are a disgrace; they're *all* so sloppy and dirty." The art director replies, "Well, look, here's a clean one!" Now, what can you say?

Avoid humor. In a conversation where a senior person is being critical of a junior person, humor can upset the delicate equilibrium that is essential to a successful result. Even when the humor is well-intentioned, it may be interpreted as satire, sarcasm, or worse. Sometimes a parting crack or even a good joke can backfire; to the individual being criticized, it may seem like a sign of managerial thoughtlessness or mindlessness. The self-assured executive need not rely upon humor to earn respect.

Several years ago I was at a highly emotional creative conference in which one writer turned to another and, holding up some copy, asked: "Jack, how would you have written this piece?" Jack glanced at the first two paragraphs and quipped, "I would have written this piece under an assumed name." The first writer froze. He has never forgiven Jack.

Outline the objectives; set a deadline. If you have been specific in your criticism, and if you have concentrated on the single most important correctable factor, then you have an obligation to establish a deadline by which you expect to see a positive change, or a positive result. Presumably the individual knows what must be done and, with your help, has developed a plan to remedy the deficiency. Work together to set a deadline. Define precisely what you expect on or before that date. Secure an individual's commitment to a positive change in the very near future, on the very next assignment, or on the revision of the deficient work.

It is my experience that creative people who are personally and professionally committed to achieving mutual objectives work very hard and derive great personal satisfaction upon achieving what might have been earlier regarded as nearly impossible or impractical.

Offer the prospect of long-range growth and career development. You can cushion the blow of almost any negative situation within the context of more positive, longer range plans. This may help to alleviate any career-threatening or talent-negating criticism you may be serving up at the moment. Today may be Black Monday. However, within the perspective of a career, today will be but a fragment of a memory.

This concept is easy to introduce into an otherwise critical conversation. At Scholastic Magazines, for example, writers, editors and other creative staff are offered opportunities to grow professionally and advance their talents by taking field trips into individual classrooms, by attending professional meetings of the Educational Press Association, and by entering the best examples of their work in professional competitions. When writers at Scholastic need to be juiced up after being criticized, they are likely to be reminded of these opportunities for personal growth, improvement and recognition. They may not leave the editor's office walking on air, but at least they know that they are on solid ground with their boss, who has confidence in their ability to do better.

How to offer praise

Like criticism, praise can be a very effective technique for managing and motivating creative personnel—when it is properly employed. Here are some suggestions.

Don't praise everything. Even though everything may be worthy of praise, save it for an unappealing job handled well, or a particularly difficult or challenging task. I know a publisher who has such a reputation for frequent compliments that one of his artists told me, "My head hurts from so much patting."

Don't exaggerate. Praise is like seasoning; a little bit is better than a lot. Competent professionals resent exaggerated or undeserved praise, and you lose their respect.

Offer praise to alleviate anxiety or concern. Be aware of the writer who recently interviewed a particularly difficult personality or the art director who is wrestling with a new design for your annual buyers' guide. They would probably appreciate a kind word at an appropriate moment.

Be specific. Your praise should be as specific as your criticism. Whereas general praise is meaningless, specific praise motivates genuine creative effort and encourages a repeat performance. So, take a moment to credit a writer for incorporating the delightful personal anecdotes and insights into an interview; and compliment the art director on the exciting graphic approach for the annual guide.

Remember that not everyone will accept your criticism or praise graciously. People hunger for an evaluation of their work; but they don't necessarily hunger for a *critical* evaluation. Like most of us, they'd rather have good news than bad.

Your consolation is in knowing that, as the responsible editorial director or publisher, your judgments are based on professional considerations, not personal ones. You can be tough-minded, but fair. Most times your decisions will be right and your batting average will be good. Even the greatest professional baseball players averaged nowhere near .500! Chances are, you are doing better than that right now.

A WISHING GAME

As a technique for motivating creative staff, try playing an informal "game" with your staff. This is particularly valuable during an otherwise tense conversation or meeting that might have started with a critical review of someone's performance, because it offers a change of pace that relieves the tension.

You find yourself discussing a problem with copy, design or mechanicals. Everything you suggest to the writer or illustrator evokes a negative response—or, what's worse, no response at all. The person just sits there and mopes or grits his or her teeth.

Start the game by asking, "What do you wish you could do with this? If you had your druthers, what would you like to do?" Such a question starts the individual thinking in more positive terms, and he is likely to provide one or two possible solutions. Don't make any snap judgments on these suggestions, just note the possibilities.

After the person runs out of ideas, he might then ask *you* the same question: "What do *you* want to do?" This gives you an opportunity to do a bit of creative problem-solving yourself, and you should have an answer ready. Between his suggestions and yours, you should be able to settle on at least one viable idea that seems likely to work.

The editor as a publisher

By J.J. Hanson

What kinds of men or women make good business magazine editors? What turns them on?

One thing, I think, is pride—pride in the ability to turn out a product that thousands of unknown readers look for week after week or month after month. Another thing is money.

After years of observation, I've decided that there are three kinds of editors: Those who make things happen, those who watch things happen and those who wonder what happened.

Most editors would like to think of themselves as belonging in the first category, but for some, this is merely wishful thinking. I'd like to suggest some ways to make this a reality—how to be the kind of editor that makes things happen—for your readers, for your magazine, for your company's profits—and for your own paycheck.

Rethink or reconsider what readers are looking for. If someone asks you what readers look for in your magazine you'd probably say something like, "News and new ideas that will help run a business better." And you'd probably be thinking in terms of editorial material alone.

But I suggest that readers of special interest or business or trade magazines are interested in total magazine Gestalt. They are as interested in the advertising as they are in the editorial.

For some reason, many editors think that readers have to be protected from the advertisers. So, they bunch some of the ads up front and bunch a lot more in back and put all their nice editorial material in the middle. It's almost as if they're saying, "If the reader stumbles onto the advertising, well and good; but it shouldn't get into the way of all the juicy editorial meat I've laid out for the reader."

Which is not very logical. In most magazines advertising pays the freight—including the editors' salaries. Wouldn't it be nice to have a bigger bundle to carve up at the end of the year? Well, why not make the advertising as easy to find as possible? Sprinkle advertising throughout the magazine. Give advertisers a better-than-even chance of being seen. Who knows? Maybe they'll find your magazine so effective that they'll be in it forever.

What about giving some advertisers right-hand page positions opposite editorial openings whenever you can? Editors always seem to want to open their features on spreads or right-hand pages. They tell advertisers that a left-hand page is just as good as a right-hand page but they're saving their right-hand pages for editorial. Who can blame an advertiser for wanting it?

In the final analysis, many advertisers are trying to do the same job you are. They're trying to present new ideas and new values to readers so that they can sell more of their products or services. Aren't new ideas, new methods, new developments and new applications your basic stock in trade? When you consider what the reader wants to be served with, you might come up with some new ways to serve that person.

Don't ignore advertisers when you're looking for good, valid sources of editorial material. Now I'm not advocating selling your soul to the devil ... or to the advertiser; what I *am* advocating is that if you haven't talked to advertisers recently or looked into what they're offering your readers, you might be missing some good editorial bets.

Advertisers are trying to solve specific problems for your readers—the same as you are. Frequently, they have a depth of knowledge that could be very useful to you.

Don't get hung up on this old bugaboo of so-called "editorial integrity"—the ostrich like attitude that says you will be forever tainted if you mention an advertiser by name in an article. Because either you have integrity or you don't. If you're simply worried that it might *appear* that you've "sold out," then you're in the wrong job. Because the only time to mention an advertiser—like the only time to mention anything else—is when it offers useful information for your reader. Don't favor advertisers, but don't discriminate against them, either.

Investigate the possibilities for special issues that offer new values to the reader. Special issues as a device to get more advertising are as old as the hills. But there are many different ways to handle the special issue.

Take, for example, *Handling and Shipping* magazine, published by Industrial Publishing Corp. Each year it publishes a thirteenth issue that isn't circulated to the regular recipient of *Handling and Shipping*. This extra issue is sent to the president of a division or the head of the regular reader's plant. It's a great opportunity for IPC to go back to advertisers it has been selling for years and secure an extra $2,300 from each advertiser, with the valid argument that the advertiser is reaching a different kind of reader in the handling and shipping field. Moreover, it's an opportunity for IPC to attract a different classification of advertising—corporate image advertising—which it may never get in the regular issues of *Handling and Shipping*.

Another kind of special issue is that which creates a body of facts or statistics that your readers can't do without. A prime example here is the Cost of Education Index, developed about 12 years ago by Paul Abramson at *School Management* magazine. *School Management,* like many other magazines, had a couple of king-size problems. Its January issue was always thin because advertisers were not ready to commit to advertising in the first issue of the year. Its August issue was equally slim because many advertisers felt that school people would not be around in

August to read it.

So Abramson conceived of a set of statistics that became the accepted yardstick for measuring educational effort and value in this country—the Cost of Education Index. Today it is universally accepted and used. This editorial idea was so successful that the January issue became *School Management*'s biggest issue of the year.

Abramson then developed the Cost of Building Index for *School Management*'s August issue and it quickly became the second biggest issue of the year.

I would warn against creating special issues that have a questionable editorial value but the potential of attracting a good deal of advertising. If they don't stand much chance of attracting the reader, it won't be long before the advertisers in such special issues perceive this.

An interesting way of publishing a special issue that has limited appeal, without hurting yourself, is to do what *Dun's Review and Modern Industry* (now shortened to *Dun's* magazine) did several years ago. *Dun's* published its regular issue with its regular smorgasbord of articles and columns. Then, as Volume II of this issue, it published a separate magazine that covered a special subject—like plant site location or distribution or air freight. The two volumes, I and II, were wrapped and mailed together. The special interest advertising went into Volume II and the regular advertising went into Volume I. Thus, in one issue, *Dun's* editor succeeded in virtually doubling the amount of advertising it normally carried in that issue.

Turn existing information or information sources into additional revenue sources. Years ago, a gifted marketing professor at the Harvard Business School named Ted Levitt published a brilliant article called "Marketing Myopia." In it he cited the reasons that such giant industries as railroads and motion pictures got into trouble. He said that the railroad industry had always considered itself as being in the railroad business when actually it was in the transportation business. Similarly, the motion picture industry was not really in the business of producing pictures; it was in the entertainment business. Had both of these two giant industries looked at their core business in a broader light, they would not have been so severely damaged by the trucking and aviation industries on the one hand or the advent of television on the other.

As editors, you are not really in the magazine business; you are basically in the information gathering and dissemination business.

If you think about your job that way, many different revenue sources will occur to you. For example, the information you now convert to articles could, in a re-edited form, be produced on tape cassettes. Books could be produced from compilations of editorial material and magazines could be converted into microfilm. Many articles, tables or sets of statistics could become salable audio/visual presentations.

A very interesting and potentially very profitable technique is to produce a newsletter. Suppose an editor conceived a newsletter describing new industrial products and circulated it to the top management of the companies he or she may now be reaching at a lower level with the regular publication. Or, he or she could conceive a series of newsletters—one for each kind of manufacturing company—and, in effect, scoop the individual's own magazine

and its competitors with a newsletter that the editor could sell to a different class of readers for $85 to $100 a year.

Not only could he or she sell it to the readers, the editor could probably sell it to the advertisers. The people who never fail to read each issue of a magazine are the advertisers who want to know what their competitors are doing. That's a whole new group of readers that could be a source of subscription revenue.

Don't get stuck in the rut of doing what you've always been doing, just because it's comfortable. There are two kinds of fools in this world. The first kind thinks that because something's old, it's good. The second kind thinks that because something's new, it's better.

I'd suggest questioning everything you do—your headlining style, graphic design, length of articles, typography, format of the magazine—at least once a year. Whether or not you change, you've at least taken a long, searching look at what you're doing to see if it can't be done better. I'd also suggest that you invite a few readers in on the exercise with you. They might reveal things you'd never guess.

Learn as much as you can about your publishing company. How often do you, as an editor, take the time to learn more about what a publisher does?

Even if you don't want to become a publisher, how well do you know what goes into the job so that you can become a more productive contributor to the profits of the company? Spend a regular amount of time to systematically learn as much as you can about the business you're in.

I'd also suggest that you go to lunch with your circulation manager and your production manager. Sit down and talk with your sales manager, your promotion manager, your business manager—even your space salespeople. Visit your printer. You're a trained interviewer. Use your skills to your own advantage and find out how you can contribute to the solution of the problems your company faces.

Consider developing special interest seminars. Say you're a magazine for the meat processing business. Why not get together with a computer organization and several computer consultants and run seminars in six or 10 or 20 cities around the country? Sell admission at $150 or $300 per person for a one- to three-day meeting. Invite readers to sit in on a discussion of how to handle accounting, personnel records, inventory reports and other areas in a meat packing company through the use of a mini-computer. Or better distribution scheduling. Or how to put some of the newer developments in operations research to work for them.

Develop a trade show service in your field. If your field doesn't already have a show or convention, this is an ideal activity for a magazine to sponsor. It lends prestige to the magazine and gives you an opportunity to learn things about suppliers to the industry, as well as readers, that can be most helpful in running a more service-oriented magazine. Even if a trade show already exists in your industry, you might run an information seminar in conjunction with the show or you could visit the trade show acting as a surrogate for readers who find it impossible to attend. You could tape record highlights of the trade show and either report in the magazine what went on or sell the cassette report to readers as a separate package.

Set up special interest tours for your readers. For several years now, Time Inc. has been running a very successful economic tour for important businesspeople. These businesspeople go abroad for three weeks to meet important heads of state, economic ministers and advisors and their business counterparts in various key capitals all over the world.

The prestige this confers on Time Inc. is immeasurable. And the service that Time Inc. provides to very important readers is also immeasurable. Through its contacts, the magazine is able to line up face-to-face meetings with renowned world leaders that individual businesspeople would be hard-pressed to contact on their own.

What about your industry? Could you arrange a tour of supplier plants in Europe or the Far East for your readers? Or a symposium on selling in South America? And how could you develop this idea so that your company receives not only recognition as a leader but also realizes substantial revenue from the trip?

Also, aside from the fact that it's nice to go on a working junket, imagine how much more you, as an editor, would learn about your industry vis-a-vis the world from a tour like this.

Set up a marketing advisory panel that advertisers could use to test new products or new service ideas. Think what could happen to your magazine in terms of stature and revenue if you set up a marketing panel of typical buyers and buying influences in your industry. You might hire a statistician to structure an adequate sample of the industry you serve and get a goodly number of people across the country to agree in advance that they will re-turn four questionnaires every year on various subjects. You then could market the panel to your advertisers.

You could charge a handsome fee simply because it would cost the advertisers a good deal more if they were to construct the sample themselves and do their own market testing.

Moreover, the results of the surveys could provide you with some valid and valuable editorial information. The rest of your readers would be interested in seeing how their counterparts make buying decisions and what products and services they deem to be valuable.

These are just a handful of ideas. I offer them as thought-starters, hoping I have stimulated you to consider some new approaches on your own.

There's still one area I haven't touched on in terms of making more money for your company—and therefore, yourself. That is cost cutting.

This may make 95 percent of the magazine consultants in this country turn white, but I don't want anybody in my company spending very much time worrying about cutting costs. I want them to spend their time thinking about how to increase revenue. It's much more fun, and it's much more rewarding. You wind up with a better product, and you're happier about it. Going forward is always a better emotional kick than searching through the haystack for cost cutting opportunities.

Get everybody in your organization to think about how to increase sales revenues and profitability and you'll have a much more exciting company to work for. You'll be an editor that makes things happen—for your magazine and for yourself.

The editor as marketer: A heretical but correct approach

By James B. Kobak

The thought of editors getting involved in marketing may seem like heresy to some. I hope, however, that those who rebel at first thought can keep their minds open enough to run through the list of "Editorial Truths." There probably are not many you disagree with.

A look at the list of "Editorial Why Don't We's" after that probably will not seem so outlandish, either. I hope, too, that a reading of these lists will spark additions to both.

42 Editorial Truths

1. A magazine is not a sacred literary event. Even if it were, it would be nice to have as many people as possible experience that event.

2. A magazine is a consumer product with a very short shelf life—and should be marketed as one.

3. Editorial integrity is important. Too often it is mouthed to avoid doing things editors don't like to do.

4. A magazine is a single product whose success is the result of the efforts of those who specialize in editorial, advertising, circulation, production and management—and sometimes in sub-areas of these.

5. The worst thing that can happen to a magazine is

over-departmentalization—each person doing his or her thing without regard to the overall.

6. Editors are the most iconoclastic of those on a magazine. There are a number of reasons for this—they don't want to be interfered with, most are not extroverts, they have no desire to know how the other operations work and they want to retain a mystique about the creative process.

7. Editorial content does more than anything else to sell magazines. Editors are in the marketing business whether they like it or not.

8. Many editors seem to go out of their way to make it hard for readers to read their products. Often it is hard for a reader to know what is in a magazine—or even what it is all about.

9. Many magazines have lots of pages of gray matter—solid blocks of long paragraphs in what seems to be set in 6 point type.

10. Reading is hard work for most of us. We are busy and have all kinds of competing interests.

11. The most important page in a magazine is the cover. Here you can make a reader—or turn a reader off.

12. The cover has several functions: (a) Identify the magazine, (b) identify the issue, (c) exemplify the overall content, (d) attract attention, (e) lure the reader inside and (f) be pleasing. If too much emphasis is placed on any one function of a cover, it is probably a failure.

13. The newsstand is an excellent place for reviewing covers. Differences in effectiveness are very apparent.

14. Covers are obviously important for newsstand magazines. They are also important for subscription or controlled-circulation magazines.

15. The contents page is used by many readers to find what is in the magazine. It can act as a further lure to the inside of a magazine.

16. People will not automatically read an article. They must be invited, enticed and often tricked into it.

17. A good picture is worth a thousand words. A bad one is negative.

18. Some art directors seem to inhibit the reader's interest rather than enhance it. Artwork is useful only if it helps reading and understanding, not for its own sake.

19. Beautiful effects can be achieved in black-and-white.

20. Type, without illustrations, can often be used to create handsome readable pages.

21. Editors' opinions are sometimes of interest to readers, but not all the time on every subject.

22. Readers' impressions of a magazine are important. A handful of letters is not sufficient to gauge their feelings.

23. Editors are not infallible in their understanding of their audiences.

24. While readers may not know what they want in a magazine, knowledge of what they actually read gives an indication of what interests them.

25. A magazine without a defined editorial rationale will fail.

26. If an editor cannot describe the editorial rationale of his or her magazine in ten words, the editor doesn't have one.

27. If the editorial rationale is not known by advertising and circulation people, they sell a product which does not exist. The actual product then does not achieve the promise.

28. The best place to sell a magazine to a reader is in the magazine itself.

29. The best place to sell a magazine to an advertiser is in the magazine itself.

30. The editor should be in the best position to define the editorial rationale of a magazine.

31. Issues should be planned editorially far in advance. They can be.

32. A good logo is very helpful. It should be used everywhere possible.

33. Editors will do a better job if they understand publishing economics.

34. An involved reader is a better reader.

35. If an editorial piece is not used right away, it probably should never be used.

36. Readers like to have a pattern to their magazine—but they want to be surprised every so often.

37. The very basis of a magazine is to have a balance of subject matter, writing styles, information and artwork. While an issue devoted to one subject may be good once in a while, it is not as a steady diet.

38. None of us really knows what a reader will like until he or she tries it.

39. Most editorial pieces are too long.

40. Too many pieces are done for the editor's or the art director's pleasure rather than that of the reader.

41. Readers really have no interest in data about the circulation department, advertising department, corporate headquarters and lists of everyone involved in a magazine.

42. The number of editorial pages has no relationship to the usefulness of a magazine.

35 Editorial Why Don't We's

1. Have regular meetings of editorial, advertising, circulation and other groups on a magazine to discuss the various activities in each area?

2. Go on "retreats" from time to time to rethink the magazine as a whole?

3. Take the marketing pages—the cover, contents page and coming attractions—out of the hands of the editor?

4. Have a package designer help develop the cover?

5. Make sure the logo on the cover is distinctive enough to stand out?

6. Have the logo on the cover large enough to be seen?

7. Develop a logo which is recognizable even if part of it cannot be seen on the cover?

8. Be sure covers are different enough from issue to issue for the reader to know quickly whether he or she has read it or not?

9. Make sure the cover tells the reader what is inside in type large enough and colorful enough to be read?

10. Develop a contents page which helps a reader determine what is inside—in type large enough to be read?

11. Put the contents page in a fixed location,

preferably on page 3?

12. Give a short description of each piece in the contents page, not just the title?

13. If it will help identify or arouse interest, include a picture or a drawing on the contents page?

14. Use headlines, blurbs, symbols or anything else to arouse reader interest in every article?

15. If necessary, use more than one page for describing the contents?

16. Make sure that all illustrations are relevant to the text?

17. Eliminate the editorial page as a regular feature? Only voice an opinion when there is something worthwhile to say and the subject is vital enough to warrant it?

18. Make sure captions are readable, relevant and help entice a reader into the article?

19. Do regular research into the actual reading of the various parts of the magazine?

20. Explore reader interest through other research, focus groups and the like?

21. Develop a brief statement of the editorial rationale?

22. Have the editor tell and retell the rationale to the reader, other departments and the advertiser?

23. Have the editor review material from other departments to be sure they are explaining the magazine he or she is editing?

24. Have the editor visit the advertiser and everyone connected with circulation, including newsstand people, to explain what he or she is doing with the magazine?

25. Use the pages of the magazine to tell what is coming in future issues, in type which can be read—possibly print the next issue's contents page?

26. Break up long paragraphs and solid pages of text matter with blurbs, boxes, short quips or anything else?

27. Make sure the type size and style have been chosen for readability and for nothing else?

28. Remember that length does not make for quality, nor does it indicate depth of coverage of a subject?

29. Use the magazine's logo whenever the name of the magazine is used—never use any other type face?

30. Put the logo on every page of the magazine?

31. Use quizzes, games, puzzles, questionnaires and anything else which will get the reader involved with the magazine?

32. Give the art director parameters within which to work—amount of color, legibility of type, spending limitations and the like?

33. Review every headline, blurb and caption to be sure it helps lure the reader into further reading?

34. Teach editors the economics of publishing?

35. Eliminate all the space wasted on lists of employees, corporate headquarters, etc., confining this to key people in the editorial area?

Getting editors involved in marketing

By Joan Silinsh

Marketing is probably the most misunderstood function in business magazine publishing. It is misunderstood because people in different phases of the publication do not know how they relate to marketing.

• If you had only editors and a circulation department, most of the readers couldn't afford the magazine.

• If you had only sales representatives, the magazine would only have ads and would be nothing more than a catalog.

• If you had only marketing people, it would be like selling a soap carton without soap.

• And, if you had only publishers, you might have a three-martini luncheon club.

Everyone is creative on a magazine: editors, salespeople, circulation, production and promotion staffers, and marketing people coordinate this creativity and help to sell the magazine. To sell it effectively, editors should know what's needed and what can be done with their product.

Why should editors care about marketing? Well, successful marketing makes for successful magazines—and that's what pays salaries. Editors should be unofficial members of the marketing team, because it can only reinforce their economic well-being.

How do *you* get involved in marketing? First, by defining your editorial rationale for your marketing people. If this rationale is not known by your circulation and advertising people, they are selling a product that doesn't exist.

The market a particular magazine serves determines its editorial content—whether it's construction, electronics, apparel, pollution control or whatever. Those within the market a magazine reaches—or is aimed at—determine what will appear within the magazine. They will also determine how the magazine compares to its competition in that market, and how it is sold, that is, the arguments, the strong points and the sales pitches that will be the most effective in convincing advertisers to put their dollars in your magazine.

The "in" people in marketing and advertising call this "positioning." It's really a refined way of fitting square pegs in square holes—or not trying to sell advertising space to a manufacturer of construction equipment when the magazine's readers are primarily concerned with construction materials and their engineering.

So, it's important that marketers clearly understand what the editors are, and will be, writing about. And it is equally important that editors understand the magazine's market, its positioning within that market and the needs of the readers in that market. That's what makes a magazine useful—sometimes even indispensable—to its readers and that's what helps sell advertising and subscriptions and generates the revenue on which a magazine operates, pays salaries, pays for postage and so on.

Sadly, such two-way understanding between editors and marketers is often lacking and the long range effects can be disastrous—such as a magazine going broke and out of business, and that happens much more often than we may want to believe.

Editorial Input for Guide

Here are some specific examples of editorial expertise used in the marketing effort.

One of the most effective marketing pieces produced by *Chemical Engineering* is an annual "Marketing Planning Guide." This is ready in the fall, the season when advertising agencies and ad managers use it to decide how they are going to spend their marketing dollars in the coming year. The guide lists all issue dates, closing dates for advertising and editorial features planned. *CE's* editors recognize the value of preparing their editorial plans in the fall, and without this editorial cooperation, the guide could not be produced.

The sales staff uses this guide to sell advertising schedules, rather than single issues for the coming year. The guide needn't be a printed document. A simple typed list that covers the same information can do the job. So, if you are short on cash and staff, the typed version is an easy way to handle this vital project.

Once the guide is out, specific promotion pieces can be produced for each special issue. Editors again play an important role in the preparation of this promotion by providing details, as complete as possible, on the issue's content, as well as an interpretation of its importance to the marketplace. And, they can provide guidance to the sales staff by suggesting the type of manufacturers who would be interested in that issue and could be potential advertisers.

Editorial plans can also be promoted in less formal ways. *Industrial Marketing,* for example, has a special section where issue topics can be listed, thus alerting the advertising community about its plans. The main thing here is to assign someone to submit the information on a regular basis and on time.

Cooperative Effort

Chemical Engineering has another promotion piece that was truly a cooperative effort. This was a manual of chemical process flowsheets, which originally appeared in the pages of the magazine. It was compiled as a circulation premium to generate more subscriptions. Editors got involved by selecting flowsheets that would be typical of the industry segments defining the market, the chemical process industries. Editors also got involved in compiling the information for an index of the equipment used in these processes. These booklets were used by the marketing people to define the market for prospective advertisers and to show how their equipment was used in the industry. This is an example of team effort, but more so it shows that the editor's expertise was essential for the preparation of these vital marketing tools.

Garbage Marketing

There's another aspect to the editor's role in marketing his or her product. I call it "garbage" marketing. Just think about how much and what kind of material, received in your editorial offices, is thrown directly into the garbage. Is it thrown away because it doesn't "fit" in your editorial plans? If so, can your salespeople benefit from it? I'm referring to new product releases, notices of promotions, company realignments, unsolicited articles. Is the news release you throw away today the harbinger of a new trend tomorrow? Should somebody know about it?

Why not go beyond the editorial selection process and scribble a note on the releases you can't use. Tell the salespeople why you can't use the items—perhaps the product is not really new, or the product is new but not applicable to the industry, or maybe you just don't have the space to run it.

On the other hand, if the release is hot enough to turn it into a feature story, let the sales representative know. There's nothing more embarrassing than having the salesperson be the last to know.

If you do develop a major story, why not suggest maximizing the article's distribution through reprints? Timing is important here, especially if the reprint can be done as an inexpensive overrun.

New product releases, personnel changes, acquisitions, plant openings, financial releases, new ventures, etc., are invaluable leads to the sales staff. It's a practical way to keep them informed on their accounts' activities. You have to remember that a salesperson cannot see every customer and prospect personally. Remember: A knowledgeable salesperson is a better spokesperson for your magazine.

Dull, But Vital

Next, consider those editorial reports all editors hate, such as listings of who makes what, construction roundups, directory-type reports. Every magazine has some. No, they don't require creative writing, but—and it's a big but—they do require creative thinking, creative organizing, creative questioning, creative followup.

So, why delegate an editorial task to a temporary clerk or a secretary who has been drafted for the occasion?

Questionnaires are usually sent out to gather the information, and as they are received back in the home office, many editors relinquish their editorial function.

Yes, these articles are dull to prepare, but they are vital and informative to the reader. Otherwise, why publish them?

The editor must assume the role of marketer in this type of project. He or she is the only one who can judge the accuracy and completeness of the information. If certain companies are not represented, but you know that they manufacture that certain product, do you alert the sales staff? Do you contact the company yourself? Or do you just let it go? A clerk or secretary can only process the paperwork; the editor has to be involved to ascertain the completeness and accuracy of the finished report.

Also keep in mind that the companies filling out the questionnaires may have asked a secretary or clerk to send in the information. Just because the company submits the questionnaire doesn't mean that the information is correct. Your expertise is needed here, too.

The Competition

Okay, what about the competition? Is your competition scooping you? Or, are you scooping them? How many other magazines compete with yours? Do you read them all? If not, the logical way to keep up with the competition is to assign an editor to monitor each publication, so that he or she can become the "expert," the always-current source of information on the competition.

What do marketing people want to know about these competitors? Well, how timely and accurate is the editorial content? Is what they print as news something your own publication ran months before? If they've covered a topic you've also run, how do the two compare side by side as to quality and thoroughness? How do you evaluate their editorial integrity?

All of this is invaluable information for the sales staff. The information can be passed on to them by informal memos, can be turned into competitive data sheets and can make for dramatic editorial presentations at sales meetings.

Value of Personal Contact

One of the things that we cannot underestimate is the value of personal contact between editors and customers and prospects. It is particularly essential in a technical publication, where an editor can play the role of educator.

Most advertising and agency people do not have educational backgrounds in the subject areas of your magazine—yet they make the decisions as to whether your publication is included in the media schedule.

Don Cramer, media supervisor of Rumrill-Hoyt, recently stated that to select a specific magazine, he must have confidence in the magazine, and to gain this confidence he likes to have a chance to meet the editors to learn how they are trying to serve their readers and to gain better insight into their businesses and industries.

Some of the most effective meetings we've had with *Chemical Engineering* advertisers consist of group sessions where various aspects of the magazine are represented—editorial, promotion, research, sales. Advertisers cannot help but be impressed by the professional team effort and balance of expertise. Each participant had a role to play in his or her own special area.

Timeliness and Awareness

Timeliness in magazine publishing is next to godliness. It's okay to schedule a major feature article dealing with a particular industry trend and then alert the marketing staff to it. But, it's not okay to allow insufficient time for the marketing and salespeople to capitalize on it in their advertising sales efforts.

The closing date for advertising may be weeks before the article appears, and it takes many weeks before that to sell the advertisers on placing an ad in that issue. The marketing staff has to get into gear many weeks before that to gather the information on the issue and prepare and distribute the appropriate promotion material to help sell the advertising.

On very special issues, such as a show issue, do you work with your marketing people to prepare the issue cover in time for them to use the actual thing in their promotion material and perhaps as part of their booth display if they are exhibiting at the show? It's important in such cases to come up with a cover that truly depicts the editorial "event," and from the graphics point of view to design a cover that will work well when put to other uses. So, it's not only a question of timeliness, but also of an awareness of the many other uses that can be made of the cover and other contents of your issues.

When it comes right down to basics, the only thing we marketers have to sell is editorial. You can do without us better than we can do without you. But, success comes only by working together.

My last example of team effort is the current campaign the McGraw-Hill Publications Company is running in *Advertising Age* and *Standard Rate & Data*. It uses "The Market/The Magazine" approach. We are working directly with editors in developing these ads, because they are the most knowledgeable about their market and how their magazine serves the market. We take their input, polish it up, select a cover that contains an element in it that can be used to depict the market, and our advertising agency doesn't get involved at all.

We are running a second campaign in *Business Week, Industrial Marketing, Sales & Marketing Management, Media Decisions* and *Advertising Age* that features industry leaders. Marsteller prepares these ads by interviewing these industry leaders to learn why the particular McGraw-Hill publication they read is essential to their jobs. The ad also features the editor of that publication and let him or her talk about how the magazine is serving his or her readers' information needs. Note how the campaign has editorial content at the core.

The role of editors as marketers is a valid one—so much so that the editor even ought to consider taking his or her magazine's marketing manager to lunch. If your budget doesn't allow it, at least let the marketing manager know that you're available. It could be the beginning of a wonderful, worthwhile and profitable relationship.

The underestimated art of editorial planning

By John Peter

Everybody agrees on one thing: Without editorial planning you can't get out a magazine.

Both the editor who does extensive planning a year in advance and the one who does the minimum amount in the most informal way will tell you that planning is essential. What they do not agree on, however, is how extensive and formalized the planning should be.

Naturally, it would be foolish to expect that a weekly newsmagazine and a monthly special-interest magazine could employ the exact same planning procedures. *Newsweek* often can't say more than a week ahead what the lead article in the "National Affairs" section will be. But if *Better Homes and Gardens* wants to have photos of new May perennials in its May 1979 issue it has to plant the flowers two years ahead in the fall of 1977 and photograph them a year ahead in 1978.

Both magazines plan, and planning has to be done by every magazine staff. Yet in my experience as a consultant, editorial planning is frequently one of the most underestimated aspects of magazine making. Although the schedules and needs are different, all top magazines have two things in common: They do a good job of planning and there are basic similarities to how they do it.

Fundamentally, there are two kinds of planning, by whatever labels you put on them—long-range and short-range planning, or strategic and tactical planning or annual and issue planning. Operationally, there is frequently some intermediate planning which is a mixture of both.

Start with a Goal

Planning starts with having a goal. As Sey Chassler, editor of *Redbook,* says, "You can't have a successful publication without knowing where you are going and who your audience is. If you take those two things together, that's what planning is."

Keith Johnson, assistant managing editor of *Money,* comments, "Everybody has to figure out what the object of his or her magazine is and how the person is going to achieve the object. When you start thinking specifically about how you're going to achieve that object, that's when you start planning. It's inescapable."

Any serious discussion of magazine goals obviously involves the entire publishing team. There is a clear relationship between a product and its sales—a magazine and its circulation and advertising. One of the dominant characteristics of modern publishing is the importance of this marketing relationship.

It is, of course, true of all products in today's world. But in some ways it is particularly true of magazines. General circulation publications—*The Saturday Evening Post, Look, Life,* as well as the old-time general circulation women's magazines, have adapted to special-interest approaches. Magazines have to be more carefully targeted today.

You can't do this without superior planning. What experts call "Lewis and Clark planning" i.e., looking back on one day's journey and planning the next, is not good enough anymore. Today's editorial product requires long-range planning.

This kind of planning ought to happen, at least, on a periodic, usually annual, basis. It is characteristic of successful magazines that they have a clear editorial goal and it is periodically reexamined, refined or redefined.

Procedures for accomplishing this vary. They often reflect the traditional systems of the publishing firm and, perhaps in publishing more than in many businesses, the character and characteristics of the people involved.

First, Planning Meetings

The discussion of and decisions on goals may or may not be a part of an editorial planning meeting, but you can't have implementation planning without them.

"We have periodic planning meetings that take place every 12 to 18 months," says Ed Kosner, editor of *Newsweek.* "We all go off to a place and talk for three days or so. It's not on an annual basis but it tends to happen. It's both philosophical and long-range planning. Before the meeting takes place I will solicit memos from the participants on things that they would like to talk about which can range anywhere from specific editorial projects to the direction of the magazine. I organize the agenda based on what people are interested in talking about plus whatever I want to talk about. The mix is different depending on the actual meeting.

"In political years, for instance, we will do a lot of planning about covering the primaries, conventions, elections and things like that. If we know there are going to be events like the Olympics or an inauguration we will have specific detailed planning about those things. We will also plan for special projects that are not related to events—a year-end issue, for instance."

At Time Inc., the magazines periodically schedule weekend meetings where the senior editorial staff gets together for more or less informal discussions on where the magazine is and what it ought to be doing.

At *Redbook,* editor Chassler has found that a series of informal meetings is helpful in keeping the staff of about 60 people in touch and informed. There is no regular schedule for the meetings; instead they are held "whenever we feel that we could use a little more.

"What we do here," explains Chassler, "is run a series of lunches with each department in the executive dining room. Then we do another series that is a random selection of people from various departments that crisscross with each other. What we are talking about, in these cases, is not so much planning as general philosophy. Are we doing what we set out to do? Is there some other direction at which we should be looking at this particular time? What's happening to young women, our audience? How are they changing and so on? The meetings tend to be more philosophical and directional than specific planning, though story ideas can grow out of such meetings."

Many magazines schedule their major planning meetings on an annual basis.

A.J. Vogl, editor of the biweekly *Medical Economics,* holds an annual editorial conference with the goals of "a better magazine, improved staff morale and more of a sense of what our purpose and objectives are. We step back and look at what we are doing and the ways we are doing it."

The meetings, which are attended by the entire editorial staff, as well as representation from the art department, the sales manager and the director of research, are held at a conference center or a resort hotel with meeting facilities. Vogl feels that the results benefit from the more relaxed atmosphere that is possible away from the office.

"Very often," he explains, "the conference is themed to something very particular. On past occasions we treated things like systems, organization and things we could do better. There was one session on article headlining. For one of the meetings we brought in a half dozen doctors whom we thought were typical, and we just sat down and questioned them about their reading habits for an entire day. It was really rather exhaustive. At times, we may make special assignments to the editors attending so that they chair different sessions. They have to prepare, investigate various possibilities and report on them at the meeting and the staff reacts to the presentation."

Industry Week, another biweekly, has an annual editorial meeting that is geared more closely towards what will be in the magazine during the coming year, but still it is general and not specific planning.

Editor Stanley Modic explains, "We review what we have done and broadly explain to the staff members what we hope to be doing in the coming year—major editorial thrusts, major editorial campaigns. Generally in that same meeting we break down into brainstorming sessions in which each man or woman contributes what's happening for the coming year. From that we get a broad feel for what's going to be happening in the next year.

"As editor, I lay out some goals, some plans, some general thinking as they reflect any circulation shift that we might have, any emphasis in marketing that we might want to do—those kinds of things we become aware of. We don't say in this particular month we are going to do this story but these are things that we are going to be following."

Planning Well in Advance

At *Better Homes and Gardens,* the annual planning covers a span of time up to 23 months in advance, with some projects started even earlier. This January it will be making general editorial plans for all of 1979. The specific issue planning is done 12 months ahead.

James Autry, *Better Homes and Gardens* editor, says, "We get into some pretty major programs. We've

done houses with the American Plywood Association, concept houses with Armstrong. We were actually controlling the design—assuring that the houses meet the criteria of low maintenance, moderate cost, energy conservation, etc. Some of these projects have to be initiated two years ahead of time."

At the regular monthly staff meeting Autry goes over any general instructions. Following the meeting is issue planning week, a solid week of individual meetings, with each of the six areas of the magazine—building, crafts, gardening, food, furnishings and the text articles.

"Six meetings, morning and afternoon—it makes for a rather disciplined week," says Autry. "We assemble the departments, from the lowest person to the highest and they present what they want to do in that issue for the next year. We discuss everything from general concept down to execution—right down to whether we are going to do it on location or in the studio, on the East Coast or the West. Depending on the season we are going to shoot, are we going to have to go south or to the mountains or whatever? At that time, we even begin to get some preliminary design ideas. Are we going to do it full bleed and reverse the type and drop in the how-to art?"

To avoid the problems of prediction involved in planning so far in advance, the *Better Homes and Gardens* editors are heavily involved in the industries represented in their departments to help the magazine be not only a trend reporter but a trend setter. Says Autry: "In our concept of service journalism, and I should say advocacy journalism, our department heads participate in industry functions, on committees and in seminar groups. We are not only able to measure what is likely to happen in that industry, we frequently influence the industry before it even gets on our pages. We are fairly accurately able to predict the trends."

"Chance favors the man who plans," quotes editor Arthur Fox, of the construction newsweekly, *Engineering News-Record.* "You can look awfully smart in a given week's issue if you say the right thing. If you anticipated what there was to be said you are more apt to say the right things. It's a matter of constantly trying to intensify our efforts to plan.

Coordinating Efforts

"You can't leave anything to chance. You have to anticipate everything you possibly can. Planning is very largely coordinating the efforts of an awful lot of people and making sure that everybody knows what everyone else is doing.

"In October," says Fox, "the senior members of our staff and I, plus our publisher and advertising sales manager—a dozen of us—had a day away from the office, a kind of retreat to think big thoughts and dream big dreams and decide what the future might hold for the readers of *Engineering News-Record.* We also talked about staffing problems and the nitty gritty of journalism, which is the most important thing we can talk about.

"Also in October or so and again in May the managing editor and I schedule a whole series of meetings with a representative group from each of our six departments. They come forward with a great laundry list of the stories that will get done in the next months. Some of them will get done, some of them won't. Some of them fall by the wayside, and other things take higher priority. But we have a notion, at least, of the major features, the trips these people intend to take, the conventions they intend to cover, the people stories they intend to write, the profiles of companies."

Annual Planning Imperative

Annual editorial planning is imperative for most business publications. Each year many publish a calendar listing the special issues and special emphasis features. Developed with the publisher and advertising manager, it represents a commitment by the editor to run a certain topic in a given issue. Special issues may range from straight reader-interest subjects like a "forecast" issue to extra supplier-interest topics such as a new products issue. Special emphasis may represent a single article. The calendar is deliberately designed to leave the editorial approach quite open.

Even publications without formal annual planning usually have some annual plans.

Lew Harris, managing editor of *Los Angeles* magazine, says, "We have certain things that happen most months. Nine out of 12 months we have an idea of what we are going to use as a basic theme that will take up maybe 10 percent of the magazine. The themes are really pretty basic. Every September we have a business forecast. That's also when we cover the new TV season. October is wine and home entertainment. Every January is self-improvement and personal economy. February is home and recreational condominium living. It runs that way."

Every long range plan in time has to be implemented by an issue plan. Issue planning procedures vary from magazine to magazine.

The issue plan is usually drawn up by the editor or the managing editor. At *Money,* however, it is done on a rotating basis to spread the work, provide different viewpoints and give all the top of the staff a better knowledge of the magazine as a whole. Assistant managing editor Johnson explains: "There is a meeting every month with the managing editor, two assistant managing editors and two senior editors. On a rotating basis, one of the assistant managing editors or one of the senior editors drafts a story list for the next issue, which is two months down the line. He circulates the list to the staff, asking for comments. A couple of days after the list is circulated, the group of us gets together for the monthly story conference."

Most issue plans represent a scheduling of features and departments which have been in the works for varying periods of time.

Harris says that at *Los Angeles* magazine, the publication is divided into two sections—features and departments. "We are constantly assigning departments so that we always have a backlog. A running list is kept of all departments we have on hand. For each issue we go to the list and decide on what things to use from each department to make the balance. That's 60 percent of the magazine right there."

When *Redbook* plans an issue, it is "probably 98 to 99 percent set," Chassler says. "An article might drop out or a writer might be working on an article and it might prove out that he or she can't make it for some reason. We

then have to do some scurrying around to replace it but, by and large, once you plan the issue, that's it. On the other hand, sometimes I might be looking at a schedule and say for some reason it sounded better at the meeting but now it looks a little soft as an issue. I might decide that we better get back together."

Medical Economics editor Vogl says: "The booking comes from the managing editor. We have a preliminary book and as it gets closer to publication day we have a final booking where the editors can see what's in a specific issue. There is also in the office a huge board where all the articles are set down by category. We can see what is there. If a story is bumped for any reason we can slip another in without making a big deal of it."

One persistent argument against planning is: "Things change so fast." Yet few hold planning more important than editors of newsweeklies who have to live with fast-breaking events.

At *Engineering News-Record,* editor Fox states, "We meet every Tuesday morning, planning the issue that is going to close the following Monday night. Some of the features in it have been committed. Some of the news hasn't even been made. Out of that meeting comes a brief of the book, a one-page list of the stories and the editor who is handling the story, and the news bureau or stringer, if there is one. It tells what the features are that have already been committed and department by department what the other possible stories are."

At *Newsweek* editor Kosner says, "The decision as to what actually goes on the cover is made the week of publication, but the planning and preparation for cover stories can go on for as much as a year in advance or as little time as an hour. We worked on the Jasper Johns cover story for a year. We knew that he would have a retrospective at the Whitney. Basically, we would work on a story like Jane Fonda for six weeks, children and TV maybe two months. That means that the reporting has been going on for a month or more. The writing takes a week or two.

"I think you have to have a lot of material in work, constantly refilling the reservoir of projects. The image I use is a plane circling over an airport. You bring down the ones that you want to bring down. You land the projects you want to land. In any given week I would love to have, and often do have, four or five wonderful things that we can do in addition to the breaking news. We decide which ones are good for the issue. Planning is important but it is not a sterile, scheduled thing."

Planning, Not Just Scheduling

Planning is often confused with scheduling. Obviously, planning does include scheduling—setting deadlines for the completion of tasks. But planning, as Kosner observes, is also developing options. Magazine planning is more like planning to play a football game than it is planning to erect a building. It has to be more flexible to cope with changing circumstances.

Dero Saunders, executive editor of *Forbes,* observes, "If you are a Platonist, you can believe that everything is knowable and that all elements can be grasped by intelligent men and women of good will and therefore shaped in an intelligent and planful way to an organized and predicted end, and that's fine.

"If, on the other hand, you believe that human experience is so diverse that it is impossible to comprehend it all and the best comprehension that you have can only tell you some of it, then the objective is to try to plan as well as you can with the material you can sensibly gather within a finite period of time. The most important objective is to leave your options open for the something that goes wrong as you inevitably expect. I would say that we are characterized by the second of these kind rather than the first.

"Understanding planning's limitations is quite as important as understanding its potential. The greater the flexibility, at least in our feeling, the better off a publication is."

The most frequent argument advanced against planning is: *We don't have the time.* The fact is that planning saves time. It reduces false starts and revisions. It reduces mistakes and corrections. It saves time at the time when you need it the most, namely, when you are close to the deadline.

It also saves money.

On the part of a few editors the feeling persists that planning, however flexible, inhibits inspirational nimbleness and engenders editorial stiffness. Ironically the specter of overplanning is most often invoked by those who need it most. Proper planning does not lock you in but sets you free. It sets you free to choose among options. With the bulk of the work completed it sets you free to bring the maximum attention, skill and imagination to bear on a better idea, the latest development, the newest opportunity.

The fine art of editorial planning represents one of the greatest opportunities for publication improvement.

Most magazines are underplanned. How about yours?

On the firing line
By Bernard Weiss

Suppose, despite the fact you thought you hired the best available talent for your publication and despite your best managerial efforts, the results have not been satisfactory. You reluctantly decide to discharge an individual because continuing the relationship would be uncomfortable for you, unrewarding for the editor or (art director), disastrous for the publication and possibly unprofitable for the company.

The first thing to do after deciding to discharge an employee is to acknowledge responsibility. This is difficult to do, for in deciding to discharge an individual you have, in a sense, admitted your own failure. Somewhere along the line you probably made a serious mistake. You may have hired the wrong person for the job. Perhaps you didn't describe the position and the responsibilities adequately to those who applied. Training or orientation for the newly hired editor may not have been satisfactory, or your supervision may not have been complete. Perhaps there was an insufficient budget to financially support the job you wanted done. Perhaps you didn't offer enough guidance or feedback during the initial period of employment.

Recognize your share of responsibility

Whatever the circumstances, as a mature manager, you must recognize that you share responsibility for the individual's lack of success under your direction.

With that recognition, you can also tell yourself that, though the person failed in this particular situation, he or she may be happier and more successful at another publication, with another publisher or editorial director. Your publication is not the only one that can give this person a chance at a successful career in publishing. There are countless opportunities.

In fact, in a large publishing organization, there might be another opportunity just down the corridor or one flight up in the same building. Therefore, before discharging someone find out if his or her particular skills can be profitably employed by another executive in your company. Thinking in terms of a transfer rather than an outright dismissal can ease the pain for both you and your subordinate.

Avoid surprises

Everyone who works for you is entitled to know how he's doing. You therefore have an obligation to periodically review every individual's work. You will not have been fair with your employee unless, over a period of time, you have given him some guidance and help on how to improve his work or mend his ways. *He must have been given a chance to improve himself under your direction.* If he fails to do better, then you have an honest basis for the termination.

In fact, if you have given satisfactory direction and made clear your concerns and your hopes for his success, you may not have to discharge him at all—he may resign. In my 20 years' experience on the editorial side of publishing, I have met many writers, editors, artists and other creative people who were very sensitive to career relationships. Some of them knew, well before I did, they weren't going to make it on my staff. They usually offered their resignations before I decided to discharge them. When forced to discharge them, I found they accepted my decision with great relief.

There is one more consideration before actually going through the procedure of termination. Do you have a qualified replacement ready, or can you find one quickly? Not just anyone will do. You must be certain that the change in personnel will result in some improvement. At least the potential for improvement must exist. Remember: The devil you know is better than the devil you don't know.

Conducting the termination interview

Here are some suggestions for conducting the termination interview, that final discussion during which you actually fire the individual.

1. Make it short. Knowing what's coming, both of you will probably approach this meeting with great anxiety. Get right to the point, say what must be said and end the meeting quickly. You should be able to conduct the entire discussion in five to seven minutes. Longer meetings simply prolong the agony.

2. Don't be critical. It's too late for criticism and complaints. Doing so now will only prolong the meeting, promote animosity and strain the already-difficult relationship between you. Most important, don't criticize anything about the individual or the individual's job performance that he can't change anyway.

3. Don't review the past. Simply state the facts: The job is not being accomplished to your satisfaction and you want to make a change. That is usually sufficient. It is hoped that in previous meetings you will have reviewed his shortcomings, your disappointments, the objectives that were not met and the opportunities missed.

4. Do not allow yourself to be conversationally sidetracked. He may beg you for another chance. He may demand to know who is going to get his job. He may blame you for long-forgotten mistakes. He may attack the company's management. Whatever his response, including tears, stand firm: "Joe, I repeat. This job is not being done to my satisfaction. I am making a change. Perhaps I did make a mistake last year. Perhaps you did start with two strikes against you. But none of that changes anything now. My mind is made up. I am asking you to leave."

5. Don't say, "You're not happy here." Attitudes and outlooks are less important than job performance. Moreover, suppose he responds, "But I *am* happy here—I *like* my work." Against this response you have no defense.

6. Give him some emotional support. This is easy with most creative people because nearly everyone has some special talent or skill that is extraordinary. Mention that to him. Keep in mind what originally intrigued you about this person. In fact, at one time you thought highly enough of his talent to offer him a job. Say so—he needs to hear it from you now. You can also be supportive by reminding him that his unique talent or style is very worthy of professional appreciation—if not here, at some other publication—and that under different circumstances he may do much better for himself. He probably wants to fully utilize his talent—and in another position where it could be recognized, appreciated and rewarded.

7. Don't neglect the formalities. Offer severance pay. If you can afford to, be generous. Giving him more than the required minimum will ease the pain (yours as well as his). Policies on severance pay vary widely, depending on such circumstances as type of publishing company, size of staff and whether there is a labor contract. In the absence of any firm policy, however, consider these broad guidelines, based on trends at several publishing clients surveyed: One week of severance pay for every six months of employment for creative staff who are discharged. In certain circumstances, where there is no profit participation for creative employees, the one week/six months rule is also applied to those who leave voluntarily.

Offer to write letters. Make phone calls to help him find another position or line up interviews with other publishers. Your intent is to help him find a spot that will utilize his assets without taxing his talent or exposing his weaknesses. Ask him to stay in touch.

8. Do it in the morning, early in the week. Firing people on Friday afternoon is barbaric because it gives them the whole weekend to do little except feel rotten and grow more depressed. I prefer to discharge people at other times so they can immediately start making phone calls to employment agencies or friends to set up interviews. They can also revise and print their resumes, put ads in the papers, get some letters out and take other positive action.

9. Don't allow him to stay until the end of the week. There is little to be gained (he surely isn't going to put forth his best efforts now) and much that can be lost (since he may want to strike back against you, your publication, your company). You can avoid that possibility entirely by stating firmly: "Joe, I suggest you leave now. Pick up your things from your office, make your goodbyes. Come back in about 10 or 15 minutes. By that time, accounting will have given me your check and we can walk out together." Walking out with him gives you another opportunity to be supportive and reassuring: "Let me know if I can help you. I still have great admiration for your creative talent and I want to see you make it big—if not here, somewhere else."

10. Be introspective. Because it represents a personal failure, the act of dismissing someone is difficult. It should be difficult. If discharging people becomes easy for you, if you are relaxed and almost casual about it, question yourself: Are you getting too much practice? Do you enjoy it? Has the act of firing someone become a substitute for other neglected managerial functions, such as supervising, directing or training your staff? Be alert to these warning signals.

Adopt a composed picture

Try to adopt a posture of professional composure. You should be firm and tough-minded. But, with a soft tone of voice and appropriate gestures and words, you can also be sensitive, humanistic and kind. Avoid the example of George Steinbrenner, owner of the New York Yankees, who once fired a secretary for failing to get him an airline reservation. He fired her from the airport, over the telephone, when he discovered that the airline had no record of the reservation. "Clear out your desk," he told her. "You're through." She didn't leave, however, and the next day Steinbrenner made his apologies by arranging to send her child to summer camp.

Few executives ever acquire much experience at discharging subordinates and even fewer are skillful at it. The best you can hope for is a clean, quick break—a painless break from which you and your ex-employee can get a fresh start.

I'm fired

Editor's note: The author of this article, a business magazine editor in his mid-forties, asks to remain anonymous.

First, the shock.

You've had a gut feeling about it for months. The refusal to communicate with you; the non-inclusion in several meetings involving most of the rest of the staff; the lack of consultation when new personnel were hired; even your exclusion from out-of-the-office social occasions which involved most of your co-workers. You wondered whether to make an issue of it and confront management head-on, but decide it smacks too much of paranoia. Besides, you tell yourself, be realistic. I'm doing far too good a job to ever give them a reason to fire me.

And, just when you've convinced yourself of this fact, the firing comes. You're not given any convincing reason and, caught at a disadvantage because the moment is of their choosing, you fail to insist on discovering the true cause.

You spend the remaining hours of that Friday hastily packing the belongings you've assembled. Then you wait. You wait until most of the people have gone home because you're too embarrassed to face them and say goodbye, and—although they already know, thanks to any office's instant grapevine—they're equally embarrassed to come to see you. To walk out in the middle of the afternoon, even though you have nothing to do, would simply not be playing the game.

While you're sitting and watching the minutes tick by, you think about all the unfinished business: the myriad instructions you would have given if you were going on vacation to ensure the smooth flow of work. Now, no one asks you anything. And, since you still have the good of the magazine at heart, you worry about future issues and how they'll look without your guiding hand.

Anger sets in

Then the anger. The first weekend is the worst. Saturday is a "nothing" day. No businesses open. No phone calls you can make. No help wanted ads to browse through.

And your anger builds up. It was the best job you ever had. You'd even been told you'd done it better than anyone else, making your firing even more implausible. If ever there's a time for "Why me?" breastbeating, this is it.

You reflect on the weekends you went into the office to play catch-up with the printer, because others had missed their deadlines. You remember the numerous weekends and evenings you spent at home behind a typewriter to build up an ever-depleted inventory of stories. And you think about the monstrous winter snows when you struggled in from 30 miles away because you had a job to do, while your Manhattan co-workers, two miles distant, stayed home. Above all, you swear to yourself that you'll never show any company such loyalty again.

Sunday comes and, with it, *The New York Times.* You haven't bothered to buy the classified section early because you know that the jobs advertised there are hardly ever geared to your level of competence or salary. But, with the arrival of the entire paper, you go through the motions of looking, circling, clipping—and organizing a plan of action for next morning. You haven't sunk to the level of writing to box numbers yet—the most despicable of all employer subterfuges. And you don't even hurry to write other letters, figuring that, if you wait a few days, your answers will stand out from the bunch.

Besides, you have no resume. You were so secure in your job that updating a resume was the last thing you ever thought of. You can write one, yes. But getting it reproduced will have to wait, like everything else, until Monday.

Finally, the depression. And Monday, almost inevitably, brings with it pouring rain, and the first of the many excuses you'll find for inaction over the weeks. No point in trying to see anyone today, you reason. You'll look like a drowned rat. So you visit the local library to consult the reference books, find names, addresses and contacts, and make a plan of action.

That's when you discover that even the best of the suburban libraries has no reference material on the publishing industry to speak of. Their stock of magazines is sparse and at least a year old. And, when you do find a so-called standard reference volume, you turn first to the area you're familiar with. There you find that virtually all the information the section contains is at least eight years out of date. Presumably, the rest of the information you wanted will be on a par.

But at least, once the week starts, you're in action. You get your resumes in order, write letters, make phone calls to everyone you know in the industry, arrange lunches and appointments. No matter that all the activity isn't geared to a purposeful end—the action is a psychological remedy to the feeling that you have nowhere to go, nothing to do.

Letters take time to deliver. Friends, when they do anything to help, need time to set up contacts. But one thing you can do immediately: make the rounds of the agencies.

Depression deepens

And that's where the real depression sets in. If you need the score on how successful they're likely to be, just take a look at some of the offices they set up shop in. The cheapest quarters in the oldest office buildings in the city: no windows, peeling paint, toilets a hundred yards away down the hall—and the staff dressed accordingly. From these firms you expect to find an executive position?

Other so-called editorial agencies are, by contrast, plush and humming with activity. The "activity" consists of dozens of young ladies in their early twenties chasing after the plethora of gal-Friday jobs, each of which always seems better than the ones they leave. You walk in, middle-aged, and looking for three times their salary—and about as out of place as a tiger in the antelope enclosure at the zoo.

But no matter where you go, they put you to work. You're given the inevitable form to complete by a bored receptionist who speaks—and probably knows—no more than ten words. You're looking for an executive editorial position in the upper twenties or above, and you're required to state your typing speed, whether you have a chauffeur's license, where you went to high school, even though your resume tells it all in great detail.

And—this exercise in futility takes place at the agencies which you carefully selected because they claim to specialize in editorial positions. (Watch out, by the way, for the two definitions of publishing. If you have trade magazine experience, you have almost no chance of breaking into book publishing, and vice versa.)

Eventually, an interviewer appears and, with a show of bonhomie, yells out your first name. You go into a cubicle the size of an average toilet stall and you hear about the same three jobs which have just opened up. Each agency will tell you the listing is exclusive with them. But by the time you've been to three agencies, you can second-guess every job opening which will be mentioned to you.

You leave with equal bonhomie, assuring each other of your undying devotion, while your resume disappears God knows where, and you know you'll never hear from them again.

In actual fact, it's three months now since I started going to agencies, 11 weeks since I hit the last of the more than dozen employment "counselors." And although, for all they know, I'm still looking, I haven't heard one word from any of them. This, despite the fact that, every Sunday, they advertise at least one position which I'd be qualified for.

Why, then, go to agencies at all? It's a game you have to play. Think of it as employment productive for the people who work there. Above all, catalog everything you've done. It vastly impresses the state unemployment authorities who won't dole out their weekly pittance without proof of "an active search for work."

The name of the game is seeing people on actual interviews. And no one can help you more than friends. Over the years in the business, you've developed quite a number. You tell them all that you're looking and, certainly, some of them will come up with people to see. But you soon realize that job hunting for you is only a secondary activity for them. And remember, if the job were as good as they tell you, they'd probably be after it themselves.

Interviews boost morale

However, scheduling appointments at least is a morale booster. Get enough of them on your calendar and you develop a micawber-like belief that the perfect job is just one interview away.

You also make your own rounds of companies you'd like to work for. Usually, there are no openings, but at least your resume has landed on the doorstep. That you believe your resume will wind up somewhere else than it does in an employment agency is irrational. But the experience of visiting actual companies is as psychologically stimulating as that of going to employment agencies is depressing.

Getting into the offices of companies you think you'd like to work for is, in itself, revealing. Sometimes, the physical surroundings where you might have to work stifle any further ambitions in that area. And, since most fringe benefits are comparable, it might be more telling if you inspected the rest rooms instead. These can speak volumes about what you could expect if you worked there.

You're a realist about your abilities, but also an incurable optimist. So, on the theory that you have nothing to lose, you also apply at the biggies—companies such as Time-Life. You don't get past the receptionist, of course, but the mere mention that you have a good resume and that you may be called gives you a psychological "high" for days. The greatest temptation, at that stage, is to stop everything else and settle back to wait for a firm offer.

That, as every job-hunting book will tell you, is a mistake. Keep looking, keep active—and never believe a soul when they assure you that they'll call you back. Each of us has a weakness when it comes to interviewing. And the interviewers share a weakness too: the absolute inability ever to terminate an interview with a "No." They all will take the coward's way out by keeping you on a string.

The waiting is undoubtedly the most depressing part of any job hunt. After a while, you've exhausted what you usefully can do. So you sleep late, don't shave, wander around the house and feel progressively more sorry for yourself. The odd jobs that you've never had time to do, you now have time for. But mysteriously, they still don't get done! Each day of your unemployment, the old American work ethic nags you a little more as you realize you're no longer a part of the economic mainstream. But each day, with enforced inactivity, your desire to work again gets progressively weaker.

You haunt the libraries, read through the shelves of material on changing your job and career. You wonder why every one of these books is written at such an elementary level, and why each book's purpose is to suggest you analyze your life and what you're doing.

If you're a true editor, it's addictive. You already know your purpose in life and have no intention of changing careers. The only thing you can't understand is why you've become derailed in mid-term, and why they're not hungering after your talents out there.

The offer comes through

Eventually, of course, the firm offer comes through. While it may seem like an eternity, it's probably only been a few weeks—not even time for your severance pay to run out. And, as luck always has it, not one but several jobs magically appear. Elation and worry share center stage with you during those days. It's great to have a job again, but are you taking the right one? (Two years from now, when normal job fatigue and boredom set in, remember your reasons for making your choice.)

I've just lived through this experience. Fortunately, it took me just five weeks to find my new job and, in fact, it is more satisfying than the one I had. My salary has gone up, I've acquired a permanent free-lance assignment from a contact I made during my search, and, along the way, I've learned a few valuable facts about myself.

If it was such a valuable experience, would I like to live through it all again? Not on your life.

Job hunting: what you can do

Resumes

The minute you land a new job, prepare a new resume. Don't be caught short without one when you need it most. Update it every few months as you acquire new responsibilities. It's elementary perhaps, but remember—you're a writer. There's no excuse at all for your resume to be badly written, contain even one typo, or be cheaply reproduced. The resume game is one that everyone plays. Be a champ at it.

Unemployment insurance

The money isn't much. The ambiance of state offices is nil. The people you meet there are unlikely to become your friends. But you're entitled to the money and at least some of it is tax-free. Don't miss out and don't wait more than a day to register. Your benefits start when you apply.

Employment agencies

By law, you have to visit the state employment office. But it's a formality. Chances of landing a job from this source are one in a thousand—or less.

Chances of getting a top position through a commercial agency are about the same. They all seem to be geared to the $8,000-a-year typist. But try it anyway, if only to discover what jobs are actually open and to develop some leads you might follow up yourself. Don't follow up confidential information from any agency, however, unless you're prepared to pay the agency's fee.

Have no faith in any recruiter who tells you that you'll hear from him. You won't. Conversely, consider highly the person who tells you there's little the agency can do for you. If any jobs are forthcoming, this will be the source.

Executive search firms

Tradition has it that they contact you, never that you contact them. Another tradition: they're not interested in you, if you're out of work. It's not necessarily true. If you've been contacted by a headhunter in the past, by all means let him know that you're actively looking for employment. He's certainly more likely to find something at your level than a regular employment agency.

Friends

Don't let pride keep you from telling everyone in the industry about your predicament. Because this is a cutthroat business, they realize that the person out of work could easily be themselves. Where they can, they'll help.

Personal visits

Visit every likely (and unlikely) company where you'd want to work, in person. You may never get past the personnel assistant assigned to screen out job-hunting nuisances, but at least you'll have established personal contact. Try to get that person's name and write it down. It's especially useful if you make later follow-up calls.

Letters

Opinions vary on scattershot letters around the country. For one thing, are you prepared to relocate if they offer you a job in East Podunk?

Opinions about enclosing resumes vary even more. My advice: Don't. A good letter (and remember, that's your stock in trade) can arouse enough interest in the recipient to make him ask for a resume.

If you decide to write, however, don't be content with only one contact. Follow it up with a reminder letter or a phone call.

Finally, don't address your letter simply to the editor or the chairman of the board. If you're interested enough to want to work there, you should be interested enough to get their names and exact titles.

Help wanted ads

Answer them if you feel you qualify at least in some areas. But never write about your past or expected salary, even if the ad calls for it. You know and they know roughly what the job pays, by its nature. Leave all money matters until the final interview when they're already expressed a willingness to hire you.

The same goes for a resume, even when the ad calls for it: Don't send one. Make your letter so intriguing, however, that the company will want to see you anyway.

Box numbers? Write only if you're desperate. If you're currently out of work, of course, there's no chance your letter will go to your present employer. But a box number relieves an employer from even the moral obligation of replying to your letter. Save the postage.

Free-lance work

It's true that nine out of 10 free-lancers are regular employees out of work. But, if you can get it, take it. It may lead to future, more lucrative work or an offer of a permanent position. It will keep you occupied and too busy to think about becoming depressed. And the earnings certainly come at a useful time.

A warning note: the unemployment authorities frown at your attempts to earn even a marginal wage while living on their largesse of about $100 a week.

Graphics

Anatomy of a magazine

By John Peter

One of the most neglected elements of a magazine is one of the most important—the positioning of editorial and advertising material. Variously described as flow, pagination or structure, it is one of the first things I study when designing a new magazine or undertaking a publication's improvement program. The right structure can do wonders for readership of both editorial and advertisements.

In most publications the pattern is set at the time of the magazine's conception. A sequence is established, usually by the publisher, based either on some competitive publication in the field or some much-admired magazine. Over the years the original plan is modified to fit new editorial notions or special advertising opportunities. These tend to persist long after the original reason for them has disappeared or been forgotten.

One of the major reasons for neglect is that responsibility for the basic structure, as distinct from issue-to-issue makeup, can fall in the cracks between the publisher, the advertising manager, the editor and the production department. They obviously have a common goal—a successful magazine—but they each view the problem differently.

The publisher focuses on income—primarily from advertising and, with a paid publication, from circulation. This does not mean he or she ignores expenses. But when it comes to structure, attention is most constantly fixed on advertising positioning. The publisher simply has to be sensitive on this score.

The advertising manager, if the magazine has one, will naturally and properly focus attention even more sharply on this advertising area of concern.

The editor's responsibility is readership. While editors appreciate the fact that advertising usually pays the bills, they are understandably more concerned about editorial exposure.

The production department generally strives, under the high pressure of deadlines, to come up with a happy compromise between editorial needs, advertising requirements and economical printing. Makeup, like politics, is the art of the possible. Some would maintain that it's more like the art of the *im*possible.

It is inevitable that this situation breeds unilateral decisions and friction. In the interest of team harmony, it usually means that nobody tends to reexamine the underlying structure, preferring not "to make waves."

Yet nothing can be more worth reexamining. A clear, consistent structure is one of the less appreciated reasons why many magazines are well read. Misinformation about positioning, unfortunately, flourishes like crabgrass on a suburban lawn.

As Far Front As Possible

A good example is the advertiser's insertion order requesting "as far front as possible." I recall one magazine receiving this request typed by a dutiful secretary on an order for the back cover. However, there is a case to be made for high readership in the front of the magazine. It's usually true—perhaps because we put our best editorial material there. But it's not always true. Many structures place high readership material in the back of the publication. The very last editorial page facing the back cover in some magazines gets higher readership than the first editorial page. Front-of-the-magazine magic makes a formidable appeal to our Western sense of sequential logic. Yet we know most right-handed readers first leaf through a magazine back to front. The Chinese and the Hebrews may be right. We put things backward.

Magazines originally were little more than periodical books without advertising. The earliest form of magazine advertising was classified notices. Display advertising as it developed was usually placed discreetly in the back of a publication as in a high school annual. In those days the reader was paying the fare for the magazine. Advertisers were added revenue in the back of the book. With the growth of advertising and the emergence of the popular-priced press, advertisements took a more prominent location. Front-of-the-book positioning often included the front cover. The effort to maximize advertising exposure has led to the innumerable arrangements of ad/ed groupings and mix.

There are many factors which determine structural patterns. Page size is one. A news tabloid, for example, means a structure often having abundant runarounds. Printing capability, such as form size and two-color or four-color signatures, is another. The type of binding—saddle-stitched or perfect-bound—is still another and proportion of full- to partial-size ads yet another. The golden factor, of course, remains editorial-to-advertising ratio.

There is also the black art of makeup practiced by

such masters as *Fortune*'s Sidney Sklar, which goes far beyond complicated technical skills. In addition to keeping extensive records of past positions for each ad and for each client as the basis for equitable rotation, his uncanny ability in positioning facing full-page advertisements on the basis of their design, bleed, typography, photography, illustration, content and the phase of the moon is widely admired. When asked what magazine term he used to describe a solid advertising area in his magazine, he replied, "I call it money."

Within all the constraints and conjuring, objectives should be pretty clear. The optimum structure must be a flexible balance between three requirements—readership, advertising and production.

Built-in Flexibility

Any pattern must have built-in flexibility for expansion or contraction depending on the size of the issue. Magazines, like athletes, usually have trouble in the joints. These flexible areas are worth watching. Does it make more sense from a reader standpoint to add more columnists in the front of the magazine or add an extra feature with turns in the back of the publication? The answer may depend on where ad positions are needed. In a business publication is it better to trim front-of-book news or new products and new literature sections? The answer may lie in the publication's posture in the marketplace—as a newsmagazine or as an inquiry book.

A key point is that reading is habit-forming. *From a reader's standpoint, the less sequential change from issue to issue the better.* A reader likes to find things in a familiar place. This should not become the excuse for never making a change. The reader can acquire a new habit, but not every week or month.

While the variations may be considered endless, all magazine editorial makeup patterns can be divided into two categories—monowell and multiwell.

The monowell structure, with what is often described as an editorial bank or solid, goes back to when magazines began with a book format. While this makeup may provide the reader with single or partial editorial pages scattered through other parts of the publication, its distinguishing feature is one single uninterrupted well of editorial matter. Perhaps the best way to appreciate this form is to examine some of the widely circulated examples. Popular publications are selected only because you probably are more familiar with them. The similar structural patterns occur in business, professional and trade publications.

Playboy is a hot publishing property for more reasons than meet the roving eye. It runs a high 67/33 percent ed/ad ratio delivering a substantial package of editorial. Its hefty cover price and healthy single copy newsstand sales make this both possible and profitable. An average 75-page editorial well, centerfold and all, opens about one-third the way back. The high editorial ratio obviates the necessity for a compensating advertising well. The advertising policy is to avoid facing advertising full pages except, of course, on spreads by the same advertiser. All half-page ads are lower horizontal halves. Consequently, these are not faced unless they are designed as a half-page spread by the advertiser. In practice, a full page sometimes faces another full page or half in metro sec-

tions, but usually ads face editorial material. Departments up front and feature editorial run over in the rear.

The New Yorker is a remarkable publishing performance. It combines an enviable journalistic reputation and steady newsstand and subscription sales with an appealing reputation as an advertising showcase. It runs an average 18-page editorial well, opening about one-third of the way back in the publication. The substantial advertising well of facing advertisements up front kicks off with retail ads to, as a *New Yorker* spokesman puts it, "set up the action, the buying mood." Back of the editorial well is a neat run of full page ads facing vertical two-thirds or one-thirds separated by editorial in the gutter. This structure, with a dozen or so other full page editorial pages scattered about, delivers a beautiful 55/45 ad/ed ratio.

Fortune also has a fortune-fostering pattern. It places its average 40-page editorial well about one-third back in the issue and does not hesitate to face ads in advertising wells up front. When the format size was reduced, however, two feature stories were detached from the solid editorial bank to float toward the rear.

Vogue, like most fashion magazines, responds to the advertisers' front-of-book request with an "everybody into the pool!" approach that positions the editorial well at the end of the magazine. The claim that the reader reads the magazine for the advertisements, which is also true in a substantial number of publications, particularly in the specialty and trade fields, permits this structure. "It's important," says *Vogue* managing editor Rosemary Blackman, "to have an editorial solid so we can convey our editorial point of view."

Put in various ways, this is the argument for a substantial editorial well. The reader feels that somewhere in the magazine he or she is receiving a substantial slice of editorial content. This can be especially important if the publication carries a high cover price like the $2.95 on home decorating magazine *Architectural Digest*. It is equally important if it bears the cachet of an institution or professional society, as do the prestigious *Harvard Business Review* and *New England Journal of Medicine*. Material in a good-size editorial well can be designed well in advance for visual excitement and paced for reader interest.

Editorial and Advertising Clusters

Multiwell magazines group material in editorial clusters. This usually means advertising clusters, as well, if the publication is to remain healthy.

McCall's was once the all-out example. The magazine was once divided into three sections—fiction, fashion and service—each with its own cover. It was promoted as "Three Magazines in One." *McCall's* today has three editorial wells. Special stock insert "Right Now" up front and book reprint in the back are built around a central editorial well. Many magazines ranging from *Sports Illustrated* to *Family Circle,* from *Money* to *True* use this structure of a major editorial well with one or two minor wells.

The most demonstrable examples of multiwell structures are described as read-throughs. This promotional phrase contains the gentle implication that publications with other structures are not really read through cover to cover. Nevertheless it describes the concept. A high advertising/editorial mix has long been characteristic of newspapers. Tabloid magazines quite naturally follow this pattern. News magazines with their newspaper inheritance are perhaps the most expert practitioners.

Time is a prototype example in which departmentalized material is spread relatively evenly throughout the publication. There is, to be sure, an average of nine grouped editorial pages at the beginning of national affairs and about five on the cover subject and some color pages for the picture essay. Each week there is a fixed amount of editorial—about 50 pages. While editorial departments follow a similar pattern issue to issue, the sequence is not locked in.

Business Week, another classic, hits a 60/40 ad/ed ratio. As on most magazines this is an annual rather than an individual issue ratio. "We make," says *Business Week*'s production manager Angelo Rivello, "a 140 editorial column minimum commitment to our readers. We never go below it; most often we exceed it." *Business Week*'s yellow stock "flash" page inserts provide extra editorial visibility and magazine identity.

There is an ultimate relationship between multiwell structure and editorial presentation. A high mix works best with a relatively restrained and structured typographic and pictorial presentation. Excessive editorial design pyrotechnics will tend to make the "editorial look like the ads." This can mean, on one hand, that the editorial material gets lost among the ads and, on the other, that it competes with the ads for attention which makes it a two-time loser with the reader and with the advertisers. Magazines with substantial editorial wells can create special visual impact with less risk of confusion. But multiwell magazines have the asset of distributing editorial interest throughout the issue.

Structure Can Make the Difference

Tactics can have a lot to do with which form or its variations you choose. Too often new magazines follow the structure of publications already in the field. *Penthouse* avoided this mistake and offered advertisers a multiwell approach to compete with *Playboy*'s monowell success. *Newsweek* went with a multiwell structure but deliberately chose a different pattern than *Time*. Structure is a fundamental advantage or difference a magazine can have over its competitor.

Trends also affect structure. High prices, particularly for paper, may mean tighter ad/ed ratios in the future.

There are definitely fewer advertising positions sold. An increasing number of publications have no contract positions except the back cover, preferring to rotate advertisers. This does not mean that advertisers will not continue to seek good positioning. It does mean they are less likely today to pay a premium price for it. Ads must be seen to be read. Advertisers expect visibility.

At the same time, publishers today are also more prone to consider the "good of the book" in placing advertising material. Editorial product is becoming the name of the game for advertisers as well as readers. The trend toward asking the reader to pay an increasing share of a magazine's inevitably rising costs means increasing attention to readership.

By now you may have gathered that *there is no one perfect structure for magazines*. Each must be custom tailored to the individual publication. Here's how to do something about yours. Call a meeting—yes, another meeting. It's worth it, because a clinical examination of your magazine's anatomy is something you won't do every week. Maybe you've never really done it before. Present at the meeting should be the publisher, advertising manager, editor and production person—namely all parties concerned—plus anybody else who can help.

Go through your magazine page by page. Also, you can take apart two copies of the same issue and pin them on the wall to see a typical issue sequence. Look through your competition and any other magazine you like. Discuss the structure of your magazine in terms of its own flow and in relationship to the others. See if there aren't some improvements you can make taking the reader, the advertiser and production into consideration.

Even if you don't change a thing, I think you will find it worthwhile to be confident you have the best structure for your magazine. It has been my experience in such sessions that you will probably discover things that can be improved and the improvements will pay off like blue chip annuity.

A structural examination is important to the health of any magazine. It is very, very unfancy, very commonsensical and *very* seldom done.

The great grid controversy

By John Peter

Chances are your editors won't like it.

Your art director may hate it.

But an increasing number of editors and art directors believe the grid to be the most important development in modern magazine make-up.

The basic magazine grid is something we are all familiar with—even if we don't call it a grid. We find it on layout or paste-up sheets. Fine lines, frequently printed in light blue, establish the exact size of the page or spread and indicate the position of the standard type columns. While the dimensions may vary depending on the size and style of the publication, this basic grid is universally employed.

It's employed, though not always followed. Feature pages of many magazines depart from it. These departures are made for understandable reasons. Yet, they are at the core of the controversy concerning the use of the more modern, more detailed grid.

After all, to the artist a magazine *can* be as unconfined as a painter's bare canvas; it is a two-dimensional blank space for the play of free imagination.

However, magazine design is not a fine art but a fine craft. The art director may be an artist possessing inventive talent and visual skills, but he or she is employed as a communications designer. The art director's aim is to get ideas off the printed page and into the minds of readers as clearly and quickly as possible. The elements are typography and graphics. Our education as well as the mechanical nature of the printing process set certain standards that can be violated only at the risk of decreasing readability and increasing costs.

The rules of readability are very arbitrary but surprisingly immutable. For example, it can be argued that we could read right to left. Roughly one-third of the people on earth do read that way. But with the Western alphabet, we are conditioned to read the other way around. We can read lines placed at an angle on the page, but we find it easier to read on the level. Type can run any length, but we find certain relationships of type size, spacing and line lengths less fatiguing.

While these things may be irrelevant to an artist, they are not to a communications designer. The blank magazine page comes with a grid defined by the dictionary as "a rectangular system of coordinates used in locating the principal elements of a plan." Magazine layout sheets are usually divided into two, three or four columns with margins, bleed and folio positions. Some have additional guide marks—for example, a special drop top margin for editorial feature pages.

A number of logically minded designers, however, have explored the possibilities of carrying this rudimentary grid system much further.

The Bauhaus Influence

Opponents usually blame these explorations on the ever-organizing Germans and the very precise Swiss. That influential post-World War I school, the Bauhaus in Dessau, Germany, which sought to unite art and industry, formulated a series of architectural patterns for typographic layout. Jan Tshichold and Herbert Bayer were the most influential practitioners.

Post-World War II Swiss designers like J. Muller-Brockmann and   pioneered a modular grid which they applied principally but not exclusively to book and catalog design. Many of today's most enthusiastic devotees of the grid have been inspired by the work of this strict Swiss school of design. It also produced today's most widely used sans-serif typeface whose name is appropriately derived from the old name for Switzerland, Helvetia. Some all-out gridders feel that this is *the* appropriate typeface to use with the modular grid. It is an interesting fact that most magazines designed to a strict grid today do use Helvetica type.

One of the most widely admired publication designs of recent times was created by Willy Fleckhaus for the late German magazine *Twen.* When I inquired about its closing from a European publisher friend he jokingly replied, "Its circulation consisted mostly of American art directors."

Yet it's a safe bet that few of the admirers were aware of the Fleckhaus grid system which contributed so much to its distinctive look. It was a twelve-part vertical grid on a large-size page allowing the designer flexibility to divide it into two columns, three columns, four columns or six columns.

An American designer, William Hopkins, who worked with Fleckhaus at *Twen,* brought Willy's brand of grid thinking to the U.S. "When I came back," says Hopkins, "and went to work as art director at *Look,* I had found a direction for myself. Instead of having every de-

520

signer on the magazine start out with a blank piece of paper, I said, 'Let's all start out with the same kind of piece of paper. Let's develop a structure for ourselves.' We started with an adaptation of the *Twen* grid. Then we made a number of variations of it and incorporated them into our basic form."

This grid, like *Twen*'s, emphasized the importance of the verticals but, like other new grids, it also made use of horizontals. It was the horizontal lines that transformed the standard layout sheet into a modern grid that looked something like modular graph paper. In its purest use, everything fit into both vertical and horizontal sections.

Arguments in favor of the grid begin with the sense of unity which it gives to miscellaneous material. "The grid," says Muller-Brockmann, "makes it possible to bring all the elements of design—typography, photography and drawings—into a relationship to each other. The grid process is a means of introducing order into design."

John Massey, director of corporate marketing and

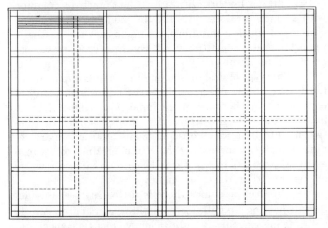

communication at Container Corporation of America, planned its magazine *CCA Today* to a grid because "it gives a sense of order."

A magazine represents a collective effort reflecting a particular point of view. Andrew Kner, art director of two tightly gridded magazines, *Print* and *Packaging Design,* put it this way: "Some editorial philosophy must unify things or why are they under one cover? The visual manifestation of this is some kind of grid."

Separating Editorial From Advertising

The grid can help solve one of the most irritating problems in magazine make-up—separating the editorial pages from the ads. Quite aside from their different objectives, editorial pages have characteristics different from those of advertising pages. The sheer number of editorial pages offers the opportunity for continuity from front to back of the magazine. Each advertisement is designed to get its message across in a variety of magazines. In fact, it is expected to work even when facing another ad. The variety of advertisements, contrasting with a distinctive editorial format which does not compete with them, works best for the reader and advertiser. The right grid offers this editorial unity while still permitting wide variety in typography, photography and graphics.

Kner also emphasizes the unifying assets of the grid in low-budget publications where the bulk of visual material is contributed. "Two sources contribute photo-

graphs which don't relate, but the stories have to. Then a grid helps to get control of the material." A grid can encourage planning and execution of stories ahead of time by assuring the visual fit. "At *Look*," as Hopkins observes, "we did all stories in advance. We did not know where they would fall in the issue. We needed a system."

Massimo Vignelli, who designed the magazines *Industrial Design* and *Dot Zero* to a modular grid, sees straightforward advantages in time and money. "There is a saving in production. First, because of the standardization of elements involved. Second, in paste-up because the people doing it have less opportunity to make a mistake. You can also design much more quickly. The art director doesn't have to make an invention on every page. He can still do inventions if he wants, but within a system."

James Leinhart, who gridded the magazines *Savings & Loan News* and *Sphere,* believes many art directors "put all of their creative energy into developing new arrangements each time rather than using a system that would allow for very simple planning, which would leave them more creative time for the development of really strong ideas. I realize coming up with ideas, developing concepts, and considering things from a more serious point of view can be kind of frustrating. It's easier to size something up another three picas."

James Kendall, managing senior editor at *Savings & Loan News,* also emphasizes time-saving. "Our adoption of the grid system has made production much simpler. We spend far less time fussing with the layouts and far more time working with the copy."

As with *Professional Engineer,* the grid system offers extra advantages on small publications where layout is handled by an editorial or production person. It provides a discipline for the inexperienced.

"A modular grid enables a person to consistently come up with an exceptionally clean and crisp design," says John Beveridge, designer of the magazines *Construction Specifier* and *Professional Engineer.* "One of the functions of the grid is to make a magazine more readable. The beneficiary is the reader, who views the information in a well-organized progression that is highly legible, logical and visually attractive. You must also set up type styles and type sizes and measures."

It's at this point that grid talk begins to sound like the dictums of the Swiss school. "The rule that text should be readable is an unconditional one," writes the Swiss Emil Ruder in *The Typography of Order.* "Uncompromising acceptance of the sizes dictated by this grid results in a correct and consistent overall design."

It is this threat of automatic layouts, with all the loss of freedom it implies, that raises the most serious questions about the grid. There is the real danger that the designer can become a slave to the system, that the words and graphics will be warped to fit a formula. There is also the danger that the designer will end up running a system, not a magazine. There are fears some art directors may use the grid perversely as a system of personal protection forbidding all that "violates" it.

Charlotte Winter, art director of *Architecture Plus* warns, "You have to keep your eye on what's beautiful. Don't get hung up on fads of the moment." William Cage, art director of *Redbook*, says, "You have to evaluate the content of the art or photograph when making a layout. This may be more important in terms of balance than working to some grid." Henry Wolfe, former art director of *Esquire* and *Harper's Bazaar*, who worked on the redesign of *Business Week*, says, "The grid is in the eye. If you have to print it on paper, forget it." Such observations reflect the opinion of many talented designers who see little to be gained by the use of the grid in the way they work. That's what makes the grid controversial.

John Kane, editor of *Professional Engineer*, who is happy with the advantages of his grid, still worries about "the boredom factor. If readers are not all out there passionately waiting for your peerless prose each month, you need to keep the layouts attractive." Other editors hold that the grid can demand writing to fit or excessive authors' alterations.

Vignelli believes, "There is a tremendous misunderstanding about the grid—particularly in this country where people have a pragmatic rather than a disciplined education. It causes a tremendous visual pollution with no sense of reason.

"Some see the grid as the bars of a prison. They would even look on the notes of the musical scale as a prison. Everyone uses the same notes, but there's a tremendous lot of variety in music. For me, using the grid is much more fun because you are playing the game within limitations and getting a higher result.

"Using a system and coming out with a poor result is the fault of the designer. The magazine probably would have been equally dull without the grid. It might also have been stupid. At least in this case the stupidity is taken out and you just get a basic dullness."

"Regimentation relates to the person using it," maintains Leinhart. "If it's a person who is a very strict believer in the ideal column width, the ideal point size, only one typography system—like Helvetica—then you are going to get that kind of restricted look. My feeling is that to be persuasive the layout should also have emotion. Anything that is communicating to people has to have a human connection."

It was this factor that first attracted Hopkins to *Twen*. "I believe in structure and order but what I was doing lacked emotion. In *Twen* there was a great deal of emotion in the use of type, photographs, and ornamentation. It had a grid, but it was by no means pure in its approach."

Right Balance of Discipline and Flexibility

A mechanical and rigid look can be caused by a grid which is too simple. The trick is to create a grid with the right balance of discipline and flexibility. The same thinking applies to exceptions to the grid. "You can make an exception," says Vignelli. "However, if you make 90 percent exceptions and 10 percent grid you are defeating your purpose. If it's the other way around I think you have a pretty good balance. I get out from the grid sometimes because the grid may be in the way of doing a particular thing. There are ways of doing this so it is still related to the previous and following pages in a publication."

Despite the ardor of their own convictions, not all gridders are convinced its use will spread in the future. Kner even saw a reaction to it. "In the underground press

movement of the sixties there was a sort of paste-pot kind of thing—a complete visual anarchy, a the-hell-with-the-system idea. This underground style is surfacing in magazines."

Lost in the clouds of controversy is the relationship of the grid to fundamental changes that are happening to the way magazines are made. As a consultant, I am designing and redesigning more magazines to a grid each year.

Part of a Total Manufacturing System

The grid makes most sense as a part of a total manufacturing system that utilizes the latest technology. This includes coded copy, optical character recognition scanners, transmittal devices, output tapes, computers, print-outs, photosetting and offset transparencies. This equipment, arriving one development at a time, is quietly revolutionizing publication production. The grid fits the picture of tomorrow. Its modular layout, for example, suits the new capabilities of making up complete pages on X and Y coordinates.

Making layouts with a grid has much in common with architectural design. Like the modular construction systems of modern buildings, it emphasizes the aesthetic importance of repetition and continuity with variety employed for emphasis.

This type of design is bound to be more important in the future as the need to create the editorial identity of each magazine becomes more important. High advertising/editorial mixes will press for stronger distinction between editorial and advertising pages. As readers are required to pay an increasing share of magazine costs, every editorial page has to register to be sure a reader knows he or she is getting his or her money's worth.

The grid presumes there is little creative satisfaction in pasting up galleys—something a machine can do with far more accuracy and efficiency. Once type specifications and space standards are set by the designer, they are automatically maintained. I am part of one client's publishing team that is putting all new-product and all new-literature items into a modular grid system that will go directly into column and page make-up.

The grid presumes that in a society with rising educational standards and employment expectations this kind of mechanical labor is going to be increasingly expensive and difficult to obtain.

In considering the grid, these are three things to bear in mind:

The nature of your publication. Benefits of the grid correlate with the complexity of the magazine. They might be minimal with an all-text publication. They are greater with a mix of text, headline, subheads, boxes, illustrations, graphics, charts and photographs. In some magazines the grid may be more useful in regular departments than in feature sections.

The quality of your production. The more sophisticated your typesetting services and make-up facilities, the more sense the grid can make. If you can't get simple copy set straight, you can forget it.

The skills of your editorial staff. A well-organized team can maximize grid benefits. It has been my experience that the key person in a grid system is the managing editor or whoever performs that organizing and monitoring function. Planning is essential. Relationship of concept and copy input to the art director and production department is critical. However, with ever-rising costs of revisions and increasingly critical press times, this kind of staff performance is becoming mandatory with or without a grid.

Creative editors, writers and designers prefer to focus on what really counts—the contents, both words and visuals. The grid is no substitute for content but it can help people focus on content. The better the editor, the better the art director, the better the editorial team, the more

they will get out of the grid.

It's like your friendly computer—no better than what you put into it. Garbage in. Garbage out. You will need the right grid, the right system, and your staff will deserve the right introduction to the grid and a part in developing it. As with the computer, you'd better expect problems and not be oversold on the benefits.

When the great grid controversy is over, the grid will prove a useful, perhaps even indispensable tool.

Magazine structures: A lesson in anatomy

By John Peter

I have been using structure charts for the past 10 years as a way of understanding the anatomy of a magazine. To me, the structure chart is like an x-ray: It reveals the often-hidden inner workings of a magazine.

Magazine structures can be reduced to five basic types. Two of these types—magazines consisting of either all editorial content or all advertising—can be immediately dismissed for our purposes here.

The remaining three structures can be described as mono-well, multi-well and high-mix.

The mono-well structure features a single editorial cluster—usually positioned somewhere near the middle of the magazine—with advertising clusters in the back and front of the book. This editorial well is generally reserved for features, with the various departments interspersed between the advertisements in the front and the back.

The advantage of the single well is that it keeps a good deal of editorial together, and the decision to use this structure is based on the attitude that the reader likes it that way. This attitude is based on two common sense premises: The fewer the interruptions to the reader, the more the reader likes it; and the more pages the reader sees together, the more value the reader feels he or she is getting for the money.

Preferred for book-like publications

This structure is a natural for a magazine which does not contain many ads and for a high-priced magazine. Actually, the more book-like the publication, the more this structure is preferred. Professional and association publications use it widely, but it is also employed in others, from "class" magazines to special interest publications.

Ads must fight for attention

The disadvantage of the single well, however, is that while keeping the editorial together, it also keeps the

ads together. Advertisers are interested in being where the magazine readership is, and they know that a position which increases exposure gives them a better chance of securing the reader's attention. In fact, the standard request of magazine advertisers has always been, "Right hand far front as possible."

But many advertisers now feel that a huge up-front ad well is not the best place to be. They would rather not be in a crowd seeking attention. They also suspect that placement near the editorial material increases their opportunity for exposure.

It is obvious, then, that the mono-well structure becomes a problem for a magazine where advertising is an important source of revenue. In addition, the central editorial well tends to suffer attrition when the ad/ed ratio is raised.

Multi-well created as alternative

To solve this problem, the multi-well structure was developed. This structure usually has two or three editorial clusters distributed through the magazine, with other editorial material in single, double or partial pages throughout the magazine. This structure has the advantage of the mono-well and, at the same time, increases advertising proximity to the editorial material.

Used by variety of magazines

This format is successfully employed in magazines where editorial display is important and is used by a wide variety of magazines ranging from service magazines to business publications.

The third type of structure is the high-mix ("read-thru") format, with editorial and advertising positioned fairly evenly throughout the magazine. This structure is most successful in newsmagazines and tabloids. Although a few editorial pages may be placed together—and some small advertising wells may develop—a relatively even

523

distribution distinguishes it from the multi-well publication.

The advantage of this structure is that it provides the advertiser with both maximum exposure and editorial adjacency, although if improperly handled, it can provoke the reader into thinking that the magazine is all ads. However, the less book-like and the more newspaper-like the content, the more natural this form seems to the reader. *Time*'s structure shows high-mix front to back.

Production factors influence choice

Production factors naturally enter into structure planning: binding—perfect or saddle stitch, special stock, inserts, etc.; printing—black and white, two-color, four-color, etc. Usually the chief production problem is to find the most economical way to meet editorial and advertising needs.

Most publishers are prepared to consider switching production arrangements, even spending more money, if it means accommodating more advertising, securing leadership in readership or substantially increasing revenue.

Evaluate design possibilities

When planning your structure, keep in mind that each structure has its own important editorial and design possibilities. The mono-well format gives the editor control of a good number of consecutive pages in the magazine. Sequence and pace can be more easily regulated, and layouts, typography and illustrations can be made much more lively since the adjacent material is under editorial and art department control.

The multi-well structure offers some of these same editorial and design possibilities—but to a lesser degree. Editorial pacing must be more flexible, and the editorial content of each well should be selected on the basis of editorial flow. Design in this structure must be carefully watched, especially when editorial and advertising pages face each other.

Position wells for even readership

Frequently, different wells contain different types of material—news, features, etc. These wells should be positioned to secure cover to cover readership and relatively even readership research figures front to back. Although this may not always be possible, having this as a goal can greatly improve the flow. The last page of the magazine can be one of the best-read pages.

High-mix needs low-profile design

The high-mix structure demands a relatively low-profile design throughout. The reader must be able to identify every single editorial page, no matter where it is placed. Editorial sign posts like labels and jump headings become more important in signaling to the reader the content and continuity. And many of the devices employed in advertising to attract attention—headlines that shout, acrobatic layouts, typefaces with a fashionably brief life —should not be used. In fact, using a family of typefaces which can be identified with a publication—a trend in all three structures—is mandatory in a high-mix structure.

Properly handled, all of these editorial devices can maximize the editorial assets of page after page flowing through a high-mix format magazine. A recognizable conversational tone can be established without competing with the advertisements proclaiming their wares.

Custom fit structure to your magazine

It is clear that each structure has its advantages and disadvantages. Our structure studies show that the trend is strongly toward the multi-well and high-mix formats, but any structure you choose should be custom-fit to your own magazine. It should also be designed with flexible spots for larger and smaller issues.

Above all, however, the structure and sequence should be maintained: Readers will read any structure, but they like to find things in the same place issue after issue.

Logos: What's in a name?

By John Peter

The title is the most important word or words in any magazine.

Plenty of thought and time usually goes into the selection of a name that will appropriately reflect the publication. Some names are naturals and come easily. Others come hard and often mean settling for the best that's still uncopyrighted. Some magazine names mean next to nothing, but eventually they come to mean a definite something to the reader.

The trial issue of DeWitt Wallace's magazine carried the name *Reader's Digest*. The reasons given for the title were characteristically direct. It was a digest and it was designed to attract readers.

The trial issue, incidentally, was sent to prospective publishers, not readers. Neither the name nor the idea attracted them. It was turned down everywhere. Two years later Wallace published it on his own.

The working title for *Time* was *Facts*. But Henry

Luce was never happy with it. One night, riding home on the subway, he saw an advertisement with the headline, "Time to Retire" or "Time to Change." He couldn't recall afterwards which "Time" stayed in his mind. After sleeping on it and trying it out on his partner, Britt Hadden, in the morning, it was adopted as the name in the prospectus.

In 1929 Luce submitted to his directors the proposal for a new magazine complete with name—*Fortune*. It was chosen from many suggestions because it appealed to his wife, Lila.

Naming a magazine an identifying color was once a solution—*The Yellow Book, The Blue Book* and *The Red Book*. The editor of the latter, Trumbell White, gave it that name because he felt red was the color of cheerfulness. His editorial in the first issue announced that the aim of the magazine was to give intelligent readers what they desire—a publication "invariably interesting, wholesome, decent and cheerful."

Some early publishers solved the title problem by using their own name—*Harper's, Forbes, Dunn's Review, MacLean's*. James McCall came from Scotland after the Civil War to sell ladies' dress patterns. As a promotion piece, he printed a four-page leaflet that became known as *McCall's*.

Such nondescriptive titles, which are defined by the content of the magazine itself, are often cited when title discussions are deadlocked. The argument runs that any name ultimately comes to have the designation the publication gives it, which may be true, but the right name is a big asset when launching a new magazine. The argument has merit in the case of a relaunching.

A short, simple one-word title has advantages. Time Inc. set the style with titles like *Time, Life, Fortune, Money, People*. The unavailability of the title *Sport* forced the only departure from the formula. However, two- and three-word title magazines have obviously proven little handicap to success.

It is the despair of editors, especially those working on business magazines where similarity of titles abound, that a competitor will frequently get credit for an editorial exclusive. It is the fond but false hope that a name change might alter this situation. Disheartening as it may be, readers tend to be more interested in content than source.

Logotypes

The design of a title is an important decision. The appropriate letter forms can reinforce the meaning of the title and increase its identity.

A logotype is also something more than the title on the cover of the magazine. It appears on stationery, in advertising and circulation promotion. It is the widely used symbol of the publication. Publication titles, to a degree, are not read but recognized.

There is no disagreement about this.

Yet I am frequently surprised at two things.

First, how little care is sometimes taken in this typographic decision. Often, few options are explored. Sometimes the designer will explore various logotypes, but submit only one or two. Sometimes there scarcely is a design and almost any imagination would improve the originality and identity of the letter combinations. On occasion, there is too much design involved. The name is virtually unreadable except to the designer.

A typeface can be too heavy for an elegant publication, too flippant for a serious one. The Didot capital letters of *Vogue*'s logo reflect the fashion and beauty of its contents. The bold upper and lower case Egyptian of *People*'s logotype fits the newsy, informal style of the magazine. Herbert Lubalin's Avant Garde logo for *Family Circle* matches the labels in a modern supermarket.

The second surprise to me is the frequency with which some publications switch their logotypes. There is a case to be made for never changing a logo. There is an even better case to be made for refining it periodically. This retains continuity and keeps it up to date. There is also a case to be made for changing the logo-style to reflect some editorial change in a publication or the market it serves. There is very little to be said for switching it because someone is tired of it or "just to have a change." In some quarters there is the illusion that a new logo on the package will substitute for improved contents.

Fortune's first title and cover were designed by Thomas M. Cleland, an artist and one of America's most distinguished typographers. The original was sketched backwards on a tablecloth by Cleland. Luce liked it so much that he took the tablecloth off the table and carried it back to the office. The classic logo was Cleland's response to the charge to make *Fortune* "the most beautiful magazine."

Fortune's logo has changed over the years, reflecting changes in the publication, but *Time*'s logo has remained substantially the same. It was made somewhat heavier about four years ago during a general typographic redesign.

Designer Milton Glaser made a similar change in the logotype of *New York*. It was first published as a supplement in the Sunday New York *Herald Tribune*. When the newspaper folded, its editor, Clay Felker, bought the rights to publish it as a magazine. Glaser redesigned the gracefully thin logo which was based on Caslon typeface to a bolder one based on Bookman. This retained the appearance of the original logo but gave it a tougher, more aggressive attitude.

Art director Kenneth Stuart explains his modifications of the *Reader's Digest* logo: "The earlier letter was a bastard letter. All I did was to base it on a classical letter, Caslon. I also changed the 'R' a little to make a design of it.

"I wanted a letter that, to my mind, would be in style forever, the way Chippendale furniture will always be stylish. If you get a good piece of Philadelphia Chippendale furniture, you don't have to worry that it was made in 1760. It looks as good today as it looked then. And it will look as good a hundred years from now.

"The type I used was the type in the Declaration of Independence. It's Caslon, designed by William Caslon in England. He used to sell it to Benjamin Franklin. Since we are an American magazine and about 20 million people buy it each month, we want something related to that. It would not be appropriate for me to design something like an IBM or RCA logo. Those are different design problems, which I love, but the answers wouldn't be fitting for us. We're like ham and eggs and a turkey dinner. We want that feeling in what we do."

When it comes to designing logotypes, it's thinking

that has to be the basis for art. The results should look right, but it's more important that they be right with the character of the magazine.

If you have the right logo, stick to it. If you don't, it

takes very little time and money to come up with the right one.

Why not?

-

Why covers fail

By David Merrill

My first boss, David Ogilvy, believed in borrowing from the "editorial look" when designing his advertisements. Consequently, most of his early efforts, and many of Ogilvy & Mather's current print ads, look like pages from *Reader's Digest*. They flag the reader with something that is important to him and then promise worthwhile information.

But because a magazine cover is an ad, an ad for your magazine, harking back to some of David's early rules probably isn't a bad exercise in magazine cover design.

Your magazine's cover is the single most important element in creating an overall image of the magazine. Unfortunately, a first impression may be the *only* impression that some people—media buyers, for instance—will have.

Obviously, a cover is of the *utmost* importance in a magazine start-up. But it is still important every time an unfamiliar reader or potential advertiser sees it.

David Ogilvy would say that the product name, in this case your logo, should be prominent, descriptive and legible. An ad agency rarely has the opportunity to name its product—but you do.

Henry Luce has a marvelous talent for labeling his products. *Fortune. Life. Sports Illustrated.* He smiles down on the latter day *People* and *Money*.

Time was pretty good too, but *Newsweek* probably would have been more to the point. However, Luce salvaged it by adding *The Weekly Newsmagazine* as an underline which stayed on the cover for about 40 years.

A descriptive underline for a magazine cover is extemely valuable, especially in the beginning, if the logo doesn't or can't say it. *Venture* used to be a travel magazine. Now *Venture* is a business magazine introduced in 1979 and is labeled *The Magazine for Entrepreneurs,* an underline that clearly identifies the magazine. Furthermore, since almost all of the single, descriptive words are already taken, underlines can be a good idea.

Designing your logo

Once your magazine has a descriptive label, with or without underline, that label should be unique and tastefully designed. After a while, a magazine logo becomes a stamp of identification for the reader browsing the newsstand or the morning mail. You could misspell it, and the habitual reader wouldn't notice. But if you change the typeface, he wouldn't be able to recognize it.

It follows, then, that your cover format ought not to

be changed without reason and forethought if you have an established readership. Improvement is good. But change without improvement might do no more than irritate your habitual readers.

Ideally, your logo is unique and totally appropriate. I had a design teacher once who said that, "Everything we design should be different." He went on: "If you take your clothes off and run naked down the street, that would be different . . . but it wouldn't be in good taste."

Having come up with a unique, descriptive and tasteful logo for long term identification, and an underline with an appropriate "promise," the next problem is to determine what to put on your cover from week to week or month to month.

A few magazines, like *The New Yorker,* don't do anything to draw people inside. Others like *Reader's Digest* say it all with a table of contents. (Of course, the *Digest* backtracks by using tip-ons with flag words prominently displayed for the check-out counter racks.)

Most magazines split the difference between the two and try to catch the potential reader's interest with a dominant cover visual, related or not to a story inside the magazine. You have to decide what your philosophy is and then effectively carry it out.

A good starting formula (middle of the road, but dripping with reason) is a primary cover story with a single illustration and a big blurb. Then, just in case the cover story isn't compelling to everyone you want to reach, add a few smaller, alternate blurbs about secondary and tertiary stories within the issue. Assuming that the cover is an ad for the magazine, give the potential reader many reasons to become an actual reader.

Most magazines, of course, aren't newsstand so it might seem that the content of the cover doesn't matter. (I've been told that by a few publishers and editors while designing or redesigning their magazines.) But even if your publication isn't in combat on the newsstand, it *is* on the coffee table and with the rest of the morning mail. How and what is displayed on your cover can (and almost certainly will) determine whether your publication is opened *now*. Or later. Or never. Therefore, in my opinion the principles of good cover design apply to every magazine equally.

Your cover has to project the image you want your magazine to have. And it has to give your readers a reason to open it as soon as possible. Since whoever looks at your cover will have his attention diverted by something else, your cover must be competitive.

The cover can get you the first time newsstand sale. Or the initial subscription. Or the media buyer's interest. If the cover succeeds while the magazine fails, it's the editor's fault. The cover is only an *ad* for your product.

Once a magazine has an established unshakable bunch of readers who know what to expect inside, additional readership can be attracted by featuring something other than the expected on the cover.

For instance, thousands of people buy *Time* on the newsstand every week. This large base of readers would buy the magazine if it had only its logo and a red border because those addicts merely want their capsulization of the week's news and they know they'll find it inside. But when *Time* puts something relatively unexpected on the cover—a movie or science story or a pretty face—they generally sell substantially more newsstand copies.

Although this is especially valuable for newsstand books, it also applies to purely subscription magazines. Following the newsstand sales barometer, an unexpected cover will get the millions of subscribers inside more quickly.

A few years ago the four best sellers of the year for *Time* were three attractive women and a shark (Jaws). None of them typical of *Time*. But the advantage of those covers was that they kept the regulars and added the special interest readers who care more about movies and people than the weekly news.

Almost always, *Time* and *Newsweek* sell more copies with a back-of-the-book cover story than they do with a predictable, hard news cover. Certainly, part of the reason is that with a back-of-the-book cover story there is less competition for the potential buyer's interest. If *Time, Newsweek* and *U.S. News & World Report* all feature a Friday night presidential address, they not only end in a three-way tie with each other, they also lose to the networks and every Sunday newspaper in the country.

All of their regular readers know they can expect the usual recap of the speech inside. So if one of them breaks away and does something unexpected on the cover, it will increase sales. At stake is their image as "newsmagazines," but in view of television news competition, there might be room for adjustment in their thinking.

If yours is a furniture or restaurant or golf magazine in competition with other furniture or restaurant or golf magazines, it might not be a bad idea to splash on the cover something other than that issue's expected furniture or restaurant or golf story, which will predictably be splashed by your competition.

The cover as packaging

A magazine cover is as much a package as it is an advertisement. If it's better than the product—the editorial content—it will sell it . . . once. If it's different than the content, it will mislead and attract the wrong audience . . . once. If it doesn't advertise your good product, no one will discover it. There are a lot more ways to fail than to succeed with magazine covers.

Should your cover, your ad, your *package,* have an illustration or a photograph? Or should it be all type?

The answer is that it ought to be whatever is in the best interests of your magazine's image and the exciting, effective communication of your cover story.

When everything else is equal, *Time* uses illustrations on its cover rather than photographs—but *Time* has a special situation. It is to their newsstand sales advantage to look different from *Newsweek*. And *Newsweek* almost always uses photographs.

Although there is both editorial and advertising research that suggests that a photograph is generally better than an illustration, I discount the findings because of the multitudinous variables. *What* you put on the cover is always more important than whether it's printed or photographed.

Of course, some subjects lend themselves better to one style of execution than the other. According to newsstand sales information at *Time,* if your cover subject is to be the president, a good photograph that communicates the tone of your story is better than an equally good artist's representation. People prefer the reality of the photo. The believability. They want to see the pores in his nose. On the other hand, if the concept of your cover story would be better served by a picture of the president wearing a dunce cap or throttling an Arab, illustration is clearly the more practical way to execute your cover.

Beyond the art versus photo controversy, there is occasionally a place for a cover that is all type (although such covers are sometimes a cop-out). If the announcement is especially startling to your readers, added illustration can be superfluous.

Quite a few years ago a *Time* cover asked the question, "Is God Dead?" and I defy any art director to enhance the impact of that question with an illustration. I did a cover a few years later near the end of the Vietnam War which simply stated, "The Shape of Peace," when Kissinger returned with the shape. Because it wasn't just another in a series of Henry Kissinger covers, it assumed a special importance for *Time*. There *was* an apostrophe-sized dove on the cover but it didn't add much. Even short of the importance of those covers, there are many other times that all type covers can be used effectively.

Your magazine should have some element of consistency to its covers, both to help your regular reader find it and to help establish its philosophical image. But if you don't vary your covers and if you don't choose the best style of execution on each issue, they can become boring.

Some magazines, notably women's magazines, have applied the slide rule to such an extent that their covers are nearly always the same. It's hard to argue if they work, but in my opinion (loosely backed by research), twists and variations within a proven cover formula add to reader interest.

There's very little reliable cover research around. While I was at *Time* the only thing we learned conclusively was that if too much of the logo is covered, some of the people who are looking for *Time* on the newsstand won't be able to find it. Therefore, common sense suggests that your logo ought to be easily identifiable and prominently displayed on every cover.

Choosing a cover subject

Your primary cover subject should be the most exciting story—from your reader's viewpoint—in your magazine. Artistic license is certainly advisable in selecting the cover story since there's no rule that the cover story has to be the longest or most painstakingly prepared story in the issue.

Project yourself into the reader's shoes and select the story which is most likely to attract his immediate attention. You can always deal with your expensively produced, "more important" story with a secondary cover line.

Another major consideration in selecting the cover story subject is that it be illustratable. Sometimes (too often) a very good story just doesn't lend itself to a gripping cover illustration and a very exciting issue dies on the newsstand or the coffee table. (It is important, of course, that the cover story carrot pays off. The old "SEX! Now that we've got your attention . . ." gambit will only work once.)

David Ogilvy, who has certainly put more rules to paper than any other advertising practitioner, used to forbid humor in his agency's ads and commercials. But recently, speaking at a conference in Frankfurt, he said, "Always in the past I've persecuted copywriters who wrote funny commercials. But, thank God, now we can be funny, too. Our new research reveals that humor can be very effective if . . . concentrated on the product."

Well. His revelation comes about two decades after Volkswagon advertising proved his point. But the point can be translated into magazine covers. A cartoon or a humorous photo or illustration can often be effective in conveying a cover story message.

Ogilvy also said that "advertising as practiced today is inefficient—grossly, extravagantly, obscenely inefficient." The same thing could be said for most magazine covers. The newsstand, the morning mail and the coffee table tend to be grey with average, run-of-the-mill covers. The occasional one that stands out and grabs the reader's attention in a positive manner greatly benefits the magazine and its advertisers.

A *Time* or a *Playboy* can probably coast for a long time on established readership, but how about the struggling new magazine or the magazine somewhere in the middle of the pack among its competition? For them, exciting covers can make a substantial difference.

Strive for efficiency

Since a magazine cover is an ad for the magazine, it, too, ought to be first and foremost: *efficient*.

Therefore, whether it's an illustration, a photograph, or all type is irrelevant. Instead it must be efficient. Every cover should solve its particular communication problem as strongly, as quickly and as crisply—as *efficiently*—as possible.

Formulas in cover design can be tremendously self-defeating for the magazine trying to carve out its share of the market. As soon as you decide to do all photographs for consistency's sake, and because there's research that "proves" they work best, you'll come up against a cover subject that screams for a cartoon . . . or an old Bettmann Archive woodcut . . . or something else.

Let the design consistency be carried by the logo and perhaps a design format, but let each cover story be illustrated in the most effective and efficient manner possible. Many magazine art directors get enamored with a style of illustration and then work backward through the solution in the general direction of the problem.

It seems obvious, but first should come a concise definition of the problem: What are we trying to communicate? Then the solution: What is the literal content of the cover art? Then the execution: Should it be an illustration, a photo or all type?

Too often, an art director or editor will say, "I'd really like to use so-and-so's work because it's so such-and-such," and then will struggle in reverse trying to shoehorn the execution into the slot for solution, regardless of the problem.

One way (and I'm not suggesting the only way or the best way) to establish a consistent look is to design a rigid format for your cover into which you can stuff any type of illustration and still look like you.

New York is a very good (and perhaps the most imi-

tated) example of this philosophy. In its favor is a very distinctive logo and an area on the cover where any type of illustration can be displayed without it looking like a different magazine every week. *Geo* doesn't look like *New York,* but its cover is designed with the same philosophy. Or you could follow *Time* and put a color frame around your cover like *Sports Afield* and *L'Express.*

The *New York* format also provides a clear, uncluttered space at the top where their readers can expect to find the alternate billings every week.

The new *Time* has a similarly conceived format: there's always the corner flap for the second most important story in the magazine. But *Time*'s format is limited (whereas *New York*'s is not) in that they *have* to come up with the second most important story in the magazine even when no single story is clearly second. And I'm sure it's often difficult to tuck a tiny illustration into that little triangular shape.

Most magazines, of course, opt for the full-page, four-color bleed cover because of the relative impact of a big picture. A disadvantage is that any minor billings frequently get lost in a busy background or interfere with the primary story. A less obvious disadvantage is that such a cover frequently forces the cover designer into a less than ideal cropping of the primary art, thereby decreasing its impact, in order to accommodate the other language.

This magazine, FOLIO, has excellent covers, and the magazine has a look that is consistent. And yet, the covers are sometimes in black and white, sometimes full color. Futhermore, the logo changes size and floats all over the cover, defying what is almost everybody's cardinal rule.

But it doesn't matter because there is a good cover designer making the decisions every month and his design philosophy is consistent.

Perhaps a good rule of thumb is that if you have a good art director or cover designer, you should leave the cover format rather loosely constructed. If not, button it down tightly so design consistency doesn't get lost.

So, what constitutes a good cover is at least debatable and certainly not the same for all publications.

Whether or not you *can* judge a book by its cover, the truth is that most people *do,* at least initially. So it behooves every publisher to make that first impression reflect his intentions. This is especially important for small magazines, new magazines and trade magazines since the average media buyer isn't necessarily going to be familiar with or interested in examining such magazines in any depth.

After a discussion of a magazine's cpm, advertisers are interested in a magazine's "editorial environment," and there are many class advertisers who won't be seen in a sloppy environment.

How a magazine looks is an important influence on the potential reader. It's easier to make a snap judgment, as many do, by the *look* of a magazine rather than its editorial content. If it *looks* cheap and amateurish, readers may never find the editorial pearls.

I don't know how to make perfect covers, and I doubt if anybody does. But I think there are a few general guidelines that apply to all publications:

•Every magazine should have a clear design identity that reflects what you want people to think of the magazine.

•The cover is the most important single element of the magazine, and the logo is the most important part of the cover. Typefaces have personalities and the one used for your logo ought to reflect the personality of your magazine. Not all logos do. Not all are good. Frequently they are arbitrarily chosen, and when they are, that magazine has missed an opportunity to suggest who and what it is. Think of Coca Cola. CBS. Volkswagon. *The New Yorker. Life.* Corporate identity is the same as magazine identity.

•A cover should be as simple as possible, but it should carry as much information as necessary. Although this leaves a lot of room for discussion, in general, a single strong cover story visual and blurb with alternate blurbs is a good working formula.

•Finally, have someone who knows what he's doing do your covers. Art directors—like editors and publishers—are like plumbers: There are good ones, not so good ones, and ones who will leave your toilet backing up into your bathtub.

I've been on the faculty of a couple of FOLIO's seminars, and a recurring question is, "But how do we get the cover done?" There's no simple answer. Good covers come from lots of information being poured on people who know how to translate it into the visual. And the possibilities are infinite.

A good art director must understand who his audience is and what he's trying to communicate. Then he should use the tools available to accomplish the communication without imitating the styles of type, illustration and photography currently in vogue. Just because those styles worked for some other publications or won awards in the design shows does not necessarily make them appropriate for your magazine.

Magazine covers are good when they envelop the editorial content in a functional, attractive manner. They are good when they mirror the words in sense and feeling. And they are good when they enhance the communication. They are *very* good when they are also efficient.

The cover story

By John Peter

Readers read a magazine for its editorial content, not because it has a beautiful, funny or sexy cover. However, the most important single page in a magazine is the cover. Whether it's on a crowded newsstand, on a busy desk or in a jammed mailbox, it's the cover that signals what magazine it is, which issue it is and what's inside that makes the issue worth reading.

There is surprisingly little research in this area which could be called scientific. Most statistics come from newsstand sales and only a relatively small percentage of magazines are sold on newsstands. Even for many newsstand magazines, single copy sales represent only a portion—frequently a small portion—of their total circulation.

Most knowledge about covers is pragmatic, based for the most part, on specific experiences with specific publications. This knowledge is frequently questioned, even within an organization. Although the thinking that goes into choosing a cover is usually guarded as proprietary information, occasional leaks indicate that there are no big secrets.

I have served on the cover committees of a number of high circulation publications. On one committee, when selecting the cover for each issue, we enjoyed a friendly cover pool by picking the newsstand sales figure. The circulation manager, who took a scientific approach, won no more often than the rest of us but he always had a better explanation for losing.

The cover game: skill and luck

Think of covers as a game—a game of skill with a few rules, some generally accepted tactics and plenty of variables and surprises. It's the variables and surprises that make judging a cover's performance so difficult.

One variable is weather. It can be a bad surprise. Tom Kenny, circulation director of *Ladies' Home Journal*, explains how it had a very positive effect on the sale of one of the issues of *LHJ*. "One of our best selling issues was the February issue of last year. It so happens that it was on sale during a big storm in the Middle West. That issue stayed on sale six weeks."

Another variable is the number of copies on the stands and the way they are displayed. Everyone knows you can increase sales to a degree by flooding the newsstands with copies and accepting increased returns. Veteran newsstand circulation people can tell countless tales of disaster and triumph with distributors and dealers.

"It's a disaster if you don't get the copies placed where you want them on the newsstand," says magazine consultant Jim Kobak. "Only if you get good display is the cover an accurate guide to what people like. For example, women's magazines normally get good display; the one with the best cover is going to win the battle almost every time.

"If you are a hot rod magazine stuck behind seven others, your cover isn't going to help you a lot. All that counts in this situation is your logo because that's all that anyone is ever going to see."

There's also an element of luck involved. Richard Smith, circulation director of *Playboy*, explains, "One of the things that can happen is that you may decide to come out with a dark cover one month and that same month the other magazines in your category come out with dark covers. When you look at the newsstand the whole section is dark and nothing stands out. If you come out with a white cover, there's a chance they will all come out with a white cover. Every once in a while, you'll guess right and you will have a cover that is so different in total concept from the others that it just pops off the newsstand. Those issues tend to do well. It's a matter of luck, and there's really nothing you can do about it."

Timing is another variable but again, luck helps. *People's* best selling cover in 1977 featured Tony Orlando. Circulation director Donald Elliman says, "Tony Orlando just happened to be the right person at the right time. He was about to make a comeback."

Keep success in proper perspective

It's wise to keep the success of an issue in proper perspective. Sometimes covers just don't matter. Frank Wolf, publisher of *Seventeen*, points out,"Our best selling issue has been the August back-to-school issue. What we put on our August issue is an attractive gal wearing the latest thing. Kids look forward to it. It sells about 300,000 to 400,000 more copies than any other issue. I would hate to think we could put my picture on it and do as well, but the truth is, we could."

As Smith of *Playboy* notes, advance publicity of an issue can sell that issue regardless of the cover. "In November 1976, we ran the Jimmy Carter "lust for life" interview. We had a 92 percent sale. I think it would be erroneous to point to the cover design and say that's what did it."

It is also wrong to point to newsstand experience and automatically apply it to all magazines. Far and away, most magazines arrive through the mail at the home or office.

The magazines may be delivered unwrapped, with a label on the cover. Too many cover designers fail to consider the label as part of the cover design. As a consultant, I have made improvements in some covers, the cover of *Prevention* to name one, by repositioning the blurbs so they are not covered by the address label.

Since most covers are viewed closeup and in full, the newsstand wisdom of positioning logos in the top left-hand corner for stacked display is not important. *Architectural Record's* logo is at the bottom. It is also not important for the cover to have the impact of a poster because it's not necessary to catch the reader's eye from a distance.

There are three basic objectives in the cover game: getting identity, getting recognition and getting action.

Identity is based on consistency

Identity is the process whereby the reader knows quickly what magazine he is looking at. Identity is based on consistency.

Size is clearly one of the quickest clues to identity. Pocket-size magazines like *TV Guide* or *Organic Gardening*, and tabloid size like *Rolling Stone* or *Advertising Age*, are recognizable in a crowd. The widespread move to a standard size, with all its economic and production benefits, means more magazines must focus on the other distinguishing characteristics.

One of those characteristics is cover stock. Stock, textured or uncoated, is clearly a recognition factor with some special magazines like *Commentary* and *Foreign Affairs*. However, most magazines today have similar coated cover stock. Some magazines, like *Audubon* or *Classic*, believe that heavier weight cover stock adds class and appeal. Increasing the quality of cover stock is the most inexpensive paper investment that can be made in terms of impact on readers and advertisers.

Color in a special hue can be a recognition factor, but extremely few magazines continue to use a single distinctive color on the cover. In the early days of magazine publishing this was in vogue. There were even matching titles—*Green Book*, *Blue Book* and *Red Book*. While a single color does aid identity, using a single color requires

more work in order to get recognition and action.

To answer the question of whether logos are read or just recognized—the unfamiliar is read and the familiar is recognized. Misspell *Mad* or *New York* but keep the typeface and format the same, and chances are the reader will identify it as the correct magazine. Cease and desist court orders have been won where a new title has been handled in such an imitative design that a purchaser might be deceived.

How distinctive the typeface is and how well it is handled contribute to making a logo out of a title. The typeface can signal that a magazine is dignified, sporty or gutsy. The right logotype can bring to the reader's mind the image of the publication and what that publication is like.

Logo must reflect magazine's image

The logotype is the symbol of the magazine. Even standing alone on letterheads, calling cards and promotional mailings it must reflect the image of the magazine. At the same time it's important to be wary of letterforms that are too distinctive. Be sure your logo can be quickly and easily read. Readability has to be an important requirement, not only in its design but in its use.

Sometimes a logo is printed in a color that gets lost in the background. Inevitably, a printer is blamed for not following the color on the progs or on the instructions. Too often a chance is taken without full recognition of the risk.

Sometimes a logo is obscured by an illustration covering part of it. This particular bit of cover bravado should be indulged in with care, like trick plays in any game. It can severely hamper identification.

Format contributes heavily to identity. *Time* magazine's red border is one clear example. A non-bleed cover, with plenty of white space for a border, as on *Architectural Digest*, is another. It is not smart to switch back and forth from one format to another if you want the reader to identify your magazine quickly.

Consistency is the basis for identification and it works for most packaged goods.

Cover should reflect content

A magazine cover is a package. It's the wrapper for the editorial content, and the design of the package should reflect that content. A cover, as Kobak says, is a marketing tool. "I don't care if it's pretty or not. The beauty of the cover rarely has much to do with the sale." Since the cover has much in common with any other consumer package, it's an obvious idea to hire an industrial design firm to develop a cover. It has been done. The most notable examples are Henry Dreyfuss for *McCall's* and Massimo Vignelli for *Industrial Design* magazine.

We investigated the industrial designer's approach with San Francisco's Landor Associates, the largest marketing design firm in the world. Vice-president Glen Gardner says, "If asked to design a magazine cover, we would be inclined to consider the overall imagery of the magazine. Rather than being specific to an article in the issue we would perhaps express some kind of statement about the total magazine. That is an objective we look for in food or any other kind of packaging."

However, magazines do have a unique packaging problem—the cover must say, "I'm the same but different." Consistency must be combined with change, the basis for the next objective—recognition. The cover must allow readers to quickly recognize that they are looking at a new and different issue.

The most certain signal is the new date. It's also a sometimes neglected signal—difficult to find and hard to read. Readers who have heard about an issue from a promotion or a friend will be looking for the date. So will the readers who are looking for the new issue.

Other recognition signals are linked to the final step, which is action. The cover must persuade the reader to pick up the magazine and look inside.

Words and illustration promote action

Two things are important in getting a person to take action—words and illustrations.

More attention is focused on the words on the cover than on any other words in the magazine. There are magazines which are successful without these cover lines, *The New Yorker* and *Audubon* to name two, but they are exceptions. Some magazines use only type. *Reader's Digest* and *Harvard Business Review* are two.

John Allen, former assistant managing editor and now director of corporate and public affairs at *Reader's Digest*, says, "Mr. Wallace, the founder of *Reader's Digest*, is big on ease of reading. He wants to make it easy for people to get the information he wants to get across. If you have to look, even for the table of contents, then it's a little more difficult to read.

"Also, we offer many more articles than other magazines. We have 35 to 36 titles that we can put there on the cover, hoping that a number of them will interest the reader."

However, most publishers avoid these pure approaches.

Single titles convey simplicity

The case for a single title on the cover is strength and simplicity. "Class" magazines favor only one "sell." A single title also makes sense for a special issue or one hot topic.

Magazines with heavy newsstand sales such as *Family Circle* and *Woman's Day* use multiple blurbs.

Circulation director Smith of *Playboy* lists the basics: "You have to say everything you want to say to get the person to pick up the magazine. It can't be too long, it has to be punchy, and it has to be legible."

A wholesaler observes, "People tend to be vain. They tend to use their glasses only for private reading. If they are in a supermarket looking over the magazine rack, the magazine most likely to get the readership is the one that can be read without glasses."

The need to sell the reader on each issue is not restricted to magazines sold on newsstands. With people getting increasingly pressed for time, and with all the alternative activities and attractions in the home, it's as difficult to get a reader to pick up a copy from a coffee table as a supermarket stand.

Well-written blurbs are one of the surest ways to get a reader to pick up a magazine. Although art directors often wish those cluttering blurbs would go away, one test of a good cover design is how well these blurbs are handled. Yet when readers talk about liking and disliking a cover, they do not mean the blurbs. They usually mean the cover illustration.

The cover illustration is generally linked to a story in the magazine. But there are successful magazines like *The New Yorker* and *Prevention* which do not use cover art relating to an inside story. These magazines are, instead, opting to build the overall image of the magazine.

A cover can do both—project an image and tie in with an article—in special interest and professional publications. After a prolonged search with imaginative graphics and typographics on *Professional Builder*, we learned that nothing appeals to a home builder like a beautiful photograph of a home. Countless other publications have also discovered the obvious—that there's nothing like the subject of the magazine to interest their readers. *Bon Appetit* shows food; *Interior Design* shows interiors.

The two big trends in cover subjects today are people and concept photography.

People are old stuff on news and fan magazines. But you now find them very often on women's service magazines. *Ladies' Home Journal* executive editor Richard Kaplan says, "Our best success is with TV personalities who have more cachet than they used to." A recognizable face tells the reader much more about what's inside.

The pace for personality covers is set by *People* magazine. Managing editor Richard Stolley says, "What we think we know is that young sells better than old, pretty sells better than ugly, sports figures don't do very well. TV sells better than music, music does better than movies and anything does better than politics."

Although lately it's been out of fashion to have people on the cover of trade and professional magazines, I look for a return to this practice. People are interested in people. They do not have to be "brand name" personalities to interest readers. They can be the outstanding people in their own business or profession. *Modern Materials Handling* has enjoyed leadership over the years with interesting industry people on its cover.

Concept photography covers reflect the move in magazines to ideas and abstractions. The idea of the cover article is dramatized by a visual concept. The more apt and simple, the better. Though they might be drawn, they are more striking in photography. *Business Week*, *New York* and many other city magazines have been top players in this area. But special interest, professional and trade magazines such as *Medical Economics* and *Modern Railroads* are now becoming skilled at this also.

Joe Ruskin, head of photography at McGraw-Hill and cover editor of *Chemical Engineering* says, "In style, a cover must be simple. It must have impact. But it must also attract attention by getting the reader involved. This is what I mean by concept—to suggest the whole story by using a symbol with which readers can readily identify."

Concept covers, however, make special demands. They require close cooperation between the art and editorial departments. They also require imagination and skill on the part of the art director.

Cover reflects marketing position

To sum up: Keeping the basic objectives in mind—identity, recognition and action—develop a cover approach that reflects your market positioning and the character and content of the magazine.

William Campbell, circulation director of *Cosmopolitan*, a magazine with a tight cover formula, observes, "As in the case of the *Cosmo* cover girl, you notice that she is strikingly addressing you. She doesn't look off into space. *Cosmopolitan* covers are strictly subjective, and even though they are all similar, there is subtle variation from issue to issue. One girl will be a blonde, another a brunette. One will have on an understated garment, another will be absolutely dazzlingly glamorous. You will never see two consecutive covers with the same color background or costume. The character of the *Cosmo* girl, and that is indeed what she is, says something to the type of person Helen Gurley Brown is trying to reach."

Keep your cover approach clear. Reach an agreement on it between yourself and the others involved and write it down. Once that's done, you may have helped solve what, in my experience, is the single greatest problem with covers—lack of planning. Most are done too quickly and too late.

A cover takes time and is worth it. The cover is the package. It's a marketing tool, a problem in communication and a problem in industrial design. No two publications are identical. To win the cover game, you have to develop your own game plan.

The new typography

By John Peter

The photo compositor, combined with the computer, has created the most significant leap forward in typesetting since Gutenberg. It is only natural that the emphasis to date has been on its technological aspects and economic benefits. The capabilities of the new machine have pushed print into the twentieth century. The savings, the speeds and the precision of the new systems have made conversion not only economically possible but compelling.

This article takes a look at the effect of photocomposition on typography itself—what the reader reads. We have scarcely begun to appreciate that we are at the early stages of a typographic revolution—the beginnings of nothing less than a new typography.

The typesetting revolution, like all revolutions, has caused us to reconsider fundamentals which have been comfortably accepted for a long time. Today we are reexamining the basic consideration of all typography—legibility.

To begin with, we have to realize what a marvel the act of reading really is. Over the centuries we have come to accept the communication of human thought and emotion by means of symbols—the alphabet and numerals—as routine. But we know from our schoolbook history lessons that this development was one of the momentous breakthroughs in the story of mankind. It comes as something of a shock to learn that today there are more than 800 million people in the world, many of them in our own land, who still cannot read.

Question of Readability

I have spent a considerable amount of time on the question of readability. As a design consultant, I have studied everything I could lay my hands on searching for "the rules of legibility." This has been less difficult than you might imagine because there has been surprisingly little time and much less money invested in research that would meet genuine scientific standards. It is not depreciating sporadic past investigations into legibility to recognize the severe restrictions in resources as well as the admitted limits and outdating of the results. When put to it, many authorities will admit that we know next to nothing about legibility except some generally held observations: All capital letters seem harder to read than upper

and lower case. There is a readable ratio between the size of type and the length of the line. Etc., etc.

We recognize that what is considered easily legible for one person may be difficult for another. We know that physical circumstances such as light, movement, noise and comfort have a lot to do with reading. We know that physical well-being—eyes, health and fatigue—are important. Interest in the content has a tremendous amount to do with what we manage to read. If we need to find a job or a home, we will willingly read 6-point type in the classified section of a newspaper.

It's clear that all legibility is based on conditioning or, if you prefer, training. Peoples of the world read a wide variety of language symbols. We can decipher a wide variety of handwritten styles in personal letters. We also read a great number of typefaces that are quite different from one another.

Reading did not start with Gutenberg, but typography did.

Ed Rondthaller, dean of Photolettering, Inc., explains it this way: "It was a marvelous idea that Gutenberg had. It was a genius of an idea to put each letter on a rectangular metal block. It not only held the letter, but it also defined the width and height of the letter. It made it possible to set type in a line and to lock it up in relation to other lines.

"In doing this, Gutenberg introduced a mechanical appearance to letters to which I am sure there were strong objections at the time. I'm certain the old scribes said, 'That's no good. That's terrible looking.' However, over these 500 years we have become accustomed to letters separated by white space."

Later, Linotype and Monotype machines mechanized typesetting but preserved the separation of the letters. The casting matrix always required space between units.

The module of the metal base, though confining, provided a certain structural discipline to typographic design. A great design tradition developed within these perimeters.

Yet the time and cost required to cut a new typeface meant the availability of only a limited number of faces in a certain number of sizes.

Availability of Typefaces

One of the first effects of phototype has been to increase the number of typefaces available. The relative ease and low cost of creating new alphabets on photographic negatives contrasts sharply with the more complicated and expensive diemaking techniques. It is a contrast so great that we hardly comprehend its effects.

Photocomposition does not represent a simple reduction in the cost of acquiring a new typeface. At a fraction of the former cost, it is a purchase of a different order. "It will create an entirely different attitude," observes Mike Parker of Mergenthaler Linotype. It's more like buying a pair of pants, instead of buying an entire wardrobe."

In recent years calligraphers and designers have introduced a record number of new typefaces. It's only the beginning of an avalanche. In magazines the bulk of these new faces has been used for titles, headlines and decks.

It ought to be admitted that some of the wilder new faces prove next to impossible to decipher at any real speed in any sizable amount. To put it generously, in exploring the frontiers of legibility some artists have crossed over the line. Many other new faces are a genuine contribution. The redrawing of some traditional faces like Bookman is equally important.

Photocomposition has also created the opportunity for an increased number of typeface weights, from hairlines to extra bolds. Properly used, these can increase reading speed and comprehension.

The more revolutionary element of the photographic approach is that the basic principles of photography are such that with appropriate lenses, it is possible to produce type in any single size and at any italic-like angle.

Obviously, such virtually limitless freedom is unmanageable. In order to have a workable system, the point size metal base has generally been replaced by a 4-to 64-unit grid. Each letter, numeral and symbol in modern photocomposition is unitized. It is designed on a grid for reduction or enlargement.

This system still allows tremendous flexibility. But for working purposes, phototype today follows the traditional point sizes. As a transitional step from hot to cold type this makes good sense. It is inevitable that this will change over the years.

Because the traditional point system indicates the size of the metal base and not the actual height of the type itself, different typefaces of the same point size varied widely in size when printed. Photocomposition has brought some measure of order to this chaos. Phototype employs uniform base line measurement.

While traditional point sizes established the height of the letters, the width has always been varied. The I has been on a narrower base than the W. Though traditionally the space between letters could always have been increased by leading, the metal base placed definite limits on the amount to which the space between the letters could be reduced. Under special circumstances, for a relative few words at considerable expense, one letter could appear to touch another, but some physical break always remained.

It is an attribute of photography that one image can actually be placed on top of another. In photocomposition, letters of the alphabet can be made to touch or overlap each other without difficulty.

It is not uncommon today to overlap certain letters in designing a magazine logotype. This can give a modern, stronger look to even conventional typeforms. There are definite perils to this practice, even in logotypes, and it must be tightly controlled.

Yet it is in the ability of photocomposition to "set tight" horizontally that we can look for the most significant gains from the new typography.

Easier Word Recognition

Typographic expert Herb Lubalin says: "The spacing of metal type has always been a big problem. My theory is that people have been reading illegible type ever since Gutenberg. There's too much space between the letters. This makes too much space between the words, therefore causing too much space between the lines. Type has never been set the way people talk—in a steady flow. There's always an interruption between every letter of every word of every line of type because of metal. Film is eliminating that because we can push letters together more tightly so that instead of words being single letters, they become units of words. We can also pull out some of the space between words and lines."

Photocomposition's ability to set tighter and more uniformly makes word recognition easier.

"Letterers have always tried to design so that letters in a word would hang together to make a word," says Photolettering's Rondthaller. "The advantage of photographic composition is that it makes words look like words instead of a string of separate letters. For some time this has been done for headline composition, but now it is beginning to be done for body composition, too. This greatly improves the page in appearance and many of us also think it improves it in legibility.

"You can do beautiful things just tightening up body compositions. You can change the whole appearance of a page. Take a traditional design like Century, for instance. Tighten it up and you get a brand new look."

Tighter setting also means positive gains in the number of words per page. At a time when magazine page sizes are being reduced and costs per page are escalating, this is important. At a time which calls for increasing visualization, this text gain can allow space for graphics. Of course, instead of saving space, you can choose to increase the size of type for extra readability.

There are obvious limits to how tight copy can be set and remain readable. It will vary from face to face and size to size. The first thing we know is what we are *used* to reading has a great deal to do with the ease and speed of reading. But we also know now of a second factor—that we do change. We become used to new things with remarkable rapidity.

Right now the rules of legibility are more than ever the rules of common sense. Typography, of course, has important aesthetic qualities. The printed page can be beautiful. Why not? But the ultimate measure of typography is communication. If you can't read it, it does not matter how artistic it is. If the type is hard for you and your staff to read, it's probably hard for your readers to read.

But we better recognize change when we see it. We

are reading tighter type today and even tighter settings will be rapidly read by the next generation.

Our children may, in fact, be reading new types which go way back to very ancient traditions. They will have the characteristics of the manuscript styles that preceded the invention of movable type.

Alphabetical letters will be connected and combined. We see the beginnings of this in the return of ligatures. With photosetting, letters can be connected. In addition to the standard 26 English capital letters and 26 lower case letters, new typefaces like Avante Garde, for example, offer as many as 26 ligatures and alternate letters in the capitals, and six in the lower case letters. Its

designer, Lubalin, contends, "It helps readability, especially when you get letters like a capital L and a capital A together. There's a tremendous hole between them that stops they eye. We overlap them to form a ligature which closes up that space."

If ligatures seem strange to us, it can only be said that they appeared even stranger only a few years ago.

A great change has begun.

The typography of tomorrow will look significantly different from the typography of the past. The new typography will have more variety, be more compact and, most important, be more readable.

About face

By John Peter

In creating or improving magazines and books today, nothing plays a more important visual role than typography. The right type handled correctly can give a publication both identity and readability.

Technological advances from hot metal to cold type, from casting to phototypesetting with the aid of the computer, have changed the economics of typesetting, and to date, the focus has been on the big savings in production time and costs. But there are some less noted effects that should also be discussed and understood.

Photocomposition has changed the typographic machine manufacturer's attitude toward typefaces, turning that view completely around. Historically, the heavy machine manufacturers who built typecasting equipment were most interested in building machines, and their profit was in selling those machines. Typefaces laboriously milled from metal were often viewed as an expensive and annoying, albeit necessary adjunct.

Today, although the manufacturers have not quite adopted the razor blade industry's approach of virtually giving away the razor to sell the blade, they do recognize that major equipment is sold only rarely while typefaces can be sold rather frequently. Furthermore, instead of expensive metal dies, the new acetate matrices can be manufactured inexpensively and sold at nice profits.

The British typeface designer, Matthew Carter, put it this way. "It's much cheaper and quicker for manufacturers to produce film faces. In the days of hot metal typefounding, the investment of time and money necessary to manufacture, stock and sell matrices of a new face were such as to require cautious planning.

"The need for a long sales life during which to repay a considerable investment encouraged conservative design. Cheaper and quicker manufacture of photocomposition fonts has led to a market for more ephemeral designs that can bring a prompt return and, if successful, a good profit; if not, no great loss."

A flood of new faces

This is one reason we are only at the beginning of a flood of new type fonts: Mergenthaler alone is producing 200 fonts a year. Never before have there been more typefaces available, and this proliferation is both a blessing and a curse.

Most of today's newly designed typefaces are considered fashion faces, with the life span of a butterfly. Some of these are considered unreadable. And most of them are display faces which can serve a useful purpose in advertising and promotion where attention getting and novelty play an important role.

Fortunately, the proliferation has also produced some very good new typefaces. The best of these maximize the built-in advantage of photocomposition to improve legibility and increase word count.

For example, though typographers could always add space between letters and words, they could not, without great skill, time and expense, reduce it. With today's unitized photocomposition, the space between letters can be reduced by what is called minus spacing. In many of the new typefaces, the lower cases are designed with large x-heights where the central body of the letter is disproportionately bigger than the ascending and descending parts. This design enables a tighter setting, both vertically and horizontally, which allows more words per page.

Trend toward bigger text type

In redesigning a magazine recently, I was able, with minus spacing, to jump the size of the text face from 9 pt. to 10 pt. without loss of words. This increased considerably the readability of the text. With more and more to read these days, and frequently less and less time to do it, I see a trend toward bigger text type in magazines.

Many of the new typefaces are also designed with letters that kern better, reducing the disturbing gaps between certain letter combinations. This, along with tight setting, enables the reader to see words as words rather than as a series of letters.

Phototypesetting also permits letters to touch and overlap one another. Though this has been largely used only in magazine logotypes, it can be used to create script faces like Snell Longhand that really connect. Look to a future trend in the return of scripts and manuscript typography.

The computer, says Matthew Carter, "is having its effect on type designing by helping with some of the more tedious and repetitive parts of the job, such as drawing additional weights. This is something that has been discussed for years but it is only recently that a program sophisticated enough to analyze the letterforms has succeeded in altering the weight of letters in a sympathetic and controllable manner."

This development is a significant one. It has initiated the production of new faces and the redrawing of traditional ones (such as Bookman, Century, Galliard and Cheltenham) in a wide range of weights in both roman and italic. It has encouraged the development of a complete range of text faces. As a result, the conventional distinction between text and display faces is disappearing, for we now have a new breed of faces equally suited to both text and display uses.

This development is also filling a long standing need for really light weights and, more important, true bold faces. With the increasingly high ratio of advertising pages to editorial pages in magazines, designers are designing publications in a single typeface to aid the recognition of each editorial page and provide a strong sense of flow from the first page to the last. Today's wide range of sizes and weights, in both roman and italic, offers sufficient variety for editorial changes of pace.

Type families are now being further enlarged with the introduction of bold condensed fonts in such faces as Garamond, Cheltenham and Plantin which enable you to get more size and impact on the page. With shrinking page sizes, and the rising cost of paper and postage, condensed typefaces are another coming trend to watch for.

Why search for new faces?

In addition to being readable, type should also attract and encourage readership. This is another important reason behind the continuing search for new typefaces.

Mike Parker, director of typographic development at Mergenthaler Linotype Company, maintains, "There are two ways of designing a type. There has been a very heavy stress, starting with Stanley Morison and Beatrice Warde, on the fact that a typeface ought to be invisible. The simile is that a wineglass should be clear so that you see the color of the wine. A typeface's characteristic should be invisible. It should just be there doing its job without calling attention to itself.

"I would say that Garamond's romans of the 16th century are a perfect example, absolutely classical, with all the details subdued and blended into the whole. They are quiet, gorgeous, invisible, everything subdued to the purpose. But you can take that too far.

"Granjon, a contemporary, went the other way. He was a baroque designer. Anywhere that he could take a little detail and give it a little flick of emphasis, anywhere he could take a rhythm and swing it a bit, he would. Matthew Carter's Galliard is based on Granjon's roman and carries that sparkle to the page. I think that approach is every bit as valid as the more obvious silent one."

Aaron Burns, president of International Typeface Corporation (ITC), says "From a designer's point of view, I have found that a designer is always looking for a new way to say something that's not much different than what was said before. The designer's task is to make tired words look a little different."

Herb Lubalin, executive vice-president of ITC says, "Very little new has been done in this century in typography. I think that's deplorable. Type should progress in design just as automobiles progress in design or anything else progresses in design."

Among the crowd of new types, there are some standouts. Most have been designed by recognized type designers and experienced lettering men: the Americans Edward Benguiat, Ray Baker, Herb Lubalin, Tony Stan; the German Herman Zapf; the Briton Colin Brignall; and the French Albert Boton, Adrian Frutiger and Albert Hollenstein. Most of their typefaces are not completely new in that many of the letterforms have earlier sources. To an extent, all typefaces represent some continuity with the past; otherwise the alphabet would not be recognizable.

Combining existing elements

Often new faces are simply a new combination of existing elements. For example, there is a group of new faces which combines the traditional serif with the modern sans serif—New Text, Serif Gothic, Quorum. There is another group which brings "more humanity to Helvetica"—Eras, Olive and Round Helvetica. There is still another group exploring the neglected tradition of comfortable round forms—Souvenir, Korina and Benguiat.

These and other new faces, ranging from American Typewriter to Zapf International, are designed for easier handling by the new designers at the keyboards and the video screens of the new typesetting systems. One of the exceptions is Avant Garde Gothic. Lubalin says, "I think the biggest mistake I made in my life was designing Avant Garde. Although Avant Garde has been one of our biggest sellers, it has been so misused. It takes a tremendous amount of skill by a good designer to do a good type job with Avant Garde. So many people misuse it that I would almost like to see it pulled off the market."

Allan Haley, a typographic consultant for Compugraphic, warns, "If we don't get smart and start educating these new people, we are going to have a proliferation of visual pollution. We are at a point where we can make some nice things happen—some nice typography—or we can go the other way."

Incidentally, Compugraphic publishes, free for customers, a typographic bulletin with basic advice on what it takes to make good typography and ITC puts out a tabloid, *U&lc*, which is packed with imaginative ideas for even the most expert.

Legibility vs. style

"There is an inevitable quarrel between legibility and style," observes Parker. "Legibility is very much a matter of custom. If you run a legibility test in Switzerland, for example, where more people read sans serif than roman, sans will test best.

"When I worked at the Plantin museum to read the archives I had to learn 16th century Flemish as printed in black letter. Learning Flemish was easier than reading the black letter. At first I couldn't understand it, then it got very easy.

"If you maintain that legibility is based on custom and that all typefaces have to fit this pattern, you are saying the whole world will use Century Schoolbook and to hell with the rest. Very quickly, however, it becomes extremely boring and visually dull. What you want to do is create visual excitement. To the degree that it departs from the norm, type increasingly gives the reader a legibility or readability problem. But by creating visual excitement, you tend to focus the reader's attention.

"It may pay to cut into legibility, particularly for a few words in the heading, in order to create the visual excitement that will put the message over even more strongly than the words, or in sympathy with the words. Americans' ideas of normal are broadening. Designers are forcing people to reach and stretch. As readers do that, a broader range is possible."

Technology outpaces inflation

In the days of hot metal type, you usually had to settle for one of the few faces available at your printer. And too often you couldn't even distinguish it from your competitor's typeface. On the other hand, it was a discouraging expense to buy a new face in all the sizes required. Typography is one of the few fields where technological innovation has outpaced inflation, however. It's cheaper to buy a new face today than ever before.

In the past, machine manufacturers produced so called "exclusive" faces: basic typefaces copied just different enough from the original to protect the manufacturer from legal infringement and to depress the art director. Today, however, machine makers are being inclusive rather than exclusive. You can usually get the same face on another system if you ever switch printers, typographers or equipment.

With computer programming and the new layout grids, it makes economic sense to get top flight design and type specifications for your magazine. It's a small investment with a large payoff, issue after issue. It costs no more money to set the right type. And at a time when many things—size, printing and paper—tend to make publications look alike, distinctive typography can reinforce the individual editorial character of your publication.

My best advice: Be very selective about all the new typefaces. Be careful not to get overenthusiastic about tight setting or condensed faces in smaller sizes. Although the rules of good typography are changing, one rule—the rule of common sense—still prevails.

Type is a means of communication, and its function is to get editorial contents off the page, into the mind of the reader. New type or old, if you can't read it, it's pretty certain your readers can't—and won't.

Making your magazine easier to read

By Allan Haley

Unless you're a rare individual, you are probably not aware of the importance of type and typography. Most people involved in magazine production or management are not concerned with the artistic concepts, and type usually falls under the artistic heading. Yet, typographic quality is vital to a magazine's circulation and its effectiveness in providing information. It doesn't make sense to put an issue together if the typography is either poor or ineffective since this will hinder your readers from reading and understanding the content of your publication. Or worse yet, it could possibly keep them from buying the next issue! Although these statements may sound extreme, they are based on sound typographic standards.

Typographic quality can be as significant to an article being read, as the cover is toward influencing a reader to pick up and open a magazine. If the inside of your publication is as inviting as the outside, the articles will be more enticing to the reader and attractive to the subconscious mind. The text should appear to be an even gray tone. If it does, you have "good typographic color." If, however, you see black spots where words and lines of type are too close or letters touch, or if there are large white areas caused by too much interword and interline space, you have one strike against the text being read. These situations inhibit readability.

Your pages should also appear neat and orderly. The use of too many typefaces which do not relate well to each other, or spatial arrangements of type with no apparent order or structure will create jumbled typography. This is visually uninviting and will cause the viewer to think twice before reading an article.

Once you've attracted someone to begin reading an article, you want him not only to understand it, but also to finish reading it with as little difficulty as possible. What is generally considered aesthetically pleasing typography is also that which is the most readable.

As you make it easier for the eye to scan a line, your article will communicate its idea more effectively. This is because the eye does not read individual words. It scans a complete line, pausing momentarily to record groups of three to four words at a time. Excessive word space, line lengths that are too long in relationship to the type size, and incorrect interline spacing all make it difficult for the eye to read a page and inhibits the communication process.

Research into legibility of print has been carried on for years. Eye movements and blink rates during reading have been recorded. Reading speed and comprehension have been researched through various mechanical and electronic devices. Reading fatigue has been studied and character visibility investigated. The results of all these endeavors are almost always in accordance with, and emphasize the need for, proper typographic design.

Displaying high typographic quality in your magazine can also give you a competitive edge. There are approximately 11,000 different magazines currently being published, each trying to expand and solidify its reader base. One way to get an edge on your competition is to put

536

together a more visually attractive package. Which would you rather read: an attractive, well composed, easy-to-read magazine—or something else?

Realizing that good typographic quality is important to the success of your magazine, you ought to be aware of the basics of good typography and be able to evaluate the typographic effectiveness of your publication. While the skills and sensitivity of a graphic designer or typographer are not easy to come by, the basics of good typographic design can be achieved through learning a few simple guidelines and practicing a little common sense.

The four most important factors contributing to good typography are: proper word spacing, correct interline spacing (leading), harmonious line lengths and sensible typeface mixing.

Word Spacing

This is probably the single most important factor contributing to good typography and effective communication. Your magazine should strive for close, even word spacing in all text settings to aid the eye in the reading process. When text composition has excessive, or uneven word spacing, the lines break into separate elements which inhibit the eye from scanning the copy in a smooth, quick manner. Not only does tight word spacing aid readability and create aesthetically pleasing text copy, but more copy will fit on a page, saving money and/or leaving more space for advertising.

A quick check to determine if typeset composition has excessive word spacing is to turn it upside down. (See illustration #1.) If it is easy to determine one word from another at a quick glance, or if you see "rivers" of white running through the copy, as illustrated in the first example, the word spacing is too wide.

Illustration #2 shows proper word spacing. The space between words should be approximately the same as that occupied by an "i." The space between words should not exceed the width of an en (a space equal to roughly one-half of the point size being used).

Excessive word spacing becomes more apparent, and can do more damage to readability when text is set with no additional interline spacing. The interword spacing can appear greater than the space between the lines. (See illustration #3.)

The handling of word spacing in justified composition (flush left and right margins) requires increased care, especially when shorter measures are being used. Also, the shorter the measure, the more difficult it is to control word spacing. It is here that the maximum of an en space between words may be a troublesome standard to uphold. Many newspaper columns will show you perfect illustrations of this difficulty.

There are situations when interword spacing can, and should, be tighter than normal, and other times when it can be a little more open. However, the bottom line is how the text is perceived. When you read the copy, are you able to scan the lines of type in a quick, even manner, or do you see individual words separated by white space?

Line Space (Leading)

"Leading" is one of those words in typography that has become outdated in the last few years. Originally it referred to the lead strips that were inserted between the lines of type to increase the space. With the advancement of phototypography, leading is now an automatic machine function. In fact, many manufacturers of phototypesetting equipment now refer to this function as "line space," which is more descriptive. Whether it's called leading, line space, or interlinear spacing, the function is vitally important to good typography.

The amount of white space between lines directly affects the legibility of the printed piece. This thin horizontal white strip serves as a guideline for the eye. Not enough white space causes the effect called "doubling" (reading the same line twice). However, too much white space slows the reading process, hinders legibility, and makes for longer (costlier) editorial copy. A simple rule for proper line space is that it should be approximately 20 percent of the point size being used for setting the text. For example, the proper line space for ten point type would be two extra points.

As with all rules, there are exceptions. Line space may vary depending on various typographic factors. Excessively long lines (fourteen words or more) increase the possibility of doubling; however additional white space between the lines will offset this tendency. Lines that are shorter than normal (eight words or less) can afford to have less white space between the lines. In fact, many times they can even be set with the line space value equal to the point size of the type. This is often referred to as being "set solid."

The design of the typeface also plays an important part in selecting the correct line spacing. As seen in illustrations (4a, 4b), faces with a small x-height (such as Bembo or Gill) require less line space than faces with a larger x-height (Times Roman or Avant Garde Gothic).

This is because the shorter x-heights create more white space between lines. Serif faces require less line space than sans serif typefaces since the serifs aid the eye's movement across the line. Sans serif designs do not have this benefit; therefore, they need a little more space to keep the eye moving horizontally rather than vertically. As seen in illustrations (5a, 5b), heavy or bold faces (Souvenir, Korinna) require more line space than faces of lighter weights (Baskerville, Univers Light). Heavy faces tend to visually dominate the space they occupy. More line space breaks up the black texture into easily recognizable lines of copy.

Line Length

The line length should relate well to the typeface and point size being used. A line length which is too long will tire the eye and interfere with referencing the beginning of the line that follows. As previously mentioned, short lines are difficult to set; they can also be difficult to read since sentence structures are often broken.

How long is the correct length for a line? Although it depends on the typeface and point size being used, generally a line length which contains an average of nine to ten words is fine. Again, this is a general guideline that can be tempered by various factors.

Basic design characteristics of the typeface must also be taken into account as some designs require shorter lines than others. Sans serif faces are a perfect example. As pointed out earlier, serifs aid the eye's movement across the page. The absence of serifs will require a slightly shorter line length. A line containing seven to nine words, in this case, seems to work best.

Typeface Mixing

This area borders on the "no-man's land" of graphic design since what is aesthetically pleasing to some, may not be to others. It is difficult to make recommendations which are acceptable to everybody. However, a few general comments can be made that will be in agreement with what most graphic designers would tell you.

First, the design of the faces used to set the text copy (the bulk of what your audience reads), should be unobtrusive to the point of being "invisible." Stylized faces should be avoided. These typefaces were not designed to be highly readable in text material. A face that stops the reader in mid-sentence to admire its fashionability or cleverness of its choice is not a good text typeface. Stick to the standard serif or sans serif book faces; they are the best choice.

A word of caution: avoid setting extended copy in a face which has strong thick and thin contrasts (such as Bodoni or Tiffany). The exaggerated contrast in stroke weights causes an effect called "dazzling," which makes reading difficult. (See illustration #6.)

One area where typographic contrast can help you is between the faces you use for text composition and those used for headlines or titles. If your body copy is in a sans serif design, set the headline in a serif face. Running heads in the copy also should be set in a heavier face than the type used for the body copy. This is especially true if the headlines are set in a different typeface. Compare illustrations 7a and 7b. Even though the head (7a) is set in a larger size, it lacks the distinction to give it the importance it deserves.

Simply changing from a medium to a bold weight (7b) corrects the problem.

Being aware of all these guidelines can help you monitor the typographic quality of your publication. Should you find problems, they should be comparatively easy to solve using current phototype technology. Good typography is not difficult to produce, and is important to a magazine's communication effectiveness and circulation. Look around you. Many magazines are changing their typographic format, and not just for the fun of it.

Illustration 1: excessive word spacing can be spotted when it is easy to determine one word from another (top) or if rivers of white run through the copy when it has been turned upside down (bottom).

The history of writing is in a way the history of the human race, since in it are bound up, severally and together, the development of thought, of expression, of art, intercommunication and mechanical invention. Indeed, it has been said that the invention of writing is more important than all the victories ever won or constitutions devised by man. The alphabet is

(set in Helios II with excessive word space)

(set in Helios II with excessive word space) [text inverted]

Illustration 2: for proper word spacing, the space between words is approximately the same as occupied by the letter "i". The space between words should not exceed roughly one-half the point size used.

The history of writing is in a way the history of the human race, since in it are bound, severally and together, development of thought, of expression, of art, of intercommunication and mechanical invention. It has been said that the invention of writing is more important than all victories ever won or constitutions devised by man. The alphabet is a system and series of symbols representing collectively elements of written language. Let

(set in Helios II proper word space)

Illustration 3: a look at type with no additional interline spacing.

The history of writing is in a way the history of the human race, since in it are bound up, severally and together, the development of thought, of expression, of art, intercommunication and mechanical invention. Indeed, it has been said that the invention of writing is more important than all the victories ever won or constitutions devised by man. The alphabet is a system and series of symbols representing collectively elements of written language. Letters are individual signs that compose the alphabet, each signify-

(set in Helios II with no additional line space)

The history of writing is in a way history of the human race, since in it are bound up, severally and together, the development of thought, of expression, of art, of intercommunication, and of mechanical invention. It has been said that the invention of writing is more important than all the victories ever won or constitutions devised by man. The alphabet is a systematic series of symbols representing collectively the elements of written language. Letters are the individual signs that compile the alphabet, each signifying primarily one thing, what letter it is—its name.

(Bem set solid)

The history of writing is in a way the history of the human race, since in it are bound up, severally and together, the development of thought, of expression, of art, of intercommunication, and of mechanical invention. Indeed, it has been said that the invention of writing is more important than all the victories ever won or constitutions devised by man. The alphabet is a systematic series of symbols representing collectively elements

(Avant Garde Gothic Medium set solid)

The history of writing is in a way history of the human race, since in it are bound, severally and together, the development of thought, of expression, of art, of intercommunication and of mechanical invention. Indeed, it has been said that the invention of writing is more important than all victories ever won or constitutions devised by

(Souvenir Medium set solid)

The history of writing is in a way the history of the human race, since in it are bound, severally and together, development of thought, expression, of art, of intercommunication and mechanical invention. It has been said that the invention of writing is more important than all the victories ever won or constitutions devised by man. The alphabet is

(Univers Light II set solid)

The history of writing is in a way the history of the human race, since in it are bound, severally and together, development of thought, of expression, of art, of intercommunication, and of mechanical invention. Indeed, it has been said that the invention of writing is more important than all of the victories ever won or constitutions devised by man.

(set in Bodoni)

National Old Style   This is a design by F. W. Goudy. The contrast of wide and narrow letters makes it similar to his other designs and follows a classical precedent.

National Old Style   This is a design by F. W. Goudy. The contrast of wide and narrow letters makes it similar to his other designs and follows a classical precedent.

Publishing in black & white

By John Peter

There are three big reasons for producing a magazine with all editorial pages in black and white: (1) money, (2) money and (3) money.

In these tight times, any publisher may want to consider the value of color to black and white. Many professional magazines and house organs have money in the budget for nothing else *but* a black-and-white publication.

Thinking in black and white can be especially important when launching a new magazine. I designed three new magazines in 1975 which are black and white except for the front cover where color is a universally accepted asset.

Dick Netzer, editor of a new magazine, *New York Affairs*, put it this way: "Being prudent to save money was very much part of our thinking. We started this on the basis of an extremely economical operation. If we were going to make a decent looking publication, we just had to stay with black and white. The financial constraints were overwhelming, but I'm very pleased with it."

Publisher Chuck Tannen, who had his *New York Business* at breakeven within its first year, relates black and white to his printing decision. "Actually, the newsprint was the major factor. Printing on newsprint off a newspaper press saves us 50 percent of the production costs on the magazine. It was the fact that we went on newsprint that really dictated that we go in black and white and not try color. Full color is very difficult on newsprint."

Other Benefits Besides Cost

Even if you are printing on good stock and have full color ads that carry the cost of four-color production, editorial black and white has other pluses besides lower printing costs that are worth considering.

One is simplicity of production. Steve Phillips, art director of *New York Business*, describes black and white simplicity as freedom. "You don't have to worry about it. That makes things easier. If you want to do a nice scene that goes across the gutter, you don't have to worry if there's color available. You always have a sense of freedom—that whatever you want to do, you *can* do. Production requirements aren't going to get in the way. It just makes it a little easier—fewer restrictions in that sense."

Art editor Lee Lorenz comments on *New Yorker*'s black-and-white flexibility. "The magazine is assembled up to the last minute. It's not a layout design. We don't use different type faces from week to week. We use essentially the same type faces we started with 50 years ago. We have and require great flexibility in the use of the editorial material which goes into the magazine and that includes the drawings. It would restrict our flexibility to be using inside color. It could only be in certain portions of the magazine to correspond with the four-color ads that were being inserted in that issue."

Robert Essman, art director of *People*, appreciates the freedom of black and white in making photo assignments. "There's no necessity to pick which stories you are going to shoot in color and which stories you are going to shoot in black and white. If you're shooting in both, there's an additional time factor."

In addition to on-the-job time saving, Essman cites a more important factor for news-style magazines. "We distribute somewhere around two million copies coast-to-coast every week. In order to produce, print and distribute that many copies every week, the time factor is pretty incredible. If we were doing color, it would have to be a very limited amount in order to maintain schedule and the newsiness of the magazine, which is of prime importance. It does take more time and more effort to produce color."

A standard printing complaint today is the quality of the black and white. It takes a good press and a good pressman to get top quality black-and-white reproduction using the black plate on high speed four-color press. In an all black-and-white magazine the problem of reproduction is certainly simpler.

Black-and-white editorial also reinforces the sense of editorial continuity. With the right typographic design, editorial pages are separated from the advertisements. This is particularly useful in read-through magazines with a high ad/ed mix.

A Classic Example

It's hard to find a more classic example of this than *The New Yorker* which enjoys both a high reputation for editorial quality and is considered an advertising showcase. Its editorial pages carry nothing but type, black-and-white cartoons and line drawings. Any advertisement with a different typeface, a reverse panel, a Ben Day, a half-

540

tone illustration or photograph, a second color, a four-color illustration or photograph is bound to get attention. In a handsomely profitable ad/ed ratio, each editorial page is signaled to the reader without competing with the advertiser.

Black and white carries associations which can reinforce the image of certain types of publications. Aside from the fact that black and white can be closed more rapidly to catch late-breaking news, black and white is associated with news in the public mind. It has an air of reportage and fact. This is inherited from the sequence of technological development. Black-and-white printing and photography was developed before full color. Given time, color television and more comparable costs of color vs black-and-white reproduction may alter this, but today black and white still means speed. The lower overhead in some cases is correlated with integrity.

Sam Antupit, designer of *New York Affairs*, underscores this. "It's a straightforward documentary-type of magazine with some kind of elegance to it. We wanted to be a believable, credible, fact-filled, honest, intelligent magazine. We just thought that if there was a lot of color in it we would be just a flashy magazine that wouldn't be taken seriously. We were proven correct. The magazine is very highly thought of It has a high renewal rate on subscriptions even though it costs $24 a year. It's a journal. It isn't a pop sociology magazine. It's closer to a periodical paperback than it is a magazine."

Essman relates *People*'s all black-and-white editorial to a news look. "I would suspect that part of the reason, outside the cost, would be to have a newsy quality, which has worked. In addition to the fact that we are extremely newsy in our approach to the magazine, I think black and white does give it that kind of design. We try to get the sense of urgency that news magazines have."

Creating a magazine in black and white involves special design considerations. It has been my experience in designing black-and-white publications that the format, typography and graphics must be more vigorous and distinctive. Extra imagination and care have to be exercised with the type specification, type rules and spacing. These elements become more important. Sometimes they are all you have to work with. Yet working with a carefully planned specification style book and a basic editorial grid, a good editor and a solicitous production manager can produce a consistently attractive magazine. The assignment of illustrations and the selection of photography naturally become more important to compensate for the absence of color.

Phillips agrees. "Yes, I try to compensate. My feeling is that to reach people with the same impact in black and white, you do have to try even harder than you normally would. Be bolder, be bigger. That's one of the things I like about the big size of *New York Business*. Because it's big, you can really be bigger in graphics and hit them in a bigger way. I'm constantly saying, 'Seeing that this is black and white, what can I do to make it have more im-

pact than I normally think about?'"

In *The New Yorker* tradition, Lorenz works differently. "*The New Yorker* has a great deal of copy in it. The graphic material complements the written copy. It's not a matter of having it separate from the written copy or making it stand out in some way. I think they naturally complement each other. You wouldn't want page after page of unrelieved typeface. That's why we also use a great many spots in *The New Yorker*. You can't have a cartoon on every page. So small, decorative drawings which are obviously unrelated to the text are there just to lighten the copy. There aren't many magazines that use spots any more, and that might be one of the distinctive aspects of the magazine."

Despite the assets of black and white, there is no trend toward black-and-white publishing. No one denies the visual appeal of full color. The success of colorful magazines from society publications like *National Geographic* and *Smithsonian* to service publications like *Woman's Day* and *Family Circle* as well as its widespread use in advertising attests to color power.

Yet four-color editorial is not an automatic prerequisite to success. It's a matter of management decision and attitude.

The decision can be budgetary. The decision can be determined by the positioning with a black and white format reinforcing the image that fits in with the marketing plan.

Attitude can be all-important.

If the attitude is cheapness, if it is combined with cheap sales personnel, cheap promotion, cheap editorial and cheap printing, the inevitable result will be a cheap publication. Black and white can mean "schlock" publishing if it is part of a pattern with economy as the only consideration.

Black-and-white publishing is not inferior publishing. It is alternate publishing. It's an option.

New York Business publisher Tannen says, "We designed it with the newsprint in mind. We didn't start off by saying, 'Let's do a magazine and then let's jam it into a newsprint format.' Steve Phillips spent a lot of time thinking of how to work within our press capabilities, within our paper capabilities, as far as graphics go. It comes off with a very graphic look."

The black-and-white question is far less important than many other decisions in publishing, but it should be congruent with them. Even when it comes to the product itself the value of color can be exaggerated.

You have heard this before: Content is more important than form. Get a good editor. Build a strong editorial staff. Emphasize good editorial with good design. Amortized over the years and related to the contribution to success, all these cost less than you might think.

The message is: Take part of black-and-white savings, invest it in good editorial and good design. You will have a good magazine on a black-and-white budget.

Read any good contents pages lately?

By John Peter

The contents page has long been surrounded by taboos and neglect. That's changing, however. Today, the contents page could just be the most important page in your magazine.

No one questions that readers look at the contents page when they are trying to find something in the magazine. However, many editors see the contents page as little more than a reference page—a straight listing for searching readers or librarians. As a matter of fact, *The New Yorker* had simply an index of its departments until some years ago when it was replaced with a table of contents listing titles, authors and page numbers. William Shawn, the magazine's editor, explains that the magazine had grown so large that it was no longer easy to find the various pieces.

Most editors who take the reference list approach feel that readers generally ignore contents pages and simply leaf through a magazine, often back to front, scanning for things they may be interested in.

Those who hold this view cite reader research which indicates that contents pages are among the least-read pages in a magazine. However, I have examined a good deal of this research and I am not satisfied with the use of the word "read." A contents page can be viewed somewhat like a telephone book. Usually people do not say they read it. They *use* it.

More than a reference list

Although many readers do just leaf through a magazine to find out what's in it, there are three important reasons why a contents page ought to be more than simply a reference list.

First, there are those logically-minded readers who do look at the contents page before reading a magazine. The number of these readers varies widely, depending on the nature of the magazine—fewer for a picture magazine like *People* and more for a journal like *Foreign Affairs*. It also varies with the nature of the audience—fewer with salespeople on the run, more with research engineers.

The second reason why the contents page should have greater importance is an often overlooked one: It can be a valuable sales tool in the hands of a good advertising salesperson. If the page is properly organized and presented, a salesperson can use it to quickly demonstrate the appeal, quality and variety of a magazine's editorial material to a busy space buyer. This is particularly true in business publications which address themselves to a wide range of readers.

Third, the contents page represents an opportunity to entice a potential reader into buying or reading the issue. "Since a title often doesn't tell the reader enough," says Robert Stein of *McCall's*, "the contents page should include a little description, giving some general idea of what the story is about. We're expanding our contents page. It used to be two thirds of a page long. Now we use a two-page spread with two thirds of each page for the contents."

Although Stein has increased the space allotted to the contents page, he still follows the convention of sharing the page with advertising. He is also concerned that "jazzing up" the contents page with illustrations is a distraction. "Once the reader is into the contents page you have to assume he or she is interested in the magazine," says Stein. "Using razzle-dazzle to attract the reader's attention reveals a certain degree of anxiety."

Although many editors, especially his competitors in the women's service field, agree with Stein's viewpoint, many others don't. Sheldon Wax, managing editor of *Playboy*, says, "Going back several years, we had a contents page that gave strictly the titles of the pieces. We redesigned it to two pages to give more importance to the contents and to make it more of a service to the reader. Today we have copy under the titles to explain to the reader what the article is about. We also have 10 color cuts—little teasers from 10 of the features—that run down the side of the contents."

Adding a second color

With an illustrated contents page from the beginning, *New York* Magazine added a second color to the illustrations about a year ago. John Berendt, the magazine's editor, reports: "Since *New York* readers are busy people, they want to know exactly what's in an issue. They look to the contents page to see exactly what's being offered. Color makes it more attractive and pulls more readers in. People tend to look at the page even more with the second color."

Edward Kosner, editor of *Newsweek*, thinks blurbs on the contents page can enhance readership once the readers have the magazine. "The illustrations and blurbs are an effort to make the contents page useful to the readers so that the contents of the magazine are as accessible as possible. Our system spotlights five or six elements in the magazine and indexes all the elements.

"We added color to the contents page some months after we started run-of-the-book color. Color suggests to the reader, as he enters the magazine, the richness of the material that's in there. In addition, since the major features are in color, it makes sense to showcase them in color."

Editors frequently have a built-in bias against "selling" the contents of their issue. Yet in conversation, they give very persuasive reasons why an issue is worth reading. What's wrong with giving the reader these reasons and sharing this enthusiasm?

Magazines frequently present their features differently on the cover than on the contents page, or describe them differently on the contents page than on the articles themselves. These discrepancies, which can create minor confusion for readers, arise from the differences in function. Cover lines usually focus on the selling point and may not be completely descriptive of the feature inside.

Don Erikson, editorial director of *Esquire*, adds, "A cover line may be dictated by a harder sell. It is also dictated by space and graphics. Design is a big part of why our cover lines have to be shorter."

The contents page titles that executive editor Dero Saunders writes at *Forbes* are usually different from the title on the article. "Sometimes the article titles are too long," says Saunders. "Sometimes they're obscure. I want to tell the reader in a hell of a hurry what the story is and what it's about."

If you want to upgrade the importance of your contents page, first look at two things—size and position.

Though some magazines have the table of contents sharing space with an advertisement, others give it a full page. Frequently this page also carries the identification statement, the information required by the post office, and a listing of the staff. Since a right-hand page tends to receive more attention than a left and is a more appropriate titling position, I favor a right-hand page. You are doing your reader a service by making it as easy as possible to get into your magazine.

A good number of magazines have increased the contents page to two pages. If this is warranted, facing pages provide increased impact and reader convenience.

Moving the contents page up

Some people are under the misconception that the table of contents must be placed within the first five pages of the magazine. However, you can put the contents page anywhere in the magazine you want it. All the post office requires within the first five pages is a magazine's identification statement. This consists only of the name of the publication and publication number, the date of the issue (unless it appears on the cover), statement of frequency, issue number (unless it appears on the cover), subscription price (if there is one), name and address of known office of publication, second-class imprint or notice of pending application, and the mailing address for change of address orders.

Though the contents page is the conventional and convenient place for this information, some publications run these few lines separately at the foot of some column or non-bleed advertisement within the first five pages. This permits the table of contents to be run further back in the magazine.

However, I urge moving the contents listing further up in the magazine. A good number of magazines with whom I work have moved it up to page one. In designing a new magazine, I always put it on page one unless it's a double-page spread; then it's put on pages two and three.

Some magazines, of course, feel that their table of contents should be even further forward in the magazine. They put it on the cover. John Allen, former managing editor and now director of corporate and public affairs at *Reader's Digest*, says, "DeWitt Wallace, the founder of *Reader's Digest*, is big on ease of reading. He wants to make it simple for people to get the information. If a reader has to look, even for the table of contents, then it's a little more difficult to read."

The problem with a table of contents cover is that it does not provide sufficient visual change from issue to issue. Particularly on a newsstand, this type of cover fails to signal a new issue. *Reader's Digest* carries a special feature sticker on newsstand copies. *Harvard Business Review* has not only a listing of contents on the cover, but also a double-page spread of contents briefings inside. Their reader research indicates that both are used. Editor Ralph Lewis observes that many readers check off articles on the cover in three ways—"must read," "want to read," "may get to." They then look inside for further description.

Fortune, which for years had both an inside contents page and a double spread of abstracts, has reduced it to a spread with a few lines describing each article. Managing editor Robert Lubar says, "We had one contents page and what we called the 'Wheel of Fortune.' The 'Wheel' contained fairly long summaries of each article. In a monthly magazine where each article was 3,000 to 6,000 words, we found it necessary to do that because readers were not expected to read the magazine cover to cover. They were going to dip and test, but they were also interested in what we were saying in the things they weren't reading.

"When we went biweekly we wanted to make the magazine readable cover to cover. We no longer felt it was necessary or even desirable to give them a full summary. Since the articles are much shorter than they were in the monthly, we now have a more typical contents page and give a brief precis with the title."

The amount of space you allocate to the contents page, as well as its position, should be determined by the size of your issues and the needs of your readers.

The frequent objection raised against enlarging or moving up the contents listing is that the position is sold to an advertiser. However, in my experience, this usually does not work out to be as difficult as imagined.

A question of trade-offs

It's a question of trade-offs. Readership in both paid and controlled magazines is becoming so important it is frequently worth forsaking a premium from one advertiser to increase the exposure for all the others. When a contract is up for renewal—or sometimes before—an acceptable alternate position can usually be found for the advertiser. Strong magazines with good advertising salespeople do not lose many advertisers over this problem.

A contents page in a good position indicates to readers and advertisers alike that you are proud of the contents in your magazine and that you think editorial contents are important.

As a result of my consulting work in Europe where both magazine newsstand sales and readership are far higher than in the U.S., I've come to view the contents page in a new light. The contents page can be a second cover, supplementing the cover with information. Properly placed and properly designed, it's a second chance to interest the reader.

For a magazine on newsstands where readers glance at issues, this can be an important factor leading to its purchase. For any magazine, it can be an important factor in getting the reader to read it and pick it up to read again and again.

In the competition for your reader's time, a good contents page in a good position can be, after your cover, the most important page in your magazine. Perhaps it's time to take a fresh look.

The second color

By John Peter

Color attracts the eye and adds appeal. While magazine advertisers continue moving from two color to four color for maximum effectiveness, editors, who of course also appreciate the advantages of four color, are often limited by their budgets.

You don't need four color to have the advantages of color, however. With two color printing, you can get a lot for your money—and it is surprisingly cost effective.

There are very few single color web presses in the United States. A normal 16-page one color form, 8-1/2 x 11, is really going on a two color press. It's not a big jump when you go to two color. (When you go from two color to four color, you go to different equipment altogether.) The only extra costs for the second color are for additional stripping plates, additional ink, and a bit more make-ready.

These small extra costs can yield large dividends, however. The consistent use of a distinctive color can give your magazine added identity. Readers can more easily recognize your publication if you use the same color on the cover and inside each issue.

You can also use a second color to signal the reader that it is a new issue of your magazine. Changing or rotating colors month after month signals a new issue in a way that is not possible in black and white.

A single second color used throughout the issue can aid the identification of editorial pages and provide editorial unity throughout the issue. In addition, a second color can give identity to a page or a section of a magazine. Bill Rosavich, production manager of *Atlas*, says, "We use a full page of color for the World Economics section. We cover the whole page and overprint black on it. It breaks the pages out from all the others which are just black and white."

A second color can add appeal. When color is used decoratively, when rules, borders, illustrations and type are run in a second color, you get a much livelier page.

Color can also add interest to illustrations and photographs. Phil Miller, designer of *Catalyst* magazine, observes, "Our photographs are mostly stock photographs. Making some of them duotones helps get our stories across better."

Color adds clarity

All these second color techniques are used to enliven your magazine's pages. However, the best way to use color is functionally—to add clarity. In tables, charts, graphs and diagrams, a second color can help organize information and establish relationships. You can get a surprising range of color and tones on a diagrammatic map, for example, if you combine screened values of the black and color plates. It communicates better than black and white because it gets more information off the page faster.

George Arthur, design director for *Consumer Report*, says, "Because there are so many categories and subdivisions in our magazine, we use color as a tool to separate things. It helps the reader find things easily."

From a production standpoint, it's easier to use two color than four color. Turnaround time is short. You can do more with a small staff. And it's just one less thing to worry about.

Depending on the press, the forms, your imagination and skill, you can produce a sparkling multi-color magazine on a two color press. You are not limited to black plus one color—and although you cannot have more than a second color on any given page, you can have a number of second colors in the issue.

There are, however, some things you have to watch out for when working with a second color. To get the maximum benefits for the least cost, you should know about press equipment, splitting fountains and printing forms.

As Ruth Kitaif, art director of *Handy Andy*, says, "Sometimes a spread is across two forms. In order to have that spread in a color we may have to have many pages in that color. A mistake was made recently where a spread was two different colors because the forms had not been designated correctly."

You also should watch the choice of color. Not so long ago, the only second color available for editorial use was a color the advertisers had chosen, usually standard red or blue. This is far less true today, but some editorial departments fail to take advantage of the opportunity to select their own colors and run with the regular red or blue. Others utilize the opportunity but fail to pick colors that work.

Color consists of two things: hue and value. Hue is what we usually call color—red, blue, yellow, green, brown, etc.; value is how light or dark the color is on a gray scale.

While picking the right hue is important, the thing to watch closely is value.

Color value mistakes

Most mistakes are made in value. If the value is too dark, the type surprinted in black cannot easily be read. If it's too light, type in reverse cannot be read.

In post mortems we often hear how the printer did not get the right color. We hear less often how clearly the color was specified to the printer. To avoid such problems, assume that the printer might not get the precise shade you wish. Dispense with some of the subtleties. Don't take chances. Pick a color with some room for error, especially when it comes to value.

One final thing to keep in mind with a second color: run enough to count or don't do it. It makes very little sense to run only a hairline rule or a bullet dot in color "just to get some color on the page." No reader will notice it and it's a waste of money.

There is a case to be made for publishing editorially in black and white (see FOLIO, October 1975, Publishing in Black and White). There's a case to be made for publishing in four color (see FOLIO, August 1977, The Color Explosion). But don't overlook the opportunity of two color publishing.

Metlfax

By John Peter

Three top-circulation magazines in the U.S.—*T.V. Guide, Reader's Digest* and *National Geographic*—are smaller than standard size. Obviously, a small-sized magazine can produce a large-sized profit, but just how small can a magazine be?

Publisher James Stewart's metalworking magazine, *Metlfax,* is just one-quarter the size of a standard magazine. But, with a giant 102,000 controlled circulation, it's making it big.

Metlfax began in 1956 when George and Ray Huebner found they couldn't profitably distribute their standard-sized magazine, *Tooling & Production,* to all the people in the widespread metalworking field who wanted it. Two pocket-sized magazines, *Machine Tool Blue Book* and *Modern Machine Shop* (both 5-7/8 by 7-5/7 inches), were already in the metalworking field, but *Metlfax* went even smaller with a 4 by 5-5/8 inch vest pocket size.

Ad potential attracts publishers

What made this quarter-sized midget look attractive to the publishers was the advertising potential. Standard-sized metalworking magazines were loaded with quarter-page ads, and the full-page ads in the pocket-sized magazines scaled down perfectly to a quarter-page size.

"We could make a big shot out of a guy that ends up in the back of a standard-sized publication by putting him up front with a full page," Stewart explains.

Although this is still one of *Metlfax*'s basic ad sales appeals, the magazine now sells some spreads and full-color pages as well as one-sixth-page ads (at 1-9/16 by 1-1/2 inches they have to be about the smallest display ads sold anywhere). And with a 102,000 BPA audited circulation, the largest in the metalworking field, *Metlfax* comes in with the lowest black and white page rate—$760. Furthermore, *Metlfax* has the highest number of inquiries in the field—an estimated 225,000 inquiries for 1978—making the magazine even more attractive to advertisers.

Like many big tabloid-sized magazines, little *Metlfax* is a monthly new products publication. On its cover it kicks off with an exclusive product, material or process and packs plenty of reader-service-numbered items inside. Editorially it breaks these items up with several mini-sized departments ranging from "Metal Mirth" (a humor page) to "Meditations" (quotes from famous philosophers and poets). Three of the 12 issues have a special editorial focus—holding, safety and welding. These special sections, running 64 to 90 pages including ads, increase reader interest and boost inquiries.

There are other advantages to a small-sized magazine in addition to its advertising potential. Since a magazine's size is one of its most instantly recognizable features, *Metlfax*'s quarter-page size makes the magazine distinctive. In addition, a small magazine is convenient. Readers can put the magazine in their pocket and read it at their convenience. Stewart maintains that "*Metlfax* has the men's room readership in America sewed up."

The small size invites readership because it does not look like a substantial investment of a reader's time. Editors must also keep the writing simple and concise.

Furthermore, production costs are reduced. Paper costs for a small-sized publication are considerably less than for standard-sized publications. *Metlfax* runs about one-fourth of the price and the press run is cut to a quarter of the time.

Drawbacks to the size

There are also drawbacks to the small size, however. Obviously, a small magazine can't offer much editorial information in depth. Also, a small magazine gets lost on a newsstand. In the fifties, several quarter-sized magazines were launched on the newsstand. They proved difficult to handle and, both figuratively and literally, they disappeared. Furthermore, it costs as much to mail a small magazine on a unit base as a standard-sized magazine.

The small size is not geared to corporate image advertising. "I tell advertisers that the magazine is a place for product presentation," Stewart says. "Advertisers shouldn't try to build a company reputation or sell their stock in *Metlfax*."

Although the small size does not provide strong visual impact, the appeal of the miniature need not be overlooked. During World War II, with the Office of War Information in Europe, I designed six monthly airborne and underground magazines in a small 4-1/8 by 5-1/4 inch format. I learned that things *are* relative. For example, if everything is scaled properly, a double-page photograph looks surprisingly large in relation to smaller photos. A small format does not rule out good design.

A publisher has to weigh the advantages and disadvantages of a small-sized format and decide what will best suit his or her needs. In the case of *Metlfax*, Stewart says his magazine has been a very profitable property. "We've had such good fun with *Metlfax* that we've announced a companion directed to the design department in the original equipment market of the metalworking industries. It will be called *Designfax*."

Production

Who cares about production?

By Warren Owens

Over ten years ago I was involved in a decision to convert a large flatbed letterpress printing plant, with complete hot metal composition facilities, to sheet and web-fed offset with computerized cold composition equipment. That's about the time I first became aware of the tremendous impact new composition methods and faster printing processes could have on an entire publication staff, not just on the production manager.

Editors would have to know how to work with photo-typeset copy and understand all of the steps to the end product; the art director would be faced with changes in his or her method of paste-up, working sometimes almost completely with camera-ready copy; production managers would have to become experts in new types of material and would have to establish new quality control procedures. No one in a publishing company could be exempt from the upheaval that a switch in process brings about. The sales staff would have to be knowledgable about the change and capable of discussing it with their customers. The promotion and marketing managers, business manager, publisher and anyone else providing support for the sales effort would have to be as cognizant as the salespeople.

Thinking further, it became apparent that a production training program should be a normal procedure even when a publisher is not making a transition from one process to another. How would he or she stack up, for instance, when the need for training is not so easily recognized? What if a key person is disabled or sick, dies, quits without notice or is fired? What if two or three of these events should hit within a couple of weeks? It happened to me. It can happen to anyone. Without a production training program I'd have been in real trouble.

Interesting, you say, but you're not presently contemplating a change in processes. You run a healthy shop, young and strong. But have you checked any bills lately? How are your editorial composition charges—and alterations? Is artwork holding the line with the economy? Are you giving away a lot of mechanical charges you really can be invoicing? Have you talked to your printer recently about the cause of those climbing make-ready costs? Are your deadlines harder to meet? It's easy to sit on your status quo. It's only the bottom line that suffers.

You Can't Rest on Your Laurels

It takes a continuing production training program to keep on top of today's changes. Not an expensive, time consuming, sometimes boring, classroom set up, but an inexpensive, time-well-spent, interesting, on-the-job program. It takes guidance. It takes instruction that is stimulating. It takes plant visits. It takes trips to trade shows and calls on both advertisers and agencies. It takes planning and a timetable.

A large publisher or a multi-publication house can justify retaining one or more production trainees at all times to replace existing personnel when necessary. A small publisher has a totally different set of circumstances and if caught short-handed usually solves the problem by having employees cover for each other.

Whether you hire trainees or concentrate on your existing production staff, there are three kinds of training programs, each with a specific purpose, each necessary and each able to run concurrently with the other:

1. Training replacements for existing production staff.

2. Training the existing staff for the processes of the future.

3. Training to keep sharp the production talents of all staff members.

Each of these programs are quite different. The goals are not the same, the cost is not the same, the teaching talent is not the same and the modus operandi is not the same. With this in mind, let's take a more detailed look at the "how-to."

Training Production Replacements

The "how-to" production training of replacements, to cover for all kinds of absences, falls in line with good management practice. Every manager should be training his or her replacement. Every manager should have a feeling that his or her subordinate is pushing hard to take over the management spot. He or she should be training an employee to know the management job as well as, or better than, the manager does individually. The practice goes right down the line. The organization of any business demands that every employee have another employee ready to take over.

The first step in training production replacements is to write out detailed job descriptions for each area of production responsibility. Ask the employee in a given job to write his or her own job description. By doing it this way, both the employee and the manager discover what it is that each expects of the other.

Once the ground rules have been spelled out, it's not difficult to enhance a job description to include training and to choose the individuals who are promotable or who can substitute for an absentee. At this stage a large publisher might hire a trainee; a small publisher selects the person who is to cover in case of absence.

Good production training programs accomplish their purpose within a time schedule. A time schedule is efficient, of course, only when there is a periodic review.

Training for a New Production Process

The "how-to" in preparing for new processes involves a totally different set of ground rules. First, someone has to be assigned the responsibility. It is logical that this person be your top production employee. He or she must have complete knowledge of the publisher's long range plans and editorial thinking and must be thoroughly informed on circulation and sales.

This person has to be extremely careful in the use of time. Visits to graphic arts suppliers and to trade shows are invaluable but can be a waste of time and money if not carefully selected. Visits to customers, particularly problem customers, can be useful. Time has to be devoted to all facets of manufacturing: Composition, presswork, binding, paper and mailing. Your production expert must become an all around expert.

Once a decision to change a process is made, usually not too many months pass before a switch is made. There may be only the balance of time remaining on a printing contract. It may be only until the next issue, if the process is to change in a limited area like composition. Or there may be only a day or two for an advertiser's problem to be solved in order to get his or her business.

Production training for a new process reaches far deeper than your own staff. Customers, both agency and advertiser, have to be trained. Unfortunately, a letter of announcement or change in copy of your mechanical requirements on a rate card does not "reach" them quickly.

Each phone call from a customer presents an opportunity to relay news of the change.

Continuous Staff Training

The "how-to" in production training to keep things running smoothly when there are no changes is the most difficult of all. Difficult because no one is really too interested. They know all about it. Difficult because it's hard to sell to management. They don't want to spend the money.

Training in what a production department does every day of the week is a difficult idea to sell to management. But somebody had better get interested and somebody had better be willing to spend the money before the money disappears. Manufacturing is a major publishing expense.

Production training for the existing staff involves a refresher course, an update of why we do it this way and an opportunity to cover those employees hired since the last time around. Again, to be successful, this training has to be carefully planned, interesting, inexpensive and scheduled. It should have:

• Plant visits included in a refresher.

• Individual sessions so people can get things off their chests.

• Inexpensive but good visuals, such as desk top flip charts which go through a procedure step-by-step.

• Full participation by not only the production staff but the entire publication staff involved with the finished product.

• Participation by the publisher and other top management.

Production training programs are rather inconclusive unless they cover both the present and the future. Not taking care of today's concerns may lead to not having tomorrow's. Today's economy refuses to accept the publisher who is not ready for both today and tomorrow. A strong production training program that includes the entire staff is a major step towards a profitable future.

Staying on schedule: How do 'other' magazines do it?

By Karlene Lukovitz

Sure you have a production schedule. It's difficult to conceive of a magazine that doesn't. But how often do you really adhere to that schedule, or even come close to doing so?

Next to controlling costs, staying on schedule/meeting deadlines was the most frequently cited problem of production managers who responded to FOLIO's 1981 production trends survey (January, page 55).

This article is based on more than 20 interviews, mostly with production managers of publications ranging from small-circulation business magazines to large-circulation consumer magazines. We asked these production managers to cite the problems most likely to throw their magazines off schedule and measures they take to keep on schedule.

In addition, FOLIO interviewed production consultants, publishers, and ad sales directors.

The identification of problems that cause or contribute to schedule derailments is complicated by frequency of publication, type of printing process, and other factors that vary from one publication to another. It is further confused by the interrelatedness of every stage in the production process. One business magazine production manager swears that he has experienced times when so many unexpected problems became entangled that he could not, to save his life, say where it all began.

But these complications aside, it is not so surprising that the major problems cited as schedule-wreckers by production managers fall into two basic categories: late advertising and late editorial. A third, infrequently-mentioned problem is with suppliers.

All of the more than 20 production people contacted said that their companies take late ad insertion orders, as well as late ad materials, and many said that editorial materials, whether in-house or free-lance, are frequently late.

Print date: the bottom line

Nevertheless, only a handful of production managers said that they had ever missed a printing date, and that this had happened only once or twice. Even production managers who admitted that the other dates within their schedules have been known to go by the wayside on more than one occasion said that the print date is the one inviolate day in their working calendar.

The reason is cold and simple: A missed printing date can mean waiting to be fit in by the printer several days later, or, depending on whether you can afford it and if the printer is willing and able, heavy overtime charges.

Either consequence is a production manager's nightmare. The production manager is the one who will have to explain to higher-ups (and sometimes to the angry ad sales and circulation managers who are fielding the calls from irate advertisers and subscribers) why the magazine was late. In the case of a magazine with single-copy sales circulation, a late issue means missing the on-sale date and losing a significant number of sales—possibly the whole first week's worth of sales.

Or, in the case of overtime bills from the printer, the production manager must explain to the publisher and/or comptroller why he has had to exceed, sometimes astronomically, the budget for the issue. Of course, one also has the option of trying to get the printer to hold the press for your magazine. This strategy, according to the corporate circulation director for a multi-magazine consumer publishing company, usually costs between $200 and $500 per hour.

This is not to say that printers are heartless. Several of the production managers who have missed a print date report that their printers have taken the trouble to work their magazines in as soon as possible, and at little or no extra charge. But most printers, particularly large-volume ones, simply cannot afford to do this. It would mean throwing other magazines off schedule. They also must keep their presses running nearly constantly to make a profit.

As one vice president of manufacturing for a consumer publishing group puts it, "It doesn't really matter, in the end, what the problems were that caused you to go off schedule, because the press schedule doesn't change. You somehow just have to squeeze whatever you have to do into that period between the time the book closes and the press date."

Once an issue has been sent to press on time, most production managers would probably prefer to forget all of the problems that had to be overcome to accomplish the job. Unfortunately, production fiascos are like history. They tend to repeat themselves until a true solution to the problem, rather than a stop-gap measure, is found.

Because this was not a scientifically-conducted survey, it is impossible to conclude with certainty whether advertising problems are more troublesome for the magazine publishing industry than editorial problems. However, because advertising problems were voted number one by most of those interviewed, an outline of the most frequently-mentioned types of advertising problems that cause scheduling foul-ups will be presented first.

Late insertions: a production reality

Production managers are clearly resigned to (if not enthusiastic about) the fact that both publishers and ad salespeople are going to get every possible ad into an issue, whether or not the official closing date has passed.

"No publisher in his right mind is going to turn down advertising business, so we'll accept ads up to the eleventh hour, if we have to," says Glenn Frazier, manager of magazine production and quality for the publishing division of the Meredith Corporation. This statement, in slightly varying forms, was made by nearly every production manager interviewed—even one advertising production manager who works on a weekly consumer magazine with a circulation in the millions.

In fact, several business magazine production directors and a few consumer magazine production directors reported that their magazines often make post-closing sales efforts when ad revenue for a particular issue is falling significantly below expectations.

Two production executives of major consumer magazine publishing companies report that continuing economic uncertainty has exacerbated the problem of late insertions because advertisers are delaying commitments as long as possible.

"Right now, the advertising marketplace is very tight. Advertisers are holding their orders until the last minute," says one. "Naturally, the agencies are trying to deal with the same problem, which wasn't as prevalent two to three years ago when the economy was in better shape."

This production director stated the major dilemma that faces every production manager when insertions orders are late: "Waiting for an insertion order holds up the decision-making process on the fixing of the magazine's size, which pushes everything else on the schedule back."

Several production managers said that their publishers might be somewhat less lenient about taking insertion orders after a closing date if they did not have to worry about advertisers going to a competing magazine. "If our competitors are lax about closing dates, then we're forced to be lax also," says the production director of a large business magazine publishing company.

A production director who has worked for both consumer and business publishing companies during his more than 30 years in the business says he has found business magazines to be "more anxious to hold the book open for an ad" than consumer magazines. Now working for a company that publishes several business magazines with unpaid circulations, he says publishers of these magazines are particularly apt to delay closings.

"Because controlled trade books derive 100 percent of their income from ad revenue, the temptation to stay open until the last gun is fired is very great," he asserts. "If some of the publishers who have come up through ad sales here had some experience on consumer magazines, they'd know what a closing is all about."

But whether acceptance of late insertion orders happens more frequently at business magazines rather than at consumer magazines, the practice itself is virtually universal—and it falls to the production manager to deal with the havoc it can wreak on his carefully-planned schedule.

Late ad materials

Breathes there an ad agency production manager with so organized a head that he never to himself has said, "This is my problem . . . I think I'll ask for an extention"?

Maybe. But late ad materials are another painful fact of life for production managers. Unlike late insertion orders, however, late ad materials (barring those that *follow* late insertions) are not likely to set back the entire pre-press production schedule. Instead, they present their own assortment of down-to-the-wire "challenges" for the production manager.

The major problem with late ad materials is that there is often no time for the magazine production staff to put them through the usual pre-press inspection to check that the materials meet mechanical specifications. Because this obviously increases the chances that ad problems will not be detected before the form goes on the press, in-line problems on press (and resultant time losses) are more likely to occur.

John Gallagher, advertising production manager for *People Weekly* magazine, notes that late ad materials can also cause a host of time-consuming positioning problems. For example, if the editorial material for a form has already closed and the late ad turns out to be incompatible with it in subject matter, layout, or design, the production manager will have to "scramble" the positioning of the editorial material, the advertising, or both.

Magazine production directors are well aware that there are some instances in which the hands of even the best advertising agencies are tied by uncooperative clients. And, in the case of highly volatile businesses such as the movie and record industries, decisions about ad content can only be made at the last minute if the ad is to be timely and effective.

But there are also many instances in which less than tip-top organization and staffing at ad agencies leads to unnecessary requests for extensions on closing dates for materials as well as unauthorized lateness, production executives say.

In contrast to late insertions orders, late submissions of advertising materials is never encouraged at any level or by any department at a magazine—at least not outrightly. But, as nearly every production person will acknowledge, many of the ad agency production people who tend to request extensions frequently have been taught by the magazines themselves that deadlines need not be taken seriously. Not only do most magazines accept late materials, some even accept them on the date the issue is to go to press.

Needless to say, such policies, or lack thereof, stem directly from the same unavoidable business reality as does tolerance of late insertion orders: Most magazines survive primarily on ad revenue.

Of course, it is the responsibility of the production manager to see that any pre-press or on-press problems that do occur as a result of late ad materials are corrected in such a way that reproduction quality is preserved, and corrected quickly, so that the issue's distribution schedule is not endangered.

Avoiding late materials/orders

No one pretends that late insertion orders and late ad materials need never occur. However, according to some production executives and consultants, there are ways to reduce the number of these schedule underminers.

One basic mistake that encourages late insertion orders and late materials is setting closing dates without checking a calendar, according to ad sales consultant Paul McGinnis.

"When you're dealing with the advertising side of the production schedule, you're going to cause problems for yourself if you arbitrarily set all closing dates for insertion orders on the first of each month and closing dates for materials on, say, the tenth of each month," says McGinnis. "If you do this, the chances are that some of these days are going to fall on weekends or holidays, and people simply will not take those dates seriously. You must look at a calendar while you're setting the closings and adjust the dates so that all closings are on business days."

The top production executive of a major consumer magazine group stresses that the publisher and advertising director must establish a solid point of closing so that advertising is fixed and production can begin making up the book.

Production must have control

If late materials are to be kept to a minimum, however, production— not advertising sales—must have control over the granting of materials extensions, according to production consultant Elaine Jaffe.

"Production must be in charge of granting extensions, and must be extremely tough about it," says Jaffe. "You need to make it known to advertising agencies, just as you do with writers, typesetters or any other supplier, that you are really serious about deadlines. When extensions are granted easily, people feel that the original deadline wasn't valid even if it was.

"I would put an agency through hoops before I would grant an extension," she continues. "I'd want to know exactly what the problem is, to see if it's valid. If it is, I would see if the magazine's production staff can help solve the problem. If it can't, and if this was the agency's first request for an extension, I might grant it."

George Woods, production chief for Charter Publishing Company, also says that putting control over materials extensions in the hands of production is "critical" to keeping on schedule. In addition, he maintains that granting extensions to advertisers on insertions orders, and so allowing postponement of their commitment to advertising in an issue "is not reasonable" unless the production department has in-house or public service ads that can be used if the order does not come through.

In dealing with cases in which an agency or advertiser has not even asked for an extension on a materials closing date, "late charges" are a useful tool, according to Pat Wise, production manager for Windsor Communications' *Impressions*.

Impressions imposes a late charge on any materials that have not been given an extension and have arrived at the magazine within four days after an issue's materials closing date. "Advertisers and agencies are aware of this policy, and it really has helped reduce the number of these problems," he says. "Very few people who have paid extra for being late are late again."

Petersen Publishing Company has a policy of billing back to the advertiser any charges that accrue (including costs of "down-time" during printing) as a result of ad materials that have been sent in too close to a press date. Louis Abbott, Petersen's director of production, like Wise, reports that advertisers' and agencies' awareness that this policy is enforced "is a good deterrent" against late materials.

Dealing with late orders/materials

Despite avoidance/deterrence tactics, no production manager interviewed could recall ever having had an issue in which there were no late insertions or materials.

The production manager of a business magazine with a circulation of 12,000 says that about 50 percent of the magazine's advertising business is usually on extension, and that that figure generally rises to 70 percent or more for one or two issues during the year. A production executive in charge of several consumer magazines, one of which has a circulation of more than seven million, reports that only about 25 percent to 30 percent of that company's advertising business, on average, requires extensions.

For many of the larger publishing companies, an advertising service department that is very similar in function to the traffic departments of advertising agencies is responsible for dealing with late insertions and materials.

"What we call our 'advertising production service department' is responsible for granting extensions, when the need arises," says Meredith Corporation's Frazier. "It follows up on materials that are not in by closing or extension date by contacting the agency or supplier." Follow-up on late insertion orders is usually done by sales, though the ad production service department will often initiate those follow-ups, since that department regularly checks insertion orders in against the closing date.

The service department also checks all materials to see that they meet the magazines' mechanical specifications to avoid unexpected problems that could throw off printing schedules, Frazier notes.

Petersen has a similar set-up to deal with ad problems. Its "advertising processing" department monitors late materials, checks materials against specifications, and performs other tasks to keep advertising on schedule. In addition, the company's production management monitors the progress of each issue through daily reports from staff members showing whether advertising and editorial materials are flowing and being processed on schedule.

If a problem with advertising occurs, Abbott says, he and other members of production management sit down with people from advertising and editorial and talk with them about what can and cannot be done to handle the problem.

"We don't interfere with the process," he explains. "But in discussing what's happened, we sometimes suggest that the problem could be handled differently. We never talk in terms of right or wrong."

Moreover, Abbott says, whenever there have been repeated problems with a particular advertiser, he makes it a point to have similar discussions with the advertiser's agency when he is making one of his regular agency visits.

"I bring along our records and discuss with them the fact that there have been recurrent problems with a particular client. I stress the importance of working together to get future materials in on time so that we can do a quality control report and deal with problems before we go on press," Abbott says. "I find this reasoned approach works very well."

Schedule-juggling at the printer

But even companies with traffic departments must sometimes do some schedule-juggling with the printer when a form scheduled to go on press is held up by a late ad.

In Meredith's case, Frazier notes, in-house printing makes it relatively easy to "put a form from one of our other magazines into a printing slot when the scheduled form isn't ready."

Most magazines, of course, do not have the luxury of in-house printing. But virtually every magazine tries to plan so that most late ads are positioned in the last form scheduled to go to press.

"Large consumer magazines close over several days, not only one day, and are in many cases printed at several different locations," says the former advertising production manager for a major consumer magazine. "So of course you try to get the later ads together in the same form for one of the later presses.

"We naturally keep the books open as long as we can, when it comes to advertising, and we can usually take materials even a week or more after deadline as long as we have the commitment, the insertion order," says Leonard Mogel, publisher of *National Lampoon* and *Heavy Metal.* "But we keep all of these late ads in one form. Were we to do it in all of our forms, we'd be in real trouble."

But even if a magazine tries to stay on schedule by positioning late ads in a form printing late in the schedule, an advertiser or agency that insists on a certain position can cause major schedule setbacks.

"Promised positions are probably one of the most handcuffing things I have to deal with in trying to stay on schedule," says John Romeo, production director of *Forbes* magazine. "An agency will call and say, 'We're going to be late, but my client must be in a certain position.' Usually, the position is in a form that closes early, so you have to get involved in trying to shuffle around ads from other forms. The whole thing is a huge time-waster."

One production executive says he avoids such problems, and even gets late materials in faster, by telling the agency whose client is supposed to get a special position that he cannot guarantee the position if materials are too late.

James Povec, an advertising sales consultant and advertising director for *Down East* magazine, has successfully used a somewhat unorthodox strategy that allows for ad sales to go on until sales projections for an issue are met—without holding up the production schedule.

He suggests that when a magazine ad director finds himself short of revenue for an issue on the ad closing date, he should simply add to the list of sold ad pages enough additional pages to meet the revenue goal and give production a list of all pages and their positions—including the unsold pages. This allows production to determine the size of the magazine and proceed with layout of editorial and sold ads. The open ads, which Povec calls "daylight pages," are treated as if they were in-house advertising.

The ad sales staff then proceeds to call advertisers and tell them that a certain position has just become available. Because two or more of the daylight pages are planned to be in highly desirable positions in the magazine, such as page one and page three (right hand, far-forward), the salespeople can often sell the space to a regular advertiser who doesn't usually get as good a position.

Povec says that his sales staff has always managed to sell the daylight pages, even when a large part of an issue's revenues have to be sold in this way. "And if, for some reason, all of the space can't be sold, the worst thing that can happen is that you have to use a house ad or a public service ad," Povec asserts.

Last minute overtime

Of course, faced with an issue that has gone off schedule because of late ads, production can make up for the time lost by having the magazine staff and/or outside suppliers such as typesetters and separators do overtime work.

Though expensive, this is one of the simplest ways of remedying an issue that has gotten off track. And making up for lost time before a magazine gets to press is generally much less expensive than paying for press overtime or for having a press slot held, according to several production managers who use the last minute overtime "method."

Some magazines ask staff members to work overtime; others also hire temporary help on an overtime basis.

"We plan ahead to bring in many extra free-lance pasteup and camera people at the end of the production cycle of every issue," says the director of operations for a consumer magazine with a late advertising closing date. "We also have tremendous overtime bills from outside suppliers, including separators and typesetters. But I've worked it all out, and it's less expensive than closing the book earlier and losing two or three pages of advertising. It's also less expensive than asking the printer to build flexibility into his schedule. That is extremely costly."

The hiring of free-lancers for the end-of-the-issue crunch has also reduced the number of this magazine's "Laurel and Hardy chases to the airport," according to the operations director. "There have been several times in the past when we've had a limousine waiting outside the offices to speed a messenger to the airport with the issue so it would get to the printer on time," he says, "and I'm not exaggerating. But we've never missed a print date."

The editorial bind

As already mentioned, fewer production managers named editorial problems than named advertising problems as being major ones disrupting their schedules. However, only a very few production managers did not mention editorial problems at all when asked to describe what causes them to get off schedule. A surprising number, while complaining that in-house and free-lance articles are frequently late, took a distinctly paternal attitude toward writers.

"I don't really understand how writers do what they do, so I can't criticize them," says one production manager. "But I do know that creative people don't seem to have a very good hold on time and the problems that late editorial can present to our schedule. Someone's got to keep track of time for them."

The production director of several consumer magazines, who says editorial does pose a tougher problem for her than does advertising, expresses a similar sentiment.

"For some reason, even though 90 percent of our editorial is produced in-house, and even though our schedules are made with the full consent of editorial, the schedules are by and large ignored by the editors," she says. "It's gotten to the point where I'd sooner divulge the actual date we go to the printer to an advertiser than to an editor. Some of the editors have been here 10 years and yet they're still flabbergasted when deadline rolls around and it's time to make up the books.

"Production people are acutely aware of time and its passage and how much must be produced each day," she continues. "But time seems to be a foreign concept to most editors."

Avoiding late editorial

Some people said that scheduling as far in advance as possible is important, but others felt that this does not make a great deal of difference because "so many editors seem to work only under pressure," as one production director put it. Others said that editors should always have the right to approve dates scheduled by production. Editors' cooperation in meeting those deadlines is likely to be grudging at best if they have had little or no say in the matter, they added.

Several mentioned that interim deadlines can help alleviate the very common problem of the editor in chief and copy editors being deluged with articles at the end of the month.

"Editors really should try to space deadlines for articles so that they aren't hit with a torrent at the end," says Howard Rauch, editorial director of Gralla Publications. "This gives them time to really do a thorough job of reading the articles. The editor of one of our magazines, for example, specifies preferred deadlines for each article on the article assignment sheets she gives out."

One of the seven people who work in Petersen Publishing Company's advertising processing department is actually a "copy expeditor" who monitors editorial flow and its relation to the flow of advertising materials, according to Abbott. This copy expeditor figures out schedule dates (called "minus dates," because he works back from the print date in setting them) for each step in the flow. He checks that manuscripts and galley type are moving according to the dates.

If the reports show problems developing, Abbott says, the same "reasoned approach" that is used in dealing with advertising is used: Production management sits down with the editors and with advertising and all discuss the problems and possible solutions.

North American Publishing, though it has no "copy expeditor" per se, has each production manager fill out a daily production update, according to director Vijay Chowdhry. Chowdhry explains that he examines each report and, if there are problems, has a talk with the editor to see what can be done.

"If there is a problem with late in-house articles, I will immediately go impress upon the editor that the late story must either be finished immediately or be held for another issue," he says.

Chowdhry notes that North American sometimes sidesteps getting late articles from free-lancers by avoiding the mailing time. The author is asked to read the article over the phone to a Petersen editor, who tapes it. The tape is then turned over to a typist for processing.

Although these techniques are used primarily by editors at large publishing companies, several people interviewed stressed that editors at small magazines can also run a tight editorial ship.

Staff adequately

"The first thing a company of any size has to do is staff its editorial department adequately and realistically," says David Jensen, a publishing consultant who was formerly in corporate production for McGraw-Hill. "Even a realistic schedule will do you no good if you don't have enough people to do the work.

"You have to consider how difficult the editorial subject matter is and how vast the industry or subject you're covering is," he continues. "If you have highly productive editors, if the subject matter is relatively simple, and if the editors don't have to locate people in places ranging from Maine to South Africa to do their articles, then you might be able to get away with fewer people than some other magazines could."

The next essential ingredient in staying on editorial schedules, says Jensen, is a good managing editor. "It's important to remember that not all good writers make good editors. In fact, most don't," he contends. "Writers are like children, who will behave to the limits that are set for them. In fact, we're all children in that we all tend to procrastinate. But the point is that people will ultimately act within the reality, once that reality is clearly defined for them. A manager's job is to manage other peoples' reality for them."

In addition to being tough on final deadlines, Jensen feels managing editors should have some way of keeping copy flow manageable. "One smart editor I know insists that all copy be typed on yellow paper. Then, when he sees yellow copy sitting on an editor's desk, he knows the writer has been holding on to an article— probably making minor changes as he thinks more and more about it."

Discipline is also a major theme stressed by production consultant Elaine Jaffe when talking about editorial's part in staying on schedule.

"Writers tend to push their limits if they are granted extensions easily," she says. "If an editor is sporadically late, I'd try to work with him and be understanding about it. But if someone is consistently late, he must be told that he's in a tenuous position. Then, if it doesn't clear up, I'd let him go."

In addition to strong management, Jaffe believes that every person on the magazine staff, including editors, should have a personal written schedule outlining exactly when he's supposed to get his assignments in and exactly when he's supposed to pass his article on to the next person in line.

When dealing with free-lance writers, editors must give them "enough time to be creative," at least four to six weeks, according to Jaffe. They must then be followed up regularly, either by phone or by mail.

Lebhar-Friedman, a business publications company, has had success in cutting down editorial lateness by offering incentives for meeting deadlines.

The incentives are based on the successful cooperation of the entire editorial staff in meeting its deadlines, rather than on individual performance.

Though Lebhar-Friedman swears by the incentive program, many other editors are skeptical about the program—and some think it would undermine professionalism among their editors. "As far as I'm concerned, an editor's reward for meeting his deadline is keeping his job," says one.

Dealing with late editorial

When disaster strikes and an article scheduled to appear in an issue falls through, there are several options.

One production person said his company's managing editor relies on a war horse—an editor who has been with the company for years and is extremely proficient at rapidly turning out acceptable copy to fill voids.

Not all magazines have that option, however. In most cases, the editorial staff will stay and work overtime when the necessity arises, one production director notes. "I really don't envy their job any more than they envy mine," he says.

Jensen does not understand why managing editors, unlike managers in other industries, make no attempt to keep "spare parts" in storage, that is, extra articles.

"Most factories keep stock in the storeroom so that they don't have to shut down the business if a machine loses a nut or bolt," he says. "If I were running a magazine's editorial operation, I'd ask for a couple hundred dollars to be budgeted each month for giving bonuses to those editors who not only finish their assigned work, but complete 'X' number of additional columns or news items."

While this might work for some magazines—particularly magazines whose content is not timely—it would not work for many magazines, says an executive in charge of operations for a biweekly. "Articles, unlike wine, do not get better with age," he says. "Moreover, at our magazine, it would cost several thousand dollars for a good feature story. Who has a budget that allows them to keep thousands of dollars worth of articles sitting on a shelf gathering dust?"

For some magazines, late editorial problems stem not from late editors, but from the need to cover events that occur late in the editorial schedule.

One very practical way of handling this problem, when the event is not an unpredictable news event but a conference or convention, is for the editorial department to have pages set aside for the late material so that planning and layout of the magazine can proceed and does not have to be redone later on, notes Rauch. Editorial turnaround time of the late articles must also be accelerated to make such pre-planning work, he adds.

Suppliers: the last link

Several production managers mentioned problems with suppliers— typesetters, separators, stripping houses, or printers—as the cause of some issues going off schedule. But nearly all said these problems occur infrequently and that the problems are usually unavoidable.

Several mentioned computer breakdowns, employee illness and other factors that they believe to be, for the most part, legitimate reasons for a supplier's occasional tardiness. "When my printer called and told me that the issue was going to be a little late because the pressman's false teeth had fallen into and broken the machinery, I knew he couldn't be lying," smiles one publisher. "No one could make up that kind of story."

But no magazine will use a supplier for long if the firm makes frequent mistakes or excuses for lateness.

"I would want a very specific and valid reason from a supplier who is late before I would even consider using him again," says Jaffee. "And if it happened twice, that would be it."

Still, most production managers said that suppliers have been more of a help than a hindrance. Some said suppliers had gotten them out of a bind more than once. Most also felt that the prices they paid for this last minute help, though high, were reasonable in light of overtime pay, rising energy costs, and other factors.

Auditing production costs

By James B. Kobak

The largest single item on most publishers' profit and loss statements is the cost of production—paper, printing and postage. Control of these costs is not easy because, even if you have a good production manager, he or she doesn't have control of all the factors that cause expenses. Every department in a magazine has a hand in making decisions which affect production.

Wasteful habits in editorial operations can lead to late copy, excessive corrections and the like. Positioning promises to advertisers can lead to expensive printing because of the difficulty of fitting color pages in economical forms. Poor estimating by circulation can lead to the printing of too many copies. Management decisions can lead to excessive numbers of pages or copies.

By the same token, decisions which are made in the production area can have an impact on operations of other departments. The type of equipment which is used can govern the amount and placement of color pages. If too long a lead time is needed for the receipt of copy by the printer, late news may be dropped—or some ads may have to be left out.

Because of this interdependence, the control of this largest area of expense often is not as tight as it should be.

Contributing to the lack of tight controls is the technical nature of the production process itself. Most people in publishing are not as familiar with paper, printing and binding as they should be—because it is not their prime worry day after day. And even a good production department cannot know all the ins and outs of the field because its primary duty is a daily one of producing the magazine well and on time.

This article will cover the major areas where production costs can get out of control, the reasons why and how publishers can set up a program for auditing this part of their business. Every magazine is different, as we all know, so some of the items will not apply to all—and others must be handled in a very general way.

An audit of production costs should be concerned with both the basic decisions about publishing operations and production processes which are made only once every few years and issue-to-issue decisions which are made in the heat of putting out each individual issue.

Basic Decisions

How many pages of editorial matter does each issue carry? Unnecessary editorial pages can be terribly costly—and good editors always want more space than they have. The best control is a previously determined written scale which the editor must adhere to—if there are 60 pages of advertising there will be 52 pages of editorial; 59 advertising, 53 editorial; and so forth, coming out to even 16s of course (unless you use a press which delivers in other multiples).

What paper should you use? Coated stock may be necessary for good reproduction for advertisers and for some editorial pages but perhaps part of the magazine can be printed on less expensive bulking stock.

What weight paper should be used? Reproductive qualities of even lightweight paper these days are very good. Money can be saved both on paper and postage costs with lighter paper. But sometimes it is more difficult to print on. (And losing some heft might hurt the magazine's image. Could a heavier cover achieve that heft?) And of course these days there is always a question of what paper you can get, no matter what you want.

What trim size should the magazine have? Half an inch on a side can amount to a lot of money. Sometimes consultations with the printer, and maybe some slight modifications on the presses, can lead to reduction in the size of the sheet or roll.

Should you buy the paper? Or let the printer buy it? Sometimes the printer can purchase more economically because of greater buying power. And often what seems a saving when you buy yourself turns out more expensive when storage, handling, financing and other charges are added.

If you are using sheet-fed presses, should you buy sheets or rolls of paper? Sometimes it is cheaper to buy rolls and have the printer sheet it.

Where should the printer be located? While it is convenient to have the printer close, even more vital is a location which will result in lower postage costs for the magazine.

In picking a printer do you insist on quality which is really unnecessary for the subject matter and audience? Often perfection is overdone—the reader doesn't recognize it and it can be very costly. The recent development of magazines on newsprint, such as *The Village Voice* and *Rolling Stone*, certainly proves this.

In picking a printer, the type of equipment available as it relates to your magazine is of paramount importance. In checking equipment remember that binding and mailing facilities are as important as presses.

These days it may be vital to decide that a printer who can get the necessary paper for the magazine may be of as much importance as anything else.

A printer's familiarity with magazines is of great importance in deciding on one printer. Magazine printing imposes certain routines and disciplines which are not normally available in the average commercial shop. Techniques are developed that not only help the printer in doing the job but also save the publisher many headaches and extra work.

The decision on a printer should not be made quickly. The review of sources of supply should start years before the contract with your present printer has run out. And it involves more than just sending out some copies and asking for bids. Sometimes printers are willing to install new equipment or alter existing machines with the assurance of your business. This may save considerable sums. Often consultations with a printer will result in small modifications in the magazine which will reduce expenses.

Printing Bills

Should printing bills be of a blanket type—so many dollars for so many copies or so much for each page of composition—or should they be broken down by the actual items performed? It always seems simpler just to get one figure and let it go at that. On the other hand, the laundry list approach, where all items are shown, has certain advantages. First, you eliminate any cushion a printer may insert into an overall figure. Second, you have control over your own destiny. If you want to save some money, you can cut out some frills. Third, the individual items often point to wasteful practices in your own shop.

Should you carry insurance on your paper which is held at the printer's? Many publishers assume that the printer insures everything which is under his or her roof. Very often this is not true. Be sure to check. A loss in this area can be sizable.

The time schedule for delivering material to the printer is very important. The speed that is necessary is, of course, different for every magazine. A newsmagazine must operate on a very tight schedule, but for most others there is considerable leeway. Strike a balance between a tight schedule that enables you to include late material and advertisements—and gives more flexibility in make-up—and the cost of having such a schedule.

Are you taking advantage of using more than one entry point for mailing, if this is advantageous for the class of mail you are using? Enormous savings can be made in postage costs this way. The large circulation magazines have made a fine art of this. Some smaller magazines also do it by gang-shipping with others which are printed in the same plant.

Are you incurring more costs than necessary by insisting on a particular day of the month for publication? A great many publishers want their magazines at the beginning of the month. You might be able to switch to another date and save because the printer is handling you in the slack time. Few readers are tuned into the fact that you are coming out on a specific date—and most really don't care.

Should you be printed web or sheetfed letterpress or offset? It is fashionable these days to print web offset. But letterpress still delivers a very fine product. If a printer does the job that way and the price is right you may be better off. And remember that any web process involves a much larger paper waste, which becomes more important every day as prices rise. Maybe you should consider gravure or other printing methods for at least part of the magazine.

There are many provisions of contracts with printers which should be reviewed, of course, but of particular importance is the one concerned with escalation of prices because of the printer's labor and other cost increases. Too often publishers, not being familiar with the ins and outs

of the calculation involved, simply accept the percentage increase offered when the time comes. You should insist on the right to audit the method of calculating this increase. This is a highly technical calculation which requires highly skilled costing techniques. But the differences in costs can be enormous.

Issue-to-Issue Decisions

Is printing being done in the most economical manner? Have larger forms been used wherever possible? It is usually less expensive to print in 32-page forms rather than 16s and then cut them up for placement in the magazine.

Are color forms being used in the most economical manner? It is easy to get a feel for this. Count the number of color pages in the color forms and calculate the percentage of usage of the color paper available. If it is not over 50 percent, further investigation is needed. On some equipment the use of split fountains can give a great deal of color flexibility.

Is the use of editorial color carefully planned? When color forms are used solely for editorial matter, investigation is needed to see whether they could have been put into forms containing advertising color at a considerable saving.

Is the advertising department promising special positions without taking into account the extra expense which the publisher must bear? Often special positions are asked for by habit rather than through need and advertisers may be persuaded to take something else.

Are covers and other special sections being run in the most economical way? Sometimes covers and inserts can be run together and then cut apart. It may be possible to gang-run covers for several magazines and save money.

Is clean copy sent to the printer or composing house? Clean manuscript copy can result in savings not only in the basic charge, but also in later corrections. Have you considered setting cold type in-house? Some publishers have developed substantial savings by doing just this.

Here are some very costly—and unnecessary—items: Overtime charges at the printer; rush work; authors' alterations and killed matter, which should not exceed 10 percent of the original composition cost; runarounds, bleeds and other special charges; and stopping the presses.

Do any of your people visit the printer to help close the issue? It should be unnecessary. If it is being done, it is a sign of disorganization and lack of planning. It takes time and usually makes living with the printer more difficult than necessary.

One of the interesting things about a high incidence of overtime, authors' alterations, the need to visit the printer to close each issue, excessive extra charges and some of the other issue-to-issue decisions which are wasteful is that they are almost always the fault of the publisher—either within the editorial or production departments, or in their coordination. A rash of these cost increases deserves careful attention and a review of the procedures and disciplines followed. It is usually true that the department which is sloppy in these matters is sloppy in just about everything else. While savings can be achieved in production costs, it may be that the savings possible in manpower and irritation within the publishing house are much greater.

The Production Cost Audit Step By Step
- Check all calculations on all bills.
- Check all prices charged against contracts.
- Verify that the bills reflect the way the magazine was actually printed—the number of forms, the binding method, extra charges, etc.
- Check paper waste against the allowances in the contract.
- Check extra charges to be sure they reflect work actually asked for.
- Check poor reproduction of advertisements to determine who was responsible so that make-good or adjustment is not automatically paid by the publisher.
- Check the consistency of the charges from month to month.

- Annually review the entire production process for possible changes that might improve service and reduce costs. You may need outside skilled help to do this.
- Compare your costs with those of other publishers of a similar nature. This can be done against the figures compiled by some of the associations, or more informally with other publishers. If there are major differences, find out why.
- Check paper usage and paper balances at the printer against your own perpetual inventory.
- Check overruns to be sure they are within contract allowances and that you are not charged for printing and paper usage above those allowances.
- Review the number of copies ordered against the number actually sent to subscribers and newsstands. Often the circulation department does not do a careful enough count of the number needed—and the free list has a way of growing without anyone knowing why.

Six cost-cutting tips
By Jeffery R. Parnau

Wasting money isn't something we deliberately practice. Many of us are professionals at it, however, and have developed quite an expertise at wasting dollars. Unfortunately, even during difficult economic times, many production professionals remain in their self-made ruts and ignore the obvious . . . the obvious, old-fashioned, reliable methods of reducing printing costs.

The following six tips may remind you of some of the tried and true techniques that can cut a dollar or two from your budget.

1. *Economize on preparation.* In particular, I'm referring to color separations. It is all too easy to hand a job to a printer or prep house and say "I want it Monday" without stating just how you want that to happen.

Is each piece of your job separated individually? Switch to group separations. Is your work being done via conventional, indirect-screen camera shots? Switch to direct-screen separations. Are you already using direct-screens and group shots? Switch to a scanner. And if you are already on a scanner with group separations, consider having your material duplicated to final size, and *then* scanned as a group.

Each of the above steps is part of a financial progression through color separations. The first is the most expensive, while the last saves the most money.

2. *Lower prep quality.* In addition to having material prepared in the most economical method, don't overlook the possibility of the economics of quality.

Do you extensively correct your color after seeing a proof? Make moderate corrections . . . or none at all. In most cases, the reason buyers make color corrections isn't

a problem with the separation, but a problem with the original. And really, just how many times has a reader complained that the skies in his magazine weren't blue enough?

3. *Switch proofing systems.* Are you paying for press proofs? They are controversial and often bear little resemblance to the finished piece. Switch to cromalins, color keys, transfer keys, or negative-acting cromalins.

For black-and-white or two-color work, the choices include dyluxes, photographic contacts, brownprints (blueprints), and electrostatic reproductions (such as Xeroxes). If you've been using one method for years, consider a switch . . . even to the bottom-line quality of electrostatic prints. The latter can be particularly economical when you have other methods of controlling quality, such as in-house production or inspection.

4. *Switch presses.* Easy to say but hard to accomplish? Not necessarily. If you aren't aware of the needs of your magazine at all times, you may be overlooking the obvious. A few examples:

Narrow (half-size) webs can produce work that competes economically with both sheet-fed and full-web presses. A four-page insert for a multi-million-run national might be best produced on a narrow web . . . as might a complete, 64-page magazine with a run of 12,000.

Full webs come in a variety of configurations. While you might be locked into thinking of 32-page signatures, there are many full-size webs which can produce 48 pages. There are also a good many which can deliver no more than 16 pages at a crack.

Generally speaking, when you consider full-web

printing, you save the most money by running the press to its full capacity. A six-unit, three-reel press is most economical when delivering 48 pages with a total of 12 applications of color. Under-using the press costs money in unused equipment and idle hands.

Wide webs (45 inch to 50 inch paper width) are a consideration for magazines which have seen excessive growth, or which have increased frequency to weekly publication. The same consideration that applies to full webs applies here: The press runs at economical tilt when it is used to its capacity.

There is more to printing than webs, however. There are thousands of sheet-fed presses throughout the country . . . and unless you consider the requirements of each job, you may put a sheet-fed product on a web press. You'll lose lots of money. As a simple precaution, if you have even the most remote idea that a job may fit on an alternative press, ask for prices. Even if you look like a fool occasionally, you'll eventually be a *richer* fool.

5. *Switch paper.* I have made this statement in the past, and I still go by it: Black ink doesn't belong on coated paper. Process color does.

In the last few years, how many pages of simple black copy have you seen printed on coated stock? Just how much more legible was it? And, of course, how expensive was it (especially when you consider that we've damn near run ourselves out of coated stock, and created a sellers' market)?

This isn't to say that a magazine must be either 100 percent coated, or 100 percent uncoated. It is simple to mix stock, from a four-page, pulpy insert, to a complicated, interleaved product composed of various papers.

Going to a cheaper stock for a special section is a common method of saving money. And, of course, you needn't wait near the phone for readers to call and say, "How come my magazine has a special, cheap-paper section this month?"

The earlier mention of using multi-reel presses to their capacity melds nicely with mixing paper stock. Technically speaking, a three-reel press with six units could run the folowing: 1) 16 pages in four-color on coated stock; 2) 16 pages in black (or any other color) on colored stock; and 3) 16 pages in black (or any other color) on uncoated white offset . . . all at the same time. An unknowledgeable buyer might easily run the same 48 pages with three different passes through the same press. He would pay dearly for the privilege.

6. *Lower quality in general.* I often get a funny look when I say, "Your quality is too high for your product." Newspapers, for example, would never consider doing extensive color corrections, using coated paper throughout, or correcting all hyphenation errors.

Yet many publishers of trade magazines give excessive attention to quality which is never appreciated. In all areas of quality, consider your market and make appropriate decisions. If paper stock, halftone resolution, editorial perfection, and general printing fidelity have little to do with your true market needs, slash everything to the bone.

And if that sounds like drastic advice, sit back and look at the state of the economy. When such supposedly drastic steps become necessary, the first ones to take them will be the last ones to fall.

Must it be 'Production vs. Sales'?

By Jeffery R. Parnau

I have a theory—an uncomfortable theory—that nobody cares about production or production managers. Consider the following:

The ad closing on a consumer magazine (where I was gainfully employed at the time) had passed. So, situation being normal, all the ad reps were out there scrambling for their last sale. Seems that these people go into automatic sales-overdrive whenever their deadline passes.

Meanwhile, I had locked up the magazine's press imposition. It was one of those beautiful layouts that make you think presses were actually designed to print periodicals: I was using every full-color printing unit to its maximum; there was no fat, no lost production dollars spent on running "dead" pages.

My production manager's dream then slowly developed into the nightmare it had historically been. First, one of the reps wants to hold a two-page, four-color spread open . . . because he was certain to sell either that, or a single-page black and white.

Then, another rep calls in with a "surefire sale," another four-color page with an insert card. "Keep a slot open, and if they don't have it ready in time, they'll run it in the next issue."

The best laid plans . . .

And what of my perfectly designed impositions? I discussed the topic with the advertising director. The conversation went something like this:

"Well, there's really nothing I can tell you until my boys get back to me. A sale is a sale . . . bucks in the pocket. If we can get them in on time, we've got to do it."

And my response? Well, what is a production manager to say? In many cases, the production manager is considered a "service" employee, on the staff to meet the needs of others. The advertising director is often a company officer, a direct superior to the production personnel.

So, my possibilities were the following:

• I could remake the book, add four color, and hope some late advertising came in.

• I could leave the book as is, and hope nothing changed.

• I could play it by ear and pretend to be ignorant, sending the imposition to the printer and later on phoning in an "emergency" re-imposition.

I wasn't too pleased with any of the choices, so I decided to come up with yet another possibility. I got out my calculator and went to work.

The cost of accommodation

First, the possible two-page spread. In order to accommodate it, we would have to either reposition several other ads (something the ad director could hardly do this late in the game) or add process color to two signatures, not one. I determined the cost of a process makeready versus a black and white, multiplied the difference by two, and came up with something like $3,000.

Second, if the other single-page ad did come in with an insert card, we'd have to add a four-color makeready . . . plus split one of the existing signatures into two, in order to provide a slot on the binder where we could insert the card.

The press makeready was $1,500 or so. But the addition of a pocket in the binder pushed us over our limit, and would cost $350 more, plus a 10 percent overall penalty on the extra card (that, too, was over the limit).

So, the first ad would cost us an additional $3,000; the second, about $2,500 . . . assuming that we would get either one or the other.

Now, crossing territorial lines, I examined a copy of our rate card and found that if we were to spend even $2,500 in order to accommodate the single-page ad, the cost of putting that ad in the book would exceed any potential profit on the ad itself . . . particularly when we hacked off 15 percent for the agency, and a hefty commission for the rep.

Yet our rate card did not accommodate the bindery pocket-break penalty, or the additional card penalty.

The two-page ad, also, would not show a profit, no matter how I juggled the figures. True, if the ads had come in much earlier, I could have juggled the book around until something worked. Something cheap. But at this stage of the game, adding color and/or pockets to the book was just too damn expensive, in my mind, and poor corporate thinking.

Feeling well-armed with facts and figures, I made one more trek to the ad director's office. I humbly explained that if we were to accept either of these ads, we would lose money . . . not make it.

It's not his problem

And he correctly explained that such problems should have been anticipated in *my* budget. His job was to sell, sell, sell. My job was to print, print, print. No middle ground. No departmental overlap. Have a good day.

I was back to three options. This guy was right: It didn't matter if such emergencies weren't in my original budget, because nobody can really anticipate them with any accuracy. It didn't matter to him that I said we were going to lose money by running the ads, because company policy would never tell him not to sell ads, no matter how late . . . as long as we met our mailing schedule.

And he really didn't care if he totally blew my budget out of the water. Maybe the year later I could put something more accurate together. Meanwhile, his profit/cost would reflect the flattering (and inaccurate) projections used in my *current* budget, because that's all he officially had to work with when the fiscal year began.

I'm not going to give you the conclusion to this story. Rather, I'd like *your* opinions on three possible scenarios:

1. The production manager has authority, so he says, "We are not accepting any more color ads. They are too expensive and will blow my budget, not to mention that they will make this issue less profitable overall."

2. The production manager has little or no authority (as is the case with most magazines, I believe), so he relies on his convincing style, and talks the ad manager into locking the book up.

3. It's none of the production manager's business. He knows that his is merely a service job.

How about a fourth option, a consideration of the total picture by a third party? By evaluating the input of both the production manager and the ad director, an enlightened publisher certainly should be able to make a sound corporate decision.

How "real" is each situation? I'd be more than happy to receive *some* insight from readers. If not, I will have a bit more evidence to add to my uncomfortable theory that nobody cares about production—or production managers—anyhow.

The mystique of prepwork

By Jeffery R. Parnau

If you're the type of person who reads those little italicized bios at the end of FOLIO columns, you may recall that I own a typesetting and preparation business in the Milwaukee area.

So much for the advertising, which isn't the purpose of this column. What I'd like to discuss is *how* my company happened to get into prep... and how you might consider doing the same.

A magic show

First of all, prep—or to be formal, preparatory activity—is one of the least understood of the printing functions. It is, in my opinion, the most complicated... and the one area which can cost you lots of bucks. Why? Because the activity of putting a magazine together involves hundreds of decisions made *on the line*, during the actual production cycle.

So, whenever a prep person decides he needs a "choke" or a "blowdown," it must be done, right there. The activity of recording these hundreds of decisions can be so cumbersome that the printer doesn't do it. Instead, he may take a look at the final magazine and simply imagine what it must have taken to produce it. The potential, of course, is that he may be wrong about what he imagines.

That's why prep is such a magic show. By the time your job is put together, you don't know what it took or what the activities achieved. Furthermore, neither you nor your printer may know exactly what the invoice should be.

Step 1: the camera

Up until a few years ago, I was content to assume that, yes, prep cannot be understood, cannot be performed in house, and must be left to the union technicians who make their living in the darkroom.

Oddly enough, I also thought that any publisher without a stat camera had his head in the sand. How could anyone assemble a magazine— assuming that paste-up is performed in-house—without a stat camera?

Next, I found myself working for a publisher who had what he called a stat camera. It was actually a high-quality Brown, the type found in print shops across the country.

Because the publisher (1) liked to save money, and (2) was paranoid about losing an issue's worth of paste-ups, he shot his own negatives. And because he could do that, he also handled the routine reverses, advertisement reductions, and even simple contact prints which the printer would otherwise have done in-house.

When I founded a typesetting firm a few years ago, it was logical to me that—after the typesetting equipment—a camera was an absolute necessity. I bought one.

So, for the next three years, we had the luxury of never worrying that our paste-ups might be lost, because we always had back-up. As time went on, we experimented with (and nearly perfected) shooting PMT half-tones and stats (photo-mechanical transfers, if you're wondering), shooting weak copy, shooting and stripping halftones, and so forth.

Well, here comes the horror story. One sunny day, my prep shop called me to advise that they were too busy for one of our magazine accounts. And although I live and work in a graphics-oriented metropolitan area, not a single shop could strip the job to meet my schedule: Ready to go to the prep house on Friday night, and ready to give to the printer Monday morning.

I admit, the schedule was absurd. The options were to either miss the deadline... or strip the job in house.

We had the templates for the press, we had the impositions, we had a stock of pre-punched Mylar bases. We had always been involved with dis-assembly and storage of the material. What could possibly be so hard about putting an issue back together?

Now I don't suggest that our entry into stripping was the smoothest or wisest, but it was sure as hell the on-timest. We met the Monday deadline, and held our breath. Would it print? Would they reject the work? Did we assume we could strip, when in fact there were hundreds of secrets to it?

It ran like a top. It looked... well, it looked like any other magazine you'd pick up.

Voila! A prep shop

I was dumbfounded. We had started with an impossible deadline, we had less-than-apprenticeship help on the light table, and the job got out on time, and complete.

To condense the next few months into a brief summary, our company immediately ordered professional stripping equipment, more darkroom supplies (a much greater variety of film than we were accustomed to working with), took some crash courses in stripping, and within a short time we progressed to complex process-color stripping.

If you're wondering why I'm harping on this subject, get this: From that first issue henceforth, we made more money on prep than we made on typesetting. Typesetting was the business we originally wanted to be specializing in... but on a given job, we bill out more in camera work and stripping than we bill in type.

Better yet, most of the printers we deal with would be more than happy for us to do their prep. For them, prep is a headache... a goblin which constantly stands between them and their profit center: printing.

So, if I could go back a few years to that publishing operation which taught me so much about cameras, I'd give them a few facts on what to do next. Speaking as both a prep manager and a typesetting producer, I can —with reasonable accuracy—make the following statements.

If you install typesetting to save money, you probably won't. It's a competitive, low-profit business in the first place. That division of our company—and remember, that was at one time our only product—generates a lower relative profit than anything we do.

So don't install typesetting unless you are willing to pay dearly for the luxury of letting your editors slough off until deadline time.

If you ever, ever get the crazy idea to purchase a printing press, go pound your head against an eight-unit web until it knocks some sense into you. Printing, like prep, is highly competitive, and generates an approximate 5 percent profit for the owners.

And if you have a camera, consider getting into prep. This area can (1) substantially reduce your printing costs, (2) give you control over your schedule, and (3) even

make your printer happy.

For the technically curious among you, here are the ingredients for an in-house prep operation.
•One camera;
•One master template from your printer;
•One assortment of contacting film;
•One big light table;
•One trained prep person (stripper/contacter).

And if you want to know how to cook the above recipe, give your printer a call and ask. If he's like most others, he'll be more than happy to help you out. And if he says you're crazy, give me a call.

Print vs. Electronics
By Jeffery R. Parnau

I've gone and gotten myself all confused. When I sat down (which now seems long ago) to write this column, I had some clear ideas in my mind.

My first premise was that the major daily newspapers will be publishing *successful* electronic editions very soon, followed shortly by the newsweekly magazines, which are notorious for last-minute news and information. Both have an apparent need for urgency, and are already using satellite transmission.

My second premise was that small regional or specialized publishers will, for the foreseeable future, remain on conventional presses. They don't have the money, the circulation, or the urgency that big weekly publishing ventures have.

But not for me

The progression of my thinking seemed logical to me. But the other day, I was asked to fill out a questionnaire for Compuserve, a home/business computer service based in Columbus, Ohio.

The questions were straightforward enough. For example, "How often do you use the service?" "Do you read the newspapers on the service?" and so on.

(I answered all the questions, in part because they used the old survey trick of sticking a dollar bill in the envelope. I always feel obligated to fill out surveys when they send that buck. Otherwise, when you spend it, you feel guilty. It's un-American *not* to fill out the surveys, after you already got paid.)

Newspapers, of all the publishing products in this country, seem the most highly suited to electronic publishing, right? They're full of useless trivia, ads, filler, hot stories . . . they're overkill in the extreme. Every Monday I toss my three-pound Sunday intruder into the fireplace.

Yet the questionnaire got a "no newspapers" from me. I did read one or two stories on the terminal six months ago, and haven't called one up on the monitor since. That meant I had to skip about a third of the form, because they asked a lot of questions about newspapers:

which ones I accessed, how much of each story I read, whether I scan articles and such.

Other questions dealt with general use. Do I use the service for entertainment? Yup. Education? Yeah, sure. Business? Of course. But why not newspapers?

The magazines on the service never caught my eye, either. True, I occasionally buy a copy of *Popular Science* but not once have I called up its electronic version on my son's computer. For that matter, Jeremy— a 10-year-old with a passion for things electronic—hasn't tapped any of these sources either. (He has yet also to go into the educational listings.)

What we use

I finished the survey, stuck the buck in my pocket (I'm *not* going to send it to my favorite charity as the letter suggested, I'm going to buy a Taco), and started making some notes. Just what *do* we do with this service? If it offers newspapers, magazines, and a slew of other stuff, where are we spending the approximate $50/month in user fees?

My notes clearly narrow our usage down to two major areas. First, we tap the system for interactive entertainment. *Games* magazine is fine . . . but to really play a game, my kid, wife, and I go for *interaction*. We play Word Scramble a lot, where the computer mixes up a word and the player guesses it a letter at a time. Jeremy plays *Adventure*, in which the player tries to find treasures while fighting off every imaginable type of monster.

The interactive part is beautiful: When we enter a guess, a built-in game-show host tells us whether it's right or wrong. The computer is the judge and jury. It's a third party; it's interactive.

Games are fun, but I certainly wouldn't tolerate a $50 monthly bill just to keep the house quiet. Any TV can do that a lot cheaper.

My second major-use area is in pulling off weather information necessary for flying a small plane. To begin with, getting weather information at all is a problem, since Flight Service is not well known for either its speed in answering a phone or for a spontaneous, thorough weather briefing. (Of course, flying through the weather itself is a problem, but that's a story for an aviation magazine.) So, I routinely use the computer to get information (in hard-copy form) which is as current as possible...and which is critical to me as a pilot.

One final use: I recently discovered an interactive flight-planner on the system. I don't mean to be lazy, but the network computer does one hell of a job in planning my business flights.

In summary, I *don't* read newspapers on the system simply because I can read newspapers *anywhere*. I can read them cheaper than the $5 hourly rate it costs me on Compuserve. I can read them slower, better. But mostly, I don't want to pay $5 for *general, passive* information. Anyhow, by the time I scan even the most current news, I've already seen it on TV or heard it on the radio.

The game-playing we do on the system attracts us clearly because of its interactive nature. The weather reports are more thorough and detailed than what I get from Flight Service, and I get the added bonus of printing a hard copy and taking it with me on a flight. The flight-planning is convenient, personalized, and fast.

Back on the track

What's all this got to do with magazine production? Consider it background as I relate a true story.

A few months ago I lost an attractive new account, not to another type/prep house, but to the ancient system the publisher had been using for years. The product happened to be a weekly magazine, with the rather skimpy circulation of less than 5,000 copies.

The magazine's type was set in hot metal on a daily basis. A mere handful of subscribers (600) received this daily information in letterpress form. Then, additional galleys were pulled, from which the weekly magazine was pasted up.

Obviously, the daily had a tight schedule, but the weekly was not much better. The last of the information would trickle in only minutes before press time, a galley would be pulled, a neg shot, and the offset process would take over.

Well, the days of letterpress and hot-metal equipment are surely numbered. My pitch to the publisher was to install computer terminals and link them to our typesetting equipment. Problem 1: The cost and speed restrictions made computerized typesetting a virtual impossibility.

In hot-metal, the copy could be shifted at the very last minute, much as a word processor would shift it. But as soon as the hot-metal forms are composed, they are inked and start running the copies off. The computerized typesetter, in making a last-minute insertion or copy change, must run the entire file off (20 minutes), then go into the camera or plate room (another 10 minutes). By the time the photo-typeset version would be ready to print, the hot-metal version would be off press. The time-lag was unacceptable.

So I took another approach: How about a high-speed line printer, which could spit the material out in 10 minutes, and go directly onto a quick-print press? Fine... but such a press would make two passes, while the hot-metal system made only one. Printing costs would double.

The publisher did what seemed logical. He decided to stay with a hot-metal system, because it was the fastest way to print and mail the material. And the material did have to go out on a *daily* basis: It was a listing of current construction bids being opened to contractors.

Likewise, the weekly magazine had a lot of loose copy until the last minute. Coupled with the fact that it used the galleys from the daily version, re-keyboarding was out of the question due to its redundancy...so we didn't get any of that work, either. The "modern, fast, computerized" method we offered was too slow, too costly, too inefficient. Gutenberg won the job.

Chart 1:
Weekly General News Magazine

General Description	Conventional	Grey Zone	Electronic
Content is or should be:	☐General/ Universal	☐Mixed	☐Specific/ personal
Usage is or should be:	☐Passive	☐N.A.	☐Active
Accessibility should be:	☐Portable	☐Either	☐Office/ home
Information cost (user/reader to pay):	☐Low	☐Unclear	☐High
Time-critical:	☐No	☐Somewhat	☐Yes
Circulation:	☐Large	☐Moderate/ fluctuates	☐Small
Ad revenue required:	☐Yes	☐N.A.	☐No
Interaction:	☐Un-necessary	☐N.A.	☐Desirable/ required
Total boxes checked	7	1	0

Chart 2:
Weekly Regional Construction Magazine

General Description:	Conventional	Grey Zone	Electronic
Content is or should be:	☐General/ Universal	☐Mixed	☐Specific/ personal
Usage is or should be:	☐Passive	☐N.A.	☐Active
Accessibility should be:	☐Portable	☐Either	☐Office/ home
Information cost (user/reader to pay):	☐Low	☐Unclear	☐High
Time-critical:	☐No	☐Somewhat	☐Yes
Circulation:	☐Large	☐Moderate/ fluctuates	☐Small
Ad revenue required:	☐Yes	☐N.A.	☐No
Interaction:	☐Un-necessary	☐N.A.	☐Desirable/ required
Total boxes checked	0	0	8

What I should have said was . . .

I finally figured out where I went wrong. My own experience with computer networks should have filtered into this publisher's situation. His product had the following characteristics:

Users were willing to pay a very healthy fee to get the information quickly. He dealt exclusively with professionals. He carried no advertising in the daily version. He had a small circulation. He could make excellent use of on-demand information or interaction with the user.

Although "conventional" publishing can't solve his problems (antiquated equipment, high personnel cost, the dying art of hot metal), electronic publishing could offer his users exactly what they need.

The rating chart

I asked myself the hypothetical question: If I were publishing several different journals, how would I—as a production manager—decide to transmit the information to the reader? On press, or via an electronic link?

Take a look at the little rating chart I drew up, and see what you think. Personally, I doubt if newspapers will ever become very popular in their electronic format. Likewise, I doubt that general-interest magazines, weekly or otherwise, are suited for magic-wand publishing. But the smaller publishers, the regionals, the special interest magazines which could enhance their offerings with time-critical, interactive information—that's where the action will be.

Take a minute to rate your own magazine, along with a few of the "hot" trade publications you read.

You might find that your product (Chart 1) will do just fine with ink on paper, or (Chart 2) that you're a likely candidate for electronic publishing, or (Chart 3) that you just don't know.

I told you I was confused.

The word processing interface

By Jeffery R. Parnau

In magazine production, the wonders never cease. The wonder addressed here is something you've more than likely heard a bit about: interfaced typesetting.

Specifically, interfaced typesetting—for our purposes—is a system which allows you, the publisher, to store keystrokes for typesetting. The benefit is, you don't have to purchase, install, maintain or operate a typesetting device. Rather, you store the keystrokes on floppy disks, or magnetic tape. Then you deliver the information to a typesetting company by one of several methods, such as the use of voice-grade telephone lines (using a modulator/demodulator), sending the tape or disk itself, or having the information rewritten by a reformatting device (such as a Shafstall or Media 500).

All well and good . . . but this field is relatively new. As publishers approach the possibility of interfacing with a typesetter, rather than installing an output machine itself, they must also be aware of the pitfalls and benefits of going "on line."

So let's take a few minutes to clear up some of the myths of interfacing, and explain just what you should be looking for.

Don't be put off

First of all, the hardware which makes interfacing possible is available, inexpensive, and hardly "magic." Most typesetting companies are at least looking at the possibility of expanding into this field.

The myths? You may hear any of the following statements:

•We aren't going in that direction just yet. The equipment is expensive; the procedures are unreliable.

•It doesn't work for the average magazine; it's more suited to catalog-type pricelists.

•It's a song-and-dance, and doesn't really save money.

None of the above is true. The obvious benefit of interfacing is that you can store any type of keystrokes, thereby eliminating the need for retyping . . . along with eliminating the need for typesetting equipment itself.

Firms which say the equipment is expensive just haven't researched the marketplace. Most typesetting machines will accept off-line keystrokes with the addition of approximately $5,000 worth of electronics. Hardly a fortune.

And magazines, more than any other type of publication, are ideally suited to interfacing. They are primarily text, which is cumbersome to type . . . but easy to program.

Pursue prices vigorously

The second area to watch is pricing. Believe it or not, you could find yourself paying *more* for interfaced typesetting than you'd pay if you let a typesetter do it from scratch. How?

Our market research has proven, unfortunately, that very few firms provide enough pricing information for the buyer to make an intelligent decision. For example, examine the following paraphrased conversation we had with a typesetter:

"How do you price out typesetting if we do the keyboarding?"

"Well," the firm says, "we'd have to see the product first."

"How about pricing it per inch? It's nine point on 10 point leading, straight text."

"We don't price things that way; we bill by the hour."

"How much can I save," I ask, "if we do the keystrokes?"

"About 25 percent."

"Twenty-five percent of what?"

"Of our hourly rates."

That tells you, the buyer, absolutely nothing. When we finally got the above firm to state just what its hourly rates were, they turned out to be better than 30 percent higher than what other firms charge customers. So the poor buyer who decides to "save money" by doing his typing internally could easily pay a 5 percent premium plus the expense of internal typing.

If you look into pricing for interfaced typesetting, be sure to get the same information from each potential vendor: Given your specifications, how much will they charge per inch, or per character, or per square inch, or per em? Per anything . . . just so you get a price which you can compare to others. And don't pay a whit of attention to hourly rates. Some machines, just like some people, are twice as fast as the others.

Review systems and equipment

The third area of importance is this: Just how much markup do you have to do when you keystroke your copy? You will probably want to be able to change to italic and bold . . . but do you want to be able to set tabular matter? Set indents? Perform run-arounds?

Worse yet, there just isn't any standard method of marking copy for interfaced typesetting. Therefore, you should—before getting involved—fully review the markup system used by the firm. Example: Any simple microcomputer is capable of "setting" type for transmission to an output unit. *How* does the firm accommodate the variety of equipment on the market? Or must you use a special terminal, which will possibly raise your costs?

Because there are no standard methods of interfacing type, each typesetting company must pretty much re-create the wheel. And some re-creations are much harder to use than others.

Finally, there is the question of the output equipment itself. Key areas: How many customers are using the service (which may affect saturation time and limit your access)? Does the equipment have discretionary hyphenation which you can control? Exception word hyphenation? Dictionary hyphenation? Does it run unmonitored, or does it require operator intervention?

How fast is it? An 800-line-per-minute digital typesetter will obviously give you better service than a 20-line-per-minute conventional photographic machine.

Keep your eyes open

Don't get me wrong. I am a strong proponent of interfaced typesetting. It does work. It does save money, and for simple reasons:

You can use semi-skilled labor, you have simpler training, faster recovery after personnel turnover. You don't invest in equipment which will become obsolete within three years; instead, you invest in a device which merely records keystrokes. Let the equipment market do what it wants.

If, after adding up the potential savings, you make the decision that you don't absolutely need to have typesetting in-house, you can consider going into the interface arena.

Just keep your eyes open and get the facts: the prices, the conversion codes, the technical abilities of the output machine. Until this new field settles down, there will be a lot of possible misinformation floating around.

Typesetting equipment guide

By Frank Romano

All typesetting equipment can be divided into two categories: big and small. This overly simplistic segmentation can help you to understand the relative capabilities of a seemingly unending variety of equipment and to ultimately compare devices intelligently.

The small machine category is generally called "Direct Input" in order to indicate the orientation of the device from an operational point of view: one person inputs and sets type. It used to be that the operator was setting type as the input was taking place, but most devices today let you store the information on a floppy disk for later typesetting. Most of these devices also have an optional off-line input/editor which can allow all functions **except** setting type.

With the advent of floppy disk recording and off-line input and editing, it was necessary to speed up the typesetter part of the direct input typesetter so that it could be setting type with data from one floppy while the operator was inputting or editing data on the other floppy (most systems have or should have dual floppy disks). This capability is called "multi-tasking," which is computerese for the ability of the machine to essentially let two things happen at the same time.

Thus, a direct input typesetter is no longer truly direct input, and we now use the term "Small Integrated System" to define its true nature. With the introduction of the Compugraphic Modular Composition System (MCS) we have seen the traditional direct input concept advanced to multi-video terminals and multi-floppy disks in an upgradable system. As the number of input and editing stations increases, it is absolutely necessary to increase the speed of the typesetter.

An average input keyboarder will produce 70,000 keystrokes of information in a day. A 25 character-per-second (cps) typesetter (also known as 50 lines-per-minute [lpm]) will take almost .7 hour to print out that data. A 75 cps unit (150 lpm) will take .3 hour, and a 250 cps unit (500 lpm) will take .07 hour. Those same 70,000 keystrokes could represent six to 12 magazine pages of 100 percent text type. (Our speed examples are for text type set in 11 pica columns. As the point size increases and the line length widens, the speeds change proportionally.)

The average direct input typesetter at 25 cps (50 lpm) could handle 2,000 pages per year, assuming that most were "partial" pages, as most magazine pages are. We are using an 8½-inch by 11-inch page as a sort of standard, so be careful to reduce tabloid pages to a common denominator.

If we had between 2,000 pages and 5,000 pages we would get a second direct input typesetter, or at least an off-line input/editor if the main unit was 75 cps (150 lpm) or higher. If you were doing 5,000 pages a year on equipment such as this, the second unit becomes important as a backup machine more than anything else. You can, of course, have as many direct input typesetters as you wish, but we would draw the line at two with an off-line input/editor. That package would cost about $50,000 (2 x $20,000 + $10,000, to use round numbers). To add another main unit would bring you to $70,000, and here we arrive at the threshold of the Large Integrated Systems area.

There is still a gray area in the $50,000 to $100,000 price range in terms of equipment alternatives. For those dollars you can have several self-contained low-end machines which can give you the ability to handle volume and provide backup. A Large Integrated System might start at $50,000 with another $30,000 (average) for the typesetter, bringing you to $80,000, with the ability to handle volume but no backup. Actually, an average large system with a digitized typesetter is going to cost more like $130,000, and a backed-up version could easily reach $200,000.

Know your needs

If you were told that you would spend $200,000 on typesetting equipment, some of you would get very nervous, yet we see many publishers who have invested almost $100,000 in low-end equipment and want to know what the next step is. Well, the next step is a large system, and since the low-end equipment can't be used, they must start all over again. Thus, an idea of your projected volume is most important in selecting equipment.

Here is one scenario. About five years ago, Publisher X purchased a 10 cps (20 lpm) direct input typesetter for $15,000. Within a year it was apparent that the speed was too low and the decision was made to buy the 25 cps (50 lpm) version from the same supplier. That gave backup and could handle the volume. The 25 cps was faster than the operator, and the publisher purchased the off-line input/editor. The second typesetter was $20,000 and the off-line unit was $10,000.

At this point the publisher had invested $45,000 but still found that there was no systems approach to his typesetting. Now he wants to buy the small system that allows four input/editors to link to one 75 cps (150 lpm) typesetter. The price tag is almost $50,000 for the version he needs. After adding about $20,000 over the next few years, this system will reach the end of its capacity and the publisher will be back where he started from.

Should he have to buy, use and discard equipment every six years or so? For now, unless he bit the bullet and entered the technology high up on the capability ladder, he would.

You get what you pay for

Large Integrated Systems are traditionally called "Front Ends" because they let you input, edit, store, retrieve and format data before typesetting. You have to think of these systems as cohesive, that is, with the typesetter attached. In almost every case today, that typesetter will be a digitized version. Digitized typesetters are usually 75 cps (150 lpm) or above. Most systems have at least four input/editors attached.

In this category, assuming a person at each terminal, you could handle 10,000 pages per year and grow to just about any volume. You can see the gray area in terms of pages—between 5,000 pages per year for the top end of the low systems and 10,000 pages per year for the bottom end of the large systems.

There are some versions of the larger systems that are smaller. These are $60,000 and under (without the typesetter). You could link the new breed of digitized typesetters that are coming out in the $30,000 area (several will be with us this year), and some will be close to $25,000. The combination of these two devices results in a system for under $100,000. The more mature systems are closer to $130,000 for both.

The major advantages of the larger systems lie in labor savings beyond the typesetting area: assembly. Although it is technically possible to exit from a direct input typesetter with fully madeup text pages, it is not practical. Operators must make many judgments as they are typesetting, thus requiring people with a good design background. However, the larger systems are designed for page makeup and can handle it efficiently.

The lower versions of the larger systems are not as efficient at page makeup as the larger versions. We must admit, you usually get what you pay for in these systems. Most of the higher priced systems do have higher levels of automation (although I would not use price as the determining factor in selecting a system).

Production vs. editorial

This brings us to a controversial area. There are two approaches to systems: production and editorial. An editorial system allows editors, reporters, and writers to work at terminals and send type off to be typeset. Usually, editorial based systems work best with magazines with a simple repetitive format or with outside services that will actually set the type.

Production systems require a more skilled person but have much more typographic capability and more pagination power. Usually you put the production system and its operator or operators in a room and give them copy. Some publishers and their staffs are caught up in the "Lou Grant Syndrome" and want terminals for everyone. Yet, a production approach may be the most cost effective in the long term.

It sounds crazy, but an editorial system feeding data to a production system can make sense. Too many publishers today are "following the leader" and buying what the others buy.

The area that is most fertile, that may hold an answer for some publishers involves word processors and personal computers. A personal computer with a screen, keyboard, floppies and text editing software could cost as little as $2,000. Although there are some efficiencies that come from linking all terminals into a central computer and central storage area, these cheap off-line units let you input, edit, store and retrieve. You can't hyphenate and justify and you can't get a line count of that data in typeset form. These functions are only available on on-line systems.

However, there are many "originators" whose job is only to create the first version. Their floppies can be input to the main system and then called up to systems' terminals. Word processors are more expensive since they have printers attached and come in at $8,000 or so each. The personal computer will open many doors for publishers, and one of them will be the ability to let every originator, inhouse or outside, create information in electronic form. They can then transmit that data to the office by phone or send the floppy by Express Mail. Both are forms of telecommunications.

All floppies are not equal

In the office, a floppy disk reader and interface will allow the data to be input to the system. The most popular unit for this is the Shaffstall (Indianapolis) interface called the MediaCom. It can take both telephone data and actual floppy disks and translate the information into the system code. Most of the direct input devices have telephone interface as options.

For inside use, however, you will want to read the floppy. Since all floppies are not recorded equally, you will need an interface which costs between $5,000 and $10,000. In the process of converting the codes from the device to the codes of another device they also convert "strings" of characters into command functions. Thus, the input person could key "*tl" meaning "use the format for text type" and the conversion will call out the proper typographic parameters to accomplish this.

It is best to interface to more sophisticated systems. To link to the low-end devices—although possible—is not practical since some of them do not have very good levels of automatic hyphenation and justification. Word processors are designed for office communication tasks and have many capabilities beyond text input and editing. They are very expensive typesetting keyboards.

The bottom line

If you added up the per year cost of the equipment, the personnel to run it, the consumables and service (leaving out other overhead and the tax credits/amortization), and then divided the total by the number of characters input by the people who input and edit on the system (production approach), you would find a range of between 80 cents and $1.11 per thousand characters for the low-end equipment, and a range of 21 cents to 36 cents for the high-end equipment. As you find ways to "capture" the information from the originators, the number of production personnel goes down and so does the cost per thousand characters. Additionally, the high-end equipment allows you to keep a minimal paste-up/assembly staff. An expensive system may not be as expensive as it appears.

All devices, low and high, will ultimately integrate increasing levels of interactive page makeup. Today, most of them are passive: you can see a simulation of the page on a screen before actual typesetting. Stand-alone page makeup devices tend to be transitional in nature, since they will be part of our systems.

Both Varityper and Compugraphix have this capability at the low end and it is installed and working in the field. AKI, Penta, Typographix, and Itek have passive approaches in the systems area. III and Bedford have interactive approaches. If you want halftones in position, see III for now. Most of the other digitized typesetters and systems will eventually handle halftones. Right now, most of the demonstrated approaches have not been efficient.

There is no doubt that publishers are moving into typesetting at an increasing rate. It is one of the few areas where technology can bring cost under control. The circulation area is probably next. Our product review has been kept simple to allow you to group devices of similar capabilities together.

We must caution you not to use price as the only criteria and to see each device considered in operation. Do not buy the machine or system because you like the people (although that is hard to do). Given the erratic nature of typesetting technology, the people you don't like may be replaced. Don't buy because you have been well treated during the decision-making period, in terms of personal attention. Find out from users how they are treated afterward. A healthy degree of skepticism goes a long way.

Word processors move into editorial: The new typesetting link

By Douglas Learner

The process of interfaced typesetting is simple: An article is written and edited on a word processing machine and then transmitted from the word processor directly into a typesetter.

Whereas the traditional electronic editing system features a central computer supporting a number of "dumb" editing terminals, a word processor's computer power is self-contained. In fact, many word processors used for editing and interfaced typesetting are actually microcomputers equipped with word processing software.

There are definite advantages to using an interfaced typesetting system. By sending copy directly to the typesetter, the step of rekeyboarding copy is eliminated. With this step gone, typesetting costs are reduced, the possibility of errors being added to the copy is eliminated, and turnaround time is shortened.

The low cost of purchasing a word processor for editing and interfaced typesetting is now bringing electronic editing into the smallest of publishing offices. FOLIO has thus taken an in-depth look at how four magazines and one multi-title publishing company are involved with interfaced typesetting.

Their experiences are illuminating. Interfaced typesetting has enabled Cliggott Publishing Company to handle tremendous growth in one of its magazines—while still reducing production costs. *TRS-80 Microcomputer News* is using word processors to eliminate paper not only from its editors' desks, but from their outside contributors' desks as well. And *Theatre Crafts Magazine* is capitalizing on its typesetter's data processing capabilities to speed production and reduce the costs of typesetting of its annual buyers' guide.

At the *Harvard Business Review,* a year and a half was spent planning and preparing a shift to interfaced typesetting—just to make sure no problems arose. And here at FOLIO, customized translation programs were written for typesetting the Folio 400, an annual research study consisting of hundreds of charts as well as text material.

The magazines in this report were chosen because they cover a broad spectrum of publishing situations. There are business magazines, consumer magazines, monthlies, bimonthlies, magazines where editors write and edit on word processors and some where the editors never touch a terminal.

Three of the magazines are using microcomputers equipped with word processing software, while the other two have opted for multi-station word processors. In each case the equipment is also used for projects other than getting magazine copy to the typesetter.

Some have in-house typesetting, and some are using outside typesetting companies. The methods of transmitting articles from the word processor to the typesetter, and the inputting of typesetting commands, vary from one magazine to another.

The five accompanying profiles, then, illustrate different approaches and solutions to the singular problem of getting thoughts into print through interfaced typesetting.

FOLIO also spoke with consultants and suppliers because our look at how different magazines approached interface typesetting does not cover the benefits, or drawbacks, of various solutions. There are three major areas of consideration in creating a word processor/typesetting interface: the word processing equipment; the translation table which enables the typesetter to understand commands from the word processor; and the means of transmitting copy from the word processor to the typesetter. Each area has its own set of decisions.

The microcomputer option

Obviously, a publisher needs a word processor for interfaced typesetting. A main frame computer equipped with word processing software can be used, as can a word processing system or a portable memory terminal, such as those manufactured by Teleram Corporation and Texas Instruments.

Or a publisher can use a microcomputer equipped with word processing software. Micros have the advantages of low price and the capacity for use beyond a word processor. For under $3,000 a publisher can go to his local computer store and purchase a micro system complete with a printer for producing hard copies of a manuscript. And even the top-of-the-line Radio Shack TRS-80 micro-

Cliggott Publishing Company accommodates magazine growth

The greatest benefit of Cliggott's word processor is that it has enabled the production department to keep up with the growth of the company's magazines. One of its magazines grew from an average size of 260 pages an issue in 1981 to over 400 pages an issue in the first quarter of 1982. "I don't know what we would have done without the word processing interface," says Donald P. Sargeant, Cliggott's production director.

Cliggott publishes three medical magazines, *Consultant, The Journal of Respiratory Diseases,* and *Psychosomatics.* All are monthlies. In addition, it produces lesser frequency publications, as well as direct mail. In February 1981 the company purchased two AB Dick word processors to handle all copy and to interface with typesetting equipment at Nortype in Norwalk, Conn.

Sargeant estimates Cliggott's investment in the system at about $47,000. Since the installation he estimates the per camera ready page cost (Nortype also does their paste-up) has dropped 15 percent, while the savings for raw copy has been about 20 percent. In 1980, the last full year before the interface was established, Cliggott paid about $150,000 for typesetting, according to Sargeant. With the 20 percent savings from the interfaced typesetting, he estimates ROI for the word processor at a year-and-a-half.

The ROI may be even less, he added, considering the added load imposed by the growth of *Consultant* magazine.

All the copy for Cliggott's magazines is transmitted to Nortype over the phone lines. The set-up between Cliggott and Nortype is unique: Once the copy has been received by Nortype's typesetter, it is transmitted back to Cliggott's Greenwich, Connecticut headquarters where it is printed out on a line printer. The printer is able to print italicized and bold text, as well as sub- and super-script. All line breaks in the printout are as the copy will appear when typeset (though the lines are not justified).

Cliggott's editorial staff, working with this computer printout, marks any corrections that have to be made and produces a layout based on the printout. The printout and the layout are both returned to Nortype, which corrects the copy, produces the typeset galleys, and pastes up the pages. Completed pages are returned to Cliggott for proofing.

When copy is transmitted to Nortype, a manuscript with notations for special typographical commands is also sent by messenger. Much of the coding for the copy is done by the editorial staffs of the various magazines.

Sargeant has worked with Nortype to create a conversion table based on the silent commands of the word processor. For example, when the word processing command for underscoring a word or words is used, that signal will tell the typesetter to set the words in italics.

"We've tried to use the background codes, such as the one for underscoring, to take advantage of typographical features," says Sargeant. "We've stayed with the traditional proofreader marks because we don't want our editorial assistants to become typesetters. I expect them to know editorial mark-up, but, for example, I don't want them to command the machine to format an article by so many picas."

Sargeant added that each magazine has its own special format, which is locked into Nortype's computer. Before any article is sent, a special code is input to alert the typesetter which format to use.

computer-based word processing system, with a letter quality printer and a large amount of memory, is priced at only $6,300.

Though a single-station word processing machine can be purchased for under $10,000, it will not have the software capabilities of a micro. By purchasing or developing additional software, a publisher can use a micro for financial planning, accounting, ad trafficking, list maintenance and so on. Micros can also be connected to databases and computer networks, such as those offered by Lockheed, Dun & Bradstreet, and *The New York Times.*

Having a microcomputer repaired is also easy: simply take it to the local computer store. There is no wait for a serviceman to arrive. And an office equipped with a number of micros offers the publisher a measure of security, since one can be used as a back-up if another breaks down.

A publisher can use any word processor for interfaced typesetting. And his word processor can interface with any typesetting machine equipped to receive text directly

Harvard Business Review required 18 months of planning

The *Harvard Business Review*'s switch to interfaced typesetting from hot metal with its January/February 1982 issue marked the end of 18 months of planning and preparation. During that time, editorial assistants were trained to use the word processor, and the typesetting house they were going to begin interfacing with became familiar with their copy flow and typographic requirements.

While G. Scott Hutchison, executive editor, production operations for *HBR*, jests that the process was done in "slow haste," he admitted that the magazine was careful to take enough time to ensure that the transition went smoothly.

"We're really babes in the woods when it comes to electronic systems," he says, "so we've tried to anticipate problems and take things slowly. The system is new, and we're working with a new supplier. Things could get very complicated if we didn't take the time to smooth everything out first."

HBR has a five-station Wang word processing system, installed in June 1980 at a cost of about $40,000. It is used for preparing editorial manuscripts and also correspondence for the business side operations. Articles for the bimonthly are entered into the system by editorial assistants, who also make revisions from marked manuscripts given to them by the editors; the editors rarely work on the systems themselves. (Virtually all of the magazine's editorial copy comes from outside authors.)

The *HBR* staff does not enter any typesetting commands onto the copy. That is all handled by the operators at Typographic House, a typesetting company located in Boston. The typesetting operators work from hand-marked manuscripts that are delivered with the floppy discs.

Hutchison admitted that the magazine might be able to save additional dollars if coding was done in-house (he had no figures concerning savings because the magazine has only recently begun to interface its typesetting), and said that in-house coding is a possibility for the future. Telecommunications was another possibility he discussed.

For the time being, though, he prefers to let his staff gain experience on the system before making any changes.

TRS-80 Microcomputer News eliminates keyboarding of outside writers' copy

TRS-80 Microcomputer News is using a microcomputer equipped with word processing software not only to interface with an in-house typesetting system, but also to receive copy from outside contributors.

Roughly half the articles appearing in the magazine each month are written by outside contributors, according to editor Bruce Elliott. Since the writers usually have a TRS-80 microcomputer (the magazine is published by Radio Shack for owners of its TRS-80 microcomputer), Elliott makes extensive use of their ability to send articles in various electronic forms—anything, it seems, other than paper.

Elliott has writers who send articles to his micro via telecommunications, over standard telephone lines. A few writers send copy on floppy discs. There is even one writer who uses CompuServe, a computer network, as an electronic mailbox. The writer will deposit his article into CompuServe under a file name, call Elliott to tell him the article is there waiting, and Elliott will call CompuServe and pull the article out of the network into his own computer.

Elliott said he prefers to receive copy on discs or by telecommunications because it saves the magazine time in the editing and production cycles. He prefers it so much that he is offering writers a special deal if they send articles on a floppy disc: They will receive two free discs in return. The offer was announced in the March 1982 issue.

It is not surprising that *TRS-80 Microcomputer News* uses TRS-80s for interfaced typesetting. The micros interface with an in-house Quadex typesetting system, which was installed to handle all of Radio Shack's typesetting needs, from advertising and promotional copy to articles for the magazine.

The micros were actually used for editing the magazine long before the Quadex system was installed. In what Elliott calls "a very frustrating process," all copy used to be edited on the micros, printed out on paper, and taken to an outside typesetting service for rekeyboarding.

Since installation of the Quadex system, floppies containing the magazine's articles are taken from the editorial TRS-80s and carried down a hall to another TRS-80 that is connected directly to the typesetter. Elliott said he has no estimates on cost savings from the interface because of the multiple use of the Quadex system.

Elliott and his staff have about two dozen string commands they insert into the body of copy to indicate typographic features such as flush left, bold face, italicize and end paragraph. String commands are used rather than silent commands because they alert the magazine's proofreaders, who work from hard copy produced on a line printer, to the occurrence of typographic features.

When each floppy is given to typesetting, it is accompanied by a printout of the article that includes instructions for type style, copy width, type size, leading and so forth. The typesetting operator inputs these commands into the typesetting machine.

"I was trying to keep the process as simple as possible," Elliott says, "and not force anybody to learn typesetting commands."

Articles received from outside contributors on paper are entered into one of the editorial TRS-80s, and the typesetting commands are added. Yes, Elliott will accept outside articles on paper. "We're trying to eliminate paper," he says, "but we haven't succeeded yet."

from a word processor. There is, however, no off-the-shelf interfaced typesetting system (word processor, typesetter and interface) a publisher can purchase: He must assemble the pieces.

If the publisher already has in-house typesetting he simply adds the interface to his typesetting equipment. If his typesetting is done by an outside company, he must make sure the type house has an interface for its equipment.

The translation table:

The interfacing of a word processor and a typesetter goes far beyond the hardware, though. Software has to be written for the typesetter that will enable the typesetter to typeset the text it receives from the word processor.

In virtually every magazine there are a variety of typographical features used, such as changing type fonts, italicizing certain words or phrases, and even simple paragraph endings, which requires a flush left command. To achieve these different typographical functions from word processor input, special codes must be entered on the word processor along with the copy. These codes are then converted by software in the typesetter's interface, called a translation table, into understandable typesetting commands and are executed by the typesetter.

Two kinds of codes are input into copy to signify typographical features. The first is string commands, which are a combination of typewriter keystrokes such as //I to indicate that the words following the code are to be italicized. When the typesetter comes to the //I command, the translation table will tell it to change to the italicized font, and then proceed typesetting. When the typesetter comes to another string code, //R for example, it will return to the regular font.

When creating such codes the key is to find an assortment of characters that are unique and will not occur in normal copy, but are understandable enough so editors will be able to remember them.

The second type of code involves silent commands which send signals to the typesetter via keystrokes that do not cause characters to be printed. These keystrokes may be line spaces, a carriage return or a word processor's super shift keys.

Suppose you have straight text, and the only typographic feature needed is paragraph endings. (A paragraph ending is simply a flush left command for the last line.) A translation table can be written to tell the typesetter that two carriage returns on the word processor mean a flush left command and a carriage return. Thus, striking two carriage returns on the word processor at the end of each paragraph will trigger the typesetter to properly end the paragraph.

There is one drawback to silent commands, which may not even affect some publishers' operations. Because no characters are output when a command is entered, there are no flags to alert a copy editor that a typographic change has been called for. With string commands, a flag exists in the copy. (It is possible to write a translation table to allow use of both string and silent commands, with the former used for irregularly occurring typographic changes and the latter for regularly occurring ones.)

While some typesetting houses may boast of generic coding for interfaced typesetting, their coding is generic only for their customers. This has been done by the type house so it only has to write one translation table for its typesetting equipment.

This does not mean that the generic code is inherently bad. On the contrary, such codes are usually es-

THE FOLIO 400; difficulties in translation tables

The decision to typeset last year's Folio 400, FOLIO's third annual ranking of the top 400 magazines in the industry, was a natural extension of the use of a Radio Shack TRS-80 microcomputer to compute and manipulate the data appearing in the study. By sending the data directly from the TRS-80 to Publishers Resources, FOLIO's typesetter, the rekeyboarding of over 650 tables, 400 magazine profiles and indices by magazine and publishing company was avoided.

Though the system worked as expected, saving both typesetting time and costs, an unexpected problem arose in the writing of the translation tables. As John O'Toole, FOLIO's managing editor, found out, writing translation tables for tabular matter of varying formats is much more complicated than writing translation tables for straight text.

"I started out using Compugraphic's recommended translation tables for tabular matter," he says, "but they were not adequate for the job. So I had to write all the tables from scratch."

Writing the tables from scratch proved to be especially time-consuming for two reasons. First, there were several different formats for the Folio 400 tables. Second, O'Toole found that in order to write a translation table to have the Folio 400 typeset, he had to think like a typesetting machine.

"The most difficult part of writing the translation tables was learning to think like a typesetter," O'Toole says. "Basically, I had to teach myself the Compugraphic keyboard.

"But the beauty of the programming was that once the translation tables were set and debugged, the system just ran. As long as the information was correctly formatted, it just ran."

O'Toole's translation table contained more silent commands than string commands. The silent commands included such codes as three line spaces, or two carriage returns—keystrokes that sent specific commands to the typesetter. When the typesetter came across two carriage returns, for example, it would automatically change to a bold font.

Silent commands worked well for the Folio 400 because it was possible to manipulate the data into consistent formats using the software developed for computing the 400.

O'Toole said he experienced few problems when transmitting the data from the TRS-80 to the typesetter over the telephone lines. In fact, he added, the only real problem he had with the whole arrangement was writing the translation tables.

"It seemed like we were the only ones using interfaced typesetting in this way," he says of the experience last summer. "There was no one I could call to ask questions."

tablished as much for user ease as operator ease. And often a typesetter will create a custom translation table for a publisher whose job cannot be handled by the "generic" coding.

Publishers interfacing a word processor with an in-house typesetter are responsible for their own translation table. Fortunately, most manufacturers of interfaces supply a recommended translation table with their interface. This table can be used as is or modified by the publisher.

Transmitting copy:

The key to interfaced typesetting is the ability to transmit an article directly from a word processor to a typesetter. There are two different ways to transmit copy —via a recorded medium or a transmission line—and a publisher considers a number of different factors when choosing a method: where his typesetting is done—in-house or through an outside service bureau; the extensiveness of the typesetting commands entered on the word processor; the amount of time in each issue's production cycle; and each method's costs.

Here are the transmission methods available to publishers:

If the publisher has in-house typesetting, he can physically carry the floppy to the typesetter, he can transmit the data over the phone lines, or he can establish a direct cable link between the two machines. (The latter two being telecommunications methods). A publisher using either an outside typesetting house or a printer with typesetters equipped to receive word processor input can use telecommunications or can deliver the floppy directly.

There are different views on which method—telecommunications or transporting the medium—is the better method. Publishing consultant Frank Romano believes that transporting discs, or other recorded media

such as magnetic tape, to the typesetter is the most efficient way to transport keystrokes—except for publishers with a time constraint or geographic limitation.

Romano has four reasons for his view:

First, phone lines tend to be "dirty" and thus unreliable for transmitting data despite means to reduce interference and outside noise on the lines. Phone line noise can interfere with transmission by adding audible tones to the signal being transmitted from the word processor's modem to the typesetter's modem. These added tones are received by the typesetter as typesetting instructions or copy to be set.

Second is the cost of phone lines for telecommunications, be it a local, WATS, dedicated or microwave transmission line. The phone rates do go down in the evening, he says, and there is an advantage of being able to transmit copy at 6 o'clock one evening and receive typeset galleys the next morning. But unless a magazine is on a very tight production schedule, Romano adds, the cost of transmission may not be worth the amount of time saved.

Third is the possibility of equipment breakdowns on either end of the hook-up: the typesetter could malfunction or the computer could "go down." Either breakdown could then require retransmission of the text, which means added phone lines and possibly missed deadlines.

Finally, in many cases, a copy of the manuscript is sent by the editor to the typesetter along with the transmitted keystrokes. This manuscript will be marked in the traditional manner, and is used by the typesetting operator as a guide for inputting commands or as a back-up should a problem arise. Since the manuscript is physically carried to the typesetter, Romano reasons, why not carry a floppy with it and save on telephone costs.

On the other hand, physically transporting a floppy is not without its own problems. Each manufacturer has a

Theatre Crafts Magazine uses typesetter's data processing capabilities

By the time this issue goes to press, *Theatre Crafts Magazine* will have completed transmission of its first issue, an annual suppliers directory, from a Radio Shack TRS-80 microcomputer to Expertel, a New York City-based type house specializing in interfaced typesetting. The directory is unique not because it is being typeset from a word processor—there is nothing new or unusual about the interface arrangement—but because *Theatre Crafts* is utilizing Expertel's data processing capabilities to create the directory.

Theatre Crafts is published nine times a year, and reaches 27,000 subscribers. Its annual directory, which encompasses the entire June/July issue, is divided into four sections: a listing and information about each manufacturer; a listing of products by trade name; a listing of products and services; and a listing of manufacturers' representatives and distributors, by geographic region.

Though a manufacturer can be listed in all four sections (and the number of listings may be much greater if the manufacturer produces a number of different products), only a single entry for each manufacturer is put into *Theatre Crafts'* TRS-80. From this single entry, Expertel's computer pulls out the necessary information for each of the directory's sections. After separating all entries into directory sections, the computer alphabetizes the listings and sends them to the typesetter.

The use of Expertel's computer in this fashion is expected to save *Theatre Crafts* both money and time, according to the magazine's general manager, Bill Yaryan. Last year, he says, each separate listing had to be typed out in the magazine's office, and then again by the typesetter. The enormity of the job caused the magazine to miss its printing deadline by a month.

The greatest savings, though, will come next year. When Yaryan is ready to solicit listings for the 1983 directory, Expertel will transmit each manufacturer's listing from this year's directory, which will be stored on magnetic tape, back to the TRS-80. A copy of this listing will be sent out to manufacturers, along with a letter asking if they have any changes. Changes will be made for each listing on the TRS-80, and then the copy will be sent back to Expertel.

"The cost will be considerably lower next year," Yaryan says, "because most of the information will already be on tape, and the programming will be done. All we will have to do to have next year's directory typeset is make the necessary changes in the listings and add any new listings that come in."

Yaryan said he hopes to eventually have each issue of *Theatre Crafts* typeset from the TRS-80.

---

different method of placing data on the disc, which means that floppies are not interchangeable from one manufacturer's word processor to another's. Some manufacturers even alter the data storage method from one of their product lines to another. A manufacturer does this to discourage users from switching equipment. To make such a switch the user must find a company that will convert the discs to the new manufacturer's method—for a fee, of course.

Given this situation, a publisher must make sure that the floppies produced from his word processor can be accepted and understood by the typesetting equipment if he plans to physically transport the disc. It is for this reason that Jack Powers, director of operations for Expertel, in New York City, rarely, if ever, accepts floppies, and speaks out in favor of telecommunications.

"With different protocols (means of transmitting data) and parity checks (to make sure what is received is the same as what is transmitted), errors created in transmission are rare," Powers says, adding that with telecommunications there is no need to worry about compatibility of systems as with floppies. The reason: The word processor reads out text from its memory or from a floppy in the order it is typeset.

The combination of low cost and the ability to be used for varied computer applications makes microcomputer-based interfaced typesetting systems attractive to a large segment of the publishing industry. Such systems will never replace dedicated electronic editing systems with dozens and dozens of terminals. But the message is clear: Interfaced typesetting is carving its own niche in the publishing marketplace.

Buyers be aware

By H. Joel Davis

There are dozens of stories told by publishers about advertisers buying space in their magazines, or in their competitors' magazines, for the wrong reasons. I would guess that almost every type of business has similar stories.

Now I'd like to tell you six stories about publishers buying typesetting equipment for the wrong reasons. The sad part is that these costly mistakes could have been avoided if the publishers had done their homework and had not relied on overzealous sales representatives, friends, hearsay and beautiful four-color brochures.

Case #1 - The unknown need

A medium-size Midwest publisher of several recreational vehicle titles recently decided to go in-house with his type—primarily to save money. He called a number of manufacturer's representatives for presentations, attended several equipment shows, and finally purchased a system he thought would fit his budget. After six months of operation, he showed little savings and only a slight decrease in turnaround time. Overall, neither his costs nor his efficiency had been greatly affected. What went wrong?

THE MISTAKE. Before purchasing his system, this publisher had little idea of how much he was actually spending on type, or how his own internal operation functioned. In essence, he bought too large a system.

THE RIGHT WAY. Before you even look at any equipment or listen to a sales pitch, you must determine your particular needs. Instead of asking yourself, "What equipment should I buy?" you should be asking "What do I need to do the job I want done?" Since every publishing organization is different, each one should have a system designed to meet its own specific requirements.

I suggest that you avoid the simple formulas for determining potential in-house cost savings (you know . . . put in the numbers, turn the crank and get an answer) and take the time to do a thorough study of your existing operation. Only then can you intelligently compare how various phototypesetting systems will affect it.

Document, step-by-step, how jobs flow through your organization, from rough manuscripts through page make-up. Determine your volumes—the number of words needing typesetting per issue and per year. Chart your production schedules on a bar graph so you can see where peaks and valleys fall on your work load. Find out exactly what your total composition costs are, in addition to the cost of type.

Determine how each system you are considering will affect your operation. This may require some time-consuming calculations and more than a little homework. But it is time well spent. You don't know what to buy if you don't know what you really need and what options are open to you.

Case #2 - The forgotten future

An East Coast publisher of several trade journals did a very careful analysis of his operation and diligent comparison shopping for an in-house system. He found one that met all of his criteria, including budgets and present needs. The purchase was made and everything seemed rosy until the next year, when he was presented with the opportunity to acquire another existing, successful magazine. His present system suddenly became inadequate and he was faced with a choice between a capital outlay for another larger, more expensive system and letting the new title acquisition pass by.

THE MISTAKE. This publisher did his homework, but he neglected an important area: the future. To his chagrin, he realized he had purchased a dead-end (unexpandable) system.

THE RIGHT WAY. When determining your needs, don't forget your future plans. Establish goals for the next two to five years and incorporate those goals into your equipment purchasing plans. You may choose to purchase just enough equipment to meet your immediate needs, but be sure the equipment can grow with you.

There are many fine systems on the market that can meet your needs now but cannot be expanded to meet future needs. In most cases, it is more economical to add to an existing system than to buy an entirely new one.

Case #3 - Too little investigation

An East Coast publisher of a health magazine was anxious to go in-house. He listened to sales presentations and demos from several manufacturers and purchased a system that looked as if it would meet his needs and his budget. Shortly after taking delivery, another sales rep showed him a machine that not only met his needs, but would have saved him several thousand dollars in initial capital outlay.

THE MISTAKE. Here's a case where too little investigation of the equipment available really hurt. In his rush to go in-house, this publisher took the first machine that met his needs and looked no further.

THE RIGHT WAY. Obviously, the answer here is to look at everything available on the market today that meets your defined needs. Although you may feel that looking at everything available is a waste of time, it will probably take less time than you think. And since most of the equipment presented to you will automatically be eliminated, the decision will not be that difficult. Better to spend the time up front looking at systems than spending it looking at a system in your back room that you wish would go away.

Case #4 - The call not made

A publisher of a quarterly who operates out of her home in New England recently converted to in-house type. She did all her homework, talked to nearly every manufacturer, and purchased just the right system for her small operation. Not too long after installation, the machine developed a problem. The nearest service depot turned out to be in Boston, some 350 miles away. After calling several other owners of this particular piece of equipment, she realized that this problem was common to the machine that she purchased.

THE MISTAKE. This publisher made two mistakes: She didn't investigate the manufacturer's service capabilities, and she didn't talk to other users of the system.

THE RIGHT WAY. Ask your representative to provide you with references and call them personally. After you have talked to the owners on his list, try to compile your own list. Call other publishers and printers. Find out who else might have the equipment you are considering and get honest statements about its reliability and the company's service record.

Ask about the availability of parts, the speed of service calls, the average cost per service call, etc. If you are going to make a major investment in equipment, be sure it can be kept in good running order, with a minimum amount of money. Good service and reliability should be near the top of your list of criteria.

Case #5 - Unexplored possibilities

A fairly large West Coast publishing company producing eight titles each month decided that their type bills were getting too high and opted to go in-house. Their attitude was, "If we're going to set our own type, we'll do the whole job and save as much money as possible." They purchased a reasonably sophisticated system in the $35,000 to $40,000 range and went to work.

Shortly thereafter, a sales rep from a competing firm showed them how they could have purchased just a front-end system for keyboarding and then pass the keystrokes stored on floppy disks to their commercial typesetter for typesetting. The initial investment would have been about 50 percent less and, in this case, the type savings would have been the same.

THE MISTAKE. As in case #3, this publisher failed to explore *every* possibility open to him. Many publishers assume that the only economical way to set in-house type is to do the entire typesetting process on their own premises, but this assumption is false.

THE RIGHT WAY. Investigate every avenue open to you to accomplish your end product. In many cases, the most economical and successful way of setting type in-house is for the publisher to handle only part of the process, leaving the remainder to a commercial supplier. Since there are many configurations that can be devised to do just that, don't overlook these possibilities when you are considering equipment. You may need to purchase only a small amount of machinery to realize your cost savings goal.

Remember that more equipment requires more capital outlay, more personnel, more space, etc. Manufacturer's representatives are a good source of information regarding these types of alternatives.

Case #6 - The unsound manager

Six months after establishing an in-house type facility, a Midwestern publisher of a scientific journal found his new department scoring low marks on performance. He had spent considerable time defining his needs and selecting the right equipment to meet them, and yet his deadlines were slipping and type quality began to suffer. Since his reasons for converting to in-house type still seemed valid and his operator seemed competent, where was the problem?

THE MISTAKE. Although our friend did everything according to the book during the selection and purchase of his equipment, he failed to provide proper leadership and management once the department became functional. An in-house typesetting department, like any other organization, needs sound management, but too often we hire a person to do a job, provide two or three days of intensive attention, then return in three or four weeks to discover that the person is well on the road to failure.

THE RIGHT WAY. During the initial three-month period it generally takes to get an in-house typesetting facility up to speed, your care and supervision is most critical. Let your new employees know your expectations. Express them clearly and in writing if at all possible. Involve yourself in the new process so that you can better arrive at realistic, achievable goals. Set aside specific time to review your new department's progress and to discuss and resolve problems. In short, manage your new function.

The editor as typesetter

By Frank Romano

One of the goals of automated typesetting—and one of its justifications—is the capturing of copy in electronic form as close to the point of origination as possible. This implies that the creator of copy uses some special device and/or special procedures.

A few years ago everyone thought the device would be a typewriter. The typewritten pages would be scanned by Optical Character Recognition devices (OCR) and converted to electronic input. The originator would be working with a familiar machine and a byproduct of its output would do the job for electronic input.

To some extent this is still true, but originators do more than originate. They edit. And much of the editing takes place *after* copy has been typed. This is a definite problem in OCR since the manuscript must be prepared within strict limits, and the amount of material that can be changed after typing is minimal.

A few years after the introduction of OCR, word processing (WP) devices matured and multiplied. With WP, a typewriter is still used but it is connected to a recorder which records on magnetic tape what is typed and then re-plays it, allowing corrections or changes to be made in the process. Since these word processors were typewriter-oriented, however, they were weak in terms of editing. Playing through the tape (or other magnetic medium) to reach the line to be edited involved techniques that required greater concentration on the methodology than on the copy.

Typewriter word processors then evolved into video word processors which added another dimension to the originator's interaction with the material. One could see and edit an entire page of copy at one time while the information was still in electronic form. Editing was easier than marking up a typewritten sheet. You run out of space on the typewritten sheet, but you can change a video screen endlessly. (And some originators did change copy endlessly in the electronic counterpart of rapture of the deep.)

Increased typographic feedback

By 1975 multiple video devices were connected into centralized copy processing systems. The copy processing system contained the typographic intelligence which eventually produced the typeset output. This capability was linked into the video terminals to provide increasing amounts of typographic feedback to the originator or other operator.

The video screen could display changes in typeface, indicate copyfitting information and give the hyphenation points that the system would produce. Originators soon became production people and management had to create a dividing line between copy origination and copy production. In some cases that line is still not clear.

New programming for available copy processing systems attempts to make production functions transparent to the person operating the video display. Underlined copy on the screen eventually outputs as italic . . . or, striking a *1 produces a headline format. We are still evolving in this area of human interaction with the typographic format.

These devices can definitely help editors become more effective, whether the typesetting is done in-house or purchased outside.

The problem, aside from the formatting situation, is that few small- to medium-sized publications can afford the kind of copy processing systems that provide a video device for each editor or originator. As soon as an editor has to wait to use the video device he or she loses a significant amount of efficiency. The publication must then centralize the input (re-keying) function as well as that of editing.

Suppliers tend to aim for the larger publications and organizations, but that market is about to be saturated. A ray of hope for the smaller publishers is the new mini floppy-disk terminal (priced under $5,000) which can be used in a stand-alone mode and eventually linked into a multi-terminal system. Inexpensive printers can also be connected to the terminal so copy can be produced in hard copy form if required.

Editors and originators of copy should do their own input and editing; if not now, then later when the systems become cost effective. The more they do themselves—or through the system—the less that specialized typesetting personnel will have to do.

Finding operators
By Frank Romano

A recent letter I received stated: "We believed the people from the company that supplied our typesetting equipment when they said any typist could operate their device. This has not been the case, at least in our experience. Where do we find operators for our equipment?"

My reply: Typesetting is more than typing or hitting keys, as you have discovered. There are many people who are skilled at character inputting—that is, striking a key for each character in the manuscript. But there are few people who are skilled at typographic inputting—that is, determining the format and having a feel for the type. Thus, you must get by with people who are less than effective, "steal" people from other firms, find qualified people on the open market or train them yourself.

Most of us are using people who are less than effective. Most of us do not spend the time to train people correctly.

There are four levels of skill in typesetting. There is *typing*, which is an essential skill, since all typesetting devices have keyboards similar to those of typewriters. There is *machine operation*, which is the specific utiliza-

tion of a particular machine. This is what an equipment supplier trains you to do.

The next level, *applied typography*, covers the use of type. This level involves the use of small caps, italics, kerning, letterspacing or any of the other areas of typographic usage. The final level is that of *page layout*. This involves the ability to create a page with both type and art elements.

Seek an accurate typist

Finding typists is easy. You should not seek simply the fastest typist, however, but a typist with a high level of accuracy. That person can be taught to operate the device by attending the training classes run by the supplier, using training personnel hired from the supplier or by using the operating manual for the equipment.

The odds are that you will indeed have to train someone to operate your particular machine. Because of the proliferation of devices, you probably will not readily find operators who happen to be trained on your equipment.

Finding people who know about type is another problem. Such a person may be an artist or art director or someone without typing skills. This kind of person could be a typist's "director"—someone who would give the typist instructions on what should be done. The cost of such a specialist, however, cannot often be justified although this person is usually the kind who is also competent at the top level—that of page layout.

In addition, skilled typesetting requires one important aspect of intelligence: abstract reasoning. The typesetter must be able to picture in his or her mind something that does not yet exist and use a machine to create some unit of typography. (There is a personnel test from a firm called Wonderlic, in Northfield, Illinois which can determine whether a person can handle typograhy.)

Turning typists into typesetters

Since you will probably not find a person with these multiple talents, you must train a person to do the job you require.

After you've found and trained your typist on your machine, send him to school to learn about type. If there are no schools in your area, have him use books from the library.

If you spend the time and money necessary to train this person, he will then have the abilities you were originally seeking. However, other publishers are seeking these abilities too. He could probably go out and get another job—possibly with higher pay.

Therefore, you must also motivate and reward this person adequately for his performance. If you think of typesetters only as typists, they will be classified as secretaries. If they do more than secretaries, they should be paid more.

During the last few years, the job market has been seriously affected by equipment overkill. All of these typesetting machines need trained people, and since no one machine dominates the market, typesetting schools have difficulty turning out specialists.

Certainly, as machines become more intelligent, we may be able to get by with a lower level of qualification. The format of a magazine may also be simplified so that it is more of a "canned format" with little need for typographic decision-making. The repetitive nature of magazines does make the training job a little bit easier, but not much.

You can advertise for typesetters through newspapers, trade journals or even associations. But other typesetting users are competing for the same people. In the long run, your best bet is to get good people and train and motivate them. Turning a typist into a typesetter is not a simple metamorphosis.

What happened to my beautiful color?

By Frank Preucil

There's nothing worse than an unhappy advertiser. Ask any publisher. And if you are running an ad that is also appearing in other magazines and your reproduction looks lousy, you can be sure of having a disgruntled customer.

This situation happened recently when an advertiser ran the same four-color ad in five different magazines. He supplied each with a high quality four-color proof. Each magazine was printed by a different web offset printer. When the results were lined up next to each other the difference in color, tone and contrasts were so marked that the advertiser was highly disappointed.

Each printer immediately assumed that the fault was in the four-color positive films he had received. But the advertiser knew that they had all received the same quality film.

What happened?

During the preparation and press run the colors changed. Even with the most sophisticated presses—letterpress, offset or rotogravure—there still is a potential for color change. Although the plate images of these three processes are physically very different, all three transfer ink to paper, and ink and paper are the heart of your color picture. Color printing is simply the controlled reflectance of colored light by colored inks. Anything that affects normal reflectance disturbs the color.

Color control bars showing standard amounts of ink were once thought reliable on letterpress photoengraved color proofs. But a Graphic Arts Technical Foundation research survey revealed that proofs with the same amount of color ink on the bars varied 40 percent in red, green or blue areas where ink printed on ink.

This problem—called trapping—is still an uncertain variable in photoengraved proofs, and during production press runs. While offset litho trapping is sometimes a headache, the thinner offset inks generally cause less of a trapping problem than letterpress inks.

To guard against the potential danger of trapping, color proofs and production press runs should have more than color bars or squares with each color on them. There should be three two-color overlap areas. More of a picture is overlapped colors than single inks, so you can control accuracy by watching color overlaps. Then you can judge the normality of the proof and the correctness of a production press run by merely studying the two-color overlap areas.

The three two-color areas should look red, blue and normal green—not orange, purple and blue-green or yellow-green. Color shifts, such as red to orange, blue to red-purple, and normal green to blue or yellow-green, expose all three causes of color inaccuracy—wrong single color strengths, weak trapping of ink on ink, and partial opacity of some ink.

Another safeguard is to study a three-color overlap

area. In four-color printing, a three-color solid overprint of process yellow, red and blue is normally not quite black but tends toward brown.

If the three-color solid area is:

• *Clean brown*—the blue ink is either too weakly printed or not fully trapped on the other two colors.

• *Greenish*—the red ink is being run too weak or is not trapping fully.

• *Purplish or maroon*—the yellow ink is weak.

Many proofs are made on single-color sheetfed presses with wet ink printing on dried ink. Some production managers are afraid that single-color press dry proofs are not a valid prediction of what can be printed on a high speed multicolor press. They insist on seeing four-color wet proofs.

If, however, production press inks are controlled for speed, trapping and proper color balance, then good color matches can be made with single color press dry proofs.

Unfortunately, not all presses print with the same pressures and water-ink balances. In fact, it used to be common for most large four-color presses to print larger halftone dots than smaller single-color presses. Orders for four-color positives from color separation houses included the requirement that four-color halftones have sharper and smaller dots than those made and proofed on single-color presses. A 15 percent smaller dot was a typical specification.

While this was once the state of the art with many printers, a recent informal survey demonstrated that new quick setting inks, finer grained plates and better press control have markedly improved this situation. Now an average of only 5 percent smaller dots is likely on four-color presses compared to single-color presses.

On long litho press runs of over 500,000 impressions, long life bi-metal or tri-metal plates are often used. Some, with copperplate images, are acid etched. Unfortunately, a lateral dot spread is often created by the acid. For this plate—where dot gain can occur during the plate-making step—it is still current practice to make sharper, finer dots on the film positives.

Excess dot gain in offset printing can also occur on short-run plates. What causes this is excess squeeze in ink transfer and low cost underpigmented inks. Pressures should be coordinated to the degree of paper smoothness. Low pigmentation in color inks requires a thicker ink film to obtain color strength. This thick film of ink on the plates and blanket spreads wider with heavy transfer pressures. Rougher papers require more pressure to transfer ink, making pictures look flatter. Using high quality, highly pigmented inks on high gloss, smooth papers will provide strong, sharp printing.

Printing papers have three variable properties that affect the color appearance of inks—gloss, absorptivity and whiteness.

Reproduction of yellow, red and blue inks is fundamentally the controlled reflection of light, which, in turn, is limited by the paper's reflectance. In order for these three colors to create the appearance of hundreds of hues and purities, they must be transparent. Likewise, they must also dry with a glossy surface that permits them to act like color filters. Good process inks work best on high gloss papers with low absorptivity.

Magazine papers are mainly in the medium gloss, medium absorptivity field. This doesn't mean they are in a narrow class by themselves. A GATF survey of 70 magazines found a difference of 40 percent in gloss and absorptivity and, consequently, noticeable differences in the hue, or purity, of some ink colors.

If there is a noticeable gloss difference between two papers, expect color variances. Even if the paper gloss is the same, there may be ink color differences because the paper's absorptivity is different. Unfortunately, absorptivity changes between shipments of the same brand of paper are common and cannot be judged by simple visual inspection. They can be discovered with a fairly standard test—the "K & N Ink Test."

Paper surface efficiency (PSE) number can be used to compare printing papers before use and predict whether colors will print normally. Just how the PSE is arrived at can be found in a Graphic Arts Technical Foundation publication, *Research Progress No. 60—A New Method of Rating the Efficiency of Paper for Color Reproductions.*

Basically, all colors look stronger on papers of higher PSE. The gloss of dried printed ink is low if paper gloss is low or if ink soaks into absorptive paper. Ink gloss is imperative for high color strength, but it is actually more dependent on the paper than on ink.

Warm and cold colors are affected differently by paper and ink gloss variations. Blue and yellow become grayer—or dirtier—and can lose as much as 30 percent in purity on a low efficiency paper.

While the same things can happen to warm colors, their hue or purity does not shift as much as blue.

Printing papers differ widely in whiteness or brightness. The survey of 70 magazines also revealed a difference of 65 to 90 percent in paper brightness.

The brighter the paper, the purer the ink colors will look on coated papers of similar average absorptivity. An exception is the bright papers approaching 100 percent reflectivity. With the help of fluorescence, these papers gain their brilliance which would be otherwise hindered by coatings. Consequently, they cannot give the highest ink purities because they have high absorbency. Colored inks, furthermore, filter out the ultraviolet which creates the fluorescent super-brightness, so the paper under the ink is not as bright as on the unprinted paper.

The press itself adds complications to getting acceptable color quality. A press startup may show satisfactory picture quality, but later impressions look flat. Sometimes roller friction gives increased ink temperature which softens the ink and results in dot spread. Likewise, unequal temperature rise in different color inks may result in trapping changes in various colors.

While improvements in machinery are constantly being made to overcome these problems, new snags develop. A production manager who is aware of, and anticipates these many color printing headaches, can make the difference between a successful press run and an unhappy advertiser and editor.

The basic guide to color separation

By Jeffery R. Parnau

As the use of four-color material increases, more buyers face the question: "Which color separation system is best for my material?" Because the printing industry is such a complex, technical field, there are many different opinions on which system is the clear-cut winner. Consequently, there is no single answer for the "average" buyer. For those who haven't yet become opinionated, however, an overview should be helpful in picking the right system for the job at hand.

In this article, we will outline the general characteristics of three common separation systems: conventional, direct, and scan. Then, we'll compare the three techniques to one another in relation to quality, cost, and limitations. And finally, we will present traditional and innovative methods you can use to get the most from your color separation dollars.

Conventional separations

In today's world of graphic arts, some people tend to think of "conventional" color separations as old-fashioned. In a sense, they are right: Technology has advanced the art to a great extent. But there is always room for craftsmanship, and conventional techniques will probably be with us for the foreseeable future.

The conventional process involves the following steps:

First, the original artwork, photo, or transparency is placed on a "process color camera," which is simply a very accurate litho camera with color-corrected lenses and filtering ability.

Four exposures are made: magenta, cyan, yellow, and black. (These colors are, of course, the "subtractive primary colors" used in printing processes.) The resulting four negatives do not have a dot pattern. Rather, each is composed of "continuous tones." But the lithographic process cannot print continuous tones, which is why you can detect a dot pattern in all printed black-and-white or color halftones. So these continuous tone negs must later be converted into screened (dot pattern) negatives.

Before they are converted, though, the continuous-tone negatives (often called intermediate negs, or internegs) can be hand-worked to correct color. Color correction at this stage is the main strength of conventional separation: Hues can be modified just a bit (to match an elusive flesh tone, for example) or dramatically changed (making a blue automobile green, etc.).

Such corrections are performed by highly skilled color artists, who have the uncanny ability to look at the four pieces of film and conjure up a mental image of what the result will be. Because of the skills involved, good correction artists are hard to find, and they command top wages.

The next step in conventional color separation is conversion into *screened* negatives or positives. This procedure breaks the continuous tones into dots of various sizes. And from the four screened negs (or positives), a proof is made (Cromalin, Color Key, or—in some cases—a press proof).

After the proof is viewed by the customer, the screened negatives can still be modified somewhat by "dot etching." This process entails the physical alteration of dot sizes by the application of chemicals. It is a local, manual process . . . which means that at this stage of the game, you can still modify only a portion of the magenta neg, or bring up the blue in the "sky." In other words, if you ask for less red on the "face" portion of a photo, the color artist will alter only that area of the magenta—and possibly yellow— negatives.

The dot etching process is not as versatile as continuous-tone alterations. You couldn't—at this point— expect to do any major alterations . . . but you do have enough control to closely match the original art.

After the final corrections, the finished negatives (or positives) are stripped into their intended positions and are used to burn the images onto the printing plates.

Direct screen separations

The main difference between conventional separation techniques and direct screening procedures is this: There are no internegs (the continuous-tone film just discussed). Instead of creating the intermediate negs, a halftone screen is placed over each piece of film during the initial exposure. (Again, four exposures are made.)

The result is that direct screen separations are produced in less time than it takes to make conventional seps. But speed has a price. While conventional separations can be greatly modified by artists who work the internegs, all post-sep color corrections for direct screen subjects must be accomplished with dot etching alone. Because dot etching is basically limited to small changes in color, no major alterations are practical once the separation has been shot.

In other respects, though, direct screening resembles conventional separations: The four shots are made, and the resulting negs (which are composed of halftone dots) are either used to make a proof or are converted into positives, which in turn will be used to make the proof. Minor corrections are made, and the film is used to expose the printing plates.

Color scanner separations

The third common separating system is the color scanner. Scanners have been controversial ever since they were introduced several decades ago. They have been accused of everything from producing lousy seps to ruining the economy. (Some units were so bad that printers had to donate them to schools just to get rid of them!)

In recent years, though, scanning has come of age. The key was the incorporation of laser beams into the scanning operation. That didn't make the process automatic, though, and a skilled operator is still required to produce acceptable seps.

The scanning process is a non-camera procedure. Here's how it works:

The subject to be separated is wrapped around the scanning drum. A light-sensing stylus travels the length of the drum while it is rotated, and senses one of the primary colors. The information is fed through a computer, modified as necessary, and directed to another stylus (this one emits light, rather than sensing it), which in turn exposes a piece of film. The halftone screen is part of the "output" unit, so the result is the same as the direct screening procedure: A screened piece of film, produced without an internegative.

Scanned subjects, then, are also limited to dot-etched color correction with one exception: Some separation houses don't do any manual correcting. Rather, they look at a proof of the separated subject, and if alterations are required, they simply re-separate it. The scanner is programmed by the operator to increase or decrease the offending colors, and new film is produced. The logic here is that it's cheaper to run a machine than it is to hire a correction artist. Other firms, though, have their scanners so heavily booked with work that they choose to have corrections done manually.

There are many different scanners available, and all have slightly different capabilities. Some will handle separations up to 11 inches by 17 inches, while others are limited to 10 inches by 12 inches. One scanner may separate a single color in 20 minutes, while the next will scan two colors simultaneously in that time.

Because color scanning is so highly automated, it is the least-expensive separation option on the market. (Cheap for the buyer, anyhow: The supplier might have a $300,000 outlay to get a scanning department set up.) And given the recent technical advances in the field, the quality of scanned subjects is meeting the expectations of more buyers every day.

How do these three techniques compare to one another in relation to quality, cost, and limitations?

Acceptable material

All three techniques will separate either reflective or transparent artwork. However, each technique— and more specifically, each machine— has limitations. For example, one camera might be capable of enlarging a 35 mm slide up to 1200 percent, while another has a limitation of 300 percent.

There are only a few basic rules covering physical specifications. For conventional and direct methods, any work which will fit on the camera copyboard can be shot. That includes thick illustration board, tissue paper, etc. Some shops can even separate three-dimensional objects (eliminating the need to photograph them beforehand). Size is not a critical problem, because if your regular vendor can't do an extremely large separation, you can always find one who can.

Scanners, though, have some built-in—and rigid—limitations. Currently there are no large scanners on the market. An original art limitation of 12 inches by 18 inches is typical. In addition, scanners cannot accept flat artwork (illustration board, books, etc.). This is because all material to be separated must be literally wrapped around the scanning drum.

The differences

Generally speaking, you can get high quality separations using any of the three systems discussed here. The results depend, of course, on the skill of the camera or scanner operators and the amount of corrections you need

performed.

Some of the finest separations have been done with conventional techniques, while equally good material has been produced with direct processes and scanners. (It takes quite a bit of training to detect—with the naked eye—subtle differences in dot structure produced by these methods.)

But there are a few significant differences. The first —and most notable—is cost, which we discussed in part one of this article. Then there is the intermediate negative step (used only in conventional techniques), which allows the color artist to make drastic color changes. Other differences are pointed out in the comparison chart (Figure 1).

Black detail: hard to get on camera

One area that is easy to overlook, though, is fine black *detail*. Both conventional and direct camera techniques have the inherent problem of bouncing light off the art, through the lens, and onto the film. By using various filters, three of the printing primaries can be reproduced quite faithfully. But the fourth—black— presents a problem. Since black pigment is basically the presence of all reflective primaries (cyan, magenta, and yellow), it is a tough one to break out.

Sometimes you'll hear the term "ghost black" mentioned. This simply means that very little black ink will be printed on the final piece, and it is being used only to add a little punch to the color reproduction. But that can create a problem.

Suppose you have a number of fine black lines (cross-hatching arrows, etc.) in the original art? A light black will possibly help the general appearance of the piece, but it won't provide detail where you want it. In addition, the other three primaries will have a light dot structure in the "fine black line" area. The result can be that your black line will appear quite fuzzy on the finished piece. It will be composed of a little black ink, and a little of the other three colors.

The scanner advantage

This is one area in which the scanners excel. (The scanners we're talking about incorporate a laser beam in the scanning process. We don't have anything good to say about non-laser scanners.)

To demonstrate this point, we've enlarged two portions of off-set-printed artwork. One of these pieces was separated with the direct-screen method, while the other was scanned. The same piece of original art was used for both seps. Our enlargement is a line shot, which means it shows only the red and black ink. Both printed pieces were in very good register. We can't, of course, print a sample of the original because we would have to separate it with one of the three systems, and you wouldn't actually *see* the original piece.

Very noticeable

As the enlargements show, there is a significant difference in the quality of the black lines. The direct-screen version shows a strong dot pattern in the window area, while the scanned version has almost no evidence of a pattern, and the line itself is cleaner and thicker. On the original art, these were simply crisp hairlines.

So what does it all mean? Basically, it means that scanners do have something to offer that you can't get on a camera. They have no lenses, and thus don't pass the reflected light across a six-foot span, through the lens, and onto the film. Because they have direct-reading color sens-

Figure 1:
Three Separation Systems Compared

	Conventional	Direct	Scanner
Technique	Original material shot on camera, producing a set of intermediate negs which must later be converted into screened negs.	Original material shot on camera, producing screened negatives. No intermediates are created.	Original material placed on revolving scanner drum, separated electronically and producing screened negatives. No intermediate negs created.
Separation cost	Most expensive of the common separation systems in use, due to the labor required for conversion of intermediate negs.	Of these three systems, this is middle-of-the-road on a cost basis.	Least expensive option of the systems discussed here.
Speed	Slowest of the systems discussed here, due to the time required for conversion of intermediate negs into screened negs.	Because no intermediates are produced, this is faster than conventional separation techniques but slower than a scanner.	Fastest separation technique available. Most machines will scan two different colors in 20 minutes.
Definition & detail	General definition good to excellent, depending on the camera and operator. Fine black detail limited due to lens distortion.	Same as conventional.	General definition excellent on laser-based scanners. (Non-laser scanners normally quite poor.) Quality of fine black detail is excellent, and is not available with other separation techniques.
Correction ability	Primary corrections: Extensive changes can be made by a color artist working the intermediate negs. Secondary corrections: Finer balance can be achieved after conversion into screened negs by dot etching the film.	Moderate color correction possible by dot etching the film. Major color changes not practical. In extreme cases of poor color, reseparation may be called for.	Major color correction possible by re-scanning the original. Moderate color correction available by back-etching the negatives.
Correction cost	Cost related directly to extent of corrections. Depends on shop rates, but intermediate neg corrections can be very costly; dot-etched corrections somewhat less so.	Cost related directly to extent of corrections.	For re-scanning, cost will normally be a flat fee (possibly same cost as the original separation). Back-etching cost related directly to the extent of the corrections.
Size limitations	Size of original art and final film size depend on specific camera in use. Some color houses can handle originals and reproductions up to 40" X 60" or larger.	Same as conventional.	Scanner technology currently limited to machines of 12" X 18" (typical). Some machines are smaller. Drum size and final film size are the same.
Thickness limitations	Thick illustrations boards no problem. Some cameras accept even thicker material, and even solid objects can be separated by some shops.	Same as conventional	Scanners cannot accept rigid material (illustration board, for example). Separation of solid objects is not currently possible.

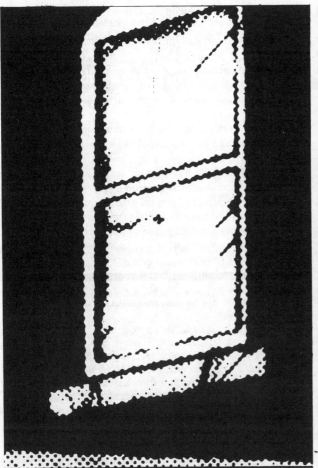

Both of the above pieces were separated from the same original art . . . but the one on the left was done by the direct-screen camera method, while the one on the right was scanned electronically. Each has been enlarged to 600 percent of the original film negative size. The black lines were fine black hairlines on the original art. Note the crisp, thick line on the scanned version, compared to the pale "ghost" black on the camera separation.

---

ing heads, electronic quality controls, and sophisticated masking ability, you can expect to get much more detail from your photos or art than you'd get with any other technique— but only if your color house is experienced in the operation of reliable laser scanners.

Making decisions

If you review the comparison chart (Figure 1), you will probably agree that no single separation system will work best for all material. But if you consider your requirements (cost, speed, detail, correction ability, physical limitations), you should be able to select the appropriate method for your work 100 percent of the time.

Reducing separation costs

Most production managers are deeply involved in the four-color explosion. The more color you use, though, the more you spend on separations, color corrections, and stripping: all expensive work.

But the number of separations doesn't have to push your final costs up proportionately. Rather, the more you have, the less each should cost.

Those cost reductions don't just happen. The buyer/manager must be aware of the techniques that *make* things happen. By combining available techniques and negotiating volume prices with your separator, you can be sure you'll get the most from your color separation dollar.

There are many traditional and innovative methods you can put to your own use.

Color separation, by any method, is a time-consuming business. Your material may get electronically scanned in 30 minutes or hand-worked for hours, which means that the cost of materials has little to do with the final price.

So if you're after economy of any sort, gone are the days of getting a single slide conventionally separated and hand worked for hours. (Conventional, by the way, means that four continuous-tone camera shots are made of the original. Each is later screened for reproduction.) Today, we talk about common focus separations, laser scanners, dupes, mounts to position, and single-page strips. Any or all of these methods can be used, depending on the type of material and number of subjects you have.

Grouping for common focus

One of the basic trade tricks is common focus separations. Common focus means that more than one subject will be separated at the same time at 100 percent or any other percentage you choose. The only limiting factor here is the camera your job is on (which may have a range of 20 percent to 300 percent, or 25 percent to 1200 percent, etc.). Check with your separator for specifications.

Common focus techniques apply to all separation systems: scanners, conventional methods, and direct screening. (Direct screening is similar to conventional camera separation, but the halftone screen is made during the initial shots.) Common focus grouping has the following advantages:

Economy: Since you're making fewer separations, your total cost will go down and your per-subject cost will be reduced.

Speed: Because you save time (which is a factor implied by economy), you get an additional benefit: When you reduce total sep time, you can work closer to a deadline.

Simplicity: Your only activity in grouping photos is to let your color separator know what you intend to do. There are no mechanical tricks for you to learn.

Requirements

Not just any group of subjects can be separated together. They must meet the following requirements:

1. *Category*. You can't group a transparency with reflective art. One gets lit from behind, the other from the front.

2. *Percentage*. Naturally, all subjects in a group must be shot at the same camera setting.

3. *Density*. You'll need to develop an eye for this. For example, a pale, white-on-white photo of a dozen eggs can't normally be grouped with a dark, campfire-type scene.

4. *Size*. Although you may have a group of subjects that meets the above requirements, you're still limited by the size of the camera copyboard which must hold your material, and the vacuum board which limits the size of final film. (Note: In the case of scanners, you're limited by the circumference and length of the machine's drum and its reproduction limits. Your material must also be flexible enough to wrap around the drum.)

If you exceed size limitations with a group, you're into another camera setup, so you're free to change the percentage of your next shot.

Compromises and costs

Naturally, grouping photos doesn't get you something for absolutely nothing. A small compromise will be made in the quality of the separations. Your separator knows this, and will probably advise you that he goes for "best overall color" or "your preference," in which case you tell him which photo of a group is most important. If you group a cover photo with a small filler shot, you'd give preference to the cover.

Usually, the cost saved by grouping subjects is significant. Therefore, you can make—and pay for—more color correcting and still come out ahead. On the other hand, if you need flawless color, you could find yourself spending more on correction time than you've saved on seps. In that case, you'd be better off paying for individual separations.

Finally, you will be charged for each additional photo you add to a camera shot. These charges vary from one shop to the next, but they are usually somewhere between 15 percent and 25 percent of the single-subject separation cost. This additional charge usually covers the time required for inspection, balancing, and possibly nominal correction. Sometimes the charge is there just to make sure you don't get something for nothing.

More compromises, lower cost

When you try to put group seps to work, you may find that your art director (or others involved in producing your material) will have several photos—all within a per-

centage or two of each other—that simply "must" be shot at those exact settings. In some cases, that is true. In other cases, however, you're just up against a bull-headed fellow employee. You'll have a better chance of winning an argument if you can show that person the bottom line.

Here's how the prices of a typical four-subject group sep might look when compared to individual shots. (These prices are realistic, but you may justifiably pay more or less in your area.)

	Grouped	Ind.
First subject	$150	$150
Second subject	30	150
Third subject	30	150
Fourth subject	30	150
Stripping for proof	25	100
Proof	35	35
Total	**$300**	**$735**

So, with a little bit of compromise, you might well be in a position to cut your separation costs by more than half. If you spend only $1,000 a year on separations, common focuses won't make you a hero. But if you spend $20,000 chances are people will notice.

Dupe to size

The most troublesome limitation of common focus separating is that all photos (artwork) in a group must be shot at the same percentage. That shortcoming can be overcome by having each subject duplicated to its ideal reproduction size *before* it is separated. When that's accomplished, your photos can all be separated with one camera setting (usually 100 percent), thus taking advantage of the money-saving qualities of common-focus groups.

That intermediate step is known as duplication, or the making of a "dupe." Each of your photos will be placed in a camera (for reflective art) or enlarger (for small transparencies) and shot at the individual percentage you require. The result will be a color *transparency* of each subject at its eventual reproduction size ready to be separated with other material on the separation camera at the same time. You are, in effect, creating a common focus group, even though the percentage requirements of the originals were initially different.

The economic factor which allows you to save money (although you are adding an additional step to the entire procedure) is the fact that *dupes* are much less expensive to produce than individual *color separations*. While making each dupe may cost you a net $20 to $30 per subject, the same percentage changes would cost you something like $100 to $150 on the separation camera.

Requirements

You'll have much more versatility when using the dupe technique as a preliminary to common-focus shots . . . but once you've duped your art and photos to the reproduction size, you still have some of the limitations that apply to common-focus grouping:

Density. Even though you may have two transparencies (of photos, art, or mixed) duped for a 100 percent shot, their densities must be similar. Very dark scenes may separate very poorly when ganged up with those brilliantly lit. However, each color separator makes these judgments individually, and each opinion will be different. After working with your separator for some time, you'll get a feel as to what he or she thinks is acceptable.

Size. All separation methods have physical limits. If the camera copyboard is 30 inches by 40 inches, that's the area limit for material to be shot at one time. So if you have a batch of material which—when laid flat—measures 40 inches by 40 inches, you will need two shots, and your separations will cost more per subject.

Compromises

There is little information available to the separation buyer about color compromises that result from multiple dupe seps. There is also little agreement among separators concerning the final quality of such work.

The reasons for the confusion are that some color sep houses are better than others, and some dupe houses are better than others. A very good photo lab can dupe and balance your work beautifully, only to have it messed up by a lousy separation. Or, a batch of poorly made dupes can be saved by a conscientious separation firm.

As you can see, there is room for mistakes, arguments, and bad feelings. But by shopping around and getting involved with problems as they arise, you can eventually create an excellent working arrangement among all involved with your work.

So back to the question: What are the compromises? Some say there are none; others say you will lose a bit of fidelity in most of your separations when you put more than one subject on a camera (or dupe a photo, thus taking the final separation one more step away from the original). You must answer the question for yourself, based on your own needs and experience. If you're really curious (and have a few dollars to spend), you might consider having several photos separated as originals . . . and then having the same material duped and separated again as a group. The proofs should give you a very satisfactory comparison.

The only real problem dupes will give you in the long run is that they demand lead time. Sure, they save *separation* time, but you must get the originals to the dupe house a week early or more. It is worth it? That depends on the nature of your deadlines and the availability of your color material.

Where and how

It is very important to get your first few jobs produced on a non-critical basis. Neither time nor quality should be of the essence until you've established sound working relationships with all suppliers.

Put your "test work" at a local color lab, one that does its own processing. (You *can* work through the mail with an out-of-town firm, but you will eventually be more comfortable with a close working relationship with your dupe supplier.)

In getting a 35-mm slide or small transparency duped, make it clear to the lab that you will give them an exact reproduction size . . . that they should not add a safety factor. (But be sure that *you* add whatever slight oversizing you will need to fill the reproduction area. For example, you might have a slide which will reproduce at 5 inches wide. Order the dupe at exactly 5-1/8 inches, and you will have a comfortable margin for final insertion into position.)

The same is true for reflective art: Determine exactly what size you want the dupe (including oversizing) and make it clear to the lab that you have already added a margin of safety. If you allow *them* to take care of such margins, they may either make the dupe too large or a shade too small. Control it yourself and you'll have less trouble.

Do expect your color separator and dupe supplier to have suggestions as to how you handle your work. Get involved, ask questions, compromise a bit if necessary, and begin formulating a stable working relationship. It will be worth it when you begin producing quality work at considerable savings.

Costs

Here again you'll find disagreement among suppliers. Your best bet will be to shop around, get the price structure here and there, place sample orders, check the quality, and put the picture together. You'll find that the following points are often brought up:

Color dupe houses may 1) charge more for reflective art; 2) have a floating schedule based on your final film sizes; 3) include some color balancing, or 4) charge for even the slightest color alteration.

Separation houses may 1) charge you for each additional photo in your group . . . and maybe they won't; 2) charge for inspection of density, regardless of additional color correction; 3) charge—either on "unit time" or per subject—for color correction. In rare cases, a sep house may refuse to accept your dupes at all. This can happen when the firm doesn't really understand your position as a buyer, or when they see too many poorly made dupes come in the door. (Rarer yet is the sep house that's just too greedy to let you save money through your own initiative.)

A cost comparison

The bottom line, naturally, best describes the advantages of duping to size. Let's say you have eight originals. For some reason, each *must* be reproduced at a different percentage, and your schedule allows you to get the work done over a two-week period. Local color dupes cost you $20, and your separator charges $20 for each additional subject on the camera. His separation charge is $150, strips for proofs are $25. Here's the final comparison:

	Individually	Duped
Dupes (8)	-0-	$160
Separations	$1,200	150
Strips for proofs	200	25
Additional subjects	-0-	160
Total	$1,400	$495

That's $905 in the bank. True, the above example is in strong favor of dupes, but that's because such situations *do* come up. Catalogs, for example, use thousands of separations, and the costs involved are staggering.

The point is, when you get into multiple-percentage work, dupes are not just an option. They're the only way to go.

Now, let's take dupes one step further and examine what happens next.

Each of those four-color photos must be stripped into its proper position. And since stripping is virtually an all-man-hours, no-materials-required operation, you are paying for the time it takes to position your material.

The separation procedure

Let's say you have a total of 15 photos to be used on a four-page brochure.

Each photo—being four color— has four separation negatives: yellow, magenta, cyan and black. Thus, the 15 photos will require the stripper to accurately position a total of 60 pieces of film.

The price schedule you will receive for this procedure will be the cost of a four-color strip (rather than one price which you would use four times per photo). Those prices vary greatly from the small printer to the big one, and from one part of the country to another.

Regardless of what that per strip cost is, if you supply 15 photos, you will pay for 15 four-color strips. But if you have only four pages in the brochure, why not cut that number of strips to four (one per page), or even two (one per printed side)? Here's how to do it.

Getting into position

The secret is to get your dupes into "page position" (meaning the positions in which they will later be printed) before they get separated. In our example of the four-page brochure, the 15 photos will print in the positions specified by the art director who created the job. If those positions are known before camera time (as they very likely are), the actual-size dupes of the photos can be placed (mounted) in their exact position on a sheet of acetate which will later be put "on camera."

The entire mounting procedure will normally have little or no effect on your group separation prices (although in odd cases, it can), but will later reduce the number of strips, and that charge will be lower. In the example above, if eight of the photos were separated "in position" for pages 1 and 4 of the brochure (one press side), and seven were mounted in position for pages 2 and 3 (the other press side), you'd only be paying for two strips rather than 15. The dollar difference is significant.

How it's done

The mounting process presumes a few things: 1) that all of your photos are of similar densities; 2) that they are of the same category (transparency); and 3) that you know exactly where they will print. Points 1 and 2 are no problem: The same rules apply to common-focus seps and the duping processes.

Point 3 won't cause trouble, either, if you're working on a "normal job." That means you have the original photos, accurate layout (or complete paste-up), and enough time to dupe (usually about a week) and mount (another day or so in this example).

If your color lab has mounting facilities, you will simply send one more set of instructions with your material. Rather than simply provide the lab with percentages or measurements for your dupes, you will also "key" each photo (give it a number, letter, or other means of identification) to your paste-up or layout. After they make the dupes, they will mount each photo on a sheet of acetate, and the result is that you'll see the photos in their exact positions relative to each other, which will coi the paste-up or layout.

On the other hand, maybe the color lab doesn't have mounting facilities but your printer or separator does. In that case, you'd supply the loose dupes and the layout to either of them. They would mount, separate, and pull a proof, so the next thing you'd see would be a Cromalin (or press proof or Color Key) of either the color work only, or the entire job (type, photos, and all). What you see at that stage will depend on the facilities of your separator, and whether or not you supplied the complete paste-ups, art, and instructions needed to fully mount, strip, and proof the job.

Some limitations

Mounting is a versatile procedure, but there are problems if you need to butt photos. (This situation occurs when one photo's margins touch another photo's margins.) The person mounting photos that butt must slice each common margin precisely, and the two photos are actually glued together (with trichloromethane, to be specific). But the problem is that the hairline glue joint may be unacceptable to you.

That problem is taken to an extreme when, for example, one photo in the shape of a circle is to print within another photo. The task of cutting two exact circles into transparencies and then gluing them together isn't just tough: It's impossible.

The solution is to make two mounts (on two different pieces of acetate) for the same page. The circular photo would be on one sheet . . . the photo in which it will print on another. Later, the stripper would combine the films with a "double burn" (which means there would be two exposures onto the plate, rather than the normal single exposure).

The problem with the solution (if you don't mind getting complicated) is that you pay for an additional separation and an additional strip. Oh, what a pleasure if all art directors were also strippers, production men, and financial tightwads!

A typical job

So, for your first try at dupes and mounts, stick to something simple. Our four-pager will be the ideal example: No photo butts another, no photo within a photo, no "cut-ins" (the corner of one sticking into another), and no complexities.

Here's the sequence of activity for our example.

1. You send your photos to the lab for duping. They return them to you; the color looks fine.

2. You mark the dupes, keying them to numbers that you also put on the paste-up. Dupes are normally delivered in plastic sleeves on which you can write with a marker or grease pencil. ("Page 1, Photo A" is a nice keying notation to use.)

3. You send the paste-ups and dupes to your printer, who in this example is also your color separator.

4. The printer first mounts the color work, separates and strips the mount instead of individual photos, shoots the paste-ups, and combines all the negatives—such as color, black-and-white headlines—into the finished film.

5. A proof is pulled and sent for your approval.

Naturally, this sequence can vary. If your printer doesn't mount or separate, you'd need to coordinate those activities with an outside source, and be sure the printer's specifications were being adhered to.

For that matter, you could take all the work—seps, stripping, and proofs—to a "prep house" and simply supply your printer with negs and a proof.

What will it save?

What can dupes/mounts do to the bottom line? Here we go:

Our example uses these variables: Dupes cost $20, each mounting procedure costs $5, and strips are $21. The example compares 15 mounted dupes on two "sides" to 15 loose dupes which will be individually stripped. Both groups will be commonly separated at $200.

	Individual	Mounted
Separations (grouped)	$200	$200
Mounts	-0-	75
Dupes	300	300
Strips	315 (15)	42 (2)
Total	**$815**	**$617**

Choosing a proof:
Color Key, Cromalin, Press proof

The Color Key

The Color Key System was introduced a while back by 3-M, and most printers still use their products. Basically, the system can be used to show a proof of anything: colored type, panels, b/w halftones, or full-color photographs.

The Color Key is, to our knowledge, the least-expensive proofing system which shows—in a composite fashion—how a printed job will look. Many ad agencies use it to proof expensive advertisements; lots of publishers even use it to proof magazine covers.

Physically, a Color Key is simply a sheet of clear acetate, which has been sensitized with a pigment (such as magenta), exposed, and developed. The result is a translucent image of the original. When four Color Keys are stacked up (yellow, magenta, cyan, and black), you can see a pretty good image of the eventual printing job.

But there are some serious limitations to using Color Keys as proofs of four-color separations (photos). First, they weren't designed for it, and don't have particularly good resolution. Second, they are often inconsistent as supplied: One sheet of "yellow" can differ from the next. Third, they are prone to operator error. And finally, they give a gray cast to the subject matter because they are composed of stacked acetate.

But one cannot overlook economy. Select the Color Key whenever you are after a "fast and dirty" proof, or when color is not critical, or when you simply need to check some complex stripping work. But don't get a Color Key if you're looking for "matched" color, and don't expect too much from this type of proof.

The Cromalin

Cromalins, when they are properly made, have often been called the next best thing to an actual press proof. That statement could be argued forever, but most people agree to this one: They give you a very good idea of what is on the film positives from which they were burned. And that is something even a press proof might not do.

A Cromalin is simply a sheet of paper, upon which has been applied an extremely thin sheet of photo-sensitive film. It is exposed, and then a pigmented powder is applied . . . yellow, for example. The powder can be mixed to match a printer's ink, and thus can get very close to what will appear on press.

Depending on the job, then, more exposures can be made (and different powders applied) until the finished product is shown in full color. A color photograph, for example, will be made up of four separate Cromalin exposures and pigment applications, which are topped off with a sheet of protective film.

Of the four systems described thus far, the Cromalin is the only one which can be used to check the true quality of four-color separations, or of critical ink matches. It will also demonstrate inconsistencies: For example, many advertisers supply a press proof and film. When the film is proofed on a Cromalin, gross color shifts can become apparent. And, if the proof was properly cre-

ated, the conclusion is that the film is bad. That's a decision that can't be solidly made when using a Color Key.

This quality can't be taken lightly: The Cromalin is probably the proof least likely to be "fudged," either by accident or deliberately. The disadvantages are that Cromalins must be made from positive-reading film . . . and they are not particularly cheap. But they're less expensive than a press proof, and certainly cheaper than a botched-up ad or a make-good.

Select a Cromalin whenever you need good control of color and/or quality. Select a Cromalin all the time if you can afford it . . . and don't want to spend the money on press proofs.

(Some printers don't request or make press proofs any more. They rely on Cromalins for all color correcting. And some publishers even have their black-and-white material Cromed, simply to ensure quality and to have something to look at in the pressroom.)

The press proof

There is still a good bit of controversy over the value of press proofs and for good reasons: They are very expensive to make, and sometimes they don't tell you a thing about the material they supposedly "prove."

A proof is, simply, a "pre-printed" printing job. Proofing presses normally run slow, and have the ability to register colors almost perfectly. They can also proof "wet" (ink on top of ink) or "dry" (colors allowed to set between applications).

In theory, a press proof is the ultimate. It doesn't show you how the job will look in a single color, or how it will look when made into a Cromalin. Rather, it shows you a printed version of the job itself.

In practice, there are two main areas where the press proof falls down on the job: First, it is almost always "pulled" (printed) on a slow sheet-fed press, while the actual job may well be printed on an ultra-fast web press. And second, it may be created from original film, while the eventual printer will be working from a duplicate set. Color shifts are to be expected.

The final area of "slop" is the ink itself. Few proofing houses actually take care to match their proofing inks to the final printer's ink. The reason is that a single press proof run is frequently used to check color at several different printers. Did you ever notice those tag lines that say, "To appear in September '77, the following magazines . . . " And the same proof will be used at a half-dozen different printers, all of whom have slightly different inks in their presses.

Press proofs just ain't what they used to be. Before the days of Cromalins, they were the only way to get a true, accurate idea of film quality. Today—in the real world, just outside the art director's office—they often cause more trouble than they're worth.

But they do have uses. Choose a press proof if you meet all the following requirements: 1) you have some money to spend; 2) you want better than a first-class job; and 3) the printer who pulls the proof will also run the job.

Looks good, yes? But what if we change the specifications for this job. Instead of a four-pager, we'll make it a 16-pager, and each of our 15 photos will print on a different page. If you mount to position, you can't get 16 pages worth of material into one separation camera shot. Rather, you would need to make four separations, and the comparison looks like this:

	Individual	Mounted
Separations (grouped)	$200 (1)	$ 800 (4)
Mounts	-0-	75
Dupes	300	300
Strips	315 (15)	84 (4)
Total	$815	$1,259

Looks bad, yes? The point is, you can't arbitrarily decide to dupe all your work, and mount all your work. Your task will be to evaluate each job based on its individual features. You can save money by using one technique today, and lose it all by using that same procedure tomorrow in a different situation.

Rest assured, though, that by using the correct procedure for the job, you can reduce your color separation costs substantially. When these tips are introduced into a firm that currently uses the "dump" method ("I got the color stuff . . . wanna dump it at the printer?"), those savings can easily be 50 percent.

Printing

What is 'good printing'?

By Jeffery R. Parnau

Are one hundred minor aggravations the equivalent of one major headache? The question comes up often in checking the performance of a printer. One month, you may have a few eyesores in an issue, along with a generally inferior printed piece. Next month, bang: The entire insert section is missing.

There are also the grey areas: Exactly what *is* a serious defect in a printed magazine? Which errors by the printer should result in a credit, and which should be thrown on the back burner?

Just how does your printer know what is important to you, as compared to routine nit-picking he sees in other clients?

Moving further back in the production schedule, how can you tell your printer in advance the areas of your prime concern?

There is a way to accomplish the above. I'm hardly a supporter of government materials—but Big Brother sometimes does print things other than pesky legislation. In the *Government Printing Office Technical Report No. 19* (February, 1979), I stumbled across an Equivalent Defect Rating System that included a five-level definition of quality.

In that the material published by our friendly bureaucrats is, in this case, in the public domain, I have taken the liberty of adapting the report for magazine publishers.

Printing and binding quality

First, it is important to understand that quality is an attribute that can be defined and discussed with a printer before a magazine goes into production. Such a discussion gives a printer direction in how to approach the work.

In a discussion on printing and binding, the following levels of quality will apply:

Level 1: Best quality. Requiring the best available materials, printing, workmanship, quality control, and commensurate production time. All films to be inspected and certified before printing. Maximum fidelity in detail, color, and resolution to original copy and/or films is required. (Example of products in this category: 300-line halftones, reproductions of detailed engravings, etc.)

Level 2: Better quality. Requiring high quality printing, materials, workmanship, quality control, and commensurate production time. Close fidelity and resolution to original copy and/or film is required. (Example: 150-line halftones.)

Level 3: Good quality. Requiring above average materials, printing, workmanship, quality control and commensurate production time. Above average fidelity and resolution to original copy and/or film. (Example: Halftones up to 150-line, crisp, clean four-color printing.)

Level 4: Basic quality. Requiring average quality printing, materials, workmanship and commensurate production time. Reasonable fidelity and resolution to original copy and/or film. (Example: Up to 133-line halftones, pleasant-looking process color.)

Level 5: Duplication quality. Requiring no information loss from original. (Example: Xerographic copies; "instant" printing.)

For most of us, levels two through four are the only viable options. There are a handful of magazines in the field which do indeed have Level 1 quality... but they pay the price. And there are a few at the bottom end that border on information loss, due to the poor quality of printing.

How do you know what's "average," compared to "the best"? If you have no comparative technique at hand, you might use my extremes: I feel that *Arizona Highways* has some of the finest printing to be seen in a magazine. The worst can be found in those publications using newsprint (or similar uncoated groundwoods). I don't mean that as an insult, however. Those publishers using newsprint for magazines realize that their halftones won't print nearly as well as they would on coated stock ... and that four-color printing on newsprint is of marginal usefulness.

Color separations

The second quality rating applies to color separations and proofs. Although this three-level system is not in the GPO report, it is in use, with a variety of modifications, by many buyers and sellers across the country.

Level 1: Matched color. I hesitate to use the word "perfect" when describing matched color, because there is no such thing. Four-color printing will not perfectly match original dyes in photographs. Process printing simply doesn't have the range.

The match can be quite close, though. In asking for a Level One color separation, you should expect the subject to be separated as an individual piece (no grouping or ganging the separations).

The film would be inspected, proofed, corrected (with either dot-etching or re-separating), and proofed again. The proofing would be done on a proof press. (There are those—such as myself—who don't believe in press-proofing, but that's another article in itself.) Press inks and papers would be the same as the finished piece.

You should expect to pay a significant amount for

Level One color separations, and to have rather long production time.

Level 2: Good color. With level two you could expect the subjects to be group separated, but with attention to compatibility and quality control. The color shifts resulting from the group separation technique would be largely compensated for in the correcting stage.

The proofing system would be either Cromalins or Transfer Keys. It is unlikely that a second set of correct proofs would be made.

Level 3: Pleasing color. As one publisher aptly put it, "Make the sky blue and the grass green." Pleasing color is often totally uncorrected, unless the balance is so dramatically wrong that the photo is unprintable. The proofing method could be Color Keys or Transfer Keys, both of which are made directly from the separation negatives.

Pleasing color is suitable for many magazines which have neither the need nor desire for better quality. Publishers using newsprint, for example, are already in the marginal-quality reproduction range, and may have little to gain by correcting their separations.

We've outlined two apparently independent quality ratings: printing and color separations. In the original government report on quality, no distinction was made between the preparatory end and a finished product.

But it seems that a magazine publisher *can* specify two different quality levels without having those instructions conflict with each other. An example:

Publisher Fred has a magazine which runs hundreds of photos per year, all of which are small pictures of new products (machinery, etc.). He sees no reason to spend the proverbial arm and leg to ensure that a tractor is printed with the proper hue of yellow . . . or that a company logotype is "Crimson Red."

Yet he will not tolerate plugged or wash-out editorial halftones, poorly trimmed magazines, or other noticeable printing errors.

So, Fred asks for Level Three color separations, but Level Two printing and binding. He is willing to pay the premium for a finely printed product, but not for elaborate work on his separations.

Classifying defects

The next quality rating applies to defects. Again, we have adapted the GPO report for magazine usage.

Critical defect. This is a defect that renders the product unfit for its intended usage. Information loss is the key factor here, and examples would be missing components (signatures, insert cards, etc.) or unreadable material.

Major defect. This type of defect is one which would be noticed by readers (such as grossly poor color balance) and which would likely result in complaints (from readers and/or advertisers). But a major defect does not make the product unfit for its intended use.

Minor defect. In this case, the problem area is one which would be noticed by the average reader or advertiser, but which would not result in complaints.

Trim variations

The final quality rating defines the guidelines for the bindery. Regarding trimming deviations, the GPO suggests the following rating system, for "Good Quality" products:

Variation of 1/16" or less: No defect. Variation from 1/16" to 1/8": Minor defect. Variation greater than 1/8": Major defect. Trim variation which results in information loss: Critical defect.

Regarding bindery trim, you can, of course, set your own standards. For a magazine publisher, a trim of 1/8" too large could result in a tremendous increase in postage costs. Thus, you might decide that any defect which adds weight to your product is critical, while under-size trim problems are minor or major (unless they result in information loss).

Although the system outlined above isn't infallible, it's a start.

Print quality: Part II

By Jeffery R. Parnau

In a recent column, we presented a modified version of the Government Printing Office's *Technical Report No. 19: The Equivalent Defects Rating System* (EDRS) which outlined five levels of print quality (from "best" to "duplication") and three classifications of defects (major, minor, and critical).

We also outlined the classes of defects in trimming a product, resulting in quality ranging from "no defect" to "critical" (trim variation of more than 1/8").

Before actually getting into the Equivalent Defect System, we'll add one *more* vegetable to the stew: revenue loss.

When errors cost money

Magazine publishers have a unique problem when it comes to print quality—the unhappy advertiser. An ad prints poorly, the publisher gets a phone call, and the negotiations start. It isn't unheard of for an advertiser to cancel a contract due to poor reproduction.

A situation where a critical defect leads to revenue loss is not limited to advertising revenue, however. What if, for example, the printer binds a publisher's insert card backwards? There is no information loss (which would automatically make the mistake critical). The error might not even be noticed by the average reader (and according

Classifying Printer's Errors

Classification	Description	Example	Value
Critical	Any information loss; trim variations of more than 1/8″; real or potential revenue loss.	Missing page or pages; reverse type not readable; lost advertising revenue; lost subscription sales.	5
Major	Noticeable by the average reader and likely to result in complaints; trim variations up to 1/16″; complaints from advertisers.	Complaints received regarding printing, but no credits given.	1
Minor	Noticeable by average reader, but not likely to result in complaints; trim variations of less than 1/16″.	Skin tones on photos off balance; correction inserted crooked.	.2
None	Noticeable by staff only.	Wrong color used in headline; photo flopped.	0

to my parameters, notice by readers doesn't classify a defect as major). However, the result could be decreased revenues for the publisher if readers can't find the house ad's appropriate order card.

For rating purposes, then, we will consider any revenue loss—either potential or real—a critical defect.

The equivalency key

The Equivalent Defects Rating System is based upon a simple premise: Some errors are worse than others.

In the accompanying chart, we've listed the various classifications of errors and added that all-important aspect of relativity. In the value column, each type of error is given a number ranging from "0" to "5".

You'll note that the bottom entry on the chart gives no weight at all to certain problems. Even though the printer may make a mistake, this system—as we've modified it—apparently lets the printer "get away with" certain mistakes. Why?

Let's be practical. You sell information. Even if your printer makes a minor mistake, such as using the wrong combination of colors for a headline, your product is hardly affected. No reader will notice the error, no information is lost, no revenue is lost, and all advertisers are happy. Why complain? Printers are human, too, and this rating system takes that fact into account.

In addition, the rating system itself is not designed to prove anything, or to punish the printer. It is designed as a vehicle of communication for quality control. It can be used to compare one printer to another. But it isn't intended to give you rock-solid evidence that your printer is good or bad. (You probably know that already.)

Obtaining a rating

With the fundamentals of the system out of the way, let's put it to work by rating a given issue.

First, you select an appropriate representation of the total printed product. There are several ways to do this:

1. Have copies mailed to "dummy" addresses so that you will get a truly representative cross section of what your readers are getting.

2. Work out an arrangement with your printer whereby you will receive hourly "pulls," or a single copy for every 10,000 bound.

3. Take a quantity of random samples from the material shipped to you by the printer.

4. Stand in the bindery and grab a magazine every 20 minutes.

Which method is best? It depends on the relationship you have with your printer (trust or no-trust), the total quantity printed, and how deeply you want to get involved in accurate quality monitoring.

And the next obvious question: How many random copies do you need?

In the original government version of rating printing, the author suggested 100 pieces. Since magazines have different press runs, 100 may be either too many or too few. In addition, you will have time constraints to work with. The objective is to select a sample large enough to provide an accurate summary of quality, but small enough to be manageable (because you or an employee will be critically evaluating each magazine, page by page).

For practical purposes, we'll suggest a random sampling of 50 books.

The review

Now that you have compiled 50 magazines which represent the overall quality of your magazine, get comfortable—now comes the hard work. You will examine each printed page of each magazine (partial insert cards count as a full page).

Let's take a walk through one of the above 50 copies for a sample review.

The first thing we notice is that the cover is slightly out of register and the color balance is out of whack. This counts as two errors. Because neither error is likely to result in complaints, and because no information is lost (due to the poor registration), we assign two minor errors (total: 4) to the cover. (To make matters easy, we'll jot the errors and value directly on the cover. We may want to go over each book later with the printer.)

Next, we notice that a four-page signature is missing—a critical information loss, to be sure. Each missing *page* is given a rating of 5, for a total of 20 points. (The missing signature is *not* counted as a single mistake because all errors are later summarized and converted into errors *per thousand pages* . . . not errors per *magazine.*)

Moving along, we notice that— just as we described

earlier—a special insert card has been inserted backwards. Readers won't have a convenient way of ordering our super-saver on Florida oranges, and by next issue they'll rot. We'll lose money, so the error gets a critical rating of 5. (Since the back half of the card didn't relate to anything in particular, it gets no error rating at all.)

Pages 32 through 39, along with an equal number of pages in the back of the book (it's saddle stitched) were apparently folded poorly. Each page is positioned slightly more than 1/16″ high. The 16 pages get a total error rating of 16 (each counts as a major error).

Fortunately, that's all we notice in this particular copy. Only 49 more to check out before proceeding to the next step!

The summary

At long last, we have 50 random magazines, each with notes on the pages with errors, and each with a summary of errors on the cover. (Keeping a chart of the errors would be easier than keeping the magazines themselves, but then you'd have nothing to show your printer.) The final step is to total all of the error ratings and divide by the total pages reviewed.

The copy we rated above had a total rating of 46.4 relative (or equivalent) points. The other 49 copies may be higher or lower, but assuming that each one had the same total rating of 46.4, the final tally would be 2,320 points.

We then determine the total pages reviewed (if each book had 120 pages, the review totals 6,000 pages) and divide 2,320 by 6 (the number of thousands of pages reviewed). And finally we have the number we've been shooting for all along: This magazine has an Equivalent Defect Rating of 386.6 per thousand pages.

That number—standing alone—is useless. It merely tells you that based on all the viewing, rating, and adding we just did, that particular printing had a score of 386.6.

The secret is to develop an Equivalent Defect Rating System and use it month after month. If the prior issue had a score of 116, and the one before it had a score of 77, quite obviously, something is wrong.

This system, as we said earlier, isn't perfect. But it is a helpful, easy-to-use tool to monitor quality. And better yet, it can be an extremely valuable tool in *reducing* the error rate. You'll never again have to use that nebulous, wishy-washy statement: "The printer is getting worse and worse, but we don't know exactly how to nail things down."

Print quality: Part III

By Jeffery R. Parnau

How bad is bad printing? How much better is one printer than another? Is the quality of your product improving or is it sliding on a predictable basis?

Such questions are common in the magazine business. Unfortunately, answers are not. However, the Equivalent Defects Rating System, explained in other articles, may be the tool that can help answer those questions. (I will assume that you have read previous articles on EDRS, so I will pick up where I left off.)

At this point, you have inspected a randomly selected batch of 50 copies of several issues of your magazine. You have made notations about the errors in each, and have finally arrived at an Equivalent Defect Rating per 1,000 printed pages. By using your own measurements to keep tabs on quality over several issues, you know whether the quality of your product is increasing or decreasing.

Now comes the communication. If you have been as objective as possible in examining the sample issues, you will have the tools to demonstrate to the printer exactly what the problems were, why they are important to you, and how a score for each issue was determined.

There are several ways to use the rating of an issue in communicating. The first is to simply compare grand totals.

Let's say, for example, that over a six-issue span, your magazine had Equivalent Defect scores of 100, 105, 112, 121, 138, and 145. If you have been objective in your ratings—and if you have kept the 50 samples of each issue—there will be little doubt that quality is on the downslide.

However, this system isn't intended to "punish" your printer. Don't even consider taking your copies to the plant and asking for credits. Instead, use the ED scores to demonstrate quality in order to improve or maintain it.

The totaled ED scores are an effective device that print management can use to communicate directly with those who produce the job. Poor quality isn't always the result of simple mistakes. If the general attitude in a printing plant is that "good enough" is equal to "great," quality will slide. It may well be that a deteriorating company morale is the reason for consistently rising ED scores.

The totals aren't the only tool you have, however. By keeping records of what the errors were, you will also be able to pinpoint specific problems.

For example: Suppose your ED scores were on the rise because of ever-increasing bindery errors. You would be able to aid the printer by identifying not only the general area, but also the specific machine at fault, which part of the machine to concentrate on, and possibly even which individual in the plant was making the mistake.

In addition to defining a problem area or machine, you would want to watch for repetitive mistakes. Recently, we used the example of an insert card being stitched backwards. If that error continued issue after issue (and kept the ED scores high), you'd be able to help the printer devise a correction, perhaps something as simple as a visual reminder for the absent-minded card feeder in the bindery.

Keeping accurate records of the types of mistakes is very important. It becomes critical when you use the ED system to compare printers. Suppose you are choosing between two printers with similar capabilities, and you have the opportunity to develop a rating system with both.

If both printers had remarkably similar total ED scores for several issues, and all other factors were equal, which printer would you choose? By referring to your records, you'd pick the printer whose Critical Error scores were lower. It's as simple as that.

Of course, most publishers find it impossible to have their magazines printed at two different plants before making a decision. However, the system can still be used if the printers give you just a hair of cooperation.

Simply ask permission to spend several hours at the plant, preferably in the bindery. Once there, take a quantity of random samples of another publisher's magazine as it comes off the machine, inspect it, make notes, and put it back. Look for errors, such as poor registration, missing signatures or inserts, varying trim, and all of the other variables we discussed in the first two parts of this series. Do the same at the plant of the competition, and voila: Months or years of guesswork boiled into a few days of observation.

How would printers react to your using a standardized system for rating quality? Ideally, they will support it. It is a far better system than most buyers use today (such as, "I heard they have crummy quality so let's print somewhere else"). Any method of objectively reviewing quality should be welcomed.

And keep in mind, the ED system should not be used solely to criticize the quality of the finished piece. If your printer cooperates, helps you out, and reduces your headaches (all of which will show in declining ED ratings), be darn sure to put your compliments into written form . . . just as you do with your complaints.

Quality in print: The manager's role

By James E. Dunne

Whether you are describing automobiles, stereos, cameras, or printing, the emphasis on the quality of a product is increasingly becoming a major factor to consumers. Most well-managed companies involved with manufacturing have had "Quality Control Depts" as part of their organization charts (it always looks good to say you have one). In many instances, however, the supervisor of that department has worn more than one hat, and when it came down to a choice, production output to meet a schedule usually got priority at the expense of quality.

Today, many companies, aware of the increased demand for quality, are finding that putting the proper emphasis on quality assurance in the initial steps of the manufacturing operation increases performance level and produces an end result that is better and possibly even less costly.

Furthermore, small magazines bent on improving the quality of production are coming to realize that they need not have a person with the title of quality assurance manager, with responsibilities specifically focused on quality. Although such a magazine might not be able to apply all of the procedures U.S. News applies, it certainly could employ some of them.

What is quality?

Perhaps one of the definitions that covers it best is "Quality is conformance to requirements." The bench marks set by a company must establish criteria for each item produced in their manufacturing operation. The guidelines are set for delivery of a product within the price range and scheduling requirements of their particular marketplace. If that "bench mark" has built-in quality flexibility, you can be sure that the end product will have some quality variations.

In the printing industry, as in many other industries, the magazines, brochures, catalogues, etc., are the by-products of ingredients bought from various suppliers and finally put together for the reading public in a finishing operation. But the paper, ink, halftones, color separations—everything down to the staples or glue that holds that printed product together—should have a measurable level of conformity to a standard set to fit the end use.

You usually do not expect a beautifully color separated 200-line screen art reproduction to print well on groundwood newsprint stock. But more and more daily newspapers are successfully running coarse screened four-color illustrations specifically prepared for that market medium. Meanwhile, the use of a high grade coated paper does not necessarily guarantee the best results for "art" subjects if the separations are not properly screened and color balanced. Why is one endeavor a success and the other a failure?

Communications is the key

You've heard it said so many times before: "Communications is the key." *Every* person involved in each step of the production line should know what is expected of him in order to attain a quality result. Don't assume that every individual knows what to look for or that someone else will eventually catch an overlooked deficiency. That "someone" may very well be a very unhappy customer!

Where should this communication begin? First of all, company intracommunication is a must. Consideration should be given to the format of the "Quality Circle" approach where management gets an opportunity to sit down with the "people in the trenches" and listens to their ideas for improvement. Management not only must give approval to this type of interplay, it *must actually get involved*. And, it's going to take time and commitment to make it work.

Second, the customer (publisher, in my case) must sit down with the supplier (printer) to discuss their mutual needs, establishing what is necessary to obtain the best quality within the limitations of schedule and cost. In the case of a periodical publication, the printer must get constant feedback on his performance to reinforce what is expected.

McGraw-Hill, *Newsweek* and *U.S. News & World Report* provide feedback routinely. At *U.S. News*, for example, a critique of each weekly issue is done on the office copies received in Washington from their four R.O.P. plants. Each ad and editorial page is compared against the proofs supplied to the printer for color match, register, alignment, trim, dirt and hickies, etc., and points are deducted from an expectancy rate figure for each defect. In the case of black-and-white or two-color, including "type" pages, the same grading is done using established inking and tonal range standards as bench marks.

The marked-up critiqued books are then returned *within two days* to the individual plant with a written report and a numerically rated "report card" establishing which printer had the "Best Book" for that week. Because of the fast turn-around, the printer knows where his areas of deficiency and acceptability are before producing the next issue. These statistics are accumulated from week to week and reviewed with the plants on a quarterly basis. The 52-week totals are then used as part of a total evaluation program designed to recognize the outstanding supplier to *U.S. News & World Report* during a given year. Each plant is encouraged to comment on the critiques of their performance so that continuing dialogue has been established. The competition and feedback have been very encouraging.

Before this procedure was established at *U.S. News*, the quality representatives from each printing plant were invited to Washington for their input and discussion. No system can be successful unless all the participants thoroughly understand the ground rules. Now each week the critiqued books from Washington are reviewed at the four individual printers at a scheduled meeting attended by a *U.S. News* plant representative along with prep, press, bindery and quality control personnel from the plant. Copies of books from the other three plants are also available for comparison against their own. At the same or tie-in meeting, the inspection reports and proofs on supplied advertising are scrutinized to determine potential problems on up-coming issues.

Inspection reports

The inspection of supplied ad material is a critical procedure that should not be assigned to a clerk or entry level personnel. It must be done by people who are qualified to analyze film and progressive proofs for dot relationship, grey balance, trap, undercolor removal, register, reverse spreads, ink densities, etc. The measuring devices must be properly calibrated and checked on a *regular* basis.

The densitometer, for instance, may have a tendency to drift a few points from day to day. With the discrepancies that do occur from instrument to instrument even when comparing readings on similar models from the same manufacturer, it is critical to keep their calibration as tight as possible to the "bench mark."

In measuring the ink densities on advertising and editorial proofs these readings become extremely significant, especially when laying out printing forms which will be incorporating material that has been produced by separators scattered throughout the country. Analyzing these numbers to minimize potential problems requires technical knowledge and a great deal of common sense.

Ten points on a densitometer are much more critical to certain colors, corporate logos and neutral greys than an illustration with a cartoon or portraying skies or seascapes, etc. And densitometer numbers conforming to an established standard don't necessarily insure good reproduction if the film supplied to the printer does not match the dot size on the proof or if the ink trap is poor. Someone with little experience and training is simply not able to make consistent judgments on what the inspections are all about.

The influence of SWOP

Up to about seven years ago each printer, agency, publisher and color separator had its own set of "standards." While there were similarities in some specifications, many were miles apart. To overcome this disparity and confusion, a number of graphic arts groups combined their efforts to produce a set of specifications in an attempt to unify this incoming material to the printer. Their efforts were successful, for the SWOP program (Specifications for Web Offset Publications) has been adopted by *every* major agency, publisher, separator, printer and graphic arts supplier in the United States. Now, it is possible to measure supplied material in order to check for conformity to these published standards.

While the SWOP project has taken a giant step for quality assurance, there is still a lot of fine-tuning to be done. Whether the cause is carelessness, indifference, or inability to match the specification because of turnaround schedules, mechanical problems or some lack of technical skills, there is still a significant amount of material produced outside of the SWOP parameters. Anyone who has stood by the side of a web press and shared the frustration of a pressman who is making inking adjustments to compensate for such deficiencies knows how the reproduction quality suffers. Equally disconcerting is the cost involved in terms of plate makeovers, excessive paper and ink waste, and lost press time, all of which may be in vain.

Check points

The checking procedure to insure quality reproduction should begin with the selection of the original illustration material. Since grainy, poorly exposed, out-of-focus photographs can be helped to only a limited degree by the cameraman at the separator/lithographer, a good original is a prime prerequisite.

If the art director is confined in his selection because of restricted availability of subject matter (very often the case in newsweekly magazines), communication with the separator/cameraman becomes extremely important (especially when time is a factor). The submit has a much better chance of being approved the first time around if the art director can tell the separator what he is looking for in the photo or transparency. He should, for example, indicate that dark areas should be opened up, a color cast removed, or that unsharp masking be used to enhance detail. Again, the SWOP specifications must be followed or the end result will be simply a "pretty picture" which cannot be reproduced on press.

The same holds true of advertising material. If the art director at the agency insists on color saturation beyond the limits of the printing medium, or if he demands that the pressman push the ink densities excessively without reworking the film, the "pretty picture" proof will often end up as a mediocre compromise in the magazine's printed pages.

The dialogue on acceptable material and the careful monitoring of deficiencies has to be an on-going procedure with cooperation between the prime components—agency, separator, publisher, printer. Each is concerned, and each is frustrated by poorly reproduced work. For the amount of time and money being spent on original art or photos—including model fees and location set ups, the typesetting and layout design plus the color separation and proofing—it just doesn't make sense to let the film and prog get all the way through the remaining steps of production without "bench mark" checks to catch deviations outside of the SWOP recommendations. And the agency/separator should be notified immediately if replacement material is required.

Pre-press proofs

As part of these checking/inspection procedures, there are several proofing systems that can be used in conjunction with the densitometer reading. Both DuPont and 3M have proofing methods which closely simulate actual ink on paper reproduction and they have proven to be valuable tools in the inspection process. If the densitometer readings of the color bars on the submitted ink-on-paper proof vary enough (more than + or - 10 pts) from the SWOP reference to raise a question about either color balance or possible in-line conflicts, etc., a Cromalin or transfer key can be used to give a visual reference determining what the proof should look like if it had been pulled to proper ink densities. They can also be used if there have been color corrections made without a reproof or if the inspection reveals a disparity between the film and the proofs.

Neither of these systems is foolproof, however, and the user should not be misled into thinking that a pre-press proof cannot be improperly made. The SWOP specifications state that there are strict procedures, which include the base stock to be used, established hues of toners or pigments matching SWOP, exposure guides, notations of color laydown and, in the case of Cromalins, specific density readings set at the individual installation to compensate for atmospheric conditions in the shop. The readings must be done for each layer of laminate in order to attain final readings which will match the SWOP color reference.

Anyone who accepts a pre-press proof without color bars and exposure guides on the proof for measurement is taking a chance on being misled by a questionably made pre-press proof. Since this type of proof has photographic sharpness and "perfect" trap, there is still some educated interpretation necessary to decide whether the supplied material can be reproduced satisfactorily or whether replacement material is required. However, using pre-

press proofs is certainly a lot better than just guessing what the erratic readings may portend.

Both 3M and DuPont are constantly fine-tuning these products for consistency and even closer matches to properly made ink-on-paper proofs. The Automatic Toning Machines and Transfer Key Laminator have helped to standardize these products. Several other companies have been introducing new methods which may be more widely accepted in the not too distant future.

If your printer or separator uses one of these pre-press systems it would be wise to do a periodic check of their procedures to assure consistency from plant to plant. This would involve taking one or two separations that have been thoroughly checked and having each supplier pull a pre-press proof from that *same* material. Be sure that the color bars and exposure guides are part of the proof.

When the round-robin is completed, a comparison can be made. If the process color hues do not match each other, or if there is a significant difference in the density readings, an explanation is in order. Very often there is a mixup in pre-press proofing procedures when a printer or separator is involved with commercial work. Both companies have several shades of magentas, cyans, and yellows for this type of work. If it doesn't meet the SWOP specifications, find out why. DuPont and 3M have technical representatives who can help in this area.

Other tools which are more costly and less practical for the average inspection set-up are the electronic previewers such as the Hazeltine or Toppan Systems. They are being used successfully in large separation houses and printers where the volume of work warrants such equipment.

Proofing stock

One of the most controversial subjects affecting quality is proofing stock. Unlike letterpress, the offset proof presses now being used at separators have limitations on the basis weight and surface characteristic that can economically and physically be put through the press.

When the recommended proofing stock for web offset publications was chosen seven years ago, it was based on the *optical* characteristics of the average magazine stock being used at that time. While the basis weight and optical properties varied from publication to publication, it was agreed at the time that the 60# Fortune Gloss was an acceptable compromise. It called for some interpretations, but at least it standardized the stock being sent to the printer as his press guide and it was available in various sheet-fed sizes on a national basis. Some inconsistencies in dry back characteristics from sheet to sheet have been encountered by the separators because of the sheeting method used at the mill, but this has been overcome by producing stock which has been sheeted from one roll at a time instead of six.

Recently there has been a combined effort on the part of the Graphic Communications Association (G.C.A.) and SWOP committees to find a more suitable replacement. As the postal and paper costs have increased since 1975, many publications have gone to lower basis weight stocks to cope with the additional expenses. This, in turn, has altered the average optical characteristics on the R.O.P. stock compared to the Fortune Gloss proofing paper. The graphic arts groups concerned are now testing a number of candidate proofing stocks which more closely resemble the R.O.P. averages.

One of the candidates is a 50# coated groundwood sheet which initially caused some problems because of surface characteristics that were primarily designed for web press printing inks and conditions. The proofing inks have been reformulated with better results. The other prime candidate is a 62# sheet coated on one side manufactured to specifications arrived at by a G.C.A. committee after almost two years of testing.

Before any final decision is made, a number of agencies, separators, publishers and printers will have evaluated live jobs under normal production conditions. If the tests are successful, the new designated proofing stock will be another step forward in the quality link. Until then, the Fortune Gloss remains the standard.

R.O.P. stock

While we're on the subject of paper, it might be well to mention another checking procedure which can help maintain quality levels.

Many printers and publishers are taking samples off the rolls of the running stocks as they are shipped from the mills and running a battery of tests either in-house or at an outside source to determine potential printing problems before the stock is actually scheduled for press. Brightness, gloss, opacity, absorptivity, and surface strength are some of the items which are analyzed on random samples from each series and measured against averages from each mill. If the test results fall outside these parameters, the mill representatives are notified and a resolution is reached based on a press runability test run. It takes some extra time, effort and dollars, but it is another measurable means of communication.

Other checks

Many people who buy printing are unaware that they are entitled to quality sample pulls taken during the course of the press run. Whether the job is run on sheetfed or web equipment, the press operator should be retrieving representative sheets or signatures on an hourly or numerical basis throughout the press run. In addition to these samples you should be getting a "start-to-save" signature, which theoretically is the first good sheet on the skid after the makeready has been completed, the register and ink balancing are acceptable, and printing units are in compensation.

The signed "color OK" sheet should also be available to you with a press count indicating at what point in the run the "best match" or highest level of quality was achieved. In addition, if the form is running more than one up on a flat, you should be receiving multiple samples from each pull and OK.

A major topic to discuss with the printer is the standard used for "acceptable to save" in relation to the color OK. Paper, ink, and presstime are going down the drain until the pressman feels he is close enough to start the good count and then fine tune. All of the quality assurance steps previously mentioned now would come together in the "moment of truth."

If no quality checks have been made, we may have ads with conflicting ink densities in line with one another, or film that doesn't match the prog, or running stock that is picking excessively requiring a softer ink, etc. In such situations, the press crew has a real challenge on their hands to satisfy the customers and their advertisers while still meeting the plant's production schedule. If the money wasted at this point with excessive makeready had been invested in an inspection set-up for incoming material, would better quality have been achieved at the same cost? I really think so!

A double-check on quality for books going through an in-plant mailing operation involves "reel books." These completed magazines are set aside because the labels contain information making them unmailable, i.e., the label comes from the beginning or end of the dick strip mailing reel, or the label had been specifically designated by Zip Code sequence or some other symbol to mark it as a bindery sample.

These bound magazines then become a cross-reference to check the quality of the signatures bound in the magazine against the press running samples. Since the bindery doesn't usually place signatures in the pockets in the same sequence as they came off the press, you are able to get a random sample as well as the chronological pulls from the pressroom.

What's the conclusion?

There is no end to this discussion because it involves an on-going process. As new technology is developed, things that we thought were impossible or impractical yesterday are being done routinely today. So any system has to be flexible to make it work.

Some old chestnuts come to mind. "Don't change for the sake of change," but don't get stuck in a rut just because "we've always done it that way." We can set up systems for checking ink, blankets, plates, exposure frames, fountain solutions—you name it—and each set of bench marks gives you a standard of performance for a specific item that will affect both quality and performance. Some of the same quality checks should be followed whether the method of printing is letterpress, offset, or gravure.

Quality doesn't just happen, it's got to be worked on...*together!* It also takes a lot of patience and persistence because many people need convincing and many others only give lip service to the concept of quality. The emphasis should be on *preventing* quality defects by measuring before the work is done. Quality assurance is an attitude of working and communicating with anyone and everyone involved in producing your product. If you are not satisfied with the quality output, you should work together to identify, analyze and solve the problem. What works in one plant, agency or publication may not work as successfully in another, but any situation can be adjusted to fit the circumstances if people have the right attitudes.

A quality program involves on-going education—attendance at seminars or special courses, in-plant training, review of procedures, selection of the proper people to do the job, reciprocal visits to sit down face-to-face to discuss mutual needs and goals. Such a program demands an investment in time, money and people. And although it has many rewards, it also involves frustration because there are certainly limitations on how much you can do.

And there are always a few surprises. Even with all the checks, there are going to be in-line problems because of conflicting positions and material that cannot be replaced or adjusted. But at least you have a good idea of where you are beforehand and can tell the plant which ad to favor if a compromise is necessary.

Last of all, don't forget feedback. People in quality control sometimes get so busy preventing fires that they forget to tell a plant or supplier they are doing a good job. If you appreciate their efforts, tell them. A pat on the back once in a while may prevent the need for a kick in the behind later on!

Assuring quality control

By Mark Dowie

The hypnotic drone of a high speed web at 4:30 a.m. can be a most assuring sound. Pressmen work efficiently. The checking of forms is almost mechanical. Pages are squared, registered, clean and in order. All's well except there's too much magenta in the illustration on page 8. Looked okay to the color operator at the press, but you hate it. Too bad, but you weren't there.

Quality magazine printing can only be assured by the active participation of the publisher throughout the entire process. Printers, in the course of selling their wares, will promise quality and quality control—from platemaking to labeling—and provide pristine, perfectly registered and bound samples to demonstrate their excellence. The promise is only as good as the publisher's participation, however.

A quick tour of a large web plant and any layman will appreciate the challenge of quality control in printing. It requires constant surveillance and educated personnel. It costs paper waste and time loss. In manufacturing a magazine, there are perhaps a thousand points at which serious mishaps can occur. With today's modern web press speeds, a few inattentive seconds can cause a minor disaster:

• A pressman starts saving the correct forms to be bound before the bad forms from a blanket wash have passed and all your subscribers from postal zones 60623 to 60678 are missing pages 5, 8, 13, 16, 57, 60, 65 and 68. Four seconds of production time = 300 irate subscribers.

• A bindery employee slips the wrong form on a saddle. It's the same size as the correct form so the caliper doesn't kick it out; 50 subscribers get to read the same story twice.

• Color register can be off for 1,000 forms before it's noticed.

The litany is endless and bad quality is costly—to the publisher who loses subscribers and to the printer who loses the publisher. The trick is to work together on quality control.

Communicating Objectives

The publisher should begin by communicating his or her quality objectives to the printer during the final stages of contract negotiations. Quality and taste are highly subjective and vary widely from publisher to publisher. Your printer has no idea what you like unless it's indicated. From somewhere in the wide quality range of publications from *Time* to *Communication Arts,* pick a few magazines that meet your standards. Show them to the printer with whom you are negotiating. Point out some qualities you particularly like in them—tone, consistency, register, trim, label placement, color, etc. Let the printer know in advance exactly how fussy you are. But remember that for the quality in *Communication Arts* magazine, you will pay more than for *Time*—all else being equal.

Learn the Technology

Most magazine publishers, along with their art and production staffs, understand magazine design and production to the point where negatives are delivered to the printer. By working closely with typesetters, color separators and lithographers, they have learned the terminology and science of the trades. To assure quality in the end product, this understanding must be extended through the entire process. Printing, like every technological profession, is mystified by its language and is simpler than it seems. There are no short cuts to becoming a journeyman printer, but a publisher can learn what he or she needs to know about printing from several competent sources:

1. The Graphic Arts Technical Foundation in Pittsburgh, Pa., publishes the most up-to-date texts and has an active seminar program.

2. Other printers: Retain as a consultant someone with first-hand working experience with the kind of press on which you plan to print your magazine. Have your consultant "walk" you through the process several times before you negotiate quality terms with your own printer.

3. There are some good general printing texts in most public libraries. Read only those published (or revised) after 1970 and study the glossaries carefully.

One caveat: Once you have acquired this new and exciting information, never treat a printer as an equal in the printer's realm. Be knowledgeable but humble. You are dealing with someone who spent as many years learning his or her trade as an architect or engineer. Be firm, informed but respectful of your printer's superior knowledge of printing. If you treat your printer like a craftsman, he or she will perform like one.

Communications

Most printing companies assign two representatives to each magazine publisher—a sales or general representative (usually residing near the publisher's office) and a technical rep at the plant. Naturally the company would prefer to have only those two people on the staff deal with the publisher and handle all complaints and problems. It's probably best to cooperate with this arrangement as long as results are satisfactory. But don't hesitate to go around your reps if you are really hot about something. Often you don't have time for "customer relations" and need to get to the heart of the matter right then. If you don't get the service you expect from your reps, write them a letter about it and send copies to their supervisors and the president.

Watching the Run

Magazine designer and illustrator Dugald Stermer says of this dilemma, "Economics have forced most of us onto web presses. While web is *capable* of producing excellent quality, speed and complexity make it imperative for us to watch the run very closely."

For *at least* the first six issues with a new printer, the publisher (art director, production manager) should physically be at the press throughout the entire process (binding included). It may mean 36 hours without sleep for someone, but it's worth it. You will learn a lot about printing as well as demonstrate your concern for quality. Besides, it's a little like childbirth—nicer if the father is there with the mother.

Though printers, for the most part, prefer to work without interference, they seem willing to have the publisher represented at the press during the run.

It is at this point that diplomacy is vital. The printer's shop is as sacred to him or her as your office is to you. And here is where your sound working knowledge of printing technology and terminology becomes essential. Long explanations of the causes of picking, inking and ghosting waste time, waste paper and frustrate the printer who wants you to initial the form so the run can start. Arguments are worse because they insult professional pride.

An additional purpose of technological understanding is to help you see the problem, identify the cause and protect you from buck-passing explanations like "It's on the negative you gave us" or "The paper, you should go up a grade." (You know that isn't true because you carefully studied the quality potential of your paper before you ordered it.)

Taking Quality to Your Printer

Be certain your printer is starting with quality material whether he or she is working from negatives, positives or mechanicals. That way the blame cannot be passed back to your separator, typesetter or production staff. Don't allow anything to be shipped from a separator to your printer before a final check by your art director or production manager, as well as your proofreader, of course.

Introduce your printer to your separator, particu-

larly if the separator is doing the stripping and flatting. They talk the same language and can save you much communication time. Your printer can tell your separator exactly how the art is to be shot to assure the best quality.

Handling of Criticism

No one likes to be criticized. Craftsmen seem to take criticism particularly hard when it comes from laymen. In order to turn criticisms of your printer to your advantage, you must lace them with recognition of the printer's problems and superior knowledge of the trade. It is also helpful to explain the impact of the printer's blunders on your business:

• A duplicate signature reaching subscribers two weeks after your first billing effort of a major new key is much more serious than if the same mistake were made four months later.

• A white line at the top of a full bleed cover can seriously damage newsstand sales.

• Bad register in one 8-page form could lose a dozen advertisers. Don't assume your printer understands your business. These things should be told.

Renegotiating Your Printing Contract

As with the original contract, quality should be a major concern in renegotiation. But trying to write quality standards into a printing contract is still going to be like writing standards for sexual satisfaction into a marriage contract. However, after a year or more you should have chronicled (with examples) each quality problem from past issues. Careful study of the mistakes may uncover a pattern or particular problem area that can be written into your new contract.

Most initial contracts have some general and generally useless agreements on quality. Usually they give the publisher recompense or the right to terminate only when an issue reaches 100,000 subscribers dripping ink, with the cover upside down and pages falling out.

From your experience in the current contract period, try to anticipate problems and include in your new contract some protective clauses and mechanisms for partial restitution in the event of poor quality.

But no matter what is written in a printing contract, consistent quality, copy by copy, issue after issue, is highly unlikely and a printer's promise of quality turns out to be only as good as the publisher's willingness to understand and survey quality controls.

Printing: The new technology comes of age

By Jeffery R. Parnau

It sits in the lobby of a Midwestern printer. It looks for all the world like a wine press, and was actually modeled after that design. Just two hundred years ago, one man would sweat as he pulled the long lever ... an action which pressed a sheet of paper into contact with metal typesetting. Another man would scramble to roll the paper bed forward, remove the sheet from the frame, hang it for drying, and place a fresh sheet in its place. Meanwhile, the lever-puller was busy inking the type, and when they both completed their respective chores, the cycle started again.

These two men had good jobs. They were printers. If they worked hard, they were able to produce 300 good impressions during their 12-hour workday.

The rumbling noise in the lobby becomes a roar as the door is opened, and there, churning out 25,000 impressions per hour, sits the new version. This one is operated by six people instead of two, but each impression contains 32 pages—16 times the output of the "wine press." In 12 hours, it might deliver almost 10 million pages.

It is tempting to look at such a modern reproduction unit—letterpress, offset, or gravure—and assume that we have finally worked the bugs out of printing. The 200-year-old press is primitive by comparison. But is the new press just as primitive when we look ahead? Wouldn't it be logical to assume that, given another 200 years of technological evolution, we will see the same depth of change as has occurred during the last two centuries?

Not necessarily. Consider that Homo sapiens first recorded information by writing on stone ... and that at the turn of this century, lithographers were still writing on stone cylinders. Not much progress in 37,000 years.

But since the turn of the century, human knowledge has increased at a fantastic rate. Indeed, we currently have but a fraction of the know-how that will be in libraries just 20 years down the road. But does that mean we have only a fraction of the printing technology that will be available in the very next generation? And that with such knowledge, printing will undergo a thorough, dramatic change?

In this article we will discuss certain changes that are bound to occur, and other changes that are possible—even desirable—but not probable. For people in publishing, the future is both exciting and frightening. And, like it or not, the future starts today.

Why reproduction methods change

Let's start with a not-too-daring blanket statement: In the printing industry, reproduction methods change only in reaction to reproduction problems. Although solutions are not sitting around waiting for problems, the industry has a good track record of solving problems when they do arise. Gutenberg invented movable type because hand-drawn Bibles could not fill the demand. Alois Senefelder invented lithography because copperplate engravings were expensive and slow. Frederick Eugene Ives

invented the halftone screen to make photographs printable.

In order to examine the future of printing, then—particularly web offset lithography—let's begin by examining the problems we face today: problems of preparation (prep), reproduction, bindery and delivery.

The first area involves all those operations which occur before a job goes on press. A decade ago, the main problems in preparation were speed, cost, and quality (of typesetting, paste-up, and color separations). There have been tremendous advances in this area over the past few years, however.

Today we have photocomposition machines which have no mechanical typefaces. We have color scanners which put out many times the volume formerly available on cameras. And we have proofing systems which don't require a full-blown press.

Have we solved the main problems? Hardly. The increased use of process color has taxed color separation capacity in many areas. Color balance is still a problem before press, not to mention while on press. And although the cost of separations has fallen on a per-unit basis, publishers find themselves spending more than ever on a per-issue basis (due to the increased use of photos).

Photographic film itself is cumbersome and fairly unreliable (ask any printer about the problems in working with duplicated film, which is the total output of many ad agencies). And although we have increased speed, publishers are still required to have the color material sent off before the balance of the issue.

Pressroom: same old problems

Pressroom problems have received some attention lately, but nothing in the pressroom has been as dramatic as what has happened in prep. For the most part, today's web press looks like its 20-year-old predecessor.

In fact, many printers actually do have presses that are that old, so we must be realistic when examining the problems in this area: although certain problems in press operations have been defined and solutions are available, the majority of printers are not using the new hardware. Thus, pressroom problems continue to be those which are the result of judgment (or error) and wasted labor.

At one end of the press, a paper roll tender guesses when to change the roll, which can affect the amount of paper used. Meanwhile, the pressman fiddles with inking keys, the compensator punches buttons and twists dials, another man or woman constantly examines and corrects registration. Then, when everybody "feels" the job is up to par, the jogger (the person who stacks things up) is told to start putting the product in the first-off skid.

The net result: A great deal of human involvement. The fact is that printing is as much an art as a science. A heartwarming thought, perhaps, but it's expensive. Results are uncannily unpredictable, and quality problems always lead to crediting some unhappy advertiser.

595

Paper problems: endless

Paper has generated more problems recently than any other printing factor. In the magazine market (lightweight coateds), the first problem is getting any paper at all. The second is the outrageous price of the stuff. The third, unpredictable performance in the lower cost (so to speak) grades. And finally, there is the ever-increasing cost to deliver this bulky substance to the customer.

Which logically leads us into binding and delivery problems: Binderies are too mechanically oriented (using tiny strips of paper to direct a magazine to its eventual owner). Regional editions get mixed up. Magazines are printed at the speed of light, only to gather a thick layer of dust while the binding equipment sluggishly puts the product together. The areas for improvement here are not so apparent as in the pressroom, but they do exist.

And when the job is finally assembled, addressed, sacked, and ready to go, it's time to pay the piper (who for most of us wears red, white and blue). By one estimate, postal costs will rise *only* 10 percent per year; other projections are better or worse.

Each of these problems cries for a solution. The solutions would, ideally, be the best technologically available alternatives. Unfortunately, since a lot of money is tied up in the hardware at the printer, we generally see only stopgap solutions—solutions specifically designed to accommodate current equipment.

In the pressroom, for example, the advances in paper handling, the development of presses that do their own makereadies and registration, and the ability to handle lighter sheets of paper, are stopgap solutions because they are designed as retrofits to the currently available printing presses. They do not even approach the ideal methods of solving problems of waste, fidelity, and speed, for these methods require entirely new techniques and equipment.

In this article, we'll discuss practical changes which are certain to occur in the industry (whether or not you get involved with them).

Pre-press: a look at the future

Let's start again with prep operations. The most obvious "missing" tool at the printing plant of the future will be the reliable old camera. We already have the ability to scan color photographs . . . and it is rather odd that it was only recently that scanning equipment was designed exclusively for black and white material. Within a few short years, you will be able to submit paste-ups to the printer, where they will be scanned (rather than photographed) along with your color photographs and artwork. The resulting film will be used to create a proof.

Moving ahead another step, the problem of bulky, unreliable film will be solved when your editorial and advertising material is completely "soft," or electronically stored. You will compose all such material on video display terminals (VDTs), create areas for photos and art, and put the entire product together without paste-ups (or paper, for that matter). This is already being done by many large newspapers; the techniques will transfer to magazines as the cost of equipment continues to fall.

Of course, if everything else can be brought up on the screen, why not advertising? In the future, you won't have to guess whether advertisements meet your standards of reproduction. The ad won't be supplied with some manipulated, error-ridden paper proof. Possibly, it won't even come with a proof at all. Instead, it will arrive as millions of bits of information stored electronically, either on a portable computer memory or recorded on a magnetic carrier. Reproduction standards will be coded into the ad, and you'll know instantly whether the color material will require electronic enhancement or alteration for proper printing.

Effects on ad sales, closing dates

At this point in the future, production changes will be feeding back into all other areas of the magazine. Consider the classic situation of selling that last ad. Today, the ad manager pleads, makes threats, lies, or begs that last day out of the production person (the oldest lie in the book being: "It's in the mail"). Tomorrow, the sales rep will routinely go right up to that last day, and when the sale is made the production department can go to the terminal (or telephone).

Because the ad is available as stored, digitized material (which is how it can be stored electronically), there is no trick to taking it over the wire (or by satellite) rather than waiting for the material to arrive. The millions of bits of information are recorded and fed into the magazine's computer where they electronically replace a filler editorial. The result: An extra ad sale.

And as long as the entire magazine is now in a digital, easily transmitted format, why bother with a trip to the printer? Rather than rely on an air carrier, the production manager will meet the deadline by sitting down once again at the terminal. Call the printer, apologize for being six minutes late (that final ad sale), access the computer, and transmit the magazine with a punch of a button. Time for a martini.

Full-color console proofing

Some of these technical advances will apply to all publishers, while others will not. For example, only those publishers who need full, last-minute control will spend the money to install color scanners which break down photographs for transmission. Those publishers will not need a final proof of the magazine because they will preview the issue in full color, page by page, on in-house terminals.

Others won't have the money for that kind of hardware, nor will they need the speed it offers. They'll be limited to generating only the black and white portions of the magazine, while color work will be done either at the printer or by an electronic prep house in their area.

For still others, there will continue to be a total reliance on outside firms to convert the product to the printer's standards. Meaning, sure . . . some smaller publishers will retain their typewriters and scissors.

The interesting point about the pre-press changes discussed here is that every concept described is either in use or is practical with current technology. *The Wall Street Journal* transmits its product to printing plants via satellite. Many of us use typewriters with electronically-generated typefaces. *Time* magazine transmits color photographs to printers at the rate of 112,000 bits of information per second. Certain newspaper plating machines scan paste-ups and use no film whatsoever. Color VDTs are in use which allow the operator to correct or alter color electronically and see the immediate results. Wide application of these techniques by magazines is virtually around the corner.

It all means that the editor, art director and production manager of the future will be of a different breed. A commercial art degree will be useless without a healthy knowledge of computer programming. The editor who is comfortable in front of a terminal will be far more valuable than the journalism graduate who skipped the electronics courses. The successful publishing employee will have the equivalent of two professions.

Changes in the pressroom

Reproduction itself will see changes, too. However, since we are limiting this discussion to those changes which will occur (putting aside a discussion of those which should occur), we will examine stopgap changes which are a simple expansion of current printing processes.

In order to reduce human error, lower the cost of makereadies, and reduce paper consumption, press manufacturers have begun to market and install a variety of equipment. The most significant is in the area of controlling color.

Within a few years—or tomorrow, if you have an ambitious printer—you will see the long awaited "standards" of printing followed automatically while the press is running.

Basically, here is how the system works: Your film material is read by a densitometer (which records values) and the numbers are fed into the press's computer. The ink fountain keys—which were, in the past, set by hand—are driven by computer-directed motors, which allow more or less ink in given areas, depending on what the film calls for.

Electric eyes continuously sense how much color is being applied and notify the computer. Color balance is thus automatically monitored, and "favoring" a specific page won't be a matter of trial and error. The computer's program will be overridden with whatever commands you ask the press operator to give it.

What does it mean? First, it will eliminate the wide variations of quality which occur. Since press operators will have the tools they needed years ago, they will no longer have to eyeball a piece.

Second, the automatic makeready ability of the press will drastically lower the cost of getting your material "up to color." Harris Corp. projects that Telecolor, the automatic registration function they now offer, will get a job to within 10 percent of its ideal printing configuration in 10 percent of the normally required time.

The benefits don't stop there. What can your picky advertiser say when you provide a press readout, proving that your reproduction was "dead on" when compared to the supplied film? You'll finally have a fancy way to prove that garbage in is, indeed, garbage out.

Not all of the above standards and techniques are here today, but we certainly can expect them shortly. In the meantime, who can expect to benefit from these changes, and what can you do to prepare yourself for them?

Economies will be available to both large and small magazines. For the larger publishers, any slight reduction in the percentage of paper used is a significant sum. For small publishers, a reduction in makeready and running costs (a relatively large chunk of the printing bill), is significant. Preparing yourself, then, is a matter of knowing what to expect and looking for it.

The addition of automatic color balance will be very expensive for most printers because the average web press doesn't have motorized inking keys. The retrofit will be a chore, but given the high cost of paper and the staggering hourly rates for press operations, we believe all publication web offset presses will eventually be outfitted for economical operation.

It is your job to maintain an awareness of what your printer is doing in this area, when it will be done, and whether or not the competition is doing it sooner. If your printer is not keeping up with current technology, let him know what you expect from his operation. He may not be aware of what his customers need in this area.

While the above system is designed for color balance, another system has been designed to control registration. It's not enough to know that someone stands at the press with this responsibility. That person needs time to absorb information (that the color is out of register) and respond to a condition. Furthermore, people can drift away from the job at hand.

Again, computers and electric eyes will take over. Each plate will print a registration mark. An electric eye will monitor these marks and feed the information into a computer which will instantly tell the proper registration motor to get in step.

Since web presses are already equipped with motorized registration controls, the problem of registration will be solved before color balance, due to the cheaper cost of this retrofit. Actually, the only reason all presses don't register automatically right now is that the cost of an on-press computer was formerly too high. Electronics to the rescue.

Other changes in the pressroom will contribute to reduced paper usage and more uniform quality, but not as significantly as those already mentioned. True-count press equipment will provide accurate delivery to the bindery, reducing the "we ran out" problem. Electronic units will automatically dictate at which point a roll of paper should be changed. Again, these tools are available —and although they are expensive, they must be introduced as quickly as time allows.

There is another interesting application of reduced makeready theory in use in this country . . . and to our knowledge, only one printer has it. The company needed a two unit web press (capable of handling two webs of paper) for production of short-run books. But they ordered a custom-built press with four printing units which could be run independently.

Special guards and motors were designed, and the press was modified so that two units are always printing while the other two units are being readied for the next set of plates. The paper passes through all four units at all times, and when the appropriate number of copies has been produced, a button is pushed and the second form begins to run.

Zero makeready. Total "bad" copies per form change: 25. Amazing . . . and technology feasible on any press in operation. The only problem is that to retrofit magazine presses to run in that manner, you'd spend nearly the cost of a new press. Paper will have to become quite a bit more expensive before the payback period on such investments becomes reasonable.

Changes in gravure

So far, we've covered only what is happening in the web offset market. Will rotogravure printing see the same stopgap tools in use? Of course. But the recent activity in the gravure rumor circle centered around a dramatic, possible change . . . a heavy hardware change that is almost foreign to the printing industry.

The theory is that expensive, heavy gravure printing cylinders could be replaced by inexpensive, wraparound plates. This would produce minimal retrofitting problems, while significantly altering the cost of getting a job on press. The goal would be to make gravure more competitive in the shorter-run magazine and catalog field—say, from 500,000 to one million.

There are different opinions as to whether this will occur and, if it will, when. We'll share our opinion with you, and you can make your own projection.

With the ever increasing use of demographic, geographic, and psychographic magazine marketing, the gravure press would compete fully with web offset only if plates were as economical and easy to make. But that doesn't appear to be the projection for wrap-around gravure plates; rather, it seems that gravure might someday be competitive at about a half million impressions.

Right now, one million is commonly used to project where web and gravure collide. We feel that even if gravure does get competitive at 500,000, by that time the typical magazine product will itself be so fragmented (with various and numerous editions) that constant plate changes will be necessary . . . for consumer magazines, possibly every 10,000 impressions or so.

If the wrap-around miracle doesn't occur at all, we still see potential problems for the gravure segment of the printing business. Distribution costs alone could force even the gravure-oriented publishers to print in plants scattered across the country. Edition A will be printed in Region A, Edition B in Region B, etc.

Advances in the prep area will make it easier to work with multiple plants (send the electronically stored magazine to five printers rather than one), and the lower makeready costs will make it more economical.

These factors—the need for more economical distribution, the need for lower paper waste, and the need for economical plate changes for regionals—could mean an ever-decreasing market for gravure (rather than the immense growth we've all read about). And without a surefire guarantee that the gravure market is growing, printers will be reluctant to expand in that area.

Changes in the bindery

If offset printing is developing the tools for the publisher who needs many versions of a single product, the bindery will have to follow suit. Again, the equipment is off the drawing board and in production . . . but to our knowledge, only at R.R. Donnelley & Sons. Several Denver businessmen have recently formed a company to produce a similar machine, and if they don't get rolling, other companies surely will.

How will automated, "personalized" binding meld with other changes? Another peek at the future: Your circulation manager waits until the last minute to freeze the mailing list for a given issue. He accesses the bindery computer and transmits each subscriber's name directly to the printer. Each name is coded with the particular geo-demo-psychographic information used by the magazine.

The bindery computer drives both the ink-jet addressor and the mechanical arms which select the appropriate sections of the magazine for each individual reader.

Since there is no set limit on how many editions you could offer, this equipment does open the door to a truly personalized magazine. The flying farmer who likes to jog will, quite possibly, get a single magazine loaded with articles and advertising directed specifically at fleet-of-foot aviating agriculturists.

Again, production will feed back into total publication operation. Since small publishers will not be in a position to expand editorially—into jogging, flying, etc.—production options will lead to increased merger activity. Huge publishing corporations or co-operatives will be the likely result. Editorial may have to be changed to reflect markets that were never penetrated before. There will, for sure, be many problems and opportunities for small magazines in the process.

The potential of the individualized magazine cannot be overlooked. The easiest way to save paper is to send the reader only the information wanted or desired, and not 50 pages of advertising/editorial that will be overlooked. Yes, marketing and ad sales will have new offerings as a result of bindery automation and selectivity, but the real importance of this production option is that it puts a big hammer in the hand of the publisher who must conserve paper (all publishers). While the presses will be chewing less of it to pieces, the publisher will be tossing less of it to the wrong reader.

As the individual magazine becomes more popular, what will happen to newsstand sales? Again, production techniques may dramatically alter marketing techniques. The supermarket rack cannot possibly offer 72 versions of *TV Guide* . . . yet, advertisers would have more than 72 to choose from if the magazine were sold only by subscription.

Will consumer advertising without psychographic breakouts become highly ineffective on a per-dollar basis compared to advertising in the individualized magazine? If so, will publishers create rates that will make selective advertising effective, but expensive? The picture gets fuzzier each time a new variable is added. Now is the time to ask the questions, though, because these options are on the horizon.

How soon you'll have the options is a tricky question. Printers know that ink-jet labeling and computer control are in their future, and they know the equipment is available. There is potential for speed, economy, and new markets, yet few printers have the equipment on order.

As the representative of one major printer put it, "What we need is someone to tell the publishers what this equipment will do for them. We'd be expanding tomorrow if we didn't face the problem of convincing our customers to use the new processes."

For example, it was hard to convince art directors that the Universal Product Code was a flashy cover design element. Now, just a few years after we shoved it down their gullets, we come back and ask them to design a nice white area on the cover where we will ink-jet the name of the subscriber. Then off to the circulation manager to do some additional convincing . . . that we now need a mag tape in the bindery rather than hundreds of pounds of paper.

If you step back, you'll agree that these transition problems are slight. The equipment would be available if publishers would demand it, prepare for it, and use it.

Some of the changes discussed here are powerful enough to alter the course of publishing. Others will simply allow it to exist in economically troubled times. But changes are coming fast and furious, large and small. Publishers themselves will have to become keenly aware of production options. And production directors will need a continuing educational program of a broad scope, covering everything from personnel management to computer operations to the mechanics of reproduction itself.

For those who haven't taken "Computer 101," your days could well be numbered. When that hot-shot kid graduates from technical school—with double associate degrees in printing and computer programming—you may suddenly find yourself answering to a rookie.

Test your production I.Q.
By Jeffery R. Parnau

Everybody likes quizzes, right? Maybe not everybody . . . but certainly enough of you are quiz addicts to warrant this month's column, which is based on the following 10 questions.

Note, however, that this particular quiz has a rather odd scoring system. If you get any one of the 10 questions wrong, you flunk. Worse yet, we can't publish the answers to the questions . . . because they differ according to each publisher's circumstances. Worst of all, if you flunk the quiz, you are running the risk of spending—or shall I say wasting—a considerable amount of your magazine's money.

With that introduction out of the way, sharpen your pencil and go to it. (By the way, this test is limited to those who have their magazines produced on web presses.)

The quiz

(1) What is the cutoff on the press you use most often in printing your magazine?

(2) What is the width of the rolls of paper used to produce your job?

(3) How much do you spend for ink on the average issue of your publication?

(4) How are your ink and paper billed to you?

(5) Are your plates burned from positives or negatives?

(6) How does the answer to question (5) affect your alteration costs?

(7) What is the speed of the press you use most often?

(8) Under which conditions would you choose to have a job run on a 50"-wide press?

(9) When can a split fountain eliminate the need to run an additional printing unit?

(10) How many pounds of paper does your printer consume for makereadies, and does the figure change from issue to issue?

Evaluating your answers

Did you have answers to all 10 questions? How certain are you about your responses? The sad fact is, many publishing executives are not technically advanced to the point that they understand either the importance of basic printing knowledge or the amount of money they might be losing. They simply do not pay enough attention to the areas discussed in the above 10 questions.

Let's briefly review some logical answers. To do that, I will assume that I am the publisher of a 250,000-circulation monthly magazine. Your answers, of course, will be different, depending on your own circumstances, including circulation, frequency, and a variety of other variables.

(1) The press cutoff dictates the amount of paper—in linear inches —used during each revolution of the printing plate. My sample answer here is that because I trim my magazine at 10⁷/₈" in height, I use a press with a 22¾" cutoff. The next common press would have a 23⁹/₁₆" cutoff, which would automatically waste about 3½ percent of the paper used to produce my work. That would translate into approximately 2 percent of my sample magazine's total annual gross income. Big bucks, in some cases.

(2) I use 34¼" in producing this sample magazine. They allow an 8¼" book width, based on my printer's specifications. I could easily order 34½" rolls by mistake (or my printer could be using that stock roll width for a variety of magazines with wider trims). Using the wider roll would needlessly waste my money.

(3) My ink bill is $4,230. Yours might be higher or lower, depending on the amount of color used in your product, along with the total page count.

(4) My ink and paper are billed on an actual basis, plus a 5 percent handling fee collected by my printer. In both questions three and four, I could easily forget about monitoring such details. Trouble is, I would be putting 55 percent of my print/paper bills in the dark, never knowing whether I was paying too much.

(5) My plates are burned from negatives. This is because my printer offers both, but my press run is short enough to be handled by the negative acting plates, which are less expensive.

(6) My alteration costs are quite inexpensive, due to the fact that I use negative-acting plates. If I were using

the positive type, by the time I saw proofs, the entire magazine would be in one-piece positive form, created from the original negatives. An alteration at that time may cause the printer to virtually start from scratch in creating the new final film.

(7) The press I use most often runs at 28,000 impressions per hour. That is up to 10,000 impressions per hour faster than some of the equipment my sample magazine might run on. Of course, the faster the press, the lower the labor cost to run it, and the better deal I get on the final invoice.

(8) I would have my job estimated on a 50″-wide press—rather than its current 38″-wide press—if it were changed to a weekly magazine, or if its circulation doubled. These factors would vary, depending again on your particular needs, size, etc.

(9) In my case, a split fountain can always save me money over adding another printing unit. But the reason is that I have limited my use of process color pages, and I split fountains only on those color forms which allow it without harming the balance of the printing signature.

(10) My printer uses approximately 1,000 pounds in making ready the average press signature. This factor can vary widely, depending on whether the printing signature is black-and-white or full color, whether more than one web is running on the press, and many other variables. Naturally, I pay for this waste . . . and I am happy to see the figure falling steadily. That's because my printer is investing in automated press controls, which reduce the amount of paper spoiled during the makeready.

Cheating on the test?

Well, there you have it. I scored 100 percent with my sample magazine. I cheated, of course. I knew what the questions were, and had plenty of time to think about the answers. I also wouldn't have asked myself anything I didn't already know.

But what about you? If you didn't have a ready answer for each question, you might also be cheating: cheating yourself out of 5- to 25 percent of your annual expenditures for printing, paper, ink, and prep work.

Unfortunately, thousands of publishers across the country are doing just that. Here is the sad predicament:

The publisher neither knows, nor cares to know, all the gory technical details involved in spending the minimum printer dollar to get the maximum result.

So he or she hires a production manager . . . but the production person has nobody to talk to, no formal method of learning the ropes. On top of that, production managers are not paid excessively in this business. My personal estimate of the average annual salary is $22,000 per year. And that salary is never augmented by the person's potential to save the company 5- to 25 percent of its most notorious expenses: printing, paper, and ink.

So while the publisher hasn't the time to learn the technical ropes, the production manager isn't given any incentive to do so. On the contrary, saving money can require some technical risk-taking. The production person has nothing to gain if he wins . . . but his job to lose if he fails. The average production manager is unfortunately relegated to the position of maintaining whatever the company happened to be doing when he arrived on the scene.

A sad situation, to be sure. And I'm afraid there is only one solution. Publishing executives will have to learn more about production in order to evaluate both their employees and their printing expenses.

Where do you learn about production? The same places your production manager does. Read the printing magazines, read FOLIO, attend seminars, get involved. It's important. Production finesse may well be the most significant factor in deciding the fate of your magazine.

And don't allow yourself to slip into that comfortable position of not knowing or caring about technicalities, simply because you can afford to make mistakes. The economy isn't getting dramatically better, so far as I can see. Even 2 percent of your annual gross—kept in your corporate pocket—might give you a competitive edge.

The fine art of soliciting printers' bids

By Bert Paolucci

If you are fortunate enough to survive as a publisher for a sufficient period of time, you will eventually be faced with the decision of whether or not to change printers. This prospect conjures up visions of printing salespeople stalking your every move, mountains of paperwork as proposals come in and the seemingly impossible task of placing all the bids on the same footing to perform an accurate evaluation.

While this process is traumatic for all concerned (the editorial staff, which has established comfortable operating procedures; production, on whose shoulders most of the evaluation work must fall; traffic, circulation, business office, ad sales, all of whom have entrenched work habits), it can be made a little less so with some advance planning.

The decision to solicit printing bids can arise for many different reasons. Your current printing contract may be about to expire. Perhaps you have acquired several publications which are produced in different printing plants and you feel that there are economic advantages to consolidating your production under one roof. You may want to change printing processes (e.g., from letterpress to gravure) or use new technology that is available elsewhere. Or you may be unhappy with your current printer's quality and/or service. In today's economy, it is not unlikely that you may be forced to look for a new printer since your current one is about to go out of business. Or you may think that you've been out of touch with the market and that it would be wise to check going market prices.

So you start grappling with the mechanics of how to go about soliciting printing bids. This is an activity which most publishers engage in only infrequently, since the majority of publication contracts are long-term, three to five years on the average. Consequently, the publisher has no organization or system set up to solicit bids efficiently (unless you are a Time Inc. or McGraw-Hill with a sizable production staff). Typically this additional work is piled onto an already burdened production staff whose primary concern is to get out a magazine.

Unfortunately, no one has yet designed a standard bid sheet which would have universal applicability to all publishers regardless of size and complexity. Any attempt to construct such an all-inclusive format would have to run several dozen pages and would be as readable as a Chinese anagram.

There are, however, some broad guidelines which can be set down to help publishers convey the proper input to the printers and to get in return the proper information for a valid cost comparison. Of course, these guidelines must be adapted to suit each individual situation.

Establishing Goals

The publisher's goals in this process should be:

1. To obtain a representative cross-section of competitive bids for the work.

2. To make sure that all bids are on an equal basis for comparison with current costs and with other bidders.

In order to avoid wasted effort later on when the bids come in, the publisher must do some homework to set up the proper specifications. It is not enough simply to list the details of how the publication is currently being put together; the publisher also looks at the long-range production needs for at least the proposed term of the contract—three years, five years or whatever. It is important for the printer to know the forecasted growth in pages, print order, color usage. The publisher must estimate the company's future involvement in new technology such as in-house composition, bindery innovation, use of ultra-violet inks, etc.

Preparing Specifications

After forecasting the magazine's future needs, the publisher should prepare a set of specifications which includes the following items:

• *Volume of work*—frequency of issue, current and projected print orders, average number of pages.

• *Composition*—type faces and sizes, type page size, column format.

• *Preparatory work*—state whether printer is to prepare mechanicals, make halftones, strip elements into position or will be supplied film from publisher.

• *Presswork*—state which printing process is required (letterpress, offset, gravure), whether sheetfed or web.

• *Paper stock*—state type of stock, basis weight, roll sizes, whether publisher supplies or buys from printer.

• *Furnished inserts*—how many and what kind, size, weight, etc.

• *Finishing*—type of binding (perfect, saddle-stitched, side-wire), final trim size, labelled or wrapped.

• *Delivery*—how to prepare copies for newsstand distribution and subscriber mailing.

• *Production schedule*—essential dates for a year's issues should be stated, i.e., ad closings, editorial closings, page proofs to publisher, print order and issue break-up to printer, on-press, start binding, start shipping, finish shipping, on-sale dates.

Select an Average Issue

The next step is to choose an average issue which fairly represents the way the book is normally made up. Use care in selecting the issue, since a too-complicated issue will slow down the bids, and a too-simple one may not provide a valid cost comparison. Prepare a package for each bidder containing:

    1. A copy of the selected issue.

    2. Imposition sheets for the forms in the issue.

    3. A copy of the actual printer's invoice for the issue with all price information blanked out but with units intact.

    4. Newsstand galleys and a breakdown of subscriber copies by SCF numbers for estimating distribution costs. The weight of a single copy and the percentage of advertising in the issue should be stated.

    By providing every bidder with the identical data on which to base his or her proposal, you have theoretically laid the groundwork for receiving directly comparable proposals. In actual practice, it never works out that well, but many time-consuming discrepancies will have been avoided.

Tell the Bidders What You Want

    Along with the specifications and sample issue packet, you should send a covering letter clearly stating the points you expect the printer to cover in the proposal. In addition, the letter should set a realistic deadline for submission of bids and set forth the desired contract term.

    The printers should be asked specifically to provide:

    • A detailed "laundry list" of prices, including paper allowances and paper prices.

    • A sample invoice for the selected issue.

    • Estimated distribution costs for the selected issue.

    • An outline of the major contract terms (price escalations, rebates for printers' errors, etc.).

    • A production schedule showing closing dates, press dates, etc., as above.

    • An equipment list.

Evaluating the Bids

    I have personally seen many instances where publishers will receive different bids, match them up against one another on a cost per copy basis or other handy rule of thumb, pick the lowest bidder and then get shocked out of their swivel chairs when the first actual invoice comes in. These people did not take the time to audit the bids, equated apples with oranges and ended up being unpleasantly surprised.

    It's a sad fact that no matter how similar the information going out to the bidders is, the playback is *never* in a directly comparable format. This step is where the greatest effort must be applied. Without it you have a meaningless jumble of numbers.

    When the bids are received, a qualified person on the publisher's staff or an outside consultant must perform these steps on each proposal:

    1. Determine that the proposals meet all the specifications.

    2. Review all sample billings for accuracy:

    • Check against actual invoice to be sure all charges have been included.

    • Check against printers' price schedules to ensure correct prices have been used.

    • Check the extensions for arithmetical errors.

    • Put all bids on the same basis.

    3. Review form layouts on sample billings to see that the book has been made up the same as original layouts, or in another way acceptable to publisher.

    4. Review distribution cost studies for accuracy.

    5. Prepare a comparison chart for all bids on an annualized cost basis:

    • Use actual cost as the base, but adjust for current printing and paper prices.

    • Adjust all bids for printers' price escalation expected in the next 12 months.

    • Combine paper, printing and distribution costs for each bidder.

    6. Prepare a comparison chart for all bids over the projected span of the contract (i.e., three, four, five years); provide for annual price escalation.

    7. Prepare a comparison chart showing production

Your Own Staff—An Untapped Resource?

    Do you involve your production personnel as much as you should before, during and after you negotiate or renegotiate a printing contract? There's a good chance that your answer is "No"—and consequently you may not have obtained the best possible contract for your publication or publications.

    Before you start in the negotiation process the next time, consider the following:

    Do you consult your nuts-and-bolts production people before seeking bids and/or negotiating with a new printer? These people have more firsthand knowledge of and experience in producing your product than anyone else in your organization. It's quite possible—especially if you publish more than one magazine—that your $100-a-week production assistant can provide as much valuable input as your $25,000-a-year production manager or director. Far too often a contract is negotiated that puts publishers at a disadvantage simply because they don't have sufficient knowledge of the day-to-day operation of their own products.

    In renegotiating with the same printer, do you check with your production people first to find out current problems and their suggestions for changes? You can be assured that the printer has sought out information from his or her personnel who deal with your people on a day-to-day basis. Shouldn't you be as well-prepared?

    Have you negotiated a schedule that is as "acceptable" to your staff as it is to the printer? Far too often, schedules are set up that are fine for the printer but are totally unrealistic to the magazine staff. And nothing eats up the dollars faster than missing your schedule. Again, communications with your staff beforehand is the best way to avoid the problem.

    After the new printing contract is signed, do you make all applicable personnel aware of the provisions of the contract—for example, what is part of the basic page cost, what is extra, etc.? More money is wasted in the production of magazines simply because the staff is ignorant of the specifics of the contract, i.e., the cheapest and/or best way to do something. "I didn't know that" can be a costly slogan.

How Easy Is It to Change Printers?

After you have evaluated the bids for your work and have selected the successful bidder, the realization hits you that now you have to move out of the old and into the new printing plant. At first glance, the problems associated with moving seem formidable:

• Will the printer losing the business be cooperative?

• What will it cost to move?

• Will the staff support the decision or fight it?

• Will your distribution pattern out of the new plant be as efficient?

• If you're changing printing processes as well, will you get the right material for reproduction from your advertisers?

It should be reassuring to know that the statistics show most publishers do change printers when their contracts expire. My own personal experience with printing contracts that have expired during the last four years has been that only one-third renewed with the same printer; two-thirds of the magazines signed on with a new printer.

The very real problems associated with a move are not enough to deter the majority of publishers from switching printers. In fact, the problems mentioned above are often resolved with a minimum of disruption.

Will the outgoing printer cooperate? Yes; the printer will want the opportunity to get the work back again in the future and will not do anything to prejudice his or her chances. Major publication printers have always behaved responsibly. The instances in which the outgoing printer has been obstructionist are few and far between.

What will it cost to move? There are some out-of-pocket costs involved for the publisher—increased travel, more communications expense, transferring paper inventory owned by the publisher. Good planning should hold these to a minimum. In no case should these one-time expenses be enough to overcome the benefits of moving.

Will the staff support the decision or fight it? You must assume that inertia will make the majority of the staff resist the move. Why should they be happy about taking on additional work, learning new ways to do things, breaking old relationships? A typical reaction is, "I've spent enough of my 25 years in publishing breaking in new printers!" To help smooth the way it is important to consult the people who routinely work with the printer to get their ideas on how the printer-publisher relationship can be improved. (Incidentally, it's not a bad idea to get input from these nuts-and-bolts people prior to soliciting bids from printers.) The legitimate criticisms of the staff must be listened to and accommodations made whenever possible; the more subjective gripes will eventually subside as the staff comes to grips with reality, especially in the current employment climate.

Can you set up an efficient distribution plan out of the new plant? Much of the distribution groundwork should have been done at the time the printer submitted a proposal; the details should be worked out between your traffic manager and the printer's shipping department. Traffic operations can be fine-tuned as the work progresses.

Can you get the correct material from advertisers if you're changing printing processes? Your new printer can be most helpful here in working with your advertising production department. After a period of familiarization, the problems in this area should be overcome by good printer-publisher-advertiser liaison.

In short, there are problems associated with moving; but these are manageable. You don't have to look far for examples of successful moves; but I cannot think of a single instance in which a publisher has been prevented from switching printers because of his or her own staff's or the outgoing printer's actions.—*Bert Paolucci.*

---

schedule dates.

Qualitative Factors

At this point you have tabulated the bids in a meaningful way and are able to compare them all, confident that they are on the same basis. The economic considerations, however, should not be the sole criteria in selecting a printer. Often the lowest bidder is ruled out on the basis of one or more of the other factors that should be considered, such as:

• Quality of workmanship
• Service
• Labor stability
• Financial stability
• Quality of management.

Unlike the cost figures, these factors cannot be weighed quantitatively but are based on a composite of your own past experience and industry gossip. A few words of caution: The printing industry is not the static business it once was. Many publication printers have been acquired by conglomerates which have supplied new investment capital and brought in new management teams. The image of two or three years ago may no longer be accurate

regarding a specific printer. You will be well advised to check with your counterparts at other publishing houses who are currently doing work in those plants bidding on your publication.

At the outset, it was postulated that this article could only cover broad guidelines for publishers to follow in soliciting bids and that these guidelines must be adapted to suit each publication. There should be no misunderstanding about the complexity of this area and I hope the process has not been made to seem deceptively simple.

Publishers who are considering soliciting printing bids should have a knowledgeable production person on their staff who can act as coordinator for the project. Publishers without such expertise on their staff are advised to look outside for help among the growing number of qualified consultants in the publication production field. Choosing a printer is one of the most important decisions a publisher must make. A wrong choice can mean long years of aggravation. The correct choice can help you meet your long range goals for growth and profitability by enabling you to offer a high-quality, competitively priced product.

Negotiating your printing contract: How to control escalation

By Edward L. Smith and Jeffery R. Parnau

Publishers who shrug off the price escalation provisions in their printing contracts as inevitable are playing a very dangerous game. A publisher's largest expense is the cost of producing his magazine. (A recent Magazine Publishers Association survey found that publishers pay out 35 percent of their revenues to produce their magazines.) If the price escalation clauses in his printing contract are not circumscribed very carefully, an unforeseen rise in printing costs could severely cut into or even wipe out his company's profits.

When a publisher signs a printing contract, he knows exactly what the printer's prices are. However, since no printer can freeze his prices for any extended time and expect to survive, virtually every printing contract permits the printer to increase those prices during the term of the contract.

Thus, negotiating the prices in a new printing contract is only half the battle for a publisher. Equally important, he must try to limit the price increases the printer can charge during the term of the contract. How well he succeeds depends not only on his negotiating skill but also on his bargaining strength. Other things being equal, a publisher can demand better terms if he orders 500,000 copies a week than if he orders only 150,000 copies a month. But every publisher, large or small, should make the effort.

To limit price escalation, a publisher needs answers to three questions:

1. What cost increases can the printer pass on to the publisher?

2. How often can the printer increase his prices to the publisher?

3. How can the publisher verify the accuracy of the printer's price increases?

1. *What cost increases can the printer pass on?*

Keep in mind at the outset that every price is made up of two elements: the printer's costs and his profits. A price increase during the term of a printing contract should reimburse the printer only for his increased *costs*. It should not increase his profits.

Furthermore, a price increase should not reimburse the printer for increases in his indirect costs, such as higher real estate taxes on his plant, or other overhead. He should be reimbursed only for increases in his direct costs—the specific expenses he incurs while performing your work.

What are a printer's direct costs? There are three kinds: 1) labor costs, such as wages and fringe benefits to pressmen; 2) the cost of materials, such as printing plates, film, stitching wire; and 3) utilities costs, such as oil, gas, electricity. (See accompanying sidebar for a discussion of paper and ink prices.)

Every price charged by the printer includes some, if not all, of these costs. And, if any of these costs to the

printer is increased, under price escalation, the prices he charges will be increased in turn.

How, then, should a contract provide for price escalation?

There are two basic ways in which a contract can protect a publisher by limiting price escalation: 1) increase each price separately, and 2) increase all prices by a flat percentage.

By far the most accurate way to pass on increases in direct costs is by increasing each price separately. Price escalation provisions in most printers' form contracts are too broad and imprecise. They leave too many questions and openings for misunderstanding. For instance, one printer's contract reads:

Beginning with the Adjustment Date and annually thereafter prices shall be adjusted to reflect changes in Printer's labor, material and related costs.

How are the prices to be "adjusted to reflect changes"? What is meant by "labor, material and related costs"? How much of each price is the cost of labor, how much the cost of material, and how much the cost of utilities? The contract does not say.

To protect a publisher, the contract should describe each cost separately and in detail. For instance:

Labor Costs consist of Printer's costs of: (a) employee compensation and direct benefits, and (b) state and federal social security taxes and other taxes directly related to labor utilization.

Material Costs consist of Printer's costs of film, plates, stripping supplies, chemicals, solvents, press blankets and packing, press rollers, tapes and adhesives, stitching wire, bundling material, skids and pallets, steel strapping and packaging materials for the work.

Utility Costs consist of Printer's aggregate cost for oil and gas, electricity and sewer and water (or any substitute) at the Plant.

In addition, the price schedule should list the cost of labor, the cost of materials, and the cost of utilities in each price. (See Example I.)

With this kind of price schedule, any increase in the printer's direct costs can be passed on accurately. Using Example I, if the cost of labor goes up 10 percent, the labor price for press plates will increase by $5 (10 percent x $50.02=$5). Thus, the total price for press plates will increase by $5, from $75 to $80.

While breaking out the direct costs in each price is the most accurate way to pass on increases in those costs, this method may be too complicated for a small contract. In that case, two simpler—though less satisfactory—alternatives may be used. Both methods increase all prices across the board by an agreed-upon percentage.

Flat percentage increase

One method is simply to agree that all prices will be increased by a flat X percent a year. In this situation,

Example I

Work	Total Price	Labor in Price	Materials in Price	Utilities in Price
Press Plates, Each	$75.00	$50.02	$17.48	$0.22
Running 8's	3.90	2.56	0.17	0.23

both printer and publisher are shooting craps, however, since neither can predict whether X percent will in fact turn out to be the printer's actual increase in direct costs during the year. Obviously, it may be more or it may be less.

The other alternative is to agree that all prices will be increased by part of the percentage increase in the cost-of-living index (or some other economic indicator) each year. This method at least bears some relationship to the printer's direct costs, because most of the increases in direct costs are due to labor increases—which in turn are often tied to the cost of living.

But not all increases in an economic index should be passed along. (For instance, the cost of living index includes increases in the prices people pay when they buy houses.) Realistically, only part of any increase—or maybe none at all—has any bearing on the printer's own increased costs.

Of course, price escalation provisions can combine methods. A publisher may be able to negotiate a provision that prices will be increased by actual increases in labor, material and utilities costs while stipulating that in no event shall the total increase in any price exceed X percent in any contract year.

2. *How often can the printer increase his prices?*

Pinpointing direct costs and laying out the method for increasing prices are only part of the answer to controlling price escalation. The publisher must also try to limit the frequency of price increases. Unless prices are frozen for some period of time, say a year, a publisher can find himself the constant target of price increases.

Here, too, form contracts will probably not solve the problem for the publisher. One such contract reads this way:

If there should be an increase or decrease in the cost of such items during the term of this contract, such prices shall be increased or decreased proportionately, as the case may be, to reflect such changes in costs effective as of dates of such changes.

The phrase "effective as of dates of such changes" allows constant increases. A publisher needs protection against them.

If the contract is for a year or less, the printer may agree to freeze all prices except perhaps labor and paper. If the contract is for more than a year, the publisher may negotiate a one-year freeze on all prices and then increases only once a year thereafter.

The following provision, for example, covers this situation:

None of the prices set forth in the Price Schedule shall be changed prior to January 1, 1982. Thereafter, the prices may be increased or decreased, in accordance with this section, for each 12-month period commencing January 1 during the term of the agreement (each such period shall be called a "Contract Year").

Effective each January 1 during the term of this agreement (commencing January 1, 1982), the Component for Labor Costs, the Component for Material Costs, and

Dealing with paper and ink costs

Some printing costs—notably the cost of paper and ink—have been rising so rapidly that, when the printer supplies these items to the publisher, their costs are often broken out separately from the other prices for the work.

Paper costs are particularly important to the printer. Approximately half his gross income pays for paper and other materials, far more proportionately than most other businesses pay. If a printer's costs for paper go up, the increases can easily slice through his profits unless he charges his customers more for that paper immediately. So printers try to pass on increased paper costs to publishers as quickly as they can.

Some publishers try to get a guarantee that the price for paper will be frozen for a specified period of time. If they get it, though, that kind of guarantee by a printer will not be what it seems. Printers *must* pass on their increased costs for paper; such costs are simply too large an expense to ignore. So, the printer who guarantees a price for a year simply anticipates all increases for that year, averages them out, prorates them, and builds them right into the price he charges on day one.

Ink costs are also increasing at a fast rate. Because ink is a petrochemical product, its cost is climbing as did gasoline prices a few years back. (Less than 10 years ago,

ink was almost an incidental expense—nobody thought twice about it—unlike paper which has always been relatively expensive.)

It makes sense, then, to break these significant variables out of the prices for the work and treat their increases in separate price escalation provisions.

Here, too, however, the printer's form agreement usually fails to protect the publisher in controlling price escalation. One such provision reads:

Rate includes handling, warehousing, investment and markup. Prices are subject to change with increases and decreases from supplier.

Since this provision does not specify what any of these changes amounts to, the printer has virtually a free hand in setting the prices he will charge.

Far more preferable is this kind of provision:

It is anticipated that Printer will provide all paper used to produce the Work, but Publisher may, by notice to Printer, elect to furnish paper itself at specifications not materially different from Printer's paper specifications. If Printer provides paper, Publisher shall pay Printer 105 percent of the invoice cost of such paper.

The same kind of provision can be applied to purchases of ink.

the Component for Utilities Costs in each price (as previously adjusted) shall each be increased or decreased, as the case may be, to reflect the net increase or decrease in the Labor Costs, Material Costs and Utilities Costs, respectively, for the Work since the preceding January 1.

3. How can cost increases be verified?

Even with this mechanism for controlling the frequency of price increases, you still need additional protection. Without questioning the printer's good faith, you need the right to verify the basis for his price increases. As the old saying goes, "Trust your mother but cut the cards anyway."

Again, most printers' form contracts provide no help for the publisher's problem. Since most do not provide for any verification at all, the publisher must, if he agrees to that contract, simply accept as accurate the price increases submitted to him.

Although a publisher should have the right to have his own accountant or other representative review the printer's records to verify the accuracy of all price increases, not all printers are willing to open their books to customers, even for this limited purpose. In that case, the publisher should try to have the *printer's* accountant certify their accuracy to the publisher. Furthermore, the publisher can argue that the printer should bear the expense of this task since he has refused to open his books to the publisher's own accountant.

This kind of provision covers certification by the printer's accountant:

Within 60 days after any notice by Printer to Publisher of a price adjustment under this agreement, Publisher may elect, by notice to Printer, to have such price adjustment verified by a certified public accounting firm selected by Printer, at Printer's expense. Such accounting firm will certify to Publisher within 90 days of such price adjustment (or, if later, within 90 days after receipt of notice of Publisher's request) that: Based upon its examination, made in accordance with generally accepted auditing standards, of Printer's calculations of all increases or decreases in the Components of the prices hereunder, in its opinion: The price adjustment has been made in accordance with this section (of the contract) and is the result of changes in employee compensation and direct benefits as evidenced by labor contracts and payroll and other applicable records; and changes in the costs of materials, supplies, energy and other costs as evidenced by suppliers' and vendors' contracts, invoices and statements.

Price escalation is a fact of publishing life. If unchecked, it can cut deeply into or even eliminate your profits in the course of your printing contract.

However, if your contract defines the kinds of cost increases your printer can pass on, if it limits the frequency of those increases, and if it lets you verify the accuracy of those increases, you can limit price escalation and defuse its potentially explosive effect on your profits.

"Lowball" bidding

By Jeffery R. Parnau

Ever since John Dean advised his boss that there was a "cancer in the White House," cancers seem to have popped up everywhere. Whenever a malevolent activity silently spreads throughout an organization, it is labeled with this catch-all noun.

What the hell, the printing industry is no exception, and we might as well talk about its peculiar disease: the cancer of deathbed price cutting.

Historically, the printing and publishing industries reflect national economic trends. If the overall picture is bleak, the percentages of rise and fall in our joint industries get into decimal-point compatibility. It's no surprise, then, that the business of printed communication is hotly competitive at this time.

In many parts of the country, print shops are collapsing, merging, or filing an assortment of bankruptcy papers. At least one major printer has closed shop entirely; another has been sold off. This kind of activity—from the tiny shops right up through the big ten—cannot be taken lightly.

Nor can it be given an instant cure: The long-term health of the publishing/printing field depends upon how the economy in general performs.

What we have, then, isn't really a problem—just a situation. A situation we'd all rather not be in, of course, but the current state of things nonetheless.

What are the effects? They are rather easy to predict. When a printing company fails, it does so with a second wind . . . and maybe a third and a fourth. Printers die with their ink-smeared boots on, and they go down kicking. Worse yet, in their final battles, they fight *dirty*.

Here's the picture.

For any of a number of reasons, a printer gets into trouble. Perhaps management was too dependent on a single account that evaporated. Or perhaps equipment purchases blindly followed historical trends while the market was shrinking.

The only short-term solution is to bring in new business. But now, it gets a bit more complex.

If this printer's problems were in any way triggered by a slow economy, the printer is not alone in his plight. Other printers—some healthy, some scrambling—are also on the prowl for new work.

You as a publisher might be pleased with the situation: a buyer's market. Because in a buyer's market, prices fall, and that's how our hypothetical printer is going to get your work. He will price it lower than all of your potential suppliers.

Just how does he go about doing this? Like this. Top management of the firm sits down and says, "Well, we can consider closing the plant . . . laying employees off . . . or getting something in here to keep the lights burning.

"True, if we price the job like that we won't make money. Matter of fact, we'll be running at a loss . . . but at least we'll be running. Then, when things pick up, we'll get back to normal."

Unfortunately, that last statement uses blind optimism to nobody's benefit.

Here's what happens next.

The healthy printer, who priced the job at normal rates, doesn't get the work. His company—if it suffers enough of these price-battle losses—will also begin to head for the brink.

Meanwhile, the panic-stricken lowballer gets the job, and runs more red ink than any of the other subtractive primaries. Because he is getting deeper into debt, he must continue to go after work at any expense, creating a financial spiral. We've all seen it happen.

On the home front, the customer is still pleased. Last year's expensive printing is being tackled, finally. The future looks a bit more pleasant, as profits will be up, costs down, etc., etc., etc.

The situation perpetuates itself until the eventual and inevitable catastrophe. The weak printer goes under, and all parties regroup.

The publisher now learns that his prices will take a sudden jump. (Unless, of course, he is approached by another printer in a panic.) The competitive printers get work which they probably should have had in the first place, and if they're not in dire trouble, they're still trying to recover from lost business.

The belly-up lithographer leaves a trail of unpaid paper bills, which will eventually be reflected by higher prices from the mills.

And who gained from the episode? The victories are few. A handful of the printer's employees got to work a little longer. The publisher got a slight—but temporary and artificial—price break.

It's my opinion that the industry would be better off without such scenes. True, they're not entirely within the publisher's control, but there is something you can do.

Ask for references. Not just the references of happy customers, which any printer can give you by the dozen, but other critical checks such as standard bank references and leasing companies. Most important of all, check the printer's paper mills. If the printer isn't cutting it with the mills, he's short for the reproduction scene.

If, on the other hand, you choose or are forced to deal with the deathbed price cutters, do so with the anticipation of moving your printing more often than necessary. And do so with the hope that, at some mythical time in the future, everything will work out.

'No' negotiating

By Jeffery R. Parnau

After months of negotiating, threatening, pleading, and calmly discussing the problem, the distraught publisher was still upset that costs for his renegotiated printing contract were 12 percent to 18 percent over the prior year.

"What are you going to do about it?" I asked.

"I've done about all I can," he replied. "I guess I'll just have to live with it."

Had he really done all he could, however?

Production is a lot of things: quality, scheduling, equipment, service. But it is, above all else, *money*. It is the area where publishers spend *most* of their hard-earned greenbacks. Production is purchasing.

Many publishers don't understand one of the fundamentals of buying printing: At the beginning of the game, the buyer has all the money. Thus, the buyer has initial control . . . but only if he or she chooses to exercise it. The unhappy publisher mentioned above is not, for whatever reason, using the ultimate tool of purchasing: The option of saying "no."

In these turbulent economic times, saying "no" could be a valuable tool for the printing industry. Consider, for example, the notorious COLA clauses—the feared Cost Of Living Adjustment built into many contracts between printers and unions.

Many printers are being hurt badly by COLA, which gives their employees non-specified raises (on top of regularly negotiated wage increases) indexed to the local inflation rate. In some cases, COLA increases (coupled with flat wage increases) have barreled through at more than $2 per hour in a year's time.

You can hardly condemn printing management for the situation. The economics of subsistence itself have changed, and laborers will do all they can to insure a decent standard of living. So when the increases come through, the printer has little choice but to pass the escalation in costs on to customers. The account might stay at the same printer for years, but with the customer's ever-decreasing enthusiasm.

What happens, though, when the buyer issues a flat "no" to skyrocketing costs? Or even a modified "no"? True, inflation is in the double-digit category . . . but that doesn't necessarily translate into the same increase for printing purchasers.

There are many variables which can soften that blow, such as increased productivity, decreased waste, competition, shorter printing contracts, labor-cost ceilings, and options to move a portion of the printing to a more economical plant.

Most of these options can (or must) be initiated by the buyer. The point, though, isn't to threaten printers with countless scare tactics. You could rattle off a dozen options over lunch, and get little more for your efforts than dessert.

The point is: Do something. Get serious. Make it clear that you are in the process of softening cost increases by exploring cost control, and that you are aggressively taking steps in that direction.

From your standpoint, controlling costs is not a devious, get-even-with-the-printer vendetta. But from the printer's side, such activity might well look like an economic threat: The buyer is considering moving some or all of the work, in order to take advantage of equipment or geography. (The printer up the road, for example, might be a few years ahead in waste-control devices.) Furthermore, other buyers might soon do the same.

The printer faced with this dilemma must act to stop an exodus, and he must act either at the bargaining table (where the question of corporate viability is put to the labor representatives) or in the shop (with increases in productivity, reduced spoilage, equipment modifications).

If all publishers were uniformly aggressive in cost control, all printers would naturally respond to the market. To survive, printers would have to become more productive, more competitive, while not allowing uncontrolled labor increases to destroy a healthy plant (which would do no good for either buyers or sellers).

Let's examine a few aggressive steps our distraught publisher might have taken.

Short-term contracts

Years ago, a printing contract could be negotiated which would, in effect, control costs for a period of time. The picture has changed dramatically. A typical contract must now include clauses for all types of material cost increases, energy increases or surcharges, and unpredictable labor-cost increases.

The publisher who prefers to continue dealing with a given printer is faced with a problem. He wants to keep the printing at the plant, but he also wants the freedom to move the work should increases become a real economic threat.

Why not, then, consider having your cake and munching on it too? A short-term contract lets the printer know that you intend to deal with him, but that you also need the freedom to reevaluate the picture on an annual basis. True, neither party will have the comfort of definitely knowing where the job will be in 12 months. On the other hand, both parties will know that cost control isn't something to be looked at every few years.

A one-year contract—automatically renewable unless notice is given—is a statement in itself.

For small publications, having any contract at all might be going overboard. Smaller jobs are easier to place, and the market is often more competitive. Rather than looking for a long-term relationship with a printer, the smaller publication might best be printed on a purchase-order basis. Should costs rise, there is always the option of checking, shopping, and moving if necessary.

Even five years ago, you could be successful in negotiating a flat ceiling on cost-of-labor increases. Now, it's virtually impossible (unless you want to work with, say, 18 percent). Labor increases, as specified in most contracts, are tied to the inflation rate of the area.

Labor ceilings

Such caps might still be somewhat useful in keeping prices from rising arbitrarily, or in allowing you to project maximum cost increases for the next few months. But in negotiating a contract at this time, it might be wiser to take labor caps a bit further: Use a specific indexed labor rate increase as cause for termination. In other words, if the cost of living rises at an exorbitant rate in the printer's town, you'd have the right to terminate the contract and take your printing to another city (with a more moderate inflation rate).

Keep in mind also that the methods of determining cost-of-living increases are under fire on all fronts. If your printer, for example, uses an index figure which includes housing costs, you've got some thinking to do. In one recent jump, housing costs accounted for 80 percent of a monthly inflation rate. Ink, paper and labor costs certainly have a limited relationship to such hikes . . . but without defining the index to be used, a publisher could find himself paying for houses rather than magazines.

For many publishers, the printer is relied upon for "total service," regardless of suitable equipment. The larger publishers have other ideas: They fragment their printing to get the best use of available machinery. A black-and-white section might be printed on a two-unit press, while the color portions are run on larger presses . . . possibly at another plant.

Split-plant printing is an option for all publishers, large and small. Are your simple forms running on four-color presses? If so, then in printers' lingo, you could be "dragging" units (not using the press to its full capability).

Insert cards are another area for investigation. While some printers will run insert cards on magazine-type presses, others will run them sheet-fed . . . or farm them out. And what about color separations and prep? Even though your printer may have in-house color-separation ability, you might be money ahead by going to a specialty shop for all your preparation work.

To ensure that you are running at full efficiency, have various segments of the product bid at outside plants. In addition, insert an option into the contract which allows you to remove a certain amount of the work (color, forms, inserts, etc.) from the main plant, even if you're not currently considering moving a chunk of the work. It not only allows you that freedom in the future, it also lets your printer know that you are ready and willing to move a part of the job should such a move become economically necessary.

If you do, in fact, find significant economies in moving a portion of the work, remember that coordinating a multi-plant production schedule requires cooperation from your printer. If your printer realizes that you are financially forced to make certain changes, he should be willing to help in the transition. But—if you project yourself as a vengeful, punishing buyer who will ruthlessly manipulate vendors, you'll be asking for (inviting) trouble.

The flat "No"

Finally, it does happen that the only option is to pack up the entire job and move to a more economical plant. At such times, honesty and firmness seem to be a nice blend: Be honest with your printer and explain the decision . . . and be firm enough to end a pleasant relationship, face the task of moving, and pull out. Your printer would not be able to keep you as a customer if he was literally losing money on your account. And if you are making errors in your production or purchasing, you are literally losing money. That's not healthy.

Prices are climbing at a ridiculous rate, true. But they needn't necessarily climb quite that quickly for individuals . . . or even in the printing industry itself. The actions of a single publisher will have an effect on his printer. And the actions of publishers as a whole will reverberate throughout the printing industry.

Tales of unsigned contracts
By Jeffery R. Parnau

During the FOLIO Face-to-Face seminars, I've often had the pleasure of working with Ed Smith—a publishing attorney—on the topic of printing contracts. One of the most commonly asked questions in these sessions is, "Why do I need a printing contract?"

This question has routinely taken a while to answer because there are many different reasons. During the past month, I have had the unfortunate opportunity to witness three separate cases that demonstrate quite clearly just how important a written agreement can be. If you're a publisher who's now working without a contract, or a vendor who doesn't demand one, this column may sober you up.

Let's start with the vendor's position. One of these cases involves a magazine prep shop (quite like the one I own, but larger); the other a printer.

No work to be done

First case: After a lengthy sales pitch, both the customer and the prep shop agreed on prices, delivery, quality, and all of the other variables. Although both agreed that a contract was the next and important step, their respective schedules suggested that they go directly into production and take care of the paperwork later. Work was scheduled to commence within two weeks.

Now, although the customer didn't know it, when they shook hands the vendor began planning a party. The owner needed one more key account, and this was it.

The work came in as scheduled but, for some reason, there was only about half of what was originally anticipated. The customer explained it easily enough, and the vendor assumed that things would pick up with the next issue.

The time for the next issue arrived. The issue didn't.

Finally, the prep shop owner called the customer and learned the news. The customer had taken certain activities in-house, and others to another vendor. They had no work for the shop.

Had a contract been signed, the vendor would at least have known that the customer fully intended to give him the work. If he had pressed the issue, he would have soon found out that no, the job wasn't coming in at all. And the poor prep manager wouldn't have hired that part-timer to help through the deadline crunch.

The prep shop lost money, time and momentum. What does it mean to you as a publisher? There's one more prep operation out there that won't consider *starting* a job without a contract. Don't be insulted if you run into the situation—and understand that one of your peers has made it a bit more difficult for you to try out a new source for prep.

Beware the spoken agreement

The second case involves another vendor—a printer. Again, the old carrot was dangling out in front; the numbers were agreed upon. But in this case, the relationship went well, without a contract, for nearly a year. Although the printer continually pressed the publisher for the signed version of their agreement, for one reason or another, the publisher just couldn't get around to it.

Meanwhile, the printer was nervous about the situation because, for this particular publisher, he needed more equipment: specifically, two more heavy-duty light tables to handle the stripping crunch, and a new film punch, in order to be compatible with the publisher's other printer. The price tag: $3,000.

The printer went ahead and invested, for two reasons. One, the publisher kept praising his work, stating that he intended to maintain their relationship. Two, they had a spoken agreement that if the relationship didn't work out, in no case would they cease working together without 45-days notice. That would have given the printer a small cushion with which to look for a replacement account.

One day, the production manager at the plant got a call from the publisher's production manager. They would be a week late with the next issue. A week later, another call: They were over their heads, and would be another week late. And 10 days later, the publisher himself called the president of the printing plant. They had selected another vendor. There would be no more work.

Add it up: The 45-day minimum notice wasn't given. Worse yet, the publisher stretched the printer out another three weeks before telling him that the job was already in production somewhere else. The publisher effectively gave notice 70 days late. But what the hell. There was no contract, so the publisher really didn't do anything wrong, right?

Just try to work without a contract with *that* printer. Just *try* to have a few sample issues done there before you sign the paperwork.

Sure, $3,000 isn't a lot of money to most printers. Sure, they plugged the work into their schedule and relaxed (for 70 days too long). That doesn't make the printer feel any better, though.

Cash in advance, please

Finally, let's talk about the third case ... about a publisher who got stung because of a contract oversight.

This publisher had a very healthy relationship with a printer for two years, producing a successful bimonthly magazine. But the relationship was gradually deteriorating: The printer wouldn't supply adequate reports on consuming the publisher's paper, and the quality of color work was sliding. In addition, although prices were not outrageous, they could easily be beaten by shops with better reputations.

So, the publisher decided to move the account. Although there was no contract, he thought it would only be decent to give the printer 60-days notice before he wanted to pull up stakes. As it happened, 60 days was right about the time an issue was to go to press.

The telegram arrived. The printer wanted the publisher to immediately send a draft for a disputed portion of an earlier invoice. Second, he wanted full payment for all of the prep work that had been completed on the issue in progress. And third, the printer wanted full payment for the printing, binding and mailing *before* he went to press with the issue. Cash in advance.

I worked with the publisher in resolving the problem, but because there was no contract, there wasn't a whole lot I could do. I advised him to pay the disputed invoice, pay for the prep work, and yank the magazine out like a bad tooth. If that printer wanted to play hardball, who's to say the issue wouldn't have suffered even worse quality—and late delivery—if we agreed to cash in advance.

I put the job elsewhere. I hope to hell I can find a way to nail the printer and drag his posterior into court, but I suspect it will all be chalked up as a lesson in publishing.

Why do *you* need a contract? There are more reasons. But for now, let it be known that if you don't have a prep contract, you may not get prep work. If you don't have a printing contract, you may not get printed. If you have a two-year-old handshake with your buddy, the printer—well, best of luck to you. And when you find out that four martinis won't let you forget that you don't have an issue coming off press, give me a call. You can use my shoulder.

Auditing your printer's agreement
By Bert Paolucci

Question: Should a publisher spend the money to audit a printer's price escalation agreement?

Answer: Probably, yes. The investment can be repaid several-fold over the life of a three- or five-year contract by eliminating misunderstandings in interpreting contract language, and assuring both parties that cost increases will be applied in a consistent manner.

Most long-term printing contracts provide for the printer to pass on cost increases over the term of the contract by raising prices. Most—but not all—printers will permit the publisher or an independent auditor to come in and audit the records supporting such price increases.

Based on my own experience in conducting such audits for publishers, I would recommend that publishers who are contractually permitted to audit price increases should do so, at least the first time around. This, of course, depends on the price escalation formula that is written into the contract.

The escalation formula is often a matter of negotiation. There are a number of different methods that can be used, ranging from a fixed percentage of increase to a completely unlimited pass-through of cost increases.

For our purposes, we might classify them into two broad categories: Those in which an audit can be useful and those in which an audit serves no purpose.

An audit will serve no purpose where:

1. Prices are fixed for the term of the contract;

2. Prices increase by a fixed percentage each year, regardless of the actual cost increases incurred.

An audit can perform a useful function in those cases where prices are adjusted as follows:

1. In relation to a U. S. government cost-of-living (or other) index;

2. Where cost increases "up to a maximum of _____ percent" get passed on;

3. Where the printer absorbs a portion of the actual increase but passes along the rest;

4. Where the printer passes on the entire amount of the cost increase.

What purpose can such an audit serve? First of all, it will assure both the publisher and the printer that the intent of the contract is being carried out properly. Contract language is often interpreted differently from its original intent by those putting it into actual practice.

Secondly, by setting up good practices in the beginning of a long-term contract, it can simplify future escalations and ensure that they are applied in a consistent manner.

Pressroom Costs—Labor & Fringes
Journeyman Rates

	Effective Dates	
	1-1-76	1-1-77
Basic Hourly Rates	$ 6.50	$ 7.15
Shift Premium	.15	.20
Total Hourly Rate	6.65	7.35
Total Labor Per Shift (7 hours)	46.55	51.45
Total Labor—Annual Rate (260 shifts)	$12,103.00	$13,377.00
Fringe Benefits—Annual Rate		
Holidays—9 days	419.00	463.00
Vacation—2 weeks	465.00	515.00
Unemployment Compensation:		
State: .5% of $4,200	21.00	42.00*
Federal: .5% of $4,200	21.00	21.00
F.I.C.A. (Social Security): 5.85% of $15,300	895.00	965.00**
Health Insurance	800.00	840.00
Workmen's Compensation (1%)	121.00	133.00
Pension ($1/shift)	260.00	260.00
	$ 3,002.00	$ 3,239.00
Total Labor & Fringes	$15,105.00	$16,616.00
Percentage Increase		10%
Percentage of Labor in Price		60%
Percentage to be Applied to Prices (10%x60%)		6.0%

New prices Effective 1-1-77:
* 1.0% of $4,200
** 5.85% of $16,500

The stakes are high. Take, for example, a $1 million annual printing contract which escalates at 5 percent per year. At the end of five years, instead of $5 million, the publisher will have paid out $5.5 million, or 10 percent more than the base cost, because of the compounding effect of the price increases. If an undetected error had been made in the original price escalation, its impact would have been doubled over the term of the contract.

What's involved in auditing a price increase? The simplest way to describe this is to follow through a hypothetical example.

A magazine publisher has a five-year contract with a printer. A clause in the contract regarding prices and price changes reads like this:

"The prices contained in the price schedule are based on salaries, wage scales, fringes, cost of materials and manning schedules as of January 1, 1976. If any of these cost elements increase or decrease during the term of this contract, then Printer is entitled to increase or decrease his prices starting on January 1, 1977, and continuing each January 1 thereafter. Such price changes will be computed in accordance with the procedures outlined in Exhibit XYZ.

"The Publisher has the right to examine all of the Printer's worksheets and records applicable to such price changes to establish that such price changes have been made in accordance with the procedures in Exhibit XYZ."

The key part of the clause is that the printer has based the prices on costs in effect on January 1, 1976. This is the base or starting point for computing future cost increases. The auditor should first verify that the base costs were, in fact, those in effect on the given date. The base costs are stated in the accompanying table. For expediency's sake, we'll look only at one wage scale in the pressroom; in actual practice, there would be a breakdown for each job category and a similar listing for the bindery.

The auditor can verify most of these costs by referring to the labor contract. Such items as base hourly wage, shift premium, vacation, holidays, health insurance and pension will normally be stated explicitly in the labor contract. The other cost factors, such as F.I.C.A., Unemployment Compensation and Workmen's Compensation, can be traced back to federal and state tax rates.

Estimated vs Actual Costs

At this point, the auditor should determine whether or not the printer has built into the base any *estimated* or *anticipated* cost increases. If *estimates* have been included, these should be adjusted to actual costs and the base cost will therefore change. If *anticipated* cost increases have been included in the base, the auditor should make sure that this is allowable under the terms of the contract; and if so, then the same procedure must be continued in all future escalations. If this is not done, the cost comparisons from one period to the next will not be consistent.

Next to the base costs in the table are the same costs as of January 1, 1977, including all the cost increases that have been incurred during the prior year. These should again be verified as before, by reference to the labor agreement and to the appropriate tax rates. The goal should be to make sure the computations are accurate and consistent.

The printer's costs, as shown in the table, have increased by 10 percent over the 12-month period. The price escalation formula provides that the proportion of labor in the presswork prices is equal to 60 percent. Therefore, to determine the amount by which presswork prices will increase due to the printer's cost increases, the formula is:

$$10\% \times 60\% = 6.0\%$$

In those cases where the contract permits a limited pass-through of cost increases—say, for example, 5 percent—then the increase must be scaled down from 6 percent to 5 percent. If there is no limit on the escalation, prices can be increased by the full 6 percent.

The auditor's checklist of things to look out for should include:

1. Mathematical errors

2. Inclusion of future cost increases not yet incurred by the printer

3. Correct application of the escalation formula

4. Cost estimate adjustments which reflect actual cost increases when known, if estimates have been used.

Where material cost increases are concerned (e.g., ink, glue, kraft wrapping), the auditor should verify the base cost and the new cost by examining suppliers' invoices on the appropriate dates. One thing to check for in this area is the quantity ordered, since unit prices can vary considerably depending on the size of the lots ordered. There are also differences in the quality of materials ordered which would affect the unit prices, so the auditor should determine that the materials are basically similar.

The cost for such an audit depends on many factors, such as the complexity of the printing contract, how comprehensive the price escalation clause is, how much detail the publisher wants to review. In most cases, a routine examination can be completed after two or three days' work. If major discrepancies come to light, more time will be necessary; but this is, after all, one of the main purposes of conducting the audit. The investment is more than offset by eliminating misunderstanding and assuring consistency.

Trade Customs

By Jeffery R. Parnau

The topic of "Trade Customs" has been getting more than its normal share of attention in trade journals lately. And it's about time. These mysterious guidelines seem to arise only when a publisher disagrees with a printer, and they have dealt nasty surprises to more than one buyer.

For some of us, Trade Customs are not a cause for concern. If a buyer has a very descriptive, lengthy, all-inclusive contract with a printer, the contract calls *all* the shots—regardless of whether it is in accord with the Customs.

Others have simple letters of agreement with printers which serve as a contract. When those letters are too short (as most are), they do not contain enough detail, and a contract without detail forces the courts to rely on Trade Customs for guidance.

Finally, most of us buy more printing than simply what is required for a magazine. There are reprints, forms, booklets, and hundreds of other items to be purchased. For these one-time buys, it is almost absurd to consider drafting a comprehensive guide to the buyer-seller relationship. Trade Customs to the "rescue" again.

It is tempting to rattle off a few horror stories as to how magazine publishers have been taken for the proverbial ride by printers' enforcement of the Customs. But to be realistic, these Customs would not even exist had buyers not manipulated printers in the past.

Drafted to protect printers

So, the 50 plus years old Customs are with us today. Because purchasers were doing all sorts of unethical things to printers, printers drafted a batch of "rules" to protect themselves. And that is exactly what many of us forget about the Customs. They were drafted by printers for their own protection.

I would like to be totally objective in discussing the Customs. But the Customs themselves are not objective in how they treat buyers and sellers. How could they be, when they were, as just mentioned, assembled by printers?

Therefore, keep in mind that the following observations are those of a buyer. If a bit of one-sidedness is present, the reason may be that the Customs were one-sided at their inception.

First of all, ignorance of the law (or in this case, Trade Customs) is usually not an excuse. All buyers of printing are presumed to know what the 17 Customs are and do. In fact, in a recent well-publicized court case, the buyer apparently "won" a deviation from a Custom. What that buyer actually won was the recognition that he didn't know the Custom existed.

So if you are unaware of these 17 rules, you can 1) check the flip side of a commercial printing bid; 2) ask your printer; 3) write the Printing Industries of America; or 4) write me in care of FOLIO.

Regarding the Customs themselves, I will limit this discussion to the four that I feel are most important to the buyer.

Custom No. 3, "Experimental Work," reads as follows: "Experimental work performed at customer's request, such as sketches, drawings, composition, plates, presswork, and material will be charged for at current rates and may not be used without consent of the printer."

I do not understand what the authors had in mind here. If I am reading correctly, the following is possible: I go to my printer and ask him to design, proof, plate, and run a test brochure for me. He does so. He charges me. And according to the above custom, I cannot use that material without the consent of the printer. Didn't I just *pay* for it?

I suspect that this Custom had an earlier version: If the buyer didn't *pay* the printer for this work (meaning it was done on speculation), it would make sense that the printer had control of it. But with payment, as the Custom now stands, I cannot imagine how any printer could defend the practice of charging for work, yet not passing title to the customer.

Custom No. 4 is related to No. 3. It reads, "Sketches, copy, dummies, and all preparatory work created or furnished by the printer, shall remain his exclusive property and no use of same shall be made, nor any ideas obtained therefrom be used, except upon compensation to be determined by printer."

At least with this Custom, I can understand what the authors were trying to do. If a printer performs work on speculation, he or she certainly doesn't want some unethical client to steal the ideas and go to another supplier.

My disagreement with this Custom is that it shouldn't exist. No buyer should approach a printer for speculative work, and no printer should be so trusting as to perform it. In addition, no work should be performed without an agreement on price *before* the job begins. As this Custom stands, the price is set after the work is complete.

Custom No. 6 is my personal favorite: "Art work, type, plates, negatives, positives, and other items when supplied by the printer shall remain his exclusive property unless otherwise agreed in writing."

The history of this custom—written in 1922, by the way—is of a different mechanical age. When Linotypes were Cadillacs and letterpress was king, it made sense. A printer might have tons of lead and tin tied up in a job. Letterpress plates were expensive, and those customers who wanted to haul the prep/plate materials out of the plant could expect a heck of a fight.

Today, the prep materials have remarkably low scrap value *compared to* their value to the customer. Let me quote from an article I wrote in the June 1980 issue of *Print Buyer & Production Manager's Newsletter*.

"Assume that for a 100-page product, a printer uses . . . 100 sheets of 20″ x 24″ film. If the average exposure of that film was 50 percent . . . the printer might recover about two ounces of silver from the scrap film. Of that, the printer might collect 75 percent of silver's market value, or about $18 based on the press-time price of approximately $12/ounce.

"Assume also that the 100-page product entailed 10 color separations at a cost of $125 each. Should the customer agree to scrapping $1,250 worth of separations so the printer can recover $12 worth of silver?"

Agreed, the price of silver has risen since those statements were made. The $18 would now be $24. Hardly a significant difference to the customer who pays for separations.

If, for some reason, the printer wants to hold the prep, he should be able to tell you exactly why.

The final Custom which bothers me is No. 11: "Overruns or underruns not to exceed 10 percent on quantities ordered up to 10,000 copies and/or the percentage agreed upon over or under quantities ordered above 10,000 copies shall constitute acceptable delivery. Printer will bill for actual quantity delivered within this tolerance. If customer requires guaranteed 'no less than' delivery, percentage tolerance of coverage must be doubled."

In effect, the latter part of the above statement means I can order "no less than" 10,000 catalogs, then pay for 12,000. If I have no use for the 2,000 overs (yet must mail to at least 10,000 persons), my costs could rise an *unanticipated* 20 percent. (There are subtleties and variations which affect the increased cost, but we haven't the space to go into detail.) It seems to me that this clause would be entirely acceptable if there were no percentages stated. Each printing job is different, and in fact a few jobs would require an even *greater* leeway than those described.

In other words, this Custom seems suited for a "fill in the blanks" exercise where the unique factors of each job would dictate the percentages of unders and overs.

You may agree or disagree with the above discussion on Trade Customs. If you disagree, no problem. Just go on with your business, and Trade Customs will cover any problems you may have with printers.

But if you agree that certain Customs do not give you entirely fair treatment, you don't have to be a wizard to design a solution. Trade Customs control the situation *only* in the absence of a written agreement to the contrary.

If you prefer to have artwork, film, and other materials returned to you, put a statement to that effect on your purchase order. Or, make the appropriate amendment right on the flip side of the printer's estimate (being sure that you both sign that side, too).

And don't get me wrong. I do not want to leave you with the impression that printers are crooks, or that Trade Customs will always be used to your disadvantage. I mean only to point out that *we* are the buyers, and should have a say as to how our money is spent.

If the Customs were prepared in a somewhat biased atmosphere, to serve printers more than publishers, we need only make the appropriate revisions before placing an order.

The printer/publisher relationship

By Hubert Gotzes

The product of any magazine publisher is the magazine! A publisher can have the finest editorial, circulation and advertising staffs and still lose. He or she must have a good printer. This means the printer has to understand the enormous responsibilities he or she has been charged with. The printer must be capable of transforming the editorial and advertising material received into a well-printed and packaged product and deliver it consistently and on time.

To do these things the printer must have a modern plant with the right equipment. Most of all, the printer must have highly competent people in all areas of the organization; not only in the sales and manufacturing departments, but also in production control, traffic, shipping, maintenance, engineering and administrative and management areas. These people must not only be competent and dedicated, they must be people who care about and are interested in the publishers' current and future needs. To be effective in preparing to meet these future obligations, the printer must know what is wanted in both general and, hopefully, some specific terms. Perhaps that is why so many recurring questions affecting the entire printing and publishing industry are being raised today. In broadest terms these questions are:

• Have we, in fact, determined exactly what our short- and long-range problems, opportunities and objectives are?

• Are publishers and printers working on the right projects?

• Have we set the proper priorities?

In a word, are we really planning or are we only firefighting?

One more question should be added: Are we, the printers and publishers, planning alone or together? If we are not planning together, are we not in serious danger of wasting valuable time, capital and even risking the possibility of working at cross purposes? R.R. Donnelley & Sons Company's experience indicates that there is considerable advantage to cooperative effort and that such effort does, indeed, reduce the number of fires that have to be fought.

Before developing the need for more cooperative planning in the future, let us review where we have been.

First of all, let me say that the mutual objectives of the printing and publishing industry cannot be met by putting ink on paper alone. A lot more must be done in the way of new and better equipment as well as the development and application of new technologies. We have made considerable investment in both what we believe will enhance our past and future capital investments and, more importantly, anticipate the economic and production requirements of the publisher, be the publisher large or small.

Recent Innovations

Many have wondered if the printing industry has become stagnant or unresponsive to publishers' needs. I think not. For example, in the last decade we have seen the introduction of far more versatile and efficient scanners and film that result in better separations for all processes; automatic platemakers in offset, nyloprint photosensitive plates in letterpress, electromechanical cylinder engravers and highly automated chemical etching systems for gravure.

In the offset press field (where the greatest growth has taken place), press speeds have doubled and wider, more productive presses are being effectively utilized. Makeready times have been shortened and running waste has been reduced. Bindery speeds have increased. The ability to bind unusual, lightweight, small signatures and gimmicks at very small penalties in speed or cost have become relatively commonplace.

I feel it is fair to say that while printing costs have gone up, a good many innovations and services, such as those just listed above, have resulted. These improvements have been instrumental in holding back the full force of inflation and are but a few of the positive things that have taken place. They tell only half the story because these efficiency gains have been counteracted by the growing need for shorter schedules, lighter weight and more difficult to run paper and regional and demographic advertising fragmented press and bindery runs. The requirements of today's modern printing plant are almost totally unlike those we knew 10 or 15 years ago. Hopefully such changes will continue to take place. I say hopefully because we recognize the publishers' need to meet change in the marketplace, as well as our own responsibility to respond to and anticipate this need.

What's Ahead?

So much for the past. What are the factors affecting the future and how can we best assess them?

Printers recognize only too well the publishers' dilemma of rising costs on every front and the need for relief. From the printer's view, building and equipment costs have already more than doubled. Continuing investment in environmental equipment and its attendant operating costs will have to be made. Labor costs will surely rise as inflation continues. Prices on publication work are already depressed, even to the point where some publication printers have gone out of business. The future will certainly see more economic pressure to improve productivity at the same time that publishers will be asking for faster schedules, cheaper preliminary work and less expensive lighter weight stock.

This is merely the recognition of almost certain

facts. Yet it is not by any means a hopeless situation. There is a great deal that can and must be done with only adjustments in emphasis. While we will undoubtedly continue to make productivity gains in the traditional sense, we see the major opportunities of the future coming from joint planning efforts that use the printer's expertise to develop production programs to best utilize the process and equipment specially developed for large and small publications. In so doing, a higher degree of standardization and specialization can be attained.

Planning and standardization may well have negative connotations to many publishers and not without good reason in some cases. I believe such concern is unwarranted in this case, however. The planning that I refer to need not be of a nature that plans are etched in stone. Quite to the contrary, plans should represent a framework from which timely and appropriate changes can be made as changes in the publishers' needs are foreseen. Any plan to be usable must become a living document.

Similarly, I can understand that "standardization" might imply that publishers will lose their identity and that we are suggesting that all publications look alike. Obviously, such an objective would destroy any publication's ability to be creative and distinctive—the very things that make a publication great. The kinds of standardization we refer to are in specifications of materials, equipment, quality standards and the like which can result in the kind of cost and quality improvements from which we believe both printing and publishing can benefit.

To meet our mutual objectives for the future, it is evident that printers and publishers need each other. They are, in fact, really totally interdependent. The publisher must find ways to use his or her printer and equipment in the most economical fashion. The publisher must work with the printer to achieve maximum economy in the design and production of the magazine. The same is true of the printer. The printer must work with the publisher to be sure he or she properly anticipates customer needs and is equipped to meet those needs within the time and economic framework that is allowed. A professional printer's representative will understand the creative requirements of the publisher and be able to marry these requirements with the mechanical requirements of the printing processes. If the representative has the ability to draw on experienced staff specialists within his or her own organization, he or she should be able to pull together a highly specialized, if not unique, production plan to meet the unique requirements of that particular publication. It is impossible to be very specific in the space allotted. Many approaches to this problem are generally known but not necessarily universally applied. Just a few of the considerations to be tested include the placement of color on one side of the web, the way forms close to eliminate bunching and minimize the personnel required and gang running forms.

Cooperative Planning

The optimization of future publishing production requirements can only be attained through cooperative long-range planning. The mutual understanding and commitments required of both parties for new technology create a strong mutual interest in insuring that the right decisions are made. The possible penalties in time and money for either doing nothing or making the wrong decision are totally unacceptable to either party. Where a proper relationship of respect, competence and trust exists between the printer and the publisher, there is no reason for such errors to be made.

What, then, are some of the areas where this planning can be of benefit?

Let's start at the very beginning. The publisher should be certain that the printer knows not only what the publisher's present schedule and makeup requirements are, but that the printer knows what direction the publisher plans to take in the future. The printer can be an extremely valuable resource in optimizing schedule and makeup considerations. For example, color placement, the use of combination forms for late closings, the selection of 2-, 4- or 6-color presses can optimize the use of the printer's work force and equipment without reducing the publisher's flexibility. Perhaps he or she can open options that were not previously considered or believed possible. When preparing for the future, such knowledge becomes an extremely important element in setting specifications for projected capital investments. And remember, the printer must be capable of providing the same planning skills to small or large publishers. Each can get a return on the time spent to develop such plans both in the short- and long-range.

There is a great deal left to do to improve not only the preliminary operation but the pressroom operation as well. Printers have certainly become a great deal more sophisticated in evaluating and correcting supplied film. Densitometry is now widely used in prepress operations. But regardless of the generation of technology, the printing press is usually incapable of making improvements over the film furnished for making plates or cylinders. As printing presses get larger and faster in order to take advantage of the economies of such design, the input material becomes even more important than it is today. Improved input, which might well cost more, will probably be more than offset by improved efficiencies in platemaking and presswork and in paper savings.

Because of the nature of advertising, there is no question but that this film input will still come from a number of sources. But in the future these sources must be capable of delivering a consistently high quality product that meets all of the standard specifications set forth by the industry. As we all know, we have only touched the surface of this problem. The industry and all of its suppliers must agree upon a set of preliminary specifications for each process and then be willing to insist that they are consistently followed. Without this kind of standardization, and discipline, we cannot logically expect a continuation of the same rate of productivity improvement in the pressroom that has been experienced in the past.

With this kind of standardization of input, economies can be realized and further improvements in quality are quite possible. Consider the effect of good input material on preliminary department inspection and correction costs, in press makeready time, in faster and better form OK time. All of these lead to reduced waste and the printer's ability to reduce the nonproductive delay time on an extremely expensive piece of capital equipment.

A mutual objective must be to lower material costs without sacrificing quality. There are two obvious ways of reducing material costs: One is by lowering the cost per pound or unit and the other is to use fewer materials. While we must work on both fronts, I am not sure that the proper effort has been put on the latter, especially when considering the relatively high cost of materials in the total production package. By working together, the printer and publisher can establish material specifications that would allow printers to properly evaluate incoming materials before they are used. These efforts, coupled with the use of computer technology, can be used to develop process monitoring and process control systems on the line equipment. That, in turn, will allow printers to obtain optimum efficient use of that equipment and establish minimum waste standards. The process monitoring systems have already made important savings in these areas.

Joint publisher-printer planning efforts can develop layouts of issues that minimize prepress and bindery preparation. The elimination of odd roll sizes and press form deliveries or small signatures will allow for more efficient use of production equipment.

Distribution planning has become increasingly important and has also been greatly aided by the use of computers to optimize pool shipping. More sophisticated systems will be needed as freight and postage costs increase. While a lot of good work has been done in this area, further innovation and sophistication can be developed.

These are not just advantages to the printer. If industry practices would allow printers to effect such economies in their operations, the savings could be passed along to customers the same as the costs of many inefficient practices must necessarily be reflected in actual price and quality levels.

The printer can also be of considerable help to the publisher in marketing his or her product. "Selectronic Binding" systems will make far greater bindery fragmentation available to the publisher. We have not yet determined how this technology, combined with ink jet label printing, can best be applied to publisher marketing programs. For example, I am not sure that we really know what the total possible applications might be, not only for reading a magnetic tape and printing a label, but how additional applications for such things as expire cards, demographic advertising or other special fulfillment or advertising purposes might be most effectively used by the publisher. This is but one example of a new marketing opportunity presented to the publisher through the continuing development of printing technology.

There has to be concern in the publisher's mind about the adequacy of technical effort in the printing industry and its heavy capital equipment suppliers. The fact is that there will never be enough. Most industry research and development budgets are limited and the many companies that have inadequate earnings cannot afford to participate at all. It is therefore essential that the available funds are properly managed and utilized on the priority projects that can be mutually agreed upon. While good progress has been made in many promising areas, a great deal more must be done. This can only be accomplished through the heavy reinvestment of profits.

In summary, printers believe that standardization and specialization can be complementary to publishers' needs for creative expression and individualism and still provide economies to both publisher and printer operations, be they large or small. It is in the interest of the publisher to choose and use a supplier in whom he or she has trust and one who has the financial stability, management, technological and dedicated craft strength and experience to become a part of the publisher's future planning. This kind of cooperative approach to publishing/ printing problems and opportunities can be the key to the efficient use of developing technology and the productivity gains that are essential for profitable future operations.

You can reduce print costs

By Roger V. Dickeson

Survival—being in business tomorrow—is the issue for both printer and publisher. In the last year, several major printing plants have closed—a situation virtually unheard of in the last half of the seventies. And more *will* close. A magazine official quoted in *The New York Times* on May 6, 1981, says: "I think you could see some well-known magazines go down the tubes this year that are going to really surprise some people."

In an economy of double-digit inflation, printers and publishers are finding that costs are rising faster than prices: Prices have been increasing at a rate of 8 percent a year, whereas costs are rising at a rate of 14 percent a year. The killer is the 6 percent gap between costs and prices.

Why don't publishers and printers immediately pass on their cost increases in price increases? (The oil companies do.) They don't for the same reason the airlines don't: competition.

Publishing and printing are extremely competitive industries, and only the fittest among publishing and printing companies will survive in an inflationary period. Thus, when enough marginal firms have succumbed to the inflation virus, maybe the remaining firms will be able to pass on cost increases more easily. Cruel but effective.

The publisher and printer, in close cooperation, must seek ways of increasing productivity in a counterattack on inflationary forces. If management takes the time to measure and pay attention to productivity, a great deal can be accomplished.

A production official at one of the national magazines that does its own type composition recently gave a startling example of what can be done.

"We had heard the slogan, 'Until you measure you don't control,' " he said. "We tried it by setting up a form that required noting the time the story landed at the composition desk and the time the proof galleys were delivered to the editor's desk. The first week, the average interval was over 90 minutes.

"After two weeks, the average interval had dropped to less than 60 minutes. It's true: 'People respect what management inspects.' "

There *are* really just two choices: We can sit quietly and hope that the tooth fairy and President Reagan will curb the inflationary spiral. Or, we can seek ways to reduce costs and increase productivity. The issue: Do we take a passive or an active role? If you opt for passive, stop reading. Turn the page to the next article.

If you choose an active role, consider the following yield enhancement strategies—strategies designed to increase productivity. It is my intention that these strategies will get the creative pot boiling, for everyone (we've learned from the Japanese Quality Circles) has to get into the act. If we all seek out every imaginable idea we can to increase the productivity of what we are doing, we will begin to find ways to bridge the 6 percent gap between cost and prices.

Finished trim size

Cut the magazine's finished trim size to 8¹/₈-inches by 10⁷/₈-inches. Many of the major magazines have already done this. It not only decreases paper costs by reducing the roll width, it also reduces postage and distribution costs by cutting the magazine weight.

Does it hurt the appearance? Doubtful. Start measuring the magazines that come across your desk.

Does it create a problem for supplied full-page ads? Not really.

Basis weight

Cut the basis weight of the body stock. Although paper mills charge a premium for the lighter weights, you'll get more linear feet per pound. Furthermore, a lighter paper will decrease postage and distribution costs.

Roll width

Have your printer check the width of the rolls being used for your magazine, if you're supplying the paper. Many mills have a habit of supplying rolls that are 1/16 of an inch over width in an excess of caution. This is costing you money.

Detailed waste reconciliation

Remember the illustration of the publisher and the composition time? If you're supplying paper for your magazine, ask your printer for a detailed waste reconciliation for each form and issue. It's your paper. Until the printer starts to measure and account for the material waste in detail, he doesn't really control it.

When he does start to measure, inspect the results and let him know that you are doing so. Magic will happen. Waste goes down! It has been demonstrated many times. You are simply forcing the printer to do what he ought to be doing for himself.

Sharing waste savings

Publishers supplying paper negotiate waste allowance schedules with the printer. On the settlement date, if the printer has consumed more paper than allowed by that schedule, the printer pays. If the printer has consumed less paper than allowed, the publisher profits. For the printer, it's a game of "Heads the publisher wins, tails the printer loses." There is no incentive for the printer to reduce waste below the allowance level. Revise the contract so the printer can share in such savings.

What price quality?

Publishing and printing, like most other businesses, have their own mythologies. One of the most devastating of these is the quality myth. Publishers and printers spend more money chasing the quality will-o'-the-wisp than is needed to support a medium-sized city.

In their quest for graphic arts quality, publishers probably add an unexpected 10 percent to print and paper costs. How? Through extended press makereadies, press running waste, "make goods," unnecessary time spent in endless argument and discussion, sending representatives to the printing plant to "approve" press forms.

Why? Because no one really hammers out a realistic definition of quality. "I can't tell you exactly what quality is, but I sure can tell it when I see it." The problem, however, is that one man's "quality" is another man's trash.

A definition of quality that is rapidly gaining acceptance is as follows: "Quality is conformance to requirements."

Read *Quality is Free*, by Philip B. Crosby (New American Library), a $2.95 paperback that is worth millions. Warning: The book may endanger your favorite myth.

The trick is to define the requirements. If you can't state your requirements precisely, then don't use the term "quality" when talking to your printer. Performance either conforms to requirements or it does not. If conformance is not economically practical, then change the requirements.

Some of the greatest fiction of the day appears in *Standard Rate and Data* as publication mechanical requirements: the statements are unrealistic and are uniformly ignored.

The attack on the printing costs starts with the publisher's statement of the mechanical requirements. This must state the "requirements" for quality advertising input. Unfortunately, the only time this statement is referred to now is when an agency rep calls to protest about the way the ad was reproduced in the magazine.

Publishers and agencies must understand that the three prime variables of graphic reproduction are a) paper; b) film; and c) ink. If the requirements for each are clearly stated, then each must conform. If they do conform, then the desired aesthetic effect will be present (assuming that the printer is capable of reproducing dots). If they are not met, then the offending party must be seized warmly by the throat and shaken until wisdom sets in.

Careful definition of requirements in place of vague references of "quality" can save a lot of money and eliminate a lot of agony.

Cost of money

The cost of money is the measure of inflation, and it is based upon time. Either the publisher pays for the time cost of money directly or he pays it indirectly. Like lunch, there ain't no free money.

Printers used to be a bit careless about money because it didn't cost 22 percent—merely 5 percent or so. In the last two years, however, the cost of money has become a prime economic factor. It is now a major raw material.

The longer you tie up the printer's money, the more it costs the printer and the more he must find ways of passing it on to the publisher. If the publisher furnishes paper, the cost of money to the printer in raw materials, work in process, and receivables is cut by about 35 percent.

Example: Assume an interest rate of 21 percent, a cycle of 90 days from receipt of paper stock to collection of print bill, and a print bill of $100,000 (including paper). The money cost is $9,000, about 9 percent of the total print bill.

Now change the assumptions. Assume the publisher supplies the paper at a cost of $40,000. The print bill is now $60,000. The money cost is now $5,400 or $3,500 less.

If you furnish the paper to your printer, you are entitled to assert this money cost reduction to the printer in bargaining.

Printers must pass on the cost of the money just as they attempt to pass on the costs of labor, energy, and supplies . . . to the extent that competition allows. If they don't, they petition for reorganization.

But, just passing on the cost of money is only a part of the problem. The other part is the velocity.

Advertisers are stretching agency billings. Agencies are stretching publication bills. Publishers are stretching print publication bills. Printers are stretching paper and ink bills. And so on.

In this continuous stretching process, management of the velocity of money—liquidity—becomes the cost of the ball game. Peter Drucker tells us that there are three things we must manage in today's economy: liquidity, productivity, and the cost of being in business tomorrow. They are closely interrelated. Liquidity is a measure of money velocity.

The publisher who manages liquidity well can reduce print costs by bargaining with a cash short printer. The publisher furnishing paper should consider the substantial cost of money being saved by the printer. The publisher who can pay his print bill in 10 days should appraise the economic value of that velocity to the printer. Managing the velocity of money is a yield enhancement strategy.

Schedules

Printers are operating with high costs of capital for hardware: presses, binders, and the plant space to house them. Replacement costs of those items is a survival issue. Since printers must utilize the expensive capital equipment to maximum advantage, idle time is a mortal enemy.

The publisher who cannot keep schedules must pay a premium for any delay time he causes. On the other hand, the publisher who is rigid in keeping schedules with the printer is entitled to preferential cost treatment.

Publishers fall into a bad habit with "rubber" closing dates. They allow materials to be submitted by ad agencies beyond the stated closing date in order to capture marginal ad revenue. This attitude of the publisher flows down to the production department. If the closing date schedule can be stretched, why not the printer's deadline?

As a result, little games are played. Agencies know which magazines are not rigid on closing dates and they stretch to the limit. Publishers believe that the printer has built a certain "slack" into his schedule and they stretch, often to the limit. To play the game, you set fictitious closing dates and printer's deadlines.

The games have to stop at some point. Think about it. There just must be some real, honest-to-goodness dates that can't be fiddled with, even if you set some "ostensible" dates for ad agencies.

"Approving" press forms

Many publishers send a representative to the printing plant to approve press forms. Some printers recognize the delays, the confusion, and the waste this provokes, and they'll tack a premium (1 or 2 percent) on their pricing for the added cost.

It's truly surprising how many of these publisher's representatives do not understand the subtractive nature of the light absorption by the inks. It often happens that ink key changes requested by these representatives provoke the opposite of the result desired.

The solution is to have the printer establish a mechanical proofing system, one that can truly predict what the press will print, and then run to this proof. The press is not the instrument to use for re-separating color.

Keep the representative in the publishing office doing something constructive. Take a hard look at this costly practice. Is it really cost effective? Can you honestly say that it contributes to results? The practice has been abandoned by many publishers.

Some publishers and representatives think that they can dictate when the printer shall start to save during the makeready process. They believe that the printer should not start keeping copies until they sign the sheet.

If you insist on having a rep at the plant, then he should *never* sign off on a sheet until the press has been up and running at full production speed and copies are being saved. The color has not truly settled down to a run status until this time.

If the publisher insists on dictating when saving shall commence, the printer is entitled to bill the publisher on a "time and materials, cost plus" basis. No one in his right mind wants that.

Impositions

To hold your print bills down, take full advantage of the press cylinders and folder configurations being used by the printer. This requires careful communication with the printer and some technical understanding. Avoid the need for burning another plate, opening another form, or creating an additional press run to accommodate a color requirement.

Avoid double proofing

Film flats for burning plates are made up of combinations of four, eight, or 16 pages, depending upon press size. When furnished materials arrive at the print plant, they must first go through a step called "image generation," where half-tones and line camera shots are made, copy is fitted, and the individual components are assembled into pages.

The next step is called "image assembly," where the individual pages are assembled into the four-, eight-, and 16-page combinations on a carrier base. Proofs can be furnished at the image generation or image assembly stages, or both.

Where possible, avoid double proofing. It not only adds to the cost of the proofing materials, it also compounds the possibility of error and increases the time required.

In the double-proofing situation, something called the piecemealing factor is involved. Every time materials are picked up, studied, and then put down again, time is lost and the chance of error is increased.

Kennel clubs

Some printers have what is called a "Kennel Club." To qualify for membership in this club, a magazine must be a "dog," yielding both a contribution to overhead and inadequate profits (profit below that necessary for adequate return on investment of the past and investment in new equipment at the inflationary levels of the future).

There are three ways publications attain this status.

First, in the original bargaining process of contract negotiation, the publisher may have squeezed too hard, or the printer may have been weak at that moment. The work may simply be underpriced for the needed contribution margins of the printer.

Second, the practices of the publisher may not be as represented . . . not conducive to efficient production in the printing plant. Or, the practices may have deteriorated through time. Or the printer may have slipped in efficiency.

Third, the price increases negotiated at contract renewal may have been cumulatively inadequate.

When the Kennel Club is reviewed in the printing plant, the plant personnel should first examine all production practices to determine if there are "valuable engineering" approaches that can be taken. Have unnecessary losses been occurring due to certain practices? Are there some short cuts that can be taken? If all else fails, the printer may be forced to make a "jump" bid, a substantial price increase demand, at the next contract opening.

If a publisher thinks his magazine is in the Kennel Club, he should request a creative, friendly session with his printer. Together, they should thoroughly examine every production practice that may be creating inefficiency.

Above all, however, everyone involved must keep in mind that the right attitude can do more to enhance productivity than any other single factor.

Example: It is well known that the "weeklies" run faster and with less waste than "monthlies." As a matter of fact, "dailies" run even more efficiently than weeklies. There is a "law" in operation: "Magazine production inefficiency expands in direct relationship to the time interval between publication dates."

Examine this law carefully. Is is etched in stone? Or is there any way that a dog publication in the printing plant can be converted into a pussycat?

The real difference lies in the *attitudes* of the publisher and printer personnel toward the publication. Printers and publishers have certain attitudes about a weekly that enable it to run faster and with less waste. They have different "requirements" that dictate a differing quality level. The makereadies are shorter. The schedules are more rigorously kept. There is a "work rhythm" that is different, more efficient. Can these attitudes be duplicated for a monthly in order to increase its productivity and thereby hold its costs down?

Conclusion

Survival is truly the issue. The cost/price gap due to the escalation of the inflationary rate in competitive industries spells the end of business as usual. Both publishers and printers must take immediate steps to establish some Yield Enhancement Strategies and make them work. Productivity increase can close a large part of the cost/price gap.

Printing priorities

By Jeffery R. Parnau

I like to run my process color on the heavy side—and I mean heavy! When I buy that ink from the printer, I want to see it layer upon layer, pigment upon pigment, until the pressman screams, "No more!" On the other hand, some publishers like to run their color on the lighter side, achieving pleasant—even somewhat pale—reproduction.

Printers, of course, have absolutely no way of knowing what kind of reproduction you are most pleased with. And presses, for good or bad, are just as adept at printing too heavy as they are capable of printing too light.

The situation becomes even more complicated when you add the variables of advertising, editorial photos, and preference (e.g., giving more attention to a photo of Bo Derek than a photo of your local tax assessor).

Because so many variables are involved, many purchasers choose to perform the traditional press check —that boring, cumbersome chore of standing in the pressroom while a problem-riddled machine confronts frustrated operators.

I happen to be a promoter of press checks. Printing is, for good or bad, a publisher's life blood. If you publish a magazine today, you are involved with printing. Assemble the words in any sequence you like; they must still roll off the press.

However, a representative at press-side can do no more than tell the printer whether the product meets the publisher's expectations.

Let me offer an example. Years ago, I began making

a regular trek to a particular printing plant for a specific customer. With each visit, the printer and buyer were a bit more in sync: on visit number three, they had a better feel for my whims because they remembered the decisions we made during visits one and two.

After half-a-dozen press okays (over a six-issue span), things became much easier for everybody. While on day one my penchant for heavy process color was looked at with a bit of apprehension, six months later the pressmen would be piling that ink on thick long before my phone rang.

In addition, it took some time before certain publisher-optional preferences became clear to the operators. For this magazine, the publisher chose to let the editorial material suffer whenever a conflict arose between house material and paid advertising. That seemed an obvious decision to me, but little did I know that some clients of this printer actually favored their editorial and let the advertising suffer. How were the pressmen to know what was more important?

We finally got the priorities straight. But what if I had written my expectations down at the outset, presenting my idiosyncrasies in memorandum form? Wouldn't that have given the press personnel some direction, thereby saving a lot of aggravation?

The fact is: memo writing can be one of the most productive steps you can take in obtaining uniform, customer-pleasing printing. It can either complement or replace the chore of standing next to those noisy, overgrown duplicators.

Suppose the printer had the following memo sent to him before I had ever stepped through his door:

"We tend to run our process color on the heavy side. We prefer glossy color over perfect matches to the proof. Advertising always takes priority over editorial. Advertiser-supplied proofs take priority over subsequent proofs. Full-color advertisers take priority over partial-color advertisers. Double-truck (cross-align) advertisers have absolute priority."

Although the instructions are quite simple, keep in mind that the printer may have 100 customers to deal with, each of whom has a slightly different set of rules.

Let's review each simple sentence from that memo, and point out the possibilities.

"We tend to run our color on the heavy side." As I mentioned earlier, heavy color happens to be one of my own personal preferences. But the fact is, some buyers run their color on the light side. They prefer a clean, crisp dot to dense, shiny color. The printer should know what you want.

You can test this out by doing a single press check, asking the printer to demonstrate the difference between a light application of ink and an extremely dense one. If you've never done this test, you will be surprised at the versatility of a press in producing a wide variety of results from the same printing plate.

"We prefer glossy color over perfect matches to proofs." This clarification can be extremely important to the press operators. Some customers are absolutely fanatic about coming as close to the proof as possible. Others show up at press-side only to say, "Hell, that looks better than what we gave you. Run it."

Of course, if the customer states that glossy color is preferred over perfect matches, that preference should not be interpreted to mean that glossy color cannot be achieved along with a perfect or close-to-perfect match. If both good gloss and a good match are possible, both should be achieved.

"Advertising always takes priority over editorial." You might think that everybody in the business knows this. Well, it ain't true. There are many publishers who prefer to concentrate on their editorial photos, even at the expense of paid advertising. Printers must cope with these widely different methods of producing a pleasing product . . . and you simply cannot expect a printer to read your mind.

Worse yet, you could be one of the publishers with a hybrid preference. Consider the following: "Advertising always takes preference over editorial unless the conflicting editorial is a full-page photo of a human face." Don't laugh . . . that's a direct quote from one publisher's preference memo.

"Advertiser supplied proofs take priority over subsequent proofs." This statement implies that there may be a difference between what the advertiser gave you and what you are getting from your film.

Again, it is entirely logical for the printer to assume that you wish to print what was on your film. It is no secret that the difference between a supplied press-proof and a subsequent Cromalin (or Color Key, or Transfer Key) can be extreme. It is also just as logical for the printer to assume that you want to match the supplied proof. With both solutions falling nicely within the sphere of printers' logic, you would do everyone a favor by putting your directions in writing.

"Full-color advertisements take priority over partial-color advertisements." This statement covers those situations where the printer has no way of knowing which advertiser to favor when you run into a compromise problem.

However, what if you had been working for years to land a national advertiser—who happens to run two-color ads—and that ad happened to conflict (on press) with a full-bleed, old-faithful, full-color account? Since you would be more concerned with the two-color printing, you'd have to alter your own instructions in this situation.

"Double-truck advertisers have absolute priority." This request says that no matter what happens on press, the printer is to favor the advertiser who occupies the most space.

Consider the following: A two-page ad is run on two different signatures (sometimes due to the need for a stitched-in insert between the two pages). On the printing of the second signature, in-line problems suggest to the printer that a compromise is necessary (in order to save some of the quality of the competing ad).

In this situation the publisher's memo would clearly tell the printer to let the one-page ad go down the drain, if necessary, to save the color balance of the two-pager.

If this all sounds complicated, just remember: As a production person, a publisher, or an observer, you have preferences which are not always the preferences of your printer's other customers. By putting those preferences in writing, your printer will be able to give you exactly what you want—with a minimum amount of fuss.

Dealing with in-line problems

By Jeffery R. Parnau

One of the most satisfying aspects of teaching at FOLIO'S Face-to-Face seminars is the opportunity to answer questions. However, I was surprised at a question posed during a discussion on press impositions at last November's conference:

"Jeff, these in-line problems you describe . . . how do you resolve them on press?"

Although these sessions always provoke questions that deal with very basic production techniques, this question in particular implied a surprising lack of sophistication concerning imposition (or in-line) problems. To put it bluntly, an in-line problem simply cannot be solved on press. That's one of the basic limitations of the modern web.

What's the problem?

An in-line problem typically occurs when you run a four-color page beneath another four-color page. In such a situation, the pressman must decide either to "favor" one of the pages to get the best color, or to compromise on both pages. Obviously, either decision can cause a problem with an ad and, therefore, a problem with a paying customer . . . an advertiser.

When an in-line problem is generated in the production department, it doesn't go away. The conventional web press simply cannot accommodate two critical-color pages, one above the other, without sacrificing something.

The only solution, then, is to avoid generating the problem in the first place.

Viewing the actual imposition

Let's look at a typical eight-page press form, as the press sees it. Figure 1 shows a side of a 16-page signature. To create the worst of all possible in-line problems on press, all one has to do is put a four-color ad on every page of this press pass. Would anyone do such a crazy thing?

Yes—a lot of publishers do. Unaware of the limitations of printing fully-saturated signatures, these publishers assume that all of the color ads—eight of them—might as well be printed with the greatest possible economy. That "economy" can be deceptive: If a single advertiser gives you heat about poor reproduction quality, you could well lose any possible savings.

What's the solution?

Since avoidance is the only answer, your production department should be equipped to properly plan for good reproduction. It's not enough to simply know which pages have available color and which ones don't. The imposition itself must be viewed in its printing format.

All web printers have imposition layout sheets available for customer use. So it's merely a matter of planning the book out, dropping the pages into their respective positions, and re-doing the entire procedure until you get something that will print, with little or no in-line color conflicts.

Figure 2 shows one solution. It's the "checkerboard" method of laying out a form. With this solution, no advertisement will run in-line with another. But to make use of the color available, you might choose to print editorial color above or below the ads.

There are two points to consider if you use this approach:

First, you must get it in writing to your printer that all advertisements take priority over all editorial.

Second, be prepared for some terrible printing on your editorial. True, many times you will luck out. But occasionally, when the printer favors a given ad, the editorial will look as bad as an early makeready, throughout the run.

There is an even better solution to the in-line situation. As shown in Figure 3, instead of checkerboarding color ads and editorial, you could checkerboard color itself. In this example, the publisher is deciding to use only four pages of process color per eight-page side.

Is such a solution practical? It would depend on just how critical you are about your color, and what you want to spend. Taken to an extreme, this solution could double your four-color makeready costs.

Be thankful

All of these examples use an eight-page side. That makes sense, because most magazines are printed on standard-width webs.

But if you think the in-line problems discussed above are troublesome, consider the poor production managers who use wide-webs. They have 16 pages to work

Figure 1.

13 4C	4 4C	1 4C	16 4C
4C 12	4C 5	4C 8	4C 9

Figure 2.

13 4C EDIT	4 4C AD	1 4C EDIT	16 4C AD
4C AD 12	4C EDIT 5	4C AD 8	4C EDIT 9

Figure 3.

4C	B&W	4C	B&W
B&W	4C	B&W	4C

with on any process-color side. The possibility of compromising on four ads running in-line can make a veteran production manager polish his or her resume to perfection.

And be jealous

On the other hand, you might envy the person who plans forms for a mini-web with only four pages to worry about at a time. Meaning, even if that person checkerboards in order to accommodate two ads, only two pages of the form are lost.

The more effort you put into avoiding in-line problems, the less often you'll have to resort to the standard explanations:

•"Gee, none of our copies were like that. You must have accidentally been shipped a makeready copy."

•"Your film was (full, weak, out of register). We did the best we could."

•"Bear with us. We're switching printers as soon as we can."

•"We fired that production director; it will never happen again."

•"What color problem?"

Press checks

By Jeffery R. Parnau

"The customer is going to press-check the job himself? Add 20 percent to the price. We didn't know he wanted to see it on press."

Say what? No kidding, a printer actually said that.

"Union rules don't allow us to have customers in the pressroom."

"We have many trade secrets, and if we allow anybody in there, our competition will figure out how we do things."

"It's dangerous in there."

"It's against company policy."

"Be honest. You don't know as much about the press as we do. Let us do our job, and you do yours."

Yup, those are the excuses. What bothers me is, how many of the excuses are related to the opening line of this column?

On the other hand, publishers have their own reasons to avoid the pressroom:

"You put the onus on the printer if he has total responsibility to run the job well."

"If I sign a press sheet, I'm stuck with the job no matter what. If I miss something important, the printer is in the clear."

"I'll be damned before I wait up all night for a form that should have run yesterday. They go out of their way to make it inconvenient."

From the sound of the above, you'd think printers spend most of their days waging out-and-out wars against publishers and vice versa.

To watch or not to watch

But there are other opinions. During a Folio Face-to-Face session last year, a printer-panelist suggested that customers should watch their job run on press at least twice a year, possibly more if the job is complicated. Why? To understand how the job is produced . . . to relate his or her preferences directly to the pressmen . . . to show interest in the job, which will generate the respect of those who run it.

Yet most publishers might hesitate to send an employee to the plant. First of all, it's difficult to know whether the employee knows his stuff. And second, assuming any mechanical responsibility for a task the printer normally performs is risky. Signing a press sheet does, in effect, bless the job.

It is my opinion that yes, you should maintain direct contact with your work. You should watch it run a few times a year at a minimum. But how do you accomplish that while not relieving the printer of his responsibility and control?

Try this. Pick the person or persons who will go to the plant, and advise them of their act: Act interested, act curious, act concerned. You are going to learn, not to teach. The following points will be helpful:

1. Admit your ignorance. Ask stupid questions.

2. Deny that you are doing a color okay. State that you are there to watch the job and learn about printing.

3. Never tell. Just ask. "Is this too blue?" carries an entirely different meaning than "This is too blue."

4. Don't sign anything. If you're not okaying the color, there is no need to put your Hancock anywhere.

5. If you see a major problem, ask about it. "Isn't this page upside down?" It might not be, you know.

6. If you have preferences, state them. "We like that advertiser" can make one ad look better than others.

Even seasoned, experienced production personnel avoid telling a pressman what to do, short of telling him to stop the press. The mere fact that a person is there is plenty of impetus for the operator to go for great color. And the presence of that customer on the spot may well bring answers to questions you've had about reproduction.

You'll never impress a pressman

What about those who think they know enough to "really" do a press check?

Such people are quite rare, and if your own employee likes to say "more yellow, less red, and wash the top blanket on the third unit," he's probably a good liar.

The most common error made by such know-it-alls is their failure to understand that good pressmen can walk that fine hairline between adding ink to *get* color and adding ink to *kill* color.

How can adding ink have either effect? Simple. Up to a point, increasing the amount of ink on a page will make it look more colorful. (We're describing a full-color photo.) After the magic line is crossed, the addition of ink will begin to absorb too much light, rather than reflect it to the eye.

Pity the poor customer who enters the pressroom at the moment the operator is applying as much ink as possible. He wants a bluer sky, and says "more blue ink." The pressman complies, and the sky gets darker. "Still needs more." Darker yet. Until he finally botches up the page so bad, he thinks the pressman is playing games.

Unless the customer literally knows more about the press and the paper and the ink than the pressman himself, it's wiser to sound like an idiot. "My boss will kill me if that sky isn't snappier and prettier. Can you help me?" And the pressman may well go and cut the red ink back a notch.

If that fixes the sky, who cares what you sound like? You will never, ever impress a pressman with your knowledge . . . so why not impress yourself by getting exactly what you want?

For those who insist on calling all the shots, I wish you luck. Doing a press check is like going to your spouse's office Christmas party. You're not on your own turf, and you are in a strictly social situation. An error in attitude is as damaging—and attention-getting—as wearing a lampshade.

And what about the printers who refuse to let customers into the pressroom . . . or, as the opening comment suggested, charge them for the privilege? Maybe it's because they get away with inferior printing when the customer isn't there. Maybe they allow customers to call too many shots, such as when to save. But until you hear the roar of the ink and the smell of the press, you'll never be sure.

Stick with open-door printers, and take a look now and then.

Production vs. sales, Epilogue

In an earlier article, I presented the question of whether production is given enough consideration . . . particularly when conflicts arise with the ad sales department.

Briefly, here's the problem: When arbitrary decisions—or late changes—are made, should a production manager have the authority to say no? Or should a third party, such as the publisher or president, take charge in settling disputes?

To be honest, I had a gut feeling I was out on a limb with the column. Historically, production managers have had as much authority as the third-shift janitor. Similar jobs, too: Both clean up after somebody else made a mess; both work after hours.

And per my offer, I suggested that anyone with an opinion should feel free to grab a few inches of this column and state it. Herewith—and anonymously—is the input.

"As a sequel, try 'Production vs. Sales and Editorial.'

"We publish two journals, both with four-color editorial (scattered) and advertising. Try holding a budget working with placement of editorial color on the same page as the reference even though you end up with several consecutive pages of color and constantly have to run four over four *(Ed. note: four colors on the top and bottom of the web)* on press. Try fitting in four-color—or even black only—advertising in smaller than full units, with a policy that calls for 'no advertising of any kind interrupting editorial except at the article's end. And every advertiser wants a right-hand page.

"The editorial director hates the ads in editorial matter. The ad director hates 'bunching up' the advertisers. The publisher flips when you present the printing bills. 'Why did you have to run four over four on every form?'

"You can't please everybody, but it helps once in a while to please somebody."

And this letter:

"You certainly hit the nail on the head. Being one of those relatively rare publishers who comes from the production department and not sales, editorial, or financial, I have tried to bring a new perspective into our operations in this regard.

"As you stated, too many publications are strictly 'sales oriented.' Failure to look at the whole picture regarding overall profitability and economics is exactly what you have described. Quite consistently we use the fourth option that you brought up. In this case, I serve as the final judge.

"Like most practical publications, we take late advertisements. Sometimes very late. From a salesman's standpoint, it is more profitable to him personally to publish an advertisement in this issue for certain, rather than be promised that same advertisement in a subsequent issue. This is where the overall picture must be carefully coordinated."

And a note:

"It's about time somebody put it in print. As the publisher, I am concerned with one thing. The bottom line. If it doesn't make sense to accept a late ad, or a spread we can't economically handle at the last minute, we simply don't run it. We're in business to make money, not pamper the ad director's ego or pad his wallet."

Well, I was a bit surprised at the above comments. Either my position makes a bit of sense, or those who disagree with me went out of business because they lost too much production money.

Ethics

By Jeffery R. Parnau

A true story:

The customer was a publisher of several small trade magazines. He was getting competitive bids for a contract, with a price range of $4,000 to $6,000 for printing and paper. When the final bids were in, one printer had a bottom line of $5,200, while another came in at $4,800.

The publisher contacted the low bidder and explained that he would certainly like to give him the work . . . but that $4,800 was too high. He asked if the printer couldn't cut it by $500, and if so the job would be his. The printer cut the price. The publisher gave him the work.

Now, the story might have ended there . . . but it so happened that the competitive bidders were not total enemies. At a cocktail party, the $5,200 bidder made the comment that something was wrong with his own pricing. He had cut everything to the bone to get that job, and still didn't get the work. And suddenly, the printer who was producing the work for $4,300 (he'd knocked $500 off his bid) realized he'd been had. A very sour relationship had just been born.

Is it ethical?

Obviously, the above situation was triggered by the publisher, who created an artificial price in order to get his work done less expensively. But is it fair?

First, let's look at the publisher's side. Suppose he suspected that the two bidders were in some sort of conspiracy. In that case, he might have tried to lower the price in order to get a fair deal.

If that kind of thinking is necessary, however, we're all in trouble. It would mean that there is virtually no way to get an honest bid in the printing industry.

Let's be a bit more realistic. Could it be that all printing prices are padded because all buyers try to squeeze a few pennies out before signing on the dotted line? And if that *is* the case, are we in a situation where we must all grind printing prices down because printers expect it?

How many of us haven't asked a printer to cut this price or that, only to learn that it is a routine practice? Lower this printing price . . . that press price . . . shave something off the bindery, and "you'll get the job." For good or bad, it does seem that there is always a tiny bit of fat in the original quotation. The quantity of fat may depend on how attractive the work is to the printer *at that time.*

So, it appears that the question of artificial prices can't be called fair or unfair based on the above facts. The printing industry can play games; prices can be manipulated. Printers can undercut a competitor for spite . . . or simply because they have more economical machinery for a particular job. That puts the question of ethics back in the buyer's lap.

The net effects

In order to get closer to a position, let's look at the possible results of creating artificial bids.

•If the printer finds out, the situation is not only embarrassing (as it was in the above example), it can also trigger economic revenge. The printer's normal reaction in such a case would be to get that money back somehow. He will take pains to make sure that particular buyer gets nailed next time. Maybe he'll change the overrun percentage on the job and deliver a quantity of sub-quality products. Maybe he'll pad a loose area of the bill, such as prep work. Or maybe he'll be painted into a corner and take his lumps.

In addition, he will tag the buyer a con man. And if the buyer pulls it too often on too many printers, he is quietly and unofficially blacklisted. He gets burned in the end.

•If the printer doesn't find out, he will have to recover the loss from all customers (assuming that the price was lowered to something less than a reasonable profit level). If the printer never realizes what happened, all of his customers—you and me, for example—get burned a little. The culprit, if he's good at creating phony bids—can then continue to have other buyers pay for a percentage of his printing. Not a fair situation, of course.

•There are some subtle, cumulative effects as well: If printers get the idea that buyers are manipulating prices and creating phony competition, they will learn to protect themselves by getting their initial bids up higher. As the bids creep up, the buyers react with more aggressive price chopping, and the cycle begins to perpetuate itself. In the long run, the printers will—as a group—still compete, and the buyers will still get printing . . . but all will be doing it under the umbrella of complicated low-balling, high-balling, and revenge.

Counter-productivity

In my opinion, there is nothing to be gained—in the long run—by knocking a bid down with an artificial price. Sure, the individual might win in an isolated situation . . . but eventually, someone pays the tab. When it's not the guilty party, it's buyers in general. If printers were consistently losing money to fast-talking customers, they'd have been out of business long ago. They're still in business, so they're not losing.

If it's unethical to mold prices as described, how can the practice be stopped? We know it goes on, and we logically fear that prices may be padded at the time . . . yet the big picture says we shouldn't play the game. The simplest solution would be for printers to bid properly from the start and to hardline the buyers. If someone asks for a quote, a printer should simply assemble the initial prices in the most economical fashion, put in the profit margin, draw the bottom line, and that's that!

Take our opening example. What if the low-priced printer had said, "If Acme has us beat, more power to you. I hope they do a good job for you. Bye-bye." What would the buyer—who didn't have a lower bid in sight—have done? Either he could have gone to the higher-priced printer and paid the premium, or he could have made up some flimsy excuse ("They forgot the paper") and returned to the original low bid.

In our example, the buyer was obviously going for the financial throat ... so chances are, he would have eaten humble pie and placed the job. At the same time, he probably would have given himself away. Chalk one up for the printer (who, in theory, makes a normal profit), another for the other customers who don't pay the tab on the underbid, and chalk up a lesson for the artificial bidder.

It would be nice, although optimistic, to assume that printers will spontaneously begin to provide clean, tight, rock-bottom unpadded prices. Is there anything that buyers could do to promote such practices? Moving from optimism to idealism, here's a possibility.

Suppose you—the buyer—put the specs together for an upcoming job and send bid requests to three printers. Suppose you explain to each of them—in a letter or on the phone—that you will make the specs as complete as need be in order to get the most accurate bids.

Keep supposing: You explain to each printer that only those companies who are fully capable of doing a decent quality job are being invited to submit a competitive price. (It's not at all uncommon for a buyer to mention just who else is bidding the work.) And finally, you tell them you will examine the final prices and select a printer, simple as that. No second tries.

Making suppositions is a fine mental exercise, but the acid test will be putting these ideals into practice. Will they work right off the bat? Probably not. But if you—and all of your peers—begin to follow through on such techniques, several things would happen.

First, you'd begin to get a reputation as a dollar-conscious square shooter. Novices in the print-purchasing field often have no idea of just how important a reputation can be.

And second, you would eventually see a trend toward consistent, competitive, bottom-line bids on the first go-around. No games, no fat to trim, and smoother sailing in picking a printer for your jobs.

In "proving" that you are dealing on the level, it doesn't hurt to release non-volatile information to those who didn't get the job. If a losing bidder calls and asks where the job was placed, why not tell him where ... and why? In my view, it doesn't hurt to give a general idea of what part (or parts) of a bid prompted you to go elsewhere.

By cleaning up this area of the purchasing act, nobody can lose. As the situation is now, far too many buyers either use artificial prices or—almost as bad—go to their favorite printer and say, "You were 4 percent high. If you can lower your price, you get the job." In those situations, you must keep in mind that the buyer is—for practical purposes—allowing the printer's competitor to create the selling price. That's just unhealthy.

Ethics, Part II
By Jeffery R. Parnau

The subject of kickbacks isn't given much attention in the printing industry. There are several reasons for this, the most obvious being the fact that people who give or receive kickbacks don't want to talk about the matter.

But using the term kickback may be a bit too broad, for there are many different ways for a buyer to pick up some sort of freebie, be it money, material, or a favor. So for the purpose of this article, this discussion will encompass "anything that doesn't show on the invoice."

Free lunch
Starting on a fairly innocent level, how about lunch? Certainly, the most common way to get something for nothing is to accept the countless invitations to lunch that most salesmen are inclined to offer. There are many valid reasons for accepting these invitations: Lunch is a good way to meet a salesperson, get a feeling for his style, learn a bit about his company, and, what the heck, get some food. Although I don't know how many martinis you should drink (remember the three-martini-lunch legislation?), I do think that the lunch hour can be a productive part of the work day.

But even something as innocent as free lunch can be taken to excess. Those excesses often occur at dinnertime. If a salesman must constantly wheel his clients to the most expensive dinnershows in the city, and the customer expects this kind of treatment routinely, it can become a form of a kickback.

As an example, I was once given a "sales pitch" from a fairly large printer in a major city. The pitch was a $300 dinner, show, and— pardon the blush—a strong insinuation that we could satisfy our every desire. All within that beautiful city ... and available *every* time we went to press. (We were never offered a complete estimate, by the way.)

The problem here is that the buyer could begin to pay more attention to the night life than the matter at hand. On top of that, keep in mind that the salesperson isn't "giving" anything to the customer. It all gets tacked on to the bill eventually ... but, of course, without a description. In summary, "free lunch" isn't too dangerous, as long as there is some reasonable purpose to the event. When it's taken to an excess, it can be a bribe.

The cash payment
Freebies can be more blatant. It is not unheard of

for a buyer to accept a cash bribe as a reward for placing a job with a particular printer. The highest offer I've personally seen was a clean, laundered $12,000 . . . but then, I haven't seen too many. The upper limit for cash kickbacks is certainly much higher than that.

We needn't spend much time or discussion on this particular freebie: It is patently unethical. For a buyer to consider taking payment such as this is dangerous, dirty, and counterproductive. It is merely stealing from one's own company, because whatever the payment is, it will show up on the invoice over a period of time. In addition, accepting a bribe will surely get around the industry, and there goes a reputation. Finally, the person who accepts the bribe can be blackmailed into accepting technically inferior work.

Softer names for bribes?

Less blatant than the above, but in the same ballpark, is the "finder's fee." This is a sum which a printer might be willing to pay to a person who is somehow responsible for placing an order or signing a contract.

There is nothing wrong with a finder's fee when it's used properly. For example, if an independent freelance salesperson places your job at a printer (with whom he has no direct ties), he may be paid a straight commission over the long haul, or he may be bought off with a lump payment. A finder's fee.

We bring this fee up only to point out the obvious. The finder's fee should never weave its way into the hands of the buyer. There is no ethical reason for this to happen, even if a salesperson says it is commonplace.

The real action: third party

So much for the up-front, here's-the-money routines. Fact is, the direct cash payment to the buyer is not the most common form of a kickback. The real action occurs when there is a third party in the picture.

Consider consultants versus brokers. A person can be one or the other, or both . . . but not at the same time on the same job.

A broker is an independent salesperson who gets bids from various printers on, let's say, your printing requirements. If he places the work for you, he may bill you directly for the printing, or he may have the printer bill you. In either case, there will be a commission paid to the broker.

This is routine, and there's nothing wrong with it. A broker can save you the time and expense of getting a series of bids. He may be more knowledgeable than you, too, in which case he would possibly do a better job.

The consultant, on the other hand, may have the same knowledge as the broker, but instead of getting a percentage of the total payment, he is paid by the client (you) to examine the job at hand, find the right production situation, and give advice. Again, there are many valid reasons to use a consultant, and it's a normal practice.

Here's the hitch: The most routine method of double-dipping in this business is for the consultant to bill the client for his advice while at the same time accepting a finder's fee (or commission, or monthly percentage of the bill) from the printer. Somebody gets taken for a ride. The customer.

This practice is more than simply unfair. If you are paying the consultant/broker to handle your job with a printer, and the printer is paying him too, what happens when something goes wrong with the job? Both paying parties will say, "Straighten this out. That's what we're paying you for." The middleman, of course, has his hands tied. Damned if he does or damned if he doesn't.

I think this topic—brokers/buyers—was demonstrated well in a mailing I received recently. The pitch was by a firm that offered its consultation and print purchasing expertise at "no charge whatsoever." You may have heard similar pitches: The firm will come in to your office, examine your printing requirements, and advise you that "Printer X" will save you $10,000 per year. That may well be the case . . . but the consultation is 1) not free, and 2) in need of careful scrutiny.

Is the consulting firm truly independent, or is it in cahoots with a particular printer? If all is on the level, fine . . . but the firm will then make their money from the printer who gets the work. They will be acting as printing brokers. The come-on of free consultation is merely an advertising trick. Any broker worth his salt offers free consultation, and spends time and money to secure new business. In comparison, any respectable consultant charges nicely for his services.

Unfortunately, the question of ethics for buyers isn't limited to the buyers themselves. When brokers and consultants enter the picture, the buyers run the risk of participating—unknowingly—in an unethical triangle. The buyer, of course, is the only one who can lose money.

The only way for you to ease your mind is to get to know the people you deal with. A consultant should have many references; a broker should have a reputation. Any third party will probably have a history of dealing with various printers. If you are entirely up front when checking out a broker or consultant, you can get honest answers (like one I received: He's a petty thief).

In the long run, buyers can collectively work to reduce the skimming perpetrated by unethical brokers and consultants by paying attention, asking questions, and making accusations if necessary. (I should mention here that I do not have low esteem for either brokers or consultants. I have acted as both.)

Free travel

There's another common inducement to the buyer—usually the novice—that's not uncommon. It's a couple of airline tickets to the printer's home base, offered so you can see the plant and meet the people. I see nothing obviously wrong in using the printer's tickets to see his plant . . . as long as it is with your company's approval, and as long as you are at least somewhat interested in working with that printer.

Keep in mind again, though, that sales expenses eventually show up on the invoice. You would be better off having your company pay directly for your travel expenses.

The complete invoice

If you eventually pay for all these little details, it might be productive to see an invoice that's more explicit than most. The sample I have produced assumes that some print user, somewhere, is paying for every down-and-dirty trick, in addition to the innocent, routine expenses. But my point is, your payment to the printer does include everything. Just because you don't normally see certain items doesn't mean you're not paying for them.

Excuses, excuses

By Jeffery R. Parnau

When you think about it, printing magazines can be pretty complicated stuff. The opportunities exist for a multitude of errors, in as many different areas.

Which leads to this column's topic: If there are countless problem areas, there are countless excuses you may hear from a printer. So let's take a light-hearted look at excuses ... and their possible causes.

•*Excuse: The film processor went down, so we'll fall behind a day or two on your prep work.*

Possible problems: (1) Somebody goofed on the job we did last week, and now we're redoing it, so we can't start your work. (2) We owe the film supplier too much money and he cut us off. (3) We're so busy in the press department, we'd have no way to run your job this week anyhow. (4) You owe us too much money, and we're punishing you.

•*Excuse: We're experiencing mysterious web breaks and losing lots of time.*

Possible problems: (1) We just hired an inexperienced roll tender, and he messes up every other splice. (2) We're running off that cheap stock we sold you. (3) That press is so weatherbeaten, you're lucky you ever get a magazine off it.

•*Excuse: Horrible folder problems; haven't saved a signature all day.*

Possible problems: (1) I told those dummies not to tell you about that imposition. It never worked before, and never will. (2) That goof-off on third shift misplaced the replacement folder pins. (3) We started the job a shift late, so of course we have nothing saved.

•*Excuse: According to union rules, you can't come into the pressroom; we'll bring samples out to you.*

Possible problems: (1) It's such a disaster in there, you'd never want to print with us again. (2) You don't know a damn thing about printing, so don't go bothering our pressmen. (3) We'd be ashamed if you saw the junk we put in the "good" skids. (4) You might notice that we have one press . . . not two, like we told you.

•*Excuse: The mill shorted us this month; we'll have to go back on press later.*

Possible problems: (1) We're yanking your job off press so we can get a head start on a new account. (2) We swiped some of your paper for another job. Now we have to replace it. (3) A pipe broke in the warehouse. The vice president will tell you how much stock you lost; that's his job. (4) The mill cut us off; we think they talked to our film supplier.

•*Excuse: We've got some trimming problems in the bindery; we'll catch up tomorrow.*

Possible problems: (1) Fred forgot to have the knives sharpened again. (2) We're still binding that job of your competitor's. (3) The Postal Service is in there giving us hell.

•*Excuse: Those magazines you saw were make-ready only. We'd never deliver that kind of work to a customer.*

Possible problems: (1) We ran a little short, so instead of going back on press, we used the makeready junk to finish the job and meet count. (2) We always have a batch of sub-quality magazines in your run, but we always

shipped them to Canada. (3) You're too picky. It's good enough for you.

•*Excuse: We had to charge you overtime because you were late with your film.*

Possible problems: (1) We're sick and tired of you missing your due date, and you're going to pay for it from now on, overtime or not. (2) Your job has such a marginal profit level, we can't afford a dime for overtime or we'll lose money on you.

•*Excuse: You had in-line problems on press. You should have anticipated color problems with your ads.*

Possible problems: (1) Gee, didn't anybody even look at this job on press? It's awful. (2) If that red printing unit keeps doubling, I suppose we'll have to break down and fix it. (3) Must have run that on second shift. If only we could find a qualified supervisor.

•*Excuse: Your insert cards ran out while we had another ten thousand magazines to bind.*

Possible problems: (1) That'll teach you to farm out your cards. Let us do them next time. (2) That drunk ran into a skid with his hand-truck and threw away everything he couldn't restack. (3) Actually, we ran out of covers, so we shut down.

•*Excuse: We had to add a man to the press because of a union agreement, so your prices are going up.*

Possible problems: (1) You'd figure out any other reason for a price hike. You'll never nail us down on this one. (2) We've been running it a man short for years, but they finally complained. (3) The man we added wipes up grease spilling from that bad red unit. We really should consider rebuilding it.

•*Excuse: We shut down . . . had a blanket problem.*

Possible problems: (1) The air conditioner went out, and when we opened the doors, June bugs flew in, got into the press, and smashed three blankets before we figured it out. (2) The boss is cheap and won't let us replace blankets until they don't print.

•*Excuse: The left widget in the lower gizmo knocked the press out for 24 hours.*

Possible problem: We didn't work yesterday.

Should you investigate?

Of course, I have failed to point out that any one of these excuses may be the only legitimate explanation for the situation. Printers *do* have problems with printing units, folders, short-count cards, and the like.

But printers, like publishers, are capable of stretching the truth on occasion. How do you know when an excuse is valid?

If an answer—a totally honest answer—is important to you, get involved. See the problem with your own eyes, talk to the equipment operators, ask for physical evidence.

But in most cases, you might be just as well off to trust that your printer is either (1) telling the truth, or (2) stretching the facts for a valid reason, such as not getting you insanely upset.

And if any ambitious printer out there wants to make a rebuttal —tongue in cheek or otherwise—I'd be more than happy to share some column space.

Lost shipment insurance

By Jeffery R. Parnau

In another column, I drifted a bit into the management process of deciding how a magazine should be transmitted to the reader: electronically or mechanically; on paper or via some computer network.

All fine and well, but if I were to take a hand count of those readers who are currently using electronic publishing techniques, I'm afraid that we old-fashioned publishers would be in the obvious majority.

So this time, why don't we drift into an area which could be easily solved by electronic publishers, but which presents a real threat to us old folks? The problem: Loss of data.

Although the term data is used loosely and widely in the electronic arena, it is largely unheard of in the mechanical publishing world. Yet if you take a moment to look at your data, you'll agree that you have a lot of it to lose.

Take the average magazine. My surveys and experience show me that most magazines are typeset and pasted up in-house. The data flow starts with either an outside contributor or an in-house writer, but is quickly transformed into digital information upon its entry to a phototypesetter. That is a form of data backup: both the hard-copy original (paper manuscript) and its electronic counterpart (tape or disk file) are intact.

But what happens next? First, the electronic output is used to create typesetting galleys. No problem, since they can be run again. But then, the galleys are the object of intensive manual labor. They are organized into the actual paste-ups.

Photographs are the next concern. While a few publishers shoot halftones in house, most do not. And when the photos are to be run in full color, virtually no publisher will have the facilities to separate them.

Obviously, all of this valuable stuff is packed into a box or stuffed into an auto trunk and sent to vendors. The question: What if it is lost?

What's involved?

Starting with paste-ups, a loss during shipment could be overcome if the publisher had the time and manpower to simply rerun the material, and reassemble it. But time—particularly in magazine publishing—is money.

What about the black-and-white photos? Replacing a candid shot is a virtual impossibility. Likewise, replacing the "perfect" color slide can be an insurmountable task.

What protection can you give yourself if you cannot afford to lose material which—as happens often—simply cannot be replaced, due to either its original nature or the time involved to duplicate it?

A few years ago, the answer would have been to invest in a complete prep shop. It would need color duplication facilities (try $15,000), a litho camera ($5,000), a good film processor ($5,000), a lot of planning and wiring (maybe $2,500), and a few skilled employees (at $20,000 annually a person).

For all that, you would get a product which cost you more to produce, and backup which—if you were lucky—you would never, ever need.

Hardly a bargain, but you might sleep better.

Well, if losing paste-ups and original photos is a concern, you can take heart in the fact that technologies have changed in the past two years, even for us simple folks who occasionally whack out a memo on a manual typewriter. I'd like to briefly describe some equipment and backup techniques which can not only prevent the ultimate catastrophe (losing the magazine), but can even save you some money.

Insurance investment that saves money

The first and unavoidable step is an in-house camera. How publishers function without one is beyond me, but I hear it is done all the time.

A simple camera—capable of producing stats, negatives, and so forth—can be purchased and installed for less than $5,000. Even less if you already have adequate wiring and a nice, dark place to put it.

I admit, $5,000 is substantial to some publishers ... but no art director who's ever worked with one will later work without one. It allows the production department to get the job done right, if not actually cheaper.

Moving along, any stat camera can also produce negatives. One of the problems in shooting your own page negatives is that you need a processor ... any common rapid-access processor. But let's back up a bit. If you set your own type, and produce anything of even moderate quality, you already have a rapid access processor. (If you set type using a stabilization processor, you aren't interested in quality anyway, so you might as well not worry about losing your material, either.)

So if you have a camera, and you set quality type, you can shoot your own negatives.

How do you then protect your halftones? The same camera will produce halftones, but they can be a bit tricky. So you could either 1) train a person to shoot a good-quality rapid-access halftone, or 2) merely shoot backup halftones—my term for a continuous-tone (no-dot) version of a photo. A duplicate photo, so to speak, shot from the original and held as backup.

There is one more option: Shooting screened PMT (Photo Mechanical Transfer) halftones. Although they do not offer much in terms of quality when pasted directly onto a paste-up, they are a viable alternative, and an inexpensive one.

That covers the paste-ups and B/W photos. What about those irreplaceable color prints and slides?

No problem with color

Believe it or not, if you have taken the matter to the point described above, you are about $200 away from total protection against the potential lost magazine. Both Kodak and Agfa-Gavert have introduced color duplication materials that work in the average, poorly controlled darkroom . . . meaning, lousy temperature control, untrained operators, and minimal equipment budgets.

With these simple systems, you can use a standard process camera to make a duplicate color print, either at the same size as the original, or scaled to its appropriate printing size.

For color slides, a simple enlarger—costing less than $200—will allow you to make prints from color slides or small transparencies. Contact-printing is also available for larger transparencies.

For the skeptics out there who would insist on a $5,000 enlarger with a suitable color-head, I dare you to buy a $100 Omega and $15 worth of filters. Prove me wrong.

And it won't take your line employees long to figure out that if you can duplicate your color material, you might as well dupe it to size and mount it in its eventual printing position, relative to other photos. The dollar savings in both separation and stripping costs will pay for the setup in as little as a half an issue.

You're terribly quality conscious at your magazine you say? Then don't put your backup material into the production cycle. But if you're that picky, you would want the backup just so you would print that particular, special photo, rather than the second-best (or a completely different) version.

What's the bottom line? In effect, for very little investment, you can do the following:

1. Ensure that your paste-ups will neither be lost nor fall apart during transit.

2. Provide either back-up or the actual printable photo for halftones.

3. Ensure that you never lose a slide or color print which cannot be replaced.

4. Save money on separations and stripping.

5. Take two full steps backward from the electronic invasion, and protect your materials in good old fashioned physical forms.

I hope I'm not sounding like a computer traitor. It's just that most of us still put ink on paper, and most of us run the common risk of losing part or all of a time-oriented product . . . one which sometimes cannot be replaced at all.

Think ink

By Jeffery R. Parnau

It is no secret that ink contains petroleum products. No secret either that petroleum products are outrageously expensive, and getting worse. And it comes as no surprise that printers are mighty cautious about billing their customers for the amount of ink used on a job.

Couple the above with today's increased amount of four-color printing (which demands far more ink than black and white reproduction), and the stage is set: Customers are getting nailed with ink bills . . . bills which can easily constitute over 5 percent of a magazine invoice.

So, it was quite logical that printers began to warm up to the idea of billing ink separately from other materials and labor. Over the past few years, several different billing methods have been developed. Some are better than others . . . which means, some will cost you less in the long run.

Per color/per page

One such billing method is the "per color/per page" system. Basically, it works like this: If you use black ink on a coated page, price "X" will cover the cost of ink for 1,000 impressions. If you use black plus a standard process color, "Y" covers the same number of copies.

Advantages: The chief advantage of these flat-rated prices is that you, the buyer, can anticipate ink costs in advance. True, the price of this petroleum-derived goo rises on a regular schedule . . . but you are given fair warning of the hikes.

Disadvantages: Unfortunately, there are several disadvantages to this particular system. The main problem is that it is, at best, an "averaging" technique. The averaged factor is obvious: You might run a headline in process yellow and process magenta, using two colors in a small area. Your cost would be the same as if you had run a full-bleed, four-color photo on the same page. One headline hardly chews up the amount of ink consumed by a full-bleed photograph.

Second, the cost-per-page/color technique does not show the cost of the ink itself. It shows only that the printer is charging a certain amount, which may have little relation to what the printer pays for the stuff.

When to use it: The color/page system isn't totally useless, however. It is the fastest, simplest method of passing ink costs directly to the customer. For those magazines that use a limited amount of process color, this billing technique would be adequate. Not terribly informative, but adequate.

Per square inch

A slightly more sophisticated method of billing ink

would take into account the approximate area covered by the ink itself. For example, the total coverage of the above-mentioned headline might be two square inches in two colors, while the full-bleed photo would occupy 93 square inches in four colors.

The resulting figures would be billed to the customer, and would theoretically cover the actual amount of ink used.

Advantages: The advantage of square-inch billing over per-page billing is obvious. It takes into account the fact that each page uses a different amount of ink. It is a better system.

Disadvantages: It's far from perfect. The main problem is that only one or two printers in the country are equipped to accurately estimate total density of ink coverage. A good estimate would be performed by a scanning densitometer, which would record the values of each piece of film. However, the usual method of estimating total coverage is by eye ... and one opinion is as good as another.

Furthermore, one customer may "paint" the page, whereas another likes light, airy, almost weak process color. The conclusion: the system is, at best, an honest guess.

When to use it: Still, it is not a useless system. On the contrary, if a printer is willing to spend the time in doing reasonably close estimates of total coverage, the customer will benefit from the effort in the end. It is closer to being accurate than color/page billing. It just isn't perfect.

Actual poundage

There are two other ways to measure the amount of ink used on a job. One is a rather clumsy method of weighing the ink itself. The other is achieved by installing flow meters on the press. In either case, the advantage of using actual consumption is obvious: You pay only for what you need on your job. If you run light coverage, the press eats less ink; if you paint each page, you gobble up the petrols.

1. Weighing the buckets: This system involves a bit of planning by the printer, but very little equipment. Basically, the printer starts your job with the ink fountains full. The barrels (or buckets) from which ink is taken are weighed before your job. Ink is removed from the barrels and added to the fountains as necessary. And when the job is wrapped up, the fountains are again topped, the barrels are weighed, and you know exactly how much ink you have eaten.

2. Flow meters: The other alternative can be slightly expensive for the printer. Flow meters, which are installed above each ink fountain, record the actual volume of ink passing into the press. It isn't exactly cheap to retrofit a press with such equipment (most new web presses have flow meters installed as a matter of routine), but it is very accurate once the setup is running.

Advantages of actual billing: Actual poundage billing is the ultimate tool for invoicing ink. Both the customer and printer benefit, because neither one of them is guessing at bottom lines.

Although the bucket/barrel weighing system is a bit cumbersome, it does provide access to true poundage used. And the ink-flow measurements will surely become more popular as buyers demand accurate ink charges—

charges we will all be paying as such costs escalate.

Disadvantages of actual billing: When compared to any of the other methods of paying for ink, this system shines. There are no obvious disadvantages to paying for what you get.

Assuming that you are currently paying for ink via one of the above methods, and assuming also that flow meters will become more popular, what do you actually pay for the ink?

Most reasonable printers offer "cost plus," when the monitoring systems are accurate enough to provide a reliable consumption figure. Cost-plus-10 percent is a fairly common number.

That sounds fine ... until your ink bill goes into the $30,000 range, which isn't uncommon for a hefty magazine. And furthermore, what *is* the printer's cost?

There are two ways to look at it, which can result in significant differences on your invoice. One printer might say, "Cost includes the time it takes to order the ink by my agent, the paperwork to track it, the floor space to store it, and the labor to haul it to the press."

And another printer will say, "Cost is what's on the invoice I receive from the manufacturer."

Whose version is correct? Both. You can say ink costs include or exclude overhead, interest charges, late payment penalties, or any other variable common to business. The critical point is that you—the ultimate purchaser of ink—know which figures your printer is using.

Your printer will probably be willing to share this information with you, even to the point of showing you his actual invoices from the ink manufacturer. After all, it is your money that is ultimately being spent.

If a printer really wants to take advantage of you, no amount of detective work will prove it. For good or bad, trust is a key factor with ink, and with virtually all other items shown on your invoice. Just one more case for a good buyer/seller relationship, bonded by optimism and faith.

Ink is so ridiculously priced that—like paper—it is drifting into the publisher-supplied category. In that there is little relief in sight, publishers are beginning to ask whether they should do their own ink shopping, and ship directly to the printer.

It seems certain that a few of the major newsweeklies will lay firm groundwork for the rest of us. They will, with sheer muscle, negotiate direct purchases of ink, matched to their specific printing requirements, and ship the material to the printer, as is currently done with paper. They will maintain their own inventories, use penalty/reward systems for consumption, and pay only for what they actually use.

But until the groundwork is complete, it would be premature for the average publisher to purchase ink directly. Before this becomes common, there will be a mountain of technical and paperwork problems to be ironed out. And after that, ink purchasing will be a likely candidate for cooperative purchasing by publishers, requiring even more coordination.

Until then, your best bet is to use one of the above systems to pay for your ink ... and at that, to use the system which will most nearly allow you to pay only for what you are actually using.

The paper game
By Jeffery R. Parnau

"If we shave a single day off our average collection time, we save $8,000 a day."

Sound crazy? It's not. In fact, that figure is already much higher. The statement was made by a printer when interest rates were hovering around 12 percent. Since then, they have risen to 20 percent, fallen to 10-3/4 percent, and scrambled back to 21 percent. By the time you read this, they could be anywhere from 10 percent to 25 percent. Such numbers make cash flow a gamble rather than a projection.

And the "collection time" that printer was talking about had everything in the world to do with magazine production. As I've said before, you can call production anything you want. For magazine publishers and printers, however, production is money, plain and simple.

So how does a printer go about saving $8,000 by reducing collection time, say, from 54 days to 53 days?

In many respects, a printer can save money conventionally: Get paid on time, put the money into an appropriate investment, and make more money with it.

But a printer has other ways to save. Considering the fact that paper costs can be equal to half a printer's gross, a printer would be well ahead by paying the paper manufacturers on time instead of borrowing money to pay them, and then having to pay interest to a bank.

Some printers *don't* pay their paper bills on time, especially the weaker firms with poor cash flow. And once into the descending spiral, it takes only a short time for a printer to become permanently fouled up in cash problems.

Consider this situation: Because you happen to be one of the unscrupulous few who pay your printing bills in 59 days, your printer must wait for your check. Meanwhile, he has payroll to think about, so when the next publisher (who pays on time) makes his deposit into the printer's account, the money first goes into general overhead. Then, to the paper people.

But because general overhead (and profit) amounts to 50 percent of the printer's funds, somebody gets shortchanged. And when the situation gets out of control, the paper company puts the printer on C.O.D.

Now, the printer waits for your check and cannot even solicit new business while he waits. (He'd have no money to pay the C.O.D. paper bill.)

Allow this situation to brew for a while, and you force your printer into bankruptcy.

Solving the problem

There is a patently obvious solution to this problem. Publishers have merely to pay their bills on time. Printers would then not be forced into the interest-rate arena and could devote their time to the business of making magazines.

But face it: You might pay on time, and I might pay on time. But some greedy little customer will take advantage of the situation and hold payment for 90 days. The good guys who pay on time, without knowing it, then pay the interest on this publisher's late check. Hardly fair, is it?

We recently saw a solution. It was, unfortunately, offered by a printer who was *forced* to do something. His customers had collectively driven him to the brink of Chapter 11.

The answer was related to the printer's most notorious expense: paper. The cycle had run its course and the printer was on C.O.D. Furthermore, since the local papers carried every rumor about corporate failure to the hilt, the reputation of this firm was long since gone by the time this simple scheme surfaced.

And simple it is. The printer finally figured out the fact that *he* had no end-use for paper. His *customers* did. So why carry the load of financing it . . . and the risk of not being paid for it?

Here's how the plan works. The printer puts each customer in contact with a particular paper manufacturer. The paper company checks the customer's credit. If all goes well, the paper is ordered as usual . . . by the customer instead of the printer.

The publisher is then invoiced directly by the paper company. The obvious results are that the printer's credit (or lack of it) and the customer's payment, are no longer linked. The printer needn't order paper, nor get caught in the middle when the invoice is due.

The results: Far-reaching

If this arrangement sounds too simple, it is because —on the surface—it *is* simple. But its ramifications are complex. Briefly, here's what such a working relationship does:

1. *Paper Markings.* It's no secret that most printers add several numbers to their paper invoices. The first is a handling charge, necessitated by the time spent in bookkeeping, and by the space devoted to paper storage. The second charge is for profit. One printer might add a total of 2 percent to his paper invoice, while the next will tack on 25 percent.

Obviously, the publisher who is currently paying 25 percent more than market price for his paper could save a *lot* of money by paying the mill directly. Then, the only additional expense would be for storage and handling . . . normally, 2 percent of the cost of stock, or a fee based on tonnage.

2. *Credit for early payment.* Unless you have total access to your printer's books, you don't really know when he pays the paper people. While one firm saves 2 percent for net-10 payment, another pays a penalty and goes 60 days. The difference could be anywhere from 2 percent on up.

When the publisher pays the mill directly, he is in complete control of the situation. Another bit of fat is identified, and the decision is made by the end-user.

3. *Identification of late payers.* Another effect of publishers' direct purchasing of paper is that they will finally be identified to the paper manufacturers.

Look at it this way. Right now, half of Printer X's customers pay before 54 days, and the other half pay after. All of the customers contribute to the mysterious "late payment kitty," but no customer can learn who steals from it.

If the industry were to generally accept and enforce publisher payment—direct to the mill—for all magazine paper, you know what would happen. Paper companies don't make a dime by seeing your product printed, while the printer *does*. While the printer might allow you to slide on materials in order to keep your manufacturing-gross alive, the paper companies will let you die.

So when Mr. Check's-In-The-Mail delays payment to the mill, wham. No paper for that magazine. It's cough up or roll over.

4. *Lower operating costs*. Finally, if the movement to publisher-purchased paper became popular, printers would have less interest to pay, less capital to cover, and generally lower operating costs. The marketplace would quickly translate that into competition, and printing prices could—during inflationary times—slow their dramatic climb, or even stabilize for a few precious moments.

Get to it?

There will be two reactions to the above proposal by publishers. "It'll never work" will be touted by those who are happily prancing around with—for all practical purposes—other publishers' money: the money we must all pay in higher operating costs due to late payers.

"Sounds fair" will be the reaction by those of us who are tired of footing the bill for our weak sisters.

And how does one get into the paper-purchasing market? The firm which conceived of the above plan made it quite easy for their customers. They supplied the specs, the technical data, and even helped customers draft purchase orders. Your printer could do the same.

Everyone gains

Fact is, this type of arrangement helps everybody. The average publisher will save money because he can control his own purchases. The printer is relieved of carrying tremendous paper overhead.

The only firms who *won't* benefit are those who are unethically "borrowing" profits from the print/publishing industry. And as far as I'm concerned, those late payers should carry the burden entirely on their own.

Management

The publishing management test

By Richard M. Koff

Although quizzes seem so sophomoric, they often provide a very real and quantitative measure of what is otherwise just another theoretical discussion. A quiz can turn a one-way lecture into a two-way communication.

This one provides a personal inventory of you as publisher and manager. It's short and relatively painless, but it will tell you a great deal about yourself as publisher and manager of a business.

1. Do you have a business plan?
   A. Yes. It's detailed and runs out five years.
   B. Yes. It's informal but runs out two or three years.
   C. Yes. It's not written down but it is clear in my head.

2. Can the editor, advertising director and circulation director explain your magazine objectives and the strategy being used to get there?
   A. They'd point to the business plan—it's all there.
   B. They'd probably disagree, but it'd be a good discussion.
   C. The ad director would say "more pages," the editor would say "more circulation."

3. When was the last time you met with your editor and art director and reviewed an entire issue page by page?
   A. We do it with every issue.
   B. About three months ago.
   C. The last time we changed our style and format.

4. How much editorial material is in inventory?
   A. We like to keep three complete issues in inventory.
   B. If we scrambled we'd probably be able to put together one complete issue from inventory.
   C. None. We run a very tight operation here.

5. Are you ever late in closing an issue at the printer?
   A. About once every six months we can be as much as a few days late.
   B. Never.
   C. Always, by a day or two. Sometimes more.

6. Can you estimate ad pages and circulation for your market?
   A. Sure, both this year and five years into the future.
   B. Sure, for this year. Who knows about next year?
   C. With the economy as it is, it's anybody's guess.

7. Do you personally call on all major advertisers?
   A. Yes.
   B. No, but the ad director does.
   C. No, but someone in the ad department does.

8. What is the toughest challenge your competitors offer?
   A. To stay ahead of them in our editorial content and look.
   B. To keep up with their flashy sales pitches.
   C. To hold our CPM under theirs but still make a profit.

9. How often do you do a detailed analysis of your monthly statements?
   A. Every month, of course.
   B. As often as I have time.
   C. Whenever the numbers begin to look unhealthy.

10. Is the budget prepared before it's due?
   A. Always.
   B. We start it early but it usually doesn't get done until a couple of weeks after the new fiscal year begins.
   C. Never made it on time yet.

11. Do you have a cashflow projection?
   A. Yes. It is never more than a couple of months old.
   B. Yes. It is updated every six months.
   C. No. Anyway, it never works out as planned.

12. Do you know the profit margin of every copy sold either through subscriptions or in single copies?
   A. Yes, by source as well as effort.
   B. Yes, by source.
   C. Yes, roughly, though response and sell-through vary by source and the state of the economy.

13. Do you know the profit margin of every advertising page sold?
   A. Yes. We have costs completely spelled out for every size and color combination.
   B. Yes. I have a rule of thumb that works very well.
   C. Yes, roughly.

14. Describe the ad sales staff.
   A. They are bright, ambitious hustlers. They wear me out.
   B. We have a few self-starters, the rest need a lot of supervision.
   C. They're all hardworking and helpful.

15. How often do you have performance reviews with the editor, advertising director and circulation director?
   A. I try to do it every six months in a long, private meeting.
   B. Once a year at salary review time.

C. When it's a new person who is obviously in trouble.

16. What happens if it's clear he or she is not doing the job?
   A. We talk and try to agree on a performance criterion that can be used to measure improvement.
   B. I'll talk to the person at review time.
   C. If it's really bad I'll pass some of the job over to others. The person in trouble usually gets the message and quits.

17. If the magazine had double the present circulation and advertising sales, how would the staff be different?
   A. The top people would be the same but they'd have others working for them.
   B. I'd have some of the same top people but there are one or two who would have to be replaced by better managers.
   C. I'd need all new people to handle that level of responsibility.

18. Do you get reliable data and statements from your accounting department, advertising department, and business staff?
   A. Of course not. I only believe half of it at best. They don't consciously lie; it's just that it is almost impossible to get hard data.
   B. I'd guess most of it is out-of-date, but on the whole I'd say it's pretty accurate.
   C. We've got an absolutely top notch information system now and I know I can rely on my statements.

19. How many new magazines have you been involved with in your professional career?
   A. Two or more.
   B. One.
   C. None.

20. You have a good second-tier job with a large publisher but are offered the top spot on a new magazine that has the potential to be a large, mass-market success. They want you to invest all your savings to show your commitment. Would you take the offer?
   A. Yes, if the odds were three to two in favor of success.
   B. Yes, if the odds were eight or nine to one in favor of success.
   C. No. I'm certainly not ready to risk my life savings no matter how good the odds.

The questions are divided among five areas of concern to the publisher. Within each area, count three points for every "A" answer, two points for every "B", and one point for every "C".

Planning (Questions 1 & 2)
A score below four means you have no interest in or respect for the business plan, updating it only when you go to backers or the bank for money. Such an attitude is unwise, however, for a business plan helps set specific objectives and direction. It is a means for measurement and control of the magazine—both qualitatively and quantitatively.

A business plan forces you to consider systematically many factors which then become a basis for better decision-making. It will tell you what your resource needs are right now and how they will change in the future. Will you need more funds? More personnel? These are questions that can be considered *before* the emergency hits.

Note that you don't have to be a "caretaker" to rely on a business plan. Entrepreneurs take more risks, it is true, but they prefer *calculated* risks, and that means analyzing the costs and potential returns of a contemplated plan of action—in short, a business plan.

Editorial (Questions 3 to 5)
A score below six means you are not paying enough attention to the quality of your product. Inventory can certainly get out of hand if editors are given free rein to buy whatever they want. Even three issues' worth of inventory may appear to be excessive (although it rarely is). However, too little inventory means that each issue of the magazine is put together from what is available, not from what is best.

Chronic late closing indicates too little planning and foresight and it obviously wastes money. On the other hand, a perfect record indicates the editors have been browbeaten by the finance department and will always sacrifice currency to cashflow.

Market (Questions 6 to 8)
Do you really know your customers and your competition? If you didn't get a score of six or more, the answer is probably no. (Remember to include more than the two or three direct competitors.)

Every other magazine your potential reader buys is taking time away from you. Every advertiser that wants to reach your reader should be using *your* pages, not some other magazine or some other medium. This may seem exaggerated, but if you don't think in these terms you are automatically limiting your growth potential.

Money (Questions 9 to 13)
Magazine publishers who come up through the advertising or editorial departments tend to be weakest in the money areas, yet there is no doubt where the profit controls come from. A score of less than 10 in these five questions means you are not making the profits you could.

Budgets, cashflow, profit and loss projections, subscription analyses, newsstand and advertising margin analyses—all are early warning signals about the health of your magazine. You should be taking its pulse no less often than every month. If you wait longer it may be too late to make changes that can help.

Cashflow (question 11) is critical for magazines. If you can't pay the printer or make a subscription mailing at the right time, it's going to be nearly impossible to produce a successful magazine.

Personnel (Questions 14 to 17)
In the last analysis, a magazine is nothing without its people. Yes, once the format is set a magazine has an enormous inertia which is not likely to run down in a hurry, and there are many fine editors and advertising directors available to take your ideas and run with them. But—do you have talent on the staff that can be relied on to do a little more than the minimum necessary, who can grow with the magazine? A score here of less than eight indicates you do not, and it is almost certainly your fault as manager and leader.

Are you willing to delegate the authority as well as the responsibility necessary to get the job done? Do you give department heads clear objectives and then the freedom to go about reaching the objectives?

Take especially long to think about question 17 because this is the pivot of all growth potential.

Entrepreneur or caretaker? (Questions 18 to 20)

It is important to realize that the management style identified in the first 17 questions of this quiz has nothing to do with whether one is a natural entrepreneur or caretaker. Either will be a better manager if the total score is 35 or higher because he or she will have tighter control and more reliable information about the magazine. These last three questions carry no value judgment. The answers simply separate the two personality types.

It's not hard to see how these three questions add up. If your score is seven or higher you are clearly an entrepreneurial personality—you tend to be a loner, have trouble working in large organizations, naturally gravitate to new magazine start-ups, are willing to play hunches if the rewards are high enough.

Entrepreneurs are not necessarily gamblers in the craps or blackjack sense. As a matter of fact, they may regard 50-50 odds as nowhere near high enough. On the other hand, the entrepreneur will sometimes leave a job before a new one has been found and would always choose to be president of a small magazine rather than vice president of a larger one.

Now if you were the majority stockholder of a company, would you hire an entrepreneur to run the company? Or would you prefer someone who will check back with the board of directors for all major decisions; someone who aims at steady, if slow, earnings growth; someone who will build a strong second-level management team ready to take over in emergencies?

A score of five or lower puts you in the caretaker class. You are a responsible executive and a good team player. You can delegate authority and take real pleasure in training younger executives and bringing them along. You have years of experience in publishing and take a lot of pride in doing your job well.

Entrepreneurs are usually, though not always, younger. They are more energetic, more willing to experiment, more accepting of change, brasher, ruder, more impatient, less people conscious, always in a hurry.

Caretakers are usually older, indeed they may be the mature incarnation of an entrepreneur. By definition they are more conservative, careful, interested in preserving what has been accumulated or made. It's no wonder that new magazines rarely start in the large, old publishing houses. The very selection process that picks the leaders of these companies was specifically designed to eliminate risk-taking characteristics.

Knowing what kind of manager you are is not just of passing interest. It is critical in the development of the strategic plan.

A magazine's life cycle and its profits

By James B. Kobak

It is my belief that the life cycles of magazines can be defined as follows:

1. *Infancy*—When the child is first born—full of sound and fury—but also at its most vulnerable, requiring careful feeding and nurturing. And maybe being stillborn or not ever living to a full existence.

2. *Childhood*—Marked by very rapid growth, but subject to major errors if not carefully guided and controlled.

3. *Adolescence*—Mature in many respects—still growing, almost taking care of itself, but subject to periods of exuberance and doubts.

4. *Manhood*—At the peak of its strength, but with the seeds of eventual destruction inherent in the very nature of the product.

5. *Middle Age*—The longest period: One of stability followed by gradual decline, which for some magazines seems to be almost forever, but for others is relatively short.

6. *Old Age*—When it is a struggle to retain enough vigor to stay alive and alert.

7. *Death*—Which can come at any point in the cycle, but which for a well-managed magazine will only occur after a long and full life.

The point of this article is to give some idea of how a publisher—or a potential publisher—should think of the profit possibilities in the magazine business. Remember that every magazine is different, is in the various stages of its cycle for different lengths of time, is of different size (in dollars), can change in form, frequency or other ways and can be run well or badly.

For example, *Magazine A* is devoted to a special interest consumer field. Its peak circulation was a little over 300,000 and it was quite prosperous for a good many years. The accompanying graph and table trace the life of *Magazine A* through its 40-year history. They can give us an idea of what happens at various stages of that life and the profit which should be attained.

The data are, of course, hypothetical, but are not too far from the actual operations of such magazines. Note that the income and cost structure are as they are today. No effort has been made to introduce the effects of inflation which would inflate all the figures—revenue, costs and profits. Nor have the profits which can be earned from byproducts of the magazine been introduced. These can often account for as much profit as the magazine itself. To simplify the situation I assumed it was a subscription magazine and did not make any allowances for newsstand income and costs.

The life span of 40 years is not abnormal; indeed it may be short for a successful magazine.

Now, let's look at the figures on the graph and table:

1. Infancy

Year 1 shows the costs involved in planning, developing a dummy, testing the concept, staffing and then doing a major mailing—the results of which will not show in the first year and are included in Year 2.

Year 2 is the typical opening phase of a magazine's operations. A charter subscription price of $6 has been offered and every effort has been made to gain respectable circulation early so that renewals will be available soon and advertisers will be impressed. A low advertising rate has been used to induce the placing of some space in the first issues, although only some 10 pages per issue were received.

2. Childhood

Year 3 continues the subscription effort at low prices. The advertising rate has been increased to some $10 per thousand and some further advertiser acceptance is seen with 15 pages per issue.

Year 4 shows the first breakeven—and indicates that the magazine can be successful. The subscription price has been raised and renewals are strong. Advertiser acceptance continues.

Year 5 continues this pattern with the first profits shown.

3. Adolescence

Years 6, 7 and 8 indicate rapid growth of circulation and acceptance by the reader even with a subscription price advanced to $10. Advertisers have recognized that the magazine is here to stay, unless it stumbles, and pages increase rapidly. Total revenue grows at a startling rate, and profits of a million dollars are realized for the first time.

4. Manhood

Years 9-15 show *Magazine A* at its strongest. Circulation continues to grow despite the magazine's high price, but the publisher is wise enough not to push too fast. The probes at more than 300,000 are done carefully and apparently do not work out. Complete advertiser acceptance has been gained with the grand figure of 1,000 pages attained in *Year 13*, giving profits of $2 million. Profit margins are well above 30 percent of revenue.

Yet even during the period of great strength the seeds of decline can be seen. Circulation over 300,000 does not seem to be economically feasible. After reaching the 1,000-page mark, advertising declines because of a contraction in the number of advertisers in this special interest field, a phenomenon which seems to occur in every field as it matures. And the decline in the profit margin in *Years 13-15* indicates that the magazine's operations have begun to be hardened and that it has accumulated some

fat which is difficult to reduce.

5. Middle Age

Years 16-31 show a long period of good profits, although declining operations are evident in all aspects of the operation. Advertising pages continue to decline as the number of advertisers continues to dwindle. Circulation is still strong, but the cost of acquiring subscribers keeps increasing. The result of these two trends is a constant diminution of profits—but still there has been a great number of dollars added to equity during these years.

6. Old Age

Years 32-37 see the inevitable. In an effort to increase profits the subscription rate is raised and circulation is allowed to drop steadily. The advertising rate is reduced, but pages continue to decline. Finally in *Year 37* we are back to a breakeven.

7. Living Death

Years 38-40 show a frantic effort to restore the magazine to its former status—with the usual futile result. The decline persists and finally, a few years too late, the owners give up.

During its lifetime *Magazine A* took in more than $95 million dollars of subscriber revenue, more than $60 million from advertisers, for a total of some $156 million. Profits over the period even after including the losses at the beginning and end of life were about $40 million or 25 percent of revenue. It sold some 10 million years of subscriptions, was read by uncounted millions of people and carried more than 22,000 advertising pages.

Lessons to Be Learned

A number of lessons can be learned from this oversimplified example:

1. Magazines do have life cycles. Magazines only exist because of the interests of people. Those interests change as time goes on and a point is inevitably reached when the publication is no longer needed. Before that happens the advertisers in the field usually contract as smaller producers are gobbled up by the major companies.

2. Magazines should aim at high profits. A creative business like magazine publishing should be highly profitable—or should not be entered. By highly profitable I

Magazine A   Revenue and Earnings During Its Life Cycle

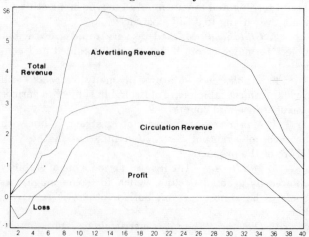

mean 30 percent or more on sales over quite a period—with a return on the capital invested of 10, 20 or many more times. If you cannot foresee this type of operation when you start, forget it. Compared to most businesses it should be golden—or else the basic idea is not good.

3. *Careful early planning is essential.* This is a long-time business. Taking more time and spending carefully at the beginning can make the difference between a great success and a so-so business. A handful of poor decisions at the beginning can reduce the chances for real success over the entire life of a magazine. I am referring to such decisions as:

● Starting with a frequency which cannot be sustained by circulation and advertising revenues. How many magazines would have been better off by starting slowly rather than immediately going weekly or biweekly or monthly? Increased frequency introduces a cost structure which is enormous and very difficult to abandon.

● Insisting on large size with all the costs that entails.

● Insisting on paper and printing quality which are expensive but which are not recognized by the public.

● Using a very low circulation rate to get readers quickly—only to find that the road to adequate prices is very long and very expensive.

● Rushing to get more circulation than can be sustained by the magazine at reasonable costs.

● Instituting an advertising rate base which cannot be naturally sustained without great cost—a cost which is not just once, but every single year as nonrenewals must

Magazine A   Revenue and Earnings During Its Life Cycle

	Year	Price (Average)	CIRCULATION			ADVERTISING			Total Revenue (000)	Profit (Less) (000)	% Profit To Revenue
			Amount (000)	Revenue (000)	Page Rate	Pages	Revenue (000)				
Infancy	1	—	—	—	—	—	—	—	$ (300)	—	
	2	$ 6	73	$ 440	$ 500	$ 120	$ 60	$ 500	(700)	—	
	3	6	104	620	1000	180	180	800	(500)	—	
Childhood	4	7	114	800	1250	240	300	1100	—	—	
	5	7	179	1250	1500	300	450	1700	200	118%	
Adolescence	6	7	189	1320	1700	400	680	2000	350	17.5	
	7	7	229	1550	1900	500	950	2500	500	20.0	
	8	10	250	2500	2500	600	1500	4000	1000	25.0	
Manhood	9	10	265	2650	2750	910	2350	5000	1500	30.0	
	10	10	280	2800	2800	960	2700	5500	1700	30.9	
	11	10	285	2850	2850	960	2750	5600	1900	33.9	
	12	10	290	2900	2900	970	2800	5700	2000	35.1	
	13	10	300	3000	3000	1000	3000	6000	2100	35.0	
	14	10	300	3000	3000	970	2900	5900	2000	33.9	
	15	10	305	3050	3100	870	2700	5750	1900	33.0	
Middle Age	16	10	305	3050	3100	850	2650	5700	1850	32.5	
	17	10	310	3100	3100	810	2500	5600	1800	32.1	
	18	10	310	3100	3100	790	2450	5550	1750	31.5	
	19	10	310	3100	3100	770	2400	5500	1700	30.9	
	20	10	305	3050	3000	780	2350	5400	1650	30.6	
	21	10	300	3000	3000	770	2300	5300	1600	30.2	
	22	10	300	3000	3000	740	2200	5200	1570	30.2	
	23	10	300	3000	3000	700	2100	5100	1530	30.0	
	24	10	300	3000	3000	670	2000	5000	1500	30.0	
	25	10	300	3000	3000	650	1950	4950	1470	29.7	
	26	10	300	3000	3000	630	1900	4900	1430	29.2	
	27	10	300	3000	3000	600	1800	4800	1400	29.2	
	28	10	300	3000	3000	570	1700	4700	1350	28.7	
	29	10	300	30`0	3000	530	1600	4600	1300	28.3	
	30	10	300	3000	3000	500	1500	4500	1200	26.7	
Old Age	31	10	300	3000	3000	470	1400	4400	1150	26.1	
	32	12	260	3100	2700	410	1100	4200	1000	23.8	
	33	12	250	3000	2500	400	1000	4000	800	20.0	
	34	12	225	2700	2250	360	800	3500	600	17.1	
	35	12	200	2400	2000	300	600	3000	400	13.3	
	36	12	175	2100	1500	270	400	2500	200	8.0	
	37	12	150	1800	1000	200	200	2000	—	—	
Living Death	38	10	150	1500	1000	200	200	1700	(200)	—	
	39	8	150	1200	1000	200	200	1400	(400)	—	
	40	8	110	880	800	150	120	1000	(600)	—	
TOTALS			9673	95810		22300	60740	156550	39700	25.4%	

be replaced.

4. *Magazines can be good earners for a long time.* With careful early planning a magazine can be put on the road to profits for a very long period of years. Middle Age is not bad, if it is recognized as being just that—and if efforts are confined to maximizing profits rather than trying to be a young lad again.

5. *Telltale signs of the cycle are easy to read.* The signs that you are moving from one stage in the life cycle to the next are readily apparent if you look for them. During the first few formative years such things as acceptance by readers and advertisers at adequate prices are relatively easy to test. And if the big winner is not there, that is the time to kill the project before the investors' funds have all been spent for what is going to be a borderline project.

As we reviewed *Magazine A* we saw that circulation resistance, advertiser contraction and hardening of the arteries within the company were also easy to spot. Even the death throes were apparent if wishful thinking had not made us hold on too long.

6. *Magazines can be good investments.* If they are well run. Our example indicated that over the history of *Magazine A* an investment of $1.5 million resulted in profits over its life cycle of more than $40 million. And this was without considering the byproducts and inflation which would have made the figures much higher. (Note that the investment in most magazines can be deducted as ordinary deductions for tax purposes in most instances. This offsets the fact that we made no provision for the payment of income taxes by the magazine itself. The earnings ratio would remain about the same.)

So, enjoy and profit from the growing pains of infancy, childhood and adolescence; have a long and healthy manhood and middle age (or, if you prefer, womanhood and middle age); and, well...

'Magazine publishing is not a management-intensive business'
By James B. Kobak

Some FOLIO readers will be startled when they hear about the magazine publishing company that is deliberately moving its four profit centers into separate buildings in different parts of the New York area.

Not only that, but the art department is being disbanded, the production activities are being performed by each individual magazine and accounting functions are handled within each profit center.

This is an organization that publishes eight business magazines, a number of directories and a few newsletters.

Some years ago the company started with just one magazine and since then has purchased several others. As is normal, it brought all the properties under one roof, developed art, production, circulation, accounting, personnel and office service functions to bring "efficiency" to these common functions.

Then the empires started to build, the departmental walls grew up and the task of management became more important than editorial, advertising and circulation.

The point was reached where there were more people in the various service functions than actively working on the publishing properties.

Breaking Up the Family
How did they get back to concentrating on publishing rather than on services? By making each profit center an independent entity. And to make the point stick and avoid future empire build-ups, physically separating the parts by locating them in different places.

Remaining in corporate headquarters are just three key people who are available to consult, control and plan for the future. They visit with each of the parts about once every two weeks, go over progress, activities and plans, but do not get into the minutiae of day-to-day activities. And not surprisingly, they are doing a better job of management than before, when everyone was physically located together.

Interestingly, the McGraw-Hill Publications Company did something along the same lines not too long ago. While the profit centers have not been physically moved apart and all services have not been disbanded, the company has developed six publishing centers, each of which is in essence a complete publishing company. Each has its own circulation expertise, its own controller, its own research and planning functions and is independent in other ways.

Finding the Optimum Size
Why does this approach work?

Because every living organism has an optimum size and a business organization is no exception. While antitrust laws were created to prevent the concentration of power, nature, in a more subtle way, may have imposed better constraints than has man with artificial means.

There are many misconceptions about efficiency. One of them is that larger numbers of people working together bring about greater and better results. This is sometimes known in management circles by those wondrous words, economy of scale. Up to a point this has to be true. Skills, talents and ideas of different kinds are needed. But after a certain point has been reached, the reverse effect sets in.

How often have we seen companies decide that they will take divisions from nine different locations around town and put them in one nice big new building? They do this for better communications and greater efficiency.

The Inward-Oriented Approach

And so nine highly-motivated groups devoted to diverse tasks are brought together under one roof. Result: An inward-oriented approach develops based on the fact that papa-company is *so* big there is no real outside world worth worrying about.

Departmental jealousy, executive warfare, protective memos and records proliferate. Creativity and the knowledge that there is a whole world out there which needs cultivating are gone. Entrepreneurial spirit, if it is allowed, is turned inward.

We have all seen the same thing happen when a large company buys a smaller one which is exciting, innovative and entrepreneurial. It is moved into the corporate building. It gets so bogged down in organizational gobbledegook that it comes to a standstill.

There *are* benefits to size—economic and other types of power and efficiencies, to a point. But there are also built-in limitations.

The optimum size for each kind of organization is different, depending on the nature of the tasks being performed, the number of specialties required, the number of people involved in any one portion of the work and the degree of skill and creativity required.

I suppose that there are instances where masses of people should be assembled to perform some tasks because the advantages outweigh the disadvantages. I refer to manufacturing operations where huge machines require large crews or where the costs of moving parts from one place to another are more of a disadvantage than great size. But even in those cases, current management thinking favors the development of smaller unified groups, each with its own identity, leadership, esprit de corps and flexibility.

The reason for the optimum size concept is obvious. The minute two people are involved in doing anything, they must communicate with each other. This is time-consuming, never results in complete understanding and is at times highly emotional. The more people involved, the more of this there is. And it increases geometrically, not arithmetically.

As people are added, the smooth operation of the organization becomes more and more important until the organization itself becomes—or seems to become—more vital than the task being performed. Such things as overlapping or undone functions pop up inevitably. Organization charts, job descriptions, controls, measurement devices and other forms of organizational minutiae take more and more precedence. Creativity, morale and team spirit are necessarily pushed into the background.

The Administrative Takeover

As this occurs, the founders of organizations can no longer be their leaders because their skills no longer *seem* to be the needed ones. Lawyers, accountants and specially trained businesspeople take over because the *organization must be run.* This is the beginning of the end.

Again, the solution lies in recognition of the very simple fact that every living organism has an optimum size.

Questions should be asked about each activity: What is its optimum size? What simple control and measurement devices are needed? They must be simple because it doesn't take much to know what is going on in a 25-person unit.

I spent a good number of years with a professional firm where the optimum size became pretty apparent. For an accounting, law or other professional group, units of 25 to 50 are the most productive. Here you have manpower enough for just about any task plus room for specialists in such things as auditing, taxes and so forth, but not so many people that the organization and its management have become the important functions rather than the practice of the profession. The best way of running a professional organization is in cells of this size, even though they may be scattered in various spots in one metropolitan area.

I mention a professional firm because there is a great similarity between that and any other people-intensive business, including magazine publishing, book publishing, advertising agencies and the like. The very talents most required for groups of this kind are those which are most easily stifled in an organizational hierarchy.

There is a famous story about our friends at Time Inc., probably the largest and most successful magazine publishing company in the history of the business. For many years it had two business publications—*House & Home* for home builders and *Architectural Forum* for architects.

These magazines were wonderful products; and in all respects, save one, tremendous successes, with advertising pages running into the thousands. That one respect was, of course, that they never made any money. They couldn't because they were housed in the Time-Life Building along with *Time, Life* and *Fortune.* They could have been highly profitable if left alone on Tenth Avenue, but they never had a chance where they were.

Three Publishing Functions

Magazine publishing involves three functions:

1. Developing an editorial product that will appeal to whatever public you are after—a highly unique and highly creative task.

2. Marketing that product to the public (commonly called circulation), also a highly creative task.

3. Marketing the product through highly sophisticated selling methods to a small number of advertisers.

These three tasks call for three different kinds of

creative people, all highly skilled, highly trained and highly motivated. To be good at any of these jobs does not require management skills of more than an elementary degree. In the process of magazine publishing there is no hiring requirement that stresses management. There is no natural upward route or training program involving management skills.

This is as it should be. Magazine publishing is not a management-intensive business.

Not only that, but overmanagement or over-organization of the people in any of these three key areas tends to stifle the creativity, the motivation, the fun of the jobs they are trying to do.

The optimum size for a magazine will depend, of course, on the type of magazine. But a typical monthly special-interest consumer magazine probably operates most smoothly with somewhere between 20 and 30 people. This gives a big enough staff for specialists in the various areas of publishing but keeps it small enough so that an informal management style will be sufficient.

The optimum size for other types of magazines will, of course, vary with their nature. If circulation is controlled, the same degree of circulation skills will not be required. If there is no advertising, this department will not be needed. If it is a business magazine catering to a small, closely-knit field, only a handful of highly knowledgeable people may be needed. If it is staff-written, more editorial people will be required. A newsmagazine will need a much larger staff.

But the principle still applies. A small, highly skilled group represents the optimum size for a magazine publisher.

Getting the most from outside professionals
By James B. Kobak

One of the least-known business arts—and it is an art—is that of using outsiders to help you understand and run your business. I start with the assumption that everyone should use whatever help can be found in addition to the talents and experience already available in-house.

I have been in the public accounting and consulting fields all my business life. I have seen clients who got the most out of me and my firm—and others who got a workmanlike job, but probably not as much as they could have gotten.

I have been on the other side, too. I have had outside professionals work for me and for my firm. And I found that when I got the most out of them, it was usually because of what *I* did.

When I talk of outside professionals, I am naturally discussing those in the recognized professions, such as lawyers and accountants. But I am also including others like:

- Production consultants
- Marketing consultants
- Editorial advisors
- Single-copy sales consultants
- Management consultants
- Investment bankers
- Subscription consultants
- Executive recruiters
- Public relations people
- Publishing consultants
- Bankers
- Magazine brokers.

And there are undoubtedly many more. The magazine industry is one of the few fields where there is a vast array of the best brains and talents working as freelancers, consultants or, perish the thought, moonlighters.

To get the most out of professional outsiders you must understand their functions, when you should use them, how they work, what kind of people they are, where to find them, how to choose the right ones, how to work with them and how to pay them.

Why Use an Outside Professional

There are any number of reasons why you might—or should—use an outside professional. These include:

- By specializing in a particular area the outside professional can become more familiar with all its aspects than an insider can.

- This person has seen how others do things—and which methods work best. By applying this knowledge and experience the "specialist" can save a great deal of time an organization might otherwise spend in "reinventing the wheel."

- An outsider brings a new viewpoint that you cannot get from inside and is not bound into the organizational structure or by the restrictions and politics that go with it.

- The outside individual has an independence in forming opinions and making plans which someone on the payroll cannot have.

- In some cases the best talents turn to consulting

because it offers a greater challenge and more stimulation than an inside job.

• By paying for only part of a person's time you can get much better talent than you may be able to afford to hire on a permanent basis.

• By using outsiders you avoid building a larger organization than necessary. This eliminates fringe benefits and the hidden costs which accompany the hiring, housing and administration of each additional employee.

• An outsider can counter the tendency toward the "not invented here" syndrome which grows up in any organization.

• An outsider has time to study a situation without the distractions which people within an organization are bound to have.

In some areas it is obvious that you must have outside professionals. Whenever anything legal comes up, you must have an attorney. Taxes can only be handled well by professionals. Accounting and auditing matters require independent accountants.

Beyond those areas, we are talking about running the business—planning, buying, selling, handling employees and all the other things needed to operate.

My feeling is that any business, no matter how small, should have regular input from outsiders concerning its overall strategy, tactics and planning. One approach is to have them on the board of directors (even in a very small company).

Whether or not you have outsiders on the board, any business can benefit from a periodic review of its activities by an outsider—every year, every other year and certainly not less frequently than every three years, depending on the nature and complexity of the business.

This type of review should be open-ended—"come look at my company and tell me how you think it can be improved." Not all outsiders are capable of doing this type of work. Some are specialists and should be used only in specific areas.

You probably need an outsider if:

• You have the feeling that profits are not as high as they should be.

• Your competitors are improving their positions versus you.

• Your people do not meet their deadlines, causing excess costs of various kinds.

• Some of your people are antagonistic to each other.

• The information you receive about operations is not very helpful in running the business; or it is always late.

• You have trouble holding good people.

• You want to develop an acquisition program.

• You want to start a new magazine.

• Your costs are higher than industry averages.

• You want to start a profit-sharing, pension or ESOP plan.

• Your salespeople are making too much money.

• Your actual figures are nowhere near the budget.

• You have no budget.

• You have no long-range plan.

• You want to sell your company.

• Your single-copy sales are declining.

• You need to hire a key employee.

• Your printing contract is coming up for renewal.

• You wonder if anyone is reading the magazine.

• The appearance of the magazine is old-fashioned.

• You want to launch by-products.

• Different departments are getting in each other's way.

• You don't like to pay taxes.

• You want to set up your estate in the best way.

Who Are These Outsiders?

What manner of people are these professionals? They are different from you. Their joys come from solving problems. They usually are not around when the results of their work come in. Most of them probably would not be very good at the day-to-day job of the following through. They get their fun from working on a number of assignments at once, whereas most people would become confused and lose their priorities if faced with this kind of life. Their eyes light up with each new challenge.

Most work alone or in small partnerships. There are only a relative handful of large firms and these are mostly in areas where large numbers of people are needed on a repetitive basis (public accounting being the outstanding example).

Professional firms often do not do a very good job of managing themselves, primarily because most of those involved are more interested in solving problems than in running a firm. Law firms are particularly notorious for their poor management techniques, but other professional groups show the same tendency. You will often find professional groups which give too much of their inventory (time) away free, estimate fees poorly and send bills so long after the work is done that you have forgotten what it was that they did. Again, there are exceptions to this, with many firms hiring professional managers or designating one or more of their best partners to manage rather than to practice.

The professional's role in life is to jump when a client calls, to work late hours and weekends and to consider your situation to be just as important as you do. (Obviously, this is impossible. Your tax return is one of the most important things in the world to you; to the specialist it is one more job—and most returns are quite routine.)

Good professionals develop a sense of when they should knock themselves out and when it isn't necessary. The best ones develop techniques for making you think they are working every minute for you when they actually are doing something else.

The basic fact is that consulting is a business with an inelastic inventory—time. This means that it is a feast or famine business. Because of this such working hours, attitudes and tactics are vital.

Most professionals belong to groups which have written ethical standards which are somewhat different from those of most businesspeople. Confidences are sacred. Quality of work must meet certain standards. Educational levels are prescribed.

To the buyer of professional services the prices charged seem enormous. But if you choose and use them correctly, it may be the best buy you can get. A good professional can make the difference between success and failure—or between great and small successes. The prices paid professionals are a function of supply and demand. With a fixed number of hours, the best command the highest fees. In fact, one of the things to watch for are professionals whose fees are too low.

There are lots of hacks and hangers-on giving advice, as there are in any field. If you are not experienced in using them, you may have difficulty differentiating the good from the bad. Here are some things to watch out for:

• The long report that doesn't seem to say anything.

• A seeming misunderstanding of the assignment.

• Missing promised deadlines because of a need for further data and analysis.

• A continuous adding-on of new projects.

• A fee reduction because of a supposed misunderstanding.

• A fee increase for the same reason.

And there are other warnings of this kind. They may be perfectly legitimate in some cases, but they always bear investigating. The good professional wants to solve your problem and get out to go on to something else. If there is nothing else to go on to, the consultant may try to drag your work on.

Don't get the idea that all professionals are the same and like to work in the same way. There are those who really know their business in one area—and nowhere else. There are a few who are truly generalists and seem to know what helps get things done, no matter the subject. Some like lots of new challenges. Others like to work with a few clients on a long-term basis. Chances are that the greatest expertise will come from someone who does lots of different jobs for lots of different people. Maybe you need that—plus someone you can see often to bounce all sorts of ideas against, but who confines his or her activities to a handful of clients.

Sources of Professionals

The magazine field, like most, is relatively small. Even strangers find that they can learn just about anything about the field pretty easily if they work at it. Leads to finding help come from pretty obvious places:

• The telephone book

• Associations—MPA, ABP, DM/MA, ABC, BPA and others

• Publications—FOLIO, *Ad Age, Industrial Marketing, Media Industry Newsletter, Gallagher Report*

• Publishers and their people

• Other professionals

• Suppliers.

Choosing the Outsiders

Choosing the right professionals is the most important step. They should be chosen as carefully as employees.

But how do you do that? You may never have hired an attorney or a consultant before. And, believe me, just because a person is called "Esquire" or has the initials "CPA" after the name, it does not make that person equally qualified to help you.

Here is a sort of standard list of things to check out.

You will find this in textbooks, association literature and in speeches:

• Reputation

• History of performance

• Clients served

• Experience of clients

• Cooperativeness

• Inventiveness

• Repeat business

• Pertinent experience

• Fee arrangements

• Independence.

I cannot quarrel with any of those points. But they really do not give you a concrete idea of how to tell the best from the others. To help simplify this process, let's restate what it is you expect an outside professional to do.

In almost every case, the professional's assignment involves the following:

1. Defining the problem or opportunity.

2. Investigating the available facts and opinions.

3. Assessing the capabilities available—money, people, facilities, organizations.

4. Being able to work with you and your people.

5. Assessing alternative solutions—their costs, benefits, risks and likelihood of accomplishment.

6. Developing the optimum plan and the steps needed in implementing it.

7. Selling you and your people on accomplishing the plan.

When you break down the job in this way, it becomes easier to know the kind of person to look for.

There are three steps in doing your investigation:

1. Checking credentials and general reputation.

2. Checking with people who have hired the outsider.

3. Interviewing the individual yourself.

As in hiring a new employee, generalities are meaningless. Here is a checklist for credentials and general reputation:

• What was the original source of the individual's name?

• Who has recommended for—or against—the individual? How well do you know them? What stature and reputation do they have?

• What professional organizations does the outsider belong to?

• How has he or she been active in those organizations?

• Who have been the outsider's clients?

• What has been that person's history, both before and after doing the present type of work?

• What is his or her educational background?

• What has been the individual's activity in civic and charitable activities?

• Have any clients given public recognition to the help given them?

• Do the outsider's clients use the outsider for repeat assignments?

• Is there any question about the individual keeping information confidential?

• Has he or she been able to work for competitive companies?

- Does the outsider often appear on association or magazine programs?
  - Does he or she contribute articles to magazines?
  - What is the person's area of expertise?
  - Is the outsider known as someone who "tells it like it is"?
  - Is he or she known as a winner?

Here are some questions to ask the specialist's clients:

- How did you come to hire the individual in the first place?
  - What was the nature of the assignment?
  - Have you hired this person again? For what?
  - If not, would you? For what?
  - Overall, has the individual's work proved successful?
  - Have you implemented those recommendations made?
  - What is this person's greatest strength?
  - What is his or her outstanding weakness?
  - Was all information kept confidential?
  - Was the work done on time?
  - Have you recommended this person to others?
  - Our problem is _____. Would you think this person would be good for this?
  - Is the individual easy to work with?
  - Did the individual work with you and your people—or alone?
  - Did the individual antagonize any of your people? How?
  - Does this person tell it like it is—or pussy-foot about hard solutions?
  - Has this person done work with any of your competitors?
  - Did you have a hassle about the fee?
  - Was the fee worth it?

These are some of the questions you should think about in personal interviews with outsiders you are considering hiring:

- Do they understand your problem?
  - Can you understand what they are saying—or are they talking in jargon?
  - Do ideas pop out as you discuss the project?
  - Will the assignment be done alone or in conjunction with you and your people?
  - Do they feel equipped to do the specific assignment you have in mind? Why?
  - Are they excited about the assignment?
  - Do you communicate well?
  - Do you think they can relate to your people?
  - Do you have the opportunity to halt the assignment if things are not working out well?
  - How deep in the organization do the outsiders expect to go?
  - Does the fee arrangement seem fair?

Then there are some other points to bear in mind in selecting a consultant:

- The good ones know the other good ones and often have developed working relationships, formal or informal. If you can find one true professional in one area, that person probably will lead you to others in different fields. If you can find one with really recognized stature, you may have it made in all areas.
- Don't hire a firm. Hire specific people within the firm. Large firms have good people, but you cannot expect everyone to be top-notch. You need one who you are sure is outstanding within the firm. That individual will lead you to others who are strong in their areas of expertise.
- Don't expect to find everything you need in one place. While some firms establish a standard of excellence, they rarely can cover everything equally well.
- Don't trust anyone who cannot be exposed to your most important information. If there cannot be complete confidentiality, don't start.
- The best professionals usually get around a good deal because they are in demand—and because it is good for their business. They will know lots of people, will get to meetings, will probably be asked often to appear on programs and to write articles. This gives you a chance to get to know about them without any commitment.
- The best professionals do not withhold ideas as if they were trade secrets. Even at an initial meeting you will find them sparking with thoughts about your situation.
- Rarely do you want an outsider to attack your situation by going into an ivory tower or a trance—and *voila*—producing a solution. You will want someone to work with you and your people. The more the outsider does this, the better the job will be and the more your people will get out of it.
- Of particular importance is the ability to do the specific task *you* have in mind for you. The outsider must understand the assignment, have the qualifications to perform it—and want to do it. The person must also relate to you—and vice versa. If not, you may have a disaster.
- Be sure the individual has the courage of his or her convictions. A mealy-mouthed professional is worse than worthless. The consultant must be willing to speak frankly, hopefully in a nice way.
- Professionals do not want to waste time. Good ones will refuse an assignment if they feel you won't seriously take steps to implement change. They are liable to ask point-blank whether you will take their recommendations seriously.
- In certain types of assignments knowledge of the specific industry is of great help. In others it may actually be a detriment because the professional may be too bound up in the system—whatever it may be—to bring any new insights. In such assignments as organization studies, marketing approaches and other broad areas, a good professional is useful no matter what the industry involved. And even if it is an industry alien to the outsider, don't underestimate the ease with which the individual will become oriented to it. The principles are common—the terminology is different.
- When in doubt about which professionals to use, choose the best you can find even if it appears that they will cost more. The cost-benefit ratio in almost every case will weigh very heavily in your favor.
- The best recommendation has to be from one or more clients who have used the professional on a somewhat similar assignment—and subsequently rehired the person for further work. The strongest endorsement

(which is sometimes difficult to find out about) is one I have seen in a few cases: An attorney, accountant or other professional represented one party in the sale of a business to another company. When the latter company had need for the same kind of representation in a similar transaction, it hired the individual who had previously been on the other side.

• In checking clients, see if you can go two or three deep in the organization. The best outsiders leave a job with the respect of lots of people—not just the one who hired them.

How to Get Started

When you have about decided to work with a particular outside professional, bring that person in to discuss the project and how to approach it. It is important to be sure that you both understand what the consultant is supposed to be doing. In many cases this can be agreed upon verbally, as can the fee and billing arrangements. In more complex assignments—and in more structured companies—it is a good idea to get an engagement letter from the professional outlining the job, the steps to follow, the method and time of reporting which the individual recommends and the billing arrangements.

If you are unfamiliar with the professional, you may want to start out on a small part of the job before you engage the person for any major assignment.

Some people in any organization will worry whenever *any* outsider is brought in. The initial introduction to them and an explanation of the assignment is of the greatest importance. Cold memos just will not do.

You should plan very carefully the precise words you will use to explain the assignment, to introduce the professional, to describe the person's background and stature in the field, the method of operating, the people who will be involved, the data which will have to be accumulated, the results you hope for and the eventual reporting methods. Emphasize that everyone will get the final results. The list of those to be informed and the order in which they are informed should be carefully developed for both operational and political purposes.

It should be emphasized, too, that all employees should be completely frank, open and honest in their remarks, no matter whose toes are stepped on—including yours. And assurances must be given that nothing anyone says will be passed on as a particular individual's comment.

If it is to be an extended assignment, make arrangements for office space, for secretarial help as needed and other amenities. Give the consultant a copy of your internal phone book.

Using Outsiders—The Basic Approach

The basic reason for using outsiders is to bring a skill, knowledge and time resource into your organization to complement those you have. Since it is a person, and not a machine, all the techniques for getting the most out of people should be employed.

It's just that simple.

The basic assignment in each case is to help you reach the best conclusion and to get action on it.

This usually means that you and the outsider (and whomever else you want) become a "Task Force," whether you call it that or not. To get the most out of the task force you must have the members excited and interested. And you must develop the greatest possible liking, respect and cooperation within it.

If it works the first time, you will have developed a permanent resource which becomes more valuable as time goes on because of the outsider's knowledge of you and the company.

But you must work at it.

You Are the Quarterback

You must position the outsider to do the job well. The individual will do well only with the proper backing, information and respect.

To achieve these ends, you must do the following:

• Make your time available. Find time to discuss not only the project, but also to break down those roadblocks which some employees will inevitably set up, to help get good information fast and to do whatever else will make the job go better. If it is important enough to hire the outsider in the first place, it is important enough to do everything you can to help that person.

One of the best working relationships I have had involved the president of a medium-sized publishing company. Every morning before office hours we would sit for a half-hour to discuss progress—from my viewpoint and from his. He also acted as my appointments secretary. Aside from making it easier to get to see people, it showed everyone on a day-to-day basis that he was solidly behind the project. It also gave him a chance to get feedback from his own people.

• Don't be hesitant to put forth your ideas. The good professional doesn't care where the answer comes from. And even if your solution is not perfect, it might lead to a better one.

• Challenge the professional. He or she is a problem-solver and will react positively to such stimulation. When discussing a difficult tax situation, my old boss, J.K. Lasser, used to say, "Don't tell me it can't be done. Tell me how to do it." With that attitude, we were able to accomplish things taxwise that no one else could. The same approach will work with any good professional.

• Make every meeting with a professional a businesslike one (as you should with all meetings). Send out an agenda and whatever background material would be useful in advance. Tell each participant what you expect to accomplish. Assign responsibilities and set deadlines. You will get better results—and faster and cheaper. You will also impress the professional. After all, the professional wants to solve problems, not socialize at meetings.

• Make sure the professional has the information needed. Withhold nothing. If you do, you are not going to get the most from your consultant. And besides, what is so secret in the magazine business? Everything you do is public. With an ABC report and a few copies of the magazine anyone can approximate your P&L. In addition to the business facts, tell the professional your personal situation and that of other key people, as far as you know it. Reveal your dreams, your hopes, your worries, too.

• No matter how long the professional is around, he or she can never know everything about your company.

Don't expect an outsider to. Tell that person more than you think he or she needs to know.

- If the professional asks for additional information, have it prepared quickly. It may be data which you should have at your fingertips if you are to manage well. Make sure to study all additional material yourself. The professional may be trying to tell you something in a relatively subtle way.

- Do everything you can to position the professional as one more member of the team.

- The professional should be exposed to as many people in the organization as possible, to learn things from them which they will never tell you. After all, you are the boss. You hire, you fire and you set salaries.

- Recognize that your people—or at least some of them—may resent the use of an outsider. They may feel it is a reflection on them, whether it is or not. On top of this, every organization is afflicted with the "not invented here" syndrome to some extent.

- When the professional reports after the specific task has been finished, make sure that everyone who was involved significantly sees or hears the report and has a chance to comment on it. Most people who hire professionals are initially afraid that criticism of them will lower their stature in the organization. They normally ask that the report be given to them alone at first so that they can censor it for the others. I cannot, however, recall when any changes were made after a first meeting of this kind.

- Invite the consultant to company functions. It helps to see people interact with each other. If there are committee meetings, let the outsider sit in on them.

- There may be some situations where the best solution cannot be found through empiric thinking, but which require a participative, maybe even a brainstorming approach. If that is the case, you may want the professional to run a meeting, chair a task force or take you and your key people off on a retreat.

- If you are using several outsiders, it is usually good to have them compare notes on how to work with you, how the organization operates, trouble spots and the like.

And just a few "don'ts" to keep in mind:

- Don't ask an outsider to help in areas where he or she is not equipped. I have seen an outside art director asked for his opinion about whether a particular magazine would be attractive to lots of advertisers or not. He gave an opinion, which he probably should not have, based on scant knowledge of the subject. Worse than nothing.

- Don't try to get it for free. The good professional will tell you lots of things for nothing. But no one likes a chiseler—subtle or otherwise. You will get something—but not the best.

- Don't try to tell the professional how to do the job. If the consultant doesn't know, you shouldn't have hired that person in the first place. Sometimes, for instance, you may be surprised to find that some people are interviewed at their desks, others in a conference room and still others at lunch or over cocktails. This is not just chance. The good professional is well aware that some people are more at ease in one place than in another.

- Don't think the professional can run your business for you. The professional is a problem solver. You still must make the decisions. (Incidentally, it is nice later to tell the professional the results of the help. The consultant might be off on the next problem and never be able to ask.)

When the Consultant Leaves

After the professional has gone, *do something!* Even if it is only to tell your staff that you have decided to do nothing—*and why*. Otherwise you have lost ground.

Most people think they know what the problem is before the outsider is called in. Usually they are looking at symptoms rather than the basic cause. It is very common for the outsider to determine a different situation than you anticipated.

As an example, in one situation there was a very long lead time between the closing dates for both editorial and advertising copy and the publication date. Everyone assumed that the schedule had been put together wrong and just needed tightening up.

It turned out that it was an organization problem at the publishing house. A production department handled every bit of copy which went to the printer. An advertising service department handled the receipt of the ads, billing and recordkeeping. This department was not allowed to follow up with the agencies. This was done by the salespeople or their secretaries, who really didn't know precisely what was needed.

The result was too much handling and confusion which resulted in excess cost as well as long lead time.

The solution—which seems simple but wasn't because it wasn't easy to break up departments—was to move the entire function to each individual magazine where there was more knowledge and more interest in the product and its advertisers.

Costs reduced—lead time cut.

Don't be surprised if the outsider's solution is something you have heard before. Almost always, someone within your organization has already thought of the answer.

There was one instance where single-copy sales were slipping badly. The people in the circulation department realized the editorial product needed improvement—cover lines, blurbs, livelier pages, etc.

The outsider saw this and successfully got changes made—something which the circulation people could never have accomplished.

Methods of Reporting

There is an infinite number of different methods for reporting on the results of an assignment. This depends on the client, the professional and the nature of the assignment. These can range from simple verbal reporting, to a letter, to presentations with slides, flip charts or even movies, to long written reports.

Some assignments by their nature require written reporting. This would be the case if you were developing job descriptions, doing systems studies, valuing a company or creating a chart of accounts. Some clients demand their reports in writing. In many cases this results in a seemingly endless number of pages which sound in many cases like boiler-plate (and very well may be).

Where it is possible I favor a visual verbal presentation rather than a written one. This is in the form of a live report using slides, flip charts or other visual devices. The reasons for this are:

1. A written report often is very time-consuming to develop and can increase the cost of an assignment tremendously.

2. A written report necessarily contains a great deal of detailed information. It is probable that somewhere in it there will be a mistake—small though it may be. This can make some people feel that the entire report and its results must be incorrect and therefore worthless.

3. The object of the assignment is to get action. A live presentation can be focused on the truly important features of the assignment and ignore a great many details which are not important. This is difficult to do in writing.

In case you feel that the visual approach is not dignified or formal enough, let me assure you that I have made many reports of this kind with flipcharts in my own illegible handwriting to some of the largest corporations in the country. After the presentation we reproduced the flip charts in reduced form for all those involved.

Methods of Paying Professionals

There are a number of ways of paying professionals, depending on the nature of the work and the desires of the parties. It all comes down, in the end, to paying for the time spent. And this comes from a limited inventory of hours available.

A professional normally starts out targeting the amount he or she thinks should be made after expenses in a year. Suppose that is $50,000. A rough calculation to arrive at an hourly billing rate would go something like this:

Net income wanted	$ 50,000
Non-reimbursable expenses (office, secretary, etc.)	25,000
Revenue required	$ 75,000
Total working hours per year (50 weeks @ 50 hours)	2,500
Less: Office, marketing, association and other non-billable hours	1,000
Billable hours	1,500
Rate per hour required	$50

Because estimates of time can be wrong—and all billable hours may not be collected, a rate of $60 an hour would probably be used. Since there is an inelastic supply of hours, the popular professionals increase their rates as long as they are in demand.

Large professional firms normally have formulas to follow to produce adequate compensation for their people plus fringe and overhead costs and a profit. Some of these become very complex but wind up at about the same place—generally, about 1.0 to 1.3 percent of a person's salary per eight-hour billable day. Thus, a $30,000 person will be billed at $300-400 per day. Figuring that the average employee runs 1,500-1,800 billable hours a year, the firm receives somewhere between $62,500 and $90,000 for the individual's time, less those hours which cannot be billed or cannot be collected.

It may appear that the large firm charges more than an individual or than a smaller group—and many times they have been accused of this. There are two important differences between the large and small groups. First,

there is a good deal of backup support, research and knowhow behind the scenes in a large firm. Second, there is usually a mixture of people working on an assignment, each billed at his own rate. Because of this, senior people do not waste time doing junior work. In the end, you come out at about the same place for similar work.

I went through this lengthy explanation because it helps make clear the various methods of paying professionals. These fall into several categories, but the most important point is that both parties understand what the arrangement is and that there are no surprises.

At the end of each billing period the client is billed for the number of hours spent. This, to me, is normally the most satisfactory method if billing is done frequently enough so that everyone knows what is being done. I favor billing twice a month. Normally rough estimates are made of each phase of the work so that both parties know about what is involved.

Firm Quotation

A firm quotation is usually estimated by the professional between a certain range of figures. One difficulty is that assignments normally expand in subtle ways which are not included in the original estimate and often not worth informing the client about. For this reason, the quotations normally have a goodly margin for error. This may seem too expensive for the client. On the other hand, where the actual time comes in lower than the quotation, the best professionals bill only for the actual time involved.

It is usually best to divide a large job into phases. Then a firm quote can be made for the early phases and quotes on the later ones made only after more is known. The client normally can stop the assignment after each phase.

Contingent Fees

Contingent fees are common in certain types of professional work:

• Executive search—normally billed at time with a total fee of 25 to 30 percent of the compensation of the person hired if successful. Some firms only charge if they are successful. If the employee does not work out, the search is repeated at no charge.

• Brokerage or finder's fees—for buying and/or selling businesses. Normally billed at a percentage of the price, but often a flat amount is agreed to either before or after the transaction. Some professionals do not like to work on this basis and bill for their time plus some kind of balloon payment if the transaction is consummated. The normal schedule which is quoted for a straight brokerage commission is:

5% on the first million dollars
4% on the second million dollars
3% on the third million dollars
2% on the fourth million dollars
1% on all over $4 million.

Because in many deals the actual price is obscured by tax gimmicks, contingent deals and other items, this scale is rarely strictly adhered to in practice, but serves as a basis for discussion.

• Cost reduction activities—in certain areas, such

as short-interval scheduling and the like, a percentage of the perceived saving per year is the fee.

In some areas contingent fees are forbidden by law or by the ethics of the profession involved.

Other Compensation Points

Retainers. Some professionals and clients like the security of retainers—so much per month for, say, 10 percent of the consultant's time—or for three days a month or the like. This type of arrangement is really a function of the people involved. It can lead to dissatisfaction and the need for renegotiation if either party feels he or she is not getting his or her money's worth.

On the come. More than most businesspeople, professionals may be convinced to work without pay on some oc-casions, to be rewarded later. This often takes place when a new venture is started, when money is being raised and the like. Professionals like to help people at these times. They also may see the opportunity for a long-term large gain. In some cases, they will take a portion of the equity of the project rather than be compensated at normal rates.

Some hours are worth more than others. Once in a while an outsider will accomplish something in a very short space of time which is worth far more than the normal billing rate. It is common, then, for the parties to negotiate a substantially greater amount.

Expenses. It is normal for out-of-pocket expenses to be added to the other charges which outsiders bill. This would include travel and the like.

Good advice on getting good advice
By Frederic C. Decker

"I am not enamoured with consultants," says Don Gussow, president and editor-in-chief of Magazines for Industry. "I am sure there must be some good ones. I don't know of any except in very special areas. I believe that the work of consultants is highly overrated and overpriced. In my experience, executives who do badly in managing a business, or cannot locate a good position, usually wind up becoming consultants. Consultants usually obtain the needed information from their clients and business magazine editors and publishers."

In the other corner is Fred Danneman, publisher of *Ladies' Home Journal*, who says: "Consultants certainly have a place in business. I think they best serve in those areas where they have a high degree of expertise in subjects that are not a daily part of a business' operation."

Another warm word for consultants comes from Donald R. Wall, president of the magazine division of Whitney Communications Corp. "I've had ample opportunity to use consultants and my experience has been largely excellent. I feel that there is any number of occasions which arise in publishing today when it may be helpful or necessary to bring in a consultant. My experience with publishing consultants has been darn good."

Ask a roomful of publishers what they think about publishing consultants and how they use them and you'll get a roomful of different answers. I know, I've just finished putting questions to 41 of them. And also, to 26 consultants.

I asked the publishers of consumer and business magazines if they use publishing consultants to a significant degree. If no, why not? If so, for what kinds of projects and problems, and with what degree of satisfaction? I also wanted to find out what the consultants think about their clients—what kinds of work they most frequently perform, how they charge for their services and whether, in their opinion, publishers know how to use them and get the best from them.

Four observations surfaced immediately.

Many publishers make profitable use of consultants. This practice seems to be increasing but not to the extent as in many other industries.

Many publishers don't understand the consultant's role. Many are fearful of outside intrusion at supposed high cost. Many believe that a consultant can't offer anything that can't be obtained from in-house staff.

There are basically two kinds of publishing consultants: The specialists in every major publishing area and the generalists, some of whom offer supervised specialized services as well as general counsel.

Consultants' services are priced at widely varying levels and the basis for payment—by project, daily fee, monthly retainer—will usually be arranged to meet the need or policy of the client.

Who Needs Consultants?

I found that publishers who don't use consultants generally say that they don't need them. The president of one of the top 10 publishing houses, for example, refers to his executive group as his "big front line," and says that nobody on the outside could be more expert than they.

He may be entirely right. But according to many other publishers, he may be overlooking the fact that a qualified consultant can offer attributes and advantages that cannot be produced by even the most complete and experienced executive line-up.

Hoyt Spelman of *The New Yorker* puts it this way: "I'm very big on consultants. Someone from the outside coming in brings with him a different way of looking at things and forces you to re-examine the way you think and how you get things done. All corporations tend to be closed and the more interchange there is with outsiders, the healthier it is."

John Peter, whose New York-based editorial and design consulting firm has been serving publishers for over 25 years, expresses the point a little differently. "I do not think it so much a matter of whether we will do it better, but rather that we may offer ideas to do it differently. It multiplies the options and by working together, the chances are that the results will be better."

According to the Association Consulting Management Engineers, three-quarters of the nation's larger businesses use management consultants, as do the federal, state and local governments.

My guess is that far smaller percentages of publishing firms seek outside counsel, except for legal, advertising and accounting matters. Research indicates that in addition to publishers who are simply not sold on the need for consultants, there are others who fear that an outsider might put management in an unfavorable light. The chairman of one of the larger multi-media houses chuckled when he said, "It takes a guy with a certain amount of guts to hire a consultant for some kinds of jobs, because he's got to be able to admit he may have been making a botch himself!"

This might make it appear that the consultant is like a fireman who only gets called when there is an emergency—or an investigator hired to look for trouble. Not true. By far the greatest amount of consulting time is spent on developmental projects.

The best use of the consultant, most publishers agreed, is when there is need for improvement in a company's operations (including the executive branch), or when the study of possible new profit centers can be done by a knowledgeable person outside without disturbing staff operations, or when discreet inquiry and negotiations are better accomplished by a respected consultant who can keep his or her client anonymous.

An ACME statement describing the role of the consultant, says, "In its full sense, management consulting is the professional service performed by specially trained and experienced persons in helping managers *diagnose* management problems associated with the goals, objectives, strategy, organization, operation, precedural and technical aspects of the principal institutions of our society; in *recommending* optimum solutions to these problems; and *helping* to implement them when necessary. This professional service focuses on improving the managerial and economic performance of these institutions."

What They Do

Translated, this means that the consultant should be a pro who comes on staff for a limited time to do a job for which there is no personnel or time within the company, or which for other reasons cannot be done by staff. That job may be a study leading to a recommendation. It may be developing improved systems or techniques, in consultation with the staff. It may be sharing problems with management and adding the dimension of diversified experience. Or it may be a combination of all of these things.

Stanley Fenvessy, whose Fenvessy Associates does consulting in computer fulfillment and processing methods, puts it neatly when he defines a consultant's contribution as "a novel recombination of inside and outside practices to produce improved performance."

A recent case in point concerns a publishing company which owned several publishing properties. One was a magazine with a rapidly dropping share of the market. Editors blamed the ad staff. The ad staff blamed the editors. Management had a good idea of where the problem lay but it wanted dependable knowledge and recommendations.

A consultant was hired after lengthy interviews, and after he had submitted a detailed assessment of the situation and proposal for the specific directions his service would follow. He was given access to all records. His reason for being in the picture was carefully explained to the very limited number of involved staff members. He studied the leading magazines in the field, their statements and their promotion. He had long talks with the editor and sales manager.

Then he built an exhaustive questionnaire to use when interviewing advertisers and agencies in substantial depth about their attitudes toward all the magazines in his client's field. Five magazines were included, effectively masking the one sponsoring the inquiry.

Interviews were made in person and by phone. Most of them lasted up to an hour. Telephone interviews were made in all parts of the country to allow for differences in attitudes in different geographical sections and, importantly, to get a reading on the effectiveness of the sales coverage of the reps and staff people in different territories.

The impressions of the consultant were merged with the tabulations of the questionnaire. From these a detailed report was written. It pinpointed the client's sales problems, analyzed them and made recommendations, supported by direct quotations from advertisers—whose anonymity had been guaranteed and was protected.

Four alternative courses of possible action were outlined, with the pros and cons of each. And, finally, the consultant made his firm recommendation of the one he favored and detailed his reasons.

The executive management of the company accepted almost all of the recommendations. The consultant was then asked to meet with the board and they, too, accepted the recommendations.

Next, the consultant was retained to search for certain key personnel which he had recommended be hired. The search was successful.

At that point his job was done. Later, he could be engaged once more to assist in implementing some of the internal adjustments and marketing developments which his report recommended.

Variety of Experiences

A consultant is in a unique position to bring a variety of experiences to bear on a problem. He or she can deal with top management with more candor than employees sometimes dare. He or she is free from the imagined restrictions and non-existent policies which often inhibit middle and lower management people. The consultant can absorb overloads and supplement the work of management. He or she has broad contacts.

In confidential investigations, only an outsider can guard the publisher's identity. A consultant can work openly and effectively while shielding the client in a competitive field which is notorious for its sensitivity to gossip.

The fee and expenses for the entire project previously mentioned came to about one-fifth of the annual cost of one good ad salesperson or one-tenth the cost of a senior executive.

No staff member could have done the job while protecting the anonymity of the publisher. Rare would be the staffer who could have made as objective analyses and recommendations.

The success of the client-consultant relationship depends upon a clear understanding by both parties of their responsibilities to each other. The publisher has responsibilities which are fully as binding upon him or her as are the professional responsibilities upon the consultant.

The publisher must have a clear understanding of the publishing objective. Vague feelings of discontent or unrest do not constitute adequate reasons for retaining a consultant. Management should think the situation through and arrive at a clear definition of the project before calling in outside help. Otherwise, the consultant's time can be wasted in investigation and planning and the client eventually pays for that time. The clearer the consultant's instructions, the more specific the assignment, the more in tune all key members of the client company are, the greater and quicker will be the yield for the dollar spent.

The publisher will be called upon for input that will place demands upon time. After he or she has reached agreement with the consultant on the scope, time frame and general cost of the assignment, the publisher usually can't dump the problem in the consultant's lap and expect a result to be placed on his or her desk at some predetermined date in the future. The consultant will usually want access to the thinking of the employer. The consultant will often want to submit interim reports, have them studied and commented upon. With this kind of cooperation from the employer he or she can do properly what he or she is being paid to do.

The publisher has a further responsibility. Says Don Scott, whose Communication and Education for Industry, Inc., of Greenwich, Conn., is one of the leading consultants in sales training, "The stranger walking briskly down the hall, with bulging briefcase, heading for the president's office, is always an object of suspicion." The publisher must prepare the staff adequately for the temporary introduction of an outsider into the official family.

Status Quo Threatened

The consultant represents change and disturbance of the status quo. He or she may even appear to be a threat to job or status. One of the first jobs of the consultant should be to counsel management on how best to smooth the way for the consultant's appearance and to keep the concerned employees clued in on the project while it is in progress. Nothing makes people resist outsiders more than incomplete information which leads to distrust.

Another essential responsibility of management is to do something about the recommendations after they are

submitted and discussed. The normal inertia of most companies tends to lead to a practice of file and forget. No consultant likes to see work dropped into a big black void. If the recommendations are not going to be followed, management owes the consultant the courtesy of explaining why.

If the recommendations, on the other hand, are put into operation, he or she will want to know the results. Sometimes included in the consultant's agreement is a provision that he or she will make one or more progress assessments after the recommendations have been implemented.

Many consultants become emotionally involved in their clients' needs and may go far beyond the call of duty to serve those needs. Whit Hobbs, who does promotion consulting to *The New Yorker*, said, "I contract for 50 percent of my time, use 88 percent of my time and get paid for 32 percent."

Consultants come in numerous sizes, shapes and forms—and degrees of ability. They also come in at least two genders. Lorna Opatow, a former Hearst executive, for example, has just celebrated over 13 years of running her own research consulting firm, which competes with such other sturdy Manhattan-based researchers as Wallace Wegge and Richard Manville.

Working Out of a Job

The usual objective of a good consultant is to work himself or herself out of a job. The consultant has earned his or her money when no longer needed. As Edgar Buttenheim, president of Buttenheim Publishing Co., says, "Consultants must realize they should help you stand on your own—and get out! Beware of firms that try to perpetuate their own fee."

Types of Consultants

There are specialized consultants in magazine financial management, design and graphics, production, newsstand sales, subscription sales, fulfillment and computer usage. Other consultants are expert in promotion, sales training, market research, editorial research, editorial development, acquisition negotiation, personnel policy. McGraw-Hill not long ago sought out a consultant in corporate identification when it hired Sandgren & Murtha, New York, to develop a new identification and graphics system for the company.

There are scores of lawyers, accountants and advertising agencies that serve publishing companies. Few, however, can be called publishing specialists. Many advertising agencies handle publishing accounts. There are happy marriages between agency and client, but some agencies grouse, and not always privately, about the unprofitability of magazine accounts and the difficulty of working with magazine people who somehow believe that publishing expertise translates automatically into advertising expertise.

Another group of consultants is the generalists, full-time professionals who usually work alone. Invariably, these people came from senior jobs in publishing or in publishing-related service organizations. Some are retirees. Most, however, departed corporate life to become consultants because they don't want to be anything else.

They enjoy the life style and the wide variety of problems, projects and people that fill their lives.

Some of the generalists do not offer services beyond the limits of their own time and specialties. Others, however, offer a wide variety of additional short-term operational services. To do so, they have developed groups of "consultive associates," as one man calls them. These are either moonlighters or specialized consultants who provide services to augment those of the prime contractor, under the contractor's guidance.

When two essential conditions are observed, this system usually works well. These conditions are: First, that the client knows that other professionals are being brought in on the assignment and second, that the consultant must not lose sight of the fact that he or she must constantly stay on top of the job.

This arrangement can have advantages for the publisher. Hundreds of skillful people in full-time jobs have the time and inclination to do a little moonlighting. They may be writers, designers, direct marketing specialists, promotion people, researchers, sales executives, production experts, publishing accountants. They may bring expertise to a project which may be greater than that which the publisher can afford on a full-time staff and, in the aggregate, greater than that which any single consulting organization can offer. The cost of their services is covered in the consultant's fee to the publisher.

This relates to one of the advantages consultants bring to publishers. They don't stay on a payroll, they don't get paid vacations or sick leave. They have no profit sharing, stock options, retirement pay and company-paid insurance. They get in, get the job done and get out. There is no continuing company liability.

John Seybold of Haddonfield, N.J., a consultant in computer applications, makes a further wry comment. He says, "Another reason management likes consultants is that during a traumatic period of changeover they may prefer to be mad at their consultant rather than at their own employees!"

While the consultant doesn't want to hang around when his or her work is done, he or she does want to be called back when the next chore that fits the individual's capability comes along. William Steiner, whose William Steiner Associates, Inc., New York, has given direct marketing services to a long list of publishers, makes the point that this element helps to assure the client that a good job will be done. Employees are forgiven for mistakes. Consultants are not. Consultants are keenly aware of how dependent they are upon good references.

There is something to be said for establishing a relationship with one consultant so that he or she is the one called on whenever outside help is needed. The consultant knows how his or her client operates, and he or she knows the people. The consultant can swing into action without wasting the client's time and money by starting from scratch.

The subject of fees always comes up, so I asked consultants how they base their charges and I asked publishers what they considered a fair day's pay for a consultant.

How Much?

A few consultants mentioned daily rates of $200.

The average for the one-person generalist is in the area of $400, plus expenses. A few of the better known people are getting $500 or more.

Some consultants, particularly those who maintain staffs or sell long-term counseling arrangements, don't talk about daily rates. They like a monthly retainer for a specific number of months.

The greatest number of consultants and the greatest number of publishers prefer to work on a project basis. Here there is an agreed-upon estimated fee, an estimated expense budget, a completion schedule and clearly stated objective. Total projects are often split into phases, each with its own budget and each successive phase undertaken only when certain objectives have been accomplished.

The question of how much a consultant is worth may be like Abe Lincoln's famous answer to the question about the proper length of a man's legs. Robert Goldsmith of *Boys' Life* comments, "A good consultant is worth almost whatever he wants to charge, as long as he can produce for you. A poor one is not worth anything."

Essentially a freelancer, the consultant often experiences severe peaks and valleys in workload and income. The consulting service organization, with its multiple employees, can usually keep the flow reasonably stable. Not so the loner. He or she probably can't count on more than 50 percent of his or her time being billable. So, even at $500 a day the annual gross may be in the neighborhood of only $50,000, out of which must come office and secretarial costs and non-billable expenses. He or she may end up with a net of only a half or a third of what the consultant has earned in the past and could earn as an employee. Consultants think they are the biggest bargain a publisher can possibly buy.

Why don't more publishers use consultants more regularly? Many apparently feel as Thomas Dempsey, president of Industrial Publishing Co., does. He says, "We have tried to build IPC as a completely self-sufficient, full-service publishing company. We have several people employed in the company who serve as corporate consultants to our magazines because of their special knowledge in such areas as graphics, writing technique and content, market research, readership, etc. This seems to work best for the specialized publishing we do. This technique has this added advantage—since these people are on our staff full time, they perform a quality control function with a regular critique of our publications."

Quality control and regular critique can also be part of the function of consultants. An example is Laurence Lustig of Irvington-on-Hudson, N.Y. He has worked as a design and graphics consultant on more than 70 publications. His arrangement with many includes a periodic review of the graphics to maintain the standards he has originally helped to establish.

Many publishers agree with Tom Dempsey. They may be right. Or they may find, as has the management of MBA Communications, that consultants are useful. MBA is a relatively youthful publishing venture which has grown from a one-book house to a multi-magazine company in a very few years. Its publications are directed to the younger practitioners in the various professional fields of law, medicine, engineering and business administration.

MBA's president, Francis Pandolfi, says, "We are now using consultants on a very frequent basis to help us in many aspects of publishing. I think we are going to continue to do so ... because we do not have to assume any overhead or fixed salary expense—and we get the added benefit of some top level expertise."

Hazards of the Business

Not every client-consultant relationship is all beer and skittles. The normal hazards of business relationships are amplified by the highly personal nature of the relationship between a consultant and the management executives with whom he or she works.

Unsuccessful consultive assignments are traceable to a few basic causes. Awareness of these causes may help both client and consultant to avoid them.

Ridiculous as it may sound, one of the most common causes of client-consultant unhappiness is their mutual failure at the outset to establish a clear understanding of the objective of the assignment. Reaching that understanding sometimes may not be easy. It is necessary, first, that the client know precisely what he or she wants to achieve, and to communicate those objectives clearly to the consultant and that the consultant clearly understand. The consultant should be fully informed of all details of any of the client's previously unsuccessful attempts to accomplish the objectives. The consultant should know about all sacred cows and preconceptions.

A consultant's proposal should play back to the client all of those preconceptions and sacred cows. It should clearly restate the objectives and specify how the consultant plans to go about accomplishing the assignment, who will work on it, what result is expected, the expected completion date, the estimated fee and expense costs to the client.

There have been cases where examination of a client's objectives has revealed that they are either not valid, too fuzzy or unreachable. In those cases, the prospective client and prospective consultant have gone their separate ways, saving money for the one and frustrations for the other!

The second major cause of unsuccessful consultive relationships occurs when the consultant is miscast in an assignment which goes beyond his or her specialty or when the consultant is just plain incompetent. There have been cases, too, when consultants have taken on too many assignments and have slighted one or more of them.

Finding the Right One

The publisher's best protection against a wasteful situation is to learn everything there is to know about the prospective consultant beforehand. A place to start is with former clients. Was their objective achieved? On time? Within the budget? Were recommendations positive, practical, carefully developed, fully documented? How did the consultant get along with client personnel? Would he or she be hired again?

Detailed dossiers on the consultant's own business background and that of any principal associates should be available, along with bank references. Is this a person who is currently involved in a variety of situations or one of those whose claim to fame is primarily experience of the past?

When the field is narrowed down to two or three people, they should be interviewed in depth by executives who have the judgment and experience to evaluate them. A competent consultant will want to make a full exploration of the prospective assignment, without obligating the publisher. He or she will often write a detailed proposal.

Another cause of client complaint is that a consultant was hired with the expectation of getting the full services of one top person—yet it seemed that underlings did all the work. Here again, the initial problem is an incomplete understanding at the outset.

Second thoughts about the cost of a project, after that project has been completed, plague some clients, particularly if they are first-time users of consulting services. They feel that "that specialist made a lot of money just by doing what I really could have done myself." But when examined, the pay of a consultant may be no more than that of an employee of equivalent skill and experience.

For example, let's say a senior executive earns $50,000 in base salary, plus retirement benefits, Social Security contributions, company-paid insurance of various kinds, club dues, bonuses. Perhaps he or she costs the company $60,000 per year. Then add on another $15,000 for a secretary and the miscellaneous supplies and overhead costs for them both. You've got a $75,000 executive. For that he or she works no more than 45 weeks or 225 days—which figure out at $333 a day.

Some publishers and some consultants suggest that publishing, more than many other businesses, needs outside help. Consultant David Hagenbuch describes publishing as a "crash-type business." In its advertising sales operations, and sometimes in its circulation development efforts, this is often true. Publishing has also been described as a relatively young business. It has not yet developed the body of precedent that exists in so many businesses. It is a business in the midst of eruptive changes.

These factors—frequent crisis situations, the climate of change and the relative absence of guiding precedent—are referred to, in one way or another, by many publishers as factors that make their business one in which professional counsel is especially useful.

Most consultants don't like the term "consultant," although John Peter thinks it is good "because it doesn't overpromise." Others identify themselves as "specialists in magazine production," "specialists in magazine promotion," or whatever. But consultants seem destined to continue to be called consultants.

And they'll continue to be the butt of gentle jokes, like, "What's a consultant? A consultant is a person from out of town."

Probably they'll live with the name and with the little jokes—and like it. My investigation showed that many publishers are agreeing that perhaps that person from out of town should be called in, asked to do a job and then sent back where he or she came from.

Long-range planning

By James B. Kobak

There are many scholarly definitions of long-range planning in management writing. Peter Drucker says it is "the continuous process of making present entrepreneurial decisions systematically and with the best possible knowledge of their futurity, organizing systematically the efforts needed to carry out these decisions and measuring the results of these decisions against the expectations through organized feedback."

But if you define long-range planning as risk-taking decision making, that really says it all.

What It Is Not

To avoid confusion it is well, too, to examine what long-range planning is not. There are three things which most people get confused about.

1. *It is not forecasting.* Forecasting attempts to find the most probable course or range of possibilities. Long-range planning means bringing about the unique event that changes the possibilities.

2. *It is not concerned with future decisions.* It is concerned with the future of present decisions.

3. *It is not an attempt to completely eliminate risk.* It means having the capacity to take greater risks and the right risks and to rationally choose among the risk-taking courses of action.

There is often talk about the difference between short-, medium- and long-range planning. That is like arguing about how many angels can dance on the head of a pin. It doesn't really matter. Time spans merge into each other as planning is being done. We are talking about planning for as far ahead as we reasonably can. And that can hardly be for more than five years on any firm basis.

Reasons for Planning

The classic arguments for long-range planning are identified in management textbooks as these:

1. The time span of the results of entrepreneurial and management decisions has been lengthening. Something decided today carries its effects much longer than it would have 20 years ago.

2. The speed and risk of innovation increases.

3. Business, the economy and society are growing more complex.

4. A business is an organization of professionals of highly specialized knowledge who exercise autonomous, responsible judgment in a great number of vital areas. The success of the total organization is at the mercy of piecemeal independent decisions. To make the most of the opportunities, all must know the direction, goals and expectations of management and management must know the decisions, commitments and efforts of all the people.

5. Solid and profitable growth should be based on choice, not change.

These reasons are all correct, but for the average businessperson, the need is even more obvious as he or she goes from day to day. Because we are always making long-range plans even when we don't mean to. In fact, when we decide to do nothing, we have a long-range plan.

The difference is that we have not done it in a systematic way. And we may be using false or unknown assumptions by doing it off the tops of our heads.

Steps to Follow

The process of long-range planning is generally described as having the following steps:

1. Set broad as well as specific goals and objectives

2. Make carefully thought-out assumptions

3. Develop realistic expectations

4. Study alternative courses of action

5. Make the decision

6. Develop guidelines and lead time

7. Set up the decision structure

8. Set firm controls—review dates for progress report to analyze, evaluate and take corrective action

9. And now—impact stage of the decisions

10. The results.

I am not sure how many people consciously go through these steps. In actual process they merge into one another and sometimes take place in a different order. Once you embark on the planning process, you will find that you will pretty much take these steps without needing a list. The one that may be forgotten is the need to review, analyze, evaluate and take corrective action. Without this, you may find that you are merrily following a plan which no longer has any validity because of changed conditions.

One last point—there is only one person in an organization who can be in charge of long-range planning. That is the boss—no matter what fancy or simple title he or she may have. If the boss is not intimately involved and behind the process, forget it. This does not, of course, mean that he or she cannot get help from others. But in the end it is the boss' baby.

Planning and Your Magazine

Enough of the generalities of long-range planning. How does it particularly affect the magazine business?

Magazine publishing, probably more than most businesses, is essentially a long-range business. Decisions you make today will have an effect tomorrow and for many years to come. Consider some of the basic decisions which have to be made and their long-term impact:

• The advertising rate base you set can determine the amount of circulation you need, the methods by which you get it, the price—and often put you in a box from which you can never get out.

• The subscription price you set can only be changed substantially over a long number of years—and may haunt you throughout a magazine's existence.

• Obtaining circulation primarily through subscriptions rather than single copies may create a cost structure that prevents you from making money for many years.

• If issues are too frequent, profits may become impossible. You can always add issues but it is very difficult to subtract them.

• The page size is very difficult to change. There are emotional reactions from advertisers, readers and, most of all, from editors and art directors.

• The basic decision of whether you are going to try to make money from advertising and let circulation be just a base for it—or the other way around—leads to results which usually can never be reversed.

• The size and salary scale of the editorial department depends on the nature of the magazine you are going to put out—and also on the amount of circulation needed to support it.

• The capabilities and salaries of the advertising staff depend on the type and amount of advertising you hope to obtain.

• The capabilities of the management team depend on the nature and size of the eventual operation.

And you can go on and on. Almost every major decision locks you into a course that is very difficult to change.

A Typical Magazine Situation

Rather than talk just about the theory of long-range planning, let's take a simple example—and one which will strike home for many in the publishing business. Shown below are the basic facts and operating statement of a typical magazine. Using these we will do a simplified long-range planning exercise.

XYZ MAGAZINE

Monthly regional magazine—City or area.

Editorial focus—How to enjoy the region, some local muckraking, listings of movies, concerts, horse shows, etc.

Circulation—55,000 subscriptions, 5,000 single copies.
    Subscription price, $5; introductory, $3.
    Single copy price, 50 cents.
    First renewal, 50 percent; subsequent renewals, 60 percent.

Average issue—50 editorial pages, 50 advertising pages.
    30 advertising pages are sold at discount.
    20 advertising pages are sold at full rate.

Average pressrun—70,000.

197— Operating Statement (In Thousands)

Income

Advertising	
Local advertising @ $600 net per page	$150
National @ $720 net per page	173
Subscription	
Renewals—30,000 @ $5	150
New—25,000 @ $3	75
Single copy @ 25 cents net	15
Reprints, etc.	10
Costs	$639
Paper, printing and postage @ 25 cents per copy	$210
Advertising department	90
Editorial department	95

Circulation	
Promotion for new subscriptions @ $5	125
Promotion for renewals	22
Fulfillment @ 80 cents per subscription	44
General and administrative	55
	$641
Net profit (loss) before taxes	($2)

Offhand almost any of us would feel that a monthly magazine with an average of 50 pages of advertising at good rates and with a first renewal rate of 50 percent and succeeding rate of 60 percent at $5 should be profitable. But we are just hovering around the breakeven point.

What can be done?

Here are some suggestions from various members of the management team.

Editor: "The real answer is to make the magazine of more value to the readers. Then the circulation will go up and the cost of getting that circulation will go down. And not only will the advertisers flock to us, but we can raise the ad rate.

"All we have to do is go weekly so that we can give more current information about local events, movies and so forth. This will give me more pages to use for those hot stories like the one on the mayor last month. And if we double the editorial color, we can really put out a good-looking book that will sell itself!"

Advertising director: "If we could just get up to 100,000 circulation, I could sell 20 pages an issue in Detroit alone. One hundred thousand is a magic figure, you know, with the big agencies.

"But when you get up to that 100,000, cut down the rate per thousand. Twelve dollars is just too much to really push on GM—about $9 would be fine.

"And incidentally, how about a special rate for book stores? They would make a huge local market but they don't have much money."

Circulation director: "Sure, I can get more circulation. Just reduce the introductory offer to $2.50 from $3 and I can sell all the subscriptions you want. And let me put free copies in all the hotel rooms in town. Just these two things and I can get you up to 100,000 in a year.

"But let's stay away from single copy sales. The dealers are just so hard to get along with—and they are not really our type of people anyway."

Controller: "The only way you can make this magazine profitable is by cutting costs. Watch those long distance calls. Everyone who travels has to go tourist. And there's no reason to spend more than $5 on dinner when the salespeople go to New York. Why, you can buy the best dinner in town here for only $3.25.

"How about considering reducing the paper weight from 60 pounds to 50? Could we run fewer editorial pages with lots less color? Maybe we should consider digest size. And that January issue is always thin. Let's have a combination year-end issue like *Life* used to have.

"There are a lot of employees who are doing almost nothing. I'll bet we could cut two out of the editorial department and no one would know the difference.

Idea	Analysis	Idea	Analysis
Go weekly and increase pages.	Increases paper, printing, postage and fulfillment costs. Requires increase in editorial force. Might be able to increase circulation prices for more frequency but not in proportion. Might pick up more advertising from those who want to be in each issue. At a basic 60 pages per issue this would add $325,000 to costs, which could not possibly be made up by increased circulation, prices or advertising.		Single copy sales are also a good source for new subscriptions—at very little cost. This area requires further study.
		Free copies in hotel rooms.	Forget it. Our advertisers are not interested in this circulation. These people will rarely subscribe.
		Cutting long-distance phone and travel costs.	Forget it.
More editorial color.	Without making any calculations, it seems doubtful that the increase in circulation strength could offset the additional cost.	Reducing paper weight.	Reduction from 60 to 50 pounds would save some $15,000 per year. Let's investigate.
		Fewer editorial pages with less color.	Would save money, but dare we tamper with a product that is selling well both to readers and advertisers?
Go to 100,000 circulation, sell 20 more pages per issue at a reduced page rate.	Adds some $310,000 to advertising income for more pages at lower rate. Additional 20 pages cost $40,000 for paper, printing and postage. Additional cost of travel and salaries in advertising department of $40,000. Real question is how much it will cost to get additional circulation. Even at current cost of $5 for each new subscription there would be $200,000 of expense—and it is probable that either lower subscription prices or higher acquisition costs would result. This would completely wipe out any increase in advertising income. Besides we haven't the money to spend for more circulation.	Digest size.	Over my dead body. But let's look at the figures anyway.
		Combination year-end issue.	What was the name of the magazine that used to do this?
		Cut employees.	Possible, but we are running a pretty tight ship now. And does the editor still speak to the controller?
		Raise subscription rate.	Single copy, too, of course. An increase to $8 from $5 would bring in $140,000. But how much would circulation fall? If it dropped 20 percent we would lose some $75,000 of circulation revenue and $80,000 of advertising revenue, cutting rates proportionately. At the same time, paper, printing, postage and fulfillment costs would decline some $50,000. Net income would increase $35,000. What would it do to renewal rates? This bears investigation.
Special rate for book stores.	Sounds like a pipe dream.		
Stay away from single copy sales.	Single copy sales net us 25 cents each. With a return percentage of 50 percent, its costs for paper and printing are about 44 cents each. Subscriptions at the regular rate net 42 cents, with paper, printing, postage and fulfillment expenses amounting to 30 cents. Subscriptions at introductory rate bring in 25 cents per copy with costs for paper, printing, postage, fulfillment and acquisition of 72 cents.	Raise advertising rate.	An increase of 5 percent would bring in some $20,000 more income—if we didn't lose any space. We have been increasing in space every year. Worth investigating.

"Why can't we raise the subscription rate? And the advertising rate, too?"

Publisher: "I just cannot invest more than $25,000 to help the magazine at this point. If it costs more than that, I'll have to raise money and I'll lose control of the property. Then all that good work we have been doing in pointing out things to the city administration will go down the drain."

The situation above sounds familiar, I am sure—at least parts of it. And the worst is that no one in management really has any facts. No calculations have been made.

It's not that calculations cannot be made. But the time and effort involved in analyzing all the alternatives can be enormous. Magazine publishing is an interacting business, with two revenue streams and all sorts of expenses which depend on each other and on the method of doing business.

It was for this very reason that I developed a computer model of a magazine: So that alternatives could be analyzed in depth and long-range planning would become feasible for publishers.

Let's embark now on a practical program for doing long-range planning for our regional magazine.

First, gather all the existing data, including all the information on subscriptions, their expiration dates, renewal rates, etc. Introduce known cost increases, such as that for postage, plus expected annual increases in printing, pages and salaries. Then run out the anticipated operating statement for five years.

With the parameters we have introduced, there is no question that there will be a growing loss each year which can become substantial if no basic changes are made in the magazine. Costs can be expected to increase by some $30,000 each year, with losses in the fifth year projecting to about $150,000.

Next, let's study each idea that has been offered to see what would happen to income and costs if it were put into practice. We have done that in a simplified way in the accompanying box.

In our study of the individual ideas we found several that seem interesting. Some research can easily be done to find how to reduce the paper weight, to learn what weight other publishers are using and to determine the potential saving.

We can easily discover whether local hotels will buy copies at a price attractive to us.

But we have three areas worth investigating that can have a major effect on the future of the magazine—raising circulation prices, raising advertising rates and pushing for more single copies. What are the advantages and disadvantages of each? What are the risks? How much could we gain? Or lose?

This is where a computer really helps. We can see what overall effect an increase in subscription price from $5 to $6, or to $7 or even $8, might have. And we can combine these calculations with a lower renewal rate and a higher cost of acquiring new subscriptions. And of course, we can make the same kinds of calculations for increasing advertising rates and promoting single copy more heavily.

All right. We have made our decisions. We will raise subscription prices to $6, increase the advertising rate 5 percent and spend money to increase single copy sales. We will also continue to increase prices in the future if resistance is not too great. If all these work, our computer tells us that we will have a $100,000 profit next year. What should we do with it? Salt it away or put it to use?

You can't live on price increases alone. Is this the time to start thinking about more issues and more pages, as our editor suggests? Should we invest in building more circulation so that we will have a better chance of getting more national advertising? Should we start working on peripheral projects related to the magazine, such as maps of the area, guidebooks and the like?

Well, back to the computer. But the computer only makes calculations—it can't make decisions or make things happen.

In planning for the future, money is not the only ingredient. Two other things are equally important—people and organization.

The decisions we reached in our planning call for skills which we do not possess in the organization: The skills of promoting single copy sales, selling national advertising, promoting hotel circulation and creating and selling products other than the magazine.

We must solve the problem of acquiring these skills, either with new employees or through outside organizations, in the same systematic way we worked out the figures.

We also have organizational problems to solve. In addition to the four new skills needed, we will need other people: More editorial and production people for more issues, more circulation people for more circulation and so forth. Are we organized to handle these new functions and added people? Do we have to become more systematic here, too?

This is typical of the long-range planning process. It's like putting together the pieces of a puzzle—answering the questions that come up in an orderly way, so that we can manage our own future.

In addition to requiring an orderly process, this also calls for some soul-searching. Such questions as these come up: Do I want to work that hard to make the company grow in accordance with our plan? Do our people *really* have the strength and the skills to take on these new tasks? Are all of our people psychologically equipped to work in the environment of a larger organization? Must I abandon some of the truisms I have lived by for years just because the computer proves them to be false?

The process is fun—and hard work. It is best to do it in sessions so you are not interrupted by the telephone or visitors and can really noodle over the basics of business and the people.

Long-range planning is not a one-time shot. It is something that should be done at least once a year in every company. In doing it, start by comparing the last long-range plan with what has actually happened. By seeing the differences and analyzing the reasons for them, you can make your new long-range plan better than the last one.

"You pays your money and you takes your choice," said *Punch* in 1846. It's just as true today. You make your decisions and you take your risks. That's what long-range planning is all about.

Do you buy, start up or do neither?

By James B. Kobak

Nature demands constant growth. In organizations this takes the form of expanding in one manner or another. Very often this involves adding properties or products either by buying existing ones or starting them from scratch. This piece is devoted to discussing the elements which should be considered in determining, for any particular organization, whether to buy, start or to do neither.

The number of seemingly good ideas for new magazines must be infinite. To start one successfully requires careful planning, clear development of the concept and the steps involved in carrying it out, skilled execution in all phases and careful testing and research. Overwhelming dedication to the idea is essential. Also needed is experience in starting new things. There are techniques to startups just as there are in every other phase of business. Application of these techniques is particularly important because one slip can kill a new project completely. So few people have started even one major project, let alone enough to be real experts, that this experience rarely exists in a company.

Starting a new magazine normally involves putting a team of people together who have never worked closely with each other before, an obvious and normal source of friction. Changes in the team at some point are almost inevitable. An entrepreneurial approach is required which is quite different from the operations of most executives whose duties are primarily to make the existing properties work as well as possible. In some companies the entrepreneur is a corporate "misfit" and has great difficulty getting cooperation from some departments. Often, too, after a new magazine is started, the entrepreneur must be replaced. There's no job for that individual once the project is launched.

The planning techniques for new ventures are different from those followed in normal operations, although they appear to be the same. This is true intensive, long-range planning involving an excursion into the unknown. Judgments must be made about the viability of every phase of the project with no experience to go on. Care must be taken to develop firm evaluation points (i.e., go-no go points) or money can be dribbled out over a long period of time without anyone being able to stop the project. As far as is possible, research and testing should be carried out to take as many of the unknowns out of the equation as possible. (Testing should be used rather than research wherever possible.) And, through it all, you must be adaptable enough to realize that nothing ever goes exactly as planned.

The dedication needed to start a new magazine is enormous. It *always* takes longer than the entrepreneur can imagine. Every part of the magazine must be considered and taken care of—from a really definitive editorial product to circulation billing letters. Doing this from scratch certainly is not easy.

If you are not really committed to the startup, you shouldn't begin. You are liable not to work hard enough on it—or to close it down before it has had a real chance for success.

On the other hand, it is also easy to be too involved in a new magazine, particularly if it is your baby. Creating something out of thin air is an awful lot of fun. But you are liable to be blinded by your own optimism and carry on too long. Many companies have one or two of these losers about which the executives keep on saying, "Wait till next year."

Obtaining money for a new magazine is never easy, whether it is done inside a company or through venture capital sources. And, as for borrowing, forget it. Most bankers do not understand publishing in the first place; and startups to them are like open sewers. Within a company a new magazine must compete for funds for a myriad of possible uses put forward by each department. Investing large sums in a new magazine may not seem as attractive to a board of directors as spending to improve a data processing system to save thousands of dollars annually.

While there are a number of accounting tricks which can be used with new ventures to conceal the true impact on the operating statement and the balance sheet, in the end the only way to view the results is by measuring the cash which will be spent before a breakeven is reached.

From a tax standpoint, expenses for new magazines can be written off as incurred so that the true after-tax investment is reduced by the tax savings which are possible. And if the magazine depends on paid subscriptions, deferring of income from these could result in a considerably smaller investment after taxes—and conceivably even a net profit.

Launching a new magazine can take an enormous amount of time, not only of those intimately involved with it, but of top management and department heads who must lend their counsel, advice and help.

And in the balance you must consider the risk-reward factors. Judging this obviously varies with each project. The rewards possible for a newsletter in a field in which you already have a publication obviously do not have to be in the same range as those possible for a *People* magazine. But unless the rewards can be large enough to justify the time, worry and expense, it is better not to start.

The buying of magazines always seems to be a lively business. Doing this in the best possible way also involves careful planning, skilled development and execution and thorough research. Experience is needed here, just as it is in starting a magazine. There are techniques, too, which, if they are not followed, can produce overpayment or can turn a winner into a loser. And few executives have been through even one purchase, let alone a good number, so that experience in all its phases rarely exists in depth in a company.

Buying a magazine (or a company) involves first finding one which has good potential, fits with your company and its people and which you know what to do with. And, of course, the price must be right. This means organizing a search for the proper property, investigating the magazine, its field and its people and negotiating for its purchase. To do it right calls for very careful planning of all these steps. And no matter how carefully the job is done, something always seems to be overlooked or some unknown surfaces after the purchase.

As in starting a magazine, all these activities are not in the normal line of most executives' skills or experience. A bad purchase can not only be costly in terms of its original price, but can also drain a company of its financial and personnel resources for many years.

Normally a company will acquire a magazine together with its management. This always brings a strain both to the buyer and the seller. Personnel on both sides have to learn to get along and to take advantage of each other's skills and experience. More than once a purchase has brought with it personnel problems which far outweighed any benefits.

Obtaining money for an acquisition can be done in a number of ways. If it is not available internally, it can sometimes be borrowed. Or the purchase itself may be on a long-term payout or contingent basis. If stock is exchanged, while there is no cash cost, you have given away part of your own company.

From an accounting standpoint, assuming a substantial price is paid, in most cases the buyer will end up with an intangible asset on the balance sheet (goodwill or some other) which will have to be dealt with. For public companies, which must jealously guard their earnings per share, the need to write off the intangible can force the apparent price to an abnormally high level. In some cases, of course, depending on the specifics of the property, this situation can be avoided.

Taxwise, a purchase normally is primarily made with after-tax dollars, although in some cases this can be avoided.

The acquisition game can be very time-consuming, particularly for the head of a company, but also for all members of top management and various department heads. This time problem goes on not only during the research, investigation and negotiation phases, but also after the purchase has been made and the putting together process is going on.

There is a danger here, too. Merging and acquiring are great fun for most executives. Because it is very exhilarating, there is often a tendency to overpay to buy properties you should not have.

And, inherently, you must consider the risk-reward factors. When you pay out substantial sums and spend lots of time in buying a property, you had better be sure the reasonably projected profits will be large enough to justify it.

So Who Should Buy and Who Should Start?

There obviously is no overall answer to this. Every company has its own personality, skills, experience, means and desires. If you don't have a burning desire to grow, you probably shouldn't do it either. If you do want to grow, a review of your company is needed to see whether it is ready to do either. The checklists below give an idea of the characteristics needed.

1. *Basic Checklist: Should You Consider Either Buying or Starting?*

Unless your company can honestly fit the description below, you would be wise not to seriously try either buying or starting without first making some changes and improvements:

• The fun of growing is important to us.

• We could use a psychological lift by doing something new.

• We are well organized.

• Our managers have real authority and responsibility.

• Our present operations are operating well.

• We are highly profitable.

• We have a good information system and controls.

• We have budgets—good ones.

• We do long-range planning on a regular organized basis.

• We have been able to make major decisions without heartache or excess time.

• Our record on major decisions has been good.

• We are not afraid of failure.

• Our key people have time to devote to new projects.

• We have real strength in every area of our business.

• The owners are willing to risk part of what they now have for growth.

• We have funds which can be used without jeopardizing the present business.

2. *Further Checklist: Should Your Buy?*

Assuming your company has passed the first test, you should be able, in addition, to fit the description below:

• Our people are adaptable enough to be able to work well with a new group.

• We are not overcentralized with departments which have become empires, making cooperation difficult.

• We have available skills in research, in investigating other properties and in negotiating.

• We have excess managerial manpower.

3. *Further Checklist: Should You Start?*

If your company got this far, to consider starting a new magazine you should also be able to fit these:

• When we try something, we see it through.

• We do not hold onto proven losers.

• We are able to plan and organize a project from scratch.

• We can think conceptually.

• We have available a manager with an entrepreneurial approach.

• We also have available a manager who can continue operations once the launch has been made.

• We have available skilled manpower in areas

657

where it will be needed.

• We know how to test and research a new idea.

• We can get information about the areas of the business we do not know.

It is apparent that to do the best job in either buying or starting requires a well-managed, psychologically prepared company. Few take the time and trouble to analyze themselves prior to considering a major step such as buying or starting. But a great deal of grief could be avoided—and profits maximized—through such an approach even though it may delay the entry for a time.

As you examine the characteristics of both buying and starting, it becomes readily apparent that most larger publishing houses find it easier, less risky to their stockholders and more fitting both psychologically and personnel-wise to buy rather than start, although there are some notable exceptions. And because of the entrepreneurial dedication which is required for a startup, it is no surprise that most of these are done by one or groups of individuals.

The anatomy of a spinoff

By Jerry R. Constantino

Question: How is a whirling dervish contest like a good publishing opportunity?

Answer: Both involve spinoffs.

The spinoff—the publishing "second car"—is not often sought and is less often successful. In theory, it should work every time, but publishers have a way of theorizing themselves out of business. The market doesn't always translate as the publisher thinks it should. The obvious benefits are only obvious to the publisher. The tie-in is no better—and sometimes worse—than no tie-in at all. Or the prospective reading audience just doesn't want the "world's greatest" magazine.

I once felt "success" stories should be written after the fact, not before. But if that were the case, there would be so few in relation to attempts, and they would not reflect the hope, awe or mystique of a just-about-to-be-born "baby."

So here's a success story before the fact from a spinoff "publisher genius" (me) who said, "We won't fall by the wayside. Others, but not us! Right? Of course—we've got a natural."

That's the case of PJS Publications, Inc., Peoria, Ill., publisher of *Shooting Times* (a 175,000 monthly consumer magazine for gun buffs), *Rotor & Wing International* (30,000 monthly for owners and operators of helicopters) and *Profitable Craft Merchandising* (25,000 13-times a year for handcraft supply retailers).

Remember that last title, *PCM*—it's the spinner and *Crafts Magazine* is the spinnee.

A little background on *PCM*. (Incidentally, this is not its first FOLIO mention. In April 1973, it was one of four featured successful do-it-yourself magazines—one-man operations by individual entrepreneurs. In the article, "The Ultimate Do-It-Yourself," *PCM*'s founder, Jack Wax, told how he took the magazine from a standing start in 1965 to $250,000 in revenues in 1974 when we bought it.)

In 1965, the handcrafts market (beads, macrame twine, paints, glue, feathers, styrofoam, etc.) was doing $65 million in retail sales. In 1974 it was up to $750 million. Today it is $1.6 billion.

So a most important spinoff criterion—a strong growing market—was met. And today *PCM* is its strongest voice doing just under $1 million in business. It serves the industry's retailers, wholesalers, importers and manufacturers. It is a bible of craft information, trade news and ads.

PJS has been looking for acquisition possibilities for several years without success. We considered the craft spinoff when, in research conducted for *PCM* by Hagen Communications of New Jersey, we asked for our retailers' interest in a consumer counterpart.

Response was overwhelmingly positive, but timing (ours particularly) was not. So we waited and made *PCM* better as we continued to analyze the craft market.

There are four or five consumer magazines regularly covering crafts of various kinds. Southern Living's *Decorating & Craft Ideas* is the biggest at 700,000 paid, published 10 times a year.

There are others too (the annuals, Christmas specials, general interest women's and shelter magazines, etc.) covering crafts (as part of their mix), but they are heavy in sewing, needlework, art crafts and craft projects that call for material from junk around the house, hardware stores and only occasionally found in (of all places) craft retail stores! And this is great for the craft world. Where, if anywhere, does *Crafts Magazine* fit?

Alas, even when our *PCM* readership, in the craft retailers, stood to benefit from large consumer features and/or promotion, so often the direct tie of consumer to retailer was never made. And many of the potential new crafters around the country were disappointed when they couldn't find material for a specific project in the craft stores.

Special Opportunity

This brings us to a key point in this and any tie-in: What makes the opportunity so special by the tie that it will work when other attempts have failed?

In this case, the lines of communication in a rapidly growing homespun industry of many small shops were never laid down and one half doesn't know what the other half is doing—or worse yet, what they are going to do. The craft industry also has many different kinds of products and changes rapidly..."trendy" is the word often used to describe it.

And inventory must be "trendy" and "turn" or it sits, and craft retailers die.

Consumer media can't afford to worry about this basic law of supply and demand situation. That's the trade magazine's bag. And to complicate craft retailing even more, its biggest association includes hobby retailers such as model trains and radio-controlled aircraft—none of which are part of the product mix in most craft outlets—and all of which are more vertical in interest and less "trendy."

Who, then, can effectively help?

Answer: *Crafts Magazine* can worry about the craft retailers because *Crafts* has the tie-in sister publication, the craft retailer bible, *Profitable Craft Merchandising*.

The first premise for a successful spinoff is now complete—real reason for existence of the new magazine using the strength of its sister publication.

How will this work from a retailer's standpoint? Well, in an industry heavy in "show-and-tell" selling, when "made-ups" (finished examples of the project) are vital, *Profitable Craft Merchandising* can keep its retail readers informed one or two months before the consumer introduction of a how-to project in *Crafts Magazine*. This is a real plus.

The retailer will read about the new project, be taught how to make it, when and how to stock for it and how to display it to maximum advantage.

When the customer (usually female) reads about it one or two months later, she will be pleasantly surprised to see her favorite craft store not only has a "made-up" of the adorable dip-and-drape doll on the *Crafts Magazine* cover, but offers all the supplies, pre-packaged to make the dolls—*plus* a free class just starting on dollmaking.

Promoting to Retailer

Here's how it is promoted to the craft retailers as we ask them to get in on the sales opportunities:

"Yes, *Crafts Magazine* will wrap it all up for you—in a big extra profit package that will help you sell more craft products.

"Just see how *Crafts Magazine* will bring you those extra sales—it's quick and easy as 1-2-3-4-5.

"Benefit 1: You get advance notice of upcoming craft projects customers will be asking about—through the pages of *Profitable Craft Merchandising*. New products—new projects—upcoming consumer advertising—will all be announced in advance in *PCM*. By keeping current on crafts through *Profitable Crafts Merchandising*, you'll be in a position to anticipate what products your customers will want to buy. *Crafts Magazine* will also enable you to have the right made-ups ready, the right classes prepared and your shelves well stocked with the merchandise consumers will want and ask for.

"Benefit 2: You get immediate extra profits by displaying and selling *Crafts Magazine* in your store. *Crafts Magazine* is being launched through craft stores so your customers can purchase copies from you. And *Crafts Magazine* is an extra, impulse sale that ties in with every other sale you make. At your request, we'll be glad to supply you with a compact display rack that you can set up right beside your cash register, and you'll be surprised at the way *Crafts Magazine* will sell itself. (You've surely noticed how all the supermarkets feature women's service magazines at their checkout counters. Now, with *Crafts Magazine*, you'll have an opportunity to pick up the same kind of extra sales at your cash register!)

"Benefit 3: Then, in every issue of *Crafts Magazine*, your customers will find stimulating, interesting craft project suggestions that they can do themselves. Not impossible or impractical projects—and not "kid" projects either! Instead...useful, beautiful, decorative, valuable craft projects they can make only with products you sell. The editorial material and the ads in every issue of *Crafts Magazine* will mean not only first sales but repeat sales—by providing exciting fresh ideas every month that will bring customers back to your store to make additional purchases!

"Benefit 4: Most important—when your customers come in eager to buy, you'll be ready! Because you'll know months in advance through *Profitable Craft Merchandising* what's coming up, you'll have time to order merchandise, set up displays and be ready when consumers walk in asking for products they've read about in *Crafts Magazine*.

"Benefit 5: And finally...by using *Profitable Craft Merchandising* and *Crafts Magazine* together as a combined sales tool you gain an important point-of-purchase plus. Made-ups are important, we're sure you'll agree. Placed next to kits or open stock they attract attention and show consumers what they can make and what they need to buy. The more made-ups you have, the more ideas you give consumers for using the same products in different ways.

"But if you're like most retailers, you're reluctant to display made-ups for which you have no printed instructions to offer.

"By using projects in *Profitable Craft Merchandising* that will later appear in *Crafts Magazine*, you'll not only have eye-catching made-ups ready when customers walk in, you'll be able to direct them to the instructions in *Crafts Magazine*. And because *Crafts Magazine* is a monthly, you'll never be out of fresh ideas!"

A more recent followup study to our craft retailers told us 78 percent want to sell *Crafts Magazine* in their shop. And why not? Crafts shops have traditionally carried instruction booklets and brochures—much like music stores carry sheet music, selling from $1.50 and up. It's a business staple.

"And *Crafts Magazine* brings you extra advantages, too! Just look at all these additional advantages you get as a free bonus from *Crafts Magazine!*

"Extra Bonus: With the very first issue you benefit from reaching eager readers, eager buyers!

"Many regular crafters will come to your store for their copies. Others will subscribe or buy them on newsstands—and the projects they find in every issue of *Crafts Magazine* will bring them to your store to buy. Either way, you're a winner!

"Extra Bonus: A natural promotion tool for your classes—the projects in *Crafts Magazine* are ideal for class projects. They give you a practical monthly program to follow. They create monthly sales for you. And of course when you use *Crafts Magazine* projects in your classes, you'll sell a copy of *Crafts Magazine* every month to every student—which brings in welcome bonus profits!

"Extra Bonus: Very importantly, *Crafts Magazine* will build up and maintain a continuing interest in crafts among its readers. By providing stimulating new ideas each month, it will keep enthusiasm running high among your customers. And that makes for repeat sales from steady customers.

"Extra Bonus: You can use extra copies of *Crafts Magazine* in many special ways to stimulate sales, profits and win customer goodwill. You might give an occasional copy to special regular customers—or as an extra gift with a big purchase—because you know that each copy does real 'missionary work' toward future sales for you.

"Extra Bonus: And finally—*Crafts Magazine* will help you achieve faster turnover of the products you stock. Because you'll know in advance which products will sell, you will be able to maintain a better inventory of fresh, active products and cut back and avoid the 'slow movers.' Also, you'll avoid the most aggravating of all retail situations—lost sales because you're sold out or don't have an item in stock.

"Every way you look at it, *Crafts Magazine* is the most exciting news that's hit your cash register in years!"

The craft retailer can obtain bulk copies of *Crafts Magazine* (minimum 10 per month and no returns) at a 48 percent discount—a little better than the 40 percent the retailer buys most of his or her goods. We supply a rack on request (and "take one" subscription stuffers on which the retailer makes $2).

It's a good tie for the retailer. It's a good tie for the customer. It's a good tie for the publisher.

And since *PCM* is published especially for retailers, it is important they have the opportunity to benefit from this new consumer publication. After all, it's their customers who are learning new crafts with every issue.

Advertising Sales

Now, how about the advertisers? The same obvious tie-in benefits for the retailers apply to the advertisers as well. *PCM* carries as many as 150 advertisers in any given issue. The basics of the trade call for the manufacturer to sell the retailer on its product and letting the retailer sell the customer.

It's not that the advertisers wouldn't like to reach the customer, too, it's that they can't—not cost effectively, anyhow.

Because of the tremendous number of craft interests and the wide diversity of craft coverage in all type of magazines and media, it is virtually impossible for a craft advertiser to make a strong consumer buy without buying (and paying) much more than the budget will stand. A page ad in a larger publication with some craft editorial content could cost five times more than *Crafts Magazine*—but the basic editorial thrust of that magazine may well be needlecraft or home decor.

The craft advertisers can first promote their products in *PCM* and subsequently create consumer demand for the well-stocked retailers through *Crafts Magazine*. And they can do it with a tie-in advertising program called "Craft Ad Pac."® This allows *Crafts Magazine* advertisers on a 12x or greater frequency a 20 percent rate discount in *PMC*. A 6x frequency earns a 10 percent discount and 3x frequency, 5 percent discount.

So the tie is made for the advertisers. So far, so good.

And the Readers

Did we leave anyone out?

Oh, yes, the readers of *Crafts*. How do we get them and how many do we want?

So we go for readers. How? Well, we know consumer publishing via our successful *Shooting Times* with 80,000 paid subscribers and 95,000 sold on newsstands monthly. So we have a basis of experience and knowledge to add to this spinoff opportunity; we know enough to realize we need a direct-mail subscription professional.

We asked direct mail consultant Walter Weintz to give us a hand. Walt's company has a great record and client list (*Better Homes and Gardens Crafts Club, Organic Garden* and *Prevention Magazine, Firehouse, Scholastic Magazines, Avon Cosmetics, National Liberty Life Insurance* and *Popular Club Plan*). We told him we wanted only 80,000 subscribers initially. We figured we might get as many as 10,000 from our retailers (if we're lucky) but didn't want to count too heavily on these as past publishing experience says to take sales like this as frosting on the cake. They come slow and hard. The net effect of the big promotion to retailers, however, certainly won't be wasted—the residual benefit is to reveal completely and promote our plans to the whole market—advertisers and all, which is exactly what this tie-in will do.

We asked Walt to get us the entire 80,000. Our list selection availability was plentiful because there are so many lists in this interest area. We mailed a 100,000 test to 20 different lists, using three different charter offers—12 issues, $9; nine issues at $6.75; and six issues at $4.95.

Crafts Magazine's basic rate is 12 issues for $12, single copy $1.25.

The mailing consisted of a four-color, four-page brochure, a four-page letter, a "token" order card, a "kicker" (a free brochure on how to make beautiful silk flowers) and a business reply envelope, all in an attractive 6" x 9" four-color outer envelope.

Our initial 80,000 paid circulation (to be handled by Fulfillment Corporation of America of Marion, Ohio) is expected from 1.6 million mailers which stress our expertise and credibility as publisher of the industry's bible, *PCM*, plus a dynamite "superspread" (a Wallace Press specialty recently promoted in *Ad Age)* four-color 12-page gatefold insert with order card in three consecutive issues of *PCM* to retailers seeking bulk magazine orders.

No Publishers Clearing House—not yet anyhow, even though the PCH remittance rate for new magazines is a larger 25 percent. And we will wait until later to test newsstands. Why?

As amazing as it may sound, we don't want to start with more than 80,000 circulation although the experience of others and our knowledge tell us it could be much greater.

One of the big disadvantages of the larger magazines covering some consumer crafts is the budget-depleting page rate for numbers—even at low CPM.

Crafts Magazine's CPM will be higher, nearly $10, for fewer but definitely involved readers. Our craft advertisers (again the tie advantage in knowing your advertisers and they, you) will pay $750 initially to try *Crafts*. The out-of-pocket cash to be in the first issues is not intended to be backbreaking.

Then, as we gain momentum and prove responses, we both will grow. Our initial projections show *Crafts Magazine* growing to over 100,000 paid at the end of year one.

Introduction to the trade will be, of course, heavily in *PCM*, the trade magazine. It also ties in nicely with the annual Hobby Industry of America's convention in January where we will emphasize the relationship of both magazines.

If publishers shouldn't kid themselves with theory as to why a spinoff will work, they surely shouldn't kid themselves with dollar bills as to how much it will cost. Computing all the variables and unique expenses that go into a new venture—especially a magazine startup—can be mind boggling.

We asked Kobak Business Models to help. Putting a new magazine on a computer model is really the way to go—it's all new and fresh—no faded history to interpret or ongoing subscription liability to evaluate for your data base.

So we did. We put *Crafts* on the computer model and gave ourselves a chance to look at half a dozen different, viable options.

You know something? We know what it should—could—cost. We know what it might gross. And we expect to be profitable in year two.

And we lived happily ever after! Right? We hope...but won't know for sure for a while.

Don't bet against this one though. As a spinoff, it has a lot going for it. I promise I'll let you know what really happens.

The dilemma of the successful publisher

By James B. Kobak

Suddenly you're in trouble—and you don't even know it!

The magazine you started ten years ago has taken off. It will earn $1.5 million before taxes this year—even after your salary of $100,000. And it's still growing! It has $2 million of cash just sitting in the bank earning interest.

Your accountant has just finished the audit for the year. His parting words were, "Too bad you are doing so well. You have just two choices now—either sell out or buy some other properties." He then mutters some gibberish which included words which sounded like Aesop, double taxation, personal service maximum, 531—and left you bewildered. He asked that you commune with yourself and come up with a list of the things you would like most out of life—an unlikely request from an accountant.

This whole conversation was somewhat disturbing, so you actually sat down and tried to sort things out.

Personal Situation and Desires:

1. I am 50.

2. I enjoy very much running my magazine.

3. I do not want to run another magazine, but would like to continue improving this one and developing its by-products.

4. I once worked for a large company and do not again want a boss looking over my shoulder.

5. If I were to relinquish control of my magazine, I want to be sure that it and the people who have helped me build it are in good hands.

6. While I have two sons, I have seen too many family businesses which end in disaster and would not want them in the business with me.

7. My employees are good at their job, but I do not believe that any of them could run the magazine without me.

8. I have no desire now to retire, but I would like to take more time off to travel. I don't know that I would ever want to retire completely.

9. I want to remain as a publisher. I don't want to become financially- or tax-oriented in my thinking.

Financial Desires:

1. Get the maximum amount of cash from the business currently.

2. At some point get the maximum amount for the business through a sale or other means for my family.

3. Keep the magazine as long as possible and, since it is my principal asset, as secure as possible.

4. While I have a lot of current income, I would like to have a chunk of cash in my own pocket now.

5. Provide a reward for my loyal employees.

6. Minimize any taxes which have to be paid.

Your accountant is startled to hear that you have done your homework so quickly and so well. What follows is a seemingly endless series of meetings with him where he tries to explain the various tax provisions you are liable to be confronted with and what they mean.

Before he has gone very far you realize that you will have to sacrifice Personal Desire No. 9 (I do not want to become financially- or tax-oriented). If you don't, you are sure to make some very costly blunders.

You learn that there are not just one or two tax rates, but a whole raft of them:

Corporation Income Tax: 20 percent on the first $25,000 profits; 22 percent on the next $25,000; 48 percent on profits over $50,000.

Accumulated Earnings Tax: 0 percent on the first $150,000 (not per year, but total); 27½ percent on the next $100,000; 38½ percent on all over $250,000.

Individual Income Tax: Graduated up to 70 percent (for personal service income, the maximum is 50 percent).

Estate and Gift Taxes: Graduated up to 70 percent.

Capital Gains Taxes: If long term, generally half the ordinary rate (up to 42½ percent).

Preference Item Taxes: Too complex to recite here.

And you find that you cannot consider each tax alone, but that they are often heaped on top of one another.

You also begin to take the approach that, not only do you regret paying any taxes, but also that rates of 60 percent and 70 percent are really confiscatory and that you wholeheartedly dislike paying them, an unpatriotic feeling which disturbs you psychologically.

It is the threat of the Accumulated Earnings Tax (Section 531) which has triggered the immediate situation. Your accountant has warned correctly that, if you have another good year like the last one, the Internal Revenue Service is sure to bring this tax up. The theory behind it is that you are keeping funds in the corporation to avoid declaring dividends to yourself and paying ordinary income taxes on them.

The rates of 531 tax on top of ordinary corporation income tax are frightening. Suppose you earned $2 million before income taxes the following year. You could face paying these taxes:

Income on first $25,000 @ 20 percent	5,000
Income on next $25,000 @ 22 percent	5,500
Income on remainder @ 48 percent	936,000
Accumulated earnings on first $100,000 @ 27½ percent	27,500
Accumulated earnings tax on remainder @ 38½ percent	367,100
	$1,341,100

Effectively this is some 67 percent of what you earned. You desperately rack your brain for solutions. "What if I pay myself dividends?"

"Fine," says the accountant, "but then you will pay up to 70 percent personal income tax when you receive the dividends—and the corporation has already paid once at normal rates."

"What if I increase my salary? Then it will be taxed only at a maximum of 50 percent as earned income."

"Fine," says the accountant, "but the IRS is liable to argue that you are receiving unreasonable compensation. Then your salary will be taxed as if it were a dividend anyway and the corporation will lose its deduction."

Your accountant patiently explains that there is, unfortunately, no simple solution, although there are some other alternatives which you should explore. Some of these are listed below together with an indication of

661

how they may or may not fit the requirements you set down before.

Alternative A. Continue as is, paying yourself the highest possible salary and declaring enough dividends to avoid the 531 problem.

GOOD	BAD
•Retain complete freedom of operation. •Avoid financial complexities. •Get a chunk of cash in your pocket each year, but not so much after paying taxes.	•Pay very high taxes annually. •Do not achieve the desire to pass the largest possible amount on to your family.

Alternative B. Convert to a Subchapter S corporation. In this case the corporation retains all the legal safeguards of a corporation, but is taxed as if it were a partnership. You avoid the corporate tax, but the income flows directly through to your individual tax return where it is taxed up to 70 percent.

GOOD	BAD
•Retain complete freedom of operation. •Get a chunk of cash in your pocket each year, but not so much after paying taxes.	•Tax problem has not been solved. You have merely changed the corporate problem into an individual one.

Alternative C. Liquidate the corporation. You then own all the assets.

GOOD	BAD
•Have gotten all the cash out of the company. •Retain complete freedom of operation.	•Can be only partial solution. •After you own all the assets, you must pay ordinary income taxes on future earnings. •Must pay capital gains taxes on the value of the company at the time you take over the assets. This could be substantial.

Alternative D. Sell to the employees through some kind of long-range plan based on future profits. This can be done directly or through an ESOP (Employees Stock Ownership Plan) using an ESOT (Employees Stock Ownership Trust). These were designed for just this purpose, but the provisions of the law do not really enable it to operate as well as intentioned.

GOOD	BAD
•Reward for employees. •Gives a future incentive to employees as part owners. •Get part of the cash each year.	•Because of the large payments which will be needed based on the large value of the magazine, it may not be possible to accomplish this, even going the ESOP-ESOT route. •You lose control. •You do not believe that the employees can run the magazine and, therefore, are not sure they will ever be able to make the promised payments.

Alternative E. Pay yourself the highest possible salary plus the maximum amount into qualified pension and profit-sharing plans (25 percent of covered salaries). These plans must, of course, include most of the other employees as well, so they can be costly. Under them the contribution is deductible to the company, income earned by the plans is not taxable and the recipients only pay taxes as they receive their benefits in the future, sometimes at capital gains rates.

GOOD	BAD
•You protect part of the income from current taxes. •Part of the profits are secure for the future benefit of your family. •The other employees have received a reward.	•This can only be a partial solution. •With commitments for large future contributions to the plans, you may find that future operations are inhibited. •If the commitments are too large and too firm, you may make it too difficult to sell the business or go public later.

Alternative F. Invest excess funds in "Tax Shelters."

GOOD	BAD
•if done correctly you will avoid a certain amount of taxes without affecting the business.	•This can only be a partial solution. •There are few really good tax shelters—and many of these involve further risk which negate their effectiveness. •The 1976 tax law went a long way toward eliminating tax shelters. Regulations based on that law have not yet been completed. There are still many hazy areas, so you may find that you have not invested in a shelter at all. •Congress is liable to go further in future years to close up shelters. •You are not really oriented toward this type of tax game-playing.

Alternative G. Invest in new projects which require large infusions of cash.

GOOD	BAD
•Uses your cash and enables you to avoid section 531 as well as ordinary income taxes. •If you invest wisely, you enhance the profitability and value of the company.	•This can only be a partial solution. •New ventures are risky and you may lose everything you invest. •You have no desire to enter into new business. •You do not get a chunk of cash for yourself.

Alternative H. Buy other properties.

GOOD	BAD
•Uses your cash and avoids 531 problems. •If you buy well, you enhance the profitability and value of the company.	•This can only be a partial solution. •You are inexperienced in buying and running anything else, so this is risky. •You have no desire to get into larger operations. •You do not get a chunk of cash.

Alternative I. Go public with part of the company.

There are lots of nice good and bad points about going public. The market for new issues, however, has been almost non-existent for so long—and appears to be dead in the foreseeable future, so it is hardly worth discussing. Some other day, hopefully.

Alternative J. Sell to another company, preferably large and well-heeled.

GOOD
•Meet virtually all your financial goals.

BAD
•No longer in control.
•Will have supervision.
•Goals may differ from yours.

As you review the various alternatives you are beginning to see that your very success has forced you into a position where financial and personal goals conflict. The tax laws force you to examine the situation very carefully and to make choices between personal and financial interests.

And you find that your accountant was correct in the first place. While you can partially solve the situation through some of the methods described, in the end the only real solution financially is either to sell the company or to buy other properties.

Pity!

(Note: The complexities of this kind of exercise are enormous. There are a great many variables to all of the alternatives listed—and there are others which were not mentioned. This article was only meant to give a perspective to an area which is so complex that it is difficult to view with any objectivity.)

Relaunching the faltering magazine

By Russell F. Anderson

What do you do when you have a magazine that was a bulldozer pushing aside all of its competitors and then suddenly begins losing power?

That's what happened to *Construction Methods and Equipment,* a 58-year-old monthly that had been the one-time advertising leader in its industry. In the mid-1970s the magazine began to skid. Ad pages fell from 1,243 in 1973 to 858 in 1976. Circulation also dropped.

Late in the spring of 1977, Gordon Jones, president of McGraw-Hill Publications, appointed a Task Force to analyze *CM&E*'s problems and make recommendations as to what to do about them.

The choices to be considered were obvious. The magazine could be sold; it could be folded; it could be merged with *Engineering News-Record* and become a demographic edition; it could be switched from paid to controlled circulation to match the competitors; or it could be restructured and revitalized.

The Task Force studied the problem and decided on a total revamp of the magazine.

To get an understanding of how this decision was reached, it is first necessary to take a quickie historical look at the magazine itself and the industry which it serves.

Magazine started as house organ

The magazine was founded in July 1919, by a group of non-competing manufacturers of construction and materials handling equipment. It was a house organ, pure and simple, published by the Manufacturers Publicity Bureau in Chicago. Its title: *Successful Methods.*

In 1926, James H. McGraw bought it, changed its name to *Successful Construction Methods* and made it a companion monthly to McGraw-Hill's *Engineering News-Record,* a weekly construction magazine. The newly-acquired publication was editorially repositioned to serve the "contractor" as differentiated from *ENR*'s "engineer-ing" readers.

It was a sound strategy. And the magazine grew like topsy and became one of the company's larger money-spinners.

No discussion of a magazine problem is valid unless you understand its reading audience. The construction industry, by its very nature, differs from rather than resembles any other business served by technical publications. The construction industry is to a significant degree made up of a multiplicity of contradictions and anomalies.

Giant in size, employing 15 out of every 100 workers in the U.S., the construction industry is the largest user of steel, aluminum, copper, cement, lumber, brick and building supplies, fuel, power and the products of a host of other businesses whose prosperity depends upon it.

So, in essence, *CM&E* was addressed to a readership with different characteristics than those pertaining to the majority of McGraw-Hill technical magazines. Construction is, on analysis, not an industry at all, but a service profession. And the contractor himself is a highly mobile person, devoid of a "factory" and constantly working himself out of a job. In short, construction above all is a "people" profession.

Construction is the largest market in America, representing over 10 percent of the GNP. A huge, complicated, and diverse industry, it is different markets to different people. It is roadbuilding, dam building, home building, and building building. Because it is so diverse, there are over 100 magazines serving some segment of it. Only *Engineering News-Record*'s attempts to serve the whole market through the medium of weekly construction news.

Industry hit peak in 1973

The construction industry hit an all-time peak in 1973, and began a downward skid in 1974. Home building in particular suffered through a disastrous decline in housing starts. But this had ripple effects through the rest of the industry. Construction of appurtenances to housing was affected: roads, shopping centers, commercial and industrial building. The general recession that affected all of industry in 1974 and through 1975 also adversely affected construction.

Construction lives on borrowed money, public and private. The high interest rates of the past several years sharply reduced the appetite of entrepreneurial borrowers. The pressing problems of city deficits (of which New York City is only one of a growing number of troubled cities) sharply reduced municipal construction activity. A declining birth rate cut back seriously on the need for new school construction. In some areas, we suffered from past over-building (condos in Florida, office buildings in New York City and Atlanta, etc.).

As the construction industry bogged down so did *CM&E* ad pages and circulation. The magazine was no longer a money tree. But McGraw-Hill did not have a patent on the problem.

The heavy construction market had seen a basic flattening of ad pages during the 1970s. This, on top of quite a precipitous decline in ad pages from the all-time record years of 1957 to 1970, spelled trouble for all construction publications. Survival for many publications came from inflation-offsetting ad rate increases and vigorous cost controls. Even so, the scramble for the available advertising dollars drove several established publications out of business.

Competitor bites the dust

An old line competitor of *CM&E*'s for over 50 years, Buttenheim's *Contractors & Engineers* bit the dust in 1975. At one time, this publication battled toe to toe for years with *CM&E* for annual ad page leadership among the monthly contractor magazines. It was down to 263 ad pages in its last full year of publishing (1974). *Engineering Construction World* also went down the tube. So did two architectural magazines.

In 1973 *CM&E* carried 1,243 advertising pages. When the industry began its skid in 1974 pages dropped to 1,091. Construction activity hit bottom in 1975; it was one-fourth below its 1973 record. And *CM&E* pages attributed to 1,001. Total advertising revenue for all construction publications hit a low of $14,205,000 in 1975—down $1,915,000 from 1974.

Then early 1976 witnessed an upswing in the con-

struction industry—which slowed down in the fall of that year—then regained momentum, surging strongly through 1977. The upturn resulted in industry advertising expenditures in 1976 of $15,506,000 in all construction magazines—a comeback of $1,301,000.

CM&E's pages, however, did not bounce back. Ad pages dropped to 858 in 1976. Its major competitors, Dun-Donelly's *Highway & Heavy Construction* (formerly *Road & Streets*) and Cahner's *Construction Equipment* meanwhile were increasing their pages. So was *CM&E*'s publishing room mate, *Engineering News-Record.*

Task Force studies options

The Task Force studied all the options and concluded that the easiest way out was either to sell or fold. Merging was not a good solution, and changing to controlled circulation at the time did not appear to be a logical choice.

To completely restructure the magazine would require an investment of six to seven figures in addition to existing operating losses.

It was clear that one of *CM&E*'s problems was the loss of its share of the market. Blame could not be put on the marketplace alone.

It was the underlying thinking of the Task Force that if McGraw-Hill did not have a magazine in the construction field, and if it were contemplating a new magazine launch, the construction-contractor concept would be high on its prospect list because of the attractiveness of the field.

A relaunch—considerably less costly than a new launch—was the obvious answer.

Before taking that step, however, it was necessary to find out what caused the bulldozer to veer off course. All of the readership studies over the years were combed for clues and new research was undertaken. As a result, some interesting things came to light.

In the 1920s, the construction business was undergoing major changes. Horses and wagons and large crews with shovels were disappearing, being replaced by mechanical equipment. There was a need for a magazine covering new construction techniques, and when *CM&E* was repositioned at the time of its acquisition in 1926, it had a clear-cut editorial objective: to supply information about equipment, give practical tips on how to use the machinery and keep the contractor informed of all step-by-step "methods" used on construction jobs.

How to sell your magazine

By Marlene Jensen

Lives there a magazine entrepreneur who hasn't recently considered selling his or her magazine?

The cash flow may be receding, the ad salesmen turning into collection agents, the circulation director throwing "I Ching," and your new financial wiz starting to laugh at odd moments. You've read all the "Hunker Down for the Recession" articles, but you can't figure out how to cut 10 percent of your staff . . . which would be three-fifths of Harry, your production guy . . . which would mean you'd have to stay even later at night . . . which would mean a divorce . . . which would mean more money down the drain.

Or you're in an industry that hasn't felt the recession. You're growing fast and picking up pages and subscribers faster than you can count them. It's exhilarating. However, you're also picking up some big guy competition. That mom and pop competitor with the amateur look and the cheap paper has just been sold to a company that rounds off their profits to the million for reporting purposes. And your printer's rep just told you the publisher of the number one book in your field was seen having lunch with Rupert Murdoch.

Your eyes water at the thought of what *you* could do with a conglomerate's millions behind you. The research lab, the direct mail testing, the crack sales staff, more four color, better paper—the list is endless. You begin to feel like David facing two Goliaths—without a slingshot.

Whether you're dreaming about an island where there's no word in the language for "magazine," or whether you're thinking of adding some expensive new weapons to your arsenal before renewing the attack, you will undoubtedly consider selling. If you've never sold a magazine before, you might want a few tips. (Although it is too late to apply the first two tips, you still have time to enact the others.)

1. *Cultivate a success image.* Two new magazines with identical numbers can have opposite images—one a "winner" and one a "loser." It all depends upon lowballing the budget.

Inside Sports, for example, finished year two with some pretty good numbers for ad pages and circulation. They'd made good inroads into a fiercely competitive field. Yet every few months the trade press had it missing another target. Missing rate base, selling fewer ads than anticipated, losing more money than anticipated. Always a loser—but a loser relative to projections. What if they had projected less?

Look at *Spring.* Maybe Rodale really thought they'd just hit a 250M opening rate base, and all those ads in the press announcing a bonus circulation—60 percent after six months—just represent good fortune on their part. Then again, maybe it was expected.

2. *Be in a hot field.* Short of being born rich, nothing else will so guarantee a comfortable future for you. If you're not in a known hot field, try to find some data that show the field you *do* cover is underrated and the hot winner of tomorrow.

3. *Be aware of the competitive situation among the larger companies.* If your competitor was just sold, look closely at the buyer's competitors. This is only partly because the buyer's competitors are, by definition, in the same business. The other part is the competitive atmosphere that develops among the large publishers. When company X decides to expand into a new field, its competitors will investigate the field thoroughly, just to find out what X is up to. The end result is frequently a desire to enter the field and compete. For example, when the first video book goes to a conglomerate, it is likely that at least two of their video competitors will be sold within a year.

4. *Check your subscriber lists.* Despite denials, not all deals are done on logic. If you publish a boating magazine and one of your subscribers is on the board of a large publishing company, you can't get a better recommendation. Make contact.

5. *Become visible.* Cultivate your trade press. Give the ad trades information from a new research study you did. Give the newsletters the results of your latest direct mail campaign. Tell them all how well you're doing, how happy you are, and how you have absolutely no interest in selling. It's like setting off a flare to a potential acquirer.

6. *Anticipate the data a buyer will want.* Your financials should be broken down into their individual components, since each prospective buyer will need to arrange your data into his own reporting format.

"Editorial Expenses," for example, says absolutely nothing. That number could include manuscripts only or any other variation on up to art, manuscripts, prep and composition, engravings, salaries and supplies for the edit and art staffs, telephone, T&E and even rent allocations for the staff's office space. Give all the detailed numbers and let each prospective buyer group them according to his own methodology.

7. *Supply neat, organized data, using computer reports where possible.* It is not true that people—at least not acquisitions teams—will believe numbers more when they come off a computer report; but it is true that disorganized, hand-written data will get a fine-tooth combing. Most important, a management that is perceived as disorganized will most certainly lower the value of the property to an acquirer who expects current management to continue with the property.

8. *Read between the lines on buyer requests.* Big companies want mountains of data, but it would be a mistake to suppose they have set demands that apply to all companies. Be alert to areas of inquiry beyond the P & Ls. You can learn which parts of your magazine are perceived to have the most value to a particular buyer. If you get several growth questions about your advertisers' businesses, the buyer may be expecting rapid growth in your field. This could clue you to do a little internal research, calling your advertisers and asking how their businesses look over the next five to 10 years.

You could prepare a report with quotes for potential buyers and raise your price expectations. If their questions focus on the demographics of your readers, they may believe your book's greatest value is to their ad network.

9. *Anticipate a buyer's problems.* If you have a video book, why not prepare in advance a listing which proves just 11 percent of your advertising is for X-rated movies.

10. *Be honest.* If your print bills for last year add up to more than your financials list for printing, it won't escape notice. The buyer will either drop you, figuring the time investment in a closer look would not be worthwhile, or recalculate your company's worth, lowering your profits or raising your losses by 20 percent.

11. *To maximize profits, you should have sold two years ago.* The "times earnings" offers of today are less than half what they were. Yet the *real* price of a magazine is still only based upon three things: the market potential of the magazine, how badly the buyer wants it, and how badly you want or need to sell.

Structuring the deal: Part I

By James B. Kobak

Structuring the deal for the purchase and sale of a property is one of the most complex, difficult, confusing, fascinating and rewarding exercises in which a businessperson can become involved.

It's an exercise which involves facts, opinions, fiction, law, psychology, accounting, taxes, creativity, judgment, ideas and often legerdemain and thievery. There are tangibles and intangibles, honest men and crooks, deal makers, deal breakers and five percenters.

If you have the opportunity to participate, don't miss it.

However, because of the nature of publishing, the qualitative and human aspects of the business usually assume a somewhat greater importance than in other industries.

Let me explain. If you are buying a CATV operation, there is a going rate per paid subscriber. No such formula can possibly apply to magazines because each is a different animal with varied economics and appealing to different readers and advertisers.

In addition, many factors must be analyzed before structuring a deal and the thinking of all the parties in the transaction—the buyers, the sellers and the helping (sometimes hindering) intermediaries and professionals—must be understood.

In typical oversimplified fashion, let's see if we can define the various factors which might be involved.

Basic types of buyers and sellers

It may seem strange to talk about buyers and sellers in the same breath, but you must understand their underlying thinking, which is the same. There are, of course, myriad ways in which a magazine can be owned, but the major categories and their basic characteristics are:

Public company—Has pressure to continuously increase profits so that earnings grow and the value of the stock increases.

Semi-public company (A small amount of stock owned by the public)—Also interested in increased earnings but not to the same extent as the public company. Can behave more like a private company.

Private company owned by those running the business—Has much greater flexibility to invest in the future, or become involved in magazines which interest them, rather than only the most profitable.

Private company owned by a trust or estate with obligations to beneficiaries—Is conservative because of the necessity to protect the assets of the entity and avoid criticism or legal action by the beneficiaries.

Private company owned by outside investors—Wants to maximize the return in the long run, or the short run, but not under the same type of pressure as the public company.

Non-profit organization—Interested in anything which might further its interests through publicity and communication with its members.

Foreign company—Wants to invest in the United States because of the basic soundness of its economy, size of its market, exchange rate and dedication to the free enterprise system.

An investor (or investors)—Interested in specific areas of publishing either for profit or other reasons.

Other characteristics of buyers and sellers

This analysis by types of ownership, however, does not exhaust the subject, which must be analyzed in other ways to be completely understood.

Magazine publishing deals in intangibles. Buildings and machinery are not needed, only ideas. Most businesspeople have difficulty dealing with such a business simply because their experience has been along other lines. The process of educating these people, when structuring a deal, is often long, difficult and frustrating. Particularly troublesome is their inability to understand unexpired subscriptions and how the biggest asset shows as a liability on the balance sheet (see "A Fool and His Subscription Revenue Are Soon Parted," FOLIO, November 1972). Yet an understanding of this concept is essential in making a deal in the magazine business whenever paid subscriptions are involved.

Companies may be conservative or venturesome. There are people who enjoy taking risks and people who are very conservative—and there are all shades in between. Like people, companies have the same characteristics. Some will only bet on a sure thing while others are much more adventurous.

The wealth of the buyer and seller greatly affects the transaction. It may, however, have little impact on the price. A wealthy buyer will want to pay cash while a buyer who is not as wealthy will want to structure some kind of long-term payout in order to use the future profits of the company to pay for it. In like manner, a wealthy seller may be willing to sacrifice current cash in the hope of getting much more in a long-term payout.

Balance sheet intangibles are important. With the purchase of a magazine, certain intangible assets (goodwill, value of lists purchased, etc.) must be put on the balance sheet. These assets must be amortized over various periods. For a private company this may not be important, but public companies usually do not want to show intangibles on their balance sheets and must consider the effect of this amortization on their future profits. While magazine publishing is a cash business, from an accounting standpoint it can give rise to all sorts of strange entries representing intangible assets and liabilities.

The nature of the magazine affects the transaction. Some buyers are only interested in magazines in specific fields or of a certain quality level. Some only want magazines in the early stages of their life cycles while others like mature properties. Some lean toward highly successful properties; others buy losing properties. Some are only comfortable with fields which are allied with other things they are doing.

Personal relationships can help or hinder a deal. Some people relate to each other and can easily reach a satisfactory arrangement, while others have a terrible time and may never be able to arrive at a good conclusion.

Reasons for buying

The obvious overriding reason for buying a magazine is to increase the value of what is owned. In some cases, however, the connection between increasing value and the reason for buying is somewhat indirect. And in a few cases, it may not come into play at all. Reasons include:

•The desire to increase profits either for the short run—or the long run—or both.

•The desire to increase the size of the business.

•The wish to gain prestige by being in the magazine business—or through the prestige of a particular magazine.

•The need for certain people not only to run the magazine being bought but also to help with the existing business.

•The desire to enhance the value of the company. This is particularly important for certain public companies when publishing stocks are selling at higher multiples than their own. The purchase of a magazine may be seen by the public as setting a new, more aggressive direction.

•The desire to kill off a competitor.

•The wish to gain circulation and advertising by buying a competitor or near competitor.

•The buyer thinking he can run a property better than the present owners and thus get a bargain purchase.

•The desire to develop higher profits through synergism resulting from the merger.

•The need to have a size and earnings base enabling the buyer to go public (when the market again permits, if ever).

•The buyer's interest in the subject matter of the magazine.

•The buyer's desire to get a job for his son.

•The need to use up excess cash.

•The wish to obtain a tax loss carryforward.

•The wish to obtain profits to help use a tax loss carryforward.

•A need for cash and other assets.

•The wish to buy out a partner or stockholder.

•The desire to diversify.

•The desire to obtain a customer for buyer's printing plant, fulfillment service or other business.

•The need to gain a foothold in an attractive geographic area.

Reasons for selling

Money is not the only reason people sell their magazines. Strangely enough, many of the reasons that motivate the buyer to buy also influence the seller to sell. These reasons include:

•The desire for cash.

•Disagreement among partners or stockholders.

•The wish to diversify investments.

•The need to obtain capital for expansion.

•Need to obtain capital for operating costs.

•The success of the magazine.

•The wish to cut losses of a magazine in trouble.

•The need to dispose of a property not wanted in the first place (it might have come as part of another transaction).

•The magazine being too small for the operation.

•The seller not liking the field of the magazine.

•The seller not liking the magazine business.

•The need for management capable of running a magazine.

•Seeing bigger opportunities elsewhere.

•Synergism.

•The fun of making the deal.

•The desire to use a tax loss carryforward.

•The seller not understanding the magazine business.

•The seller's son's inability to run the magazine.

•The owner's desire to retire or the owner's death.

•The seller's belief that magazine publishing is too risky.

•The desire to get cash out of the company.

•The need to get rid of a property that cannot be supervised because of its location.

Deal must be good for both sides

It has often been said that a good deal must be good for both sides. Unfortunately, not all the people who mouth these words believe them. No matter which side you are on, a deal which is not good for both parties just won't happen. (See "Buying Magazines" and "Selling Magazines," FOLIO, September 1974 for approaches and techniques for making deals.)

There are many reasons why a potential deal does not take place. Most of the reasons do not become apparent until the parties involved are deep in negotiations. There are, however, a number of early-warning signs which make it obvious it is a waste of time, money and skill to try to make a transaction:

Reasons for buying and selling don't match—If the seller wants cash and the buyer is only able to offer some type of stock, nothing can happen. If the seller wants to retire and the buyer is looking for skilled managers, there is no sense going further.

Wide differences in values—There are always differences of opinion about a property's value. If the differences are not too wide, it often is possible to reach a compromise or to utilize certain deal techniques to bridge the differences. If they are very wide, however, there usually is no sense in getting into negotiation (see "How Much Is Your Magazine Worth?," FOLIO, July/August 1973).

People who are only lookers—There are lots of people—both buyers and sellers—who are perennial lookers, but who never really make a deal. At the other extreme are those who always seem to be able to make things happen. If you find you have a looker on your hands, you'd better call the conversations off quickly.

Incompatibility of people involved—You can tell rather quickly whether you are dealing with your type of person. If you are not dealing with your type, stop conversation early before you get too upset. Nothing will ever happen, in any case.

Other people involved

A great many people may get involved before most deals can be completed. These are of various types:

The principals and their people—These are the principals themselves, their partners and stockholders, boards of directors, key employees, wives, relatives and others. The financial people, particularly, become very much involved.

Outside helpers—Sooner or later most transactions require a host of experts of various kinds. These include brokers, investment bankers, lawyers, outside accountants, tax experts, valuation experts, consultants, negotiators and other advisors.

Outside influences—Whether you like it or not, there are often third parties whose views must be considered: the SEC and state securities regulatory bodies, the FCC, FTC, and other regulatory agencies, securities exchanges, industry associations, bankers, IRS and on and on.

The most important thing to recognize about all the people who will get involved is the role each should play in order to structure the best deal. Most principals have never been through even one deal. Some may have done one, or at best, a handful. Their major function should be to try to specifically determine just what it is they want in terms of price, method of payment, future activity and the like. This is not easy, but the earlier and more thoroughly it is done, the easier it is to structure a workable deal.

When they are used correctly, the outside helpers can be very valuable in structuring the deal. While ideas can come from any of them, it is usually good to predetermine the function of each. Each should be viewed from the standpoint of his purpose in the specific transaction without regard to his title or training. For instance, the person who brings the parties together can be a broker, banker, lawyer, investment banker, accountant, consultant or anyone else. Some of the outsiders may be capable of playing more than one role, but not necessarily. The principal functions are:

•Introducing the parties—finding buyers and sellers with mutual interests. The intermediary may have a built-in desire to see a deal take place for emotional reasons, because a fee depends on it, or both.

•Determining the price—Both buyer and seller normally require help in determining what is a reasonable price. Either an outsider or someone within the company is needed to do an analysis of what should be paid or received.

•Researching the tax consequences—This is necessary for both buyer and seller. Often a deal which seems to be falling apart can be saved through shrewd tax thinking.

•Developing the legal documents—Both sides require attorneys to be sure they are protected and to be sure all the legalities are attended to.

•Structuring the deal—Working out the deal which will give each side close to what it wants. This can be a very creative exercise.

•Negotiating the deal—Working out the tactics to be followed in obtaining the best deal.

One of the common difficulties is that each of the outside helpers—whether qualified or not—has a tendency to want to be involved in all these functions. This can lead to disaster. It's better to confine each person to those areas where he can be most effective.

To work best, it is good to have a team of "can do" types. Negativism and lack of imagination have killed many deals.

Tools available for structuring the deal

There are an infinite number of ways to structure the deal. The method is only limited by the ingenuity of the participants.

Because of the different ways these tools can be combined, it is rare that the price announced for a purchase reflects the actual amount paid. There are too many pluses, minuses, tax tricks and intangibles involved for the published price to be the actual price.

Some of the financial and other tools which may be used include:

Cash—immediate payment.

Cash—paid in installments over a long or short period.

Notes or debentures—paid over a long or short period.

Interest—on future payments on notes or on debentures. The interest can be varied to increase or decrease the total amount.

Common stock—voting or non-voting.

Preferred stock—with whatever provisions are desired. Provisions include warrants, guaranteed payments and other clever items.

Dividends on stock—can be varied to increase or decrease the total amount.

Employment agreements which can convert part of the price into salary over a long or short period.

Non-compete agreements over a long or short period.

Royalties on future sales or earnings.

Renting the magazine with an option for future purchase.

Providing capital or guarantees of loan with an option for future purchase.

Providing fringe benefits of various kinds for key people.

Supplying certain services at a price which is reduced or higher than normal.

Paying the fees of certain intermediaries and professionals.

Paying to keep a purchase option open.

Assuming contingent liabilities or hidden liabilities.

What is sold

The sale may be of:

The entire company.

All the assets and liabilities of the company.

Certain assets of the company plus the assumption of certain liabilities—for instance, all those pertaining to one magazine.

All the assets of the company with the seller retaining certain liabilities, such as the liability for unexpired subscriptions.

A portion or percentage of the company.

Price paid

The price paid may be: the actual purchase price.

However, it could be a contingent purchase price or option to buy, based on future sales, future profits or achievement of certain goals. This price may be either a direct reflection of these or a multiple of future earnings or based on a more creative approach.

Legal vehicles used

In structuring the deal, it is frequently possible to accomplish otherwise impossible things by using different legal forms or combinations. Some available forms are:

Corporation—Limits the liability of the owners to the assets it holds. It can develop considerable flexibility through the use of various classes of common and preferred stock. Profits are taxed to the corporation. It may have any number of subsidiaries.

Sole proprietorship—Owned by one person; profits (or losses) are taxed to him.

Partnership—Can have individuals, corporations, trusts, estates or other partnerships as partners. Great flexibility is possible since the partnership agreement can be written to include any desired provisions. Profits and losses flow through to the partners for tax purposes. There is unlimited liability for the general provisions. Profits and losses flow through to the partners for tax purposes. There is unlimited liability for the general partners.

Limited partnership—The liability of some partners is limited to the amount stated in the agreement. There must be at least one general partner who has unlimited liability. If the limited partners participate in management they can be considered to be general partners.

Joint venture—Really another term for partnership. However, this is usually between operating entities rather than individuals.

Subchapter S. Corporation—A corporation which has the protection of the corporate shell, but whose shareholders are taxed as if they were partners, with the profits and losses flowing through to them. Limitations are placed on the number of shareholders, the identity of shareholders and other areas.

Nonprofit organizations—Nonprofit organizations benefit from lower postal rates than companies without the nonprofit status. Once in a while it's discovered that an existing magazine could be very useful in carrying on the work of the nonprofit organization. In structuring the sale of a property in this case, calculations of the savings in postal costs on future operations are made. The nonprofit organization will probably be in a position to pay a substantially higher price than any other potential buyer.

Trusts and estates—Including profit-sharing and pension trusts. Some of these can take advantage of the Employees Stock Ownership Plan (ESOP) which has certain advantages in the tax law.

Investment companies—Including Small Business Investment Companies (SBIC) and Minority Enterprise Small Business Investment Companies (MESBIC) which have tax advantages.

Cooperatives—Can be of various kinds.

There are further complications, most of which result from special provisions of the income tax law, provisions such as the Domestic International Sales Corporations, Western Hemisphere Trade Corporations and personal holding companies. Most business forms, too, can be either domestic or foreign, with differing tax treatment sometimes offered.

And in any deal it may be useful to use a combination of various forms, which complicates things even more.

Structuring the deal: Part II

By James B. Kobak

Both buyer and seller are vitally interested in the potential of the property involved. At some point generalities must be reduced to hard numbers, usually covering a period of five years.

These figures are needed so that both sides can have a better feel for what a proper price should be, so that the return on investment, return on assets and return on equity plus other calculations can be made, and so that a basis for any contingent payouts can be developed.

Obviously, the seller should have the best information for developing the first set of future projections. Unfortunately, a great many companies are not involved in long range planning and are actually not capable of developing really meaningful figures. Other sellers sometimes fear that any projections they might make will be used as their predictions of the future and result in legal action if they are not met. In these cases it is not unusual for an outside helper to develop figures.

A buyer has to be aware that the seller's projections may be overly optimistic although this may not in fact be true. He will usually redo the figures, taking this expected bias into account. His figures will also reflect the operation as it will be changed under his ownership. This may involve different overheads, the use of different suppliers (often at lower cost) or completely changed methods. Not infrequently his figures project better future profits than those of the seller.

To get the most out of this exercise, both sides should be as reasonable as possible in their approaches and share their thoughts with each other. It is rather difficult to structure and complete a deal without general agreement on future projections. It is often good to develop three sets of projections—optimistic, pessimistic and realistic.

Mathematical techniques used

Most very large companies—and some smaller ones—have formulas in order to judge the attractiveness of a purchase or sale. While these can be set aside by other considerations, it doesn't often happen. It is necessary to understand what they are and how they are used.

Discounted cash flow (or present value)—This is simply a calculation to determine what the value of a dollar paid in the future is worth vs. the value of a dollar paid now. There are tables which make this calculation very easy, but remember, they depend on the interest rate assumed.

Return on Investment (ROI)—Most major corporations weigh projects against each other—and against preordained standards they have set for themselves. One large corporation, for instance, aims at an ROI of 20 percent per year for any acquisition. This is a very high figure, but, considering slippage in many purchases, it helps them hold to continuously growing earnings.

The precise formulas used vary from company to

company. Magazine publishing is somewhat difficult for some analysts to understand because it is so different from other businesses. What, for instance, do you do with the unexpired subscription liability and the various ways it can be handled?

Usually it is best to look at a transaction on a cash basis in making the calculation (with future payments discounted, of course). If it is anticipated that future losses will be incurred in strengthening the property, these expenditures are also considered as investment.

Return on Assets (ROA)—This formula calculates the return on the assets used in the business. Magazines usually upset this calculation because few hard assets are involved. The return ratios get so high that they run off the normal scale and some analysts become frightened by the entire deal.

Return on Equity (ROE)—This calculates the return on the equity required to carry on the business. As in the ROA, this is a meaningless number in the magazine business.

Liquidation Value—Every buyer should consider the most disastrous conceivable result—a complete failure. Many a deal has foundered because this was not considered early enough. Any magazine with large numbers of paid subscribers confronts a buyer with the specter of a huge amount of potential liabilities.

In some cases the usual explanation—that from a practical standpoint the liability is very small—prevails. The argument is, of course, that magazines have always been able to get other publishers to take over the liability and that, in any event, if disaster seems imminent, the liability can be worked down to manageable numbers at much less expense than refunding subscribers.

Dealbreakers

There are many reasons why deals fall apart, but most of these breakdowns are unnecessary. A description of some of the more common breakdowns may be helpful.

Company not as represented—The sale of a property is usually the largest sale a person can ever make, yet most sellers approach it in a very off-hand manner. This can often result in exaggerated claims about important facts with the potential buyers being given a series of unrelated documents and financial statements. It may even result in the potential buyer being told some outright lies.

Nothing could be more disastrous. When a buyer who is far along the negotiating path finds that some of the facts he has been counting on are not true, he feels cheated and wonders whether he can depend on *any* of the data he has been given.

To guard against this, it is wise to carefully write up an unbiased description of the property, its history and its prospects. Any additional information, given either verbally or in writing, should be carefully checked.

Buyer unable to raise capital—On the other side of the sale is the buyer who represents himself as capable of purchasing a property, but is unable to develop the necessary assets. In this case it is the seller who is upset—particularly because this fact is normally not known until steps are taken to close the deal.

The method of avoiding this problem is the same as in avoiding misrepresentations by the seller. A good buyer will provide a written description of his company and financial references.

Misunderstanding by the buyer about the seller —The buyer can honestly misunderstand the business of the seller. This most often happens with people who have little knowledge of the nature of the business they are buying. A manufacturing company moving into the publishing business needs extensive education about all aspects of the company.

The way to avoid this misunderstanding is by the seller providing information about how the magazine business operates, perhaps with reprints of articles, or providing access to people who are familiar with the business. Obviously, the earlier this is done, the better.

Goodwill (or other intangibles) on the balance sheet—Because of the nature of magazines, there are few tangible assets. When a company is purchased, the excess of the purchase price over the net tangible assets must be shown as an intangible asset on the purchaser's balance sheet. This asset must be expensed against profits over various periods in the future, depending upon its nature.

This is particularly disturbing for public companies. Most of these do not want intangibles on their balance sheets at all because investors tend to discount the value of intangibles. Furthermore, the amortization of these assets reduces earnings for a number of years. This can result in a decline in the price the public is willing to pay for the stock.

Intransigence by buyer or seller—If one of the parties wants only one price, and is inflexible about how to structure the deal, the transaction will probably never take place.

This can often be remedied by attitude and approach. Relatively small concessions, if handled nicely, can lead the other side to feel that the right spirit still exists.

Professional advisers affecting the deal—We have all heard countless tales of how, in a misguided effort to protect his client, a lawyer has killed a perfectly good deal. (While lawyers are most often cited in this regard, all the other outsiders can be just as blameworthy.) However, the professional may be correctly pointing out misrepresentations and other problems which should have been faced earlier. It has been my experience that outsiders (including lawyers) normally do much more to make a deal work than not work.

The best advice is to very carefully choose the outsiders for their abilities in their respective fields—and then use each only for the functions for which you hired him.

On the other hand, principals have used their advisers more than once as excuses to kill deals they didn't want to make.

Economic conditions—It goes without saying that a recession, a radical increase in interest rates, a major change in the foreign exchange rate, major inflation in postage and paper prices or any other major economic event can break a deal. In the same way, poor economic conditions in a specific field or area of interest can turn off a buyer.

Change in price of public company's stock—A major change in the price of a public company's stock can kill a deal, whether that change is down or up. If the price goes down, the value to be paid the seller will decrease, unless the seller offers more shares. If the price goes up, the opposite effect takes place. In either case, you really have a new negotiation.

On the other hand, many deals provide for an automatic adjustment in the number of shares (within limits) if there is movement in the price of the stock.

Location—Some buyers insist on moving the properties they buy to their headquarters, while most sellers will kill a deal if it involves moving all their key people. There are ways of solving this problem which require give-and-take on both sides.

Time—Timing is always important, but it is rare that a deal dies because everyone is moving too fast. More often a deal dies because someone, usually the buyer, does not follow up quickly enough and thoroughly enough. A stale deal rarely goes through.

Illness or death.

Inability to find people to run the business—Some deals depend on the buyer being able to find people to run the business and replace the seller. This is not always possible, in which case the deal falls through.

Key people leave—Often, because they hear rumors of an impending sale, the key people leave. This may happen because they do not feel adequately protected or because they wanted to buy the property themselves. This leaves the buyer without the management he expected to have and the deal dies.

The deal is too complex—Some deals die because they just get too complex. The seller may not fully understand what is happening, or there is fear of continued or future litigation. Or there is a question of what the IRS, the SEC or other regulatory bodies will do. Or, it just smells.

Control—Both sellers and buyers often express the most sincere feelings toward giving the other side "real" control of the business after the sale. But it is a fact that the owner is the owner and no one else can really be sure of controlling anything.

Many a deal has all the earmarks of being completed—and then breaks down when the seller realizes he can no longer decide how many pages will be in an issue of the magazine or what the editorial content will be. This is an emotional issue which even the seller is not aware of until he gets down to the final line.

Lack of experience and skill in making a deal—A buyer or seller who does not possess or have with him others who possess top-flight knowledge of structuring and negotiating a deal is at a great disadvantage. Half the deal-making ability is missing from the transaction. If the other side uses sophisticated techniques, he is liable to feel they are trying to put one over on him.

Don't try to "wing it." It is too important and too complex.

Seller decides not to sell—The number one deal-breaker can happen just as all the signatures are to be put on the contract. Sometimes the seller just cannot do it. The years of starting, building and nurturing his "baby" mean too much to him.

Discomfiting though this may be, the wise buyer accepts this gracefully without counting the hours and dollars spent. The best approach is to keep in close touch after the deal breaks so that you will be first in line when the seller is able to come to grips with the sale.

Recession tactics

By James B. Kobak

So you're having a recession. Good idea.

Now you have an excuse to do all those things you knew should be done to maximize profits—but haven't done because you were having more fun thinking about new magazines, launching by-products, buying properties, hiring geniuses, developing long-range plans, and the like.

Well—back to business—and to basics—like turning out a good product, selling circulation and advertising, and reducing costs. Not so much fun for the time being, but enormously rewarding in the long run.

Here are 72 items to consider. (There are undoubtedly 72 others just as useful.)

Some eternal truths

1. There are no problems—only opportunities. Some opportunities are insurmountable, but they are opportunities nevertheless.

2. The recession will not last forever, even though it may feel like it at times.

3. Magazines normally fare better during recessions than most other businesses, unless they are in those fields that suffer complete disaster.

4. The effects of recessions are normally experienced by magazines several months after other parts of the economy feel them, which gives a false sense of security at the early stages. On the other hand, recovery also lags behind the other parts as well—so you can anticipate hard times even after the economy as a whole starts to pick up.

5. You cannot radically change the way you do business in a short recession. Don't try. You will just waste time and money. Leave that for a lusher age. Just tighten the reins.

6. Any ad budget can be canceled with a brief telephone call.

7. Sometimes a whole field will evaporate. If it does, don't fool around. Get out fast.

8. Nothing in publishing costs more than paper, printing and postage—in other words, putting out the issues.

9. Sometimes the whole economy evaporates. If that happens, be the first one on your block to know. Get out fast.

10. Don't try to upgrade your staff with new people in a hurry. There isn't time to do it well—and there is always a training period. Make do with what you have.

11. To get the best results, be dramatic about the moves you are making to weather the recession. Do this with readers, advertisers, suppliers—and, most of all, employees. You will find techniques for this in later points.

12. You won't know what to do when trouble comes if you have not made long-range projections about what will happen to the economy in general, your particular field, and your magazine.

13. Keep in mind that unless your field evaporates

completely, for its own particular reasons, your first duty is survival. Everything else is secondary.

14. Do not expect your sales incentive system to take care of reducing costs in line with the reduction in advertising income which you will suffer. Your people will have built-in living costs which you must help them meet.

Quick cost savers and cash generators

15. Reduce the number of editorial pages.

16. Reduce the amount of color on the editorial pages.

17. Switch to less-expensive artists, writers, photographers.

18. Reduce editorial travel. Use the telephone instead.

19. Reduce advertising travel. Use the telephone instead.

20. Eliminate the least effective advertising salespeople in favor of independent representatives.

21. Do what your advertisers do during a downturn—make a few phone calls to reduce your advertising and promotion.

22. Limit attendance at conventions, seminars, classes, etc.

23. Let the circulation decline. Promotion to obtain it and the cost of fulfillment is expensive. Reduce the ad rate too if you must.

24. Make all color separations en masse.

25. Eliminate the profit sharing contribution.

26. Make sure your pension plan contribution is being calculated on the most favorable mortality tables. You may find that you can skip a year or two.

27. Take all cash discounts.

28. Delay paying all other bills.

29. Renegotiate contracts with your major suppliers for lower prices and better terms. Now is the time they need you.

30. Ask your suppliers for help in finding ways to reduce costs.

31. Fire any consultant who is not effectively saving money or producing revenue *now*.

32. Reduce the number of complimentary and promotion copies of the magazine.

33. Reduce telephone expense. Try one of the cheaper long-distance systems. Hire a telephone consultant to find less expensive ways of doing things. Stop personal use of the phone.

34. Establish specific allowances for travel and entertainment, precise amounts allowed for meals and hotel rooms, geared to the cost of living for different cities, of course. Airplane coach and red-eye specials for everyone.

35. Cancel the company outing. No one wants to go anyway.

36. Skip an issue—or two—or three.

37. Reduce the paper weight.

38. Get your nephew off the payroll—finally.

39. Cut out all perquisites.

40. Cut the freebies—coffee, lunch, etc. Install machines. Make a profit on them.

41. Fire the least productive 10 or 20 percent of your staff. You should do this every year anyway.

Temporary measures

42. Realistically assess the situation for the field you serve and what might happen to it—and to you.

43. Develop a new budget based on the best information you have. Change it quickly as events change.

44. Develop another budget—a disaster plan which can be put into effect quickly if it appears to be necessary.

45. Change the thrust of your editorial material to tell your readers how to cope with the recession.

46. Step up editorial research to be sure you are in tune with your readers as their interests change.

47. Abandon the old method you have had for predicting advertising sales. Those pat formulas do not work in a recession.

48. Develop a campaign designed to convince advertisers that the only intelligent thing to do in a recession is to increase their advertising.

49. Develop a special recession discount for circulation—newsstand and subscriptions.

50. Develop a special recession discount for advertisers.

51. Test new sources of circulation instead of depending on direct mail.

52. Use subscription agents—mail, school plan, field, etc.—for the duration.

53. Try a special recession issue. Sell lots of one-time advertisers.

54. Stop all new projects. Everyone works on the magazine. Anyone who is not good at working on the magazine goes.

55. Go back to work yourself.

56. Reduce the payroll. Use outsiders instead. Change your relationship with some employees into independent contracts. This reduces your fixed costs and saves payroll taxes and fringe benefits. They will probably work harder too.

57. Fire all secretaries. Everyone answers his own phone and types his own letters.

58. Hire a consultant skilled in reducing costs.

59. Set up a "quickie" suggestion system—a one-month best idea—and offer a big, interesting prize. Give out special awards for anyone who has a good idea.

60. Start a newsletter for the people most interested in your field. Charge a lot.

61. Run "employment wanted" ads free in your magazine.

62. Go after foreign circulation. The world is a small one now. Charge a lot.

63. Give each employee an egg-timer to cut down on long distance phone calls.

64. Cut all salaries 10 percent.

Disaster measures

65. Prepare a disaster budget quickly. You had better know where you stand.

66. Change your magazine into a newsletter. Charge a lot.

67. Sell to a competitor. You are worth more to him than anyone else.

68. Buy a competitor.

69. Go controlled.

70. Go paid.

71. Go non profit.

72. Go to Brazil. Take your deferred subscription income with you.

What's in a magazine's name?

By James B. Kobak

I don't know whether anyone has ever tried to make a scientific study of the naming of magazines. I am not sure whether it is possible, or would even be worthwhile.

In any case, herewith is a highly subjective report on the subject.

To start with, I question whether the name picked for a magazine has ever been a major factor contributing to its success, while I hasten to suggest that a name could be a major factor in the failure of some magazines. In any case, it certainly can make the launch of a new title much more expensive than it might be.

A poor name, too, often indicates that the concept for the magazine has not jelled sufficiently—and this can lead to disaster for other reasons.

The title should be:

1. *Descriptive of the subject matter*—*Apartment Life, Firehouse* and *TV Guide* tell you almost precisely what their subjects are. *Cosmopolitan, Grit* and *Sphere* could be discussing anything.

Some magazines may have a descriptive name but still suffer because the reader does not, at first, know what it is describing. *Organic Gardening and Farming* is completely descriptive, but until you know what organic gardening is, it is meaningless. *Mother Jones* says it all for its constituency, but if you have never heard of her, it does little good. *A.D.* (Anno Dominum—in the year of our Lord) says it all, but very few people catch on until they are told what it is and what it means. If a magazine needs a subhead to describe itself, there is a weakness—*Time*, the weekly newsmagazine; *Playboy*, entertainment for men.

2. *Distinctive*—*McCall's, Tiger Beat* and *Rolling Stone* are certainly distinctive, even if you have no idea what they are about the first time you hear the name. *Popular Science, Sports Afield* and *Car Craft* can too easily be confused with other titles.

3. *Attractive*—This is, of course, completely subjective, but *Better Homes and Gardens, Glamour* and *Decorating and Craft Ideas* all bring out visions of something nice happening. Few magazines have titles which are actually unattractive—those that do probably don't last.

To me, *Working Woman, Us* and the former *Intellectual Digest* all suffer because of the unattractive connotations of their names.

This attractiveness aspect is one which a number of magazines have improved by applying the word "new," "popular," "today," "good" or the like; the idea being that "psychology" is pretty dull unless it is *Psychology Today* or that "housekeeping" isn't much fun unless it is *Good Housekeeping.*

4. *Lend to good graphics*—A good magazine designer can develop a good logo for virtually any name. The only criteria which can be applied are names too long or too short to come out well. *Better Homes and Gardens, Ladies' Home Journal, Oui, U.S. News & World Report* and *W* all make design difficult.

5. *Capitalize on already existing reputation*—Most magazines do not have the opportunity to take advantage of a reputation which has already been built. *Smithsonian, Rona Barrett's Hollywood* and *Harvard* have done so. When it can be done, of course, it is a great plus.

Rating the Magazines

Having defined the key ingredients to *my* satisfaction, at least, I then proceeded to rate the magazines with over a million circulation to see how accurate this kind of analysis might be, using a scale of 1 to 5 for each of the characteristics—descriptive, distinctive and attractive—and then adding or subtracting for those which can capitalize on an existing reputation or those with graphic difficulties. The results are in Table A included with this article.

With these ratings I learned several things:

• It is very difficult to rate titles of existing magazines with which you are so familiar. It may be impossible.

• Relatively poor scores do not inhibit a magazine's eventual success.

• It is hard to find a name which is both descriptive and distinctive. For this reason there are few which totaled 10 or more.

• Rating of the descriptive quality is relatively easy. Distinctiveness gets a little harder. Attractiveness is very difficult. I presumed that unless the title was actually unattractive, it deserved at least 3. The only one fitting that category was *Hustler* and, of course, this is part of the image it is trying to create, so maybe my rating is incorrect.

• Attractiveness, too, has to be judged in light of the potential readers of a magazine. *Seventeen* may mean little to us older characters, but to younger girls it is very attractive.

Having proved that a good magazine can overcome a poor title, I still believe that the name can help or hinder a new magazine. With that in mind, I rated a group of new, semi-new and planned publications. This is shown in Table B.

Favorites

My favorites are pretty easy to see from the ratings. If you can be descriptive, distinctive and attractive—and then build on an existing reputation, you certainly have an advantage. *Who's Who* (a new magazine now in the test stage), *Rona Barrett's Hollywood* and *Smithsonian* fit these criteria best. *Mother Earth News* and *Mother Jones* almost make it. *Ms.* would join except that graphically it has difficulty.

Table A	Descriptive	Distinctive	Attractive	Existing Reputation + or Poor graphically –	Total
American Home	4	1	3		8
Better Homes and Gardens	4	1	5	-3	7
Cosmopolitan	2	4	3		9
Ebony	3	3	3		9
Esquire	3	3	3		9
Family Circle	4	1	3		8
Field & Stream	4	1	3		8
Glamour	4	2	5		11
Good Housekeeping	4	1	4		9
Grit	—	5	3	-1	7
House & Garden	4	1	3		8
Hustler	4	1	1		6
Ladies' Home Journal	4	1	3	-3	5
McCall's	—	5	4		9
Mechanix Illustrated	4	1	4		9
Midnight Globe	—	2	3		5
National Enquirer	—	2	4		6
National Geographic	4	2	3		9
Nation's Business	4	2	3		9
Newsweek	5	1	3		9
Oui	—	4	3	-3	4
Outdoor Life	4	1	3		8
Parents	5	1	3		9
Penthouse	3	1	4		8
People	4	4	3		11
Playboy	4	1	4		9
Popular Mechanics	4	1	4		9
Popular Science	4	1	4		9
Psychology Today	5	2	4		11
Reader's Digest	4	1	3		8
Redbook	—	4	3		7
Seventeen	4	2	5		11
Smithsonian	3	5	3	5	16
Southern Living	4	1	4		9
Sport	4	1	3		8
Sports Illustrated	4	1	4		9
Star	—	1	3		4
Sunset	3	4	5		12
Time	2	4	3		9
True Story	3	1	4		8
TV Guide	5	1	3		9
U.S. News & World Report	5	1	3	-3	6
Woman's Day	4	1	3		8
Workbasket	3	2	3		8

Table B	Descriptive	Distinctive	Attractive	Existing Reputation + or Poor graphically –	Total
Motorboat	5	1	3		9
Money	2	1	2		5
Backpacker	5	1	3		9
Outside	3	1	3		7
Family Food Garden	5	1	3		9
Plants Alive	3	3	4		10
Popular Gardening Indoor	5	1	4	-2	8
Book Digest	3	1	3		7
Harvard Magazine	—	5	4	5	14
Human Behavior	3	1	3		7
I-AM	3	3	3	-1	8
Mother Earth News	4	5	4		13
Natural History	4	1	3		8
New Times	2	1	3		6
New West	3	1	3		7
Quest	1	4	3		8
Skeptic	1	4	3		8
Us	3	1	2	-3	3
You	3	1	2	-3	3
Americana	5	1	4		10
Blair & Ketchum's Country Journal	4	3	5	-1	11
Early American Life	5	1	4	-1	9
Houston Home & Garden	5	1	3		9
Classic	—	4	4		8
Byte	3	5	3		11
Personal Computing	5	1	3		9
Firehouse	5	1	5		11
Rona Barrett's Hollywood	5	5	4	3	17
Country Music	5	1	3		9
Petersen's Photographic Mag	5	1	3	2	11
A.D.	1	5	3		9
Apartment Life	5	1	3		9
Mariah	—	4	4		8
Ms.	5	5	4	-3	11
Soap Opera Digest	5	1	3		9
Sphere	—	4	3		7
W	—	4	3		7
Working Woman	3	—	2		5
L'Officiel/USA	—	5	5	1	11
Folio	1	3	3		7
Mother Jones	3	5	4		12
Rags	3	5	4		12
Moment	—	3	3		6
Food & Wine	5	1	3		9
Who's Who	5	5	4	5	19

Other good names are of several different types.

Some are highly descriptive and also attractive— *Americana, Firehouse* and *Psychology Today.*

Some are very distinctive and also attractive— *Byte, L'Officiel, Mother Jones* and *Rags.*

Some are highly attractive to the audiences they are wooing— *Glamour, Seventeen* and *Sunset.*

Some gain from a previously established reputation— *Harvard* and *Petersen's Photographic.*

And then there are a couple which seem to fit all around but don't quite make the first rank— *Plants Alive, People* and *Country Journal.*

At the other end of the scale are some names which don't seem to make it at all— *Money, New Times, Us, You, Working Woman* and *Moment. Ladies' Home Journal* and *U.S. News & World Report* fall down because of the length of their names—and maybe this has been overemphasized. The three tabloids— *Midnight Globe, National Enquirer* and *Star* don't score well. Perhaps the name is not important in the case of tabloids.

I have purposely avoided all the new sophisticated men's magazines because it doesn't appear that anyone looks at the name—just the pictures.

What does this mean if you are choosing a name?

First, an attempt should be made to cover the three basic characteristics and to add the help of an existing reputation. Rarely will it be possible to do all of this, so that concentration on a very descriptive, very distinctive or very attractive name should be your main effort. And the addition of an attractive catchword—new, today, good, popular—seems to help.

I now await letters from those of you who know I am out of my head for saying that *Ladies' Home Journal* with over 6 million circulation and 94 years of existence has a poor name. I also anticipate kudos from those of you who scored high and letter bombs from the others.

'Creative' creative management

By Bernard Weiss

Directing a creative staff is a great challenge for an editorial manager. Since creative people are often unconventional in their thinking, their language, their dress or their behavior, I have found that the best way to effectively manage a creative staff is to tolerate the foibles, recognizing that a certain amount of eccentricity and non-conformity is acceptable and may even be essential to the creative process.

Luckily, most editors never had to try managing these three creative geniuses:

•The author D.H. Lawrence, who liked to take off his clothes and climb mulberry trees.

•The poet A.E. Housman, who was able to write whole stanzas of his best poetry "with sudden and unaccountable emotion" only after consuming vast quantities of strong ale.

•The choreographer Bob (*All That Jazz*) Fosse, who dresses totally in black. One of his three ex-wives, Gwen Verdon, says that "his eyes sink into his head and it looks like a death mask. Inmates in asylums don't look as weird as Bob. He's driven, jumpy, crazed and psyched up."

If creative people are working under your direction, your management approach should be to simply channel their talent and their energy into a productive and worthwhile effort. In making assignments, your objective should be to assign projects in such a way as to maximize an individual's creative talents while minimizing the risks of failure. Such wisely assigned projects not only enhance the editorial product but also promote the professional growth of both the staff and yourself.

How to make assignments

•*Identify the individual's strengths.* We all have strengths and weaknesses that are related to personal interest, experience, training and education. Dedicate yourself to knowing the strengths and weaknesses of everyone on your staff. William Shawn, editor of *The New Yorker*, says: "Each writer has his own kind of talent, own kind of sensibility, own inclinations . . . So often, there's only one writer right for the subject."

When in doubt, ask. I have yet to meet the writer or designer who wasn't quick to express personal preferences for projects, assignments and professional challenge. "The best way to motivate a writer," says *Good Housekeeping* editor John Mack Carter, "is to find out what he wants to write, then tell him to go write it."

•*Convey enthusiasm.* Creativity is based on enthusiasm, and as far as I can tell, nothing worthwhile was ever achieved without it. Remember this couplet from Goethe:

Whatever you can do or
   dream you can, begin it.
Boldness has genius, power,
   and magic in it.

On your staff, enthusiasm should be a lingering infection that everyone catches from you.

•*Appreciate the person.* Respect your staff as individuals as well as professionals—as people who have personal interests and concerns. Social analyst Daniel Yankelovich says that creative people refuse to subordinate their personalities to the work role; they demand humanitarian recognition of individuality and self-fulfillment, in addition to professional challenge. "When an individual is subordinated to his work role," says Yankelovich, "he is somehow turned into an object, and his humanity is reduced in some indefinable but all-important sense."

So, talk to a staff member as if he were the president of your company. Don't just reel off a list of instructions. Do your homework. Know something about his outside interests, his family, his past, his ambitions for the future. Conduct the conversation accordingly as you ease your way into the heart of the discussion.

•*Provide background.* As you explain the assignment, provide the staff member with appropriate background. Tell him about the research you've done, the insights or hindsights that led you to this discussion, the contribution this course of action can make to the magazine's editorial objectives.

In general, give staff members as much information as you can. Don't play poker with your people. Don't hold your cards close to your vest, laying down just one card at a time. Don't keep your staff guessing about your game plan, forcing them to bet on what's coming. That style works in politics and petroleum, but rarely in publishing.

Remember, most creative people are—if not geniuses—at least brainy, and brains are like hearts: They go where they are appreciated. Although a full, clear explanation may not persuade someone to act against his will or help him to develop enthusiasm for a tough assignment, it will at least let him know that the assignment was made after some editorial planning and consideration.

•*Be precise.* When possible, be explicit in your explanations. Use plenty of analogies and examples to ensure that the message you're sending is the message he's receiving. This is particularly important in discussions about graphic or editorial abstractions.

One publisher, while planning the pilot issue of a new magazine, said to his editor and art director: "I think we need a futuristic, contemporary look." That non-specific suggestion sent the art director off on two weeks of design and logo revisions. What the publisher really wanted was a larger, bolder photograph on the cover.

•*Listen.* It's easy to be so enchanted with your own ideas and your presentation of those ideas that you forget to listen. But listening is important. Listening encourages creative people to communicate freely with you, promoting their own ideas and suggestions. Listening also gives junior staff members the courage to ask questions.

•*Anticipate objections and problems.* When someone is asked to accept an assignment (particularly if it is called a "creative challenge"), his first thoughts are usually about the difficulties in getting the job done. This is part of the natural thinking process: considering the idea to see if it *can* work, or how it can be *made* to work.

You should anticipate the problems your staff member may have in accomplishing the assignment. Furthermore, you should be prepared with answers. If you demonstrate your understanding of the difficulties and help your staff member think through some of the problems, you can be very convincing as his creative leader.

Suppose you encounter the most common of all negative responses: "I don't like that idea. I don't think it will work. We've never done it before." Try this for starters: "Well, every worthwhile achievement was, at one time, considered impossible—but perhaps you're right. What are some of the problems?"

Deal with the specifics: people, time and money. As the boss, you should be able to *find* the people, time and money to make your ideas work.

What if the objections to your proposal are based on new information or a new perspective you didn't have earlier, and you are unprepared? Here's one good way to respond: "I see your point. In other words . . ." and go on to re-state his position as convincingly as possible. Remain noncommittal, however. Your decision can wait until you have studied the issue and are prepared to discuss it intelligently.

• *Encourage feedback.* If the person doesn't voluntarily verbalize his understanding of your assignment, ask him to do so: "Just to be certain that we understand each other, and that we both clearly understand this assignment (idea, concept, project), would you mind summarizing it for me, in your own words?"

If he misunderstood you, you can avoid bruising his ego by saying: "I probably didn't make myself clear—perhaps I presented it badly. Bear with me while I try again, with some elaboration."

• *Watch for tacit signals.* As you talk about the assignment, look for the subtle signals of acceptance or rejection. Such signals will surely reveal whether you are succeeding or failing to sell your idea.

Some positive signs: He starts to sketch or take notes; he starts asking pertinent questions; he seems to be catching your infectious enthusiasm.

Some negative signs: He sits back with arms folded across his chest; he appears fidgety or impatient to get on with it; he simply remains silent or looks away.

If he's tuning you out, you need to figure out why and how to overcome his resistance. Otherwise, you're wasting your time. When people are disinterested, coldly unresponsive or hostile, there's almost nothing you can do to engage their support until positive communication is re-established.

• *Practice yielding.* Especially if your subordinate accepts your broad concept, concede on some of the relatively minor points, thereby allowing him to embellish the basic idea with his own ingenuity. That's what creative conferencing is all about. If he tries to interrupt you, let him. If your art director prefers photography to illustration, let it be his choice. If the illustrator prefers charcoal to pen and ink, yield.

The point is, no one on your staff will feel a true commitment to the success of a project unless at least some of the ideas are his.

• *Avoid coercion.* It's difficult (and sometimes risky) to persuade someone to take your ideas and make them work. After all, creative success is usually a matter of judgment. If you have hired competent staff, their individual judgments in certain areas may be equal to—or better than—your own. To take advantage of that judgment, I advise against coercing people to do things your way. Ask for their judgment.

I participated in a creative conference with an editor and two art directors of a major business magazine. The editor led the discussion and began by proposing several random ideas for a special-issue cover. Then he asked, "What do you think?" Later, he asked, "What can I do to help you make this cover work?" These questions elicited several design suggestions and artistic judgments that contributed to a highly successful special edition, which later was spun off as a separate publication.

Other conversational techniques to maximize your creative staff's ability and judgment:

"Do you think it would help if . . . ?"

"What would happen if we . . .?"

"Let's assume that we want to try it; what next?"

Yes, this is professional flattery—and some may call it manipulation—but your intentions are honorable. Moreover, it encourages your staff to discuss new assignments and creative challenges with you. They'll be glad they did.

• *Seek commitment.* Ask, for example:

"How soon can you get started?"

"Will you handle this yourself, or will you get freelance help?"

"When will you be able to get back to me?"

Until there is some positive response from your staff member, indicating a commitment to action, you haven't succeeded in making the assignment. There may be questions, problems or hangups with which he's wrestling, any one of which may give him some excuse to delay an emotional commitment (as well as a time and professional commitment) to executing the plan.

When the commitment has been made, put it in writing: a memo reviewing the plan of action or key points of the discussion; a schedule showing deadlines and other important dates that represent progress checkpoints; an announcement for the staff bulletin board. Putting the commitment (agreement) in writing is a subtle way of applying mild pressure to fulfill the commitment as agreed.

• *Stay involved.* Be available for consultation, guidance and direction, especially if the writer or artist is uncertain about the assignment or even slightly insecure about his ability to fulfill it successfully. Check on progress frequently, especially with young or inexperienced staff. Demonstrate your interest and willingness to help a faltering creative effort before a failure becomes evident. Be prompt about reviewing outlines, drafts, sketches.

Above all, don't ignore those first efforts. Remember Phyllis McGinley's rhyme:

Sticks and stones may break my bones
When thrown with accurate art.
Words may sting like anything
But silence breaks my heart.

• *Avoid arguments.* As the old expression goes, a man convinced against his will is of the same opinion still. Worse, an unconvinced and reluctantly dragooned art director or writer will almost surely doom your assignment to failure. Don't force the issue, and above all—don't argue over it.

Why have you reached the point of argument? Have you not thought through the assignment carefully? Did you not present it well? Is there something else, something more important, that is preventing this writer or artist from appreciating your suggestion?

Avoid arguing over a creative suggestion by asking questions that evoke a "Yes" or other positive response. "Yes" answers can often soften someone's negative feelings because they are evidence that there are at least a few areas of agreement between the adversaries:

"Do you agree that we need to do *something* about this cover?"

"Don't you believe that we have an opportunity to do this story now, while it's still in the news?"

"I'm convinced—aren't you? —that we can somehow get better service on our separations."

If you do find yourself unavoidably embroiled in a hot discussion, let the other person know that you understand his position and that you are thinking along the same line, no matter how unreasonable it may seem: "You know, I'd be pretty upset, too, if you came into my office and insisted that I do something your way." When he sees that you've really been listening and understanding, he'll probably cool off and be a little friendlier. That will enable you both to attain some compromise.

•*Say "No" graciously.* Inevitably, there will be times when contrary ideas are presented by your own writers or other creative staff. If these ideas are unacceptable and if you must say "No," don't do it as a conditioned reflex. Take the matter under advisement (the art of business diplomacy). Later, indicate that you've given the suggestion some serious consideration, and if you must indeed reject it, explain your reasons for doing so.

I recently overheard an editor denying an art director's request for an increase in his free-lance budget. The editor began: "Up to a point, you're probably right. We aren't getting the best available talent. But that talent is very costly. I wonder if our publication can justify the increased costs . . . if it will make a difference to the readers, or the advertisers." The editor then went on to explain that the graphic improvements with higher-priced free-lance talent would be noticeable only to insiders on the staff, and that these costs would not be recoverable through increases in subscriptions or advertising rates.

He never actually said "No."

Dealing with creativity
By Bernard Weiss

I agree with Carl Ally, the ad agency president, who believes that good creative people provide their own discipline, and don't respond well to stern directives. "The way to keep good creative people happy and productive," he says, "is to give them interesting things to do and leave them alone."

I also agree with Hemingway, who maintained that true creativity cannot be forced. Hemingway said that if a good writer knows the juice is there, the juice will flow; if the writer has to force the juice, it's time to stop.

But I'm a realist, and one of the realities of our industry is that there just aren't enough good creative people to go around. There's a chronic need for creative geniuses with inventiveness, vision, organizational ability, drive and sensitivity. Only a few of the creative people I know are really something special, and in any publishing company, there may be no more than one or two.

Most publishing companies are staffed by people who doggedly pursue creative careers with only the trappings and fantasies of true creativity. Such people lack the insight, ingenuity and inspiration that make up true creative talent, and so they have not yet risen to the tops of their professions.

Meanwhile, sitting at the typewriter or drawing board, they are the troops that help us win our daily wars.

For these people, the guidelines of Ally and Hemingway don't work. In my experience, these people must be stimulated by judicious application of two factors: a special kind of managerial motivation, and a modest amount of firm discipline.

Motivation

Creative people are most motivated by personal recognition, the feeling that their work is valued, that there is a need for the particular talent that they possess. Personal recognition reinforces their generally high regard of their own worth. Stature in the organization's hierarchy and pride are other motivating factors.

The needs of salary, growth in the job, and job challenge—needs regarded by most managers as traditional motivating factors for all employees—do not necessarily motivate truly creative people and often exist for them only incidentally. Rather, the overriding principle that guides their day-to-day attitude toward job performance is the relationship with the *immediate* boss—the one who provides the recognition, prestige, reward, feedback and guidance. It is these elements that outweigh every other aspect of the creative person's job.

Discipline

Many creative people go through manic-depressive cycles. The periods of mania are brief but intensive times of high creative output; the depressed periods are usually longer and characterized by little creative output. Some wait for the flash of inspiration they "feel" is coming; typically, this inspirational flash signals a manic period.

But the vast majority of creative people I've observed trudge along from one assignment to the next—and often do so without much enthusiasm. There are many famous artists and writers who admit that if they had to wait until inspiration came, they would never get their work done. Most creative geniuses put themselves on work schedules—long, hard hours. James Gould Cozzens, a two-finger typist, worked from eight a.m. to noon for eight years to write *By Love Possessed.* "For every three pages I wrote," he says, "I threw away two. On a good day, I got two pages done."

Creativity—developing an entirely new idea or concept—is hard work. The great musicians, artists, writers and inventors of history were disciplined in their thinking and well-directed in their activity.

The point is, if the creative minds on your magazine are unable to discipline themselves to produce quality efforts on a schedule that is realistic in a business environment, then it is *your* responsibility to discipline them.

You do it with deadlines.

Most people work better when they have a deadline. Creative people have a certain amount of inertia and a deadline gives them the discipline and sense of urgency they need to conquer it. Also, setting a deadline helps them get started on a plan. Sometimes interim deadlines that require progress reports are also necessary.

Stimulating Creative Effort

It's one thing to set a deadline for a star, a creative genius whose talent is recognized and whose record for on-time delivery is 100 percent dependable.

But for the person on the way up, and for the large number of "mediocre" creative talent, and for the lazy or unenthusiastic writer or illustrator, you'll need to apply some management skills. I have found the following techniques useful in directing writers and artists for a variety of business and professional magazines.

1. Jointly agree on the time frame. Deadlines which are established arbitrarily and without consultation are likely to be ignored. "That's an unrealistic deadline—I'll just do the best I can" is a common reaction. You are most likely to achieve positive results if you meet with the person at the inception of the job and agree on the work to be done; the help he or she may need from others; the limitations of budget; approximately how long the job should take; a firm date on which the job is due, and an interim date (or dates) on which you'll expect to see draft copy, rough sketches, progress reports, etc.

When everything has been agreed upon I make up a job calendar or daily schedule, working backwards from the target date, and secure agreement on every critical date leading up to the final one. As each date is recorded on the schedule I ask: "Are you sure you can make this date?" or "Is this realistic?" If there is some resistance I try to compromise; if more time isn't available, I explain the urgency of the situation.

2. Explain the need. Many creative people are narrowly focused within their own areas of interest. Therefore, an orientation is frequently essential—without it, they may never understand what you ask of them. Be certain that they see a clearly recognized need for the product of their creativity. Each of them must believe that you want, or your audience wants, whatever it is that only he or she can create, because it will help solve a genuine problem or answer a genuine need.

3. Explain the problem. It's important to help writers or artists learn as much about the problem (and its particular circumstances) as possible, before challenging

them to come up with a creative solution. They may need input from many sources, perhaps some outside the department or company. Moreover, from you they will also need a frame of reference—the parameters of their authority, for example, or the travel restrictions. Leave room for their innovation and ingenuity, but explain the ground rules.

4. Maintain contact. Since good supervision is a critical factor in a creative person's productivity, don't lose contact with your staff. At the very least, use those interim dates and checkpoints on the work schedule to talk over unexpected problems that may be interfering with progress. Many disciplined creative people prefer to be left alone, and in fact perform exceptionally well under those circumstances. That's fine if the individual is reliable and has a good performance record with you. Most, however, need to be reminded of their agreement to stick to the schedule that you both agreed upon.

5. Let them know where they stand. Guidance must be supplied—constructive criticism, for example, or praise. To create is to agonize, and creative people hunger for evaluation of their efforts. But this is often difficult because results may be indefinite or long-postponed. So watch for signs of brooding resentment, even more than for outright complaints. Talk informally with each creative person from time to time, demonstrating your interest in the problems. Let them know your reactions to their efforts as promptly as possible. Share with them the reactions of readers, audience, advertisers, whenever such information becomes available.

6. Give them some time off, or with their peers. Many of a creative person's best ideas occur during idle periods immediately following periods of intense concentration. The problems and solutions, previously bothersome, may become clear. Ideas and insights suddenly emerge from a subconscious mind that, until recently, was totally occupied.

Also, several creative people coming together spontaneously after working individually will frequently stimulate each other's thinking and accomplish more than they could individually. Those bull sessions *may* waste time, but they may also trigger the bright ideas. A successful international advertising agency regularly brings creative people from the international offices to New York for sharing and cross-fertilization of ideas.

7. Support those manic episodes. Sometimes there will be bursts of creative activity, and during these periods of near-mania, a creative person will feverishly produce a torrent of ideas, sketches, copy or whatever. Then these periods will be followed by periods of relative quiet, when little or nothing is produced. Some creative people work on this kind of manic-depressive cycle.

The points to remember are that the individual's work cycles should be taken into account when planning schedules, deadlines, etc.; creative performance should be maximized. When he or she hits the depressed phase of the cycle, that's the time to give the person a few days off.

8. Listen to problems. It should be readily apparent that creative people need a sympathetic ear, someone who is tuned in and who listens to their troubles. Creative people are concerned about their own futures and their own selves, and they must feel that you, too, are concerned about them as an individual. Moreover, people whose contribution is principally in the realm of ideas rather than action are normally at their best when their creativity, not their security of self, is challenged. They can't function well if frightened and insecure. So, pay your creative personnel well, give them security and satisfaction in their jobs, and grant any reasonable requests that they make.

9. *Don't deny their quirks and foibles.* Creative people are often maligned because they are unconventional in their thinking or behavior, but of course, this is what makes them special. Many writers and illustrators insist on a desk-top radio. I know a brilliant writer who read *The New York Times* for an hour each morning, drinking coffee and producing nothing but cigar smoke, much to the annoyance of everyone within 50 feet of his office. Chronic tardiness is another common idiosyncrasy among creative people. All these foibles are likely to cost you little or nothing, and yet they may be essential to creative functioning—for reasons I can't explain. I only know that sometimes it is necessary to defend the creative employees against the attacks of others who think and act in more conventional ways—assuming they are worth defending.

While researching this article, I learned of an advertising art director who, after working hard all morning, takes off for a gallery or museum every day at lunch and rarely returns to his desk before 3 or 3:30 p.m. That's how he generates many of his ideas, says the agency creative director, who defends the art director's behavior based on the quality of the man's work and his level of productivity—both of which are spectacular.

10. *Show tolerance for failure.* Remember, all effort isn't good effort. When you ask a person to create, you must allow a greater margin for error than you give others. If you don't, fear of failure may prevent true initiative. Obviously, in planning your time frame for the job, you must allow sufficient time to revise or start anew following potential failure.

One technique that works well for me: When a writer and I can't agree on an approach to a new assignment, and neither of us honestly knows which is better, I'll say something like this: "Look, obviously we are at an impasse. Here's a compromise—try it your way first. Start now. I'll give you until (interim deadline date). If your approach works, fine. If it doesn't work—and you'll probably know before I do—then try it my way."

Delays and Disappointment

Suppose, despite all your best managerial efforts, a creative employee just doesn't produce on time or within acceptable limits of quality. What now?

Dealing with delay is easier. If the person has no reasonable excuse for missing the deadlines, if the problem is a chronic one, and if your schedules don't permit flexibility, you have no alternative but to terminate the arrangement. After all, you have deadlines, obligations and responsibilities of your own.

Moreover, I have never known a habitual deadline-misser who reformed in response to a lecture, threats of dismissal or anything else. In my experience, though they may sincerely promise, swear and guarantee, most creative people are simply unable to change such habits except for very short periods. Eventually, the problem will recur.

Unacceptable quality and disappointing performance are more difficult to deal with. Appraising the performance of creative people is difficult at best, and is often poorly done because there may be no previously established criteria or standards with which to compare the present effort. Performance judgment frequently comes down to a personal judgment, fair or unfair. Often I am able to avoid this problem entirely when I first make an assignment by generalizing verbally what I expect in terms of research, time expenditure, basic approach to the task, general content and writing style.

Recently the articles editor of a major consumer magazine told me how he evaluates creative writing efforts: "Unless I have previous experience with the writer, who is someone proposing a piece of fiction, for example, I take him to lunch and ask him to complete this sentence: 'This will be a fantastic story if it . . .' In effect, he is setting up his own standard of performance. It means that we both know what we want, and it's rare that good writers will bring me something that doesn't meet their own clearly stated standards. The bad writers either won't set high standards, or will simply drop out—I'll never hear from them again."

In summary, I think it is fair to say that some creative people are essentially "servants" of manager and supervisors who themselves are noncreative. For these "creative servants," many of the suggestions in this article may be helpful. For the truly professional creative person, blessed with inventiveness, genius, sensitivity and other useful virtues, the suggestions in this article are unnecessary.

Stop wasting time

By Bernard Weiss

Looking for ways to lengthen your days, to save time, to make the most of every minute?

Most of us don't have the patience to bother with gimmicks such as time logs or 15-minute-interval analyses of what we are actually doing. That's for people who "don't know where the time flies." We *know* where the time flies, don't we?

As a consultant in creativity and management, I've watched dozens of publishing executives at work, and I've been able to observe how they conserve a few minutes here, a few minutes there. The total amount of time they saved was enormous.

Here's a collection of these time-saving techniques. They may not all work for you, but they work for some publishers and some editors some of the time.

Conserving time in meetings

"Stand-up" meetings. When the editor of a major medical journal calls a meeting of his staff, he provides no seating other than what's already in his office. Most of the staff stand. "Not being comfortably seated, they tend not to prolong the discussion," he says.

Scheduled brevity. Knowing his people like to get out of the office promptly at noon for luncheon appointments and promptly at 5 o'clock to connect with car pools and public transportation, the publisher of a Florida construction magazine schedules most staff meetings for 11:30 a.m. or 4:30 p.m., often on Fridays. "All our meetings start on time," he says, "because people are anxious to be on their way—and we usually move through the agenda with dispatch so we can adjourn promptly." This publisher also acknowledges, however, that when there are matters of real controversy or substance, staff meetings are scheduled at times that are more convenient for thoughtful discussion, policy review and decision-making.

Infrequent meetings. One editorial vice president of my acquaintance schedules almost no meetings, except for quarterly and year-end reviews of budgets and personnel. "My theory is that if meetings are scheduled, someone will talk long enough to fill the allocated time. Most of the problems and decisions that come up in my organization are resolved in what I call 'parking lot presentations' and 'corridor consultations' that rarely last more than a few minutes."

Planned meetings. "I have a few simple rules that save me lots of time during and following meetings," says a San Francisco publisher.

"Generally, I make up an agenda and circulate it to the meeting participants in advance. The reasons for the meeting are therefore clear to everyone. At the meeting, if a topic that is not on the agenda comes up, we don't discuss it unless it's urgent.

"I take notes during the meeting about every item on the agenda—the recommendations, options, decisions, responsibility, what's to be done, and so forth. I do not trust my memory.

"After the meeting, I dictate a brief report to be distributed to all who attended. For each item I note the decisions made, who is to take what action, when it's to be completed, etc. In effect, this sets up the agenda for the following meeting."

Small meetings. At any worthwhile meeting, the greater the attendance, the greater the time consumed as each participant makes a verbal contribution. One small-meeting advocate explained to me that his company holds meetings with the entire staff just once a year—at the company's annual "birthday party."

Terminating the meeting I. Adjourn every meeting before the discussion slowly peters out, on the premise that most participants will simply repeat or elaborate on previous points. Let them do this individually, after adjournment. Recently I saw one publisher end a meeting of circulation personnel in a most expeditious fashion. He restated the purpose of the meeting, summarized the discussion, and stood up to say, "Thank you for coming; this has been very productive. Now let's get back to work."

Terminating the meeting II. Often a non-verbal clue—such as rising from your seat—will signal adjournment. But if that doesn't work, move toward the door, shake a few hands along the way and thank people as you pass them, then walk out of the room even if it is your own office. Your people will get the message, especially when you return moments later ready to tackle the next item on your list of things to do.

Terminating the meeting III. The vice president and circulation director of a national newsweekly cues his secretary on the intercom to buzz him when he wants to adjourn. She announces clearly enough for all to hear, "Your next appointment has arrived," or "They're waiting for you in Mr. Johnson's office." *Then* he stands up. It never fails.

Terminating the meeting IV. As a meeting begins in her own office, one fashion editor pointedly tells her secretary in a loud voice, "Please hold all my calls for the next 10 minutes." That's her signal to the meeting participants that adjournment will take place at a specified time—and that time is limited. Ten minutes later, the secretary enters with several calls to be returned.

Conserving personal time

Appointments. "I don't make appointments with my own staff," says one editor, "I just tell people to come by if they want to see me. This has worked pretty well, because most of my writers and other staff just need a brief response to proceed with an assignment. Making writers or art directors wait for an appointed meeting leaves them with nothing to do in the meantime."

This editor does schedule appointments with outsiders, and allows a few minutes within every hour for interruptions by his own staff. That's why his technique works—he's available.

No freebies. The high-visibility editor of a fashion magazine, who is much in demand for public appearances, has developed a very narrowly defined position on such requests: "I don't write anything or speak anywhere unless there's a fee," he says. The insignificant requests, the ones that sap his time, disappear. The other requests are worth fulfilling.

Establish personal priorities. First thing in the morning, tackle the most important item on your daily list of things to do. That works for the editorial department director of a religious publishing company. "I don't go on to the next item on the list until I'm either stone-walled or finished with it," she says. "Also, we have an editorial 'quiet-hour' between 8:00 and 10:30 a.m. which gives us all time to get organized and get to the most pressing items without interruptions."

Establish priorities for others. "First I do those things that set others in motion," says the executive editor of a business newsletter service. "Later, that minimizes interruptions at times that are inconvenient for me."

When traveling. Take manuscripts, reports, correspondence and a mini-tape recorder and cassettes along with you. Dictate during your stopovers, delays and—on long trips—mail the cassettes and related papers back to your office for follow-up and action by your staff. The secretary of one publisher prepares large self-addressed, pre-posted envelopes that the publisher drops in airport and hotel mailboxes.

Sort your own mail. The editorial director of an engineering publication keeps two briefcases by his desk. As he reads and sorts his own daily mail, he tosses into briefcase "A" all the low-priority reading material for his trips out of town. Briefcase "B" is his repository for high-priority reading later in the day, that evening, or over the weekend at home.

Fill-in jobs. Some publishing executives use the minutes between appointments to return telephone calls or read the day's mail, but the publisher of a Midwestern shelter magazine keeps a pile of papers on his desk. Whenever he gets two minutes—say, an appointment is late or he's holding on a call—he goes right to those papers. He responds to a memo and bucks it back; he checks his preferences for cover titles; he looks over a resume; etc. He uses a shoulder bracket for the telephone so both his hands are free.

Do not schedule breaks. There are no planned breaks in the offices of a Chicago agricultural publishing company. Says the president and publisher, "There are usually enough unscheduled interruptions to break the routine and bring some relief, so we discourage planned breaks for coffee. In fact, we schedule very little in terms of office routine. Left to their own devices, our staff—including myself and the other executives—work longer and harder than I would have any right to expect."

Use rubber stamps. The vice president of a Boston book publishing company uses a rubber stamp as he reads his paperwork. When he forwards or re-distributes a memo, letter or clipping to his staff, he stamps the papers:

To: _____

FOR YOUR INFORMATION
No Reply Necessary

He claims it saves him time writing, and later, reading unnecessary acknowledgments and comments.

When hiring. If you've screened job applicants and are down to the three or five best candidates, give them a trial assignment—copy editing a rough draft, for example, or writing the headline and introduction of a feature article, or sketching a layout for a cover story (see FOLIO, February 1978, "A guide to hiring creative people").

Applicants who aren't seriously interested in your company or this particular job will screen themselves out. They just won't execute the assignment. Others, upon getting a closer look at a realistic sample of the work that's expected of them, will disqualify themselves. And, of course, the results of a trial assignment may, in your judgment, disqualify a job candidate.

All of this contributes to fewer hiring mistakes and less time lost in training and orienting new staff. In my experience, applicants who are serious about a new job will follow up the trial assignment with some extracurricular homework. They will join your staff professionally prepared to make good on their initial favorable impression.

Saving telephone time

Minimize interruptions. The publisher of a Washington, D.C. trade association journal takes almost no telephone calls during the entire day unless he is alone at his desk. His philosophy is that the telephone is a device to be used at and for his personal convenience. His secretary screens all calls except those from his family, his boss, or his managing editor—all of whom have been asked to call him only for the most urgent of reasons.

"I'm frequently in meetings," he explains, "and it is rude and wasteful of time to keep people waiting in a meeting while I take an outside call." He returns calls *after* the meeting, while waiting for the next one to start, or at the end of the day.

Time your telephone calls. The fiction editor of a New York science magazine gets many calls from agents and writers, and "most of those people are long-winded," she says. "When I start a conversation with them, my opening words are: 'Sam, I want to talk to you, but I have just four minutes before leaving for a meeting (or lunch, or a plane, etc.). Can we keep it short?'"

Schedule your calls. Another editor who talks to long-winded writers and agents suggests that they call him back when long conversations are more convenient and less likely to be interrupted. "I always ask them to call me on a specific day at a specific time, when things are likely to be quieter around here and I have the time to spare."

Terminating a conversation. There are polite but firm ways to close a prolonged telephone conversation. I recently observed this technique, which I have myself begun to use effectively: Early in the conversation, get a clue to the other person's activity at the moment. Asking "Did I interrupt you?" or "Are you jammed?" might yield, "No, I'm just reading a manuscript" or "No, I'm just outlining a presentation." Later, as business talk degenerates into social talk, you end the conversation with "Thanks, I'll let you get back to the manuscript now."

You can play the opposite role by giving a clue to your own activity before the conversation, then referring to it as the dicussion gets off track: "I've got to be getting back to my presentation now . . . please excuse me for cutting this so short."

Now, if you'll excuse me...

Managing the privately-owned magazine

By Frank Butrick

Small publishing companies, usually owned and managed by one person or a single family, become almost human; often, they are literal extensions of the president. In many ways, this very personal atmosphere makes them nice to work for and nice to work with. The president looks upon his associates and employees as "my people." As he becomes older, he often calls them "my family."

There is nothing in the world wrong with this—except that the firm, as an extension of the president's personality, not only displays all his entrepreneurial strengths, it also incorporates his human weaknesses. And these weaknesses, multiplied by the number of employees involved, can undermine the entire venture.

By weakness I do not mean faults of personality such as procrastination or a violent temper. Instead, I am referring to areas of business ability where the president is not strong. A good organizer, for example, may be indifferent to people management, or a sales type may be weak in appreciating editorial concepts.

Even the smallest business is a complex affair, involving in microcosm almost everything done by the publishing giants—hiring, personnel management, training employees, keeping old advertisers, finding new ones, selling, purchasing, editorial planning, production control, equipment maintenance, financial management, graphics/creative development, and so on. The president of a small publishing company—whether he has two employees or 20—must oversee every one of these activities. If he is reasonably successful, his firm grows and more activities are added—planning for succession, development of management teams, long-term financing, acquisitions.

Now, no matter how smart or how ambitious (or even how successful) one man may be, it is naive to expect anybody to be an expert in all these different fields. Most publishers and business owners, because of inclination, early training, or simple necessity, specialize in one facet of the firm, be it sales, editorial, circulation, or finance. Very rarely does a man consider himself a competent expert in more than two of these four.

Being human, but smart enough to recognize what he does not know, the founder structures the company as much as possible to capitalize on his strengths and evade his weaknesses. So, a man who is strong in editorial but weaker in selling will gravitate naturally to magazines which require little advertising support—technical, sponsored (association, etc.), specialized hobby, and similar fields. A man strong in financial management is likely to look toward acquisition of other successful firms. The salesman type might gravitate toward product tabloids, since he mistrusts his own judgment in developing sound editorial content.

Obviously, a magazine exists in a certain field; nonetheless, its development over the years is a result of the president's inclination. No two magazines are ever quite alike.

But somewhere along the line of company growth, actual management/supervision becomes too much for one man and the president must hire his first "management" person. This is a momentous decision which will affect his firm for years, for he will either hire a person who reinforces his own strengths, thereby locking the firm into concentrating in his stronger areas, or he will hire a man who complements himself, who fills one of the gaps in the president's own experience and professional ability.

Consider, for example, the situation of a person with a strong editorial concept for a relatively uncrowded field who develops a successful, reader-supported magazine. When he hires his first key man, he has four choices: 1) a financial man, who could help maximize potential profits from the president's editorial ability; 2) a circulation man, who could cut costs and smooth preparation and printing tangles; 3) a sales type who will make the sales calls which the president avoids; or 4) an editorial type like himself, thus producing more and more editorial strength whether or not sales and profits mount satisfactorily.

Fortunately, most entrepreneurs recognize their own weak areas, know that a magazine is a complex entity which requires competence in a number of fields, and hire men to manage activities that they will not or cannot manage themselves. This first move toward developing a management team occurs early in the development of most publishers and is necessary for growth. However, it also lights slow-burning fuses to two bombs, one or the other of which is almost certain to blow up eventually.

The first bomb is creeping incompetence. If you recognize your own weak areas, you must try to find just the right man to complement your own strength. Above and beyond the obvious problem (how to judge a man's abilities in an area which you yourself do not know well) is the problem of finding a man who is a professional, as strong (in his area) as you are in yours.

Don't hire a Caspar Milquetoast who will be so grateful for his job that he will bow and scrape and let you tell him how to run his own show. Hire a professional, a strong man, who will argue and fight for what he knows is best for the book.

But do insist upon performance; require written plans and projections which you can approve and then use to measure accomplishments. And, since this man stands where you are least strong, insist upon constant improvement.

Don't become lulled into a dangerous complacency just because you hired "good men" to take care of these areas for you. Never assume that they run as fast as you do. Don't hire others to manage facets of your business and then permit them to become lazy, lapsing into the worst habit in business.

Don't let them evolve into experts at pacifying the boss. Make them keep their departments up-to-date, growing, and efficient. And never assume that which you do not know—that the other parts of the firm are well managed, or that your managers are as ambitious as you are. And remember, the apparent absence of problems is not the answer. In fact, the less friction in these areas, the more likely it is that your managers are devoted purely to satisfying you—to telling you what you want to hear.

So—insist upon a continuing program of improvement, of written plans, of measurable accomplishment. All procedures, methods, systems, and policies that are over a year old should be automatically suspect. Otherwise they become cast-iron habits, hide-bound operations that can undermine and rot out your entire business.

The second bomb has a longer fuse, but it can create shambles out of any business. It is the fact that since the founder and his son (daughter, son-in-law, nephew, or whoever follows when the founder retires) are not carbon copies of each other, the personal strength/weakness pattern of the founder will probably not be duplicated by the successor.

The owner may hire managers to handle the areas of his own weaknesses or indifference—or he may encourage his successor to become strong in these areas, thereby "learning the business." But since it is not likely that a strong editorial type (for instance) will hire equally strong editors (who might argue with him), the editorial vitality of the magazine will probably remain locked up in the owner's head. Then when he retires, a gaping void appears in the firm.

The new president may recognize this critical situation and hasten to hire a man to fill the gap. However, not only will he be hiring a key manager whose ability he cannot judge, he probably doesn't even know what the previous owner did or how he did it. Furthermore, the newcomer is expected to fill impossibly large shoes, and if he fails, so does the firm.

When the owner develops a successor, but develops no one to succeed in his own technical specialty, he seriously undermines the new president's chances; there will be no magazine for the younger man to manage if it collapses from the loss of the founder's skills. If the founder does not recognize this double training task, the successor is forced to attempt a restructuring of the magazine around his own personal strengths and weaknesses. To successfully accomplish such a complex transition requires either managerial skill or experience. Unfortunately, many publishing companies fail under second-generation management because the successors have neither.

So, Mr. Publisher—take time to study your business. Is it really a business built to last, or it is just an overgrown personal venture?

The personalized magazine

By M.J. (Chip) Block

Publishing is a game of inches. Very often, good management of margins is the difference between profit and loss. However, the inch has shrunk to a millimeter because we are living in a new world—a world of inflation, accelerated change, costly non-renewable resources, expanded video, high technology, and new areas of editorial interest. Thus, any publisher who wants to stay in the game must carefully examine any innovation that might stretch publishing margins, and implement those innovations that are feasible.

Ten years ago, as I began my career in publishing, I learned of an idea that quickly captured my imagination: the personalized magazine. I now believe that the personalized magazine is possibly the greatest technological innovation of the 1980s in terms of its impact on publishing economics. In effect, personalization offers new hope to this game of publishing.

Before examining this concept in depth, however, let's take a look at what doesn't work any longer.

Traditional leverage eroded

Publishing margins are to a large degree controlled by a few key leverage points: single-copy sales percentage, ad/edit ratio, subscription renewal percentages, readers-per-copy circulated, and all pricing. Unfortunately, each of these leverage points has been affected negatively by the changes that have taken place both in the economy and in our industry.

Consider the effect of inflation, for example. Consumers today have less discretionary income to spend, and with few exceptions, magazines are discretionary items. Nobody needs a magazine. I often hear people say a magazine failed because it wasn't needed. I can't think of a single consumer magazine the public actually needs.

This lack of discretionary income also means that it will be harder to raise prices. Publishers have been very successful in raising prices to the readers over the last 10 years, partly because they were starting at a very low base price.

Many magazine subscription prices have been raised from, say, $2 a year in 1971 to $10 a year in 1980. Anybody who believes we're going to be able to raise the price to $20 a year by 1990 is in for a surprise, even given the fact of inflation. The same thing is true on the newsstand.

In terms of leverage with the advertiser, the pricing problem is compounded by the fact that we compete not only with each other, but with other media as well. As the other media expand, especially cable TV, the advertising pie is going to be split up even further. The result is an ever-increasing pressure on publishers to hold down their cost-per-thousand.

In addition, the advertising/editorial ratio can't go much further. If we continue to increase the advertising ratio, the perceived value of the service we provide the reader is undoubtedly going to decline. Furthermore, the advertisers don't like it. Many advertisers are already

683

complaining about clutter in magazines.

One way out of this jam is improved operating efficiency. No doubt we have made some strides, especially in subscription marketing. The use of computers in generating information on promotion effectiveness and in refining direct mail efforts, for example, has enabled many publishers to increase subscription net income even faster than sub prices.

However, such examples are the exception. In other areas, operating efficiency is deteriorating. The total copies sold in retail outlets as a percentage of copies distributed has decreased over the last 10 years. MPA estimates the *absolute* drop at about 10 percent. This, despite increased automation by wholesalers, publisher field forces, and more sophisticated distribution by the national distributors.

The solution: personalization

Obviously, if publishers are to survive in this economic climate, they must find new ways to expand operating margins. The key to survival, I believe, is the personalized magazine: an editorial service that offers a range of materials to readers who then buy only those discrete elements that interest them.

To conceptualize the product, think of segments (newsletters or specials) growing out of a base product (the magazine), each one an entity with a constituency of its own.

In 1972, when I first learned of the concept, the technology required was in the development stage. The key element, the computer driven bindery line, was not available. That element—along with the equipment to address copies on line, also crucial to personalization—is now available. I am going to make two major, unverified assumptions about that technology.

First, I assume that the technology will work: that is, a system from order entry of subs, to file maintenance, to tape format, to the bindery, ink jet addressing on line, and into the mail. There is no reason why such a process will not work successfully.

Second, I assume that the implementation of such a system will be economically feasible. Actually, the system should eventually cost no more than current methods, given the opportunity for computer-generated promotion material, greater control of the bindery process, and postal savings.

Leverage through personalization

The personalized magazine has tremendous implications for publishers because it provides several interesting new leverage points.

First, a publisher will be able to charge a premium price to the reader. For example, if *Better Homes and Gardens* were to offer readers the option of subscribing to a special interest signature on indoor gardening, the results—in terms of prices to the reader—could be very favorable because of the reader's special interest in the area.

Second, a publisher need spend virtually nothing on the promotion that goes to the reader. He'll be promoting the magazine's special interest signatures both in the magazine and through the media that he already has to send out—renewal letters for example.

And third, personalization can provide some leverage with advertisers. By providing selectivity, he can charge a higher cost-per-thousand. And although an advertiser who might have purchased a full run might buy only a segment (albeit at a much higher CPM), the benefits will outweigh such effects by far.

In spite of these potential benefits, publishers have been rather slow to make moves in the direction of personalized magazines. The obvious candidates for personalization, the large magazines, are most often published by big companies where the decision-making process can be rather cumbersome. Furthermore, most people don't like to take responsibility for doing something that's terribly innovative.

Editorial franchise ignored

I also believe that publishers are dead wrong when they persist in seeing personalized magazines as an advertising gold mine. The economic structure of magazines as they exist today is geared toward the advertiser. However, although personalization has great potential benefits for space sales, such benefits should not be the raison d'etre for segmentation.

Publishers who look to advertising income to pay for this kind of program will find problems similar to those of magazines that are designed primarily to deliver an audience segment to advertisers, particularly a demographic segment: a true commonality of interests among readers does not necessarily exist. Therefore, if reader interest is difficult to sustain, circulation becomes costly to maintain. The result: ad revenue must cover most if not all of the publishing nut.

Another fallacious concept has also been promulgated as a framework for personalization: creating an entirely new magazine around the process itself. Some people in Colorado have developed an interesting technology called U-Stat and are trying to promote the idea of a magazine in which the reader can select subject matter he or she desires.

I believe this is an incorrect approach, however, because no editorial franchise exists. Starting a new magazine with a viable editorial foundation is difficult enough. To attempt to do so simply on the basis of a delivery system ignores both the premise and reality of periodical publishing.

Expanding functions

Undoubtedly, the role of editors will change with the advent of such editorial services.

Now, editors produce material they think will interest and entertain readers. Ten years from now, it's entirely possible that editors will be producing material that readers have chosen.

In addition, personalized magazines are going to expand the focus of specialized magazines and narrow the focus of even the most broadbased magazine (*Reader's Digest* or *Better Homes and Gardens*, for example).

This development will result in less waste in publishing because publishers will be targeting their markets a lot better, both in terms of the editorial product and the advertiser's message. And, since advertisers will be closer to the audiences they're looking for, they will pay a premium on a cost-per-thousand basis in order to reach such a highly targeted audience.

In addition, since editors will be forced to communicate with readers, they will get a lot of feedback from them, not in letters to the editor but in terms of marketing information. In fact, readers will be creating new products constantly, and publishers will be obtaining psychographic information about the readers' interests and buying habits.

The first personalized magazine

Because I believe that the personalized concept has

a great potential to expand operating margins, we have begun to implement personalization at *Games*.

Games is a true special interest magazine, so it's probably not the best magazine to be the first one to personalize. However, since I've long been in love with the idea of a personal magazine, I've decided to go ahead and try. The technology is there, nobody else is going to do it, and we think we can make a lot of money.

Our approach is probably unusual. (The only thing I can say about it is that it's safe and that's why we're confident about going ahead.) We're starting simply by offering a series of special sections to our subscribers, narrowing our editorial scope in each case into very special interests.

The first monthly special is called *The Four Star Puzzler*, and it is geared to readers who want more puzzles than the magazine itself offers. Ultimately, we will produce a series of these specials, rated in terms of the difficulty of the puzzles in each newsletter.

We have ideas for three other specials that will be published and tested during 1981. These will be completely different from the puzzler idea, but each one has some tie-in with the magazine. Furthermore, since each special is designed to be profitable as an entity in itself, the program will be profitable even if the personalized magazine concept doesn't work out.

As the system develops, we will offer readers the option of having the specials bound into the magazine. (In fact, some people may want only the specials and not the magazine.) Since several signatures will be available, and since each one will be viable individually, the reader will be able to define for himself what he's interested in.

Implications of personalization

With such a system in place, a publisher can create a family of mini-magazines around the base product at a low cost, thereby getting pricing leverage. Equally important, if this is done by much of the industry, we will have changed the perceived value of magazines in the minds of the consumer:

- Base product = $12 (per year)
- Special #1 = 8 " "
- " #2 = 8 " "
- " #3 = 6 " "
- " #4 = 6 " "

* Total value $40 " "

(Offer for total package: $30 per year, a 25 percent savings.)

With personalization, a publisher can also segment his audience for ad sales purposes. In the case of *Games*, we will be developing a special signature for people who want a Christmas shopping guide for games. Obviously, any games manufacturer in his right mind would want to reach people who are willing to pay for such information since there will be virtually no waste in that market.

Personalization also makes print a more exciting medium for both the advertiser and the reader. When this technology is used in a creative way, there will be a whole new aura around publishing, especially if it is promoted properly to the ad community and to the consumer.

Another implication: personalization will enable us to compete with the new developments in television which are a tremendous threat to publishing. Advertisers will be attracted to multichannel cable and special interest programming on television and publishers will have to compete with that kind of technology and segmentation.

The future is now

There are many problems to overcome. However, I believe that publishers must begin to explore the process, to at least attempt to use technology that holds such promise. And, after all, if personalization doesn't work out, a publisher will simply be left with a set of profitable specials (or newsletters) that are mailed separately to subscribers.

I believe that the process will work and will yield excellent margins to publishers. I will report on the results at *Games* as we progress. If I'm right, we will have performed great feats in a world of inches.

Think small

By James B. Kobak

The best organization is the one-person shop.

Why?

Because every time you add an employee, you add a management task. And every time you add another employee, you have multiplied that task not by two, but by four. The more people, the more you are in the management business rather than the magazine business.

A basic flaw in most people's thinking is that everything that can be done by your own people—employees or whatever—is automatically good.

Exactly the reverse is very often true.

Let me explain.

Man's basic philosophy is to build. And if he builds bigger, then he automatically must be building better. To build bigger obviously means having more people.

As organizations grow, the tendency is to add people to do things which could just as easily be bought outside. You know, "We do it cheaper that way because Joe is already on the payroll and we don't have the overhead and profit we would have to pay an outsider."

Phooey.

Of course, every organization needs a certain core of people to do the essential parts. But the more skills that can be purchased outside, the better. In the magazine business we need editors on the premises. But when we want some unusual editorial or artwork done, it is normally best to have it done by real specialists on a part-time basis.

Long ago most publishers realized that printing and circulation fulfillment are not really the prime work which should be carried on in a publishing house. Printing today, for almost all publishers, is done by independent companies. And a great many publishers have their fulfillment done by others.

But what about the design of mailing pieces and mailing campaigns? And what about the development of advertising promotion materials? And what about that redesign of the magazine itself? And what about the development of ancillary products which enhance the profits of the company by taking advantage of the aura of the magazine? And what about the long-range planning function itself? And what about development of salespeople's compensation schemes? And on and on.

The basic fact is that these tasks, and many like them, are rarely done by the average publisher. The publisher cannot be skilled in everything, so he or she should not try to do everything internally.

When you get your own people to do things which can be purchased outside, you are not necessarily getting the best. I would rather have a $50,000 a year person who spends his or her life designing mailing pieces help me for two weeks than have a $20,000 employee who will never be a whiz.

Besides, once a person is on the payroll, flexibility is lost. It is hard to fire someone who is not doing the job as well as you wish, so you just put up with it. If, on the other hand, you find you have the wrong outsider, simply change.

You are paying more, too, because you have to keep that employee busy all the time. You pay the outsiders only as you use them.

One area in just about every large company which gets out of hand can serve as a wonderful/horrible example. It is the internal printing area.

Each department has some forms or interoffice memos or sales literature—or something else—to be printed. So they graduate from the Xerox to the Multilith.

After a while some systems people come in and decide that all this can be centralized to save money. (It never does save money. It just creates another department and more management tasks.)

As several areas of printing get centralized, it then occurs to good management thinkers that they should be together in one location for even more "efficiency."

And now the company has created its own printing plant, whether it realizes it or not. But it is a plant which has neither the understanding nor the interest of management. The employees do not have an adequate profit incentive, no matter what schemes are developed, because it is not owned by those operating it—and the people in it realize that they are just a service to the rest of the company. Flexibility is almost nil—"let's print it in our shop since we have it"—even though it may be wrong kind of equipment. There is not top management talent because the shop is not in the mainstream of the business. There is not the ability to scrap old equipment readily in order to keep up-to-date because top management is really not very interested.

A monster has been created—and no one knows how it happened or what to do about it.

How much better if some wise person had said, very early: "Let's buy all our reproduction work outside."

We have been discussing printing, but the same is true of so many other areas—data processing, legal services, house advertising agencies, in-house consultants and many others.

The simple point is that each company should stick to what it knows how to do, keep the payroll as small as possible and buy everything it can from outsiders who specialize in various areas. You get better work *cheaper*.

What's so bad about conglomerates, anyway?

By James B. Kobak

At one Magazine Publishers Association meeting in Bermuda, my friend, Lew Young, editor of *Business Week*, gave a talk in which he deplored the purchase of publishing companies by large conglomerates. His reason: it hurts quality magazines and freedom of the press.

In some cases, ownership by conglomerates may, indeed, hurt publishing properties. However, Young's blanket attack was, in my opinion at least, both uncalled-for and inaccurate in many respects. Let me quote and refute the points in his talk, for I see the situation from a totally different perspective. Lew—please feel free to argue back.

Young: *The publisher who prizes the property over profits is disappearing.*

This statement may be the crux of the whole matter, for Lew is implying that profits and quality publishing cannot go hand-in-hand.

Exactly the opposite is true. The better the product and the publishing techniques, the better the profits—as in any business. Good magazines beget more circulation at higher prices—and more advertising at higher rates.

Magazines are products designed to appeal to the public, and it is the marketplace which makes the purchasing decision, not the few editors who think they know best. The best editors constantly watch their renewal rates and have surveys made of readership.

This is the constant argument that rages within all the communications arts. Is Public Broadcasting better than commercial because it is more erudite—and because it doesn't make money? Was "Roots" bad because it was popular and made a lot of money? Are book publishers who force obscure poetry titles out of their shops at a loss doing a better job than the publisher of Michener's books?

Are *The Nation, The New Republic, Washington Monthly,* and *National Review*—magazines which don't earn profits because of their difficulty finding readers—necessarily good because a handful of people think they are needed? A great product and high profits are not mutually exclusive: *Time* magazine is superb—and it makes money.

Young: *Publicly-owned corporations are taking the place of the proud publisher.*

There is no prouder publisher than Harold McGraw, head of the publicly-owned corporation for which Lew works, who successfully fought a takeover bid by American Express.

And what about Kay Graham of *The Washington Post*, owner of *Newsweek*? And Punch Sulzberger of *The New York Times*, owner of several magazines? Although their properties are public, believe me, they are as proud of those properties as anyone could be.

Young: *There are two main reasons: The impact of the tax laws on family-owned enterprises. Death duties are so high the survivors can't keep the operation in their own*

hands *unless they have tremendous outside resources with which to pay the taxes. The costs of publishing have risen so much—particularly the mechanical costs and the costs of acquiring circulation—that an editor with a good idea no longer can start publishing.*

I agree that tax laws make it attractive to sell out—not only publishing companies but any business. But what evidence is there that this is bad? There is no history indicating that the second and third generations of publishing families are as dedicated to good publishing as the founder was. The record on the other side is overwhelming.

I also agree that publishing costs have risen, but the industry—so far at least—has been able to maintain its equilibrium and even forge ahead. There have never before been as many magazines, as much circulation, as much advertising, and as many different publishing companies as there are now. And, I might add, profits have never been so high.

And the idea that "an editor with a good idea no longer can start publishing" just is not true. Have you heard of *Book Digest, Firehouse, American Photographer, Ms., Working Woman, Backpacker, Mariah, Venture, Country Music*—and on and on. These are all magazines that have been started by editors with ideas who *have* been able to raise money to launch their babies. Furthermore, each month I meet a hundred aspiring publishers trying to start others.

Young: *In their abortive effort to increase* Saturday Review's *circulation from 400,000 to one million, while producing four different monthly publications issued once a week, John Veronis and Nick Charney lost nearly $28 million in a little over a year.*

Sure John and Nick made a gigantic mistake with *Saturday Review*. But they were not the public corporation you are discussing. And they were the same guys who started the very successful *Psychology Today* and *Book Digest*.

Young: *So, like it or not, public corporations are taking over publishing. And public corporations have to think in terms of profits. More significant, public corporations have to think of earnings per share because they have to worry about the price of their stock; and Wall Street tends to react to earnings per share.*

Agreed.

Young: *If you understand that, you understand a lot of what is going on in publishing today. With public corporation ownership come some operating trends that are anathemas for editors: (1) A decline in interest in the product and product quality by the management. Lip service is given, but not investment—and money talks. The phenomenon, incidentally, is not confined to publishing. The number of big corporations whose managements are really interested in the quality of the product are few. Have you ridden on an airline lately?*

That just isn't true. *No one* spends more on the product than Time Inc. And if you think that Conde Nast, Hearst, Meredith, Playboy and CBS are niggardly, just look at their magazines or review their salary structures.

Besides, as Lew knows, what you spend for editorial material does not always determine its quality. It *is* a creative business, after all.

Consumers do not *have* to purchase magazines, and if the product isn't good, consumers won't buy. When a magazine outlives its life cycle or loses its editorial way, it dies. Very different from an airline—or most other businesses.

Young: *This trend comes out of the growth in financial management in the top management. A lot of the CEO's today like to boast that they are financially-oriented. They tend to be rigid on budgets and the heroes of American business today are the people who can squeeze another 1/4 percent return out of the corporate cash—not the marketers or product designers or manufacturers.*

Hey—don't talk about us CPA's and other financial types that way. Sure, some of us do not understand the creative world as we should—but that's true of any group of people.

However, because we *do* understand that you cannot live without the editors, marketers, product designers, or manufacturers, we bring realism to a company. Since we are not afraid of numbers, we can use them to help run the business. Just because an editor or a marketer thinks something is great doesn't make it so. Remember, it is the public that decides.

Young: *With a growth in financial management has come a desire to level the dips and peaks of profits through diversification. In publishing, it means acquiring other publications, other media, or other businesses. Cox Communications has just purchased an oil and gas exploration company.*

Right.

Young: *Diversification breeds its own forms of evil. One is called bottom-line management. This is a technique by which the management decides the company will earn xx profit or profits will increase by ab percent. If the normal operations do not achieve this bottom line, the management gets there by (a) cutting investment in editorial, in promotion, in people or (b) accounting tricks, such as deferring costs, postponing expenditures or advanced billings. In a diversified company, bottom-line management often means if publication R has unexpected profit troubles, publication S will be tapped to produce more profit than it budgets to make up the shortfall.*

Sure you work to keep the bottom line happy. Don't you think that a private company like Ziff-Davis does the same thing, deferring growth in one area for a time in order to keep the whole thing working?

Consider the situation if you are not diversified. Suppose publication R is your *only* source of profit. What do you do then? Sell out, go bankrupt, or just stagger along?

Young: *The hottest tool in the executive suite is a new management technique called strategic planning. In this technique the management has to determine where every product falls in its life cycle. They do this by first comparing the growth of the product's revenues and profits to the growth of the economy, and then measuring the product's position in the industry. If the product is determined to be mature, it becomes a cash cow. That means no investment should be made in it; and its profits should be siphoned off to acquire new properties that are growing faster. Strategic planning can be a useful way to examine a business, particularly a highly diversified one. But it has ruined more products than anything but a fire or earthquake. The problem is determining the maturity of a product—and the maturity changes.*

What's so bad about that?

Should you keep trying to increase the sales of a product after it has reached maturity? That's just throwing money (and talent) away.

Sure you can make errors in judging a product's maturity; but, once again, the public will do that for you in the magazine business. And conglomerates have no monopoly on making bad judgments.

Young: *This leads naturally to risk aversion—an unwillingness to take a chance because of the loss of money or reputation. That's why . . . someone like Seth Baker, president of ABC Publications, would say, "I'd rather drill for oil in Central Park than start a new magazine." Finally, and sadly, I report that some of the chief executives of publicly-owned media companies don't like the media.*

There you go again, Lew. Seth Baker doth not an industry make. And after he has a few acquisitions under his belt, you may even find him taking what you think are risks.

And how do you define risk? Some people would consider paying $50 million for Chilton a terrible risk. But ABC did it. (Please forgive me, Chilton friends.)

But back to public companies, conglomerates, diversification, risks, or whatever. Are you aware that:

• Conde Nast started *Self.*

• Meredith started *Apartment Life.*

• Time has a constant stream of new magazines being studied, and some—like *Sports Illustrated, Money, Fortune* and *People*—are eventually launched. Bless them.

• McCall's, Charter, Hearst and Meredith have each started many special interest publications.

• ITT tested a "Who's Who" magazine. It didn't work, but they were willing to take the risk.

• Litton is launching *Next.*

• McGraw-Hill tested *Muse.*

• Newsweek launched *Inside Sports.*

• Capital Cities started "*W.*"

Young: *Let me close by coming back to the corporate interest on earnings per share. There is a good reason why corporate top management looks so hard at this number. It has the greatest impact on the sale of stock. Important enough is the fact that the management may have the bulk of its personal wealth tied up in the stock. But if the share price falls too low, the company becomes attractive as a takeover candidate. Media companies are the current darlings of conglomerates. Despite what I said about how the cost of entry in publishing has risen, a going publication is attractive to an acquirer because it has little in the way of assets—unlike a steel mill or an auto company—and a high cash flow. Another measure that financial managers use to evaluate a business is how many times its assets are earned in revenues. In this measure, publishing companies tend to stand out. Because of this, you are going to see more non-publishing companies buy publishing companies.*

Right. But isn't it nice that all those publishers who start things know they can cash in—and often handsome-ly—when they want. And that their babies will be nicely cared for by those corporate types.

The compleat strategist:
Forecasting failure

By Richard M. Koff

The one thing you'd think we'd all be able to recognize is failure, yet it is amazing how far past reason many publishers take their mistakes. Of course no one wants to give up on a loved one, and it always seems as if the turn-around is just about to arrive. Why then does it stay so tantalizingly out of reach—and for so long a time?

A recent article in *The Harvard Business Review* offers some interesting statistics. The authors polled 200 of the Fortune 500 for their experiences with new products—not merely extensions of their current lines of business but genuinely new ventures to which they applied all of their considerable marketing skills. The results were amazing, even to the executives themselves, since these were companies which certainly could not be accused of undercapitalization or lack of managerial skill.

It turns out that only four out of 10 new ventures reached profitability in the first four years. Only one out of the four paid back all start-up costs in the first four years. And the average time to pay off the initial investment was eight years. This means that fully half of all new ventures started by major corporations take more than eight years to pay off their initial investments!

It's difficult to face the fact that your new magazine isn't going to make it, that still one more financial transfusion will probably be another wasted year. Furthermore, you know that more lies to your backers (and your wife) will only make your nose grow longer and longer, like Pinocchio's. You know you have to make a tough decision—probably the toughest decision you'll ever make—and no one will love you for it.

I was asked to take a look at a magazine recently and found it to be in just such a hopeless situation. It was costlier than its competition, offered less to the consumer, and for political reasons could not be changed in any important way. I advised the client that either they consider it a promotional expense and accept the losses, or fold. They locked my report in a file cabinet and continue to hope for profitability—next year.

We are dealing here with an area so charged with emotional energy that I suspect this article can only help you after the fact—post mortem, literally. But look at it this way: the experience of a failure, like the experience of getting fired, is an important addition to your fund of knowledge. You'll be a better publisher for it next time.

In any case, the challenge to the publishing strategist is to recognize an impossible situation early enough to keep the losses to a minimum. The technique isn't any different in principle from what we have been doing up to

now. You still look for a point of maximum profitability. However, if the point of maximum profitability is a negative number, there is no profitable strategy—and at that point, you're well advised to get out.

Let's take a typical situation, a subscription magazine with 90,000 one-year, $12 subscriptions. The renewal rate was 60 percent, and it is assumed it will fall only if the subscription price is raised.

To make up the 36,000 non-renewers last year, the publisher dropped 1,600,000 direct mail pieces, and the gross response was a tolerable 3 percent before 25 percent bad debt. Net paid subs acquired from the mailing totaled 36,000, just enough to maintain the 90,000 circulation.

Here is last year's performance in the critical areas we will be discussing:

Sub prc	Pcs mld (000)	CPM	Sls exp (000)	Circ (000)	Ad pgs	Profit ($000)
$12	1,600	$20	$300	90	600	−78

You know that if you raise the price the return will drop. Here is what happens to circulation over a range of subscription prices (Figure 1 shows the same data in graphic form):

Sub prc	Circ (000)
$ 8	126
9	119
10	112
11	105
12	97
13	90
14	82
15	75
16	68
17	61
18	55
19	48
20	43

Note you can go to $13 next year without affecting the number of subscriptions because inflation will have driven the prices of other magazines and books so high that yours will look good by comparison. If you leave the subscription price at $12 and check with your subscription manager about a range of mailing levels, the estimate is (Figure 2):

Sub prc	Pcs mld (000)	Circ (000)
$12	500	78
12	600	80
12	700	83
12	800	85
12	900	87
12	1,000	89
12	1,100	91
12	1,200	92
12	1,300	94
12	1,400	95
12	1,500	96
12	1,600	97
12	1,700	98
12	1,800	99
12	1,900	100
12	2,000	101

On the advertising side, you sold 600 pages last year at an average cost per thousand (CPM) of $20 or $1,800 per page, for your 90,000 rate base. If you were to raise your CPM more than 7 percent you'd lose pages. The advertising director estimates as follows (Figure 3):

CPM	Ad pgs
$20	674
21	619
22	567
23	516
24	469
25	424
26	381
27	342
28	305
29	271
30	240

Your advertising director tells you he could sell more pages if you allowed him to hire another salesperson and maybe spend some money on promotion. His guesses are (Figure 4):

CPM	Sls exp (000)	Additional ad pgs
$20	$100	295
20	125	356
20	150	412
20	175	465
20	200	513
20	225	558
20	250	600
20	275	638
20	300	674
20	325	707
20	350	738
20	375	767
20	400	793

All in all it is not a hopeful situation. Increasing prices will reduce circulation or ad pages fairly steeply; increasing mailing efforts or advertising sales expenses won't produce important changes in sales. What should you do—particularly looking into a recession which may hurt ad and circulation sales, and a continuing inflation in all costs?

A stubborn publisher would trim costs—probably for the third or fourth time—and hold the line on prices. But by this time cost cutting is likely to hurt sales. A cautious publisher would do the same and get the word around town that he's ready for another job.

A curious publisher would call the local university that has a management school and get a couple of bright young graduate degree candidates to convert these figures into equations which they can then program on a thousand dollar home computer. There are only a few additional pieces of data they would need—things like the ratio of net ad income to rate card gross (75 percent); mailing cost per piece ($.33); editorial and administrative costs ($825,000); manufacturing cost as a function of the number of pages printed ($3/M); the expected impact of inflation on these costs and on the buyer's acceptance of price increases. A student with some mathematical facility should be able to put it all down and get it running in a couple of weeks.

You'd then buy a computer and run the programs to explore each of the strategic decisions in turns. For example, suppose you wondered how profits would change as you changed subscription price:

Sub prc	Pcs mld	CPM	Sls exp (000)	Circ (000)	Ad pgs	Profit ($000)
$ 8	1,600	$20	$300	126	674	-149
9	1,600	20	300	119	674	-114
10	1,600	20	300	112	674	-98
11	1,600	20	300	105	674	-100
12	1,600	20	300	97	674	-119
13	1,600	20	300	90	674	-154
14	1,600	20	300	82	674	-204
15	1,600	20	300	75	674	-265
16	1,600	20	300	68	674	-337
17	1,600	20	300	61	674	-417
18	1,600	20	300	55	674	-503
19	1,600	20	300	48	674	-593
20	1,600	20	300	43	674	-685

Not wonderful, even though pages increased because you kept the CPM constant despite the inflationary pressure. You'd probably now be tempted to drop the price to $10 and then see what happens at different levels of direct-mail effort:

Sub prc	Pcs mld (000)	CPM	Sls exp (000)	Circ (000)	Ad pgs	Profit ($000)
$10	500	$20	$300	89	674	-69
10	700	20	300	93	674	-56
10	700	20	300	95	674	-47
10	800	20	300	98	674	-42
10	900	20	300	100	674	-40
10	1,000	20	300	103	674	-41
10	1,100	20	300	105	674	-45
10	1,200	20	300	106	674	-51
10	1,300	20	300	108	674	-60
10	1,400	20	300	110	674	-71
10	1,500	20	300	111	674	-83
10	1,600	20	300	112	674	-98
10	1,700	20	300	113	674	-114
10	1,800	20	300	115	674	-131
10	1,900	20	300	116	674	-150
10	2,000	20	300	116	674	-170

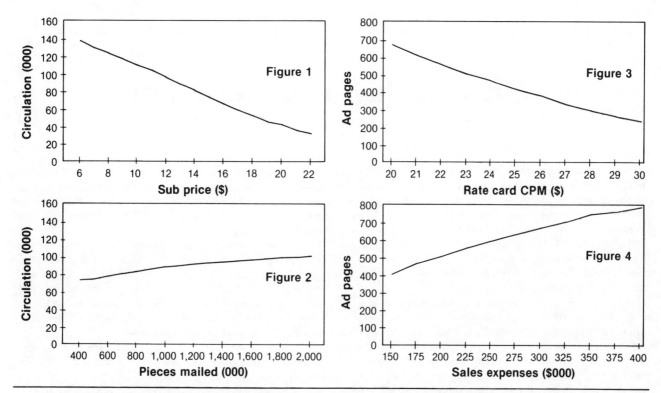

A little better, but still not profitable. Well, maybe the CPM is pegged too low. You'd try a range of CPMs:

Sub prc	Pcs mld (000)	CPM	Sls exp (000)	Circ (000)	Ad pgs	Profit ($000)
$10	900	$20	$300	100	674	-40
10	900	21	300	100	619	-30
10	900	22	300	100	567	-27
10	900	23	300	100	516	-30
10	900	24	300	100	469	-38
10	900	25	300	100	424	-50
10	900	26	300	100	381	-66
10	900	27	300	100	342	-85
10	900	28	300	100	305	-106
10	900	29	300	100	271	-129
10	900	30	300	100	240	-154

Ugh. Okay, kick the CPM up to $22 and give the advertising director a range of money to spend:

Sub prc	Pcs mld (000)	CPM	Sls exp (000)	Circ (000)	Ad pgs	Profit ($000)
$10	900	$22	$100	100	248	-91
10	900	22	125	100	299	-74
10	900	22	150	100	347	-60
10	900	22	175	100	391	-48
10	900	22	200	100	431	-39
10	900	22	225	100	469	-33
10	900	22	250	100	504	-29
10	900	22	275	100	537	-27
10	900	22	300	100	567	-27
10	900	22	325	100	595	-29
10	900	22	350	100	620	-33
10	900	22	375	100	644	-38
10	900	22	400	100	667	-45

Nothing seems to help. Even at best, you'd wind up

losing another $27,000 this year—and it can only get worse. We've assumed inflation at 10 percent in all of this. If costs rise 15 percent next year, as they well may:

Sub prc	Pcs mld (000)	CPM	Sls Exp (000)	Circ (000)	Ad pgs	Profit ($000)
$10	900	$22	$200	100	431	-110
10	900	22	225	100	469	-105
10	900	22	250	100	504	-103
10	900	22	275	100	537	-102
10	900	22	300	100	567	-103
10	900	22	325	100	595	-106
10	900	22	350	100	620	-111
10	900	22	375	100	644	-117
10	900	22	400	100	667	-124

There's no doubt about it, is there? FOLD!

Total cost to fold—maybe $5,000 for the computer and programming, separation allowances for the staff, legal fees in bankruptcy, if that's necessary, and pride. On the plus side, you take the computer home for your kids to play with and you sell the 90,000 subscriber names plus expires to your competitor for enough to pay your creditors, the IRS, and give you a luxurious summer in Florida.

It's certainly better than going in the hole for another $100,000 next year.

The publisher as a mortician

By James B. Kobak

Virtually every business person, no matter the field, tends to carry losing projects on longer than he or she should. He or she does it, of course, in the very human hope that the corner will be turned soon. The practice may even be more prevalent in the magazine field, because magazines so often take on a living quality which not many businesses have. It always seems a shame to see one die. It's like losing a friend. Yet, carrying on beyond the point of no return has ruined more than one company.

Professional morticians—or at least people who can play the role for part of the time—would be useful in almost any publishing house. They could point out the telltale signs of deterioration; project what results will be if something isn't done; combat the natural enthusiasm of publishers, editors and, most of all, salespeople; and arrange a decent burial before the patient has suffered so much that there is little good left.

The morticians have to be at the highest echelons of the company or nothing will happen. They can be the chief executive officer or other highup employee, or a director, or a consultant. They probably should not be the controller because many of them seem to take on the role of doom and gloom (because of the nature of their work) so often that no one would pay any attention to them.

Annual Examination

The examination of each publishing property should be done about once a year. The best time to do this is about three months before the budget process gets going—in June or July for most companies. This is late enough in the year so that an indication of results is available—and early enough to avoid getting involved with the budgeting process. Once budgeting starts it is difficult to make major decisions to change things—or to cut properties off.

The steps in the process are:

1. Gather basic (not detailed) information about the magazine for the past five years. This includes operating statements; comparisons with competition (advertising pages, circulation, advertising rates, circulation prices and editorial pages); copies of promotion material (both advertising and circulation); renewal rates (by original source if possible) and results of new subscription efforts.

Note that if the magazine is circulated free some of these items do not apply. It also becomes more difficult to judge reader reaction.

2. Analyze this material for trends, for competitive position, for basic weaknesses. A list of the type of thing to look for is in the accompanying box. The analysis should employ both ratios and other statistics—but should not neglect a very subjective evaluation.

3. Project operations for three years forward based on the present methods of doing business.

4. If it appears that there are really basic troubles, assemble a team of bright open-minded people to study the situation. This group preferably should include people from all areas of the business—editorial, advertising, circulation, business.

A truly creative study can rarely be done in the office during business hours. It's better to hold a retreat in some hotel where the group can really concentrate. It might be helpful to have facilities to project results under different assumptions about future operations—this can either be done by some pencil-pushing accountants or by putting the magazine on a computer.

But whatever you do, don't put such a study off—and do it thoroughly when you do approach it. Nothing else you can do can be as important.

There is no sense in getting this far just as an exercise. This is decision-making time. And remember—just going along as before is a decision even if it is done by inertia.

What Might the Examination Show

The number of alternatives which you might arrive at after the annual examination are, of course, infinite. And the chances are that if they are drastic there will be a need for further study. But basically they come down to a few:

- Carry on very much as you did before.
- Employ drastic action to resurrect the property. This might include reducing circulation, raising prices, drastic cost-cutting, reducing frequency, changing to a newsletter—or any of many other possibilities.
- Dispose of the magazine.

How To Dispose of a Magazine

Here is where our mortician uses real skills. Basically there are two choices—sell it or bury it.

There are three most-likely prospect types to whom to sell a magazine which you no longer want:

1. Competitors—More than once a magazine has been sold to a competitor with both sides coming out ahead. Frequently two magazines reach a position where neither can make profits—or make a major move to get way ahead of the other.

A sale and then a merger of the magazines often has these results: Circulation is increased so that advertising rates can be raised; not all advertisers were in both magazines (with the merger the number of pages is increased), major moves which could not be done in a competitive situation can be accomplished.

Frequently the sale price is determined as a split of future profits of the merged magazine over a period of years. And both sides benefit.

2. Another publisher—Who thinks he or she knows how to operate a property profitably, even though you

could not. Sometimes this is a mistaken concept, but in other cases losing magazines have been turned around relatively quickly. This frequently happens with a small magazine which might lose money in a large publishing house, but freed of high overhead designed for big properties, can be a money-maker.

3. To employees—Who may have concepts of operation which you may not believe in—or who may operate on a very reduced budget if they are the owners.

This article is not designed to delve into the valuation of magazines. It is obvious that in most cases where you want to dispose of a property because it is a loser, your bargaining position is not very good. Often, in order to get more than a token payment, a price dependent on future profits is agreed to.

Burying a magazine may have more complexities than you might imagine. These are primarily in the areas of subscriptions, employees and taxes.

Unexpired subscriptions really represent payments a publisher has received for future delivery of the magazine. Legally the subscribers have a claim for their money back, even though the amounts involved may in any single case be very small.

Until recently the situation was relatively easily solved. Other magazines were willing to fulfill the subscriptions—and sometimes even paid the publisher for the privilege. Cash refunds were not even offered.

The rise of consumerism, however, at about the same time *Look* went out of business, brought the federal government into the act. *Look* had to offer cash to many subscribers as an alternative to the other magazines which were willing to fulfill in its place. And there are indications that in the future even more drastic action may be contemplated.

With the death of a magazine, too, there are personnel problems. What to do with all the people who have loyally worked for it? Such questions come up as these. How much severance pay? What becomes of their pension rights? Is there some way to help them find other jobs either in the company or somewhere else?

And then there may be tax problems. Believe it or not, the killing of a magazine may trigger taxable income. If the company defers subscription income over the life of the subscription, the act of having other publishers fulfill those subscriptions results in income to the folding magazine.

We have been talking in terms of a mortician, not a very pleasant approach. What you have obviously read between the lines is this—to merit top management responsibility requires the strength to face unpleasant situations and deal with them, even if you feel like a mortician at times.

Signs of Failing Health

It looks and feels more like a pamphlet than a magazine.

Advertising pages have been declining.

The editor has been changed three times in three years.

The editor has been the same for 25 years—and is not up-to-date.

Subscription renewal rate has been declining.

Classified advertising has been declining.

Unable to sell advertising on all the covers.

Circulation promotion is selling a different magazine concept than the editors are editing.

You aren't making any money.

Your projections show you will never make any money.

You chronically fall below budget.

It is getting more and more costly to obtain new subscriptions.

This is the fifth year in a row that you said, "Wait till next year."

You skipped some issues.

Subscribers are being carried in arrears.

Competition is gaining on you—in advertising or circulation—or just in general.

You have not been able to increase the advertising rate.

Other publishers have stopped asking if you would be willing to sell the magazine.

Your mother-in-law says the magazine is terrible.

About all the advertising you have is mail order.

Rental of subscription lists has fallen off.

Some advertisers are paying less than card rates.

The stockholders are restless.

You gave the magazine a face-lifting—but it didn't do any good.

Gallagher and *MIN* don't talk about your magazine any more.

You are not invited to be on industry panels.

Newsstand sales are half what they were five years ago.

The number of qualified job applicants has dropped.

The key employees want to know if they can buy the magazine.

The key employees have stopped asking if they can buy the magazines.

You get very few letters to the editor.

Key people are looking for jobs.

Employees have become more interested in the pension plan than in a "piece of the action."

How to destroy a magazine: Let me count the ways

By James B. Kobak

I started writing this piece by putting down the most common publishing errors I have seen. When I reached 16, I figured that was enough. There is no magic in 16. The possibilities for error are limitless—and the creativity of my publishing friends in finding new errors is to be marveled at.

Most of these errors do not always represent the underlying trouble. This often is a lack of understanding of magazine economics, a lack of basic management knowledge or some other deeper problem. But a discussion of these more esoteric points would go far beyond this article.

There is no magic in the order with which the errors are listed either. And, of course, any resemblance to any person or magazine, living or dead, is purely coincidental.

Starting a Magazine No One Wants

The basic error, which has been made time and time again—and will be made often in the future—involves actually starting the magazine in the first place.

Magazines exist because the interests of a number of people need satisfaction or communication. Too often those involved with the launching of a magazine fall into a common trap—they believe that if they are interested in a subject, everyone must be. Examples are legion of magazines started by a few people who are intensely interested in a subject, only to find that there are not enough others to make it economically feasible. I just wish they would do some intelligent testing before the launching.

Sometimes there are lots of people interested in a subject—but they don't want to read about it. Consider exercise machines. Lots of people ride them. Many are purchased. But interest in reading about them is very low. The same is true for many other human interests.

And then there are fields which require communication but another medium would do it much better than a magazine.

Keeping a Magazine Going That No One Wants

When a magazine reaches the point in its life cycle where it no longer interests enough people to remain profitable, it should be killed.

That point is difficult to determine. Changes take place slowly. Other confusing things may be going on in the company, in the economy or in the field which is served. These may hide the fact that the magazine is no longer needed. Add to this the difficulty those involved have in facing the fact that a once-profitable magazine has outlived its usefulness. To kill it seems almost like killing a good friend. Recall the tears at *Life* and *Look* when their final issues were announced.

The skills required to sell advertising are unique.

They require a knowledge of the product, of the market, of the advertisers. They also involve self-confidence, persuasiveness, charm, persistence and a number of other intangible qualities.

An advertising director needs many of the same qualities. But he or she needs the skills and talents of a manager—the ability to see the overall picture, plus the ability to organize, to train, to motivate.

Selling and managing qualities are not often found in the same individual. The success formula in our country, of course, is based on the idea that anyone can do anything if that person just wants to and tries hard enough.

It just isn't so.

More good people—and good magazines—have been ruined by unwisely promoting good people into management than you can count. Not only have you lost a good salesperson, but you have also created a management disaster. The error has compounded itself.

Let's not leave the impression, however, that this only happens in the advertising department. It can occur in editorial, circulation, accounting or anywhere else.

The fault, of course, lies in a system which puts a premium on management ability over other kinds of abilities. Or maybe it is just that the managers determine the compensation levels.

Belief in the Infallibility of the Editor

How many editors have you ever known believe it is possible to measure their performance?

I haven't met any, either.

If the circulation or renewal rates decline, then the circulation people have goofed up—again. If readership scores deteriorate, then there was something wrong with the way the measuring was done—and you cannot measure editorial impact anyway.

That's a lot of hooey!

An editor can—and should—be measured just like anyone else. So let's have more readership surveys and develop all sorts of other ways of measuring editorial content. We just don't have enough geniuses editing magazines to be able to depend completely on them. (We never did in the past and never will in the future either.)

Once again, this is not confined to the editorial area. The ace advertising salesperson, the leading circulation director and the nastiest budget manager don't want to be measured, either. It just isn't as obvious in these areas as it is in editorial.

Charging the Reader Less Than He or She Should Pay

Recent history in the business is replete with examples of magazines that have not charged the reader enough. I feel that I am beating a dead horse by mentioning it.

Nowadays everyone seems to know that the reader should pay his or her share (even though few magazines live by this rule). But it wasn't so long ago that the drive to give advertisers a great many warm bodies pushed publishers into cut-rate offers which could only result in suicide.

Why should *Life* and *Look* have sold copies via the cut-rate subscription offer for less than 10 cents—while paperback books were moving well at over a dollar? And newsletters were sold for $10 to $35 a year?

The basic economics of the magazine business require substantial payments by readers, either to support the magazine or to prove to the advertising community that the readers really are involved with the magazine. And if you cannot get enough from the readers, maybe there shouldn't be a magazine in the first place.

Neglecting the Profits Which Can Be Made Through Marketing the Aura of the Magazine

Often mentioned is the emotion—the warmth—that a magazine generates within its own staff and in its readers. Yet it is only in recent years that magazines have taken advantage of this by serving their readers in other ways, such as selling them products that the magazine, and then the readers, believe in.

It should be obvious that the readers of a woman's service magazine are interested in greater depth in cooking, sewing, children, husbands. But until recently little was done to supplement these interests. And even today only a few magazines, and generally in a small way, are selling other items.

Readers believe in their magazines. The field for selling other things to them is scarcely touched. While it isn't easy, any magazine which is not taking advantage of the aura it has built up is missing a big profit opportunity.

Executive Warfare

Common to any organized enterprise is the desire for many of those below to be on top. As long as human beings are involved, this is natural.

But there is nothing which can kill a magazine as fast as executive warfare. One of the prime causes of the failure of new magazines is fighting among newly joined partners. Instead of paying attention to making a very difficult project work, getting on top becomes the goal—and disaster is the result.

The same thing happens in going enterprises. But in these there seems to be a father figure, the magazine itself, which is bigger than all of us. But a magazine is nothing but people. And if they cannot get along, the magazine cannot continue to succeed.

Allowing Editors to Choose Covers

For some magazines the cover design is vital to the sale of copies on the newsstand. For *all* magazines covers are important in getting readers to read the copy inside.

Most editors are not experts in color, in design, in display, in marketing, in packaging. That this most important function of choosing covers should be in their hands has always amazed me. The packaging of products is a high art which is practiced by experts. That art has been recognized in other consumer marketing organizations, such as Proctor & Gamble, General Foods, etc.

Since single copy sales are of such great importance to some magazines (the most profitable circulation which they can obtain), why not use every source available to sell them?

Reducing Advertising Rates—One Way or Another

Compared with radio and TV, where buying time is a high art worthy of the finest Oriental bazaar, advertising rates for magazines are remarkably solid.

There are some magazines, however, where the rates charged are subject to bargaining. And there are many which construct their rate cards as to favor a happy few advertisers.

Just as in the circulation area, prices that are too low can lead to disaster. The economies of the business simply won't permit it for long. And the word that there is room for negotiation on rates has harmed many a magazine.

Selling Subscriptions Instead of Single Copies

Some magazines can be sold in quantity on newsstands. For these magazines single copy sales are by far the most profitable—more so than any form of subscription.

And still the trend over the years has been to abandon the newsstand in favor of subscriptions, presumably so that the advertising rate base will be secure.

This kind of thinking is backwards. Not only does the publisher receive more money from single copies, but there are many side benefits. Advertisers, too, like single copy sales. They indicate the vitality of the magazine. Newsstand sales give a valuable sampling method for obtaining subscriptions and yield loyal readers at a very low cost. And they give a valuable indication of the appeal of the editorial material.

Publishing Magazines in Large Complex Organizational Structures

A magazine is basically a very small, self-contained business. Most can be put out by fewer than 30 people.

The siren call of the large organization is strong. It can supply support services which may yield cost savings and high-level skills which a single magazine cannot support. But in the long run, a magazine is better off if it is run by a handful of people as a complete unit, buying skills as it needs them.

Magazines depend on a small number of highly specialized and creative people working in great harmony. If they are burdened with administrative detail, corporate politics or unnecessary controls, the very spark that makes the magazine can easily be extinguished.

This does not mean that all large organizations are bad. It is possible to develop an atmosphere in a large corporation where individual magazines can be operated autonomously. But it is hard. And if the accounting types become involved, the people who put out the magazine can become enmeshed in an administrative morass. We have all seen it.

Marketing Magazines as Sacred Literary Products

A magazine is a literary product to the editors. It is a literary product to the buyer when he or she reads it. But in between it is something else.

There is no sense in spending the time and effort to put out a great product if you cannot get it into the hands of those who should read it.

So between its development and its consumption, a magazine is nothing more than a consumer product—one with a very short shelf life.

There should be no hesitation about marketing a magazine just as any other consumer product is marketed. All the tricks, all the contests, all the promotion, all the public relations, all the package design, all the retail outlets that are used in consumer marketing should be used. In fact, they should work even better with a magazine because it has a warmth that a box of dog food can never have.

Insufficient or Inaccurate Data

A magazine is a pretty simple thing to measure. If you want, you can just about develop the profit picture of most magazines from information which is available to the public. Accounting for magazines is a relatively easy process compared with most industries.

And yet how many publishers really know what is going on in their own publications or how their advertising salespeople are doing or which areas of circulation are most profitable?

The health of a magazine, as well as the areas of internal trouble, can be determined with a very simple two-page monthly accounting statement (including a number of obvious statistics about pages, copies, etc.).

Virtually every cost of a magazine is subject to simple control. And yet, for many magazines, such an obvious area as the number of pages in an issue is determined without real reason.

Too Much Circulation

It is hard for any publisher to realize that there is a limit to the number of people who are interested in his or her magazine. An yet there is one for every publication.

When the advertising department is constantly breathing hard down your back for just a few thousand more readers and "then we will really make a breakthrough," it becomes even more difficult.

And yet, when a magazine gets beyond its natural circulation level, there is not only the very high initial cost of acquiring those additional readers—there is a never-ending cost of replacing them because they do not renew.

Lack of Definition of the Purpose of the Magazine

Too often, as time goes on, excessive departmentalization in a magazine results in the lack of a common definition of what the magazine's purpose and method of fulfilling it are.

The editor may be editing a magazine for one group of readers while the circulation department is selling a magazine with a different slant. What happens? The circulation department sells lots of copies but the buyers find that they have a different product than was advertised and don't renew.

The same can be true about the advertising department. It may be selling a type of reader which neither the editors nor the circulation people are delivering. Again, disillusionment.

A common thrust and a common definition of what is the nature and purpose of the magazine are needed by everyone involved.

Insufficient Capitalization

No business interprise has ever felt that it had enough capital to do its job correctly. But in some cases in the magazine world over-optimism has led to the start-up of magazines which could not possibly achieve success with the capital available.

The economics of magazine publishing normally call for spending money fast because it leads to the most rapid success, as well as the smallest requirement for capital. "Bootstrapping" is almost impossible in this business.

Spending slowly results in dribbling money out over a long period of time without really making progress. Experience has shown that when things are carried on in this way the magazine never makes it—and often fails after spending much more than would have been used if done correctly in the first place.

Curing the sick magazine

By James B. Kobak

Your magazine is sick.

You have been publishing for 10 years (or 20 or 100) and, until now, everything had been going beautifully. You've never faced such a situation before.

The once-weekly offers to be bought out by conglomerates and European publishers haven't come through for several months.

The employees are no longer seeking "a piece of the action." In fact, you wonder where they spend their lunch hours.

Gallagher and *MIN* mention your magazine, but somehow differently from before.

Phil Dougherty of *The New York Times* is no longer asking for interviews.

No one from Wall Street has called about investing or going public.

Your biggest competitor wants to know if he can take over your subscription liability.

And finally, you lost money last year, you're losing money this year, and you'll probably lose money next year.

Little tell-tale signs like these tell you that something is wrong. But what?

There are only a few major difficulties that can beset a magazine:
- Circulation is harder to obtain.
- Advertising is harder to obtain.
- Competition is gaining on you.
- Everything seems fine, but profits are declining.
- All of the above.

But citing one of these difficulties is like saying "I have a headache" or "I have a stomach ache" or "My leg hurts." About all it does is describe the symptoms and localize the problem.

Then how can you find out what is really wrong? And what can you do about it?

If you have not routinely had an annual check-up, you are ready for a Mayo-type job now. Can you do it yourself? Sure. Or, at least, you can do part of the work.

The first step is to diagnose the disease.

The good news is that there are only a few diseases that can afflict a magazine. Figure I gives a quick view of the possible diseases which can produce the basic problems we started with. The symptoms are listed across the top and the diseases which could yield such results run down the side. You may categorize them differently, but these will cover 95 percent of the cases.

The bad news is that some of these diseases are fatal even before you make the diagnosis, determine the cure, and make the needed changes.

Disorders of the magazine

•The field being served is declining or disappearing.
Magazines exist because people have interests. When those interests change, there may no longer be a need for the magazine. This usually is the result of outside events over which a publisher has no control.

For example, the continued rise in gasoline prices has almost killed the RV and trailer business—at least until vehicles of a much smaller size are developed. Magazines serving this field have been badly hurt.

A couple of years ago the FCC made some very arbitrary (and unwise) rulings which resulted in bankruptcy for most CB set manufacturers. Magazines in this field have suffered.

In the business area, new products are rare in a mature industry (most industries contract when they reach maturity). The result: only a handful of suppliers remain to advertise. When the railroad industry was in its heyday, steam locomotives (there were lots of different types) were made up of lots of parts made by many manufacturers. Along came the diesel engine—and there are now only two manufacturers. Since this scene was duplicated in other parts of the industry, the effects on many of the magazines serving this industry were disastrous.

• *The product ceases to interest the public.*

The editorial product, of course, is a very fragile thing—and difficult to measure. In the friendly war among circulation, editorial and advertising people, it is very easy to blame every illness on editorial—right or wrong. There have been, however, a number of cases where it was clear that the editorial product no longer pleased the audience, either because the editorial direction had been changed—or because it hadn't.

Saturday Review, for instance, has changed hands at least nine times that I know of. And each of the new buyers thought he knew how to fix the product so that it would have more appeal. But so far nothing has seemed to work. *Harper's* and *The Atlantic Monthly* seem to be in the same boat. *Esquire* suffered for many years from humdrum editorial direction (in my opinion). It took years to really hurt—but in the end it did. (This does not mean that the new owners of these magazines will not be able to find the formula.)

• *Circulation efforts are weak.*

There may be nothing wrong with the field—or the product. It may simply be that the best methods of acquiring and holding readers are not being followed.

I recall that *Book Digest* was struggling some years ago to build its subscription base. A new circulation director was hired and, through the simple process of using a sweepstakes approach, lifted return percentages four times.

It is also a truism of the business (not terribly well-recognized) that too much reliance is placed on sending out millions of pieces of direct mail—and not enough on more creative, and possibly more difficult, but more effective methods. A few years ago, *McCall's* was paying too high a price to acquire those last few subscribers in order to keep its rate base up. By putting more emphasis on single-copy sales, not only was much of the cost eliminated, but the magazine actually made profits from the copies sold on the newsstand.

And we have all seen cases where a new renewal

series, or collection series, or copy approach has made worlds of difference.

• *Advertising effort is weak.*

It is easy to say, "All we need is 10 more ad pages per issue and everything will be fine." Usually it is not that easy to achieve. However, there are many instances where a new hot ad director like Henry Marks, Pete Bonnani, John Veronis or Carlo Vittorini (to name only a few) have literally changed the course of a magazine.

And remember what the slogan "Young Mamas" did for *Redbook* for so many years—or what a change in the rate structure has done for a number of magazines—or what Ed Miller's research techniques accomplished for the old *Life* way back when television first appeared.

• *Strong competition is having negative effects.*

Sometimes competition is a blessing. For instance, in the food field it appears that the addition of *Cuisine, Bon Appetit* and *Food & Wine* have created a field where only *Gourmet* existed before. Result: they all do well.

But consider the men's outdoor field where *Field & Stream, Outdoor Life,* and *Sports Afield* constantly beat each other over the head in every way they can. Ad rates have remained so low that it is very difficult to make an adequate profit.

And do you think Rona Barrett's *Hollywood* didn't have an impact on the old movie magazines?

• *Circulation has been pushed beyond its natural level.*

One of the major hidden dangers of the magazine business is to try to make a successful magazine more successful by increasing circulation, thereby raising the ad rate. Naturally the profits will just roll in.

Great thinking! But what happens if you push too far? You have to keep on buying readership—not just once, but every single year, because those last subscribers renew terribly.

Want examples? Look at the old *Life, Look* and *Saturday Evening Post.* Or *Book Digest*, more recently.

• *Lack of cost control is eating up profits.*

On the surface, magazines do not seem to be subject to runaway costs. After all, prices for paper, printing, postage and most everything else are relatively fixed and well known.

Don't you believe it. When Warren Erhardt went to run the three magazines for the Boy Scouts, he managed to save over $2 million a year in paper, printing and other costs without cutting the payroll or the quality of the magazines. How? Simply by buying better.

You can pay if you don't know what you are doing. Negotiating a printing contract is a fine art.

Classic died—but only because the cost structure didn't fit with the possible revenue. I believe that it could have been profitable.

Time Inc., it is rumored, cannot make really good profits on monthly magazines because of the costs they throw at them. I also remember when *Architectural Forum* was as thick as a phone book with ads—but lost money.

• *The reader is being given too little.*

Too little can be given in lots of ways—too few pages, too little good stuff, poor paper or printing, not enough color, rotten graphics, lots of pages but no substance, and on and on.

We all depend on the editorial department, but we also know that it is the least expensive part of most magazines. Usually an improvement in editorial quality costs very little, if anything.

The real question is the reader's perception of the magazine itself and the price of the magazine. There are several subjective tests which must be met.

First is the "heft" test. Does the magazine feel like two dollars' worth? In some cases, publishers have introduced heavier weight paper—or bulking stock—to solve this.

Second, is there enough editorial matter? Every magazine, except weeklies, should have at least 60 editorial pages. And if there is a lot of advertising, there should be even more—otherwise the editorial gets lost. Take a look at the women's service magazines, which have lots of edit material—much more than is apparent because of the way the advertisers play checkers and other games around the editorial material.

Of course, some business magazines in small fields can run fewer pages. On the other hand, very expensive magazines like *Geo, Town & Country* and *Realities* must carry more material.

Third, the number of different pieces and departments must be sufficient to attract different readers. Remember—we don't expect anyone to read everything, so the more variety, the better. *Reader's Digest,* of course, does this beautifully.

Fourth, the material must be quality material. If it's not, the reader will feel cheated no matter how many pages there are.

In any case, the slogan should be (as in any business): "Give the reader more—and better—than he expects."

• *The reader is being given too much.*

It is also possible to give too much—so that the reader is turned off. The "too much" is usually the result of running pieces which are too long. Both *Playboy* and *The New York Times Magazine* do this, in my opinion. (Please don't bother to send letters to the editor about this. I know they are two of the great successes of the business—but it doesn't work for everyone.)

Pages cost money—and lots of it. It is cheaper to edit better and reduce the length of articles than to pay for useless words which may turn readers off.

• *The magazine is suffering from schizophrenia.*

Magazines can have mental disorders; after all, people operate them. For example, a magazine becomes schizophrenic when the editor is putting out one product while the ad and/or circulation people are promoting another. Or circulation is acquiring one type of reader and advertising is touting another. This is more common than you can imagine.

The late *Intellectual Digest* suffered from schizophrenia (plus a terrible title). Mailings went out by the millions, but when the magazine came out, it was not what had been advertised. Cancellations poured in.

Even worse, of course, is the magazine with an undefined editorial thrust. Then no one can sell it either to readers or to advertisers.

• *Pricing is too aggressive.*

Although magazines are less price sensitive than most products, there is always a point where people will not pay even one penny more.

It is possible that *Geo* has gone too far, although indications are that readers will pay a lot for editorial products they like.

And, of course, it is possible to overprice from the advertisers' standpoint. *Woman's Day,* for instance, cannot sell advertising for any appreciable amount more than *Family Circle.* And both must worry about TV, radio, newspapers and other media used by their mass-market advertisers.

Figure I — **Magazine Disorders**

	Circulation Symptoms			Advertising Symptoms		Competitive Symptoms		Profit Symptoms
	Declining renewal rate	New subscription acquisition difficult	Weak single-copy sales	Advertising pages declining	Reader demographics declining	Competitors gaining in circulation	Competitors gaining in advertising	Situation stable, but earnings declining
Field disappearing	☐	☐	☐	☐				
Product no longer of interest	☐	☐	☐	☐	☐	☐	☐	
Weak circulation efforts	☐	☐	☐		☐	☐		
Weak advertising efforts				☐			☐	
Strong competition						☐	☐	
Circulation pushed beyond natural level	☐	☐	☐		☐	☐		
Lack of cost control								☐
Reader given too little	☐	☐	☐			☐		
Reader given too much								☐
Schizophrenia	☐	☐	☐	☐	☐			
Pricing too aggressive	☐	☐	☐	☐		☐	☐	
Pricing not aggressive enough								☐
Lack of planning	☐	☐	☐	☐		☐		☐

•*Pricing is not aggressive enough.*

A more common ailment is prices not advancing fast enough. Most publishers are amazed at the prices that readers and advertisers will pay when they like a product.

To price too low is committing hara-kiri. If you cannot charge enough to make good profits, you are better off admitting it and closing up, rather than suffering a long, painful expensive death watch.

I recall back in 1971 when most subscriptions to *McCall's* (and the *Journal, Good Housekeeping,* etc.) were sold at $3.97. When it was no longer possible to stay profitable at that price, subscription (and newsstand) prices began to rise regularly, after careful testing, with little resistance from the reader. *Time* magazine over the past five years has increased subscription prices from under $10 a year to close to $30.

Advertising rates, too, have constantly been raised. Advertisers know that they need magazines.

•*Planning and research are poor or non-existent.*

Characterizing all these diseases is a lack of thinking through what is being done and why. Unfortunately, few publishers are trained in planning techniques, and many are unfamiliar with all aspects of the business.

The planning tools exist—although not everyone takes advantage of them. I am constantly amazed by the number of publishers who have inadequate accounting . . . or who don't supplement the raw accounting numbers with helpful statistics . . . or who don't take advantage of the various computer models and systems which make planning so much easier . . . or who don't research every aspect of their magazines regularly.

There are no magazine mysteries. The tools exist—and they are well known.

Diagnostic resources

OK—so now we have the various diseases and their basic symptoms. What next?

Making the diagnosis is really very easy. Of course, every field and every magazine are different, but there are many resources available that will enable you to make a correct diagnosis. Here are the major ones:

1. *Financial statements.* I always find that the first clues—and they may be the only clues—to what is going on in a company come from a review of old financial statements. If nothing else, your review will lead you to the best places to do some digging.

By financial statements I mean not only the raw accounting figures but also budgets and key statistics (See FOLIO, February 1975, "Making the Numbers Work for You;" and FOLIO, June 1976, "Budgeting for Fun and Profit"). I also include any projections which may have been made, both short and long term.

2. *Data about the field.* Most fields are well researched, either by government, by industry associations, by business magazines serving it, and in other ways. Your own magazine may have done studies for advertisers which will indicate the trends.

Carefully examine the data on: the people involved (the number employed, number using, number attending); revenue; profitability; number of producing units; and changes in distribution patterns.

3. *The magazine itself.* Even if you are in love with your magazine and have difficulty seeing that anything is wrong, you can determine such things as: the number of editorial pages; amount of editorial color; number of different articles; balance of articles in each issue; marketability of the editorial treatment (See FOLIO, February 1976, "The Editor as Marketer"); length of articles; number of advertisements and pages by category; and quality of advertisers.

4. *Readership research.* Magazines may be the most researched objects in the country. Techniques of all kinds have been developed, not only for the benefit of obtaining advertising, but also for editorial purposes.

Research either has been, or can be developed to determine: Who are the readers? What are their characteristics—demographic and psychographic? What do they read in the magazine? How often do they read it? Do they save it? Why? How many other people read it? What other magazines do they read? What would they like to see more of in the magazine?

Techniques for doing this type of research are well-known. They include mailed questionnaires, focus groups, telephone interviews, and personal interviews. Sometimes this research is syndicated by a number of magazines participating jointly.

5. *Advertising records.* The past records of your advertising in dollars and pages—and versus competition—should include breakdowns by advertiser; agency; product; size; frequency; salesman; and color, bleed, and position.

There are many other things to look at, however: rate cards—and changes made in them over the years; pro-

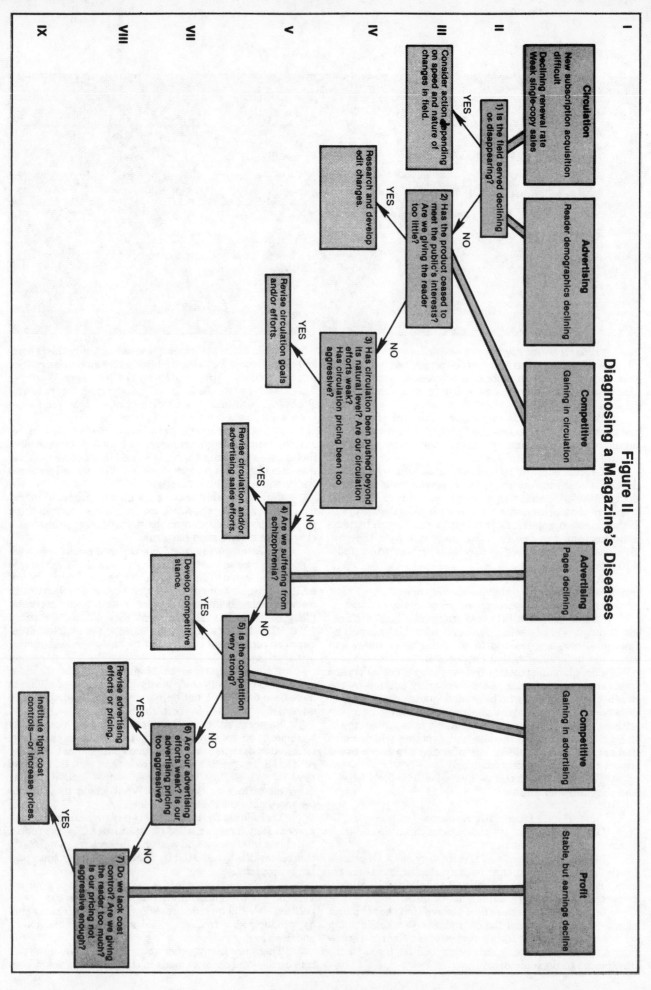

Figure II
Diagnosing a Magazine's Diseases

I Circulation
New subscription acquisition difficult
Declining renewal rate
Weak single-copy sales

Advertising
Reader demographics declining

Competitive
Gaining in circulation

Advertising
Pages declining

Competitive
Gaining in advertising

Profit
Stable, but earnings decline

1) Is the field served declining or disappearing?
YES — Consider action depending on speed and nature of changes in field. (III)

NO

2) Has the product ceased to meet the public's interests? Are we giving the reader too little?
YES — Research and develop edit changes. (IV)

NO

3) Has circulation been pushed beyond its natural level? Are our circulation efforts weak? Has circulation pricing been too aggressive?
YES — Revise circulation goals and/or efforts. (V)

NO

4) Are we suffering from schizophrenia?
YES — Revise circulation and/or advertising sales efforts. (VII)

NO

5) Is the competition very strong?
YES — Develop competitive stance. (VIII)

NO

6) Are our advertising efforts weak? Is our advertising pricing too aggressive?
YES — Revise advertising efforts or pricing. (VIII)

NO

7) Do we lack cost control? Are we giving the reader too much? Is our pricing not aggressive enough?
YES — Institute tight cost controls—or increase prices. (IX)

700

motion; sales techniques and aids; cost and profit per salesman; lost advertising—and why; and share of market in space and dollars.

All this material can be supplemented by further research—either your own or by an informed outsider—into advertiser and agency attitudes toward you, the magazine, the competition, the field, the promotion, and the individual salesmen.

6. *Circulation records.* Circulation sometimes seems to have more information than one can handle—and often the data are put together in ways that don't tell you much. It is worth spending time to develop meaningful reports so that you can quickly determine trends in both subscriptions and single-copy sales over a period of years.

For subscriptions, you will want information by source (and don't forget that each list in the mail is a separate source), by effort, and by time of year on the following: price and offer; return percent; pay-up percent; renewal percent; conversion percent; revenue versus cost; and results effort (for conversions and renewals).

For single copies you should have data on the draw, returns and net sale by: issue; section of the country; wholesaler; city; chain; individual outlet; and price.

You will also want to be able to find out such helpful information as: promotional support—when, where, how much and what type and cost; prematures; skimming; local weather conditions or other outside events; and nature of display.

Of course, this type of information is needed for both the single-copy "system" sales and for direct sales through other outlets.

It may be necessary to have reviews by your own people or outsiders in the single-copy arena to find out what is really going on. This would involve visiting newsstands, retailers, wholesalers, etc. in addition to just reviewing records.

7. *Cost data.* Financial statements are fine as they go, but very often you must look at the underlying material from which they are developed:

• Paper, printing and postage are usually the major costs in most magazines. A thorough review can often produce great cost savings (See FOLIO, September/October 1973, "Auditing Production Costs").

• Payments to suppliers for: composition; separations; manuscripts; art work, photos, cartoons; advertising promotion and research; circulation promotion; occupancy costs; consultants; telephone; stationery; fulfillment; professional fees.

• Travel and entertainment.

• Employee salaries, commissions and bonuses.

• Number of employees by department—measured against their productivity.

• Fringe benefits.

• Everything else.

8. *Industry data.* Some of the associations in the field develop data about different types of magazines, their revenue, and their cost patterns. The American Business Press does extensive work in this area for its members. From time to time the Magazine Publishers Association has developed similar material, although it is more difficult because of the wide diversity of size and type of publications.

In addition, FOLIO publishes The Folio 400, an annual industry-wide study of consumer and trade publication performance. This study concentrates on newsstand revenue, subscription revenue, and ad revenue.

It is also not unknown in the industry for competitive magazines to compare some of their numbers. And once in a while a magazine will conduct a study comparing salaries or other costs at similar magazines. Usually this is done by giving the participating publishers the results, to everyone's benefit.

9. *Competitive information.* Information on just about everything done by your competitors is available to you. In addition to Dun & Bradstreet and other public information, you can count advertising and editorial pages, read their circulation reports, get copies of their advertising and circulation promotion material which usually includes results of research they have done, inspect their rate cards, and read their magazines. If they are sold on the newsstand, you can usually get their sale and return percentage figures as fast as they can.

If you are smart, you will regularly develop operating statements for your competitors so that you will have some idea of how they are doing financially. This is not as hard to do as it may seem. After all, they face the same cost factors you do.

And if there isn't enough information open to public view, chances are that you, or one of your people, have friends over there. But don't forget—they can know just as much about you.

Steps in diagnosing the disease

Because many diseases exhibit the same symptoms, each case must be examined individually. Figure II illustrates the steps to take in diagnosing the disease.

In reading the chart, please note that you can start with the first question that is relevant to your magazine. For instance, if your magazine's competition is gaining in advertising, start with question 5.

You might, of course, want to go through *all* the steps. In that case, you will find that the investigation starts with an analysis of the field, because if there is no field, there is no need for a magazine.

If the field has declined, there is still a need, but different from the one you are delivering.

If the magazine does not fulfill the needs of the field, or does not deliver enough to the reader, no amount of skilled circulation and advertising effort will do the job. Furthermore, the cost structure is unimportant if there is something radically wrong with the other factors.

When your business outgrows you

By Robert H. Fowler

Let's say you started your magazine a decade or so ago, when you were young, full of energy and, maybe, very lucky. Your wife may have pitched in to help as secretary or circulation manager. Your first headquarters probably were in your basement or spare bedroom.

Those first few years were magic ones, at least in retrospect. You had an intense interest in the field your magazine serves but were blissfully ignorant about the publishing business. You rose early, worked through mealtimes and long past bedtime. Weekends too. You made do with second-hand office equipment and furniture.

Soon you outgrew your space and rented a small building. As you expanded, you hired friends and relatives to keep your own circulation records.

Only later did you learn that you overcame nine-to-one odds in reaching your third birthday. By then you had incorporated. You had a lawyer and accountant who knew no more about the magazine business than you. But you had the common sense to keep your overhead low and plow profits back into circulation growth. You added to your staff in a hit-or-miss way. By joining the Magazine Publishers Association and reading FOLIO you learned more and more about the magazine business, but even so you paid more attention to your magazine's field of interest than to the business of publishing.

Perhaps in time you spun off a second magazine, again successfully, and added new profit centers. You recruited a board of directors, wise people, all, but as ignorant about the magazine business as you had been in the beginning.

As the years rolled by, your sales increased, your staff grew and your reputation improved. And, alas, so did your notions of infallibility. Let's say your luck held, though. Your sales may have grown past five million or even 10 million dollars. What did it matter that your payroll and other overhead grew even faster, that you never made your enthusiastic profit projections because, as an entrepreneur, you couldn't say no to yourself or staff members when "targets of opportunity" popped up?

After all, you are a closely held corporation with no stockholders clamoring for dividends. Better to grow than pay income taxes. So you became cavalier about letting jobs out to bid, sloppy about legal agreements.

The first time a big New York company came a'courting, you were flattered but turned them down because you saw yourself as another Henry Luce or DeWitt Wallace.

The years grind on. Barnacles appear on the hull of your craft but you don't see them. You press on for growth. The first failure of a spin-off takes you by surprise. Your cash reserves stop growing. Sales remain strong, but maybe for the first time in years your company experiences a net loss.

What has happened? Well, you were a great bush pilot, very good at flying a Piper Cub at low altitudes by the seat of your pants. But without your realizing it, your business has developed into a jet plane. Not only do you lack the skills necessary to fly a 737 at 550 mph, most likely you are temperamentally unsuited to submit to the necessary routine. And, to carry the analogy a bit further, you may have a wonderful crew but they, too, probably need professional instruction to service this larger craft.

A pilot flying a Piper Cub can't get in much trouble as long as he keeps his gas tank filled and his windshield clean. The same man at the controls of a 737 is headed for disaster. He should either sell the plane or hire himself a competent pilot and crew and let them operate the craft.

Know your limits

Rare indeed is the man or woman who can switch in mid-life from an entrepreneurial to a managerial role. Although this is true in most businesses (the company Henry Ford built nearly collapsed before operations were turned over to professional administrators), it is especially true in the magazine business. The instinctive drive that turns an inspired idea into reality can develop that reality only to a certain point.

Possessors of this rare talent usually lack the patience for detail required for big business. Careful budgeting, tight controls, realistic projections, personnel policies: these only frustrate the true entrepreneur. But they are basic to proper management of a sound business.

So what do you do when, to put it bluntly, your business has outgrown you? One thing you should *not* do is thrash about desperately trying to hit a home run. You can destroy what you built up overnight.

If you are too young for retirement, you might replace yourself with a top-notch executive officer and give him full operational control. Get out of the cockpit and let him run things. Ask only that he not savage the people who helped you grow and that he keep you fully informed of what is going on.

There are problems with this course, however. Experienced, able managers are not all that easy to find. And they may cost more than you are able or willing to pay, or they may not live up to their resumes.

Also, you may find it impossible, psychologically, to turn over full control and refrain from meddling. In that case, your best bet is to find a compatible buyer for your company now while it has value. If you don't give a hang about your employees, are interested only in taking out as much money as you can, then you can pass the word of your availability and spend several hectic months of negotiation with some pretty sharp operators.

Most people who have created something out of nothing love that something very much and want to see it preserved and improved. Rather than turn their creations over to the hatchet men of a vast corporation, they will prefer a firm that understands or anyway appreciates the field of interest of the magazine, perhaps one that will want them to continue in some advisory connection while paying a fair price for the property.

We all have our pride. To a strong-willed entrepreneur, it might seem like a cop-out to relinquish control to a new CEO or to sell the magazine even to the kindliest of new owners. But the fact remains that your baby has grown into adolescence. And a wise father knows that this is the point where he has to let go if his child is to grow into strong adulthood.

Repositioning

By Karlene Lukovitz

Attempting to reposition a magazine —that is, changing it in order to maintain or improve its position within its current market, or shifting it into a different market—is probably the riskiest move a publisher can make.

Even if a magazine is failing, there is a lot to be lost in an attempt to reposition it, because every repositioning effort, successful or not, requires a major investment. One publisher who is a veteran of several repositioning efforts estimates that the cost usually ranges between half a million dollars and $5 million, but can go as high as $15 million if the magazine being repositioned is one that serves a very large market and has a circulation of several million.

There is even more to be lost in an attempt to reposition a successful magazine. In addition to the possibility of losing the repositioning investment itself, there is the very real possibility of losing the magazine's current readers and advertisers while failing to attract new ones.

Obviously, this would mean the extinction of the magazine, unless the publisher is in the rare situation of being able to afford (and willing to attempt) another repositioning effort— or can find a buyer for the magazine. (In either case, a second repositioning attempt tends to further confuse the reading public and the advertising community, at least initially, and is therefore even less likely to succeed than the first attempt.)

Yet, *Saturday Review, Metropolitan Home* (formerly *Apartment Life*), *Dun's Business Month* (formerly *Dun's Review*), *California* (formerly *New West*), and *Home* (formerly *Hudson Home*) are only a few of the more recent examples of magazines that have been repositioned.

Why reposition?

In light of the major risks inherent in repositioning why would any publisher even consider trying it?

The most obvious reason is that the magazine is in trouble, or is headed in that direction, and nothing short of a repositioning seems capable of turning it around.

Some publishers feel that attempting to reposition in such a circumstance is a serious mistake. "I would say that a good rule of thumb is 'Never make major changes in a magazine from a position in which it already has big problems,'" says Robert Potts, publisher of *Dun's Business Month*, "because if the magazine is dying, you don't have the momentum for successful change that you'd have had if you had repositioned it while it was still healthy. If you're going to reposition a dying magazine, you'd better have lots and lots of money and lots of time, too. And you'd better be right."

But the hard truth is that trouble *is* the motivating factor behind the majority of repositionings, according to several industry sources.

"A magazine can, of course, be changed from a position of strength, but the reality is that the idea of repositioning is more likely to come up *after* the magazine is already in trouble," says publishing consultant John Peter.

"If I bought a healthy property, I probably wouldn't reposition it," says Robert Weingarten, publisher of *Saturday Review*. "Tampering with a magazine that has found its audience is just too risky."

"In my opinion, the need to do something as drastic as a repositioning means that you somehow lost your way somewhere along the line— that you lost track of your market," says Alan Waxenberg, publisher of the recently repositioned *Sports Afield*.

Market changes

As Waxenberg's comment suggests, a magazine's failure to monitor and adjust to changes in the market it serves is very frequently the problem that eventually leads to the need for repositioning.

An extreme and classic example is the "old" pre-Helen Gurley Brown *Cosmopolitan*, which had become so out-of-sync with its market that everything about it but its name had to be changed in order for it to survive.

Some in the industry believe that many of the established women's service books that are now experiencing slumps in advertising and single-copy circulation would not be in that situation if they had been more aware of changes in the women's market and had repositioned accordingly several years ago.

"It seems to me that the downturn in many of the more established women's books may be due more to sociological changes than to a general economic downturn," says one publisher now in the midst of a repositioning.

"A publisher of one of those older women's books could have responded to the changes in the women's marketplace five years ago and turned his magazine into *Self* instead of waiting for someone else to come up with *Self*," he adds.

"The women's books have reduced themselves to commodities —they have no position at all," says the head of promotion for a major men's magazine. "They are sold by the pound and they're completely interchangeable."

According to John Peter, it is quite common for business magazines to shift positioning in reaction to changes in their markets. Because they tend to have exceptionally close links to their markets, they are quickly affected by and aware of such changes.

He cites as an example Cahners Publishing Company's *Electronic Business* which changed, in response to electronics industry trends, from an industry-wide publication to a management publication for original equipment manufacturers. "It's now the *Business Week* of the electronics industry," says Peter.

The former *Apartment Life*, now *Metropolitan Home*, is one example of a consumer magazine that repositioned while still successful in order to meet the changing needs of its audience, according to the magazine's editor, Dorothy Kalins.

Although *Apartment Life* was meeting or exceeding its 800,000 advertising rate base, and both its ad pages and ad revenue reached record highs in 1980, Kalins says she and publisher Harry Myers determined that major changes in the lifestyle of many of the magazine's readers necessitated a re-evaluation of its editorial thrust.

Apartment Life was launched in 1969 to meet the needs of the baby boom generation, and had already been changing to suit the needs of those readers, becoming more sophisticated as the 1970s progressed, she explains.

"Recently we realized that a growing segment of our readership had become even more committed to their careers, and very concerned about equity—about owning things and learning about tax shelters," Kalins says. "So we had a choice: We could try to serve the part of our constituency that still wanted do-it-yourself articles about how to make book shelves out of bricks and boards, or we could edit more directly to the movers and shakers in order to be their magazine for the eighties, as we had been for the seventies. We chose the latter direction."

The magazine's name was changed in recognition of the fact that, while some of its readers continue to live in apartments, many now live in houses, condominiums or townhouses, Kalins says.

As of the magazine's April issue, its physical appearance, as well as its name, was changed to reflect the more sophisticated editorial content: its paper stock has been upgraded (The Meredith Corporation is spending $1 million more annually on the paper), the binding method has been switched from saddle-stitch to perfect, and a more streamlined design is being used.

Although the changes were accompanied by a substantial decrease in the magazine's ad rate base (from 800,000 to 700,000), the combination of the superior four-color reproduction (allowed by the new paper stock) and the promise of reaching a more "upscale" audience more effectively (the advertising rates were lowered in tandem with the rate base) has apparently impressed agencies and advertisers a great deal. Ad pages for April were up by an astounding 69.5 percent, while pages for May, June and July were up by 12.9 percent, 15.4 percent and 32.7 percent, respectively.

At least one industry observer points out, however, that the real effects of a repositioning, in terms of audience demographics, cannot be proven for at least a year, since this is the minimum time it takes to get reasonably accurate syndicated research.

"*Apartment Life* was always a high-quality magazine, but it was caught in a circulation numbers game—its circulation had become inflated in competing for advertising to the point where it was losing money," he claims.

"What they did to correct this situation was utterly brilliant," he continues. "They said they were now going to keep those readers who spend the most money on their homes, and they lowered the rate base by saying they got rid of the 'bricks and boards' people. I'm not sure even *they* know quite how brilliant it is to finesse a rate base roll back and manage to increase advertising at the same time the way they did."

Bewildering the audience
A magazine can also find itself in need of repositioning if it changed at a time when its audience's needs and wants had *not* changed.

A prime example of a magazine that found itself in this type of self-created predicament is *Saturday Review*. *SR* successfully expanded from being a literary review to covering the whole spectrum of arts—a logical and appropriate expansion because it suited the interests of the magazine's audience. But subsequent attempts to expand the magazine's subject matter even further—to travel, politics, current affairs and other subjects that its readers had not bargained for—threw *SR* into a tailspin.

"It's very dangerous to take a successful magazine and walk away from its franchise in an attempt to make it even more successful, because the chances are that you're going to lose that franchise in the process," says Weingarten, who purchased *SR* last year and immediately set about restoring the magazine to its former niche by re-infusing it with articles about events and people in the arts, and exorcising all else. "That's exactly what happened to *Saturday Review*, over a period of many years and several owners."

New opportunity a factor
But as is often true of repositionings, Weingarten saw the effort not only as a way to salvage a magazine in trouble, but also as a way to tap a new market.

"We felt the magazine had moved away from culture at the very same time the country itself was moving very much more in the direction of culture," says Weingarten. "The Harris study of attitudes about the arts in this country had shown decisively that many, many more Americans are participating in cultural events and our own studies indicated that attendance of events in each cultural area is up significantly."

Weingarten had considered starting a new magazine to fill the gap he perceived in the cultural publications, but decided that the credibility demanded by readers of such publications would be too difficult to build from scratch. "*Saturday Review* already had the established name and credibility, so by buying it and once again making it a 'cultural umbrella'—a monthly round-up of the arts—we felt we could win back the old readership while attracting the rapidly-growing new segment of the market."

Sports Afield is another example of a magazine repositioned as a result of a combination of trouble and opportunity, according to publisher Alan Waxenberg.

Waxenberg freely acknowledges that *Sports Afield*, by 1977, had become a victim of the circulation numbers game. "We had a circulation of 1.5 million and were constantly trying to attract a larger and larger number of readers, in a specialized field, for the sake of advertising," he says. "The magazine was being sold at reduced prices to maintain that overblown circulation, which, to understate the case, is not highly profitable," he adds.

Moreover, Waxenberg says *Sports Afield*'s editorial content "had become stodgy and tired, and it was hard to distinguish us from any other magazine in the market."

Although one might assume that these problems

alone should be enough to motivate a repositioning, Waxenberg says it was a new market opportunity that provided the needed opening for such a move.

"There was an explosion taking place, with more and more people becoming interested in conservation and in the whole panorama of outdoor living, recreation and activities," he says. "So, we decided to drop out of the numbers race and produce a high-quality magazine aimed at this special, new segment of the market, rather than carry on with a concentration on the traditional 'outdoor magazine' sports—hunting and fishing."

Since the repositioning began, the magazine's newsstand sales have zoomed from 70,000 to 135,000 (at the same time the cover price has been raised from 70 cents to $1.50), its total circulation has been reduced to 500,000 by the elimination of cut-rate subscriptions, and its advertising picture is better than ever (ad revenue for 1980 was up approximately 28 percent, and pages were up 8 percent).

Leaving a no-growth market

The right opportunity to reposition can also extricate a magazine from a no-growth market or from a no-growth position in a particular market.

When the Litton Industries Publishing Group bought the Hudson Publishing Company in 1977, Hudson was publishing *Hudson Home Magazine* in the form of four special interest publications (*Custom Homes, Home Improvements,* and *Kitchens, Baths & Family Rooms,* each published twice a year, and *Building and Remodeling,* published six times a year).

Last February, the magazine was repositioned out of the specials field, becoming one monthly shelter magazine with a completely different design than it had as a four-piece special interest magazine. And, as of the July issue, it has a simpler name: *Home.*

"*Hudson Home* was 26 years old when Litton bought it, and it had been making and losing money on and off for years," says Thomas Wolf, publisher of *Home.* "At the time of the purchase, it was marginally profitable, but there was no potential for growth in the specials field; the field was and is stagnant. For example, the whole specials field had a total of about $111 million in revenue for 1980, while the shelter field had revenue of about $311 million.

"We saw a chance to fill a new niche in the shelter market when I studied the *Hall Reports* on the other shelter books. I found that those magazines devote more than 70 percent of their editorial content, on average, to home topics other than the physical home, such as pets, recipes, and crafts," he explains. "So, in repositioning *Hudson Home,* we decided to stick strictly to the physical home: the frame, walls, floors—anything that would be left if a family had just moved out."

Since the repositioned magazine came out in February, its total paid circulation has increased to 500,000, as compared with the specials' average monthly total of 85,000, and advertising is steadily on the upswing (when the specials were being published, 30 ad pages was average for an October issue; this year, the October issue had more than double that number).

(It should be noted that Thompson International, which purchased Litton Industries, has announced plans to sell *Home* because the company wants to concentrate on business, rather than consumer magazines.)

Dun's Review, now *Dun's Business Month,* which has been firmly entrenched in fourth position in the business magazine market for years, decided recently to change its editorial format in an effort to pull out of that position.

"Although we had already completely revamped and revitalized *Dun's Review* just a few years ago, we were still the fourth magazine in the field and some of the others have the advantage of a greater publication frequency," says publisher Robert Potts. "So we decided that instead of continuing along as a typical monthly, a fine editorial product with no great sense of urgency about it, we'd find a new way to serve our readers.

"A readership study clearly showed a need among corporate business people for a publication that capsulized news, enabling them to keep up with the overwhelming amount of information that comes their way," he continues. "We decided to do just that—report on and briefly analyze news instead of doing long articles that are time-consuming to read. We become the 'catcher's mitt' for those businessmen—we're behind them catching information that they might otherwise have missed."

Making the decision

Clearly, there are as many reasons for repositioning as there are reasons why a magazine is in trouble or not reaching its full potential.

"A magazine should be repositioned whenever a publisher feels it's not achieving the goals he set for it," says Charles Mandel, publisher of *Science Digest,* which was repositioned after the appearance of many slick new magazines in the science field. "Obviously, if you're not selling enough copies of the magazine, or you're not selling enough advertising, or both, something basic is wrong and should be corrected."

Waxenberg of *Sports Afield* agrees that it's not difficult to know that repositioning should be considered when standard yardsticks of a magazine's health are indicating poor performance. "A reduction in profit, a circulation slowdown, a loss of vitality at the newsstand, a cut in advertising, a cutback in mail from readers —all of these are warning signs, and the sooner you sense them, the better the chances that you can do something about it."

But Waxenberg and several others interviewed acknowledge that it is not always possible to save a magazine, or even improve it, by repositioning—and in such cases it would obviously be a big waste of money to even attempt a repositioning.

A publisher's chances of making the right decision on whether or not to attempt to reposition—and on how to do it, if a repositioning seems feasible—are greatly improved by research and testing, according to most people interviewed.

"I know of a few publishers who have taken the seat-of-the-pants approach, blindly embarking on a repositioning without doing research— but I know of *very* few who have succeeded that way," says a publisher who has repositioned several magazines.

"No one in his right mind would consider redirecting a magazine without doing *considerable* research," says Wolf of *Home* magazine, "because you could easily go out of business in one or two wrong moves."

Many interviewed agreed that audience-related research should take precedence over advertising concerns, although the implications of a repositioning for advertising must eventually be dealt with.

"A lot of people look at repositioning as an advertising marketing proposition, and it is, of course," says Weingarten. "But the basics of repositioning must start with the editorial content—the magazine must be written for and designed to attract a certain kind of audience. It all starts with the product and the real need, or lack of need, for a repositioning from the point of view of the *reader*."

"Some people try to do it backwards," he continues. "They try to position from the basis of the *advertiser's* viewpoint—but you can't just ask yourself which advertising category you'd like to get and design a magazine to serve that. It doesn't work, because a publication has to serve an *audience* before it can serve an advertiser."

"Today, the real battle is readership, and most people realize that now," agrees John Peter. "It's easy to send people a magazine, but it's tough to get them to read it—and if they don't read it no advertiser wants it, either."

"It's terribly important to understand the needs of your market. If you don't service a need or fill a void for your readers, you'll lose them, and then you'll lose your advertisers, too," says Waxenberg. "You've got to find out if there is a need for change, and if there *is*, you've got to ask yourself and your readers, '*Why* isn't this magazine better than it is? What could be done to *make* it better?' "

Current readers not always a priority

Several publishers noted, however, that before readers' reactions are solicited, it is important to decide *which* readers will be of most importance to the repositioned magazine: current readers or potential readers?

"When you're planning to change from a small circulation magazine to a much larger circulation magazine, you don't have to worry so much about existing readers because they will represent only a small portion of your overall readership," says Wolf. "In fact, if you're increasing your circulation considerably, you can't *afford* to direct *too* much of your time and energy, or too much of the magazine's content, to the old readership. The thoughts and wants of the much larger *new* part of your readership are of primary importance."

Most magazines, however, cannot afford to lose too many of their current readers immediately, even if a whole new audience is envisioned as the eventual goal of the repositioning. And some magazines, such as *Dun's Business Month*, which as a non-paid circulation magazine is already distributed to its optimum audience, would like to lose as few readers as possible.

Therefore, most publishers interviewed said that after weighing the importance of current and potential readers in the overall circulation goals of the magazine, they planned research and testing for both groups, but invested significantly more time and money in the more important group of readers.

Focus groups recommended

Some publishers cite focus groups as being one of the best ways to get insight into how current and potential readers of a magazine feel about it and how, if at all, they feel it should be changed.

"When it comes to repositioning, most smart magazine publishers conduct focus groups as a major part of their research effort—or, if they can afford it, they have one of the big research firms conduct personal interviews with readers," says Potts. These methods are useful, he says, because they elicit readers' needs, likes and dislikes in a setting that allows for follow-up with more probing questions.

In fact, Potts points out, he has found that films of focus group sessions can also be useful tools for advertising sales calls once the repositioning reaches that stage. "We're actually showing agencies a 15-minute film of the

spontaneous discussions we had with businessmen about what they need," he says. "These films show interplay between our claims and aims and the needs of readers as they themselves express those needs."

Potts and others also listed several other types of methods that can be used alone or in conjunction to obtain feedback. These include mail questionnaires and telephone interviews.

Wolf of *Home* magazine points out that much of the reader attitude research and other research needed before embarking on a repositioning can be done by magazine staff members, if the magazine cannot afford professional outside help.

For example, for quite some time, *Home* staff members sent out 2,000 questionnaires per month and tabulated the responses in order to obtain reader feedback for editorial purposes.

In addition to obtaining readers' reactions to a magazine, a publisher considering a repositioning should research how the planned editorial objectives of the magazine relate to trends in the general population, according to Wolf.

"You can learn a great deal about where your magazine should be going by comparing your editorial objectives to information on trends in the U.S. population. Such information is available from major research firms such as Yankelovich, Skelly and White and from government statistics," he says. "If a research piece tells you that 28 million people will be taking up hang gliding over the next four years, then you certainly know you're on the right track if you're repositioning your magazine to cater to hang gliders.

"In the case of *Home*, we are a special interest magazine, but that interest is so broadly based that we can get very useful statistics for our research from the Department of Commerce," he adds. "I'm sure that many other magazines would benefit from getting existing statistics from the government, or from associations serving the same interest groups as their magazines."

A good example of how such statistics can be used is that of *Health* magazine (formerly *Family Health*) which used government data on the health and medical fields in repositioning.

Family Health first began considering a repositioning when syndicated research indicated that the median age of its audience was decreasing, according to Milt Lieberman, a consultant who helped position the magazine.

An examination of available government statistics on health provided the insight for understanding the change in the audience age, Lieberman explains. "The statistics showed that the Federal Government, which until a few years ago had allocated the lion's share of health funds to curative projects, had shifted to the point where it now spends the great majority of these funds on preventative projects, including education and research. It was clear that consciousness of the importance of prevention was growing rapidly, and that people were concerned at younger and younger ages about taking care of themselves."

Understanding this trend, Lieberman says, *Family Health* changed its editorial focus from a stress on the curative to a stress on "a more positive, preventative approach to health." In addition, the magazine changed content by shifting away from telling parents how to take care of their children to providing articles for every member of the more health-conscious modern American family.

Circulation testing

Another area in which a good deal of research should be done when considering repositioning is circulation, according to those interviewed.

"You've got to do a *lot* of testing in circulation—you cannot mail out an untested subscription effort and expect any kind of reasonable response," says Wolf. "As far as circulation research goes, time is as important as money—you've got to have time to evaluate a subscription test after you do it—which means you need at least six months."

Any magazine that expects a significant portion of its circulation to come from single-copy sales should be ready to do newsstand tests, according to several publishers.

Young Miss, which has recently been repositioned (via a more sophisticated design and articles geared to somewhat older teens) from a subscription magazine read by 11- to 13-year-olds to a subscription and newsstand magazine read by teenagers aged 12 to 17, conducted a major newsstand test, with a special issue, before committing to the repositioning.

"We prepared a test issue in March to test the magazine on the newsstand," says Milton Franks, the magazine's publisher. "We felt that if the magazine sold on the newsstand, it would not only strengthen our belief that a need existed for it in the marketplace, but would also allow us to cut distribution costs by gradually shifting much more toward single-copy sales.

"When the results came back, showing a 60 percent sale in the nine major cities in which we tested, we really knew we had something," he says. "It's highly unusual for a magazine to sell that well its first time out on the newsstand."

Some publishers also advocate doing cover tests as part of repositioning research, particularly if the magazine is to be heavily dependent on single-copy sales. The "easiest and cheapest" way to test covers, according to Wolf, is to employ companies that measure galvanic skin response tests. "But," he adds, "the problem with those is that they only measure *reaction*—you can never be totally sure whether the viewer's reaction to the cover was negative or positive."

Selling the repositioning

Once the decision to reposition has been made, and the types of changes that should be made have been worked out, the next major problem the publisher faces is how to introduce the repositioning to current and potential readers and advertisers.

"The two big bottom lines for any magazine are, of course, its reader franchise and its advertiser franchise," says Weingarten of *Saturday Review*. "It's a very, very delicate thing to try and change the magazine and yet retain those franchises —sometimes it's easier to just start a new magazine."

Readers: hold their hands, or hit 'em?

As has already been pointed out, not all publishers *want* to hold on to all current readers when a magazine is being repositioned. It is an extremely rare publisher, however, who can afford to lose most of his magazine's current readers in a short period of time, jeopardizing the magazine's rate base and circulation revenues.

"Let's face it—you can't come up with an entirely new set of readers in a period of a few months, even if you change the whole magazine," says one publisher.

Schools of thought on how to handle current readers so as not to lose too many of them during a repositioning range from kid glove treatment to "shock" treatment.

New West's handling of its readers while in the process of becoming *California* is an example of the kid glove treatment.

"*New West* had been evolving naturally toward becoming *California* —it was really for and about California for several years before we bought it," says Ted Siff, president of New West Communications Corporation. "So we've intentionally been making changes in an evolutionary way."

"The purchase, which occurred in August 1980, was mentioned in the editor's column in one early issue," reports editor William Broyles, "but that was about it." Also, the magazine's former Northern and Southern California editions were abandoned early on in favor of a single edition.

Four months later, the words "The Magazine of California" were added above the *New West* title, in preparation for the final change to *California*, which wasn't made until last month. "We figured the worst thing we could do was to change the name immediately and start talking about how the magazine is new and how great it is, before any real changes had been made," says Broyles. "Our readers would've known that the changes were only cosmetic. A supposedly transformed magazine has to speak for itself."

The magazine's redesign, although total, has also been introduced in stages. The last major design changes were introduced, along with the new title, in the October issue in a "final push," says Broyles. "But we've protected ourselves from losing our current readers by giving them a lot of notice of the changes taking place in October," notes Siff. "We sent mailings to them in August and September." Copies of the October issue also contained cards explaining the name change and offering readers the opportunity to renew, he adds.

In contrast, Weingarten completely changed *Saturday Review*'s design, as well as its editorial content, within four weeks of purchasing it.

"We bought *SR* at the end of May, and as of the July issue, it was a new magazine," Weingarten says. "I think that if you have to reposition and you really believe the position you are moving to is valuable, you do it in one shot. You hit your readers with it. It'll take three or four months for them to adjust, but then it's over with. If you attempt to change gradually, you have a bastardized product during the interim period—it's neither the old publication nor the new one. You might just turn *everyone* off that way—your old readers *and* your potential new readers."

Though *SR* did little to prepare readers for the sudden transformation of the magazine, once the move had been made, it was explained to them in the pages of the magazine itself.

Potts, of *Dun's Business Month*, believes there is no one correct approach to readers. "It depends on the magazine," he says. "In a case like ours, when you're with fast-moving businessmen, you've got to tell them what you're doing to the magazine in a concise quick way—and bang!— they either immediately like or hate what you're doing." To reach its current readers, *Dun's* used eye-catching, to-the-point ads in the other major business publications, he says.

"But," Potts continues, "I suppose that if you're the publisher of one of the established shelter magazines and you're repositioning, you'd have to use a much less abrupt and more reassuring approach to your current readers. After all, members of the quilting bee society are quite a different breed than businessmen. If you hit them over the head suddenly with major changes in their magazine, you're likely to spook some of them."

Whether the actual changes are made rapidly or gradually, however, Potts contends that proper promotion of such changes is always a must.

"In my opinion, the biggest mistake anyone can make in repositioning—and it is a mistake made frequently—is not to do enough promotion," he says. "A lot of publishers just go ahead and bring out a repositioned magazine as a fait accompli. If you give the reader something new all of a sudden, particularly if it has a new name, he's going to be very confused and you'll probably lose him.

"You've got to do promotion both before and after the actual changes are made, to let the reader know that it *is* still his magazine, but it's been changed, improved," he continues. "You have got to make sure he understands that. With effective pre-promotion, the reader will actually be looking *forward* to the change, anticipating it with enthusiasm."

Potts says pre-selling of a repositioning to readers can be done in many ways, including space advertising in other publications the readers are likely to see, direct mail efforts, and efforts in the magazine itself. The last method, which can include house ads and explanations in the editor's or publisher's column, is one of the most effective and least expensive, Potts says.

Selling the advertisers/agencies

No one interviewed advocated springing repositioning on agencies and advertisers after the fact.

"Your agencies are going to get very upset if you make your repositioning a big surprise, and they have a right to be," says Potts. "After all, they've put your magazine on their schedules and all of a sudden it's a different magazine."

Potts asserts that promotion before, during and after the repositioning is as important in dealing with advertisers and agencies as in dealing with readers. "In addition to preparing advertisers and making them look forward to the changes, promotion can help you benefit from the curiosity value of a repositioned magazine," he adds. "As with the first issue of a new magazine, advertising agencies know that everyone will be looking at the first issue of your repositioned magazine, and some will buy it for that reason."

Several people did recommend, however, that agencies and advertisers not be made aware of an upcoming repositioning until all of the problems involved in the repositioning have been thought out and solid plans for proceeding have been drawn up.

Kalins of *Metropolitan Home* says even the magazine's advertising sales staff was kept unaware of the planned repositioning until three months before the major changes were introduced in the April issue.

"On December 8, the day we closed the February issue, we called everyone on the staff together and showed them what we were going to do with the magazine," she says. "At the same time, we broke the news to the advertising community through *The New York Times,* inserts in *Advertising Age,* brochures, and so forth.

"We kept it quiet until then because, if word had leaked, we would've lost our February ad business. Our salespeople would have been confused about what to do, and the advertisers would have been unsure about what was going to happen to the magazine," Kalins explains.

"But after all the decisions had been made, we had a story of such strength, our salespeople were extremely excited and ready to go out immediately and sell it to the advertisers."

Though a few magazines, such as *Metropolitan Home,* report that their repositioning efforts were accepted almost immediately by agencies and advertisers, most publishers say that the repositionings of their magazines were followed by a period of advertising limbo in which neither current nor potential advertisers seemed willing to accept or reject the changed product.

"In almost all cases, repositioning is like introducing a new magazine," says Waxenberg. "And, as with a new magazine, there is an investment period that must be expected. It takes time for people to understand what you're doing."

"You must be prepared for a 'wait and see' attitude on the part of current advertisers, and even more on the part of potential advertisers," says Wolf. "In budgeting, you must be aware that some of the months after a repositioning will be softer in advertising than you'd hoped."

"The biggest problem in dealing with agencies is that they tend to wait until someone else has made a commitment—no one wants to be the first," says Weingarten. "There's a real time problem when you first reposition, because you're in Never-Never Land," he adds. "Your old advertisers know it's not the same magazine *they* liked, and you're coming in and saying, 'Well, *I* didn't like it, but here, advertise in this new product.' The potential advertisers don't know what to expect, either."

"When you really think about it, a radical change in the magazine is an insult to your long-time advertisers and their agencies, unless the repositioning was caused by a sudden change in the market, which is obviously beyond your control," says one publishing executive who doesn't care to be identified. "What you're really saying is, 'Hey —we've been publishing a bad or just so-so magazine for the past two or 10 or 20 years, and now we're going to publish a good one.' Or, in some cases, what you're really saying is, 'We used to have a lousy audience, but now we're going to get a good one.' Either way, you're insulting the intelligence of your advertisers and agencies. After all, *they* obviously liked the magazine, and its audience, as it was, and now you're telling them that they were wrong. Up to this point, of course, you've been telling them they were *right.*"

Moreover, there is a long period after a repositioning during which there are no hard data to demonstrate to current or potential advertising accounts that the repositioning has in fact produced the intended results. "You've got to wait six months to get ABC figures, and at least a full year to get syndicated audience research that means anything," says Waxenberg of *Sports Afield.*

"Let's say you get your spring MRI analysis, and then you reposition the magazine in July," says Weingarten. "All you have to show to agencies are those old, invalid spring statistics. You may feel sure that certain things will happen to the audience as a result of the changes, but you can't *prove* it with statistics at this point—it's really only a guess.

"We knew, for example, that our passalong readership would be greater as a result of changing *Saturday Review*'s publishing frequency from twice monthly to monthly," he says. "But we didn't have the statistics to prove it."

These publishers said that the only way to deal with the initial post-repositioning hesitancy of agencies and advertisers is to make as many sales calls as possible and truthfully but forcefully convey what the goals behind the repositioning are and why you feel those goals will be achieved.

"It comes down to being a sales proposition," says Weingarten. "You say, 'We have reason to believe that this will happen, because this is what we did with the magazine.' Some will believe it and understand it and some won't.

"By definition, you become less important to some advertising categories and more important to others when you reposition," he stresses. "Before you reposition, it is *very* important to analyze who your advertisers are going to be and how big they are, and then measure this against the advertising *losses* you're likely to sustain so you'll know where you're headed."

Publishers can sometimes deal with even a rapid change in a market by repositioning their magazines. But what can a publisher do if a magazine's market all but disappears overnight?

That was the nightmarish situation in which TL Enterprises, Inc. found itself in 1973, when the advertising market of its magazine, *Trailer Life,* was suddenly devastated by the Arab oil embargo against the United States.

"We call the day the embargo hit 'Black Monday' around here," says Rick Rouse, president of TL Enterprises. "Manufacturers and dealers of recreational vehicles and suppliers of related products were all hit so hard so fast that there was more than a 70 percent drop in advertising business overnight. Prior to the embargo, *Trailer Life* had been one of the top magazines in the entire country in ad lineage; we were carrying 220 pages an issue. Today, the magazine's biggest advertising issue carries 90 ad pages, although the market is coming back, slowly."

Trailer Life's pre- and post-embargo ad page figures tell the whole story: The magazine carried 2,023 ad pages in 1973 but was down to 1,134 in 1974.

It was clear to Rick Rouse, his brother Denis, who is publisher, and his father, Arthur, who is chairman of the board, that the family's publishing business might not survive unless something major was done. But it was equally clear that the recreational vehicle, or RV, market crisis could not be successfully circumvented by changing *Trailer Life* in an attempt to reposition it. So instead, the Rouses decided to reposition the *company* by expanding and diversifying.

And diversify they did, although not radically at first. The expansion began with the launching of *Rider*, a magazine about motorcycle touring. "We saw that there was a major influx of people into the touring part of the motorcycle market, and that the oil embargo was having the opposite effect on motorcycles as it was on trailers—more people were buying motorcycles because of the cycles' fuel efficiency," Denis explains.

TL started and purchased several more recreational vehicle magazines throughout the early and mid-1970s, and also purchased an RV club (which then had 5,000 members and now has 400,000).

During an ocean cruise for club members, the Rouses saw a market opening that led them to begin a publication quite unlike their others. "There were no publications on the ship such as the ones that are on airplanes," says Denis. "So we decided to start a publication for the Princess Cruises company which we called *Embark.*"

TL Enterprises now publishes magazines for six different cruise lines. The magazines have a total readership of more than 1.4 million, and are expected to bring in ad revenue of $1 million in 1982.

Most recently, TL Enterprises purchased Leisureguides, Inc., which publishes city guidebooks for distribution in hotels in major cities. The Rouses are now concentrating on adding three more major cities to the large list of those already served by the magazines. The hotel and cruise publications are marketed nationally, for ad sales purposes, as the Leisureguides network.

"With the leisure group magazines, we finally went beyond special interest advertising and got into mass marketing," says Denis. "It was a tough transition, going from marketing to people in the industry that we were familiar with to huge liquor and jewelry companies, but we've done it successfully. We're not a little family business anymore."

This is something of an understatement. TL Enterprises has been transformed, in 10 years, from a one-publication company with annual revenues of about $6 million to one that publishes 18 magazines and will achieve revenues of $20 million this year.

Clearly, TL Enterprises is a good example of how a company can be successfully repositioned in a situation in which many publishers would have simply folded.

Saving your magazine
from a fate worse than apathy

By Kent McKamy

It's my observation that most magazine publishers are unaware of the value of a continuing public relations program. This is regrettable, because for exactly the same reasons that most magazines take time to promote themselves at their launching, they should sustain their public relations activities as they grow. If they do not, they may not prosper and grow as fast as they'd like—and they may not prosper and grow at all.

This is not to say that an active public relations program will spell the difference between success and failure. It won't. But it can greatly enhance the possibility of success in some very tangible ways. A strong, imaginative public relations program, at the very least, can lend substantial support to your sales promotion and subscriber promotion efforts.

From my experience as editor of a national magazine, as well as a professional public relations counselor, I know that a good public relations program can deliver the following results:

• *Make your magazine stand out.* Some publishers believe that readers and advertisers easily perceive the differences between their magazine and all its competitors. Sadly, they don't. Adroit publicity and other promotion efforts can hammer home the differences.

• *Make more recipients readers.* Whether a person pays for it or receives it free, the person who receives your magazine is not automatically a reader. When the individual learns from other sources he or she respects that yours is an interesting or useful or vital or amusing or important magazine to read, the person's much more likely to become—and stay—a steady reader. Moreover, you can win back readers whose interest has begun to wane.

• *Convince more advertisers to advertise.* Audience, reach and responsiveness are reasons advertisers use the magazines they do. It's no secret, however, that they advertise in the magazines they think they should be in. Public relations can help communicate the importance or significance or even snob appeal of your magazine—and create the subtle impression that it cannot be ignored.

• *Attract better personnel.* Good people are attracted to winners and repelled by losers. Public relations can communicate the fact that your magazine is the best in the field to work for.

• *Attract strong contributors.* The best writers, photographers, designers, illustrators, researchers and other freelancers want to work for the best magazines. Imaginative public relations efforts can make sure your strengths are recognized.

• *Attract new readers.* Whether your magazine is paid or controlled circulation, you may be missing a whole army of readers who simply don't know about your magazine, or who don't realize how useful it could be to them.

• *Improve stature of your magazine and its personnel.* In many ways, some subtle and some overt, a magazine creates an impression—slick, sleazy, overdone, well-researched, crisply written, irreverent, whatever. Public relations activities that recognize the problems and identify your strengths can help overcome negative impressions and reinforce positive ones.

• *Increase importance of publishing house.* Whether for purposes of merger or acquisition, increases in the stock price, the ability to attract better people or any other corporate objective, a publishing company's reputation is invaluable. It is often subject to the shifting winds of public opinion.

These are some of the specific objectives that can be attained with a public relations program that is well-conceived, well-planned and well-executed. These are the goals I suggest publishers consider when they sit down to map out the themes and approaches for an effective publicity campaign. (Although many public relations achievements are dependent on good publicity, publicity and public relations are not interchangeable terms. Public relations is a broader term, embodying publicity and a host of other efforts.)

Before delving into the steps you might follow in putting a public relations campaign together, let me first mention a problem peculiar to magazine publishers, and an opportunity that is unique.

The problem is that magazines are among the few commodities in the world that must be sold twice. They must be sold to advertisers and to readers. Typically, quite different programs are used. Public relations can work to achieve both goals simultaneously—assuming, of course, that your product is genuinely useful to both "markets."

The unique opportunity is that magazine publishers are among the few businesspeople who are perpetually developing new products. The very fact that each issue of your magazine is new, different from the last issue, offers unique promotion possibilities.

One caution: Magazine promotion does not depend for its long-term success on the flamboyant, the notorious or the startling. It depends more on the attention to the day-to-day details that make any effort a success.

There are seven basic steps to public relations programming for publishers.

Set Objectives

Given the several goals public relations can help you accomplish, determine which are the most important and will have priority in your PR efforts. For example, you may want to increase readership among a certain class of readers. Or attract a certain kind of advertiser. You may want to accomplish both, and you may want to build your magazine's reputation for editorial innovation at the same time. Level with your inside (or outside) public relations person, and be as specific as possible. Merely saying, "I'd like to get the magazine's name in the paper as often as possible" isn't very helpful. Your PR person may do it, but to what end?

Determine a Promotion Theme

Having once edited a business magazine that was competitive with *Forbes*, I noted with envy and admiration the promotion theme *Forbes* has used effectively for years: "Do you know an important man in business who does not read *Forbes?*" It's a beautiful embodiment of what the magazine is all about, and it has appeal to readers (and, more important, potential subscribers) and to advertisers. Just look at all the things *Forbes* is saying in those 12 succinct words.

A promotion theme is more than a slogan, of course. But if you can capsule your theme in a few well chosen words that will appeal to both readers and advertisers, you will find it much easier to separate appropriate promotion ideas from inappropriate ones.

Once you have a theme, stick to it and be patient. It takes a long time to identify a feeling or a characteristic for a magazine.

A good promotion theme can sometimes lead to a good editorial idea. Suppose, for example, your theme was "The magazine that talks to leaders." That communicates to the readers' interest and to the advertisers' impression of the magazine. As a follow-up, your editor might schedule an ongoing series of interviews with the leading thinkers or doers in your field.

Identify Promotion Opportunities

The opportunities to promote editorial material each month are almost limitless. Newsworthy or innovative articles are natural promotion fare.

You can also promote circulation innovations, such as new delivery methods, faster servicing of address changes, faster handling of inquiries. You can promote cover changes . . . new contributors . . . new service departments . . . new personnel . . . circulation increases . . .

Where To Send Your Publicity Releases: A Checklist of Sources

This guide can be used to evaluate the most effective outlets for publicity material on an article, a research report, a speech by your editor or any of the myriad subjects available to you for promotion.

Local newspapers	Never overlook promotion in your own backyard. Helps attract good employees. Local editor may file your story on state or national wire service.
Major metropolitan newspapers	Read by reader and advertising prospects. Builds your stature through "third party" endorsement of your material.
Wire services	A story on AP, UPI or Reuters can mean nationwide, perhaps overseas coverage. Check paid wire services like PR Newswire.
News, feature services and syndicates	There are hundreds of news services, feature syndicates and foreign news services.
Columnists	Promoting to columnists who cover subjects your promotion material deals with (pollution, politics, advertising, finance, human interest, etc.).
Federal legislators	Copies of your promotions that reach legislators dealing with the subject of the material you're pro-

moting often travel far. Mentions in the *Congressional Record* are worthwhile for openers, but mentions of your magazine or article or reputation by these legislators in speeches or even conversation can carry a lot of weight.

State and local legislators	Publicity releases should always go to state senators and representatives, local mayors, selectmen, councilmen and officials, especially those politicos whose area of concern touches the subject matter of the material you're promoting.
Public speakers	Many businesspeople, professors, government officials, consultants and other "professional" speakers hunger for research or background material. The major source for speakers is *Encyclopedia of Meeting & Convention Speakers* (available from American Society of Association Executives, 2000 K St., N.W., Washington, D.C. 20006).
Consultants	Consultants abound in every field, and are frequent speakers, as well as writers. *Who's Who in Consulting*, published by Cornell University, Ithaca, N.Y., lists thousands.
Noncompetitive magazines	If you publish *Leaf Mulcher's Monthly* it's a fair bet that *Compost Quarterly* won't print your publicity

demographic or geographic regions ... new columnists ... changes in paper, magazine size, type ... new statistical studies in your field ... even letters to the editor from prominent people. However, what you choose to promote and the way you promote it must be consistent with your overall theme and objective.

Determine Frequency

How often do you want promotions going out? Every week? Every month? Every quarter?

It's not enough to say you'll issue news releases when there are news breaks. By scheduling frequency, you'll be able to maintain a consistent program and still schedule special promotions when the opportunity presents itself.

About the only guide to keep in mind is this: Too many releases, too often, can give the media a tin ear toward your magazine. Too few, however, too far apart, are not likely to work well for you either.

Fix a Promotion Budget

You can achieve a regular monthly promotion, made up of a series of press releases each month, for as little as $7,000 to $10,000 a year, and even less if your promotional plans called for less work. Or you could spend as much as $500,000 a year, if you wanted to schedule a motion picture, some television appearances and heavy printing of four-color brochures as part of your public relations program.

The best starting place, however, is with your objectives. Determine what you want to do, and what it is worth to you to accomplish it.

Assign a Coordinator

Promotion plans are frequently derailed because there isn't one person in the company who is responsible for coordinating and approving promotion activities. Or, equally bad, one person is appointed, but he or she is usually impossible to find for a decision.

Especially if you are hiring an outside public relations firm to handle your promotion work, assign an inside

	releases. But many other magazines may, particularly the news magazines, if the subject you are promoting is of sufficient interest to the general population.
Newsletters	Like consultants, there are thousands of newsletters around these days. They're well read, in the main, and seek new material on which they can comment. List of newsletters by category is available from *Newsletter on Newsletters*, 370 Lexington Ave., New York, N.Y. 10017. Ask for *Standard Directory of Newsletters*.
Authors	Freelancers who write articles and books in the area with which your promotion deals should receive the publicity.
Publishing, journalism magazines	These are your trade journals, and they should receive your publicity as a matter of course.
Local, regional, state organizations	Publicity sent to the president of the local Kiwanis Club or the state cancer fund could result in an invitation to you or your editor or your sales director to address the organization.
National organizations, associations	Send publicity material to organizations or associations in or close to your field of publishing.
Educational institutions	Releases sent to appropriate departments or people in universities, colleges, junior and community colleges, and high schools (elementary schools, too, if your subject is appropriate) can create classroom mentions, mentions in research papers, citations in speeches—and perhaps invitations to your staff to lecture.
Radio and television	The obvious first choice is to blanket local network and radio and TV news departments. Consider releasing 30-second to 2-minute tapes for radio stations; 30- to 90-second film clips (with removable sound strip and script) for TV stations. But also consider talk or interview show hosts, news commentators and syndicated "columnists of the air." Public or educational television is most important; frequently overlooked, these outlets can be very helpful.
Foreign news media	Virtually every major foreign newspaper and a few foreign magazines have news bureaus in New York City. This is a handy outlet when your subject has international import.

coordinator who has sufficient stature to give the agency representatives access to the editorial, sales, circulation, business and company personnel with whom he or she will be talking to each month to develop specific promotional ideas and approaches.

Then, make sure the coordinator is empowered to make a decision when called upon. Sometimes hot ideas cool while one waits for the return of the head person.

Develop Yardsticks

What do you consider a successful effort? Having your editor on one late night talk show a year? Hitting the UPI feature wire twice a month? Being featured in a *Wall Street Journal* article?

And how do you equate these kinds of results with progress toward the objectives you set in the beginning?

Frankly, it's not terribly difficult getting a client's name in the paper. Getting it in the right paper with the right kind of message can be.

By far the most popular form of public relations is the press release. It's effective, quick and relatively inexpensive. It can be short or long, depending on what you are promoting.

However, there are many other techniques open to you and you should consider them all in putting an effective program together.

Press releases aside, there are several other mailed formats that can be effective. You might issue a press newsletter a week prior to each issue's publication, summarizing the high points (or the newsworthy points) of each of your editorial features. If a story is particularly hot, consider sending long night letters or Western Union's Mailgrams to key media. You could send printed, but personalized, letters to media you want to reach, as well as to key advertisers and agencies, publicizing a new development or a change you want them to know about quickly and personally. You could send along preprints or reprints of newsworthy or interesting articles; you might even consider sending galleys to give the promotion a sense of informality and immediacy. One promotion that was particularly effective for me some years back was to send key media copies of the original manuscript from a prominent figure, with all the editing and type specs showing on it. Lastly, don't overlook sending issues of your magazine as promotions to important media and influence leader contacts; they're very effective, especially with a short covering note directing his or her attention to a specific article.

Many magazines tape record interviews as background for article material. Sometimes excerpts from these tapes can provide excellent promotional devices, particularly while they're relatively new and uncommon.

It can be very useful to have your editors, sales personnel and the publisher available as speakers for key trade shows, association meetings, conventions on subjects within your magazine's purview, industry meetings—even as guest speakers for a large company's quarterly or annual meeting. It is a fine way to promote the knowledge, experience and expertise of your key people—a technique which can't help but reflect favorably on the magazine.

If you have an especially hot article or news break, don't hesitate to get on the phone and call key press contacts at newspapers, radio and TV stations and the wire services. Offer to send them background later, but impress them with the immediacy of the phone. You also can use it to inform key legislators of an important development, particularly if you can give them advance knowledge of something that will break publicly in a day or two. These people are opinion setters, and even their casual mention of your magazine publicly or privately can do you a world of good.

If your editors have put together a useful piece of research, or have investigated areas that might personally interest a key group of readers or advertisers or press contacts, put a tour of the area together and invite as many people as you can afford to handle. This is a fine way to take the breadth of your company beyond the printed page.

If your magazine deals with new products in an industry, consider setting up a sample panel of readers who would agree to act as a "test marketing" panel for the new products and services of your advertisers. It's an added way to attract advertisers to your pages and it could develop into an intriguing editorial feature—not to mention an excellent promotable activity. It's also an excellent and unusual service to advertisers.

Many magazines that cover certain industries make sure to report on the trade shows in those industries. But how many magazines actually exhibit there, especially if they want to get greater advertiser and reader interest?

Finally, whatever promotional avenues you elect to take, the list of media and other contacts that will be important to you is critical. It takes time and care to isolate all the areas, as well as develop the specific names for each list and type of promotion.

A few parting words:

If you publish a special interest magazine, don't think your opportunities to promote your material are limited. While the basic thrust of one of your articles might be too technical or too specialized to draw much generalized press attention, some information might not. Bear in mind that many newspapers carry story after story about the findings in highly complex electronic, medical, space, oceanographic and biological fields. If your public relations people can translate the article's thrust into nontechnical jargon, identifying the general import or meaning for the general public, it stands a good chance of being picked up.

Don't expect everything you mail out to be used. It won't be. But even the material that's read, considered and tossed aside makes an impression on the person who received it. That is a worthwhile result, since it may well predispose that person toward your next release. Moreover, a steady stream of news and information from your company—whether used or not—creates in the mind of the press the impression of a dynamic, innovative magazine (or publishing company) on the move.

Don't expect your material to be used right away. Just as your editors tuck useful material away for use in a larger story or a roundup article, so might that be happening to your releases.

Don't isolate your public relations efforts from your regular subscription promotions and advertiser promotions. *Look* magazine did a tremendously effective job some years back when it coordinated the promotion of the impending publication of William Manchester's book, *The Death of a President.* The subscription promotion resulted in hundreds of thousands of new subscribers; the advertising promotion added hundreds of thousands of advertising dollars—and the press pickup of the book's excerpts was phenomenal.

Finally, encourage the people in your company to think about promotable opportunities. When editors, circulation people, salespeople, business managers and even you, as publisher, are thinking about ways to put the magazine on the map, you'll be thinking about ways to improve it.

Not-for-profit magazines needn't be losers

By Willis M. Rivinus

Not-for-profit magazines all too frequently take their taxable status literally. Not only are their operations not for profit, they generate sizable losses which appear to be escalating even faster than the postal increases.

Some not-for-profit organizations charge off the publication losses to "the mission"—spreading the Gospel, inspiring the needy, educating the membership, serving as a forum for specialized knowledge—with the costs assigned to membership dues or contributions from the faithful.

But a growing number of executives are beginning to challenge these annual "cost overruns." They ask why the deficits are so great and what can be done about them. They wonder whether they can afford the luxury of losing money every year in return for doing good. They consider whether the money might be spent more wisely on some other project.

In a few cases the losses on a magazine may be fully justified in terms of an overall program. In many cases, however, the losses highlight more fundamental problems related to the reader need for the publication and the business competence of the organization.

Too often the product is weak. The selling price is too low. The production costs are uncompetitively high. Meanwhile, those responsible for ultimate management have not set up realistic objectives and controls. The business runs out of control and everyone wonders what to do next. In due course there is an operational crisis—with one alternative being to cease publication.

Before that doomsday, in fact every year or two, each not-for-profit publishing operation should undergo a rigorous physical examination to identify its problems and adjust to the changing world. Ten areas are vital in the examination of a not-for-profit publication.

1. Financials should break even

The magazine or publication program may not be designed to make a profit, but there is rarely any excuse for it to lose money consistently or in great amounts. The managers should ask:

Is there a reliable management information system? Are there budgets and controls? Is the accounting system consistent with industry standards?

What have been the long-term financial trends? Is there a reliable financial forecasting model or system in place? Do the publication financials fit logically into the organization's overall financials?

Is the cash flow being managed effectively? Are the accounts receivable pursued aggressively? Are the accounts payable settled to best advantage?

It is essential that the financial position of the publication be managed efficiently to insure that it serves the overall organization goals. Then the financial department becomes the clearinghouse and control point for the other departments of the publication.

2. Editorial vitality should be measurable

Some not-for-profit publications have outlived their usefulness. They are out of touch with their audiences. Their editors are removed from the practical realities of their constituents. The coverage is obsolete or innocuous. But, how can the management know this in an essentially non-competitive environment?

Circulation is the primary measure of editorial vitality. Is it growing? Is there a healthy program to promote new readers? How are renewals? A 90 percent renewal rate may sound good, but in the face of a negligible new-reader promotion it may mean that the publication is slowly dying.

Surveys measure reader interest, and additionally provide valuable editorial content. So also do letters to the editor and subscriptions received by white mail. So do contests, games and sweepstakes.

Advertising, particularly classified advertising and mail order advertising, is an effective measure of reader interest. People who believe in a magazine use it in a variety of ways.

The layout should be vibrant and exciting. The pictures should be clear and full of action. Here is an easy way to improve the editorial content at an almost insignificant cost.

There should be a healthy level of editorial ferment, new ideas, new writers, strong personal opinions, lots of job applicants. The department should have a reputation for constructive excitement.

The positive results of editorial vitality will show up in renewals, industry awards, quotations carried in other publications, maybe even a little copying and healthy competition.

3. Circulation should grow

Circulation in the not-for-profit world is deceptive in that there is usually no direct competition of publications in the field as there is in consumer magazines. But, that doesn't mean that these readers are lacking for other activities and interests. A not-for-profit publication should be working to build and to hold circulation just as diligently as a profit-making one.

Share of universe is the first measure of circulation effectiveness. If the universe of members or people actively interested in the field is 300,000 and the publication goes to only 25,000, something is wrong. Conversely, if the primary distribution to the same universe is 250,000, it is probably time to expand the universe, raise rates, add new products, or all three.

As the universe grows and fragments, the circulation should keep pace with expanded promotions, special offers and appeals, and new products. Direct mail, space ads, agency sales, bulk sales, and gift sales should be pursued actively.

Billing and renewal notices are as important here as anywhere else, and just as rewarding. A not-for-profit organization sometimes feels sensitive about asking for money. Don't, unless money doesn't matter.

Fulfillment is a critical area where costs frequently mount far higher than industry averages. Fulfillment should be bought just as competitively as any other phase of the business.

4. Circulation pricing must keep pace

Few areas are as sensitive to a not-for-profit as pricing its publications. In part this occurs because of a missionary zeal which can drive a publisher to give away the magazine if only he can make a convert. In part it derives from the desire to hold on to long-time readers who first subscribed at low rates per year. In part it comes from innate conservatism and rejection of the high inflation rates which plague all businesses. And, in part it comes from inadequate planning and wishful thinking.

Whatever the reasons, a not-for-profit must charge realistically for its product because this is virtually its only source of revenue. In a world full of general interest publications with vast circulation and big advertising incomes, the special interest, low circulation, low advertising publication must charge in relation to the uniqueness of its audience and its proportionately higher production costs. If the audience values the publication, it will pay. If it does not, no price breaks will save the business.

A not-for-profit publisher should compete enthusiastically with healthy rates offset with discounts. Bulk orders are normally a must. Even premiums and sweepstakes are appropriate. All the tricks and gimmicks which work for profit-making magazines are fair game for the not-for-profits. In some rare instances a voluntary subscription rate can produce more revenue than a fixed one, especially if the organization periodically asks for funds.

5. Advertising can make the difference

Not-for-profit publications have a problem with space advertising. They normally have too small a circulation to command the attention of the big name advertisers. Their very specialization of editorial interest turns off most general advertisers. They sometimes consciously prohibit certain types of products and advertising. They cannot afford a significant advertising sales staff. They end up with trade ads and institutional ads—and relatively few of those.

That does not say that advertising cannot be an important financial contributor. If the audience is unique and affluent, the advertiser should pay for the privilege of reaching these potential buyers.

In addition there are all those specialized service ads for the membership—employment ads, classified ads, special interest group ads, cookbook ads, hobby ads, and lots more. If the audience is responsive, these ads can grow to carry a big share of the book's cost. In addition to their financial contribution, these ads build and sustain readership.

6. Printing and paper must be competitive

The printing business is changing. There are new techniques for typesetting and composition, new web presses, new techniques with color printing, new bindery equipment and direct addressing. There are even new postal regulations allowing for attached mail.

Printing is a very competitive business. So are the prices. Many not-for-profit publications feel a loyalty to a long-time printer. This is admirable. Just be sure that this feeling of loyalty does not cloud an unnecessarily high printing cost. The easiest way to be convinced is to solicit printing bids at least every three years.

Paper is a different matter. Some organizations adopt an elegant paper because they believe their journals will be treasured forever. Is this realistic in today's information explosion? Would not a "publication grade" in a standard size work just as well for 99 percent of the need?

Other organizations use a very inexpensive newsprint which produces a poor printing image and a poor organization image. Would the audience prefer, and be willing to pay for, a somewhat better-looking product? It might be worth testing.

7. Distribution is a challenge

The Postal Service has changed the economics of not-for-profit publishing. Not that this should come as any surprise. There have been steady and significant rate increases scheduled for a number of years now. What came as a surprise was the acceleration.

Now that higher rates are a fact of life, what is to be done about them? First, there is a variety of postal sorting, bagging, and tagging regulations which will improve delivery. Is the printer taking advantage of them?

Attached mail can allow for a significant cost reduction in mailing invoices and renewal notices. Is this being implemented?

Bulk shipments and newsstand shipments can frequently be consolidated into fewer truck shipments from a large printer. This saves money. Even alternate delivery carriers can work effectively in some situations.

8. Ancillary products can be gold mines

Sell a general interest magazine to the general readership as a "loss leader" and make up the difference through the sale of special-interest journals. This financial approach works well for some, provided that the journal "profits" can keep up with the magazine "losses."

The number of ancillary products which are potential moneymakers is impressive. The first and most logical is books published by the same editorial staff, or acquired from others. The audience interest is established. It remains only for the publisher to cultivate it profitably with technical pieces, tests of new editorial directions, old potboilers, calendars, notebooks, and dozens more.

Gifts and gimmicks sell, notwithstanding the

qualms of the editorial gurus. Even a book/gift catalog can generate funds.

Conventions, seminars, tours, trips can raise money if they are appropriate to the interests of the audience, and they are managed with the intent of making money.

9. Outside help must help

All not-for-profit organizations have on their boards and committees successful businessmen and women who contribute ideas and guidance. These people can be very helpful.

The problem the outsiders consistently run into is that they have difficulty motivating and moving the insiders who know that the good ideas are only advisory. Then, there are those well-meaning outsiders who seem to suspend their wisdom honed in the marketplace when they enter the aura of the not-for-profit organization. The result in both cases spells trouble.

Trade associations in both the organization's field and in the magazine field can be immensely helpful. They provide industry standards, and education and understanding of the business, news of impending changes in the industry, and invaluable contacts for the solution of particular problems.

Consultants can help periodically by providing objectivity, fresh ideas, and experience.

10. Management is critical

The management of a not-for-profit organization and its publication is just as important as the management of an organization in the profit-making world. The rules of business are the same if success is the objective.

Probably more than anything else, the organization and its publications must have concrete goals and objectives: bench marks to measure effectiveness and success; targets to shoot for which will provide motivation and inspiration for the team. Without these goals the publication will drift slowly but inexorably into extinction.

The staff of the publication must be as alive and vibrant, decisive and dynamic as anywhere else in business. A not-for-profit magazine should not become a final home for retirees regardless of how little they are willing to work for. If the staff is not "mean and hungry," just like the rest of the marketplace, the magazine will suffer sooner or later.

Not-for-profit magazines tend to become insular over time. Without the competition of the marketplace they tend to become complacent. The unique nature of their special interest tends to isolate them from what others are doing in different subject areas.

At the same time they are forced to compete in their business, in the printshop, in the mails. It comes as a shock that the world does not help them with the same enthusiasm with which they seek to help the world. They are forced to operate with two standards—their intellectual discipline and the business discipline.

The business discipline offers great challenges and also great opportunities for the not-for-profit publication. If it can operate efficiently and economically, it can advance "the cause" and provide expertise to the organization as a whole.

One of the most effective ways to insure the business health of a not-for-profit publication is to perform an operational audit of these 10 areas every few years. The ultimate benefit will be a more dynamic magazine and a balanced budget.

Keeping up with database publishing

By Barbara Love

Many magazine publishers are sitting on gold mines and don't even know it. Very often, publishers have valuable information in their editorial, marketing and circulation files that could be repackaged and resold for additional profit.

The key to developing these new revenue streams is the computer. The computer provides the ability to store, access and manipulate information. Around it has grown the concept called database publishing.

More conceptual than actual at this point in time, database publishing is still a new and boggling concept for many publishers. However, some of them are beginning to realize not only that there is vast profit potential in database publishing, but that their market franchises, and even their magazines, could be threatened if they don't get involved in it.

Unfortunately, most publishers don't know much about database publishing—they don't have a clear definition of what it is, and they don't know what other publishers are doing in this area—because most of what goes on in database publishing is taking place quietly behind the scenes.

What is database publishing?

Database publishing is the process of providing facts and figures to industry, government agencies, and individuals from information that has been stored in computerized data banks.

This definition would not please everyone, however. "I dare say that if you go to 20 people, you'll get 20 different definitions," says Seth H. Baker, president of ABC Publishing. "And if you ask 20 people how it is going to evolve in the publishing industry, you'll get at least 20 different versions. Nobody really knows. Everybody's groping."

Perhaps the best way to approach the subject of database publishing is to see how it relates to activities already familiar to publishers.

As recently as 10 or 12 years ago, a publisher generally used the information published in his magazine only once. As soon as he became involved in his next issue, he would forget about the material he had already published. Although some publishers would occasionally use previously published information for books or catalogs, this was relatively rare.

Today, however, many magazine publishers are storing their published information and finding new uses for it. They are repackaging it and selling it to the market that bought the original product (the magazine)and to new markets as well.

By reusing information, publishers can increase profit opportunities and take minimal risks doing it. If a publisher already has both the raw material (stored information) and a market, the cost of putting out a second product from that raw material is relatively low and the prospects for income relatively good. This use and reuse of information is called multi-media publishing.

The similarity between multi-media publishing and the somewhat advanced phenomenon of database publishing is that both produce a variety of products from one information source. The difference, however, is that the information used in database publishing is computerized: it is machine-readable; it can be manipulated; and, if it's going to be on-line, it is continually updated.

Since computers can store, update and access information quickly, and since the amount of information available on any subject (particularly business subjects) is growing rapidly, publishers are in a position to move into database publishing. Furthermore, since computers can manipulate information, new products can be created quickly and efficiently. For example, a database on the broad subject of music can be accessed in minutes for information on chamber music—a specialized sub-topic.

Although the concept of database publishing is just beginning to gain widespread attention, it is not new. People like Robert Birnbaum, a publishing consultant known for his work in database publishing, and Paul Doebler, a publishing consultant now working with R.R. Bowker, have been explaining its potential to publishers for a decade.

"The field of database publishing is only now just beginning to take shape," says Doebler. "Everybody's experimenting, trying to solve problems. Often it's not clear what's going on."

The circular concept

To illustrate how database publishing works, Doebler drew up a chart showing how publishers can use information today. The chart also explains some of the reorganization going on within companies and the many strange company marriages taking place today.

Working with Doebler's chart, Birnbaum developed a concept he called "closing the marketing circle" (Figure 1) that evolves from the central resource, the basic store of information. An outer circle, the "marketing circle," shows the various media options as links in a chain, each lending strength to the others while maintaining its individual identity as a profit center.

The circular concept shows actual working relationships that could not be visualized as easily in the conventional organization chart. It also shows that the same information can be used by any medium.

"The market is truly 360 degrees," Birnbaum explains. "It includes all of the possible ways of communicating with people—books, magazines, newsletters, seminars, on-line transmission, etc."

It is not necessary for a publisher to have in house all of the operations necessary to produce the different products, Birnbaum points out. A publisher would not need a book division, for example, to publish books. He or she could draw upon outside talent (experts or freelancers) who could "package" books for that publisher, if desired.

Linkage and leverage

What Birnbaum finds most important in multi-media/database publishing is the "linkage and leverage" gained by publishers who go this route. The linkage, he explains, comes from the fact that the communications vehicles are all around the same database. The leverage comes from the fact that a publisher can often use the same customers and marketing facilities (as well as the same information) in a different media "package."

As you connect the links, you gain market leverage. You can sell more to the same customer. Making a profit becomes easier and easier as you add links. Eventually, customers of one product delivered by one communications vehicle become customers of other products delivered by other communications vehicles.

Birnbaum's favorite example of how a publishing company "closed the marketing circle" is Billboard Publications. The illustration was given by Birnbaum 10 years ago and it is still good today.

Billboard, he explained, found a new identity in the marketplace rather than in the media. They placed market identity in the position of central importance, and by pooling the strengths of various media divisions toward serving the common market, they evolved considerable leverage.

According to Birnbaum, Billboard formed a new division serving the art instruction market. The new division included both a magazine and a book publishing operation. The pooled information and strengths were used to spin off related products and services for the art instruction market, including a book club and even a travel service.

The same information and markets were tapped over and over again in shaping new products. The product lines were packaged in whatever medium was appropriate, and each was designed to gain from and give support to the other.

The book club, for example, opened new markets for their established line of books. The books themselves offered an immediately marketable product, and the subscription list of the magazine that serves the same audience supplied an immediate source of book club customers.

A contemporary example that everyone would accept as database publishing (because it is on computer) is ABC Publishing. ABC has a company called NILS Publishing (National Insurance Law Service) which puts out a loose leaf compilation of the insurance codes and regulations in 50 states. NILS information is now being computerized. When that is accomplished, the same information will be disseminated in print form and on-line to CRT equipment in offices of people who want it instantaneously.

Making the transition

The thought of getting involved in database publishing is often met with anxiety rather than excitement. "The term database is feared by top management," says Tom Moran, corporate circulation director for Penton/IPC. "They think they are going to lose control totally, when, in fact, they are going to gain control. Furthermore, it's frightfully expensive, fraught with all kinds of pitfalls and requires a pretty smart group of people to make it user-oriented, simple, and flexible."

The move into database publishing can be problematic if the publisher moves too fast, Birnbaum points out. But a publisher can go slowly, taking one careful step after another to establish firm ground.

"The business of feeling one's way and going slowly is particularly advisable for small companies," he says. "A large company can afford to gamble and try two or three things at once."

The least painful, least risky way a small publisher can begin to explore the potential of database publishing, says Birnbaum, is to become a multi-media publisher first, developing revenue sources that could justify the expenditure needed to pay for a true database. In Birnbaum's opinion, publishers should find ways to repackage information before they get into computerized database publishing.

For example, a magazine might be better off developing a market for a directory, actually producing it before putting all the directory information on computer. That way, the publisher will have customers built in when he creates the database of information in the computer. The income that the directory creates will help justify the cost of the computer.

"If you went cold turkey from a magazine into a database, you would be faced with the problem of how to justify the cost of creating and maintaining the database," he says. "The fact that you have all this information stored is worth nothing unless you have previously started to create a market for it. If anything, it's a liability because it begins to die as soon as it's created and you have the problems of keeping it current."

The cost becomes easier to justify when a publishing company has two or three or more operations that successfully use the same information.

Some publishers have suffered because they have not adequately developed other markets for their information before making the transition to database publishing. These publishers now contend that the cost of creating and maintaining a database is disproportionate to its use and return on investment.

"In those instances where a database has been a lodestone around a publisher's neck," says Birnbaum, "I think it's because he moved too quickly into capturing information on computer without developing his markets."

In one case, according to Birnbaum, a magazine started to get beyond areas in which it had expertise. The magazine used only the name and the market when developing new products and did not sell products related to its information franchise, which is a magazine's greatest strength.

A common approach

In addition to developing new markets through new products using the same raw materials, there are other ways to ease into database publishing. A common approach is to use a computer for traditional functions in the company where the cost can be justified apart from database usage.

Birnbaum cited two areas where the computer could be used in traditional operations. First, a mini computer can handle subscription fulfillment and accounting internally without a major expenditure. Second, a publisher can introduce computer typesetting into his company and save money over typesetting outside.

Both of these forays into computers may be cost-justified on their own. They can also be viewed as tentative and careful steps toward database publishing.

When the time comes that the publisher has developed additional markets for editorial information, for example, he can begin indexing information as it is typeset

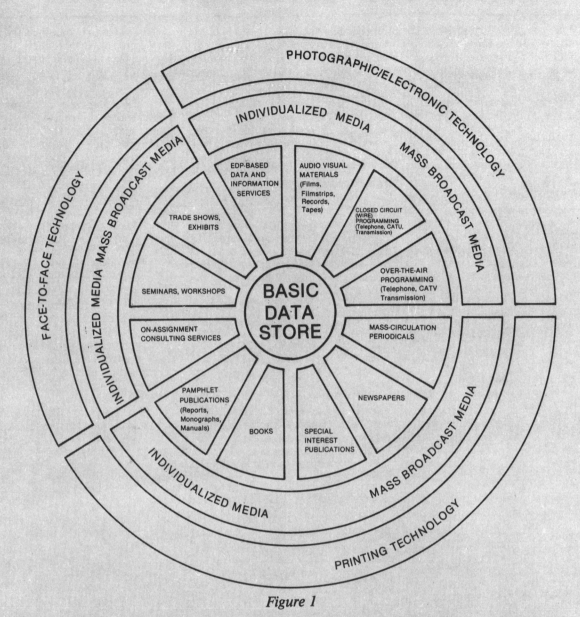

Figure 1

Patterns for Tomorrow in Multi-media Publishing

The ways publishers are publishing are multiplying rapidly today. And publishers are surprising themselves with how many ways they can find to publish once they break with traditional ideas. A picture of the publisher of tomorrow is emerging from all this multi-media activity, and this chart is our attempt to sketch this concept. The first—and perhaps most important—change a publisher must undergo is breaking with the old idea that his business should be oriented around the medium or media he deals in. Rather, the publisher of the future will see the common interests of audiences as his prime focus; his basic store of information and data as his prime resource; and all the possible means of communicating as his array of tools. Here, we've pictured the basic data store in the center of a wheel, from which the publisher radiates informational packages to his audience via a variety of media. These can be conveniently grouped under three fundamental types of information-carrying technology used to create media packages—printing technology, personal contact or face-to-face technology,

and photographic/electronic technology. To add another dimension, media can be ranked approximately according to the size audience they are most suited to serve. Thus, in each technology spectrum, media most suitable for individual or small-group service fall at one end, and broadcast media for reaching large numbers of people fall at the other end. Such a view of publishing activity suggests some important ideas about publishing house organization for the future. Being information-market oriented, tomorrow's publishing organization might be made up of several divisions, each dealing with a single subject area and producing information packages in all of the above media. Thus, rather than having a magazine division, a book division, a seminar division, tomorrow's publisher might have a metals division, an electronics division, a homemaking division—and each division might publish its own books, periodicals, seminars, television programs, *etc.*, working from its own central data bank and reaching its own audience.

Developed by Paul Doebler, publishing management consultant

and keep it in storage, where it can be called up.

With computer typesetting, the publisher has the ability to store all the copy in his magazine and recall it. A number of publishers are storing their magazines' contents in the computer and selling it. *Newsweek* and *U.S. News & World Report*, for example, have an arrangement with Mead Data permitting Mead Data customers to have access to all the magazine's editorial (except for the current and prior week's issue) on-line through terminals.

A database would not normally consist of just the articles a magazine is publishing, however. To give the database the breadth and depth it should have, the publisher would have to capture information from other sources as well.

Sitting on a gold mine
One of the best justifications for a database occurs in the storing of circulation and market data—names and other information about companies, subscribers and suppliers.

A number of firms, such as Penton/IPC, McGraw-Hill, Technical Publishing, Cahners and Hitchcock feel that they are sitting on a gold mine of such information.

"Right now all this information is used to make up audit statements; it's used to sell space; it's used to make up promotion pieces; and it's used a little bit for list rental," says Moran about Penton/IPC. "But other people can use it and will pay for it.

"We'd like to get all our information up on computer and accessible," he says, "because when we do we'll have all the data needed by anybody who wants to sell to 17 markets. We'll have those markets sewn up."

Moran says he sees tremendous revenues coming from such databases. "There'll be applications we never dreamed of," he says. "I can't even tell you what they are because I don't know yet."

Moran stresses that many magazines have valuable data and are struggling to create a database system.

"McGraw-Hill's trying to do it; Chilton's trying to do it," says Moran. "Cahners tried 10 years ago but gave up. It was too hard. The hardware wasn't there and people weren't smart enough back then."

Southam Publishing Company, a Canadian publishing company with 28 magazines, has come the closest to preparing for database publishing in terms of a computer system, Moran feels. "The company has succeeded in getting all of its circulation systems into one standard, streamlined system," he says. "It's the most beautiful thing I've ever seen, but the company isn't using it as efficiently as it could."

One of the questions that is frequently asked of Birnbaum when he talks about database publishing is, "Does the marketing circle or database organization chart mean that you can have only one database and one subject for each company?"

The answer is "no," says Birnbaum, who envisions a corporation having a cluster of databases. One publisher could be in charge of one database or several.

Indeed, a database task force at McGraw-Hill identified 70 databases five years ago and concluded that it would be profitable to exploit 40 of them.

The definition of a database used by McGraw-Hill, according to Joseph L. Dionne, vice president, McGraw-Hill Inc., is an information source that the user accesses directly, not necessarily requiring an editor as an intermediary between the user and the data. "We use a broad definition of a database," says Dionne. "We have a slightly different interpretation for each division because we have different kinds of products."

Much of McGraw-Hill's efforts in database publishing are directed to developing on-line products. It has spent $10 million to develop such products, in addition to $103 million for Data Resources, Inc. The new subsidiary was bought not only for its information in econometrics, but also for its expertise in packaging and selling computerized information. McGraw-Hill can use that expertise in exploiting their massive amounts of information.

To more effectively exploit its many databases, McGraw-Hill has a person at a high level in each of its seven companies who is in charge of database publishing operations.

"We're working very hard to ensure that each company remain marketing oriented and does not become media bound," says Dionne.

Changing role of publisher
Traditionally, we can say that the title "magazine publisher" implies a primary obligation to getting a magazine out.

In database publishing, the words "to publish" mean to disseminate. This does not necessarily mean by print on paper. As a disseminator of information, the publisher's stock in trade is not any one medium like a magazine. It's information.

There will still be traditional magazine publishers in the database era, but they will be on the spokes of the marketing or organization wheel. They will create and distribute a magazine from the information that comes out of the database. But they will be specialists.

A corporate executive or database publisher will be in the center of the wheel, making decisions on which medium—magazines, books, newsletters, etc.—will be most profitable for delivering information.

The great advantage to organizing around a circle is that the corporate executive or database publisher has no allegiance to any one medium.

"If you are a traditional magazine publisher, the great problem in diversifying is that you are already committed up to your ears to getting a magazine out," says Birnbaum. "Occasionally, a magazine publisher will say to me, 'I've got too much to do. I've got a magazine to put out and I'm too busy. Someday we'll diversify.'

"In fact, his job is structured in such a way that what he says is true," Birnbaum continues. "He *doesn't* have the time. So it behooves a corporation that really wants to get into database publishing in a big way to position a database person in the center of the marketing circle and say, 'You have 360 degree options on how information is going to be disseminated. The only thing we want you to do is make money.' "

Such a change may put new people in top management above the publisher, unless the publisher is versatile enough to make the transition to database publisher.

The move from traditional magazine publisher to database publisher might be tough for some people and duck soup for others, says Birnbaum.

"I'm always fascinated by the learning process," he says. "Some people stop learning when they reach some degree of professional proficiency. They have become 'a magazine publisher' and they know how to put out a magazine. They stop learning and resist anything that interferes with that occupation. Then there are other people who are constantly searching. They are intellectually curious. They never lose that. They are excited by change. These are the people who will make the transition to database publishers.

"A person who sees himself only as a magazine publisher thinks of database publishing as 'off the subject, a total waste of time,'" says Birnbaum. "The magazine publisher who is interested in growing gets excited by the idea and responds with, 'That's great, exciting, pertinent.'"

The editor's role

The editor's role will also change when database publishing comes of age for magazines. But again, it is not clear how.

"Typically, the editor makes the decision on what the reader will find in the magazine," says McGraw-Hill's Dionne. "But with database publishing, the 'reader' may interact directly with the database. In this situation, there's no editor involved."

In traditional publishing, an editor uses files to prepare the product, another McGraw-Hill executive says. In database publishing, the editor prepares the files to be used as the product.

Doebler, who has been exploring database structures for years, has some interesting theories on how editors will be affected. He points out that magazine editors today have two functions: 1) to obtain stories and prepare them for publication (Doebler calls this the manufacturing function); and 2) to determine what the reader wants. Sometimes this is done by talking to readers, taking readership surveys, and analyzing circulation. But often, Doebler points out, it is done by instinct.

With database publishing, these two functions may be given to two different people, Doebler speculates. "In industrial manufacturing, the manufacturing division is completely separated from research and development," he adds.

Manufacturing editors

Doebler sees the possibility of "manufacturing" editors—essentially research and reference editors—who are trained in detail work, structuring things, and getting exactly what the readers say they want. He or she would be going out and executing the ideas.

The other type of editor would be the research and development editor, who might also be thought of as a market research planner or product planner, according to Doebler.

"Think of it, most published products—books, magazines, newspapers—rely on the editor to pull in material he or she thinks somebody might want, package it, and put it out on the market," says Doebler. "People either buy it or not, and that's the end of the editor's responsibility. The editor doesn't know what readers do with the magazine or why they are reading it.

"A good editor must stay attuned to the audience," he continues. "That's the only thing that weds the publication to the market. But with database publishing, you just can't have a few random people who are good or better than others at doing things by instinct. Database publishing simply can't work that way. You can't have people operating on instinct on something that is critical."

The business side of the magazine is even more unprepared for database publishing, according to Doebler. "You get to the business side where advertising is sold and these people have no understanding of what it's all about," he adds. "They have no background or training for selling the product to users."

Doebler, like others, can only speculate on how database publishing will affect structures and job functions.

"The publishing industry is not fully aware of all the implications of this important development," he adds.

There is more than one market for much information that is accumulated; there isn't for other information. The value of a database, Doebler stresses, really comes from understanding the need for it. A publishing company may have a great deal of stored information, especially if it is producing one or more magazines through computer typesetting and can easily store everything being printed in the magazine. But that doesn't mean the information is valuable to others.

"For seven or eight years, the newspaper industry has known that there is an enormous amount of information going through its electronic editorial systems," Doebler relates. "And that's true, there is. But the industry never thought, 'Who wants to buy yesterday's news?' Newspapers, like magazines, are going to have to think creatively about what's going through those systems. Management is probably going to have to say, 'If we take this raw material, pull certain elements out of it, and package it in a certain way to fit this need over here, then we can sell this to them.'"

However, a lot of information that goes through systems is useless in terms of resale value, Doebler adds. "It's not easy to determine what is valuable, who wants it, and in what form," he says. "We're going to have to get beyond the point of simply saying, 'Well, let's just make it available and we'll see who uses it.'"

Edward W. Green, vice president, computer services, Data Resources, Inc., recently warned business press executives not to think of data simply as data, but to concentrate on how that data can be used. "It's the packaging and the promotion and tying the data to user applications that count," he said.

"Lots of people have data," he added, "The U.S. government has a lot of information but doesn't know how to package or present it."

Overwhelmed by options

With the growing understanding that it's the distribution of information that is the focal point in database publishing, and therefore any medium can be used, publishers are overwhelmed by the many media options available.

"Most people have not gone to the trouble of thinking through what information should be put out on what medium," says Doebler. "People are still doing this by gut instinct, not by rational analysis."

Once information is stored on a computer, new electronic media (such as on-line transmission) can be used. However, because the electronic media are the new and glamorous media, Doebler warns publishers not to get carried away with them.

"Publishers have to be careful not to jump right into the new media that they think are going to take over the world," he says. "This is a typical problem with any new technology coming into a field. People into a new technology see some glimpse of the future, but they don't have the whole thing put together."

The publishing industry has been through new-media frenzies before, such as the microfiche rage, and has gotten over it, Doebler points out. "You still hear people saying, 'Why don't we put that on microfiche? It will be cheaper.' That was a big sell in the 1960s. People were saying you could put a $10 book on microfiche for 50 cents, but they forgot that the cost isn't in the physical product but in the editorial work and marketing. They didn't understand the economics of the business.

"Even on-line, the current rage, will eventually take its place in the media mix," he says. "Some people are saying on-line is going to replace every other medium, but that's just not going to happen. It never does."

Birnbaum, like others, believes there will still be plenty of room for traditional magazine publishing in the database age. "The difference is that now publishers see that they can use the information contained in their magazines in a variety of ways to get a maximum return on investment and secure a franchise on supplying information to their markets."

Competition for that franchise will come not just from magazine publishers. Any type of company that has a bank of information and a group of customers can publish that information. And if that company were to develop a big part of an established magazine's market, it would definitely be a threat to the magazine.

Unexpected competition

Let's take an example of how a relatively unknown company to magazine publishers—Cordura Publications—can become a competitor.

Cordura Publications (San Diego, California) is structured as a database company, with no allegiance to any medium in particular. The company organizes and markets technical and pricing information in three industries: automotive afterparts, computer components, and plastics materials. It has three publishers, each in charge of one database. None of the publishers is identified with any particular medium. Each one looks at all the different ways of communicating with the marketplace and decides which can deliver information most profitably.

Keep in mind that each of the fields served by Cordura is also covered by established business magazines. Although Cordura does not publish books, it does market books. It also markets microfiche and audio visual materials, and it expects to market information through on-line transmission soon.

Now let's look at Cordura's position vis-a-vis one magazine publisher in one market—the electronic components market.

Through its subsidiary, D.A.T.A. Inc., Cordura supplies the electronics industry with a series of books describing the characteristics of thousands of electronic components. These publications are used by design engineers and purchasing agents throughout the world to select the optimum components for their products.

Cordura's market infringes on the market for *Electronics Components News,* a Chilton magazine which publishes information on new products in the electronic components field.

"D.A.T.A.'s book project is certainly the kind of thing we might have done," comments Peter F. Sprague, who recently left his post as director of corporate planning at Chilton. "The question is what options you choose to develop."

Sprague points out that Cordura and Chilton have different approaches to the market. Cordura puts out reference books, which have a longer shelf life and rely heavily on subscriber revenues, but they also take advertising. In contrast, Sprague says Chilton's magazine is published from the point of view of what advertisers want and concentrates on new products and pictures.

But Chilton is now storing information on electronic components for annuals, much the way Cordura does.

When asked if Chilton would not eventually store the same type of referral material on electronic components as Cordura does, Sprague replied, "The thought has occurred to us. The crunch will come when on-line electronic publishing becomes a reality. Both the D.A.T.A. books and the information in our tabloid lend themselves to electronic publishing."

The question in this case, and many other cases that are expected to arise, is "Who will develop the market for electronic transmission first, and who will be seen by the market as having the franchise on electronic components information?"

"Every publisher has a franchise. Whether he exercises that franchise, whether he protects it, whether he utilizes it—it's up to him," says Birnbaum.

Whatever it takes to make the transition from traditional publishing to database publishing, Birnbaum believes magazine publishers had better start exploring such a move. "I think publishers will have to make the transition just to survive in the electronics information age," he says. "If publishers don't consider database publishing, they are shortchanging themselves and could, conceivably, put themselves out of business."

ABC Publishing's Baker agrees: "Database publishing is not going to evolve as quickly as everybody thinks," he says. "It's not going to be highly profitable in the beginning. But everybody has to start getting involved in it because it will be important 10 years from now. A lot of people are going to lose a lot of money, and a lot of people are going to make many mistakes. But everyone who is in the specialized information business will inevitably be involved in database publishing."

Moran feels more urgency: "We're going to be left out in the cold if we don't hop on that bandwagon. Databases are being built all over the country. We have to establish and be able to market our own."

Not everyone feels magazine publishers should be moving into database publishing, however. There are publishers who contend that database publishing is the most overworked and overrated buzz word in publishing today. And there are publishers who think the whole subject is irrelevant and may even be a diversion from the business they know best, which is putting out a magazine.

At the trade show

By Barbara Love

Why should a publisher want to get involved in a trade show? At first glance, a trade show looks like a beehive or a circus. It is not easy to figure out what is going on and how a publisher can relate to all the activity.

The questions of "how" and even "if" a publisher should market a magazine at a trade show are difficult not only for those with no experience in the area but also for publishers active in many trade shows already. To answer these questions effectively, a publisher must be observant and creative, and obviously a little sharper than his competitors.

For many years, a show issue or booth exhibit were the only activities that publishers were involved in at trade shows, and publishers felt they were getting a lot of mileage out of these activities. Show issues are very satisfying since they usually are the fattest issues of the year. And exhibit booths provide salespeople and editors with a base of operations right in the center of the action.

But today, publishers work trade shows in a more sophisticated manner. They pay for television coverage of trade shows, hold tennis tournaments and disco parties, install wire services, and do many other things—all in the pursuit of winning over potential advertisers. They are constantly finding new ways of bringing together the valued advertiser and the influential reader.

Picking the show

The decision on whether or not to promote a magazine at a show, and to what extent, depends on many factors. If the show is the biggest gathering in the industry, the most important show of the year, and national in scope, publishers are likely to go all out with a booth, special issue, cocktail party, and possibly a special project that will make a splash. If the show is smaller, perhaps regional in scope or directed at a peripheral market, the publisher may just send salespeople and extra copies of the magazine, which often contains some show coverage.

For some publishers, numbers play a key role in the decision to put time and money into marketing a magazine at the show.

Robert Sward, vice president and general manager of the publications division of Chilton Co., who has 22 promotion managers reporting to him through the publishers, thinks numbers are a critical element. "We've gone to some shows where you could throw bowling balls down the aisles and they wouldn't hit anyone," he says. "We didn't go back to these shows."

On the other hand, the associate promotion director at another company, with 14 business magazines, claims the decision to promote magazines at trade shows has nothing to do with numbers. Instead, the decision is based on the buying influence of attendees.

"We'd promote the magazine at a show where there are only 1,000 attendees if all of them were leaders in the industry. We don't feel it's a numbers game at all."

This promotion executive says the decision to promote a magazine at a show, with at least a booth, depends on the publicity given the show, the group that is running

it (an industry association or not), and feedback from readers. But, in the end, he admits, "It's really a gut feeling."

Exhibiting at a new show is no problem for this publishing company. "In most cases, we will exhibit at first-time shows," says the executive.

Selecting a project

Trade show marketing projects for magazines meet certain needs. While there are many possibilities, the best projects or special events accomplish the following:

(1)*Supply some missing element in the show or convention.* A magazine can examine the convention schedule and plan events that will complement the schedule.

For example, if a show does not have seminars, the magazine might put on seminars. If no social event is planned, the magazine might plan one. If all the social events are held at the convention center, a social event could be held elsewhere, which would allow participants a refreshing change.

A magazine would be wise to avoid doing something similar to what its competition is doing. Through the years, some magazines have become so strongly identified with a particular event—a closing or opening convention party, for example, or a tennis tournament—that other magazines might not be able to follow without looking like me-toos.

This is not always true, however. Nearly everybody has cocktail parties, for example. And, at some big shows, there can be as many as five business magazines putting out successful show dailies, even though such a project might appear to be limited to only one magazine.

The promotion director for one big magazine publishing company says flatly that he does not consider what the competition is doing when planning an event at a trade show.

"When we stage an extra event, we certainly make sure we don't conflict with what the association is doing," he says. "But as far as the competition goes, we really don't concern ourselves with that."

(2) *Display some selling point of the magazine.* Some projects can be particularly well-suited for certain types of magazines. For example, a newsweekly could display an Associated Press or United Press International wire service to keep showgoers up to date with what's going on outside the exhibition center. Such a project not only gains visibility for the magazine, it also demonstrates that this newsweekly has the news.

(3) *Plug into trends or interests of advertisers and potential advertisers.* Some successful promotion projects center around activities that have nothing to do with a magazine's unique selling point; instead they tap some trend or area of personal interest.

For example, *Supermarketing Business* and *Health Care Product News* run tennis tournaments, which are very successful in gaining the goodwill of advertisers. "Tennis is very popular and many executives are into it," says a promotion executive working with these magazines. "We're capitalizing on that."

Another example: *Meeting News* rented a restaurant and a cable TV hook-up to show an important football game on the Sunday afternoon of a trade show. The event was a sensation. There were no exhibit hours that afternoon and advertisers really wanted to see the game.

Although these events were not show-related, they obviously fulfilled certain needs and interests of people at the show.

(4) *Take advantage of the city where the convention is being held.* The special attractions of the city where the show is being held offer opportunities for magazines.

In St. Louis, one magazine located a great bar in the warehouse area which had good bluegrass music. The magazine held a beer bash there on the last night of the trade show and the place was jammed till the wee hours of the morning. "Exhibitors really let their hair down and had a good time," says the publisher.

Other possibilities: A Country and Western show at a convention in Nashville, a riverboat cocktail party in New Orleans, a museum party in New York—all put on with prominent identification of the magazine.

Since an activity sponsored by a magazine should not conflict with a major official event, it is important to have the show's schedule as soon as it is available.

One publisher tells of his experience when he had to schedule an event without knowing the official schedule. (The association putting on the trade show failed to supply an advance schedule early enough.) It turned out that his event conflicted with the show's big, official social event—a night at Disneyland with free tickets for all—and participation in the magazine's activity was cut in half.

Official tie-ins best

Some publishers find that working with show planners in scheduling an official event can be very successful.

"From a promotion point of view, a magazine will greatly increase mileage by tying in officially with the show producers, perhaps as a co-sponsor," says Pete Shure, editor and co-publisher of *Meeting News*.

"If you are going to spend the money to do something at a show, you might as well get all the publicity for your event you can," he says. "By being an official part of the show, you get on the program that the convention planner sends out, and it's as if you are getting 50,000 or 60,000 direct mail pieces."

It is not that difficult to tie in with a show or convention, according to Shure, who attends many convention-planning sessions. Many co-sponsorships are made available by show planners.

A show manager often looks for others to pick up some of the costs in order to make a show more profitable. At the same time, a publisher can gain tremendous exposure by picking up those costs and supplying some essential and visible show element.

A magazine could sponsor any one of perhaps two dozen projects that are on the show planner's list, including the official program, entertainment, awards, bus transportation and door prizes.

Sponsoring the program at the Hotel Sales Management Association (HSMA) Convention is considered a very successful project by *Newsweek*. For the last two years, the magazine has printed the official program in a format that looks like a miniature *Newsweek*.

The program has the *Newsweek* name and logo on the cover with the picture of the current HSMA president. The back cover carries an ad for *Newsweek*.

"Everyone at the convention gets the program; people receive it when they check in," says Robert McMur-

try, director of travel advertising for *Newsweek,* who handles the project. "We get tremendous exposure from the program. People carry it everywhere and refer to it constantly."

The cost of sponsoring a show program is about $5,000, which is also the amount the association saves.

For another publisher, absorbing the cost of the official entertainment paid off. The publisher was asked to put in $1,000 to sponsor the major entertainment event at a show.

"We got good mileage out of it," says the publisher. "Our sponsorship was announced at the event and the hall was filled with our advertisers and potential advertisers."

Because show elements such as the program or hotel transportation are part of the show planner's responsibility, magazine projects in these areas are obviously open only to publishers who are able or willing to work with the sponsoring group. Where magazine publishers are in competition with the sponsoring group (perhaps an association has its own trade magazine), such projects would be impossible.

Many opportunities exist

There are many opportunities for the publisher who works alone.

At exhibit-oriented shows, a publisher might present a seminar, a slide presentation, or a panel discussion covering the state of the industry. A magazine is presumably an expert in the field it serves, and the industry is eager for information from the magazines it relies on all year long.

For example, a few years ago, a magazine realized that a convention in its industry was offering no seminars. The magazine decided to put on five one-hour seminars on a Sunday afternoon and charged $75 to $100 for the seminars. The seminars made money and the magazine got good exposure.

Here was a situation where a magazine saw a gap in the show schedule and filled it.

There are also opportunities in making presentations. The fact that one group—even the official group—is making a presentation on the state of the industry does not preclude the possibility of a magazine doing a status report on some specific aspect of the industry.

In the supermarketing industry, for example, the official industry association and two business magazines have all put on well-attended presentations on the industry. But each focused on different kinds of information and on different aspects of the industry.

Presentations capture the attention of attendees and demonstrate to potential readers the editorial quality of the magazine.

Presentations can be costly or inexpensive, depending on how lavish the publisher wants to get. Although production costs for a slide presentation may be as little as $300 or $400, the publisher must figure in the cost of the original research, the individual co-ordinating the project and, of course, the room rental. (Some of these costs can be charged to editorial, however, and the material reused as a main feature in the magazine.)

There are other ways to impress convention-goers with the quality of your editorial. *Newsweek,* for example, has been successful for years with its Periscope Panels of top editors, which are requested at many conventions.

Show issues

Show issues, the heart of many magazines' show

marketing efforts, often contain double or triple the advertising of a regular issue.

Selling advertising in a show issue is normally very successful for four reasons:

• Show issues will (ideally) be seen by show attendees prior to their arrival at the show. The attendees will have a better grasp of which exhibits they would be most interested in at the show.

• Bonus circulation of the show issue at the show itself will provide advertisers with extra readers.

• Product line round-ups for expanded reports will prompt readers to keep the issue and refer to it many times during the year.

• Package deals give advertisers a tie-in with other marketing opportunities, such as show dailies.

Most show issues offer the following types of editorial coverage: a greatly expanded new products section, a program schedule, a list of exhibitors, an interview with the president of the association putting on the event, interviews with the industry leaders on trends, and perhaps a special statistical survey.

New products get special emphasis in many publishers' show issues.

Plant Engineering includes a special four-color section on new products. It also carries reader service cards on each advertiser included in the new products section. Because there are hundreds of exhibitors at the Plant Engineering Show, the magazine does not attempt to include everyone's new products in this section. Instead, it invites only past and present advertisers to send in four-color pictures and write-ups.

Home & Auto expands its new products section from about 25 items to about 300 items for its big issue covering the Automotive Parts and Accessories Show in the fall. It also devotes a large section to all booth spaces, listing them alphabetically.

There are variations in the ways publishers handle new product information for readers. *Housewares*, in its January 1980 issue covering the National Housewares Manufacturers Association Show, ran product trend information for 21 product classifications, such as electric, baked goods and rubber.

"We guarantee that the issue will be on the readers' desks the first of the month, 10 days or two weeks before the show, so that readers will have time to think about the products they want to see," says *Housewares* associate publisher John M. Hard.

"These product sections help readers pinpoint where their needs are so they don't need to thumb through all the pages," says *Housewares* editor Ian Gittlitz. "And, from a sales viewpoint, they enable us to better tie in ad placement to appropriate editorial."

The contents of a show issue need not duplicate already existing ingredients of a show.

Gittlitz at *Housewares*, for example, does not include an exhibitors list in the housewares show issue because the NHMA, which puts on the show, has a 700-page program that exhausts that information.

Closely associated with show issues, but not to be confused with them, are the one-shot show issues. A one-shot show issue is only about the show and is published in addition to the magazine's regular publication.

Pre-, post-show issues

Although most magazines put all their efforts into promoting the show issue and related activities, a few magazines market pre- and post-show issues.

Health Care Products News is one of the magazines that successfully markets two issues around a show—in this case, the American Hospital Association Convention.

By buying both the pre-show issue (the July issue) and the show issue (the August issue), an advertiser also gets literature distributed along with the magazine at the show.

The pre-show issue and the show issue each draw an extra 25 to 30 percent more advertising pages than regular issues, says *HCPN* co-publisher Gil Numeroff. "These are our biggest issues because people buy the package."

Some big publishing companies do not see potential in marketing two issues around the same show. None of the Harcourt Brace Jovanovich magazines, for example, are doing it, according to George Glenn, vice president-editorial.

"We have no major pre-show or post-show editorial packages," he says. "From my own personal experience, most magazines put everything into the show issue. After the show, they are into special marketing issues not related to the show. These issues might feature some special merchandise area for retailer-oriented magazines, for example."

Show dailies

Show dailies are considered to be real money-makers. Some publishers make as much or more from show dailies as they do from show issues. Furthermore, the tie-in of a show daily with the magazine's show issue greatly increases revenue for the parent publication.

What are show dailies? They are publications that contain news of the show's events and exhibits along with interviews with industry leaders attending the show. They are put out at the show, often in a matter of hours, and distributed early in the morning at key convention hotels, convention hall registration areas, and on the convention floor.

One reason show dailies are so profitable is that advertisers can put an ad that is running in the show issue in one, two, three or even four show dailies. The sales people selling the show issue can sell the show dailies at the same time with a minimum of extra effort.

Furthermore, costs of show dailies are extremely low. There are no new advertising materials, no fulfillment costs, and no postage. Editors are usually at the show anyway, and some publishers even bring their own typesetting equipment to the shows.

These show dailies are often very big and of very good production quality, despite the very fast production required. Many are produced on coated stock, and have color, although color is pre-printed on a wrap-around section or insert.

As mentioned earlier, conventions can often support several show dailies. The Consumer Electronics Show, for example, which has about 1,000 exhibitors and 60,000 attendees, supports five show dailies.

How successful are these show dailies? The first of four editions of *Consumer Electronics Show Daily*, put out at the January show, contained 232 pages and was reportedly bigger than anybody's monthly at the show.

The four editions at the show carried a total of 350 advertising pages. With a four-time rate of $925 an issue and a one-time rate of $1,000, the total ad revenue for the January show was just under $350,000. Since the June show dailies for this publisher were expected to gross another $450,000 in ad revenue, the total for the year could be about $800,000.

Consumer Electronics Show Daily is put out by CES Publishing, which has two profitable magazines—

Consumer Electronics and *Audio Times.* However, according to *Consumer Electronics* publisher Richard Ekstract, the show dailies are even more profitable than either magazine.

The production of the dailies is "a killer and a half," Ekstract says. The show opens at 9:30 a.m. The writers have staggered deadlines, but all copy is due in by 4 p.m. A waiting car then takes the production manager and copy to a waiting plane that flies from Las Vegas, where the convention is held, to Los Angeles, where the daily is produced. By midnight, the publication is printed on coated stock and perfect bound, and copies are back at the convention hotels by 5 a.m.

"It's like a James Bond movie," says Ekstract.

When the Consumer Electronics Show is held in Chicago, the show dailies can be put out even faster. Pictures taken at the show at 8:30 p.m. appear in the next day's edition.

One publishing company—Gordon Publications, Inc.—has had such success with show dailies that it has set up a separate division to handle them. In 1980, three Gordon magazines published a total of six show dailies, along with the regular convention issues. The magazines are *Laboratory Equipment, Chemical Equipment* and *Metalworking Digest.*

Gordon ties in the show daily advertising rate with advertising in the regular show issue of the magazine. If an advertiser buys the regular show issue, he is eligible for a black-and-white ad in each of the two show dailies for an added cost of 20 percent. That is, a four-color ad in *Chemical Equipment* costs $4,000. An advertiser taking such an ad could run the same ad in black and white in the two show dailies for $800 or more.

Gordon's show dailies by themselves are profitable, reports Kenneth M. Nelson, president of the company.

More important to Nelson is the fact that the show dailies help build ad sales for the magazine. The Chemical Show issue of the magazine billed $400,000. When the magazine had no show dailies, the magazine's show issue billed only $95,000. Nelson attributes the hike to the show issue's tie-in with the dailies.

"We're not going to get rich on show dailies," says Nelson. "Although $120,000 a year in income might make a profit center, I'm not really interested in making money on show dailies. I'm interested in building ad sales in show issues of the magazine."

Gordon has outside writers for its show dailies. The writers gather information all day and write their stories at the printer. Nelson says the company does not use magazine printers for this work. "We use newspaper printers," he says. "They can turn around a page in hours."

Nelson doesn't see a publisher without a magazine in a field getting into show dailies. "The income for an individual show daily alone isn't worth it," he says.

Nelson also believes that magazine publishers could not handle the complex production involved in putting out a show daily. "It took us two years to perfect show dailies," he adds.

Hospitality

Personal contact is very important—perhaps the most important thing for magazine sales people at a trade show.

Hospitality events provide warm, friendly face-to-face contact with advertisers in a relaxed setting.

Once again, when deciding on what kind of hospitality event your magazine should sponsor, other events should be noted. Analyze the program. If you cannot secure this year's program, look at last year's. See what's covered and what's missing in terms of rest and relaxation—food, sports, a place to sit down—and supply it.

The tried and true hospitality suites and cocktail parties are still very successful, and they have become increasingly elaborate at some shows where there is strong competition for attention.

"A lot of magazines put on a big hoopla," says Julie Laitin, promotion director for Harcourt Brace Jovanovich. "They'll have exciting, romantic parties. The more people they can draw in, the more impact, the more credibility the magazine has. People throw around thousands and thousands of dollars on such events."

A full-blown party—complete with printed invitations with special artwork, a band, door prizes—could cost over $100,000, according to Laitin. Such big affairs are not usually necessary, however, and the simple cocktail party is still more common.

The benefits of a luncheon are pointed out by *Plant Engineering,* which serves about 700 people a show. *Plant Engineering* salespeople distribute tickets during the show to those exhibitors who advertise in the magazines.

"If you've ever worked a show, you know it's very hard to find time to eat," points out *Plant Engineering* editor Robert Baldwin. "People appreciate our hot and cold buffet in the convention center. The restaurants are too far to walk to, and there are only hot dogs on the floor."

Tennis tournaments

A tennis tournament is one way to get exhibitors alone for a few hours in a quiet, friendly environment. One magazine executive running tennis tournaments at trade shows reports that tournaments attract potential advertisers whom sales people have never been able to meet before.

While selling is not done during the tournament, important introductions can be made, linking the advertiser more closely to the magazine and its staff.

Two magazines that hold tennis tournaments at shows are *Health Care Product News* and *Supermarketing Business.*

"We invite the chief operating officer, the company president, vice president and sales manager to the tournament, but we are not strict about who enters," says *HCPN* co-publisher Gil Numeroff. "We usually get 45 to 75 people.

"Basically, many people in upper level positions like tennis," Numeroff continues. "They also enjoy getting away from the show for a few hours."

HCPN turns the tournament into a constant reminder of the magazine. Participants wear *HCPN* T-shirts, trophies are given out, and winners get their pictures in the magazine.

"We feel the tennis tournament is a lot better than a luncheon or a cocktail party," says Numeroff. "The participants are with us for hours and there is plenty of time to talk between matches."

The only problem with such tournaments is a minor one: If the magazine has a sales person, editor or publisher who is an exceptionally fine tennis player, he or she has to figure out how to lose without appearing to throw the game. The attention and the victories are, of course, intended for the advertisers.

Exhibit booths

A common and very important element in almost

any magazine's trade show plans is the exhibit booth. Exhibit booths enable a magazine to gain visibility. They also act as a base of operations for sales people and editors.

Hardware Retailing's bird dog committee was conceived as a marketing tool. Every manufacturer whose product was selected for the report is given a bird dog symbol that can be used in ads—even in ads in competing magazines. They are also sent information on the magazine's advertising program. Some of these manufacturers buy quarter- or half-page ads that elaborate on the small descriptions of their products in the magazine's editorial.

About 80 to 100 products are chosen by the bird dog committee, and about four or five manufacturers of those products become new advertisers, according to the magazine's editor, Robert Vereen.

Message centers

Several magazines gain visibility at trade shows by running relatively inexpensive message centers.

Newsweek runs a news and message center at two major consumer electronics shows and a news center at the National Appliance Retail Dealers Association Convention. The magazine installs two telephones and staffs the center with local people who take messages, pin them on a board, and sometimes deliver them to exhibitors and attendees.

The "news" part of the message center consists of wire service output, which attendees like because it keeps them in touch with the outside world.

"The center pays off for us," says Eugene Waggaman of the marketing services department. "We have the name *Newsweek* prominently displayed, and people come by all day long to see if they have messages or to check the news."

Waggaman says the cost of such a center is low, somewhere between $2,000 and $3,000.

Catalog Showroom Business also provides a message center at major shows. Again, the name of the magazine is prominently displayed and a telephone operator takes messages.

Awards presentation

Many in an industry eagerly look forward to awards ceremonies. Such events inevitably generate publicity. *Playthings* has an annual awards dinner at the American Toy Fair where awards are given by the magazine to those retailers who have the most creative merchandising ideas.

The American Toy Fair was chosen for the awards ceremony because it is the biggest annual show in the industry, with the largest number of toy retailers gathered in the same place.

Coffee carts

A rather off-beat but apparently successful trade show project for *Food Engineering* and *Instruments and Control Systems* is the coffee cart.

"Before the show opens, exhibitors are in their shirt sleeves setting up their booths," says Chilton's Sward. "They really appreciate a cup of coffee."

Of course, as with all the other activities, the name of the magazine is displayed on the cart to gain exposure.

In conclusion, the publisher planning a trade show marketing project should observe, observe, observe. Observe what the show planners already have scheduled. Observe what competitors are doing, and observe what other magazines in other industries have done.

At the exhibit booth, show issues of the magazine can be handed out, along with packages of flyers about advertisers.

About half of the 14 Gralla publications distribute "Hotlines"—economical versions of show dailies—at exhibit booths. "Hotlines" are usually two or four pages, all black and white, without pictures, and mimeographed or printed. They cover show highlights and often mention something about what advertisers are exhibiting at the show. Two of the "Hotlines" even have "help wanted" and "positions desired" notices for reps.

Some magazines use the booth to give out promotion items, such as shopping bags with the name of the magazine on them. In the case of *Plant Engineering*, about 15,000 plastic orange hard hats bearing the magazine's logo are handed out. "You can see the orange hats all over the convention and it makes quite an impression," says Baldwin.

Sometimes subscriptions are promoted at the exhibit booths. One magazine calls in its telephone subscription sales people to run its booth, whenever a show is in Chicago, where the telephone service is located. "These people are articulate and know the magazine," says the publisher. "They are good at the booth."

Television spots, coverage

Television, often thought of as a competitor of magazines, can be used to promote magazines at trade shows. Magazines that have television projects at shows impress advertisers, who see the results of the magazine's efforts in the morning in their hotel rooms while they are shaving or fixing their hair.

A television project is considered particularly appropriate for a magazine trying to make its presence known at very large shows. Such a magazine can arrange TV spots on morning shows for its advertisers. One magazine offered advertisers in its show package (show issue, plus two show dailies) a free 10-second spot with one of the three network affiliates during an industry-wide show in Chicago.

The spots included a picture of the advertiser's product and a voice-over by the advertiser about new products. The announcer then mentioned both the booth number at the show where their products could be found and the magazine in which the product was advertised. Finally, several spots at the end of the show were used exclusively to promote the magazine.

"The TV spots were seen by many exhibitors at the show," says the magazine's editor. "The manufacturers were excited when they saw their new products on television."

The magazine's associate publisher says that TV spots are a very important part of the magazine's promotion because of the size of the industry's show. "Approximately 2,000 exhibitors are on the floor at this show. It's impossible for our sales people to reach all these people in four days," he says.

The spots cost between $150 and $300 each, but they are well worth it, according to this publisher, who will offer major advertisers the same bonus at the July show.

There are other ways to use television at a show. *Hardware Age* and *Iron Age* do television coverage of events at their respective shows. They videotape seminars and interviews with key show personalities and put the coverage on closed circuit TV in official show hotels the next morning.

Something similar is done at the Consumer Electronics Show. "The Consumer Electronics TV Show Daily" put out by *Sound Arts* magazine even carries advertising.

Chilton's Sward notes that TV coverage of a show makes sense only if there is a lot of activity. "There is nothing to televise at shows that have simply exhibitors in an exhibit hall," he says. "On the other hand, shows that have workshops on current problems and trends are excellent prospects for TV coverage. Since attendees usually can't get to all of the workshops, they appreciate seeing the highlights the next morning."

Bird dog committees

Two magazines—*Sporting Goods Dealer* and *Hardware Retailing*—have bird dog committees comprising subscribers who volunteer to "sniff out" and report on noteworthy products and trends at shows.

Sporting Goods Dealer publishes its committee's findings, along with pictures of committee members, in an issue following the show.

Your lists are like money in the bank
By James B. Kobak

Although they rarely appear as assets on the balance sheet, a magazine's lists, particularly those related to circulation, are vital to the magazine's existence. These lists, in fact, often represent the greatest value the magazine has.

Ironically, because of the accountants' fiction of deferred subscription income, they normally appear only as liabilities.

There are a number of different circulation lists. For a majority of publishers the most important is the list of paid subscribers. A paid subscription is a contract in which the publisher agrees to deliver copies of a magazine for a consideration paid in advance.

The principal value of a subscriber list is normally in connection with the magazine itself. The lists actually exist, however, and have value independent of the magazine. They can be sold, rented, used to sell other products, exchanged for other lists or other media and used in other ways.

Even when a magazine goes out of business and the list has no further existence connected with the magazine, the list has great value. In virtually every case in which a magazine has died, other magazines have assumed the obligation to serve the subscribers (with their approval, of course). And often payment has been given for the opportunity to assume the contracts with the subscribers. This is usually less expensive than obtaining new subscribers in other ways.

Life magazine probably affords as good an example as any of the enormous value of a subscriber list. When *Life* died, other magazines agreed to service virtually the entire unexpired portion of the existing subscriptions, several million of them. In addition, over the years Time-Life Books and others used the *Life* list for the sale of other products. Indeed, the very founding and existence of Time Inc.'s book enterprise was based on this and other magazine lists.

When to Determine Value

While it is not an everyday occurrence, there are a number of times when it is important to determine the value of a subscription list. Frequently in the sale of publishing properties the assets required for publishing are sold rather than the company as a whole. When this happens, the value of each asset must be determined. The list of subscribers usually represents the largest value.

There are times, too, when a publisher might want to indicate, either on the balance sheet or elsewhere, a value for the lists owned. This may serve to impress on a banker or a potential investor that there is real measurable value in a magazine—often a hard thing to prove, particularly when a large deferred subscription liability appears.

This treatment coincides with the current trend in accounting circles to develop present value concepts rather than the traditional historical values. It is really no different from indicating the current value of securities, land, buildings, machinery, leases, inventories or anything else.

If a value has been put on the books for the subscription list, it can be expensed either over the life of the subscription—or over the life of the subscriber, taking into account the probability of the subscriber renewing. In some cases circumstances dictate more complex formulas.

Its Potential Earning Power

The basis for arriving at the value of any asset is, in the last analysis, its potential earning power. As in the case of a magazine itself, a number of factors must be considered.

There is, unfortunately, no rule of thumb or pat formula. The major factors which are normally considered are these:

1. Size of the list (number of names).
2. Unexpired portion of the subscription.
3. Attractiveness of the market.

4. Portion of the market covered by the list.

5. The profit—or potential for profit—of the magazine itself. Even if the magazine has no value, the list may have value.

6. Amount which has been earned through the sale of other products—and the potential for such earnings.

7. Price paid by the subscriber for the original and renewal subscriptions.

8. Renewal history of the subscription.

9. Future renewability of the subscriptions.

10. Original length of subscriptions.

11. Channel of sale—whether by direct mail, field sold, catalog agent or whatever.

12. Quality of the subscriber in terms of demographics, location, income, etc.

13. Amount which has been earned through rental—and the potential for rental.

14. Ability to exchange the list with other publishers or other list owners.

15. Original cost to obtain the subscriptions.

16. Cost to replace the subscriptions.

17. Availability of alternative lists—or other ways to reach the market.

While a list may, in some cases, have enormous profit potential and therefore a huge value, it would be difficult to assign a value to it greater than the cost of replacing it, if that were at all possible.

Different portions of the list, too, have different values. A subscription sold at full price is worth more than one sold at a reduced rate. A subscription which has been renewed is more valuable than a first-time subscriber.

And so on.

As with most assets, a subscription list has different values for different people. Most frequently, it is purchased by someone who wants to continue the magazine, buys assets and assigns values to each of them. Sometimes it is purchased by someone who sees an opportunity to sell other products to the subscribers.

A competitor might find a greater value than anyone else. By adding the unduplicated subscriptions to its own, the magazine can increase its circulation and, probably, increase its advertising rate as well. There are times, of course, when doing this would be detrimental to the magazine, increasing circulation to a point which could not be sustained without enormous cost.

And for just about all subscription lists there are other magazines for which there is value, even if they do not cover the precise field. Almost any magazine can use some subscriptions which are obtained at lower cost than that for adding the last incremental readers.

Other lists publishers own have value, although normally these are worth substantially less. Among these are:

- Expired paid subscribers
- Potential paid subscribers
- Controlled (free) recipients
- Potential controlled recipients
- Former controlled recipients.

To the extent that they apply, the same factors are considered in valuing these lists as in the case of paid subscribers.

A basic guide to magazine research

By David P. Forsyth

Magazines thrive when they bend and adapt to the needs and desires of their fickle audiences. Change is the life-blood of magazines. Yet research, the one tool that can gauge the change and provide early warnings, is too often shunted aside. In fact, magazine research has probably been the most maligned and neglected of the basic tools available to people in the magazine business.

Admittedly, there are good reasons why this has been the case. Magazine research is often conducted poorly, generating figures so inconsistent that decision-making would be better off based on the flip of a coin. The result: many publishing people are turned off by "bean counters."

In addition, magazine research is often biased and self-serving. There are media buyers who simply will not look at another piece where the sponsoring publication takes first place across its own circulation in a poorly designed study.

Furthermore, even when the research has been objective and the data adequately gathered, the numbers are often left crying for interpretation. If the rows of inert numbers are discarded into the bottom left drawer or circular file, no one can possibly know what the information means. It might show why a non-reader isn't reading, why a writer is missing the needs of the target audience, or why a salesperson lost the last sale. But the data continue to gather dust.

Despite these negatives, today's knowledgeable—and successful—publishers, editors, circulation managers, and advertising sales directors know that there is no substitute for magazine research, objectively conducted. They understand that when a study is conducted with proven procedures and tied together with the marvels of computer tabulation analysis, the resultant research can supply valuable information that can literally dictate success or failure for a magazine.

Valid and reliable

Magazine research, like any marketing research, must be both valid and reliable to be acceptable. It must measure what it has been designed to measure, and it must be consistent from study to study.

Information for magazine decision-making must be obtained through correct use of the basic tools of data gathering. (A magazine executive need not be an expert with these tools, but he should have enough understanding of the techniques to instill confidence in the results.)

Proper research planning involves outlining the kinds of information wanted, determining what is to be accomplished, and deciding who is to be queried.

Correct procedures must then be followed, preferably by a knowledgeable research professional. These procedures include minimum standards for drawing representative samples, construction of questionnaires, use of the proper data-gathering method, a high response rate, and proper analysis of final results.

Only by sticking to these basics, no matter what the study, can the executive obtain the data that will improve his magazine.

The method of magazine research data gathering—personal interview, telephone, mail, panel, focus group—is dictated by the nature of the information needed, the kinds of people to be interviewed, and the budget available.

Personal interviewing—the most expensive method, with individual interviews ranging from $50 to $150 each—is probably the best method since the interviewer has plenty of time with the reader and can control the interview format.

Telephone interviewing—currently the most popular method because it is less expensive than personal interviewing—ranges from $15 to $50 per interview. It is faster and permits a fine degree of control. Furthermore, through monitoring, the questionnaire can be upgraded as the study progresses. Telephone interviews normally are shorter than personal interviews, however, since a tired respondent can simply hang up.

For economic reasons, mail surveys are most often used, costing from as little as $5 per return up to $25, depending on the incentive offered (if any) and the kinds of people being questioned. Since more returns can be obtained for the money through mail, the data can be broken down into more statistically significant units. For example, 200 interviews may be sufficient to evaluate a total group of readers, but at least 100 in each category, or 500 total, may be required to break out readers by five job functions; or up to 1,000 or more to separate consumers by multiple age classifications.

On the other hand, mail questionnaires might reveal the main objective of a research study in the first several questions, thus biasing the remainder, whereas key questions can be delayed in personal and telephone data gathering. Lengthy mail questionnaires, moreover, tend to reduce respondent cooperation.

Mail panels, another method, are occasionally helpful in improving reader cooperation, thus cutting costs substantially (sometimes under $5 per respondent) while increasing response.

In a panel, a select sample of readers agrees to answer a group of questions from time to time. Care must be taken to replace panel members regularly so they won't become conditioned or sensitized, supplying information they think the magazine would like rather than information that expresses their true feelings. Furthermore, a panel may not be representative because a true cross section doesn't take part.

Diary research, similar to panels, carries somewhat the same problems and opportunities. First, a sample of readers or potential readers agrees to maintain diaries for a certain period of time. If, for instance, the data desired relate to magazine exposure, the respondents report on what they did with the magazines every day. The advantage is that the burden of thinking back over a long period of time is eliminated and extensive lists of publications are not required. On the other hand, as with panels, there is a possibility that the respondent will anticipate what the sponsor wants.

Aim for high response rate

Whatever data-gathering technique is used, a large percentage of the sample must respond to ensure that the information is representative of the audience. Major research organizations prefer 70 percent to 80 percent projectability; 60 percent is often considered acceptable. Under 40 percent may result in a distorted reflection of a group of readers, unless a follow-up of non-respondents is conducted to determine whether their answers are similar to respondents' answers. Incentives and follow-up interviews are often used to encourage sufficient returns or to increase response rates.

Sample error and confidence levels can be calculated to determine mathematically the accuracy and precision of study. But this can be done effectively only if the quality of the research is maintained—that is, if some form of unbiased sample selection is used, if the questionnaire is carefully written and pretested, if care is taken with the gathering of data, and if the response rate is high.

Focus groups

Occasionally, a magazine problem calls for a qualitative rather than a quantitative approach. The answer could very well be a focus group, usually consisting of eight to 12 people representing one or more kinds of readers or potential readers. Conducted by an experienced moderator, focus group sessions can be useful in obtaining information when representative data aren't required. The end-use materials are more on the order of ideas, produced in "brainstorming" sessions. Costs range from $1,000 to $2,500 per session.

Focus groups can be helpful in developing new story ideas, considering new magazine concepts, and in framing questionnaire outlines to be used later in personal, telephone, mail or panel studies.

Five kinds of magazine research

There are five major categories of magazine research: research available to an editor, research on magazine audience, research on advertising/marketing, circulation research, and new publication feasibility research.

• *Research available to an editor.* Editorial research for product improvement (which is different from research by an editor or writer to obtain information for an article) is conducted primarily to evaluate if and where a publication must be improved editorially to better fulfill the needs of its readers.

Perhaps the most valuable research for an editor is a reader profile, a detailed description of the typical subscriber or reader. For a business publication, such a profile may detail the reader's function, title, type of business, and responsibility for buying various products for the company. These responsibilities are in themselves indices of interest in articles about those products.

For consumer magazines, a profile might include age, level of education, marital status, size of family, etc. When all of these characteristics are evaluated carefully, an editor will know his audience and understand how he must direct his writing.

Reader interest and need studies are natural follow-ups to profile surveys. Unfortunately, readers are generally vague in describing areas of interest, especially those they will actually read later. One way around this problem is to develop a file of information needs by asking readers about the major problems they face on the job.

A reader acceptance study is a way to determine use of a magazine, while the more detailed involvement study, an investigation in depth by personal interview, plumbs the role played by a magazine in the life of a reader.

Publication positioning, of additional value to a publisher and salesperson, assists the editor by pinpointing where his magazine is situated in the minds of his readers in comparison with competitive magazines. Which magazine, for example, is doing the better job, as evaluated by the regular reader of each, in supplying work-related information?

What about the non-reader, the person who is on the subscriber list but spends little or no time with the magazine? What can be done by an editor to get the non-reader involved? A non-reader study might help the editor answer the question.

• *Research on magazine audience.* The counterpart of the editor's profile study is the subscriber or recipient study developed from the standpoint of the advertiser. This study includes industrial or consumer demographics, depending on the kind of publication, and can go so far as to include lifestyle data.

A natural follow-up is a product/service usage survey—or a determination of purchase decision-making within a family. On the industrial or business side, the counterpart is a purchase decision study describing how a reader gets involved in the buying patterns of products bought by his or her company.

Syndicated studies, developed to measure the total audiences of magazines, are probably responsible for the greatest part of the research dollars expended today by the larger publications. Conducted by SMRB and MRI, these studies have evolved during the past 25 years to answer the competitive pressures of television and radio. Always controversial and exceedingly complicated, today's surveys are no exceptions as "through the book" and "recent reading" methodology discussions hog the media limelight.

Generally, a range of useful qualitative data about readership, other media, and product usage is obtained while the magazine readership data are being collected.

For magazines with circulations too small to appear in syndicated studies, primary circulation surveys are often substituted for the total audience approaches. Also, since total audience includes both primary and pass-along readers, special surveys have been developed to determine the value of each type.

Specialized magazines covering easily measured total audiences such as medical doctors and farmers are also studied by syndicated surveys.

On the other hand, some magazines which serve significant, yet vertical, audiences (such as construction workers, coal miners, or discount retailers) have circulations too small or complicated to be covered by national syndicated studies and have to be described in other ways. Moreover, because a complete definition of the intertwining audiences serving similar industries is both complex and expensive, primary subscriber studies or semi-sophisticated pass-along studies often have to take the place of total audience evaluation of industrial audiences.

Difficulties associated with total audience data gathering have been instrumental in the use of special diary studies wherein readers daily describe media and product usage.

Apperception, media image or media comparability—all these terms describe a similar kind of audience study which can be conducted for magazines. Apperception is the concept that a magazine can provoke certain kinds of reader involvement, beyond perception or seeing.

It tells us what a reader brings to the publication such as established expectations, moods, sentiments and beliefs. An apperception study shows that these elements influence the way in which a reader reads articles and advertisements.

Media comparability compares publications covering similar fields by screening regular readers of two or more of the magazines, then having the reader evaluate how well each publication rates on special attributes such as "authoritative" or "timely."

A popular type of audience study in business publishing is reader preference or readership studies, as they are often erroneously called.

Reader preference surveys are occasionally sponsored by agencies or advertisers to assist in media selection, more often by individual magazines for competitive purposes.

After a list is compiled covering purchase decision makers across a specific market (the circulation of the publication, customers/prospects, directory list, etc.), a sample is sent the questionnaire requesting such information as receipt, readership and preferences for the publications covering the market. A randomized aided-recall list of reproduced magazine covers works best.

This kind of study, perhaps the most widely abused of all magazine research, can easily be biased by poor selection of lists, self-serving questions, non-inclusion of important magazines, and poor response. When carefully done and accompanied by full disclosure information, it can prove valuable to media buyers.

An extension of the above magazine comparison studies is some of the work done by the Magazine Publishers Association in determining intermedia involvement, or how people perceive, use and respond to different media such as magazines and television.

Audience accumulation, still in the experimental stage, attempts to describe how magazines accumulate the audience of a given issue on a daily basis. It has been found, for example, that newsweeklies accumulate 60 percent of their audience within seven days of publication.

Closely related to audience accumulation is issue life, the amount of time that a particular issue is kept and used.

• *Research on advertising/marketing.* Research which measures readership of advertising and coverage of specific markets is perhaps the most readily available to a publication today.

Magazines, for example, using Starch-style recognition techniques will probably total 440 during 1981 with more than 1,800 separate issues being covered. While a number of independent suppliers provide the bulk of the reports, major publishing companies such as McGraw-Hill supply objective surveys to both inside and outside publications, and a number of individual magazines offer their own, generally conducted through the mails.

One of the more useful off-shoots of advertising readership studies are the data bases developed as a result of the large number of studies conducted over time. Correctly analyzed data can supply useful insights to an agency's creative department on the physical characteristics of advertising, including use of color, size, bleed and ad placement.

Not only are ad readership surveys useful for the study of advertising in regular issues of the magazines, but similar techniques can be used to evaluate special issues and directories.

Somewhat more sophisticated for evaluation of advertising in magazines are recall techniques available both to magazines and agencies. Here there is little or no reliance on recognition (determining whether a reader recalls an ad by showing it to him), with more dependence put on what a reader recalls about something he or she previously read.

Advertising page exposure (APX) studies, developed in the late fifties by the Politz organization and later improved by ensuring multiple exposures to the same advertisement, have given magazines a different approach to measuring advertising. Now used primarily by medical publications and some industrial magazines, an APX study involves sticking a reader's name or a check made out to the reader on a randomized ad in an issue. A follow-up study or analysis of cancelled checks gives an indication of how many issue readers were exposed to the ad message.

Magazines can contribute to advertising effectiveness by providing agencies with pre-testing and post-testing capability. Circulation lists are generally classified by zip, function, or buying responsibility, thus making target audiences readily accessible.

Follow-up studies of inquiries and coupons for advertisers provide continual analysis of actions and buying patterns. Similar surveys can be developed for actions taken as a result of reading non-coupon advertising, especially if the follow-up is tied into an advertising readership study.

Before and after, or benchmark, studies, when properly controlled, can help measure how well the objectives of a campaign are communicated. Care must be taken to ensure that the magazine readers who have had the best chance to be exposed to the advertising are brought into the study; that the people interviewed have responsibility for purchasing or are in the market for buying the product advertised; and that the questions relate to the communications objectives. Campaigns can be tracked over longer periods with similar research controls.

Evaluations of promotion tools, such as advertising, trade shows, direct mail and sales calls, particularly in industrial and merchandising marketing, can be useful to publication management and potential advertisers. In an advertising's reach study, on a case study basis, establishments or locations are visited by personal interviewers who track down all people in the plant with purchasing responsibility for a specific product. Retention of direct mail messages, attendance at trade shows, calls from salespeople and publications read which carry advertising about the advertised product are investigated and compared.

Brand preference and acceptance studies measure the current levels of awareness and preference for products, services, and companies among readers of a magazine. On the business side, purchase plans and supplier evaluations among buyers of specific products can also be measured.

• *Circulation research.* First, a circulation manager should avail himself of all the editorial, audience, and marketing studies conducted for his publication. An evaluation of this material will provide information on readers which will give direction as to kinds of lists and which audiences should be approached as potential subscribers.

Other circulation survey research could include pinpointing functions and titles of prospective subscribers in a sample of manufacturing plants to determine how many names in the plant, and therefore in the universe, would qualify in the circulation market. Total circulation potential can then be evaluated.

Subscribers who don't renew can be contacted to find out why and to discover what editors could do to retain them as readers. Similar studies can be conducted to determine why people don't pay when they are dunned for non-payment.

Many managers draw samples of subscribers in different regions and check on delivery dates and the physical condition of the magazine when received.

In the consumer area the traditional research methods can be applied to single-copy purchase behavior studies wherein interviewers approach magazine buyers at the newsstand and interview them there or obtain names and home addresses and follow up later by telephone or personal interview.

Various other kinds of circulation research take a different tack from traditional data-gathering methods and rely on testing rather than survey techniques.

Subscription mailing tests, for example, may consist of targeting special demographic or regional audiences, developing special mailings, and testing which wave pulls better across the various segments. The main emphasis is on careful record keeping.

Testing subscription price works in essentially the same manner, using either demographic or specific locality audiences.

Tests of magazine covers or price on single-copy sales may follow regional breakdowns with records kept of where specific prices or covers were consigned.

• *New publication feasibility research.* Evaluating the potential of a new magazine or publishing concept may take different directions. One of the most common in testing concepts is to use the focus group approach. Here, focus panels with pre-selected groups of potential readers are set up in major target markets across the country, region or industry most representative for the potential idea. Trained moderators explore various approaches and direct participants to "brainstorm" their views and attitudes on publication concepts.

Quantitative studies are logical follow-ups of focus groups with questionnaires developed from data obtained from the focus sessions. Here the magazine concept might be described to a large segment of potential subscribers, perhaps by telephone, and quantitative evaluations obtained. Or prototype copies can be sent to selected audience segments and follow-up interviews conducted.

Whatever the outcome of the above initial research, you cannot be absolutely sure you have a winner until you find out what your audience really thinks of the new magazine. Test mailings help to provide this answer. A well-designed testing program directed to various potential readers is imperative.

Starting
the new magazine

Starting a new magazine

By James B. Kobak

I have the impression that every man, woman and child in the United States has an idea for the one magazine that is "needed" (which is much stronger than "wanted") by the American public.

This isn't really surprising since magazines are a communications device for people who have an interest in a subject, and the range of different interests seems to be unlimited. Whoever thought that there could be magazines serving such diverse areas as tall people (*Max.*), parapsychology (*Psychic*), or Civil War buffs (*Civil War Times*)?

But this is not going to be an esoteric treatise on new magazines. Rather it is a "how-to" approach to starting a new magazine based on the experiences of a great number of people who have tried.

Starting a New Magazine Is Not Like Anything You Have Ever Done Before

Starting any new venture involves basic ways of thinking that are different from any you have experienced before. It requires such diverse activities as:

1. Doing detailed long-range planning about every aspect of the magazine, including both its start-up and its eventual operation.

2. Finding and assembling a team of people with highly developed diverse skills who are as excited about and as dedicated to the idea of the magazine as you are.

3. Getting these people to work together smoothly even though they start out as strangers.

4. Raising small and large amounts of money—partly from your relatives, friends and neighbors, partly from individuals or institutions devoted to the venture capital business.

5. Getting involved in every aspect of the magazine—advertising salespeople salaries, where the coatrack should be placed, what printer to use—and on and on.

6. Choosing consultants and professionals in areas such as design, circulation acquisition, legal and tax matters, accounting, and then getting the most out of them.

7. Exhibiting the kind of dedication which will make you quit your job so that you can spend nights and days working on the magazine for many months, maybe years, before it is hatched and in business—and keeping your family happy while this is going on.

8. Having the persistence and strength to be turned down often, reach the brink of disaster a few times and carry on anyway.

9. Having the strength of character to drop the project if you find that the world was not waiting for your magazine after all.

Each magazine is different. It is appealing to a different group of people. It has a different set of advertisers. The editorial product is different. The people involved in the project are different. Techniques and the world have changed since you did it last.

In fact, the worst assumption you could make is that you know the formula. There is no formula.

And if you try to apply the same methods over again you are doomed to failure. Time Inc. recognized this. *Money* and *People* were launched in completely different ways—and neither followed the pattern of its last previous product, *Sports Illustrated*. John Veronis and Nick Charney see it too. Their *Book Digest* is being done very differently from the way *Psychology Today* was started.

There are lots of human interests. And for almost any one of them there are quite a number of devotees. But that doesn't necessarily mean that communication is required, or even desired.

For instance, a great many people buy exercise cycles. But the requirement for communication about them is virtually nil. Can you picture a catchy series by an exercise buff on "How to Decide the Best Room for Locating Your Exercise Cycle."

Even though we are supposed to be an audio-visually oriented society, the vast majority of people seem to think in terms of print when communication is required—and most turn to the magazine format.

In truth, however, radio, TV, movies, newsletters, books or skywriting may be better for the subject, the audience, the frequency of communication needed and the commerical viability of the project. Print is not always the answer

Crystallizing the Editorial Product

The first step is the hardest — deciding what to say, how to say it and how to visually present it.

You have no idea how many editorial plans sound like this:

New Magazines and Existing Publishing Companies

A good deal of this article is devoted to the requirements of obtaining financing from private investors. The situation within an existing publishing house presents a number of important differences, although the steps involved in developing the concept, the business plan, testing and staffing are essentially the same.

You might think that the most logical place for new magazines to start is in existing publishing houses. Financing, manpower, publishing knowhow, supplier contacts and just about every other needed capability is there.

Yet, publishing companies rarely are the founders of major new magazines, with some important exceptions. For the most part, the approach has been to let others take the initial risks and buy them out when profits have been assured.

Very few existing businesses, whether in publishing or not, are devoted to starting new projects. So the level of knowledge in these areas is little different from that of the entrepreneur who strikes out on his or her own.

Most managements are structured and tuned to operating a going business most profitably rather than starting new things.

The entrepreneurial type does not necessarily fit into many organizations. He or she can be upsetting to a good number of employees who are satisfied with their normal duties.

Methods for adequately rewarding entrepreneurs are difficult to establish in most compensation plans without upsetting other people.

Existing companies are rarely big risk-takers. This is logical. The smaller, private company often does not have the capital to take major risks. If it does, it may not want to jeopardize the normal profit picture of the company. Public companies have a built-in need to maintain earnings, which makes ventures difficult to justify. Further, such ventures, if they fail, can have an adverse effect on the public image of the company.

In some ways, too, there may just be too much knowledge about the magazine field. There is that remembrance of the big failure of 20 years ago. Agreement on the concept and specific plans may be difficult to achieve. Perhaps the overhead of the company as normally applied will doom any new venture.

It is not surprising, considering all this, that few magazines are started in existing publishing companies.

Yet, for a company to maintain its relative position, either startup of new magazines or purchase of properties from others is essential. The very existence of the life cycle for each magazine virtually ensures that every property will mature at some point and eventually die.

The infusion of new things is needed to maintain an adequate growth rate in this field. By the same token start-ups can be great for the morale.

And it is quite possible that a few carefully handled and watched new ventures will be less costly and less risky than one big purchase.

"The magazine will be bright, witty and chatty— serious without being ponderous. Graphics will be used liberally and will be designed to complement the text without being obtrusive. Headlines will be lively and catchy. We will take a stand, but not go out of our way to be controversial. Among the regular features will be an Editorial Column, Letters to the Editor, Book Reviews, Interviews with the following people in the field and short newsy items, in addition to the major pieces."

What did it say?

Nothing.

Even a law review tries to do all that, but the editorial content, spirit and qual y have not really been defined.

I remember when Vincent Drucker had an idea that a new magazine was needed for teachers because of rapid changes taking place in teaching methods. Going from this basic concept to what the magazine would really be took more than a year. In fact, we reached the conclusion that it could not really be done well enough without the participation of the eventual editor. This entailed a search for the person best suited for the spot, arousing his or her interest and getting that person to participate.

The editor, Frank McColloch, and Vincent then developed tables of contents for an entire year's issues together with the titles of articles, the probable authors and a brief precis of the thoughts to be included in each.

Then—and only then—did we really know what the magazine was really going to be all about. Eventually, of course, *Learning* was launched and has been successful.

In that case an experienced editor was on hand. There was no question about his ability to translate the table of contents into a professional magazine which lived up to the promise of the basic concept.

This development of tables of contents for a number of issues is really the minimum required for crystallizing a concept. Depending on the skill and experience of the people involved and the nature of the subject matter, even more must often be done.

Allen Bennett, then on the launching pad with *American Photographer*, developed 48 actual pages of the first issue with Sean Callahan, his editor, because this was really the only way to demonstrate the visual concept involved. The same has been done with a number of other magazines.

And, of course, it often happens that during the crystallization process you discover that the concept does not jell, or becomes too narrowly defined, or would be too expensive to produce, or is a newsletter or a book or something else, but not a magazine.

You Must Develop a Detailed Business Plan

Once the editorial concept is crystallized, the next step is a well-thought-out, detailed business plan showing prepublication costs, anticipated losses before achieving break-even and potential profits which can be earned.

This is normally prepared on a cash-flow basis because in a new magazine the cash investment is the only really important financial fact. Usually such plans are projected for at least five years.

Development of the business plan involves deciding on every aspect of how operations will be carried out. For instance, in the editorial area, you must formulate the number of editorial pages needed, the size of the editorial staff, salary levels, what outside editorial or design consultants are needed, what manuscripts, artwork and photos will have to be purchased and at what cost.

This becomes a big, complex project. Because it is hard to come to grips with it in the abstract, it is normally formulated through the technique of detailed financial projections. In developing these projections you necessarily must make decisions about every aspect of the business.

What Does the Business Plan Tell Us?

The first thing we want to know from the business plan is, "Do we have a possibly profitable magazine based on reasonable assumptions about circulation response, advertising support and cost factors?"

We very often find that major profits are impossible to achieve no matter what is done or that major changes have to be made in the plans to reach a profitable point.

Frequently a would-be publisher drops the grand plan for publishing weekly, compromising at six issues for the first year and a gradual move up to 12, or reluctantly agrees that 50-pound stock reproduces color as well as needed even though he or she really wanted 70-pound, or sees that the idea would be a better newsletter than magazine, or decides that he or she doesn't need many ad salespeople during the first year because there won't be much advertising for a while.

Many seemingly good projects must be dropped at this stage because it is impossible to anticipate a profit return large enough to justify the capital needed. It is at this planning stage when you had better find this out, not after business has started.

The Most Important Document You Will Ever Write—The Business Plan

The key to raising money, recruiting future employees, developing the interest of suppliers, consultants and others is the well-documented business plan. The basic information which should be contained in the business plan is outlined below:

The Concept—State the idea for the publication as simply as possible, ideally in one sentence. Also very briefly state who the people involved in the venture are. Keep to one page if possible.

The Editorial Need—Expand in this section on the editorial idea for the publication, offering substantial evidence of this need and discussing how this need has or has not been fulfilled up to this moment. Be very specific on the types of articles and editorials.

The Market—All the facts that can be mustered about the proposed audience for the magazine. Include facts that will demonstrate why they will be interested in the proposed editorial product, and be willing to subscribe if subscriptions are to be sold. Add facts that will demonstrate that the audience will be attractive to advertisers if advertising is going to be accepted.

The Advertisers—All the specifics that can be spelled out on the types of products and services which would logically be advertised to the audience. Also clearly spell out the degree of importance advertising revenue is to the success of the venture. If the venture is projected to break even on circulation revenue with advertising revenue the key to big profits, spell it out. If success or failure is based primarily on advertising revenue, say it.

The Company—Describe in detail how the company would be organized. If products other than the magazine are envisioned, explain them.

The Competition—The specifics about other magazines and other media serving the market. Give facts on their audience, rates, degree of success, and anything else that clearly presents whom this new magazine will be competing against. If information is available regarding the shortcomings of competition, use it only if it is factual and accurate. Leave out hearsay and opinions unless those offering them are recognized authorities in the area.

The People Involved—This is extremely important because a magazine is a product of people. The key individuals involved are the essential ingredient. Spell out in detail who will handle the editing, who will be the financial and business manager, who will have the overall direction of the operation and who will be advisors. And if you already have investors, name them. Include some pertinent background (but not too much) on each principal.

Financial Projections—Show for the startup period plus the first four years a forecast of cash receipts and disbursements. Indicate the basic assumptions upon which the forecasts are based (i.e., estimated circulation, percent return mailings, average ad rate, number of advertising pages, number of total pages, renewal percentages, subscription prices, etc.). Include any facts that will help the reader judge the validity of financial projections. But keep it short.

Write the Business Plan for the Audience You Are Trying to Interest—Big Investors

I have seen business plans which run anywhere from 10 pages to more than 200. A few try to explain the entire magazine business in detail. If that is what you want to do, write a book, but don't try to raise money for a magazine with it.

Some are full of indecipherable charts. Many look like a slick Madison Avenue sales promotion. Rarely do they contain good understandable financial projections done in normal accounting style.

If you consider that the most likely source of major financing is from venture capital groups (described later), you can easily understand that you must tailor your presentation to them. And remember that they may review as many as 10 ideas in a single day. With this in mind here are some things to remember:

• The basic concept must come through very clearly and concisely. (Once again, crystallizing the editorial concept is vital.)

- The document should tell the whole story, but very briefly. If it can be kept to 20 pages, all the better. If you arouse interest, you will be asked more questions than you have ever heard before.

- The flavor of the magazine should come through in the writing style and in the description of the editorial content.

- It should be very businesslike and professional. Good typing, no typos, simple cover—like a business report. At this point you want to come across as a thoughtful businessperson. Tomorrow you can be the colorful editor or salesperson.

- Financial projections should be shown simply and understandably. Follow normal accounting style. Do not give too many figures—it confuses. But have them all in your briefcase when you need them.

- Profit projections should be the ones you realistically expect. Don't blue-sky it. No one will believe you. But don't be overly conservative either. The reader will automatically reduce your figures anyway.

- Build in several go/no-go points. In every magazine project there are a number of key factors which must take place or failure is inevitable. One might be the results from the first big mailing; another, the ability to get a certain number of advertising pages by a certain time. There should be evaluation dates at which these key indicators are reviewed. If certain minimums have not been achieved, then the project should be stopped and the investors will not lose their entire investment.

- An experienced and skilled team should be available to make the project work. Particularly important is the existence of a good financial person to make sure there is careful control of the funds.

What Kind of People Do You Need and When?

A new magazine is successful because of the hard work and dedication of a very small number of people. But when should you hire them? Unless the publisher is also the editor, an editor must become involved very early. If advertising is vital at the early stages, an advertising director must be involved early. Otherwise he or she is not needed until several months before publication. If complex circulation planning is needed in the early stages, the circulation director must be involved then. Otherwise you can wait until several months before publication. The business manager is usually needed shortly before publishing operations begin.

This sounds as if just the publisher and possibly the editor are needed full-time in the early stages. This is true. At the beginning the publisher is probably the only person who must be completely immersed in the project. But input of the whole future team is invaluable in developing the business plan and in learning to work together. And if money-raising is required, the existence of a full team of skilled people has often made the difference between getting or not getting funded.

Using Consultants, Professionals and Others

With the skeleton staff outlined above, the need for using outsiders in some places is obvious. You just cannot know everything about every phase of the business. And there are lots of good consultants in just about every phase of the business. In fact, it would normally be impossible for a starting publisher to hire anywhere near the same caliber people on a full-time basis that he or she can obtain as consultants.

There is one important point to bear in mind in choosing consultants in the magazine field. Most of the areas where they are used are essentially creative—art direction, circulation, direct mail copywriting, editorial and the like. Here the most important ingredient may not be the reputation of the person, but rather his or her understanding of and excitement in the concept of the magazine. If he or she isn't really turned on, if he or she does not relate to the project and to you, that person probably is not the right one. Try another.

Capital Can Be Raised

Raising capital for any new venture is unbelievably time-consuming, frustrating and difficult. It is particularly so for a new magazine.

A magazine is intangible—there is no factory, no machinery. It is a disposable product. There are not many financially-oriented people that have been trained to understand intangible businesses, and even fewer who understand the economics of magazine publishing. There are few public companies which are big in magazine publishing, and normally these operations are mixed with books or printing or are completely overshadowed by other types of businesses. So there are very few analysts who devote themselves to publishing.

In addition, the general public has watched *Collier's, The Saturday Evening Post, Look* and *Life* die without really understanding why, and a number of individuals and institutions have lost money on magazine startups which were poorly conceived, poorly planned, badly executed or all three.

But while it is difficult, capital has been raised for new magazines, is right now being raised and will be raised in the future.

Capital—Seed Money

The testing technique discussed later fits very well into a two-step approach to capital. The first step (seed money) is used for developing the concept and business plans, for conducting the test and, in some cases, for keeping the entrepreneur alive.

This is money which very rarely can be obtained from normal capital sources. The venture is too risky at this stage for them. Capital usually has to be obtained in the most difficult possible way—from relatives, neighbors, friends. And more than one venture has made it only because the entrepreneur unhappily went hat-in-hand to in-laws and cousins.

The amount of seed money required obviously varies with the nature of the magazine, the size and the type of test and the financial staying power of the entrepreneur. A relatively typical list of expenses, including a direct-mail test, might look something like this:

Legal costs for formation of corporation or
partnership and other documents $ 5,000

Preparation of business plan—printing, consultants, etc.	5,000
Direct mail test—100,000 pieces—circulation consultant, artwork, copywriters, paper, printing, postage, lists, etc.	40,000
Incidental expenses	5,000
Total	$55,000

This is the bare minimum.

You will note that nothing has been included for other costs the entrepreneur may have incurred over a period of many months to bring the project to this stage. Quite a bit may have been spent in developing the editorial approach—artwork, dummies and the like. This rarely is recovered by the entrepreneur at this point, but may be later.

And I have included nothing for living costs of the entrepreneur during the testing and money-raising phases. Normally it is expected that he or she will exist meagerly on his or her own resources. Sometimes, however, additional seed money is raised so that a salary and ongoing expenses can be paid.

Testing Is Imperative

No matter how clever or intelligent you may be—or how good the idea may seem—you cannot be sure you have a winner until you have had the opportunity to find what your audience really thinks of it.

Testing, of course, cannot give the complete answer. Only the actual production of the magazine over a period of time can do that. But a well-designed testing program can get you over the first hurdle. In fact, this ability to test audience reaction is one of the beauties of the magazine business. Without it, raising capital to publish new magazines would become almost impossible.

Different magazines can be tested in different ways. *Money* was tested through a direct-mail appeal; *People* on the newsstand; Norman Cousins' *World* (later merged with *Saturday Review*) primarily by telephone. In some cases the use of a "one-shot" on newsstands will indicate whether there is an audience for a full-fledged magazine. But for most magazines the mail approach is the most suitable way to test whether there is really an audience that wants the magazine.

Design of the Direct Mail Test

Each potential magazine must be tested in its own way for its particular audience. In general, however, the following basic approach is followed. If you do not have in-house direct-mail skills, it is best to hire one of the highly experienced direct-mail consulting firms to help develop the mailings, choose lists, etc.

Depending on the nature of the magazine and the size of the potential audience, a test mailing of anywhere from 100,000 to 200,000 pieces should be ample to determine the viability of the project. For smaller magazines, however, this may not be possible. A special interest magazine might be confined to 20,000 or 30,000, since the larger numbers might well cover the entire prime audience.

While it is always desirable to have as large a test as possible, the money available normally limits the size.

Besides determining the basic viability of the project, the test is designed to learn a few other things like what price is best, what lists pull best, what copy approach pulls best. Normally it is better to test only a few different variables for price and copy approaches—to try to get too complex at this stage may be confusing and may negate the value of the test itself. Three mailing pieces and three copy approaches are plenty.

In the copy area it is best to get several of the best direct-mail copywriters to try their hands. But don't forget to include one very simple direct explanatory approach which fully defines the magazine, or you may end up not knowing whether the project is saleable or not.

I am talking here about a full-fledged direct-mail offer to buy the new magazine—asking for the order and, in some cases, for payment. This means that the mailing pieces must be as professionally done as those for magazines that actually exist. Indeed, normally one of the mailing packages is used just as it is when larger mailings are made.

And here again we see the importance of having crystallized the editorial concept. It is impossible to develop a mailing piece which adequately describes the magazine if the editorial approach is vague. And, even worse, if you describe one product and then come out with a magazine which is different, the results are meaningless.

Timing of the Direct-Mail Test

The entire timing of a new magazine launch is often dependent on when good mailing seasons exist. Unfortunately the magazine business seems to be subject to only two good mailing seasons—right after Christmas (January through March) and in late summer (July through October). Different mailing experts have their preferences as to the best time, but in general they agree with these dates.

What everyone will agree on, however, is that it is foolish to test in periods which are known to be poor. No matter what the results then, you haven't really learned anything.

With this kind of timing you can see that if you are going to send your first big mailing out in, say, January 1977, you must have your test out early enough to enable the results to be evaluated. This requires time for reserving the lists you want plus printing, inserting and mailing. To be sure you can get the big mailing out in January you must send the test out as early in the summer as possible.

In recent years an entire industry has grown up devoted to venture capital. It includes such types as SBIC's (Small Business Investment Companies), operated by virtually every major bank in the country and a few others; firms which have raised capital devoted to venture businesses; funds devoted to ventures by some large companies; funds set up by wealthy families and individuals; funds set up by Wall Street firms and other groups.

These are professionally operated venture funds, with paid managers in many cases. Their business is devoted to helping entrepreneurs get started—or to keeping moving at later stages. They are experienced in reviewing plans, judging people, anticipating trouble, assisting in the early stages, developing financial plans and all the other aspects of high-risk ventures.

Their business involves investing in order to obtain several times their investment within three to five years. The nature of this type of investment means that they cannot be successful in every case—and they know it.

Those running venture firms are intelligent, open-minded, easy to approach, innovative and probably overall the best businesspeople—as a group—that exist. They take the time to examine virtually every opportunity which is shown to them.

Once in a while major financing comes from other sources, but in the last few years, the venture capital firms have been the major source for new projects. While many of the firms will not go into publishing ventures, a good number have in recent times. Unfortunately, not every magazine they have invested in has been soundly conceived and managed so that a number of the venture firms have soured on the field.

There is an added complication in the magazine business. When people invest in most fields they do it on a strictly financial basis—what makes sense as an investment. If it is a steel mill, they don't really care what color you paint it.

Magazines are different. Although the return on investment is still important, the investors also want to relate to the magazine itself. Too often potential investors say, "I wouldn't read it," or, "I don't think the public will go for it," or, "It looks cheap, so I don't want to get connected."

Though this personal appeal aspect is often a foolish reaction, it exists.

On the other hand, there are often times when the investors take an interest in a particular concept—again, possibly foolishly—and put their money where the return may not be so good.

I suppose in the end it all averages out for would-be publishers. The personal "feel" helps in some cases, hurts in others.

How and When to Approach Potential Investors

Investors are busy people. They usually travel a good deal, either for business or pleasure. Although they usually have an open-minded approach to seeing people with ideas, it is often difficult for them to find the time.

Since they are experienced in looking at ventures, they almost always want to see the business plan before meeting the people involved. If the concept as a whole does not interest them, it is better for everyone not to waste time in conversation.

When you get into money-raising, you will find that it is the hardest and most discouraging kind of activity there is. It *always* takes longer than you had imagined. Just getting together with these people takes a lot of time.

Since you don't know which of the potential investors currently has money for new ventures and will spark to your concept, it is best to contact as many prospects as you can to find who might have some interest. Then you can concentrate on these. I leave it to your attorney to tell you what approach to use and what the limits on numbers of people might be.

When sizable amounts are to be raised for any type of venture, you will find that there are often several investors who say they will go along for a substantial hunk if you can find a "lead" investor.

I am not sure there is any precise definition of a lead investor. But in general, it is a person or institution who will invest a large percentage of the total—but, more important, has the respect of other investors. Usually, too, he or she will take on the job of "monitoring" the venture on behalf of the investment group. This means having the skill and time to become very immersed in the business—without interfering with the operations unless disaster strikes. He or she sits on the board and talks with the entrepreneur frequently. If more money is needed later, he or she will take the lead in organizing for it.

Without a lead investor, it becomes very difficult to raise money, so it is best to concentrate effort there.

In terms of timing, the sooner potential investors can be contacted, the better. That is, however, only after the business plan is thoroughly polished.

If a test of some kind is being made, I advocate developing the business plan before the test and making the investor rounds early. In this way, you can determine soon who shows interest in the idea.

Then, assuming that the test proves successful, you can get back to the interested investors, update the financial projections and move that much faster. It also adds credibility to have equalled or surpassed your predicted test results.

Time Schedule

It is advisable to make up a timetable so that you can concentrate on the most important areas at any particular point. The length of time before actual publication begins always seems incredibly long. But the considerations of good mailing periods, the fact that advertising budgets are designed on a calendar year basis, Christmas holidays, the difficulty of reaching investors when you want and all sorts of other contingencies seem to make everything take longer than necessary.

For example, here is an actual startup situation for one magazine.

January 1972—Entrepreneur started to work on magazine concept.

July 1972—Entrepreneur reached conclusion that magazine concept was good and needed publication. Went to venture capital firm, was told it was not in good enough form to consider.

July-December 1972—Working on business plan—many revisions and rewritings.

January-February 1973—Tried to raise $60,000 seed money from individual investors he had anticipated would be interested. No sale.

March 1973—Realized editorial concept did not come through and found editor who could make it more meaningful.

May 1973—Revised business plan to include better editorial material.

May-July 1973—Raised $48,000 from people closely connected with the field covered. Limited partnership set up. Direct-mail test planned.

January 1974—Direct-mail test of 200,000 pieces made. Results spectacular.

February 1974—Started round of fund-raising for

major financing.

April 1974—Business plan revised to reflect test results, latest cost increases on postage, paper, etc.

May 1974—Staff members hired.

August 1974—Big subscription mailing made and other promotion begins.

October 1974—First issue of magazine.

If major financing had not been completed quickly, the entire program would have been advanced six months, with a major mailing January 1975 and first issue in March 1975.

Financing Arrangements

In the final analysis, there are several parties interested in the ownership of a venture: The entrepreneur, the investors (who may be divided into two groups—seed money and major financing) and the employees.

The portion each group ends up with is the result of negotiation. These negotiations take place early with the seed money investors. Later, the major investors come along at a time when they are indispensable and because of this have great bargaining power.

This makes it sound as if the poor entrepreneur and employees will have a hard time of it. Fortunately, venture capitalists are realistic about the fact that the operators need a sizable piece of the ownership or the project won't work. And the investors know they have neither the knowhow nor the experience to do it themselves.

The number of different arrangements which have been made is enormous. To give some idea of the general relationship that eventually results, here are some rough ranges of percentage of ownership:

Entrepreneurs (and others who may have contributed time and talent in the early stages)	25-40%
Seed money investors	10-15%
Major investors	45-60%
Employees	5-10%

The bargaining power of the entrepreneurs varies with their skill and experience and the attractiveness of the concept.

Seed money investors generally get three to five times the percentage of ownership of the major investors for each dollar they invest.

The employees' share depends on their skill and experience. In many cases options are offered employees rather than outright stock.

The legal form of the venture can vary considerably. Since the startup expenses in publishing can be written off for tax purposes, many ventures are launched as Subchapter S corporations or limited partnerships at the beginning. The seed money investors can then take current ordinary deductions for their investments.

When you get to the major investment phase, the form it takes can vary all over the lot, with convertible debentures, preferred stock, short-term notes, guaranteed bank loans and just about everything else used from time to time.

All of this, at first, may seem incomprehensible. But remember that thousands of entrepreneurs have been through all of this before and have survived. Once the magazine starts you will face even tougher business decisions—it is a never-ending education process. But that's another story.

Alan Patricof

By Charles I. Tannen

Alan Patricof invests in magazines. As president of Alan Patricof Associates, New York, he has examined hundreds of new magazine proposals and, more importantly, the people behind them. Most noted for his financing of New York Magazine, *he recently has lined up the financing for* American Photographer. *Here, from an interview with* FOLIO *editor Charles Tannen, is Alan Patricof on starting a magazine.*

On entrepreneurs:

"I'm interested in people who think about how to use all the cleverness available to them. That means stretching themselves and going out on the limb a bit. The biggest mistake that entrepreneurs make is not thinking of the many ways available to raise money besides equity. I see too many proposals which carry the magic figure of $1 million as the capital requirement. Many of these entrepreneurs haven't put enough effort into exploring all the obvious alternatives. Unfortunately, these alternatives are usually available only to individuals who have some credibility or track record in the industry. In other words, they have the first essential characteristic for a successful new venture; namely, they have experience in the field. They don't realize all the IOU's they should be collecting for all their years in the business."

On replacement of equity:

"One of the major things I look for is how imaginative the entrepreneur is in developing sources of financing that are not traditional. I often see proposed budgets with editors' salaries of $40,000, publishers' salaries of another $40,000, large well paid staffs and all the normal relationships with creditors. These entrepreneurs then discover the hard fact that either they can't raise that much money, or that they have to give away 70 to 80 percent of their company. I look for proposals that can do it for less, and that doesn't mean they have to do a poor quality job.

"One magazine I invested in started out with one paid employee the day after the financing, and that was the assistant to the editor. They are now up to four people as they get close to publication, with a lot of other people working on a per diem or retainer basis. But they've reduced their overhead and their telephone bill and all the other expenses that build up very quickly.

"Normally printers want payment in advance from new publishers. But with the right credentials, previous relationships and a certain amount of cajoling and trading, you can come up with a printer who will give you 30 or 60 days credit. If you can't arrange credit for all of the print bill, at least try for everything but paper.

"The next source of equity replacement might be your direct mail house. Although you'll probably have to pay for your direct mail test in advance, if the test is successful it is conceivable that you could convince the direct mail house to accept a payment schedule for everything but postage. You could even set up a lock box arrangement with them to escrow the first funds collected. The same arrangement might work with your printer, too.

"Another source is advertising. Advertisers pay their bills, for the most part, on a regular 30-day basis. The more advertising you can sell in advance, the more of an element you have to finance against, since receivables can be assigned to a financial source. The rate of interest may be high and the percentage that they will lend against the receivables may be low, but it is a source of funds."

On realistic management:

"Why should one magazine cost under $500,000 to start and another comparable magazine cost over $1 million? *Texas Monthly*, for example, has a 200,000 circulation—it's one of the largest city/regional magazines. Yet similar magazines spent twice as much to get started and have smaller circulations. It all has to do with the economics and the viability of the magazine. If someone is spending $1 million they should look very carefully at the market, how their product fits into it and what it costs to get that market. I think the real difference, though, is the people and their attitudes toward running the business."

On investor control:

"I think control is always in the hands of the entrepreneur, regardless of how the equity is divided. An investor depends on the good graces and wise actions of the en-

trepreneur. I accept that. But there are some elements of control that can be put into a document, such as the approval of an annual budget and the requirement of a certain number of board members to decide on large expenditures, or mergers, or acquisitions or raises. Too many entrepreneurs become mesmerized by the obsession of owning 51 percent, as if that were a magic number. They often fail to get off the ground because the financial realities require them to cede a greater amount to the investor. Never forget, the ultimate objective is to get launched with proper capitalization."

On return on investment:

"I think that anyone who invests in a private, high risk venture, excluding tax considerations, should be looking to make three to five times on their money over a period of five years. That's the objective in any private, illiquid, high risk situation. I don't think it should be any more or any less except that sometimes there is a psychic income involved with magazines that motivates people to sacrifice some of their potential return. But there is a big difference between what you're looking for and what you get. If an investor gets two or three times his money, he can be happy. Sometimes, if he gets his money back he's satisfied. I've known situations where over $2 million have been invested in a magazine ending up with less than 100,000 circulation, and it loses even more money. There's no way the economics on that could ever work out. I think people forget the economics of the alternative use of capital."

On keeping investors happy:

"I think the best way to make investors happy is to give them their money back. Then they're less concerned with selling or getting their profits out. If I could work out a partnership arrangement where the first cash flow retires the investment, then I wouldn't mind riding with the deal with nothing more risked. And, of course, there is always the possibility of selling out the magazine or merging it. But I don't start out with that approach. I'd be happy if each of my magazine investments became its own publishing empire, each with its own entrepreneur. There was a day, and it doesn't exist now, when you hoped the magazine would go public. I think that is unrealistic today. I don't think a single magazine could go public. Maybe a multi-publication company could be successful, though. I think you have to look at magazines as an illiquid investment and that investors have to know they are in for a long term situation. That should be mutually understood before going into financing.

"Another way of keeping investors happy is by keeping them informed. Don't exaggerate the future or disregard the unpleasant realities of today. Investors can be patiently cooperative—even supportive—if they feel loved and respected. Don't take them for granted."

Starting a consumer magazine

By Irvin J. Borowsky

Irvin J. Borowsky, founder and president of North American Publishing Company, launched his first consumer publication in 1948. It was a weekly guide to television programs, which later became the cornerstone of the present TV Guide.

He is one of a handful of publishers who are comfortable in both the business and consumer fields. His company published Cue *magazine from 1975 to 1980 and* Audio, *which it sold to CBS in 1980. It currently publishes numerous magazines, from* ZIP *and* Marketing Bestsellers *to magazines for educators, medical labs, the export industry, and the printing and publishing industries.*

Why do practical, highly successful entrepreneurs and sophisticated investors finance inexperienced editors and publishers—with investments totaling millions of dollars—to start consumer magazines, many that are *doomed* to fail from the start?

And why do so many respected business publishers take the plunge, only to find that losses are four to 10 times more than they had budgeted or dreamed of investing before reaching break-even?

What seduces everyone? Although there are probably as many answers to this question as there are views to a statue, I believe the fundamental attraction is the big pot of gold—the potential massive contribution to corporate profits when a new idea works.

Many new titles introduced in the past 25 years have become more than magazines—they have become major corporations. *TV Guide, Playboy* and *Penthouse* are but a few. Less spectacular but still significant are the numerous smaller and medium-sized consumer special-interest publications that are producing excellent cash flow.

These success stories make it difficult to turn a deaf ear to the bright, young person with a plausible new idea. After all, many successful magazines have been started by people with no prior publishing experience.

Rumors further inflate the image of the pot of gold. While we don't know if *TV Guide* really did reject an offer of $500 million a few years ago, any amount near $100 million or more for a single magazine is staggering to a business publisher.

Indeed, consumer magazine publishing, when compared with business magazine publishing, does offer an opportunity to make it big. But it also has been the graveyard for many. A great deal of money can be lost funding new consumer titles.

What's the problem?

The major trap that ensnares highly successful business publishers who move into consumer publishing is the deep, dark hole of building profitable circulation, both in newsstand sales and subscription sales.

The key to the survival and growth of most consumer magazines is single-copy sales. However, most *business* magazine publishers are not accustomed to a magazine distribution system that operates exclusively on a consignment basis. There are no exceptions: *All* magazines are shipped on a fully returnable basis to 500 exclusive wholesalers, who tell the publisher how many copies were sold. Furthermore, unsold inventory is returned only if the publisher pays extra for handling the returns.

(Fortunately, the publisher doesn't have to bill and collect from each of these 500 wholesalers. There are about a dozen national distributors in the U.S. who will take over the billing and collection process for a fee of 6 percent to 10 percent of the net receipts.)

Another problem for the new magazine building single-copy sales is the shortage of rack space in retail outlets. Up-front displays are vital to the success of a new magazine, but chewing gum, stockings and film are all competing for limited display space.

Because of the shortage, the large retail chains must limit their stores to handling only 100 to 200 magazine titles. This limitation prevents over 1,000 titles from being displayed or sold at these important outlets that now account for an impressive percentage of all single copies sold.

Subscription sales also has its problems. Consumer magazines use a variety of methods (e.g., bind-in and blow-in cards, subscription agencies, sweepstakes) to sell subscriptions to meet circulation guarantees. However, alternative sources other than the publisher's own direct mail and blow-in cards have one major disadvantage: Returns on renewals secured from alternative subscription sources are considerably less than those sold through the publication's own efforts. Unfortunately, consumer publishers are often forced to use these alternatives or short cuts, especially when their circulations fall below the guarantee promised advertisers.

There is a positive side, of course. Once you gain the momentum of a 60 percent to 70 percent sale of all copies shipped, your profit zooms. Think of how profitable it is to pay your printer 40 cents to 50 cents per copy (based on end of run printing costs) while receiving $1 per copy for 100,000, 500,000 or 1 million copies per month.

Start small

In a recent survey conducted among business publishers who stuck their toes into the competitive pool of consumer publishing, the following guidelines for getting into consumer publishing emerged:

1. For your first venture, it is much less risky to acquire a *small* established consumer magazine than to launch a new title.

2. Unless you are prepared to invest seven figures, think small: regardless of how competent you think you are, consumer publishing is as different from the business press as a book club is from marketing co-op post cards.

3. There is a learning period that cannot be avoided. Pace yourself during this time by committing yourself to smaller chips.

4. Whatever figure you have projected for development costs—double it, and then double it again.

5. Get the right people: Special interest business publishing personnel who have no background in consumer publishing must go through a costly learning period.

6. Don't publish for professional organizations or societies. They are too political. You have to contend with board members who have no background in publishing and who become authoritative—especially if they were once editors of their school newspapers.

7. It is easier to succeed in the special interest fields than in the broader-based markets. Titles such as *Audio* or *Bicycling* are clearly defined, whereas magazines such as *New Times, GEO* and *Quest* require a lot of market explanation to media buyers.

8. One business publisher stated: "If you are planning a start-up, think about it for five years. Circulation never comes up to your expectations."

My own view? I believe that if you have the desire and money, plus the cash flow from profitable business magazines to support developing costs—why not try it? It's exciting, and it can be fun. I've done it seven times, and I'll do it again.

I guarantee that the experience will widen your overall publishing scope—and just maybe you'll develop a mammoth new profit center that will broaden your personal horizons as well as augment your company's bottom line.

Now that you've raised money for a new magazine...

By James B. Kobak

Congratulations! You have raised $30,000—or $300,000—or $3 million—to launch your magazine.

What happens now? That's up to you!

You are embarking on the second hardest job there is—starting a new business. (The hardest, of course, is raising money. You've already done that.) The next phase is very different.

First, let's agree on a few basic assumptions:

• Not many people have successfully started a new business of any kind.

• You have never started a new business.

• The business of magazine publishing involves attracting a part of the public to your product. And who can predict what the public will like?

• You are familiar with some aspects of publishing but others are foreign to you.

• The team you have assembled—or will assemble—has never worked together before.

• You are not really sure how good each member of the team is.

• You have rounded up some money—and some investors—but you do not know them very well.

• You will only get one shot at the project.

• You get hurt worse than anyone else if things don't work out.

• You are exhausted—and to some extent frustrated—from the money-raising activities.

Congratulations!

Now what? Now comes organizing, planning, hiring, directing, buying, selling, negotiating, dealing and doing all sorts of other things you probably have never done before.

Will you be good at them? Who knows?

Anyway, below is a checklist of 186 things to do after you've raised money for the new magazine. (Of course, every item may not pertain to every venture. But, taken as a whole, this list will certainly provide a useful checklist—for the publisher of a well-established magazine, as well.)

1. No matter how exhausted and discouraged you get, continue to resell the investors. You may need more money later.

2. No matter how exhausted and discouraged you get, continue to resell your staff. They may not always remember that it is better to work longer and harder for you than they would elsewhere and to receive less pay than they think they can get elsewhere.

3. No matter how exhausted and discouraged you may get, continue to sell the suppliers. They must continue to understand the importance of being connected with such a successful and prestigious magazine—and you may need them for extended credit at some point.

4. No matter how exhausted and discouraged you may get, continue to sell advertisers and agencies on the idea that they should place their ads in your magazine (even though they normally do not do this for new magazines).

5. No matter how exhausted and discouraged you may get, continue to sell your banker. When you need money later your banker may be able to furnish it.

6. No matter how exhausted and discouraged you may get, continue to sell everyone else you can find on the concept. Who knows when they might be helpful?

7. Work an 18-hour day every day including Sundays and holidays. You will probably only be able to do this for two to three years.

8. Don't let the investors have any surprises. Tell them everything, even if they think you are the greatest bore in the world.

9. Never, never, never find the need for midnight calls to investors for money you need tomorrow.

10. Get to know your competitors.

11. Overcommunicate with employees, suppliers, investors, advertisers, readers and everyone else—or at least try.

12. Expect surprises in the quality of your employees. Some may even be pleasant surprises.

13. Listen to advice from your investors. Don't necessarily act on it. Remember, just because they have money doesn't mean they are dumb. And some of them may have experience in starting things.

14. Keep investors from forcing you to hire their ne'er-do-well relatives.

15. Listen to publishing people and their advice. But remember that very, very few of them have ever been connected with a startup—and even if they have, no two new magazines are the same.

16. Get your spouse interested and useful in the project. It's cheaper and less time-consuming than a divorce.

17. Delegate authority and responsibility as much as you can—don't abdicate anything.

18. Review every plan and every decision anyone makes.

19. Develop an organization chart and short job descriptions. Review and update them regularly.

20. Don't fritter your time away with minor projects. Keep your eye on the ball.

21. Stay flexible.

22. Get wired into your company's grapevine. Be sure you have a way to plant rumors, too.

23. Remember that *everything* is important when you start a new business—what kind of wastebaskets to buy, where the coffee machine is located, etc.

24. Make sure that you have good accounting and statistical records and that each month's results are known quickly.

25. Sell advertising even if you don't think you are a good salesperson. No one else has the same enthusiasm and dedication.

26. Budget on both the cash and accrual basis. As you learn more, change the budget, as often as monthly if it is helpful. Use a computer model to make it easier. Keep investors informed of any change.

27. Project operations for several years ahead. Make changes as you get more information. Keep investors informed.

28. Join MPA, ABP, DM/MA and/or other useful associations. Get to know others in the business. You can learn things, make friends and find prospective employees.

29. Subscribe to FOLIO, *Ad Age* and other periodicals.

30. Send yourself and your employees to programs run by associations and magazines as they fit your situation. Maybe your investors would be interested too.

31. Have a board of directors. Be sure you have knowledgeable people who will speak up to you on it.

32. Investigate, negotiate and make arrangements with a law firm.

33. Investigate, negotiate and make arrangements with an accounting firm. Be sure you are audited every year.

34. Investigate, negotiate and make arrangements with an executive recruiting firm and employment agencies.

35. Investigate, negotiate and make arrangements with an advertising agency.

36. Investigate, negotiate and make arrangements with a subscription consulting firm.

37. Investigate, negotiate and make arrangements with a single-copy sales consulting firm.

38. Investigate, negotiate and make arrangements with a marketing consulting firm.

39. Investigate, negotiate and make arrangements with a public relations consulting firm.

40. Investigate, negotiate and make arrangements with an overall publishing consulting firm.

41. Investigate, negotiate and contract for composition.

42. Investigate, negotiate and contract for separations.

43. Investigate, negotiate and contract for printing.

44. Investigate, negotiate and contract for paper.

45. Investigate, negotiate and contract for subscription fulfillment.

46. Investigate, negotiate and contract for a national single-copy distributor.

47. Investigate, negotiate and contract with various catalog, mail, telephone and other subscription agents.

48. Investigate, negotiate and contract for office equipment, supplies and other necessaries.

49. Investigate, negotiate and contract for computer modeling.

50. Investigate, negotiate and contract for other outside systems—payroll, general ledger, advertising, etc.

51. Organize an editorial board if it will be helpful.

52. Seek out and hire the editor and the editorial staff.

53. Seek out and hire an advertising director and salespeople.

54. Seek out and hire advertising promotion people.

55. Seek out and hire advertising research people.

56. Seek out and hire publishers' representatives.

57. Seek out and hire subscription promotion people.

58. Seek out and hire subscription fulfillment people.

59. Seek out and hire single-copy salespeople.

60. Seek out and hire production people.

61. Seek out and hire a controller and other accounting people.

62. Seek out and hire an office manager.

63. Seek out and hire writers.

64. Seek out and hire an art director and artists.

65. In seeking out and hiring, remember the equal opportunity laws.

66. Seek out and hire secretarial and clerical people.

67. Get to know reporters for *The New York Times, Chicago Tribune, Ad Age* and other publications covering the field.

68. Organize and carry out a carefully thought-out public relations program for the magazine and advertising community.

69. Determine the location of your main office. New York is by far the center of the magazine business. People and services are easier and more expensive to obtain and the principal advertisers and agencies are there. But there are lots of successful magazines published in all sorts of other places around the country.

70. Determine where the actual office will be—and what kind of effect you want. Remember that nobody visits the publisher—and investors appreciate the frugal approach.

71. Investigate, negotiate and contract for space and facilities for your main office.

72. Investigate, negotiate and contract for office layout and decoration.

73. Determine if and where you will need branch offices.

74. Investigate, negotiate and contract for space and facilities for your branch offices.

75. Determine the phone system you will need.

76. Develop rough pay scales for employees.

77. Develop incentive plans for as many employees as possible.

78. Set up a routine for changing salaries.

79. Determine what fringe benefits you will offer—holidays, vacations, working hours, etc.

80. Investigate, negotiate and contract with insurance people for fringe-benefit packages. Don't forget the plans set up specifically for publishing groups.

81. Develop stock purchase, option or other plans for key employees.

82. Decide whether you will have pension or profit-sharing plans.

83. Determine expense account policies and procedures.

84. Get your employer's Social Security number and do other necessary steps to comply with federal and state requirements.

85. Investigate, negotiate and contract with insurance people for business insurance of various types.

86. Establish your fiscal year.

87. Obtain the necessary copyrights.

88. Consider company life insurance for you and other key people.

89. Name the magazine.

90. Have a logo designed. Be sure it is distinctive, related to the magazine and prominent on the newsstand.

91. Have a design for the inside of the magazine developed. Be sure it is designed with the reader in mind.

92. Determine pay scales for outside manuscripts, artwork and photographs.

93. Develop a contract for outside authors.

94. Set up schedules of things to be done by you and by everyone else.

95. Develop a system for checking on the meeting of these schedules.

96. Establish a reading file where copies of every letter and memo are placed. Read it regularly.

97. Decide on the best post office entry points for the magazine.

98. Make the necessary arrangements with the post office.

99. Determine when the first issue will be published.

100. Determine the publishing schedule thereafter.

101. Determine advertising closing dates, editorial schedules, printing schedules, mailing dates, single-copy on-sale dates and other related schedules.

102. Decide on paper weight and quality.

103. Open bank accounts. Decide who can sign checks.

104. Have investors and staff get to know each other.

105. Set up a regular reporting schedule for investors.

106. Develop a schedule for the number of pages in each issue depending on the number of advertising pages.

107. Decide whether to offer charter rates—or some other schemes—to get early advertising.

108. Develop advertising rate cards.

109. Decide whether to guarantee a circulation rate base and what it will be to start.

110. Decide on subscription and single-copy prices.

111. Decide on reduced introductory prices.

112. Decide whether to be perfect bound or saddle-stitch.

113. Decide on size of magazine.

114. Decide on titles for the staff—and the layout of the masthead.

115. Decide on design and layout of your stationery.

116. Decide whether to do your own typesetting.

117. Decide on how to train your employees.

118. Decide whether to do in-house or outside data processing.

119. Organize to develop classified advertising.

120. Make arrangements for renting your lists.

121. Be sure to take advantage of all the tax opportunities offered to magazine publishers.

122. File all required tax returns.

123. Instill in all employees the attitude that the reader is a customer and should be treated as such. Review all material sent to readers with this in mind.

124. Work to get the most out of the suppliers and professionals you use.

125. Set up committees and task forces to study and execute difficult projects.

126. Don't let any piece of advertising promotion, public relations or research get out of the shop without your OK.

127. Frequently get an updating of the status of advertising sold.

128. Be sure you have a good call report system for advertising salespeople. Monitor it frequently.

129. Establish contacts with the key accounts and agencies, not only to help sell, but also to be able to monitor both the sales force and the attitude of the ad community toward your magazine.

130. Set up a credit-checking system for advertisers and agencies.

131. Set up a billing and collection system for advertising.

132. Be sure you have a complete file of advertising prospects. See that they are intelligently assigned to salespeople.

133. Review all subscription sales plans.

134. Study the results of subscription efforts and tests regularly.

135. Push the fulfillment house for fast and accurate data. Be sure you understand it yourself.

136. Move into single-copy sales gingerly. Confine to specific areas to start with.

137. Get to know the single copy wholesalers in the areas where you have heavy distribution. Get to know their marketers, route people and distribution clerks too.

138. Set up direct sales outlets with logical retailers who are not served by wholesalers.

139. Read every word of every issue before it is put out. Don't hesitate to insist on changes.

140. Review each issue after it has been published. Mark it up to show how things could have been improved.

141. Do reader research on each issue to find out what has been read.

142. From time to time focus group sessions with readers to try to find ways to improve editorially.

143. Make sure excess cash is invested wisely and safely. Ask the investors to help with this.

144. Have your circulation audited if you carry advertising.

145. Develop audience research for advertisers.

146. Keep on testing for subscriptions. You may find a breakthrough—for at least small improvements.

147. Set up regular structured meetings with the staff.

148. Know what to say when certain newsletter writers call.

149. Decide whether to have a company outing in the summer and/or a Christmas party. If so, decide what they should be like, whether spouses should be invited and where they should be held.

150. Review each issue for printing quality.

151. Have regular directors' meetings at logical decision points.

152. Negotiate with foreign publishers for international editions of the magazine.

153. Start planning for byproducts.

154. Go over the layout before closing each issue for the least expensive printing imposition.

155. Review all printing and paper bills.

156. Decide when to change advertising rates and/or the rate base.

157. Decide when to change circulation prices.

158. Insist on editorial plans at least six months ahead.

159. Hold a retreat with key members of the staff annually to rethink the entire project.

160. Review competitors' magazines—personnel and operating methods.

161. Remind the editor that the editor too is a marketer.

162. Remind the circulation director that he or she is really a marketer.

163. Explore other ways to get subscriptions.

164. Realize that you and the other founding partners may not get along. When that happens, face up to it.

165. If one or more of your partners has to go, so be it.

166. If you must get out to save the project, so be it.

167. When you find that the editorial product is not turning out as well as you had anticipated, do something. Fire the editor, get a new art director, hire a consultant.

168. Or go off and rethink the whole editorial approach.

169. When you find that subscriptions are not coming in at the rate you had anticipated, do something. Get a new subscription director, hire a new consultant, have a new letter written.

170. Or go off and rethink the entire circulation approach.

171. If single copy sales are not coming in as anticipated—or if you cannot find out how many are sold—do something. Get a new single copy director, get a new national distributor, hire your own field force, try new promotion devices.

172. Or go off to rethink whether you have a newsstand magazine or not.

173. If advertising sales are disappointing, do something. Hire a new ad director, change the promotion, try a new research approach.

174. Or go off to rethink whether your ad sales approach is right.

175. The office is in chaos. You wonder how the issues get out. Get a new office manager—or hire a new publisher to replace you.

176. Get rid of anyone who is not doing his or her job whether that person is an employee, a consultant or a supplier.

177. If you are the misfit, take yourself out of the picture—fast.

178. You have already developed go/no-go points. Don't be so excited that you carry on even though the stop signal is there.

179. Something big is sure to go wrong. When it does, don't hide it. Tell investors, suppliers and anyone else who might be helpful.

180. Have a party when an issue gets into the black. Make sure it isn't such a good party that you go back into the red.

181. Make sure to see your children on Christmas, Thanksgiving and their birthdays.

182. Make sure that the investors know early that

you have a need for more money because things have not quite worked out right.

183. Let your investors know early that you will need more money because of your tremendous success.

184. If it looks as if you will run out of money, don't dribble away what you have. Stop publishing and cut all other drains on it until you can raise money.

185. If things look as if they will not work out, be the first to know it—and the first to admit it.

186. Forget about ever starting another business. Once is enough.

Chart of a New Publisher's Regular Duties

Meetings	Times a year	Hours devoted	Review Activities		
			Financial reports	12	36
			Advertising sales status	52	52
Key staff for updating	52	156	Advertising call reports	52	52
Retreat with staff	1	20	Subscription plans	12	48
Company parties	2	6	Subscription results	52	52
Board of directors	4	12	Read issue before publication	12	60
Subscription consultant	4	8	Review issue after publication	12	36
Single copy consultant	4	8	Reading file	52	52
Marketing consultant	4	8	Layout of magazine	12	12
Public relations consultant	4	8	Editorial plans	12	36
Publishing consultant	4	12	Reader research	12	12
Printer	2	4	Focus group research	2	6
Paper supplier	2	4			454
Fulfillment house	2	4			
National newsstand distributor	2	4	**Performance Activities**		
Insurance agent	1	2	Sell advertising	52	520
Editorial board	1	4	Develop budget	4	10
Competitors	4	8	Develop long range projections	4	10
Associations	2	30	Revise organization chart, job descriptions	4	8
Seminars	2	20	Communicate with investors	12	24
Attorney	2	6			572
Accounting firm	2	6			
Advertising agency	2	4			
Banker	4	8	TOTAL		1,368
		342			

Writing the proposal

By James B. Kobak

This is the first of a new series of articles describing the steps involved in starting a magazine. Back in 1974 I wrote an article on this topic, but it has become apparent that it was not specific enough. Some people also feel that it is a bit out of date.

Rather than write more articles describing the process, I, along with my devoted wife, Hope, decided to show by example—invent a magazine and develop a business plan for it. Then everyone can do their own magazine without us.

Our idea is for a magazine devoted to our favorite sport—body surfing, an increasingly popular pastime. (Some may think of body surfing as simply using your body as a surfboard and riding in on a wave, but we connoisseurs know it is much more.) Here is the story of how the magazine idea was developed.

It was a quiet Sunday afternoon and I was trying to watch yet one more football game. The Jets were only down 21-0 in the second quarter and had reached their own 30-yard line for the first time that year. It was a tense moment.

"Hey," Hope said, "let's start a magazine."

"Oh God," I replied, "not you too!"

"What's the thing you most like to do?"

"Well, I used to—but—in the afternoon? In the middle of a game? Besides, I'm 57 years old!"

"Oh, I didn't mean *that*. I meant what you really like—body surfing," she answered helpfully.

I looked at her quizzically. "But Hope, there are only about 12 other people in the world who know what body surfing is. Who would advertise? All you need is some water. No equipment. You don't even need a bathing suit. In fact, it's better that way," I said, confident that that would be the end of the matter.

It wasn't. This conversation was to continue for another two months.

Finally, I told her to do what I tell everyone else to do—define the editorial concept and develop editorial plans, very detailed tables of contents, for the first 12 issues. I thought that should keep her out of mischief for at least a year.

The next week during the Jets-Cowboys game, she handed me this:

THE BODY SURFER PERSON
The concept

The Body Surfer Person will be about all aspects of body surfing. It will be witty, urbane, folksy, whimsical, naughty, newsy and gossipy. It will have superb graphics, with great photographs and terrific original paintings. It will be au courant. Articles will be gutsy as well as entertaining. It will be fun, not pedantic. Informative without being dull. America—and the world—*needs* this magazine and has been waiting for it!

"Sorry, Hope," I said. "It says nothing." A mild tantrum followed. I returned to the game—the Jets were winning.

Four months later. The season is over. Hope has conquered the concept.

"It's all a learning process," she says. "After four tries at writing the concept, I realized I hadn't formed a detailed enough plan. Tables of contents aren't enough. You must be more specific, almost as if you are directing your writers toward exactly what you want in your book. Finally, I learned that if your thinking is the least bit fuzzy beforehand, it will only become more so.

"It's only after you've struggled through a half dozen-or-so attempts that you begin to know your magazine, what it's really about and who it's for. Then, surprisingly, the concept just about writes itself. And I see now that the editorial plan is not simply a list of ideas for articles. It must give a specific diagram of how an issue will look: a detailed diagram."

I nodded. I had told her this at every half-time, but I suppose it must be experienced. She then handed me this:

THE BODY SURFER PERSON
The concept

The Body Surfer Person magazine is for everyone who has ever body surfed—or ever wanted to. It is for men, women, teenagers and older children. It describes the experience, tries to be helpful in giving advice on beaches, travel to and from beaches, techniques and other relevant information.

But particularly, *BSP* attempts to recapture the simplicity of a lifestyle in the sun, sand and surf.

BSP is for the expert. *BSP* is for the novice. Or even the armchair traveler. Though at times *BSP* adopts a tongue-in-cheek style, *BSP* really tells you what's going on in body surfing all over the world.

Here is the first editorial plan Hope was able to develop. Note that she gives the numbers of pages and suggested authors (which helps define the tone of the magazine) and she specifies the graphics to be used with each piece. She also chose to put some departments (fashion, health) in the "editorial well" rather than in the front or back of the book. That is her prerogative. In this case it works. It may not work in other magazines.

THE BODY SURFER PERSON
The wave-lover's magazine

November—Table of contents
(editorial plan)

Waveback (reader letters)

Understanding the waves (four-page feature). Suggested author: Jacques Cousteau.

A detailed treatise on what makes good surf; understanding how the wind, the sun and the moon all play a part in creating waves; and how to test for ocean currents and undertow. The clouds can tell you what's going to come rolling in soon. This knowledge may one day increase your fun—or save your life! Diagrams and underwater photographs.

Meeting a girl at a macho surf beach (four-page article). Suggested author: Ann Landers.

Best way—politely hand her the top/bottom of her bikini. Landers gives tips on what to do and what not to do. It turns out that the technique isn't too different from the one used in the school library. Landers has done her homework—she gives you the lingo and tells you to memorize it, then take off! We supply a handy pull-out glossary of terms.

Robert Redford discusses the ecological threat to our beaches (eight-page interview).

BSP leads a lively exchange with the superstar who is widely respected for his determination to preserve the wildernesses of the world. While Redford speaks of his love of the sport of body surfing, the interview covers all aspects of his life: his childhood, his love of nature, his Hollywood trials and triumphs. Through his cogent replies to searching questions, you will gain new insight into the character of this multi-faceted man. Many interesting photographs of Redford talking and surfing.

The seaweed quiche (one-page department). Suggested author: James Beard.

There are many varieties of seaweed and almost all of them are edible. Some are tastier than others. Beard leads you step by step through a seaweed quiche recipe. There are even bits of chopped seaweed in the crust! Colorful photographs of the delicious result in rich greens and purples.

Teaching your parents to body surf (two-page department). Suggested author: Soupy Sales.

Eventually they will thank you for opening their eyes to the Greater Life out there, but you must be prepared for resistance. Keep a firm authoritative tone of voice. Repeat: "Nonsense, those sharks are just being friendly." "Undertow? A myth." "Now, try again. You can't expect to master this sport after riding only 212 waves." And, finally, explain with great care that it really isn't important at all that they don't know how to swim! *You* are there.

Beware your travel agent—Lake Erie is not good for body surfing (four-page article). Suggested author: Arthur Frommer.

A serious discussion on how you can be misled by supposedly good advice. Most people think surfing means board surfing, and they wrongly assume that it's the same as body surfing. It decidedly is NOT, as you'll discover when you get to the beach. Frommer tells you what questions to ask. He also lists many little known body surf beaches of the world and their dangers. He offers to give you his personal advice if you send a stamped envelope. Now you can forget your travel agent! Color photographs of Lake Superior at sundown.

A photographic portfolio (eight pages).

This month BSP takes you to the famous Palm Beach of Sydney, Australia. Twelve color photos show you an aerial panorama of one of the world's loveliest beaches, the famous volunteer lifeguards at work and in one of their colorful contests, a shark watch in progress with helicopters overhead and the patrol boat with spear guns and rifles at the ready and those beautiful long-legged Australian beauties.

. . . . . For Christmas giving . . . . .
How to measure your wife for a new bikini without her knowing! (one-page department). Suggested author: Diana Vreeland.

Forget it! She'd rather have one of the splendidly designed new one-piece suits. The shoulder straps never slide down and they come in luscious colors. Vreeland lists accessories such as beach caftans, totes, sunglasses, beach towels—all the paraphernalia for body surfing. Photographs of each item. On page 82 we list the stores where all this loot will be available.

Surfpacking the grandchildren (three-page article). Suggested author: Dr. Benjamin Spock.

Surf's up and you're babysitting. What to do? Assuming the little tykes are at home in the water and are at least beginner swimmers, this article teaches (with illustrations) the basic techniques of beginning surfing—with a special section devoted to the increasingly popular practice of infant surfing. Dr. Spock also makes a case against allowing children to use inflated rubber rafts and mattresses. He states the pros and cons of this issue.

The gin game (one-page department). Suggested author: Dr. Paul Swimmersear.

Next to sunburn, the surfer's biggest complaint is earache. Dr. Swimmersear discusses how to prevent it and explains that there is no need for expensive prescription preparations. As a preventive, a dropper full of gin from your picnic basket into the ear after swimming will do just fine! He discusses what medication to have on hand should your ear become infected. He gives his forthright views about nose plugs and ear plugs. Diagrams of the inner ear and channels to the nose are included.

Where to go, where to stay, how to get there (12-page department). By our round-the-world correspondents.

Specific data about six of the world's great surf beaches. This month we cover Copacabana, Rio; Biarritz, France; Palm Beach, Sydney, Australia; Newport Beach, Rhode Island; Curtain Bluff, Antigua; Davis Bay Beach, St. Croix, U.S. Virgin Islands. This is a factual section of listings including:

Weather you can expect at different seasons of the year and the nature and size of the surf. Average wave heights as well as air and water temperature.

Facilities at each beach including numbers of lifeguards (if any), lockers, towels and chair rentals, snack bars, rest rooms. Prices are given, but they are frequently out of date.

Hotels, guest houses, campsites and villas for rent. Quotes prices and lists addresses.

Information about local transportation that will get you to the beach. Bicycle, motorcycle and car rental agencies are listed and prices quoted. Availability of taxi service.

This section is perforated for easy tear-out.

Win the skin game (one-page department). Suggested author: Dr. Saul Blister, surfing dermatologist.

Protective sunscreening lotions that work (listed by degree of protection and price). The doctor discusses what to do if those wave-awaiting shoulders get burned. He offers home-made, economical sunburn salves and a moisturizer you can make yourself from coconut milk. It does wonders for those sun wrinkles.

Letter from Washington (four-page cover story). How decisions at Camp David will revolutionize body surfing. Suggested author: Jack Anderson.

The Begin-Sadat accord has opened 627 miles of surfing beaches previously denied to the aficionado. A secret pact—secret until *BSP* uncovered the story—spells out that future disagreements will be settled by body surfing contests judged by representatives from the non-aligned nations.

Special feature: photographs of the leading body surfers of Israel and Egypt in action!

Do-it-yourself surf (four-page article). Suggested author: Edward Wagner.

There are devices on the market that can create surf in your lake or swimming pool. Body surfing will be commonplace sooner than you think! The availability of these devices, their cost, practicality and maintenance problems are discussed at length. Also covered is the expense of padding the swimming pools with a special bounce-off foam rubber product to prevent injury. Illustrated.

You know you always wanted to look like a seal—now you can! (one-page department).

Wet suits—how practical are they? At what temperatures do you need them? What do they cost? Where do you find them? Best buys listed by location and price.

Crossword (one-page department).

A marine life first. You'll need your dictionary for this one!

Horoscope (one-page department).

You sure need to know what's in store for you in that next wave!

What's new (one-page department).

Halston, that inimitable innovator, describes his new bikini—that schlepped-in look. It's not fashion—it's survival! Illustrations.

After reading all this I sat back in my armchair and surveyed Hope. I was really quite impressed.

"Not bad," I said. "Now all you need are 11 more editorial plans just like it and you're on your way." She looked at me forlornly. I continued. "But of course, even then, you have to remember it probably won't work. There are still only 12 people in the world who need or want this magazine." She didn't take my comments well, as she calmly poured my drink into my lap.

Writing the business plan

By James B. Kobak

Since my wife Hope had done such a superb job of developing the editorial concept of *The Body Surfer Person* (See "Writing the proposal"), we were sure that at least from the editorial standpoint the magazine could be done—and done well.

Now we had to make a business plan to see whether the idea had commercial possibilities. Too many publications claiming to have avid followers just cannot make it economically. We certainly didn't want to be involved in one of those—bad for the reputation, you know.

The next step: defining the market for readers. How many are there? What is their degree of interest? Where are they? Who are they? When do they think about body surfing? And how would they view the usefulness of this new magazine?

Some of the information needed is statistical; the rest is an educated guess. Here is how we finally described the market in the business plan.

The market for readers

While there are no reliable statistics on the number of body surfers (the Bureau of the Census neglected to include this question in the last count), there is conclusive data indicating that the total number of body surfer persons in the United States is 20 million—with the worldwide total at least ten times that.

Support for these figures is available in some relatively simple statistics:

•Swimming is the largest participation sport in the country with approximately 130 million people active in 1977. Twenty-five percent of these people swam five or more times in that year.

•On a typical summer weekend, more than 4 million people visit ocean beaches in the New York area alone. While not all of them are ardent body surfers, at least 20 percent do surf, either on purpose or inadvertently.

•Estimates are that more than 500 million visits are made each year to the ten major beach areas in the United States (Coney Island, Jones Beach, Riis Park, Jersey Shore, Miami Beach, Ocean City, Laguna Bay, Waikiki, New Beach and Virginia Beach). This number can be doubled for the great many lesser beaches, giving a total of more than one billion visits.

•Assuming average attendance to be ten visits, a total of 100 million people each year go to ocean beaches. A conservative estimate that only one in five is a body surfer yields a total of 20 million.

•An indication of the size of the market can also be gleaned from an analysis of the circulations of the magazines presently serving the fringe areas of the sport—sailing, diving, canoeing, board surfing, swimming:

Motorboat	103,000
Motorboating & Sailing	131,000
Sail	164,000

Boating	192,000
Cruising World	74,000
Powerboat	69,000
Sea	177,000
Yachting	131,000
Skin Diver	166,000
Surfer	119,000
Surfing	114,000
Swimming World	40,000

(This list, of course, does not include smaller publications and those serving regional areas.)

• A further indication is shown by the circulation of the major travel magazines, all of which devote substantial space in every issue to data and pictures of beaches in an effort to lure the body surfer persons to read:

Carte Blanche	556,000
Signature	631,000
Travel/Holiday	751,000
Travel & Leisure	781,000

It is obvious, then, that the market in the United States alone is huge. And beyond that, of course, is the rest of the world.

Since there are so many people interested in the subject, it is possible to find them in virtually any group of people, although they tend to congregate on the East and West Coasts, Hawaii, Puerto Rico and the Bahamas. (The Middle West, Southwest and Alaska, for some reason, seem to be very low in body surfing activity.)

It is not enough just to know that there are a large number of people interested in a subject, however. Their interest must be sufficient to guarantee purchase of our product.

While there is no published research on the subject, it stands to reason that a body surfer is intensely interested in his or her sport. An informal survey among surfers at Montauk Point showed that the average surfer traveled over 60 miles to participate, and that 82 percent of the surfers wanted more information about the sport. After all, when you risk your life with each wave, you want to know every technique—old and new. So far, this huge audience has been starved for information, relying only on word-of-mouth.

We then decided to conduct focus group interviews, to develop qualitative rather than quantitative information. Focus group research, when used as a technique for analyzing the viability of a new magazine, involves discussing a project with a group of 15 or so potential readers for two or three hours to determine the depth of their interest, their response to the editorial approach and other intangible factors. Often, a publisher can avoid a bad mistake or add a vital feature as a result of these interviews. (A dummy copy or pilot issue is very helpful in doing this type of research.)

Our focus group interviews, conducted by marketing professors at four different locations, indicated that the potential reader had a great interest in vacationing by the ocean, an avid desire to improve body surfing skills and a tendency to stay at the beach too long—which resulted in frequent exhaustion and sunburn.

Everyone expressed a need for more definitive data about body surfing techniques, best locations, body surfing clubs and wave analysis. When shown a pilot issue of *The Body Surfer Person*, just about everyone in the groups said that they would subscribe. Price did not seem to be important.

Research uncovers huge market

Our research, indicating the size of our universe of potential readers (the estimated number of people interested in the magazine's subject matter) and the intensity of interest, convinced us that there is a huge market hungering for our magazine and other related products—a market which is not sensitive to price. We were also convinced that we had a viable editorial product and, thus encouraged, we decided to press on to complete the business plan.

Please understand that, while all signs seemed good, we had no thought of launching the magazine based on the research available to us at this time. We knew full well that the only research that counts must involve people *actually buying the magazine.*

While our approach to *The Body Surfer Person* was based on the assumption that the magazine could be highly profitable through circulation alone, we felt that advertising could add in several ways: It would provide additional revenue and profits. It could improve the appearance of the magazine—and add to its heft. It would probably be of interest to readers who are always on the lookout for new equipment, new beaches and other allied items. And classified advertising of beach trips, body surfing schools, world class competition, etc., can be read and enjoyed almost as thoroughly as the editorial matter.

At first, we were afraid that there would not be a great many potential advertisers, but further research and conferences with a number of agency media buyers led to a very different conclusion.

The advertising market

Advertising prospects for *The Body Surfing Person* are substantial because the audience is large and attractive to advertisers.

The magazine is aimed at an upscale, affluent, well-educated audience of readers in the 21- to 39-year-old age group. It is interesting that our survey showed that some 40 percent of body surfers fit that group. Further, this elitist group, which is of greatest interest to advertisers, consider themselves "body surfers," while the others, the downscale group, call the sport "riding the waves." This difference makes identification easy, and the continued efforts of the downscale group to advance into the higher-class group means more readers in the future.

The major characteristics of the upscale portion of the audience to which *The Body Surfer Person* will appeal are:

Sex—male	66%
female	34%
Median age	28.4
Median family income	$29,650
Managerial and professional	67%
Cars owned (average)	2.8
Own house	92%
Total trips for body surfing 1977	27
Trips abroad for body surfing	6
Highest level of education	
some college	82%
graduate school	51%
Active in religious or community affairs	98%
Hospitalized because of accident during the past year	67%

The advertising market divides into three major areas:

Equipment for surfers, their families and friends: bathing suits, bathing caps, ear plugs, wet suits, umbrellas, picnic baskets, beach towels, sunburn cream, portable hi-fi, CB radios (for help), wheelchairs, automobiles, books, cameras and bandages, splints and crutches.

Services for surfers, their families and friends: beach resorts, ambulance services, fast food, medical groups, insurance, subways, airlines, rental cars, credit cards, travel agents, hospitals and weather services.

General advertisers: cigarettes (body surfers live dangerously), fashion, greeting cards, and liquor, beer and wine.

Advertising prospects totaled approximately 1,078 companies. Publisher's Information Bureau reported on 522 of those companies, indicating a total of $876 million spent on magazine advertising during 1977.

People involved

Important to any project—possibly most important—is a team of people who have the experience, knowledge and enthusiasm to turn the project into a profitable operation. A brief description of their backgrounds should be in the business plan. We described our team for *The Body Surfer Person* like this:

Publisher and editor—Hope and James Kobak form one of those rare and legendary husband and wife teams whose talents complement each other, much in the manner of some other publishing pairs—Clare and Henry Luce, Lila and DeWitt Wallace, Blanche and Alfred Knopf.

Both are avid body surfers. Their sport has taken them all over the world to learn different techniques, to meet with fellow surfers and to cope with local wave conditions.

Hope was the founder, editor and publisher of the *Pine Orchard, Connecticut Post* in 1941 at the age of only 16. She worked for a time as a reporter for the *Annapolis News*. Her written works include one novel, one screenplay, one theatrical play, one short story, one essay and one poem—all unpublished to date. She has taught several writing courses at the New School in New York. She is a graduate of the school of journalism at Syracuse University.

Jim Kobak has worked in the editorial departments of the *New York Sun* and the *Boston Herald-Traveler,* both now out of business. For three months he was publisher of *Casket & Sunnyside,* a business magazine for the funeral profession and for a like period was publisher of *Tobacco,* a trade paper for the industry. He later practiced public accounting for 25 years, a profession he no longer follows. He now gives advice.

Circulation director—Coleman Boyd has been circulation director of *Ballyhoo* magazine for 25 years. He has competed unsuccessfully in body surfing contests worldwide.

Advertising director—(Name withheld) has been senior advertising director of an existing special interest magazine. While he is not a body surfer himself (indeed, he cannot swim), his five-year-old son is prominent in the Red Bank, New Jersey, Pee Wee Body Surfing Club.

Controller—Peter Rathbone is a C.P.A. and partner in the Los Angeles office of Touche, Ernst, Waterhouse. He has worked with many clients in the magazine industry.

Attorneys—Lord, Sherman, Hughes—New York.

Accountants—Haskins and Lybrand—New York.

Circulation consultant—Walter, Eliot, Dick and Jim, Incorporated.

The timetable

By James B. Kobak

This is the third part of the story of the planning Hope and I did for the launch of our favorite magazine, *The Body Surfer Person.* You may recall that we previously had defined the editorial, outlined the markets for circulation and advertising, discussed the competition, and given a rundown of the very talented group we had gathered together to run the magazine.

We now faced a critical question: Exactly how would we go about it?

Typically, Hope wanted to start immediately. She described her schedule to me like this. "Here it is March 1, 1979. Let's get going right now! I can dive into the project as soon as I finish buying the grandchildren Easter presents. We'll have the staff on board by April 1 and the first issue on the stands by July 1, just in time for the big weekend."

Patiently, as always, I explained that the surest way to disaster in starting a new magazine is to rush. I did this in words of one syllable to be sure she would understand completely. In fact, I did it in words of one syllable 22 times that day.

"It is barely possible," I pointed out intelligently, "that not many people will want to buy our magazine."

"You're kidding! We did the market study.

Americans want and *need* our magazine. I can feel it deep down!"

"Agreed—but let's test it first."

Since FOLIO is a family magazine, I will refrain from repeating the rest of this conversation verbatim and simply describe the planning of our time schedule.

The pilot issue

First, we needed a pilot issue—5,000 copies—as soon as possible. There are several reasons for a new magazine to develop a pilot issue:

1. To fix the logo and the design of the magazine.

2. To show potential investors what the magazine will be like.

3. To help attract staff by showing them how professionally the magazine will be done.

4. To use in focus groups and other research with potential readers to help refine the editorial contents.

5. To act as a base from which the test mailing can be designed.

6. To help sell advertising.

What should a pilot issue be like? The overriding rule is—the more it is like the real magazine, the better. People who see a pilot issue are usually unable to visualize what the final product will really be like from sketches, drawings, paste-ups, slides, or anything else. This is obviously true for the potential investors, but also holds to a greater extent than you might think for those in the magazine business.

The ideal pilot is a complete issue just as it might be published—editorial material written, set in type and printed. Typical advertisements should also be included. It should contain the same number of pages with the same paper-weight that will be used in the actual magazine: In addition to looking like the product, it should have the same feel.

The ideal, of course, is expensive. It is costly to write, develop artwork, set type, make separations, and print a complete magazine.

The alternative, then, is to print only part of the magazine. That way, everything is much cheaper (but it's not nearly as good).

I have seen pilot issues in various forms:

•Slides—a little unfair because the artwork may look better on the screen than on paper. They do not have the feel of a real magazine.

•Boards—artwork does not have the look of printing. The size of the boards confuses. And again, there is no feel.

•Pasted dummies—same problems. They also get dog-eared if used often. If you have to do it this way, put pages in glassine in order to preserve them.

In addition, a disadvantage to all of these forms is that you cannot have enough copies for all the people who should have them.

For *The Body Surfer Person*, Hope and I decided that we would do it right—within the obvious cost constraints. In addition to the usual reasons for a printed pilot, we felt that the true beauty and excitement of body surfing could not be captured any other way.

Timetable—ideal

We figured that the pilot issue could be completed by March 1. Assuming we had raised seed money for a direct mail test, we could do the test by May 1.

Here we faced a problem. Since we will probably have only one chance to launch *The Body Surfer Person*, if

our test bombs, we are out of business—forever.

May is known in the direct mail business as a bad month. Even though we thought May would be fine for our magazine, we didn't want the test to be bad because we mailed at a bad time. We wouldn't have learned anything about whether anyone wanted our magazine, and we would be out of business. So we knew we would be smarter to wait until July (one of the best months) to test.

Assuming a successful test mailing on July 1, we would know the results in about two months, say September 1. We could then put out a big mailing in October (but not later—gets into Christmas mail) and another one right after Christmas.

It would make sense to start hiring the staff as soon as we knew the test was successful. But, given the lead times for preparing, printing and distributing the magazine, the earliest we could get a really good issue out would be April 1980. This would be a good time because by then we would have a lot of subscribers from the test mailing and the two large mailings. It also would give us time to sell some advertising in the first few issues.

Ideal time scheduling

1/1/79	Business plan completed
3/1/79	Pilot issue completed
4/1/79	Seed money raised
7/1/79	Test mailing
9/1/79	Test mailing results
9/1/79	Major financing available
10/1/79	Hire staff
10/1/79	First large mailing
12/26/79	Second large mailing
4/1/80	First issue

This is the timetable we planned and to which we would like to adhere. But it's tight—and we have to be prepared to push it forward if necessary.

Alternative 1

There are a number of things which could go wrong and delay us:

1. Unable to raise money for test mailings.

2. Unable to develop the mailing packages we wanted. (No sense in going out with one we didn't think would work.)

3. Unable to get all portions of the mailing printed, collated, etc., on the date we wanted. (Envelopes, particularly, are almost always difficult.)

4. Unable to get some of the lists we want to test in July.

5. Post office holds up shipping of test mailing.

6. Unable to develop good pilot issue.

If any one of these things happens, the schedule is changed—although not drastically.

Suppose the mailing does not get out until August, September, or October. The result is that we will not know if our test is successful in time to do a major mailing in October. The answer is to scratch that mailing completely and do the first big drop in December. We can schedule publication in May, but we'd probably have to have another major mailing in March.

Alternative 1—Time Schedule

9/1/79	Test mailing
11/1/79	Test results
11/1/79	Major financing available
12/1/79	Hire staff
12/26/79	First large mailing

3/1/80   Second large mailing
5/1/80   First issue

Alternative 2

Suppose one or more of the above problems takes place—but the time spread is even greater and we cannot get our test out before the end of October. Answer: push the test mailing to December and move everything else forward like this:

Alternative 2 — Time Schedule

12/26/79   Test mailing
3/1/80   Test results
3/1/80   Major financing available
4/1/80   First large mailing
5/1/80   Hire staff
7/1/80   Second large mailing
10/1/80   First issue

One of the distressing problems as we thought about this was that even very small difficulties would result in major delays of at least three and maybe six months. And if snowstorms or something else unforeseen happened, the whole schedule would have to be pushed forward another three months—and we would be a full year later than our original schedule.

Alternative 3

Our test goes off successfully in July 1979—but we haven't raised the major capital to launch the magazine.

If we can get hold of money by December, we could still do a major mailing then and publish the first issue in May, following the schedule in Alternative 1. If not, we could move on to Alternative 2.

Alternative 4

Our test is successful in July 1979, but we have great difficulty raising big money and are unable to do a major mailing in January 1980, or even March. A major mailing in April, May or June would not be wise, however, because these are traditionally bad months for direct mail.

We could make a big mailing in July—but it is now a year after our first test. That test may not be meaningful anymore and we don't want to waste our investors' money. Besides, they won't let us.

The solution—test again in July 1980. This would reaffirm the initial success and enable us to test other prices and lists. Theoretically we would be in an even better position because we would know more about what works best.

But here we are—back to our first time schedule—a year after we thought we had it all solved. But through this process, we learned that starting a magazine can be long, slow and frustrating. We not only had to develop a good product, assemble a team, raise money and design mailings, we also had to worry about the seasonal characteristics of the direct mail business. This meant that every change in plans moved the schedule back at least three or six months.

We also realized that since it is better to do it right (despite the frustration), Hope had better get a job. This could go on forever.

Pilot ready

We finally completed our pilot issue, which contained 96 pages plus cover, the size we hoped the first issue would be. (Not all of these pages were printed, how-

ever—just 40 pages and the cover.) Editorially it contained 24 pages, including the cover, the contents page, two columns as well as several features.

We included headlines, artwork, sub-heads, captions and blurbs with real material, but we did not actually set the editorial stories in type. Instead, we used material from other magazines in the same type face and size we planned to use. We thought of using "Greek" type but discarded the idea because any we felt did not have the appearance of real text.

To give as much flavor of the eventual magazine and its varied contents as possible, we had cover lines for one issue on the cover, a contents page describing another issue, actual articles from a third issue, and coming attractions from a fourth.

Advertising consisted of 16 pages of typical ads, the separations for which were lent to us. We found that advertisers and agencies were happy to do this once we explained the concept of *The Body Surfer Person* and its tremendous potential. Naturally they did not pay for this.

Timing and public relations

There were certain timing problems that bothered us. Obviously, we were terribly excited about *The Body Surfer Person* and wanted the world to know about it as soon as possible. Hope thought she should appear on the *Today* show immediately—or better yet be interviewed by Barbara Walters. I suggested *The Gong Show*.

We finally decided to do nothing publicly until we had a successful test and the money to publish. There is nothing worse from a PR standpoint than to announce something and then have nothing happen. (Many politicians have discovered this bit of wisdom too late.)

We reasoned that the media, which are always happy to discuss a new magazine (or a failing one), would get tired of us by the time the magazine appeared if we started too early. The public would go looking for our magazine and, not finding it, would become disillusioned. And, worst of all, the advertising community would think we were an old magazine which hadn't made it by the time our first issue finally appeared.

Timing and the staff

Another major timing worry involved the people we had assembled who were ready and eager to join and start working. We had painstakingly searched for them and had them at a fever pitch of enthusiasm. We did not want them to fade away.

Hope, of course, would be the editor, and I the publisher. But we also had a group of people who knew what they were doing. Coleman Boyd was to be circulation director; (name withheld), advertising director; and Peter Rathbone, controller. Fortunately, none had left a well-paid job to start with us.

We also had a number of famous writers in various parts of the world ready to go: George Seltzer, winner of the Sydney (Ohio) Body Surfing Championship; Hyman Kahn, leading exponent of the Gaza Strip body surfing technique; and Vladimir Perkowski, coach of the new Russian entry into the body surfing event of the Olympics. These, we felt, we could replace if we had to.

With the others, however, we did have a problem. Having assembled the team, we didn't want it to break up.

In the end, we didn't have much choice. Without a specific date, it would have been unfair to tie any of them up (and we probably couldn't have done it anyway). We finally decided that we would have to rely on our persuasive powers (Hope is very good at this) and hope that they would all still be available when we needed them.

In the meantime, we would continue to be out and around the industry, running into people who could replace them if it became necessary.

Designing the new magazine

By John Peter

No magazine launching is failure proof. But most expensive design mistakes can be avoided. The key is the product development role of management as well as the practical knowhow and creative talent of the designer.

Looks are not everything, but they are seldom so important as with a new magazine. The visual appearance strikes both the reader and the advertiser first, and it's difficult to alter first impressions. Content will be appreciated later, and in the long run will prevail. However the right design can accelerate the speed of success. A new magazine needs everything going for it.

All agree that the task of design is to make manifest the editorial character and content of the magazine. The design of a communications vehicle is a problem-solving process.

The late Sam Goldwyn once had the bright idea of buying movie rights to all George Bernard Shaw's plays. He flew over to see Shaw about it. Shaw turned him down. A reporter pursuing the story visited Shaw and asked him why. Shaw said, "Mr. Goldwyn spoke only of art. I spoke only of money."

Beware of the designer who speaks only of art. The good designer will give you reasons. Where aesthetic judgments are involved it makes sense to take seriously the designer's recommendations. But designing a magazine is a commonsense project and you should not, out of any deference to "art," run and hide. You ought to have a good idea of how potential advertisers will look at your new magazine and you should be able to put yourself in the position of a reader. If you can't read the typeface, say so. If you don't like anything else, say so, and say why.

This advice may be unnecessary. You may not be afflicted with an "I-know-nothing-about-art" syndrome. Presumably you don't have an "I-know-everything-about-art" complex or a penchant for do-it-yourself design.

Although few publishers speak of design only in terms of cost, a tight budget usually goes hand-in-hand with a new magazine. But the money invested in design is so small in terms of the total budget, that it pays to go first class. But first class becomes expensive if the more important investment of top management's time isn't made.

The development of a new magazine, like the development of any other new product, demands time from management. By management, I mean the executive officer, the publisher and the editor. You might also like to include the advertising manager and circulation manager.

The designer must have a clear idea of the objectives—editorial concept, audience, circulation goals, distribution plans, potential advertising areas, competition. If all this isn't crystal clear, a good designer will ask questions. For each new magazine I design I spend half my time in these research and development briefings. A designer must thoroughly understand the problem before he or she can come up with the answers.

Sometimes production decisions are made before the design phase—like choosing the printer, the trim size, average number of pages, paper and structure. A designer can be helpful in making some of these decisions, but if they have already been made, it's important that he or she understand the reasons behind them. From the beginning, the designer's link to the realities of the production department is important.

Design work should be integrated from the very beginning into the realistic timetable for the launching. This can range from two years to four months. But be certain to allow sufficient time to see the design as a whole. Avoid piecemeal or rushed decisions that do not allow the opportunity for revisions.

Starting with the Cover

The first thing designed is usually the cover. It is the most important page in the magazine. It's the package. As such it's the natural focus of most design discussions. The good cover is a happy combination of elements that stay the same and elements that change. The title, size and format provide the continuity, issue to issue, so readers quickly recognize the magazine. The date, illustration and sell lines change so readers recognize each new issue.

The most important design element on this most important page is the logotype. The logo should typographically position the magazine for its audience and in its market. It should signal style, quality, impact, character and mood. It should be distinctive but not at the expense of readability—despite the loose talk that people don't read logos but only see them. The logo is a lot more than something for the cover of your magazine. It's a trademark to be recognized on your letterhead, calling cards, labels, promotion and advertising. It's surprising how often these aspects get neglected. Logo possibilities should be reduced to card and letterhead sizes as part of the decision-making process. There are usually not too many good solutions to the logotype design problem, but you should see the options.

Typographic elements on the cover like the date and price seldom present problems. But sell lines often do. If you have them—and you nearly always should—they are the toughest and often most neglected problem. Nobody likes them as much as the readers. Another problem that can be neglected is the cover illustration. Some approach ought to be pinned down early, rather than dreaming that it will solve itself on an issue-to-issue basis.

Some of the new magazines introduced recently give us a look at the direct relationship between the editorial concept, marketing positioning and the design.

On Time Inc.'s *People* magazine the key editorial idea, says Richard Stolley, managing editor, is "to deal exclusively with human beings and not with causes, trends, arguments or issues—only people. It is almost unavoidable that magazines like *Time* and *Newsweek* concentrate on issues. People become anecdotes or quotes or statistics. What we have done is reverse the trend and let the issues take care of themselves."

Designed for newsstand and supermarket distribution, *People*'s cover logo is bold, the cover illustration is a closeup portrait of a personality with plenty of big-name sell lines.

With the new subscription-sold magazine, *Cricket,* "The editorial objective," says assistant editor Marcia Leonard, "is to provide high-quality literature to children, to reintroduce children to the pleasures of reading. *Cricket* is designed to be kept, collected and even put on a book shelf." All the design thinking followed from this premise. The first answer was to make it paperback format. The cover carries a book-like script logo and a colorful children's book illustration within a neat frame.

On *Viva*, design director Art Kane wanted to establish a sophisticated image on the cover. "I wanted very provocative, photographically interesting women looking straight at the buyer. I studied newsstands and everybody was in full color. I decided to go with a limited color range. We are the only cover running sepia tone or one color. That seems to be effective."

The quarterly *Backpacker* is a special interest publication in the recreation field. On the cover art director Ron Zisman used only a distinctive bold logo and issue numeral with an uncluttered scenic photo "to get the feeling of wide open spaces." On *Gamblers World* art director Pasquale DelVecchio and designer George Lois crowd the cover with swinging activity and selling blurbs topped with a riverboat style logo.

Designing the Insides

The basic page format of a magazine with position, width, height and number of columns per page is more important than it might initially look. It's at this point when production considerations again enter into the design. Correlation with advertising units can be too easily overlooked. In a new magazine you may find that keeping the number of ad sizes down can benefit the appearance of the magazine and save money in makeup. Of course, the existing number and size of ads in your potential advertising universe often determine how far, or even if, you are able to move in this direction.

On the biweekly newsmagazine, *New Times,* art director Steve Phillips has two types of stories. "In the news section we attempt to be simple, not overdesigned, to let the stories and the news-type photos speak for themselves. We have to stick to a pretty set format because there is no time to really design a news story. In the feature section we have a little more time. There's more character to it because the stories have more character."

Choosing Body Type

It's the choice and use of type that give the pages of a magazine their character. This is the characteristic "look" with which readers become familiar. Surprisingly little of this look is created by the face in which most words are set—the text face. It's generally selected on readability, word count, availability and outright preference. Most of the magazines in the United States use one of a favored few body faces.

Elton Robinson, *People*'s design director, picked the sans serif face Helvetica for text even though all other Time Inc. magazines are in Times Roman. "The magazine was scorned by a lot of people at Time Inc. There was a little culture shock involved ... but now even those people are coming around and saying they really like it a lot. It hasn't changed, it's just that they have become used to it."

For the magazine *Investing,* designed for franchise distribution through brokerage firms, art director Herbert Rosenthal picked something distinctive—a recently designed typeface with a touch of the past called Souvenir.

It's the headlines along with the decks, subheads and captions that usually establish the typographic character of a magazine. They ought to work out well for the editor as well as look right to the designer. The trend today is towards one headline type family throughout, rather than many faces. The reason is that with a high mix of advertising and editorial pages, it's easier to maintain editorial identity. However, this will depend on the type of magazine.

At *Gamblers World,* many different headline faces add excitement. "We are looking for a very 'now' thing," explains Bill Hartney, senior editor. "We can change because we have not done a complete identification with the reader."

The styling of special pages like contents, editorial, columnists or departments, deserves real attention. The contents page not only can sell the reader on the issue, but in the hands of a good space salesperson it can also sell the advertisers. The trend is towards illustrated contents pages but some magazines stick to an index for reference only. In a magazine it is often the columns and departments that attract regular readership. They deserve a distinctive style so they can be spotted even when surrounded by busy advertising.

Photographs and graphics are usually very eye-catching in the dummy issue presentation. The quality is often superior to what a publisher may be able to actually produce, or afford. What's more important to judge is whether they are the right prototypes. The character and style of illustrations, as well as the often neglected charts, graphs and maps, constitute the visual communications of editorial content.

You can expect designers to vary in the way they present a dummy, but within a sensible budget the more closely it represents the finished product the better. All the key members of the publishing team should be at the design presentation, and it's best to do it at one time. Obviously only a few people will make the final decisions. There should be no hesitation in requesting revisions to resolve any problems before the first issue.

A stat dummy with potential ads stripped in will give you a chance to judge how the design really works. Properly used it can be a valuable research vehicle as well as a potent sales tool.

For reader testing as well as ad sales, many publishers print a prototype issue. How definitive and complete this need be depends on the budget and the magazine. A while ago I helped produce a complete issue of a proposed magazine for a W.R. Simmons reader research study months before the actual launching. In this case it was before investors gave a Go/No-Go signal on the project and any full-time staff was hired. A test issue also often points out bugs in production and design. It will also take a lot of the guessing out of projecting real costs.

The design phase is not over with the first issue. Revisions and adjustments can be made based on the experiences of the early issues. If all things were done right before, however, there will be far less to do later.

The point to know about designing a new magazine is that it almost always *can* be done right before launching. It's expensive to make your mistakes in public. This may seem elementary, but several new magazines launched this year have already switched their designers or art directors and others are still searching for a format.

The advantage rests with the magazine that does it right the first time out.

Ten Questions To Ask When Interviewing An Art Director or Designer for Your New Magazine

1.*Ask about publication experience.* Experience isn't everything, and it's not a matter of age, but the person who is this important to the success of your publication ought to have it. Magazine knowhow, not just design ability, is what you are buying.

2.*Ask for references.* Though a designer's talent may appear evident, he or she may have been only partly responsible for the result. It may have been whom the person worked with. On the other hand, a talented designer may not have a record of working well in an editorial team. You should know it. Good designers expect to supply references.

3.*Look at the magazines the designer has worked on.* This will give you a chance to size up ability. There may be an advantage if the publications happen to be in a similar field to the one you are entering, but this is not nearly as important as the talent displayed.

4.*Ask about the thinking behind these magazine designs.* Some things may be a matter of aesthetics and difficult to explain. Good designers have reasons for their designs, however, and most do a good job explaining them.

5.*Ask about format and layout.* This will give you a chance to learn more about the candidate's thinking in relation to the overall goals of magazines. These elements establish the image of the magazine with the readers and advertisers.

6.*Ask about typography, photography, illustration and graphics.* This is what a designer employs to get ideas off the page into the reader's mind. Remember, the designer should be a communicator. The designer's work can play an important part in your readership.

7.*Ask about paper, printing and production.* A good publication designer will maximize the potentials of the production process. This means both a creative and practical approach on the designer's part.

8.*Ask about scheduling and budgets.* This should give you an idea of the administrative and organizing abilities of the designer as well as his or her understanding of costs.

9.*Ask about the designer's procedure in designing your magazine.* You should not expect free samples of design, but it only makes sense to inquire how the designer would go about doing the job. This will give you an appreciation of the designer's working practices as well as the timetable involved.

10.*Ask about the designer's interest in your project.* The designer's response may reveal more than you might guess about his or her enthusiasm for your particular magazine. Depending on the temperament of the individual, it need not be wildly enthusiastic but it should be, at least, very firmly positive. You will need all the confidence and extra effort you can get launching your new publication.

Selling the first issue

Remember the McGraw-Hill ad with the guy staring straight at you and saying: "I don't know who you are. I don't know your company. I don't know your company's record. I don't know what your company stands for," and so on?

Well, it's often just that sort of guy that salespeople for new magazines face each day as they make their rounds with attache cases filled with intangibles—unproven and/or unprovable charts, surveys and sundry other selling tools.

These salespeople are often the new people on the block, so to speak. They have a lot of proving to do.

"Advertisers look into more than just the demographics of a new magazine; they look into its entire concept and operation," says George Hirsch, publisher of *New Times*, a newsmagazine.

"You won't get an advertiser into a new book simply with demographics or introductory offers. They're quite secondary. They do provide an incentive, but only after an advertiser has thoroughly looked into the concept of the magazine, its viability, how it is financed and if it meets a particular marketing need," Hirsch explained. "Only then, when the advertisers have been satisfied with the answers to these questions, does the equation add up."

But no matter how much information a salesperson puts before the advertiser, there is no way of insuring that the magazine is going to live up to its promotion. The advertiser, then, must often act on instinct and faith.

Offering Incentives

One way that many publishers deal with this situation is by offering some special incentive to place an advertiser in a brand new magazine. There are dozens of variations.

For example, Hirsch offered charter advertisers three free ads if they signed a 13-time contract (*New Times* is a biweekly). *Diversion*, a leisure magazine in the health field, offered advertisers a free ad for each paid ad in any of the first three issues. *Pension and Investments* gave away two, three or four ads in its four charter issues in 1973. The number of free ads was determined by the size of contract advertisers signed for 1974.

The main thing, many publishers agree, is getting the advertiser into the magazine. The first issue must look impressive, even if no revenue comes from it.

"You find that some new magazines have a thick and successful feel while others have a thin and struggling feel. Advertisers and readers sense this and quickly categorize a magazine, and these categories stick unless there are some drastic changes," said Robert Dowling, former publisher of *In-Service Training and Education*.

Advertisers in Dowling's magazine were offered a free ad in the first issue if they contracted to buy space in the second and third issues. There was no penalty if an advertiser cancelled after the first issue, but they were on

contract and the burden of cancelling was on them.

Harcourt Brace Jovanovich Publications does the same sort of thing with all its new magazines except its advertisers sign a four-time contract in order to get the first one free. Robert Edgell, HBJ Publications president, bristles at the mere mention of the word "discount," however, and insists that giving away the first ad if the advertiser agrees to buy the next three at full price does not mean he discounted anything.

Aside from looking healthy—even though it may produce little revenue—the first issue supplies the magazine's salespeople with an excellent selling tool—the magazine itself.

Instead of making calls with just brochures, or a dummy mocked-up issue, the salespeople can produce a thick actual magazine, which they can explicity talk about and leave behind.

But there are many publishers who refused to give any kind of discounts or deals to advertisers in their first issue.

Starting with Full Rates

"When we started we didn't make any advertising offers at all and I'm glad we didn't," said Michael Levy, publisher of *Texas Monthly*. "I feel that once you start making deals the advertisers will expect you to continue. We offered the regular agency and cash discounts and provided rate protection, but that's standard industry practice."

Even in highly competitive fields, many publishers feel that starting with full rates is best. For instance, *The Journal of Legal Medicine* started in 1973, the same time that more than a dozen other medical magazines were starting. But still it stuck to its one rate for its first issue.

"We felt it was worth it," said publisher Marvin Tobin. "We were able to maintain a reputation for holding to our rate card. We felt that it was very important."

Establishing a New Magazine's Worth

But setting a rate for the first issue is only part of the problem. The proving still needs to be done. New magazines are unaudited and have no readership studies to show. But they can produce the research that went into conceiving and funding the magazine. They *can* show studies and reports that illustrate the need, or their niche, or the validity of their concept.

"But you have to give advertisers more than just numbers," said William J. Miles, Jr., executive vice-president of *Playgirl*. "They want to know what the intended audience is like, what its interests are, its education, things like that."

At *Ms.* Magazine before making any sales calls they set certain standards that advertisers would have to meet. According to Cathleen O'Callaghan, then ad director of

Ms., "When we first started making sales calls we went after a particular type of advertiser. We stressed that we appreciated creative advertising that reflected the real world of products and services that women use today. When we saw an ad campaign that measured up to our standards we went to that advertiser with our sales story. Now that *Ms.* is better established, the advertisers and agencies recognize what *Ms.* wants."

But no matter how good the sales story, however, there still is no substitute for lots of hard work, and it often is the publisher that not only sets the pace, but ends up making many of the initial sales calls.

Many say that advertisers like to see the publisher's face, particularly when they are placing an ad in a new magazine. There is nobody who knows more about the magazine and can get more genuinely excited about the concept than the publisher. So it is natural that on many magazines the publisher goes out with the salespeople on many initial calls.

"A publisher can't be on top of affairs if he or she doesn't know them from the inside out," insists Alfred Malecki, publisher of *Pensions and Investments*. Malecki says that the publisher must go out and be familiar with accounts and learn the field. And talking with advertisers is one of the best ways of learning it.

But other publishers disagree. They feel that they can be most useful staying on the inside, running the *total* operation while leaving the sales to the sales manager and salespeople. Of course, as with every other aspect of starting a new magazine, there is no one correct way to do it. But on one thing they all seem to agree—new magazines, no matter how brilliant the concept, don't sell themselves.

The launch package

By Eliot DeY. Schein

A circulation promotion mailing for a magazine that hasn't hit the newsstand, or probably hasn't even been printed yet, can be compared to an empty shelf in the supermarket: There's no product and there's no benefit. How, then, assuming your list research was done intelligently, do you provide the proper blend of benefits, advantages and titillations to qualified prospective subscribers? How do you get them to order something that nobody ever heard of until your envelope arrived?

For the launching of a new publication, the test direct mail subscription solicitation package should be somewhat different from the usual new business package sent out by already-existing publications. Management should be aware of the differences in advance and not fall into the trap of thinking (as many have) that if the package looks like the usual new business package, it's good enough to launch a new magazine.

Certainly, the results of any test mailing are affected by many variables such as timing, copy, offer, field of interest and list selection. Because these results often spell the difference between whether or not a publication is started, the facts that follow are of even greater importance to a new publisher with no previous publishing experience.

We must look at the prospective subscriber as someone who is sitting around minding his or her own business when the mailman delivers a third-class piece of sales mail. The prospect now, on a one-to-one basis, is going to make a "buy" or "no buy" decision, without benefit of any previous knowledge of the product's existence.

To enlighten that prospect, a magazine launch package must present a full and comprehensive description of the magazine's contents. This presentation often takes a lot of copy because it has to familiarize the potential subscriber with everything pertinent about the magazine. It's almost like describing an elephant to someone who's never seen one.

Show "the elephant"

To give that prospective subscriber some idea of what "the elephant" looks like, use pictures as well as words. Show a cover (in color, if the magazine will be in color) and sample spreads utilizing the typeface and showing the proposed page format.

One note of caution here: Time after time, publishers come out with direct mail packages that say, "I've got the greatest magazine idea in the world and the world's going to beat a path to my door to buy it!" Not only doesn't the world beat any paths, but the mailman with the business reply mail doesn't beat much of a path either.

Why? Familiarity. By the time the people responsible for the launch test have the go-ahead (and the money for it is in the bank), management has probably been living with the editorial concept for a number of years. The publisher and editor, so thoroughly familiar with the magazine, often feel it's unnecessary to go to great lengths to describe it. They assume everyone knows the magazine as well as they do, which, of course, is not the case.

To ensure a comprehensive description of your magazine, a clear presentation of the subject to the direct mail creative team is necessary. For the copywriter who is doing the package or packages, the problem of a launch is massive. There are no previous packages to look at in terms of what worked and what didn't work, and there are no back issues of the publication because it hasn't been published yet.

(Note to management: Be sure to read the copywriter's first draft as well as the final draft. Very often the copywriter develops some ideas for features or departments for the new publication while writing the letter. There may be some ideas worth incorporating into the eventual publication.)

The first announcement seen by prospective subscribers is the carrier envelope. It should announce the hallmark event with great fanfare. "This terrific new magazine is going to make your life easier and happier, and you can have it at a special price." The words "FREE" and "Charter Subscriber" often have a positive effect on the test results. Charter-year subscriptions can be offered for the first year-and-a-half to two years.

Ask for payment

And remember, you can ask for payment on a test, even if you have no intention whatsoever of sending out the publication. Federal Trade Commission regulations require that if there is no fulfillment of the product within 30 days, the subscriber must be offered his money back. Asking for advance payment is probably worth the extra work involved in order to get an idea of how many people will pay.

Another technique, the "soft" or trial copy offer, allows the consumer to request a sample copy of the publication. That copy is part of his subscription, assuming the consumer eventually pays for the subscription.

The order form wording is usually something like, "I accept your offer of a free trial copy of *Elephant Magazine*. I understand if I am not fully satisfied and don't agree that it is the greatest publication in the history of the world, I may write 'cancel' across my invoice and send the invoice back to you and the free trial copy is mine to keep without cost or obligation."

(If the publication is eventually going to be an Audit Bureau of Circulations [ABC] audited publication, some care must be taken to avoid the phrase "free sample issue." ABC has traditionally allowed a publisher to say your free *inspection* copy will be sent to you without cost if you decide not to be a subscriber.)

Although the soft offer approach usually increases up-front response, it also reduces pay percentage. Depending upon the quality of the publication when it is finally fulfilled, the net subscription generation sometimes dips as low as 50 percent of gross. While each magazine's experiences are different, a publisher should deduct 40 percent from the gross percentage response of a soft offer to get an idea of the final paid subscriber percentage. Naturally, there is no substitute for the real information, but that takes more time than most publishers are willing to invest.

Many are the news stories that tell of a publisher pulling 10 or 12 percent on a launch test mailing. After reductions for things like free trial copy offers, regular bad pay on credit options and people canceling because the product didn't meet expectations, the published 10 or 12 percent (which probably was an inflated figure anyway) shrinks to a more realistic number somewhere between 2.5 and 4 percent.

No doubt the most critical item of all for a publisher to keep in mind when sending out a launch test mailing is the renewability of the subscribers that are captured by that mailing. If the claims and benefits enumerated in the package are not accurate, if the package does not provide full disclosure of the contents of the publication, or if promises are made that just cannot be kept, the renewal rate will be a disaster.

A new publisher, in an effort to satisfy investors, will often build in "promises" of this nature that cannot be kept. Although these promises increase the up-front response percentage, they destroy renewability. (Sometimes publishers don't care enough about this as long as the investors can be comfortable in thinking they have a winner on their hands.)

For solid, honest, intelligent and projectable results from a launch mailing, you must follow the rules of good direct mail in general. Specifically, be very careful about renewability, benefit promises, proper exposition of the total theme, thrust, appearance and attitude of the publication. If the selected consumer area at large likes the editorial premise and the test mailing package, the test results will satisfy the publisher and the investors. The test results will also have a projectability in terms of renewal that will enrich the lives and coffers of all concerned.

There is probably no activity more exciting than launching a new publication. It's a risky activity at best. But a well-thought-out marketing plan, editorial package and test program can and will provide the thrill of a start-up for a viable product.

Launching a magazine on less than a $million

By Ronald T. Scott

Is it possible to start a new magazine without a million dollars? Based on what I have read and heard over the past few years, this question would seem to be naive. Numerous articles suggest that only the largest companies can even consider starting new magazines. And one hears with some regularity: "He is starting his new magazine with only $2 million. I doubt that he can last."

During the past few years of inflation distorted economics, many of us seem to have lost sight of one of publishing's greatest attractions—that entering the business is easy because it's inexpensive.

Let me qualify that last statement: It is not expensive to enter the *newsstand* publishing arena. (Entering the *subscription* publishing arena is, in fact, expensive.)

During the past 20 years, I have been involved in launching several hundred new magazines—as a publisher, as a national distributor, and as a consultant. Of all the titles I've worked with, only five were initially capitalized for over $1 million, and all five emphasized subscription circulation heavily. All of the remaining titles were launched with minimal capitalization because their primary circulation emphasis was newsstand sales.

The economic equations of newsstand sales are simple, direct, and highly disciplined.

Determining the risk

The most critical of these equations is the break-even percentage, the percentage of the copies printed for newsstand distribution which must be sold to recapture all of the costs of publishing each issue of the magazine. This break-even percentage enables the publisher to determine the degree of risk that he is taking with his new (or old) magazine each time he publishes. Obviously, the higher the break-even percentage, the higher the risk the publisher is taking.

To illustrate the process of launching a new magazine using the newsstand as the primary source of circulation, let us develop the following scenario:

After examining existing titles and market potential, a publisher decides to publish an 80-page magazine at a $1.75 cover price with a press run of 175,000 copies. He must now calculate how much of that $1.75 he will actually get.

First, his national distributor will bill the local wholesalers at less 40 percent of the cover price: $1.05 ($1.75 x 60% = $1.05). In addition, the national distributor will incur additional costs on behalf of the publisher—for retail display agreement incentives, shipping and special allowances to local wholesalers in high labor cost areas— which will approximate 5 percent of the cover price, further reducing the net income to the publisher to $0.9625 ($1.75 x 5% = $0.0875; $1.05 − $0.0875 = $0.9625). Finally, the national distributor will require a commission of 7 percent of the cover price for the services he will render, which brings the net income to the publisher to $0.84 per copy sold ($1.75 x 7% = $0.1225; $0.9625 − $0.1225 = $0.84).

The publisher now knows that he will receive 84 cents for every copy of each issue shipped and billed to the newsstand system and not returned within the specified time. If he then multiplies that figure by the press run (175,000), he will know the maximum income from newsstand sales for that issue ($0.84 x 175,000 = $147,000).

If the costs of producing the issue, less such revenue as advertising, licensing, etc., are $73,500, the magazine has a break-even percentage of 50 percent ($147,000 ÷ 73,500). If the costs are $58,000, his break-even percentage is 40 percent ($147,000 ÷ $58,800). If his costs are $88,200, his break-even percentage is 60 percent ($147,000 ÷ $88,200).

It is important to remember that the break-even percentage is a bench mark of risk. Since the newsstand industry has an average 50 percent sale, a break-even percentage of 50 percent would put our publisher in an average position. A break-even percentage higher than 50 percent means a higher-than-average risk, and one lower than 50 percent means a lower-than-average risk.

Now, when our publisher negotiated his distribution contract with his national distributor, he agreed on a commission for the national distributor of 7 percent of the cover price on copies sold. As part of that negotiation, our publisher also requested an advance payment from the national distributor in anticipation of sales.

In our scenario, the national distributor made a business judgment that the title had good potential and agreed to advance on completion of shipping 30 percent of the gross charges, or $44,100 ($147,000 x 30% = $44,100). If our publisher had a cost of $73,000 to produce his issue (a 50 percent break-even), he would need only $29,400 in capital for the first issue of his magazine ($73,500 − $44,100 = $29,400).

Now, I am not in any way saying that one can start a new magazine for under $30,000. At least three if not four issues would have to be published before the national distributor would account for the final sale of the first issue. Furthermore, I have not included in these calculations such items as start-up costs prior to publishing, preproduction inventories, etc.

I am saying, however, that it is possible to start a new magazine without being a millionaire. And I am saying that doing it through the newsstand sales channel is probably the better way to go.

Many publishers believe that all new magazines should be started via the newsstands and not offered through subscription channels until they have proven consumer demand. The theory here is that an initial subscription sale proves only that one has convinced a subscriber to buy a promise and not the actual product, and that only at renewal time does one find out if the consumer actually wants and needs the title.

Although I believe the above to be a sound theory for many new magazines, I believe that such a judgment depends upon the degree of specialization of a new magazine.

A publisher must determine the characteristics of his target consumer, including his buying habits and the intensity of his interest. Newsstand sales and subscription sales should be complementary rather than competitive, and each magazine ought to have its own unique mix of each.

But for a new magazine, or an older one for that matter, the newsstand channel of distribution can be an inexpensive method of entering the marketplace of ideas, information and entertainment.

Problem solving: Starting <u>another</u> magazine

By James B. Kobak

Logic tells us that the obvious place for starting a new magazine is in a company already in the business. After all, an established publisher knows the ins and outs of advertising, editing, circulation and management of magazines. He has long-standing relationships with printers, fulfillment houses and other suppliers. He knows people in the field. And, in terms of keeping his people happy and stimulated, it is to his benefit to continue to start new properties.

Yet, with a few notable exceptions, such as Time Inc., most publishers do not want to get involved in starting new magazines. More often they are started by individuals who may not even have a passing knowledge of the publishing business or by companies which have never been in the business.

As illogical as this idea may seem at first, on examination it is not so puzzling. In most publishing companies, there are many road blocks preventing the start-up of new ventures—and there is an almost universal lack of knowledge of how an existing publisher should go about it.

Problems of starting magazines in publishing houses

Likes and dislikes—When it comes to magazines, people become irrational. They only want to get involved with magazines which they can relate to and enjoy publishing.

Within a company, no two people have the same likes and dislikes. One person may like to sail and another to golf. If the sailor ignores the opinions of the golfer and launches a sailing magazine, the golfer may be upset. Multiply this situation by the total number of key employees and you can have a big problem. In an organization, morale is all-important.

Everyone too busy—Parkinson's law (Work expands to fill the time available) operates in publishing as it does everywhere else. Within a company, there never seem to be people available who can work on a new project.

This often happens because a publisher knows only his or her very best people should be entrusted with the planning of a new venture—and those people are the ones who are most indispensable to current operations.

Not entrepreneurs—People, not companies, are entrepreneurs. The very purpose of most companies is to maximize the profits from already existing properties.

Most employees are hired to efficiently and carefully carry out their day-to-day duties. Their orientation is toward doing the same job well, or better, than they have in the past, but not to spend their days innovating. In most companies the entrepreneur fits badly, if at all. And in some companies, the politicians will cut him up into shreds.

Insufficient rewards—Starting a new magazine is an exhausting job which requires dedication and long hours. In addition, the people involved risk losing their more secure jobs if something goes wrong, whether or not the error was their fault. While they may be tempted to drop their current duties for a new project, it may be too much to ask of them.

Never did it before—We all resist doing things we have never done before. Even if you have been involved in one start-up, each one is different. There is always fear of the unknown.

Lack of certain skills—The business magazine publisher may lack experience in consumer magazine publishing. These areas of publishing are very different in virtually every aspect. To some degree, every new field is different from every field you are accustomed to.

Risky—The stories of failure and the costs involved are legion. "Why jeopardize the successful business we have built up for some hare-brained scheme?" is a common question.

Financial conservatism—Financial people—people who are and should be very conservative—can find all sorts of ways to stop the start-up of a new magazine. They can spew out arguments on return on investment, return on equity and return on assets if the cashflow argument does not kill the project first.

Timing—There are times when ideas for new magazines should be proposed—and times when they should not. If other properties are suffering, a brilliant new magazine concept which would probably be greeted with open arms a year from now would be turned down. Resurrection, historically, is virtually impossible.

Idea becomes stale—Companies usually have decision-making processes. Because of the pressure of daily business, getting a new project through the decision makers is often a very time-consuming process. The very length of time a project is under consideration can lead to its downfall.

No decision procedure—Most companies have structured ways of evaluating the need for new typewriters. These companies try to adapt their normal methods of making decisions to new projects. Often this means that the wrong people are involved in the decision-making process and, in a case like this, it is unlikely that a new magazine will get off the ground.

Other companies are too casual about considering a new magazine, and therefore the people involved always have a haunting doubt that they have studied the idea thoroughly enough. They probably haven't.

Why non-publishing companies invest in new magazines

So it isn't so strange that existing magazine publishers shy away from starting new magazines within their own shops.

Why, then, are other companies so anxious to get into the publishing business—and, in many cases, to enter the business with start-ups. For instance, American Can, Control Data, IT&T, Christiana and others are involved. It might be interesting, therefore, to examine the thinking of outsiders who are willing to invest in new magazine properties.

Cash business—The money invested today comes back very quickly. Cash is not tied up in slow-to-move inventory, receivables or other assets which may look good on a balance sheet but which take a long lead time before profits are realized.

Not capital intensive—There is no need for buildings, machinery and other assets which may tie up capital for many years. There is no need to continuously renew and update equipment—a requirement in most businesses.

Easy to monitor—You can monitor most magazines by counting the number of advertising pages, looking at the ABC statement and reading the magazines themselves. Accounting concepts are simple in the publishing industry—there is no worry about depreciation policies, inventory valuations or other exotic concepts which can distort what is actually going on.

Fun—Publishing is a fun business which deals with ideas—and most of the people in the business are intelligent, verbal and interesting.

Low-risk—Compared to most businesses, publishing is low risk because just about everything which is done can be tested before large amounts of money are spent.

Low fixed costs—Since publishing is a cottage industry, most magazines require only a handful of people. Fixed costs are quite small.

By-product opportunities—Because of the nature of magazines, a number of profitable by-products can normally be developed.

Recession-proof—No business is completely recession proof; but compared to most, magazine publishing comes very close. Most industries are beset by major cycles of disaster and euphoria. Because of this, a stable property, such as a magazine, can be very helpful.

Profits can be high—Once a magazine reaches its break-even point, it is often possible to earn very high profits over many years of its life cycle.

High leverage—The cost of starting most magazines is small compared with the cost of starting most businesses. Because of the tax practices in the industry, substantial tax write-offs are often available at the beginning of operations. In some cases, the start-up costs the investor nothing after taxes. Even when there is cost, the profits which can be earned later become very high when measured against the required investment.

Easy to realize gains—The market for magazine properties is very lively and has been for many years. There are many people looking for magazines—and some of these people have a lot of money. There is no problem selling a property if that is a future goal.

How to handle the starting

When you combine the problems existing publishers have with the interest other companies have in starting magazines, the answers for publishers become apparent.

• Do it offline. Starting a magazine is very different from an existing business. It is foolish to try to put a start-up into the normal business set-up.

• Put someone in charge. Someone must be in charge of reviewing and evaluating new ideas. This person must be given sufficient time to perform the activity and he must be very high in the organization, or he won't have enough clout to make things happen. Perhaps it should be the president. His major duties should consist of eliminating those ideas which do not fit the company's philosophy and making sure each worthwhile concept is explored intelligently and fully before it is presented.

• Organize decision-making. A committee or task force is needed to judge each concept presented. This group will probably be different from any other group in the company. It should work with predetermined criteria of what fits in with the company, the investment available, method of proceeding, etc.

• Start with what you know. The easiest magazine to start, of course, is one in a field very close to the field served by the existing magazine. For instance, *Guitar Player* has recently started *Contemporary Keyboard*, *Sail* started *Motorboat*, and *Better Homes and Gardens* started *Apartment Living*. There have been many cases where business magazines have started other properties in contiguous fields or in splinter areas of the fields they serve. After you have done one or two of these, your confidence may make it easier to move out further.

• Prepare. The tendency to engage in casual conversations about new projects, while walking down the hall should be resisted. Starting a new magazine is one of the major efforts to be made in a company and it should be organized with that in mind. It is just as difficult to raise venture capital within a company as it is to raise it outside. The same business planning and other steps taken by an entrepreneur should also be followed within a company.

• Assign each project. A committee cannot develop a new magazine. If a magazine is being started in house, its planning and direction should be assigned to one person so that he can bring the same dedication and interest to the project an outside entrepreneur would bring. It becomes his "baby."

• Pay adequately. Whether the start-up is the result of the efforts of an insider or an outsider, it requires activity far and above normal duties. A person involved in a start-up should be adequately compensated. This compensation means a share of profits—or maybe even more.

• Locate employees elsewhere. A new magazine should be insulated as much as possible from the day-to-day operations and politics of the existing company. The people running the magazine are in an entrepreneurial mode. They are being paid differently than other employees. It is best to put them in a separate location so they will not get caught up in day-to-day operations.

•Don't kid yourself. Many people involved in new ventures do not assign the full range of costs that are applied to all other operations. They may let different departments work for the new property without charging for that labor, omit the application of overhead or hide costs in other ways. It's better to treat the property as if it has to stand on its own feet. If you don't, you may find that you are carrying a loser much longer than you should because you do not have a real handle on the costs.

•Get all the help you can. The investment in a new magazine is a major one in terms of cost, people's time and personal involvement. There is no need to use only people who may be on your payroll, just because they are there. Do everything you can to insure success—it will be more worthwhile than a few hurt feelings. If you don't have adequate circulation strength, hire outsiders. If a different printer can do this job better than your normal printer, get him. If you are entering a part of the publishing business with which you are not familiar, get help.

•Inside or outside. Concepts for new magazines can come from either inside or outside a publishing house. While one would think that people in the business would constantly be coming up with good ideas, more ideas actually come from outsiders. This is not as strange as it may seem.

Insiders are often so immersed in what they are doing that their imaginations become limited. And they may suffer from "groupthink" by working with the same bunch of people. There are also not as many "insiders" as there are "outsiders."

Almost every organization looks inside for its new concepts. After all, the organization has confidence in its people. This thinking often results in locating a market and then trying to develop a magazine to fit it. This procedure can work at times, but the creative spark may never emerge and the best that can be done is pedestrian.

More often, the truly innovative concepts come from people who are not working on a particular magazine (although many may have at one time been in the business). These people have an added advantage of having a far greater dedication to the project than insiders have. Many of these people have quit their jobs, nearly starved, and suffered in other ways to get their brainchild into print. There is no substitute for these kinds of sacrifices.

While the tendency for magazine publishers has been to avoid starting new magazines, this trend does not have to continue. Publishers have missed a great many opportunities for profit and will miss many more if they continue in their current direction.

The answer lies in understanding that a magazine should be treated differently from the existing business and that its organization should be treated very differently. A publisher must be willing to accept ideas and help from outside, to change ideas about compensation and to act in other ways which are foreign to the basic business. The result may mean starting a magazine inhouse—or simply investing in new concepts.

Start-up research

By Ronald T. Scott

Is it possible to successfully launch a new magazine in today's highly competitive newsstand marketplace? If it is possible, what are the ingredients of successful newsstand sales?

I have been asked these two questions very often during my 20-plus years of active participation in newsstand publishing and, surprisingly, the answers have remained the same. First, it *is* possible to successfully launch a new magazine today, just as new magazines have been launched successfully for a lot longer than the 20 years of which I speak. And second, successful newsstand sales require careful planning, a clear understanding of the consumer audience to which the magazine will appeal, and a well-packaged editorial product.

No matter how different a publisher thinks his new magazine is, there probably are magazines already on the newsstands which appeal to somewhat the same consumer audience. And, because the subject matter of today's magazines is becoming more and more specialized, the audience for most magazines is very sharply defined. Thus, a publisher who estimates a potential audience of five million readers must rely on the newsstand circulation system (national distributor, local wholesaler, retailer) to locate that special consumer group.

Sales information freely available

Fortunately for publishers of newsstand magazines, all sales and return information by retailer and local wholesaler—on all magazine titles—is freely available to all national distributors and all publishers. In fact, national distributor field sales people gather and report such information on a daily basis for magazine titles they represent as well as for their competitors' titles.

Thus, the publisher of a new magazine can accumulate a vast amount of newsstand sales information on those existing magazine titles which are directly competitive or partially competitive to his new magazine.

By carefully analyzing this information, he can find the retailers who attract the type of consumer he feels will buy his magazine. He will learn something about the volume of newsstand sales he can realistically expect, the range of sales efficiency, or sales percentage, he can expect, and the number and types of retailers who sell these competitive titles.

He will become aware of the regional nature of the sales pattern (if such a pattern exists), and, if the competitive titles have different manufacturing specifications and different cover prices, he will learn the various consumer responses to these formats.

This sales information will also indicate the best type of retailer to sell his new magazine and identify the type of chain retailer who must first authorize his new title. This is important because most major retailers require approval of new titles before local wholesalers are allowed to deliver copies to their individual stores.

Plan carefully, don't rush

Because it takes time to accumulate all of this detailed information from some 500 local wholesalers and a sampling of the 140,000 retailers, careful planning is necessary. In fact, it will take at least four months to accumulate the information, form an action plan based on it, and execute the plan. (Please note that this four months is before the press run is set and after the contract is signed with a national distributor.)

The procedures shouldn't be rushed, condensed or avoided, however, since the alternative to this carefully planned and disciplined approach is the uninformed allocation of copies to local wholesalers. Too often, a new publisher will base his allocation decisions on another title distributed by the national distributor and give only cursory attention to the critically important authorization of the title by the major chain retailers.

Another critical factor in the success of a magazine on the newsstand is packaging. I make a distinction between packaging and content just as do almost all producers of consumer products. Unfortunately, the presentation of the information and entertainment contained in the magazine is at least as important as the contents, and here I speak specifically of the cover design, cover treatment, and cover lines.

A new magazine faces competition from hundreds of successful, established magazines with proven editorial formulas and carefully crafted cover packaging. If a new publisher has accumulated the sale and return information discussed above, he can easily determine the more successful titles. By carefully studying their cover lines and cover designs, he can get a general idea of how to sell to his target consumer audience.

Realistic evaluation is essential

After a new publisher has analyzed the newsstand situation, he faces a critical challenge: how to be realistic in evaluating the potential level of success. Unfortunately, many publishers who accumulate and analyze the sales information will still print far too many copies and expect far too high a sales percentage. The result of such unwarranted optimism is almost certain disappointment and all too often leads to the demise of the title—not because there were no consumers who would buy it nor advertisers who would support it, but because the publisher had reached for a circulation level beyond his grasp.

The successful newsstand publisher combines his sensitivity to consumers' needs with good information from the distribution channel—and realistically evaluates the situation. Hundreds of new magazines are launched successfully each year using this new formula.

Diversion

By Stephen Birnbaum

The inauguration of *Diversion* as an independent leisure and travel publication for physicians was actually somewhat of an accident. Of course, it still had all the editorial and financial problems that every new magazine seems to endure, but a history of prior publication was able to slightly cushion the growing pains (emphasis on the word "slightly").

Diversion had its first incarnation in April 1973, as a sort of glorified house organ for the Johnson & Johnson pharmaceutical organization. Johnson & Johnson provided professional advertising from its family of companies, and advertising solicitation for consumer products was undertaken by J&J's publishing partner in what was essentially a co-venture.

That partner, Family Health Communication, did the best it could while *Diversion*'s offices remained in New York City. But when Johnson & Johnson decided to move *Diversion* to Titusville, N.J., consumer advertising solicitation became difficult.

I became editor of *Diversion* in April 1975, and inherited a first-class editorial product—though one with a severely limited advertising constituency. Johnson & Johnson's pharmaceutical advertising alone could not make *Diversion* profitable and consumer advertising was erratic at best. I can remember wondering just how successful *Diversion* might be if only it could solicit advertising from the numerous other drug companies.

At the beginning of 1976, Johnson & Johnson recognized the dilemma of *Diversion*, and the opportunity arose to purchase the magazine on very favorable terms.

Magazine represented unfamiliar focus

Although the price for *Diversion* was relatively low by market standards, a substantial amount of working capital was definitely needed. The magazine was attempting to establish itself in a pharmaceutical market dominated by literally hundreds of strictly scientific clinical journals.

The group that was formed to purchase and sustain *Diversion* wisely recognized that its main advertising thrust would have to be directed towards pharmaceutical companies and that inroad into this market might be a lengthy and costly process. In all candor, the fact that funds were available enabled the magazine to weather a very lean first 18 months as an independent publication.

Part of our initial confidence in the magazine was based on the precise and well-defined nature of its readership, and our conviction that this readership would enthusiastically embrace the concept of leisure and travel editorial material.

It took all of that first year and a half for the pharmaceutical industry to even begin to recognize *Diversion's* impact on its physican audience, and for independent syndicated research to confirm its wide readership among a very select audience. The ultimate result of this recognition by advertisers was a quantum jump in advertising pages from 138 for the first half of 1976 to a blessed 579 for the first half of 1978. Hallelujah!

Ignorance and faith bring success

So much for the realities of the *Diversion* experience, for I suspect that its success is attributable in equal parts to ignorance and faith. The ignorance was that of the editor and publisher (me), who didn't have enough real publishing experience to realize that a leisure magazine directed solely at doctors could not possibly succeed. The faith was that of an unusual group of investors who, time and again, put their money where their minds told them they shouldn't.

Time is an incredibly important element in any new magazine's success. Ideas for magazines at least as good as ours have foundered and died because the money ran out before the advertisers and the reading public could recognize what a valuable publishing property was in their midst. We were lucky enough to have enough time to succeed.

One other thing: At all times, we assumed our audience would accept only the finest editorial and graphic material we could produce. Every time we even considered the possibility of cutting quality to keep costs down, our financial backers vetoed the idea.

I'm very glad I didn't know then what I know now, because I might not have promoted this venture as enthusiastically as I did. I can't think of a more perilous situation for a fledgling publisher to be in than one of under-capitalization. Given today's economic environment, no magazine can possibly survive without sufficient funding to carry it well beyond initial projections of profitability. With enough money, at least you have a fighting chance.

Country Journal

By William S. Blair

This article is written for the benefit of someone like myself—a small businessman who wants to start a magazine of his own and doesn't have as much money as he should.

When a big company like Time Inc. plans to start a magazine, it faces many of the same problems which face the small entrepreneur—problems like reader acceptance, renewal rates and advertising response. But there's one problem they do not share. If the projections say "Spend $10 million and don't worry—it'll all come back," finding the $10 million is no problem for the big company. For the small entrepreneur, however, a solution that involves spending $10 million is no solution at all.

Virtually all new magazines are under-financed. The reason is very simple: Entrepreneurs don't have enough money themselves; and they learn very soon that the more capital they look for, the more stock in the company they are going to have to give up in exchange.

Consequently, the most important aspect of running the business end of a new magazine is cash flow. You must plan it ahead in minute detail, and you must watch the actual figures month by month and modify your plan as you go.

When friends, well-wishers and even other publishers ask the following questions: "How are you doing? Are you breaking even?" or "Are you making a profit yet?" my usual answer to these questions is that I don't know. And sometimes I'm even tempted to add that I don't care. Profit and loss are hypothetical concepts put together by accountants (in the case of small companies like this) for the benefit of the IRS. You can make your profit larger or smaller by using different accounting procedures.

Abstract concepts have limits

But you cannot make the amount of money in the bank larger or smaller by applying abstract concepts. If you have $50,000 worth of bills that have to be paid today, and only $10,000 in the bank, you have a problem that no accountant can help you with.

For many businesses, the difference between cash flow and P&L is negligible. If a restaurant owner pays his help weekly and his rent monthly, if his suppliers insist that he stay current with his bills and if he wisely refuses credit to his customers, he'll find at the end of the month that the difference between what he's taken in and what he's spent is his profit.

But in magazine publishing it isn't so simple. The

principle reason is the prepayment of subscriptions.

Suppose you plan to start a magazine. Your first subscriber is your mother-in-law, who gives you $12 for a one year subscription. You spend $10 of this printing up some letterheads. At that point you say to yourself, "I'm in pretty good shape financially. I don't owe anybody anything, and I've got two bucks in the bank."

"Nonsense," your accountants will tell you. "You received the $12 on the promise that you'd send the old lady 12 magazines, and you have not fulfilled any part of this promise. You don't earn that money until you deliver magazines. Far from being in good shape financially, you have incurred expenses of $10 and earned no income. Your enterprise therefore has a *negative* net worth of $10."

Even financial people sometimes fail to grasp the importance of cash flow in magazine publishing. Many of them believe that the health of a company is measured exclusively by its P&L statement. For example, when I went over our balance sheet figures with the field interviewer for Dun & Bradstreet, he couldn't understand why we weren't bankrupt.

Even some bankers have trouble understanding the situation, and it's a tribute to the Vermont National Bank that they were willing to lend money to a company that not only was "losing money" in the traditional sense, but was budgeted to lose even more in the future.

Deal foiled by P&L misconception

One more example. At one point it became necessary for us to find a new printer. We negotiated with several. The treasurer of one of them looked over our disastrous balance sheet and told us that he'd have to have cash in advance. This, of course, would have put a fearful crimp in our operations.

I tried to explain to him that any publishing expert looking at *Country Journal's* record—its renewal rates, its advertising trends and so on—could see immediately that there was virtually no danger of its going out of business. We could pay our bills so long as our cash flow was healthy, regardless of P&L. The very worst thing that could happen would be so pressing a need for cash that my partner and I would have to sell our controlling interest.

This, though a disaster to us, presented no risk at all to the printer. But since I could not get him to see beyond the P&L statements, we did not do business together.

Absolutely essential to our start-up was the formulation, month by month, of detailed and precise cash flow projections. We came on the scene just before computer models were generally available to magazine publishers, so all of our original projections were made by hand. This was a valuable exercise for me (I did them all), for it compelled me to go over, in detail, every item of income and expense and specify exactly when the payment would take place.

If I were to do the exercise again, I would use a computer model. But I would also back it up by hand calculations to see whether I came up with the same answers.

How accurate have our projections been? They have been remarkably close in most respects. Each time I make a budget I find myself saying, "Well, the next year is going to be touch and go, but just wait for the year after that." A year later I find myself saying exactly the same thing. It's much like climbing a mountain, when you say to yourself that if you just get to the top of that next rise it will all be over; but when you get there you find there's another hill beyond.

Four years bring four disasters

The biggest mistake I made in projections was not allowing for things that can go wrong. Murphy's Law ("if something can go wrong it will") is of course a facetious over-statement. But the fact is that if a number of things can go wrong, *one of them* almost certainly will. Here are four things that have gone wrong in our four years.

First, after about a year of publishing, our printer decided to go out of business. He announced this decision on a Saturday. Our upcoming issue was scheduled to go to press on Monday.

Second, we have had a series of disasters in the fulfillment area. Adding the cost of unnecessary mailing of invoices and renewals to the lost revenue from forgotten or alienated subscribers, I come up with a figure of over a quarter of a million dollars.

Third, a mailing was due to come out of our Boston letter shop when that city was closed down for a week by a snow storm. When it finally got to the post office it was delayed further by the crush of mail.

Fourth, in another mailing the merge-purge house forgot to run the names against our list. And so on.

I simply did not make enough allowance in my projections for disasters of this kind. In most cases, however, my figures were remarkably realistic. But if I were to do it over again, I would make the expenses 5 percent higher and the income 5 percent lower—simply to accommodate Mr. Murphy's hypothesis.

Making projections is one thing, however. Controlling the figures that go into these projections is something else. Here again I will illustrate from our own history.

Country Journal has two founders, Dick Ketchum and I. He edits and I publish. We are exactly equal partners and have been since the beginning.

Raising start-up capital

We financed a test mailing with our own money (about $40,000). We worked for a year without salary and agreed to work for the next few years at less than half what we had been earning before. We decided that this was the extent of the financial contribution we could make, so we went out to raise the necessary start-up capital from other people.

Our overriding consideration was that we did not want to give up control of the company. In other words, we wanted to end up with a corporation in which Blair and Ketchum together owned more than 50 percent of the stock. What we aimed for, and got, was two thirds. (By giving stock to employees, we have since reduced our 67 percent ownership to 60 percent.)

It wasn't an easy job. For one thing, our timing was terrible. We were out looking for money in the winter of 73-74, which was a period of economic disaster. We had also been conservative in our estimates of the potential market for *Country Journal*. This, in turn, limited the potential profit, and therefore the amount of capital that was worth investing in the project. This was a major problem, for as the magazine entrepreneur soon learns, it costs just as much to start a small magazine as it does to start a big one.

What we finally raised from friends and relatives was a grand total of $224,000. For this the investors received partnership interests which later converted into about one third of the total stock in the corporation. In fact, we started publication with only $16,000 of this money actually in hand. It turned out that after we published a couple of issues it was easier to get the rest, and we charged the later investors a higher price.

Once we had produced a few issues, the atmosphere became a bit easier. Many people could see we had a viable project on our hands. Consequently, in our first year we were able to negotiate with our local bank for a line of credit up to $150,000.

Ketchum and I had to "go on the note," as they say, meaning that we had to co-sign. In a sense, we were risking all our property and our homes on the success of our magazine. But I didn't lose much sleep over it because again, the gamble was not whether the roofs over our heads would be sold but whether we would be able to keep control of the company.

The two hundred twenty-four thousand dollars with which we started was an absurdly small sum of money for a major publishing venture. In case some of you are not familiar with *Country Journal*, I should say that we print on good quality 50-lb. stock, using a good deal of color. We have never printed less than an 80-page issue and, after our first year, never less than 100 pages. An expensive product.

Speed receipts, delay disbursements

With such a small sum of money at our disposal, there were immediate restraints on what we could and could not do. It was of vital importance to look for every means of accelerating receipts and delaying disbursements. Let me cite some examples.

In our initial mailing—and indeed for the next two years—our standard offer to new subscribers was payment in cash or credit. We thought we would get a higher total response, even after bad pay, from a "first issue free" offer; but our cash or credit offer turned the money around much faster.

Our initial mailing produced 50 percent cash with orders—enough to pay for the entire cost of the mailing. The credit collections came in later and helped to pay for printing and distributing magazines.

After we had published two or three issues, it became apparent from letters, conversations and press reactions that the people who were getting *Country Journal* really liked it. So we looked to our subscribers as a source of financial support.

Our first issue came out in May 1974 and in October we were in the mails with an advance renewal. About 25 percent of our subscribers sent us money for the second year when the first year was scarcely half over. Eventually 80 percent of those original subscribers renewed. We encouraged them to renew for periods longer than a year, and many of them did, giving us more money up front.

We also recognized that the magazine had considerable appeal as a Christmas gift and we promoted it as such to our subscribers. Gifts will normally produce a very high proportion of cash, and this was true for us. We still offer last year's Christmas donors a fifty cent reduction if they renew and send cash in the summer.

Another thing we did was offer our readers lifetime subscriptions at $100 (since raised to $150). Today we have 480 lifetime subscribers. This isn't a vast number, but it represents $50,000 of working capital that we raised from our subscribers rather than from greedy investors who might want more stock.

One thing we did not do, and something I certainly would do if we were starting a magazine today, is use bind-in and blow-in envelopes rather than cards. They bring in a much higher proportion of cash.

Minimize expenses

One way to improve your cash position is to minimize expenses. This is an obvious piece of advice, but I really do suggest that you look at every expenditure with the eye of a zero-base budgeter.

Do you need to have offices in a high-rent location? Do you need a *new* desk? In fact, do you need a desk at all? At *Country Journal* some of us use folding tables, and others use secondhand desks. Our budgets show an income of just under $3 million, which makes us a bit more than a "mom and pop" operation. Yet our balance sheet shows a total investment in physical objects—which include furniture and fixtures for 20 people, lighting table, file cabinets and typewriters—of $9,000.

Similarly, a small business in which everybody can communicate face to face is an ideal place in which to abolish the inter-office memo. And you can keep a log of statistics and other records in your own handwriting. We found that a small company like this does not need proportionately as much secretarial help as a big one.

Experience is expensive, and if you insist on having experienced employees in every position, you can run up the payroll very fast. We have been able to find quite a few young, able, energetic people. Such people are attracted to small new businesses, and publishing has a special appeal of its own.

With supervision, they were able to become highly effective in a short time. For example, selling advertising—especially to small local advertisers—requires skill, tact and perseverance, but it doesn't require years of experience.

Where you should not scrimp, of course, is in the quality of the product you are offering to your readers.

One thing I would certainly advise is an attitude of complete candor with your suppliers. If possible negotiate terms of payment with them beforehand so that you know precisely when you must pay each bill and what interest (if any) you should pay. Let them know if you are going to be late, and, if you do drag out payments beyond the customary time, when you expect to catch up.

Throughout this entire period of minimizing and delaying expenses, and attempting to maximize and speed up income, my paramount consideration was that each $7,000 dollars we had to raise by selling stock represented 1 percent of the total capitalization of the enterprise.

This realization was a powerful incentive to keep costs down: When you're spending your own money, you watch it carefully.

Equus

By Ami Shinitzky

After publishing *Polo* magazine for a year and a half, I was itching to start a new publication with greater potential. Although *Polo* has impressive demographics, the marginal size of the sport necessarily limits the journal's growth. Months of systematic thought yielded no attractive ideas. But then one evening came the idea for *Equus*..

The field of horse publications is a crowded one. There are countless regional and breed publications and more than a dozen major ones, each with over 30,000.

Because of such competition, the new idea had to have, first and foremost, an unquestionable editorial validity—not the kind of validity one could explain to a friend over dinner, but rather one that could be conveyed to the ever-besieged potential subscriber by letter or space ad.

Beyond that, there were other major considerations: Was there easy access to the universe? Could promotion be efficient? Were there sufficient advertisers who would feel at home with the given editorial product and the magazine demographics? And the last question (really the first question): What size investment would be needed, would the idea be profitable as a business proposition and could the necessary monies be raised? Whatever else a magazine is, it is above all a business, and that means watching a bottom line. Any editor and/or publisher who forgets this is asking for trouble.

Magazine uses common denominator

The validity of *Equus* is that, unlike any other horse magazines, it focuses on the only common denominator of all horse aficionados—the generic horse. It transcends breed, use, region and orientation. It deals only with those aspects of a horse as they apply to every horse: health and care, behavior, his relationship to man. Such a concept makes every horse owner a potential reader.

Armed with this argument and many more, I set out to raise money. My pursuit of cash was much like everyone else's except that rather than going for seed money to finance a test and then going for the rest, I went for the whole sum at once. The amount of money needed was only in the low six figures, rather modest compared to sophisticated start-ups; but having no previous success story with which to lure money, even that amount seemed beyond reach at times. It was only a strong conviction in my idea that kept me going.

Fearing a loss of time between the testing stage and start-up, and hence a loss of momentum and accumulation of overhead costs, I set up the deal so that only a certain amount of money would be allocated for the test. The balance was to be held in an escrow account to be released to me or returned to the investors when the go/no-go decision was made.

Another less common feature of this limited partnership is investor returns on a sliding scale. This enabled me to retain maximum ownership yet make the deal attractive to investors. Their initial returns exceed their ultimate share, and with every installment paid back, mine increases. Thus, there is a strong incentive for the entrepreneur and the hope of quick returns for the investor.

A proper business plan was, of course, prepared. A start-up circulation of 40,000 was projected, with a leveling off at 150,000 in four to five years. The March 1977 test, however, clearly showed that our expectations would be exceeded.

Test proves magazine's viability

This test was composed of 96,000 pieces—four representative lists and eight different packages. With 32 variations, it was quite manageable and demonstrated that the magazine was indeed a viable proposition and a strong pulling package at $12 per subscription. Ten dollars and fourteen dollars were also tested. Moreover, we discovered that we could encourage payment with the order and still have above average returns.

Through thrifty buying, we finally went out with a direct mail package that cost us only $165 per thousand and, in addition to the credit orders, we received back more cash (27 percent) than we invested. We were thus able to do two more direct mailings before our publication date in October of 1977 and ultimately delivered some 100,000 copies of our first issue for which the final pay-up was 85 percent.

Since beginning publication, we have introduced a softer offer and have continued to mail. Our rate base is now 150,000 and we have revised our original growth projection to 250,000.

On the advertising side, our performance is more conventional, having sold the first two issues well with the aid of a carefully prepared eight-page dummy. As time brings greater recognition, we look forward to a larger share of the equine-related market as well as some contracts from horizontal advertisers.

Our financial planning is circulation oriented, based on our realization that securing advertising revenue is an uncertain undertaking. Circulation variables can be thoroughly tested, projected, and—given cash flow consideration—manipulated in a hundred different ways. With the variety of sophisticated reports available from good fulfillment houses, a calculator, patience and perhaps a computer model, a publisher has a good bit of control over the situation and should rarely face major surprises.

Higher price lowers response

If advertising is to be the main source of revenue, the circulation department will be preoccupied with circulation numbers. On the other hand, if circulation is to be the financial backbone, then maximizing dollars becomes the goal—and that is by no means synonymous with maximum circulation. Although today's magazine reader is usually willing to pay more, a higher price will generally lower response.

Because we are committed to maximizing circulation revenues, our editorial product is primarily designed to give readers value for their money. It is never, of course, an either-or situation between advertising and circulation, and there is no reasonable way to test how elaborate the editorial product should be. It is rather a matter of judgment and emphasis where more is probably better than less as a sound investment toward better renewals.

There are four reliable objective indicators which

will tell a publisher how good his product is. However, these indicators are not letters to the editor, returns on initial promotion or friends. So when the first glorious issue is in hand, don't rejoice yet in the feeling of success. A publisher and his staff never mirror the market . . . the market must speak for itself.

Using objective indicators

Three of the four objective indicators will tell their story within a few weeks while the fourth, renewals, will obviously remain unknown for nearly a year. First, what's the pay-up rate compared to industry norms and your own projections? Clever promotion will sell almost anything, but to enjoy a good pay-up rate the product must be equally good. Second, how are bind-in cards doing? Is the magazine selling itself? And third, how do those readers who weren't motivated to write to the editor feel about the magazine? A reader questionnaire will reveal the true, across-the-board reaction from the market. In fact, such a study could be a constructive feature in any magazine, new or old.

If thumbs are up on all of the above, a sigh of relief and a pat on the back are in order.

Here are some additional thoughts, based on things we did and did not do. Talk to everyone in the business who will stand still long enough to hear your questions, but "listen" to your own intuition. Always make up your own mind after a thorough analysis and understanding of all the possible consequences of your decisions. You are responsible for your magazine, and no one knows it as well as you do.

Be cautious. No matter how well things seem to be going, leave a good bit of margin for error. Don't over-promise either advertisers or investors. That cushion might just make the difference between peace of mind and a never-ending hassle. Putting some cash in reserve, of course, falls under this advice, too.

If you are working toward a large subscriber file, immediately hire a competent circulation manager, construct a system and simulate the worst that could happen, because it will. You don't want unhappy subscribers and a less than maximal cash collection system.

Don't compromise on quality and, finally, constantly study and revise your business and circulation plans as new information becomes available. You are in this business to make money, not just to publish a magazine.

Vegetarian Times

By Paul Obis

Trying to write about my own success is like trying to look at the back side of my head—I know it's there, but no matter how fast I turn, I still can't see it.

When I was 22, I started a magazine called *Vegetarian Times*, in my spare time with money from my nursing salary. It was a single-sheet newsletter folded to make four pages, and it was typewritten and distributed free. Total circulation was 300 at a production cost of $17.

Four and a half years later, we became the largest periodical for the growing population of vegetarians in the U.S. We're a 64-page bimonthly, bound in a four-color, 70-lb. cover with a paid circulation of 32,000. Our annual dollar volume of $150,000 supports a four-person, full-time staff, divided between an office in Chicago and one in New York.

In an industry where typical start-up costs run from $250,000 to $3 million, our annual dollar volume may seem modest, but the potential for growth is excellent. In 1978 our circulation increased 320 percent despite a 50 percent increase in our cover price and renewals remain at 75 to 80 percent. Ad linage was up 700 percent for the same period, despite a 250 percent increase in our rates.

Our dedicated base of readers was established while the magazine grew from 4 to 56 pages—without advertising—under the direction of a person who had not one ounce of previous magazine, marketing or business experience.

Sometimes the desire to succeed took extraordinary efforts, such as carrying home 1,500 copies of a 24-page magazine on a bicycle six miles through city traffic, then addressing, sorting and bundling them by hand. It was this kind of determination which played the most important role in my first three and half years of publishing.

Need for more capital arises

After three and a half years a critical point was reached—a point where a large influx of capital became necessary. Ironically, I found it in a company whose beginnings were not unlike my own—Associated Business Publications. In exchange for a majority of the stock, I received salaried personnel, some cash and about $30,000 worth of advertising support. I retained editorial control, got the job I always wanted and retained a percentage of the ownership.

Selling controlling interest was a humbling experience initially, but it was tempered by the infusion of money and the knowledge that in many cases publishers trade off 70 to 80 percent of their ownership at the start in exchange for venture capital. Thus, my position is no different than that of many others who have started magazines, although my first three and a half years in publishing were very extraordinary.

The fact remains that I succeeded in reaching a long-time goal by the age of 26, and I did it without experience or financial backing for the first years of publication. I recount my story not to laud myself, but to encourage others by saying that it can be done. If your determination is strong enough, you will succeed.

My experience has been rewarding. By coming into publishing through the back door, as I did, I was able to see the whole business—from editorial to fulfillment to production. In the process, I learned many things and drew some conclusions from my own experiences and observations.

One conclusion I reached is that although money is a valuable commodity, its importance has unfortunately been over-emphasized, particularly in the beginning stages of publication. Many successful publications have been started on a relative wing-tip shoe string. Consider the following magazines and their start-up costs: *Playboy*—$16,000; *Nursing '78*—$20,000; *High Times*—$25,000; *Rolling Stone*—$6,500; *Mother Earth News*—$1,500.

Plan your budget to last

I do not mean to understate the importance of capital, but I feel money is better spent when spent on promotion and development after the base has been built and the kinks have been worked out. If one is fortunate enough to have substantial backing from the beginning, that money should be made to last. The likelihood is that it will take two to four years for the publication to turn a profit. Plan your budget to last. Many magazines have started with a bang, only to go under in a matter of months.

"Write for the readers" is another sensible but often forgotten rule. Too often the magazine is directed at advertisers—unintentionally or otherwise. However, it won't go in a consumer book. It is better to build a loyal, dedicated base of readers rather than reach for numbers in hopes of attracting advertisers. If your readers are loyal, the advertisers will follow as surely as flies are attracted to honey.

Be realistic in your marketing plans. How many people will really want to read your magazine? Will putting 100,000 copies on the newsstand be the best way to spend your money? Once the presses are running, it costs an average of 25 cents per copy for a magazine. Each unsold copy is 25 cents out of pocket, plus shipping, distributor fees and retail display allowances, if any.

All of this assumes your magazine will have something useful to say. It should be either informative or entertaining—preferably both—with the copy presented in an attractive manner. Editorial quality and overall design are, of course, extremely important. But *all* of the elements are important.

Creative Computing

By David H. Ahl

Back in 1973, the use of computers in schools was really taking off, but the amount of information available to teachers concerning their effective use was lagging way behind the technology of the hardware.

Several manufacturers and educational computing projects were issuing newsletters, but there was no single publication for exchanging information. There was nothing that discussed the social impact of the computer—its effect on jobs, medical care, privacy and the like. Even more important, there was nothing that focused on the users and sheer fun of computers in the classroom.

Thus was born the idea for a vibrant and lively, but educationally sound, magazine for educational computer users. I looked at over 50 proposed names that said "fun," and it finally came down to *The Purple Peanut Butter Computing Magazine*. Unfortunately, that was a mouthful and a half—besides, it wouldn't fit on the cover very well. So I fell back to the number two choice, *Creative Computing*. The name being decided upon, the next thing was to publish it. Right?

In my blissful ignorance, having had no experience in the publishing industry whatsoever, I figured all I had to do was print a promotional flyer telling people about *Creative Computing* and they would beat a path to my door. I printed such a flyer and then, not knowing any better, I set out to contact good authors for articles and to typeset, print and mail the magazine—all with a total investment of $600!

It seemed simple enough on paper but then came the reality. The period between July and September of 1974 was incredible! Virtually simultaneously, I was writing 150 potential advertisers (two responded), distributing flyers at six conferences (a waste of time), preparing and mailing four different press releases to 224 magazines (printed eventually by 19) and purchasing mailing lists. I was contacting writers, artists, reviewers and contributors. I was editing the first issue, finding and getting price quotes from printers, laying out the magazine and answering an average of 30 letters a week.

At the same time, I was selling a house in Concord, Mass., purchasing a home in Morristown, N.J., moving, getting settled, finding schools for my kids and learning the ropes of my new position as marketing manager, education with AT&T. (At that time, *Creative Computing* was just a hobby with me.) Whew! Disaster and/or divorce loomed nearer with every minute of every day.

By the time I was ready to print the first issue I had 850 subscribers at $8 each (for six bimonthly issues). So I used all that subscription money to print as many copies of the first 48-page newsprint issue as I could afford.

First issue gets off the presses

On Oct. 7, 1974, the first issue rolled off the presses. There were 43 cartons at 52 pounds each—8,000 copies which equalled one basement plus one family room. Junior high school kids worked in the house around the clock, labeling each magazine, rubber stamping "ATTN: So and so," "Dear Computer Center Director," or "Dear Librarian," inserting letters while keeping them in ZIP Code order (ha!). Okay, sort again, tie into bundles, cart to the post office (oh, for a large truck!), weigh and mail.

As time went on, I hired people, most of whom were as ignorant about the publishing industry as I was. But we shared two things in common—we were willing to learn and we were determined to succeed.

Are we successful? Today we're the leading computer magazine for educational computing. More important, however, we've broadened our coverage to include personal (home) computing, electronic and video games and small business computing as well.

We've graduated to slick paper, four-color illustra-tions, a respectable amount of advertising, monthly frequency (as of January 1979), a paid circulation in excess of 60,000 in 50 states and 24 foreign countries, a full-time staff of 20 people and we just bought *ROM* magazine, one of our competitors.

We've branched out into publishing books (eight titles so far) and computer software, and we also run a book service. And, oh yes, we've been profitable since our third issue.

Our goals are more ambitious than they used to be —we're shooting for 200,000 circulation by 1980. We're sure we can make it because we're still willing to learn and we're determined to succeed.

Fishing Tackle Retailer

By Spencer H. Longshore III

There are a lot of good ideas for magazines floating around out there. You just have to be lucky enough to have the right idea at the right time and place, or smart enough to recognize a genuine opportunity, grasp it, and make it work.

The concept of our new trade magazine, *Fishing Tackle Retailer*, was probably on the minds of many people at Bass Anglers Sportsman Society, without their ever being aware of it. B.A.S.S., a $25 million sales company, is the largest fishing organization in the world. Our publishing division publishes *Bassmaster Magazine*, the largest fishing magazine published in the world, and *Southern Outdoors Magazine*, the largest regional outdoor magazine in America. We also publish college alumni directories and freshman yearbooks.

As do most people, we read the industry trade books to find out what is going on, spot new manufacturers, and so forth. We had come to believe that the editorial content of these magazines was unresponsive to the changing marketing conditions of the fishing tackle industry. Because of our leadership position in the industry, we felt we could do certain things better than anyone else. One of these things involved publishing a new trade magazine.

A major question that kept confronting us as we developed the concept for *Fishing Tackle Retailer* was, "How often should this new trade magazine be published?" The need for "business press" information certainly did not dictate a monthly trade magazine, and after discussions with major manufacturers, jobbers, and others, we didn't feel even six issues were required to do a good job publishing to the fishing tackle trade.

Eventually we settled on four issues a year (August, which is our trade show issue; November, January, and March), a frequency that covers the four major trade buying cycles that exist within this industry. We felt it was more important to publish four big, thick, slick, impressive issues than six skimpy ones. The seasonality of freshwater fishing also influenced our frequency decision. We also found in measuring our competitor's magazines that the big space ran during the period we intended to publish our four issues. We would also rather publish four issues and make a profit than six or eight and start at red ink. Eighteen months down the road, our decision has proved to be a wise one.

The importance of editorial

One essential that an aspiring publisher must keep firmly in mind is the absolute necessity of producing the finest editorial product available to a specific marketplace. Most trade magazines within an industry address identical audiences; the big difference lies in the editorial and advertising messages within the magazines. The editorial content of a magazine is everything.

We understand the value of editorial at B.A.S.S. Publications and have built our consumer magazines on that premise. Furthermore, our editorial attracts the type of audience that advertisers want.

How did we position *FTR? Fishing Tackle Retailer* was not conceived to be a people and places, gossipy, chit-chatty, trade book. Instead, we positioned the magazine as a merchandising/marketing primer for a basically non-marketing-oriented group of fishing tackle retailers across America.

For example, our trade show issue doesn't devote page after page of exhibitor listings. We take that same space and talk about new products, and interview retailers across America and discuss what they need from the industry.

In lieu of running long manufacturer-generated editorial copy, we use freelance writers (several hold MBA's in marketing). These people write about such subjects as how to run in-store fishing tackle promotions, and the role of the minicomputer in today's small retail shop.

How did we find 20,000 retailers that we could BPA qualify and send this never-before-published trade book? We scratched our heads many times trying to answer that question. We knew that our primary competitor had only 10,000 qualified names; that was just about half as many as we should have. We tried to rent or buy mailing lists, but when we couldn't find any that gave us the needed numbers or quality, we knew we had to search elsewhere.

We then looked to the fishing tackle industry itself—which has two distinct and identifiable traits in the flow of product from manufacturer to consumer. The majority of the manufacturers in our industry, whether regional or national, depended on jobbers, distributors, or wholesalers to move product to the retail level. However, those manufacturers with direct sales staffs have some record of their retailers, and most were willing to provide us with computer tapes of their retail customers.

We keyed all of these names and addresses into our computer, then did a merge/purge—and came up with only about 10,000 names. (Our research had shown us that there were about 20,000 retailers out there selling fishing tackle.)

We approached our next source, the jobbers/distributors/ wholesalers, and were able to obtain many of their customer lists. After keying literally hundreds of lists containing tens of thousands of names, we produced an unduplicated listing of 20,000 names and addresses of fishing tackle retailers.

We have just recently received our initial audit report from BPA. It reflects a qualified circulation of 18,679, out of a total circulation of 22,098.

Attracting ad dollars

Because our circulation is controlled and advertising our only source of revenue, we knew we had to sell a ton of advertising. Fortunately, in selling the concept for this new magazine, our sales staff had on their side not only the credibility that we already enjoyed in the industry, but our sales story as well.

We sold the *Retailer* on the basis of its being the largest circulation trade magazine in the fishing industry, and on its editorial excellence.

The fishing tackle industry was, and is, experiencing problems competing with other sports—jogging, racquetball and tennis, for example. These sports were pirating customers from our industry. So we led our target group of potential advertisers through these competitive magazines and pointed out incident after incident of non-fishing editorial surrounding their fishing ads. When our sales platform addressed our competition directly, many manufacturers began to re-evaluate how they were spending their trade advertising dollars.

I think our methodology and approach to selling *Fishing Tackle Retailer* was a textbook study in how to take a concept and not only sell it, but quite possibly set an all-time record for ad page production in a premiere issue of a new trade magazine. Our premiere issue had a total folio of 232 pages, and contained 138.41 advertising pages. Our first year of publishing produced 308.7 pages of advertising in just four issues.

Fishing Tackle Retailer, now almost 20 months old, is outperforming our initial projection. It has been profitable from day one, and fits so compatibly with our consumer titles that we all wonder why we didn't do it years ago. (Perhaps we didn't because that proverbial "void in the marketplace" all of us love to speak about didn't exist.)

The industry has reacted so favorably to the editorial position of our magazine that we see nothing but a bright, profitable future ahead for the first, but certainly not the last, trade magazine to be published by B.A.S.S. Publications.

Sheet Music Magazine

By Ed Shanaphy

The idea for *Sheet Music Magazine* grew out of my experience in the direct marketing of music products.

About 12 years ago, I was selling records and songbooks by mail to a market that could not get enough. Music buyers cannot get enough music; they cannot get enough books; they cannot get enough how-to materials. Furthermore, there are not nearly enough music stores to service this market.

My initial concept was of a mail-order songbook continuity series—a series of books containing the words and sheet music for pop songs. Warner Bros. Publications was willing to lease us copyrighted songs (they were the only music publishers willing to do so) but required our delivering 18,000 subscribers with the third issue. (Newsstand and in-store sales were forbidden by contract at that time.) If we didn't deliver the paid subs, Warner Bros. would pick up all their songs and go home, and we'd be left with a cover.

Cash up front

Realizing that I needed a lot of up-front orders, I decided to call the series a magazine, since magazine buyers are used to paying up-front for a continuing product.

The approach to the magazine, therefore, was similar to that of a mail-order product, be it a record package, a waistline slimmer, or a banana tree: Charge full price for a whole product and get cash with the order. No check, no banana tree.

Furthermore, the idea had to work in print advertising. We shunned direct mail at that time because direct mail required too much cash. Print advertising required the least amount of time and cash before the flow would start, and I knew a couple of publications that would tell us if we had a viable product.

We hired a copy pro to prepare our first ad. I had my own idea stashed away, but avoided using it for fear of closeness. Mistake number one. Closeness to the product is less a villain than distance.

The pro's ad bought subscribers at $10 per. Since our subscription price was $11, this was a disaster from a mail-order-product point of view. When I brought my "publisher's" ad out of the trunk, our average cost per sub shrank to $4. This was in national media, general editorial and special interest *other* than music publications. (Five years later, this ad is still our control ad. It has nothing to do with copywriting. It's paternal. Any publisher who doesn't test talking about his baby is making a serious error, I think.)

The cycling-in technique

I wanted every new subscriber to be bowled over. To insure this, we made certain they all received a blockbuster first issue—a "cycling-in" issue which we used for three years. It was filled with such good stuff (everything from "As Time Goes By" to "The Hustle," a biggie at the time) that even the most skeptical subscribers would be kept happy and quiet for two months at the very least.

The first shipment of this issue went out approximately six weeks after our initial subscribers had responded. And our first regular issue did not go out until 10 weeks after that. Fortunately, we never heard a complaint about delay, and this timing, together with the impact of such a heavy-hitting introductory issue, enabled us to buy four months' time between initial testing and the first *regular* issue. Enough time to gather lots of subscribers and lots of cash. Remember, we had no editorial staff but for George Gershwin, Cole Porter, Gordon Lightfoot and company. So there was no added salary drain during this period.

We accomplished a great deal more with this issue, however. Remember, we had to deliver 18,000 with the printing of the third issue. When we printed 25,000 copies of this cycling-in issue, the heat went off at Warner Bros. And it was this issue that helped give us the necessary time to reach 18,000 with issue number three.

(Note: the "cycling-in" issue was tested as a freebie in addition to the nine regular issues per year, versus having it count as one of the nine issues. No difference.)

Don't count on next year

From what I could gather as a newcomer to the field, most magazines are constructed around a "come" bet: renewals and advertisers yet to be won. As far as I was concerned, however, a renewal is something that may or may not happen next year. (Brimming with confidence!) Besides, I was never the type who could wait for the residual sales, the second efforts, the conversions.

In addition, potential advertisers (piano and organ manufacturers, record companies, music publishers) were very apathetic. It was the beginning of tailspin time in Tin Pan Alley, and I didn't want to build a business based on their ability to stem the tide. Yessir . . . this would be a circulation magazine. And it would break even or better in the first year . . . just on circulation! (Ha!)

Needless to say, this was not quite the case, but the attitude kept us very healthy. The "product-by-mail" philosophy governed all our marketing. Blow-ins and bind-ins were always envelopes to carry cash. They still are. Only recently did we begin testing a bill-me offer.

The initial results of this testing are interesting. In direct mail, where the consumer is accustomed to magazine solicitations with soft offers, our bill-me seems to be working. In print, where consumers are conditioned to cash-with-order mail-order ads, our cash-up-front offer out-performs the bill-me.

From bop to Bach

Anyone observing our success would have realized that an exact knock-off in the classical music area —*i.e.*, a magazine with music for classical music/piano buffs—was our next step. Discussions with people in the classical music "communications" business rerouted me from this plan to one calling for a magazine aimed at the general classical music audience, not just keyboard, and one, therefore, that did not include music in it.

We tried it, but it failed miserably and we quickly converted it to the original idea. *Keyboard Classics* now has a paid subscription total of 40,000. The beauty of this magazine is that there are no royalties due to Beethoven, Chopin, Bach.

It is interesting that so many of our *Sheet Music* subscribers are taking on a subscription to *Keyboard Classics* in addition to their *Sheet Music* subscription. Music buyers simply cannot get enough music!

Magazines as testing areas

Our list of music buyers by mail, which includes our active subscribers (200,000 plus), expires, and buyers of various offers we have made, now stands at one million, and as such is the only significant list of these people. The magazines are a perfect vehicle for advertising related products, but should not be thought of as the only way of advertising them.

I regard the magazines as test areas for direct mail. If an offer generates a certain amount of response in the magazines, we immediately create a very basic direct mail piece. And that's where the big numbers come in for related product offers. The same art and typography that is used to create ads and/or mailings for the various products is reproduced in mini-catalog form as a bounceback stuffer for each and every package going out.

The magazines are not an end product, but rather the basis of a music direct-marketing company. The staff and I are just back from a cruise to Bermuda where we taught our subscribers how to have more fun playing music. In the spring, we are off to Vienna to take them to concerts and operas. We are creating an audio/visual series of master classes from some of the leading musicians in the world. (It's surprising that such a project has never been done.) On the hardware side, we're offering everything from music boxes to piano lamps. Of course, they're not buying all of it—but they do buy most of it.

The biggest mistake I made? Not starting this music direct-marketing concept on the very first day.

Natural Foods Merchandiser

By R. Douglas Greene

Like many entrepreneurial tales, this one is a story—not to mention a labor—of love.

The idea of starting a natural foods trade magazine occurred to me—as have most of my better ideas—in a totally unbusinesslike manner. Actually, I was in a sailboat off the coast of Malibu, which my wife (who's now editorial director) was piloting in a somewhat carefree manner. We still run our magazine that way—a spirit of risk-taking keeps it all from getting stale.

My interest in natural foods had been stirred about a year earlier during a meeting with my first hard-core natural foods enthusiast at a dinner table at Club Med in Mexico. The enthusiast also happened to be an M.D. with impeccable credentials. Since I was 27 at the time, and felt like 50, it seemed an intelligent decision to give the whole thing a try.

To give you a bit more perspective on my consciousness-raising, I was then head of a publishing rep firm in Los Angeles, which I'd founded some three years earlier, and which was providing me with a wonderfully comfortable living—about $100,000 per year. Among the companies we worked with were Gralla Publications, United Technical Publications, Walker-Davis, and many others.

My wife, Karen, and I were one of those couples—and surely one of the few to marry—who had first met in the aisles of a trade show, while working for Gralla.

In 1978, after a year of personal experimentation with natural foods, we decided we'd like to become involved in what we perceived as a somewhat more meaningful business than the one I was in. We both believe in taking gambles—so we did.

Room for a fifth

At first we thought of starting a retail store in the industry, or launching a product line, but after reviewing the four trade magazines in the field, we felt there was a tremendous need for a strong, business-oriented book.

Scanning *SRDS* gave us a shock, though, since the full-page ad rates in the industry magazines were less than the commissions I was receiving for a page in my rep business. This necessitated my staying part-time in the rep business for the first six months. Once I had dreamed I could actually do both. We found this workload a torturous proposition.

Luckily, I was foolish enough to give it a try. In October, the two of us struck out—alone. By day, I sold space for my clients (I let them know ahead of time what I was doing, and they agreed that it was fine as long as my market share remained satisfactory), while Karen answered the phone and typed all the correspondence. One or two days a week, I'd sell *Natural Foods Merchandiser* while she worked on the editorial.

From the beginning, I made it a point to spend as much time with retailers (our primary audience) as with the advertisers. It's a practice I found extremely informative, and one which I continue to this day.

Offers they couldn't refuse

I hit the road with our dummy front cover glued to a copy of a Gralla book, and with a "charter advertiser" package which incorporated six offers:

1. Seven ads for the price of six, with the first ad in the premiere issue and a free ad in the second issue. Too often, a new book comes out with a smashing first issue, while the second issue looks as if bankruptcy is close behind. If for any reason an ad schedule was canceled, the free ad was billed at the one-time rate. There was also a half-page minimum with this offer.

2. The advertiser's logo to be listed each month during our first year in a special charter advertiser section.

3. A copy of our newly organized independent sales rep directory.

4. A mini-research study, which involved our mailing a questionnaire to 500 retailers and splitting the cost of postage and printing with the advertiser. They were limited to seven questions and we would add three more for editorial purposes. The data were confidential, and we provided analysis of the information.

5. A merchandising mailing to their wholesalers and/or sales force. This included a copy of the premiere issue with a cover letter, which I signed, promoting their ad program. (This is actually a great way to get wholesaler names and build publicity for your new magazine.)

6. Easels displaying their ads at all major trade shows.

Within 90 days, I'd sold 180 pages of space, with 44 lined up for the first issue.

The next step was financing. We knew we had a viable concept on our hands after meeting with so many retailers and suppliers. Through friends, I found a young, creative banker (yes, they exist) to meet with. Following the Boy Scout motto, I wanted to be prepared, and gathered up everything I could think of except the family photo album. Style is every bit as important as information when it comes to financing, I've found.

Changing lanes costs money

I'd figured that the difference between my rep commissions and cash outlay would at most be $10,000 per month once a good cash flow set in. We'd already decided to sell our beautiful new house in the hills of Malibu in order to help pay for this opportunity to experience "life in the alternative fast lane," though real estate at the time was moving at a brisk crawl. I might also note here that economic indicators were bordering on the pessimistic. Naturally, we were undaunted.

In any case, my creative banker said he'd not only loan me $10,000 for each of three months, but he'd give me a $50,000 unsecured line of credit for the corporation, which, I might add, had an extremely good track record from the rep firm.

We used the line of credit to negotiate maximum credit terms with our suppliers. We also opened discussions with a major midwestern bank with trade magazine experience in case we needed additional cash flow financing for growth. (We didn't, as it turned out.)

We also made it clear to our advertisers that we were producing a quality product that would be important to their marketing efforts, and that our 2-10-net 30 terms *did not* mean 2-*20*-net. (Little did I know that cash flow from advertisers and agencies comes about as rapidly as summer in Maine.)

Anyway, we were really off and sailing. We knew advertising sales would go well. We'd found a good printer. We'd found retail lists to buy. And we even had several large companies in the industry offer their customer lists to us—a real blessing. All we had to do was turn out a magazine and get it to the printer. That, of course, is the tough part.

Tunnel vision

One of my biggest criticisms of trade magazines (I've got about 1,000) is that they think awfully small. They don't see the scope of the industries they're involved in, much less the large creative role they can play in an industry's development.

It's critically important when you're starting up to analyze a marketplace from the standpoint of real issues and real activity. Not the *politics* of the marketplace, but the *actual* marketplace. This necessitates primary research. Don't ever depend on second-hand information.

Above all, remember that often senior magazines in a field tend to focus more on the politics than the realities of any marketplace.

Most magazines could benefit from the courage to take stands on important industry issues, especially in the area of product quality, even though they may be deemed controversial.

The retailer's agent

We decided from the beginning to position *Natural Foods Merchandiser* as an information-gathering agent for the retailer, not a selling agent for the suppliers and advertisers—as is usually the case.

We also decided that our editorial department would have first priority in terms of travel dollars and personnel. In fact, we utilized three full-time writers and only one salesperson, until recently.

We also decided after our first issue to bring typesetting in-house. It not only saved money, it gave us a tremendous flexibility that most small magazines don't have, along with as few turn-around problems as possible. We found that freelance typesetters, art directors and paste-up personnel work out quite well.

The same doesn't hold for sales and editorial staffers, I strongly feel. Trade magazine publishing is a very specialized field, and with rare exceptions (actually I can't think of one) should not be left in the hands of an employee with less than a full-time interest and commitment to your particular industry.

The single most difficult task for a trade publisher is recruiting quality employees—they are the company's major asset. We have always held off opening any new po-

sitions as we grew until we could pay at or above current market salaries.

Pride in the product

Editorial vitality is a topic oft mentioned but seldom delivered in trade publishing. Many publishers feel that it's enough to stay one small step ahead of the competition—any more is a waste of money. But in turning that equation around, and striving to deliver an editorial product that we could be tremendously proud of, and which would attract personnel who want the excitement of producing a challenging, quality product, we feel our success came far faster than it otherwise could have.

Trade magazine graphics are another Pandora's box that is best left unopened—they're nearly always abominable—but suffice it to say that a continuing effort to deliver a graphically vital product has also paid off.

Probably one of the most critical decisions we had to make came with our third issue, when we began doing a bit of "investigative reporting." We ran a front-page article, not to mention a full-page editorial, calling into question the efficacy of a product category—timed-release vitamins—which then constituted about 25 percent of our advertising.

Sparks flew (to say the least), and the whole subject was egged on by our competitors. To hear a few of our advertisers talk, you'd have thought we were espousing communism, or worse. We lost some advertising, but gained a lot more in the end. It turned out we were right, our readers loved it, and overnight everyone was talking about us.

The bottom line on this is that we decided there were already four unadventurous publications in the industry, and we had no intention of becoming a fifth. If the industry wouldn't support an honest, independent journal, we'd spend our time elsewhere.

We're very careful, however, to keep opinions to the editorial page. All other material is written with a strict eye to reporting—not evaluating—data. That function is always best left to the readers, we believe.

Obviously, an ex-sales rep could drag on here with lots of stories. But I'll just close by saying that we're about to embark on our fourth year of publishing in an industry we strongly believe in and that has a tremendous growth potential.

Financially, we've experienced such a rapid growth that we have never had to touch our credit line. And our suppliers will vouch for our paying our bills on time. (Sometimes too fast, I feel.)

We now run over 1,200 ad pages per year and are headquartered outside of New Hope, Pennsylvania, in our own building that's listed in the historical register, in a lovely rural setting. We also have offices in Malibu, California, and Eugene, Oregon. We also produce a national business conference and exposition in the natural foods industry, which 3,500 professionals attended last year. And, we're researching starting or buying a new magazine.

Anybody want to buy a house?

Solar Age

By Bruce Anderson

Although mankind has been tapping solar energy for millions of years in the struggle to survive, the modern appreciation of solar energy began with the infamous oil embargo of 1973-1974. The resulting tenfold increase in the price of oil—coming as it did on the heels of a decade-long national dialogue on the deleterious environmental, social and political consequences of using conventional energy sources—set the stage for a much-needed interest in alternative energy sources.

It was in this context that the solar dawn broke with a vengeance, and with it came the need for a magazine to deal with such an important subject.

Several months earlier, after having completed my Master's thesis on the social, engineering and architectural issues of solar energy, I had started a solar-oriented architecture, engineering, research and education firm—Total Environmental Action, Inc.—in Harrisville, New Hampshire (population 450).

That fall, Kurt Wasserman, president of his own small firm, Barrier Industries, Inc. in Port Jervis, New York, a manufacturer of environmental and institutional control cleaning and costing products, called me. Kurt, a graduate chemist and energy buff, was thinking of starting a magazine called *Solar Age*.

Would I edit it if he supplied the feed money? Since I had been having similar thoughts, I said yes, and we became partners in the new publishing company, Solar-Vision, Inc., he as part-time publisher, and I as part-time editor. (I remained as president of T.E.A. and was writing *The Solar Home Book*. Kurt remained as president of Barrier and began to get involved with developing new solar devices.)

Believe it or not, together we knew less about magazines than most publishers know about solar energy. But we did know about solar energy, and we knew that solar energy's time had come and that it was the only real long-term solution to our energy future.

We also knew that such an important subject would require a magazine. Simply stated, a large number of people need to stay abreast of fascinating, burgeoning fields. Solar was no exception. And we knew it was best to come out first.

Besides, we had a personal approach we wanted to take in presenting the subject. There are solar applications that make sense—economically, environmentally and socially—and there are those that don't. Our mission was and is to help our readers sort out the good from the bad, not just to promote solar as an all-purpose panacea.

Creating a staff

In an effort to pinch pennies, we didn't hire an experienced publisher. In retrospect, had we hired a general manager experienced in running a business, we would have avoided many of the problems that eventually befell us.

Hiring staff members was a matter of chance. Because I was considered one of the few "solar experts" at the time, I was occasionally visited by journalists. I hired the first two who walked through the door—part time, of course.

The first, the editor (then called assistant editor), hired a free-lance paste-up artist two hours down the Hudson Valley from her, in New York City. The second, six hours east of her on the New Hampshire seacoast, sold advertising. How? He just picked up the phone and started calling people who were in the business. That all happened in October.

Boy, was our overhead low! But try having a directed, trouble-free operation when five people are working full-time in other jobs in five different places scattered all over New England. Three strikes before walking to the plate.

To make matters worse, we then discovered that after our premiere issue in January (yup, little more than two months after we started), there was February, then March, then April . . . We certainly had not constructed an organizational system that would sustain such an effort.

The content? That was the easy part, or so we thought. *Solar Age* would "cover solar energy," not just the technology of it, but also the way in which it was bound to affect our lives. And not just solar energy for heating buildings, but also solar energy as it drives the winds, the tides, photosynthesis and hydropower.

As simple as that sounds, however, clearly defining editorial policy is a never-ending battle. The rapid development of solar energy requires continually evolving editorial policies. Each department interprets guidelines differently. New staff members bring new preconceptions. Furthermore, good content and good authors are still hard to come by.

Attracting readers and advertisers

We didn't know a thing about direct mail, not even how to prepare the right kind of piece or to whom to mail. We just assumed that the whole world would beat a path to our front covers. Little did we know that at the time most people couldn't differentiate "solar energy" from their leaky plate-glass picture window.

A year-and-a-half into the life of our magazine, we were adopted as the official publication of the American Section of the International Solar Energy Society, and their membership immediately doubled our circulation to 7,000. Affiliating with a not-for-profit association has ramifications all of its own. In this case, the Society's slow growth proved disappointing and did not appear to attract advertisers.

In a moment of unwarranted self-confidence during our second year, we had acquired regional advertising sales representatives covering the entire country. It was a disaster. With our small circulation, our rates were too low to provide much incentive to the reps. We also discovered that ad reps just couldn't communicate with the solar industry. And because we ended up selling most of our ad space ourselves, we still had to pay commissions to the reps—due to our lack of knowledge about contracts.

As soon as we could, we terminated the contracts and began selling exclusively by telephone from our offices. We were better able to communicate our more focused editorial content to an embryonic industry that was itself still learning how to market. More than that, we had learned how to sell advertising ourselves.

We also came to the realization that mail, telephones, buses, cars, trains and airplanes just couldn't compensate for the disadvantages of a dispersed operation. The complexities of publishing demand communication that only side-by-side desks could provide. The challenges of monthly deadlines require full-time people.

We therefore began geographical consolidation to Harrisville, first the publishing and then the editorial functions.

We set up operations on the second floor of an old mill building which lacked many of the basics, such as warmth, potable water, and peace and quiet. The weaving loom manufacturer pounding and sawing just below us for about six hours of the day provided us with a constant humming to work by, not to mention the fine layer of sawdust that would settle nicely on our mechanical boards. Fortunately, in spite of the discomfort, we have always been able to attract top-notch talent eager to join our hardworking staff.

Talent, experience, and energy prices

Finally, in mid-1979, three-and-a-half years after start-up and a year after the completion of the consolidation, we found our stride. Although we had a disappointing 20 pages per month of advertising and a circulation of less than 20,000, management, finance, editorial, circulation and advertising started to fall into place. New talent and the growing experience of existing staff, accompanied by soaring energy prices, cold winters, nuclear catastrophies and a somewhat supportive President Carter, enabled us to flourish.

Managerially, we had deciphered the publishing puzzle. Financially, we were turning the corner on the negative cashflow curve and upgrading our budgeting and bookkeeping practices. Editorially, we were preparing content for a more carefully defined audience—specifically, professionals interested in solar, plus energy-conscious homeowners.

Our circulation efforts became more scientific. Sophisticated testing and analysis, along with careful attention to scheduling, became the rule. We began rolling over positive cashflow from small mailings into ever larger ones.

It wasn't an easy road—those first three-and-a-half years contained many nightmares. Finances were always tight. There were many times when we were not sure whether we'd be able to keep our doors open. One major ingredient would have made it all much easier—money. It seems that you just can't have enough of it, particularly during adolescence.

Over the years, we have dabbled in other publications. In 1977, we combined our July and August issues into a large *Solar Age Catalog.* Two years later, a similar publication, the *Solar Age Resource Book,* captured a nomination for Best Paperback Reference Book of the Year.

Our *Solar Products Specifications Guide,* a product reference book for solar professionals, contains highly specialized, technical information on over 700 products. The only book of its kind in the field, this high-ticket item is composed of two three-ring notebooks and is updated with new information every two months. Now nearly three years old, sales and renewals are thriving. Our own readership is by far its best market.

At this point, I cannot say I wish I knew then what I know now, because I may not have answered "yes" so eagerly to Kurt's question. But now, as *Solar Age* closes its sixth year, its paid circulation is breaking 100,000, representing one of the largest readerships in the building industry, reaching those architects, engineers, contractors and other professionals most concerned about solar energy, and energy conservation.

The solar industry has reached the critical mass necessary to sustain itself well into the future. Solar Vision, Inc. is becoming profitable and has a positive cashflow (usually). The magazine is now positioned to be a guiding light of education and information into the solar age.

And I must say, I enjoy it.

On Cable

By Peter Funt

When the established publishing giants launch a new magazine, it is usually because voluminous research indicates that *someone* will want to read it. But when small entrepreneurs start a magazine, it is probably because *they* want to read it. *On Cable* fits into the second group.

As a marketing consultant to Omni Cable TV Corp., a medium-sized cable operator with cable systems in 18 states, and as a video buff who had reported for years on the TV-radio scene, I was frustrated by the lack of consumer coverage in the rapidly growing cable TV field. At that time (spring 1980) *TV Guide* was just discovering that cable existed; *Panorama* was attempting, with little success, to cover all aspects of the video revolution—from VCRs to disks to cable; and a few regional publications were providing sketchy cable program listings, but without any national perspective.

Meanwhile, Omni and other cable operators were bombarding their subscribers with all sorts of new program channels, but, in most instances, viewers had no idea what was carried on those channels, much less when.

On Cable, a monthly magazine combining locally-tailored cable listings and features about cable programs and personalities, could fill this need.

Although taking this publishing concept to an outside firm was briefly considered, we concluded that the risks in implementing it ourselves were modest compared with the potential rewards.

Our resources for getting out the first issue (October 1980) consisted of myself and two young assistants working with typewriters, paper and pencils at a conference table in Omni's Norwalk, Connecticut, office. There we decided to use small batches of Omni's own cable subscribers in Georgia and Illinois as test markets.

The total distribution of the first issue, sent free to the test groups, was roughly 8,000. Readers were informed that two issues would be sent for free, after which a $1 charge would be added to their cable bill each month for *On Cable*—unless they notified us to cancel. By January it was clear that at least 80 percent were willing to pay.

Seize the moment

At this point, a more conventional publisher would have pronounced the test a success and shut down for a year or two to plan actual publication. We, however, had cable subscribers in 18 states who presumably wanted our magazine as badly as did subscribers in Georgia and Illinois. And because we sensed that our plan was one that others might be working on, there was simply no time for a conventional approach.

We decided to maintain continuous publication—meaning that issues had to be produced each month while such basics as circulation strategy, ad sales and editorial format were still in the developmental stages. For additional financial support we turned to Connecticut Telephone Corp., already a major investor in Omni and a believer in what we had conceived. A staff was gradually assembled, and separate offices were opened in Norwalk.

Although we had now budgeted several million dollars for each of *On Cable*'s first few years, a financial squeeze would have occurred had it not been for a major savings in circulation. Our plan was to bypass newsstand and conventional subscription sales in favor of direct dealings with cable operators like Omni who, in turn, would deal with the public. This is the marketing plan we developed:

We negotiate a three-year contract with local cable systems. We agree to supply a locally-tailored edition for their subscribers. They, in turn, agree to pay us for each copy. Furthermore, they pledge not to distribute any other magazine or program listing.

The cable systems are then free to sell the magazine to subscribers, as Omni succeeded in doing, or to provide it as part of their overall services to their subscribers. Systems with fewer than 15,000 subscribers, for which a tailored edition would be too costly, receive one of our "national" editions, which list most of the programming carried by national cable networks.

Editorial quality

After refining our marketing approach, much effort was needed to mold our editorial content, which is more than 50 percent program listings. The listings could have been purchased in camera-ready form from existing computer firms, but we elected to write, edit and produce all listings ourselves—primarily to achieve editorial and quality control.

The same logic guided us in the preparation of our features and columns. Because we were determined to offer cable viewers a magazine that exceeded their own expectations of what a "program guide" should include, we set our sights, and budgets, on producing a serious, entertaining product free of public-relations hype.

Our greatest challenge came in the area of production, since separate listings sections had to be produced for the different regions. Ultimately, we devised a three-section format.

The outer section, including cover, contains full-color editorial and national ads, with no splits. The middle section contains color program highlights and is printed in at least six versions for different programming combinations. The inner section, which contains the actual program listings and local ads, is printed in any number of versions—depending on how many editions we are able to sell.

Although we opted from the start for in-house typesetting for text and ads, the program listings could be handled only by a large computer house. The one we selected, in Stratford, Connecticut, takes our channel-by-channel input and produces type (in galleys or paginated) that reflects the proper sequence, channel name and number, and time zone for each edition. This is a complex task, one which we must study constantly if we are to keep pace with the technological demands of profitable publishing.

Advertisers like upscale audience

Because *On Cable* evolved in a prove-as-you-grow pattern, we found it took longer than we would have preferred to generate national advertising. Our specialized content and unusual method of distribution made advertisers wary at first. But, over time—and thanks to independent research—they were persuaded that *On Cable* is a highly attractive buy, delivering an upscale audience that spends a remarkably long time with each copy.

Selling local advertising was a problem because our editions serve markets of varying size, spread throughout the country. Fortunately, Continental Telephone has a wholly-owned subsidiary in the yellow page publishing business, Leland Mast Directory Co., that was able to place salespeople in some of the more remote areas where conventional reps were not available. Properly handled, our local ad program has proved capable of pre-selling an edition, thereby cutting our initial costs of entering a new market.

That, in general, is the *On Cable* story. Today our paid circulation is over 400,000. Because many of our affiliated cable systems are in the early stages of construction in major urban markets, it is certain that our circulation will more than double this year—even if we fail to sign any new business. We have also embarked on a direct-subscription campaign as a supplement to our normal distribution to ensure that *On Cable* is available to all cable viewers.

Was it worth it? It was for those of us who could tolerate 18-hour workdays, seven-day workweeks, and months—perhaps years—of chasing a dream. But in those respects, I suppose, *On Cable*'s launch was a normal magazine launch after all.

Trouser Press

By Ira Robbins

The magazines that attract the attention of the media and generate the bulk of the publishing industry's excitement seem to be the ones that do everything at high speed—the overnight successes, the enormously impressive launches, the spectacular first-year failures. However, although it's clear that only big money can buy quick growth (or speedy oblivion), many small publishers have learned that you can start a magazine with *no* money—as long as you have the time to invest.

My experience of seven years as publisher of *Trouser Press,* a rock music monthly with a current circulation of 60,000, verifies my claim: Thanks to the spare time that the people involved could devote to it, *Trouser Press* took the slow, arduous route to its current position with an initial budget of only $100. And I wouldn't have wanted to do it any other way.

Given a large enough investment of money, it would not be difficult to establish a 60,000 circulation monthly in a matter of six months. But the potential profit would hardly offset the expense. And the intrinsic quality of editorial product, staff, and reputation as well as the loyalty of a long-standing readership cannot be hurried in any case. Only the application of hard work, some common sense, and a dash of luck over a long period of time can achieve those strengths. That's what time, not money, can buy a magazine.

The value of time is only one of the general lessons that my seven-plus years in magazine publishing have taught me. Another is the importance of timing, knowing when to use an outside firm instead of doing a job yourself. I have learned how to gauge when the product is ready for a broader audience, and I have learned how to analyze the benefits and risks of going to a more sophisticated system. It's a fine line to walk—between doing things prematurely that will backfire, and holding off doing what's necessary to move the magazine forward. I'm sure I've made some mistakes in this area, but that's what's nice about being completely independent as a publisher—no one is looking over my shoulder.

Shared love; shared ignorance

Trouser Press was conceived in late 1973 by myself and two friends who shared with me a love for rock 'n' roll music and a reckless desire to try our hands at putting out a magazine. Of course, we also shared a complete unfamiliarity with both business and publishing.

I was in engineering school at the time but really wanted to be a rock critic. When breaking into the established magazines as a writer proved frustrating, the idea of starting a magazine of my own became more attractive.

The way we planned it, *Trouser Press* would champion bands that we liked and who were not, in our view, getting enough coverage in the existing rock press. We wanted to avoid the self-serving "critic-as-star" attitude that seemed prevalent and give record consumers some objective information that would be both useful and entertaining. Our aspirations were not great, and our plans were not developed beyond doing a first issue, which we

scheduled for March of 1974. Planning consisted of coming up with a name, arranging for a mimeograph machine, and selecting our topics for that first issue. That was all we saw was needed.

Trouser Press #1 ran 24 pages on hand-collated and stapled mimeo bond. The press run was 400 and the cover price 25 cents. The extent of our marketing strategy was to peddle the magazine in front of New York concert halls (a practice we later discovered, the hard way, requires a license). Our business plan was that if the first issue's sales were enough to recoup our investment (13 reams of bond, two tubes of ink, a box of staples and two dozen stencils), we would try a second issue two months later. That was 68 issues ago, and *Trouser Press* is still growing and going strong.

Trouser Press never benefited from the top-to-bottom planning that is an essential part of a "proper" magazine launch (*i.e.*, one where cash money is involved). Instead, the magazine has been the product of a constant learning process with countless small mistakes, small victories, improved procedures, and growing budgets. Every step forward has been the result of every cent of income being plowed right back; at no time have I risked the existence of the magazine on a major gamble.

Do-it-yourself publishing

In this type of publishing, doing everything yourself at one time or another is both a valuable tool and a financial necessity. Because we couldn't afford a fulfillment house when we started getting subscriptions, we developed our own notion of file maintenance, and we learned a lot about the post office. Then, when we did turn the job over to an outside agency (at about 2,500 it became unmanageable for us), we were able to tell them exactly what we wanted them to do.

Similarly, typesetting was another inside/outside decision, but it went the opposite way. When we first decided to have the magazine typeset (after a dozen issues of typewriter composing), we had no choice but to use an inexpensive outside firm. After a while it became obvious that we were spending a lot of time running back and forth with copy, and that our creativity was being lost to the availability of our typesetter. We looked for and finally found a situation that would allow us to do type in-house, and we have never regretted the change. Any small publisher can economically do in-house typesetting, and the non-monetary rewards are justified by themselves.

Also under the heading of when to make a move, we postponed acquiring a national distributor until *Trouser Press* was free of the self-indulgence and narrowmindedness that characterized our early issues. There was no point giving a big push to a magazine that was not in the league to compete with other rock publications, so we worked with independent distributors and alternatives, as well as with direct accounts (record stores, primarily) until we felt we were ready.

One of the major decisions for a small publisher is choosing a printer. We have had some interesting ones in our day, including a glue-bound web shop near the ocean that couldn't print when the salt-air was too heavy, and another outfit that balked after doing all the prep on our first issue with them because they had found a four-letter word in our copy! We have finally graduated to a major publication printer in the Midwest that is fully adequate for our needs now and for quite some time to come.

Publishing a magazine as a part-time job had its own unique problems, and I was very relieved when we were finally large enough to afford salaries for the essential employees—publisher, editor, art director—in 1977. Although we had to move from a six-time annual frequency to a ten-time frequency in order to adequately amortize the cost, the extra work was a bargain in exchange for the bother of being at another job when something important is happening to your magazine.

Our first distribution break—a record importer that had several thousand retail accounts and had decided to carry *Trouser Press*—came while I was at lunch in a pizza parlor near my other job. It wasn't until someone tracked me down there and gave me the good news that I was able to return the call from a pay phone and arrange the deal. The luxury of going to work at the magazine every day was (and, when things are smooth and quiet, still is) a treat.

From difficult to routine

From our current position, where ad sales and subscription promotions are a regular aspect of day-to-day operations, it's hard to remember how difficult it was to sell that first ad or write a renewal letter. Everything that now seems so routine once presented an obstacle that appeared insurmountable.

I was also fortunate in that I received a lot of helpful advice from generous acquaintances at other magazines who were willing to listen, discuss problems, and offer solutions, shortcuts and better ways. An experienced advisor can be of great value to a small publisher.

On the other hand, some advice may be totally inapplicable; a lot of what works for a large magazine may have no bearing whatsoever for a small operation. Realizing when advice is useless is important.

The future for *Trouser Press*, now that it's established as a junior competitor to the magazines that make up the majority of the rock field, presents a whole new set of challenges. Having gotten the easy stuff out of the way—setting up a staff, finding the right suppliers, developing a systematic way of handling the administrative work needed to keep a magazine—the next step is a hard one.

We are constantly reevaluating goals, planning new ways to further widen the magazine's popularity and success. I want to see *Trouser Press* reach the 100,000 circulation mark before the end of 1982, with a lot of that increase coming from new subscriptions. Although we've had a very high renewal rate (70 percent), we have not been able to convert a substantial portion of single-copy buyers (in rock publishing, the purchase is impulse-based to a large degree) to subscribers. Through a new project that began in January, we're including a free musical soundsheet featuring the artists covered in *Trouser Press* as a bind-in for subscription copies only, with the hope that we can turn a lot of occasional buyers into steady and renewable subscribers.

If we reach our circulation goals, we will be able to sell a much wider spectrum of advertising. At our current circulation, most of our advertising is from record companies, retailers, and mail-order distributors of related products. At 100,000 we should be able to interest manufacturers of audio equipment and other related fields in our select readership.

Finding out the hard way

Figuring out how to publish a magazine has been the most challenging task of my life. Whenever things start to run a bit smoothly, I start to look for new areas that I've postponed investigating, or I compare our methods with other magazines' methods to see if we might improve our work. I had to find out a lot of things the hard way, like every publisher, but with a little care and forethought, it has been possible to keep disasters to a manageable level.

Trouser Press has achieved enormous success in the light of our original intentions, and the future looks bright.

I would be less than honest if I didn't admit that going the time-extensive route has had its drawbacks. There have been projects that I wanted to pursue but was stymied by the lack of available cash. However, from a whim whose time had come to a contender in the rock field, *Trouser Press* has gone against the odds, and not just survived but prospered. Where we'll be two or three years from now (when I'm 30) is beyond the range of my annual planning, but as long as there's rock music worth listening to, there'll be *Trouser Press* covering it.

Direct

By Mark M. Evens

My first mail-order purchase was a Captain Midnight ring that sent secret signals and glowed in the dark. From the moment I opened the package, I was hooked, and my ensuing addiction to the wonders of shopping by mail explains my involvement in *Direct*—America's first magazine for people who love to shop by mail.

Direct is not a trade book or a catalog, but rather a magazine containing information on products and services either not generally available in retail stores or priced lower than in stores. Its articles cover a variety of topics, such as "Building a house by mail"; "Weddings by mail"; "Shopping by television"; "How to buy 30,000 brand-name products by telephone at 20 percent to 30 percent savings." And the magazine features extraordinary savings on special items for *Direct* subscribers only.

The idea for *Direct Magazine* was born in April 1980; the first issue came off the press in September 1981. Like most advertising sales managers, I assumed I knew the entire publishing cycle. During those 19 months, I began to learn my trade.

Those months were filled with joy, fear and love for an idea. Early on, one of my advisers told me that starting a magazine must be a total commitment . . . 12-hour days every day, with one purpose only: getting out that first issue. He was wrong; they were 16-hour days.

Direct was launched partly because we found a market void and partly because, at the age of 40, I felt it was time to be *on my own.*

A market needing a voice

During the fall of 1979 the retail pipeline was backed up. As interest rates rose, retailers were ordering inventory monthly rather than by season. While retail sales were static, the direct mail industry had grown from $7 billion in sales to $30 billion in a seven-year period. Shoppers were faced with higher gasoline costs, less service and selection at retail stores, and less time to shop. Catalogs seemed to be the answer for an increasing number of American families.

There were over 10,000 companies selling products and services by mail or telephone, and over 2,000 active catalogs finding their way into homes. Even discounting those who purchased magazines by direct mail, 30 million Americans bought other merchandise items from catalogs and other direct mail solicitations. Of this total, six million purchasers accounted for 80 percent of the total dollar volume purchased by direct mail. With those figures behind us, we felt we had a market.

This market needed a voice. Someone had to comparison shop these catalogs and present the best. If one were looking for energy-saving devices, which of the 100 catalogers selling such items offered value, how did the product differ, what products were unique?

It is impossible for a consumer to shop hundreds of catalogs. *Direct* would do that for them. Our original concept was to be the "Consumer Report" for the direct mail industry, but we quickly discarded that idea in favor of a service magazine presenting only quality products that are unique and have value.

In August of 1980, after six months of reading every book and article I could find on direct marketing, I left my job at *Playboy* and, with my secretary, Maria, opened Evens Publishing Corporation. The name sounded impressive, but after seeing our headquarters, 300 square feet on East 44th Street in New York City, the reality of the situation hit home. With my limited funds, we started.

I talked to scores of people in the direct mail industry for ideas and support. Some thought *Direct* would never work. Why would people buy a magazine on how to shop by mail? One industry leader asked me if I would buy a magazine called *Department Store Shopper*? I said I would, and I do. Magazines like *Vogue, Architectural Digest, New York* always send readers to department stores.

Package inserts a natural

One of our earliest supporters was Mike Slosberg, president of Wunderman, Ricotta and Kline. After learning what a package insert was from the people at L.L. Bean, Mike counseled me about why such inserts would work for *Direct.*

These inserts, offers sent with ordered merchandise, have become our largest circulation source. It was logical that package inserts would work for us. After all, they would go to hot-line direct-mail buyers and be received when the buyer is in a most positive frame of mind. They had just received their gift to themselves, and it was already paid for.

My wife and I wrote the first package insert. Those 1,500 words, mostly picked up from other promotional copy written for us, took two weeks to get on paper. Finally, in October of 1980, we tested three insert programs—L.L. Bean, Adam York, and Country Loft. All three paid out. Our test panels were only 6,000; it was all we could afford at the time.

In March 1981, with capital provided by early partners of *Direct Magazine* (now a limited partnership), we tested nine more package insert programs with three creative approaches and two price tests; 180,000 pieces were sent out.

We found a winning package as well as our price point. Of prime importance, we found that we were going to develop an upscale audience because the higher the average sale of the cataloger carrying our inserts, the higher our response.

We developed a premium, "*Direct Magazine*'s Catalog of Mail Order Catalogs." This premium offered the potential subscriber highlights of over 1,000 of the most interesting catalogs from all over the world, as well as valuable mail-order shopping information. We thought at first that we had a one of a kind, but after we started promoting our premium we found four others in the market. Ours came *FREE*!!! with subscriptions, however, whereas the others cost money. Our premium worked and became the focal point of our winning circulation offer.

Advertisers eager

In January of 1981, the publicity on *Direct* broke. We received over 100 requests for advertising rate cards. It was then that we realized our advertising potential. Where else could mail order advertisers find prospects willing to pay for a magazine to guide them in buying even more items by mail? We then decided to accept only advertising which included a coupon or other direct response mechanism (such as sweepstakes, contests and premium offers). The ads were to be a true extension of the editorial product . . . every page of *Direct* would be acted upon. (Our first issue came out with 53 pages of advertising in a 116-page issue. Our second issue carried more than 65 pages of advertising.)

The direct marketing trade reacted favorably to the news of *Direct*. After all, we were to function as the meeting place where mail order suppliers, advertisers and consumers could come together in an area of mutual trust. *Direct* was to broaden the national base of mail order buyers, and its editorial would encourage current customers to increase the frequency of their buying.

Catalogers were cooperative. They helped us with our package insert program. Now, over 40 companies (who collectively deliver more than 100 million packages annually) are part of our circulation program. Our job is to continually test packages for response, creative compatibility and seasonal variations of our offer.

With the results of our October 1980 test and a handful of letters from potential advertisers, I began a business plan. At that time I assumed we would have our plan in one month and all our financing one month later. I was convinced we would have an April 1981 issue. Well —the business plan took nearly three months to complete, and raising the money took more than a year.

The October 1980 issue of *Magazine Age* had given us a big boost. John Mack Carter wrote a piece on us, "Only the Best New Magazine Idea Since . . . *Ballyhoo*?". John believed we had a great idea and his enthusiasm for *Direct* gave us an emotional lift and credibility when we most needed it.

No money/no drop

At that time it was still just Maria and me. We were cooped up in that tiny office, now filled with boxes and mail bags. We learned to deal with printing suppliers, list brokers, and investors. It was an education. We interviewed editors and circulation directors, and we convinced Marshall Feldman, who worked with me at *Playboy*, to be our ad director.

Everyone was to start in January, but come January, we still had no money in the bank. The employees came on board in April and May.

Our business plan had to be restructured five times. The delays in raising money kept delaying our circulation drop. Beatrice Jones Hanks, our circulation director, threatened to jump out of our 23rd floor offices more than once. I promised her that if she jumped, I would be holding her hand on the way down. She must have valued my life—she never made the leap. She did, however, keep sanity in our operation by day and rewrote the business plan by night.

We were fortunate in finding editors who had written some 20 books on mail-order buying. They shaped the first issue of *Direct*. We are still searching for the perfect editorial format. (Our second issue looked much different from our first—more graphics, less verbiage.) We receive dozens of letters from our readers each day expressing their likes and dislikes. Friends in our business are calling. Some say we should look more like a catalog and emphasize the ads. Others suggest more lifestyle editorial. Ain't publishing fun?

A cataloger's delight

We sent out a four-page survey form to 1,000 of our early subscribers. With over 500 returns, with no incentive other than "we would like to hear from you," we began to get a fix on our audience. Fifty percent have household incomes of more than $25,000. Seventy-three percent made 11 or more mail-order purchases in the last year. Sixty-eight percent spent more than $250 through the mail last year. And 42 percent were college graduates. We were pleased.

Direct is unique in two ways. First, there has never been a magazine like it before. Second, no other magazine ever had a circulation plan that relied so heavily on package inserts. This makes the work exciting, but without a prototype we have had no one to learn from except ourselves.

Financing remained the problem it was in the beginning. After several false starts, we met the people at Diversion Communications who not only arranged our financing, but gave us the publishing backup we needed as well. Good accounting and cost control, production skills, and efficient editing were some of the gifts my new partners contributed.

In the beginning, I believed I could own the whole thing. How quickly we learn when we look for outside monies. I have no regrets. We are financed and have able assistance from our partners.

I lost my Captain Midnight ring along the way, but I have replaced it with *Direct,* and I'm still hooked.

Contributors

William Abbott, marketing director of *Self* magazine, was associate publisher, marketing for *New York* magazine. He was also vice president of the National Retail Merchants Association and promotion director for CBS Publications.

Jules Abend was previously manager of news operations for McGraw-Hill World News, dealing daily with correspondents. Currently, he heads his own specialized news service called Clarion Business News and Feature Service, Inc. Among his clients are *Purchasing World, Datamation, Banking* and *Factory* magazines.

David H. Ahl is publisher of *Creative Computing.*

Herb Ahrend is president of Ahrend Associates, Inc., a direct advertising agency and consulting firm with headquarters in New York. He has created successful programs which have won 45 national and international awards.

Bruce Anderson is executive editor of *Solar Age.*

Russell F. Anderson, publishing consultant, previously was senior vice president of the McGraw-Hill Publications Company, which he joined in 1945 following a career as a foreign correspondent for International News Service. He has launched co-venture magazines throughout Europe, South America and Japan. He also has served as publisher of some of McGraw-Hill's wholly-owned overseas-based magazines including *International Management.*

Roger Appleby is sales promotion director for American Baby, Inc. He previously was advertising director for *Weight Watchers* and has had careers as an ad agency head, consultant to magazine publishers, musician and restauranteur.

Jim Atkins is co-owner of Information Telemarketing, Inc., a consulting firm in New York City specializing in telephone sales.

Dick Barnett was associate editor of *Mechanix Illustrated.* Previously, he was an editor with *Outdoor Life.*

Ted Bartek is a management consultant specializing in magazine circulation and advertising sales planning and promotion. During the past few years, he has been associated with *Progressive Grocer* magazine, *Forbes* magazine, CBS Publications and Doubleday Bookclubs in various financial, marketing and advertising capacities.

Richard V. Benson began his direct marketing career at Time Inc. He is now a direct marketing consultant and has worked for more than 40 publishers and more than 60 magazines. He is also the publisher of *The Content News-Letter.*

Bob Birnbaum, after 30 years of highly diversified experience as a consumer and business magazine and book publishing executive, launched his own publishing management and marketing consulting company, specializing in new profit opportunity development.

Stephen Birnbaum is editorial director of *Diversion* Magazine.

William S. Blair is publisher of *Blair & Ketchum's Country Journal.*

M.J. (Chip) Block is head of Redwood Communications, Inc., a publishing consulting firm. Previously, he was publisher of *Games* Magazine, associate publisher of *Ladies' Home Journal* and director of circulation at Downe Publishing, Inc.

Irvin J. Borowsky is founder and president of North American Publishing Company, which currently publishes magazines ranging from *ZIP* and *Marketing Bestsellers* to publications for educators, medical labs, the export industry and the printing and publishing industries.

Ed Burnett is a direct-mail consultant with 20 years' experience working with Mobil, Exxon, Polylok, Pioneer Electronics and other Fortune 500 firms. He is widely recognized as the pioneer on many of the list marketing concepts and techniques utilized today throughout the nation.

Frank Butrick is managing director of the Independent Business Institute of Akron, Ohio, a consulting and publishing form, and president of Butrick Manufacturing Company, which produces tools and machine accessories for the metalworking industry.

E. Daniel Capell is president of Capell & Associates, a consulting firm specializing in publishing and direct marketing. He is also publisher of *Capell's Circulation Report.* Previously, he was with Newsweek, Inc., as vice president and circulation director of *Newsweek* and vice president, new magazine development. He has also been an executive with Ziff-Davis.

Jerry Constantino is executive vice president and publisher of PJS Publications, Inc.

C. Lynn Coy has been president of C. Lynn Coy & Associates, a publisher's rep firm in New York City, since 1962. Prior to that time, he was eastern sales manager for Peacock Business Press.

Stepen M. Curran is an account supervisor with the publisher's rep firm of Galavan, Hatfield & Kittle, Inc. Steve, who began his advertising career in 1965, has been a sales rep for Family Travel Guides and national sales magazine, vice president and editor of Mar/Com West, Inc.

H. Joel Davis formerly was Compugraphics Corporation's marketing manager for both magazine publishing and advertising agencies.

Frederic C. Decker is president of The Frederic C. Decker Company, Inc., Brookfield Center, Connecticut. He is a former publisher of consumer and business publications, newsletters and texts. Since 1972 his firm has been consultant to scores of publishers in this country and abroad in areas of management planning, sales positioning, and development, feasibiliity analysis, personnel search and motivation.

Milton F. Decker has been prominent in the avertising and publishing field for over 40 years. He has been a media director and account supervisor in leading agencies on major accounts such as Procter & Gamble, Westinghouse, McGraw-Hill. More recently he has worked in sales management and promotional capacities with major media, including Time Inc., *The New York Times*, Scripps-Howard and, for more than 15 years, with *Life* magazine. For the past ten years, through M.F. Decker Associates, he has conducted a sales and promotional consulting practice serving leading magazines including *Architectural Digest, Audubon, Bon Appetit, Promenade, Smithsonian* and *World Tennis*.

Roger V. Dickeson is founder and president of Printing Efficiency Management Corporation. He is a tax attorney, past president of two web-offset printing companies and author of numerous print industry publications.

Robert E. Dimond has been editing and publishing business magazines for 26 years, the last 20 of them in the computer and office products industries. Previously publisher of *Office Products Dealer* (to the retail trade), and of *Inforsystems* (edited for the computer user), Dimond now serves as consultant to publications, trade associations, vendors, retailers and other organizations in the office products and computer industries.

Mark Dowie is managing editor of *Mother Jones*, a national monthly published in San Francisco.

Hal Duchin, national sales manager for Playboy Enterprises, was previously advertising director of *Book Digest*. Prior to 1974, he was with *Psychology Today* for six years, rising to director of advertising sales.

George Duncan is a freelance direct-response copywriter/consultant, specializing in magazine, newsletter and book promotion. A former secretary of the Direct Marketing Creative Guild and winner of the John Caples Copy Prize, Duncan held senior copy positions with Ziff-Davis Publishing Company, Columbia House and Xerox Education Publications before establishing his own business in 1976.

William Dunkerley is a publications consultant based in New Britain, Connecticut. He has been president of a technical publishing company, publications manager of a national non-profit organization, and served as a director of the Society of National Association Publications.

James E. Dunne joined *U.S. News & World Report* as

quality assurance manager in 1979 serving in a similar function at McGraw-Hill for 13 years. He has been involved with the production committee of the American Business Press and the Association of Publication Managers. He has been an active member of the SWOP committee since its founding in 1975.

Ira Ellenthal is executive vice president/marketing of Folio Publishing Corporation. Previously, he was executive vice president of Charleson Publishing Company, as well as publisher/editor of two of its monthlies, *Product Marketing* and *Food & Beverage Marketing*. He is author of the book, *Selling Smart*.

Mark M. Evens is publisher of *Direct Magazine*.

David P. Forsyth, vice president-research, McGraw-Hill Publications Company, has helped pioneer the use of specialized magazine research.

J. Wendell Forbes has been a publishing and direct marketing consultant since 1970. Before that he worked at Time Inc. for 22 years and was circulation director of *Life*. He was also circulation director of *McCall's* and was with Young & Rubicam. He is a past chairman of the board of DM/MA and has served on the boards of numerous circulation and direct marketing related companies.

Robert H. Fowler is founder and chairman of the board of Historical Times, Inc. He was a newspaperman for 10 years before he and his wife launched their first magazine, *Civil War Times*, in 1959. Historical Times, inc. now publishes three other magazines of popular history, *Early American Life, American History Illustrated* and *British Heritage*, with combined circulations of 600,000. The company also publishes books and conducts a travel service for its magazines' readers.

John Fry is director of publciations development for Times Mirror Magazines, Inc. Previously, he was editorial director of *Outdoor Life, Ski* and *Golf*.

Peter Funt is editor and publisher of *On Cable*.

George A. Glenn has been the editorial director for Harcourt Brace Jovanovich Publications since May 1976. During his 30 year career in publishing, he has served in every editorial capacity in business publication journalism, starting as a business magazine editorial assistant.

Dave Gotthelf is the co-owner of Information Telemarketing, Inc., a consulting firm in New York City specializing in telephone sales.

Hubert R. Gotzes is a group vice-president of R.R. Donnelley & Sons Co. and director of the company's book group. He began his career with Donnelley in 1947 as a bonus estimator and since then has served in a variety of sales, manufacturing and administrative positions.

Milton Gralla is executive vice president and partner in Gralla Publications, New York, publisher of 14 national business/trade magazines.

R. Douglas Greene is chairman of the board of *Natural Foods Merchandiser*.

Morton E. Grossman is a media consultant, specializing in the development of marketing strategies to improve advertising sales performance. Previously, he was director of marketing for Ziff-Davis Publishing Company and has held marketing management positions at *TV Guide, The*

Washington post and *The Journal of Commerce.*

Henry A. Grunwald was appointed editor-in-chief of all Time Inc. publications in 1979, after serving as corporate editor of Time Inc. since 1977. Grunwald is a director of the World Press Freedom Committee and a member of the Council on Foreign Relations.

Dave Hagenbuch is president of Dave Hagenbuch & Associates, Inc., a consulting firm specializing in publishing, communications and sales development programs.

Allan Haley is a typegraphic consultant at International Typeface Corporation. Previously, he was a typographic consultant at Compugraphic Corporation. Since 1971 he has contributed in type design supervision and corporate graphic design, winning numerous National Composition Association awards in typographic excellence.

John Hall is an executive at Ogilvy & Mather Direct Response, Inc. He was formerly circulation director and then director of TV marketing at *Country Music* magazine.

Joseph J. Hanson is president and editor-in-chief of Folio Publishing Corporation.

Denison Hatch heads Denison Hatch Associates, Inc., of Stamford, Connecticut, a firm specializing in direct response copy and design for a wide variety of clients, including many magazines. He was director of book clubs at Macmillan and Meredith and, for 3½ years, was a vice president and copywriter with Walter Weintz & Company.

Frank Herrera is the vice president, director of distribution for the Hearst Magazine Division of the Hearst Corporation, a position he assumed in January 1980. He has three divisions reporting to him: International Circulation Distributors, Periodical Publishers Service Bureau, and Eastern News. Before joining Hearst, Herrera was president of Independent News Company, now Warner Publisher Services.

Marlene Jensen, publisher of *Audio* Magazine, formerly was Director of Magazine Acquisition and Development for CBS Publications. Previously with ABC Leisure Magazines, Jensen survived the sale of her own startup, *Sportswoman*, in 1975. She is on the government committee of Ad Women of New York, and is a member of International Mensa Society.

The senior editor of *Plant Engineering*, **Jeanine Katzel**, is also a member of the American Society of Business Press Editors and Women in Communications, Inc. She has previously done technical research and writing for the American Medical Association and the University of Wisconsin Sea Grant Program.

When it comes to reader service, **Joseph Kelleher** knows that it doesn't cost that much to please the customer. He's gained this knowledge from over 20 years at Publishers Clearing House, Port Washington, N.Y., one of the largest magazine agencies in the world. Before joining PCH as its vice-president for operations, Joe was subscription manager for Scholastic Magazines. He is a former member of the ethics committee of the Direct Mail/Marketing Association, serves on the executive board of the Long Island Better Business Bureau and is past president of the Fulfillment Management Association.

John D. Klingel is a magazine consultant specializing in circulation and financial planning, direct-response promo-

tion and new magazine development. Based in Palo Alto, California, he works with a variety of magazines located throughout the country and has been involved in the startup of a number of magazines.

James B. Kobak of Darien, Connecticut, has been a magazine management consultant since 1971. Previously, he was administrative partner of J.K. Lasser & Company and international administrative partner of Lasser, Harmood Banner and Dunwoody.

Richard M. Koff is a management consultant to publishers and other magazine executives concerning strategic and tactical problems. Previously, he was vice president, business manager and assistant publisher with Planboy Enterprises, Inc., for 11 years and was with McGraw-Hill for 10 years. Koff is also the author of the book, *Strategic Planning for Magazine Executives.*

Benedict Kruse is president of Frank Associates, Tujunga, California, and is also a principal and creative director of *information/education*, a multimedia publisher of educational programs. Since 1950, his work includes the writing of more than 2,000 magazine articles, two dozen books and scores of self-study-type learning programs. He has also worked extensively as an editorial consultant for magazines, has started several magazines for industrial and professional clients and is involved in the complete packaging and publishing of professional and educational books.

Julie A. Laitin is president of Julie A. Laitin Enterprises, a firm specializing in sales promotion and advertising for magazines. Before forming her own company, she was promotion director for Harcourt Brace Jovanovich Publications and sales promotion and advertising director for Bill Communications and Lebhar-Friedman Publishers.

Melissa Lande is a founding partner of Chacma, Inc., a promotion and public relations agency in New York, specializing in campaigns and audiovisual presentations for publishers.

Douglas Learner, former associate editor of FOLIO: THE MAGAZINE FOR MAGAZINE MANAGEMENT, is currently its circulation manager.

Spencer H. Longshore III is advertising director of B.A.S.S. Publications, publishers of *Bassmaster, Southern Outdoors* and *Fishing Tackle Retailer*. Prior to joining B.A.S.S., he was director of special promotions for the Advertising Company and publisher and vice president of Baldwin County Publishing Company.

Barbara Love is executive editor of FOLIO: THE MAGAZINE FOR MAGAZINE MANAGEMENT.

Robert Luce is a publishing and direct-response marketing consultant with offices in Westport, Connecticut. He was associated with *Changing Times* and *The Kiplinger Washington Letters* for 10 years. Luce was also publisher of *The New Republic* and was director of planning for Time-Life Books and editor-in-chief of the Time-Life Book Clubs.

Karlene Lukovitz, previously senior editor of FOLIO: THE MAGAZINE FOR MAGAZINE MANAGEMENT, is managing editor of *Catalog Age*.

Angus Macaulay is regional sales manager of *Inc.* Magazine. Previously, he was advertising sales manager of *Chemical Engineering*. He joined McGraw-Hill in 1968 as

787

a sales trainee for *Chemical Week* in New York. In 1969 he was appointed a multi-pub district manager in Dallas. He subsequently, in 1971, was named district manager for *International Management* in Cleveland, and in 1973, he became district manager for *American Machinist* in Chicago.

Theresa P. MacDonald is senior vice president and director of communications development at Young & Rubicam, Inc. She has worked in several capacities there, including supervisor of media analysis and assistant to the media director.

James MacLachlan is assistant profession of marketing at the New York University Graduate School of Business Administration.

Jim Mann of Jim Mann & Associates, Ramsay, New Jersey, is a consultant specializing in product-development and market-positioning of communications media. Prior to 1974 he was editor and president of *The Gallagher Report*, having been associated with the newsletter for 15 years. He is also the author of the book, *Solving Publishing's Toughest Problems.*

Edward McCabe, formerly editor of *Group Travel*, currently does freelance work in the magazine field. His background includes editing *Premium & Incentive Product News* and helping to rewrite Gellert Publications' professional photographic catalog.

Paul J. McGinnis is president of the Paul McGinnis Company, a publishers' sales and marketing company in New York City. He previously was associated with McGraw-Hill Publications, Cahners and Ziff-Davis Publishing Company.

Kent McKamy is president of The McKamy Partnership. Previously, he was executive vice president of Manning, Selvage & Lee.

David Merrill is a New York City-based magazine design consultant. Previously, he was senior art director of Ogilvy & Mather and the art director of *Time*, where he designed morek than 500 covers. His recent clients have included Bill Communications, CBS Publications, Fairchild Publications, McGraw-Hill, Playboy Enterprises, Times Mirror Publications and Venture Publishing Company.

Mark F. Miller is vice president and business manager of Hearst Magazines. Previously, he was director of circulation planning. And prior to that, he was assistant to the director of circulation and assistant to the vice president and resident controller of the company.

Douglas Mueller is president of Gunning-Mueller Clear Writing Institute, Inc., Santa Barbara, California. In the past year, the Clear Writing Institute has conducted over 50 seminars for large Fortune 500 companies, universities and publications. He is former newsman, teacher and corporate public relations executive.

Paul Obis is associate publsher of *Vegetarian Times*.

David Z. Orlow is president of Periodical Studies Service, Inc., a management consulting firm serving upper management in magazine and directory publishing. Prior to that he was senior vice president at Media Networks, Inc. and held a number of positions at Ziff-Davis Publishing Company, including vice president corporate planning, director of marketing and director of sales development.

Earlier he was marketing director and publisher of various technical and business publications.

Warren Owens is the production manager of the Chilton Book Company and was previously director of production for Chilton Publications.

Charles Pace was postal affairs director at *Newsweek*. He was previously with the Post Office Department in the transportation and economic development division. He now has his own postal consulting firm, Charles L. Pace Associates, in Wilton, Connecticut.

As a management consultant in the field of publication production, **Bert Paolucci**, Larchmont, New York, has a background that includes helping both large and small publishers find ways to reduce production costs, install cost control systems for paper and printing expenditures, evaluate capital investments and draw up new printing contracts.

Jeffery R. Parnau is an independent printing consultant, president of Parnau Graphics, Inc., and publisher of several printing-related journals. He has served as editor, art director, and production manager for various publishing operations over the past 15 years.

S. William Pattis is head of The Pattis Group, a large publishers' rep firm headquartered in Lincolnwood, Illinois, with offices throughout the United States, Canada and Europe. Bill was executive vice president of United Business Publications and publisher of five of the company's magazines prior to forming The Pattis Group rep firm in 1959.

John Peter is head of the New York City-based John Peter Associates, Inc., leading international publishing consultants. He was previously art director of *McCall's*, former president of the New York Art Directors Club and former editor of *Life* and *Look*. His client list includes a broad spectrum of the publishing industry in this nation and abroad.

Robert Potts is vice president and publisher of *Dun's Review* and was formerly vice-president. Conover-Mast Division, Cahners Publishing Company.

Before becoming a graphic arts color consultant, **Frank Preucil**, Evanston, Illinois, was director of color reproduction studies at the Graphic Arts Technical Foundation, director of photography at Gerlach-Berklow Co. and at Chicago Rotoprint Co. He is the author of over 100 articles on color reproduction and has conducted seminars in many foreign countries and dozens of American cities on printing and production problems.

Howard S. Ravis, former editor and associate publisher of FOLIO: THE MAGAZINE FOR MAGAZINE MANAGEMENT, currently heads his own consulting firm, Howard S. Ravis & Associates.

Jerry Reitman is president of Scali, McCabe, Sloves Direct Response. Previously, he was president of Ogilvy & Mather Direct Response, vice president/magazines for Publishers Clearing House and president and publisher of Academic Media.

Shirrel Rhoades is publisher of *Family Computing* and corporate vice president of Scholastic, Inc. Previously, he was vice president/consumer marketing for Charter Publishing Company, vice president and associate publisher of *Harper's*, vice president and general manager of the magazine division of Carus Corporation and president and publisher of *Directions*.

Willis Rivinus is a broad-based consultant specializing in magazine publishing. He combines seven years as a business planning consultant with eight years of publishing, editing and circulation management. Most recently, he has been involved with two magazine startups and the introduction of a major electronic test editing and photocomposition system.

Ira Robbins is publisher of *Trouser Press*.

Frank Romano is president of Graphic Arts Marketing Associates. Hee is a publisher and a typesetter, and the author of five books in the field of automated typographic systems.

Stephen Sahlein is a newsletter and direct response copywriting consultant based in Larchmont, New York. He has started successful newsletters in a number of different fields. All are still in publication.

Robert Sbarge is president of Seminar Management International, Inc., New York, a seminar management company serving magazine publishing and selected associations. Prior to forming his own company, Bob served as seminar director of the Young President's Organization.

Eliot DeY. Schein is president of Schein/Blattstein Advertising, Inc., a New York-based agency with specialties in direct marketing and circulation promotion.

Ronald T. Scott is former president of the Capital Distributing Company and a past president of the Periodical and Book Association of America (PBAA). He is currently an independent consultant.

Robert Sgarlata, former associate editor of FOLIO: THE MAGAZINE FOR MAGAZINE MANAGEMENT, is currently conference manager for Folio Publishing Corporation.

Ed Shanaphy is publisher of *Sheet Music Magazine*.

Ami Shinitzky is editor and publisher of *Equus* and president of Fleet Street Corporation.

Joan Silinsh is district manager of *International Management* Magazine, a McGraw-Hill publication. Previously, she was associate director of marketing communications for McGraw-Hill, and was an associate with Maurice Feldman Public Relations.

J. Wesley Silk is publisher and advertising sales director of *Better Homes and Gardens*. He came to the publication in 1971 as New York sales manager and two years later became advertising sales director. The title of publisher was added in 1979. Mr. Silk began his magazine career in 1952 and has worked as New York sales manager for *American Home* and national advertising sales manager at *Life*.

Eugene Slawson has been in the circulation business for over 17 years. For the last seven years he has been with Davis Publications. Prior to that, he was with Ziff-Davis, *Redbook* and Prentice-Hall. He holds a doctorate degree from the School of Law and Administration, University of Krakow, Poland.

Edward L. Smith, a New York attorney in private practice, specializes in the business and editorial legal problems of publishers. He was previously vice president and counsel of *Newsweek* and, earlier, the corporate attorney of *The New York Times*. Before entering the law, he was an editor and reporter for the Associated Press.

Leo Spector is the editor of *Plant Engineering*, a certified plant engineer and a member of the American Society of Mechanical Engineers. Formerly Chicago regional editor of *Machine Design* and editor of *Assembly Engineering*, he is also chairman of the American Institute of Plant Engineers' Professional Relations & Certification Committee.

The late **A.C. Spectorsky**, editorial dirrector and associate publisher of *Playboy*, always had very definite ideas aboout what makes a successful magazine. His thoughts on magazines and the magazine industry are valid for every magazine—consumer or business, large or small.

Mary Staples is general manager of 3M Media Services, Inc., formerly KBM. She started out with IBM, where she was involved in professional recruiting and customer education and has since installed computer systems in several industries.

William Steiner is the president of William Steiner Associates, Inc., a direct marketing and mail order agency. Over the course of his career, he has been the director of promotion and public relations for *The Washington Post*, business manager of *American Girl*, director of mail order sales for Eton Publishing Company, director of market research for Topics Publishing Company and publisher of *Garden Magazine*.

William Strong, vice president/circulation of Crain Communications, is responsible for all circulation operations on 12 Crain Communications publications, Corporate Computer Center, List Rental Profit Center and Subscription Fulfillment Service Bureau operation. Strong is past president of Chicago Circulation Roundtable and past chairman of ABP Circulation Committee. He is currently serving as chairman of ABC's Business Publications Industry Committee.

Charles I. Tannen is editor and publisher of FOLIO: THE MAGAZINE FOR MAGAZINE MANAGEMENT and executive vice president/publishing of Folio Publishing Corporation.

Howard B. Taylor, retired editorial consultant for the Copley Newspapers, was also a professional lecturer in copy reading and editing at the Medill School of Journalism at Northwestern University for 10 years. He has also been a copy reader for the *Des Moines Register* and the *Chicago Tribune*, managing editor of the *San Diego Union* and editorial-training director for the Copley Newspapers.

Tom Tully is currently general manager, distribution operations and business activities of McGraw-Hill Publications Company. He joined McGraw-Hill in 1971 after serving as traffic manager for Select Magazines and Popular Library Inc. He was formerly assistant traffic manager of Art Color Printing Co., a division of W.F. Hall, Chicago.

Henry Turner is a publishing consultant in Cold Spring, New York. Formerly, he was president of American Family Publishers, vice president and circulation director of *McCall's Magazine* and later *Book Digest*.

Jerry Ward is circulation director at Meredith Corporation. Previously, he was with Ford Motor Company in sales and distribution.

David Webber is technical director of 3M Media Services, Inc., formerly KBM. Webber designed its computer systems, including a Magazine Publishing Model and Advertising Information System. Previously, he was with IBM in England and later transferred to the United States to become manager of its Mathematical Optimization Systems.

Bernard Weiss conducts in-house management training programs, workshops and seminars for magazine and book publishers. He is president of Bernard Weiss & Associates, an international consulting firm specializing in motivating and rewarding editors, art directors and other creative staff; hiring and firing creative personnel; and reviewing and appraising creative performance. Based in Stamford, Connecticut, Weiss is on the faculty of New York University.

Chris Welles' professional career began in 1962 as a reporter for *Life* magazine. He was promoted to business editor in 1965, a position he held for three years. In 1968, he became business editor of the *Saturday Evening Post* and remained with the magazine until it ceased publication in 1969. He has been freelancing ever since, specializing in business, finance and the media. Welles is director of the Walter Bagehot Fellowship Program in Economics and Business Journalism, a mid-career program of study for professional journalists administered by the Columbia University Graduate School of Journalism. He also teaches economics and business journalism to students at the Columbia journalism school.

Loy Wiley, president of Wiley Associates, Inc., is an independent editorial consultant in Dayton, Ohio. Her company provides production-ready copy for two national business magazines.

Milton Williams is the president of Hayes-Williams, Inc., a public relations firm in New York. Prior to opening his public relations agency, he was at Fairchild Publications for 17 years as corporate circulation director and news editor of *Home Furnishings Daily*.

Michael M. Wood is president of Hanley-Wood, Inc., a Washington D.C.-based firm which manages magazines and provides management advice for magazine publishers, and is publisher of *Builder* magazines.

Philip Wooton is an advisor to major publishers on editorial problems and concepts. He was executive editor of the old *Life* Magazine before becoming associate director of research and development for Time Inc.